W9-AOB-258

ED & WOODY'S 10-MINUTE OFFICE XP TUNE-UP

You've just installed Office XP. Now what do you do? Before you get to work, why not tweak a few settings? In 10 minutes, you can clear away clutter, add the toolbar buttons you really use, and generally make yourself more productive.

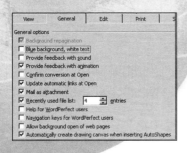

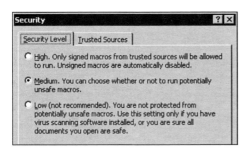

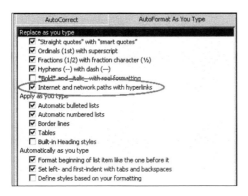

Step 1: Overall Adjustments

For any Office program you use regularly, start by opening the Options dialog box. Choose Tools, Options and go through all the tabs, paying special attention to these crucial settings:

- **General Settings**—Change the number of files on the Recent list to 9 from its default setting of 4. For Excel, choose how many workbooks you want to create in a default workbook and set the standard font and size for Normal text.

- **View Settings**—Decide whether you want to see rulers, scrollbars, status bars, and other widgets.

- **Edit Settings**—Turn off the annoying "click and type" option in Word and disable Excel's AutoComplete function.

- **Security**—In general, the options shown on the Security tab apply to individual files. Click the Macro Security button to control whether and how macros execute. Expert users can choose Medium security; if you're paranoid about macro viruses, choose High. You must set this option separately for each program.

Step 2: Set AutoCorrect Options

Office programs include an array of tools designed to check spelling, automatically correct common mistakes, and display information about certain types of data using Smart Tags. Choose Tools, AutoCorrect Options and configure these settings:

- **AutoCorrect Settings**—Office can clean up after you if you inadvertently begin a word with two capital letters or make one of the misspellings it recognizes. These options are available in Outlook 2002 as well, even if you're not using Word as your editor. You also can enter custom corrections of your own.

- **AutoFormat As You Type Settings**—If you don't want Word, Excel, or PowerPoint to convert Internet addresses to hyperlinks, clear the check box shown here. Word and PowerPoint include a slew of options here; adjust as needed.

- **Smart Tag Settings**—Word gives you the most options for displaying Smart Tags; Excel offers a handful. No options are available for PowerPoint.

Step 3: Tweak Those Toolbars

Choose Tools, Customize to display a list of all available command buttons. While this dialog box is visible, you can drag buttons off any visible toolbar or move them around. Drag new buttons from the dialog box and drop them on a toolbar to add them.

Step 4: Get Organized

- **File Locations**—Tell each Office program where you store data files. By default, this is your My Documents folder, but you can tweak the setting on a per-program basis. Choose Tools, Options; then click the File Locations tab (Word), the General tab (Excel), or the Save tab (PowerPoint).

- **Favorite Places**—In common Open and Save As dialog boxes, you can customize the Places Bar, which gives you one-click access to common file locations. From any Office program, open this dialog box and right-click to switch to small icons. Choose any folder icon and choose Tools, Add to "My Places."

- **CYA**—Tell each Office program how often you want to save AutoRecovery files and whether you want to back up previous versions automatically when you save a new version. From Word, Excel, or PowerPoint, choose Tools, Options, and click the Save tab.

- **Printers**—Open the Print dialog box and set options for all currently defined printers.

Special Edition Using

Microsoft Office XP

Ed Bott

Woody Leonhard

201 W. 103rd Street
Indianapolis, Indiana 46290

Special Edition Using Microsoft® Office XP

Copyright © 2001 by Que

International Standard Book Number: 0-7897-2513-4

Library of Congress Catalog Card Number: 2001087728

Printed in the United States of America

First Printing: May 2001

04 03 02 01   4 3 2

Trademarks

Warning and Disclaimer

Associate Publisher
Greg Wiegand

Acquisitions Editor
Stephanie J. McComb

Development Editors
Rick Kughen
Mark Reddin

Managing Editor
Thomas F. Hayes

Project Editor
Heather McNeill

Copy Editor
Julie McNamee

Indexer
Erika Millen

Proofreader
Harvey Stanbrough

Technical Editor
Doug Klippert

Team Coordinator
Sharry Gregory

Interior Designer
Ruth Harvey

Cover Designer
Dan Armstrong
Ruth Harvey

Page Layout
Heather Hiatt Miller
Mark Walchle

CONTENTS

ABOUT THE AUTHORS

Ed Bott is a best-selling author and award-winning computer journalist with more than 15 years of experience in the personal computer industry and on the Web. For the past decade he was responsible for *PC Computing* magazine's extensive coverage of every conceivable flavor of Microsoft Windows and Microsoft Office. If you lined up every book Ed has written (all published by Que), they'd take up more than six feet of shelf space. Ed is a three-time winner of the Computer Press Award, and he and Woody Leonhard won the prestigious Jesse H. Neal Award, sometimes referred to as "the Pulitzer Prize of the business press," in back-to-back years for their work on *PC Computing*'s "Windows SuperGuide." He lives in an extremely civilized corner of the Arizona desert with his wife, Judy, and two amazingly smart and affectionate cats, Katy and Bianca.

Woody Leonhard describes himself as a "Certified Office Victim." With 17 (or is it 18?) computer books under his belt, he's seen parts of Office that would curl your hair. Woody's best known as the publisher of *Woody's Office Watch*, the feisty, weekly, no-holds-barred (and absolutely *free)* electronic newsletter that specializes in holding Microsoft's feet to the fire. More than half a million people subscribe to WOW and Woody's other newsletters on Windows, Palm-like handheld computers, and more (`http://www.woodyswatch.com`). He and his cohorts are also responsible for "Woody's Office POWER Pack," the number-one add-on to Microsoft Office. Woody has won eight Computer Press Awards and, with Ed, two American Business Press Association awards. He and his son recently gave up the Colorado mountain scene, and now bask in the glorious sun on Phuket Island, Thailand.

DEDICATION

To Judy, who has kept me healthy and sane throughout the many sleepless nights and frantic days that a book like this demands.

—Ed

To Namtip Chompuseang, my most amazing lady from Isa'an, the kindest person I've ever known. And to Justin, who's made me so proud I could pop. We've been through some mighty tough times together, but having the two of you with me has made all the pain worthwhile.

—Woody

ACKNOWLEDGMENTS

Thanks to Susan Daffron, who came up with the outstanding "Three Dog Delight" sample files. The WOPR programming team—Mike Craven, Claude Almer, Vince Chen, Scott Krueger, and Eileen Wharmby—contributed their school of (very) hard knocks advice. Doug Klippert gave us the ultimate backup, with his outstanding technical edits. And the many loyal readers of *Woody's Office Watch* provided the complaints and questions that inspired our pull-no-punches style.

SPECIAL THANKS TO

Doug Klippert is an independent contract trainer living in Tacoma, Washington. He is an MCSE and an Expert Microsoft Office User Specialist (MOUS) in Word, Excel, and PowerPoint. Doug has been working with Word/WinWord since 1991. He's the Credit Manager for a public utility and has a BA in Accounting and an MBA.

TELL US WHAT YOU THINK!

As the reader of this book, *you* are our most important critic and commentator. We value your opinion and want to know what we're doing right, what we could do better, what areas you'd like to see us publish in, and any other words of wisdom you're willing to pass our way.

As an associate publisher for Que, I welcome your comments. You can fax, email, or write me directly to let me know what you did or didn't like about this book—as well as what we can do to make our books stronger.

Please note that I cannot help you with technical problems related to the topic of this book, and that due to the high volume of mail I receive, I might not be able to reply to every message.

When you write, please be sure to include this book's title and author as well as your name and phone or fax number. I will carefully review your comments and share them with the author and editors who worked on the book.

Fax: 317-581-4666

Email: feedback@quepublishing.com

Mail: Greg Wiegand
        Que
        201 West 103rd Street
        Indianapolis, IN 46290 USA

INTRODUCTION

In this introduction

Arguably, Microsoft Office XP is the most important software upgrade in the history of personal computing. Consider the evidence:

- Microsoft Office is the best-selling business application in the history of personal computing, with more than 70 million copies sold.
- More than 2.6 million developers have built custom applications that tie directly into Office programs.
- The two oldest Office programs—Word and Excel—are undisputed standards in the business software category.
- Newer members of the Office team—notably FrontPage and Outlook—are among the best choices in their categories as well.

In Office XP, Microsoft has largely delivered on its promise to integrate the different programs that make up Office—toolbars, task panes, and other interface elements don't just look alike, they use the exact same code—and when you learn how to customize one application you can generally transfer the same skills to other Office programs.

Yes, Office XP still has odd inconsistencies, as well as bugs, features that don't work as advertised, and basic interface elements guaranteed to drive expert users crazy. But there are also startling usability improvements, including major improvements in some of the most basic features of Word and Excel, the oldest and most popular Office applications.

The deeper you go into Office XP, the more you find, including a sophisticated programming language—Visual Basic for Applications—that lets you automate tasks and tie together business processes in ways that are literally limited only by your imagination. Office XP also speaks fluent Internet, with superb support for Internet standards—a remarkable achievement when you consider that the World Wide Web didn't even exist when Office debuted less than a decade ago.

Given the considerable changes in Office XP, we worked long and hard to completely revamp our previous edition of this book. What you see in *Special Edition Using Microsoft Office XP* is meticulously reworked, sentence by sentence, to bring you the latest, most accurate, most complete information available.

WHO SHOULD BUY THIS BOOK

If you need an Office XP reference book you can rely on—one that won't bore you with the obvious, pull punches when Office comes up short, or turn mealy-mouthed when you hit the really hard parts—you have the right book in your hands.

As with other titles in Que's best-selling *Special Edition Using* series, this book focuses on the unique needs of business professionals and business users. We assume you're experienced with Windows, the Web, and, for the most part, previous versions of Microsoft Office. We know that Office is an absolutely essential part of your everyday working life. We're also certain you've experienced your fair share of Office bugs and annoyances firsthand. Because we're confident you've already figured out the basics, we've spent our time figuring out how these programs *really* work. Trust us—Office has plenty of bugs and poorly designed features, and Microsoft doesn't always make it easy to see how you can combine features or customize applications to increase productivity.

What you'll find documented here is the raw Office, in all its glory, seen through the eyes of experts who have been pushing Office to the limit for years and years. We don't gloss over the rough spots. We show you what works and what doesn't—giving real-world examples and advice for the former and, whenever possible, workarounds for the latter.

We built this book from the ground up as the first Office reference category killer. You'll find page after page after page of previously undocumented material—key details, insight, and real-world advice you can't find anywhere else. And it's all arranged so that you can get in, find the answer you need, apply it to your work at hand, and get out, in record time. There's never been a computer reference book like this: dead-on accurate, encyclopedic, but accessible and usable. It may weigh a ton, but if you need the straight scoop on anything related to Office, this is where you should look first.

If you use Office every day, the book should pay for itself in the first hour—maybe in the first ten minutes. As far as we're concerned, the only correct answer to Microsoft's "Where do you want to go today?" is "Home"—you want to get your problem solved and get home on time. We know that. Even if it seems that Microsoft doesn't.

To top it all off—to seal this book's reputation as a category killer and the best value on the market—we've included a full license of the award-winning Office add-on "Woody's Office POWER Pack," or WOPR (pronounced "Whopper") XP/2002, which you can download from Que's Web site. Tens of thousands of copies of WOPR have been sold for $49.95. The latest version, WOPR XP/2002, is available only on Que's Office XP Web site.

We hope you agree that *Special Edition Using Microsoft Office XP* "raises the bar" for Office reference books.

HOW THIS BOOK IS ORGANIZED

Special Edition Using Microsoft Office XP is organized into 8 parts. Naturally, each of the major applications in the Office suite gets its own section. Before diving into specific features of Outlook, Word, and Excel, however, we recommend you read through the sections that cover the techniques common to all applications.

Part I, "Common Tasks and Features," covers the essentials of Office, including techniques you can use to transform the Office interface into your own personal productivity center. We show you how to customize Office XP's Open and Save As dialog boxes so that you can find your working files with the fewest possible clicks (an innovation that Microsoft, er, borrowed from the WOPR 2000 utility we introduced in the previous version of this book). This section also covers Office XP's stellar graphics and document-scanning tools. Clippit, the annoying Office Assistant, has a diminished role in Office XP; if the pesky paper clip somehow survived the upgrade process on your computer, we show you how to make it disappear, permanently, in Chapter 6.

Office 2000 was no slouch at creating and editing Web pages; Office XP is even more skilled at HTML editing tasks. Turn to Chapter 7, "Using Office on the Web," for in-depth instructions on how you can create, edit, and publish sophisticated Web pages without having to tangle with HTML tags.

Outlook 2002 earns the award for most improved Office application. After you master its sometimes overwhelming interface, you'll use it to tie together contacts, calendars, tasks, and e-mail. In Part II, "Using Outlook," we'll help you tame the flood of e-mail, banish spam forever, keep your address book up to date, and set up reminders so that you never miss another appointment.

Part III, "Using Word," covers the oldest and most polished productivity application in Office. We'll walk you through every customization option (including a few you probably never even knew you needed). We'll show you how to supercharge your text-editing and formatting skills, how to manage long documents, and how to automate everyday documents so that they practically write themselves.

Part IV, "Using Excel," shows you tricks you never realized you could perform with this incredibly versatile tool. Check out the examples in our formatting chapters to see how you can turn drab rows and columns into eye-catching data graphics. We'll explain how to master any of Excel's 300+ functions, as well as which ones are worth memorizing. If you struggled with PivotTables in previous versions of Office, turn straight to Chapter 27. PivotTables (and their graphics cousins, PivotCharts) will change your life—we promise. And we'll show you how to use Excel to create bulletproof worksheets and data-entry forms that you can safely share over a network, with even the most clumsy co-workers.

Of all the Office applications, PowerPoint is probably the least appreciated. In Part V, "Using PowerPoint," we explain how this program really works, and we'll help you create compelling presentations that you can deliver in front of a large audience or a small one—or completely unattended over the Web.

In Part VI, "Other Office Applications," we focus on two extra-strength programs found in selected Office versions. Access is Microsoft's industrial-strength database management program. Beginning with Chapter 34, we explain how to build tables, forms, and reports, as well as simple (and not-so-simple) queries to find and filter data. We'll also clue you in on techniques you can use to automate everyday business tasks without having to become a programmer.

FrontPage, another high-end Office application, makes the grade as a comprehensive, useful tool for Web site designers at almost all levels of expertise. In Office XP, its integration with the rest of the suite is complete, and every serious Office user with Web aspirations should take the time to learn it. Check out Chapters 36 and 37 for details.

If you've tinkered with Word and Excel macros in previous Office versions, Part VII, "Automating Office with Macros and VBA," will take you to the next level. We explain the core concepts of VBA, and we'll help you build up a library of useful macros and mini-programs that you can use to become more productive.

If you need to install Office on one PC or several hundred, we'll run through all your options in one of two appendixes at the back of the book. In the last appendix, we'll show you how to use the valuable utilities you'll find in *Que's Special Edition WOPR XP/2002 Pack* (available exclusively over the Web to purchasers of this book).

What Is Que's Special Edition WOPR XP/2002 Pack?

WOPR XP/2002 (pronounced "whopper") is available exclusively through Que books. WOPR is the #1 Office add-in, providing a custom set of tools to enhance Office XP. The copy of WOPR XP/2002 available on Que's Web site is fully licensed at no additional cost to you, the owner of this book. This isn't shareware, freeware, trialware, demoware, or limited in any other way.

For more information on WOPR, see Appendix B, "What's on Que's WOPR XP/2002 Pack."

Conventions Used in This Book

Special conventions are used to help you get the most from this book and from Office XP.

Text Conventions

Various typefaces in this book identify terms and other special objects. These special typefaces include the following:

Type	Meaning
Italic	New terms or phrases when initially defined. An italic term followed by a page number indicates the page where that term is first defined.
Monospace	Information that you type, Web addresses, or onscreen messages.
UPPERCASE	Typically used to indicate Excel objects, such as functions and cell references.
Initial Caps	Menus, dialog box names, dialog box elements, and commands are capitalized.

Key combinations are represented with a plus sign. For example, if the text calls for you to enter Ctrl+S, you would press the Ctrl key and the S key at the same time.

SECRETS OF THE OFFICE MASTERS

While using Office, you'll find many features that work well together or others that simply don't work well at all without some poking and prodding. We've used this chapter-ending element to point out some key areas in which you can combine features or find startlingly productive new uses for everyday features.

SPECIAL ELEMENTS

Throughout this book, you'll find Tips, Notes, Cautions, Sidebars, Cross References, and Troubleshooting Tips. These elements provide a variety of information, ranging from warnings you shouldn't miss to ancillary information that will enrich your Office experience, but isn't required reading.

ED AND WOODY'S "SIGNATURE" TIPS

Tip from

Ed & Woody

Tips are designed to point out features, annoyances, and tricks of the trade that you might otherwise miss. These aren't wimpy, run-of-the-mill tips that you learned the first week you used Office and don't need us to tell you. Watch for our signatures on the tips to indicate some industrial-strength—and in many cases never-before-documented—information.

NOTES

Note

Notes point out items that you should be aware of, although you can skip these if you're in a hurry. Generally, we've added notes as a way to give you some extra information on a topic without weighing you down.

CAUTIONS

Caution

Pay attention to Cautions! These could save you precious hours in lost work. Don't say we didn't warn you.

TROUBLESHOOTING NOTES

We designed these elements to call attention to common pitfalls that you're likely to encounter. When you see a Troubleshooting note, you can flip to the "Troubleshooting" section at the end of the chapter to learn how to solve or avoid a problem.

CROSS REFERENCES

Cross references are designed to point you to other locations in this book (or other books in the Que family) that will provide supplemental or supporting information. Cross references appear as follows:

→ For a full discussion of the wonders of PivotTables, **see** "How PivotTable and PivotChart Reports Work," **p. 274**.

SIDEBARS

Want to Know More?
Sidebars are designed to provide information that is ancillary to the topic being discussed. Read these if you want to learn more about an application or task.

COMMON TASKS AND FEATURES

CHAPTER 1

AN OVERVIEW OF OFFICE XP

In this chapter

WHAT'S NEW IN OFFICE XP

In a world that moves at Internet speed, it's difficult to believe that Microsoft Office has been around, in one version or another, for more than a decade. With a user base that's measured in the tens of millions, it's also difficult to imagine that anyone is seeing Word, Excel, and the rest of Office for the first time. But absorbing the changes in a new version can be a daunting task.

If you work for a large corporation or just never found a particularly compelling reason to upgrade, you might have skipped over a version or two to get to Office XP. If you've previously used Office 97, you have a lot to absorb, because Microsoft has made dramatic changes to Office in the four years since that program was released.

For the sake of this book, we're going to assume you have at least a nodding familiarity with one version of Office or another. If you're upgrading from Office 97 or earlier, you'll see a completely new interface, with different toolbar buttons and redesigned dialog boxes that are immediately apparent. If you're upgrading from Office 2000, on the other hand, the differences aren't so obvious—at least not at first boot. Many of the basic Office interface elements—including toolbars, menus, and the individual applications that make up Office—should look refreshingly familiar. And with the exception of Access, the file formats in Office XP programs are identical to their Office 2000 counterparts; so you should be able to open, edit, and save all your documents, worksheets, and presentations without any hitches.

> **Note**
>
> As we explain later in this chapter, the XP label applies only to the Office package itself. Individual programs in the suite are identified with the 2002 label—Word 2002 and Excel 2002, for instance. And to make things even more confusing, the internal version number of each program is 10.0.

Still, it should only take a couple of clicks in Office XP to uncover some pleasant surprises as well as a few irritating flaws—sometimes on the same screen. So what's new? In general, the changes fall into three broad categories: improvements designed to make everyday features easier to use; changes that allow Office programs to recover from errors more gracefully; and new Office tools, including slick utilities that let you scan documents directly into Office programs.

CHANGES IN THE OFFICE INTERFACE

You'll probably notice dozens of small changes in Office XP programs, all designed to enhance usability. The common Save As and Open dialog boxes, for instance, include new options to customize the *Places Bar* on the left, which gives you one-click access to common locations where you're likely to store files you've worked with previously. Instead of being limited to 5 shortcuts, as in Office 2000, you can add your own shortcuts to this list and shrink the icons so you can see 10 at a time.

→ For details on how to use and customize the Places Bar, **see** "Customizing Toolbars," **p. 30**.

Other usability-inspired interface improvements include reorganized dialog boxes and more helpful messages. But two interface innovations in Office XP stand above the rest.

Smart Tags are small indicators that appear in Word documents, Excel workbooks, and PowerPoint presentations when the program recognizes a certain type of data. Each time you paste text from the Clipboard, for instance, you see a Paste Options Smart Tag (see Figure 1.1), which lets you tweak the format of the pasted data. Excel uses Smart Tags to identify possible worksheet errors. PowerPoint tags AutoFit and AutoLayout decisions.

Figure 1.1
Smart Tags save you time by allowing you to adjust pasted data instead of manually reformatting it.

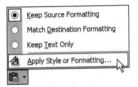

The pop-up menus available from Smart Tags can save you a tremendous amount of time be eliminating the need to continually undo and redo actions to get the formatting you're looking for.

Task panes are the second huge usability improvement used in all Office programs. These small vertical panes, which usually appear at the right side of the program window, are used for opening new files, showing styles and formatting in a Word document, and working with the enhanced Office Clipboard (see Figure 1.2).

Figure 1.2
The task pane at the right of this program window adjusts to show different types of data, including items copied to the Clipboard.

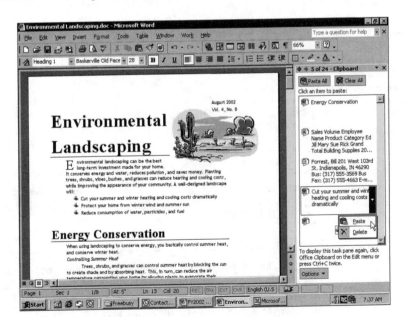

→ For an in-depth discussion of the Office Clipboard, see "How Office Extends the Windows Clipboard," **p. 132**.

SPEECH AND HANDWRITING RECOGNITION

Microsoft researchers have been working on alternate data-entry technologies for years, including the ability to recognize and respond to speech and handwriting. In Office XP, these new technologies are interesting, but frankly they're more of a parlor trick than a productivity booster. If you're unable to work with a keyboard or mouse, you might find the complex setup and training procedures worth the return. Most Office users, however, should wait until a future Office version.

→ For a quick overview of how to enter text with a microphone, see "Using Speech Recognition to Enter Text," **p. 90**.

RELIABILITY AND RECOVERY FEATURES

Anyone who's ever lost hours of work because of a program crash knows what pure, unadulterated frustration feels like. The bad news is that Office XP programs still crash. The good news is that your chances of recovering the file you were working with at the time of the crash are dramatically better in Office XP.

For starters, when any Office program hangs—that is, it refuses to respond to keystrokes, mouse clicks, swear words, or blunt objects—you can call on the Microsoft Office Application Recovery console (see Figure 1.3). This new utility provides a safe way to shut down a program and recover the document currently in memory. Although it's not completely foolproof, we've been amazed at the number of times this feature has come through in a crisis.

Figure 1.3
Is an application refusing to respond? Shut it down gracefully and recover your unsaved data using this utility.

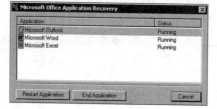

Recovered documents appear in a pane to the left of the main application window (see Figure 1.4). You can view each recovered file and decide whether to save it as a new version, replace an existing version, merge the recovered document into another document, or discard the recovered file.

Tip from

EQ & Woody

If an Office program stops responding to input but Windows is still working, don't use Ctrl+Alt+Del to close it. Instead, open the Programs menu, choose Microsoft Office Tools, and click Microsoft Office Application Recovery. Choose the Recover Application option to attempt to save the current file and restart gracefully.

Figure 1.4
After a crash, Office programs can often recover the files you were working with at the time of the crash.

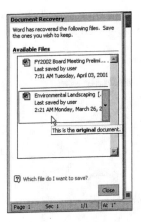

AN OVERVIEW OF OFFICE XP APPLICATIONS

The basic lineup of programs in Microsoft Office XP is essentially identical to those that have made up every Office version since Office 97. Overall, the package consists of five core applications—Word, Excel, Outlook, PowerPoint, and Access—as well as a handful of smaller programs. FrontPage is available in high-end editions, and Microsoft tosses a free copy of Publisher into some Office boxes. The sections that follow describe what's new in each of these applications.

Note

> This book covers most of the applications found in the Professional Special Edition of Office XP. If you've purchased a different Office edition, the program code for individual applications is the same and our advice applies just as well. In particular, if you use the Standard edition of Office, you'll find everything you need in here. The only commonly found Office component we don't cover is Publisher (included in the Small Business Edition of Office XP, bundled with some new PCs) and the high-end programming tools in the Developers Edition.

OUTLOOK 2002

The biggest news for Outlook users is that Microsoft has finally cured the program's split personality. You don't have to deal with the confusing split between Corporate/Workgroup and Internet Mail Only modes that made setting up Outlook 98 and 2000 so tortuous. Instead, you can set up connections to Internet accounts, Web-based e-mail such as Hotmail, and Exchange mailboxes from one convenient dialog box (see Figure 1.5).

→ For details on how to configure e-mail access in Outlook, **see** "Setting Up E-mail Accounts and Connections," **p. 190**.

Generally, Outlook gets an overall usability polish, with improvements such as AutoComplete for addresses in new messages you compose. Outlook 2002 also does a better job of cutting back on screen clutter. In previous versions, each reminder popped up in its own window; Outlook 2002 consolidates them in a single Reminders window, where you can deal with them all at once. Managing accounts is easier too, with a wide array of online and offline synchronization options.

Figure 1.5
You can set up any account type from this redesigned Outlook dialog box.

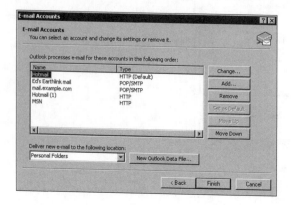

WORD 2002

The oldest and most mature of the Office programs, Word is also the most popular. It's an extremely versatile tool—ideal for creating short documents, such as letters and memos, with enough layout and graphics-handling capabilities to also make it suitable for sophisticated publishing chores. Thanks to its HTML-editing capabilities, it's also an excellent starting point when you want to create a Web page—a topic covered in great detail in this book.

More than any other Office program, Word takes full advantage of Smart Tags, such as those used for AutoCorrect options. If you've been baffled by the thicket of formatting options in previous versions, you'll be impressed by two new task panes that let you see Styles and Formatting and Reveal Formatting in the current document (see Figure 1.6).

→ For full details on how Word's formatting options work, **see** "Applying and Modifying Formats," **p. 338**.

Other usability enhancements in Word 2002 include a new Mail Merge Wizard that uses the task pane, and improved tools for working with bulleting and numbered lists. You'll also find big changes in document sharing, such as a new markup view that shows comments in bubbles in a document's margin.

EXCEL 2002

As an all-purpose number-crunching tool, Excel is incredibly useful for tasks as simple as balancing a checkbook or as complex as modeling a hostile takeover of a Fortune 500 corporation. Experienced Excel users will notice small usability improvements in Excel 2002, such as tiny cell markers that highlight possible worksheet errors with Smart Tags (see Figure 1.7) and an easier interface for inserting functions into the formula bar.

Figure 1.6
Working with styles and other formatting options is easier in Word 2002 than in previous versions, thanks to this task pane.

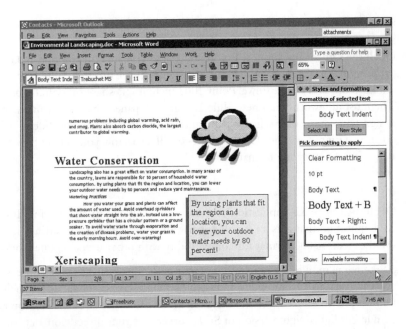

Figure 1.7
On-the-fly error-checking capabilities make Excel 2002 worksheets more accurate.

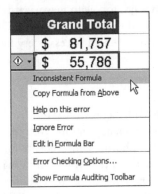

Most of the improvements in Excel 2002 fix longstanding annoyances from earlier versions. For instance, you can now color-code worksheet tabs, find and replace text and numbers across an entire workbook, and add pictures to headers and footers.

POWERPOINT 2002

PowerPoint has always been an effective way to create PC-based slide shows for presentations in front of a large audience. Recent versions add the capability to create effective Web-based presentations as well. You can't truly appreciate the effectiveness of Web-based presentations until you create one. PowerPoint can turn slide titles into a table of contents in the left pane of a frame, and then display each slide on the right, with the viewer pointing and clicking to drive the show.

→ For step-by-step instructions that will help you get a PowerPoint presentation into Web format in record time, **see** "Creating a Presentation," **p. 748**.

Of all the Office applications, PowerPoint has earned a reputation as the most user-friendly, probably because many PowerPoint users dust off the program only every few months, unlike Word and Excel. PowerPoint 2002 includes its share of usability improvements, too. The most noteworthy is a new Slide Design task pane, which lets you see and preview design templates, color schemes, and animation effects while the slide is visible. Unlike the documentation—or other Office books—we'll also show you exactly how to use each of PowerPoint's many file formats.

ACCESS 2002

Of all the Office XP applications, Access is by far the most challenging. It's the only Office XP application that gets a new file format (although the default settings let you continue to use the Access 2000 format for compatibility with other users on a network).

As the name implies, Access lets you tap into data from a variety of sources. For example, you can use it as a front end to industrial-strength corporate databases such as SQL Server. Or you can install a new component called the SQL Server 2000 Desktop Engine, a compatible but lightweight version of SQL Server that runs directly on a client machine, and save data locally. The connections work both ways, too, with new wizards that help you create HTML documents that are directly bound to data in a database. Using these Data Access pages, you can let anyone on your network run an Access query by opening a Web page and clicking a button.

FRONTPAGE 2002

Although it's possible to create good-looking Web pages with Word, you'll quickly run out of gas if you want to build sophisticated pages or manage entire Web sites. FrontPage is now firmly entrenched as the leading HTML authoring and Web-site management tool you can buy. FrontPage 2002 is a full-fledged member of the Office family, with the same editing tools, menus, and customizable toolbars you'll find in the other Office programs. (It's included in the Premium Edition of Office only, although it's also available as a standalone program.)

The coverage of FrontPage in this book includes full instructions on how to create world-class Web pages and maintain a complex Web site.

ONLINE HELP FOR EXPERT USERS

Office XP includes a sophisticated and remarkably thorough help system with content for any Office user, regardless of his technical sophistication or experience level. The help system has three interdependent components:

- **The Help Content Itself, Including an Extensive Index**—All the individual Help topics look and behave like Web pages (one-click "hot" links, the back button for navigation, and so on) because they are written in HTML.

- **A Natural Language-Based Search Engine, Called the *Answer Wizard*—**In some circumstances the Answer Wizard will find relevant information that doesn't turn up in keyword searches.
- **The Office Assistant Character—**This "social interface" to Help information is the single most provocative Office feature: You either love that %$#@! paper clip, or you hate it.

This rich set of interface tools gives you a variety of choices in how you approach the search for answers. You needn't use the Office Assistant to take advantage of the natural-language search engine, for example. You can also use the help system, with or without the Office Assistant, as a quick way to search through a list of keywords. And if you don't find the answer in the online help system, you have several advanced support options.

Tip from

EQ & Woody

Of course, sometimes the best interface is no interface. If all you want is answers, without having to deal with dialog boxes or a cartoon character, type a keyword or phrase into the tiny box at the top right corner of any Office program window. (You can't miss it; look for the light gray "Type a question for help" prompt.)

When fully expanded, the Office Help engine includes two panes, as shown in Figure 1.8. The Navigation pane (left) includes three tabs that offer different ways of locating help information. The topic pane at the right displays the contents of the currently selected topic. Two buttons at the top left of the Help window control whether the Navigation pane is visible and how the Help window docks with the program window. In a default Office installation, however, you have to get past the Office Assistant to get to this view.

Figure 1.8
Office XP uses this two-pane hypertext Help engine to display Help topics.

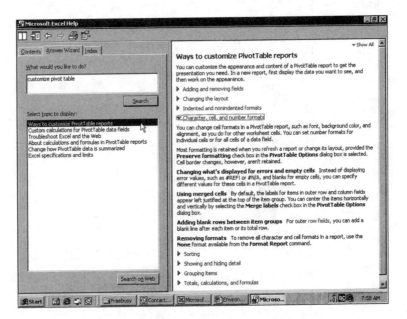

Normally, when you open a Help window, Office resizes the currently active program window and tucks the Help pane into a window just to the right of the program window. When you close the Help window, the program window returns to its full size again. On a high-resolution system, you'll probably appreciate this arrangement, but if desktop space is at a premium, or if you want to keep the Help window open but minimized while you work, you'll need to make an adjustment. Click the Untile button at the top left of the Help window to allow the Help pane to float; click it again to restore the AutoTile configuration.

USING THE OFFICE ASSISTANT

The Office Assistant in Office XP gives you simple and quick entrée to Help's Answer Wizard and keyword searches, but only if you want it. By default, this helpful (and occasionally annoying) cartoon character is hidden. You can hide it for good by right-clicking and choosing the Hide button. After a few tries, the Assistant will get the hint and offer to disappear permanently.

To search for help on a topic, click the Office Assistant, type your question or keywords relevant to your topic, and click Search. Assuming there are six or more "hits" associated with your query, the Assistant presents five answers in the first balloon, with a See More button. Click See More, and the Assistant displays the next four hits. Regardless of how many hits the Assistant actually registered, at the end of the nine topics in this list you'll find a button that says None of the Above, Search for More on the Web (see Figure 1.9).

Figure 1.9
The Assistant returns a limited number of hits to your query, even if it finds a wealth of information.

Tip from

Ed & Woody

The Office Assistant shows you a maximum of nine hits from the Answer Wizard. Period. If you don't find the answer you're looking for in this set of nine topics, do *not* automatically jump onto the Web and look for more information. Instead, follow the instructions in the next section to review the full set of answers available from the Answer Wizard–the topic you're looking for is most likely in that list.

USING THE ANSWER WIZARD

The Answer Wizard, Microsoft's natural-language Help search engine, lets you pose questions in full sentences or by typing keywords. The Office Assistant, the Answer Wizard, and the Help box at the top of the program window all use the same program code to find answers; the key difference is the number of answers they're willing to cough up in response to your question.

If the Office Assistant is enabled, bringing up the Answer Wizard is a needlessly complex task: Ask the Office Assistant a question, click Search, and choose a Help topic (any topic will do). When the Help window appears, click the Show button to display the Navigation pane. Then—finally—click the Answer Wizard tab. As Figure 1.10 demonstrates, the Office Assistant and the Answer Wizard use the same search results, in the same order, but the Answer Wizard lets you see the entire list.

Figure 1.10
The Answer Wizard displays far more results than the Office Assistant, even though both use exactly the same program code.

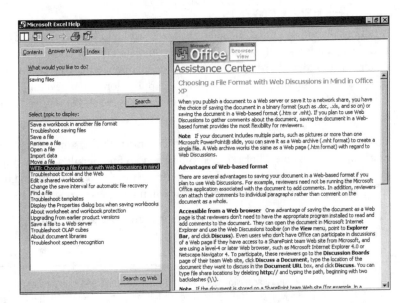

Tip from

EQ & Woody

If you prefer to work without the Office Assistant, you can disable it without uninstalling it. Right-click the Office Assistant, choose Options, and uncheck the Use the Office Assistant box. With this option disabled, clicking the Help button or pressing F1 takes you straight to Help. (To turn the Assistant back on, choose Help, Show the Office Assistant.) If you frequently use the Answer Wizard, Help Contents, or Index, but you also want the Office Assistant to be readily available, check the Use the Office Assistant box and uncheck the Respond to F1 Key box. By using this option, you can click the Help button to show the Office Assistant or press the F1 key to bypass the Assistant and go directly to Help.

When you type in your query and click Search, the Answer Wizard fills the box marked Select Topic to Display, ranking each hit according to its own internal (frequently inscrutable) criteria: The hit deemed most likely to answer your question appears at the beginning of the list—the one least likely is at the bottom.

Note

The Office Assistant latches on to the nine hits with the highest scores. Because the algorithm frequently fails to recognize the keywords in a natural-language query, those highest scores might go to hits that have nothing to do with your question.

BROWSING THE HELP CONTENTS

A full installation of Office XP splatters dozens of Help files throughout various locations in your Program Files folder. Each one has a complete table of contents, organized by topic in a more-or-less logical order, not unlike the table of contents you would find in a book. (In many cases, asking for Help from within an application opens several Help files, in which case the Help engine combines the contents list from each file to give the illusion of a single table of contents.)

Browsing the Contents pane for information can be cumbersome—pages break at the end of a topic, for example—but it can also be a way to find detailed information you didn't even know to look for. Searching through this list can also help you find information related to a particular topic that might not appear when you use other search techniques.

To search the Contents pane, open a Help window, display the Navigation tab, and then click the Contents tab (see Figure 1.11).

Tip from

EQ & Woody

If you're browsing the table of contents for a broad overview of any Office program, make it easier by expanding the full table of contents. With the Contents list visible, right-click on the Navigation pane and choose Open All. To collapse the list again, right-click and choose Close All.

Figure 1.11
Each Office Help topic contains a full table of contents.

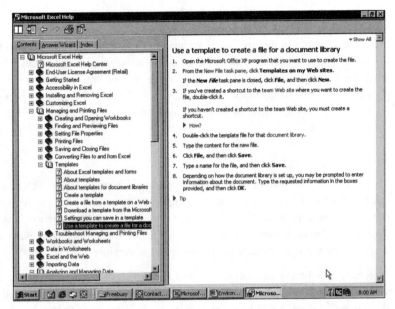

USING THE INDEX TO FIND KEYWORDS

To perform a quick keyword search, or to browse through the Help system's alphabetical index (which resembles the index in a book), open the Help window, show the Navigation pane, and click the Index tab (see Figure 1.12).

Figure 1.12
The Help system's extensive Index will frequently help you find details overlooked by the Answer Wizard.

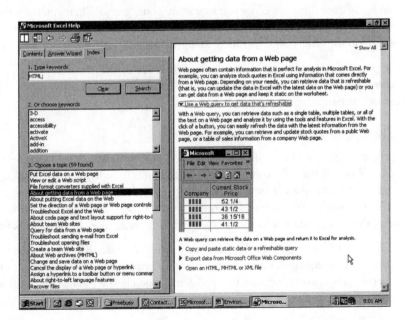

ADVANCED SUPPORT OPTIONS

Microsoft delivers an extraordinary amount of support information for all Office versions on the Web. That commitment doesn't extend to answering individual questions free—if you purchase a retail version of Office, you get two free assisted support incidents, over the phone or via Web-based support options, while all other personal support options cost at least $35. But if you're willing to search long enough, chances are good that you'll find the answer yourself.

USING THE OFFICE RESOURCE KIT

Microsoft sells its *Office Resource Kit* as a heavy and high-priced book/CD combination. You can buy the book if you insist, but we suggest that you save your money and download only the pieces you need from the Web. Every word in the printed version is available online from `http://www.microsoft.com/office/ork/`, as are several special-purpose utilities. And the Web version is up to date, unlike the printed version.

In general, the Office Resource Kit isn't for end users or even power users; rather, it's for system administrators and information-technology professionals who need tools to help them deploy Office XP in large organizations. Still, some of the tools are extremely useful in small offices and even in one-person shops. If you want to be an Office power user, this site is a must.

USING HELP ON THE WEB

When you click the Office Assistant's None of the Above, Search for More on the Web option, Office does not allow you to modify your query. When you click the Send and Go to the Web button, Office connects you directly to the Office Web site, formulates a search based on the criteria you specified, and presents you with the search results.

(If you bypass the Office Assistant and choose Help, Office on the Web, you'll connect directly to the home page for the Office program you're currently using, without sending a search as part of your page request.)

SEARCHING THE MICROSOFT KNOWLEDGE BASE

The mother lode of all Office information, *Microsoft's Knowledge Base* (also known as the MSKB or just the KB), contains tens of thousands of individual articles, ranging from succinct overviews of features to detailed bug reports to exhaustive technical-reference material. The Knowledge Base is updated continuously. When you talk to a Microsoft tech support rep, this is the online reference book in which they're most likely to look for information.

The fastest way to get into the KB is through Microsoft's Knowledge base Search page (`http://search.support.microsoft.com/kb/c.asp`). Make sure you select Office XP (or the specific program that's giving you problems), and choose the option to ask a question using a free-text query.

MSKB articles are all identified by number, generally a Q followed by six digits: Q233529, for example. MSKB article numbers serve as a kind of techy shorthand: "To solve that problem, check out article Q174293." If someone gives you an MSKB article number, type it into the search criteria box on the Knowledge Base Search page, choose the Specific Article ID Number option, and click Go. The article (and any others that refer to the article by number) will be listed.

OTHER RESOURCES

Microsoft maintains dozens of newsgroups on the Internet that provide peer-to-peer assistance. (In other words, the answers come from other users, Microsoft doesn't necessarily monitor them, and you have no guarantee the information you receive will be accurate.) Most of the heavy lifting in the newsgroups is performed by MVPs—people chosen by Microsoft because of their knowledge and dedication to the newsgroups. Although the MVPs deserve kudos for keeping the newsgroups going, they're all volunteers, and they don't have Microsoft's extensive support resources at their fingertips. For the most part, you can expect them to search the exact same online sources that are available to you. if you can get the attention of an experienced MVP with a well-stocked collection of bookmarks, you may save some time.

To subscribe to the Microsoft newsgroups, use a newsgroup reader (such as Outlook Express, which can be launched from Outlook 2002 by choosing View, Go To, News). Look for newsgroups starting with the name *microsoft.public*.

An even bigger bargain is Microsoft's TechNet, an incredible online resource that is also available on CD and DVD. TechNet includes the following content:

- The entire Microsoft Knowledge Base
- White papers, technical notes, tips
- Resource kits, drivers, patches, service packs

At $300 per year (USA), a monthly TechNet subscription might not sound cheap, but for system administrators and PC professionals, it's a lifesaver. If you don't need monthly updates, almost all TechNet content is available free at http://www.microsoft.com/technet.

Tip from

EQ & Woody

Your most important source of up-to-date information about Office is *Woody's Office Watch* (if we do say so ourselves). WOW delivers weekly updates on every aspect of Microsoft Office. If you want to know what's happening in the Office realm—from the latest freebies, to bug reports, to tips and workarounds, and more—WOW brings it to your e-mail inbox, free, every week.

Woody, Ed, and WOW Editor Peter Deegan also keep you abreast of changes, errors, and updates to this humble tome. It's like an update subscription to *Special Edition Using Microsoft Office XP*—and it's free.

More than 100,000 Office users rely on WOW to keep them up-to-date. You should, too. To subscribe, send a blank e-mail message to wow@wopr.com, or drop by www.wopr.com/wow.

CHAPTER 2

Customizing the Office Intertface

In this chapter

CONTROLLING AUTOMATIC INTERFACE CHANGES

Each Office application includes hundreds of customization options. Because Office uses shared program code to display toolbars and menus, the techniques for customizing these elements are absolutely consistent from one application to another.

Just as in Office 2000, the single most controversial customization option is the personalized menus and toolbars feature. Unlike other Windows programs in which toolbars and pull-down menus are fixed, Office menus and toolbars change from day to day. Unless you specifically disable this feature, each Office program monitors your usage patterns and "personalizes" menus and toolbars. The idea is to reduce clutter in each menu by showing you only the choices you use regularly, rather than potentially confusing you with a long menu that contains many choices. In practice, however, personalized menus can add confusion by causing menu choices to disappear and reappear, seemingly at random—especially for expert users who know an application's menus inside and out.

You can configure the precise way that personalized menus and toolbars behave, and if you don't like this feature, you can disable it completely. This section explains how the process works, and how you can take charge of it.

Note

You can customize all Office settings for all users on a network, or for various groups of users based on a network directory. This option typically is found on managed networks that use system policies, which are stored on a Windows NT/2000/XP server. For detailed instructions on how to configure and enforce system policies in Windows 2000 Server, check out *Special Edition Using Microsoft Windows 2000 Server,* published by Que (ISBN: 0-7897-2122-8).

HOW PERSONALIZED TOOLBARS AND MENUS WORK

When you first begin working with an Office XP application, the personalized menus option is enabled. When you click any item on the menu bar, you'll see only a subset of the choices available under that menu. (You might see short versions of cascading menus as well.) If the choice you want isn't on the short menu, force the full menus to appear by using any of the following three techniques:

- Click the chevron character at the bottom of the short menu.
- Leave the short menu open for more than three seconds without making a selection.
- Click a specific menu item twice in a row; the first click displays the short menu, and the second expands it to the full menu.

Tip from

EQ & Woody

If you detest personalized menus, but you find yourself working at another user's machine where this option is enabled, here's how to keep your sanity: Get in the habit of double-clicking top-level choices on the main menu bar. By double-clicking, you'll blast right past the short menus.

Don't confuse the grayed-out choices on a menu with hidden choices. As in all Windows applications, grayed-out menu choices mean that an option is unavailable in the current context; Office applications use 3D effects to display the difference between visible and hidden menu choices.

Office uses an extraordinarily complex algorithm that examines usage patterns over time to define which buttons appear on short toolbars. In general, personalized menus and toolbars follow these rules:

PART

I

CH

2

- When you first install Office XP, you see a default short selection for pull-down menus in each application. If you leave the Standard and Formatting toolbars on a single row, you'll see a default short selection for each of these toolbars as well.

- Default menu items remain visible for at least six different application sessions on six different days in which you use other items on the same menu. If you use Excel every day, but you use the Data menu only once a month, for example, it might be six months or more before the default choices on that menu change.

- Each time you use a hidden menu item or toolbar button, it is promoted to the list of visible entries. In the case of toolbar buttons, Office might hide a button to make room for the newly promoted button.

- Menu items remain visible for at least three different sessions on three different days after you use them.

- The more you use a menu item, the longer it stays around. If you work on a complex PowerPoint presentation for several weeks and regularly use the Action Buttons choice on the Slide Show menu, that option will remain visible for much longer than if you clicked it one day as an experiment.

- Office never changes the order of items on toolbars and menus (although you can use customization options to do so). When an Office application promotes a menu choice or makes a toolbar button visible, it appears in the exact same position (relative to other menu choices) as when you display full menus.

DISABLING ON-THE-FLY INTERFACE CHANGES

If you're an Office expert, you'll probably find this constant shifting of menus and toolbars more confusing than helpful. If that's the case, you can disable personalized menus and toolbars. Select Tools, Customize, click the Options tab, and check both boxes in the Personalized Menus and Toolbars section, as shown in Figure 2.1.

RESTORING DEFAULT MENUS AND TOOLBARS

You might be one of the rare expert users who actually prefers personalized menus. Or maybe you're setting up Office for a novice user and you feel this option will make her work easier. To restore personalized menus and toolbars to their default settings, select Tools, Customize, click the Options tab, and click the Reset My Usage Data button. Then clear both check boxes in the Personalized Menus and Toolbars section.

Figure 2.1
To force Office to display full menus and toolbars at all times, check both boxes in the top section of this dialog box.

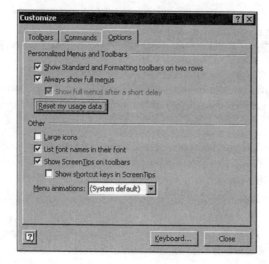

You also can select this option if you shift a machine from one user to another without setting up a new user profile or after a training session in which users explore a large number of features they're unlikely to use regularly.

Note

This option has no effect on buttons you add or remove using explicit customization options. It also has no effect if you've chosen the Always Show Full Menus option.

CUSTOMIZING TOOLBARS

Each Office application includes an assortment of toolbars in addition to the Standard and Formatting toolbars. Some, such as Word's Outlining toolbar and Excel's PivotTable toolbar, appear automatically when you begin performing specific tasks. You can show specific toolbars and arrange them onscreen when they're needed and then hide them when you're finished working with them. In every Office application, you can also customize toolbars by adding and removing buttons, and you can create new custom toolbars that contain exactly the buttons and menu choices you specify.

Tip from

EQ & Woody

On a monitor with limited resolution, you might prefer to toggle between the one- and two-row settings for the Standard and Formatting toolbars. In Office XP, this option is always available by clicking the arrow at the right of either toolbar. This is a welcome change from Office 2000, which required that you dive into dialog boxes to adjust these settings.

SHOWING, HIDING, AND ARRANGING TOOLBARS

To display or hide toolbars, right-click any visible toolbar or right-click the menu bar to see a list of commonly available toolbars, similar to the one in Figure 2.2. Click any item in the list to display that toolbar; click a checked item to hide the toolbar.

Figure 2.2
This list of toolbars shows only a subset of those that are actually available; use the Customize dialog box to see a more complete listing.

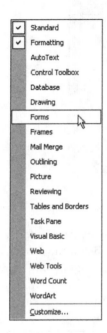

Curiously, not all available toolbars are shown on this pop-up list. If you work with a Word document in Normal view, for example, you'll see a selection of only 19 toolbars on this list, although 30 are actually available. To make any of these additional toolbars available, select Tools, Customize, and click the Toolbars tab (see Figure 2.3). Check the box next to any item on the list to make that toolbar visible.

Tip from
EQ & Woody

If you use the Customize dialog box to display a nonstandard toolbar, you don't need to go through all those clicks to hide it again. If the toolbar is docked, grab its left edge and drag it into the program window so it floats, and then click the Close (X) button in the upper-right corner of the toolbar.

Figure 2.3
This list of available toolbars offers more choices than the simple pop-up menu you see when you right-click a toolbar.

When working with toolbars, you have three positioning options:

- You can dock any toolbar to any side of the screen. By default, for example, the Standard and Formatting toolbars are docked just below the menu bar in every application, and the Drawing toolbar attaches itself to the bottom of the screen. Click the sizing handle (the thin horizontal bar at the left or top edge of a docked toolbar) and drag the toolbar to any edge of the screen to snap it into its new position.

Tip from

EQ & Woody

Not all toolbars actually work properly when docked to the side of the screen. Some drop-down list controls, such as the Font and Style choices on the Formatting toolbar or the Line Style selector on the Borders toolbar, aren't visible on a side-docked toolbar, and pull-down menus can be harder to read when displayed sideways. Toolbars that contain only buttons, such as the Reviewing toolbar in Word, Excel, and PowerPoint, work best in this configuration.

- You can dock two or more toolbars on the same edge, side by side, or one over the other. Drag the sizing handle to move a toolbar on its row.
- You can also drag any docked toolbar into the application window to let it "float." This option is best suited for controls you use when designing forms and charts, creating macros, working with objects in the drawing layer, and editing PivotTables. In fact, Excel's PivotTable Field List toolbar does not allow you to dock it to the bottom of the screen because doing so would render it practically useless.

When you add more buttons to a toolbar than will fit in the current screen width, or when you dock two or more toolbars on the same row, there might not be enough room to display all buttons. In that case, the application shows only those buttons you have used most recently; click the down arrow at the right of the toolbar to see additional choices.

If you regularly use specific sets of toolbars, create macros that display and position the toolbars you want, and then clear them away as needed. Assign the macros to menus or buttons on the Standard toolbar for quick access.

Use the following code, for example, to show the Web and Drawing toolbars, with the Web toolbar floating and the Drawing toolbar docked to the bottom of the screen. The .Left and .Top properties define the starting point, in pixels, from the left edge and top edge for a floating toolbar:

```
Sub ShowFavoriteToolbars()
    With CommandBars("Web")
        .Visible = True
        .Position = msoBarFloating
        .Left = 300
        .Top = 400
    End With
    With CommandBars("Drawing")
        .Visible = True
        .Position = msoBarBottom
    End With
End Sub
```

To hide all toolbars except the Standard and Formatting, use the following code:

```
Sub HideAllToolbars()
On Error Resume Next
For Each cmdbar In CommandBars
    If cmdbar.Name = "Standard" Or cmdbar.Name = "Formatting" Then
        cmdbar.Visible = True
    Else
        cmdbar.Visible = False
    End If
Next
On Error Goto 0
End Sub
```

→ For a thorough introduction to the art and science of macros and VBA code, **see** "How Macros Work," **p. 964**.

ADDING AND REMOVING BUTTONS

Instead of using personalized menus and toolbars, most expert users prefer to customize built-in toolbars, adding and grouping buttons they use most often. Click the Toolbar Options arrow at the right side of any toolbar and select Add or Remove Buttons to display the list of buttons available for that toolbar, as in Figure 2.4 (if you add a button, it appears on this list as well). A check mark next to any item on the list means that button is currently visible; click to toggle this check mark and display or hide the button.

When customizing the selection of buttons on a toolbar, you're not limited to choices on the Add or Remove Buttons menu. In any Office application, you can add any command, macro, or existing menu to a toolbar. In Word, you can add fonts, styles, and AutoText entries as well. Access users can also select from tables, queries, forms, and reports in the current database, plus Web pages and ActiveX controls.

Figure 2.4
Click the drop-down arrow at the right of any built-in toolbar to add or remove buttons easily.

To add a command to a toolbar, follow these steps:

1. Select Tools, Customize (or right-click any toolbar or menu and choose Customize from the bottom of the shortcut menu). The Customize dialog box opens.

2. If the toolbar you want to customize is not visible, click the Toolbars tab and check the box for that toolbar.

3. Click the Commands tab, select an entry from the Categories list on the left, and then select the command you want to add from the Commands list on the right, as in Figure 2.5.

Note

The items in the Categories list typically correspond to top-level menu choices, built-in toolbars, and some collections of tools. Only Word includes an All Commands category that consists of an alphabetized list of every available command. If you're not sure what a particular command does, select it from the Commands list and click the Description button.

4. Drag the command from the Customize dialog box to the toolbar where you want to add the button. When you see a thick black I-beam in the correct position, drop the button to add it.

Figure 2.5
Drag items from the list on the right side of this dialog box to create new toolbar buttons.

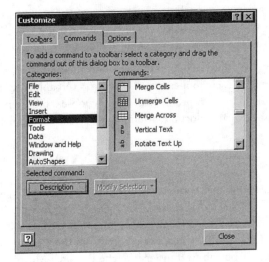

5. Repeat steps 3 and 4 to add more buttons to any toolbar.

6. When you've finished working with the toolbar, click Close to put away the Customize dialog box.

If you never use certain toolbar buttons, clear them away to make room for the buttons you do use. It's ridiculously easy to remove a button from a toolbar: Point to the button you want to remove, and then hold down the Alt key as you drag it off the toolbar—when the pointer displays a tool icon with an X, release the mouse button to delete the item. If the Customize dialog box is open, you can remove any button or menu item by dragging it off the menu bar.

Tip from

EQ & Woody

Use these same drag-and-drop techniques to move buttons and menu items, either on the same toolbar or between toolbars. From any editing window, hold down the Alt key and drag a button to move it to a different place on the same toolbar or to a different toolbar altogether. With the Customize dialog box visible, hold down the Ctrl key and drag any button to create a copy. And here's an undocumented shortcut we guarantee you haven't read anywhere else: Hold down the Ctrl and Alt keys simultaneously as you drag a button to create a copy, either on the same toolbar or on another toolbar, without opening the Customize dialog box. This technique is especially effective if you want to create slightly different versions of the same toolbar for different tasks: Base one toolbar on an existing toolbar, and then modify the new copy and use macros to switch between them for different tasks.

CREATING A NEW TOOLBAR

You're not limited to the selection of built-in toolbars—you can also create custom toolbars in any Office program, adding your own selection of buttons and menus to each new toolbar. Use custom toolbars to give yourself one-click access to styles, fonts, macros, and built-in commands. To create a new toolbar, select Tools, Customize, click the Toolbars tab, and click the New button. Give the new toolbar a name and click OK to save your changes.

How do you make a new toolbar available for all new documents and worksheets? The procedure is slightly different for each application. Use Word's Organizer to copy a toolbar from one document or template to another. Unless you choose a different location, Word stores a new toolbar in the Normal document template, `Normal.dot`, to make it available for all documents.

→ To learn more about copying elements between templates, **see** "Copying Styles and Settings Between Templates," **p. 482**.

If you open an Excel workbook that contains a custom toolbar created by someone else, you can copy it to your Personal Macro Workbook (`Personal.xls`). Open both workbooks, and then switch to `Personal.xls` and select Tools, Customize. Click the Toolbars tab and click the Attach button. Select the toolbar you want to copy from the Custom toolbars list on the left, and then click the Copy button to transfer it to the Personal Macro Workbook.

To move toolbars between Access databases, open the database to which you want to add the custom toolbar. Select File, Get External Data, Import. Select the database file that contains the toolbar or toolbars you want to copy, and then click the Options button and check Menus and Toolbars under Import. Select any other items you want to import and click OK.

Note

Outlook allows you to create custom toolbars. Because the program stores all customizations as part of the program options rather than associating them with data files, there's no need to copy these toolbars to a different location.

ADDING MACROS TO A TOOLBAR

One of the best uses for a custom toolbar is to hold a collection of macros you use for specific tasks. To help manage an Excel list, for example, you might construct a set of macros that filter and sort the list to five or six specific views. By placing all those macros on a custom toolbar, you make switching to any view at any time easy. Use a custom toolbar in Word to hold macros and AutoText entries you use when creating a specific type of document, such as an invoice or a sales report. (Skip to the end of this chapter for an example of how we created a custom toolbar for use in writing this book.)

Adding a macro to a toolbar requires slightly different techniques for each application:

- In Word, PowerPoint, and Outlook, follow the same steps as you would to add a command button; select Macros from the Categories list and the name of the macro from the Commands list. If you have macros stored in different Word templates or in the document itself, you must select the correct location from the Save In drop-down list.

■ In Excel or FrontPage, select Macros from the Categories list and drag either the Custom Menu Item or Custom Button choice onto the toolbar. Right-click the new button or menu item, select Assign Macro from the shortcut menu, and select the macro you want to use.

■ In Access, select All Macros from the Categories list and the name of the macro from the Commands list.

→ For more suggestions on how you can create shortcuts for running macros, **see** "Creating Toolbar Buttons, Menus, and Key Combinations," **p. 1015**.

CUSTOMIZING THE APPEARANCE OF TOOLBAR BUTTONS

You'll encounter unique design challenges when you create custom toolbars that mix built-in commands with macros, styles, and AutoText items. If the toolbar includes standard button and menu options, you can decide whether you want to see only an image, only text, or both.

For buttons you use infrequently, the default icon might be utterly inscrutable. By showing both the icon and the text, you don't have to constantly scan ScreenTips to see what each icon does. (Outlook, for example, uses this option effectively to show the Find and Organize buttons on the Standard toolbar in the Inbox.) Select Tools, Customize to display the Customize dialog box, and then right-click any button to display the shortcut menu shown in Figure 2.6.

Figure 2.6
Use this shortcut menu to change the text and icon that describe a toolbar button or menu choice.

The four choices on this menu let you decide whether to show icons only, text only, or a combination of both.

Most built-in commands include their own images that Office programs can use as the icon on a toolbar button. You can change the image on any button, and if you're a decent icon designer, you can use Office XP's built-in Button Editor to create your own custom button images.

Tip from

EQ & Woody

Although you can create an icon from scratch, it's usually best to start with an existing button image. If you see an image that you like on a built-in toolbar button, copy it to your custom icon using the Copy Button Image and Paste Button Image choices on the shortcut menu for each icon; then edit the pasted image. If you make a mistake, click Reset Button Image and start over.

When you have a group of buttons that work together, use a separator line to define the group. If the Customize dialog box is open, right-click the icon that begins the group and select Begin a Group from the shortcut menu. To quickly add a separator line without leaving the normal editing window, hold down the Alt key, click the button to the right of the place where you want the line to appear, and drag slightly to the right. To remove a separator line without having to go through a dialog box, hold down the Alt key, click the button to the right of the line, and drag the button over the line.

EDITING A TOOLBAR BUTTON'S ICON AND LABEL

To edit the text and icon associated with any button, first make sure the toolbar is visible. Then open the Customize dialog box and click to select the button you want to change. Click in the Name box to enter the text that will appear on the button when you select any display option other than Icon Only. The text you enter here will also appear as a ScreenTip for that button.

To edit the existing icon, right-click again and select Edit Button Image. This opens Office XP's Button Editor (see Figure 2.7). Click any color in the color box, and use the pointer to paint that color over any pixel.

Figure 2.7
Use the Office Button Editor to create images for use on toolbar buttons. Each image is limited to this palette of colors and a total size of 32 pixels square.

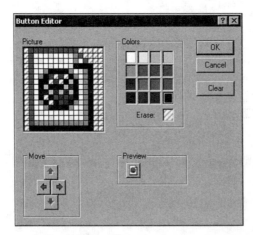

To create a custom icon, right-click the button and select Change Button Image. You can start with any of the icons shown in Figure 2.8 or build a new icon from scratch.

Figure 2.8
Office lets you choose from this assortment of somewhat hokey custom icons, or you can cut, paste, and edit an icon from an existing button.

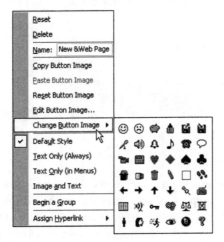

ASSIGNING A HYPERLINK TO A TOOLBAR BUTTON

All Office programs allow you to attach a hyperlink to a toolbar button, although the procedure for doing so is cumbersome. You can create a hyperlink to a Web page or to any file, on your machine or on a network. You can also assign a graphic file to a toolbar button, so you can click a button to insert a logo or other graphic you use regularly.

To attach a hyperlink to a toolbar button, you first must create a toolbar button and then customize it. Only Excel and FrontPage enable you to create a blank button or menu item; in other programs, you first must add a button—any button—using an existing command, and then customize it.

With the Customize dialog box open, right-click the button to which you want to assign the hyperlink. Select the text in the Name box and replace it with a short description of the link you want to create. Then select Assign Hyperlink. Click Open if you want the button to open a file or Web page, or click Insert Picture if you want to create a link to a graphic file.

In the Assign Hyperlink dialog box (see Figure 2.9), click the Existing File or Web Page button and select the item you want to link to the button. Click OK to create the link.

→ To learn more about using the Office hyperlinking features, **see** "Maintaining Accurate Hyperlinks," **p. 945**.

→ Use AutoText to enter large blocks of text and graphics with a few simple keystrokes; **see** "Entering Text and Graphics Automatically with AutoText and AutoCorrect," **p. 376**.

To remove a hyperlink from a toolbar button, open the Customize dialog box, right-click the button, and select Edit Hyperlink, Remove Link.

Figure 2.9
Select a file or Web page and assign it to a toolbar button as a hyperlink, and then open the file or insert a picture with a single click.

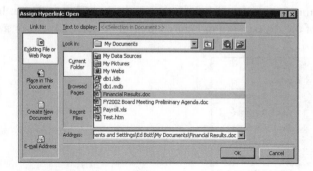

CUSTOMIZING BUILT-IN MENUS

If you've mastered the art of customizing toolbars, you already know how to modify menus. That's because Office menus are simply toolbars without icons. You can mix and match menus and buttons on any toolbar; in fact, the default menu bar in each Office application is actually just another toolbar, and you can rearrange top-level items as well as menu items and even submenus.

In this section, we show you how to rearrange the built-in menus in any Office application; how to add new menus to any Office toolbar (whether it's the built-in variety or a custom toolbar you create); and how to modify right-click shortcut menus in Word, PowerPoint, and Access.

REARRANGING PULL-DOWN MENUS

Customizing the default menus for any Office application is a tricky proposition. Yes, you can remove menu items to simplify the range of available choices—for yourself or for other users—but when you take items off the menu, you make it extremely difficult to gain access to those functions if you discover you need them at a later date. Likewise, if you drastically change the order of menu items or add new items, you risk confusing users (including yourself) who expect to see each menu choice in a standard location.

 For tips on how to recover if you customize a menu or toolbar a little too much, see "Back to Square One" in the "Troubleshooting" section at the end of this chapter.

To add, remove, or rearrange menus, follow the same steps as described in the previous section, "Select Tools, Customize," and then click and drag to add commands, macros, and other items to a menu, or to move an item to a different location within the pull-down menus. Drag items off the menus to remove them. Right-click any item and change the text in the Name box to rename it.

Tip from

Ed & Woody

All Office applications give you quick access to top-level menus through the Customize dialog box. Click the Commands tab and select Built-in Menus to select from a full list of top-level menus and add them to any toolbar; the Excel version of this list includes not only all top-level menus but cascading menus under them as well.

CREATING NEW MENUS

Adding a new cascading menu item to an existing menu or toolbar is an excellent way to organize macros and other shortcuts for quick access, without cluttering the interface. For example, you might create a new cascading menu called Favorites on Word's Format menu and use it to hold a collection of shortcuts to the handful of fonts and styles you use most often. Or, you could add a similar menu to the Drawing toolbar containing hyperlinks to pictures you can insert in any Office file.

To add a new menu to any toolbar (including the default menu bar), be sure the toolbar you want to customize is visible, and then select Tools, Customize. Click the Commands tab and select New Menu from the bottom of the Categories list. Drag the New Menu item from the Commands list and drop it in the correct position on the toolbar.

Right-click to rename the new menu. Then add buttons and menu items by dragging and dropping commands, macros, and other objects from the Customize dialog box or from other toolbars. When you drag an item over a pull-down menu, the menu drops down so you can drop it in the correct location.

PART

I

CH

2

Tip from

EQ & Woody

For Word users, one of the most powerful menus you can add is buried at the bottom of the Built-in Menus list and is completely undocumented. The Work menu lets you build a list of files you work with regularly so you can get to them anytime. Drag the Work menu onto the menu bar or any toolbar; when you open a file that you know you'll want to work with again, select Work, Add to Work Menu. To quickly remove a file from this list, press Ctrl+Alt+- (hyphen) and point to the file on the list.

MODIFYING SHORTCUT MENUS

The context-sensitive shortcut menus found throughout Office are powerful timesavers, but they're not perfect; for example, Microsoft's interface designers chose not to add the Paste Special command to the shortcut menus that pop up when you edit a Word document or a PowerPoint presentation. Customizing these shortcut menus can make you more productive by placing the commands you use most frequently within easy reach and removing those you don't use.

Word, PowerPoint, and Access allow you to customize shortcut menus; unfortunately, there's no easy way to customize shortcut menus in Excel, Outlook, or FrontPage.

To add the Paste Special command to Word's shortcut menus, follow these steps (the techniques are virtually identical for PowerPoint and Access):

1. Select Tools, Customize, click the Toolbars tab, and check the Shortcut Menus box. The Shortcut Menus toolbar appears (see Figure 2.10). Note that these menus are organized by category; Word, for example, uses separate shortcut menus for editing text, working with drawings, and managing tables.

Figure 2.10
Use the special-pur-
pose Shortcut Menus
toolbar to customize
right-click menus in
Word, PowerPoint,
and Access (but not
Excel or Outlook).

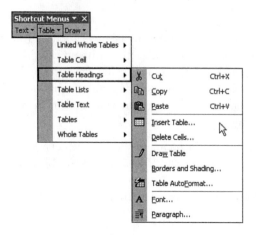

Note

Even if you leave the Shortcut Menus box checked, this special toolbar disappears when you close the Customize dialog box. This toolbar is available only for customization, not for regular use.

2. Click the Commands tab, select Edit from the Categories list and Paste Special from the Commands list, and then drag the command over the Text choice on the Shortcut Menus toolbar. The full list of shortcut menus appears; drag the new menu item down to the Text menu, which will cascade to the right. Drop the Paste Special item on the menu, beneath Paste.

3. Repeat this process with other menus you want to customize from the drop-down lists on the Shortcut Menus toolbar. At a minimum, add the Paste Special choice to the List and Headings menu under the Text group. If you want the Paste Special command to be available when you edit tables as well, add this choice to every shortcut menu under the Table group.

4. Click Close to close the Customize dialog box and return to Word.

 If shortcut menus don't work as you expect, see "Broken Shortcut Menus?" in the "Troubleshooting" section at the end of this chapter.

BYPASSING MENUS WITH KEYBOARD SHORTCUTS

Office includes a literally overwhelming number of keyboard shortcuts for nearly every task. Some mnemonic shortcuts, such as Ctrl+B (Bold), Ctrl+U (Underline), and Ctrl+I (Italic), are common to every Office application. Others follow Windows standards, such as the universal Ctrl+X (Cut), Ctrl+C (Copy), and Ctrl+V (Paste) shortcuts. Still others give you access to commands that are nearly impossible to access any other way. For example, there's no menu choice in Word to convert field codes to their results; you have to know the shortcuts: Ctrl+6 (from the numeric keypad, not the row of numbers above the QWERTY keys) or Ctrl+Shift+F9.

Office applications are remarkably consistent in their use of keyboard shortcuts, with one notable exception: Outlook is the black sheep, with many, many nonstandard keyboard shortcuts. Throughout every other Office application, for example, you use Ctrl+F to display the Find and Replace dialog boxes; in Outlook, however, that key combination forwards an item via e-mail. To find text in Outlook, press F4, which works as the Repeat key everywhere else in Office.

Only a savant could memorize every Office keyboard shortcut, but learning a select few can dramatically increase your productivity, especially for commands and functions you use regularly.

PART

I

CH

2

Tip from	To make discovering keyboard shortcuts for a particular Office program easier, turn on the option that displays keyboard shortcuts along with ScreenTips. Select Tools, Customize, click the Options tab, and check the Show Shortcut Keys in ScreenTips box.
Ed & Woody	

Of all the Office-wide keyboard shortcuts, one stands out as by far the most useful. F4 is the Repeat key, which repeats the previous action; it comes in handy in a wide variety of situations. For example, you can use F4 to apply a new style to a series of paragraphs scattered throughout a Word document. Click in the first paragraph and select the style from the drop-down list. Click in the next paragraph and press F4 instead of going back to the Style menu; F4 will continue to apply that style until you perform another action, such as typing or formatting. Add or delete a row in an Excel worksheet, and then move the insertion point and press F4 to add or delete another row, again without using menus.

Printing out an exhaustive list of shortcut keys for each Office application would take hundreds of pages. To see a generally complete list organized by category, search in each application's online help for a topic called "Keyboard Shortcuts."

Of all Office programs, only Word enables you to easily customize keyboard shortcuts. Select Tools, Customize, and then click the Keyboard button to select a command, a macro, an AutoText entry, a font, a style, or a common symbol. The Customize Keyboard dialog box displays the current key combination assigned to each item you select (see Figure 2.11).

To add or change a key combination, first select the item you want to assign; then click in the Press New Shortcut Key box and press the key combination. Check the text just below this box to see whether the key combination you've selected is already assigned to another function; if the option is available, click Assign. Look in the Current Keys box to see whether a key combination is already assigned to that function; to remove that definition, select the item and click Remove.

For details on how to restore default keyboard shortcuts if you inadvertently reassign the wrong key, see "Restoring Default Shortcut Keys" in the "Troubleshooting" section at the end of this chapter.

Figure 2.11
Only Word enables you to easily customize keyboard shortcuts.

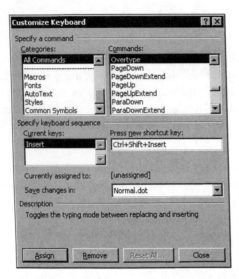

CONFIGURING COMMON OFFICE FEATURES

In every Office application, you'll find most customization settings on the Options dialog box. Select Tools, Options to adjust these settings. Although the available settings vary widely, you can typically customize the following:

- Control the number of files on the recently used file list. The default is four, and the maximum is nine for most Office applications.

- Set spelling preferences (Word and PowerPoint), as explained in the following section.

- Enter user information, including your name and initials, for use with comments.

- Control whether you see and hear animation and sound effects when you use menus and other interface elements. If sound effects annoy you, turn them off here.

- Set AutoRecover options (Word, Excel, and PowerPoint) to automatically save snapshots of files in memory at regular intervals so that the program can recover them in the event of a system crash. (This is not a substitute for saving your work regularly!)

- Hide or show status bars at the bottom of each program window. These typically display information about the current document, worksheet, presentation, or other data file.

- Hide or show rulers, scrollbars, and other interface elements.

→   For a discussion of text entry, editing, and formatting options used throughout Office, **see** Chapter 4, "Editing and Formatting Text," **p. 81**.

CUSTOMIZING TASK PANES

Task panes, a new interface element in Office XP, are small windows that dock within an Office program window to provide easy access to commands and program functions. Task panes fuel search functions, the Office Clipboard, clip art, and file management tasks throughout Office XP.

Despite their widespread use, task panes are mostly fixed and barely customizable. The one and only task pane option lets you make the task pane visible each time you start an Office program without opening a saved document. From the bottom of the New Document, New Workbook, or New Presentation task pane, check the Show at Startup box to enable this option.

PART

I

CH

2

Tip from

Ed & Woody

Although most task panes can be docked only to the right side of the program window, you can move the pane—point to the pane's title bar and drag it so it floats over the window. You can also change the width of the pane by dragging the left edge; this option is especially useful with the Insert Clip Art task pane.

CUSTOMIZING SMART TAGS

Smart Tags are a welcome addition to the Office XP interface. These tiny button/menu combinations appear automatically after certain types of actions. For instance, Smart Tags appear whenever you use the AutoCorrect or Paste function in any Office program. If the results aren't what you expect, you can use options on the Smart Tag menu to change the way the data appears. Smart Tags assist in error checking in Excel worksheets and are used for layout functions in PowerPoint. They can also automatically identify blocks of text that meet certain criteria. For instance, you can configure Word to automatically recognize addresses and names (as in Figure 2.12), or ask Excel to recognize stock ticker symbols.

Figure 2.12
Word automatically adds a Smart Tag to names in a document. Click the button to add the name to your Outlook Contacts folder, paste in the contact's address, or perform other tasks.

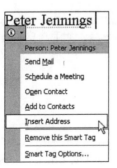

Subtle indicators mark the positions of each Smart Tag in an Office document. In a Word document, a faint purple line under a name means a Smart Tag is buried there. In Excel, triangular indicators in the corner of a cell mark the presence of a Smart Tag. Hover the mouse pointer over the Smart Tag to display an Action Button; click the button to see a list of actions you can take in response to the tag.

A wide array of options is available for customizing Smart Tags. To adjust these options for any Office program, select Tools, AutoCorrect Options, and click the Smart Tags tab. Figure 2.13, for instance, shows the full range of options available in Word. Using this dialog box, you can specify which types of data will be recognized or turn off Smart Tags completely.

Figure 2.13
If you find Smart Tags more annoying than helpful, clear this check box to turn them off for good.

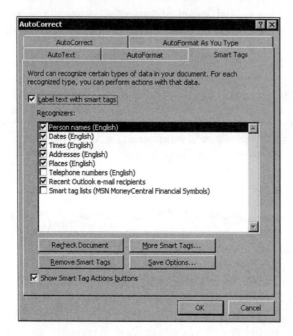

Tip from

E Q & Woody

Because Smart Tags use industry-standard XML, third-party developers can easily create Office-compatible add-ins that work as Smart Tags. Check the Office Update Web site (select Help, Office on the Web) for a selection of available Smart Tags.

SETTING UP SPELL-CHECKING OPTIONS

All Office applications use a common spell-checking module, based on the exact same dictionaries. When you add words to your custom dictionary, regardless of which Office application you use, your changes are stored in a single text file, which you can easily open and edit.

To adjust spelling options for each application, use the following techniques.

For Word, select Tools, Options, and click the Spelling & Grammar tab. Use the dialog box shown in Figure 2.14 to adjust options.

Figure 2.14
Word's spelling
options are by far the
richest of any Office
program.

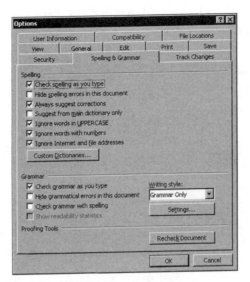

Word has the most extensive set of spelling options, including the capability to add supplemental dictionaries for specialized vocabularies, such as those used in a medical or legal practice.

 To tame some of Word's aggressive spell-checking tendencies, see "Word Changes Text Mysteriously" in the "Troubleshooting" section at the end of this chapter.

→ For more details on how Word automatically uses suggestions from the spelling-checker, **see** "Checking Spelling and Grammar," **p. 395**.

Excel and Access offer identical Spelling options (see Figure 2.15). In both programs, you can specify the language you want to use, as well as which dictionary file you want to use when adding words.

Figure 2.15
Excel users might
want to create sepa-
rate custom diction–
aries to recognize
specialized financial
terms in worksheets.

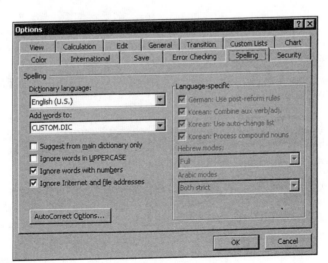

PowerPoint's spelling options are far less comprehensive. Select Tools, Options, and click the Spelling and Style tab to display the dialog box shown in Figure 2.16.

Figure 2.16
PowerPoint's spelling options are far less extensive than those in other Office programs.

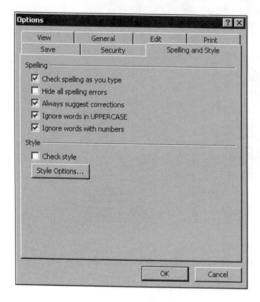

To hide the red squiggly line under spelling errors for a given presentation, check the Hide All Spelling Errors box. To turn off automatic spell-checking completely, clear the check mark next to the Check Spelling As You Type box.

In Outlook, select Tools, Options, and click the Spelling tab to set spelling options. Outlook lets you check spelling on any message you compose, including replies. It doesn't allow on-the-fly spell-checking, however, unless you use Word as your e-mail editor.

All Office spelling tools share the following dictionary files:

- A main dictionary, as determined by your language settings; on a system configured for U.S. English, for example, this file is `Mssp3en.lex`.

- A custom dictionary, which stores words you add while spell-checking; the default name for this file is `Custom.dic`.

Where will you find these dictionary files? The exact location depends on how you installed Office and how you've configured Windows. In most cases, the main dictionary file will be in `C:\Program Files\Common Files\Microsoft Shared\Proof`.

The custom dictionary file, on the other hand, should appear in a personal data folder, such as `C:\Documents and Settings\`*Username*`\Application Data\Microsoft\Proof`. Because the custom dictionary file is a simple text file, shared by all applications, you can use any text editor to edit it. Outlook makes this task easy—click the Edit button on the Spelling tab to open the custom dictionary in Notepad. In Office XP, however, Microsoft has added a much simpler interface, which is accessible only from Word. From the Spelling & Grammar dialog box, click the Custom Dictionaries button, select the correct file from the list if necessary, and click Modify. This opens up a neat dialog box where you can add a word at a time, as in Figure 2.17.

Figure 2.17
To edit the Office-wide Custom dictionary, click the Modify button in Word's Spelling & Grammar dialog box.

SETTING SECURITY OPTIONS

In earlier Office versions, security settings were scattered throughout each program in a variety of locations. In Office XP, all security options are consolidated in a single dialog box. To see the security options for any Office program except FrontPage, select Tools, Options, and click the Security tab. Figure 2.18 shows this dialog box for Word, which offers the most extensive set of options of any Office program.

In general, you'll find three categories of options in this dialog box:

- **Password Protection**—These options apply to the current document, worksheet, or presentation only. You can assign a password, set encryption levels, and add a digital signature here.

- **Privacy Options**—Office documents typically include information about a document's creator and company, as well as other details that might be added during editing. For documents you intend to publish outside your organization, you might want to delete this information. Excel and PowerPoint allow you to check a box to remove this information when saving a file; Word goes a step further, letting you remove this information before printing or e-mailing a file.

■ **Protection from Macro Viruses**—Click the Macro Security button to select one of three levels for determining which macros will run in each Office program (see Figure 2.19). By default, macro security is set to high, meaning only macros from trusted sources will run properly.

Figure 2.18
Every Office program except FrontPage includes a Security dialog box similar to this one. Word's privacy options are more extensive than other programs.

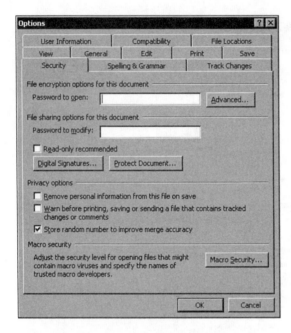

Figure 2.19

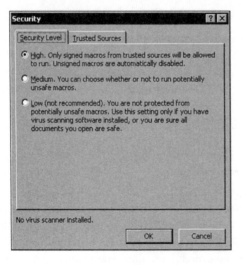

→ For a full discussion of macro security issues, **see** "Macro Security," **p. 976**.

Tip from

EQ & Woody

If you don't use antivirus software, you're simply begging to lose data or suffer cata-strophic loss. The best antivirus programs integrate tightly with Office to protect you from infection when you open a document from the Internet or received as an e-mail attachment. Check with the maker of your antivirus software to determine whether you need an update for compatibility with Office XP.

SAVING AND RESTORING PERSONAL SETTINGS

After you've painstakingly customized every Office application, what happens if you get a new PC? System backups can preserve your data files, but you need to take an extra step to ensure you capture all options and preferences in a format you easily can restore to a new machine. Microsoft makes two utilities that can assist in this chore:

- **Save My Settings Wizard**—The best choice for Office users in small businesses, home offices, and other environments not managed by full-time IT staff. This simple utility (a free download) saves your settings in a file and stores that file on a server at Microsoft's Office Update site.

- **Office Profile Wizard**—Intended for administrators who want to save an Office user profile that represents a standard or semicustom configuration, which they can then deploy to multiple desktops. This utility, also free, requires extensive manual configura-tion but is highly customizable. It's included as part of the Office Resource Kit.

To download either of these utilities, visit Microsoft's Office Update site by selecting Help, Office on the Web from any Office Program.

Note

Windows XP includes a Files and Settings Transfer Wizard that is Office aware.

TROUBLESHOOTING

BACK TO SQUARE ONE

You've customized menus and toolbars a bit too much, and now you can't find several key commands.

You can restore any toolbar, including the main menu bar, to its default settings. Select Tools, Customize, and click the Toolbars tab. Choose the toolbar whose customized settings you want to remove (select Menu Bar for the main menus) and click Reset. Word users can specify whether the change applies to the current document only or to the template in use.

BROKEN SHORTCUT MENUS?

You've customized shortcut menus in Word, PowerPoint, or Access, but they don't behave as you expect.

Be sure you customized the correct menu. When you edit tables, for example, Word uses different shortcut menus depending on whether you're working with a table heading, text within a table cell, an entire cell, or the whole table. If you want the Paste Special command to be available in each of these instances, you must customize the shortcut menus for each of these specific contexts.

RESTORING DEFAULT SHORTCUT KEYS

You inadvertently replaced a useful system shortcut and want to reset the default shortcut.

When you assign a keyboard shortcut to a specific function, it removes that shortcut for any other function that uses that combination. To restore the shortcut, select the original function and assign the proper key combination. To restore every default Word key combination, select Tools, Customize, click the Keyboard button, and click the Reset All button in the Customize Keyboard dialog box.

WORD CHANGES TEXT MYSTERIOUSLY

As you create a document, you discover that Word is consistently changing some words or abbreviations you type. You've checked thoroughly, and you know the text that triggers the change is not in the AutoCorrect list. What's up?

Word is aggressively changing text, using a well-hidden spell-checking option. To stop this behavior, select Tools, AutoCorrect Options, click the AutoCorrect tab, and clear the check mark from the Automatically Use Suggestions from the Spelling Checker box.

SECRETS OF THE OFFICE MASTERS: CUSTOM TOOLBARS FOR QUICK HIGHLIGHTING

While working on this book, we regularly used Word's yellow and green highlighters to mark text for specific tasks and then cleared the highlighting when the task was complete. Because Word's Highlighter icon remembers the last color you select, this routine often takes two clicks—one click to display the drop-down list of available colors and a second click to select a color (or None, to erase highlighting).

To make highlighting a one-click process, we first created three nearly identical macros, using the following code:

```
Public Sub NoHighlight()
Selection.Range.HighlightColorIndex = wdNoHighlight
End Sub
Public Sub YellowHighlight()
Selection.Range.HighlightColorIndex = wdYellow
End Sub
```

```
Public Sub GreenHighlight()
Selection.Range.HighlightColorIndex = wdGreen
End Sub
```

We then created a new toolbar and assigned each macro to a button on the new toolbar, with a brightly colored icon and text label to clearly identify each highlighting option, as in Figure 2.20. (Note that this toolbar also includes buttons to add strikethrough formatting, show field codes, update field codes, and unlink field codes—all tasks that are difficult or impossible to do using Word's menus.)

Figure 2.20

Although you can't tell it from this page, the button next to each toolbar label is the same color as the highlighting choice. Creating the icons was simple—we started with the "happy face" icon and used the Button Editor to cover the inside of the face with the highlight color associated with each macro.

PART

I

CH

2

CHAPTER 3

OFFICE FILE MANAGEMENT FOR EXPERTS

In this chapter

SETTING UP OFFICE FILE STORAGE LOCATIONS

Office XP works especially well in the typical well-connected office, making it easy to store and retrieve Office files in a wide variety of locations. You might keep some files on your local hard disk, others on a network file server, and still others on a Web server with Microsoft's SharePoint extensions installed. In an environment this complex, having a well-thought-out storage system is the only way to stay organized.

CHOOSING A DEFAULT LOCAL STORAGE LOCATION

Three Office versions ago, Microsoft introduced the My Documents folder. The idea was simple: to create a default location for personal data files, making it easier for users to find and back up files they create. In practice, however, the first implementations of this idea were poorly thought out, and most expert Office users simply ignored the My Documents icon on the desktop—or quickly figured out how to delete it. Since its first appearance in 1995, the My Documents folder has evolved into a standard feature of Windows; if you deleted the My Documents folder supplied by Office, you might have been startled to see it reappear when you upgraded Windows. Beginning with Windows 98, in fact, and continuing with Windows ME, 2000, and XP, the My Documents folder has become an integral part of Windows, and that icon on the Windows desktop and in the My Computer window is much more useful.

Office XP makes extensive use of the My Documents folder. Advanced users might cringe at the name, but this system folder is the default starting point for common Open and Save As dialog boxes in Office applications. It's also hard-wired to one of the default icons on the Places Bar in those dialog boxes. If you're willing to reorganize the way you store data files to take advantage of this location, you can substantially increase the odds that you'll find files you're looking for when you need them. You can also change the default location that individual Office programs use for data files; it's slightly more difficult, but still possible, to redefine the location of the My Documents folder. (Oh, and if the name bugs you, just change it.)

The exact physical location of the My Documents folder varies, depending on which Windows version you have installed:

- On a system running Windows 95, Windows 98, or Windows Me without user profiles, the My Documents folder appears in the root of the system drive, usually C:\My Documents.

- On a system running Windows 95, Windows 98, or Windows Me with user profiles enabled, the My Documents folder appears in the user's local profile folder, typically C:\Windows\Profiles\<*username*>\My Documents. (Note that you can override this option by clearing a check box in the Users dialog box of the Control Panel.)

- On a system running Windows NT 4.0 or earlier, the My Documents shortcut opens the Personal folder in the user's local profile, typically C:\Winnt\Profiles\<*username*>\Personal.

■ On a system running Windows 2000 and XP, the My Documents folder appears in the Documents and Settings folder, normally C:\Documents and Settings\<*username*>\My Documents.

Tip from
EQ & Woody

If you use Windows 98 or Windows Me, you can safely (and quickly) eliminate the My Documents icon from the desktop: Right-click the icon and choose Remove from Desktop. Because this icon is only a shortcut with a few special properties, eliminating it does not have any effect on files stored in the physical folder to which it points. To restore the My Documents icon to the desktop on a Windows 98 system, right-click any empty space on the desktop and choose New, My Documents Folder on Desktop. In Windows Me, open the Folder Options dialog box, click the View tab, and check the Show My Documents on the Desktop box.

PART

I

CH

3

In all 32-bit versions except Windows 95 and NT 4.0, the My Documents icon on the desktop and in Explorer windows is actually a *shell extension*—a virtual folder like the My Computer and Network Neighborhood icons, not an actual physical location. Opening this shortcut opens the folder that's registered as the current user's My Documents location. To change the folder that this icon points to, right-click the My Documents icon, choose Properties, and enter the folder name in the Target text box.

Tip from
EQ & Woody

Changing the default file location in FrontPage 2002 requires hacking the Registry. Navigate to the following key: HEKEY_CURRENT_USER\Software\Microsoft\FrontPage and change the value DefaultSave to the full path of the folder you want to use.

Then, open the following key:

HKEY_CURRENT_USER\Software\Microsoft\Frontpage\Explorer\FrontPage Explorer\Settings and change the value for Default\WebName to the same folder name.

Finally, you can change the default working folder for any individual Office application (with the exception of FrontPage), although the exact procedure is slightly different, depending on the program you're working with. Follow these steps, for example, to adjust the default document folder in Word:

1. Choose Tools, Options, and click the File Locations tab. The dialog box shown in Figure 3.1 lets you specify a wide range of system folders.

2. In the File Types list, select the Documents option.

3. Click the Modify button; then use the Modify Location dialog box to browse through drives and folders. Select the correct folder and click OK.

4. Click OK to close the Options dialog box and save your change.

Figure 3.1
Use the Options dialog box to adjust the default working folder for any Office program.

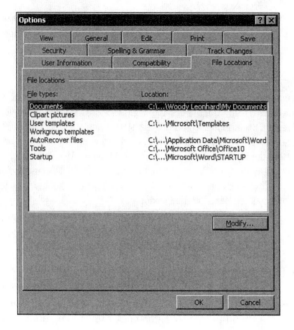

Follow the same basic procedure for Excel, PowerPoint, and Access, with the following exceptions: In Excel and Access, click the General tab; in PowerPoint, click the Save tab. In the box labeled Default File Location, enter the full name and path of the folder that you want to specify as the new default. Unfortunately, only Word lets you browse through drives and folders to find the one you want; with all other Office programs, you must enter the full directory path manually.

The default file location setting for each application is independent. If you set Word's default Documents folder to a location on the network, for example, Excel and PowerPoint continue to open to the default My Documents folder.

Tip from

EQ & Woody

Curiously, several other settings in Word's File Locations dialog box apply across the board to all Office applications. If you change the location of the Templates or Workgroup Templates folder in Word, that change applies to Excel and PowerPoint as well. Specifying the Workgroup Templates folder here is an ideal way to make sure that individual users always have access to the most current corporate templates in the three main Office applications. Users can continue to save and open personal templates in their own folders, but any Word, Excel, or PowerPoint template in the Workgroup Templates folder will "automagically" appear in the New dialog box of all three applications.

Behind the scenes, Office creates and uses one additional standard location, creating a group of subfolders in the Application Data folder. On a default Windows 98/Me setup without user profiles, you'll find these files at C:\Windows\Application Data\Microsoft. With user profiles enabled, this location is typically C:\Windows\Profiles*<username>*\Application Data\Microsoft or, in Windows 2000/XP, at C:\Documents and Settings*<username>*\Application Data\Microsoft. Office keeps separate folders for each application, special-purpose folders for use by all Office programs, and a folder for Office itself. This location is where Office stores customization data, such as your Excel Personal macro workbook, any custom templates that you create in any program (stored in the Templates folder), custom dictionaries (in the Proof folder), and Word startup templates (in the \Word\STARTUP folder).

OPENING AND SAVING FILES OVER A NETWORK

Office XP lets you work with files over a network or on the Web in much the same way that you access files and folders on a standalone PC. If you are connected to a network, contact your network administrator to find locations on the network where you're permitted to read or write files. You should get a network share address for the location, using *UNC syntax* (*Server_name**Share_Name*\). Unless the network administrator has restricted your rights, you can create and manage your own subfolders in this location.

Although you can type UNC-style network addresses directly into File Open or File Save As dialog boxes, doing so is usually more trouble than it's worth. For easier access, browse to the My Network Places folder (in older Windows versions, this is the Network Neighborhood) and navigate to the correct server, share, and folder.

Aside from the additional navigation steps, there is no difference between using network shares and using local drives, assuming that you have proper authorization from your network administrator.

STORING FILES ON THE WEB OR AN INTRANET

Storing files on the Web—whether to a Web server or to an FTP server—is almost as simple as working with files on a local network. As long as you're connected to the Web, you need only the URL for the location (for example, http://www.mydomain.com/someplace or ftp://microsoft.com/incoming) and approval from the site operator to read or write to the location. You can even copy the URL from your favorite Web browser's Address box and paste it into the File Name box.

To open or save a file to a Web server or an FTP site on the Internet or an intranet, display the New Document/Worksheet/Presentation task pane and click Add Network Place (at the bottom of the pane). Follow the steps in the Add Network Place Wizard to create a shortcut to the location (see Figure 3.2).

PART
I

CH
3

Figure 3.2
The Add Network Place Wizard lets you set up Internet or intranet locations so that they work just like regular folders.

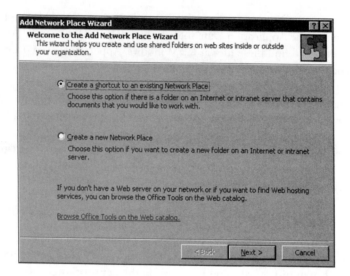

You can also reach the Add Network Place Wizard from the My Network Places or Network Neighborhood icons in any common dialog box.

> **Note**
>
> From a technical standpoint, there are almost no differences between publishing to an intranet Web server and publishing to one on the Internet. The format of the URL that you use likely will be different—intranet servers are typically identified with a one-word name (such as http://marketing) rather than a fully qualified domain name (such as http://www.example.com). You'll likely encounter different security issues, including password-protected logins and possibly disk quotas (which limit the amount of disk space that a user can fill with Web content) on both types of server.

WORKING WITH SHARED FOLDERS ON A SHAREPOINT SERVER

Some editions of Office XP include an add-on called SharePoint Team Services. This software is a stripped-down version of a more powerful package called SharePoint Portal Server. You can install the SharePoint Team Services add-in on any Windows 2000/XP machine that is also running Internet Information Services. With a SharePoint server available (usually on an intranet), co-workers can share and discuss files on a Web server, using an attractive Web-based front end.

Office XP integrates exceptionally well with SharePoint servers. Depending on how the SharePoint administrator has configured the network, you can access SharePoint document libraries directly from Office XP common dialog boxes. Any document stored on a SharePoint server is available for Web Discussions as well. Use the My Network Places folder from an Office Open or Save As dialog box to work directly with a SharePoint shared folder.

CREATING NEW FILES

When you use the New File task pane or New dialog box to select from available templates in Word, Excel, or PowerPoint, Office builds the tabbed dialog box on the fly from two (and, in some cases, three) sources:

- The default collection of Office templates is stored in a subfolder that corresponds to the system's current language settings; on a default U.S. English installation, this is C:\Program Files\Microsoft Office\Templates\1033. All users of the current system see these templates.

- Each user's custom templates are stored in the location specified for User Templates. On a Windows 98/Me machine with user profiles enabled, this is C:\Windows\Profiles*<username>*\Application Data\Microsoft\Templates; on a Windows 2000/XP machine, it's C:\Documents and Settings\<username>\Application Data\Microsoft\Templates. The actual location can be changed in Word's File Locations dialog box, accessible by choosing Tools, Options, and, on the File Locations tab, clicking User Templates and then Modify.

- If you've used Word's File Locations dialog box to specify a Workgroup Templates folder, Office displays templates from this location in the New dialog box as well. If a template in the Workgroup Templates location and one in the User Templates location have the same name, the Office program displays and uses only the one from the User Templates location.

PART

I

CH

3

Note

> The default Office installation does not install all available templates; instead, you'll find shortcuts to some templates in the task pane and New dialog box. The first time you use one of these templates, Office attempts to install the supporting files. Word, Excel, and PowerPoint templates are covered in Chapter 18, "Using Styles, Templates, and Themes"; Chapter 21, "Excel Essentials"; and Chapter 28, "PowerPoint Essentials," respectively.

 If you're having trouble finding templates that you've saved, see "Putting Templates in Their Place" in the "Troubleshooting" section at the end of this chapter.

→ For more details on how to install templates and other Office components, **see** "Adding and Removing Office Features," **p. 1069**.

Although you can manage the contents of template folders in an Explorer window, the easiest and safest way to make new templates available to an Office program is to save the file in Template format. After creating the Word document, Excel workbook, or PowerPoint presentation that you want to use as a template, follow these steps:

1. Choose File, Save As.

2. From the Save As Type drop-down list, choose Document Template (Word), Template (Excel), or Design Template (PowerPoint). The dialog box displays the contents of your User Templates folder.

3. To add the new template to one of the existing tabs, click the Create New Folder button and add a folder with the same name as the existing tab. If you want to create a custom tab for the New File task pane and New dialog box, specify a new folder name. If you don't select a subfolder here, your new template will appear under General templates on the New File task pane or on the General tab of the New dialog box.

4. Type a name for the template and click Save.

USING AND CUSTOMIZING COMMON DIALOG BOXES

The Office File Open and File Save As dialog boxes have a series of shortcut icons on the left side, called the *Places Bar* (see Figure 3.3), designed to speed navigation through common file locations:

Figure 3.3
The Places Bar on the left of the Open and Save As dialog boxes can be easily customized. Put commonly used data folders here for quicker access.

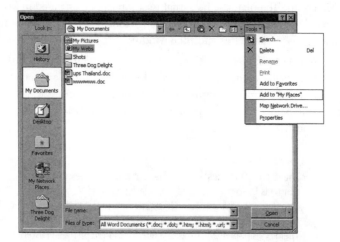

- **History**—Opens the Recent folder, which contains shortcuts to files and folders that you've worked with. Office maintains up to 20 shortcuts for each file type in this folder. When you click this icon from within an Office program, Office displays only shortcuts appropriate to the application you're using.

Note

Don't confuse the Office Recent folder with the Windows system folder of the same name. Office manages a separate Recent folder for each user profile on a system. To manage the Office shortcuts from an Explorer window, open the user profile folder (on a Windows 98/Me machine, this is typically C:\Windows\Profiles\<username>; in Windows 2000/XP, it's C:\Documents and Settings\<username>) and look in \Application Data\Microsoft\Office\Recent.

- **My Documents**—Opens the personal data folder for the user currently logged on. As noted earlier, Windows enables you to change the target folder that Office opens when you click this icon.

- **Desktop**—Opens or saves files on the Windows desktop. Use the desktop as a holding area when you want to create a file and move it elsewhere using the Windows Explorer. Using the desktop as a permanent storage area is generally a bad idea because most Office applications have a tendency to create temporary files in the same location as the file you're working with.

- **Favorites**—Displays the contents of Internet Explorer's Favorites menu.

- **My Network Places**—Lets you manage files stored in shared folders on your network or on Web/FTP servers.

In Open and Save dialog boxes, Office includes two features that make it easier to find a file by name:

- As you type in the File Name box, the *AutoComplete* feature suggests the first name that matches the characters that you've typed so far. Keep typing, or press Enter to accept the suggestion. Note that the list of files does not scroll as you type.

- If you click in the list of files and then type a character, Office selects the first file that begins with the letter or number that you typed. If you quickly type several characters in rapid succession, the selection moves to the first file that begins with those characters. If you pause for more than a second between characters, this type-ahead feature resets. Note that as you select files in this fashion, Office does not fill in the File Name box.

To adjust the display of files in the Open and Save As dialog boxes, use the Views button. The drop-down arrow lets you choose from a list of views, or you can click the button to cycle through the following four icon arrangements:

- Large Icons, Small Icons, and List mirror their counterparts in Windows Explorer.

- Details displays size, file type, and other information, as shown in Figure 3.4; click any heading to sort the list by that category. (If you think that the information in the Type column is useless, we agree. Skip to the "Secrets of the Office Masters: Details, Details" section at the end of this chapter for details on how to make the Details view much more useful.)

- Properties displays summary information about the selected document in the right half of the dialog box.

- Preview displays a thumbnail version of the document in the right half of the dialog box as you move from file to file in the list. In general, you should avoid this option because of the performance penalty you pay: As you scroll through a dialog box, the program that you're working with has to open each file; find an import filter, if necessary; and generate the preview. Switch to this view when you want to quickly verify that the file you're about to open is the correct one, and then switch back to List or Details view after peeking at the file.

■ Thumbnails displays a thumbnail image of all graphics files and some Office documents.

Figure 3.4
Click the Views button to change the arrangement of icons in the Open and Save As dialog boxes.

Some files, especially certain Excel worksheets, can't be seen in the Preview pane. For suggestions on the possible reasons, see "No Preview in Common Dialog Boxes," in the "Troubleshooting" section at the end of this chapter.

Tip from
EQ & Woody

To manage files in Open and Save As dialog boxes, select the filename and right-click. Shortcut menus here work just as they do in an Explorer window. You can move, copy, delete, or rename a file, for example, as long as the file that you select is not currently open.

CUSTOMIZING COMMON DIALOG BOXES

The Places Bar can be customized to make it easier and faster to get to frequently used folders. To add your own folders to the Places Bar, select the icon for the folder that you want to add, and then choose Tools, Add to "My Places." To remove a custom location from the Places Bar, right-click its icon and choose Remove from the shortcut menu. (You can't rename or delete the five default locations on the Places Bar.)

Tip from

EQ & Woody

If you add more icons than can be displayed in the Places Bar, small scroll arrows appear at the top and bottom of the list. You can see more icons in the Places Bar if you right-click it and choose Small Icons. Put no more than 15 locations in the Places Bar; with any more, you'll spend too much time scrolling.

To rearrange folders in the Places Bar, right-click an icon that you want to move, and choose Move Up or Move Down.

Tip from

EQ & Woody

Both the Open and Save As dialog boxes can be resized by clicking and dragging on any of the edges or corners.

PART

I

CH

3

NAMING DOCUMENTS

Office documents must follow these file-naming rules:

- A filename may contain any *alphanumeric* character, including the letters A to Z and numbers from 0 to 9.

- A filename may be as short as 1 character and as long as a total of 255 characters, including the full path—drive letter, colon, backslashes, and folder names included.

Caution

The rules governing maximum length of a filename include the full path. For this reason, moving a file with a long name can cause problems, especially when the destination folder is deeply nested. In practice, you can avoid this problem and still have descriptive names if you keep filenames to a maximum length of about 40 characters.

- The following special characters are allowed in a filename: $ % - _ @ ~ ` ! ( ) ^ # & + , ; =.

- You may use spaces, brackets ([ ]), curly braces ({ }), single quotation marks, apostrophes, and parentheses within a filename.

- You may not use a slash (/), a backslash (\), a colon (:), an asterisk (*), a question mark (?), a quotation mark ("), or angle brackets (< >) as part of a filename. These characters are reserved for use with the file system, and you'll see an error message if the name that you enter includes any of these characters.

- Office files typically include a three-letter *extension*, which is added automatically by the application that created the file (such as .doc for files created by Word). However, a file extension is not required, nor are file extensions restricted to three characters. To force an Office program to use the exact name and extension that you specify, enter the full name, including the extension, between quotation marks.

Caution

> If you use a nonstandard file extension, you might be unable to open the file from an Explorer window. Also, files that include unregistered file extensions do not appear in the Open dialog box unless you choose All Files from the drop-down list of file types.

- A filename may contain one or more periods. Windows treats the last period in the name as the dividing line between the filename and its extension.

Note

> Windows filenames are not case sensitive. Office ignores all distinctions between upper- and lowercase letters when entering a filename in an Open or Save As dialog box.

 If you encounter problems when sharing files with coworkers who use 16-bit Windows or DOS programs, see "Dealing with Short Filenames," in the "Troubleshooting" section at the end of this chapter.

USING ALTERNATIVE FILE FORMATS

By default, Office applications save data files in their own *binary* formats. That's the correct choice in most circumstances, but when you share files with a coworker who does not use a recent version of Office, you might need to open or save a file in a different format.

Tip from

> In previous Office versions, *Rich Text Format* (RTF) was often your best choice for saving a file and using it with other programs, especially from software companies other than Microsoft. No more. Nowadays you'll probably find that the easiest way to share data is HTML, which is virtually guaranteed to be readable by any other person, even on a computer without a single byte of Microsoft code.

Office includes a wide range of file converters to help translate files into other popular formats, including those for earlier versions of Office. Normally, Office programs open any file created in a compatible format without requiring any extra work on your part. The file that you want to convert might not be visible in the Open dialog box if it ends with an extension that the Office program doesn't recognize. To see all files with extensions normally associated with a given file type, such as WK1 and WKS files for Lotus 1-2-3 spreadsheet files, select the appropriate entry from the Files of Type drop-down list. (If you can't see any extensions in Explorer windows or dialog boxes, open Explorer's Folder Options dialog box, click the View tab, and uncheck the Hide File Extensions for Known File Types box.

Tip from

> To see all files in the Open dialog box, regardless of their extension, choose All Files from the Files of Type drop-down list. Some other distinctions in this drop-down list are less obvious but still useful. For example, selecting Word Documents filters the list

to show only files with that file type and the *.doc extension, whereas All Word Documents includes Web pages (*.htm) and Word templates (*.dot), as well as ordinary Word documents. Likewise, the All PowerPoint Presentations choice includes any HTML file in addition to PowerPoint presentations and shows.

To save a file in an alternative format, choose File, Save As. In the Save As dialog box, choose an entry from the Save as Type drop-down list.

Office displays the full range of compatible file types in both the Open and Save As dialog boxes. In some cases, you might need to supply the Office CD to install a particular converter before opening or saving a file in that format.

→ To help ensure that Word files that you create can be accessed by users with other versions of Office, **see** "Avoiding Compatibility Problems," **p. 330**.

→ To learn more about Excel file compatibility, **see** "File Compatibility Issues," **p. 539**.

PART

I

CH

3

STORING DOCUMENT DETAILS

The Windows file system keeps track of details about each file: its size, when it was created, and when you last modified it, for example. Windows enables you to store extra details about Office file types; these *properties* include the author's name, a title and a subject for the file, and comments or keywords that you can use to search for documents later. A Custom properties sheet lets you track more than two dozen built-in categories or add your own.

Maintaining file properties takes a fair amount of up-front work, but it can have a profound pay-off, especially in a networked office where many users share documents.

- When you use the Search task pane, you can specify any property of any Office file by choosing Advanced Search at the bottom of the task pane. If you've trained an entire department to enter details about a client, project, or product line in the Properties dialog box, it's trivially easy to locate all the files associated with that activity.

- If you use Outlook's Integrated File Management features, you can create custom views that include any properties in this dialog box. By adding the Author and Title fields to an Outlook view, for example, you can group the contents of a folder by author and by title—something you simply can't do with the Windows Explorer.

→ For a brief overview of how Outlook enables you to manage files, **see** "Managing Outlook Data Files," **p. 199**.

- All file properties are available to macros that you create by using Visual Basic for Applications. As a result, you can create simple but effective document-management routines that are limited only by your imagination. For example, you can create AutoNew macros that prompt users for key information every time they create a new document based on a particular Word template. You can then use that information to file or route the document when the user saves it.

→ For more ideas and techniques using VBA, **see** Chapter 40, "Building Custom Applications with VBA," **p. 1005**.

To view and edit details for the current file, choose File, Properties. The dialog box that appears resembles the one in Figure 3.5.

Figure 3.5
The Properties dialog box displays summary information about Office file types.

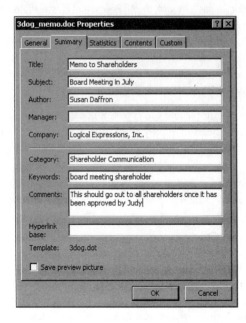

The Properties dialog box for an Office file includes the five tabs described in Table 3.1.

TABLE 3.1 OFFICE FILE PROPERTIES

Properties	Description
General	Basic information from the Windows file system: name, location, size, and so on.
Summary	Information about the current file and its author, including fields for company name, category, and keywords. The Comments field is particularly useful when you use Outlook's file management capabilities because the text appears beneath each filename when you turn on AutoPreview.
Statistics	Details about the size and structure of the file, such as the number of words in a document or the number of slides in a presentation; also displays revision statistics and total editing time. This information is frequently incorrect, especially when you inspect it from the shortcut menus in an Explorer window. Professional writers and students who rely on these statistics should always inspect them from within the document itself to guarantee that the information is up-to-date.
Contents	The parts of the file: the outline of a Word document, based on heading styles; worksheet titles in an Excel workbook; or slide titles in a PowerPoint presentation.
Custom	Twenty-seven built-in fields that you can choose from, including Client, Document Number, and Date Completed. Alternatively, you can add a field of your own. Custom fields can contain text, dates, numbers, or Yes/No information; they can also be linked to Word bookmarks, named Excel ranges, or PowerPoint text selections.

> **Note**
>
> For data files located on a Windows NT/2000/XP disk formatted with the Windows NT file system (NTFS) you'll see a sixth tab that contains security settings.

For simple projects, you might choose to ignore file properties; in these cases, a descriptive filename can tell you everything you need to know about the file. For more complicated documents, however, adding file details—including keywords and categories—can help you or a coworker quickly find a group of related data files, even months or years after you last worked with them. Use the Comments box to add freeform notes about a given file.

To enter additional details about an Office file, you must open the properties dialog box before you save the file. If you use this feature regularly, you can configure Word, Excel, and PowerPoint to display the File Properties dialog box every time you save a file.

→ To learn more about the common features found within the Office applications, **see** "Configuring Common Office Features," **p. 44**.

DEFAULT DOCUMENT PROPERTIES

By default, Office applications save only a few document properties when you save a file. Properties saved vary by application:

- Windows stores standard file details, including the name, size, and date and time the file was modified.

- All Office applications add your name in the Author field and your organization's name in the Company field.

- Word and PowerPoint fill in the Title field as well, using the first few words of a Word document or the title of a PowerPoint presentation.

> **Note**
>
> In Word documents in particular, this capability can lead to embarrassing consequences if you're not careful. By default, if you fail to enter document properties, Word picks up the opening line of your document and plops it in the Title field—up to the first paragraph mark or 126 characters, whichever comes first. For example, if you begin composing an angry memo and save it, your initial angry words might survive in the Title field, even if you tone down your rhetoric considerably in the final version. That fact alone is an excellent reason to configure Word to pop up the Properties dialog box whenever you save a new document. You can also guarantee that this information is not saved with a file by choosing Tools, Options and using the Privacy options on the Security tab.

If you want to add categories, keywords, or comments to any Office file, do so on the Summary tab.

USING CUSTOM PROPERTIES TO ORGANIZE FILES

In an office where a large number of people create and share files, custom file properties can make it easier for workgroups to share files. In a legal office, for example, you might use the Client, Status, and Recorded Date fields to track the progress of Word documents. Members of a team producing budget worksheets might use the Checked By and Forward To fields as part of a document management system. Use the Office applications' Search task panes to find files whose properties match a particular set of criteria. Figure 3.6 shows a Word document that includes several custom properties.

Figure 3.6
Record additional file properties on the Custom tab; later, use the Find tool in Office common dialog boxes to search for files that match these criteria.

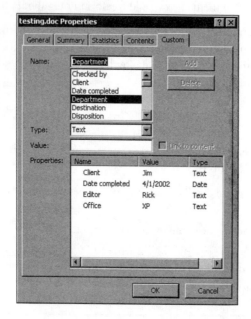

To enter custom criteria for any Office file, follow these steps:

1. Open the file and choose File, Properties.
2. Click the Custom tab to display the dialog box shown previously in Figure 3.6.
3. Choose a field from the Name list. To create a new field, type its name here.
4. Choose one of the available data types from the Type drop-down list.
5. Type the data for the selected field in the Value text box.

Caution

If you specify Number or Date as the data type for a custom field, you must enter the value in a matching format. If you enter dates in a nonstandard format or you include text in a field that should contain only numbers, Office enters the value as text.

6. Click Add. The new entry appears in the Properties list at the bottom of the dialog box.

7. Repeat steps 3–6 for any additional custom fields. To remove an item from the Properties list, select its entry and click Delete. Click OK to close the dialog box and return to the program window.

USING EXPLORER TO VIEW FILE PROPERTIES

To view any Office file's properties without opening the file itself, open an Explorer window, right-click the file's icon, and then choose Properties. If you're using Windows 98, Me, NT 4.0, 2000, or XP, you can edit most file properties for Word documents, Excel spreadsheets, and PowerPoint presentations directly from an Explorer window. If you're using Windows 95, you can view properties on the General, Summary, and Statistics tabs, but you must open the file with its associated program to change those properties. Regardless of which Windows version you use, only the most basic summary information is available when you view the properties of an Access database from an Explorer window.

If you've configured Explorer to use Web view, you can see some Office file properties, such as the author's name, in the info pane along the left side of the Explorer window, as shown in Figure 3.7. You can also see a thumbnail of the file itself in this region, but only if you checked the Save Preview Picture box on the Summary tab of the Properties dialog box. By default, this box is unchecked for Word documents and Excel workbooks and is checked for PowerPoint presentations.

PART

I

CH

3

Figure 3.7
In Web view, Explorer windows display some information drawn from an Office file's properties. The thumbnail preview is available only if you check an option when saving the file.

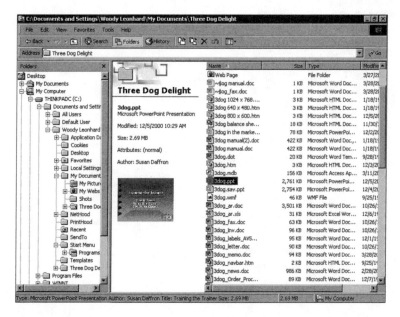

 To save a preview of an Excel workbook, you must check this box when you first save the file; see "No Preview in Common Dialog Boxes" in the "Troubleshooting" section at the end of this chapter for more details.

SEARCHING FOR OFFICE FILES

The Open dialog box displays a list of all files in the current folder. Searching for a specific file can be tedious if the folder is full of files with similar names, or if it's organized into many subfolders. Office includes a powerful Search tool, available in the Search task pane, that enables you to search for files or Outlook messages—even Web pages—by using almost any criteria. If you can remember a few scraps of information about the file—part of the name, a date, or even a word or phrase that you remember using in the document—you can probably find it.

For example, a sales manager might look on a shared network file server for all presentations that have been updated in the past week. Or, a legal secretary might search for files that include a specific case number and that are not marked as completed. If space is at a premium on your local hard drive, you can search for all Office files that were last modified more than six months ago, and then move them to a new location.

Compared to previous Office versions, the Search tools in Office XP are dramatically improved and far more usable. To display the Basic Search task pane (see Figure 3.8), click the Search button on the Standard toolbar, or choose View, Task Pane, and select Search from the drop-down list at the top of the pane.

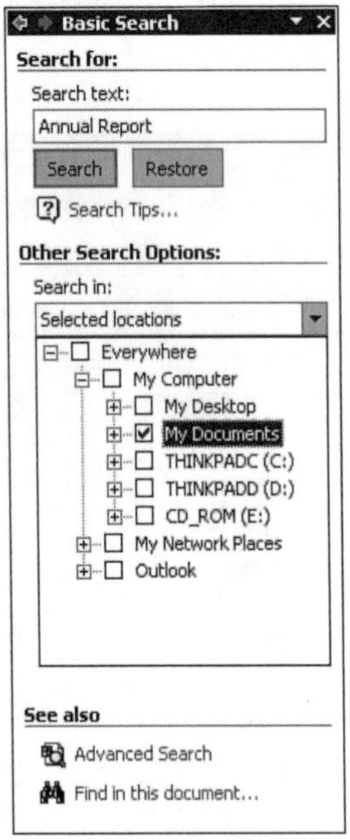

Figure 3.8
Search for a file or Outlook message by using simple search criteria in the Basic Search task pane.

Caution

Office XP, unlike its predecessors, does *not* allow you to save and reuse search criteria. You can bring back the most recently used Search by clicking the Restore button, but there is no capability to store searches within Office XP programs. For that task, run your search in Windows Explorer instead, and save the search as a shortcut.

Basic searches are quick and simple. Advanced searches, on the other hand, can be complex, with sophisticated logic and multiple criteria. To switch to the Advanced Search task pane (see Figure 3.9), click the Advanced Search entry at the bottom of the Basic Search task pane.

Figure 3.9
Be careful when using AND/OR logic in the Advanced Search task pane. The correct order affects your search results.

You construct a search by adding criteria to a list. Each entry in the criteria list consists of three pieces:

- **Property**—Includes file system properties (name, date created, and file size, for instance), statistics (such as the number of slides in a PowerPoint presentation or the number of paragraphs in a Word document), and Office custom properties.

- **Condition**—Defines the comparison that you want Office to make. The list of available conditions depends on the property you selected previously.

- **Value**—Defines the specific text, number, or other data type for which you want Office to search.

A pair of buttons (And, Or) at the left of the criteria definition boxes enable you to combine criteria, and you can specify that Office search multiple folders and subfolders.

Criteria can be extremely simple—for example, all files last modified this week. For more sophisticated searches, combine criteria to quickly filter a huge group of files into a manageable list. After you enter the first set of conditions, click the Add button. After you've entered all your search criteria, click the Search button. Options at the bottom of the pane let you restrict file types and locations using check boxes.

FINDING FILES OR MESSAGES BY CONTENT

To conduct a simple search by content—whether you're looking for a file, a message, a contact, an appointment, a task, a note, or a Web page—bring up the Basic Search task pane and follow these steps:

1. Type the text (content) that you're looking for in the Search text box. You can use wildcards: ? stands for any single character (m?t searches for *met* or *mat*, but not *meet*); * stands for one or more characters (b*m searches for *bam* and *blam* but not *ban*).

2. In the Search In list, specify where you want Office to look. You can narrow the search to specific drives or folders in My Computer, or Outlook; you can also limit search to specific locations in My Network Places.

3. In the Results Should Be box, specify which types of Office files and Outlook items to look for; you can also search in Web pages.

4. Click the Search button. The matching items appear in a list. If you click once on a filename, the appropriate Office application opens the file. You can also choose from a drop-down list to the right of the filename if you want to create a new file based on the selected one.

USING DOCUMENT PROPERTIES TO LOCATE FILES

Use the Search task pane in conjunction with file properties to construct a powerful document-management system. It takes training and discipline for a group of workers to routinely enter the correct information in file properties. You can automatically add some of these details by customizing templates or using Visual Basic for Applications. For example, you might use simple AutoNew, AutoOpen, and AutoClose macros, which run automatically when you open or close a document, to prompt the user to enter specific details about a document.

All built-in file properties are available from the Property drop-down list in the Advanced Search task pane. To search for properties that you've added to the Custom tab, you need to manually enter the name of the property.

WORKING WITH MULTIPLE FILES

Word, Excel, PowerPoint, and FrontPage enable you to open more than one file at a time. Access does not, and you can't open multiple files directly by using the New File task pane. To open multiple files using the common dialog boxes, follow these steps:

1. In the New File task pane, click More Documents. Equivalently, you can press Ctrl+O or choose File, Open to display the Open dialog box.

2. Hold down the Ctrl key and click to select multiple filenames.

3. Click the Open button or press Enter to open all selected files.

To open multiple files from an Explorer window, hold down the Ctrl key and click each icon; then right-click and choose Open.

You can also open any file by dragging its icon from an Explorer window into an Office program window. When you drag an Excel or PowerPoint icon from an Explorer window into an open program window, Office opens the new file in its own window. On the other hand, if you drop a Word icon into an open document window, Word assumes that you want to insert the file at the point where you dropped it. The same thing happens if you drop a Web page icon into a FrontPage window in which you're editing another Web page. To open the document or Web page in a new window instead, drop the icon onto the title bar of the Word or FrontPage program window.

In Office XP, each new data file gets its own button on the Windows taskbar, and you can switch between document windows the same way you switch between programs.

Unfortunately, Office's techniques for handling multiple document windows are wildly inconsistent among applications. Unless you change its default behavior (see the following tip), each Word document exists in its own window; there's no way to display two or more Word documents in the same window, and closing one Word document has no effect on other windows. Excel and PowerPoint, on the other hand, enable you to rearrange document windows within a single program window, and if you click the Close (X) button on an Excel or PowerPoint window, you close all open workbooks or presentations.

PART

I

CH

3

Tip from

Ed & Woody

You can have Word put multiple documents inside its window like the other Office applications do (the so-called "multiple-document interface"). With Word in this condition, you can, for example, choose Window, Arrange All to have multiple documents appear inside Word without multiple copies of the menus and toolbars hanging around cluttering up the screen. To do so, choose Tools, Options; on the View tab, clear the box marked Windows in Taskbar. Unfortunately, when you do this, individual documents no longer appear in the Windows taskbar.

SETTING UP AUTOMATIC BACKUP AND RECOVERY OPTIONS

Office XP comes with "air bags"—a sophisticated set of programs that are designed to make crashes less frequent, to make crashes less devastating when they do occur, and to increase your chances of recovering a document when Office does crash. These are the important points to keep in mind:

- If an Office application "hangs"—goes out to lunch and doesn't come back—you should shut it down using the Office Application Recovery program. Click Start, Programs, Microsoft Office Tools, and choose Microsoft Office Application Recovery. Avoid using Task Manager or the other Windows tools—Office is one of the few Windows programs that ships with tools specifically designed to dislodge a "hang." We will note with appropriate irony that it's also one of the few Windows programs that needs one.

- When you restart an Office application that has crashed, chances are good that you'll be presented with the Office Document Recovery task pane (see Figure 3.10). Documents that are listed as [Original] probably aren't as up-to-date as those marked [Recovered]. Choose the version that you want to keep, click it, and then Close the Document Recovery task pane.

Figure 3.10
Office's Document Recovery task pane appears on the left side of the screen.

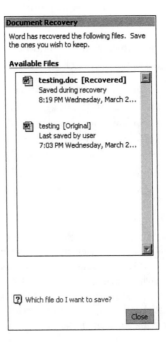

- It might be worthwhile to save several [Recovered] documents and compare the versions to see which (if any) have worthwhile changes. To do so, click the down arrow to the right of the [Recovered] filename and choose Save As.

Tip from

E & Woody

Automatic Backup and Recovery—the "air bags for Office"—should be treated with the kind of skepticism usually reserved for "version 1.0" Office features. Sometimes it works; sometimes it doesn't. If you find yourself with crashed Office documents that aren't resurrected by the "air bags," consider using a dedicated document descrambler, such as those offered by OfficeRecovery (`http://www.officerecovery.com`).

TROUBLESHOOTING

PUTTING TEMPLATES IN THEIR PLACE

I created a group of templates and saved them along with the standard Office templates in the C:\Program Files\Microsoft Office\Templates\1033 folder. But when I choose File, New, none of my custom templates are visible.

Microsoft designed the folder that stores system templates so that users cannot add templates to it. Instead, you should save your templates to the default User Templates location. The safest way to save templates to this location is one at a time. If you choose Template from the Files of Type list in the Save As dialog box, all Office programs will save your work to the correct location. If you want to add a large number of files to this location, open Word and choose Tools, Options; then click the File Locations tab and verify the User Templates location.

NO PREVIEW IN COMMON DIALOG BOXES

I selected Preview from the drop-down menu of views in an Office common dialog box, but when I click a file in the pane on the left, Windows displays the words Preview not available instead of showing my file.

The preview pane shows a static snapshot of the document as it existed the last time you saved it. By default, this option is not selected because it tends to add roughly 60KB to every file that you create. To make this preview picture available, you must choose File, Properties and check the Save Preview Picture box on the Summary tab. You can do this at any time with a Word document or PowerPoint presentation. However, this option is effective with Excel workbooks only if you use it when you first create the file. Checking this box on an Excel workbook after you've saved it with this option off has no effect at all. To enable the preview, check the box, save the file under a new name, and use Windows Explorer to delete the old version and rename the new one with the old name.

DEALING WITH SHORT FILENAMES

Several co-workers in my organization use Windows 3.1 and Office 4. When they browse through shared folders for files I have created, they have a difficult time telling which is which because all the files have names like Letter~1.doc.

Saving files in the correct format is only half the battle. If you routinely share document folders with coworkers who use 16-bit Windows or DOS programs that don't recognize long filenames, you need to follow some common-sense rules. For starters, try to restrict filenames to a maximum of eight characters, not counting the extension. If you must use longer names, make sure that the first six characters in the name will provide a clue to the file's contents when viewed in a 16-bit common dialog box. As you've seen, Windows will add a two-character numeric tail to the short version of each filename, making only the first six characters significant. (Although some well-meaning Windows experts have published a tip that enables you to hack the Registry and change this behavior, we strongly recommend that you not follow this advice; as an unfortunate side effect, you might end up with duplicate Program Files folders.)

When naming files that you expect to share with users of 16-bit programs, avoid using anything except letters and numbers in the first eight characters of a filename. When creating the aliases that 16-bit programs use, Windows substitutes an underscore for special characters such as semicolons, plus signs, and brackets, and the effect is to make the filename nearly indecipherable to those users.

SECRETS OF THE OFFICE MASTERS: DETAILS, DETAILS

In common dialog boxes, trying to use information in the Type column is an exercise in frustration, thanks to Microsoft's marketing machine. After a default installation of Office XP, you'll have 75 registered file types, each starting with the word Microsoft—Microsoft Word Document, Microsoft Excel Worksheet, and even Microsoft HTML Document 5.0. The effect is to make it impossible to distinguish the types of documents in a detailed list unless you expand the Type column to a ridiculous width.

Making all file extensions visible is a crude solution to this problem, but Explorer windows don't allow you to sort by this information anyway.

So here's a better idea: Regain control of the file types that you use most often, removing the useless Microsoft tag at the beginning of each one and making extensions visible for selected file types, such as HTML documents, where you might want to edit that change on demand.

In Windows 98, Windows Me, Windows 95 with IE4's Windows Desktop Update, or Windows NT 4.0, 2000, or XP, follow these steps: Open any Explorer window (the My Documents or My Computer folder is a good choice), choose View, Folder Options or Tools, Folder Options, and then click the File Types tab. Scroll through the list of registered file types until you reach the Microsoft block, and begin editing each file type. Select a file type (Microsoft Word Document, for example) and click the Edit or Advanced button. In the Edit File Type dialog box, remove the unnecessary "Microsoft" from the Description of Type box. Click the Always Show Extension box to ensure that .doc extensions are always visible (and editable) in Explorer windows.

Repeat this process for other file types, such as Microsoft HTML Document 5.0 and Microsoft Excel Worksheet. Now, when you use Details view, you'll really see the details that matter.

Figure 3.11

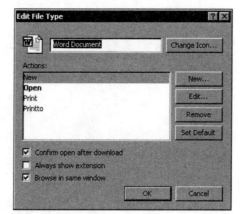

CHAPTER **4**

EDITING AND FORMATTING TEXT

In this chapter

ENTERING TEXT

Most Office users don't think about entering text until they encounter a character that's not part of their daily repertoire: a currency symbol such as ¥, perhaps, or a Greek character such as π.

In fact, Office XP contains full support for the *Unicode standard*, a universally recognized character set containing tens of thousands of letters, ideographs, and other symbols, which spans the majority of all written languages. If the operating system you are using supports the characters used in a specific language, those characters are available in Office.

INSERTING SYMBOLS AND SPECIAL CHARACTERS

Office supports three relatively easy methods to place a single symbol or other special character in an Office document:

- The Symbols tab in the Symbol dialog box (choose Insert, Symbol) gives you a magnified preview of every character available in normal or decorative fonts (see Figure 4.1). This comprehensive list of symbols should be your first resort.

Figure 4.1
The frequently overlooked Subset list for Insert Symbol's normal text option offers quick access to different groups of characters.

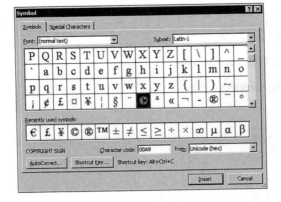

Tip from

When you click a symbol, a short description of the character, as well as its character number and shortcut key (if any) appear at the bottom of the Symbol dialog box.

Note

The Symbol dialog box is easy to use and comprehensive, but it doesn't close after you've inserted a character. You must press Esc or click Close (X) or Cancel to dismiss it.

- The Special Characters tab in the Symbol dialog box (see Figure 4.2) gives you quick access to the most common punctuation characters (also known as *special characters*). The tab is only available in Outlook, Word, and Excel. If you are tired of scrolling through the Symbol dialog box's detailed lists, this is the place to turn.

Figure 4.2
The Special Characters tab includes only a small subset of the characters listed on the Symbols tab, but the ones that are there are easier to find and (in Word and Outlook) include Shortcut key reminders.

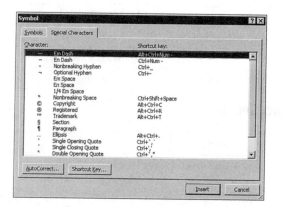

- If you know that you're going to be using a specific symbol or special character repeatedly, set up an AutoCorrect entry for it by clicking the AutoCorrect button on the Symbol dialog in Word or Outlook, or by choosing Tools, AutoCorrect Options in Excel, Access or PowerPoint. For example, if you use the ¥ (Japanese Yen) symbol frequently, tell Office to AutoCorrect the two characters "Y"="" to ¥. The entry will work in Outlook, Word, Excel, or PowerPoint, but not in FrontPage.

→ To learn more about saving and reusing text, **see** "Using AutoCorrect to Automate Documents," **p. 91**.

Note

To find various dashes, "curly" quotes, daggers, ellipses, and many more common marks quickly, choose General Punctuation in the Subset box.

More ways can be used to insert symbols into your documents. For example, you can use the Windows Character Map applet, or you can follow the buttons on Word and Outlook's Symbol dialog to create AutoCorrect entries or Shortcut keys. You can write a macro in any Office application that inserts a specific character and assigns it to a toolbar button or key combination. You can also fall back on ancient but reliable utilities such as Sidekick, the key-swapping, do-anything program with roots dating back to the early days of DOS.

ENTERING ACCENTED AND INTERNATIONAL CHARACTERS

If you use the U.S. English version of Office XP and you have only occasional need for an accented, inflected, or otherwise altered character common in European languages, Word and Outlook recognize the shortcuts in Table 4.1.

PART
I

CH
4

Table 4.1 Word and Outlook's Accented Character Shortcuts

To Type Any of These Accented Characters	First, Press This Key Command	Then Type the Desired Letter
ÀàÈèÌìÒòÙù	Ctrl+ `	AaEeIiOoUu
ÁáD´dÉéÍíÓóÚúÝý	Ctrl+ '	AaDdEeIiOoUuYy
ÂâÊêÎîÔôÛû	Ctrl+Shift+ ^	AaEeIiOoUu
ÄäËëÏïÖöÜüŸÿ	Ctrl+Shift+ :	AaEeIiOoUuYy
ÃãÑñÕõ	Ctrl+Shift+ ~	AaNnOo
ÆæŒœß	Ctrl+Shift+ &	AaOos
Çç	Ctrl+ ,	Cc
Åå	Ctrl+Shift+@	Aa
Øø	Ctrl+/	Oo

To enter an inverted question mark or exclamation point (¿, ¡) for use with Spanish text, press Alt+Ctrl+Shift+? or Alt+Ctrl+Shift+!.

Entering Text in Another Language

Office interprets the keys on your keyboard according to the conventions established inside Windows. To change the mapping of keys to characters, use the Control Panel's Keyboard applet: Click Start, Settings, Control Panel, double-click Keyboard, and then click either the Language (Windows 95) or the Input Locales (Windows 98, ME, NT, 2000, XP) tab.

Tip from

EQ & Woody

It's easy to set up a keyboard shortcut that changes languages. On the Keyboard applet's Language or Input Locales tab, use the Switch Languages (or locales) option. In Windows 2000 and XP, you'll need to click the Change Key Sequence button in the Hot Keys for the Input Locales section.

When you switch keyboards, Word automatically switches fonts to those that are designed for the language and sets the proofing language for spell checking and grammar checking.

Before you can edit text in those other languages, you need to have Office install the features demanded by that particular language. To do so, click Start, Programs, Microsoft Office Tools, Microsoft Office Language Settings. On the Enabled Languages tab (see Figure 4.3), check whichever languages you want Office to recognize.

The actual tools involved vary from language to language. For example, if you install Thai language support, the Font dialog box (choose Format, Font) will, from that point on, include a selection for complex scripts (that is, text that includes Thai characters; see Figure 4.4).

Figure 4.3
Office 2002 supports a wide variety of languages, even if you have only the U.S. English version.

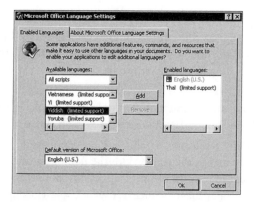

Figure 4.4
Choose to enable Thai language support, and the Font dialog box enables you to specify a font for Complex scripts. Note the "Sample" in Thai at the lower right.

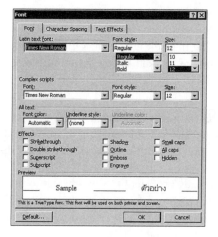

Some languages require additional tools. Arabic, Hebrew, and Farsi, for example, need *bi-directional support*, because they are input and read from right to left. Ideographic languages need the Microsoft Input Method Editor to make it possible to type "text" (ideograms) at all. (*Ideograms*, the cornerstone of several written Asian languages, are symbols more related to ideas or things rather than a spoken sound. Ideographic languages are notoriously difficult to input into a computer because they typically contain thousands of "characters".) For more details, consult the online Help topic "About Multilingual Editing and the Microsoft Proofing Tools Kit."

SELECTING TEXT

Certainly the most fundamental of Office activities, it's amazing how each of the Office applications handles text selection shortcuts so differently.

When you select text with a mouse, the following shortcuts apply:

- Double-clicking a word selects the word in all Office applications. In Outlook, Word, PowerPoint, and FrontPage, double-clicking also selects the word's trailing space(s), if any; in Excel and Access, it does not. That can be confusing when switching between applications.

- Triple-clicking selects an entire paragraph, but only in Outlook, Word, PowerPoint, and FrontPage. Triple-clicking in Excel does not select an entire cell.

- Word enables you to move your mouse pointer to the left margin, where it will turn into an arrow pointed up and to the right. With the pointer in that state, you can click once to select the current line; twice to select the paragraph; or three times to select the entire document. FrontPage behaves similarly, except triple-clicking selects only the line. Oddly, Outlook does not have a similar capability.

- In addition, Word, Outlook, and PowerPoint automatically force you to select entire words when you click and drag over more than one word. All three applications enable you to turn this feature off using the Edit tab on the Options dialog box (choose Tools, Options to get there); clear the box marked When Selecting, Automatically Select Entire Word.

→ To learn more ways you can customize Word, **see** "Customizing the Word Interface," **p. 354.**

- When working with text boxes in the drawing layer, Office takes on the clicking conventions of the underlying application: Triple-clicking in a paragraph in an Excel text box does nothing; the same action in Word or PowerPoint selects the entire paragraph.

Many advanced Word users—especially proficient typists—prefer to use the keyboard to select characters and words. By memorizing a few simple commands and avoiding the round trip to the mouse, they can plow through text much faster. Keyboard-selection techniques stay fairly uniform throughout Office (see Table 4.2).

TABLE 4.2   KEYBOARD SELECTIONS VALID IN ALL OFFICE PROGRAMS

To Select	Press
Next character to right	Shift+Right Arrow
Next character to left	Shift+Left Arrow
To end of word	Ctrl+Shift+Right Arrow
To beginning of word	Ctrl+Shift+Left Arrow
To end of line	Shift+End
To beginning of line	Shift+Home
Entire document	Ctrl+A

In addition, Outlook and Word have two important shortcuts that experienced users will want to memorize (see Table 4.3). These shortcuts come in handy when you're trying to select blocks of text in large documents, "from this point to the beginning" or "from this point to the end." No menu or toolbar button equivalents exist for either.

TABLE 4.3   KEYBOARD SELECTIONS VALID ONLY IN OUTLOOK AND WORD

To Select	Press
To end of document	Ctrl+Shift+End
To beginning of document	Ctrl+Shift+Home

In Outlook and Word you can select discontiguous characters—that is, characters that are not next to each other—by holding down the Ctrl key as you select. In Excel you can select discontiguous cells the same way. In PowerPoint, you're allowed to select discontiguous slides. But you can't select discontiguous text in Excel, PowerPoint, or FrontPage.

FINDING AND REPLACING TEXT

When you want to find or replace a piece of text in an Office document, the method varies depending on which application you use to find a particular text string, do the following:

1. Choose Edit, Find. Type the text you want to locate in the Find What box. Word's (and Outlook's) Find and Replace dialog box is shown in Figure 4.5.

Figure 4.5
Word and Outlook have the most comprehensive Find and Replace options.

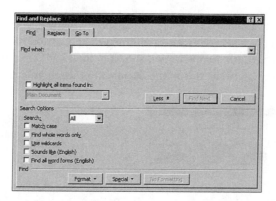

2. Set up the parameters, known as *criteria*, for your search. Depending on which Office application you are using, the process of setting up your search criteria will vary:

   - In Outlook, Word, or FrontPage, you can choose whether you want to search Up (toward the beginning of the document) or Down (toward the end). In Access, you can choose Up or Down as well, but to do so you must click the More button in the dialog box. In Excel (see Figure 4.6) or PowerPoint, you have no choice as to direction—the first Find uncovers the first occurrence of the string; subsequent Find Next selections move to later occurrences. The Search All option in Access also finds the first occurrence, the same as an Excel or PowerPoint Find.

Figure 4.6
Excel's Find and Replace is remarkably different from Word's.

- Excel enables you to choose whether you want to search *row-major* ("Search By Rows" going across the current row before dropping down to the next one) or *column-major* ("Search By Columns" going down the current column before looking at the next one to the right). Make your choice in the Search box. Excel also enables you to look at formulas or values (that is, formula results). If you have a cell that contains the formula =SUM(A1:B3), for example, searching the formulas for B3 results in a hit, whereas searching the values doesn't.

Note

Excel enables you to easily search for text in comments. This feature can come in handy if you're scanning for comments from a specific individual or those that apply to a given topic. To do so, select Comments in the Look In box.

- All the Office applications enable you to specify that you want to Match Case (the accelerator key varies from application to application, see Figure 4.7). With this box checked, the capitalization shown in the Find What text box must match the capitalization of the text in the document precisely to get a "hit".

Figure 4.7
PowerPoint's Spartan Find dialog box is limited.

- Outlook, Word, FrontPage, and PowerPoint enable you to restrict the search to Find Whole Words Only, by checking a box. In that situation, the text in the Find What field must appear in the document preceded and followed by a space or punctuation mark: beast, for example, will match beast but not beasts. Excel has a comparable check box that limits hits to cells where the entire cell contents matches the text in the Find What box. Similarly, Access can limit hits to those that match the entire field.

3. With the find criteria established the way you want, click Find Next and the application selects the next occurrence of the text.

Outlook, Word, Excel, and Access accept wildcards:

- * matches one or more letters. For example, s*ap will turn up hits on snap or strap, but not on sap.

- ? matches one single letter. For example, b?t will match bit or bat, but not boot.

- In Excel only, the tilde character (~) followed by a ~, ?, or * matches ~, ?, or *. So hop~* matches hop*, but not hop? or hope, and tr~?p matches tr?p but not tr*p or tr-p or trip.

Word has an enormous number of additional search features; the other Office applications pale in comparison.

→ To learn more about Word's powerful search features, **see** "Finding and Replacing Text and Other Parts of a Document," **p. 370**.

CONVERTING SCANNED DOCUMENTS TO TEXT

Although you wouldn't want to depend on it for mission-critical applications, Office comes bundled with a surprisingly good Optical Character Recognition system. Converting hard-copy to a Word document is a two-step process:

1. Scan the document and turn it into a TIF file. To do so, from Windows, choose Start, Programs, Microsoft Office Tools, Microsoft Office Document Scanning, and follow the instructions.

Tip from

EQ & Woody

The Document Scanner includes an option to "re-stitch" documents that are printed on both sides of the paper. You scan one side and then the other, and the software puts the two halves together, in sequence. It's a very handy feature.

2. Turn the TIF file produced by the Office scanner (or any other TIF file, for that matter), into a Word document. Click Start, Programs, Microsoft Office Tools, Microsoft Office Document Imaging. Open the TIF file. Click the Send Text to Word icon. It can take a few minutes for the OCR engine to analyze a page, but the results can be quite good.

In experiments scanning a pristine printout employing typical business text in 12-point Times New Roman font, recognition rates were in the high 90s. On a faxed tabular report, originally printed on an impact printer, complete with (nonsimulated) coffee cup stains, Office still managed to recognize much more than 80% of the characters.

Whether that's good enough for your business is largely a matter of how the scanned documents will be used. If you're relying on sophisticated indexing to retrieve all the documents that include specific phrases, recognition in the high 90s might not be good enough. On the other hand, if you want electronic copies of documents to get the gist of what was said, Office's tools are much more than adequate.

PART

I

CH

4

USING SPEECH RECOGNITION TO ENTER TEXT

Speech recognition is still in its infancy, and Office's implementation only underscores that fact. Speech recognition can be a godsend to those who are physically challenged; however, text input using dictation rates as little more than a novelty to serious Office users. Voice Command mode doesn't fare much better.

Before you even attempt speech recognition, make sure you have the following:

- A PC running at 300MHz or faster (Microsoft's recommendation). In tests run for this book, corn grew faster than dictation on a 500MHz machine.

- At least 96MB of memory.

- A high-quality microphone that comfortably sits within an inch of your mouth.

Start using speech recognition by choosing Tools, Speech. You will go through a 15-minute "training" exercise, where the speech recognition software learns to recognize the words you speak (see Figure 4.8). Training is required even if you're only going to use speech recognition for commands. When you finish the training, Office connects to the Web and runs a video.

Figure 4.8
Start by training the Speech Recognition system to understand words as you speak them.

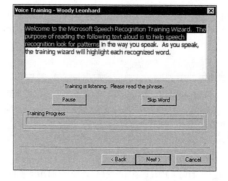

When Speech Recognition is activated (choose Tools, Speech), a free-floating bar called the Language bar appears in the upper- right area of the screen.

Note

The Language bar might look like a plain-vanilla Office toolbar, but it isn't. You can't hide it or make it appear by choosing Tools, Customize, Toolbars. It won't dock. It's available to all of Windows, so the toolbar doesn't travel with an application's window when it's minimized. To get rid of the bar, right-click the left or right ends, and choose Close the Language bar.

Clicking Voice Command on the Language bar sets up voice recognition so you can choose menu items: File <pause, pause, pause> Open <pause, pause, pause> will reliably bring up the Open dialog box, for example. After the dialog box appears, you can navigate to a greater or lesser extent by using the names of tabs on tabbed dialog boxes, or drop-down lists. For example, if you want to open the fifth document in your My Documents folder, you would say: File <pause, pause, pause>, Open <pause, pause, pause>, Down <pause, and so on>, Down, Down, Down, Open. (Assuming all your commands were understood, and you didn't end up opening the Views list, for example.)

Note

On a 500MHz PC, we could disconnect the mouse from the back of the PC, open the mouse up, blow off the ball, put it back together, reconnect it, and then use the mouse to open the fifth document in the My Documents folder in about the same amount of time that it took to use Voice Command. And the mouse would do it reliably, whereas the Voice Command sequence frequently sent us off into Office never-never land.

Choosing Dictation on the Language bar enables you to dictate into the document. Microsoft claims an initial recognition rate of 85%–90%, providing you use a high-quality microphone, you're working in a dead-silent room, and you consistently keep the microphone in the same location close to your mouth. Our tests didn't measure up to that claim, but your results might vary.

Tip from
Ed & Woody

Do the math. If you commonly put 2,000 characters in a typical single-page business letter, and your error rate is 15%–20%, you'll have to change 300–400 characters on that page before it's usable. Right-click spell checking and grammar correction help speed up the process, but using the built-in Word tools don't help "train" the voice recognition system.

Microsoft claims a recognition rate of 95% if you devote a sufficient amount of time to "training"—and you can go back to training at any time. Every time you use the Correction tool on the Language bar, you're helping train the speech recognition system, as well.

Tip from
Ed & Woody

The most important fact a typical Office user needs to know about speech recognition is how to remove it. Go into Control Panel (Start, Settings, Control Panel), double-click Add/Remove Programs. Choose Microsoft Office, click Change. Choose Add or Remove Features. Pull down the list under Office Shared Features and under Alternative User Input, turn the icon in front of Speech to a big red X (Unavailable). Click Update, and speech recognition goes away.

USING AUTOCORRECT TO AUTOMATE DOCUMENTS

No doubt you've seen the result of AutoCorrect when you type a word like teh and it comes up the. Don't take AutoCorrect's name too literally. Yes, it's true that AutoCorrect watches over you, correcting typos in Outlook or Word—for example, type `isn;t` and AutoCorrect converts it to `isn't`. But it does much more:

- AutoCorrect also works in Excel, PowerPoint, and Access—surprisingly, however, it doesn't work in FrontPage. Entries in one application work in all the others (with one exception discussed later in this section); if you tell Access to change `mouses` into `mice`, the correction applies in all other Office applications.

- You can create your own AutoCorrect entries to supercharge your typing—say, changing your shorthand `tpfp` into the `Party of the First Part` or `otoh` into `on the other hand`.

- If you commonly work with boilerplate text, AutoCorrect can handle it for you. If you have an addendum that you add to the end of most contracts, you can set up a code you can remember—such as `addend1`—so it expands into paragraphs, even pages, of text, footnotes, and the like.

- In Word and Outlook, AutoCorrect entries can include graphics. This is handy if you frequently reuse the same graphic image. For example, you might want to scan your signature and turn it into an AutoCorrect entry called `mysig`. Then, wherever you type `mysig`, your scanned signature appears.

- AutoCorrect can even help you with odd capitalization. For example, if one of your company's major customers is called `ZapItInc`, you might have trouble getting the caps right when you type the company name. Set up an AutoCorrect entry for `zapitinc` (all lowercase) and have it corrected to `ZapItInc`. Then every time you type `zapitinc`--or `Zapitinc, ZapItinc, Zapitinc,` or even `zApitiNc`--AutoCorrect automatically changes the word to `ZapItInc`.

Word has a similar feature, called AutoText, which can be more appropriate than AutoCorrect in certain situations.

→ To learn when you should use AutoText instead of AutoCorrect, **see** "Entering Text and Graphics Automatically with AutoText and AutoCorrect," **p. 376**.

Tip from

EQ & Woody

In all the applications except Excel, whenever AutoCorrect changes something you've typed, you can hover your mouse over the changed text and a lightning bolt icon will appear below it. Click the icon for easy access to all AutoCorrect options—including, most specifically, the capability to undo, or even permanently turn off, whatever correction was made.

HOW AUTOCORRECT WORKS

The AutoCorrect engine watches as you type. Whenever you press the Spacebar, type a punctuation mark, or press Enter, it looks to see whether the preceding characters match one of the AutoCorrect entries. If there's a match, the old text is replaced by the contents of the AutoCorrect entry.

For example, in Figure 4.9 you can see an AutoCorrect entry that changes acommodate to accommodate. Because of this entry, if you ever type acommodate followed by a space, punctuation mark, or Enter, it will be automatically changed to accommodate.

Figure 4.9
An AutoCorrect entry to change acommodate to accommodate, from the Tools, AutoCorrect dialog box.

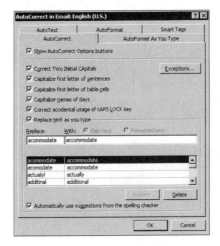

The entry must match precisely. In Figure 4.9, acommodated would not be changed to accommodated—unless, of course, you set up a custom AutoCorrect entry to make the correction.

If you ever have a word changed and you want the original back, hover your mouse next to the change, and use the lightning bolt icon to undo it, by choosing Undo Automatic Corrections. Alternatively—and much more quickly—you can immediately press Ctrl+Z, or you can choose Edit, Undo AutoCorrect, or click the Undo button. Any of these actions will reverse the change made by AutoCorrect and restore what you typed to its original state.

SETTING AUTOCORRECT OPTIONS

In addition to replacing one string of text with another, Office has four additional AutoCorrect settings:

- When you check the Correct TWo INitial CApitals box, Office examines each word you type and if a word starts with two consecutive capitals and the word appears in the dictionary, Word changes the second letter to lowercase. For example, if you mis-capitalize AHead, Word changes it to Ahead; but if you type JScript, CDnow, or XYwrite, Word leaves it alone. You might want to override AutoCorrect on certain two-capital combinations such as GOpher. To do so, click the Exceptions button.

  You can bypass this dialog box and automatically add words that begin with two capital letters to the Exceptions list by immediately undoing the change. If you type GOpher, for example, and Word, Outlook, or PowerPoint"corrects"" the entry to Gopher, hover your mouse over the changed text and choose Stop Automatically Correcting GOpher (or you can press Ctrl+Z in any application) to undo the change. Office restores the second capital letter and adds the word to the Exceptions list in one operation. To disable this feature, click the Exceptions button on the AutoCorrect dialog box and clear the Automatically Add Words to List check box.

■ The Capitalize First Letter of Sentence box presupposes that Office can recognize when you're starting a new sentence. That's not an easy task, and if this setting causes Office to mis-capitalize more frequently than you like, turn it off. Office identifies sentences by the presence of a period followed by a space, but tempers that judgment by a lengthy list of exceptions including approx. and corp., which rarely signal the end of a sentence (see Figure 4.10).

Figure 4.10

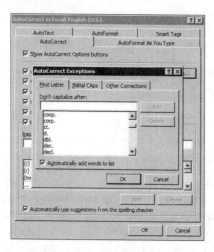

■ The Capitalize names of days check box works as you would expect.

■ The Correct accidental usage of cAPS LOCK key check box, however, comes into play only when you type one lowercase letter, followed by pushing the Caps Lock key, and then continue typing. With this box checked, Office turns the first character into a capital, makes the other characters lowercase, and turns off the Caps Lock function.

Word and Outlook have two more AutoCorrect check boxes. The first, Capitalize first letter of table cells, works much like the Capitalize first letter of sentences setting. The second, named Automatically use suggestions from the spelling checker, has Word do the usual AutoCorrect lookup and, if it doesn't find the word in question in the AutoCorrect list, it consults the spell checker. If the spell checker comes back with one—and only one—suggested correct spelling, the word you typed is replaced with the one offered by the spell checker.

PART

I

CH

4

Caution

You could have an embarrassing mistake if Word substitutes the absolute wrong word for a misspelled one. However, Word's automatic substitution routines don't seem to generate vulgar expressions; capitalized words are left alone (so, for example, if you type Mr. Turkye, it will remain Turkye, and not be AutoCorrected to Turkey).

→ To learn more about spell checking your documents, **see** "Checking Spelling and Grammar," **p. 395**.

If you type tiime, and there's no entry for tiime in the AutoCorrect list, Word consults the spell checker. The spell checker offers only one correct spelling—time—so, with this box checked, tiime is replaced by time.

CUSTOMIZING THE AUTOCORRECT LISTS

Office maintains two AutoCorrect lists. The first one includes all unformatted Word and Outlook AutoCorrect entries, plus all the entries for the other Office applications. The second AutoCorrect list exclusively handles formatted Word and Outlook entries.

Use a formatted AutoCorrect entry whenever it's important that formatting be applied in the replaced text. For example, if you always want the term Congressional Record to appear in italic text, you might set up a formatted AutoCorrect entry called cr that always produces Congressional Record (see Figure 4.11).

Figure 4.11
Formatted
AutoCorrect entries
are available only in
Word and Outlook.

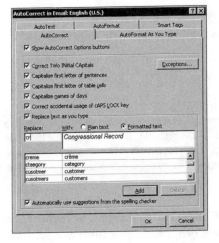

Adding your own formatted entries to the AutoCorrect list is easy:

1. Select the text you want AutoCorrect to produce. Apply whatever formatting you want.

2. Choose Tools, AutoCorrect. The text you've selected appears in the With box. Click the Formatted text button.

3. Type the text you want to trigger an AutoCorrect replacement in the Replace box. In Figure 4.11, we instructed Office to replace cr with Congressional Record.

4. Click Add.

Formatted AutoCorrect entries apply only to Word and Outlook. If you add the formatted *cr* entry shown earlier in Figure 4.11 and then type *cr* in Excel, PowerPoint, or Access, nothing happens. The text *cr* is AutoCorrected only in Word and Outlook.

To add an unformatted AutoCorrect entry, choose Tools, AutoCorrect, and type the entry name in the Replace box and the replacement text in the With box. Click Add.

Caution

When Word and Outlook search for AutoCorrect entries, they look for formatted entries first. Building on the previous example, if you have a formatted entry for *cr* and an unformatted (plain text) entry for *cr*, typing *cr* in Word or Outlook will bring up the formatted entry, but typing *cr* in Excel or PowerPoint will bring up the unformatted (plain text) entry. It's potentially very confusing.

You can also add AutoCorrect entries while performing a spell check. Right-click a word with a red squiggly underline, choose AutoCorrect, and select the correct spelling. An AutoCorrect entry is generated automatically.

Deleting AutoCorrect entries is just as easy as adding them. Bring up the AutoCorrect dialog box, scroll down and select the entry you want to remove, and click Delete.

If you type the name of the entry you want to delete in the Replace box, Office jumps immediately to that part of the list.

Caution

Referring to the previous example where the same replace text has both formatted and unformatted (plain text) entries, if you try to remove the formatted entry by using Tools, AutoCorrect, it won't appear in the list. Your best bet is to remove the unformatted entry. That causes Office to remove *both* the formatted and unformatted entries.

Word fields can appear in AutoCorrect entries, but only as Formatted Text. If you switch to Plain Text when creating an AutoCorrect entry that contains a field, Word converts the field to its field result before storing the entry.

Unformatted AutoCorrect entries are stored in *.acl files and can be moved from machine to machine along with other Office personal information. Formatted AutoCorrect entries are in Word's global template, Normal.dot.

→ To return Word to its original, out-of-the-box condition, **see** "Saving and Restoring Personal Settings," **p. 51**.

Also consider adding words you commonly type that have odd punctuation—Yahoo! comes to mind—so the capitalizing routine will operate properly. You might have other abbreviations that appear frequently in your writing: tb. perhaps, or exec.. To add these exceptions, choose Tools, AutoCorrect, and then click the Exceptions button. Type Yahoo! and click Add. Type tb. and click Add again; type exec., and click Add one last time.

The AutoCorrect list is filled with hundreds of entries—not all of which might be to your liking. Consider removing the ones you find obtrusive (choose Tools, AutoCorrect, select the entry, and click the Delete button). For example

- Several combinations of colons, semicolons, dashes, lines, and parentheses are automatically turned into smiley faces. If you don't particularly want to have smiley faces appear at odd points in your documents, delete those entries from the AutoCorrect list. They're all near the beginning of the list.

Tip from
EQ & Woody

Outlook will not replace emoticons such as :-) with smiley faces in your e-mail messages if you work in Plain Text mode (select Plain Text from the Message format drop-down box). Working in Plain Text also short-circuits AutoCorrect entries that would generate odd characters, such as the copyright symbol.

- If you commonly create numbered lists by hand, and use (a), (b), (c), and so on within the numbers, you'll quickly discover that (c) is automatically turned into a copyright symbol. To override that behavior, use the lightning bolt icon that appears when you hover over the copyright symbol and choose Stop Automatically Correcting "(c)".

- Another AutoCorrect entry turns a standalone lowercase i into an uppercase I. That, too, can be problematic if you create numbered lists by hand. To get around it, use the lightning bolt icon.

- One AutoCorrect entry changes three consecutive periods (...) into an ellipsis. The ellipsis is a single character that looks like three periods, squished close together (…). As long as your documents are destined to be used only by Office, the ellipses pose no problem. But when you copy the text into an e-mail message, for example, or post the document on the Web, the ellipsis character can turn into something totally inscrutable. To keep Office from changing three periods to an ellipsis, use the lightning bolt icon.

PART
I

CH
4

ADVANCED AUTOCORRECT TECHNIQUES

Any situation that involves boilerplate text is a likely candidate for AutoCorrect. If you commonly construct letters that contain five or six paragraphs selected from a pool of many dozens—or hundreds—you can set up AutoCorrect entries for each of the possible paragraphs and, based on a printed list that's memorized or easily accessible, construct the letter rapidly.

In fact, by using {fillin} fields, you can prompt for specific pieces of text to further customize the boilerplate text.

→ To learn more about creating user input forms using Word fields, **see** "Prompting for Input," **p. 507**.

If you commonly write consumer response letters, something along these lines

> *Thank you for your letter of* {fillin}. *We appreciate your taking the time to write to us.*
>
> *I have looked at the suggestion you sent and regret to say that we won't be able to implement it in the near future. However, we do keep suggestions such as yours on file, and refer to that file every time we go through a design change. If we decide to use your suggestion at some future date, I'll be in touch.*
>
> *Thanks once again for writing.*

you can set up the first paragraph as an AutoCorrect entry called *intro17*, the second paragraph as *body23*, and the final paragraph as *close3*, then you can "type" that entire letter with three simple lines:

```
intro17

body23

close3
```

In addition, if you set up the {fillin} field at the indicated location in the first paragraph, when you type intro17, Word prompts you for the date of the letter. You type in the date and it appears in place of the {fillin} field.

Add a final AutoCorrect entry for your scanned signature and title, and you can produce customized boilerplate letters quickly, accurately, and with little effort.

AUTOCORRECT DO'S AND DON'TS

The most common problem with AutoCorrect entries arises when you create an entry that has unexpected side effects. For example, you might create an entry called prn that AutoCorrects to insert the paper in the printer. Then, weeks or months later, you might type a line like this:

```
…create a file called Output.prn and…
```

and the AutoCorrect entry kicks in:

```
…create a file called Output.insert the paper in the printer…
```

 If you find it difficult to locate some AutoCorrect entries, see "Finding Obscure AutoCorrect Entries"" in the "Troubleshooting" section at the end of this chapter.

To minimize the chances for side effects like these, many Office experts use punctuation marks in their AutoCorrect entries. You might be tempted to set up an AutoCorrect entry called usr, for example, to "correct"" into United Steel & Resources, Inc. Unfortunately, every time you misspell use as usr, AutoCorrect kicks in and you get gibberish. If you define the entry as usr., on the other hand—note the trailing period—you can type the entry almost as quickly as usr, and the chances for accidental side effects are greatly reduced.

AutoCorrect entries can be transferred from machine to machine, or swapped around on one specific machine. In theory, you might want to swap out AutoCorrect entries on one computer if you spend part of the day working on office correspondence and the rest of the day rewriting the Human Resources manual. You can download a tool for managing AutoCorrect entries from `http://office.microsoft.com/2000/downloaddetails/supmacros.htm`. Although the tools were developed for Office 2000, they appear to work with Office XP (and updated tools might be available by the time you read this).

Tip from

Ed & Woody

You should avoid swapping around AutoCorrect lists, unless it's absolutely necessary. Instead, use AutoText entries attached to the appropriate template. Although you lose a few of AutoCorrect's niftier features, you'll find it far easier to keep track of the entries if you store and move them with their appropriate template(s).

USING AND MANAGING FONTS

The first law of *typography*: Don't use more than three different fonts (typefaces) in any single document—one for the body text, one for headings, and at most one more for the masthead or main titles. Using these guidelines, you might settle on Garamond for body text, Arial for headings, and Verdana for the title page.

The second law of typography: Nobody follows the first law.

Unless you have a compelling reason to flout convention, most business letters and memos use at most two fonts: one font for the logo, return address, or any other fixed text at the top and bottom of the first sheet; and a second font for all the rest. In the United States, it's customary to use a *serif* font as the main font (for body text), and *sans serif* fonts are commonly used for heading text; in Europe, sans serif is almost as common as a body font, with serif fonts frequently used in headings.

PART

I

CH

4

Tip from

Ed & Woody

A serif font, such as Times New Roman, has curlicues on the ends of the letters, sometimes referred to as feet; a sans serif font, such as Arial, has straight ends.

For example

This is Serif.

This is Sans Serif.

You can mix and match as you like, of course, but be aware that each font you add to a document increases the likelihood that typography will obscure, not enhance, your message. The sure sign of an amateur is a wild mixture of fonts, of varying sizes, with *lots* of italic and **even more** bold italic (unless you're John C. Dvorak, in which case you can even toss in underlines for `dramatic effect`).

When you include the fonts that come with Windows and the fonts included with different Office applications, you have at least 200 fonts at your disposal. That's enough to overwhelm all but the most dedicated font aficionado.

If you find your collection grows unmanageable (and it surely will by the time you hit 300–400 fonts), invest in a third-party font management program. These programs enable you to load and store groups of fonts, bringing them up when they're needed.

At this writing, the best, easily available font management program is Bitstream's Font Navigator. See http://www.bitstream.com/products/world/fontnavigator/index.html for details.

Tip from

ER & Woody

The world of fonts changes constantly. To keep up-to-date on all the latest news, reviews, utilities, and the like, read Peter McDonell's Font Pharos articles in Woody's Windows Watch, the free weekly electronic newsletter, available at http://www.woodyswatch.com/windows/subscribe.asp.

COMMON FORMATTING OPTIONS

Although each Office applications enables you to modify font formatting, and those with paragraphs (Outlook, Word, FrontPage, and PowerPoint) enable you to change paragraph formats, only Word and Outlook use the same dialog boxes to do so, and each application has its own quirks.

CHANGING CHARACTER ATTRIBUTES

To change character formatting, follow these steps:

1. In all Office applications, select the characters you want to change.

2. In Word (see Figure 4.12), Outlook, Publisher, FrontPage (see Figure 4.13), Access, or PowerPoint, choose Format, Font. In Excel (see Figure 4.14), choose Format, Cells, and click the Font tab.

Figure 4.12
Word and Outlook offer, by far, the greatest variety of font-formatting options of any Office application.

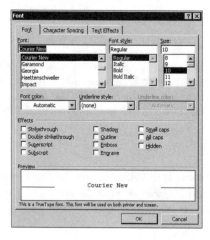

Figure 4.13
FrontPage's options tie directly into Web browser (HTML) standards, as you might expect.

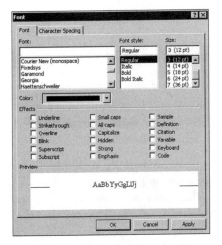

Figure 4.14
Excel, by contrast, offers a more limited selection of font options.

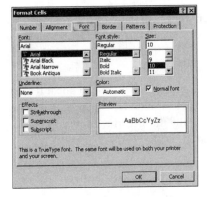

PART

I

CH

4

3. Set the characteristics. All Office applications enable you to change the font (that is, the typeface), size (in fractional increments), style (regular/roman, bold, italic, or bold italic), color, and single-line underline. Excel has several different kinds of underlines, strikethrough, superscript, and subscript. PowerPoint enables you to specify the super/subscript distance, shadow, and emboss. FrontPage enables you to define character styles by selecting one of the check boxes in the final column.

Tip from

EQ & Woody

In theory, the Automatic color (available in every application except Access and Outlook) tells Office to choose a color that contrasts with the color of the background. If you choose Automatic for the text color, for example, and then change the background to black, the text color changes to white and you can still read it. Unfortunately, thanks to a wide-ranging bug in Office, this feature works only in Word documents and tables. If you specify the Automatic color in a PowerPoint text placeholder, an Excel worksheet cell, or a text box in any application, Office ignores your request and formats the text as black. If you then change the background to black, your text disappears from sight.

4. Click OK to change the selected text.

To see the types of character formatting available only in Word, see Chapter 15, "Expert Text-Editing Techniques."

→ To learn more about adding different formatting to your text, **see** "Changing Text Formatting," **p. 380**.

Three Office applications—Word, Excel, and PowerPoint—have check boxes that refer to the Default or Normal font. Each of these boxes works in completely different ways; only Word's actually changes the default font for new documents:

- In Word, the Default button sets the properties you want to use for the default font in all documents created in the future, from the current template. When you click the Default button, Word asks whether you want to use the font settings for all new documents based on the current template. Click Yes. That sets the character formatting for the Normal style in the current template.

→ To see how you can put templates, styles, and themes to work for you, **see** Chapter 18, "Using Styles, Templates, and Themes," **p. 465**.

- In Excel, by contrast, whenever you check the Normal Font box, Excel sets the font, style, and size in this dialog box to match the characteristics of the workbook's Normal style. To change the standard font used in Excel, choose Tools, Options, and on the General tab, modify the Standard font entry.

- In PowerPoint, you can set the font, style, size, and so on, and then click the box marked Default for New Objects. That merely sets the default font for newly created items in the drawing layer—basically the size of the font in new Text Boxes and Auto Shapes in the current presentation.

USING BULLETS AND NUMBERS TO SET OFF LISTS

Bulleted and numbered lists come in handy both to emphasize and to organize. In general, you'll use bulleted lists to draw attention to important members of collections, and you'll want to save numbered lists when there's some sort of internal hierarchy (for example, a top-ten list), or when you might need to refer to one of the points (for example, "see step 3").

Word, Outlook, and PowerPoint all offer *Bullets and Numbering*, and the implementations are remarkably similar: In each case, you choose the paragraphs you want to bullet or number, and then choose Format, Bullets and Numbering.

They all enable you to choose a picture or any character as a bullet. These implementations give you control over whether the numbering is to continue from the previous number or start again from one. They enable you to start AutoNumbering by typing a number followed by a period and space or tab. The primary differences:

- Word and Outlook have outline numbering, where you construct numbering schemes such as 1.A.3, 1.A.4, and so on. Word and Outlook also create AutoBulleted lists if you type a *, >, or a similar character, followed by a space or tab.

→ To learn more about constructing customized numbering schemes, **see** "Formatting Simple Lists with Bullets and Numbers,"**p. 392**.

- PowerPoint enables you to easily scale the size of the bullet so you can select the best size for your presentation.

→ To learn how to create effective bulleted and numbered lists in PowerPoint, **see** "Working with Bulleted and Numbered Lists," **p. 775**.

UNDOING AND REDOING CHANGES

All Office applications have Undo features. If you make a mistake, click the Undo icon, or choose Edit, Undo, or press Ctrl+Z. Every Office application supports at least one level of Undo, and some enable you to undo a number of successive changes. If you discover you made a mistake five minutes ago, you might be able to recover by clicking the Undo button repeatedly. If you close your file, however, all bets are off—all Office applications clear the Undo history when you close the document.

Word and Outlook have a virtually unlimited number of Undo levels. As long as you don't close the document, you can undo anything you've done. (There are some physical limitations to the size of the Undo file, but in practice they aren't significant.)

Word and Outlook's tremendously powerful Undo capability enables you to bring back material that you might have thought was lost. For example, if you're working on a speech and you decide the opening paragraph you started with is better than the one you ended with, you can easily restore it. First, save your current document! If anything goes wrong while using Undo in this way, you can exit without saving and reopen your document to start over.

PART

I

CH

4

Tip from

EQ & Woody

Click the drop-down Undo list and scroll all the way to the bottom, selecting every action on the list. When you release the mouse button, Word undoes everything you've done in the current session, restoring your document to the state it was in when you first opened it. Next, select the text you want to restore and copy it to the Clipboard (do not, under any circumstances, use the Cut command). Now scroll to the bottom of the drop-down Redo list and click to redo every action you just undid. Your document is now back to the state it was in before you performed the multiple-level undo, and you're free to paste in the paragraph from the Clipboard.

⚠ *If you've lost the ability to Redo changes in Word, **see** the Troubleshooting tip "Cutting Text Clears the Redo List" in the "Troubleshooting" section near the end of this chapter.*

Excel, on the other hand, limits you to 16 levels of Undo. This relatively severe limitation has been part of Excel for years, since the Undo feature was first introduced.

→ To overcome this limitation, you need to hack the Registry; **see** "Customizing Excel," **p. 566**.

PowerPoint enables you to select the number of levels of Undo you want to support. (Choose Tools, Options, click the Edit tab, and spin the Maximum Number of Undos box.) The default value is 20, but you can increase this to a maximum of 150.

FrontPage enables you to undo up to 30 operations.

TROUBLESHOOTING

FINDING OBSCURE AUTOCORRECT ENTRIES

A rogue AutoCorrect entry is causing unwanted text to appear in my documents, but I can't find the offending entry in the AutoCorrect list.

Most of the time, it's fairly easy to figure out which entry is causing the problem. Unfortunately, AutoCorrect isn't always so simple. In particular, note that AutoCorrect entries can have embedded spaces so, for example, an entry for any time might correct to anytime. That behavior can be puzzling until you realize that you might be the victim of an AutoCorrect entry that begins with "any".

CUTTING TEXT CLEARS THE REDO LIST

I used Word's multiple-level Undo capability to roll back a large number of changes, and then cut a block of text. But when I wanted to restore my document to its previous state, the Redo button was grayed out.

Did you save your changes before you performed the Undo operation? If so, exit the document without saving, and restore your saved copy. If not, you're out of luck. When you use Word's multilevel Undo, you can copy anything you want to the Clipboard; if you use the Cut command, you wipe out the Redo list, and nothing will bring it back.

SECRETS OF THE OFFICE MASTERS: USING AUTOCORRECT TO ADD A DIGITAL SIGNATURE TO YOUR DOCUMENTS

If you have a scanner, it takes only a few minutes to set up an AutoCorrect entry that will replace the text you type in Word with a scanned image of your signature. For example, you can have Word replace the text sigWL with a scanned image of Woody Leonhard's signature. A signature slug can be useful for "signing"" daily correspondence, and it's indispensable if you want to sign a fax that is sent out electronically.

Start by scanning the signature into a Word document by choosing Insert, Picture, From Scanner or Camera. Use your scanner's software to crop the image and insert it into the document. Select the scanned image and choose Tools, AutoCorrect. Make sure the Formatted Text button is selected, and type the text entry in the Replace box.

Make sure you don't allow others to use the scanned signature without your permission.

Figure 4.15

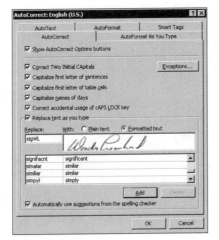

CHAPTER **5**

CREATING AND EDITING PROFESSIONAL-QUALITY GRAPHICS

In this chapter

USING OFFICE DRAWING TOOLS

Every version of Office XP includes an assortment of applications designed to help you insert, edit, and manage graphics. But some surprisingly powerful graphics tools are built directly into Office, and you can access them directly in Word, Outlook, Excel, and PowerPoint (and, to a lesser extent, FrontPage). With a few clicks you can insert one of six basic prebuilt diagrams, each with many options. With the help of the Drawing toolbar, you can add geometric shapes, lines, arrows, and text boxes to a document, worksheet, or presentation, and then add colors, shadows, and backgrounds to create images with impact. These aren't simple one-dimensional shapes, either—you can stretch, layer, and combine Office *AutoShapes* to create complex flowcharts and diagrams.

If you're a graphics professional, you'll quickly outgrow the basic capabilities of the Office Drawing tools. But for most business purposes, they're a welcome way to avoid the typical dull, gray report or presentation.

WORKING WITH THE DRAWING LAYER

Before you can even hope to harness the power of Office's Drawing tools, you need to come to terms with a fundamental concept: Word, Excel, and PowerPoint documents, as well as formatted (HTML) Outlook e-mail messages, are *layered*. FrontPage enables you to insert pictures into a Web page and supports rudimentary operations on the pictures (crop, contrast, forward/backward, rotate, and a Web-centric capability called thumbnailing), but there is no FrontPage drawing layer.

Note

When the term *document* is used in this chapter, it's referring to any Office data file that includes a drawing layer, including formatted (HTML) Outlook e-mail messages, Word documents, Excel worksheets, and PowerPoint presentations. Access also has drawing tools, but they are integrated into its object creation mechanism in a different way. Drawing in Access isn't discussed in this chapter.

It's tempting but misleading to think of an Office document as the two-dimensional (2D) piece of paper that emerges from the printer or the visual display on the screen. Actually, that finished product is only a snapshot of the real document, which consists of multiple layered drawings in addition to the main layer of the document itself; by changing the order, grouping, and arrangement of these drawings and the main layer you can dramatically change a document's appearance.

The main layer is called the working (or text) layer. The graphic material is in a *drawing layer*, which exists independently of—but can interact with—material in the working *text layer*. Technically, just one drawing layer is present; however, because you can position each object within the drawing layer independently, from front to back—and the text layer can be set at any depth—it's more useful to think of each object as a layer unto itself.

Think of the layered transparencies that you probably saw in your high school biology book. As you peeled back each layer, a dissected frog appeared, with each layer revealing some additional aspect of the frog's anatomy. The drawing layer works like that: Drawings are arranged from top to bottom (called the *Z order*), one drawing per sheet, and each drawing can be moved independently toward the top or sent toward the back.

When you begin working with the drawing layer, it helps to visualize a complex document as consisting of many transparencies, each with its own data and properties:

- Because each layer, including the text layer, is transparent, you can see the contents of any one layer through all other layers.

- Although the main text layer is normally at the bottom of the stack, with individual drawing objects in front of it, you can also position a drawing object behind the text layer.

- The contents of the working text layer can be wrapped around a drawing layer.

- You can reorder and reposition virtually every object in the drawing layer; you can also group drawing items together and treat them as a single object, and then ungroup them to work on each individually.

The various capabilities for massaging data in Office—everything from search-and-replace to master formatting functions—apply only to the working text layer. The information in drawing layers will not appear in your table of contents, nor will the appearance of the drawing layers change if you alter the formatting of your document.

You generally work with the Drawing layer through the Drawing toolbar. You'll also find a button on the Standard toolbars in Word and Excel that opens the Drawing toolbar. To display the Drawing toolbar, right-click any toolbar or the main menu bar and choose Drawing from the list of available toolbars (see Figure 5.1).

PART

I

CH

5

Figure 5.1
The starting point for Office Drawing objects is the Drawing toolbar and AutoShapes.

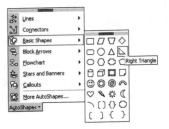

WORKING WITH A DRAWING CANVAS

Frequently you want to treat several drawings as a group so they can be moved or resized together, or so you can be sure that they will always appear on the same page together. That's the reason for the Drawing Canvas. The Drawing Canvas only appears explicitly in Word and Outlook, although you'll see vestiges of its design in Diagrams throughout the other Office applications.

Consider the analogy developed in the preceding section, where drawing layers are equated with sheets of transparencies in a book. If you use scissors to cut a transparency down to size (almost any size, as long as it is rectangular), you'll see how drawing layers work. They're rectangular bits of transparent film on which you can place any number of drawings. All of the drawings will be handled together as a single unit.

If you select a Drawing Canvas by clicking it, the corners and edges take on a distinctive bold outline (see Figure 5.2).

Figure 5.2
The short, bold corner and edge lines distinguish a Drawing Canvas.

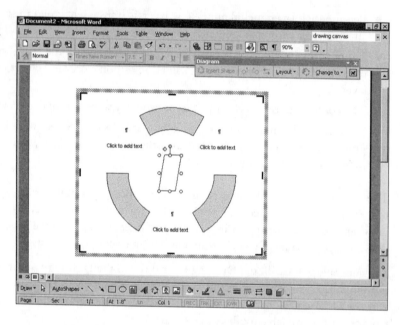

Click and drag on a Drawing Canvas's edge or corner, and you'll change the size of the Canvas, but you won't change the size of the drawings or their relative positions. When the document is printed, all of the drawings in the Canvas will appear on one page.

After a Drawing Canvas is selected, if you insert a drawing (picture, AutoShape, and so on) into your document, the drawing is placed inside the Canvas. From that point, it's treated like any other drawing on the Canvas, moving and resizing along with the rest. To remove the drawing from the Canvas, click it and drag it off. Easy.

If no Drawing Canvas is selected, when you insert an AutoShape into a document—for example, if you click one of the icons on the Drawing Toolbar—Word creates a new Drawing Canvas for you, and places the AutoShape on the Canvas.

Tip from

EQ & Woody

You can disable this behavior by choosing Tools, Options and then on the General tab, clear the box marked Automatically create drawing canvas when inserting AutoShapes.

The Drawing Canvas toolbar, which appears whenever a Drawing Canvas is selected, has the following options:

- **Fit**—Make the Canvas as small as possible, without moving any of the drawings on the canvas
- **Expand**—Increase the size of the canvas in small increments, moving the drawings along with it
- **Scale Drawing**—When this button is "pushed," any resizing of the Drawing Canvas increases or decreases the size of the drawings on the canvas proportionally
- **Text Wrapping**—Enables you to control whether (and how tightly) text flows around the Canvas

To apply formatting to the Drawing Canvas (outline, background color, and so on) right-click the border and choose Format Drawing Canvas.

DRAWING SIMPLE SHAPES

The Drawing toolbar makes it easy to draw simple geometric shapes: lines, rectangles, arrows, and more.

Tip from

Ed & Woody

For many shapes, holding down the Shift key while you drag makes the shape symmetrical. For example, Shift+drag with the rectangle shape to produce a square; use the same technique with the oval to draw a circle.

You are not limited to Microsoft's four choices of default shapes. For example, to add an octagonal stop sign shape to the main part of the Drawing toolbar, do the following:

1. Click the AutoShapes button and choose Basic Shapes.
2. Click and drag the horizontal "tear-away" line at the top of the Basic Shapes list. You'll get a free-floating Basic Shapes toolbar.
3. Hold down the Alt key, and drag the octagonal "stop sign" icon onto the main part of the Drawing toolbar.

When you no longer want the stop sign on the main Drawing toolbar, choose Tools, Customize, and then click and drag the button off the Drawing toolbar.

WORKING WITH AUTOSHAPES

One of the easiest ways to add professional-quality graphics to a document is through the use of *AutoShapes*, geometric shapes that form the basis for graphics and charts routinely used in business reports.

In addition to rectangles, ovals, and other basic shapes, the library of AutoShapes covers most of the important bases in diagramming: flow-chart symbols, generic geometric shapes, and display arrows. You can also add callouts, balloon-shaped drawing objects typically used

PART

I

CH

5

to provide information on specific items in a document; for example, you might add a callout to a sales table or chart to show the spike in sales when a new product was introduced. PowerPoint goes even further, providing Action Buttons—not unlike controls on a form—that can be set to execute commands or macros when clicked.

Tip from	Put related AutoShapes into a single Drawing Canvas so you can move or resize all of them in concert.

If you're creating a diagram that includes several instances of the same AutoShape, a useful approach is to create one example of the graphic item you need, and then copy that AutoShape to the Clipboard and paste it in position as needed.

Tip from	When you click on the AutoShapes button on the Drawing Toolbar, don't overlook the More AutoShapes entry. That choice takes you to a good sized collection of shapes in the Insert Cip Art task pane.

Tip from	Instead of having to eyeball a shape, you can set specific dimensions for it. The best approach is to start by drawing in the rough dimensions of your shape with the mouse, right-click the shape, choose Format AutoShape, and click the Size tab. Options in this dialog box enable you to specify a precise size for the shape.

USING LINES AND ARROWS

After you have your basic shapes down, you'll frequently want lines, dashed lines, and arrows to connect them all, and illustrate the relationships in your charts.

Excel and PowerPointprovide true charting *connectors*—lines that stay connected to preset positions on shapes—for every shape in a document. As you move the shapes, the connectors move with them without requiring you to manually redraw them. Word and Outlook have connectors, too, as long as all the connected shapes sit in the same Drawing Canvas.

To create a connector, do the following:

1. Draw the shapes you want to connect. In Word or Outlook, make sure all of the shapes are in the same Drawing Canvas.

2. On the Drawing toolbar, choose AutoShapes, Connectors. Pick the type of connector you want to use. Your mouse pointer turns into a square with four radiating lines.

3. Hover your mouse pointer over one of the shapes. The predefined connection points for the shape turn into colored dots on the perimeter of the shape. Click the point you want your connector to go "from."

4. Repeat the process at the desired connector point on the "to" shape.

To change a connection point, click the connector, and then click and drag one of the red connection boxes at the beginning or end of the connector. Move it over the second shape until you see the colored dots that indicate automatic connection points, and then pick one of those points to snap the connector into position.

Tip from

EQ & Woody

If you've moved an AutoShape so that its connectors are on the incorrect side of the shape, let Office make a more logical connection for you; right-click the connector and choose Reroute Connector.

In addition to the connector capability, Excel and PowerPoint also include *snap* and *grid* settings—crucial tools for placing lines and other shapes. Word offers similar capabilities, although they are implemented differently.

When you use the drawing layer, you can take advantage of a hidden layout grid. By default, drawing objects align to this grid. Although it's usually a helpful shortcut, this *snap to grid* feature can be a problem when you're drawing a line manually. Because the edges of shapes are tied to grid positions, they might not line up visually with other shapes that are arranged in slightly different positions on the grid. The fix is to *snap objects to other objects* (in Excel it's called *snap to shape*) so, for example, the end point of a line connecting two shapes ends up at a reasonable point on each shape.

Note

Snap objects to other objects is off by default in Word and PowerPoint, but Snap to shape is enabled in Excel.

PART

I

CH

5

To set the snap to grid and snap to shape values in Excel, choose Draw from the Drawing toolbar, and then Snap, and toggle the To Grid or To Shape settings.

To set the snap to grid and shape values in Word, Outlook, and PowerPoint (and to make the grid visible, re-set the grid, and much more), choose Draw from the Drawing toolbar, and then choose Grid. In Word, you'll see the Drawing Grid dialog box shown in Figure 5.3. The options in PowerPoint are more limited, but analogous. Check the Snap Objects to Grid and Snap Objects to Other Objects boxes.

Figure 5.3
Normally, the grid is hidden in Office applications; make it visible in Word, and then "snap" drawing objects to the grid for precise alignment.

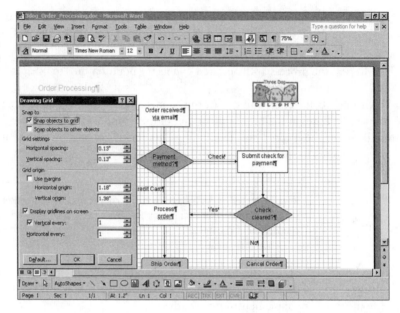

Note

Don't be confused by the terminology. In this case, a "shape" in Excel is identical to an "object" in Word, Outlook, and PowerPoint.

It's possible to move one or more objects in very fine increments without completely disabling the grid. Hold down the Alt key as you drag the object, and it moves freely rather than following the grid. You can also use the keyboard to move objects. Normally, when you select one or more objects and press any arrow key, the selection moves to the next point on the grid. If you make a selection and then hold down the Ctrl key while pressing any arrow, the selection moves in much finer increments.

CHANGING BACKGROUND COLORS AND LINE FORMATS

Office enables you to draw shapes and lines galore, but they won't accomplish much unless you make them blend in with your document.

AutoShape backgrounds can have their own colors. (A background color is called a "fill" color.) By default, the fill color is white—rarely a good choice because it obscures everything underneath the AutoShape.

Color backgrounds can come in handy if you're working with a color medium—color printer, onscreen documents, or Web pages. But the same technology that makes background color inviting can also jump up and bite you: Unless you choose high-contrast color combinations to differentiate text from background, your message can be lost completely. Remember that PC monitors in particular are notorious for not reproducing colors accurately. A carefully crafted color scheme on one monitor can morph into an illegible splotch on another.

In addition to the fill color, all AutoShapes have borders around the outer edge. You can adjust the border width, style (dashed lines, for example), color, and size. In many cases, the border is superfluous and detracts from the appearance of your document; don't hesitate to get rid of it.

To edit an AutoShape or line, follow these steps:

1. Select one or more of the shapes or lines in the drawing layer.

2. Right-click and choose Format AutoShape. You see the Format AutoShape dialog box (see Figure 5.4). Click the Colors and Lines tab.

Figure 5.4
Use the Format AutoShape dialog box to add colors and change the appearance of lines and borders.

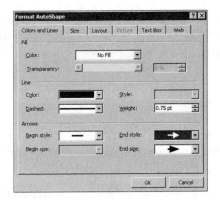

3. Adjust the fill color, lines, and arrows per the dialog box. If you want to be able to see through the shape, make sure you change the Color setting to No Fill, or check the Semitransparent box. A semitransparent shape makes the objects underneath fuzzy; for example, it will turn black text to a fuzzy gray.

Tip from
EQ & Woody

If you want Office to use the new formatting settings—fill color, line size, arrow types, and so on—for all new shapes, apply the formatting, right-click the object, and choose Set AutoShape Defaults.

PART
I

CH
5

ADDING SHADOWS AND 3D EFFECTS

3D effects rarely add to, and frequently detract from, the effectiveness of a document. Before you consider using a 3D effect, ask yourself—repeatedly—whether the inherently 2D medium you're working with will be able to properly convey that third dimension. The answer is usually no.

Shadows, on the other hand, if applied consistently and with attention to detail, can add depth to a document without detracting from the main story.

To apply Shadow or 3D effects, follow these steps:

1. Click once on the shape you want to modify, or Ctrl+click to select several.

2. Click the Shadow or 3D icon on the Drawing toolbar.

3. A tear-off menu of effects opens up. Click the effect you want, and Office transforms the selected shapes.

In addition to the choice of effects, the two menus also each have a "settings" button for fine-tuning the effects. For example, you can change the depth and "lighting" of a 3D object, or the extent and placement of the shadow.

Tip from

Ed & Woody

A few effects go a long way. A business chart is not abstract art; if you use a red 3D rectangle for one particular item, then similar items also should be red 3D rectangles.

ADDING TEXT TO A DRAWING

In many cases, you will want to put text inside your AutoShapes, to identify the steps in a flowchart, for example, or the decision points in a decision matrix. All the AutoShapes (except lines) can be converted to text boxes, if you know the trick.

Most books (including this one) and many other documents use callouts to draw your attention to specific locations in a picture. Although the terminology varies a bit depending on where you work, a callout in Office parlance is a text box with a line attached to it. Several of the built-in Office callouts look like dialog balloons, like you would see in a comic strip. Here's how to use them:

1. On the Drawing toolbar, click AutoShapes, Callouts, and then choose the callout type you want—in this case, the callout in the upper-left corner.

2. Click in the drawing layer where you want the point of the arrow to appear, and then drag to form the rest of the callout.

3. Immediately begin typing; the text you type appears in the callout.

4. Right-click the callout and set its formatting. In the example in Figure 5.5, we set the balloon to have no fill (so you can see through it), but retained the border line (so that it looks like a dialog balloon), turned it white, and then selected the text and made it white, too. Click anywhere outside the callout to continue with your document.

Figure 5.5
AutoShape callouts come in many different forms. This one looks like a dialog balloon from a comic strip.

> **Tip from**
>
> *EQ & Woody*
>
> Don't worry about getting the text or formatting in a callout perfect the first time. To change text in a callout, click once in the callout text, and then add, delete, or edit the text. To change formatting in a callout, right-click the text and choose an option from the shortcut menu.

ALIGNING AND GROUPING GRAPHIC ELEMENTS

Depending on the naked eye to center shapes in a drawing isn't always reliable. Office has built-in drawing tools with the capability to bring symmetry out of chaos. When *aligning* objects, the key is to do it one step at a time, carefully planning out what you need to do to redistribute or align them, and in which order.

If you have four objects on the drawing layer above an Excel worksheet and you want to organize them as shown in Figure 5.6, follow these steps:

Figure 5.6
Use the Drawing toolbar's alignment tools to make your graphics line up.

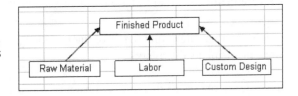

1. Select the bottom three rectangles by holding down the Shift key as you click each one.

2. To evenly space the three shapes, click the Drawing toolbar's Draw menu, and then choose Align or Distribute, Distribute Horizontally.

3. To line up the three shapes, click Draw, Align or Distribute, Align Top.

4. Now align the top rectangle with the middle one. Select both shapes, and then choose Draw, Align or Distribute, Align Center.

After you have properly formatted, connected, aligned, and distributed all your AutoShapes, you can take one more step to *group* them all into a single graphic object. This step is crucial; it enables you to preserve the relationships between objects and it helps prevent the chance that you'll accidentally move or resize a shape.

Select all the elements you want to group, and then choose Draw, Group.

Tip from
EQ & Woody

> When you're creating complex drawings that consist of several AutoShapes, it's easy to leave one out accidentally. After selecting multiple items for grouping, it's always a good practice to drag the collection left and right just a little; you can see whether any odd pieces are hiding behind other shapes.

The individual elements in a group can't be edited independently. For example, if you have a text box in a group, you won't be able to change the text in the box as long as it remains grouped.

If you find you need to make a revision, you can ungroup, make your edits, and then regroup. To ungroup a composite graphic, select the graphic, and then choose Draw, Ungroup.

WRAPPING, LAYOUT, AND STACKING

Let's say you copy a complex graphic into a Word document. When first placed, the text in your report is shoved out of the way by the graphic.

To improve the look, you can use layout options to adjust the placement of graphics relative to the text layer, thus changing the way text *wraps* around drawing objects. Right-click the graphic and choose Format, Object. In the Format Object dialog box, choose the Layout tab:

- For a light-colored graphic, choose only Behind Text or In Front of Text. Otherwise, the graphic will completely overwhelm the text on the page.

- Use the standard Square method to wrap text around the rectangular borders of the graphic.

- Use Tight wrapping if you want the empty spaces of the graphic ignored, so the text comes up to the drawing elements themselves.s

You can also change the order of objects so that one is in front of another. By default, when you create or position a graphic element so that it overlaps another graphic element (including a Drawing Canvas), the new element appears on top of the old one. To change the front-to-back ordering, right-click the graphic element or Drawing Canvas you want to move, and choose Order. At that point, you can

- Float the graphic all the way to the top (Word calls it Bring to Front) or sink it all the way to the bottom (Send to Back).

- Bring the graphic up one level (Bring Forward) or push it down one level (Send Backward).

- Move the graphic so it's on top of the working text layer (Bring in Front of Text), or place it behind the working text layer (Send Behind Text).

When should you use each wrapping option? The simplest rule of thumb is this: If you want to turn a single graphic into a background or an overlay for your document, use the Layout tab. If you have multiple graphic elements or Drawing Canvases you want to arrange in the document, go with the Order tools.

Tip from

Ed & Woody

Adjusting the order also enables you to create sophisticated effects interweaving the text and graphics. For example, you can use the Bring in Front of Text layout option to place a group graphic on top of the text, and then ungroup and move some elements of it under the text.

CREATING GRAPHICS FROM TEXT

In addition to pure graphics, Office also enables the use of text as a graphic tool, enabling you to add some personality that far exceeds standard font formatting.

USING TEXT BOXES TO CREATE PULL QUOTES

One well-known technique for livening up text is to throw in a *pull quote*—an excerpt from the text, but in a box and with large-sized type. You'll often see pull quotes used in newspapers, magazines, and book covers. Pull quotes are visual cues designed to draw the reader's attention to the text. Word has an exceptionally cool technique to do this:

1. Select the text excerpt you want to use and copy it.

2. Click the Text Box button on the Drawing toolbar. Word immediately creates a text box containing the selected text (see Figure 5.7).

3. Format the text box, resize, and move it to your desired location.

4. Word actually moves the text you selected into the text box. To get the text back in the main part of your document, click in the document in the appropriate location and paste the text from the Clipboard.

Figure 5.7
Word can create an instant "pull quote" by using a text box in the drawing layer.

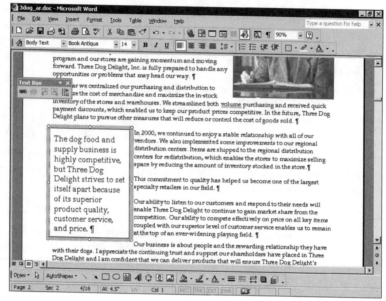

Text boxes can be used to put free-standing text of any kind in your document. The device works for a short sidebar; for example, to highlight a point, you can use the method described in the preceding section to combine a text box with an AutoShape.

The term *text box* is a bit misleading, at least in Word, Outlook, and PowerPoint. More accurately, this drawing object is a subdocument that appears in the drawing layer over (or under) the working text layer of the document. In Outlook, Word, and PowerPoint, you can paste anything into a text box, including graphics. In Excel, however, a text box can contain only text (although you can group text boxes with other shapes).

Tip from

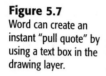

If you want to make it easy to move and position a picture on a Word document or PowerPoint slide, insert the picture into a text box. Move the text box, and the picture goes along for the ride.

USING WORDART FOR LOGOS

WordArt is an Office application that enables you to manipulate TrueType fonts. The resulting picture can be dropped into the drawing layer of documents, charts, or slides. Don't let the name fool you—the WordArt application is available in Outlook, Excel, FrontPage, and PowerPoint as well.

For the small business without a graphic arts department, WordArt can form the basis of a simple logo. You can take advantage of WordArt's capabilities to lay text out vertically, curve it, and add 3D effects.

To create a WordArt picture, follow these steps:

1. Click the Insert WordArt icon on the Drawing toolbar or click Insert, Picture, WordArt. Office responds with the WordArt Gallery shown in Figure 5.8.

Figure 5.8
WordArt makes for attention-getting text effects or easy logos.

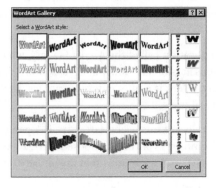

2. Choose the basic style of WordArt you want to construct, and then click OK.
3. In the Edit WordArt Text dialog box, type the text you want to use as WordArt; select the font, font size, and treatment, and click OK.

Tip from

Ed & Woody

WordArt uses only TrueType fonts, meaning that your PostScript fonts can't be used as WordArt. Start with a simple font, such as a basic serif font. Decorative fonts produce horrible WordArt.

4. After the WordArt object appears in the drawing layer, click and drag any of the sizing handles to change its appearance, or use the Free Rotate icon on the Drawing toolbar to slant the WordArt object up or down.

The WordArt toolbar includes a large collection of shapes under the WordArt Shapes button that you can use to further bend, stretch, and modify existing pieces of WordArt. Additional buttons enable you to move and size text and adjust character spacing. A shortcut also exists for wrapping text around the WordArt. If the WordArt toolbar isn't visible, right-click any toolbar or the main menu bar and choose WordArt from the list of available toolbars.

PART

I

CH

5

USING THE MEDIA GALLERY

Clip art—reusable drawings, photos, and the like—derives its name from the not-so-distant past, when designers actually clipped images from a book and pasted them into documents. The electronic versions of these tools are easier to use, but the effect is the same: to enliven an informal document. Much depends on the audience you want to reach and the effect you want to achieve.

A dynamite piece of clip art can tell a story worth a thousand words. A really poor piece of clip art hinders communication, leaving people scratching their heads about the possible obtuse meaning of it all.

Gratuitous clip art—that is, clip art that doesn't relate to the topic at hand or otherwise impedes the flow of your documents—distracts your audience and often detracts from the point you're trying to make.

Office comes complete with an application called the Media Gallery, which has ties to the Web where you can download thousands of additional images, sounds, video clips, animated graphics, and the like. The Media Gallery is a fully indexed graphics database that lets you search for images in a wide variety of ways.

At its simplest, you can search for relevant images by category. To open the Media Gallery in Outlook, Word, Excel, PowerPoint, or FrontPage, choose Insert, Picture, Clip Art. You'll go through some preliminary steps to catalog pictures that are already on your hard drive.

You'll probably find it easiest to proceed in this order:

1. Choose Insert, Picture, ClipArt to open the Insert Clip Art task pane.
2. In the Results should be box, choose the media type you're looking for (see Figure 5.9). Click the + buttons to narrow your search to very specific types of media (for example, JPEG files).

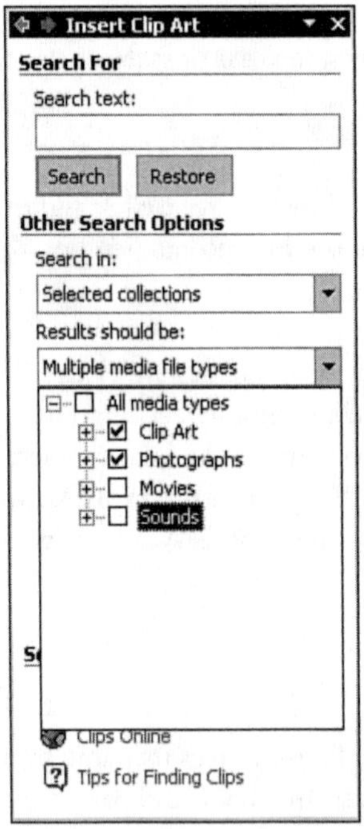

Figure 5.9
Start by specifying the types of files you're willing to consider. Generally, this is the easiest criterion to establish at the onset.

3. Pick the "collections" that you want to scan. As a first stab, you should probably uncheck the box marked Web Collections. Search the Web after you've exhausted your local possibilities.

4. Type keywords in the Search text box, and click Search.

You're not bound by the built-in keywords. To set your own keywords for a particular clip, follow these steps:

1. Right-click the clip and choose Edit Keywords. The Keywords dialog box opens(see Figure 5.10).

Figure 5.10
The Keywords dialog box enables you to set your own keywords and caption for the clip.

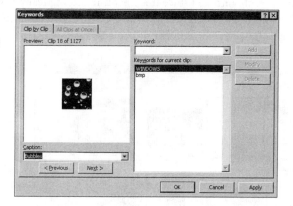

2. In the Caption box, type a descriptive name for the clip. It can be virtually any length, and include punctuation marks and other special symbols. The caption text will appear as a ScreenTip when you hover the mouse pointer over the clip in the task pane.

3. In the Keywords for Current Clip box, add or remove keywords for the particular clip.

PART
I

CH
5

Caution

Office helps you maintain consistency in your keywords by use of the drop-down list. If you're careful to use uniform keywords, your efforts will pay off later with more effective searches.

You can also add clip-art images from graphics files on an individual computer or on the company network, with the Gallery providing an option to move or copy a graphic onto a user's PC, or link the Gallery item to the original file. Click Clip Organizer at the bottom of the Insert Clip Art task pane.

IMPORTING, EXPORTING, AND COMPRESSING GRAPHICS

Clip art has its place, especially in presentations and informal documents. But professional-quality corporate reports typically require graphics such as photographs or image files produced by professional graphics artists. To add graphic files to Office documents, choose Insert, Picture, From File.

Office can read any graphics file format for which it has "filters," the software that converts the graphic format into data usable inside the Office application. This is a particularly good illustration of the practical value of Office's Installed on First Use setup option.Install those filters you know for certain you will use, and if you encounter a different one, Office prompts you to install the necessary additional filter.

CHOOSING EMBEDDING OR LINKING

When you place a picture file into an Office document, it automatically goes in the working text layer, not the drawing layer. As Figure 5.11 shows, Word gives you three choices; PowerPoint and Excel offer a smaller number of choices:

Figure 5.11
Word lets you Insert, Link to File, or Insert and Link a picture in a file.

- **Insert**—This choice *embeds* the picture, physically placing it in the document. If you aren't overly worried about file sizes, don't need any history telling you where the picture came from, and don't care whether the picture gets updated, this is your best choice. This choice is available in PowerPoint, FrontPage, and Excel as well.

- **Link to File**—This choice puts a pointer to the picture in the document. The picture itself is never placed in the document. Instead, it's brought in as needed to display on the screen, or print on the printer. If there's a chance the picture will be changed, and you need to reflect those changes in your document, this is your only option. This menu choice is available in PowerPoint and Access but not in Excel or FrontPage.

- **Insert and Link**—This hybrid option (available only in Word and Outlook messages) puts a copy of the picture in the document, but maintains a link as well. That way, when the picture is needed, Office can try the link. If the picture isn't found, it reverts to the copy stored in the document. This is especially useful for documents stored on portable computers because it ensures that graphics will be available when you are away from the office and your network, while still allowing the option to update the image when you reconnect to the network.

Office frequently uses fully qualified filenames as the links, which can cause problems if you move either the picture file or the document. If you link the picture C:\My Documents \My Pictures\3dogs.pcx in a document and move the document to a second machine, the picture must be located in the same folder hierarchy or Office won't be able to find it, and will substitute a meaningless placeholder (see Figure 5.12).

Figure 5.12
The dreaded "missing link" placeholder graphic. If you see this placeholder, it means Office couldn't find the picture.

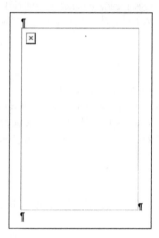

When should you embed graphics and when should you link? Follow these guidelines:

- If you repeatedly use the same graphic—for example, a letterhead logo—link to it and make sure it doesn't move. Otherwise, your document archive will explode in size.

- In a networked environment, linking works if the graphic is in a *shared network folder* that's accessible to all persons who use the document. If you don't have ready access to the shared folder, insert the graphic.

- If you plan to distribute documents externally, you must insert the graphics, unless all the files reside in the same folder as the document, or the recipients are savvy enough to replicate the folder structure on the machine where the document was first created.

PART

I

CH

5

 If you discover broken image links in your document, see "Fixing Broken Image Links" in the "Troubleshooting" section at the end of this chapter.

RESIZING AND CROPPING

When you insert a picture into a document, it appears full size. If the picture file is six inches wide, that's what you'll see in your document.

More often than not, you'll need to resize the picture, which you do by selecting it and maneuvering the sizing handles. The corner handles enable you to resize it proportionally; the other handles alter the picture's proportions, or *aspect ratio*.

The Picture toolbar also gives you a fast way to *crop* the picture; that is, select the portions of the picture that will be visible in the document. To bring up the Picture toolbar, right-click any visible toolbar or the main menu bar and choose Picture.

The Picture toolbar also enables you to make a few adjustments in picture quality: contrast, brightness, color, and the like.

Tip from

EQ & Woody

In Word, you can avoid some sizing hassles by drawing a text box where you want to place the graphic and then inserting the graphic into the text box. The graphic is resized automatically. If the picture is already in the document, click it once, and then click the Text Box button on the Drawing toolbar to surround the image with a box.

COMPRESSING GRAPHICS FOR WEB PAGES AND PRESENTATIONS

Unless you're going to print a graphic on a high-resolution printer—in which case you can probably use all the detail you can get—chances are good that you can use Office's built-in Compress feature to squeeze down the size of the graphic. This will reduce the size of the document without any significant detrimental effect. To compress a graphic, follow these steps:

1. Click the graphic to select it.

2. Right-click and choose Format Picture.

3. On the Picture tab, choose Compress.... You'll get the Compress Pictures dialog box (see Figure 5.13).

Figure 5.13
Office includes built-in tools to shrink the size of embedded graphics, thus reducing the size of a document or presentation.

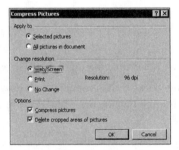

Choose from Web/Screen resolution (at a nominal 96 dots per inch, which is fine for most monitors); Print (nominal 200 dots per inch, which will produce a fuzzy but legible picture); or No Change (which you would use if you wanted to delete cropped portions of the picture without affecting the resolution of what remains visible). Click OK.

Although PowerPoint doesn't have this specific feature, it does enable you to specify a low-resolution alternative to the chosen picture. To use the option, right-click the picture, and choose Picture Properties to bring up the General tab.

USING ADVANCED PICTURE EFFECTS

Inserted graphics can be grouped, ordered, wrapped, layered, and given colored backgrounds, borders, 3D, or shadow treatments, just like other Office graphics. They can also be placed inside a Drawing canvas. Note that in Word, assigning layout formatting to a linked graphic breaks the link.

AutoShape 3D effects are not available for pictures (both clip art and imported files) when they are in the working text layer, but a limited number of shadow effects are. The full complement of effects is available if you put a text box around the picture. This enables you to frame your art in a way that can spell the difference between a document that looks routine and one that looks professional.

One popular professional graphics effect in Excel involves replacing colored or textured bars, wedges, and other chart components with pictures. Follow these steps to do so:

1. Create the chart. Right-click the chart object where you want to use a picture (a data series in a column chart, for example) and choose the appropriate Format option—Format Data Series, in this example.

2. Click the Patterns tab, and then click the Fill Effects button. On the Fill Effects dialog box, choose the Pictures tab.

3. Click the button marked Select Picture, and choose the picture you want to use.

4. If you want the picture to be distorted so a single image fits on the chart object, click Stretch. If you want pictures to be placed one on top of the other, choose the Stack option. Click OK twice to place the picture on the chart object (see Figure 5.14).

Figure 5.14
You can use a picture to "paint" any component of an Excel chart.

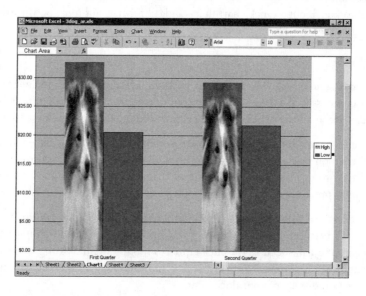

PART

I

CH

5

WORKING WITH SCANNED IMAGES

Word, Excel, Publisher, and PowerPoint directly support scanners and digital cameras that include *TWAIN* (Technology Without an Interesting Name) drivers (the industry-wide scanner standard). This option does not require any separate image-editing software.

To scan a picture directly into an Office document, choose Insert, Picture, From Scanner or Camera. The dialog box you see next varies, depending on the capabilities of your input source. Typically, the TWAIN driver enables you to choose the image type and resolution; some software also lets you choose the image size.

Tip from

E & Woody

The scanning capability, in combination with Office's graphics layer, provides a solution to a relatively new problem: How do you type up a printed form when you don't have a typewriter anymore? The answer: Scan the form into a Word document, and then insert it as a picture in the document header. Crop and resize the image as needed, and format the picture layout as Behind Text. Exit from the header, and you can type over the form.

Alternatively, scan the form and place the image in the main text layer. Crop and resize as needed, and then format the graphic object by using the Behind Text option. Add a text box on top of each field in the form; use the ordering options to place this layer in front of the form and make the box semitransparent.

CREATING AND EDITING CHARTS AND DIAGRAMS

Office ships with a handful of generic charting and diagramming tools. They can come in useful to knock out a quick chart in a standard format, but most power users will find them lacking, rather quickly.

SIMPLE CHARTS

Last, and quite possibly least, Office's portfolio of graphics tools includes Microsoft Chart. You can access it in Word and PowerPoint by choosing Insert, Picture, Chart. It also appears automatically when you create PowerPoint slides with chart placeholders.

The number one bit of guidance to give you on Chart is: If you have more than just a few numbers, don't use it. Chart is a leftover from the days in which customers typically purchased Word or PowerPoint alone rather than the full Office suite, and it was available so you could pretend you were incorporating Excel material in your documents.

Now, of course, you do have Excel, and there is nothing Chart can do that can't be done easier and better in Excel. If you do give Chart a try, you'll see that it starts out with a prefab chart and datasheet. Right-click either to modify them, putting in your own data and selecting the chart type. Normally, you would then toggle away the datasheet, leaving only the chart on display in your document.

It is just as easy to click Insert, Object, select Microsoft Excel Chart from the pull-down list, and insert a real chart into Word or PowerPoint. You'll get the same model chart to adapt to your needs as with the limited charting module, but you'll have the full power of Excel at your command.

ORGANIZATION CHARTS

It's physically possible to put together organizational charts with AutoShapes. Drawing charts this way is exhaustingly tedious, but if you're persistent and patient, the results can be aesthetically pleasing.

A much easier alternative is to use the Organization Chart applet included with Office. To use it, choose Insert, Picture, Organization Chart.

After the Microsoft Organization Chart Canvas has been drawn (note the use of Drawing Canvas technology—even in Excel, which doesn't have explicit Drawing Canvases), click once on each placeholder to add names and titles. Add ready-made boxes for Managers, Assistants, Co-workers, and Subordinates by clicking the appropriate icon in the toolbar, and then clicking the associated block in the organization chart. Limited formatting tools, covering fonts, box styles, shadowing and lines, are available.

Tip from

Ed & Woody

The Insert Shape toolbar can be "torn off" and floated to make it easier and faster to add new people to the chart.

The standard Drawing Canvas tools—Fit Canvas to Contents, and so on—are available under the Layout drop-down box.

Tip from

Ed & Woody

If you're sketching a quick organization chart for a 10-person organization, the Microsoft Organization Chart application will suffice. As soon as you get to 40 or 50 people, however, it's practically useless, or worse. Get a more powerful package. Visio (http://www.microsoft.com/office/visio/), for example, can handle organization charts suitable for huge corporations. BillG liked them so much he bought the company.

DIAGRAMS

Office comes with five additional prebuilt diagramming tools, similar to the organization chart tool mentioned in the previous section. These tools can be used for constructing any of the following:

- **Cycle diagrams**—Bits of text arranged in a circle, with lines or arrows between the blurbs (for an example, refer to Figure 5.2)
- **Radial diagrams**—Bits of text with one blurb in the middle, and the rest arranged around it, with lines emanating from the center to the outside blurbs
- **Pyramid diagrams**—A triangle in the background is adorned with evenly spaced blurbs down the middle
- **Venn diagrams**—Overlapping circles with blurbs arranged outside the circles (note that the amount of overlap cannot be adjusted)
- **Target diagrams**—A bullseye has superimposed callout lines and spaces for blurbs in a single heap at the side

The tools here are rudimentary, but they can be useful, particularly if your intent is to convey a general idea, as opposed to a mathematical exactitude. Other tools, notably Visio, give you much more control over the appearance of your diagrams.

TROUBLESHOOTING

FIXING BROKEN IMAGE LINKS

I created a link to an image stored on a networked computer and everything worked fine. When I opened the document later, however, the image link was broken.

If links get messed up, you have one tool at your disposal, short of directly editing Word field codes to fix the broken links. Choose Edit, Links, and use the tools provided by the application to change or correct the links. You also can use this approach to changed linked files to embedded files.

SECRETS OF THE OFFICE MASTERS: A PROFESSIONAL WORD FLOWCHART

Office AutoShapes give you the opportunity to create almost any kind of basic business-related diagram. Note how this flowchart emphasizes clean, simple phrases, and places them in color and shape-coded boxes. A simple, clean flowchart can do wonders for explaining an otherwise difficult procedure.

Figure 5.15

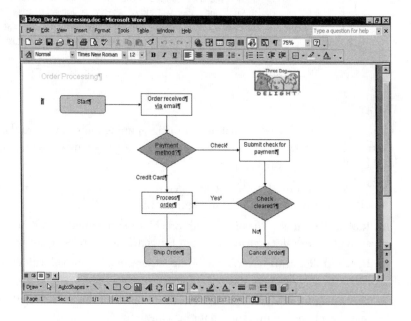

CHAPTER **6**

SHARING DATA BETWEEN OFFICE APPLICATIONS

In this chapter

USING THE OFFICE CLIPBOARD

In Office 2000, Microsoft tried to improve the standard Windows Clipboard by augmenting it with an enhanced toolbar called the *Office Clipboard*. Unfortunately, the Office 2000 Clipboard toolbar was plagued with bugs and an annoying, half-baked interface that made it nearly useless. In Office XP, this feature is improved, although still not perfect. If you detested the Office Clipboard in its previous incarnation, we recommend trying it again in Office XP; you might find it more useful and manageable this time around. If not, we'll show you how to make it go away.

HOW OFFICE EXTENDS THE WINDOWS CLIPBOARD

Using the Office Clipboard, you can gather as many as 24 Office objects (that's twice as many as the Office 2000 Clipboard allowed) and then paste them—one at a time or all at once—into an Office document. The enhanced Clipboard can hold any data type that will fit in the Windows Clipboard, including text from a Word document; a dataset from an Access database; graphics (even the animated variety) for use in PowerPoint presentations or forms built in Word, Excel, or Access; and Excel charts or ranges.

Using the Office Clipboard, you can tackle any of the following tasks:

- Pull together excerpts from a large report to create an executive summary, talking points, or a press release.
- Gather background information from scattered files and assemble the appropriate parts into the first draft of a memo or report.
- Take a collection of briefing memos, one from each member of your committee, and stitch them together into a single report.
- Quickly collect a list of names or figures you expect to use repeatedly in a document.

The enhanced Clipboard is available in any Office application. It appears automatically (see Figure 6.1), if you copy or cut two Office items in sequence without an intervening paste—by pressing Ctrl+C twice in a row, for instance. To display the Office Clipboard pane manually, choose Edit, Office Clipboard.

→ To learn more about working with the task pane, **see** "Configuring Common Office Features," **p. 44**.

Each item on the Office Clipboard is represented by an icon that depicts the application from which the item was copied. The Clipboard pane also displays a thumbnail view of the copied item, whether it consists of text, numbers, or a graphic.

When you start an Office application, the first entry on the Clipboard toolbar consists of the current contents of the Windows Clipboard. After an Office application is active, any item you cut or copy to the Clipboard (even from a non-Office program) creates a new entry on the Clipboard toolbar. The contents of the Clipboard toolbar remain available as long as any Office application is running.

Figure 6.1
Use the Office Clipboard to copy up to 24 items, and then paste them, one at a time or all at once, into any Office document.

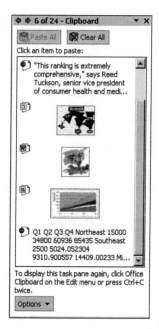

Each new item appears at the top of the Office Clipboard pane. When the Office Clipboard is visible and reaches its maximum of 24 items, cutting or copying another item drops the oldest item on the Clipboard.

To paste the contents of one specific copied item, position the insertion point where you want the item to appear, and then click the button for that item. To paste all the copied items into a document in the exact order they appear on the Clipboard toolbar, click Paste All.

 If you're frustrated because the Paste All button is grayed out, see "Paste All and the Office Clipboard" in the "Troubleshooting" section at the end of this chapter.

To remove an individual item from the Office Clipboard, click the arrow to the right of the item and choose Delete. To clear all the Clipboard contents at once, click the Clear All button.

Note

The Windows Clipboard continues to operate just as it always does, without regard to the contents of the Office Clipboard. Every time you cut or copy a new item, it replaces the current contents of the Windows Clipboard. Whenever you use the Paste command in a non-Office program, the Windows Clipboard uses the last item you cut or copied.

PART

I

CH

6

CUSTOMIZING THE OFFICE CLIPBOARD

Click the Options button at the bottom of the Office Clipboard pane to display a shortcut menu that lets you customize its operation in any of the following ways:

- If you find the Clipboard pane annoying, clear the Show Office Clipboard Automatically checkbox. In this configuration, the Clipboard pane will appear only when you specifically choose to display it.

- If you want to collect a number of items but don't want the Clipboard pane to clutter up your workspace, check the Collect Without Showing Office Clipboard option.

- When the Office Clipboard is active, a small icon appears in the notification area (also known as the system tray) at the right of the taskbar, and a brief message appears each time you copy an item. The two items at the bottom of the Options menu let you hide either or both of these indicators.

- To stop the Office Clipboard from collecting any additional items, right-click the icon in the system tray and choose Stop Collecting from the shortcut menu. This immediately closes the Clipboard pane and removes the tray icon.

CONVERTING CLIPBOARD DATA INTO ALTERNATIVE FORMATS

When you paste an item from the Clipboard into an Office document, the Office application examines the item to determine its data format—simple text, HTML, formatted text (so-called Rich Text Format), worksheet data, or one of many picture formats, for example. Before the Office application pastes the Clipboard contents, a negotiating procedure takes place in which the application attempts to discover the format that's most appropriate for the current contents.

In some cases, however, you might want to translate the Clipboard contents to a different format when pasting into another application (or even within the same application). For instance, when copying formatted text from one Office application to another—for example, the contents of an HTML-based Outlook e-mail message into Word—you typically don't want the original formatting to appear in the document where you're pasting the data. Instead, you want to transfer just the text, letting it take on the paragraph formatting defined in the Word document.

In Office XP, you have two opportunities to override the Office defaults and switch formats when using the Clipboard:

- Instead of using the default format, choose Edit, Paste Special, and select any available format from the As box (see Figure 6.2). In this case, Unformatted Text is the best choice.

- After pasting the data, you can change its format by clicking the Paste Options Smart Tag (see Figure 6.3). In this example, we copied a range of cells from an Excel worksheet and pasted them into a PowerPoint slide. The Smart Tag shows additional formats available for the pasted data.

Figure 6.2
Use Paste Special when you want to choose the format of copied data before pasting it into a new document.

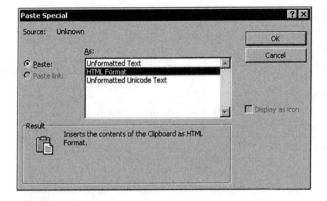

Figure 6.3
After pasting data into an Office program, click the Paste Options Smart Tag to change the format of the data.

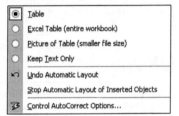

Tip from

The Paste Options Smart Tag is one of the most useful improvements in Office XP. Whenever you use the Clipboard to copy data from one place to another within Office, it pays to check the Smart Tag to see which options are available.

With an Excel worksheet range on the Clipboard, for instance, you can choose any of the following formats when pasting into a Word document:

- **Microsoft Excel Worksheet Object**—This is a good choice if you plan to update the data in the worksheet and you want to ensure that the latest numbers appear in the Word document whenever it's opened.

- **Formatted Text (RTF)**—This option converts the Excel range to a Word table, retaining text formatting such as fonts and colors from the original data.

- **Unformatted Text**—This option forces the text to take on the surrounding formatting in Word.

- **Picture, Bitmap, Enhanced Metafile**—Choose one of these formats to enable scaling and cropping, and to allow other kinds of picture formatting.

PART
I

CH
6

Tables 6.1–6.8 show the most common reformatting options when you paste data between Office 2000 applications.

TABLE 6.1 PASTE SPECIAL CONVERSION TABLE—PASTING TEXT FROM WORD INTO WORD

Paste Special Format	Result
Microsoft Word Document Object	Embedded Word document with source file formatting.
Formatted Text (RTF)	Formatted the same as in the source file.
Unformatted Text	Formatting stripped; inserted text picks up paragraph style as defined at the insertion point.
Picture	Formatting the same as in the source file; text cannot be edited, and any resizing or cropping will cause the picture to be distorted.
HTML (default)	Uses styles and other formatting as defined in the source file; if target document includes styles with identical names, formatting adjusts accordingly.
Word Hyperlink	Inserts text using hyperlink character format and paragraph formatting from target, with link to source file.

Note

The Paste as Hyperlink choice on Word's Edit menu has the same effect as choosing the Paste link option in the Paste Special dialog box, and then choosing Word Hyperlink.

TABLE 6.2 PASTE SPECIAL CONVERSION TABLE—PASTING A TABLE FROM WORD INTO WORD

Paste Special Format	Result
Microsoft Word Document Object	Embedded Word document using formatting of source file.
Formatted Text (RTF)	Formatted as in source file.
Unformatted Text	Converts table to text, separating cells with tab characters, using paragraph formatting as defined at the insertion point.
Picture	Converts text to picture using fonts and other formatting from source file; table spacing not exact.
HTML (default)	Uses table formatting and styles as defined in source; if target document contains styles with identical names, uses those formats.
Word Hyperlink	Table is hyperlinked to source file.

TABLE 6.3   PASTE SPECIAL CONVERSION TABLE—PASTING TEXT FROM WORD INTO EXCEL

Paste Special Format	Result
Microsoft Word Document Object	Embedded Word document with source file formatting.
Picture (Enhanced Metafile)	Picture in source file's formatting; text cannot be edited, and text might be distorted if picture is scaled or resized.
HTML (default)	Text is pasted into workbook using source formatting; each paragraph occupies one Excel cell.
Text or Unicode Text	Each paragraph occupies one Excel cell, using cell formatting. For bulleted or numbered paragraphs, each bullet or number appears in one cell, with text in cell to its right.
Hyperlink	Text is all in one cell, hyperlinked to source.

TABLE 6.4   PASTE SPECIAL CONVERSION TABLE—PASTING A TABLE FROM WORD INTO EXCEL

Paste Special Format	Result
Microsoft Word Document Object	Embedded Word document with source file's formatting.
Picture (Enhanced Metafile)	Picture in source file's formatting.
HTML (default)	Table contents pasted into worksheet using source file's formatting. Cells might need to be resized.
Text or Unicode Text	Table contents pasted into worksheet using worksheet's formatting. Cells might need to be resized.
Paste as Hyperlink (on Edit menu)	Contents of table pasted into single cell and hyperlinked. (Thus, if the copied cells have the values 1, 2, and 3, Excel pastes the value 123 into a single cell.)

TABLE 6.5   PASTE SPECIAL CONVERSION TABLE—PASTING TEXT FROM WORD INTO THE BODY OF A POWERPOINT SLIDE

Paste Special Format	Result
HTML (default)	Pastes text into slide using formatting from source document. Text appears as single bullet point, regardless of paragraph marks.
Microsoft Word Document Object	Embedded Word document with source file formatting.
Picture	Picture of Word document with source file formatting.
Formatted Text (RTF)	Pastes text into slide with source file formatting; if source data contains paragraph marks, each paragraph becomes a bullet.

TABLE 6.5 CONTINUED

Paste Special Format	Result
Unformatted Text	Pastes text into slide with target file's formatting.
Attach Hyperlink	Text is pasted; hyperlink doesn't work.

Note

If you choose Edit, Paste as Hyperlink, the effect is the same as selecting the Attach Hyperlink option from PowerPoint's Paste Special dialog box.

TABLE 6.6 PASTE SPECIAL CONVERSION TABLE—PASTING A RANGE FROM EXCEL INTO WORD

Paste Special Format	Result
Microsoft Excel Worksheet Object	Embedded worksheet in source file format.
Formatted Text (RTF)	Embedded worksheet in source file format.
Unformatted Text	Pastes as text, with contents of each cell separated by tab character and a paragraph mark at the end of each row.
Picture	Picture of worksheet range.
Bitmap	Picture of worksheet range, with gridlines.
Picture (Enhanced Metafile)	Picture of worksheet range, centered on Word page.
HTML (default)	Inserts as Word table, using fonts, column widths, and other formatting as defined in source range.
Word Hyperlink	Inserts as Word table, hyperlinked to source.

TABLE 6.7 PASTE SPECIAL CONVERSION TABLE—PASTING A CHART FROM EXCEL INTO WORD

Paste Special Format	Result
Microsoft Excel Chart Object (default)	Embedded chart, formatted as in source.
Picture	Picture of chart.
Picture (Enhanced Metafile)	Picture of chart, centered on Word page.
Paste as Hyperlink	Not available.

TABLE 6.8   PASTE SPECIAL CONVERSION TABLE—PASTING A CHART FROM EXCEL INTO BODY OF A POWERPOINT SLIDE

Paste Special Format	Result
Microsoft Excel Chart Object (default)	Embedded chart, formatting as in source, centered on slide.
Picture	Picture of chart; to edit, must be converted to Microsoft Drawing and then grouped.
Conventional Paste	Same as Microsoft Excel Chart Object.

DRAGGING AND DROPPING DATA

All Office applications support standard Windows drag-and-drop actions. Dragging with the left mouse button within a document, worksheet, or presentation moves the item from one place to the other. All Office applications also enable you to drag with the right mouse button; when you do, you see a shortcut menu from which you can choose the correct action. For example, in Word, right-dragging a selected item enables you to choose whether to copy or move it to the new location, or to insert it as a link or hyperlink (see Figure 6.4).

Figure 6.4
All Office applications allow you to drag text or objects with the right mouse button; in Word, use this technique to move text.

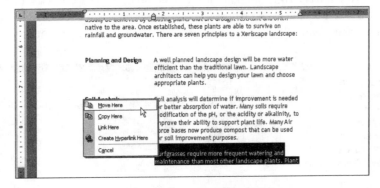

Excel allows right drags and provides even more choices than Word: Move Here, Copy Here, Copy Here as Values Only, Copy Here as Formats Only, Link Here, Create Hyperlink Here, Shift Down and Copy, Shift Right and Copy, Shift Down and Move, Shift Right and Move, Cancel.

If you hold down the Ctrl key while dragging, the default action changes. In Excel, for example, use this technique on a worksheet tab to create a copy of the sheet. In PowerPoint's *Slide Sorter view (page x)*, Ctrl+drag copies the slide.

→ To learn more about moving and copying Excel data, **see** "Moving, Copying, Inserting, and Deleting Worksheets," **p. 535**.

Drag and drop is not limited to single documents or even single applications. By arranging document windows on your screen (in Excel, choose Window, Arrange, as shown in Figure 6.5), you can easily drag-and-drop data from one window to the other.

Figure 6.5
Excel gives you multiple choices for arranging document windows.

Word's Arrange Windows function is dreadful—you can only arrange windows one on top of the other, and Word displays toolbars in all the arranged windows, leaving virtually no text visible.

 If you'd like to be able to have three or more Word documents open at once and still have room onscreen to work with the documents, see "Viewing Three or More Word Documents at Once" in the "Troubleshooting" section at the end of this chapter.

It's unfortunate that the Word document windowing capability is botched so badly, because right-dragging between documents in Word is powerful and quick. For example, if you select a phrase in one document, right-drag it to another document, release, and choose Create Hyperlink Here, you'll create a fully functional hot link between the two documents.

PowerPoint has terrific drag-and-drop capability in Slide Sorter view (see Figure 6.6). Drag or Ctrl+drag a slide from one presentation to another and you not only move or copy the slide, it automatically takes on the master style of the target presentation.

Figure 6.6
When you drag and drop in PowerPoint's Slide Sorter view, slides you move between presentations are transformed to the target presentation's style.

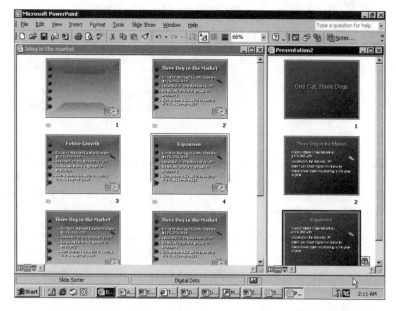

To drag and drop between Office applications, arrange the windows on your screen so you can see both, and then drag some Word text into an Excel cell or a PowerPoint slide into Word.

Tip from

EQ & Woody

> If you have a Word outline that's properly formatted, you can import it directly into PowerPoint and turn it into a presentation. But if your Word document doesn't conform to the official formatting rules, you can still assemble a presentation quickly: Set up a Word window next to a PowerPoint window, and click and drag text from Word to the PowerPoint outline.
>
> When you want to drag between Office applications, but you want to work with each program at full size, use the Windows-standard *drag and hover* technique. Click and drag the data from the target application and hover your mouse pointer over the target program's icon on the Windows taskbar, but don't release the mouse button. After a moment, the target application appears. Move the pointer to the correct location and release the mouse button to complete the drop.

CONVERTING AND IMPORTING FILES BETWEEN OFFICE APPLICATIONS

For almost all Office users, the most common intra-Office data sharing involves retrieving contact names and addresses from Outlook to put in a Word letter. Unfortunately, both Word and Outlook conspire to make that common activity uncommonly difficult. This book contains a little-known method for simplifying the connection.

→ To learn how to retrieve Outlook addresses for use in a Word document, **see** "Addressing Letters with the Outlook Contacts List," **p. 425**.

→ For more information on working with Outlook Contacts, **see** Chapter 12, "Managing a Contacts List," **p. 293**.

One way to share information among multiple Office applications is to open one application's file in another. You can:

■ **Open an Excel workbook in Word**—All the worksheets appear as Word tables, but charts do not appear; you must add those as objects.

■ **Open a Word file in PowerPoint**—PowerPoint attempts to construct a presentation based on the file structure.

Note

> If you try to use an Office application to open an HTML file generated by any of the Office applications, the file opens—but Office reads the XML tag in the file and launches the originating application to load the file.

Numerous built-in methods are available for data sharing:

- Access enables you to bring in an Excel worksheet as an Access table (choose File, Get External Data, Import).

- Excel can import an Access table by using Microsoft Query or the Pivot Table Wizard (choose Data, Pivot Table Wizard, or Data, Import External Data, New Database Query).

- Word exports to PowerPoint through File, Send To, Microsoft PowerPoint.

- Word can use information stored in Outlook, Excel, or Access as the *data source* for a mail merge.

→ To see how Word can help you create mass mailings, reports, envelope labels, and more, **see** "Using Mail Merge to Personalize Form Letters," **p. 516.**

COMBINING TWO OR MORE DATA TYPES IN ONE DOCUMENT

After you get beyond the simple letter-writing or number-calculating aspects of Office, *compound documents*—such as a Word document with an integrated Excel worksheet or a PowerPoint presentation with an Excel chart—become more and more essential to effective business use of Office XP.

The most common example, of course, is a corporate report, in which financial data from Excel (or tabular material from Access) is blended into a Word document, as shown in Figure 6.7. Or you might use Word to generate explanatory text for an Excel worksheet. You can store résumés from job candidates as Word documents in a field in an Access database. PowerPoint presentations almost routinely are compound documents with slides containing charts and tables from Excel.

Figure 6.7
Compound documents like this one, which embeds an Excel worksheet and chart in a Word document, let you use the best tools for each type of data.

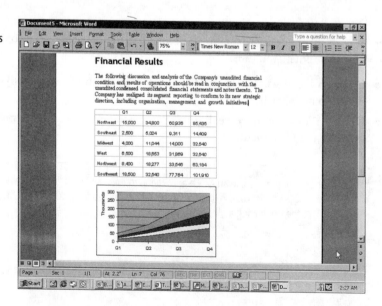

Creating compound documents lets you use links between data so that each element is available for updating. When you click in a résumé stored in Word format in an Access table, for example, Office automatically opens Word for you to read and modify the document. You can continuously revise those Excel data ranges in the annual report, even as co-workers edit the text around them.

This all works because Office has an *object design*: Each Office document is essentially a container into which several kinds of information can be poured.

You'll see references to *OLE objects*, *COM objects*, and *ActiveX objects* in the online documentation and elsewhere. For everyday use, these terms all refer to the same thing. For simplicity's sake, we call them "objects" in this book.

Note

> You'll also see *OLE container*, *ActiveX container*, and *COM container* in the Help files and Knowledge Base articles. Don't be confused. These terms refer to Office files—documents, workbooks, and presentations.

EMBEDDING VERSUS LINKING

Office offers two very different methods for putting objects (such as text, charts, pictures, or a worksheet range) into a Word document, Excel worksheet, Access database, Outlook item, or PowerPoint presentation. The two methods are called *embedding* and *linking*:

- Embedding stores the data as an object inside the document, including an indication of which application made the object. So, if you embed an Excel chart in a Word document, all the data for the chart resides inside the Word document and Word "knows" it can be edited with Excel. Because all the data for the chart is inside Word, you can't start Excel and edit the chart directly. Instead, you must start with Word and edit from there.

- Linking, on the other hand, inserts a pointer to data stored in an external file. When you create a link, the document that contains the link might include a snapshot of the data, but the container document attempts to update the link whenever necessary. Thus, if you insert a named range from an Excel worksheet called `C:\My Documents\Salaries.xls` into a Word document, the document stores a code that instructs Word to retrieve that range whenever you open or print the document. Because the data exists in an external file, you can use Excel to update `Salaries.xls` at any time, and your changes will be reflected the next time you open or print the Word document that contains the link.

Note

> Pictures frequently appear in documents as, simply, pictures—they're neither embedded nor linked.

Embedded objects are edited in-place: If you double-click an Excel chart embedded in your Word document, for example, Excel's menus and toolbars replace the Word equivalents—even though you're still working in the Word window (see Figure 6.8).

Figure 6.8
When editing an embedded Excel worksheet in Word, note that the window title says Word, but Excel takes over the menus and toolbars.

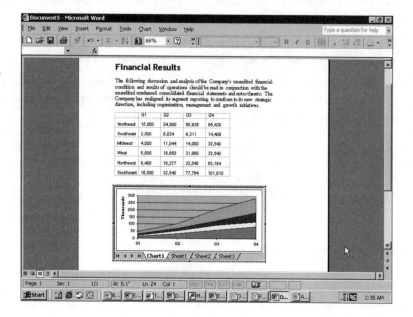

On the other hand, if you double-click a linked object, the originating application opens and loads the data from the linked external file. If you double-click an Excel chart linked in a PowerPoint presentation, Excel starts with the chart ready for work.

When you consider whether to link, embed, or place objects in documents, you must juggle three competing considerations:

- **File Size**—Will the objects bloat the document? Office does an excellent job of compressing pictures—in fact, you'll rarely get much additional compression by using Zip compression—but a document with 50 pictures that compress to 20KB each will still be more than 1MB in size.

- **Update Capability**—Will the object change? If so, you need to keep your options open. Yes, you can paste an Excel range into a Word document as a table, and then convert it back to an Excel range for updates. But if you plan to update the data frequently, it's easier to embed or link the data.

- **Portability**—Will the document and objects stay on a single machine or in easily accessible network locations? Or do you plan to move them to a portable PC, or distribute them to one or more people who are not connected to the same network?

Note

If you're creating Web pages, linking is usually your best option. For complex Web sites, use FrontPage, which has the best tools of all Office programs for maintaining and repairing links.

→ To learn more about maintaining and repairing links in Web pages, see "Managing Hyperlinks," **p. 924**.

With those three goals in mind, here's how to select the best method for putting an object into a document:

- If you're not particularly worried about file size, and you won't need to update the object, forget about linking or embedding. Insert the data—picture, table, chart, whatever—into the document.

- If file size is the overriding concern, use links to external data such as pictures and charts. You might encounter problems when moving documents, but if you duplicate the folder structure for document and objects on all the machines, linking will work.

- If portability is the main concern, and it's possible you'll need to update the object or move the file that contains the source data, use embedding. That way, you'll always have the object at hand—the object and its data travel with the document.

- In a workgroup, linking is the best way to handle items on which you plan to collaborate: One person or group can be working on the document while another person or group works on, say, the linked chart. When both groups are ready, update the document to bring in the latest version of all linked objects.

Tip from
EQ & Woody

You can quickly tell whether an object in Word is embedded or linked. Choose Tools, Options, and check the Field Codes box. An embedded object appears with an {Embed} field code; a linked object appears as a {Link} field code. Pictures that are part of the file won't have any field code, and you can see the picture.

→ To learn more about putting field codes to work in your Word documents, **see** "Using Fields Intelligently," **p. 488**.

CREATING AND EDITING EMBEDDED OBJECTS

The general method for creating any kind of new embedded object in Word or Excel is as follows:

1. Click to place the insertion point where you want to add the object.

2. Choose Insert, Object, and click the Create New tab. You'll see the Object dialog box shown in Figure 6.9.

PART

I

CH

6

Figure 6.9

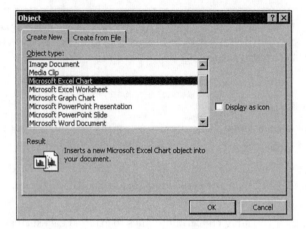

3. Scroll through the Object Type box until you find the type of object you want to insert. Select it, and then click OK.

4. The program associated with that particular object appears so you can edit in-place. When you're done, click outside the object area to return to the main document.

When you're back in the document, right-click the object and select Format Object to set text wrapping, colors, size, layout, cropping, and the like.

PowerPoint works similarly, although the dialog boxes are labeled a little differently.

 If you become frustrated trying to format or resize an embedded object, see "Formatting or Resizing Embedded Objects" in the "Troubleshooting" section at the end of this chapter.

If you want to embed an existing object into a Word document or Excel worksheet, you have two reliable choices:

- **Use the Clipboard**—Select the object and copy it to the Clipboard. Then click to position the insertion point at the location where you want to embed the object, and choose Edit, Paste Special. Select the correct Object format (Microsoft Excel Worksheet Object, for example), click the Paste option button, and click OK.

- **Use the Insert Object Dialog Box**—Click in the document where you want to embed the existing object. Choose Insert, Object, and click the Create from File tab. Use the Browse button to find the object, make sure the Link to File box is *not* selected, and click OK.

Again, the PowerPoint dialog boxes aren't exactly the same, but they perform similarly.

In some cases, you can right-click and drag to create an embedded object. For example, if you right-drag a picture file from the Windows Explorer and drop it onto a Word document, Word displays a shortcut menu. Choose Copy Here to embed the picture.

CREATING AND EDITING LINKED OBJECTS

You can create a link to an existing object in many ways. The easiest way to reliably create a link is to follow these steps:

1. Click to position the insertion point at the location in the document (worksheet, presentation, and so on) where you want to add the link.

2. Choose Insert, Object, and click the Create from File tab. You'll see the Object dialog box shown in Figure 6.10.

Figure 6.10
If the object already exists, you can embed or link to it from this dialog box.

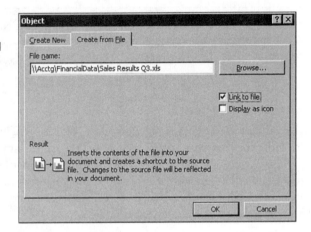

3. Use the Browse button to find the object, make sure the Link to File box is selected, and click OK.

Other ways to link to objects include the following:

- **Place the Object on the Clipboard**—Click in the document where you want the link to appear and choose Edit, Paste Special. Select a format, choose the Paste Link option, and click OK.

- **Choose Insert, Picture, from File and Select a Picture**—Instead of clicking the Insert button, click the down-arrow next to it and choose Link to File.

- **In Word, Choose Insert, File**—Instead of choosing the Insert option, click the down-arrow next to the button and choose Insert as Link.

In Word, if you choose Insert and Link from the Insert Picture dialog box, you'll get an embedded picture that's linked to the source file but uses Word as the picture editor. That way, a copy of the picture travels with the document, but each time the link is updated, Word goes out to the linked file and refreshes the picture.

PART

I

CH

6

Tip from

EQ & Woody

If you edit the picture from inside Word (right-click, and choose Edit Picture), the file itself isn't changed, but the new picture is stored in the document as an embedded–*not linked*–file!

It's all done with something called an {includepicture} field, which implements this strange hybrid of embedding and linking you won't find anywhere else in Office.

Tip from

EQ & Woody

If you're trying to link to a picture from the Clip Art Gallery, you're out of luck. Microsoft doesn't have any capability for linking or embedding clips in the Clip Art Gallery.

MANAGING LINKS BETWEEN DOCUMENTS AND OBJECTS

Try as you might, links break easily. Because a link is just a pointer—a fully qualified file-name, possibly with some ancillary information such as a range name—any time the path to the file changes, the link goes kaput. If you change the name or folder location of the object, the link breaks. If the link extends over a network and you break the connection to the server or individual PC on which the object is stored—for whatever reason—the link breaks as well. This is a particular concern on portable PCs.

 If you have placeholder links instead of the pictures that should be in your document, see "Broken Links to Image Files" in the "Troubleshooting" section at the end of this chapter.

When you have a linked item in a document (Word document, Excel workbook, or PowerPoint presentation), the Edit Links menu item becomes active. Click it, and you see the Links dialog box shown in Figure 6.11.

Figure 6.11
When a link has broken, use this dialog box to fix it.

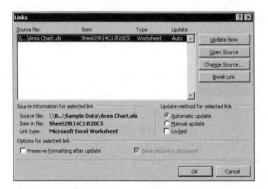

From the Links dialog box, you can change the object (using the Change Source button), update the linked object manually, or break the link altogether. If you have a document you're about to take on the road or send to a client, you should consider breaking the links prior to sending the document.

When you break the link, a format conversion takes place, changing the linked object into a picture, which is then placed in the document.

TROUBLESHOOTING

PASTE ALL AND THE OFFICE CLIPBOARD

Why is the Paste All button on the Office Clipboard grayed out?

When you click the Paste All button, the effect is the same as if you were to paste each item individually, pressing Enter (if necessary) between items. In some cases, the data types are incompatible with the current location of the insertion point. For example, if you've selected a chart or title placeholder in a PowerPoint presentation, you won't be able to paste a collection of text items. In that case, Office disables the Paste All button.

VIEWING THREE OR MORE WORD DOCUMENTS AT ONCE

I want to view three Word documents at once, so I can cut and paste data between them, but the document area is nearly impossible to see.

Try disabling any toolbars that aren't absolutely necessary (right-click any toolbar and uncheck the names of the toolbars you don't need). Turn off the horizontal scrollbar and status bar by choosing Tools, Options, and unchecking the appropriate entries in the View tab of the Options dialog box. Repeat for each document.

FORMATTING OR RESIZING EMBEDDED OBJECTS

An embedded object is the wrong size, but there are no obvious options for reformatting or resizing it.

Formatting, resizing, and cropping an embedded object is difficult because embedded objects use formatting from their native application and generally ignore formatting from the host application. To complicate matters, the inserted object is frequently sized arbitrarily. If you can't get the formatting correct from outside the object, double-click it and see whether you can change settings in the application that created it.

BROKEN LINKS TO IMAGE FILES

There are placeholder icons in my document instead of the pictures that should be visible there.

Those placeholder icons are broken links to image files. Ask the network administrator to check the permission on the shared drive or folder. If it's necessary to move the linked files, you might need to re-create the links.

SECRETS OF THE OFFICE MASTERS: REPLACING THE OFFICE CLIPBOARD

Conventional wisdom says Microsoft always gets it right on the third try. If that's true, it's going to take one more try before the Office Clipboard is ready for prime time. The first version, introduced in Office 2000, was so infuriatingly unusable that most sensible Office users made disabling it their top priority. Office XP's Clipboard is better, but still suffers from too many limitations to be truly useful.

If you really want to put some power in the Windows Clipboard, we recommend replacing it with a third-party utility. Search any well-stocked shareware site and you'll find dozens of candidates. Our favorite is the $20 ClipCache Plus, from XRayz Software (`http://www.xrayz.co.uk`). It includes these worthy improvements over the less-capable Office Clipboard:

- Unlike the Office Clipboard, this utility works with any Windows program.
- You can save favorite clips for reuse later—when filling in forms, for example. With the Office Clipboard, your saved clips stay in memory only as long as you have an Office program open, and you can't save the list.
- ClipCache Plus can save hundreds or even thousands of clips, instead of the arbitrary limit of 24 that Office imposes.
- You can assign keyboard shortcuts to any saved clip and use it in any program, not just Office.
- This utility enables you to clean up clips—removing e-mail forwarding indicators, for instance, or converting the case of text in a clip.

CHAPTER 7

USING OFFICE ON THE WEB

In this chapter

OFFICE AND THE WEB

Office XP is truly Web-enabled, with HTML, the language of the Web, serving as a native file format for Office applications.

This means that the long-elusive "round-trip" is a reality: You really can take a Word document, Excel workbook, or PowerPoint presentation, save it to the Web, then open it in a browser, and end up with the same document you saved. You can create and modify Web pages with confidence, knowing that what you see in an application is what you'll get when surfing.

Word 2002 also incorporates the capability to save "clean" HTML, at the expense of round-tripping: You get an HTML file that's slightly smaller and less complex than Word usually produces, but you lose the capability to read the file back into Word and retrieve all the formatting.

Tip from	Although it sounds good in theory, the "clean" HTML generated by Word is still loaded with extraneous tags and flotsam; if you're an HTML-savvy Web designer and you absolutely need standard HTML for your Web site, use a different editor.

This chapter is designed to show how Office works with the Web. It won't make you an expert on Web-page design or managing Web sites—for that, you should look at Chapters 36, "FrontPage Essentials," and 37, "Developing and Managing a Web Site," which cover FrontPage, Office's premiere Web-centric application.

USING HTML

HTML (Hypertext Markup Language) is the fundamental language behind all Web activity. It defines a set of operators, called *tags*, that control how information is displayed in a browser, and how the browser is to react to certain events. There is (at least in theory) only one correct way to display each tag: An <H1> heading in one browser should look the same as an <H1> heading in all browsers.

HTML is the basic (some would say "old") technology that drives the Web: Any browser will support early versions of HTML, and most HTML pages based on the classic (read: "old") tags will display perfectly well in any browser. But like so many other components of the Web, HTML has evolved on Web time, mutating so quickly that it's difficult to keep track of the various standards from day to day.

Office applications take advantage of many advanced HTML features, including those that go way beyond the traditional HTML tags. The following features in particular are likely to cause some document formatting to display incorrectly when viewed in particular browsers:

- *Extensible Markup Language* (XML) incorporates tags that go beyond the capability of standard HTML to describe and present data. It takes HTML further by introducing the concept of a *style sheet*. Style sheets add a new dimension to HTML. They allow an individual user to specify how the browser should interpret a tag. If your machine has a style sheet that declares all <H1> headers appear in blue, then they'll always appear in blue—on your machine. Most advanced Office features rely on XML to help them survive the round trip between the application that created them and the browser.

For more details on the XML standard, point your browser to `http://www.w3.org/xml`.

- *Cascading style sheets* (CSS) make style sheets more flexible by allowing inheritance (similar to Word's "Based On" styles), and automatically generated text and graphics. They extend basic HTML with style properties that define fonts, colors, margins, and other formatting properties. If you view a Web page that contains a CSS in a browser that can't interpret it, the browser displays the page using its default fonts and layout properties.

- *Dynamic HTML* (DHTML) allows a Web page designer to add effects to text and images, such as hiding or displaying a block of text when the user clicks it.

The structural differences between HTML and XML are extensive. For example, in HTML you specify where you want a paragraph mark (with the <P> tag), and the browser puts a carriage return/line feed in that location. But in XML, you specify where a paragraph starts and ends (with <PARA> and </PARA> pairs), and the style sheet tells the browser how to format the paragraph.

HOW OFFICE HANDLES HTML DOCUMENTS

All the major Office applications include a Save As Web Page command that lets you translate a file into HTML format and save it locally or publish it to a Web server. In addition, Word allows you to save in Web Page, Filtered format, which generates comparatively clean HTML, at the expense of retaining all formatting information.

When you create a document in Word, Excel, PowerPoint, or Access and save it as a Web page, the resulting file uses HTML as a companion format along with the application's native format. (FrontPage, of course, has always used HTML as its native file format.) As a result, all your formatting and most features survive the "round trip" from Office application to browser and back; when you open the file for editing, all your formatting and document features survive the round trip.

The requirement for 100% HTML compatibility is so stringent in Word, Excel, PowerPoint, Access, and FrontPage that Microsoft has adopted HTML as its primary format for use on the Clipboard. If you copy data from Excel to PowerPoint, for example, the data is translated into HTML as an intermediary format. If you copy anything from a Web browser into one of those Office applications, it should come across completely intact.

HTML compatibility and round-trip capabilities aren't the whole story. If you create a Web page in Word, for example, then you edit the page manually, then open the page and save it again in Word, there is *no* guarantee that Word will maintain your manual edits (although it leaves tags intact that it doesn't understand). The possibility of Word modifying a handwritten tag can be confusing and frustrating to experienced Web-page designers.

Because FrontPage was designed from the ground up as an HTML editor, it does a superb job of maintaining the integrity of tags and edits you construct manually. If you're an experienced HTML editor and you want the freedom to edit tags by hand at any time, stick with FrontPage.

VIEWING OFFICE DOCUMENTS IN A BROWSER WINDOW

Word, Excel and PowerPoint let you easily see how a Web page will appear in your default browser window: Choose File, Web Page Preview. As you can see in Figure 7.1, Office is smart enough to apply all the changes that it would normally incorporate for output as HTML into the browser window.

Figure 7.1
Documents can be previewed in your default browser by using Web Page Preview.

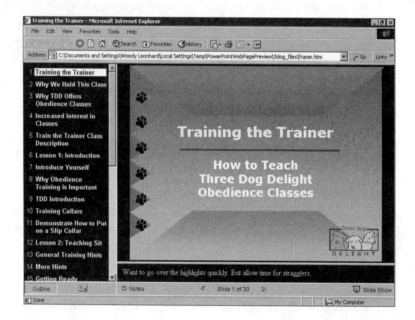

If you want to modify your document so it looks better in a specific browser, choose Tools, Options; then click the General tab. Click the Web Options button. On the Browsers tab, select your preferred browser from the offered list of Target Browsers.

CHOOSING THE RIGHT TOOL FOR THE JOB

Which Office program should you use to create Web pages? There's no universal answer to that question. Instead, the correct answer varies, depending on the task you're trying to accomplish and your level of Web sophistication.

Each application, however, has its own strengths, weaknesses, nuances, and gotchas. If you're trying to maintain a complex Web site, with a constantly changing lineup of links, or if your pages contain scripts and custom HTML tags, FrontPage is your only reasonable choice. On the other hand, if you just want to slap together a simple Web page with minimal fuss, Word might be able to handle it—and the Web Page, Filtered format will trim down some of the bloat so often associated with Word documents on the Web.

Word's Web Page, Filtered format is a one-way trip: Much of your formatting can be lost if you open the "clean" page in Word. If you want to make changes to the Web page, you have to open the original document, make your edits, and then choose Save As Web Page, Filtered again.

WORD

With a few small exceptions (such as diagonal cell borders, weird text formatting, and shaded paragraph backgrounds), anything you can put in a Word document will appear on a Web page, as in the example in Figure 7.2. Even the items that don't appear on the page will survive a round trip: Write a VBA/Word macro for a document, save it as a Web page, then open the Web page in Word, and the macro works just fine.

Figure 7.2
Word can handle small Web sites, and pages that include frames.

Word is an excellent choice for creating and maintaining relatively simple Web pages. Although it has no features for tracing or maintaining hyperlinks across a site, experienced Word users will find it easy to use and understand. The extensive frames capabilities (available when you choose Format, Frames) make it easy to create framed Web pages.

Word ships with a handful of useful templates and a wizard devoted exclusively to creating Web pages.s

→ To learn more about creating Web pages using Word templates, **see** "Using Word's Built-In Templates," **p. 476**.

EXCEL

As with Word, a few Excel features won't appear when you save a workbook as a Web page: custom views, nested functions, scenarios, and some advanced formatting don't appear on the Web page. Nonetheless, those features all survive a round trip, and Excel does a good job of not clobbering tags it doesn't understand.

Although it's true that you can use Excel to publish almost anything to the Web—entire workbooks go up easily, and static tables and charts pose no problem with any version 3.0 or later browser—the most interesting Excel Web pages provide interactivity. To create an interactive Web page, use the Add Interactivity check box on Excel's Save As dialog box, as shown in Figure 7.3.

Figure 7.3
Interactive spreadsheets, charts, and PivotTables start with the Add Interactivity box on the Save As dialog box.

This interactivity comes in two different forms:

- You can allow the viewer, using her browser (Internet Explorer 4.01 or later), to manipulate the data, just as the user would if she were running Excel itself. She can change data, move or copy cells, change formulas, and the like, and see the impact of those changes in spreadsheets, charts, or PivotTables.

> **Caution**
>
> If you expect that some persons will use Internet Explorer 3.x or any version of Netscape Navigator before 6.0 to open a Web page you create in Excel, do not use Web components to add interactivity. Only Internet Explorer 4.01 or later correctly displays content using these browser components.

- You can have Excel tap into a database on the server, so the data is updated in real time. Using this "data binding," the latest data is reflected on the Web page.

If you want to add interactive spreadsheets, charts, and PivotTables to a Web page, create the page in Excel, and then import it into FrontPage or Access (as a data access page) for additional polishing. The person who ultimately views the interactive Excel pieces must have Excel (or the Office XP Web Components) installed on their machine to take advantage of the interactivity.

POWERPOINT

PowerPoint is suitable for generating Web pages if you are willing to abide by its strict structure: PowerPoint creates a slide show on the Web, and not much else.

Although a great deal of flexibility exists in the format of the slide show—you can put slide titles in a pane, as shown earlier in Figure 7.1, and you can set up your own navigation buttons if the ones at the bottom don't ring your chimes—the end result is a slide show, pure and simple.

→ If you want to publish your PowerPoint presentations to the Web, **see** "Using a Browser for Your Presentation," **p. 845**.

ACCESS

Access's primary means of working on the Web involves a database object called a *data access page (DAP)*. (Figure 7.4 shows an example.) When you place data on a DAP (as opposed to an Access form or report), it can be viewed and edited by anyone with Internet Explorer 5.0 or later. DAPs in other browsers are static. The data on the page can be bound to a database residing on the server.

Figure 7.4
An Excel spreadsheet is embedded in an Access DAP.

PART

I

CH

7

Only consider DAPs if you know that all your users will be running Internet Explorer 5.0 or later, and that all of them will have valid licenses for Office 2000 or later (a Microsoft legal requirement). Providing you can meet those stringent requirements, you can use DAPs to

- Enter, view, and edit data using standard Access controls.

- Bind any of the three interactive Excel Web components—spreadsheets, charts, or PivotTables—to underlying data on the server.

OUTLOOK

Outlook uses the Internet and the Web for all sorts of things—meeting schedule conflict checking; to-do list status reports; vCard dissemination of Contact information; and much more—with one exception; it isn't designed to create Web pages.

That one exception is a humdinger. However, Outlook will publish a professional-looking calendar, encompassing all your appointments, as a Web page(see Figure 7.5) .

Figure 7.5
Outlook will publish your (or an organization's) appointment calendar to the Web.

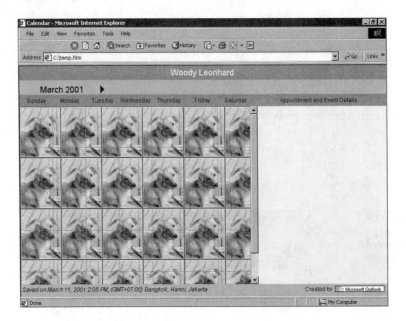

→ To learn more about using Outlook to publish your calendar, **see** "Publishing a Calendar as a Web Page," **p. 324**.

FRONTPAGE

FrontPage, by contrast, does anything and everything with Web pages, from easy visual placement of page elements to sophisticated support for HTML tags and script coding. It also enables you to manage even a large Web site, using comprehensive maps of links like the one shown in Figure 7.6. FrontPage also supports sophisticated management features so groups of people can work on a site simultaneously without getting in one another's way or inadvertently overwriting one another's pages.

Figure 7.6
FrontPage's Hyperlinks view gives you a concise picture of all the hyperlinks in a Web site.

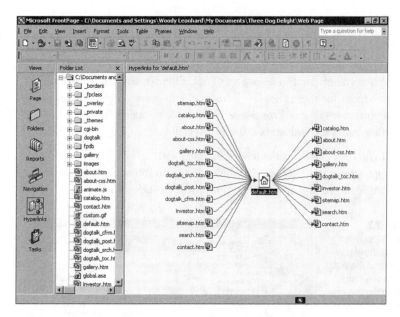

FrontPage uses all the Office import filters, so it's easy to open almost any kind of file and turn it into a Web page. Because Word, Excel, PowerPoint, and Access support HTML as a native file format and common copy format (and FrontPage's native file format has always been HTML), copying and moving data among these Office applications is a breeze.

In general, if you're serious about page design and, especially, Web-site management, you should always use FrontPage, unless

- You already know one of the other Office applications well, and your needs don't exceed the capabilities of the application.

- You want the specific controls provided by Excel (spreadsheet, chart, and PivotTable). Even then, it's a good idea to run the data through Excel, and do everything else with FrontPage.

- You require the data binding available in Access's DAPs. Again, running the pages through FrontPage for everything but the data-specific work can save a lot of time.

- You want a special feature in one of the Office applications (Outlook's calendar publisher, for example, or one of the Word Web Wizards) that precisely meets your needs.

MOVING BETWEEN HTML AND OFFICE FORMATS

When Office applications create HTML files, they usually store the identity of the creating program in an XML tag at the beginning of the document. For example, a Web page created in Word 2002 will have these tags:

PART

I

CH

7

```
<html xmlns:v="urn:schemas-microsoft-com:vml"
xmlns:o="urn:schemas-microsoft-com:office:office"
xmlns:w="urn:schemas-microsoft-com:office:word"
xmlns="http://www.w3.org/TR/REC-html40">
```

When you attempt to open an HTML file with any Office application, the File/Open routine looks for these tags; if it finds one, it automatically launches the associated program. So if you're working in FrontPage and you try to open a Web page created in Word, FrontPage launches Word and feeds it the HTML file.

If you look closely at the icon associated with an HTML file created in one of the Office applications in the Open File dialog box, you can see a tiny icon in the upper-left corner that identifies the originating application, as shown in Figure 7.7.

Figure 7.7
A tiny icon superimposed on the upper-left corner of the Web icon tells you which Office application originated the HTML file.

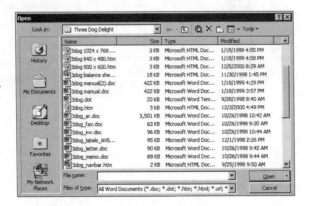

 If you need to open an HTML file in an Office application other than the one that originated it, see "Opening Office-Generated HTML Files" in the "Troubleshooting" section at the end of this chapter.

Not all browsers support the advanced features that the Office applications use. FrontPage gives you great flexibility in specifying precisely which features you want to include in generated Web pages, by choosing Tools, Page Options; and then clicking the Compatibility tab. Word and Excel give you a lesser (but still useful) range of compatibility choices. To access them, choose Tools, Options; click the General tab; and then click the Web Options button. You see a dialog box like the one in Figure 7.8.

Figure 7.8
Word and Excel let you "dumb down" your pages so they'll look better in less-capable browsers.

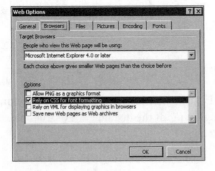

Traditional HTML files are plain text files; they cannot contain graphics. If you construct a Web page in Word, Excel, PowerPoint, Outlook, or Access, and the page contains a picture or other item (such as a macro or an embedded Excel interactive control), the application has to store the picture (or other item) outside the HTML file, and create a link to the picture within the text of the HTML file.

Tip from

EQ & Woody

You can save files in Web Archive (*.mht) format, although not all browsers will be able to cope with the format. Web Archive files combine traditional HTML files with their associated graphics, so they can all be handled at once (thus eliminating the problems described here). To save a file in Web Archive format, choose File, Save As Web Page. Then choose Web Archive in the Save as Type box.

All the Office applications will translate the graphic, if need be, into a GIF or JPEG file, which can be readily viewed on the Web. The rest of the story, however, isn't so simple.

Word, Excel, PowerPoint, and Access solve the problem in an elegant (if potentially dangerous) way: They create a folder with the same name as the file, and put the graphics (and other items) in the folder. Say you create a graphic-laden Web page in Word that's called 3dog.htm, and save it in the folder \Intranet\public. If you look at the folder, you'll find the original Word file, \Intranet\public\3dog.htm. You'll also find a folder called \Intranet\public\3dog Files, which contains all the graphics from the original page, translated (if necessary) into GIF or JPEG format.

Caution

The links between the HTML file and the graphics are hard-coded to refer to an appropriately named subfolder. (For those of you who might have encountered this problem in other guises, Office stores relative addresses, not absolute addresses.) If you move an Office-generated HTML file—in this case, 3dog.htm—you must move the supporting folder—3dog Files—and all the contents along with it. Otherwise, the links will be broken. If you use PowerPoint to move HTML and graphic files, the program will maintain the proper links.

Word, Excel, and PowerPoint (but not Access) let you change this behavior, if you like, so all the files—main page and supporting files alike—go into a single folder. To do so, choose Tools, Options. Click the General tab, and then click the Web Options button. Click the Files tab (see Figure 7.9), and clear the Organize Supporting Files in a Folder box.

Outlook's calendar pages are different. The calendar main page and all its supporting data are dumped in the same folder. The initial page of the calendar is given the name of the folder. So, if you save a calendar called Status Meetings, all the supporting data is placed in a folder called \Status Meetings. The main page goes in the same folder, and it is called Status Meetings.htm.

Figure 7.9
Word, Excel, and PowerPoint let you choose whether supporting files should be placed in their own folder.

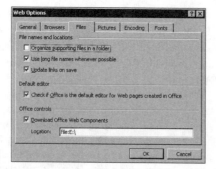

Note

Office saves VBA projects in a binary file called Editdata.mso and stores it along with associated files for that page. Similarly, Word, Excel, and PowerPoint store XML-formatted lists of support files in Filelist.xml, and PowerPoint and Outlook store cascading style sheets in various *.css files.

WEB-PAGE DESIGN ESSENTIALS

Web-page design is an art unto itself, with a broad array of graphic considerations that don't apply when you're working with printed media. Most computer magazines run design articles from time to time, and no two seem to agree on what constitutes an outstanding design. A topic as simple as frames versus no frames can trigger flame mail worthy of a barroom brawl.

That said, all would-be Web-page designers should keep a few simple tips in mind:

- Obey the Web design corollary to the KISS principle—Keep It Small, Stupid. Nobody likes to wait for downloads.

Tip from
EQ & Woody

FrontPage has a handy reminder, down on the status bar, that tells you approximately how long it will take to download the page you're constructing, using a 28.8 modem.

- Avoid ransom note typography. Two different fonts on a page make your point. Three annoy anyone trying to read the page. Four convinces them to click another link and go read something else.

- Make colors work together. Magenta text on a red background might be (barely) legible on some monitors. It won't be legible at all on many.

- Don't break the law. Copyright protection applies in cyberspace, too. It might be easy to reproduce copyrighted work on your page, but that doesn't make it legal.s

→ To learn more about creating Web pages, effective design, and so forth, **see** Chapters 36, "FrontPage Essentials," **p. 915** and 37, "Developing and Managing a Web Site," **p. 941**.

Browser-Compatibility Issues

When you publish a Word document, PowerPoint presentation, or a Web page that contains interactive Office Web components on a corporate intranet, you know exactly what software is running on the server. Generally, that means you can predict or even control which browsers your users will view the pages with, minimizing the possibilities for compatibility problems.

On the other hand, when you post an Office-generated page to a server that's widely accessible on the Web, you have to anticipate problems. Many of these problems can be traced back to fundamental differences in the way various Web browsers work.

Specific, known limitations include these:

- When you use Access to create DAPs, they can be viewed only with Internet Explorer 5 or later. Microsoft makes no claim for compatibility with earlier versions of Internet Explorer or any version of Netscape Navigator (although the folks at Netscape might beg to differ).

- If you use Excel to create interactive Web pages, they can be viewed only with Internet Explorer 4.01 or later.

- Word and Excel save documents and worksheets in HTML format with XML markup tags. Thus, at least in theory, the content of Word- and Excel-generated pages should be visible in almost any browser, although some formatting might be lost, especially in older browsers.

- Some Office document elements—most notably drawing layer objects, including organization charts—don't look very good in any browser, including Internet Explorer 5. Be cautious of how the various browsers render carefully crafted graphics in the drawing layer.

Adding VBScript or JScript Code

Web pages in general can contain embedded programs written in *VBScript* or *JScript*. Office provides good support for writing and deploying those programs in Web pages generated by Office.

Office allows you to attach two completely different kinds of programs—two different kinds of macros—to documents. The kind of macro you want to create depends on when you intend to use it:

- If you want to run the macro while viewing the document in Office—that is, you want the program to work while you have a Word document open in Word, or an Excel workbook open in Excel—you must use Visual Basic for Applications. VBA is a robust, thorough, often complex programming language, which is covered in several chapters later in this book.

→ For an extensive introduction to these kinds of macros, **see** Chapter 38, "Using Macros to Automate Office Tasks," **p. 963**.

PART

I

CH

7

■ On the other hand, if you want to run the macro while viewing the document with a Web browser—that is, you save the document in HTML, post it to the intranet or Internet, and look at it with a browser—you must use VBScript or JScript as your macro language. Both VBScript and JScript are designed to be small, quick, and limited in their capabilities.

To look at it in a slightly different way: VBA runs within Office; VBScript and JScript run within your browser. VBA has a sophisticated development environment and strong ties into Office. From a developer's point of view, VBScript and JScript are held together with a little (but not a lot) more than baling wire and chewing gum, and can nudge your browser around a bit, but they might still be the solution when used in the right situation.

For example, if you want a macro that scans and reformats a document, and you're going to use the macro when you're working in Word, you have no choice but to use VBA.

But if you want a macro that rearranges some data on a Web page and prints it, and you want to use the macro when viewing the data through a Web browser, you need either VBScript or JScript.

VBA's capabilities are discussed extensively in Chapters 38–41 of this book. Although a thorough discussion of VBScript lies beyond the scope of this book, you might find it instructive to see a sample VBScript program, and how it can be tied in to COM objects on a Word-generated Web page. Let's say you want to put a timer button on a Web page—click the button, and it responds with the current system time. You might want such a button if, for example, you're tracking response time on your company's intranet. Here's how you create one in Word:

1. Right-click any visible toolbar and select Control Toolbox from the list of available toolbars. You'll see the Control Toolbox, which contains Word's built-in COM objects.

2. Click the Command Button icon in the Control Toolbox. That places a command button labeled CommandButton1 in the upper-left corner of the document. Click and drag the button so you can see all the text, as in Figure 7.10.

Figure 7.10
Start by placing a Command Button control in the upper-left corner of your Web page.

3. Choose Tools, Macro, Microsoft Script Editor. That brings up a VBScript/JScript macro-editing environment remarkably similar to the one in FrontPage (see Figure 7.11).

Figure 7.11
The Microsoft Script Editor provides support for programming in both VBScript and JScript.

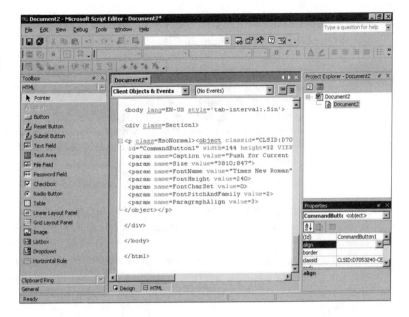

4. Click View, Other Windows, Document Outline to bring up the Document Outline pane (which you can dock). Then double-click CommandButton1. That brings up the properties for CommandButton1 in the Properties window, at the lower right. Click once, in the HTML pane, in the <param name=Caption ... > tag. Locate the property called Caption and change it to Push for current time (see Figure 7.12).

Figure 7.12
Set the CommandButton1. Caption property by typing into the Properties window.

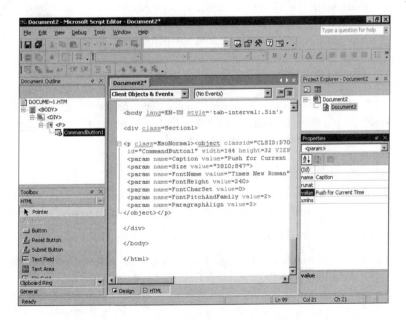

5. Set VBScript to work with HTML version 4.0 features by choosing View, Property Pages and, on the General tab, changing the Target Schema drop-down list to HTML 4.0.

Caution

Many advanced VBScript capabilities rely on HTML version 4.0, and every modern browser will work with HTML 4.0. Word 2000, by default, supports HTML 4.0. For reasons known only to Microsoft, Word 2002 ships with the Target Schema set to the earlier version, HTML 3.2. If you learned to program VBScript with Word 2000, make sure to change the Target Schema as outlined above, or you'll be faced with all sorts of problems.

6. In the object drop-down box at the top of the HTML pane, choose CommandButton1. In the Event box, choose Click. Word responds by creating a subroutine called CommandButton1_Click. If you've used VBScript before (or any version of Visual Basic, for that matter), you'll recognize that as the name of a program which will be run when the user clicks on the button called CommandButton1. Word even provides the Sub/End Sub pair, so all you have to do is type in the middle line of the three-line program:

```
Sub CommandButton1_Click
CommandButton1.Caption = Time()
End Sub
```

7. Choose File, Exit to leave the Script Editor. When asked if you want to save changes to Document1, click Yes. In the Save As dialog box, choose a name and a location for your new Web page. Choose File, Exit to leave Word.

8. Open your new Web page, either by locating it in Windows Explorer and double-clicking it, or by launching your Web browser and navigating to it. Click the command button. The current time should appear (see Figure 7.13).

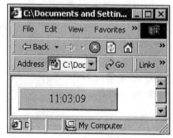

With all the controls in the Control Toolbox at your disposal, it's possible (although not easy) to build full-fledged VBScript applications inside Word or Excel.

Figure 7.13

PREVIEWING AND TESTING WEB PAGES

As the most important—and most frequently overlooked—step in creating Web pages, testing is a necessity after you go beyond a single HTML page with no attached graphics.

If you work on a corporate network, you will probably have four or five options for testing:

- If you have a good Web page design tool, such as FrontPage, the Web preview available in the tool will probably suffice for layout and general debugging. FrontPage also has a Preview in Browser feature (File, Preview in Browser), which pulls up the browser of your choice. Failing that, the Web Page Preview command on the File menu in Word or Excel will do in a pinch.

■ At the next level, you can double-click an *.htm or *.html file, and your browser will attempt to load it. (Equivalently, you can start the browser and type the filename, or drag and drop the file onto the browser.) This is a good quick-and-dirty approach for verifying VBScript code, and if you've carefully constructed internal file links so they're relative, you might get some feedback on mislinked graphics.

Tip from

EQ & Woody

If you flip between, say, FrontPage and your browser to check on the status of your page, make sure you save your changes in FrontPage before opening or refreshing the page in the browser.

■ As a final staging area prior to release on the Web, it's hard to beat an intranet. If you have a client/server network running Window 2000 (or NT) server, you might have one already. Contact your network administrator, or look for the folder C:\InetPub\Wwwroot\Intranet.

■ After you're on the Web, you might find it advantageous to "hide" the main page for a few days, to shake out any final bugs. You can do that by calling the main page in the default folder Index0.htm, for example, and instructing your testers to use that page instead of the default Index.htm or Index.html.

WORKING WITH HYPERLINKS

All the Office applications allow you to put a hyperlink in your documents using the same Insert Hyperlink dialog box (choose Insert, Hyperlink), shown in Figure 7.14.

Figure 7.14
The Insert Hyperlink dialog box allows you to create "hot" links to Web pages, files, or locations within files, with a few simple clicks.

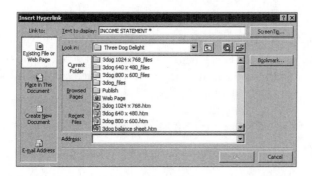

It's important to realize that hyperlinks in Office aren't limited to Web pages: They can just as easily specify files located on a server, or locations within files on your hard drive, or even mailto: links for e-mail addresses.

Hyperlinks are implemented differently in each of the Office applications. That can lead to some bizarre, and confusing, differences:

- In Word, if you don't select any text before invoking the Insert Hyperlink dialog box (and Word doesn't automatically select any for you), Word creates a hyperlink with display text that shows the name of the destination. The hyperlink doesn't change if you alter the displayed text. So, if you insert a hyperlink to www.mcp.com and then you edit the hyperlink text in the document so that it reads www.m.com, the link still points to www.mcp.com. Click the edited www.m.com and you'll end up at the Web site www.mcp.com. Very confusing.

- In Excel and PowerPoint, if you don't select any text before invoking the Insert Hyperlink dialog box, you'll also get the name of the destination as the displayed text for the link. But in Excel and PowerPoint's case, if you edit the text, the link changes. So if you change the hyperlink text www.mcp.com to www.m.com, and then click it, Excel and PowerPoint look for www.m.com.

Although these odd exceptions might throw you, in general, hyperlinks can be copied, moved, or deleted, much as you would copy, move, or delete text.

You can find advanced discussions about hyperlinking as it pertains to each individual Office application throughout this book.

TROUBLESHOOTING

OPENING OFFICE-GENERATED HTML FILES

I created a Word document and saved it as a Web page, and now I want to edit it in FrontPage. Every time I try to open the HTML file in FrontPage, however, Word opens instead.

You have several options; the following two are the easier:

- Open the Web page in IE5, click the arrow to the right of the Edit button on the browser's Standard toolbar, and then choose Edit with Microsoft FrontPage.

- From FrontPage, choose File, Open; in the Open dialog box, right-click the icon for the file you're trying to open, and choose Open in Microsoft FrontPage.s

SECRETS OF THE OFFICE MASTERS: KEYS TO EFFECTIVE WEB PAGE DESIGN

When designing a Web page, keep in mind some of the techniques used in the following page, the home site for Que Publishing.

In particular,

- The most important information appears at the left, where it's both easy to find and fast to load.

- The Search function—what most users are looking for—stands out. There's no clutter. *Special Edition Using Office* appears prominently.

- Different fonts are used sparingly: All the text (outside the graphics) is simple Arial.
- Colors blend together well, and color contrasts highlight changes in emphasis.
- There's no question about how to navigate from this page, no ambiguity about what clicking a particular element will accomplish.

Figure 7.15

CHAPTER 8

SHARING OFFICE DOCUMENTS

In this chapter

KEEPING SHARED DOCUMENTS SECURE

Before you share an Office document with anyone else—whether by giving an entire department access on your corporate intranet or on the Internet at an FTP or Web site—you should first consider how you're going to protect the document, both from prying eyes and from unwanted changes.

PROTECTING OFFICE DOCUMENTS WITH PASSWORDS

Your first line of defense is to protect the document file itself with a password. That simple precaution will usually keep out casual snoops, and with a little extra attention, you can scramble a document so effectively that only a determined cryptologist could unlock it without knowing the password.

Password protection works by *encrypting* a file—scrambling its data so it can't be read without being unlocked. Office XP's encryption options are significantly improved over the password-protection options in earlier Office versions: Word documents, Excel workbooks, and PowerPoint presentations can be password protected, with separate passwords for read-only and read-write access. The default encryption option for Word and Excel is the same as in Office 2000 (allowing users of earlier Office versions to open those files with the correct password); you can add stronger protection using the CryptoAPI support in Office XP. To select a stronger encryption technique, choose Tools, Options, click the Security tab, and click the Advanced button.

→ For more details on Office security settings, **see** "Setting Security Options," **p. 49**.

By default, Office documents are protected with 40-bit RC4 encryption, which is pretty darn hard to crack on a typical PC. If the password is more or less random (that is, it doesn't appear in a typical cracking dictionary), it can take a day or more of PC time *per character* to crack the password.

Note

Of course, the people who work for "those" agencies (the ones with three-letter acronyms for names) crack 40-bit RC4 encoded documents in the time it takes to down a tall latte. Supercomputers and massively parallel processors hardly break a sweat. They have a considerably tougher time with longer key sizes.

→ To learn more about sharing Word documents with other members of a workgroup, **see** "Sharing Documents," **p. 396**.

→ To keep sensitive Excel worksheets safe from prying eyes, **see** "Using Passwords to Restrict Access to a Workbook," **p. 704**.

That's the good news, if you're concerned about security (or the bad news, if you've forgotten your document's password). Password protection used elsewhere in Office is much, much simpler.

Tip from

It's important that you know which passwords are easy to break, so you don't rely on an "easy" password protection scheme to keep your documents private. Believe us, the bad guys know all about password crackers.

The forms of password protection vary slightly from application to application:

- Word allows you to password-protect documents to track changes, only allow comments, or for forms, on the Protect Document dialog box (choose Tools, Protect Document). All those passwords are trivial to break.

- Excel allows you to protect individual worksheets (contents, formats, objects, and scenarios), workbooks (structure, windows), and the logs that track changes to a shared workbook, all by choosing Tools, Protection. These passwords are also easy to crack with any commercial password cracker.

- PowerPoint lets you protect a presentation file using the new CryptoAPI support. A password-protected presentation cannot be opened in earlier versions of PowerPoint.

- Outlook offers password protection for individual *.pst files. These passwords are also easy to break.

- Access security differs from the other Office applications. You can set a database password that locks out anyone who doesn't have that key. You can also encrypt a database using the Tools, Security, Encrypt/Decrypt Database menu commands, but you can't select encryption levels. If user-level security definitions are in the database, being able to open the database won't accomplish much. Database passwords are easy to crack, but the internal security definitions are much more difficult.

- FrontPage has no document password security, period.

- Visual Basic for Applications modules can be password protected (VBA calls it "locked for viewing"). VBA passwords can be cracked easily.

Note

Although macro software developers decry VBA's weak password protection, there's a hitch: Some macro viruses are designed to encrypt VBA modules. If the VBA password protection were stronger, antivirus products would have a much harder time rooting out viruses.

If you've forgotten your password, see "Forgotten Passwords" in the "Troubleshooting" section at the end of this chapter.

For maximum file security, lock the document using one of the advanced encryption options available in Word, Excel, or PowerPoint, and dial up the encryption-key length from its default 40-bit setting to the maximum of 56. Note that this option locks out users of older Office versions, and that it isn't available for Access users.

CREATING A BACKUP COPY AUTOMATICALLY

Each time you open or save a Word document or Excel workbook, you can protect the original file. From the Save As dialog box, click Tools and choose Save Options; then check the Always Create Backup Copy check box. This option saves a backup copy of the original version every time you open or save a file, using the previously saved version of the file.

Caution

This protective measure is of limited value. It's designed to protect you from incredibly obvious mistakes, and it's useful only if you discover your mistake immediately. Let's say you open a Word document, make some changes, and save the changed document under the same name. If you then discover to your horror that you've altered the master copy of a crucial document, you can open the backup copy and recover the original. However, if you make some more changes and save your work a second time, Word creates a backup of the first set of changes you made, replacing the backup it created when you opened the file. At that point, the original document is history, and you better hope you have an alternative backup copy to restore.

HOW OFFICE LOCKS DOCUMENTS TO PREVENT CONFLICTS

Office keeps track of which documents are open on the network. If you try to open a document that's already in use by someone else, you'll receive a warning message such as that in Figure 8.1.

Figure 8.1
Word and PowerPoint won't let two people change the same document simultaneously. At best, one can edit the document while everyone else can only view a Read Only copy.

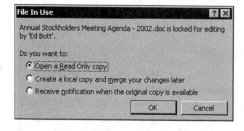

This kind of protection is necessary to keep unsynchronized changes from compromising the document's integrity. If you and your partner are simultaneously working on copies of your business plan in Word, what happens when she changes a paragraph that you're working on? For collaborating on documents in this fashion, you're better off using Word's revision-tracking features or Web Discussions (discussed later in this chapter). Better yet, use NetMeeting or a similar conferencing program to share the document in real-time on a virtual whiteboard.

→ For more information on how to work with shared Office documents on a Web server, **see** "Office Web Discussions," **p. 180**.

→ To learn how and when to use revision tracking in Word, **see** "Tracking Revisions," **p. 396**.

⚠️ *If you get File in Use messages when you're the only user attempting to use a document, see "Hidden Applications Lock Files" in the "Troubleshooting" section at the end of this chapter.*

Excel allows more than one person to work on a workbook simultaneously, but you have to set up the sharing before others on the network start opening the workbook.

→ To learn how to set up network-based file sharing in Excel, **see** "Sharing a Workbook," **p. 708**.

OPENING DOCUMENTS IN READ-ONLY MODE

You can help (or force) yourself and your co-workers to open particular Office files in read-only mode. As the name implies, applying the read-only attribute allows anyone who opens the file to view its contents. To make changes, you must save a copy of the file under a new name, and then make changes to the copy.

You have the following read-only options in Office XP:

- When saving a file, you can discourage users (including yourself) from making changes to a Word document. In the Save As dialog box, choose Tools, Security Options; then select the Read-Only Recommended check box. (For an Excel workbook file, choose Tools, General Options.) This technique is particularly useful when you frequently use the same document or worksheet as the base for new files, and you occasionally forget to use the New from Existing Document option in the New file task pane. When you try to open a file saved with this option, you'll see the dialog box shown in Figure 8.2. Click yes to prevent accidental changes to your original file.

Figure 8.2
When you try to open or save a Word or Excel file saved with the "Recommend read only" attribute, this dialog box appears.

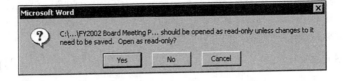

Tip from
EQ & Woody

If your goal is to prevent other users from damaging an important file (especially users who might not be sophisticated enough to understand the consequences of this option), use a Modify password instead. This option is unavailable if you save a document in Word 6.0/95 format.

- When you open a document in Word, Excel, or PowerPoint, you can choose to open it as a read-only file. Click the Open icon, or choose File, Open. From the Open dialog box, click the arrow to the right of the Open button and choose Open Read-Only from the drop-down list.

- For most Office documents, you can assign separate passwords for full read-write (modify) access. If you assign a read-write password and no read-only password, your correspondents will be able to open read-only, but will require the password to make changes to the file.

CONTROLLING FILE ACCESS WITH WINDOWS PERMISSIONS

You can also use Windows to restrict access to Office files or the folders in which they're stored. File-level and folder-level restrictions are highly dependent on your Windows version:

- Windows NT, 2000, or XP Professional Edition running the NT File System (NTFS) provides the only secure Windows environment for controlling access to files. Although it isn't absolutely perfect, NTFS lets you restrict access to files or folders by individuals or groups. In Windows 2000 and XP with NTFS, you can also encrypt files and entire folders for maximum security.

- Windows XP Personal Edition allows you to make folders (but not individual files) private.

- On a computer running Windows NT4 Server Edition with the FAT16 or FAT32 file system, you have some degree of control over access, although a knowledgeable user can bypass these controls.

- The basic peer-to-peer networking in Windows 95/98/Me provides minimal access control using password-based security on shared folders only, not on individual files.

ROUTING, REVIEWING, AND REVISING DOCUMENTS

Sometimes server-based collaboration just doesn't have the urgency of e-mail: You can tell people over and over that they need to connect to the server and make their comments, and some never will. But if they receive the document by e-mail, the immediacy can help spur them to action. Add a routing slip that details how long an individual has been procrastinating, and you might have enough incentive to move mountains.

Office includes several tools that help you mail, route, and control your documents.

SENDING A DOCUMENT AS E-MAIL

The simplest way to send a document to an individual or group is by sending it as an e-mail message, in HTML format. You can do that in Word and Excel, but not in PowerPoint:

1. Open (or create) the document.
2. Click the E-mail icon on the Standard toolbar (or choose File, Send To, Mail Recipient). The application responds with an e-mail "send" bar, as in Figure 8.3.
3. Fill out the To, CC, and Subject lines, just as you would in Outlook.
4. Click Send a Copy on the E-mail toolbar. The application attempts to send the message immediately, using your default e-mail application and its default e-mail account.

Figure 8.3
You can send a document as an e-mail message, in native HTML format, while working in Word or Excel. From PowerPoint, you can send a presentation as an attachment

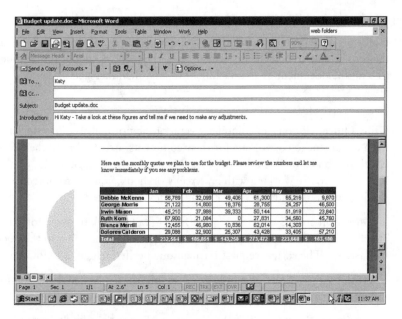

If the message cannot be delivered immediately, you will see a warning, but no reminder will be stored for you in the e-mail application. You have to remember to resend the message at a later date.

When the document is sent as an HTML message, each recipient can modify the document directly, as long as the recipient's e-mail reader can handle Office's particular version of HTML (this includes most modern mail clients, including Outlook 98/2000, Netscape mail 4.5 or later, and Eudora 5 or later; Outlook 97, AOL, and many older mail programs cannot). The recipient can then send the message back, and you have the challenge of assembling the HTML messages, converting them to native Office file formats, and comparing the results.

Tip from

EQ & Woody

Expect many minor inconsistencies. For example, characters as simple as "curly" quotes aren't legible on many HTML e-mail readers. And complex formatting can cause no end of trouble—up to and including General Protection Faults on your recipients' computers.

If you decide that you don't want to send a copy as a mail message after all, click the E-mail button again to make the message header disappear.

SENDING A DOCUMENT AS AN E-MAIL ATTACHMENT

If all your correspondents are using Office 97, Office 2000, or Office XP, and you want them to be able to edit the document properly, you'll no doubt find it much more reliable to send the document as an attachment to an e-mail message.

SENDING OFFICE DOCUMENTS FOR REVIEW

Using Office XP, you can combine several of the normally tedious steps involved in forwarding a document to co-workers for their comments. After opening the Word document, Excel workbook, or PowerPoint presentation, choose File, Send To, Mail Recipient (for Review). If you're working with an Excel workbook, you're prompted to turn on workbook sharing, which is required as part of the reviewing process.

The program creates a review request form—an Outlook message form that includes a file attachment (if the file is stored locally on your system) or a link to the document on a network server. The review request form automatically includes a follow-up flag ("Review").

Insert the names of one or more reviewers into the To box, add any comments or additional instructions in the message body, and click the Send button.

When your recipients receive the message and open the file, the reviewing toolbar is automatically displayed, and change tracking is turned on. After they add comments and make changes, they can send the document back to you. When you open the reviewed document, Office prompts you to accept or reject any changes. You can end the reviewing process at any time by clicking the End Review button on the Reviewing toolbar.

ADDING A ROUTING SLIP

For simple collaboration between two or three people, e-mail messages and attachments are all you need. Coordinating a larger group of collaborators can be a more daunting task, especially for important legal and financial documents in which following a formal set of procedures is crucial. Office allows you to route a document to a series of people for review, either sequentially (one after another) or all at once.

Routing slips let you control who receives the file, and in what order, providing the recipients are willing and able to forward the document properly. They are available in Word, Excel, and PowerPoint. To create a routing slip:

1. Create or open the document you want to route.
2. Choose File, Send To, Routing Recipient. After a security dialog box that prompts you to allow access to your Outlook Address Book, you'll see the Routing Slip dialog box shown in Figure 8.4.

Figure 8.4
Word, Excel, and PowerPoint let you choose a predetermined routing order for a document.

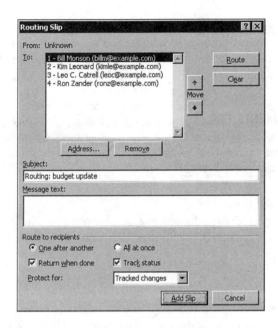

3. Add recipients by clicking the Address button and choosing from your Outlook Contacts list. Change the order of recipients with the Move buttons.

    -   Use the One After Another option when it's important that edits proceed one person at a time, in a set order—so that Legal sees the document after Finance, for instance, and the project manager sees the document after all comments have been added.

    -   Use the All at Once option when you plan to incorporate all the changes yourself, and you want each routing recipient to read the entire document but concentrate on just their section.

4. If you want the document to be returned to you after the last person on the routing slip has finished, check the Return When Done box.

5. If you want to receive an automatically generated e-mail message each time the document is forwarded, check the Track Status box.

6. If you're ready to send the document to the first person on the routing list, click the Route button. Word generates a message, attaches the document, and places the message with attached document in your Outlook outbox, so it will be sent the next time you send mail.

7. If you're not ready to send the document, click the Add Slip button. Make any final corrections you like to the document and, when you're ready, choose File, Send To, Next Routing Recipient.

The document itself is attached to a message that contains easy-to-follow instructions for routing the document to the next recipient on the routing list.

The key point, of course, is that each person in the routing chain has to know, understand, and follow the protocol for forwarding the message to the next person on the routing slip. To do so, the recipient might save the document or open it directly from Outlook. But when his edits are complete, he must choose File, Send To, Next Routing Recipient.

Note

If you receive a routed document and want to route it to someone not on the routing slip, choose File, Send to, Other Routing Recipient; then select the new recipient. When that person is done with the file, she can resume the routing slip sequence by choosing File, Send to, Next Routing Recipient.

Anyone along the chain can change the order of people on the routing slip. To do so, choose File, Send To, and choose Other Routing Recipient. Then move the names up and down with the Move arrows. Click the Route button and the document is routed immediately, via Outlook.

COMPARING, REVIEWING, AND MERGING CHANGES

When multiple Office users work on the same document, workbook, or presentation, you can compare the contents of each version and merge the changes into a single document. Word and Excel allow you to review each change individually or merge all changes at one time. PowerPoint does only a full comparison and merge between two presentations.

→ For details on how to track changes in Word documents, **see** "Sharing Documents," **p. 396**.

→ To learn how to share Excel workbooks and consolidate changes, **see** "Sharing a Workbook," **p. 708**.

OFFICE WEB DISCUSSIONS

Office XP includes support for a feature called *Web discussions*. Using this capability, which was introduced in Office 2000, members of a workgroup can share comments about Office documents and Web pages, even when the members of the workgroup are scattered across wide geographic locations and don't have the capability to directly modify the documents themselves. Like many debuting Microsoft technologies, this feature is a classic 1.0 release—it's easy to see its promise, but also frustratingly difficult to configure and use.

USING A WEB SERVER FOR DISCUSSIONS

To participate in a Web discussion, you must have access to a Web server running Internet Information Server 4.0 or later with Office Server Extensions or SharePoint Team Services on a computer running Windows NT 4.0, Windows 2000, or Windows XP. You can also use Personal Web Server 4.0, included with Windows NT Option Pack 4.0, or Windows 2000's Personal Web Manager.

Tip from

Ed & Woody

It isn't necessary to have access to a Windows NT or Windows 2000 server; you can effectively maintain a Web discussion database in a small workgroup by using the Workstation version of Windows NT 4.0 or the Professional editions of Windows 2000 or XP. (Windows XP Personal Edition does not offer this capability.)

It's important to understand the architecture of Web discussions. As Figure 8.5 shows, comments are not stored within the Office document or Web page itself; instead, a Web server stores the comments and a pointer to external documents and Web pages in an *SQL database*. When you open a Web page or Office document, you can click a button or choose a menu option to display those comments within the application or browser window.

Figure 8.5

Office stores comments in one location and displays them in the same window as a document or Web page, without changing the original file.

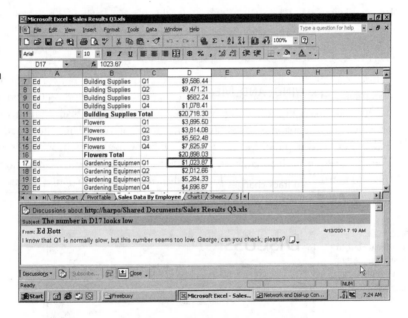

Anyone with access to the server that contains the discussion database can participate in a discussion, either in a browser window or in a program window. In either configuration, the Web Discussions toolbar lets you navigate through discussions. Comments appear in threaded form, and you can rearrange, regroup, and filter on comments.

When should you use Web discussions, and when is it more appropriate to embed comments directly in Word documents and Excel workbooks, or to use the revision-tracking features in either program? Of course, the most significant limiting factor is access to a Web discussion server; if you don't have a location to store discussions, the option isn't available to you.

- Consider Web discussions when you want to have a group discussion of a document to which some or all users do not have write access. For example, you can use Web discussions to critique a competitor's Web site and discuss strategies for adopting some of its features for your own. Or you might post a draft of a new policies manual to an intranet server and encourage employees to comment on it. Because the discussion does not affect the document itself, you can encourage comments without worrying about the integrity of the document.

■ Skip Web discussions and use the built-in collaboration tools in Word and Excel when you want a small group of people to actively collaborate on the creation or editing of a document or workbook. These tools are most useful when the document is under construction and users are adding and changing content. In this case, the fact that comments and changes are part of the file is a benefit. Whoever is responsible for coordinating all changes can use the Track Changes feature in Word or Excel to produce a final file.

→ For details on how to track changes in Word documents, **see** "Sharing Documents," **p. 396**.

→ To learn how to share Excel workbooks and consolidate changes, **see** "Sharing a Workbook," **p. 708**.

CONFIGURING OFFICE FOR WEB DISCUSSIONS

Before you can participate in a Web discussion, you have to create a connection between the document and its discussion server. If you open the document directly from the server, this happens automatically. To configure this manually, open the Web page or Office document on which the discussion is based. From Internet Explorer 5, click the Discussion button; from within an Office document, choose Tools, Online Collaboration, Web Discussions. From the Web Discussions toolbar, click the Discussions menu and choose Discussion Options. Click the Add button to display the dialog box shown in Figure 8.6. Enter the name of the server that contains the *discussion database*, give it a descriptive name, and click OK.

Figure 8.6
Use this dialog box to establish a connection with a Web discussion server.

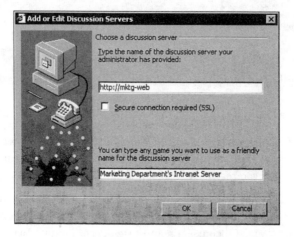

After this crucial configuration step is complete, use the Discussion Options dialog box (see Figure 8.7) to specify options that apply to the specific document under discussion. Each comment in the discussion database includes a number of fields. To keep the screen uncluttered, you can hide some of these fields in your browser or application window.

Figure 8.7
Use this dialog box to configure options for the specific document or Web page under discussion.

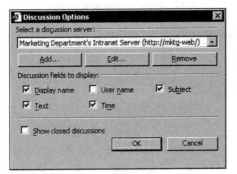

PARTICIPATING IN WEB DISCUSSIONS

When the Discussion toolbar is visible, any comments in the current document or Web page appear as *embedded note markers*. You can start two different types of discussions, depending on the file type:

- In Word documents and Web pages, you can carry on *inline discussions* relating to a specific paragraph, table, or graphic. Click the Discussions button and choose Insert in the Document; Word adds a comment marker at the point where you clicked and opens the Enter Discussion Text dialog box (see Figure 8.8). Enter a subject and the message text, and click OK to save the comment to the discussion server.

Figure 8.8
Every comment includes these two elements. The subject line is important, because it's used for maintaining threaded conversations.

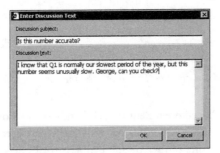

- In Word documents, Excel workbooks, PowerPoint slides, and Web pages, you can add discussions about the document, workbook, slide, or page itself. Click the Discussions button and choose Insert About the *<file type>* to display the Enter Discussion Text dialog box and add this sort of comment.

The discussion pane shows each comment in a threaded discussion, so it's easy to see original comments and replies. At the end of each comment is a marker; click the marker to display a shortcut menu, like the one in Figure 8.9, that lets you reply to the comment.

Figure 8.9
As the author of a comment, you can use this menu to edit or delete an existing remark.

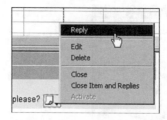

To hide the discussion pane, or to show the discussion pane if it's currently hidden, click the Show/Hide button, just to the left of the Close button on the Discussion toolbar. Hiding this pane does not remove comments from the discussion database or break your connection with the discussion server; it merely removes the display of comments from the current screen.

You can also *filter* discussions in a document—to see only comments added by a particular co-worker or within a certain interval. For example, you might choose to show only remarks inserted by your boss since Monday. To filter a discussion, click the Discussions button and choose Filter Discussion.

If you want to receive e-mail notifications when new comments are posted to a Web discussion, start by opening the document or Web page and connecting to the discussion server. Click the Subscribe button on the Discussions toolbar to use the Document Subscription dialog box.

TROUBLESHOOTING

FORGOTTEN PASSWORDS

I saved a document with a password months ago. I tried to open the document, but I forgot the password. What can I do?

If you forgot the password for a Word document, Excel workbook, or PowerPoint presentation, brace yourself: It's going to take a long time to recover the password, if it can be recovered at all. Start by ordering one of the commercial password-cracking programs at http://www.accessdata.com or http://www.lostpassword.com. If you need to crack only one document, ask the manufacturer for a money-back guarantee that its product will be successful.

On the other hand, if you lost a different kind of password, your task is much simpler. You can check with either of the previously mentioned companies, or search on the Web for many other "crackers."

HIDDEN APPLICATIONS LOCK FILES

When I try to open a Word document or Excel workbook, the File in Use dialog box appears. I know no one else has the file open. Sometimes, the dialog box even accuses me of being the one using the file. The program only allows me to open the file as Read Only.

If you know that nobody else on your network has the file open and you get the File in Use dialog box, a hidden instance of one of the Office apps might be holding on to the file. Or, if the program that had the file open crashes, it might not correctly remove the file that tracks the lock.

When this happens, use the Windows Task Manager (Ctrl+Alt+Del) to find any hidden instances of the program in question and end them. If the dialog box appears after Word crashed on your system, look for an owner file in the same directory as the file that refuses to open. This temporary file has a .doc extension; the filename itself is the same as the original file, except the first two letters are replaced with a tilde (~) followed by a dollar sign. This temporary file holds the logon name of the person opening the file. Delete it to remove the lock.

SECRETS OF THE OFFICE MASTERS: TIPS FOR MANAGING AN INTRANET SERVER

Are you responsible for managing an intranet server on which members of a busy workgroup constantly post documents, workbooks, and other Office files? Here are some tips that can make your life easier:

- Make sure all users have shortcuts to the server. If necessary, create a shortcut on your desktop, and then e-mail that shortcut to other users. When they open the shortcut, Windows automatically creates a matching icon in their My Network Places folders.

- Install and configure the Office Server Extensions (or ask the Web server administrator to do this for you). Although users will be able to post documents to the server by using the older FrontPage extensions, the Office version adds significant new capabilities.

- Use the Discussions toolbar to set up daily e-mail notifications so that you can see any changes to a folder. These alerts will let you know when a user has added a new document, modified an existing one, or deleted a file. Use these notifications to quickly check that the document opens properly and contains the right content and formatting.

- Use Word or FrontPage to create a Web page that contains instructions for using the intranet. Make sure this link is prominent on the home page that users see when they connect to the site. Use Word's Frequently Asked Questions template as a jumping-off point; you'll find it on the Web Pages tab when you choose File, New.

- Manage discussions themselves from the Web server. Look on the server for a page called the Office Server Extension Administrator, which allows you to see all the discussions and remove entries for those that are no longer active.

USING OUTLOOK

OUTLOOK ESSENTIALS

In this chapter

Is Outlook the Heart of Office?

Outlook is the newest member of the Office family, but it's rapidly become the most popular. If you use Outlook as your e-mail client at work or home, it's probably the first program you open when you start Windows, and it's the last one you close at the end of the day. To reflect its popularity, we've decided to move Outlook to the front of this book, ahead of its well-established Office-mates, Word, Excel, and PowerPoint.

Thankfully, Outlook also deserves the Most Improved Application award for Office XP. In previous versions, its shortcomings and idiosyncrasies made it difficult to set up and a source of endless frustration for support professionals and (ahem) computer book authors. If you've been using a previous version of Outlook, pay special attention to the following sections on setup and configuration. You might discover that some of your pet peeves have vanished in this version.

Setting Up E-mail Accounts and Connections

Outlook 2002 eliminates the frustrating split personality that plagued Outlook 98 and Outlook 2000. Configuring those earlier versions required that you make a choice between two modes—Corporate/Workgroup (CW) and Internet Mail Only (IMO)—with different menus, feature sets, and options for each one. In Outlook 2002, the confusing CW/IMO split is gone. You can connect to any combination of accounts from any supported mail server, including Internet-standard (SMTP/POP3/IMAP) accounts, Exchange Server mailboxes, Hotmail accounts, and older third-party servers with MAPI transports.

The first time you run Outlook 2002, it scans your system for compatible e-mail client software. If it finds a previous version of Outlook (97/98/2000), Outlook Express, Netscape Mail or Netscape Messenger, Eudora Pro or Light, Microsoft Internet Mail, Exchange Inbox, or Windows Messaging, it offers to import your account settings (server information, username, and so on) and any existing mail messages. If you accept this option, you're done—Outlook sets up mail accounts and copies all your messages to your Inbox. On a system with no existing e-mail settings, you jump straight to a wizard that offers to set up an e-mail account.

If you're setting up Outlook on a system where you haven't previously used an e-mail client, or if you have a new e-mail account, you'll need to go through a fairly painless setup process. Start by clicking the Mail icon in Windows' Control Panel, which opens the dialog box shown in Figure 9.1, and then click the E-mail Accounts button.

You can also set up a new account from within Outlook, by choosing Tools, E-mail Accounts.

Regardless of which of these options you choose, choose the Add a New E-mail Account option and you'll end up at the dialog box shown in Figure 9.2.

Figure 9.1
To configure Outlook accounts, data files, or profiles, you can use the Mail icon in Control Panel, which opens this dialog box.

Figure 9.2
When setting up a new e-mail account, Outlook gives you these options. For typical Internet e-mail accounts, POP3 is the correct choice.

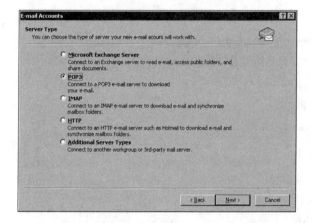

> **Note**
>
> Like all previous Outlook versions, Outlook 2002 is incompatible with AOL e-mail accounts.

In Outlook, you can configure multiple e-mail accounts, but you must designate one of those accounts as your default account. You can configure each account's connection options individually, so that you check for new mail automatically, or only on demand.

CONFIGURING INTERNET STANDARD E-MAIL ACCOUNTS

Before you can send or receive e-mail over the Internet, you have to configure Outlook to communicate with incoming and outgoing mail servers. Outside of the corporate world, the most popular e-mail configuration by far is an Internet-standard SMTP server that supports POP3 connections.

Note

On mail servers that use IMAP, messages are stored on the server itself rather than in your Personal Folders file. If you check this option, you will see an additional tab (IMAP) on the <*Account*> Properties dialog box, and the account name will appear in your folder list as a new icon at the same level as your Personal Folders file.

The IMAP protocol offers options that are especially useful over slow connections, but it also creates some configuration headaches when using Outlook. You can't automatically save copies of sent messages, for example, and you won't receive notifications of new mail, even if you've set up Outlook to do so. For a detailed list of problems and possible solutions, see Knowledge Base article Q185820, "Using an IMAP Server with Outlook."

When you choose POP3 or IMAP as the account type, you enter information on the Internet E-mail Settings dialog box shown in Figure 9.3.

Figure 9.3

Fill in the basic information here and click the Test Account Settings button to set up a POP3 account in Outlook.

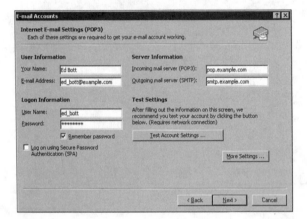

The Internet E-mail Settings dialog box fills in only the most basic account information. For required information like the names of mail servers and the username and password you use to log on, fill in the information exactly as it's provided to you by your mail system administrator. In the User Information section, enter your name and e-mail address, exactly as you want mail recipients to see these details in the From: line on messages you send.

Tip from

EQ & Woody

If you use more than one mail account, enter slightly different information in the Name field for each one. For example, in the account you use to send and receive mail through a corporate server, add your company name in parentheses after your username. When you receive replies to messages you sent through that account, you'll be able to spot them quickly just by looking at the name in the To field.

In the Server Information section, you must specify fully qualified domain names for both incoming and outgoing mail servers. At some Internet service providers, both names are identical, usually in the form `mail.example.com`. Other common configurations use `smtp`, `pop`, or `pop3` as part of the full server name, with separate server names for incoming and outgoing mail servers. MSN users with POP3 access should specify `pop3.email.msn.com` and `smtp.email.msn.com`, for example. Most ISPs provide this information when you establish an account, and those that care about their customers also make it easily available on the Web.

Outlook automatically fills in the User Name box in the Logon Information section, using the first part of the e-mail address you entered earlier. If your logon name is different, change this value. If you want Outlook to supply your password automatically each time you connect to the server, enter it in the Password field and check the Remember Password box.

PART

II

CH

9

Note

Leave the Password box blank if you want to eliminate the possibility that another user can send mail from your computer using this account; in that configuration, Outlook prompts you for your password the first time you connect to the server after starting Outlook.

On mail systems that use *Secure Password Authentication (SPA)*, a separate security package prompts the user for credentials when logging in to a server. This option is extremely rare at ISPs, with two noteworthy exceptions—The Microsoft Network (MSN) and CompuServe. If you use either of these ISPs, here's how to configure Outlook to authenticate passwords using SPA:

- If you have an MSN POP3 account that was created before November 2000 and has not been converted to a Web-based mail account, leave the User Name and Password fields blank and check the Logon Using Secure Password Authentication option. When you first attempt to connect to an MSN mail server in an Outlook session, you'll see an MSN password dialog box.

- CompuServe users might choose this option or the simpler POP login. See the CompuServe configuration instructions for more details.

After you use this dialog box to create a new account, click the More Settings button and adjust the information on the General tab (see Figure 9.4). In particular, give the account a friendly name (the default is the name of the incoming mail server) and fill in the Organization and Reply E-mail fields.

After you've entered all the details, click the Test Account Settings button. This option, new in Outlook 2002, logs on to the POP3 server and sends a test message using the SMTP server. If you receive an error message, check your username, password, and server names carefully. If the test succeeds, click the Next button to add your account.

Figure 9.4
If you have multiple
e-mail accounts, be
sure to change this
default account name
to something more
descriptive.

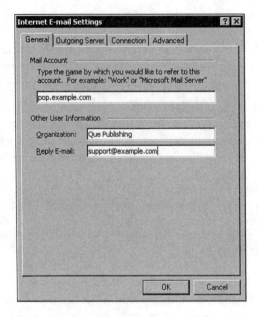

HOTMAIL AND OTHER HTTP ACCOUNTS

If you have a free Hotmail account or an MSN account that has been set up for HTTP
access, you can read and send messages from within Outlook—a feature that was not available in previous versions. Choose Tools, E-mail Accounts, select Add a New E-Mail
Account, click the HTTP option, and select Hotmail or MSN.

> **Note**
>
> Microsoft disingenuously offers an "Other" option that allows you to enter the URL of
> an HTTP server from a non-Microsoft provider. As of this writing, no other Web-based
> e-mail providers are compatible with this option.

As with a POP3 account, you need to specify your username and password for an HTTP
account. However, the server details are filled in automatically for you and you have limited
connection options.

You can set up multiple HTTP-based Hotmail and MSN accounts in a single Outlook profile. If you have more than one Hotmail account, use the technique described in the previous section to give each account a descriptive name so you can identify it easily.

→Hotmail accounts work differently from POP3 accounts. For more details, see "Managing Multiple
E-mail Accounts," **p. 238**.

ACCOUNTS ON AN EXCHANGE SERVER

If you have an account on an Exchange Server, your setup options are dramatically different
from those on a POP3 server. You must be online and able to connect to the Exchange

server to perform this setup. Make sure you have the server name, your username and password, and any other required information before starting.

PART

II

CH

9

> **Caution**
>
> On corporate networks that use Exchange Server, administrators typically handle the work of setting up user accounts, and they typically have a low tolerance for users who screw up their mail settings. Before you change any of the details in your Exchange Server account settings, we recommend you contact your mail administrator.

To set up an Exchange account, choose Tools, E-mail Accounts, and select Add a New E-Mail Account. After you select Microsoft Exchange Server from the list of e-mail account types, Outlook presents the dialog box shown in Figure 9.5. Enter the name of the Exchange Server and your username, and then click the Check Name button. After making the connection to the server, Outlook changes the username display to include the correct form of your mailbox name and underlines it.

Figure 9.5
Click the Check Name button to verify your settings. After connecting with the Exchange Server, Outlook displays the username with an underline.

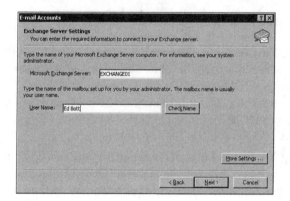

CONNECTION OPTIONS

For each Internet e-mail account you set up, Outlook lets you specify separate connection options. These options are most useful when you have a full-time dial-up connection or a network connection that is sometimes not available—on a portable PC, for example. To change settings for an Internet e-mail account, choose Tools, E-mail Accounts, and select View or Change Existing E-mail Accounts. In the E-mail Accounts dialog box, select the account name, and then click the Change button. Click More Settings and select the Connection tab of the Internet E-mail Settings dialog box. Then adjust any of the three options shown in Figure 9.6:

Figure 9.6
Use the Connection page to specify connection options for each account separately.

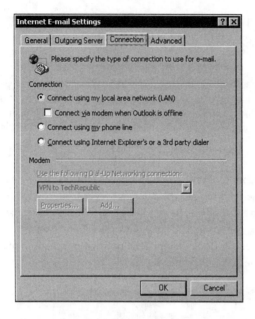

- **Connect Using My Local Area Network (LAN)**—The LAN option assumes you have a full-time connection to the Internet through a *local area network*. Unless you choose to work offline, Outlook checks for mail every 10 minutes. If you work in a corporate environment with a constant connection to a mail server, this most likely will be the best option for you. It's also the right choice for anyone with an "always on" Internet connection, such as a DSL line or cable modem.

- **Connect Using My Phone Line**—This option uses the *Dial-Up Networking (DUN)* features in your version of Windows to make an Internet connection every time you send or receive e-mail. Choose an existing DUN connection from the list at the bottom of this dialog box, or click the Add button to create a new one. When Outlook attempts to connect with your mail server, Windows displays the DUN dialog box for the connection you selected.

Note

For detailed instructions on how to configure a Dial-Up Networking connection in Windows 2000, including hands-free options, see Chapter 16, "Connecting to the Internet," in *Practical Windows 2000*, by Ed Bott (also published by Que, ISBN: 0-7897-2124-4).

See *Special Edition Using Microsoft Windows XP Home Edition* and *Special Edition Using Microsoft Windows XP Professional Edition*, both published by Que, for details on setting up a Dial-Up Networking connection in Windows XP.

- **Connect Using Internet Explorer's or a 3rd Party Dialer**—In this configuration, Outlook does not dial or disconnect automatically. This option is your best choice if you use the same phone line for voice calls and Internet access and you want to control exactly when you connect to the Internet.

On a computer that is permanently connected to the Internet through a corporate network, you can set all accounts for LAN access; this option allows you to receive mail from any Internet account.

On a notebook computer that is occasionally connected to the Internet via a corporate network and at other times uses a dial-up connection, choose the LAN option, and then check the Connect via Modem When Outlook Is Offline box (refer to Figure 9.6). This sets up a hybrid LAN/Dial connection option; if you attempt to check your mail and Outlook cannot find the specified server, you see a dialog box that offers to make a dial-up connection for you.

On a computer that uses more than one dial-up connection, you can configure a variety of dial-up options. Choose Tools, Options, and then click the Mail Setup tab to display the dialog box shown in Figure 9.7. Use these options to control whether Outlook dials and hangs up automatically after it finishes sending and receiving mail. Note that these options apply to all dial-up connections; you cannot apply separate dial-up options to individual accounts.

Figure 9.7
Use the options shown here to create a hands-free connection for checking Internet mail.

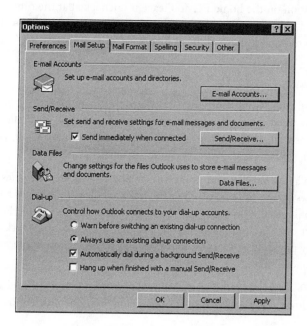

⚠ *If you experience problems sending mail through multiple accounts from a single connection, see "Working Around Anti-Spam Filters" in the "Troubleshooting" section at the end of this chapter.*

ADVANCED OPTIONS

For POP3 and IMAP accounts, click the Advanced tab of the Internet E-mail Settings dialog box to adjust any of the following options:

- If your mail server uses nonstandard *TCP/IP* port numbers or requires a *Secure Sockets Layer (SSL)* connection to send or receive mail, use the boxes in the *Server Port Numbers* section. Outlook's default settings use widely accepted Internet standards, and the overwhelming majority of users will never need to change these settings; do so only if your mail server administrator provides specific instructions.

- Use the Server Timeouts slider to control how long Outlook attempts to connect to the server before timing out and displaying an error message. The default is 1 minute; you can adjust this setting in 30-second increments to any value between 30 seconds and 5 minutes. Set a longer value if you get frequent error messages when trying to send or retrieve mail over a slow connection or a poor-quality phone line.

- Check the Leave a Copy of Messages on Server box when configuring a copy of Outlook to retrieve mail from a location other than the one at which you normally receive mail. For example, if you occasionally check your office mail from a home PC, but you want to maintain a complete archive of messages on your office computer, check this option on the home PC and leave it unchecked at the office. Any messages you download at home will remain on the server; when you return to the office and retrieve your messages, they will be available for you.

SETTING UP ALTERNATE E-MAIL PROFILES

In Outlook 97 and when using Corporate/Workgroup Mode in Outlook 98/2000, you were required to set up *profiles* to manage groups of accounts. Outlook 2002 allows you to set up multiple profiles as well, although this is rarely required. For virtually all users, a single profile containing all accounts is the correct configuration.

When you set up a new profile, you associate e-mail accounts and data files with that profile. This option allows you to use one profile to access mail directly from an Exchange server with another profile set up for remote access synchronized to an Offline Folders file. You might want to set up separate profiles if you have highly confidential work e-mail and you want to avoid any possibility of mixing messages and accounts between your work connection and your personal files.

To set up an Outlook profile, double-click the Mail icon in Control Panel and click the Show Profiles button. This option displays the dialog box shown in Figure 9.8.

Figure 9.8
Use the options at the bottom of this dialog box to select a profile when you start Outlook.

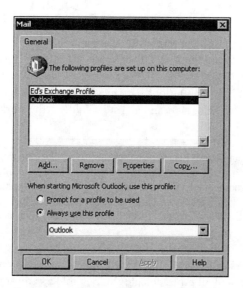

Click the Add button to create a new profile. A wizard will prompt you to add e-mail accounts and specify a data file. Click the Remove button to eliminate an existing profile. To work with a profile without opening Outlook, choose the profile and click the Properties button.

Normally, Outlook creates a single profile and uses it automatically each time you start. Choose the Prompt for a Profile to Be Used option if you want to select from a list of available profiles every time you start Outlook.

MANAGING OUTLOOK DATA FILES

Outlook stores all information in a *flat-file* database—a simple list. In Outlook parlance, each record is an *item*, and the type of item—e-mail message, contact, appointment, and so on—defines which fields are available for entering and displaying information. Each of Outlook's default folders displays items of a single type, and you can create new folders as well.

CHOOSING WHERE OUTLOOK STORES YOUR DATA

When new mail arrives, or when you create and save a new item in one of Outlook's default folders (Contacts, for example), Outlook adds the new item to the location specified as the *primary store*. That location might be a local file, or it could be a set of folders on a Microsoft Exchange Server. The exact location depends on how you (and, in some cases, your network administrator) have configured Outlook. In most of the examples in this book, we assume that your primary store is a Personal Folders file (with a .pst extension) stored on your local PC.

PERSONAL FOLDERS FILES

A *Personal Folders file* is the basic storage format for a single user's data. These files use the extension .pst. When you configure Outlook 2002 for use with one or more Internet-standard e-mail accounts (no Exchange servers), Outlook creates a single Personal Folders file called Outlook.pst and stores it in the Outlook data files location. This file holds all Outlook data—messages, attachments, the Contacts and Calendar folder...the works.

Tip from

Where are your Outlook data files and settings stored? The exact location depends on your operating system and whether you've upgraded from a previous version. For a remarkably complete listing of these locations, open the Help system and search for the topic "Outlook file locations." Even easier: Open Outlook, choose File, Data File Management, and view all current settings in a convenient dialog box.

In this configuration, the Personal Folders file is the primary store: New messages are delivered to the Inbox in that file, and all other default Outlook folders are stored there as well. If you connect to an Exchange Server, a Personal Folders file is optional. Regardless of your e-mail configuration, however, the file format is identical.

Typically, Personal Folders files are stored on a user's local hard drive, although it is possible to store a file on a network server. You can also create multiple Personal Folders files and access them at the same time. In this configuration, the additional Personal Folders files are defined as *secondary stores*. Outlook does not save new items directly in these files, but you can move items into a secondary store by dragging and dropping them from your primary store, or you can define rules that automatically move incoming messages into the secondary store based on their content.

Tip from

Outlook's default settings bury data files in odd locations that aren't easy to back up. If you administer your own computer and regularly back up the entire folder that contains all your user documents and settings, you're OK. For home and small business users who administer their own computers, we recommend moving data files to their own subfolder in the My Documents folder. Create a folder called My Mail, for instance, and move the PST and/or OST files there so that they're properly backed up with the rest of your data. Note that you must close Outlook before moving data files. After moving the file, reopen Outlook and choose File, Data File Management; use the dialog box to open the data file.

Although there are limits on the size of a Personal Folders file, in practice, most users won't ever come close to hitting the maximum size. A Personal Folders file can be up to 2GB in size and can contain up to 16,384 folders, with each folder containing a maximum of 16,384 subfolders. If your Personal Folders file reaches even a few hundred megabytes, you should seriously consider breaking it into multiple files for ease of management. This is especially important with archive files, which can grow to unmanageable sizes over time if they contain many large file attachments.

To create a new Personal Folders file, choose File, New, Outlook Data File. Choose Personal Folders File (.pst) from the dialog box. Give the file a name, choose a location, and click OK. You'll see the dialog box shown in Figure 9.9, which allows you to define the name that appears in Outlook's Folders List and set compression and encryption options.

Figure 9.9
Outlook uses the name you enter here to identify the top-level folder for a Personal Folders file.

Tip from

EQ & Woody

There's no relationship at all between the name of the Personal Folders data file and the text label that appears in the Folders List. If you create a second file that you intend to use for messages from mailing lists, for example, you might choose to use a filename such as Lists.pst, and then change the top-level folder name to My Mailing Lists.

After creating the additional Personal Folders file, Outlook automatically opens it. To close the file, right-click its icon in the Outlook Bar or the Folder List. You can also use this shortcut menu to adjust the properties of any Personal Folders file.

OFFLINE STORE FILES

If you connect to a Microsoft Exchange Server, you can create one (and only one) *Offline Store file* and store it on your computer. This file type, which uses the extension .ost, closely resembles a Personal Folders file.

Items in an Offline Store file can be synchronized with your Mailbox folder on a Microsoft Exchange Server. As the name implies, Outlook compares the items on the server with those in your Offline Store file and adds, updates, or deletes items in both places so they always contain the same information. This enables you to read and compose e-mail or other items when the server is unavailable—for example, when you're reading mail from a home PC or from a notebook computer on the road. When you connect to the server via remote access, or when you return to the office and reconnect your notebook computer to the network, click the Send/Receive button to transfer changes in both directions. Follow these instructions to set up offline access:

1. Choose Tools, E-Mail Accounts.

2. Choose the View or Change Existing E-Mail Accounts option and click Next.

3. From the list of e-mail accounts, choose Microsoft Exchange Server and click the Change button.

4. In the dialog box that lists your server and usernames, click the More Settings button.

5. On the Advanced tab of the Microsoft Exchange Server dialog box (see Figure 9.10), click the Offline Folder File Settings button.

Figure 9.10

6. In the File box (see Figure 9.11), enter the complete path to the file you want to use as the Offline Folder file. Use the Browse button to select a location other than the default data files folder.

Figure 9.11

7. The default filename is Outlook.ost; however, you can give this file any name.

8. Click OK to save your changes.

When you set up an Offline Folders file, items remain in your local file and messages you compose remain in your Outbox until you click the Send/Receive button and synchronize the folders.

You control exactly which items are available in which folders when you synchronize with the Exchange Server, using any of the following techniques:

- To control whether a particular folder is synchronized with an Exchange Server, select the folder and choose Tools, Send/Receive Settings, Make This Folder Available Offline. This menu choice is a toggle; a check mark means it's on.

- To filter items in a folder so only some of them are synchronized, right-click that folder's Offline Store icon and choose Properties. Click the Filter button on the Synchronization tab to change settings. For instance, you might want to synchronize only messages that are less than 30 days old to avoid clutter.

- To work directly with the server files and bypass the Offline Store file temporarily, click the Disable Offline Use button in the Offline Folder Settings dialog box (shown previously in Figure 9.11).

When your primary store is an Offline Store file, you can still create and use any number of Personal Folders files. All such files will be secondary stores. You might choose this strategy if you want to save network space or reduce synchronization time by archiving messages to a local file for ready access.

MAILBOX FOLDERS ON AN EXCHANGE SERVER ONLY

If you use Outlook to connect to a Microsoft Exchange Server, you can access mail and create calendar and contact items in your Mailbox folders on the server. If you lose the network connection, you lose all access to your data. This option is typically found in highly managed corporations where administrators are concerned about security and/or local storage space on users' computers.

DELETING AND ARCHIVING OUTLOOK INFORMATION

By default, Outlook automatically moves items out of your Personal Folders file after a specified amount of time has passed. Using this AutoArchive feature, Outlook checks every item in your Personal Folders file at intervals. When it finds appointments, tasks, and e-mail messages that exceed the age limits you specify (by default, it looks for any items that are more than six months old), it automatically moves them to an *archive file*. You can also force Outlook to archive items instead of waiting for its next scheduled archive operation.

Tip from

EQ & Woody

Cleaning up and archiving mail folders is easier if junk mail and other nonessential messages never get there in the first place. Use Outlook's Rules Wizard to delete specific types of messages and move other types directly into folders as they arrive. The folders you specify as the destination in each rule can be in a different Personal Folders file; if you use rules to move messages into different folders in your primary Outlook data file, you can specify custom AutoArchive options for those folders.

Configuring AutoArchive options in Outlook 2002 is a much simpler process than in previous versions. From a single dialog box, you tell Outlook how often you want it to scan your Personal Folders file (or files) and perform AutoArchive options. Then, optionally, you can set different archiving options for individual folders.

By default, Outlook performs an AutoArchive operation every two weeks. To adjust AutoArchive options, choose Tools, Options, click the Other tab, and click the AutoArchive button. This action displays the dialog box shown in Figure 9.12.

Figure 9.12
By default, Outlook scans all Personal Folders files every 14 days. Click the Apply These Settings to All Folders Now button to change settings for all folders.

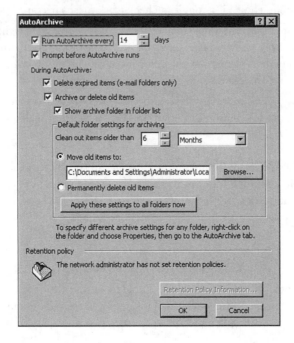

Use any or all of these AutoArchive settings:

- To enable the AutoArchive option, make sure a check mark appears in the Run AutoArchive Every *n* Days box.

- To adjust the AutoArchive interval from its default of 14 days, pick a new number between 1 and 60 here. Choose a smaller number if you want Outlook to aggressively manage your data.

- If you want the AutoArchive operation to occur unattended, clear the check mark from the Prompt Before AutoArchive Runs box.

- Specify a filename and location in the Move Old Items To box. Unless you change this setting, Outlook creates a new Personal Folders file called Archive.pst and stores it in the default Outlook data files location, along with your main Outlook data file.

Tip from

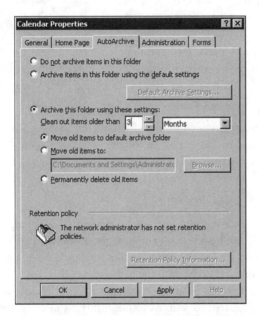

By definition, the archive file includes data you don't need every day, so it doesn't make sense to keep this file open. If you want to search for an item in this file, choose File, Open, Personal Folders File (.pst), and select the Archive.pst file. Then use the folder list to display the contents of individual folders in the archive file.

Each time Outlook runs its AutoArchive check, it performs operations on each folder separately, using the default settings. To adjust AutoArchive options for an individual folder, right-click its icon in the Outlook Bar or in the folders list, and then choose Properties. The AutoArchive tab of the Properties dialog box (see Figure 9.13) lets you enable or disable archiving for that folder. This dialog box also lets you specify a location where you want Outlook to move items (the default is the file you specified in the global AutoArchive options), or you can choose to delete all items that are older than the specified time.

Figure 9.13
The Properties dialog box lets you set different AutoArchive options for each folder.

Note

Because items in the Contacts folder do not have a date associated with them, there is no AutoArchive tab in this folder's Properties dialog box, and AutoArchive operations do not affect this folder.

In many cases, you'll want to radically adjust these default settings. For example, if you never refer to your Calendar folder to look up old meetings and appointments, you can safely specify that you want to delete these items when AutoArchiving. On the other hand, if you live and die by e-mail, you might want every message you send and receive in the same file so you can search for information easily. In that case, right-click the Inbox folder, choose Properties, and remove the check mark from the Clean Out Items option.

RECOVERING FREE SPACE IN OUTLOOK DATA FILES

Deleting items from your Outlook data files is only a first step. When you toss the items, Outlook doesn't automatically recover the space the deleted items used. (Old database developers are familiar with the syndrome, in which the database file continues to reserve space long after the data is gone.) In fact, even after you delete every single item from a 200MB Personal Folders (.pst) file, that file continues to occupy the full 200MB. To squeeze this wasted space out of your files, you need to *compact* the files manually, using the following steps:

1. Make sure the file you want to work with is open. (If necessary, choose File, Open, Outlook Data File.) Then, from the main Outlook menu, choose File, Data File Management.

2. In the Outlook Data Files dialog box, select the file you want to compact and click the Settings button to open the Personal Folders dialog box shown in Figure 9.14.

3. Click the Compact Now button. Depending on the size of the file and your available system resources, this action might take some time.

4. Click OK to close the Personal Folders dialog box.

5. To compact another open Personal Folders file, select it from the list and repeat steps 2–4. When finished, click OK to close the dialog box.

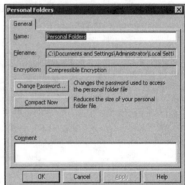

Figure 9.14

REPAIRING A DAMAGED PERSONAL FOLDERS FILE

If you begin encountering error messages or suspect that a Personal Folders file is damaged, a well-hidden Outlook tool can help you set things right in short order. Search your hard drive for a file called Scanpst.exe. As the name implies, this utility can scan a Personal Folders file, report any damage it finds, and repair the errors with your permission. Double-click the file and follow the wizard's prompts; note that this process might take several hours on a large PST file, so be prepared to wait. (Another utility, Scanost.exe, works with Offline Folder files.)

Caution

Personal Folders files are remarkably resilient, but not indestructible. If you keep irreplaceable information such as important e-mail or contact information in one of these files, back it up regularly—preferably to a tape or server stored in a different physical location. You must shut down Outlook before you can copy a Personal Folders file.

USING AND CUSTOMIZING THE OUTLOOK INTERFACE

Outlook's interface resembles that of other Office programs with one noteworthy exception: Along the left edge of the main program window is the Outlook Bar, which contains icons that you can click to display any of Outlook's default folders. At the top of the Outlook Bar is an icon that lets you jump to the Outlook Today page, which summarizes current tasks, appointments, and messages. Although it's not immediately obvious, you can also see an Explorer-style folder list by clicking the heading just above the window that displays the contents of the current folder. Figure 9.15 shows all these interface elements.

Figure 9.15
Normally, the Folder List shown here is hidden; click the Inbox label to drop it down, and then click the pushpin icon to lock it in place.

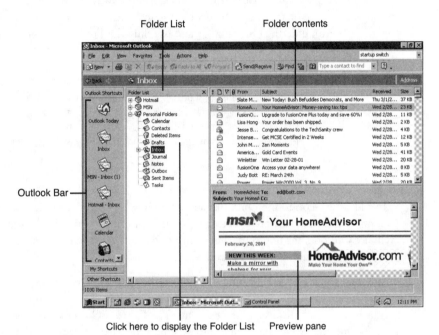

CUSTOMIZING THE OUTLOOK TODAY PAGE

Outlook Today is a Web-style view of selected items in your primary store; it shows upcoming appointments, current tasks, and unread messages in a single convenient Web view. If you like this "day-at-a-glance" style, you can make Outlook Today your default view. You can also customize this template, but only in limited ways.

To customize the Outlook Today page, click its icon in the Outlook Bar, and then click the Customize Outlook Today link on the page itself (the exact location of this link varies depending on the style you've selected). You can set startup options, define which folders appear on the page, and customize Calendar and Task lists.

> **Note**
>
> The Outlook Today layout is based on an HTML template. You can create your own custom pages called Digital Dashboards that display a custom mix of Outlook data and pieces of Web pages. For more information on how to create Digital Dashboards, see the Digital Dashboard page at `http://www.microsoft.com/business/DigitalDashboard/`.

CUSTOMIZING THE OUTLOOK BAR

The *Outlook Bar* is fully customizable. You can add new icons and delete existing ones, change the name or rearrange the order of icons, and reorganize icons into groups. For that matter, you can hide the Outlook Bar and use only the Folder List for navigation, if you prefer that view.

> **Tip from**
>
> *Ed & Woody*
>
> Outlook Bar icons are shortcuts, and as with any Windows object, you can right-click to see a full range of available options. Use shortcut menus to rename or remove an Outlook Bar icon; drag and drop icons to rearrange them in the Outlook Bar. To see more icons in the same space, right-click in any empty space in the Outlook Bar and choose Small Icons.

To add a new icon to the Outlook Bar, drag any icon from the Folder List and drop it in an empty space. Alternatively, you can right-click any empty space in the Outlook Bar and choose Outlook Bar Shortcut; the resulting dialog box lets you select any existing Outlook or Windows folder and add its icon.

Although the most visible group of icons on the Outlook Bar is the default set of folders, there are actually three different *groups* of Outlook Bar shortcuts, and you can add groups of your own as well. To display the contents of a different Outlook Bar, click its title. To create a new Outlook group, right-click any existing group heading and choose Add New Group. You can create up to 12 groups on the Outlook Bar.

As you'll see shortly, icons on the Outlook Bar serve one other important function. You can drag any item out of the main Outlook window and drop it onto one of the Outlook Bar icons to create a brand-new item, using the original item as a starting point.

CUSTOMIZING THE FOLDER LIST

If you've organized your Outlook items into a large number of folders, you might find it easier to work with Outlook's Explorer-style Folder List instead of the Outlook Bar. Drag-and-drop actions work identically regardless of which shortcuts you use. Click the Folder List button on the Advanced toolbar or choose View, Folder List to open the complete list in its own pane.

To display the Folder List temporarily so you can switch to a different folder or move items, click the folder name just above the contents window. As the arrow to the right of the folder name suggests, this action displays the drop-down version of the list; click anywhere outside the pane to hide it after switching folders or dropping an item on a folder. Click the pushpin icon to lock the Folder List into position.

If you prefer to use the Folder List instead of the Outlook Bar, clear the check mark next to the Outlook Bar entry on the View menu. Click the Close (X) button to hide the Folder List.

CREATING, EDITING, AND MANAGING OUTLOOK ITEMS

When you create, view, and edit items, Outlook uses a variety of standard and custom forms to control which fields are visible. When you double-click any item, it opens using the default form for its type.

MOVING, COPYING, AND DELETING ITEMS

To move or copy items between Outlook folders, you can use many of the same techniques you use to manage files in an Explorer window. Drag an item out of one folder and drop it into another to move the item; hold down the Ctrl key while dragging to make a copy. Or use shortcut keys to cut (Ctrl+X), copy (Ctrl+C), and then paste (Ctrl+V) the item into the destination folder. Curiously, although Outlook's pull-down Edit menu includes all three choices, the shortcut menus available when you right-click on any item (such as a mail message) don't allow you to cut, copy, or paste.

 If you try to move an item into a folder and it opens a new item instead, see "Dragging Doesn't Always Move an Item" in the "Troubleshooting" section at the end of this chapter.

Although it's possible to create multiple folders for other types of items, you'll most commonly use subfolders to manage e-mail messages. To do major message management, open the Folder List by clicking the folder name just above the display of items; click the pushpin icon to lock the list in place, and drag messages directly onto folders as you would in Windows Explorer.

To move one or more selected messages into folders without using the Folder List, click the Move to Folder button on the Standard toolbar. This displays a menu showing the folders you've used most recently. If the folder you want isn't listed, choose Move to Folder from the bottom of the menu. (This option is also available if you right-click selected items to display the shortcut menu.) The dialog box shown in Figure 9.16 appears.

Select the folder you want to move the selected items to. Click the plus sign next to any folder to see its subfolders. Click the New button to create a new folder in any open Personal Folders file. Click OK to move the selected items and close the dialog box.

Figure 9.16
Drag and drop or use this dialog box to move Outlook items (typically e-mail messages) to another folder.

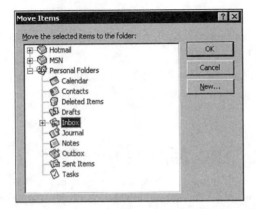

Tip from

Ed & Woody

You can drag any item onto the Windows desktop or into a folder to create a copy of that item. This is a convenient way to keep a contact's personal information at hand or to keep a copy of a mail message at hand. When you create a copy using this technique, you create a new file containing only that item. Be careful when using such a copy, however: Because there is no link between the item you create on the desktop and the one that remains in Outlook, any changes you make in either place are not reflected in the other.

To delete any item or items in any Outlook folder, click the Delete button on the Standard toolbar, use the keyboard shortcut Ctrl+D, or drag the item and drop it on the Deleted Items icon in the Outlook Bar or the Folder List.

By default, Outlook saves the contents of the Deleted Items folder until the next time you archive. To empty this folder manually, right-click its shortcut in the Outlook Bar and choose Empty_ "Deleted Items" Folder. If you prefer to empty this folder automatically every time you close Outlook, choose Tools, Options, click the Other tab, and check Empty the Deleted Items Folder Upon Exiting.

To create a new folder at any time, choose File, New, Folder. In the Create New Folder dialog box (see Figure 9.17), enter the name of the new folder, specify the type of items you want to store in the folder, select the folder in which you want to store the new subfolder, and then click OK.

To move, copy, delete, or rename a folder, open the Folder List, lock it in place, and use the right-click shortcut menus.

ENTERING DATES AND TIMES AUTOMATICALLY

One of Outlook's most impressive time-saving features is its capability to interpret dates using almost any text you enter. To enter a date in any date field in any type of Outlook item, use any of the following techniques:

Figure 9.17
When creating a new folder, be sure you specify the correct type of item you want to store in the folder.

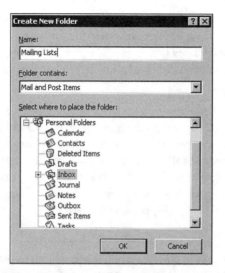

Tip from

These techniques are useful throughout Outlook, not just in appointments or meetings. For example, you can use AutoDate shortcuts to define the dates for follow-up flags on e-mail messages, or to specify the due date for an upcoming task.

■ Type the date in a format that Outlook recognizes, such as 9-29-02, 9/29, or Sep 29. If you omit the year, Outlook automatically fills in this year's date if that date is in the future; if appending the current year to the date results in a date that has already passed, Outlook uses next year's date instead.

■ To pick dates from a calendar, click the drop-down arrow to the right of the date field and use the control showing the current month (see Figure 9.18). Use the arrows to scroll backward or forward, and click to insert any date in the current field. Clicking the Today button quickly returns you to the current date.

Figure 9.18

■ When you enter dates and times for appointments, you can also use words and phrases and let Outlook use its AutoDate feature to interpret your meaning.

Outlook can recognize text such as next Thursday, one week from today, or tomorrow, substituting the correct date for you. To schedule a staff meeting for next Wednesday at 2:00 p.m., for example, click in the Start Time box, enter next wed, and then press Tab and type 2 (Outlook assumes that times you enter are during the default workday unless you specify otherwise).

AutoDate understands dates and times that you spell out or abbreviate, such as 6a (for 6:00 a.m.), or first of jan. If you type 30 days in the Start Time box, Outlook converts it to the date 30 days from today; if you enter that same text as the end time, Outlook adds 30 days to the start date you specified. AutoDate recognizes holidays that fall on the same day every year, such as Halloween, New Year's Eve, and Christmas. It can also correctly interpret dozens of words you might use to define a date or an interval of time, including now, yesterday, today, tomorrow, next, following, through, and until.

Caution

You can't use AutoDate to define a recurring appointment. If you enter every other Wednesday in the Start Time box, for example, Outlook will appear to accept your entry, but it will ignore the first two words, setting the appointment for the coming Wednesday and ignoring your attempt to create a recurring appointment.

ASSIGNING ITEMS TO CATEGORIES

You can assign most Outlook items, including e-mail messages, contacts, appointments, meetings, and tasks, to *categories*. Using categories can be a powerful way to extract groups of information from a list of contacts or to categorize e-mail messages by client or project.

By default, Outlook includes a Master Category List containing 20 entries. You can add your own categories to this list, and then assign items to categories individually or in groups. In the case of e-mail messages, you can assign categories automatically, by defining *rules*.

→For more details on how to create rules for handling incoming mail, **see** "Using the Rules Wizard to Sort and Process Mail," **p. 262.**

Tip from
EQ & Woody

You can assign a single item to multiple categories. This flexibility lets you work with the same item in multiple contexts—for example, you might assign a contact to the Key Customer, VIP, and Holiday Cards categories to make sure that her name is included each time you assemble a mailing list based on any of these categories.

To assign a single item to a category, open the item and click the Categories button; you can also select the item, right-click, and choose Categories from the shortcut menu. Either action displays the Categories dialog box shown in Figure 9.19.

Figure 9.19
To assign categories to Outlook items, use the check boxes in this list.

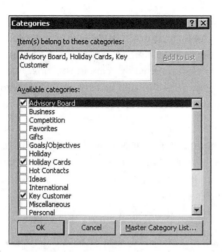

Check the box to the left of the categories to which you want to assign the item. To add a new category and make it available to all items, click the Master Category List button; in the Master Category List dialog box, type the name of the new category and click Add. A category name can contain up to 255 characters, including spaces, but in practice you should keep category names much shorter.

> **Caution**
>
> It's possible to assign categories directly by typing in the box to the right of the Categories button in each item. We recommend avoiding this practice, however, because even a slight difference in spelling or style (VIPs instead of VIP, for example) will result in inconsistent categories and will cause errors when you try to filter or group by category.

CREATING REMINDERS AND FLAGGING ITEMS FOR FOLLOW-UP

Outlook allows you to attach pop-up *reminders* to any type of item except a note. In the case of appointments and tasks, the default form allows you to define the date and time when you want to see a reminder. For an e-mail message or Contact item, you must create a *follow-up flag* before you can set a reminder.

 In some cases, reminders and follow-up flags simply won't work. For an explanation, see "Alarms Fail to Go Off," and "Alarms Work Only in Four Key Folders" in the "Troubleshooting" section at the end of this chapter.

Reminders help you avoid the embarrassment of missing a meeting because you forgot to check your calendar. By default, Outlook adds a reminder to all meetings and appointments, set for 15 minutes before the scheduled time. To change this setting, choose Tools, Options, click the Preferences tab, and set the preferred interval by using the pull-down list (or typing an entry) in the Default Reminder box.

You can enter or edit the reminder for an appointment or meeting by opening the item and selecting or entering a time from the drop-down Reminder list. This time is always relative to the start time of the appointment or meeting; you can request a reminder by entering any number of minutes, hours, days, weeks, months, or years in this box. For example, if you enter 1 week, Outlook dutifully pops up a reminder exactly one week before the meeting is scheduled to start. You cannot, however, enter a specific date or time when you want to receive a reminder.

Outlook automatically includes reminders for tasks as well, using the date you enter in the Due Date field and a default time of 8:00 a.m. If your workday begins earlier, you can change this default: Choose Tools, Options, click the Preferences tab, and select a new time from the drop-down list in the Tasks section.

Tip from

EQ & Woody

To prevent Outlook from automatically setting a reminder on every new task, you must dig through three layers of dialog boxes. Choose Tools, Options, click the Other tab, and then click the Advanced Options button. Click the Advanced Tasks button and clear the Set Reminders on Tasks with Due Dates check box. Click OK in each of the three open dialog boxes to return to Outlook.

To set a reminder for an e-mail message or a contact, you must first assign a follow-up flag for that item. Unlike task and appointment reminders, which display the Subject line of the item, you can define custom text that appears in the pop-up reminder notice.

If a coworker sends you a status report via e-mail, for example, you might want to set a reminder to yourself to follow up on unfinished items next week. Or, if you want to call a handful of key customers next Monday after your company makes an important announcement, you can select the corresponding items in the Contacts folder and flag each one for a phone call.

To flag an open e-mail message or Contact item, click the Flag for Follow Up button on the Standard toolbar. To flag one or more messages or contacts, select the items, right-click, and choose Flag for Follow Up. In either case, you'll see the dialog box shown in Figure 9.20.

Figure 9.20
To flag a message or contact, choose one of the canned messages in this drop-down list, or enter a text message of your own.

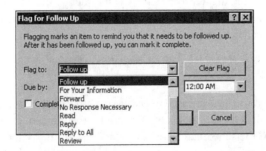

The default text in a flag is Follow Up. You can choose from other alternatives, including Call, Read, or Review. If none of the canned alternatives is suitable, you can enter your own text. For example, if you're expecting a shipment of catalogs from the printer next Monday and you want to make sure your best customers get a copy ASAP, you can flag a group of contacts with the text Send Catalog and set a reminder for next Monday.

The reminder date and time are optional parts of a follow-up flag. Enter a value here if you want a reminder to pop up at a specified date or time. By default, if you enter a date, Outlook adds the time 5:00 p.m. You can enter a specific reminder time for any follow-up flag by using the exact date and time or any text that Outlook's AutoDate feature recognizes. If you received an e-mail from a key customer and you need to follow up first thing next week, for example, enter next mon 9am in the Due By box and Outlook translates the date and time for you.

In table views, flagged items include a flag icon and appear in red text. The follow-up message text and date appear in the information header at the top of a flagged message or contact item, whether you open it in its own window or use the preview pane.

PART

II

CH

9

Tip from

EQ & Woody

> You can use follow-up flags in mail you send to other people as well; if they use Outlook, they'll see the flag text and due date in the info bar at the top of the message when they read it. (Sending a flagged message with a due date does not set a pop-up reminder for the recipient, however.) Several of the choices in the Flag for Follow Up dialog box, in fact, are available precisely for this purpose. While composing a message, click the Flag for Follow Up button and choose For Your Information or No Reply Necessary to alert the receiver that they needn't act on the message. Or choose Review and add a due date; even if the text of your message includes a request to reply by a certain time, this technique adds emphasis.

Regardless of how you set a reminder, when the specified time rolls around, Outlook plays a sound (if you selected that option) and pops up a reminder message. In earlier Outlook versions, each message popped up in its own window, and the constant barrage of pop-ups could be annoying. In Outlook 2002, all current reminders are consolidated in a single window, as shown in Figure 9.21. The icon to the left of each item shows which folder it came from.

When you see a reminder, you can dismiss it so you don't see it again, or open it so you can view the item itself. This option is especially useful when you want to review notes for an upcoming appointment or look up the phone number of a contact you plan to call.

Use the Snooze button to hide the reminder for a while. The default setting is five minutes, but you can use the drop-down list to select a new reminder time as much as one week later. If you have a major event coming up, you can set an initial reminder six or eight weeks out, and then reset the reminder a week at a time to jog your memory every week.

Figure 9.21
This Reminder dialog box can stay open while you work with items in Outlook folders.

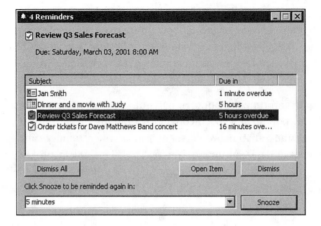

If reminders don't appear when you expect them to, see "Alarms Fail to Go Off" in the "Troubleshooting" section at the end of this chapter.

Tip from

EQ & Woody

To see all flagged messages or contacts, display the Inbox or Contacts folder and then switch to the built-in By Follow-up Flag view. This table view shows all items that include flags at the top of the list.

After you've finished working with a flagged item, you have two choices to remove the flag. Flag the item as complete if you want it to show in views that include flags, or clear the flag completely. Either option is available from right-click shortcut menus or in the Flag for Follow Up dialog box.

USING CUSTOM VIEWS TO DISPLAY INFORMATION

Outlook uses *forms* to display the data in individual items. To see groups of items within a folder, you use *views*. By default, every Outlook folder includes a selection of built-in views available to all folders containing that item type. For specific tasks, create custom views to sort, filter, and group items as required.

USING VIEWS TO DISPLAY, SORT, AND FILTER ITEMS

Every folder starts with a default view. For example, when you first open the Calendar folder, you see today's appointments alongside a list of tasks; you can switch to Recurring Appointments view to see a list of all recurring items, grouped according to whether they repeat Daily, Weekly, Monthly, or Yearly. Likewise, items in the Contacts folder appear by default as address cards with minimal details, but you can choose to see more detailed cards or a simple Phone List view with one contact per row instead.

Tip from

EQ & Woody

The Organize button on the Inbox toolbar offers a useful set of shortcuts for creating mail-processing rules, but in all other folders, this button slows you down. All it offers is an oversized interface for applying views and categories and moving contacts and tasks to other folders. To switch views with maximum efficiency, use the drop-down list on the Advanced toolbar. Advanced users who frequently modify views should remove the Organize button from the Standard toolbar in the Contacts, Tasks, and Calendar folders and replace it with the Define Views button.

To switch between built-in views, use the drop-down list on the Advanced toolbar, or choose View, Current View and select an entry from the list of defined views. Outlook remembers the view you used most recently and reapplies that view whenever you return to that folder.

CUSTOMIZING AN EXISTING VIEW

If none of the built-in views offers the arrangement of data you're looking for, you can customize the current view. As you'll learn shortly, you can change some aspects of a view directly, without using dialog boxes. To see all your customization options, choose View, Current View, Customize Current View. The View Summary dialog box appears, as shown in Figure 9.22.

Figure 9.22
Use this dialog box to customize all available options for the current view. Depending on the view type, some options will be unavailable.

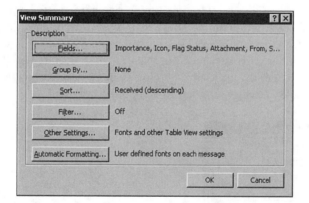

The sections that follow explain how to modify each characteristic of the selected view; note that some of these options will not be available for specific view types. For example, you can't group items in the Contacts folder's Address Cards or Detailed Address Cards view. In Table-based views, you can also apply changes to the current view interactively.

⚠ *If you've customized a built-in view and you need to undo your settings, see "Resetting the Standard Views" in the "Troubleshooting" section at the end of this chapter.*

CUSTOMIZING FIELDS

You can add fields to the current view. If many of your contacts have mobile phones, for example, you might want to include that field in the Address Cards view of the Contacts folder. You can also remove fields from any view.

Using the View Summary dialog box, click the Fields button to display the Show Fields dialog box (see Figure 9.23). Select fields from the list on the left and click the Add button to add them to the current view. Select fields from the list on the right and click Remove to eliminate them from the view.

Figure 9.23
Use this dialog box to control exactly which fields appear in a custom view.

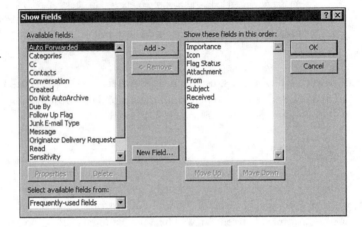

If you're customizing a table-based view, such as the Messages view of the Inbox or the Phone List view of the Contacts folder, you can drag and drop to add or remove fields. Click the Field Chooser button on the Advanced toolbar or right-click the field headings and choose Field Chooser to display a list such as the one shown in Figure 9.24. Drag fields onto the headings in the current view to add them to the view; to remove fields, drag column headings down onto the list itself, and release when you see the large X. Drag headings from side to side to change their left-to-right order in the list.

Figure 9.24
The Field Chooser lets you add fields to a view by dragging and dropping.

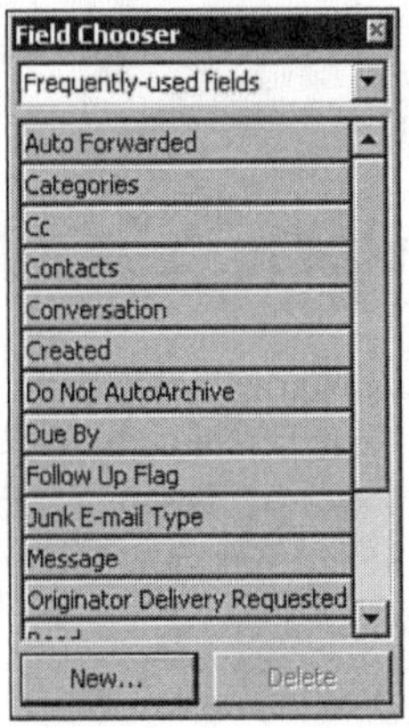

Tip from

EQ & Woody

When you add fields to a view using either the View Summary dialog box or the Field Chooser, Outlook displays only its limited selection of frequently used fields. To see a broader list of available fields, use the drop-down list in either dialog box. For example, if a folder contains Contact items, you can see all Name fields, all Phone Number fields, or an enormous list of all Contact fields.

GROUPING ITEMS

Outlook's grouping options let you arrange the contents of a folder in outline style, with each item in the outline corresponding to a field you select. Most folders include ready-made By Category views—such as the one in Figure 9.25—which allow you to collapse or expand a list of items according to categories. The Contacts folder also includes three additional built-in views that use grouping—By Company, By Location, or By Follow-up Flag.

Figure 9.25
Use the plus and minus signs to the left of each group to expand or collapse the list of items in that group.

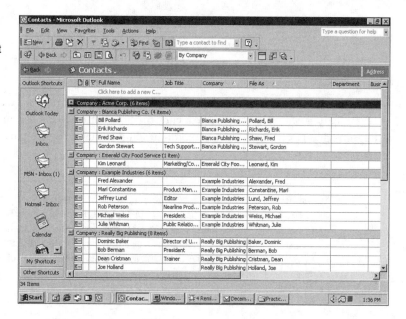

For maximum control over grouping options, click the Group By button in the View Summary dialog box. This displays the Group By dialog box shown in Figure 9.26.

You can group by multiple fields; for example, if you're planning a business trip you might want to group by State and then by Category to see all the contacts in a particular area organized according to categories you've defined.

In any table-based view, you can change grouping on-the-fly. To group by any field that's visible, right-click its column heading and choose Group By this Field. You can also drag headings into or out of the Group By box, which appears just above the column headings. Click the Group By Box button or right-click the column heading and choose Group By

Box from the shortcut menus to show or hide this area. To move an item between groups in this type of view, just drag it out of its old group and drop it under the new group heading.

Figure 9.26
Use this dialog box to define grouping levels; note that you can choose whether the view starts with all items expanded or collapsed.

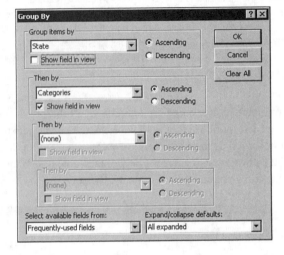

SORTING ITEMS

In any view, you can *sort* your data in a specific order—by due date, for example, or by last name. In the View Summary dialog box, click the Sort button to choose up to four fields for sorting. In table-based views, click a column heading to quickly sort by that column. Click again to sort in reverse order.

Tip from

Normally, the Messages view of your Inbox shows all mail sorted by the date and time it was received. Want to find mail from a specific person in a hurry? Click the From heading to sort the folder's contents by the sender's name, and then quickly type the first few letters of the sender's name as it is displayed in this list. Outlook jumps immediately to the first message in the list, and you can scroll to see all other messages from that person, sorted by date received.

FILTERING ITEMS

Filters show a subset of the items in any folder, based on criteria you define. The Overdue Tasks view in the Tasks folder, for example, displays only those tasks that you should have completed by now; if you inspect this view, you'll see that it uses a filter consisting of two items: Complete equals no, and Due Date on or before Yesterday. Likewise, the Annual Events view of the Calendar folder shows all the birthdays and anniversaries you've defined using a custom filter that shows only all-day events that recur yearly.

In combination with custom views, filters are a powerful way to manage information. In the Contacts folder, for example, you can define filters that show you only people who work for a specific company or who belong to a category you define. If you have a large family, you can create a filtered view of your Contacts folder that includes only people who share your last name or who belong to the Family category.

To define a filter for any view, open the View Summary dialog box, click the Filter button, and select the criteria you want to use in your filter. This dialog box is identical to the one used in the Advanced Find dialog box.

→For more information about how to define filters and searches, **see** "Advanced Search Techniques," **p. 226**.

FORMATS AND OTHER VIEW SETTINGS

You can define custom display formats for many items in many views. In general, these options are available from shortcut menus. For example, in a table view, you can right-click any column heading to set its alignment (left, right, or center), change its column size to automatically fit the widest entry in the view, or change the column heading. Font changes apply to all fields in a section (card body or a row in a table); you can't pick out one field and format it separately.

From the View Summary dialog box, you can also set a variety of other options. Click the Other Settings button to see a dialog box like the one in Figure 9.27. The specific options vary by the type of view selected; in table views, as shown here, you can control whether or not it's permitted to edit in rows and whether gridlines appear.

PART

II

CH

9

Figure 9.27
Use this dialog box to set overall formatting options for a table or other type of view.

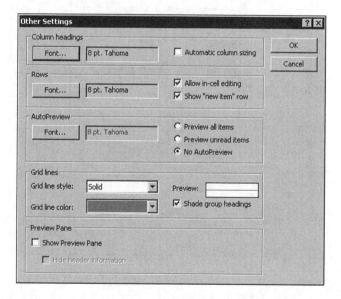

The AutoPreview option is a useful way to see additional information about items that contain details. In your Inbox folder, it shows the first three lines of each message so you can tell at a glance what's inside without having to open and read each message. In other folders, you can use it to see details—notes about each person in your Contacts folder, for example, or the beginning of an appointment's description.

To add the AutoPreview option to a view's settings, use the View Summary dialog box, or click the AutoPreview button on the Advanced toolbar to hide and show this information on-the-fly.

Note

Don't confuse AutoPreview with the Preview pane. When the Preview pane is visible, you can read an entire mail message in a window just below the message list; by contrast, the AutoPreview feature shows only the first three lines of a message, and it disappears after you've opened and read the message. If you use AutoPreview in other folder types, the text remains visible at all times.

CREATING A NEW CUSTOM VIEW

Sometimes the fastest and surest way to create the view you're looking for is to start from scratch. To begin defining a new custom view, switch to the folder that contains the items you want to view, and then choose View, Current View, Define Views. Click the New button to display the dialog box shown in Figure 9.28.

Figure 9.28
When defining a new view, you must start by defining a view type.

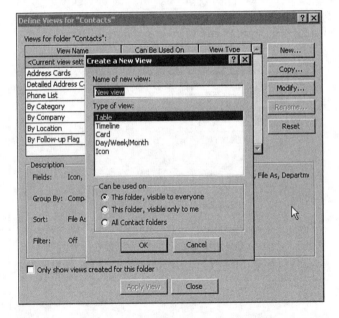

Note

You can't change a view's type after you create it—you can't convert a Card-style view to a Table-style view, for example. When you first create a new view, you have one, and only one, opportunity to make this choice.

All views start with one of the following arrangements.

Type of View	Description
Table	Default view for Tasks folder and Inbox, although you can use it with any folder. Displays data in worksheet style, with each item in its own row, each field in its own column, and headings for each column. Useful for displaying simple lists.
Timeline	A bar along the top displays days or hours; tiny icons underneath show all the items in the folder according to when they were created, received, or started. Especially useful with Tasks folder.
Card	Displays item title in bold, with selected details underneath. Most useful in Contacts folder, which includes two built-in Card views.
Day/Week/Month	Available for all folders, but appropriate only for the Calendar folder. Options determine how many days you can see at once; more days mean less detail for each entry.
Icon	Displays each item as a large or small icon with title text underneath, as in an Explorer window. You can't add fields or group by different fields. Default view for Notes folder is inappropriate for other item types.

After you select a view type, choose where you want to use the view from the set of three options at the bottom of the dialog box. Choose either the This Folder, Visible to Everyone or This Folder, Visible Only to Me options if you do not want the view to be available from the list of named views in other folders that contain the same type of data.

Note

This Folder, Visible to Everyone is applicable if you're creating a view for a public folder on an Exchange Server, or if you've chosen to share a particular personal folder with other Exchange users. This option has no effect if you're not connected to an Exchange Server.

If you want the custom view type to be available for all folders containing the same type of items as the current folder, choose All *<Item Type>* Folders. In general, this is your best choice; make an exception when you've defined a view that is relevant only to a specific folder.

After completing this step, the process of creating a new view is identical to the procedure for customizing an existing view. Add fields, set grouping and filter options if necessary, and save the view under a new name.

MANAGING CUSTOM VIEWS

Outlook gives you a complete set of tools for managing custom views you create. Choose View, Current View, Define Views to display a dialog box listing all views available for the current folder. Select any entry in this list and use the following buttons to work with that view:

- Click Copy to make a copy of the selected view. Give the view a new name to add it to the list. This technique lets you experiment with view options without worrying that you'll mess up a view you've carefully constructed.

- Click Modify to edit any available view setting for the selected view. Note that you cannot change the view type, and some settings are unavailable for certain views.

- Click Rename to give a view a different name; the name you enter is the one that appears in the drop-down list on the Advanced toolbar.

- Click Delete to remove a custom view completely. Note that you cannot remove or rename Outlook's built-in views, although you can edit their settings.

- Click Reset to remove all customizations from a built-in Outlook view. This option is not available for custom views.

OPENING A FOLDER IN A SEPARATE WINDOW

If you use a single Outlook window, you'll notice after switching to a new folder that the Back and Forward buttons are no longer grayed out. These buttons are identical in function to those on the Internet Explorer toolbar: Click the drop-down arrows to the right of either button to see a list of previously viewed folders.

On a fast PC with sufficient memory, Outlook is quick to switch the display of information between folders. However, if you use Outlook regularly, you might prefer to open multiple windows—for example, one window to show your e-mail, another for your Calendar, and a third for Contacts. Outlook lets you open an unlimited number of windows at any time, and each can display any folder using any view.

To open an Outlook folder in its own window, right-click its icon in the Outlook Bar or in the Folder List and choose Open in New Window. Second and subsequent windows don't include the Outlook Bar, and each window gets its own taskbar button.

FINDING OUTLOOK ITEMS

If you use Outlook regularly, your collection of personal data will eventually become so large that you won't be able to find information simply by browsing through items. Outlook offers two tools to help you track down items based on their content. The Find pane, accessible via a button on Outlook's Standard toolbar, is fast, simple, and greatly improved by its Outlook 2000 predecessor. The Advanced Find dialog box requires much more work, but it allows you to pinpoint a single item or snag an entire group of items with precision.

For some tasks, using built-in or custom Outlook views is faster and easier than performing a search. For example, if you use categories in the Contacts, Calendar, and Tasks folders, switching to the built-in By Category view makes it easy to locate all related items. Likewise, try the By Sender view in the Inbox folder to see all messages from a specific person, or the By Company view in the Contacts folder to organize all contacts based on the companies they work for.

FINDING CONTACT INFORMATION FAST

By far, the fastest way to open any Contact's record is with the Find a Contact text box at the right of Outlook's Standard toolbar. Enter a part of any person's name or e-mail address, and then press Enter. If only one item matches the text you entered, Outlook opens that record. If more than one contact's name includes the text you specified, you'll have to pick from the full list of matching names in the Choose Contacts dialog box. If multiple matches appear in the e-mail address field, you'll see the Check Names dialog box from the Outlook Address Book; pick a name and click OK to open that contact's record.

PART
II

CH
9

USING THE FIND PANE FOR SIMPLE SEARCHES

To use the Find pane, first switch to the folder in which you want to search, and then click the Find button on Outlook's Standard toolbar or choose Tools, Find. Unlike its huge and obtrusive predecessor in Office 2000, this version of the Find pane occupies a single row just above the Contents pane, as shown in Figure 9.29.

Figure 9.29
Use the Find pane to search for items in the current Outlook folder.

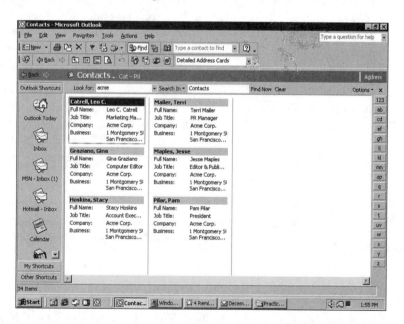

Enter a word, phrase, or alphanumeric string in the Look For box. By default, the current folder is selected in the Search In box; click the arrow to choose a different folder. To search through all text in all items in the folder, click the Options arrow and choose Search All Text in Each Message. Click the Find Now button to begin the search.

Note

In Outlook 2000, you couldn't stop a search in progress. In this version, Microsoft fixed that annoyance. While a search is under way, look for a Stop button just to the right of the Find Now button.

Outlook searches for the exact text in the Look For box; if you enter two or more words separated by a space or punctuation, all the words you entered must appear in the same field. The search results replace the contents below the Find pane. Unlike in Outlook 2000, you can change the view of the search results; click the Clear button to the right of the Find Now button to restore the full view.

Tip from

EQ & Woody

Searches are not cumulative. Each time you click the Find Now button, Outlook searches the entire folder and replaces the results of your previous search. If you want to perform a series of searches to narrow down a large group of items, use the Advanced Find dialog box instead.

ADVANCED SEARCH TECHNIQUES

If the Find pane doesn't turn up the information you're looking for, use the more sophisticated (and complex) Advanced Find dialog box. This option lets you find items that contain specific types of information; you can also use it to search for virtually unlimited combinations of *criteria*. For searches you run regularly, you can save and reuse any set of Advanced Find criteria.

The Advanced Find dialog box is most useful when you want to search using multiple criteria or within specific date ranges. When filling out an expense report, you might search for appointments that include the word "Dinner" in the description and that occurred in the current month. Before a business trip, you might search for contacts that you've assigned to the Business or Key Customer category who are located in the cities or states you're planning to visit.

Tip from

EQ & Woody

If you regularly use Advanced Find, learn its keyboard shortcut—Ctrl+Shift+F—or add an Advanced Find button to the right of the Find button on Outlook's Standard toolbar.

→ For more details on how to add buttons to Office toolbars, **see** "Customizing Toolbars," **p. 30**.

To open the Advanced Find dialog box, choose Tools, Advanced Find. If the Find pane is visible, you can click the Advanced Find link on the Options menu. In either case, you'll see the dialog box shown in Figure 9.30.

Follow these steps to use the Advanced Find dialog box:

1. Use the drop-down Look For list to specify the type of items you want to search for—messages or appointments, for example. By default, this value is set to the type of item stored in the current folder. For the widest possible search, choose Any Type of Outlook Item—this option is useful if you want to search for all messages, contacts, appointments, and tasks related to a specific company, for example.

2. By default, your search covers only the current folder. To change that folder or select more than one folder, click the Browse button and check or uncheck boxes as needed.

Figure 9.30
Use this dialog box to search for Outlook items using a combination of criteria.

Note

You can search multiple folders within only a single Personal Folders file. Thus, to search for related messages in current and archived folders, you'll need to perform two searches. Open a second copy of the Advanced Find dialog box if you want to see all search results simultaneously.

3. Fill in your search criteria using one or more of the three tabs in the Advanced Find dialog box.

• The most common options appear on the first tab; the name of this tab and the exact choices available vary slightly, depending on the type of item you're looking for. For example, when searching through mail messages you can look for text in the subject field only, in the subject field and message body, or in frequently used text fields.

• Click the More Choices tab to see additional options that are specific to the type of item you're looking for. When searching for Outlook items, this tab always lets you select from the Categories field or find items based on their size. As Figure 9.31 demonstrates, you can use this tab to recover space in your Inbox by selecting messages that contain file attachments over a specified size, and then deleting them or moving them to a new location.

Figure 9.31

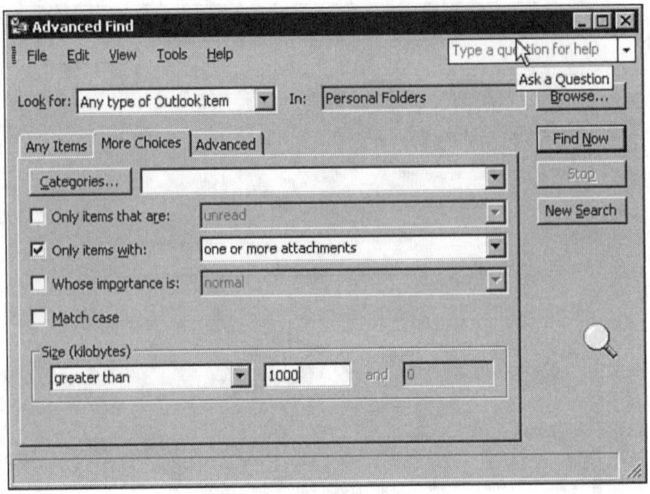

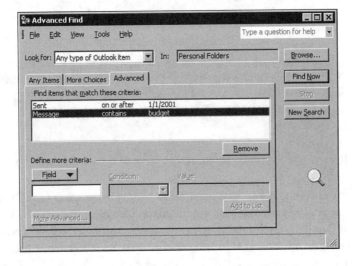

- Use the Advanced tab (see Figure 9.32) to define criteria based on any Outlook field. Click the Field button to select a field, and then enter a Condition and (if necessary) a Value. Click the Add to List button to insert the criteria in the box above the button.

Figure 9.32

4. Click the Find Now button to begin the search, using the criteria you entered. The results of the search appear in a simple list below the Advanced Find dialog box. Click the Stop button to interrupt the search at any point.

Double-click to open any item in the search results list. You can move, copy, delete, or edit items in this folder as well, using right-click shortcut menus (or click and drag to folders in the Outlook window). You can't choose a view other than the Table view; however, you can customize the fields that appear in the search results, change the sort order, and apply grouping. Right-click any column headings in the search results to display these options.

Tip from

EQ & Woody

> The settings in the Advanced Find dialog box are identical to those in the Filter dialog box that you use to define a custom view. Unfortunately, you can't transfer settings between these two dialog boxes. When you use the Advanced Find dialog box, you can view the results only as a simple list; if you want to see the search results in a different view, such as Address Cards, define a new view and create a filter for it.

Click the New Search button to clear all previously defined criteria and start from scratch.

One trick that even many Outlook experts don't realize is that you can customize the display of found items in the results pane at the bottom of the Advanced Find window. Right-click the column headings and use the Field Chooser to add or remove columns; you can also group messages in this display. When you save the search, these settings are saved also.

→ To learn how to save and reuse complex searches, **see** "Secrets of the Office Masters: Building a Library of Saved Searches," **p. 235**.

INTEGRATING OUTLOOK WITH EXCHANGE SERVER

If you use Outlook as the *client software* on a network that includes Microsoft Exchange Server, many administrative tasks are performed by the server administrator and cannot be controlled by the client. Depending on the server configuration, you can also perform the following tasks within Outlook itself:

- **Work with Public Folders**—As the name implies, these folders are accessible to other users across the network. You can share your contacts, Calendar items, and task lists; participate in public, online discussions; or share files. Before you can create and manage *public folders* from Outlook, the Exchange server administrator must first delegate access to you.

- **Delegate Access and Folder Permissions**—If the Exchange Server administrator allows it, you can give another person (a co-worker or assistant, for example) *access permission* to work in your Outlook folders and send messages on your behalf. You can also assign *folder permissions* to other users so that they can read, modify, or create items in your public and private folders on the server.

Note

> For a full list of the connections between Outlook and Exchange Server, search for the Help topic, "Outlook features available when you use Microsoft Exchange Server." Also, pick up a copy of *Special Edition Using Microsoft Exchange Server 5.5*, also published by Que (ISBN: 0-7897-1503-1).

If you're responsible for setting up and administering an Exchange Server, you'll find excellent resources to help you configure server options so that Outlook users can make the most of public and private folders. Start with Microsoft's BackOffice Server Web site: http://www.microsoft.com/backofficeserver/.

If you're an Outlook user on an Exchange Server network, you can read more details about how to customize your client setup in *Special Edition Using Microsoft Outlook 2002*, also published by Que (ISBN: 0-7897-2514-2).

IMPORTING AND EXPORTING OUTLOOK INFORMATION

You can also use the Import and Export Wizard to transfer data between Outlook and other programs. The most common use of this feature is to help you migrate your data to Outlook from a contact-management program such as ACT! or Lotus Organizer. If the Import and Export Wizard doesn't include the specific name and version number of the program you use, you need to export the data to a delimited text file or a database format and then import it into Outlook.

Tip from

EQ & Woody

If you use multiple Personal Folders files to maintain your mail, use the Import and Export Wizard to effortlessly move items from one file to another. Choose File, Import and Export, and then select Export to a File or Import from Another Program or File. In either case, you'll find a Personal Folders File (.pst) option. Follow the wizard's prompts to select the folder or folders you want to move—defining a filter if necessary, so you move only items that match criteria you specify—and choose the name of the destination file.

IMPORTING DATA FROM EXTERNAL PROGRAMS

Outlook makes it relatively easy to import personal information, including contacts and appointments, from other software. Using the Import and Export Wizard, choose Import from Another Program or File, and then select one of the following supported file formats. Outlook 2002 recognizes data files created by a number of older contact-management programs, but this list has not been updated in years.

If Outlook can't work directly with the native format of the program that contains the data you want to import, you'll have to first export the data to a supported format. Comma Separated Values and Tab Separated Values are the most common, but the import utility can also read Access, dBASE, and FoxPro files as well as Excel lists.

Note

Both delimited text formats (*Comma Separated Values* and *Tab Separated Values*) offer DOS and Windows alternatives. The DOS version uses the ASCII character set, while the Windows versions incorporate the *ANSI character set*, which includes international and publishing characters. When in doubt, always choose the Windows option.

To import the data, follow these steps:

1. Choose File, Import and Export.

2. In the Import and Export Wizard, choose Import from Another Program or File; then follow the wizard's prompts to select the specific data format and the file that contains the data.

3. In the Import a File dialog box (see Figure 9.33), specify how you want Outlook to handle items that duplicate those in the current folder. You can replace the existing item with the imported one, ignore the duplicate item, or allow Outlook to create duplicates. When in doubt, allow Outlook to create duplicate items and manually resolve the differences later.

PART

II

CH

9

Figure 9.33
Specify whether you want to create duplicate items (based on the title) when importing information. Regardless of your choice, Outlook does not warn you whether it created or rejected any duplicates.

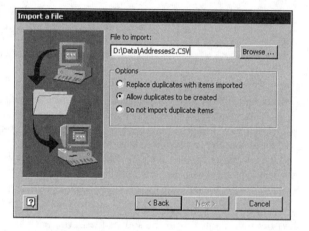

Tip from

When you import data, Outlook doesn't give you any feedback as to how many new items it created, or whether it dealt with any duplicate items. If you want to know how many new items were created, open the destination folder before importing and check the status bar (just below the Outlook Bar) to see how many items the folder contains. After completing the import, check the new count to see how many items were added.

→ Under some circumstances, Outlook can help you merge duplicate items that creep into your Contacts list so that you don't inadvertently keep outdated information; **see** "Merging Duplicate Contact Items," **p. 303**.

4. Select the *destination folder* into which you want to import the data, and then click Next.

5. In the last step of the Import and Export Wizard, click the Map Custom Fields button if you want to verify that Outlook plans to stuff information from the source file into the correct folder. The Map Custom Fields dialog box (shown in Figure 9.34) reads the *field* names from the *source file* and makes its best guess at matching them in the destination file.

Figure 9.34
The pane on the left shows the field names from the source file; drag names into the pane on the right to match them with Outlook field names.

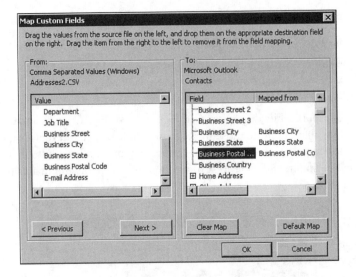

Whenever you import any amount of data, large or small, into your primary Outlook data file, we strongly recommend that you first create a new, temporary folder. Give the folder a name that describes the data, such as "Imported Addresses," and then start the import. This precaution lets you inspect the imported items for errors and correct any information that was damaged during the import. When you're satisfied that the new items are correct, drag them into the proper destination folder.

6. Outlook displays the field names from the source file in the left pane. Scroll through the list of mappings on the right to see how Outlook has matched the field names in the source file to Outlook fields. Drag field names from the left pane and drop them on the corresponding fields in the right pane to create a mapping. For example, if your source file includes a field called Full Name, drop it onto the Name field in the right pane.

7. Click Finish to import the data.

You don't need to map all the fields from your source file to Outlook. If your original database includes hundreds of fields for each record, but all you want to import is the name and business address so that you can prepare a mailing, click the Clear Map button to eliminate all mappings. Then drag just the handful of fields you want to use into the destination pane.

EXPORTING OUTLOOK DATA

When you need to export data, Outlook offers fewer options than on the corresponding import side. In most cases, you'll need to export the data from one or more folders into a file using a standard data-interchange format.

Outlook enables you to export to an Excel worksheet or a database format (Access, dBASE, or FoxPro); choose the Excel option if you want to manipulate the data using Excel's list-management features.

→ To learn more about working with Excel's list-management features, **see** Chapter 25, "Working with Lists and Databases," **p. 673**.

If you plan to export the data into a non-Office program, choose one of the comma- or tab-delimited text formats. To export data to a file, choose File, Import and Export. In the Import and Export Wizard, choose Export to a File, and then follow the prompts to select the folder you want to export from, the file format you want to create, and the name and location of the resulting output file. As with the import version of this wizard, you can map custom fields. This is an excellent way to quickly export selected information from your Contacts folder into a format that other programs (including Word and Excel) can readily use.

 If your exported data contains stray characters that cause problems when you try to open the file in another program, see "Removing Multiline Addresses from Your Contacts Folder" in the "Troubleshooting" section at the end of this chapter.

Synchronizing Outlook Data with a Handheld Device

If you own a handheld computer such as a Palm PC, Handspring Visor, or Pocket PC, you can *synchronize* data between your Outlook Personal Folders file and the handheld device. Don't use Outlook's Import and Export Wizard, however—instead, use the synchronization software included with the computer. In most cases, this software can exchange data directly with Outlook data files.

To set up and synchronize with a Pocket PC running Windows CE, use the Windows CE Inbox Transfer utility, available from Outlook's Tools menu. This dialog box lets you move files between your handheld device and a desktop or portable PC; you can also configure space-saving options, such as restricting the size of messages on the handheld device and ignoring attachments.

To synchronize with a handheld device running the Palm OS, you must first install Chapura's PocketMirror software. This software adds a button to Outlook's Standard toolbar and also makes a PocketMirror Settings option available on the Tools menu.

Note that this option only synchronizes the Calendar, Contacts, Tasks, and Notes folders. If you set up e-mail on your Palm device, only the Outlook Inbox is synchronized. In addition, some information is lost during synchronization. For instance, recurring appointments are typically split into individual appointments on the handheld device.

Troubleshooting

Working Around Anti-Spam Filters

I have two Internet service providers. One is a local provider I use at home, because I like their speed and service. For business trips, I use an account with a national Internet service provider, to avoid having to access the Internet via a long-distance call at exorbitant hotel rates. While on the road, I have no trouble receiving mail from your regular ISP, but when I try to reply to e-mail, I get an error message that says something like This server does not allow relaying.

Most ISPs restrict access to SMTP servers for sending outgoing mail—typically, the mail server checks your IP address before allowing you to connect to the SMTP server. This step verifies that you are an authenticated user on the network, as is the case when you dial in directly. If you connect from another ISP, the server doesn't recognize your IP address and blocks your attempt. This configuration prevents unauthorized users from hijacking the mail server to unleash a flood of spam, but it also prevents you from connecting to the outgoing mail server to relay messages. On the road, set up another Internet mail account, and adjust your configuration so you send mail through the SMTP server that belongs to the account you dialed in with, but receive messages on your regular POP3 server. To make sure that recipients send replies to the right address, be sure to specify your regular (home) mail account as the Reply-To address on this new account.

ALARMS FAIL TO GO OFF

I set a reminder on an Outlook item, but I never received a pop-up reminder.

It sounds obvious, but Outlook must be running if you expect to receive reminders. Outlook displays past-due reminders the next time you start the program, but these reminders don't do you much good if you've already missed an important meeting or appointment. To ensure that Outlook runs every time you start your computer, place a shortcut to the program in your Startup group. And if you use reminders, avoid shutting down Outlook except when you plan to turn off your PC.

ALARMS WORK ONLY IN FOUR KEY FOLDERS

Outlook was running, but I still never received a pop-up reminder for an item.

Check the folder the item is stored in. This problem is most common when you use rules to automatically move incoming messages to a folder other than the Inbox. Outlook monitors only four specific folders for reminders and follow-up flags: Inbox, Calendar, Contacts, and Tasks. And it monitors only the data store that is designated as the one to receive incoming messages. If an item is in another folder, even if it's a subfolder to one of these folders, Outlook will allow you to set the reminder, but it won't pop up the notice when you expect it. When you move the item back to one of these four folders, you'll see an Overdue reminder immediately.

RESETTING THE STANDARD VIEWS

When I view information using a built-in Outlook view, some fields are missing, or the sorting and grouping options aren't what I want.

Outlook makes it too easy to customize the built-in views, which is usually the cause when fields disappear from standard views. Fortunately, it's also easy to return a built-in Outlook view to its original settings. If you've messed up the Messages view of the Inbox or the Address Cards view of the Contacts folder, for example, just choose View, Current View,

Define Views, and then select the view name and click Reset. This option is not available for custom views.

REMOVING MULTILINE ADDRESSES FROM YOUR CONTACTS FOLDER

When I open the Outlook data I exported to another program, the file contains stray characters that I didn't put there. What's happening?

Your exported data contains stray characters that cause problems when you try to open the file in another program. The culprit might be multiline addresses from your Contacts folder. In some export formats, Outlook includes carriage return characters with each line of the address, and the program you're using to import the data interprets these as end-of-record markers. Try exporting your data again, this time using the Comma Separated Text format, which adds carriage returns only at the end of a line.

DRAGGING DOESN'T ALWAYS MOVE AN ITEM

I tried to move an item from one folder to another, but Outlook opened the form for a new item instead.

You can move items only to folders capable of storing that type of item. If you try to move one type of item (such as an e-mail message) to a folder intended for a different item (such as the Contacts folder), Outlook assumes you want to create a new item, just as if you had dropped the original icon on the folder's shortcut in the Outlook Bar. Choose a different destination folder.

SECRETS OF THE OFFICE MASTERS: BUILDING A LIBRARY OF SAVED SEARCHES

One way to dramatically increase your productivity is to build a library of saved searches that you can reopen easily. Even if you need to modify one or two details of a saved search, it's usually much easier to do so than to start from scratch.

Create a subfolder in the My Documents folder or on the Start menu and call it Saved Outlook Searches. Whenever you create and save a search, store the shortcut here so you can access it again.

Open the Advanced Find dialog box and begin building a library of universal searches starting with the list shown here. For each search, establish the type of item to look for: Messages, Contacts, or Tasks, for example. Specify which folders you want Outlook to search. If you've set up rules to process incoming messages into multiple folders, be sure to select all those folders; remember to create separate searches to cover archived messages in separate PST files.

After selecting all search settings in the Advanced Find dialog box, choose File, Save Search. Give each file a name; you could use the bold text at the beginning of each item in the following list. Choose the location you set up for your saved searches and click OK. Each saved search is stored in a small (about 4KB) Office Search shortcut file with the extension .oss. To reuse a saved search, double-click its icon, or open the Advanced Find dialog box and then choose File, Open Search and select the shortcut.

- **Messages Received Since Beginning of Last Month**—Choose Messages from the Look For list, and then choose the Inbox and any other folders you use for incoming messages, especially those included as part of rules. Click the Advanced tab and add two criteria: Received This Month and Received Last Month.

- **Messages Received Since Beginning of Last Week**—Same as the previous item, but use Received This Week and Received Last Week as the criteria on the Advanced tab.

- **Messages Sent Since Beginning of Last Month** and **Messages Sent Since Beginning of Last Week**—Same as previous two items; specify the Sent Items folder as the location in which to search.

- **Company Mail**—Specify Messages as the Item Type. Choose the Inbox, the Sent Items folder, and any other commonly used message folders as the locations in which to look. On the Advanced tab, use criteria that search for a specific domain name in the To and From fields. For example, if you work for Que Publishing and your e-mail address is at quepublishing.com, add the criteria `To contains quepublishing.com` and `From con-tains quepublishing.com`; this will find all messages to or from other people in that domain. Use the Field Chooser to remove unnecessary icon fields and show both the To and From fields in the results pane; then group the results by the In Folder field.

CHAPTER 10

EXPERT E-MAIL MANAGEMENT

In this chapter

MANAGING MULTIPLE E-MAIL ACCOUNTS

How many e-mail addresses do you use? Between work, home, and Web-based accounts, it's not unusual for even a casual e-mail user to have 3 or more accounts to check. If you're an e-mail addict, you could easily have more than 10 e-mail addresses to keep track of.

Outlook includes a variety of tools and features that you can use to manage multiple e-mail accounts effectively:

- Unlike previous Outlook versions, Outlook 2002 offers full support for Microsoft's Web-based mail accounts, Hotmail and MSN.com.

- You can define multiple Send/Receive Groups with separate connection settings for each mail account. This allows you to check your favorite mail accounts regularly while downloading from infrequently used mail accounts only when you want to do so.

- You can define rules to process incoming and outgoing mail automatically—moving it to folders, color-coding it, or assigning a message priority, for example.

In this chapter, we'll explain how to use each of these options most effectively.

CREATING, MANAGING, AND USING E-MAIL ADDRESSES

In terms of complexity, Outlook's address-book structure falls somewhere between baseball's infield-fly rule and the U.S. tax code. What looks simple on the surface quickly becomes baffling, thanks to the many locations in which Outlook can store e-mail addresses and other contact information, and two completely different interfaces for viewing and editing that information. More bad news: If you mastered this stuff in Outlook 2000, you'll have to start over again, because several key Address Book details have changed.

Where are your e-mail addresses stored? Depending on your configuration, Outlook might use any of the locations listed in Table 28.1.

TABLE 28.1   OUTLOOK ADDRESS BOOK OPTIONS

Location	Description
Global Address List	This is the master address book on a network running Microsoft Exchange Server.
Offline Address Book	Available only on networks running Exchange Server; by default, it includes all addresses from your site, typically a subset of the Global Address List. To create an Offline Address Book, you must be connected to an Exchange Server; choose Tools, Send/Receive, Download Address Book.
Contacts folder	The default location for addresses in your primary store; you can create additional folders containing Contact items and make them available for use with e-mail messages as well.

Location	Description
Personal Address Book (*.pab)	The original address-book format for Exchange clients; this option is still available in Outlook 2000/2002, primarily for backward compatibility. You can have one and only one PAB file per Outlook profile.
Windows Address Book (*.wab)	This application, included with Outlook Express and all versions of Windows since Windows 98, can store addresses in its own file format (WAB) or can share information with Outlook's Contacts folder.
Other MAPI-based address books	Third-party software developers can hook into Outlook as services, using their own file formats to store address information.

Did you notice that we didn't mention the Outlook Address Book? In Outlook 2002, the Outlook Address Book is not a physical location for storing addresses. Instead, it represents an important alternative method for viewing the contents of the Contacts folder and any other folders that contain Contact items. As you'll see shortly, this is a crucial concept in understanding how to configure Outlook addresses.

PART

II

CH

10

Tip from

Ed & Woody

When you install other programs, they might take over functions you expect Outlook to handle, including e-mail and address-book management. To specify that you want to use Outlook as your default e-mail, calendar, and contact manager, choose Tools, Options; select the Other tab; and check the Make Outlook the Default Program box.

Outlook includes the Contacts folder as a default store for contact information, but you might find it useful to create additional contact folders. For example, at work you might want to segregate information about friends and family in one folder and reserve your main contacts folder for business contacts. If you're a frequent traveler, put listings for hotels, airlines, restaurants, and other on-the-road resources in a Travel folder. If your collection of contacts is particularly large, you can subdivide it even further, into separate folders for Customers and Suppliers, for example, all stored as subfolders under the Contacts folder.

CONFIGURING THE OUTLOOK ADDRESS BOOK

Savvy Outlook users do most address management from the Contacts folder. Its default data-entry form is the most flexible way to enter new items, and its support for custom views and filters makes it the best choice for quickly viewing information. But Outlook also offers another view of the Contacts folder; click the Address Book button on the Standard toolbar to display a window on your Contacts like the one shown in Figure 10.1. Unlike folders that contain Contact items, this view shows only items that have an e-mail address or a fax number.

Figure 10.1
If you've configured
Outlook correctly, the
Address Book view
shows information
that's stored in your
Contacts folder.

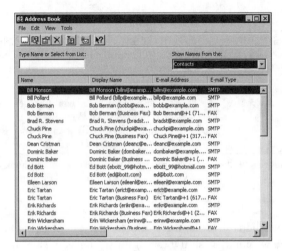

→ For full details on how to use the Contacts folder, **see** "Managing Your List of Contacts," **p. 294**.

It's possible—no, make that way too easy—to inadvertently configure Outlook so that you have more than one address book. We strongly recommend that you double-check your Outlook setup to make sure you've eliminated the possibility of creating duplicate addresses in more than one address book. In particular, if you have a Personal Address Book folder, do whatever it takes to get rid of it. Working exclusively with the Outlook Address Book (and your Global Address List, on an Exchange Server) is much simpler.

Follow these steps to safely migrate addresses from your PAB file and remove it from your Outlook profile:

1. Choose File, Import and Export, and use the wizard to import the contents of your Personal Address Book into your Contacts folder.

→ For step-by-step instructions on how to import information into Outlook, **see** "Importing and Exporting Outlook Information," **p. 230**.

2. Choose Tools, E-mail Accounts. Select View or Change Existing Directories or Address Books and click Next.

3. Select Personal Address Book from your list of directories and address books and click the Remove button. Click yes to confirm that you do want to remove the PAB.

4. If the Outlook Address Book is not in your profile, click the Add button in the Directories and Address Books dialog box and install it. Close and restart Outlook if prompted.

5. Right-click the Contacts folder icon in the Outlook Bar and choose Properties. On the Outlook Address Book tab, check the Show This Folder As an E-mail Address Book box. Click OK to close the dialog box. Repeat this step for any other folders that contain contact items with e-mail addresses.

> **Tip from**
> *Ed & Woody*
>
> You don't have to designate all contact folders as address books. Reserve this honor for folders filled with items that have e-mail addresses or fax numbers. If you create a folder with contact items that identify restaurants, hotels, airlines, and other travel-related institutions that you typically contact over the phone rather than through e-mail, don't designate this folder as an address book.

6. Open the Directories and Address Books dialog box again. Select Outlook Address Book from the list of address books and click the Change button. Make sure the Contacts folder and any other folders you specified in step 5 are listed here (see Figure 10.2). Adjust the way names display if necessary in the Show Names By section of the dialog box.

> **Note**
>
> If you receive e-mail through an Exchange Server, your profile might also include an Offline Address Book. Do not remove this entry from your profile.

7. Close all dialog boxes and choose Tools, Address Book to verify that the folders you specified are the only ones shown in the Address Book.

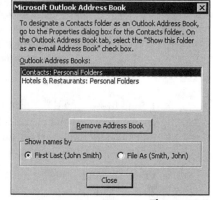

Figure 10.2

INTEGRATING OUTLOOK WITH THE WINDOWS ADDRESS BOOK

The Windows Address Book was originally designed primarily to store e-mail addresses for Outlook Express. You can configure the WAB so that it draws addresses from your Outlook Contacts folder instead of from a WAB data file; this allows you to use your Outlook Contacts folder from within Outlook Express, without having to worry about keeping two address books in sync. Even if you never use Outlook Express, we recommend that you enable this integration, because it allows you to access your Contact information quickly, even when Outlook is not running.

To enable integration with the Windows Address Book, click the Start button, choose Run, type WAB, and press Enter. The Windows Address Book opens. Choose Tools, Options; then select the Share Contact Information option. This allows all contact managers to share address book data stored in the Contacts folder.

> **Note**
>
> This option is only available on a system with Outlook 2002, Outlook 2000 (configured in Corporate/Workgroup mode), or Office 97. On a machine without Outlook, the Options menu is missing from the Windows Address Book.

Some people find it easier to use the Windows Address Book to edit e-mail addresses and other personal information, such as the name of a contact's spouse and children, as well as birthdays and anniversary dates. If you've configured the Address Book and Contacts folder to share information, entering or editing an item in either window changes the information in the Contacts folder.

ADDRESSING AN E-MAIL MESSAGE

When addressing an e-mail message, you have several options:

- The most reliable way to make sure you address each message correctly is to reply to an e-mail message you've received. In this situation, you can almost always be certain that the address is accurate.

 If you reply to a message and get a delivery failure, see "When Your E-mail Bounces" in the "Troubleshooting" section at the end of this chapter.

Tip from
EQ & Woody

Although it's not immediately obvious, all address information in the header of a message you receive is "live." Right-click any address to display a shortcut menu. Choose Add to Contacts to create a new item in your Contacts folder using the name and e-mail address displayed in the header, or choose Look Up Contact to search your Contacts folder for an item that contains a matching e-mail address. You can also use the shortcut menu to copy the address and paste it in the To or CC box in another message.

- For addresses you don't plan to reuse (such as a request for information from a merchant), enter the full e-mail address in the To, Cc, or Bcc box. If the e-mail address you enter matches one in the Contacts folder, Outlook replaces the information you typed with the display name from that item.

- Open the Address Book and choose Action, Send Mail, or open the Contacts folder and choose Actions, New Message to Contact.

- Click the To, Cc, or Bcc buttons to display the Select Names dialog box, which is actually a different view of the Address Book (see Figure 10.3). Use the buttons shown here to add addresses to any of the three envelope fields, or to create a new item or open an existing one. This is the easiest way to add a large number of addresses to a message quickly and accurately.

- For people you send mail to most frequently, enter any portion of the recipient's name in any envelope field (To, Cc, or Bcc) and let Outlook's AutoComplete feature resolve the address for you. (To enter multiple names this way, separate each name with a comma.)

AutoComplete is a power user's dream. It searches in your Contacts Folder and other Address Book locations; it also remembers addresses you've recently entered manually or by replying to a message. If Outlook finds one and only one matching item, it completes the name automatically, using the default email address. If Outlook finds multiple matching names, it shows a drop-down list of matching names so you can select one.

Figure 10.3
Select one or more
names from the list on
the left; then click one
of the three buttons
to add the selected
addresses to the fields
on the right.

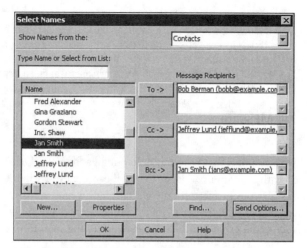

Caution

AutoComplete can also cause nightmares, if you're unaware of how it really works. Because the list of AutoComplete possibilities includes addresses you've entered manually, Outlook may "remember" a name and suggest it to you. The name looks all right in the To field, so you accept it; unfortunately, you don't realize that the message is going to a rarely used email account for that contact, rather than the address they check 10 times a day. To avoid this possibility, double-click the name in the To field to display a dialog box that shows the Display Name and E-mail Address fields.

To configure AutoComplete options, choose Tools, Options, click the E-mail Options button, and click the Advanced E-mail Options button. The Suggest Names While Completing To, Cc, and Bcc Fields choice at the bottom of the dialog box (see Figure 10.4) lets you turn off AutoComplete.

Figure 10.4
Use this shortcut menu
to resolve names when
the text you enter
matches several
entries in the Address
Book.

Advanced E-mail Options	? |X
Save messages
Save unsent items in: Drafts
☑ AutoSave unsent every: 3 minutes
☐ In folders other than the Inbox, save replies with original message
☑ Save forwarded messages
When new items arrive
☑ Play a sound
☑ Briefly change the mouse cursor
☑ Show an envelope icon in the system tray
When sending a message
Set importance: Normal
Set sensitivity: Normal
☑ Allow comma as address separator
☑ Automatic name checking
☑ Delete meeting request from Inbox when responding
☑ Suggest names while completing To, Cc, and Bcc fields
☑ Add properties to attachments to enable Reply with Changes
OK Cancel

Tip from

EQ & Woody

Most Outlook experts don't even know this tip: Every contact item includes a field called Nickname that you can use to make name matching more precise. To find this field, open the contact's record and click the Details tab. Enter the text you want to use as a shortcut when addressing mail to that person; try to find a nickname that isn't also part of other names. For example, if one of your contacts is named James R. Jones, enter JRJ as his nickname and you can avoid seeing the red wavy lines in the future.

How do you deal with contacts that have multiple e-mail addresses? Don't create multiple Contact items, each with a different address; that will cause a mess when Outlook tries to resolve the addresses for you. Instead, enter each different e-mail address as part of the same Contact item. When you use the Contacts folder, you can enter up to three e-mail addresses; the first is the default address that Outlook uses when sending mail to that person.

→ If you've inadvertently created multiple Contact items for the same person, you might be able to merge them into a single record; for details, **see** "Merging Duplicate Contact Items," **p. 303**.

CREATING AND USING PERSONAL DISTRIBUTION LISTS

Outlook enables you to create a single alias called a *Personal Distribution List* that represents a group of e-mail addresses. Use this option to avoid having to repeatedly enter a slew of addresses when you routinely send mail to the same group of people. For example, if you're on the board of a local charity, you can create a Personal Distribution List that includes all the other members of the board, and then name it Board. When you type that name in an envelope field on a message form, Outlook recognizes the list and resolves it for you. When you send the message, Outlook substitutes all the individual names so that your message is delivered correctly.

To create a Personal Distribution List in the Contacts folder, choose File, New, Distribution List. From the Address Book, choose File, New Entry, New Distribution List. Both methods lead to the dialog box shown in Figure 10.5.

Figure 10.5
Use this dialog box to add names to a Personal Distribution List.

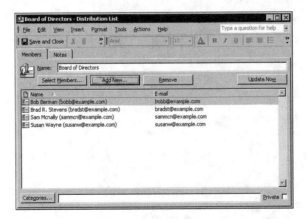

Enter the name you want to use for the list in the Name field. Click the Select Members button to add names from the Address Book. Click the Add New button to open a dialog box where you can enter a new name that isn't currently in your Contacts folder; check the Add to Contacts box to store that new item in the Address Book as well as in the Personal Distribution List. After you finish adding names to the list, click the Save and Close button to save the list.

If you need to change the lineup of names that make up the list—if a member of the board quits and another takes her place, for example—open this dialog box again and use the Remove button to get rid of the names you no longer need.

Tip from

Ed & Woody

> If you routinely send messages to a large number of recipients—more than 10, for example—think carefully about how to address the message. If it's not necessary for any of the recipients to respond to all others on the list, address the message to yourself and add the other recipients' names to the Bcc field. Your message is far more likely to be read in this format, especially by people using mail software that displays the entire message header—a list of 20 or so names takes up the entire screen and pushes your message completely out of sight otherwise.

PART

II

CH

10

Personal distribution lists appear in the Outlook Address Book as boldfaced entries.

USING WORD AS AN E-MAIL EDITOR

Outlook enables you to choose Word as the default editor for composing new messages and reading messages received in Rich Text Format. In Outlook 97, this option was known as WordMail, and Office veterans remember its unfortunate tendency to slow down your system and cause data-destroying crashes. In Outlook 2000, the integration between Word and Outlook was much improved, but still far from perfect. With Outlook 2002, Microsoft finally might have gotten the integration between Outlook and Word good enough for most people to seriously consider using Word in place of Outlook's built-in message editor.

If you configure Outlook to use Word as its default editor, you have to deal with the following tradeoffs:

- On the plus side, you get to use Word's much more sophisticated editing tools to compose messages. That means you can take advantage of AutoText and AutoCorrect in messages, and you can use macros and templates to automate message creation. If your default format is HTML, you'll appreciate Word's editing tools, especially because you can use Word tables and text boxes to organize an HTML message. You can use themes to add personality to your messages. And Word's unlimited undo feature is a godsend when composing messages.

- On the downside, you have to load Word to compose a new message; that slows down performance initially and uses more memory than Outlook alone. Word is overkill for editing plain text messages. And despite dramatic improvements in this version, you can expect the Word-Outlook combination to be less stable than either program would on its own.

To use Word as the default editor for all new messages, replies, and forwards, choose Tools, Options, click the Mail Format tab, and check the Use Microsoft Word to Edit E-Mail Messages box. (A second check box lets you use Word to read messages you receive in Rick Text format.) Figure 10.6 shows the result: a Word window with one extra toolbar and a set of address headers at the top of the document.

Figure 10.6
When you use Word as your e-mail editor, you get a richer set of editing tools, but you also lose some options.

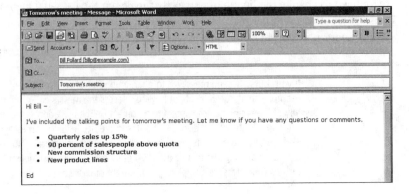

If you're not willing to configure Word as your full-time mail editor, you can still get most of the benefits of this configuration and choose exactly when you want to use it. Instead of using Outlook to compose a new message, open a new Word document instead, and then click the E-mail button on the Standard toolbar. This adds the address toolbars to the document, enabling you to create and send a message in HTML format. You can't use this option for replies or forwards, however.

CREATING AND SENDING MESSAGES

After successfully addressing a message, composing a message is a reasonably straightforward process. If you've chosen Plain Text format, enter text and add attachments (you can drag any file from an Explorer window into the message window to attach it, or choose Insert, File to choose items from a dialog box). For Rich Text messages, you can also use font and paragraph formatting. HTML messages give you the option to add pictures, background colors and graphics, and other Web-style formatting. Depending on the message type you've selected, you can also choose several advanced options.

CHOOSING A MESSAGE FORMAT

When you compose a new message or click the Reply button, Outlook lets you choose from three distinct message formats. In some circumstances, it makes the choice of format for you, and you have to specifically override that decision. If you're picky about which message format you send out, pay attention to the fine details in this section, because the obvious options do not always behave as you expect.

- **Plain Text**—Transmits nothing but letters, numbers, and symbols in the character set you use to create the message. Outlook strips any formatting, including colors, fonts, and inline pictures, when it sends the message.

- **Outlook Rich Text**—This format, the default on most Exchange servers, was developed by Microsoft years ago, before HTML became popular. Using Rich Text format enables you to specify fonts, colors, bullets, and other text attributes, with one major caveat: Only recipients who use Outlook or another Exchange client will be able to correctly view that formatted information. Rich Text is the default format on Exchange Servers. If you send a Rich Text message to a recipient who is using another client program, he will see most of the text in your message as well as an attachment called Winmail.dat, which contains useless information. Outlook automatically creates messages in Rich Text format when you use group-oriented features such as meeting invitations, and task requests.

PART
II
CH
10

Tip from
E Q & Woody

> Outlook 2002 lets you specify that you want Rich Text messages to automatically be converted to HTML or Plain Text when sent over the Internet. If you send and receive some e-mail through an Exchange Server but also an Internet-standard SMTP/POP3 account, choose Tools, Options; click the Mail Format tab; and click the Internet Format button. Choose a format from the drop-down list

- **HTML**—Offers the same text formatting options as Rich Text format, plus the capability to specify styles, automatically number lines, and add horizontal rules. Because the underlying format is the same as a Web page, you can also define background graphics and insert images into a message. Most modern Internet mail client programs are capable of reading HTML-formatted messages, including all versions of Netscape Mail and Outlook Express, as well as most recent Eudora versions. If the recipient's mail client software can't interpret HTML, the recipient sees a plain-text version of the message with an attachment that can be viewed in any Web browser.

Which of these three formats will Outlook use when you create a message? As with so many configurable settings throughout Office, the correct answer is: It depends.

Tip from
E Q & Woody

> The name of the current message format always appears in parentheses in the title bar of an open message.

When you create a new message from scratch, Outlook uses the default format; choose Tools, Options; then click the Mail Format tab to choose any of the three supported formats.

When you reply to a message, Outlook ignores the preferences you specified as your default and uses the format of the original message. This isn't as rude as it sounds: If you receive a message that was composed in HTML or Rich Text format, you can be certain that the sender is capable of reading messages in that format. On the other hand, when you receive a message in Plain Text format, the most conservative response is to assume that the sender either can't work with other formats or chooses not to use formatted mail, and respond in kind.

Caution

Pay close attention to message formats when you reply to messages. If the original message was in Rich Text format, your reply to the original sender uses that format as well; if you add recipients and they use mail client software that is incapable of reading Rich Text format, they might have difficulty reading the original message or your reply.

You can switch on-the-fly to a new message format. From the Format menu in Outlook's editor, choose Plain Text, HTML, or Rich Text. The same options are available as a drop-down list on the E-mail toolbar in Word. Note that you can't switch directly from HTML to Rich Text or vice versa; in either case, you have to first convert the message to Plain Text format, losing all formatting, and then choose the other format.

FORCING OUTLOOK TO USE PLAIN TEXT FORMAT

In one specific circumstance, Outlook uses Plain Text format, regardless of whether you are creating a new message or replying to an existing one. This option is useful when a particular contact has made it clear that he absolutely despises formatted messages; if your boss says "No HTML messages," you have to comply.

If you want to avoid sending HTML messages to a particular recipient over the Internet, you need to set an additional option. Open that person's Contact item and double-click the e-mail address you want to configure. This opens the E-mail Properties dialog box (see Figure 10.7). In the Internet Format box, choose the Send Plain Text Only option instead of the default (Let Outlook Decide the Best Sending Format). Repeat this process for other e-mail entries in the same Contact item, if necessary.

Figure 10.7
Setting this option guarantees that you won't accidentally send an HTML-for-matted message to a particular recipient.

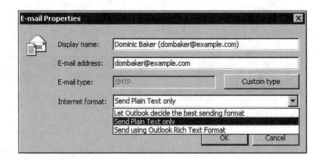

When you set this option, Outlook automatically converts messages to Plain Text format when you send to the specified recipient. You do not see any confirmation dialog boxes or warning that the message format has changed.

ADVANCED MESSAGE FORMAT OPTIONS

Both Plain Text and HTML formats include advanced settings that can make your messages easier to read. (If you mess with these options too much, you can also turn outgoing text into garbage, so be careful.) To see and adjust these settings, choose Tools, Options; then click the Mail Format tab. In the Message Format section, choose your default format for outgoing mail, usually Plain Text or HTML. Click the Internet Format button to set other options, as shown in Figure 10.8.

Figure 10.8
In general, most Outlook users should leave these settings at their defaults.

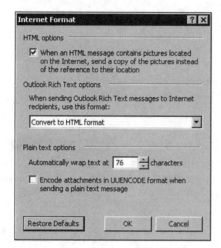

USING A SPECIFIC ACCOUNT TO SEND A MESSAGE

Normally, Outlook sends replies using the same account with which you received the original message. On new messages, forwards, and replies, you can choose which account to use for sending. From Outlook's message editor or from Word, use the drop-down Accounts button on the Standard toolbar (just to the right of the Send button) to select a different account.

USING SIGNATURES

Outlook allows you to create a *signature*—a short block of text (and, optionally, graphics or HTML code) that identifies you and perhaps supplies some information about you or your company.

If you use Outlook as your message editor, you can create one or more signatures for use with all outgoing messages. Outlook maintains separate text, Rich Text, and HTML signatures.

1. Choose Tools, Options, click the Message Format tab, and then click the Signatures button. The Create Signature dialog box (see Figure 10.9) shows all the signatures you've created so far.

Figure 10.9
Create multiple signatures for use with different types of messages.

2. Click the New button. In the Create New Signature dialog box (see Figure 10.10), enter a descriptive name for your signature and specify whether you want to create it from scratch or base it on an existing signature or file. Click Next to continue.

3. In the Edit Signature dialog box (see Figure 10.11), enter the text you want to use for your signature.

Figure 10.10

Figure 10.11
Your signature can include just your name and title, your e-mail address, or complete contact information.

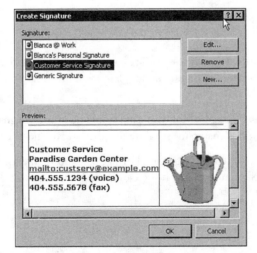

4. Click the Font and Paragraph buttons to add formatting to selected text. To add advanced formatting using an HTML editor such as FrontPage, click the Advanced Edit button.

5. Click Finish to save your signature.

When you specify a default signature on the Mail Format tab of the Options dialog box, Outlook automatically adds that text to the end of every new message you create. A check box lets you specify whether you want to include the signature with replies and forwards. To choose which signature you want to use on each new message you create, choose <None> as the default signature. When creating a new message, choose Insert, Signature; then select an entry from the list of available signature files. Note that if you use a default signature, you must delete that text before you insert a new one; this routine dumps the new text into your message body without deleting the old signature.

To create a signature when you use Word as your e-mail editor, open Word and choose Tools, Options. Click the General tab, and click the E-mail Options button. Although this dialog box (see Figure 10.12) differs slightly from the Outlook version, the basic steps are the same.

Figure 10.12
If you use Word as your message editor, use this dialog box to create and edit signatures.

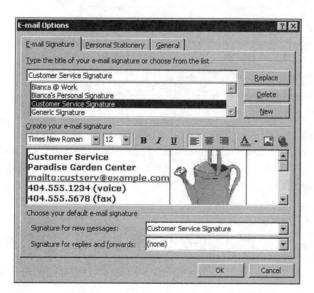

USING STATIONERY AND FONTS IN FORMATTED MESSAGES

Want to impress some message recipients and annoy others—sometimes even in the same message? Use a graphic image and predefined fonts as *stationery* for an e-mail message. Like a Web page theme, stationery adds consistent formatting to an e-mail message that you compose in HTML format. If you stick with a simple color and font selection, the effect can subtly enhance your message; if you go too far, it adds unnecessary distraction and can make message text nearly impossible to read. Outlook's stunningly inconsistent collection of built-in stationery choices offers plenty of examples of both.

The procedures for using stationery are slightly different, depending on whether you use Outlook or Word as your e-mail editor.

If you use Outlook as your message editor, you can make a particular stationery selection your default for every new message. Choose Tools, Options; select the Mail Format tab; and click the Stationery Picker button. Select a background image from the Stationery Picker dialog box and click Edit to adjust stationery options (see Figure 10.13).

Figure 10.13
You can adjust fonts and backgrounds for Outlook's stationery selections.

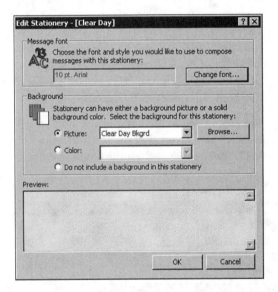

If you use Word as your e-mail editor, personal stationery is tied to your collection of Web themes. To choose a default background image or color and matching fonts for messages you create using Word, first open Word. Then choose Tools, Options; click the E-mail Options button; and set options on the Personal Stationery tab.

SETTING MESSAGE OPTIONS

When you click the Send button after composing a message, you tell Outlook to deliver the message using all your default settings: The message goes to your default mail server, you get a copy in your Sent Items folder, and that's about it. If you want the message to have special handling, click the Options button and adjust any of the settings in the Message Options dialog box shown in Figure 10.14.

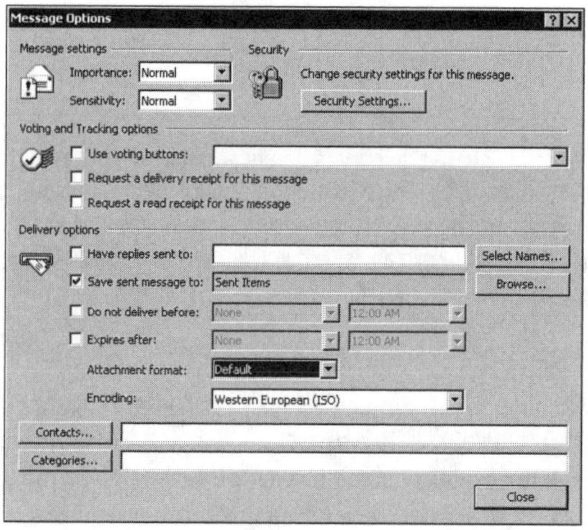

Figure 10.14
Several options in this dialog box, such as the capability to defer sending a message, can be extremely useful in business.

In the Message Settings section, use the Importance and Sensitivity drop-down lists to change these fields from their default setting of Normal to Low or High. Other Outlook users will see a blue down-arrow in the message list for Low Importance messages, and a red up-arrow for High Importance messages.

Tip from

If you encourage co-workers to use the Low and High Importance settings for messages, you can use the Rules Wizard to automatically highlight or file messages based on this setting. Skip the Options button and use the High and Low Importance buttons on the Standard toolbar when composing a message.

The choices in the Delivery Options section of the Message Options dialog box are probably the most useful:

- Check the Have Replies Sent To box and enter an alternate Reply-to address. This option is especially useful when you want an outgoing message to go out under your name, but you want to redirect replies to a different address. As the president of a company, for example, you might want to announce a new benefits plan for your employees; if you specify the human resource director's name in this box, employees can reply directly to your message for more information.

- Clear the Save Sent Message To box if you don't want to save a copy of the current message, or click the Browse button to select a different folder.

- Check the Do Not Deliver Before box and enter a date if you want to compose a message and send it automatically at a time you specify. This option can be extremely useful when the timing of a message is crucial but you won't be physically present to send the message. For example, say you're planning an important announcement for Monday at 10 a.m.; go ahead and prepare the press release, and then enter Monday 10am in this box. Make sure to leave Outlook running with the option to automatically send and receive mail every 10 minutes or so, and your message will go out within 10 minutes of the time you specify, even if you're out of the office.

> **Note**
>
> If you use the deferred delivery option to schedule messages far in the future, be prepared for an annoying side effect of this option. Every time you close Office, you'll see a dialog box warning you that there are still messages in your Outbox and asking whether you want to exit anyway. If you know you'll restart Office before the message is due to be sent out, click OK.

→ For more details on how to enter dates using plain-English equivalents in any Outlook item, **see** "Entering Dates and Times Automatically," **p. 210**.

- Check the Expires After box if you use Exchange Server and your message has a time element to it. For example, if you're sending a reminder of a meeting that starts in an hour, add an expiration time that matches the start of the meeting. Recipients who check their e-mail before the start of the meeting will see the message. In the case of recipients who haven't picked up the message by its expiration time, the Exchange Server automatically deletes it, and you avoid cluttering up their Inboxes.

Are you tempted by the check box in the Voting and Tracking Options section that enables you to request a receipt when your message is delivered or read? Temper your expectations. If your message is going over an Exchange Server to another user on the same server, this option works exactly as you expect: The server can send you a delivery notice when the email lands in the recipient's Inbox, and another when it's opened. If your message has to pass through an SMTP server before reaching its destination, it's extremely unlikely you'll see a receipt—support for this feature is hit-or-miss on the Internet, and the recipient can choose to ignore the request for a receipt.

SETTING REPLY AND FORWARD OPTIONS

When you reply to a message, it's customary to include some or all of the original message to give the recipient a context for your answer. Outlook lets you choose from several formatting options to help make the original message text stand out. You can also define how Outlook identifies the original message text when you forward a message to someone else. Regardless of which option you choose, the insertion point appears at the top of the message window, with the original message below it.

To set either or both options, choose Tools, Options; click the Preferences tab; and click the E-mail Options button. If you routinely use HTML format, you can include the original message, or include and indent the original message. If you use Plain Text as your default format, we recommend that you choose the Prefix Each Line of the Original Message option and select the default quote character, a greater than (>) sign, as shown in Figure 10.15.

Figure 10.15
If you send mostly Plain Text messages, use the options shown here to prefix the original message in replies and forwards.

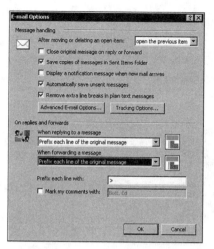

Caution

Avoid two options available in this dialog box. Specifying Do Not Include Original Message for replies makes it difficult (and sometimes impossible) for recipients to figure out what you're responding to. (It is good etiquette, however, to try to trim extraneous matter from replies and forwards.) The Attach Original Message option forces recipients to go through the additional step of detaching and opening an attachment to read the original message. They won't thank you for the extra work.

CHECKING YOUR MAIL AND READING NEW MESSAGES

Some experts recommend that you check e-mail only twice a day—any more often, they say, and you won't be able to concentrate on what's really important. At companies that live and die by e-mail (including many in the computer and Internet industries), following that advice would be a classic career-limiting move.

Still, the general point is valid: Figure out how often you need to check e-mail, and use Outlook to do as much of the work as possible. You have a variety of manual and automatic choices that control how you check messages.

SETTING UP SEND/RECEIVE GROUPS

By default, Outlook assigns the same mail-checking options to all your e-mail accounts. To adjust these settings, choose Tools, Options; click the Mail Setup tab; and click the Send/Receive button. This opens the Send/Receive Groups dialog box (see Figure 10.16).

Most of the options here are fairly self-explanatory. You can create a new group; edit, copy, or rename a group; or remove a group from the list. Note that you can also define separate online and offline settings, which are controlled by the Work Offline choice on Outlook's File menu. These options are especially useful if you have a dial-up connection; users with always-on broadband connections can safely ignore offline settings.

Figure 10.16
Using offline settings is especially helpful for notebook users; in this configuration, for instance, Outlook checks for new mail every three hours.

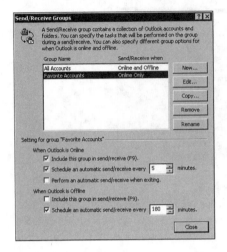

To set up a new group, click the new button. Give the group a name and click OK to display the dialog box shown in Figure 10.17.

Figure 10.17
Adjust settings for each mail account in a Send/Receive group.

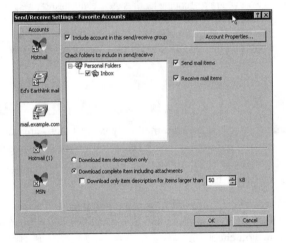

In each Send/Receive Group, you can define whether to send or receive mail items, whether you want to download headers only or retrieve complete items. In the case of Web-based mail accounts, you can specify which folders to download—typically, this is the Inbox only.

Each Send/Receive Group you create appears on the Tools menu, under the cascading Send/Receive list. Using this menu, you can select all accounts, choose a group you've defined, or check messages for a single account.

CHECKING MESSAGES AUTOMATICALLY

By default, Outlook offers to check messages every 10 minutes when you have a permanent Internet connection. You can adjust this setting by choosing options on the Mail Setup tab of the Options dialog box.

Tip from

Ed & Woody

If you have a dedicated line for dial-up Internet access and you want to check your messages automatically every two hours without disturbing a current connection or leaving a connection open unnecessarily, create a LAN/Dial configuration for the account. Set up a Send/Receive group and specify that you want to check for new messages every 120 minutes. Next, choose Tools, Options; click the Mail Setup tab; check the Always Use an Existing Dial-Up Connection option; and choose Automatically Dial During a Background Send/Receive.

CHECKING FOR MESSAGES MANUALLY

Under several circumstances, you might prefer to check your e-mail manually rather than setting an automatic option:

- If you're on a business trip and using Outlook on a notebook computer, you can't predict when you'll have an Internet connection. Configure Outlook's Send/Receive Groups to skip automatic mail checking when you work offline.

- For secondary mail accounts that you use only sporadically, you might choose to check your mail once every few days or even less frequently. When setting up a mail account in this configuration, clear the Include Account in This Send/Receive Group check box.

- If you're expecting an important message and your next scheduled automatic connection is hours away, make a manual connection.

- If you have only one phone line at home, you probably want to check for mail only when you're certain other family members aren't on the phone.

When you click the Send/Receive button on the Standard toolbar, Outlook checks all accounts for which you've specified this option. To check a single account, choose Tools, Send/Receive; then select the correct account or group from the cascading menu.

SETTING NOTIFICATIONS

Outlook offers to notify you in several ways when you've received new mail:

- The two most subtle options play a sound and briefly change the mouse pointer when you receive new mail. To adjust either setting, you need to burrow several dialog boxes into the Outlook interface. Choose Tools, Options; click the Preferences tab; click the E-mail Options button; and click the Advanced E-mail Options button. If you're not at your computer, you'll completely miss both these cues.

- A more persistent but still subtle reminder is the icon that appears in the notification area to the right of the Windows taskbar (this area is also sometimes called the tray). An envelope icon here means you've received new mail; double-click the icon to open the Inbox and read the messages. You can't eliminate this icon.

- The most intrusive form of e-mail notification is a pop-up message that takes over your screen when new mail arrives. By default, this option is off, thankfully. Although we don't recommend enabling it, you can do so by opening the Options dialog box and clicking the E-mail Options button on the Preferences tab.

SPEED-READING NEW MESSAGES WITH THE PREVIEW PANE

As noted at the beginning of this chapter, heavy e-mail users sometimes get hundreds of messages a day, and dealing with them all means you have to make decisions in seconds. When time is of the essence, we suggest you use the Preview pane to blast through messages at lightning speed:

1. Switch to Unread Messages view. We recommend keeping the Advanced toolbar visible at all times so you can use the Views drop-down list to switch views anytime.

2. If the Preview pane at the bottom of the message window isn't visible, click the Preview Pane button. Using this pane lets you quickly scan any message without having to open it.

3. Choose Tools, Options; click the Other tab; and click the Preview Pane button to display the Preview Pane dialog box shown in Figure 10.18. Check the bottom two boxes here to mark mail as read when you view it in the Preview pane; if you want to be able to skip over some and leave them marked as unread, check the top box instead.

Figure 10.18

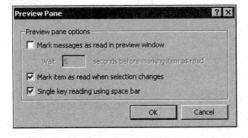

> If you're unable to view some messages in the Preview pane, see "When Active Means Invisible" in the "Troubleshooting" section at the end of this chapter.

4. Begin reading your mail. Use the spacebar to move through each message without using the arrow keys. As you finish with each message, press Ctrl+R to compose a reply, Ctrl+Shift+R to reply to all. Press the Delete key to trash the message, or press the spacebar to move to the next message. When you do so, Outlook marks the previous message as read, removes it from the current view (but leaves it in the Inbox folder), and jumps to the next message.

WORKING WITH ATTACHMENTS

Outlook 2002 is ruthless with file attachments. With some file types, in fact, it simply refuses to allow you to access attachments at all. This is not a bug; it's a controversial security feature designed to protect users from possibly dangerous attachments.

Every time you receive an e-mail message with an attached file, Outlook 2002 checks the file extension for that attachment, using a list of extensions stored in the Registry. If the extension is on that list, Outlook may force you to save the file before opening it, or it may forbid you to access the attachment in any way.

The attachment security list divides potentially dangerous files into two levels. So-called Level 1 files—executable files, shortcuts, scripts, Access databases, and other objects that can conceivably carry viruses or other harmful content—are considered the most dangerous. When Outlook finds a Level 1 file, it displays a banner in the Info pane that tells you it has blocked access to a file; the message includes the full name of the attached file. (To see a full list of the blocked attachment types, search the Help files for the topic, "Attachment File Types Blocked by Outlook.")

If you have an account on an Exchange Server, your administrator can change any Level 1 file type to a Level 2 file type. In that case, when Outlook detects that file type, it forces you to save the file to your hard disk, where, presumably, it will be scanned for known viruses using the antivirus software you have installed.

Part

II

Ch

10

Tip from

EQ & Woody

You *do* have antivirus software installed, right? It has been updated recently, hasn't it? Do yourself a favor—if you don't have an up-to-date antivirus program installed, download one now (we'll wait right here) and protect yourself. Windows users have dozens of choices in antivirus software, including some that are absolutely free. For an excellent list of available alternatives and links to useful information, visit the Antivirus site at About.com (`http://antivirus.about.com`). If you have installed antivirus software, make sure you keep its definition files up to date so you're not bitten by fast-spreading new viruses.

Although Exchange administrators can customize this behavior, Outlook users can't easily tweak these settings using the Outlook interface. However, it is possible to change this behavior by editing the Registry. Look for this key:

```
HKEY_CURRENT_USER\Software\Microsoft\Office\10.0\Outlook\Security
```

Under that key, add a new string value, name it `Level1Remove`, and fill in its value using a list of file extensions, separated by semicolons. Entering `url;hlp` allows Outlook to launch Internet shortcuts and Help files directly from a mail message.

Tip from

Ed & Woody

You don't need to hack the Registry to fix this Outlook annoyance. Outlook MVP Ken Slovak has written a free add-in program that adds a new tab to the Tools, Options dialog box. You can pick and choose file extensions that are included or excluded from the Level 1 category or click one button that tells Outlook 2002 that you want to be able to make your own decisions about *all* file attachments. Get Ken's program from http://www.slipstick.com/outlook/esecup/getexe.htm#ol2002.

Attachments that Outlook deems safe (including Word documents, Excel workbooks, and Zip files) appear in the Preview pane and in message windows, where Outlook displays an icon and filename for each attached file. These details appear in the Attachments line, just below the Subject. You can't drag and drop these attachment icons, but you can Right-click any icon and use shortcut menus to open, print, save, or remove that attachment. To quickly save an attached file in an open Explorer window, for instance, right-click on the attachment icon and choose Copy. Then right-click in the Explorer window and choose Paste. The same technique works for copying attachments between e-mail messages.

Tip from

Ed & Woody

Want to work around these restrictions? Get in the habit of using Zip compression on all attachments. Outlook waves Zip files right through, without stopping, without checking the archive file's contents. Presumably any user who's smart enough to use a Zip utility will also be responsible enough to have antivirus software.

ORGANIZING YOUR E-MAIL

In some organizations, e-mail is the preferred mode of communication, and it's not uncommon for a busy manager to receive hundreds of messages per day. Trying to process that tidal wave of mail can be an overwhelming task if you're not in front of a computer constantly.

Over time, experienced Outlook users usually develop the ability to blast through a crowded Inbox at warp speed, using the Preview pane and message headers to quickly make snap judgments about which messages are worth reading and which can safely be tossed.

You can drag messages into folders to keep them organized, but it's smarter still to create Outlook rules that process messages automatically. In less than the time it takes to read a day's e-mail, you can create a set of rules that can easily help you avoid wasting time on junk e-mail, file messages by category or project, and also ensure that you never miss an important message because it was buried in your Inbox.

Tip from

Ed & Woody

Two built-in shortcuts are especially useful for locating related messages or for finding all messages from the same sender. From the message list, right-click any message and then choose Find All. Choose Related Messages to find all messages that are part of the same conversation (the original message and all replies); choose Messages from Sender to display a list of all messages in the current folder from the sender of the selected message. In either case, Outlook opens the Advanced Find dialog box and displays the results there.

To launch Outlook's most basic message-processing tool, open your Inbox and click the Organize button on the Standard toolbar. The Organize pane slides into position just above the message window, as shown in Figure 10.19. Under the right circumstances, three of the options shown here are useful:

Figure 10.19
The Organize pane lets you create one specific type of rule to sort mail to or from a specific address.

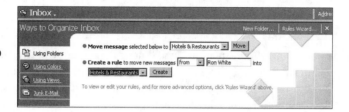

→ For details on how you can highlight contacts, mail messages, and other items, **see** "Assigning Items to Categories," **p. 212**.

- Select a message, and then click the Using Folders option to create a rule that moves mail from the sender of that message to a folder you specify. This option is especially useful for dealing with messages you receive because you subscribe to a particular mailing list; if you receive daily digests from the Doberman Fanciers list, use this option to file them in their own folder automatically. In some cases, you might need to click the drop-down arrow and define a Sent To rule. This option is appropriate when you subscribe to a list in which the sender's name differs each time but the recipient is always the same.

- Click the Using Colors option to specify that you want all messages from or sent to a specific person to appear in your Inbox in a certain color. Use this option to format messages from your boss in bright red, for example.

- Click the Junk E-Mail option to turn on Outlook's automatic rules for filtering suspected junk mail and so-called adult content, such as come-ons for X-rated Web sites. (We'll explain how junk-mail filters work a little later in this section.)

The Organize pane is a bare-bones tool with virtually no options, designed to build a rule from the current message. As long as you understand its limitations, you can make good use of it. It's most effective for mail that is highly predictable, always arriving in exactly the same format from the same sender. Rules you create this way will search for text that precisely matches the entry in the current message. If you receive mail from a correspondent who uses multiple e-mail accounts with different Sender names, you'll need to define multiple rules to process the mail correctly.

Tip from

EQ & Woody

Don't dismiss the Organize pane out of hand. Although its utility is limited, it has one praiseworthy feature: When you create multiple rules to move messages from different senders to a common folder, it consolidates those rules into one. So if you determine that some people in your company never, ever send you important messages, create a folder called Boring Company Mail (BCM). Each time you identify another coworker who's consistently wasting your time with trivial e-mail, select a message from that person, click the Organize button, and create a rule to send all future messages from that dullard to the BCM folder. Eventually, this rule will define a list of the least interesting people in your organization!

USING THE RULES WIZARD TO SORT AND PROCESS MAIL

For the bulk of mail-handling situations, you'll need greater control over the conditions and actions defined in rules. To use these more advanced options, choose Tools, Rules Wizard. The Rules Wizard dialog box (see Figure 10.20) shows you all the rules you've previously defined and lets you create new rules and manage existing ones from a central location.

Figure 10.20
The Rules Wizard builds mail-processing rules one step at a time; the Rule Description pane (bottom) shows details of the selected rule.

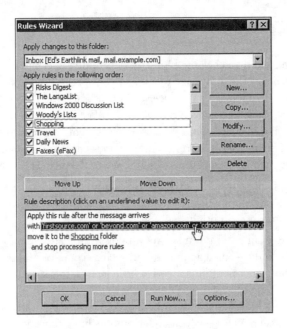

Note
Note that rules you create using the Rules Wizard do not apply to HTTP (Web-based) accounts such as Hotmail or MSN.

Use custom rules to handle the following categories of messages you send and receive:

- **Urgent Mail**—If you sometimes receive messages from key contacts who need immediate assistance, you want to know ASAP. Create a rule that pops up a dialog box as soon as messages containing hot-button words—urgent or problem, for example—arrive from particular senders.

- **Personal Mail**—Move personal messages from family members and friends into a designated folder when they arrive in the Inbox.

- **Posts to Mailing Lists**—Delete messages you send to mailing lists instead of saving them in your Sent Items folder, because you'll receive your message when you receive the next edition of the list.

- **Mail from Other Accounts**—Move all mail you receive from a particular account (a personal account you check at work, for example) into a special folder so you can clearly segregate it.

- **Commercial Mail**—Identify commercial e-mail from companies that you truly want to hear from. If your favorite online bookstore, music dealer, or travel agent occasionally sends you notices of deals you might be interested in, you can flag these messages for special handling.

- **General Clutter**—Create a set of cleanup rules you run periodically before archiving messages, such as one that identifies messages with large attachments and moves them to a special folder. Set these rules so they don't run automatically on new messages you receive in the Inbox; instead, use the Run Now button in the Rules Wizard to apply them to selected folders, including your archive folders, when you're ready to perform major cleanup operations on a Personal Folders file.

PART

II

CH

10

Tip from

Ed & Woody

> Outlook stores all rules you define in a file called Microsoft Outlook Internet Settings.rwz, in a subfolder of your personal profile, if applicable (on a system running Windows 2000, for example, you'll find this file in C:\Windows\Profiles\<*username*>\ Application Data\Microsoft\Outlook). It's always a good idea to back up your current rules to a new file; as a bonus, you can use this feature to share mail-handling rules with other people or with multiple systems. To save rules in a file, choose Tools, Rules Wizard, click the Options button, and choose Export Rules. To restore rules from this file or to add rules that a friend or co-worker defined and sent to you, choose Import Rules.

To begin creating a rule, choose Tools, Rules Wizard. The wizard walks you through five steps. As you check options in the top of the dialog box, the rule appears in the bottom pane; when you see underlined text in the condition or action, click to pop up a dialog box to add more details. (Editing a rule works the same way; open the Rules Wizard dialog box, select a rule, and click the Edit button.)

If you've defined a rule and it doesn't work properly on incoming messages, see "A Rule Isn't Working as You Expect" in the "Troubleshooting" section at the end of this chapter.

Step 1: Specify the Type of Rule

You can choose from nine templates (see Figure 10.21), most of which are predefined combinations of options available in succeeding steps. If your rule doesn't fit into any of these predefined categories, choose the Start from a Blank Rule option and start with one of the two general-purpose rules: Check Messages When They Arrive and Check Messages After Sending.

Figure 10.21

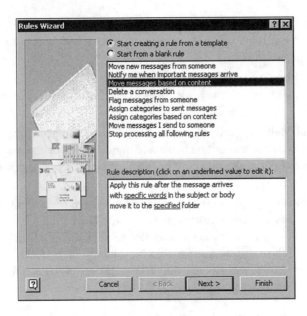

STEP 2: CHOOSE CONDITIONS

The Rules Wizard offers a list of 28 options you can use to define almost any combination of *conditions*. Your range of options is impressive:

Tip from
Ed & Woody

> You can enter multiple data items for any condition that requires you to specify items. Enter each item individually and click the Add button after each one. Outlook will add them to the list, separated by a logical "or."

- By account (choose the Through the Specified Account option).
- Is an incoming message addressed specifically to you? Rules can determine whether your name is or is not in the To or Cc box, for example, or when a message is sent only to you. Fine-tune combinations of conditions to highlight mail that is indisputably for you (Sent Only to Me, especially when you add conditions that test who sent the message) or identify less important mail (Where My Name Is Not in the To Box).
- Attach conditions that test for a specific sender or recipient: From People or Distribution List or Sent to People or Distribution List. These conditions depend on Outlook's capability to resolve an address in your Address Book.

→ To learn more about handling Personal Distribution Lists, **see** "Creating and Using Personal Distribution Lists," **p. 244**.

- Use two extremely powerful conditions to fine-tune rules that search for mail from a specific person or group of people, regardless of whether they're in your Address Book. Check With Specific Words in the Recipient's Address or With Specific Words in the Sender's Address, and then enter any part of the e-mail address you want to test for.

Tip from

Ed & Woody

Use this option to identify all mail that arrives from anyone in a particular organization or domain. While working on this book, for example, we created a rule and applied special handling to any message that arrived from any recipient whose address contained `quepublishing.com`.

- Search for specific words in the subject or body, or in the message header. Use this condition in combination with those that search for messages from a specific person to look for hot-button words: With `quepublishing.com` in the Recipient's Address and With `deadline` in the Subject or Body, for example.

- To create cleanup rules, or to identify messages that might bloat your mail file on a system with limited storage, use the conditions that test whether a message has an attachment or has a size in a specific range.

STEP 3: SPECIFY ONE OR MORE ACTIONS

Outlook applies actions you choose here to messages that meet the conditions you specify. Note that if you've selected one of the prebuilt rules from Step 1 of the wizard, some options will already be checked.

- One of the most powerful options available is Notify Me Using a `Specific Message`. Using this option, you can tell Outlook to interrupt whatever you're doing and display a dialog box that alerts you to important incoming messages. If you're working on a group project under deadline pressure, for example, you might define this type of rule for messages from any address in your company that contains an attachment. If your stockbroker uses e-mail to alert you to important developments in the stock market, you can tell Outlook you want to know immediately whenever you receive a message from that address. Figure 10.22 shows an example of a dialog box generated by an Outlook rule.

Figure 10.22

- One of the most interesting options available here is the Stop Processing More Rules choice. Use this option to avoid unintended consequences when rules collide. For example, if you want to be notified when you receive a message sent only to you from your boss, check the proper conditions and actions; then scroll to the bottom of this dialog box and click this option. Make sure rules using this option are high on your list.

- You can move messages that match your defined conditions to a specified folder, copy them to a folder (including a public folder on an Exchange server), delete them (move to Deleted Items folder), or permanently delete them.

Caution

Never, ever use the Permanently Delete It action on rules that apply to incoming messages. No matter how carefully you define a rule, it's possible that the Rules Wizard will inadvertently apply it to the wrong message; use the Delete It condition to move messages to the Deleted Items folder instead, where it's possible to recover messages moved by mistake. Reserve the permanent option for cleanup rules only.

- Forward messages to an address you select, either as an e-mail message or as an attachment. Use the latter option if you want the recipient to see the message exactly as it was received.

- The Reply Using a `Specific Template` option is powerful and potentially dangerous. You might be tempted to use this option to send a message automatically to anyone who sends you mail, alerting them that you've gone on vacation. Unfortunately, if you apply that option to all incoming messages, you risk creating an e-mail loop with automated message senders. If you receive a message from a mailing list and Outlook replies automatically to the list, for example, the list server might send a message telling you that you're not authorized to post to the list; if Outlook replies to that message, the loop begins. Craft this type of rule carefully and test it before deploying it in a production environment.

- Flag a message for action in a specified number of days (or clear a flag, useful in a cleanup rule), assign it to a category, change its Importance setting, play a sound, or start an application.

Note

Most Outlook users can safely ignore the Perform a `Custom Action` option, which applies only when you have a third-party add-in that defines special actions for incoming messages.

STEP 4: ADD ANY EXCEPTIONS

In general, the 25 built-in categories here mirror the conditions you specify in Step 2 of the wizard. Defining exceptions is a powerful way to fine-tune rules: "Delete all messages from John Smith except if my name is in the To or Cc box" will squelch posts from particularly annoying senders who post to mailing lists you receive.

STEP 5: SAVE THE RULE

In the Rules Wizard's final step, give the rule a name and check all conditions, actions, and exceptions in the dialog box shown in Figure 10.23. Use the two check boxes here to specify whether you want to run the rule on the contents of the current folder immediately and whether you want to enable the rule. Clear the second check box for "cleanup" rules you want to run occasionally.

Figure 10.23
The final step of the Rules Wizard lets you confirm all the steps in your rule and run it on the current folder.

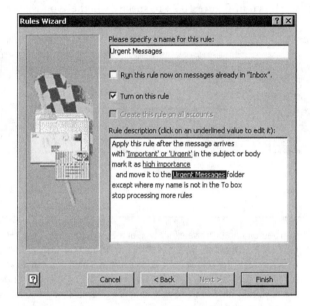

USING OUTLOOK'S JUNK AND ADULT CONTENT FILTERS

As mentioned earlier, Outlook includes two built-in junk-mail filters that try to identify adult content (solicitations to visit pornographic Web sites, for example) and junk mail (also known as Unsolicited Commercial E-mail, or *spam*). These filters use lists of known attributes and keywords common to both types of unwanted messages. A message with the subject $$$ MAKE MONEY FAST! is nearly certain to trigger the junk-mail filters, for instance.

Note

To see the full list of built-in junk mail and adult content filters, search for a file called Filters.txt. In a default Office installation using U.S. English, this file is located in C:\Program Files\Microsoft Office\Office10\1033.

You can add specific addresses to the list of senders you want to process using these filters; you can also define exceptions to avoid false positives. If your baby sister can't resist adding exclamation points to her subject line and your accountant routinely puts dollar signs in his messages, add both addresses to the Exceptions list.

Both the Junk Mail and Adult Content filters are turned off by default; enabling either or both options adds new rules in the Rules Wizard: an Adult Content rule, a Junk E-mail rule, and an Exceptions List rule. To enable and configure either or both filters, follow these steps:

1. Switch to the Inbox, click the Organize button on the Standard toolbar, and click the Junk E-mail link.

2. Use the options shown in Figure 10.24 to specify whether you want to color-code messages that match either filter or move them to another folder.

Figure 10.24

Outlook uses color-coding to identify messages that match junk and adult content filters; if you're certain they work properly, move messages to another folder instead.

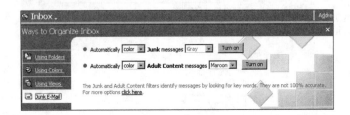

Tip from

Don't automatically move either type of message to the Deleted Items folder—at least not until you're certain the filters work reliably for you. Instead, start by color-coding each message; the default for junk mail is gray. Later, you can move each type of message to its own folder. For the first few weeks after enabling either of these filters, you'll typically need to do some fine-tuning to avoid inadvertently detecting messages you want to read as junk e-mail.

3. Click the Turn On button to the right of either filter type to enable the specified filter. (This button changes to read Turn Off after you've applied the filter.)

To add a sender to either list, regardless of the content of messages they send, select a message from that sender in the Inbox; then right-click and choose Junk E-mail, Add to Junk Senders List or Add to Adult Content Senders List.

Tip from

In fact, you can add an entire domain to the Junk Senders or Adult Content list. If you routinely receive unwanted messages from different senders at the same domain, you can add the entire domain to the list. Choose Tools, Organize, and click the Junk Mail option. Click the link at the bottom of the pane to display additional options. Click the Edit Junk Senders or Edit Adult Senders list to add addresses manually. Enter a domain (like example.com) to filter out all messages from that domain.

To add any sender's name to the Exception list so that it is not inadvertently trapped by these filters, open a message from that sender, right-click the From address, and choose Copy. Then open the Rules Wizard, select the Exception List rule, and click the underlined text in the description pane at the bottom of the dialog box. Click the Add button and paste the address you copied into the text box. Close all dialog boxes.

Occasionally, Microsoft issues updates to its junk-mail and adult content filters. Click the link at the bottom of the Junk Mail Organizer pane to download this update.

TROUBLESHOOTING

WHEN ACTIVE MEANS INVISIBLE

The Preview pane says it can't display the message because it contains active content.

That's Outlook's maddeningly roundabout way of telling you the message is in Rich Text format and contains a script. Open the message to read it.

WHEN YOUR E-MAIL BOUNCES

I replied to a post on an Internet newsgroup via e-mail, but my mail server bounced the message back to me, saying the recipient doesn't exist.

More than anywhere else, people who post to public newsgroups are likely to disguise their true e-mail address. The reason is to prevent bulk-mail artists—spammers—from harvesting their address and reselling it to scam artists. Check the header on the message carefully to see whether the true e-mail address is hidden. Sometimes the solution is as simple as removing the phrase *no.spam* from an address such as *bianca@no.spam.example.com*.

A RULE ISN'T WORKING AS YOU EXPECT

I used the Rules Wizard to define a mail-processing rule, but Outlook isn't processing the message as I expected it to.

This problem is almost always the result of conflicting actions from multiple rules. First things first: Check the order of rules, and pay special attention to any rule that contains the Stop Processing More Rules action. You might have defined two rules that apply to the message in question (it's from a specific person and it contains a certain phrase, for example), and each rule wants to move the message to a different folder. When the actions in two or more rules conflict in this way, the one that's higher in the list wins. Try changing the order of the rules, using the Move Up and Move Down buttons. Finally, be especially careful with rules that create message flags with reminders; if another rule also moves that message to a different folder, you'll never see the reminder, because Outlook monitors flags only on messages in the Inbox. Rules that attach message flags should always be high in the list, and they should include a Stop Processing More Rules action.

SECRETS OF THE OFFICE MASTERS: EXPERT STRATEGIES FOR OUTLOOK RULES

Outlook rules follow a rigid set of logical standards. Knowing how rules work can help you troubleshoot problems:

- When rules contains multiple conditions, they are always treated as logical AND statements: The subject contains "budget" AND the sender is "Bill Green." You must create separate rules to apply OR logic.

- Within a condition, items you specify are always treated as though they are joined with a logical OR: The sender is "Woody Leonhard" or "Ed Bott" or "Bill Green."

Note

If you are connected to a Microsoft Exchange Server, you can create rules using the Out of Office Assistant. These rules are applied at the server rather than on arrival in your Inbox. Your Exchange administrator can offer more information on how these rules work with your server.

In general, you'll get best results from Outlook rules when you follow these guidelines:

- Deal with your most important messages first. Identify messages you definitely want to receive and handle them with rules at the top of the list, ending each such rule with the Stop Processing More Rules condition. This guarantees that a less important filter doesn't inadvertently catch a message that you want to keep.

- Try to combine similar rules to reduce clutter. For instance, if you subscribe to daily updates from several online newspapers, you can create a single rule that moves all those messages to a Daily News folder. Use AutoArchive options to clean all messages out of this folder after a week or two.

- Give each rule a meaningful name. A descriptive name can help you sort through a list of rules more quickly.

- Back up your Outlook Rules regularly. The more work you put into constructing them, the more you'll appreciate being able to recover them in the event of a problem.

CHAPTER 11

TRACKING APPOINTMENTS AND TASKS

In this chapter

MANAGING YOUR PERSONAL CALENDAR

Outlook's Calendar folder can keep track of any number of appointments and meetings, whether they're one-time-only events or recurring appointments that repeat on a regular schedule. Although you can print a calendar for reference, Outlook's calendaring features are best suited to people whose duties keep them close to a computer screen most of the time, or those who have a handheld Palm or Pocket PC that can synchronize data from Outlook's Calendar, Task list, and Contacts folder.

If you've been using Outlook 2000, one improvement in this release is worth noting: As explained later in this chapter, you can color-code appointments manually or using automatic rules.

The default view of the Calendar folder (shown in Figure 11.1) displays a day's worth of appointments and a short list of tasks. It also includes a two-month calendar control called the Date Navigator; as the name implies, you can click here to quickly jump from today to any date in the past or future.

Figure 11.1
Use the Date Navigator, to the right of the Appointments list and above the TaskPad, to quickly jump to a different date.

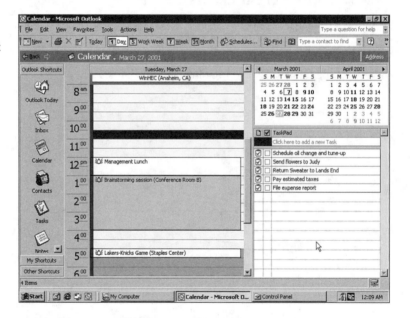

Use the left- and right arrows to move backward and forward a month at a time in the Date Navigator. For long-distance jumps, however, there's a secret, undocumented shortcut. Click the name of a month above the Date Navigator and hold down the mouse button to see a list that includes the three months before and after the current month. Drag the pointer below or above the list to scroll to any month, and then release the mouse button to jump to that month.

CREATING A NEW APPOINTMENT OR EVENT

You can create three similar types of items in the Calendar folder. *Appointments* have starting and ending times blocked out in your schedule; *events*, such as vacations and business trips, last 24 hours or more; and *meetings* are appointments to which you invite other people.

→ To see how Outlook can help you coordinate meetings, **see** "Planning a Meeting with Outlook," **p. 318**.

If you want to add a new item to your personal calendar and you know the date and time of the appointment or event, you can open a new appointment form with those details already filled in. Open or switch to a window displaying the contents of the Calendar folder, and then use any of these techniques:

- From any Day view (including multiday views), use the Date Navigator to select the correct date, and then double-click a time slot to open a new appointment. Outlook uses the default appointment interval of 30 minutes. To use a different interval, click and drag the mouse pointer from the start time to the end time, and then right-click and choose New Appointment.

- In Week or Month view, select the date of the appointment, and then right-click and choose New Appointment; this creates an appointment with a start time that is the default starting time for the day. If you select multiple dates, Outlook creates a new event on the selected dates, with no start or end times.

- To open a new event form from any view, right-click and choose New All Day Event.

You can also create an appointment instantly by dragging an e-mail message from your Inbox and dropping it on the Calendar icon in the Outlook Bar. This shortcut can be a true time-saver when you receive a message that includes essential details about an upcoming event. The subject of the mail message becomes the subject of the appointment, and the message text appears in the Notes area of the appointment form. You'll probably need to adjust the date and time, however, because by default Outlook uses the next available block of time in today's schedule.

If you've looked up a name in your Contacts folder and you want to create an appointment that includes a link to that person, don't just drag the item onto the Calendar icon—that action creates a meeting request addressed to the selected person. Instead, hold down the right mouse button and drag the item from the Contacts folder, drop it on the Calendar icon, and then choose Copy Here As Appointment with Text. If you drag two or more Contact items into the Calendar folder, Outlook assumes you want to include all the information in a single appointment.

To see the maximum amount of information in an appointment you create by dragging and dropping a Contact item, switch to Detailed Address Cards view in your Contacts folder first.

You can create a new appointment from scratch by using any of the following techniques:

- Click the New Appointment button.
- Press Ctrl+Shift+A.
- Choose File, New, Appointment.

Enter a name for the appointment in the Subject field, and then tab from field to field and add more details. Click the Save and Close button when you're finished. Add details about the meeting in the Notes area just below the Reminder field. You can also add attachments here, including files, copies of Outlook items, or shortcuts to files or Outlook items. Figure 11.2 shows a filled-in appointment form.

Figure 11.2
Like most Outlook items, appointments can include file attachments and links to Contacts.

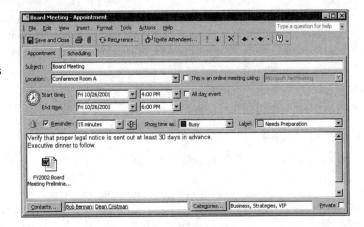

→ To learn how Outlook will fill in times and dates for you, **see** "Entering Dates and Times Automatically," **p. 210**.

→ To learn how to organize Outlook items using categories, **see** "Assigning Items to Categories," **p. 212**.

→ To learn more about instructing Outlook to remind you of important activities, **see** "Creating Reminders and Flagging Items for Follow-Up," **p. 213**.

TABLE 11.1   STANDARD APPOINTMENT FIELDS

Field Name	Description
Subject	Enter the text you want to see in Calendar view. Although you can enter up to 255 characters, you should keep the Subject line much shorter—preferably 30 characters or fewer. Subject lines over about 150 characters will not print correctly in Tri-fold format.
Location	Enter a location; the drop-down list lets you choose from among the 10 locations you entered most recently (you can't customize this list or change its order).

TABLE 11.1   CONTINUED

Field Name	Description
Start Time, End Time	Enter starting and ending times and dates by using any common date and time format or an AutoDate description; click the arrow to the right of a date or time field to select from a calendar control or a list of preset times.
This Is an Online Meeting Using	Check this box to create a link to NetMeeting or other online conferencing software.
All Day Event	Checking this box removes the Start Time and End Time fields from the form; when you enter an event, Outlook's default settings show the time in your shared schedule as Free.
Reminder	Appointments can pop up reminders at times you define; unless you change the defaults (as described in Chapter 9, "Outlook Essentials"), Outlook adds a reminder 15 minutes before every appointment.
Show Time As	Specify how others view your calendar by designating the time an appointment takes as Busy, Free, Tentative, or Out of Office. Each of these four descriptions uses a different color in Calendar views. You cannot add new descriptions to this list. This option is useful when you use the Delegate option on an Exchange Server; other people can't see details of your schedule, but they at least know whether you're in the office.
Label	This option, new in Outlook 2002, lets you color-code appointments using one of 10 labels. You can apply a label manually or use rules to color-code appointments on-the-fly.
Contacts	Click this button to link an appointment to one or more items in your Contacts folder.
Categories	Assign appointments to categories, just as you do contacts and tasks. See Chapter 9 for a list of standard categories and instructions on how to create new ones of your own.
Private	Check to designate an appointment as private so no one who looks at your shared schedule will know that you've gone to the ballgame. Details of private appointments do not appear on shared calendars, although the time is blocked out; when printing, you can choose to hide details of appointments marked Private.

PART
II

CH

11

ENTERING A RECURRING APPOINTMENT

Some appointments and events are one-shot deals, but others—like it or not—happen over and over again. When you enter details for a recurring appointment, Outlook manages the entire series from a single appointment form. You can specify recurring patterns on a daily, weekly, monthly, or annual basis. The options for recurring appointments are surprisingly flexible

→ To learn more about setting up recurring tasks, **see** "Entering Recurring Tasks," **p. 286**.

To set up a *recurring appointment* or event, create the item from scratch or open an existing item, and then click the Recurrence button to display the Appointment Recurrence dialog box (see Figure 11.3).

Figure 11.3
Use this dialog box to schedule even complicated recurring appointments, like this one every Tuesday and Thursday at 4:00 p.m. for the next 5 weeks or 10 occurrences.

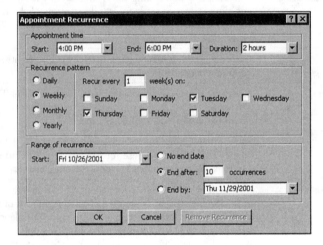

Adjust the options as needed to match the schedule of your event. Enter an ending date or a fixed number of occurrences, if appropriate, and click OK. Then click Save and Close to add the recurring appointment or event to your Calendar folder. Outlook adds a recurrence icon to the left of the event description in all Calendar views.

To edit a recurring appointment or event, open the item. A dialog box lets you specify whether you want to change the entire series or just the selected instance. If your production department moves this week's status meeting from its regular slot of Wednesday at 2:00 p.m., you can change the times for that occurrence without affecting the rest of the items in the series. On the other hand, if a new production manager decides to move the meetings to Monday mornings, you can edit the entire series, and you need to change the details only once to reschedule all future occurrences.

Tip from

To see a list of all recurring appointments and events (and edit one or more of them, if necessary), switch to Outlook's predefined Recurring Appointments view. Note that this list includes birthdays and anniversaries, which Outlook treats as recurring annual events.

RESCHEDULING AN APPOINTMENT OR EVENT

The most labor-intensive way to change the date and time of an appointment or event is by opening the item and manually adjusting the entries in the Start Time and End Time fields. Try these time-saving shortcuts instead:

- To change the scheduled starting time for an appointment in any Day view (including multiday views), point to the left border of the item until the pointer turns into a four-headed arrow, and then drag the item to its new time.

- To move an item to a different day, point to the left border until the pointer turns into a four-headed arrow; then drag the item and drop it on the selected day in Week or Month view or in the Date Navigator. (If the date you want is not visible in any of these places, you must use the Cut, Copy, and Paste options on the Edit menu instead.)

- To copy an item to a new date and time, hold down the Ctrl key and drag the item to the new date by using the Week or Month view or the Date Navigator. This technique is particularly useful when scheduling a follow-up appointment; because copying the appointment item also copies all its details, you eliminate the need to search for your notes from the original meeting when it's time for the follow-up.

Tip from
EQ & Woody

If you want to edit the description of an event or appointment, without adjusting its date, time, or details, click its listing in any daily, weekly, or monthly Calendar view and edit the text directly. As soon as you click the text to begin editing, the location (in parentheses after the description text) disappears; the only way to edit location information is to open the form.

PART

II

CH

11

VIEWING A DAILY, WEEKLY, OR MONTHLY CALENDAR

When you first click the Calendar icon in the Outlook Bar, you see today's schedule in Day/Week/Month view. The default view of your appointments shows just one day at a time, but you can expand the view to cover appointments that span multiple days, one or more weeks, or a full month at a time.

USING THE DATE NAVIGATOR

The Date Navigator is the small calendar that appears on the right side of the Calendar window, just above the TaskPad. Like similar controls elsewhere in Office, the Date Navigator lets you quickly jump to any date to see the appointments and events scheduled for that date. Bold numbers in the Date Navigator tell you that appointments or events are scheduled on those days.

By default, the Date Navigator is visible in Day and Week views; it displays the current month and next month. To change the number of months shown in the Date Navigator, drag the left border, the bottom border, or both. To see four months at a time, for example, drag the bottom border of the Date Navigator down until you see two rows of two months each.

SWITCHING BETWEEN DAY, WEEK, AND MONTH VIEWS

Four buttons on the Calendar folder's Standard toolbar let you quickly switch between Outlook's built-in views.

Click the Day button to display one day's events. Use the Date Navigator to show another day's schedule, or click the Go to Today button to jump back to today's calendar. Press the Page Up and Page Down keys to scroll through that day's calendar; use the left- and right-arrow keys to move through the Calendar folder one day at a time.

Tip from

Ed & Woody

In any Day view (including the built-in Work Week view and others that include multiple days), pressing Home takes you to the beginning of the workday and End jumps to the end of the workday—8:00 a.m. and 5:00 p.m., unless you adjust these defaults. Press Ctrl+Home or Ctrl+End to jump to the beginning or end of the day—midnight in either direction.

Click the Work Week button to show a side-by-side view of five days at a time, leaving off weekends, as in the example in Figure 11.4. Because the display for each day is extremely narrow, don't expect to read the full description of each event; point to any item to see a ScreenTip that includes its time, subject, location, and up to the first 12 lines from the Notes field.

Figure 11.4
Use the Work Week view to see five days at a time (customize the display if your work week is different). ScreenTips help you identify each item without opening it.

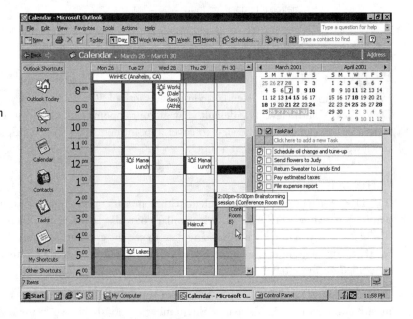

Click the Week button to display a full week's schedule (see Figure 11.5), with each day's appointments in a box; Saturday and Sunday listings are half the size of other days. As in other views, all-day events appear in a banner at the top of each day, with multiday events extending over the tops of several days. Press Page Up and Page Down to move through the calendar a week at a time.

Figure 11.5
Unlike daily views, the Week view shows only scheduled items and events in the block for each day.

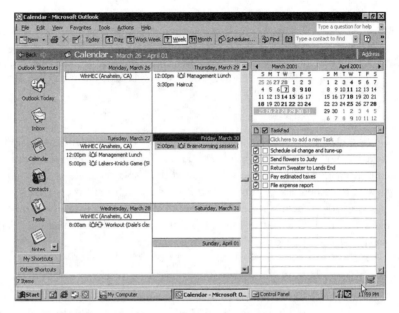

Click the Month button to see a month-at-a-glance calendar (see Figure 11.6), with event descriptions truncated to fit; the Date Navigator and TaskPad are normally hidden in this view, although you can drag the right border of the calendar to make them visible. To jump a month at a time in either direction in this view, use the Page Up and Page Down keys, or the vertical scrollbar at the right of the window. The Home and End keys jump to the beginning and end of the current week.

PART

II

CH

11

Figure 11.6
In this monthly view, as in all other views, clicking an appointment selects it, and double-clicking opens it.

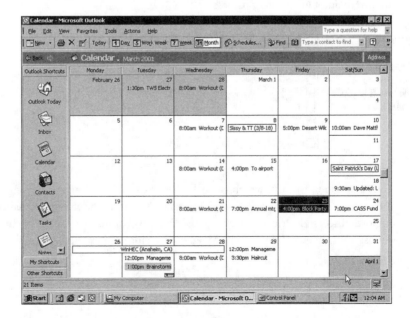

Tip from

EQ & Woody

In any Day/Week/Month Calendar view, press Alt+Page Up to go to the first day of the current month or Alt+Page Down to jump to the last day. Each time you press either key again, you'll move one month in that direction. If you start on March 15, for example, pressing Alt+Page Down repeatedly takes you to March 31, April 30, May 31, June 30, and so on.

Use the Date Navigator to create a custom view of your calendar that's different from the standard day, week, and month views. Hold down the Ctrl key while you click two or more dates (they don't have to be adjacent), and the display changes to show you a side-by-side view of the schedules for the selected days. This technique is especially useful if you're checking your schedule to see which day works best for a meeting or business trip. A multi-day view can display up to 14 days at a time, side by side, although it's nearly impossible to see details because each day's display is so narrow.

COLOR-CODING IMPORTANT APPOINTMENTS

If you use Outlook's Calendar to track large numbers of appointments and meetings, it's easy to lose track of individual items. Because each one looks the same on the screen, you might have trouble distinguishing between important meetings (with your boss or your most important client, say) and trivial ones.

A new feature introduced in Outlook 2002 lets you solve that problem by using color codes to highlight items in the Calendar folder. Outlook 2002 includes 10 predefined and color-coded text labels. When creating or editing an appointment or meeting item, use the Label drop-down list (see Figure 11.7) to apply a color coding. By default, for example, red means Important and blue means Business.

Figure 11.7
Use this drop-down list to assign any of the 10 colors to appointments in your Calendar folder.

You can't add to this list, which is hard-wired to exactly 10 entries. But you can change the text associated with each color. For instance, you might change the label on red from Important to High Priority or change Birthday to Family. To work with the list of labels, choose Edit, Labels, Edit Labels. Make your changes in the dialog box shown in Figure 11.8.

Finally, you can tell Outlook to automatically apply a specific color code to an item based on conditions you define. For instance, you might create a condition that applies the Important label to any meeting whose Subject includes your boss's name, or use the Needs Preparation label for any meeting that includes the word Status.

Figure 11.8
Be careful–changes you make here apply to all items, past and present, to which you've assigned that color.

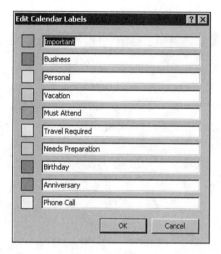

To define an automatic color code, follow these steps:

1. Choose Edit, Automatic Formatting. The Automatic Formatting dialog box (see Figure 11.9) shows all rules you've created previously.

2. Click the Add button to create a new rule. Outlook gives it the default name Untitled.

3. Choose a color and matching text label from the Label list.

4. Click the Condition button and define the criteria that an item must match to be subject to automatic formatting. This dialog box works exactly the same as the Advanced Find dialog box.

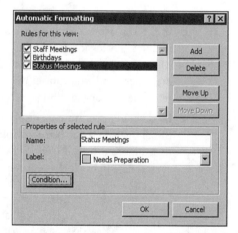

Figure 11.9

5. Click OK to save the rule and apply it instantly to the contents of the Calendar folder.

Note that rules are applied according to their order in the Automatic Formatting dialog box. Rules that are higher on the list prevail over those beneath them. Note, too, that manual formatting always overrides automatic formatting.

CUSTOMIZING THE CALENDAR DISPLAY

To change options for Outlook's built-in Day, Week, and Month views, right-click any unused space in the calendar display and choose Other Settings. The resulting dialog box (shown in Figure 11.10) lets you change the fonts and font sizes used in each of the three views:

Figure 11.10
Adjust these options to change the way Outlook's default Day/Week/Month views display your schedule.

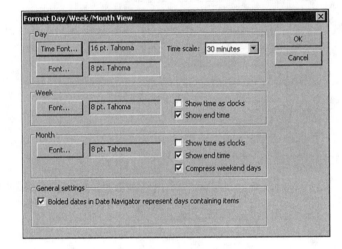

- In the Day view settings, you can adjust the Time Scale from its default setting of 30 minutes. Professionals who bill in 5-, 6-, 10-, or 15-minute increments might want to choose one of these values from the drop-down list; if your schedule is usually light, on the other hand, you can set this value to its maximum of 60 minutes and see your entire schedule without scrolling.

- By default, appointments displayed in Week view include only a starting time. Check the Show End Time box to display end times for each appointment as well. If you want to see more text, check the Show Time as Clocks option, which uses icons to display each time—light clocks represent a.m. and dark clocks are for p.m.

Tip from
EQ & Woody

If your vision is less than 20/20, we recommend that you pass on the option to use tiny clocks to show appointment times in Week and Month views. Trying to identify the position of the microscopic hands, especially against the dark background for p.m. times, is difficult at best, and possibly a painful cause of eyestrain.

- Options for the Month view are the same as those for the Week view, with one addition. Checking the Compress Weekend Days option shows each week in a row of six boxes, beginning on Monday, with Saturday and Sunday sharing a box. Clear the check box to display each day in its own box, for a row of seven boxes for each week. The latter option makes sense if you have busy weekends and you're willing to surrender some screen real estate for weekdays to see a full display for each day of the weekend.

CUSTOMIZING OTHER CALENDAR OPTIONS

Outlook includes another batch of calendar options that let you adjust the basic look and feel of this folder. Choose Tools, Options, click the Preferences tab, and then click the Calendar Options button to display the dialog box shown in Figure 11.11.

Figure 11.11
If you don't follow a Monday-to-Friday schedule, use these options to redefine your work week and its starting date.

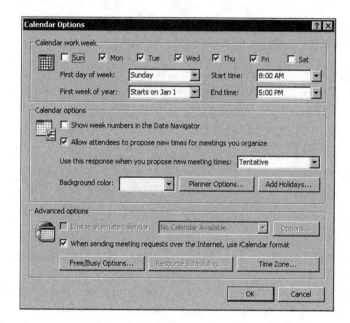

■ In the Calendar Work Week section, check the days that correspond to your work week. In the First Day of Week drop-down list, select the day you want to see at the beginning of Week and Month views. You can also define the Start Time and End Time for your typical work day here.

> **Note**
>
> When you double-click to add an appointment in Week or Month view, Outlook opens a new appointment form using the starting time as defined in this dialog box.

■ Check the Show Week Numbers in the Date Navigator box if you want to see small numbers to the left of each week. This option is most useful for people who work in retail and other industries that measure performance weekly.

■ The Background Color option lets you choose from a limited selection of pastel colors to use behind Day and Work Week views. The default Light Yellow is the most readable.

- If you regularly travel long distances on business, or if you work with people in another part of the world, you can also specify a second time zone to display in daily views of the Calendar folder. That option lets you see at a glance whether you're trying to call Moscow at midnight or Hong Kong at 3:00 a.m., when no one's there to take the call. Click the Time Zone button to open the dialog box shown in Figure 11.12, and then check the Show an Additional Time Zone box. Select the second time zone and give each one a label, and then click OK. (Be sure to read the section at the end of this chapter before changing your time zone, however!)

Figure 11.12
Frequent flyers can click the Time Zone button to add a second time zone along the left side of a Daily calendar view.

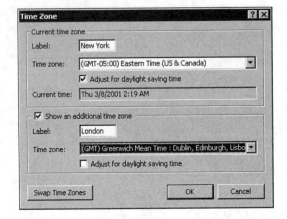

- Click the Add Holidays button to incorporate a list of common holidays into your Outlook calendar. Surprisingly, this feature doesn't use a sophisticated set of calculations to determine when Easter, Thanksgiving, and Yom Kippur fall each year. Instead, Outlook looks at the contents of a text file called Outlook.hol; in a U.S. English installation, this file is stored in C:\Program Files\Microsoft Office\Office10\1033. The Add Holidays dialog box lets you choose which country's holidays should be added to your calendar—a handy option if you routinely travel around the globe.

Tip from
EQ & Woody

To customize the holidays list, open this text file in a text editor and get started. Each group of holidays (organized by country) starts with a name in square brackets; each item in the list includes a name, followed by the date in yyyy/mm/dd format.

- The Resource Scheduling button lets you define options if you're responsible for processing meeting requests for resources, such as conference rooms and slide projectors.
- Click the Free/Busy Options button to display a dialog box that lets you publish information about your calendar to an Internet location for other people to use when scheduling meetings.

→ To learn more about making your Outlook schedule available to other members of your workgroup, **see** "Sharing Group Schedules," **p. 314**.

MAINTAINING A PERSONAL TASK LIST

In Outlook, *tasks* are essentially to-do items. They can be as simple as a note to yourself ("Pick up milk on the way home") or you can add start dates, due dates, and detailed notes, and then track your progress on a complex task over time. Outlook lets you define *one-time tasks* or *recurring tasks*, such as weekly status reports. A list of current tasks appears on the *Outlook Today* page.

→ To learn how you can modify the Outlook Today page to meet your needs, **see** "Customizing the Outlook Today Page," **p. 207**.

ENTERING TASKS

The absolute simplest way to create a task is to view the Tasks folder in Simple List view. To do so, click where you see the gray letters Click Here to Add a New Task, press Tab, enter a due date, and then press Enter to record the task.

To create a new task with more details, choose File, New, Task or press Ctrl+Shift+K. In the Task form (see Figure 11.13), enter the task text in the Subject box and fill in any of the additional fields, all of which are optional.

PART

II

CH

11

Figure 11.13
The only required field for a Task item is the Subject line; enter date and status information if you plan to produce status reports.

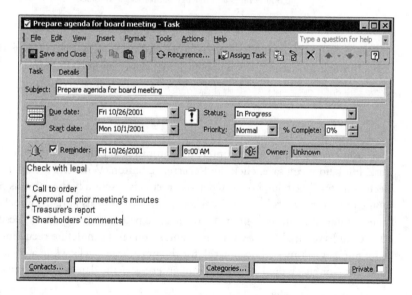

Enter the Due Date first, and then fill in the Start Date. Fill in the Status, Priority, and % Complete boxes only if you want to be able to sort a complex list of tasks using this information. By default, Outlook creates a *reminder* for every task on its due date; if you don't want to set reminders automatically, choose Tools, Options, and click the Preferences tab.

Then click the Task Options button and clear the Set Reminders on Tasks with Due Dates check box.

Add details, notes, and file attachments (including document shortcuts) for the task. Click the Contacts button at the bottom of the form to link to one or more persons in your Contacts list. Click the Categories button to assign the task to *categories*. If you're on a corporate network with an Exchange Server, you can check the Private box to prevent anyone with shared access to your Tasks folder from seeing the details of this item.

→ Sorting your Outlook items by category is essential to managing your appointments, contacts, e-mail, and so on; **see** "Assigning Items to Categories," **p. 212**.

If you plan to use the Tasks folder to track items from which you'll generate billing reports, click the Details tab. Boxes on this region of the Task form let you enter the amount of time you spend on a task, as well as Mileage details and additional notes in the Billing Information box. Click the Save and Close button to add the new item to your Tasks folder.

Tip from

To create a billing statement with Outlook, create a custom Table view that includes the fields you want to use on your billing report. Sort or filter the list to show only the clients or companies for whom you want to generate the report. Select the rows and press Ctrl+C to copy them to the Windows Clipboard; then open a new Excel workbook and paste the copied rows into a blank worksheet range. Use formulas to translate hourly rates and mileage allowances into totals.

Items on your task list show up in red when they're overdue, and in gray, with strikethrough formatting, when you click the Mark Complete button.

⚠ *If the due dates on some task items mysteriously change, see "You Want It When?" in the "Troubleshooting" section at the end of this chapter.*

ENTERING RECURRING TASKS

For tasks that repeat at regular intervals, enter the data just as you would for a one-time task, but before you save, click the Recurrence button. With one noteworthy exception, the technique for specifying how often a task recurs is essentially the same as for a recurring appointment or event. You specify whether the task repeats at daily, weekly, monthly, or annual intervals, and then enter the recurrence pattern—every other Tuesday and Thursday, the second Wednesday of each month, and so on. You can define recurring tasks that occur a set number of times—once a week for the next three weeks while a co-worker is on vacation, say—or check the End By box and enter a specific date when the task ends.

→ If you must complete the same task on a regular basis—such as a weekly sales report—use Outlook's recurring appointment feature; **see** "Entering a Recurring Appointment," **p. 275**.

Unlike recurring appointments, you can define an interval for recurring tasks that are based on completing the previous instance. Let's say you want to stay in touch with a valued but hard-to-reach customer by calling roughly once a month, but you don't want to seem overly aggressive by calling too often. If you define a recurring task to call on the 5th of each month, and you don't actually connect until the 20th, you'll end up making your next call only 15 days later.

Instead, use the dialog box shown in Figure 11.14 to specify that you want to generate a new task 30 days after you complete the previous instance. Click the Regenerate New Task box, and then fill in the number of days, weeks, months, or years you want between instances. Each time you mark a task complete, Outlook creates a new Task item using the specified settings. So if you connect with your customer on the 20th, your next reminder occurs one month later, on the 20th.

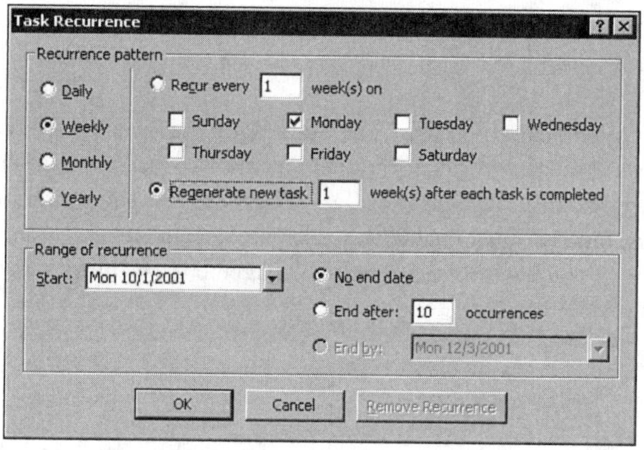

Figure 11.14
Use the Regenerate New Task check box to specify that you want the due date of the next recurring task to be based on the date the previous one was completed.

Outlook adds recurring tasks to your task list one at a time. When you mark one occurrence of the task complete, the next occurrence appears in the list. If you look at your task list for the next month, you'll see only one instance of a recurring task, even if it recurs daily or weekly. When you mark each task complete, Outlook creates a new item with a new due date. If you try to delete a recurring task, you can delete just the specified instance or all recurrences.

SORTING AND FILTERING THE TASK LIST

Outlook's built-in views for the Tasks folder include table views—Simple List or Detailed List—that let you see all tasks regardless of due date and status. You can create custom filters and views for items in the Tasks folder as well. The following views are built-in:

- Switch to the Active Tasks view to see all tasks except those where the Status is Complete or Deferred.

- The Next Seven Days view shows all tasks due in the next week. It does not include overdue tasks.

- Choose Overdue Tasks to see only those items for which the due date has passed. This view excludes tasks that have no due date.

■ Click the By Category view to see an outline style view of tasks organized according to categories you assign.

Tip from

EQ & Woody

You can assign a single task to multiple categories; switch to By Category view, and then hold down the Ctrl key and drag to assign an item to a new category.

■ The Assignment and By Person Responsible views are relevant only if you assign tasks to other persons.

■ Choose the Completed Tasks view to see only those tasks you've marked as completed.

→ Use Outlook's Views settings to organize your Outlook data; **see** "Using Views to Display, Sort, and Filter Items," **p. 216**.

If you scrupulously update the Due Date, Start Date, Status, and % Complete fields, you can use the Tasks folder to perform rudimentary project-management tasks. But when we say rudimentary, we mean it. Outlook's Task Timeline view shows start and end dates for individual tasks, but it doesn't enable you to create dependencies, balance resources, or link related projects. If you need robust project-management capabilities, look at a product such as Microsoft Project instead.

PRINTING A CALENDAR

Outlook's calendar works best for those who sit at a desk all day long. Unfortunately, most of us leave the office often enough to make it impractical to look up each event on the PC. If you're not willing to synchronize with a handheld device, then do the next best thing and put your schedule on paper.

You can print Outlook calendars in a variety of styles and formats. What's the easiest way to keep the paper and electronic versions in sync? If you get in the habit of printing out a daily or weekly calendar, you can jot notes and record new or revised appointments on that printout. When you return to your desk, transfer the handwritten notes to Outlook so that they'll appear the next time you print out your calendar.

To print your schedule for one day or for multiple days, weeks, or months, first switch to the Calendar folder, and then follow these steps:

1. If you plan to print one day, week, or month, select the corresponding view for the period.

2. Click the Print button. Outlook displays the Print dialog box shown in Figure 11.15.

Figure 11.15
Choose the Calendar Details Style option to print all the notes you've added for individual appointments and events on your calendar.

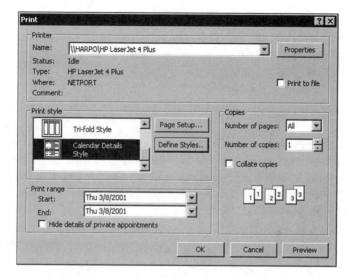

3. Choose one of the five page formats from the Print Styles list:

- **Daily**—Shows appointment and event descriptions for 7:00 a.m. to 6:00 p.m., a two-month calendar such as the Date Navigator, TaskPad, and room for you to write notes. Only a few lines from the Notes field for each appointment are visible.

- **Weekly**—Shows one week per page, with the Subject field only. This format includes a two-month calendar that resembles the Date Navigator, but no Notes field and no TaskPad.

- **Monthly**—Shows an entire month's events and appointments, with Subject lines truncated at approximately 50 characters. If the print range spans two or more months, Outlook prints a calendar for each month in the range.

- **Tri-Fold**—Prints a three-paned view in landscape mode on 8 1/2×11-inch paper. The left pane shows today's appointments, the middle includes the TaskPad and room for handwritten notes, and the right shows a compressed view of the week's schedule.

- **Calendar Details**—If you've added detailed notes such as driving instructions or agenda items to an appointment, choose this format so your printed pages include all details, not just the description, time, and location. This style uses the full width of the page.

4. In the Print Range area, adjust the Start and End dates, if necessary. If you're printing the paper version for someone else, such as a co-worker or assistant, check the box that lets you hide details of private appointments and show only that those times are booked.

5. Click the Preview button to see what your page will look like when printed. Use the Page Up and Page Down keys (or the corresponding toolbar buttons) to see additional pages.

6. Click the Page Setup button to adjust layout options, paper sizes, fonts, headers, footers, and other settings.

7. Click Print to send the schedule to the printer.

If none of the built-in print formats is exactly right, try creating a custom format. The safest way to explore print formats is to choose File, Print, and then click the Define Styles button. Choose the format that you want to modify, and click Copy. In the Page Setup dialog box (see Figure 11.16), enter a name for your new layout, and then adjust options on the three tabs of the dialog box:

Figure 11.16
Instead of designing a new print format from scratch, modify an existing layout and give it a new name.

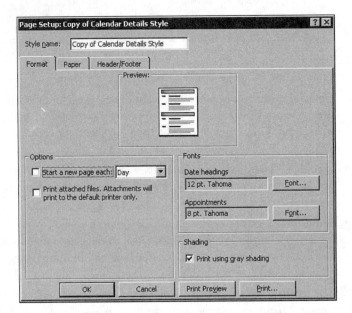

■ Use the Format tab to set options that are specific to the layout you started with. For example, in a Tri-fold format, you can choose which parts of the calendar go in each of the three panes. In Daily and Weekly styles, you can define the starting and ending times for the day's appointments. This tab also lets you select fonts and shading options for all views.

■ Use the Paper tab to define the dimensions, paper source, margins, and orientation for each page. Scroll through the Size list in the Page box to see a collection of layouts intended for use with Day-Timer, Day Runner, and Franklin Planner products.

■ Click the Header/Footer tab to customize the text at the top and bottom of each printed page. You can add literal text, or click any of the five buttons to add fields that insert the page number, number of pages, date printed, time printed, and username.

Tip from

E.Q & Woody

If you regularly print out monthly calendars, visit Slipstick Systems (http://www.slipstick.com) and search for Outcal. This package includes a Word document template and instructions for producing good-looking printable calendars using Outlook data.

TROUBLESHOOTING

RESETTING THE FORMATTING OPTIONS

I customized a built-in calendar layout without making a copy first. How do I start over with the default form?

Choose File, Print, click the Define Styles button, and select the built-in format from the Print Styles list. Click the Reset button to return all formatting options to their default settings. This option does not affect your custom layout.

YOU NEED IT WHEN?

The due dates of some Task items changed, even though I never touched the Due Date field.

That's not a bug; it's a design decision. Did you change the value in the Start Date box at any point? If so, Outlook automatically changed the value in the Due Date field by the exact same interval. By design, Outlook assumes that tasks take a fixed amount of time, and delaying the start date delays the finish as well, even if you know you can meet your original deadline. Always check the Due Date field—and adjust it if necessary—after you change the Start Date.

SECRETS OF THE OFFICE MASTERS: JUGGLING MULTIPLE TIME ZONES

Sooner or later, every world traveler who works with Outlook discovers the peculiar way it deals with changes in time zones. Microsoft's engineers designed Outlook so that, when you change time zones on your computer, Outlook adjusts all appointments, past and present, to match the new time zone.

How does that cause problems? Imagine you've scheduled your regular staff meeting for Monday, October 1st, at 10 a.m. You've added the appointment to your Outlook calendar with a few notes about the agenda. A few days before the meeting, you're called away to London on a business trip. You book your return flight on Tuesday, October 2nd at 10 a.m. and dutifully enter the time in Outlook.

You bring your notebook with you to London. What happens next depends on what you do with your computer's clock:

- If you adjust the time zone to Greenwich Mean Time when you land in London, Outlook changes the entry for both appointments from 10am to 3pm. If you phone your office, you'll be able to participate in the meeting via conference call. Unfortunately, when Tuesday rolls around, you'll miss your flight if you rely on Outlook's reminder instead of your ticket.

- If you don't adjust the time zone, Outlook will leave both appointments at 10am in your Calendar folder. When you try to phone in for the status meeting, it will actually be 5am in New York and no one will be there to take the call. But you'll be right on time for your flight the next day.

Microsoft claims that Outlook is working exactly as intended. You're expected to adapt by adding a second time zone to your Calendar, using this simple shortcut: Switch to Day view, right-click the time display along the left edge of the calendar, choose Change Time Zone from the menu, and check the Show an Additional Time Zone box. Enter a label for each time zone, click OK, and you'll see two time displays at the left side of the Day view. Whenever you enter an appointment or meeting, make sure you choose the correct time scale.

This solution is cumbersome, but it works well enough if your trip takes you to only two time zones. When you reach your destination, open the Time Zone dialog box again and click the Swap Time Zones button. The time on the system clock changes, but you can still stay on time as long as you don't succumb to jet lag and look at the wrong scale. If your trip takes you to three or more time zones, however, using this technique is a one-way ticket to hopeless confusion. If you can't handle this date arithmetic—especially with jet lag—leave Outlook's time zone alone and add a note about the time zone in the Subject of every appointment.

Oh, and if you move across country, all your records of previous appointments will be changed to reflect your new time zone. So if you consult the Calendar folder to determine exactly when you had a particular meeting, you'll discover that Outlook's records are off by several hours. Outlook is irritatingly insistent on making these changes, too. If you move from New York to Los Angeles, every holiday, birthday, and anniversary will be shifted three hours earlier on your calendar; to set each of these recurring events right, you'll have to open it, change the time, and click the Save and Close button.

CHAPTER **12**

MANAGING A CONTACTS LIST

In this chapter

MANAGING YOUR LIST OF CONTACTS

Outlook's Contacts folder serves a dual purpose: For Internet mail users, it's the primary storage location for e-mail addresses. It's also a useful place to store names, addresses, phone numbers, and other important information about friends, family members, and business associates. If you use the Contacts folder only to manage e-mail addresses and occasionally print an address book, it will certainly be worth the minimal effort it takes to enter and update contact information. But if you're willing to learn Outlook's secrets, you can make it do much more. For example, you can

- Quickly add addresses to letters and envelopes you create with Word. After you master the quirks of the Outlook Address Book, you can configure each entry so names and addresses appear in the correct format.

- Build lists of related contacts for use in mail merge projects.

- Dial your phone and log calls automatically. If you provide professional services and bill by the hour, Outlook can track the time you spend on the phone with each contact, for later billing.

- Flag one Contact item or a group for a follow-up reminder.

- Use categories to print specialized phone books. If you frequently travel to another city, for example, enter names, phone numbers, and notes for your favorite restaurants in that city, and then print a list of just those items before you leave.

→ The Contacts folder and the Outlook Address Book offer different views of the same information; for full details, **see** "Configuring the Outlook Address Book," **p. 239**.

By default, the Contacts folder opens in Address Cards view, shown in Figure 12.1. This view includes the contact's name (as defined in the File As field), plus the mailing address and as many phone numbers as you've defined for the contact. This view lets you see a fairly large number of records at one time, but it doesn't display company or job title information.

To see more information about each contact, switch to the Detailed Address Cards view, which displays virtually all fields in each contact record.

→ Outlook provides a variety of options for sorting and filtering your Outlook items; **see** "Using Views to Display, Sort, and Filter Items," **p. 216**.

Figure 12.1
The default Address Cards view packs the maximum number of records onto the screen by displaying only essential address and phone information.

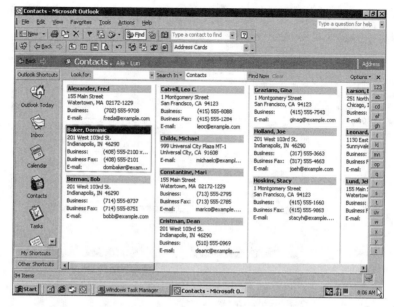

ENTERING AND EDITING CONTACT INFORMATION

To begin creating a new contact from scratch, use any of the following techniques:

- Click the New Contact button.
- Press Ctrl+Shift+C.
- Select File, New, Contact.

Outlook's form for creating a new item in the Contacts folder includes a number of smart features that help you enter properly formatted information quickly and accurately. Start in the Full Name field and use the Tab key to jump from field to field. After you've entered all the information, click the Save and Close button at the top of the dialog box to store the new item. Figure 12.2 shows a filled-in Contact form.

In all, each Contact item includes more than 140 fields of information. Most Outlook users, however, work with only a small fraction of these fields—those that are visible on the General tab of the default Contact form. To see more information, click the All Fields tab. Use the drop-down list to filter the collection of fields so you see a manageable subset, such as all Address fields, all Name fields, and so on. Select All Contact fields to see (and edit) the entire list of available fields, in alphabetical order, as shown in Figure 12.3.

PART

II

CH

12

Figure 12.2
Outlook automatically fills in some of the blanks when you create a new item in the Contacts folder, and it checks the rest to make sure that you left nothing out.

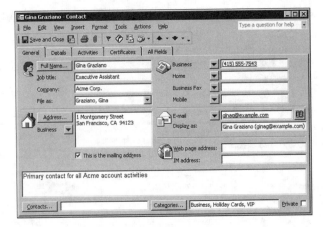

Figure 12.3
The last tab of the default Contact form lets you scroll through (and edit) more than 140 fields in each item.

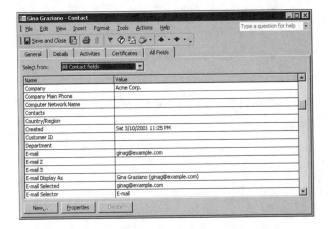

If you're having trouble selecting or deleting a field's contents, see "Selecting and Deleting Field Contents" in the "Troubleshooting" section at the end of this chapter.

ENTERING AND EDITING NAMES

When you enter a new contact's name in the Full Name field (or change an existing one), Outlook slices and dices your entry into as many as nine separate fields. You will rarely see most of these fields, but knowing how Outlook *parses* names—that is, breaks them into their component parts—lets you control the process. This will pay off later when you use items from the Contacts folder as the source for e-mail, letters, envelopes, and mail merge projects.

Tip from

EQ & Woody

Don't bother with the Shift key when you enter Contact names. If you enter a name in all lowercase letters, Outlook automatically capitalizes each name as soon as you Tab out of the field.

As soon as you enter the full name, in any order, Outlook attempts to break it into five sub-fields: First Name, Middle Name, Last Name, Title (Ms. or Dr., for example) and Suffix (Jr. or M.D., for instance). To view (and edit) the contents of these fields, click the Full Name button, which opens the Check Full Name dialog box, shown in Figure 12.4. If any information is incorrect, edit it here.

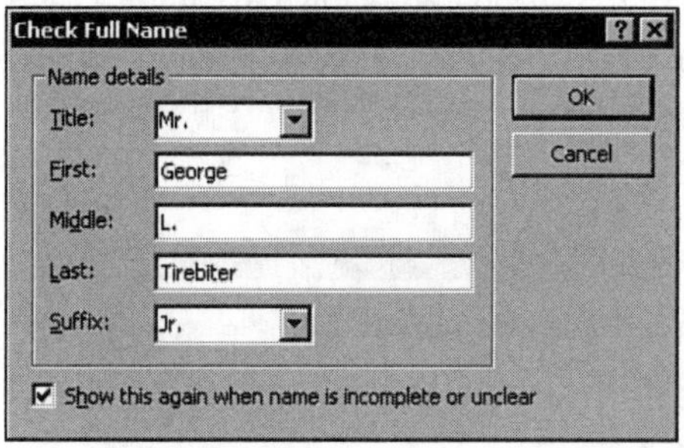

Figure 12.4
When you enter a full name, Outlook automatically breaks it into these subfields; if any information is incorrect, edit it here.

How do you include a courtesy title such as Mr., Ms., or Dr. in each new Contact item? Get in the habit of entering the title at the beginning of the Full Name field. Outlook recognizes the following titles, which are also on the Title drop-down list in the Check Full Name dialog box: Dr., Prof., Mr., Mrs., Ms., and Miss. Even if a title is not available on the drop-down list, it still might work. For example, beginning a name with Sir, Herr, Fraulein, Monsieur, Madame, or Signore will correctly fill in the Title field. If you're not sure a prefix will work, try it in a new, blank Contact form.

Based on what you type in the Full Name field, Outlook also fills in two additional fields automatically:

- **The File As Field**—Controls the order in which the Contacts folder displays items when you switch to Address Cards or Detailed Address Cards view. Although Outlook automatically fills in this field using its default format, Last Name first, you can easily change it.

- **The Subject Field**—Does not appear on any built-in forms but is accessible on the All Fields tab. It defines how each Contact item appears when you display the Address Book. By default, Outlook fills in this field with the First Name field first.

→ To learn more about how Outlook files your Contact items, **see** "Changing the Way a Contact Item Is Filed," **p. 300**.

 If you don't want Outlook to automatically (and incorrectly) split company names in your Contacts Folder into first and last names, see "Using Company Names in Your Contacts" in the Troubleshooting section at the end of this chapter.

WORKING WITH ADDRESSES

Just as with name fields, when you enter a mailing address in the Address field on the default Contact form, Outlook splits the address into component parts and stores the information in as many as 31 separate fields. You can store up to three addresses per contact; click the drop-down list just below the Address button to select Business, Home, or Other.

When you enter an address, Outlook parses the address into separate fields for the street, city, state, and other fields. If you enter information in a format Outlook doesn't recognize—if you omit the city or state, or if you accidentally leave a digit off the ZIP code—Outlook pops up the Check Address dialog box shown in Figure 12.5 (you can also click the Address button to display this dialog box). This display shows how Outlook proposes to divide the information into subfields. Click OK to save the record as typed, or edit the contents of any field.

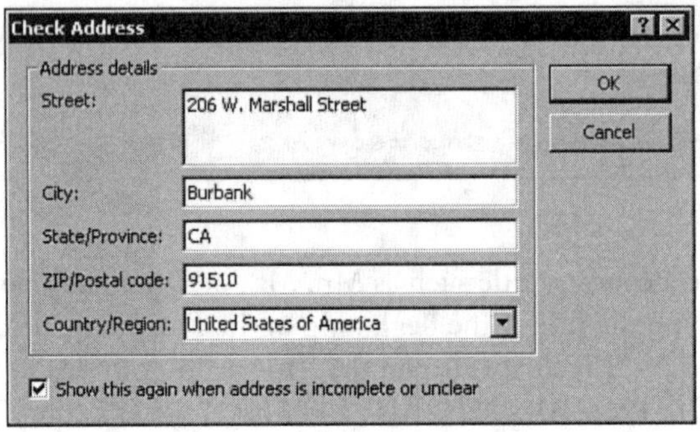

Figure 12.5
This dialog box shows you how Outlook proposes to parse the address you entered into subfields.

When you check the This Is the Mailing Address box, Outlook copies this address to the fields that are used when you create letters, envelopes, or mail merge lists in Word.

→ To learn more about using Word's mail merge capabilities, **see** "Using Mail Merge to Personalize Form Letters," **p. 516.**

ENTERING JOB AND COMPANY DETAILS

On the General tab of the default Contact form, you'll find two boxes for entering work-related information about a contact: Job Title and Company. Click the Details tab to enter other work-related information, such as Department and Manager's Name.

Although the Details tab includes a field for Assistant's Name, the field for Assistant's Phone Number is buried in the full list of fields on the last tab of the dialog box. There's a much easier way to enter this information, however: Click the drop-down arrow to the left of any of the four phone number boxes and select Assistant, and then enter the number. After you enter the number, it is visible in both Address Card views.

MANAGING PHONE, FAX, AND OTHER NUMBERS

The General page has room to enter up to four phone numbers—by default, you can fill in Business, Home, Business Fax, and Mobile numbers. You're certainly not limited to those options, however; you can actually enter as many as 19 separate phone numbers, using the drop-down lists at the left of each number to select different fields.

Note

Both default Address Card views display as many phone numbers as you've defined for a contact. These appear in an order determined by this form, with most business-related numbers at the top. Curiously, however, the Business Fax field appears at the bottom of each list, and we can't find any way to change this order.

You can enter phone numbers any way you like, with or without punctuation; when you exit the field, Outlook automatically reformats the numbers using its standard punctuation scheme—parentheses around the area or city code and a hyphen after the first three digits of the phone number. If you omit the area code, Outlook assumes the number is in your local dialing area and adds your area code to the entry. If Outlook parses this information incorrectly, or if you need to add a country code to the number, click to select the phone number field and then click the button to the right of the field. This action opens a dialog box that allows you to enter or edit this information.

If a contact's phone number includes an extension, add this information at the end of the phone number, preceded by a space and the letters x or ext. Outlook ignores this information when formatting the phone number or using the AutoDial feature. You can also add text before or after a phone number; for example, if one of your contacts is bicoastal, you might enter a number in both the Business and Business 2 fields, and then label them LA and NY.

ENTERING AND EDITING E-MAIL AND WEB ADDRESSES

You can store up to three e-mail addresses per contact. Click the drop-arrow next to the E-mail box to select any of these three blanks, and then enter the address. Click the Address Book button at the right of this box to view e-mail addresses in the Outlook Address Book, which uses a different form to display information.

→ For an authoritative explanation of how the Outlook Address Book works, **see** "Configuring the Outlook Address Book," **p. 239**.

→ To find out how Outlook uses Address Book information to fill in addresses on e-mail messages, **see** "Creating, Managing, and Using E-mail Addresses," **p. 238**.

In a welcome usability improvement, Outlook 2002 lets you see and change the text displayed in the To and From fields of message windows for each address. When you enter an e-mail address in any of the three boxes on the Contact form, the Display box beneath it shows how the name will appear in messages you send to or receive from that address. By default, the Display value is set to the value of the Full Name field, followed by the e-mail address in parentheses. Edit this address to show whatever you want—you might want to replace the e-mail address with a Company name or the word *Personal* in parentheses, for instance.

The General tab of the default Contact form also includes input boxes where you can enter a Web page address; if you enter a recognizable URL, Outlook converts it to a hyperlink so you can jump to a contact's personal or corporate Web page.

PART

II

CH

12

> **Note**
> Click the Details tab to add other online information, including settings for NetMeeting calls and the server where the contact publishes his Internet Free/Busy Time.

If you use MSN Messenger, enter the Instant Messaging address for the contact in the IM Address field.

→ For more information on how Outlook integrates with MSN Messenger, **see** "Using MSN Messenger to Communicate with Contacts," **p. 305**.

ENTERING PERSONAL INFORMATION AND OTHER DETAILS

Click the Details tab to add some personal information about each contact. Fields on this tab include Nickname, Spouse's Name, Birthday, and Anniversary. You can see still more fields in this category (including one in which you can enter the names of children or specify a contact's hobbies) by clicking the All Fields tab.

As in virtually all Outlook items, the Notes area at the bottom of the Default Contact form lets you add extensive notes and comments, as well as shortcuts to other Outlook items, files, or file attachments. Click the Categories button to assign each entry to one or more categories; the long list of built-in categories includes a Holiday Cards choice that lets you quickly print a list of friends, family, and business associates to whom you'll send season's greetings.

If you click the Contacts button, Outlook pops up a dialog box that lets you link one Contact item to another. You might want to do that with business partners, for example, or to link the individual records for a married couple to a third record that contains their family details. Use that last record in your holiday cards list.

→ To learn more about categorizing Outlook items, **see** "Assigning Items to Categories," **p. 212**.

WORKING SMARTER WITH CONTACT ITEMS

Most Outlook users are perfectly content to enter one item at a time in the Contacts folder. If you have a bulging address book, though, you'll want to employ the secrets and shortcuts described in this section.

CHANGING THE WAY A CONTACT ITEM IS FILED

In both built-in Address Card views, the field used for sorting and displaying information is the File As field. By default, Outlook fills in this field by using the information you type in the Full Name field, displaying it last name first. If you don't enter a name here, Outlook assumes the record refers to a business and uses the information from the Company field. You can accept the default, or you can change the information displayed here.

Although organizing an address book by last name is traditional, you might choose to mix different filing orders within the Contacts folder. For example, when you enter a record for a person who serves as your main contact with a company, file the record under the company name, with the person's name in parentheses. In some cases, you might even use simple generic descriptions such as Drugstore or Travel Agent.

If you can't remember how you filed a Contact item, click the Find button on the Standard toolbar. A simple search looks through all Name, Company, and Address fields. Click the Options drop-down arrow and check Search All Text in Each Message to look for specific information in a Contact's Notes field.

To change the way a specific Contact item is filed, double-click to open the item. In the File As field, click the drop-down arrow. If both the Full Name and Company fields contain data, Outlook offers the following five choices:

- Full name, first name first
- Full name, last name first
- Company name
- Full name, last name first, followed by company name in parentheses
- Company name, followed by full name, last name first, in parentheses

To file the item using any other text, replace the contents of the File As field. Whatever you type appears in alphabetical order in all views of your Contacts folder.

To change the default order for all new contacts, select Tools, Options, click the Preferences tab, and click the Contact Options button. Two drop-down boxes let you select a default for the Full Name field and the File As field—they don't have to be the same.

ENTERING SEVERAL NEW CONTACT ITEMS AT ONCE

Have you ever returned from a meeting or trade show with an inch-thick bundle of business cards? Typing the details from those cards into Outlook can be a tedious process. Here are three time-saving shortcuts to help make shorter work of that stack:

- Enter data by using a table-based view instead of the default Contact form. Click in the empty box in the top line to begin entering a new item. Press Tab to move from field to field. When you press Enter, Outlook stores the record and moves the insertion point back to the beginning of the first line, where you can begin a new item immediately.

  If you just want to get a few crucial names, phone numbers, and e-mail addresses into Outlook, create a custom Table view that contains only the fields you need and no more. Be sure to include the Categories field so you can identify the trade show or meeting where you met this person (ABC Conference 2002, for example).

- If you prefer to use a Contact form, enter the information for the first card in the stack; then select File, Save and New. This hidden menu option saves the item you just entered and clears the form so you can begin a new contact immediately. After you enter the last card in the stack, press Esc to clear the blank form.

- When you have two or more cards from people who work in the same office, let Outlook copy key information to the new Contact item. Open the item, click the

Actions menu, and select New Contact from Same Company. Outlook creates a new item, entering the company name, address, and phone number from the previous item, but clearing all other fields.

EXCHANGING CONTACT INFORMATION

It's extremely easy to exchange items with other Outlook users. For example, if you've asked a co-worker to follow up with a customer on your behalf, you can make the job easier by forwarding a copy of that person's item from your Contacts folder. If you're certain the other person uses Outlook, the procedure is easy: Drag the item from the Contacts folder and drop it in the message window to send it as an attachment. Your co-worker can add the item to her Contacts folder by opening the message and dragging the attached item onto the Contacts icon on the Outlook Bar.

To exchange information with someone who doesn't use Outlook, use the *vCard* format (short for virtual business card) to translate standard name, business, address, and phone fields into a simple text file that other compatible programs can import. When you send your vCard to another person via e-mail, that person can easily add your address information into Outlook, Lotus Organizer, the Netscape Personal Address Book, or any compatible contact-management program. You can also turn any item from your Contacts folder into a vCard and attach it to an e-mail message.

Tip from

Ed & Woody

Unless you're absolutely certain the person to whom you're sending a mail message uses Outlook, you should send contact information in vCard format. In fact, because this card uses plain text, your recipient can read its contents even without a compatible contact manager—just open the file in a text editor, such as Notepad.

EXPERT EDITING TECHNIQUES

If you want to change an address or phone number or edit a misspelled name, you don't need to open a Contact item. You can edit directly in any Card view (Detailed Address Cards, for example) or Table view (such as Phone List). Click the letter along the right side of the window that matches the first letter of the item you're looking for; use the scrollbars, if necessary, to find the name you're looking for and then just click and start typing.

It's also possible (although difficult) to update the same field in a group of records, all at one time. Let's say XYZ Corp. merges with ABC Industries to form a new company, A to Z Industries. If your Contacts folder includes a few dozen records for people who work at XYZ and ABC, you can change the company name for all those records in one operation, instead of having to open and edit each one individually.

Unfortunately, this technique has some serious limitations. It will not allow you to update phone numbers when an area code changes, for example—an increasingly common situation in the United States—because the area code is not stored in a separate field from the rest of the number. Nor can you sort and update using fields based on formulas.

1. Switch to a view that shows all Contacts grouped by the field you want to change. In this example, you can use the built-in By Company view; to change another field, you might need to create a custom view.

→ To learn more about using Outlook's built-in view or to create your own custom views, **see** "Using Views to Display, Sort, and Filter Items," **p. 216**.

2. Select View, Expand/Collapse Groups, Collapse All. Find the group that contains the items you want to change and click the plus sign to expand only that group.

3. Select one item in the group and edit the Company field so it contains the correct information—in this example, change XYZ Corp. to A to Z Industries. As soon as you save the change, you'll see a new group in your list, containing the item you just changed.

4. Drag the Group bar from the group of records with the old Company name and drop it onto the Group bar for the item you just changed. As you drag the Group bar, a ScreenTip will alert you that you're about to change the Company name to A to Z Industries.

You don't need to use this technique to assign multiple contacts to categories, however. Instead, select a group of records, either individually or by using filters; then right-click and select Categories from the shortcut menu.

MERGING DUPLICATE CONTACT ITEMS

How do you deal with duplicate Contact items? This problem is particularly prevalent if you use incoming e-mail as the basis for a Contact item. When you drag a message from the Inbox and drop it in the Contacts folder, Outlook creates a new Contact item using the sender's name as it appears in the From box. If one person occasionally sends messages using a different display name, eventually you'll wind up with two, three, or more Contact items for a single person—most consisting of just an e-mail address.

In some cases, Outlook can combine duplicate records for you. If you attempt to enter a record using exactly the same name as an existing Contact item, Outlook displays the dialog box shown in Figure 12.6.

PART
II

CH
12

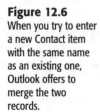

Figure 12.6
When you try to enter a new Contact item with the same name as an existing one, Outlook offers to merge the two records.

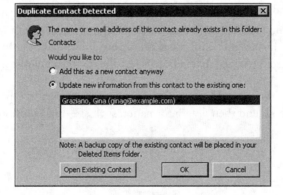

If you intended to create a duplicate record, or if this is a new contact that happens to have the same name as another item in your Contacts folder, select Add This As a New Contact Anyway. If you select the default option, Update New Information from This Contact to the Existing One, Outlook replaces every field in the existing item if the new item contains information in that field. If you're not sure whether to update the record, click the Open Existing Contact button and compare the contents of the two items.

Caution

Think before you automatically update a contact record. Outlook does not show you what it's going to do before you merge items, and there's no record afterward of which fields changed and which stayed the same. If you enter even a single character in the Notes field for the new record, for example, it will completely erase any notes and file attachments or shortcuts in the existing record. If you inadvertently delete important information by merging contact records, look in the Deleted Items folder, where Outlook keeps a copy of the original item when you use the merge option.

The merge function is smart about e-mail addresses. Each contact item can contain a maximum of three e-mail addresses. If the original item contains one or two e-mail addresses, Outlook will add e-mail addresses to the unused address field rather than replacing an existing address.

Outlook offers to merge items only when the name you enter in the Full Name field is absolutely identical to an existing item, and the offer is good only when you create the duplicate item. If you've added several items to your Contacts folder that refer to the same person with slightly different names—William Gates and William H. Gates, for example—you can use a sneaky workaround to merge the data:

1. Open the master item—the one that contains the record you want to merge other information into. Copy the contents of the Full Name field to the Clipboard and close the item.

2. Open the second item—the one that contains information you want to merge into the master item. Paste the contents of the Clipboard into the Full Name field in the second record, and then click the Save and Close button.

3. Select the second item and press the Delete key.

4. Select Edit, Undo Delete. Outlook restores the contact item from the Deleted Items folder. Because this has the same effect as creating a new item, Outlook displays the Duplicate Contact Detected dialog box. Select the option to merge information.

You can also merge information from two or more records manually. Open each contact item in its own window, and then drag information such as e-mail addresses from one item to another.

Tip from

Ed & Woody

If you never, ever want to be prompted to merge contact items, turn off this feature. From the main Outlook window, select Tools, Options, and select the Preferences tab. Click the Contact Options button and clear the Check for Duplicate Contacts check mark.

USING MSN MESSENGER TO COMMUNICATE WITH CONTACTS

Outlook 2002 integrates with the MSN Messenger Instant Messaging utility, enabling you to communicate with contacts immediately, in a Messenger window, rather than through e-mail.

Before you can take advantage of this Outlook feature, you must enable MSN Messenger integration. To do so, select Tools, Options, click the Other tab, and check the Enable Instant Messaging in Microsoft Outlook box.

With this option, Outlook will look for a value in the IM Address field for any Contact item. When you open a contact record or an e-mail message, Outlook checks to see whether that person is available via MSN Messenger. If so, you'll see a bar at the top of the message or contact record; click to open a Messenger window and begin composing an instant message.

ADDRESSING LETTERS AND ENVELOPES USING YOUR CONTACTS LIST

Word and Outlook can work together with varying degrees of success to help you generate properly addressed letters and envelopes. Outlook's Actions menu, in fact, includes a New Letter to Contact choice that ostensibly does exactly that. What it actually does, however, is kick off Word's Letter Wizard—an option that always works better when started from within Word. We don't recommend that you select this option from Outlook; instead, always start with Word when you want to create a letter or envelope with the Letter Wizard.

→ For full details on the only effective way to use Word's Letter Wizard, **see** "Creating and Editing Letters," **p. 421**.

You can, however, kick off a Word mail merge from Outlook. This process can be surprisingly effective, especially if you're willing to create a custom view and filter your Contacts list first. Start by opening the Contacts folder, and then select View, Current View, Define Views. Click the New button and define a Table or Card view that contains all the fields you need for your merge. For example, if you're planning to mail letters to customers, be sure

PART

II

CH

12

the list of fields includes Title, First Name, Last Name, Suffix, and all the Business Address fields. Don't use the Full Name or Mailing Address fields, which might contain home addresses or names that are formatted incorrectly. Save the view with a name such as Business Mail Merge.

→ For instructions on how to create a new view, **see** "Creating a New Custom View," **p. 222**.

1. If you want to send the mailing to a subset of your list, select the individual items manually, using Ctrl+click, or select View, Current View, Customize Current View and define a filter.

→ For details on how to create a filter in Outlook, **see** "Customizing an Existing View," **p. 217**.

2. Select Tools, Mail Merge. The Mail Merge Contacts dialog box opens, as shown in Figure 12.7.

Figure 12.7
Use these options, combined with a custom Outlook view, to quickly create a Word mail merge document.

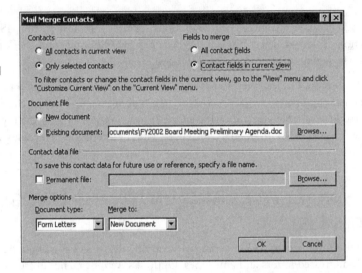

3. From the Contacts section, choose whether you want All Contacts in Current View or Only Selected Contacts. From the Fields to Merge section, choose whether you want All Contact Fields or Contact Fields in Current View. If you've created a custom view as we recommend, select the latter option.

Tip from
Ed & Woody

You can merge using the entire list of fields from the Contacts folder. If you do that, however, the list of merge fields will include all 140-something fields from Outlook, and scrolling through the list will be a chore. Trust us—creating a custom view will save you a lot of time.

4. From the Document File section, choose whether you want to use a New Document or an Existing Document. Use the Browse button to select a file. If you want, you can

pause here, create your document in Word, save it and close it, and return to the dialog box to continue.

> Using an existing document is a great way to print custom envelopes easily, using a return address of your choosing. Run this mail merge routine and create an envelope that contains the First Name, Last Name, and appropriate Business Address fields. Add a text box containing your return address (with a logo, if you want), and save the file using a name such as My Business Envelope.doc. The next time you want to create an envelope, select one or more items from your Contacts folder, and use Outlook's mail merge features with the document you just created. The results are nearly foolproof—and you can use the same technique for letters as well, producing much better results than the Letter Wizard.

5. In the Contact Data File section, check the Permanent File box if you want to save the filtered data from your Contacts folder in a separate file for reuse later. If you've defined a custom view, this step is not necessary; it's most applicable if you want to share the data file with another Word user who doesn't have access to your Contacts folder.

6. Select a Document Type from the Merge Options section of the dialog box; normally, you'll use the Form Letters option, but you can also select Mailing Labels, Envelopes, or Catalog. These options are the same as those available using Word's Mail Merge Wizard. Select one of three Merge To destinations as well: a new document, the printer, or e-mail.

7. Click OK to launch Word with the document and data you specified ready to merge. If you started with a new document, you must add merge fields and text; if you began with an existing document that already contained merge fields and text, you're ready to go.

→ For more details about how to use Word's mail merge capabilities, **see** Chapter 20, "Merging Data and Documents," **p. 513**.

PART
II
CH
12

PRINTING PHONE LISTS FROM YOUR CONTACTS LIST

You can print contact lists in a variety of styles and formats, using all the items in your Contacts folder or only a subset of them. You can even turn your address list into a booklet printed on both sides and small enough to fit in a shirt pocket—although you must be willing to hover over the printer while it spits out pages. (You also must resign yourself to wasting many sheets of paper while you figure out the precise order in which to perform each step.) This feature can be useful when you're heading off on a business trip, for example, and you want to print the addresses and phone numbers of contacts in that area.

The steps required to print an address book or phone list containing items from your Contacts folder are nearly identical to those for printing a calendar. If you want to print a subset of the folder's contents, use one of the following techniques:

- To select a contiguous block of items, click the first item; then hold down the Shift key and click the last item in the group.

- To select individual items that are not adjacent, hold down Ctrl while clicking each one.

- To show only items that match specific criteria, use the Find button or the Advanced Find dialog box.

- Customize the current view or switch to another view and filter the list.

→ To learn more about using views to control how you work with Outlook items, **see** "Using Views to Display, Sort, and Filter Items," **p. 216**.

→ To learn more about Outlook's search capabilities, **see** "Finding Outlook Items," **p. 224**.

→ For an explanation of the techniques for printing calendars, **see** "Printing a Calendar," **p. 288**.

1. Switch to any Card view and select the items to be printed. If you want to print the entire list, you do not need to make a selection.

2. Click the Print button. Outlook displays the Print dialog box shown in Figure 12.8.

Figure 12.8
Select the Phone Directory Style option to print all the names and phone numbers in your Contacts folder, with no company or address information.

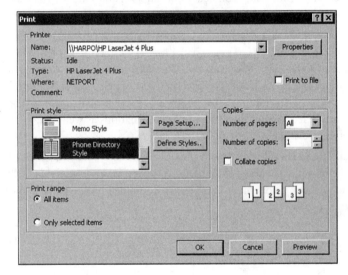

3. Select one of the five page formats from the Print Style list.

 Are you having problems seeing all the Print Style choices in the Print dialog box? If so, see "Setting Print Styles" in the "Troubleshooting" section at the end of this chapter.

4. In the Print Range box, choose whether you want to print All Items or Only Selected Items.

Tip from
EQ & Woody

Have you used the Notes field to keep track of a lot of information about some contacts? To extract the maximum amount of information when printing, select Memo Style, check the options to start each item on its own page, and print all attachments.

> Be careful, however; this option can chew through a ream of paper faster than you can say, "Save the rainforest."

5. Click the Preview button to see what your page will look like when printed. Use the Page Up and Page Down keys (or the corresponding toolbar buttons) to see additional pages in the Preview window, as shown in Figure 12.9.

Figure 12.9
Preview an address book or phone list before printing to ensure the format matches what you expect.

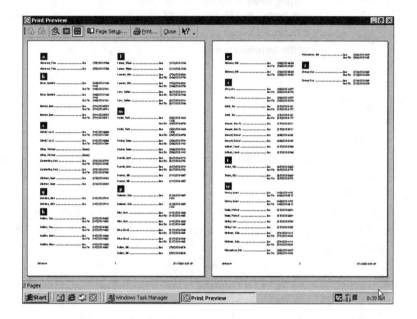

6. Click the Page Setup button in the Preview window or in the Print dialog box to adjust layout options, paper sizes, fonts, headers, footers, and other settings.

7. Click Print to send the job to the printer.

When you print your phone book, select from the following five formats:

- **Card Style**—Shows all the details from the underlying Card view. Switching to Detailed Card view adds more fields to each item but also extends the size of your printed book.

- **Small Booklet Style**—Prints in Card view, with each page shrunk to 1/8 normal size. Default settings suggest you should print this booklet using both sides of the paper. If you don't have a printer capable of handling two-sided printing, you can get the same effect, tediously, by using the manual feed option in your printer and feeding each sheet through individually.

- **Medium Booklet Style**—Also prints a two-sided booklet, but each page in this style is only 1/4 the size of the printed page. Experiment with a four-page sample before printing your entire phone book.

- **Memo Style**—Prints every bit of information about a contact, including all notes. To print a single contact in Memo Style, bypassing all dialog boxes, open the item and click the Print button.

- **Phone Directory Style**—Prints the name and all phone numbers for each contact in a two-column format that takes up the full width of an 8 1/2×11-inch sheet of paper. Although you can change the number of columns and the fonts used in this style, you can't add new fields.

→ If none of the built-in print formats is exactly right, try creating a custom format using the same techniques as with a calendar; **see** "Printing a Calendar," **p. 288**.

TROUBLESHOOTING

SELECTING AND DELETING FIELD CONTENTS

When working with the All Contact fields list on the last tab of a Contact form, Outlook won't let you edit the File As field, the names of e-mail entries, and several other fields. So, how do you select or delete the contents of these fields?

Outlook won't let you edit a handful of fields in this list; most of these are fields Outlook generates automatically based on the contents of other fields. Use the General tab of the Contact form to change this information.

USING COMPANY NAMES IN YOUR CONTACTS

You've entered a company name in the Contacts folder, but Outlook insists on splitting it into first and last names—so that Acme Industries becomes Industries, Acme.

When entering a new Contact item for a company, leave the Full Name field blank and instead press the Tab key twice to jump to the Company field. Whatever you type in that field also appears in the File As and Subject fields, exactly as you typed it.

SETTING PRINT STYLES

You clicked the Print button, but you see only one print style choice in the Print dialog box. Naturally, it's not the one you want.

This occurs when you click the Print button while displaying the Contacts folder in a Table view, such as Phone List view. Exit the Print dialog box and switch to a Card view, such as Address Cards or Detailed Address Cards, and then try again.

SECRETS OF THE OFFICE MASTERS: MAPPING A CONTACT'S ADDRESS

One of the coolest features of Outlook 2000/2002 is so deeply buried even some Office experts aren't aware of it. Using Microsoft's Expedia Maps service, you can use the Internet to automatically look up a contact's address and generate a detailed map.

Open any Contact item and make sure the address you want to map is visible; then click the Display Map of Address button or select Actions, Display Map of Address. This option sends you to Microsoft's Expedia Maps page, where you'll see an interactive street map. You can zoom in or out, print the map, save it as a URL or graphic, e-mail it to another person, or get driving directions.

Figure 12.10

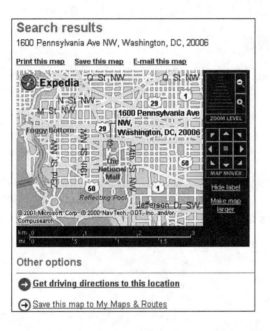

PART

II

CH

12

If Expedia tells you there's no address to map but you're certain the street exists, check to make sure the correct address is selected. This option uses the address that's visible in the current window, so if necessary, switch between Home, Business, and Other addresses until the one you want is visible and then try again. If that still doesn't work, try editing the address in the browser window. Pay particular attention to abbreviations, which can confuse Expedia Maps—for example, if the address is on N. E. 20th St., try entering it as NE 20th Street, instead.

CHAPTER 13

SHARING SCHEDULES AND PLANNING MEETINGS

In this chapter

SHARING GROUP SCHEDULES

Outlook is more than a personal organizer. If you work closely with a team of people who also use Outlook, you can coordinate schedules among group members to streamline the process of organizing meetings. As a meeting organizer, your job is much easier when you can see at a glance what times are available for the other group members.

Outlook 2002 is significantly more capable than earlier versions when it comes to working with group schedules. In the office, you can view details from calendars on a Microsoft Exchange Server or on a corporate Web server. For Outlook 2002 users only, Microsoft offers an Internet server on which you can publish a list of Free/Busy times and share them with friends, family, and co-workers over the Internet.

Caution

The basic concepts behind group scheduling are simple, but the reality is not so easy without an Exchange Server close at hand. Support for Internet Free/Busy information sharing was notoriously buggy and unreliable in Outlook 2000, and as this is written, Microsoft's public Free/Busy server is too new to assess fairly. If you choose to use this emerging technology, be prepared to endure some configuration headaches as well as some glitches in day-to-day operation.

To use Outlook's automatic scheduling features, everyone in your office needs to publish details of their schedules so that Outlook can identify free and busy times for each meeting attendee. If you're connected via an *Exchange Server*, this process is relatively easy. If you choose to use an Internet or intranet-based Web server, the process is slightly more complicated.

Tip from

Ed & Woody

Group scheduling works properly only when everyone in a workgroup actively participates. In particular, you need to make sure that every appointment you make is entered in your Calendar folder; if you don't, Outlook constantly reports to other people that you have free time, even when you're booked solid. Make sure that you check the Show Time As box for every appointment. You can select any of four options: Free, Tentative, Busy, or Out of Office. Check the Private box if you've published your Calendar folder on an Exchange Server and you want others to see only that you're busy, without being able to view details.

SHARING CALENDARS ON AN EXCHANGE SERVER

To allow other users to share your calendar on an Exchange Server, you must meet all the following conditions:

- You must use Microsoft Exchange Server as your mail service.
- Your Calendar folder must be stored in the Exchange Server mailbox.

- You must assign access permissions to the Calendar folder. Right-click the folder icon, choose Properties, and click the Permissions tab. Click Add to add the name of a user or group; choose Default to assign rights for all persons who have access to the Exchange Server. Set the desired permissions and click OK.

Caution

When assigning rights to others to view your Calendar folder, be careful. For the default access, choose the Reviewer role, which enables others to view items in your Calendar but not add, edit, or delete items. Remember that unless you check the Private box, other people will be able to read the Subject line of any appointment or meeting on your Calendar.

USING MICROSOFT'S PUBLIC FREE/BUSY SERVICE

If you use Outlook outside of a traditional office, you can use Microsoft's Internet-based Free/Busy Service to store information about your schedule. If the other members of your team do the same, you can easily share schedules with one another when you're halfway across the country or even on different continents.

Tip from

Ed & Woody

If you share schedules with people in other time zones, it's crucial that you configure Outlook to reflect your time zone accurately. Don't forget to do the same in your Passport account.

To set up the connection, choose Tools, Options, and click the Preferences tab. Click the Calendar Options button, and then click the Free/Busy Options button. In the Free/Busy Options dialog box, check the Publish and Search Using Microsoft Office Internet Free/Busy Service box. To set up the service or change settings, click the Manage Button. The management controls are Web-based; this button opens your Web browser and takes you to the correct page.

To use the Microsoft Office Internet Free/Busy Service, do the following:

1. Log in with a Microsoft Passport account. This account is based on an e-mail address, although not necessarily the one you use with Outlook.
2. Sign up for the Microsoft service.
3. Enable Outlook to work with the service. This process uses an ActiveX control.
4. Authorize other users to access your Free/Busy information. They can do so using Outlook 2002 or by accessing the Microsoft Office Internet Free/Busy Service directly over the Web.

Note that this option is not compatible with Outlook 97, 98, or 2000. If your team uses a mix of new and old Outlook versions, you can still share Internet Free/Busy information using the option described in the next section.

PUBLISHING FREE/BUSY INFORMATION ON A WEB SERVER

If you don't have access to an Exchange Server, you can still publish your Free/Busy information to a Web server for sharing over a company intranet. This option lets other people see the times you've marked as busy on your calendar, but it doesn't allow them to view details about individual appointments.

Outlook publishes Free/Busy information as a simple text file in HTML format. To publish your information, follow these steps:

1. Choose Tools, Options, and click the Preferences tab. Click the Calendar Options button, and then click the Free/Busy Options button. You'll see the dialog box shown in Figure 13.1.

Figure 13.1
To publish your free and busy times on a Web server, enter the details here.

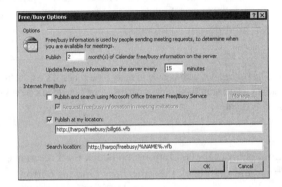

2. Check the Publish at My Location box.

3. In the Publish at My Location box, enter the full address of the page where you want to publish your Free/Busy information.

Tip from

Eℓ & Woody

You can define any page name for your Free/Busy information, but we suggest that you use the following standard naming scheme. Start with the full name of the server, and for the page name, use the first portion of your e-mail address (up to the @ sign), followed by the extension .vfb. Thus, if your e-mail address is jsmith@example.com and your administrator has set up a folder called Freebusy on a Web server named Groucho, enter the URL `http://groucho/freebusy/jsmith.vfb`. Using this naming convention makes it easy for other people to find your information without customizing your contact record, as explained in step 5.

---

4. Specify the number of months of information you want to include on the Free/Busy page, as well as how often you want to update this information. By default, Outlook

publishes two months' worth of information and updates details every 15 minutes. You can enter any number between 1 and 99 in either box.

5. In the Search Location box, enter the following URL: `http://<servername>/<pathname>/%NAME%.vfb`. Substitute the actual names of the server and path where your company's Free/Busy information resides, but type the remaining text exactly as shown here. When searching, Outlook substitutes the first part of each contact's e-mail address for the %NAME% variable, followed by the .vfb extension. If everyone in your organization uses the standard naming conventions defined in step 2, you'll be able to pick up Free/Busy information automatically.

6. Click OK to close the dialog box and begin publishing your Free/Busy information on the schedule you specified in step 4.

If some of your contacts have published information using nonstandard naming schemes, or on servers other than the default location you defined, you can enter a custom URL that identifies this information. Switch to the Contacts folder and open that person's item; then click the Details tab and enter the full URL in the Internet Free-Busy Address box.

WORKING WITH GROUP SCHEDULES

In previous Outlook versions, comparing group schedules was a fairly cumbersome process. Outlook 2002 provides easy access to a group schedule window, where you can save settings for any number of groups and open them by clicking a button.

From the Calendar window, click the Schedules button (or choose Actions, View Group Schedules). This opens the Group Schedules dialog box (see Figure 13.2), which shows groups you've already created. You can create a new group or work with an existing group; to add or remove names from a group, for instance, click the Open button. You can also remove a group from this window.

Figure 13.2
This dialog box shows groups you've already created and saved.

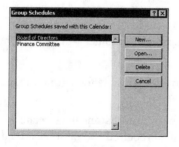

PART

II

CH

13

To create a new group, click the New button, enter a name for the group, and click OK. To add new members to the group, enter their names in the Group Members box and let AutoComplete suggest the correct name for you; or click the Add Others button to add from any Address Book or public folder. When you're finished, the dialog box should resemble Figure 13.3.

Figure 13.3
When creating a new group, you can enter names directly in the Group Members box or pick from an address book.

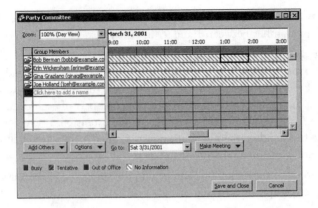

Click the Save and Close button to save the settings for the new group you just created. When you do, Outlook updates the Free/Busy information for the people on the list. If schedule information is not currently available for any person in the group, you'll be prompted to save a link that invites the group members to sign up for the Microsoft Office Internet Free/Busy service when they receive an invitation or e-mail from you.

After creating a group, you can use it as the basis of a meeting request or e-mail. Open the group schedule and click the Make Meeting button to see your options.

PLANNING A MEETING WITH OUTLOOK

In the world according to Outlook, there is a crucial difference between an *appointment* and a *meeting*. When you create an appointment, you set aside a block of time on your own personal calendar. Although an appointment might involve other people, it's your responsibility, not Outlook's, to coordinate your schedule with theirs.

An Outlook meeting, on the other hand, consists of identical items in the Calendar folders of two or more people. Although these items closely resemble appointments—with a subject, start and end times, and the option to set a reminder—there are several crucial differences:

- Every meeting has an *organizer*, who is responsible for setting the time, location, and other details.
- The organizer fills in a meeting request form that includes details of the meeting as well as the names and e-mail addresses of all required and optional attendees; Outlook sends the invitations automatically when the organizer saves the meeting request.
- When you receive a meeting request, you can accept, tentatively accept, or decline the invitation. If you accept, Outlook adds the meeting to your calendar; Outlook sends all responses to the meeting organizer and tracks the meeting's status automatically.
- As part of the planning process, the meeting organizer can reserve a conference room and other resources, such as overhead projectors or presentation equipment.

- If you and other members of your workgroup publish the details of your schedule on an Exchange Server or a Web server, Outlook can automatically pick a time when all proposed attendees are available.

CREATING A NEW MEETING REQUEST

You can begin scheduling a meeting by opening a meeting request form directly, using any of the following four techniques:

- Choose New, Meeting Request; or press Ctrl+Shift+Q to open a blank meeting request form.

- If you've already selected the exact date and time of the meeting, switch to a Calendar view of that date and select the block of time; then right-click and choose New Meeting Request from the shortcut menu. This option opens a meeting request form with the date and time already filled in.

- To open a meeting request form with the invitees' names already filled in, select one or more names in the Contacts folder; then right-click and choose Actions, New Meeting Request to Contact.

- To create a meeting while viewing a group schedule, click the Make Meeting button and choose New Meeting with All. (You can also Ctrl+click to select individual names from the Group Members list; choose Make Meeting, New Meeting to use only the selected names.)

- If you've already created an appointment in your Calendar folder and you want to turn it into a meeting, open the item and click the Invite Attendees button. This option uses all details you defined previously, adding a field in which you can enter the names of other attendees.

As Figure 13.4 shows, a meeting request form closely resembles an appointment form, with the crucial addition of the To field. Fill in the prospective attendees' names, and then add the remainder of the meeting details—Subject, start time, end time, notes, and so on—as you would for an appointment, and click Send to deliver the invitations.

PART

II

CH

13

Figure 13.4
A meeting request form resembles a cross between an e-mail message and an appointment form.

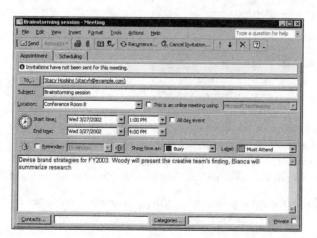

Tip from

EQ & Woody

Because the meeting request form is delivered via e-mail, you can use any of Outlook's addressing shortcuts, including automatic name checking. Click the To button to open the Address Book and select names directly.

Don't forget to include details in the Notes box at the bottom of the Appointment tab. Text you enter here appears in the Meeting item added to each attendee's Calendar folder after your invitation is accepted; it also serves as the text of the e-mailed invitation.

Tip from

EQ & Woody

To help attendees prepare for a meeting, you might want to send one or more files with the invitation—an agenda or a background memo in Word format, for example, or a worksheet for attendees to review before a budget-planning meeting. Drag a file icon directly into the Notes box on the meeting request form, or choose Insert, File, and select the file from the Browse dialog box.

When preparing a meeting request, you can designate some attendees as Required and others as Optional. By default, anyone you invite to a meeting is a Required attendee. To change their status to Optional, click the Scheduling tab and choose the Show Attendee Status option to display a dialog box as shown in Figure 13.5. Click the icon in the column just to the left of any name and use the drop-down arrow to adjust an invitee's status.

Figure 13.5
Use this tab on a meeting request form to designate an attendee as optional rather than required.

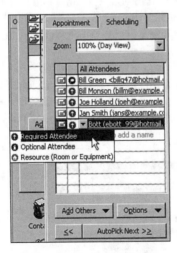

As the meeting organizer, you can change the status of any attendee at any time. When attendees open a Meeting item and click this tab, they see only the list of attendees and their status, without the capability to change the designation. On the meeting organizer's calendar only, this tab also summarizes the responses from prospective attendees.

After you've finished entering all details in the meeting request form, click the Send button. Outlook delivers the requests via e-mail to all prospective attendees.

If many of your recipients use contact-management programs other than Outlook, including Lotus Organizer, consider sending all meeting requests in *iCalendar* format. To set this global option, choose Tools, Options, click the Preferences tab, and click the Calendar Options button. Check the Send Meeting Requests Using iCalendar by Default box. Outlook recipients will still see all meeting requests exactly as they normally do, but users of other contact management programs will be able to deal with them as well.

USING GROUP SCHEDULES TO CHOOSE A MEETING TIME

One of the most frustrating aspects of scheduling a meeting is the lengthy exchange of e-mail messages and phone calls over schedules. If everyone in your group shares their calendars over the office network or over the Internet, Outlook can help you automatically pick a time when every prospective attendee is free. To work with an existing group schedule, open its window. If you've already started a meeting request form, click the Scheduling tab.

The list of attendees appears in the column at the left. To add new invitees to the list, enter a name directly in the blank box just below the last name in the list; click the Invite Others button to select additional people or resources from the Outlook Address Book.

On an Exchange Server where you've been granted permission to view another person's calendar, you'll see details about the other person's appointments. If you don't have access to calendar details for another person, color-coded blocks In the right side of the window show free and busy times on each attendee's schedule. The white zone is the block of time set aside for your meeting; click a new time to move the meeting, if necessary, or drag the left and right borders to change the start or end time and make the meeting longer or shorter. You can also set start and end times by using the controls at the bottom of the dialog box, and then see whether the time you selected works for all attendees. If your meeting includes a large number of people and only one attendee has a conflict, your easiest course of action might be a quick phone call to that person to see whether they can reschedule their conflicting appointment.

Click and hold the Options button to choose from a menu that controls the display of times. By default, you see only working hours for a two-day period, but you can change the display to show all hours. Another option on this menu lets you refresh the Free/Busy times for all attendees instead of waiting for the next scheduled synchronization. Use the Zoom control at the top of the window to see additional days or greater detail.

Use the AutoPick Next button to instruct Outlook to select the next free time in the calendars of all prospective attendees automatically; click the left- or right arrows to pick an earlier or later time that fits on every attendee's calendar.

CHECKING THE STATUS OF A MEETING YOU'VE ARRANGED

Outlook uses special scripts embedded in meeting invitations to process responses. As the invitees accept or decline the meeting request, they return a message to you; when it arrives in your Inbox, Outlook uses the script commands to update the status of the list. As the meeting organizer, you can check a meeting's status at any time by opening it. Look at the information bar at the top of the Appointment tab to see a running tally of the number of prospective attendees who have accepted, declined, or failed to respond.

 If you continually fail to receive updates from specific people, see "The Case of the Missing RSVP" in the "Troubleshooting" section at the end of this chapter.

For a more detailed view of responses, click the Scheduling tab and select the Tracking tab. This list lets you see at a glance which invitees have failed to respond to your invitation, allowing you to send a follow-up message quickly, if necessary.

RESCHEDULING OR CANCELING A MEETING

Handling changes to Outlook meetings requires a delicate balancing act. After the initial round of invitations and responses, each prospective attendee has a separate meeting item on his calendar. Communication of any changes is crucial. In previous Outlook versions, only the meeting organizer could trigger a new round of Outlook messages that ensures every calendar is properly updated.

As the organizer, you can change the date or time of a meeting, change other details (such as its location), or cancel it outright. To make any changes, open the item in your Calendar folder, click the Appointment tab, and change the meeting details; then click the Send Update button. To cancel the meeting, open the meeting item and click the Cancel Invitation button on the Standard toolbar. If you change the date, time, or other details, Outlook prompts you to send an Update message to everyone on the list; if you cancel a meeting, Outlook generates a cancellation request.

An Update message looks exactly like the original request. Everyone who receives it will see the Accept, Decline, and Tentative buttons, just as if it were an original meeting request.

Tip from

Ed & Woody

When you send an Update message, be sure to include text in the Notes box that explains the changes you've made—that text becomes the body of the update message. If you omit this step, attendees who don't read the message carefully might assume they're receiving a duplicate of the original meeting request and fail to notice the change in date or time.

RESPONDING TO MEETING REQUESTS

When you receive a meeting invitation via e-mail, it resembles an ordinary message, with the following key differences:

- The Meeting Request icon to the left of the invitation in the message list is different.
- The message header shows the sender's name, Required and Optional attendees, and the location and time of the meeting.
- Special-purpose toolbar buttons are visible in the Preview pane and in the message window, as shown in Figure 13.6. Using these buttons, you can accept the invitation, decline it, or propose a new time. Click the Tentative button when you want to reserve the right to change your mind later.

Figure 13.6
Use these buttons to accept or decline a meeting invitation. Click the Calendar button to open your Calendar folder and check details of your schedule.

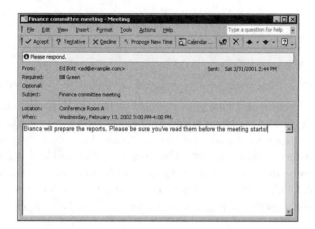

If you accept the invitation, Outlook adds the item to your calendar. You can add a note to your response or send a default notification to the meeting organizer.

If you're not the meeting organizer, you can propose an alternate date or time for the meeting. Choosing this option opens a form in which you can respond to the meeting organizer. As the organizer, you can see all proposed changes in a single window and choose the one that works best for you.

If a meeting organized by someone else is on your calendar, you can change its time—for that matter, you can delete it outright. There's nothing wrong with this course of action if the meeting organizer stops you in the hall or calls on the phone to cancel or change the time. If you change the item in your calendar, Outlook does not update the original item on the meeting organizer's calendar.

Caution

If you attempt to change the time of a meeting organized by someone else, be sure to click the Propose New Time box. If you click Accept or Tentative, the Office Assistant displays a warning dialog box urging you to send a message to the meeting organizer, but Outlook's response-handling script ignores the changes and marks the original item on the organizer's calendar to show that you've accepted.

PART

II

CH

13

To decline an invitation after you have already accepted the meeting request and added it to your calendar, open the item and click the Decline button. Outlook offers to send a message to the organizer; add text explaining that your schedule has changed, and click the Send button.

If you are the meeting organizer, you can also cancel a meeting at any time by deleting it from your calendar. Outlook offers to send a cancellation message on your behalf to all the attendees you previously invited.

TROUBLESHOOTING

THE CASE OF THE MISSING RSVP

Every time I plan a meeting involving a specific person, I fail to receive a response from that person.

Make sure the recipient is receiving your e-mailed invitations. If there's a problem with her e-mail address, the invitations might not be arriving. If she doesn't use Outlook, you might need to send the invitations in iCalendar format. To use this option, open the meeting request form and choose Tools, Send As iCalendar. It's also possible that the recipient is consistently choosing the Don't Send a Response option when acting on meeting invitations. If you can't break recipients of this habit, you'll have to follow up (preferably by phone) and manually update their status on the Attendee Availability tab of the Meeting item.

SECRETS OF THE OFFICE MASTERS: PUBLISHING A CALENDAR AS A WEB PAGE

If you don't have access to an Exchange Server and you don't want to publish your Free/Busy information to a Web server, you can still give other people access to calendar information by saving your Outlook Calendar folder in HTML format.

Tip from

EQ & Woody

This option is especially useful if you maintain an events calendar for an organization. Choose File, New, Folder and create a folder that contains Calendar items. Enter details of the organization's activities as appointments in this folder, and then publish the contents of the calendar periodically as a Web page.

Switch to the Calendar folder and choose File, Save as Web Page. Outlook opens the following dialog box.

Figure 13.7

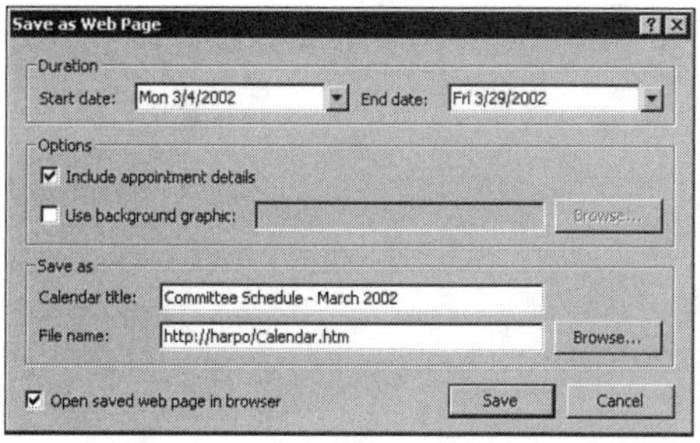

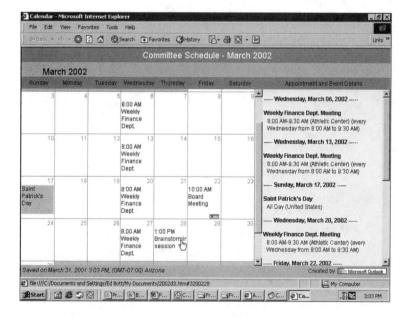

Choose the start and end dates you want to publish and specify whether you want to include details about each appointment from the Notes box. Give the calendar a title, specify a file location, and click Save. If you've set up a shortcut to a Web server in your My Network Places folder, you can publish the page directly to the server by using this technique. The result, as shown in the following figure, is a slick, frame-based page that lets you click individual dates in the month view at left and see details in the frame on the right.

Figure 13.8

USING WORD

CHAPTER 14

WORD ESSENTIALS

In this chapter

AVOIDING COMPATIBILITY PROBLEMS

If you commonly exchange Word documents with people who use other versions of Word, or other word processors in general, one of your first concerns is file compatibility.

USING DIFFERENT WORD FILE FORMATS

The default file format for documents you create with Word 2002 is fully compatible with Word 97 and Word 2000, although there are some minor differences. For example, if you create a nested table in Word 2002, and then open it in Word 97, the nested table is gone. The data's still there—in a single cell, with paragraph marks after each item that had been in its own cell—but if you make any sort of change to the document in Word 97 and save it, the nested table won't reappear in Word 2002, either.

In general, if you and your coworkers all use Word 2002, 2000, or 97, there should be just a few minor file compatibility problems. If you share documents with Word 6 or 95 users, compatibility concerns are a bit more serious. Here's a list of the most common problems:

- Side-by-side tables, diagonal lines in cells, and text that wraps around graphics in table cells (features in Word 2002 and 2000) won't be visible when you open a document in Word 97.

- Word 97 doesn't support 24-bit colors in borders and shading, or WordArt as bullets.

- Word 95 and Word 6.0 (the version in Office 4.x) use a file format that is dramatically different. It doesn't compress graphics well, so a graphics-laden document in Word 6/95 can be nearly twice the size of a similar file in Word 97/2000/2002.

- Word 6/95 documents are limited to 32MB in size; Word 97/2000/2002 files have no such artificial restriction.

- The Word 6.0/95 file format does not support any of the following features in Word 97/2000/2002: page borders, character shading, multilevel bullets, embedded fonts, animated text, versions, and Unicode characters. It also fails to recognize some types of merged table cells, paragraph and text borders, underscores, hyperlinking, tracked changes/revisions, drawings, and text wrapping around pictures.

In addition, passwords are lost in the transition to Word 6.0/95 format. To password protect a Word 97/2000/2002 document that's been saved in Word 6.0/95 format, you have to open the saved document in Word 6.0 or 95, and save it with password protection (File, Save As, Options).

STRATEGIES FOR MIXED WORD ENVIRONMENTS

It's common, especially in large companies, to have working environments where significant numbers of people are using different versions of Word. This causes a number of problems:

- Word 6.0/95 users cannot open Word 97/2000/2002 files, unless they have a specific filter.

- If a Word 6.0/95 user installs the filter, opens a Word 97/2000/2002 document, and subsequently saves it, Word drops all the Word 97/2000/2002 features.

- Word 97/2000/2002 users might open Word 6.0/95 documents and unwittingly save them in Word 97/2000/2002 format, which can make the file inaccessible to Word 6.0/95 users (unless they have installed the import filter described later).

If some members of your workgroup use Word 95 or Word 6.0, you have two choices to reduce compatibility problems:

- Users of Word 97, 2000, and 2002 can save documents in Word 6.0/95 format. That means everyone in the workgroup will be able to open and work with the files, but you lose all the Word 97/2000/2002-specific features.

- Users of Word 6.0 or Word 95 can install an import filter to allow them to open and work on Word 97/2000/2002 files. But as soon as the Word 6.0/95 user edits and saves the file, all the Word 97/2000/2002-specific features disappear.

CHANGING THE DEFAULT DOCUMENT FORMAT

To change the default document format for Word 97, 2000, or 2002 to Word 6.0/Word 95 format, choose Tools, Options, and click the Save tab. In the Save Word Files As box, choose Word 6.0/95 (*.doc).

In Word 2000 and 2002, every time you save a document, Word scans the document to see what features will be lost (see Figure 14.1). Click Continue to save in Word 6.0/95 format.

Figure 14.1
When you save a document in Word 6.0/95 format, Word 2000 and 2002 warn you of any features you're about to lose.

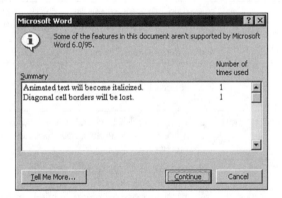

Is the standard word processor in your company something other than Word 2000 or 2002? If most of the people in your office use Word 95, and you save files in Word 95 format even though you're using Word 97, you can force Word 2002 to behave like Word 95. In fact, if most of the people you exchange files with use WordPerfect, other early versions of Word for Windows and MS-DOS, or Word for the Macintosh, you can make Word 2002 change how it displays your document, so it looks more like how it will appear with other word processors. To do so, choose Tools, Options, Compatibility, and select the other word processor in the Recommended Options For box.

PART

III

CH

14

INSTALLING THE WORD 97/2000/2002 IMPORT FILTER FOR WORD 6.0/95 USERS

To install the Word 97/2000/2002 import filter so Word 6.0/95 users can open and edit files you create in Word 97/2000/2002 format, copy the Wrd97cnv.exe file (for Windows 3.x users) or Wdcnv97.exe (for other versions of Windows) from Microsoft's Office Update Web site (officeupdate.microsoft.com) to a temporary folder on the machine using Word 6.0 or Word 95. When you run Wrd97cnv.exe, it automatically detects the version of Word in use, installs the proper filter, and makes necessary adjustments to the Windows Registry. Using this filter, Word 6.0 and Word 95 users can open Word 97, 2000, or 2002 documents directly (although, as noted earlier, they can't save in Word 97/2000/2002 format).

EXPORTING DOCUMENTS IN OTHER FORMATS

Word 2002 contains dozens of export filters, which enable you to save Word 2002 documents in other file formats. To change the format of a file, choose File, Save As, and pick the format in the Save as Type box. Most of the file format descriptions are self-explanatory; see Table 14.1 for a list of those that aren't as easily understood.

TABLE 14.1 SAVE AS FILE FORMATS

Format	Meaning
Rich Text Format (*.rtf)	A general-purpose format that generally retains all formatting. Can be read by many programs.
Plain Text (*.txt)	Straight text with no formatting, using the ANSI character set. Section breaks and page breaks convert to paragraph marks (that is, carriage return/line feeds). The "lowest common denominator" format.
Text with Layout (*.ans)	Same as Plain Text, but also places a paragraph mark at the end of every line, and inserts spaces to approximate indents and tabs.
MS-DOS Text with Layout(*.asc)	Same as Text with Layout, but uses the extended ASCII character set (which contains a few characters not in the ANSI character set).
Word 6.0/95 (*.doc)	Save in Word 6.0/95 format. (Actually, it's in Word 95 format, because there are slight differences between Word 6 and Word 95 formats; for example, highlighting doesn't appear in Word 6.)
Word 97-2000 & 6.0/95 – RTF (*.doc)	When you save in this format, Word actually saves the file in Rich Text Format (see first entry in this table), but it places a *.doc filename extension on the file.
Web Archive (*.mht, *.mhtml)	Saves all the components of a Web page, including text and graphics, in one HTML file.

Format	Meaning
Web Page, Filtered (*.htm, *.html)	Saves the document as an HTML file, with most HTML tags removed. If you save a document in standard HTML format, you'll be able to open the HTML file and edit it normally in Word (the so-called "round trip" feature). If you save in this special, trimmed format, the file will be much smaller and less complex, but you lose the round-trip feature: open a filtered HTML file in Word and many Word features (for example, bulleted lists) are lost.

Caution

When you save a Word document as RTF, but with a *.doc filename extension, third-party programs might fail to recognize the file (indeed, some will trigger a General Protection Fault). In addition, the file will be much larger than the same file saved in Word 2002 *.doc format. Unless you have a specific, pressing need to use this odd hybrid, avoid it. Remember, this was the original default file format for Word 97. This caused so many compatibility problems that Microsoft quickly released a fix.

To remove extraneous export filters from the list, use the Office 2002 CD-ROM to uninstall the ones you don't need.

→ For details on how to remove features after installing Office, **see** "Adding and Removing Office Features," **p. 1069**.

STRATEGIES FOR NON-WORD ENVIRONMENTS

If you want to exchange documents with people who use other word processors, you have several options:

- Save your files in a format the other person can open. Although few word processors read Word 97/2000/2002 format documents directly, many can handle RTF or WordPerfect 5.0 format.

- Use a third-party format-conversion routine. There are several on the Web. WordPort has a free evaluation version available at www.fileconverter.com.

- Have your correspondent use a Word 97 document file viewer. Although he won't be able to make changes to the document, he will be able to see it as you intended. There's a free viewer available from the Microsoft Web site, www.microsoft.com. See Knowledge Base article Q165908 for a detailed description of platforms and installation instructions.

BATCH CONVERSIONS WITH THE CONVERSION WIZARD

Word 2002 includes a wizard that you can use to convert any number of files to or from Word 2002 format in a *batch* operation. This could come in handy if, say, you've already converted an entire department to Office 2002, and you have a shared folder full of large Word documents with graphics. A batch conversion could significantly reduce disk space demands. (On the other hand, if you have a large number of Word 6.0/95 users still working on those files, it's probably smartest not to convert them.)

To use the Batch Conversion Wizard, follow these steps:

1. Choose File, New (or bring up the New Document task pane). Under New from Template, choose General Templates. On the Other Documents tab, double-click Batch Conversion Wizard.

2. The wizard (see Figure 14.2) asks whether you want to convert the files from Word 2002 format to a different format, or whether you want to convert a different format to Word 2002. Select the format you require.

Figure 14.2
The Batch Conversion Wizard converts entire folders of files from one Word format to another.

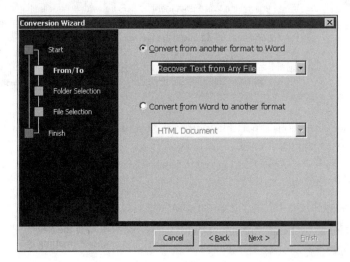

3. Choose a folder containing the files you want to convert and click Finish.

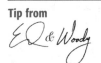

Tip from

Use the Recover Text from Any File converter (see Figure 14.2) to salvage corrupted documents. This remarkable option reaches into files—even scrambled Word documents—and salvages any text it can find, discarding binary characters.

UNDERSTANDING YOUR FORMATTING OPTIONS

Every Word document consists of components arranged in a strict hierarchy that is unrelated to the way you create a document. Every Word document follows a predictable hierarchy, consisting of one or more sections, which in turn contain one or more paragraphs, each of which consists of one or more characters. Although it's possible to select an entire document and apply formatting to it, Word doesn't actually format at the document level; instead, it applies your changes individually to characters, paragraphs, and sections within the document.

Word allows you to apply formatting directly, by making a selection and then using the Styles and Formatting task pane, the Format menu, or the Page Setup dialog box. You can also re-use formatting that appears elsewhere in your document via the task pane in an ad-hoc fashion. Or you can define collections of character or paragraph formatting choices, save them as named styles, and then apply the style to selected characters or paragraphs.

CHARACTER FORMATS

Character formats apply to letters, numbers, and punctuation marks. The most common formatting options that apply to characters are font-related: the font name, size, and color, for example, as well as attributes such as bold, italic, underline, and strikethrough. If you copy or move a formatted character from one part of a document to another, the formatting travels with it.

→ To learn more about formatting, **see** "Common Formatting Options," **p. 100**.

Three special characters merit close attention:

- Each space is a character. Although you can't see its color, you can easily note its size: A 10-point space takes up much less room on a line than a 48-point space.

- Within a Word document, a tab is a character. When Word encounters a tab character, it shifts to the next tab stop before continuing to lay down text.

- A paragraph mark is technically a character as well, although you can't print a paragraph mark. By default, Word does not show paragraph marks on the screen, but they're always there. You can select, copy, move, or delete paragraph marks.

→ You can check the Show All Formatting Marks box at the bottom of the Reveal Formatting task pane or click the Show/Hide button to make paragraph marks and other formatting characters visible; **see** "Using the Show/Hide Button," **p. 355**.

The most common character treatment options are available via toolbar buttons and keyboard shortcuts. For example, you can click the Bold, Italic, or Underline buttons on the Formatting toolbar, or use the shortcut key combinations Ctrl+B, Ctrl+I, Ctrl+U, respectively, to toggle these formatting options for selected text.

Tip from

EQ & Woody

Here's a formatting shortcut even many experienced Word users don't know about. If you position the insertion point within a word and click a formatting button or key combination, the formatting applies to the entire word. In this case, a "word" is any series of characters delimited on each end by a space or punctuation mark. Use this option to change the font, size, or attributes of a word without selecting it first.

When you start typing in a new, blank document, Word's default setup uses 12-point Times New Roman. To change the default font and size, choose Format, Font, select the font you want to use as a default, and click Default (see Figure 14.3).

PART

III

CH

14

Figure 14.3
Change the default font for all documents by selecting the font you prefer and then clicking the Default button.

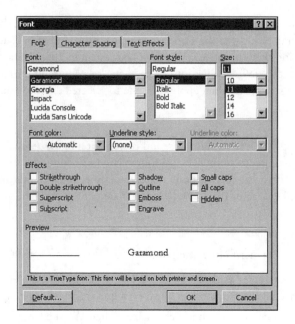

For normal correspondence, consider changing the font—Garamond, for example, is much more striking visually—and reducing the point size down to 11, or even 10. Although 12-point is the Word default, many people find it too large for business correspondence. Many experts feel 11-point type is an excellent compromise.

Tip from

E&*Woody*

If you usually share documents with other users instead of printing them, make sure you pick a default font that others are likely to have, such as one of the default Windows or Internet Explorer fonts.

Character spacing can be changed in any number of ways: moving characters above or below the baseline (superscripting and subscripting); magnifying or reducing selected groups of characters (scale); and even squishing together predefined pairs of letters that fit well together—such as VA—to minimize the whitespace between them (kerning). All these are discussed in the next chapter.

→ To learn more about fonts and character formatting, **see** "Using and Managing Fonts," **p. 99** and "Changing Character Attributes," **p. 100**.

Word also supports highlighting, a method of changing the background color much as you would with a highlighting pen. Although highlighting is rarely used in final documents, it's a handy way to draw attention to text during reviews, or to emphasize pieces of text for your own scanning.

If you're exchanging drafts of a document with a coworker, for example, use a yellow highlighter to flag sections where you have questions or comments. If several people are reviewing the same document, each one can use a different color so others can see at a glance who marked up specific sections. Although you can formally track changes to a document, highlighting comes in handy in informal situations.

→ To work with documents in a group, **see** "Sharing Documents," **p. 396**.

Although highlighting isn't, strictly speaking, a character format (because it really affects the character's background), it behaves much like a character format: If you copy or move highlighted characters, for example, the highlighting travels with the character.

Caution

Highlighting is *not* removed when you use the Clear Formatting option on the Styles and Formatting task pane. Internally, Word does not treat highlighting as if it were character formatting.

To apply highlighting to characters within a document, you can either make a selection and then click the Highlight button on the Formatting toolbar, or click the Highlight button, and then "paint" the highlighting on characters. Click the drop-down arrow to the right of the Highlight button to choose one of 15 available colors. The pointer changes to a highlighting pen with insertion point; to turn off highlighting and return to normal editing, click the Highlight button again, or press Esc.

→ For advanced formatting tips, **see** "Changing Text Formatting," **p. 380**.

If you open a document that contains fonts that you don't have on your machine, Word provides a way to specify which fonts should be substituted for the missing ones. Choose Tools, Options, Compatibility, and then click the Font Substitutions button. In the Missing Document Font box, select the font you want to change. Then, in the Substituted Font drop-down list, choose the font to replace it.

Tip from

EQ & Woody

Although the fonts you specify won't be, literally, substituted for the missing ones—the document file itself isn't changed—Word uses the fonts you pick to display the document onscreen, and to print it.

PARAGRAPH FORMATS

Each time you press Enter, Word inserts a paragraph mark and starts a new paragraph. By definition, a paragraph in Word consists of a paragraph mark, plus all the characters before the paragraph mark, up to (but not including) the preceding paragraph mark. Paragraph marks are a crucial part of Word, because they contain all paragraph formatting. When you copy, move, or delete a paragraph mark, the paragraph formatting goes with the mark.

Paragraph formatting includes alignment (left, center, right), indenting, bulleting, and spacing—both between lines within a paragraph and between paragraphs. It also covers

PART
III

CH
14

background colors and shading, and boxes and lines drawn around and between paragraphs. Surprisingly, tab stops are also considered paragraph formatting—you don't specify a set of tab stops for each line on a page, as you would with a typewriter; instead, tab stops remain uniform throughout an entire paragraph.

When you press Enter to create a new paragraph, the new paragraph usually takes on the formatting of the earlier paragraph. For example, if you position the insertion point with a right-justified paragraph and press Enter, the new paragraph will also be right-justified.

DIRECT FORMATTING VERSUS STYLES

For simple, short documents, it's often easiest to apply formatting directly to paragraphs and characters, either through the Format menu, or using the Styles & Formatting task pane. But when a document extends beyond a few pages, or when consistent formatting is crucial, you should use styles instead. Styles have one great advantage over manually applied formatting: If you change the style, those changes ripple throughout the document.

Word supports two kinds of styles: character styles, which include only character formatting; and paragraph styles, which combine paragraph formatting information with character formatting.

→ To learn more about styles, **see** "Formatting Documents with Styles," **p. 468**.

For example, you might establish a paragraph style for a marketing report called ChapterHeading, and make it Arial 24-point bold (that's the character formatting part), with 6 points of space after the heading (the paragraph formatting part). As you're typing, every time you start a new chapter, you type in the title of the chapter and apply the ChapterHeading style. The day before your marketing report is to be sent to the board, you decide it will look better if you use a different set of fonts, and you decide to change the chapter headings to Garamond 20-point italic with 12 points of space after the heading.

If you know that every chapter heading in the marketing report is formatted with the ChapterHeading style, you can change all the chapter headings in a few seconds, by changing the settings for the ChapterHeading style. On the other hand, if you had applied formatting manually, you would have to scan the entire document and change the formatting of each chapter heading manually; you run the risk of missing a chapter heading, which results in an unprofessional look for your document.

→ Line and page breaks, indents, tabs, and other paragraph formatting are covered in depth in "Changing Paragraph Formatting," **p. 383**.

APPLYING AND MODIFYING FORMATS

Word 2002 includes two nifty task panes that make it easier than ever to understand why and how formatting has appeared in your document, and to apply formatting quickly and reliably.

REVEALING FORMATTING WITHIN A DOCUMENT

WordPerfect diehards won't be impressed, but Word 2002 includes a feature that's meant to mimic the "reveal codes" capability found in WordPerfect.

Bring up the task pane, and choose Reveal Formatting at the top. Word responds with a comprehensive list of all formatting applied to the current selection (see Figure 14.4).

Figure 14.4
Word can show you full formatting information for any part of a document.

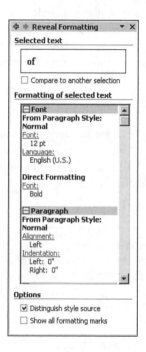

If you check the Distinguish Style Source box at the bottom of the Reveal Formatting task pane, Word shows you precisely why specific formatting appears in the selection. For example, in Figure 14.4, you can see that the base font for the paragraph is 12 point, and bold formatting has been applied directly. This kind of detail can be useful if you're trying to sort through exactly why and how text appears in a particular format.

COPYING FORMATS

There are three ways to copy specific formatting from one place in a document to another:

- Set up a style to reflect the formatting, and apply the style (either character or paragraph) to the text you want to change. This is the most consistent and reliable approach, and it allows you to change formatting throughout a document by modifying the style.

- Use the Format Painter icon on the Standard toolbar. In general, you select the text (or paragraph) that includes the text that's formatted to your liking, click the Format Painter icon, and then "paint" the formatting elsewhere in your document. The process is slow, cumbersome, and error-prone, especially if you accidentally select a paragraph mark prior to "painting." This method should only be used if you don't have enough room on your screen to use the task pane.

- Use the Styles and Formatting task pane. If your document already contains the formatting you want, select the text you want to format, and then click the formatting in the Pick Formatting to Apply box on the task pane. Note that the Styles and Formatting task pane isn't limited to formally defined styles: it also includes entries for all the manually applied formatting that exists in your document.

The Styles and Formatting task pane also makes it easy to set up formal styles, then modify and apply them.

REMOVING TEXT FORMATTING

Novice users can make a thorough mess of a document by randomly applying direct formatting to characters and paragraphs. To remove all manually applied formatting from a selection so you can start fresh, bring up the Styles and Formatting task pane and choose Clear Formatting. Doing so removes all manually applied formatting, both at the character and the paragraph level.

Tip from	Although the key combination is a bit arcane, you can also remove manually applied formatting by selecting the text, pressing Ctrl+Q to remove manually applied paragraph formatting, and then press Ctrl+spacebar to remove character formatting.

PAGE/SECTION SETUP OPTIONS

Most simple Word documents contain just one *section*. Usually, you'll add sections to a document when you want to change the header or footer in the same document, or to alter the number of columns—perhaps to print a long list. You can also change sections to switch from one paper size or orientation to another—for example, to print a table in landscape orientation in the middle of a document.

Each section in a document has its own headers and footers, page size, margins, number of snaking newspaper-like columns, and paper source—a designated paper bin on your printer.

→ To properly format sections, **see** "Formatting Documents by Section," **p. 407**.

Sections are separated by section break marks, which are visible only in Normal view (see Figure 14.5).

Section formatting is stored in the section break mark; the formatting for the final section in a document is in the document's final paragraph mark. When you select a section break mark and copy, move, or delete it, the section formatting stored in the mark goes with it.

Figure 14.5
To see section breaks, switch to Normal view.

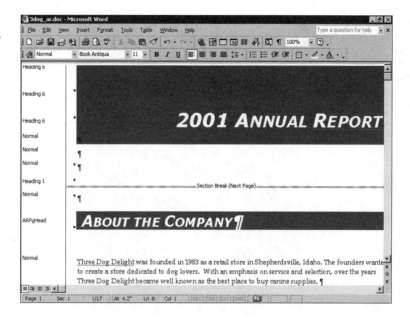

The safest way to add a new section to a document is to insert a new section break manually—choose Insert, Break and choose from the list of available section break types:

- Next Page starts the next section on a new page.
- Continuous lets the new section follow the current one, without a page break.
- Even Page forces the next section to start on an even-numbered page.
- Odd Page forces the next section to start on an odd-numbered page.

Word automatically inserts section break marks in a document if you choose File, Page Setup, click the Layout tab, and choose This Point Forward (see Figure 14.6). Word adds the section break as a consequence of changing the layout. Similarly, if you choose Format, Columns and choose This Point Forward from the Apply To drop-down list, Word automatically inserts a section break to mark the point where the number of columns changes.

Tip from

EQ & Woody

Editing and formatting documents with multiple sections can be extremely confusing. If you inadvertently move or delete a section break mark, you can make a mess of the document's headers and footers, for example, and it's nearly impossible to recover except by starting over. When you work on documents with more than one section, it's strongly recommended that you work only in Normal view, and that you insert section break marks manually by choosing Insert, Break.

PART
III

CH
14

Figure 14.6
Choosing This Point Forward inserts a section break mark in the document, and then formats the newly created section.

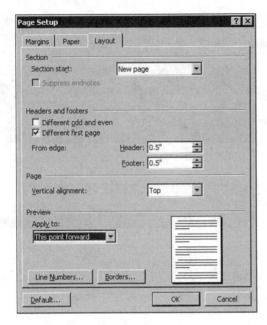

The most common reason for using multiple sections in a document is to alter headers and footers. Each section in a document has its own headers and footers, although you can specify that a section "link to" the preceding section, and carry forward the preceding section's headers and footers.

→ To customize headers and footers, **see** "Creating and Editing Headers and Footers," **p. 417**.

Sections also allow you to organize snaking newspaper-like columns, whether they're for an entire document, or for a list of items you want to appear in the middle of a document.

→ If you need to change the number of columns, **see** "Formatting a Document with Columns," **p. 414**.

FLOATING VERSUS INLINE OBJECTS

Like other Office applications, Word includes a *drawing layer*, which can contain pictures, text boxes, and other drawing objects. When you specify that text should wrap around a picture, for example, Word places the picture in the drawing layer.

→ To change text-wrapping options when you use floating objects in the drawing layer, **see** "Working with the Drawing Layer," **p. 108**.

Note

When you place a picture inline in the document itself, Word treats it as though it were a single character. Thus, you can choose Format, Font and use the resulting dialog box to place an animated border—say, Marching Black Ants—around a picture.

Word also allows you to insert an object called a Drawing Canvas onto the drawing layer. The canvas constitutes a "sanctuary" for drawings: Everything you place on a canvas sticks together; objects on the canvas stay in the same relative location, and the canvas as a whole is not allowed to break across a page. To place a canvas on a page, choose Insert, Picture, New Drawing. A canvas also appears the first time you select an AutoShape on the Drawing toolbar. (To access this setting, choose Tools, Options to open the Options dialog box. Then select the Automatically Create Drawing Canvas When Inserting AutoShapes box on the General tab.)

AUTOMATIC FORMATTING

Unless you make a special effort to turn them off, Word applies automatic formatting in a wide variety of situations, sometimes for no apparent reason. The effect is guaranteed to annoy anyone except a Microsoft marketing manager, for whom these automatic changes are a trademarked feature called IntelliSense™. The most obvious paragraph AutoFormatting options are listed in Table 14.2.

TABLE 14.2   PARAGRAPH AUTOFORMATTING

If You Type Any of These...	Followed by This...	You'll Get...
* - -- > -> =>	A space or tab, and then text, and Enter	A paragraph formatted as bulleted
A symbol (Insert, Symbol)	Two or more spaces, or a tab, followed by text, and Enter	A paragraph formatted as bulleted, using the symbol as the bullet character
A picture (Insert, Picture) slightly larger than the height of the line	Two or more spaces, or a tab, and then text and Enter	A paragraph formatted as bulleted, using the picture as the bullet character
0 1 I i A a	A period, hyphen, closing parenthesis, or > sign, then a space or tab, and then text and Enter	A paragraph formatted as numbered, using standard, Roman or alphabetic numbers
Three or more - _ = * ~ #	Enter	Applies a border to the paragraph above (or below)
Series of plus signs and hyphens, ending in a plus sign; for example, +----+----+	Enter	Creates a one-row table, with columns defined by the plus signs

As soon as Word applies AutoFormatting, you're presented with a "lightning bolt" icon that gives you quick access to various options for undoing what Word hath wrought (see Figure 14.7).

Figure 14.7
Word gives you the tools to undo AutoFormatting as soon as an piece of text has been changed.

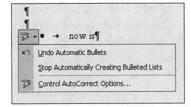

To undo automatic paragraph formatting quickly, press Backspace or Ctrl+Z immediately after Word applies the AutoFormatting.

In the case of AutoFormatted numbered or bulleted lists, if you press Enter twice, the bulleting/numbering is removed from empty paragraphs. To turn on bullet/numbering formatting again, either start the list numbers over, or go back to the end of the last bulleted or numbered paragraph where you left off, and press Enter. Auto bulleting and numbering can also be turned off by clicking on the appropriate icon on the Formatting toolbar.

The most obvious types of character AutoFormatting:

- If you type an ordinal, such as 1st, 2nd, 3rd, 4th, 30th, 175th, and so on, Word superscripts the characters: 1st, 2nd, 3rd, 4th, 30th, 175th.

- The specific fractions 1/4, 1/2, and 3/4 are changed into ¼, ½, and ¾.

- Internet addresses such as www.mcp.com and woody@wopr.com are automatically converted into hyperlinks. The hyperlinks are "hot," so Ctrl+clicking a Web address brings up your Web browser and takes you to the site; Ctrl+clicking an e-mail address invokes your default e-mail program and sets up a message.

In all three of these cases, if you click the Undo button or press Ctrl+Z immediately after Word performs its AutoFormatting, the formatting returns to normal. In addition, automatically created hotlinks come with full drop-down instructions on various means of their removal.

To turn off this kind of character AutoFormatting, see "AutoFormat As You Type Options" later in this chapter.

CHOOSING THE RIGHT DOCUMENT VIEW

Select a document view by clicking the View menu. Different document views have their own advantages. Most advanced Word users will find themselves switching views as they work on documents—particularly more complex documents—depending on what they're trying to accomplish.

NORMAL VIEW

Normal view (see Figure 14.8) shows section breaks, fonts and other character attributes, page breaks (shown as a dotted line), and, optionally, the names of paragraph styles. Normal view doesn't show headers or footers, or place pictures in the locations they will ultimately occupy when the pages are printed.

Figure 14.8
Normal view shows most formatting, but reduces overhead by not showing pictures in their ultimate location.

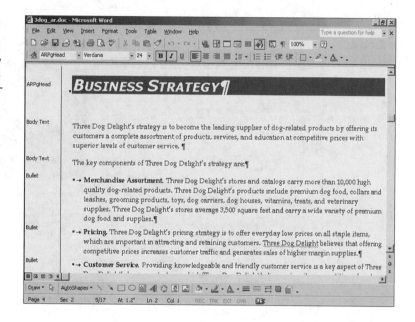

Normal view has three advantages:

- You can see section breaks. If you have more than one section in a document, you should seriously consider working in Normal view when formatting or entering text.
- You can see style names for all paragraphs. Normally, this area is hidden; to make it visible, choose Tools, Options, click the View tab, and use the Style Area Width spinner control to set a width greater than 0. If you're scanning a document to ensure that style standards are being observed, Normal view and Outline view are your only choices.

PART

III

CH

14

- Because it doesn't attempt to place pictures, Normal view runs considerably faster than Print Layout view. On slower machines, or with large complex files that contain many graphics, the difference in scrolling speed can be considerable.

PRINT LAYOUT VIEW

Print Layout view (see Figure 14.9) shows the document precisely as it will be printed, with page breaks, headers and footers, and pictures arranged correctly onscreen. (In previous Office versions, this view was called Page Layout view.)

Figure 14.9
Print Layout shows a true WYSIWYG (What You See Is What You Get) view of your document.

Many advanced Word users work in Print Layout view unless they specifically need one of the tools available in the other views because there are no surprises: The rendition on the screen closely mimics what will appear on paper.

WEB LAYOUT VIEW

Of course, if you aren't going to put the document on paper, but instead intend to publish on the Web, it's important to see how the document will look when viewed as an HTML file. That's where Web Layout view comes in.

In Web Layout view, Word wraps text to fit the window, shows backgrounds, and places graphics on the screen the same way they would appear in a browser.

OUTLINE VIEW

Outline view (see Figure 14.10) allows you to see an outline of your document while you're working on it. This view can be particularly helpful for rearranging sections of large documents, or promoting and demoting headings.

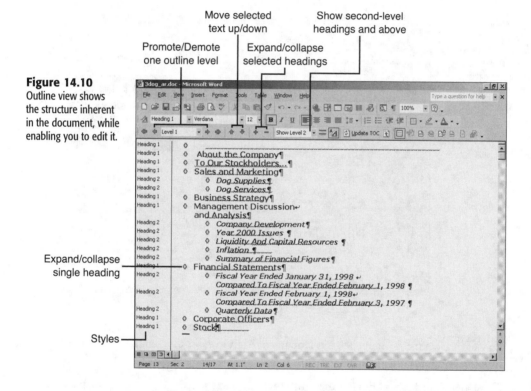

Figure 14.10
Outline view shows the structure inherent in the document, while enabling you to edit it.

PART

III

CH

14

Of course, all the normal editing techniques are available in Outline view: You can select, drag, copy, cut, and paste, as you would in any other view.

Master Documents are generally maintained in Outline view.

→ To work in Outline view, **see** "Outline View," **p. 347**.

DOCUMENT MAP VIEW

Word has one more method for keeping track of a document's structure while you edit it. The Document Map (see Figure 14.11) shows the document's outline, using the same outline levels employed in Outline view.

Figure 14.11
If you have enough room on the screen, Document Map offers one-click navigation to any heading in a document.

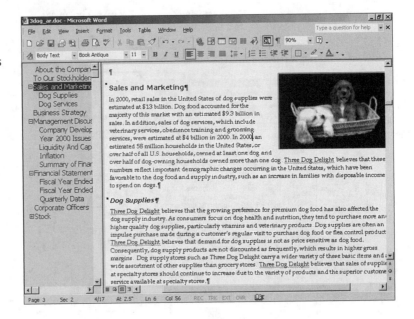

To view a Document Map, click the Document Map icon on the Standard toolbar, or choose it from the View menu.

The Document Map is "hot" in the sense that you can click anywhere in the map and be transported to that location in your document. Although it isn't as active as Outline view—you can't promote or demote headings in the Document Map, or set a single uniform outline level for viewing—experienced Word users who commonly deal with long documents can readily navigate with it.

Caution

If you apply outline levels to a Word 2002 document and then open that document in Word 97, chances are good that an annoying Word 97 bug will destroy all your work. Word 97 automatically scans documents as it opens them, and arbitrarily reassigns outline levels, thus destroying the Document Map.

Three additional important settings are under the View menu, as described in the sections that follow.

ZOOM OPTIONS

Word lets you "Zoom" a document, making it appear larger or smaller on the screen, by choosing View, Zoom (see Figure 14.12), or the Zoom button on the Standard Toolbar.

Figure 14.12
Zoom in (higher percentage number) to see more detail; zoom out to see more of the page.

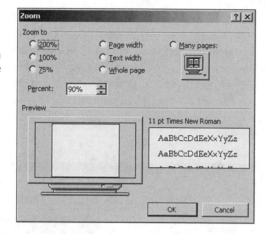

Tip from
EQ & Woody

Fine-tune the Zoom percent to make your fonts more legible. For day-to-day use, you want the largest zoom factor that lets you see your most commonly used fonts without straining. Also, double-check to ensure that your zoom setting lets you easily distinguish, visually, between normal, bold, and italic characters.

If you have an IntelliMouse, you can zoom in 10% increments by holding down the Ctrl key as you rotate the wheel up or down.

FULL SCREEN VIEW

Full Screen view shows you a larger part of your document without changing screen resolution, at the expense of making menus and toolbars harder to access. It's particularly useful for people working at low-display resolutions.

When you choose View, Full Screen, Word gets rid of most interface elements—including the title bar, menus, toolbars, status bar, rulers, and scrollbars—showing you only the document along with a lone toolbar that contains the Close Full Screen button.

In Full Screen view, you can reach the pull-down menus by sliding your mouse to the top of the screen, but toolbars that were previously visible are hidden. If you lose the Close Full Screen button, you can restore it by pressing the Esc key.

Tip from

To display other toolbars in Full Screen view, right-click the Close Full Screen button and choose the toolbar from the list. After making the toolbars visible, you can dock them to any edge of the screen or allow them to float. The Close Full Screen toolbar is also fully customizable. If you regularly work in Full Screen view, consider adding buttons to this toolbar for common tasks.

SPLITTING A DOCUMENT WINDOW

Word allows you to split the document window, giving you two independently scrollable panes looking in on the same document, one over the other (see Figure 14.13). Although each of the panes operates independently—you can even have Normal view in one pane, and Outline view in the other—it's important to realize that you have just one copy of the document open: Changes made in one pane are reflected immediately in the other. This can be useful because it allows you to compare parts of a document side by side, even when they're widely separated in the document.

Figure 14.13
Split the document window into two separately maintained panes. Split panes enable you to view different parts of the same document simultaneously.

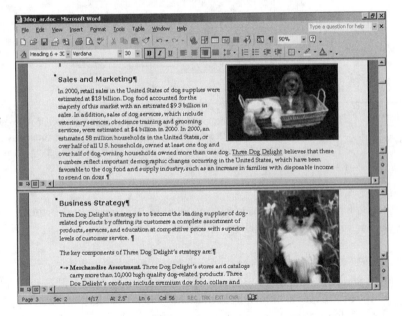

To split the document window, choose Window, Split, and click where you want the split to appear. Click and drag the split bar to resize the document panes. Double-click the split bar to restore the window to a single pane.

Note

You cannot split the document window when Document Map is active.

PRINTING WORD DOCUMENTS

When you get right down to it, most Word documents are destined for the printer. Word offers many features to give you extensive control over how pages print.

PREVIEWING PRINTED PAGES

If you're looking at one page, Word's Print Preview mode offers no advantage over the standard Print Layout view. But there are two situations in which Print Preview is extremely useful. Click the Multiple Pages button and drag to show as few as two or (depending on hardware) as many as 60 pages at one time (Print Layout view's Zoom setting goes up to only 6 pages). This view is especially helpful when you want to see at a glance where headlines, graphics, tables, and other nontext elements fall in your document. Although it's possible to edit text and move objects on the Print Preview screen, this screen is most appropriate for getting a bird's-eye view of your entire document.

To enter Word's Print Preview mode (see Figure 14.14), click the Print Preview button on the Standard toolbar, or choose File, Print Preview.

Figure 14.14
Word's Print Preview mode shows you precisely how the printed page will appear—but Print Layout view does almost as well, with none of the limitations.

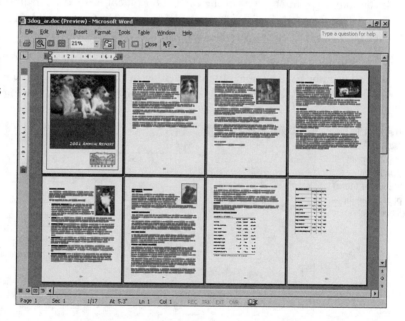

Tip from

EQ & Woody

In Print Preview mode, the default mouse pointer lets you toggle between a 100% view of the page you click or back to a view of the number of pages you selected. Click the Magnifier button to toggle between this pointer and an I-beam insertion point you can use for editing.

PART
III

CH
14

In Print Preview mode, you also have access to the Shrink to Fit button. Use this feature when the last page of your document includes two or three lines, and you want to force those leftovers to fit on the previous page.

Click the Shrink to Fit button and Word alters font sizes to reduce the number of pages in the document by one. Note that changing the font size sometimes doesn't affect the spacing between paragraphs, so the resulting document might have an inordinate amount of white-space. Also, the Shrink operation makes no changes to margins. Word won't reduce font sizes below the range of 6 or 7 points.

> **Caution**
>
> While in Print Preview mode, you can click the Undo button or press Ctrl+Z to reverse the Shrink to Fit operation, but after you've closed and saved the document, it's impossible to return the document to its original state.

CHOOSING WHAT TO PRINT

If you want to print one copy of the current document using the defaults established on the Print tab of the Options dialog box (see the Print What Choices table later in this chapter), click the Print icon on the Standard toolbar.

Word also allows you to print the currently selected page(s), or to specify the pages you want to print by page number. To invoke either of those options, choose File, Print, and select Current Page or type in the page numbers in the Pages box (see Figure 14.15).

Figure 14.15
Word 2002's Print allows you to print "thumbnail" images, two or four (or more) to a page, using the Pages per sheet box.

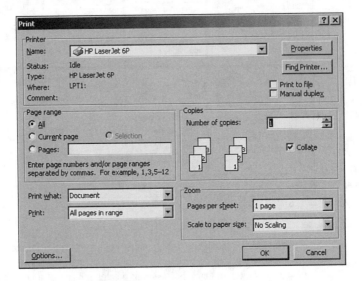

The Print box lets you print all pages, or odd or even pages only. If you know how your printer feeds sheets, you can use this setting to print "duplex"—where pages alternate on the front and back of each sheet.

Tip from

EQ & Woody

> If you check the Print to File box in the Print dialog box, Word prompts you for a file-name. If your printer is currently unavailable, but you want to produce a hard copy of a document you're working with now, it can be a good option. Later, when the printer is available, you don't need to reopen Word; just copy the file you created directly to your printer by, for example, dragging it onto the printer icon in Windows Explorer.

Ever wonder what AutoText entries you have set up in a particular document or template? How about the styles, or many other hidden parts of your document, for that matter. Choices in the Print What drop-down list let you find out (see Table 14.3).

TABLE 14.3   PRINT DIALOG BOX'S PRINT WHAT CHOICES

Option	What Prints
Document Properties	Some of the information found in the dialog box that appears when you choose File, Properties: all the Summary information, and some of the General and Statistics
Document Showing Markup	Prints the document with track changes items, including comments, in the margin; it does *not* print the style area
Styles	All the styles that you can see if you choose Format, Styles, and select Styles in Use
AutoText entries	All AutoText entries available in the document, whether they originate in the document's template or the Normal global document template, Normal.dot
Key Assignments	Only custom keyboard assignments for the current document, template, and global

PRINTING THUMBNAILS

The Pages Per Sheet list in the Print dialog box (refer to Figure 14.15) offers you the opportunity to print thumbnails of your documents—2, 4, 6, 8, or 16 pages—on a single sheet of paper.

Tip from

EQ & Woody

> If your primary reason for printing is to file away a hardcopy record of your documents, consider printing 2-up or 4-up, duplex if possible. Although you might need a magnifying glass to read the resulting printout, the storage space savings are enormous.

COLLATING

If you choose to print more than one copy of a document, Word's default settings *collate* the copies for you—printing one copy from start to finish, and then printing the next copy from start to finish, and so on. That's convenient if you want to pull the pages right out of the printer and pass them around without any additional work.

CUSTOMIZING THE WORD INTERFACE

Many components of the Word interface—menus, toolbars, keyboard shortcuts, and the like—work precisely the same way as the other Office applications.

→ For the Office-wide overview, **see** Chapter 2, "Customizing the Office Interface," **p. 27**.

In this section, you learn how to take control of features that are specific to Word.

Much of the rest of the way that Word works can be customized, as well. If you find that a specific "feature" in Word gets in your way, more often than not there's a simple check box that will disable the feature—or enable an alternative that might work better for you.

Word's customizing settings fall into two main groups: Options settings and AutoCorrect settings. You'll find both menu choices on the Tools menu; in addition the "lightning bolt" icon that appears whenever an AutoFormat change has taken place allows you to delve directly into the AutoCorrect settings, by choosing the Control AutoCorrect Options item. Although most of the settings are quite obvious, the more confusing and most important ones are covered in the following sections.

Tip from	Take a few minutes to review your settings, with these advanced user suggestions in mind. Then save the settings with the Save My Settings Wizard so you can restore them if you have to reinstall Office or switch to a new computer. To get to the Save My Settings Wizard, choose Start, Programs, Microsoft Office Tools, Save My Settings Wizard. Run the wizard and follow the instructions to store your settings in a convenient location.
EQ & Woody	

CONTROLLING HOW WORD DOCUMENTS APPEAR ON THE TASKBAR

Until the appearance of Word 2000, all previous versions of Word used the Windows "Multiple Document Interface" or MDI. Under MDI, Word appeared on the Windows taskbar just once, no matter how many documents you had open. Word 2000 took a different approach, introducing a variant of the "Single Document Interface"—SDI—which produces one taskbar icon for each open document.

The MDI versus SDI debate has many facets; neither is clearly superior to the other. For example, under MDI, there's very little screen real estate overhead inherent in displaying multiple documents simultaneously. Under SDI, however, all the toolbars and other screen overhead is duplicated for each open document, leaving precious little room available to show your documents.

Word 2002 allows you to switch between MDI and SDI, by choosing Tools, Options, going to the View tab, and either checking or unchecking the Windows in Taskbar box at the upper right. (Check the box for MDI; uncheck it for SDI.)

Tip from

EQ & Woody

If you commonly show more than one document on the screen at a time, its strongly recommended that you uncheck the Windows in Taskbar box, and stick to SDI.

It remains to be seen if Microsoft will finally resolve the MDI versus SDI debate in the next version of Word by allowing users to choose whether to show multiple documents on the taskbar but only a single set of toolbars with multiple open documents—the combination most advanced users would take. Third-party add-ons have been doing this for years.

OPTIONS SETTINGS

The View tab controls what appears on the screen. When you create a new document, it takes on the View tab settings in effect when it was created. You can subsequently change View tab settings for the document, and they "stick" when you open and close the document. These are the main considerations for making View tab options more useful:

- Consider showing tab characters, so you can see why and how text lines up on tab stops.

- Many advanced users insist on showing paragraph marks, to reduce confusion over copying, moving, and deleting them. If paragraph marks aren't shown on the screen, it's difficult to tell when you have selected one.

- If you have trouble with drawing layer items moving around on a page, show object anchors to see where the drawings are tethered.

USING THE SHOW/HIDE BUTTON

No doubt you're wondering why you would go through this dialog box to turn on paragraph marks, tabs, and object anchors, when clicking the Show/Hide + button on the Standard toolbar makes all three appear on the screen (clicking the Show All Formatting check box at the bottom of the Reveal Formatting task pane does, too). Unfortunately, clicking this button also puts a dot on the screen for every space—a distraction few Word experts will tolerate.

You can make the Show/Hide + button work the way you want by writing a macro to take over its function:

→ For more details on setting up VBA macros to take over built-in Office features, **see** "Substituting for Built-In Commands," **p. 1015**.

1. Start the VBA Editor by choosing Tools, Macro, Visual Basic Editor. If you've already read Chapter 41, "Advanced VBA Tools and Techniques," and have a template ready to hold your custom macros, navigate to it. Otherwise, use the Project Explorer (in the upper-left corner of the VBA Editor) to navigate to and double-click \Normal\Microsoft Word Objects\This Document.

2. Choose Insert, Procedure, type ShowAll, and click OK. VBA creates a new subroutine called Public ShowAll(), and provides both the first and last lines of the subroutine.

PART

III

CH

14

3. Type the macro into the editor, so it looks like this:

```
Public Sub ShowAll()
With ActiveDocument.Windows(1).View
    .ShowParagraphs = True
    .ShowTabs = True
    .ShowObjectAnchors = True
End With
End Sub
```

4. Choose File, Close, and return to Word.

Back in Word, click the Show/Hide + button on the Standard toolbar or, equivalently, bring up the Reveal Formatting task pane and check the Show All Formatting Marks box at the bottom. You should see paragraph marks, tabs, and object anchors (if any exist) in the current document—and you won't see those pesky dots for character spaces.

Tip from

EQ & Woody

You can adjust this macro to show or hide whatever you like in the View tab of the dialog box that appears when you choose Tools, Options. To see how, click once inside the word .View in the macro, and press F1.

SETTING OPTIONS ON THE GENERAL TAB

The General tab contains a hodgepodge of settings:

- If a specific document has links that you want to update only manually (perhaps because the updating takes a long time), uncheck the Update Automatic Links at Open box.
- There is no penalty in rolling the Recently Used File list to nine, aside from a little lost screen space when the File menu is displayed.

SETTING OPTIONS ON THE EDIT TAB

The Edit tab controls how Word reacts when you edit text:

- If you check Typing Replaces Selection, Word overwrites any selected text whenever you press a key on the keyboard. Many advanced users turn this off, to avoid accidentally deleting text.
- Normally, the Insert key toggles Word into and out of Overtype mode (where characters you type at the keyboard overwrite characters on the screen). You can turn off that behavior by telling Word to use the Insert key to Paste, although the side effect might be just as bad: If you hit the Ins key by accident, Word dumps the contents of the Clipboard at the insertion point.

Tip from

EQ & Woody

> If you find yourself pressing the Insert key accidentally all the time, there's a much better way to disable the key entirely. Choose Tools, Customize, then click the Keyboard button. On the left, choose All commands. On the right, pick Overtype. Click Insert and then the Remove button. Click Close twice to permanently prevent Insert from shifting you into Overtype mode.

- Use Smart Paragraph selection will drive many advanced Word users nuts. If you have this box checked, and you select only part of a paragraph but include the paragraph mark, Word drops the paragraph mark automatically and without warning.

- Use Ctrl + Click to Follow Hyperlink is one of the truly great improvements in Word 2002. Keep this box checked and you'll never accidentally chase a hot link by accidentally clicking it.

- Similarly, the When Selecting, Automatically Select Entire Word setting drives some careful advanced users nuts, because it forces Word to select an entire word plus the following space when only part of a word is actually selected. Keeping this box checked can make it hard to select portions of words and sentences.

Setting Options on the Print Tab

The Print tab contains default printer settings:

- Consider checking the Update Fields box if you want Word to automatically update all the fields in a document before it's printed. In some cases, it's beneficial to update all the fields so they have the most recent information (times, dates, and so on). But in other cases, you might want Word to skip the updating—for example, if you've gone in and modified several field results (perhaps Table of Contents or Index entries), manually.

→ To learn about fields in depth, **see** "Using Fields Intelligently," **p. 488**.

- Specify whether Hidden Text should appear on the printout by checking or unchecking the Hidden Text box.

Tip from

EQ & Woody

> Printing hidden text can come in handy if you need to print two different versions of a document. For example, a teacher might set up an exam so the questions are in regular text, and the answers are marked as hidden. Printing hidden text would produce a key for graders.

Setting Options on the Save, User Info and Locations Tabs

The Save tab includes settings for both saving and AutoRecover:

- Check the Allow Fast Saves box only if you have huge documents that take enormous amounts of time to save. Even so, you should weigh the time you might save against the potential risks of losing data.

Caution

Fast Saves are the single greatest source of corrupt Word documents. If something goes wrong in the middle of a Fast Save—the power goes out, or your hard drive controller hiccups—the entire file can be rendered illegible. Fast Saves also save old remnants of documents; a sufficiently motivated snoop could see data you've deleted from a document by using a file viewer to inspect the hexadecimal text.

- Word can automatically save an AutoRecover backup copy of the currently active document—a so-called *.wbk file—at time intervals you specify in this dialog box. If Word crashes or freezes, the next time it starts, it automatically looks for and open any *.wbk files. With a little luck, the automatically recovered file will contain all your edits, up to the most recent AutoRecover time. This protection is in addition to—and, in our experience, far more reliable than—the built-in crash protection.

Tip from

EQ & Woody

Don't disable AutoRecover unless you find the backup process terribly onerous. And if you do disable it, make sure you periodically save the current file. Word *does* crash—it isn't a question of whether, only of when.

The User Information tab contains the user's name, initials, and address. These settings are used for identifying tracked changes, comments, envelope return addresses, and much more. Take a moment to make sure they're correct.

The File Locations tab lets you change the location of all Word's key data files: My Documents, templates, AutoRecover files, and more.

DISABLING AUTOFORMAT SETTINGS

Advanced Word users should also periodically examine their Tools, AutoCorrect Options settings to ensure that they aren't getting in the way. There are five tabs in the AutoCorrect dialog box:

- The AutoCorrect tab consolidates all AutoCorrect entries.

→ For an overview of how AutoCorrect works, **see** "Using AutoCorrect to Automate Documents," **p. 91**.

- The AutoFormat As You Type tab contains a number of settings that advanced users, in particular, might want to disable, per Table 14.4.

TABLE 14.4   GETTING RID OF AUTOFORMATTING

To Disable This Kind of AutoFormatting	Uncheck This Box
* - -- > -> => symbols or pictures to create bulleted paragraphs	Automatic Bulleted Lists
0 1 I i A a to create numbered lists	Automatic Numbered Lists

To Disable This Kind of AutoFormatting	Uncheck This Box
Three or more - _ = * ~ # to put a on a border paragraph	Borders
+----+----+ to create a table	Tables
1st, 2nd, 3rd, and so on converted to 1st, 2nd, 3rd	Ordinals (1st) with Superscript
1/4, 1/2, 3/4 converted to ¼, ½, ¾	Fractions (1/2) with Fraction Character (½)

Also on the AutoFormat As You Type tab, by default Word automatically detects Web addresses and e-mail addresses and turns them into hyperlinks. If you're going to publish your document on the Web, that can be useful. In almost every other case, it isn't: Many publications print an embarrassingly large number of underlined Web addresses and underlined links because of Word's over-eagerness.

To turn off this intrusive setting, uncheck the Internet and Network Paths with Hyperlinks box.

- The AutoText tab controls all AutoText entries.

→ For the full story on AutoText, **see** "Entering Text and Graphics Automatically with AutoText and AutoCorrect," **p. 376**.

- The AutoFormat tab controls what Word does when you choose Format, AutoFormat.

→ To learn more about Word's AutoFormatting features, **see** "Formatting All or Part of a Document Automatically," **p. 394**.

- The Smart Tags tab controls whether Word looks as you type for something that appears to be an Outlook Contact. The only downside to enabling the full look-up capability is the performance hit: If you feel that Word is unnecessarily sluggish, try disabling these settings to see if performance perks up.

WORD STARTUP SWITCHES

You can control how Word starts with *command-line switches*. These switches work from a command line, the Start/Run box, and as switches in Windows shortcuts. For example, to start Word with the /a switch enabled, click Start, Run, type winword /a, and press Enter.

 If you are frustrated because you can't get Word to start, see "Word Won't Start" in the "Troubleshooting" section at the end of this chapter.

The available switches are listed here:

- /a keeps Word from running any Auto macros stored in the Normal document template, Normal.dot. It also keeps Word from loading any add-ins in the \Startup folder. For example, if you want to start Word and keep it from running add-ins, you might click the Start button, choose Run, type winword /a, and press Enter. Use this switch if you are having trouble getting Word to start.

- /n starts Word normally, but doesn't load the usual "Document1" first document.
- /mMacroname starts Word, then runs the specified macro. (Note that there is no space between the "m" and the macro name.) For example, the following line starts Word and runs the macro File1, a built-in macro which loads the most recently used document:

```
c:\Program Files\Microsoft Office\Office\winword.exe /mFile1
```

To set up a shortcut that starts Word and restores the last used document, try this:

1. Right-click the Windows desktop and select New, Shortcut.
2. When the Create Shortcut Wizard asks for a command line, type the following, taking care to put a space before the /m, but no space in /mFile1:

   ```
   "c:\Program Files\Microsoft Office\Office\winword.exe " /mFile1
   ```
3. When asked for a name, type Open Last Word Doc and click Finish.
4. If you like, you can copy or move this shortcut anywhere—the Start menu, say, or (if you're using Internet Explorer 4 or later) the QuickLaunch toolbar on the taskbar.

Similarly, you can use /mFile2 to open the second file in Word's most recently used list, and so on. This line

```
"c:\Program Files\Microsoft Office\Office\winword.exe " /mFile1 /mFile2
```

starts Word and opens both the #1 and #2 files on the most recently used list.

Note

The Word documentation says that the /t switch opens a document as a template, but actually that startup switch opens the specified file as a document. Unfortunately, this is a bug that has been around in Office for some time.

Of course, you can always put the name(s) of document(s) on the command line, and Word will load them when it starts:

```
"c:\Program Files\Microsoft Office\Office\winword.exe " "c:\My Documents\some.doc"
```

Tip from

Ed & Woody

If the filename—including the path—includes any spaces, be sure to put quotes around the entire filename. Otherwise, Word won't interpret the command line correctly.

TROUBLESHOOTING

WORD WON'T START

When I try to start Word, a dialog box appears telling me there's been a General Protection Fault (or some other error) in file Winword.exe. Even after uninstalling and reinstalling Office, Word just won't start.

There are many reasons why this could happen, but there's one easy solution that works at least half the time. Click Start, Run, type

```
winword /a
```

and press Enter. Word almost always starts. If it does, your problem probably lies in a corrupt template. Shut down Word and rename Normal.dot (to Old-normal.dot, for example). Then see whether you can start Word in the usual manner. If not, rename Old-normal.dot back to Normal.dot. Then try renaming *.dot files in your Startup folder, in a similar way, one at a time. You can usually isolate the corrupt template in this manner.

SECRETS OF THE OFFICE MASTERS: STYLES AND MANUALLY APPLIED FORMATTING

To understand the interplay between styles and manually applied formatting, consider the character highlighted in Figure 14.16. As discussed in this chapter's section, "Direct Formatting Versus Styles," a paragraph style was created called ChapterHeading and applied to the heading, "How *Not* to Run a Store."

Consider what Word goes through to display the letter N properly. First, it picks up the paragraph formatting from the ChapterHeading paragraph style—flush left, page break with Auto space before, and so on. Second, it picks up formatting that's been applied manually to the entire paragraph—in this case, a 5% gray pattern that appears in back of the letter N.

Third, Word picks up the font formatting defined in the paragraph's style—here, that's Arial 24 point bold, kerned at 16 point. Fourth, Word applies any formatting associated with a character style. Because the letter N does not have a character style applied to it, there's nothing new at that level.

Finally, Word looks for font formatting that's been applied directly to the character. In this case, the letter N is italic because it's been formatted manually this way.

Every time Word displays a character, it goes through a complex process just like this, to sort out exactly how the character should appear. You can see precisely how Word came up with the formatting of any specific character by following along closely in the Reveal Formatting task pane, particularly if the Distinguish Style Source box is checked. Shift+F1 will bring up the task pane.

Figure 14.16

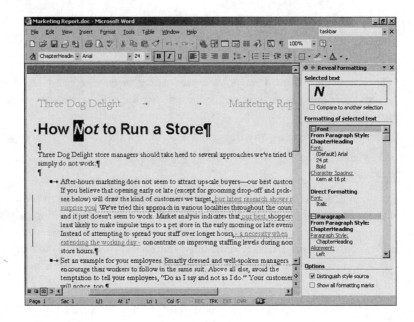

CHAPTER **15**

EXPERT TEXT-EDITING TECHNIQUES

In this chapter

NAVIGATING THROUGH A WORD DOCUMENT

Word offers an enormous number of ways to move through a document, and most people can increase their productivity by learning some of the shortcuts.

You needn't memorize dozens of key combinations or obscure mouse tricks to boost your productivity. Rather, if you concentrate on reducing the effort you expend on the two or three navigational techniques you use most, your productivity will soar, and the amount of time invested is negligible.

Not all the best navigation tricks are well known, either. Some of them aren't even documented. Instead of merely throwing lists of shortcuts at you, you'll learn some tricks for memorizing the most important ones.

USING THE KEYBOARD TO MOVE THROUGH A DOCUMENT

Aside from the obvious up-, down-, left-, and right arrows, the most useful keyboard shortcuts for navigating around a document are listed in Table 15.1.

TABLE 15.1 NAVIGATION KEYS IN WORD

To Move	Press
Next word to right	Ctrl+Right Arrow
Next word to left	Ctrl+Left Arrow
One paragraph up	Ctrl+Up Arrow
One paragraph down	Ctrl+Down Arrow
To beginning of line	Home
To end of line	End
Up one screen	Page Up (PgUp)
Up one page	Alt+Ctrl+Page Up
Down one screen	Page Down (PgDn)
Down one page	Alt+Ctrl+Page Down
To beginning of document	Ctrl+Home
To end of document	Ctrl+End

Most experienced Word users would benefit from memorizing three groups of shortcut keys from those in Table 15.1, and they're all based on the Ctrl key. Here are the combinations, and the way the Ctrl key changes the keys you're probably accustomed to:

- Ctrl+Home/Ctrl+End go to the beginning/end of the document (instead of beginning/end of line)
- Ctrl+Left/Right Arrow move by words (instead of characters)
- Ctrl+Up/Down Arrow move by paragraphs (instead of lines)

Tip from	Possibly the most useful, but obscure key combination in Word is Shift+F5. Word keeps track of the last three locations where you edited text. Pressing Shift+F5 cycles through those three locations. When you open a document, if you want to return to the last location you were editing, press Shift+F5.
Ed & Woody	

WOPR XP/2002, at www.quehelp.com, contains a sophisticated program called QuickMarks that enables you to quickly set and return to navigation points that you define in a document by using your number pad.

→ To find out more about this WOPR XP/2002 utility, **see** Appendix B, "What's on Que's WOPR XP/2002 Pack,"**p. 1077**.

USING THE MOUSE TO MOVE THROUGH A DOCUMENT

Word follows most of the standard Windows mouse navigation techniques, with a few interesting twists, as described in Table 15.2.

TABLE 15.2   MOUSE NAVIGATION TECHNIQUES IN WORD

To Scroll	Do This...
Up one screen	Click above the scrolling box
Down one screen	Click below the scrolling box
To a specific page	Drag the scrolling box and watch for page number
In Normal view, scroll	Press Shift+Left Arrow Left, into the margin

If you have a mouse with a scroll wheel, such as the Microsoft IntelliMouse, many additional mouse navigation options are available.

NAVIGATING WITH THE DOCUMENT MAP

By far the most powerful way to navigate through a long document with the mouse is via Word's Document Map. After several false starts, Microsoft has finally made DocMap reliable. It's particularly valuable for advanced Word users who have to navigate through moderately long documents (say, five or more pages).

The Document Map is a "hot" outline of the document's contents—similar to a Table of Contents—which appears in a pane to the left of the document itself. If you take a little care in applying heading styles, the entire structure of your document appears in DocMap, and each important point is directly accessible.

Because the DocMap table is "hot," you can click a heading—"Chapter 7," for example—and the document immediately jumps to the beginning of Chapter 7. Click the heading "Sales Goals for 2003" in the DocMap pane, and Word jumps to that location in the document.

Word constructs the Document Map based on outline levels in each paragraph. If you stick to the standard Word heading styles—Heading 1, Heading 2, and so on—the outline levels are automatically applied by Word (level 1, level 2, and so on). If you use your own styles, they can have whatever outline level you want to apply.

→ For more details on styles, **see** "Formatting Documents with Styles," **p. 468**.

→ Outline level is part of paragraph formatting. For details on setting the outline level and what it entails, **see** "Adjusting Paragraph Alignment and Outline Level," **p. 384**.

Using the Keyboard and Mouse to Select Text

In general, Word parallels the rest of Office in methods for selecting blocks of text. The wonders of Extend mode, however, remain unique to Word.

→ Think you know all there is to selecting text? Think again...and while you're at it, **see** "Selecting Text," **p. 85**.

Word allows you to select multiple, noncontiguous blocks of text. Hold down the Ctrl key as you drag across the text you want to select, or double- or triple-click as you would with a single selection.

Tip from
EQ & Woody

> You can change one single selected block of text without deselecting everything. Hold down the Ctrl key and click once inside a previously selected block. That specific selection, and only that selection, is deselected.

In addition, Word enables you to extend the selection:

1. Click once at the beginning of the text block you want to select.
2. Double-click the grayed-out EXT box on Word's status bar (or press F8; see later in this section). This puts you in *Extend* mode.
3. Click again at the end of the text block you want to select. If you make a mistake, continue clicking until you get it right.
4. Double-click the EXT again, or press Esc, to leave Extend mode.

This technique can be particularly useful if you need to select large blocks of text. Although you can always click and drag across the text you want to select, Word frequently scrolls pages by so quickly that it's hard to stop. Use Extend mode or Shift+Click to scroll at your own pace.

Tip from
EQ & Woody

> You can even use Word's Find feature while in Extend mode. To select everything from the insertion point to the next occurrence of the word "Corporation," for example, double-click EXT, click Edit, Find, type Corporation, and click Find Next. The selection is extended automatically for you.

Word has one additional keyboard-related method for selecting text that doesn't have a parallel in any other Office application: the F8 key.

Press the F8 key once, and Word goes into Extend mode. Press it a second time to select the current word. Press it a third time and you select the current sentence. Press it a fourth time, and you highlight the current paragraph. Finally, press it a fifth time and you select the whole document.

Conversely, at any point in the F8 expansion process, you can press Shift+F8 to shrink one level: If a paragraph is selected and you press Shift+F8, the selection shrinks to a sentence.

Tip from

Ed & Woody

F8 has one more trick up its sleeve. Say you want to select all the text from the current insertion point location up to and including a specific letter. Press F8, and then that letter. To extend the selection from the insertion point to the next *r* in the document, for example, press F8+r.

BOOKMARKS

In the real world, a *bookmark* is a piece of paper that marks a location in a document. In Word's world, a bookmark is a selection—a piece of text, a picture, or just an insertion point—with a name.

Bookmarks come in handy in two different situations:

- They provide a location to which you can navigate. For example, you can put a bookmark in a document called "StartOfChapter17." Then you can tell Word "go to the bookmark called StartOfChapter17" and you're transported to that location. Similarly, you can use bookmarks as the destination for hyperlinks setting up a link, say, to the bookmark called TermsAndConditions in the document c:\My Documents\Contract.doc.

- Word provides several tools for retrieving the text covered by a bookmark. For example, if you put a bookmark called CustomerName over the name of a customer in a contract, you can sprinkle {REF CustomerName} fields throughout the contract, and everywhere the field appears, that customer's name will show up.

→ To learn more about Word's {Ref} and {PageRef} fields, **see** "Referring to Document Contents," **p. 498**.

To set a bookmark, do the following:

1. Select the text you want to have bookmarked, or click in your document in the location you want to bookmark.
2. Choose Insert, Bookmark. The Bookmark dialog box appears (see Figure 15.1).

Figure 15.1
Bookmarks can cover text, pictures, paragraph marks, and almost anything else in a document—or they can be as small as an insertion point.

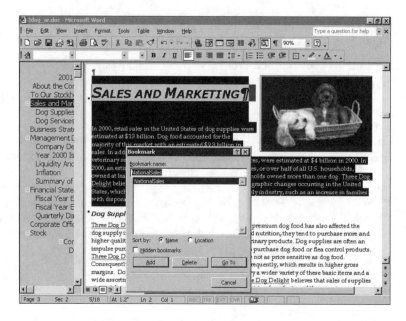

3. Type a bookmark name. Names must start with a letter and can include letters, numbers, or the underscore character (_), but not spaces.

4. Click Add and Word establishes a bookmark with that name at the indicated location.

Word has a woefully inadequate method for displaying bookmarks (which are usually invisible). Click Tools, Options, click the View tab, and check the Bookmarks box. Word displays bookmarks as [ ] brackets surrounding the bookmarked text.

 If you're wondering why you're having trouble making heads or tails of your bookmarks after you've chosen to view them, see "Which Bookmark Is Which" in the "Troubleshooting" section at the end of this chapter.

If you move a block of text that includes a bookmark, the bookmark goes along. If you delete a block of text that includes a bookmark, the bookmark is deleted. If you copy a block of text that includes a bookmark, however, the bookmark stays put.

Word has no built-in method for renaming bookmarks. You must use the Bookmark dialog box to first delete the old bookmark name, and then establish a new bookmark with the required name.

Be careful when adding or deleting text near a bookmark. Text that's typed at the beginning of a bookmark is added to the bookmark. Text that's typed at the end is not added.

NAVIGATING THROUGH DOCUMENTS WITH THE OBJECT BROWSER

In the lower-right corner of the Word window—down below the vertical scrollbar's down arrow—you'll find a remarkable collection of three buttons known as the Object Browser.

Word's Object Browser has absolutely nothing in common with Visual Basic for Applications' Object Browser. The latter is a real Object Browser. The former is a marketing buzzword.

The Word Object Browser generally works best if you use it this way:

1. Click the circle in the middle (the Select Browse Object button) and tell Word what you want to look for. You can have Word cycle through all the pictures in a document, for example.

2. Click the double-down arrow to search toward the end of the document for the next occurrence (say, the next picture). Click the double-up arrow to search toward the beginning of the document. Of course, after you've selected the type of object you want to use for browsing, you can skip trying to hit these undersized buttons and use the keyboard shortcuts instead: Ctrl+Page Up and Ctrl+Page Down.

You can search for the following "objects":

■ **Fields**—Word moves from field to field, although it skips hidden fields (such as {XE}, the field that creates entries for a document's index).

→ To learn how you can empower your documents with fields, **see** "Using Fields Intelligently," **p. 488**.

■ **Endnotes**—Word jumps from endnote to endnote. If you start in the body of the document, Word stops at each reference to an endnote, in the main part of the document. If you start in an endnote, Word cycles through each of the endnotes.

■ **Footnotes**—Similarly, if you start in the body of the document, Word goes from footnote reference to footnote reference. If you start inside a footnote, the footnotes themselves are selected.

■ **Comments**—Surprisingly, Comments don't work the same way. If you position the insertion point inside a Comment (for example, by choosing View, Comments), and you scroll down, you'll go to the next Comment. But if you scroll up, you'll end up in the body of the document, at the reference point for the preceding Comment.

■ **Sections**—Word moves from the beginning of one document section to the next.

→ Ever used sections before? Many Word users haven't, at least knowingly. **See** "Page/Section Setup Options," **p. 340**.

■ **Pages**—Word moves from the top of one page to the next.

■ **Go To**—As shown in Figure 15.2, Go To includes most of the options in the Object Browser (Fields, Endnotes, Footnotes, Comments, Sections, Pages, Heading, Graphic, Table), plus Line, Bookmark, Equation, and a confusingly named "Object" option, which goes to the next OLE Object.

Figure 15.2
Go To lets you navigate to absolute locations such as "Page 137," relative locations such as "120 lines down from here," bookmarks, and the like. The Go To options are accessible both from the Object Browser and by choosing Edit, Go To.

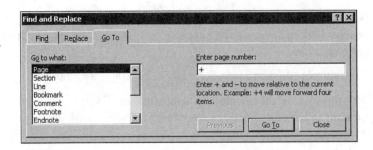

The easiest way to jump to each of the bookmarks in a document is to click the Select Browse Object circle, and then click Go To (or choose Edit, Go To). In the Go to What box, select Bookmark. Click the Go To button. From that point on, each time you click the Object Browser's double-up arrow or double-down arrow (or press F5), you'll go to the next bookmark in the document.

- **Find**—Same as choosing Edit, Find from the menu bar. Find is discussed at length in the next section.

  After you've set up a Find or Replace, the easiest way to repeat the Find or Replace is to clear the dialog box away and use the keyboard shortcut Ctrl+Page Down (or Ctrl+Page Up to search backward).

- **Edits**—Word automatically keeps track of the last three locations in the document where you've made changes. This setting lets you cycle among the three edits (the same as the Shift+F5 keyboard shortcut).

- **Headings**—Cycles to the beginning of each paragraph in the document that is formatted with a "Heading n" style, where "n" is any integer between 1 and 9.

- **Graphics**—Moves to the next picture in the document (whether linked or embedded), or the next Drawing Canvas, but ignores pictures and Drawing Canvases in the drawing layer.

- **Tables**—Cycles through all the Word tables in the document. (That is, tables created by the Table menu or the Tables and Borders toolbar.)

→ To learn more about which objects are stored in the drawing layer, **see** "Working with the Drawing Layer," **p. 108**.

FINDING AND REPLACING TEXT AND OTHER PARTS OF A DOCUMENT

If you want to find something simple, Office's standard Find features suffice. You can have Word look for m?ne (matches mane and miner, but not manner) or bo*t (matches boats or bought, but not bat).

→ To sharpen your finding text skills in any Office application, **see** "Finding and Replacing Text," **p. 87**.

Sometimes you need a more powerful search capability. Perhaps you're looking for all the words in a document that end with "ing." Or you can get complex—say you have a list of license plate numbers and need to find the ones starting with the number 1 through 9, followed by the letters "QED," and then four numbers ending in "9."

Word contains a flexible, powerful mini-language that lets you specify precisely what to find. To use it, choose Edit, Find, click the More button, and check the Use Wildcards box (see Figure 15.3).

Figure 15.3
The wildcard specification <[1-9]QED [0-9]{3}9 solves the license plate number problem mentioned in the text.

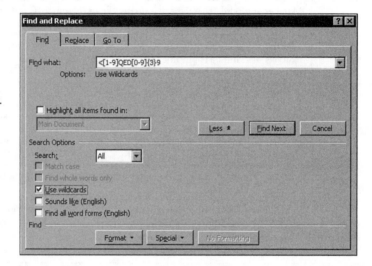

As detailed in the next section, this search string will find all those license plates:

`<[1-9]QED[0-9]{3}9`

The < signifies that the following characters have to start a new word (or, in this case, a license plate number). The [1-9] matches any single number between 1 and 9. The QED forces an exact match on the letters QED. [0-9] matches any single number, but when you put a {3} on the end, it's repeated three times: thus, you must have three numbers to match. Finally, the 9 on the end will match only a 9.

FINDING TEXT

In addition to the ? and * wildcards, Word recognizes the symbols in Table 15.3. (See the preceding section for a detailed example for matching license plate numbers.)

TABLE 15.3 WILDCARDS FOR FIND

Symbol	Meaning
[xyz]	Matches exactly one of the listed characters. b[aioe]g matches bag and bog, but not bug.
[A-Z]	Matches any single character in the range. Case sensitive. b[A-W]g matches bAg and bUg, but not bug or bARge.
[!xyz]	Matches any single character except the ones listed. b[!au]g will match big and bog, but not bag or bug or bring.
[!A-Z]	Matches any single character that doesn't lie in the range. Case sensitive. b[!a-m]g matches bog or bug, but not bag or big.
<	The following character(s) must appear at the beginning of a word. <[a-c] matches act and cat, but not react. <bl matches blue and blech, but not able.
>	The preceding character(s) must appear at the end of a word. ing> matches hiking and writing but not singer. [a-c]> matches Alma and tab but not read.
{n,m}	The preceding character must appear between "n" and "m" times. blec{3,7}h matches blecccch and blecccccch, but not blecch. If the "m" is omitted, the character must appear "n" or more times.
@	Same as {1,}: the preceding character must appear one or more times. bo@t matches bot and boot, but not bat.
\	Search for the following character, even if it's a wildcard. wh[ae]t\? matches what? and whet? but not whether or whatever.

Caution

The Word documentation says that the {n,} and {n,m} wildcards work for any expression. They don't. They work only for a single character. For example, b[a-n]{2,}g does not match bang.

Word also includes a handy list of special symbols—tab characters, em- and en dashes, page and section breaks, and so on—under the Special button of Figure 15.3, shown previously.

All this wildcard-matching business can be confusing, but it gets worse: Word supports two different kinds of pattern matching. All the wildcard matching discussed so far in this chapter applies when you check the Use Wildcards box shown in Figure 15.3. A different set of symbols is available if you do not check the Use Wildcards box.

Perhaps the easiest way to illustrate this is with the paragraph mark. If you leave the Use Wildcards box unchecked, and you type ^p (a caret, then a p) in the Find What box, Word will dutifully find the next paragraph mark.

However, if you have the Use Wildcards box checked, there is no apparent way to tell Word to find the next paragraph mark! If you type ^p in the Find What box, and the Use Wildcards box is checked, Word will stop only if it finds, literally, a caret followed by a p in the document.

It's difficult to tell, offhand, whether a particular character or symbol is included in one group or the other. The safest approach is to use the Special button shown in Figure 15.3. If you're trying to match an odd character, start with the Use Wildcards box unchecked, and see whether you can find the character. If that doesn't work, check the Use Wildcards box, click Special, and look again.

Although the online documentation encourages you to paste text from a document into the Find What box, in fact, some characters (most notably paragraph marks) can't be pasted.

There are two more search options that you should use with caution:

- Sounds Like catches some simple homonyms (new, gnu, knew, for example, or fish and fiche), but it also makes odd matches (rest, according to Word, sounds like reside) and bizarre mistakes (oh sounds like a, according to Word, but not owe). It also fails the Woody test: According to Word, Leonard does not sound like Leonhard. Woody's parents would beg to differ.

- Find All Word Forms is supposed to catch noun plurals, adjective forms, and verb conjugations: tell Word to replace heavy with light and, with Find All Word Forms checked, heavier will be replaced by lighter, heaviest will be replaced by lightest. This, too, has problems. For example, tell Word to replace bring with take and, with Find All Word Forms checked, "I have brought it" will be replaced by "I have took it."

REPLACING TEXT

Replace behaves much the same as Find, except the entry in the Find What text box is replaced by the entry in the Replace With text box (see Figure 15.4).

Figure 15.4
The Replace tab of the Find and Replace dialog box lets you use all of Word's powerful wildcard mini-language.

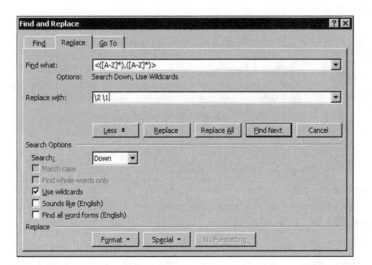

When performing a replace, you can use parentheses in the Find What box to specify groups of characters, which are then referenced in the Replace With box. The contents of the first pair of parentheses in the Find What box becomes \1 in the Replace With box; the second becomes \2; and so on.

This can be handy if, say, you want to replace all the occurrences of American style dates (perhaps 10-20-51) with their European day-first equivalents (20-10-51). Make sure you have the Use Wildcards box checked, and then in the Find What box, type

`<([0-9]*)-([0-9]*)-([0-9]*)>`

to force Word to recognize the American style date: the day (inside the first set of parentheses) becomes \1, the month (in the second set of parentheses) becomes \2, and the year becomes \3. In the Replace With box, type

`\2-\1-\3`

and the dates are swapped around.

Few people realize that you can use Word to change a list of names that looks like this:

`Lastname, Firstname`

Into a list that looks like this:

`Firstname Lastname`

To do so, click Use Wildcards and in the Find What box, type

`<([A-Z]*), ([A-Z]*)>`

and in the Replace With box, type

`\2 \1`

Tip from

E Q & Woody

You can tell Word to "Replace With" the contents of the Windows Clipboard. That can be handy if, for example, you want to replace a word, such as STOP with a picture (perhaps a stop sign) throughout a document. To make it so, uncheck the Use Wildcards box, and type ^c in the Replace With box. Word interprets ^c as being the contents of the Windows Clipboard.

FINDING AND REPLACING FORMATTING

Word doesn't limit you to searching for and replacing text. You can specify formatting, as well—say, replace all occurrences of the italicized words *current month sales* with the bold number **$12,345,678**. Here's how:

1. Choose Edit, Replace (or equivalently click the Object Browser circle in the lower-right corner of the screen, select Find, and choose the Replace tab). Click the More button to expose the Format selections.

2. In the Find What box, type `current month sales`. With the insertion point still in the box, click the Format button and choose Font. Under Font Style, click Italic, and then click OK (see Figure 15.5).

Figure 15.5
In formatted searches, Word tells you that you're searching for formatted text by including the Format: line under the Find What or Replace With boxes.

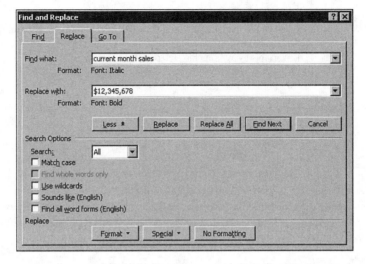

3. In the Replace With box type `$12,345,678`. With the insertion point still in the box, click the Format button and choose Font. Under Font Style, click Bold, and then click OK.

4. You can now proceed with the replace: Click Replace to verify each match by hand, or Replace All to make the update throughout the document.

Advanced Word users frequently find it easier to Find/Replace the first instance of a particular piece of text, and then close the dialog box. That way, you can click the down arrow in the Object Browser (or press Ctrl+Page Down, or Shift+F4) to Find/Replace the rest.

Tip from
Ed & Woody

Closing the dialog box clears clutter off the screen, and you can better see what you're doing. You can also quickly edit the found text without having to click outside the dialog box, and then press Ctrl+Page Down to continue searching.

In addition to Font formatting, you can specify Paragraph formatting, Styles (either character or paragraph), Tabs, Language, Frame type, or Highlight.

If you want to clear the formatting for either the Find What or Replace With boxes, click once inside the box and then click the No Formatting button at the bottom of the dialog box.

Both the Find and Replace formatting settings are "sticky": If you set Find to look for "Heading 1" style paragraphs, for example, the next time you perform a Find or Replace, Word continues looking for "Heading 1" style paragraphs.

> **Note**
>
> When you're done looking for a particular kind of formatting—or replacing with a particular kind of formatting—you must manually clear the formatting from the Find or Replace boxes by using the No Formatting button.

INSERTING FOOTNOTES

Footnotes in Word are straightforward, although the terminology is a bit difficult to fathom.

To put a footnote in a document, click Insert, Reference, Footnote. The Footnote and Endnote dialog box appears, allowing you to choose whether you want a footnote (at the bottom of the page or bunched after the end of the text on the page) or an endnote (at the end of the current section or the end of the document). Word numbers the footnotes (or endnotes) for you, automatically, or you can specify your own footnote reference character.

Word draws a horizontal line between the text on a page and the first footnote. The line is called a Footnote Separator. If the footnote is too long to fit on one page, Word continues it onto the next page and uses a longer horizontal line, called a Footnote Continuation Separator. You can work with the separators by moving into Normal view, choosing View, Footnotes and, in the footnote pane, selecting Footnote Separator or Footnote Continuation Separator.

→ If you need to create two references to the same footnote, **see** "Inserting Cross-References," **p. 433**.

ENTERING TEXT AND GRAPHICS AUTOMATICALLY WITH AUTOTEXT AND AUTOCORRECT

Word has two main features for entering text and graphics automatically: AutoText (the older feature that's available only in Word) and AutoCorrect (newer, and available throughout Office).

→ To learn how to speed up repetitive text entry, **see** "Using AutoCorrect to Automate Documents," **p. 91**.

When you type an AutoCorrect entry followed by the Spacebar, Enter key, or any punctuation mark, Word swaps out the text you've typed and replaces it with the indicated text (and graphics) in the entry. For example, you can set up an AutoCorrect entry to change `tpfp` into "the `Party of the First Part`." You see no warning that the change will take place; it just happens.

On the other hand, when you start to type an AutoText entry, after the first four letters Word puts a ScreenTip on the screen reminding you that an entry exists: type `octo`, for example, and a ScreenTip saying `October (Press Enter to Insert)` appears. If you want to accept the AutoText entry—in this case, replace the octo you've typed with the word October—you need to press Enter, or the Tab key, or F3 (they're all equivalent).

In addition, you can insert an AutoText entry into a document by clicking Insert, AutoText, and either choosing the entry directly (they're grouped into categories) or by choosing Tools, AutoCorrect Options, and choosing the AutoText tab (see Figure 15.6). You can also put an AutoText toolbar on the screen by right-clicking any blank spot on a toolbar and choosing AutoText.

Figure 15.6
The Add button creates a new AutoText entry. The Insert button inserts the selected entry into the document.

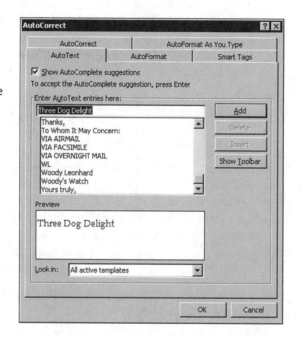

> **Tip from**
> *EQ & Woody*
>
> AutoText category names are taken from the style of paragraph in which the entry was originally created. To see it, try this: Type an AutoText result, format the paragraph as style "Company," select the AutoText result, and then click Insert, AutoText, New to create a new AutoText entry. That entry will be in a category called "Company."

The current date, days of the week, months of the year, your company name, username, and initials are all picked up automatically by Word and turned into AutoText entries.

AutoText entries are stored in templates, so you can have separate "global" entries stored in Normal.dot, and "local" entries that apply only to documents based on specific templates.

Both the AutoText toolbar and the lengthy Insert, AutoText menu command change depending on the style of the paragraph you're working on. For example, if you create an AutoText entry in the "Company" category (see preceding tip), and the insertion point is in a paragraph formatted as "Company" style, both lists are limited to "Company" category entries.

Note

You can get at all the accessible AutoText entries by clicking Insert, AutoText, AutoText to open the AutoText tab on the AutoCorrect dialog box (refer to Figure 15.6).

If you can't find a specific AutoText entry in the list, chances are good it's stored in a template that isn't currently accessible.

In most cases, you'll find AutoCorrect superior to AutoText:

- AutoCorrect entries (at least unformatted entries) are available to all Office applications.
- When AutoCorrect is done, if you hover your cursor over the AutoCorrected entry, the "lightning bolt" icon gives you access to the full array of AutoCorrecting options, both for this individual entry and for AutoCorrect in general. That's handy.
- It takes an extra keystroke—Enter, Tab, or F3—to put an AutoText entry into a document. Many typists, especially fast typists, find that distracting.

However, in some circumstances AutoText is superior:

- You can create AutoText entries for words without fear of accidentally triggering a replacement. For example, you could create an AutoText entry called pater that expands into The Paternal Order of Ornery Fellows. If you had an AutoCorrect entry with the same name, should you type the Latin phrase pater familias, you would end up with The Paternal Order of Ornery Fellows familias.
- AutoText ScreenTips warn you about the contents of the replacement. AutoCorrect gives no warning.
- AutoCorrect entries are global. Super-global, in fact, in that they take effect throughout Office. AutoText entries can be localized to specific templates.

To create an AutoText entry:

1. Type and, optionally, format the replacement text (or graphics) that you want.
2. Select the text. Include the paragraph mark, if you want to include it and the paragraph's formatting in the AutoText entry.
3. Click Insert, AutoText, New. Give the new AutoText entry a name and click OK.

To add your AutoText entry to a document, type the AutoText entry and press Alt+F3.

Word includes tools for copying and moving AutoText entries in the template organizer (choose Tools, Templates and Add-Ins, Organizer, AutoText).

USING HYPHENS AND DASHES

Word automatically changes some hyphens into em- and en-dashes (an em-dash, as the name implies, is the width of a lowercase m, and an en-dash is the width of a lowercase n).

For example:

- Type a letter, followed by two hyphens, followed by another letter, and Word changes the hyphens to an em-dash. It's nicely done, because the em-dash has a little bit of space to the left and right, and a line can break before or after an em-dash.

- Type any letter, followed by a space, a hyphen or two, and any other letter, and Word transforms the hyphen(s) into an en-dash.

This behavior is controlled by Word's AutoFormat As You Type feature.

→ For instructions on how to disable this and other AutoFormat options, **see** "Disabling AutoFormat Settings," **p. 358**.

In addition, you can always type an em-dash into a document by pressing Alt+Ctrl+- (minus) on the Number pad. An en-dash is Ctrl+- (minus) on the Number pad.

Caution

Don't use the - (minus, or hyphen) that's to the right of the zero on most keyboards. If you accidentally hit Alt+Ctrl+- (to the right of the zero), check the "Troubleshooting" topic at the end of this chapter called "Removing Menu Shortcuts."

→ For instructions on how to customize keyboard shortcuts for dashes and other characters, **see** "Bypassing Menus with Keyboard Shortcuts," **p. 42**.

As your columns become more narrow, good hyphenation becomes crucial to minimize the vast expanses of whitespace that characterize unhyphenated or poorly hyphenated text. Word offers three different methods for hyphenating:

- **Automatically**—Most experienced Word users who work in Print Layout view avoid this method because the constant sliding of lines makes it hard to concentrate on the screen. To turn on automatic hyphenation, choose Tools, Language, Hyphenation. In the Hyphenation dialog box (see Figure 15.7), click the Automatically Hyphenate Document box. Hyphenation takes place immediately when you click OK, and Word continues to automatically hyphenate as you type or edit text. The Hyphenation Zone is the maximum allowable whitespace at the end of a line; the Limit Consecutive Hyphens To box specifies the maximum number of consecutive lines that can be hyphenated.

- **Manually, Whole Document**—Choose Tools, Language, Hyphenation, and then click the Manual box. Word steps you through each hyphenation, allowing you to accept or reject each.

Note

Generally, you'll want to undertake a manual hyphenation only after the text is in its final form. Making any changes to the text will probably throw off the hyphenation, at least in any changed paragraphs.

Figure 15.7

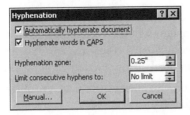

- **Manually, One Word at a Time**—You needn't turn on automatic hyphenation to have Word hyphenate an occasional word. Instead, use a "soft" or "optional" hyphen by clicking where you want the soft hyphen to appear, and then pressing Ctrl+-. Word uses the hyphen if it's required to balance out the line; if not, the hyphen won't appear.

Sometimes you want to prevent Word from breaking a line at a hyphen. For example, the word CD-ROM should never be broken. Tell Word that you don't want it to break at that point by using a "hard" or "nonbreaking" hyphen: Ctrl+Shift+-.

Tip from

EQ & Woody

Word will not hyphenate paragraphs that have either of two types of formatting. In the Paragraph dialog box (choose Format, Paragraph), you can check the Don't Hyphenate box. Or in the Language dialog box (choose Tools, Language, Set Language), you can check the Do Not Check Spelling or Grammar box.

CHANGING TEXT FORMATTING

When you're typing, each new character you type takes on the formatting of the character before, unless you do something (such as pressing Ctrl+I to turn on italic formatting) to change it. The first character you type in a paragraph takes on the formatting of the paragraph mark.

To restore character formatting—that is, to make it match the formatting of the current paragraph's paragraph mark—bring up the Styles and Formatting task pane, select the text, and click Clear Formatting. (Equivalently, you can press Ctrl+Spacebar.)

Select a character or characters, click Format, Font (or right-click and choose Font), and you will see Word's main font formatting options (see Figure 15.8). Most of the character (Word says "font") formatting you'll commonly encounter is applicable to all the Office applications.

→ To learn more about character formatting, **see** "Changing Character Attributes," **p. 100**.

Figure 15.8
Most of the Font dialog box's options match up with options in other Office applications.

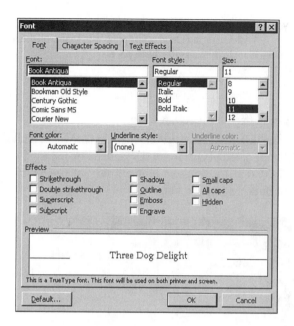

Word has a few formatting options that aren't quite so straightforward. On the Font tab:

- Superscript reduces the size of the characters about four points, and moves them above the baseline by about three points; Subscript also reduces about four points, and moves the characters below the baseline about two points.

- Small caps shows and prints lowercase letters as capitals, reduced about two points (so, for example, a lowercase letter in 11 point will print as a cap in 9 point). Some fonts have specific small caps characters, in which case those will print.

- Hidden text is displayed onscreen and/or printed only when you specifically request it (choose Tools, Options, View and Tools, Options, Print).

Tip from

Hidden text can be useful when you want to keep details handy, but show them only occasionally. For example, teachers frequently type exams in Word, and place the answers inside the document as hidden text. That way, they can print the exam normally for distribution to students, but then print a second copy with answers for graders.

The Hidden Paragraph Mark
Sometimes Word forces you to have a paragraph mark, whether you want one or not. For example, if you have a document that ends in a table, Word insists on placing a paragraph mark after the table. Sometimes those extra paragraph marks get in the way—in the worst case, Word might print an extra, blank page at the end of the document to accommodate the invisible paragraph mark.

If that should happen to you, remember that the paragraph mark is just like any other character. In particular, you can format it as Hidden. A Hidden paragraph mark won't print, won't show on the screen, and one at the end of a document won't force Word to print an extra, blank page.

Formatting options on the Character Spacing tab (see Figure 15.9) include the following:

- Scale applies a zoom effect to the selected text.

- Spacing controls the distance between characters. In particular, it allows you to add space after each of the selected characters (Expanded), or reduce the amount of space between characters (Condensed). Use it to unobtrusively expand lines that need to be longer, or shorten lines that are too long.

Figure 15.9
Character spacing allows you to squish, elevate, lower, and push together fonts.

- Position controls how far above or below the baseline of text the selected characters will appear. This is similar to Superscripting and Subscripting, discussed earlier in this section, except it doesn't change the font size, and this box gives you fine control over the positioning.

- Kerning squishes matched pairs of letters together. The most dramatic example in English is AV. If AV is not kerned, there's a considerable amount of whitespace between the letters. If it is kerned, they're squished together so the leftmost part of the V appears to the left of the rightmost part of the A. Kerning doesn't have much effect at smaller point sizes and, for letters smaller than 10 points or so, it even inhibits your ability to read the type. If you want to kern letters, select them and tell Word the point size at which you want kerning to begin.

Can't Kern

Kerning must be defined in the font itself–the people who design the font have to set up pairs for kerning and tell Windows how much space can be squeezed out between each pair. Most common text fonts have defined kerning pairs; many fonts do not.

If you tell Word to kern selected text, and you can't see any effect on obvious kerning pairs such as AV, first check to make sure the type size is equal to or larger than the "points" setting on the Character Spacing tab. If it is, chances are good that the font you're using doesn't support kerning.

Word has one more automatic character-formatting capability that some people love, and many hate: If you type an asterisk, followed by text, followed by another asterisk, the text between the asterisks is made bold. Similarly, if you type an underscore, text, underscore, the text between the underscores is made italic. To turn off this feature, uncheck the *Bold* and _italic_ with Real Formatting box in the AutoCorrect dialog box (accessed by choosing Tools, AutoCorrect, and clicking the AutoFormat As You Type tab).

In fact, when Word detects the asterisk-text-asterisk combination, it formats the text between the asterisks with the formatting defined by a character style called Strong. (The text remains in Normal style—it isn't turned into Strong—but the formatting defined by the Strong style is applied to it.) The underscore-combination is formatted with the formatting dictated by the character style called Emphasis. If you like, you can change the characteristics of the Strong and Emphasis styles; for example, you can change the style so that *text* makes the text red, or _text_ makes the text Arial 14 point.

Tip from

EQ & Woody

If you check the *Bold* and _italic_ with Real Formatting box and then use asterisks to create bold text, the style Strong suddenly appears on the Styles and Formatting task pane. From that point, it's easy to change the style definition. This works similarly for Emphasis.

→ To learn more about working with styles, **see** "Saving Formats as Named Styles," **p. 471**.

CHANGING PARAGRAPH FORMATTING

Word lets you change the indenting and spacing of paragraphs. Word also gives you control on a paragraph-by-paragraph basis over whether to keep entire paragraphs together or to force one paragraph to "stick to" the next, so they both appear on the same page.

The key concept: Paragraph formatting is stored in the paragraph mark. When you copy or move a paragraph mark, the formatting goes with it. When you delete a paragraph mark, the new paragraph takes on the formatting of the deleted paragraph mark.

Tip from

EQ & Woody

It's almost impossible to tell whether you've selected a paragraph mark unless you have paragraph marks showing on the screen. Many advanced Word users won't even look at a document unless paragraph marks and tabs are showing. To make them appear, click Tools, Options, and on the View tab check the Tab Characters box and the Paragraph Marks box.

To restore default paragraph formatting—that is, the formatting mandated by the paragraph's style—select the paragraph and click the style name on the Styles and Formatting task pane.

ADJUSTING PARAGRAPH ALIGNMENT AND OUTLINE LEVEL

Word includes simple tools for aligning your paragraphs to the left, center, right, or "justifying" to both left and right margins. If you click inside a paragraph, or select one or more paragraphs, and click Format, Paragraph (or right-click and select Paragraph), you'll get the Paragraph dialog box shown in Figure 15.10. Set the Alignment box to reflect the alignment you like.

Figure 15.10
Use the Paragraph dialog box to set a paragraph's relative outlining level, for both Outline View and Document Map. Body Text is the lowest level; Level 1 is the highest.

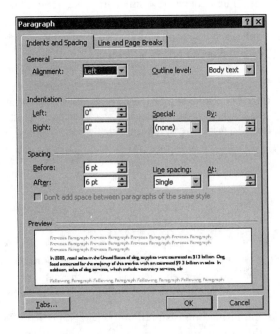

→ Word helps you navigate through large documents by using headings. To learn more, **see** "Outline View," **p. 347** and "Navigating with the Document Map," **p. 365**.

Equivalently, you can use the Align Left, Center, Align Right, or Justify buttons on the Formatting toolbar to set alignment.

Tip from

EQ & Woody

To justify the last line in a justified paragraph, click just before the paragraph mark, and press Shift+Enter.

Word has another text-aligning technique called "Click and type," which allows you to click anywhere on the screen and start typing text. Although it should be called "Double-click and type," the paragraph alignment part of the concept is straightforward:

- If you double-click somewhere near the middle of an empty line (that is, halfway between the left and right margins), Word converts the line to Center alignment. You can tell the area is "hot" because Word puts centered lines below the usual I-beam pointer.

- If you double-click somewhere near the right end of a line (that is, near the right margin), Word converts the line to right-justified. Again, you know the area is hot because Word changes the I-beam pointer so it has lines to the left.

Caution

Unless you're careful and watch the lines around the I-beam closely, Word might insert tabs and tab stops instead of changing the entire paragraph's alignment. Although the tab stops might fool a novice, paragraphs with tabs don't act like aligned paragraphs, as a few moments' work will demonstrate. This is yet another reason for showing paragraph marks and tab characters on the screen.

INDENTING PARAGRAPHS FOR EMPHASIS

You might think of it as a margin change, or a way to set off quotes or other material for emphasis. In Word terminology, an "indent" moves the left edge of a paragraph to the right, or the right edge of a paragraph to the left. The paragraph shown in Figure 15.11 has been indented on the left and the right.

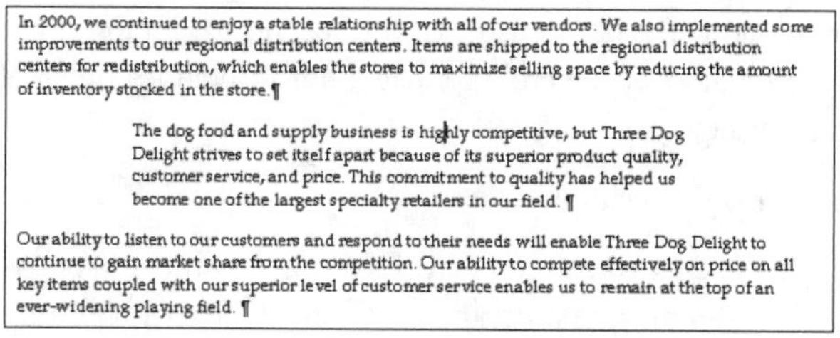

Figure 15.11
In Word, an indent moves the entire left or right margin of a paragraph. To move only the first line of a paragraph to the right, use a first-line indent.

In 2000, we continued to enjoy a stable relationship with all of our vendors. We also implemented some improvements to our regional distribution centers. Items are shipped to the regional distribution centers for redistribution, which enables the stores to maximize selling space by reducing the amount of inventory stocked in the store. ¶

The dog food and supply business is highly competitive, but Three Dog Delight strives to set itself apart because of its superior product quality, customer service, and price. This commitment to quality has helped us become one of the largest specialty retailers in our field. ¶

Our ability to listen to our customers and respond to their needs will enable Three Dog Delight to continue to gain market share from the competition. Our ability to compete effectively on price on all key items coupled with our superior level of customer service enables us to remain at the top of an ever-widening playing field. ¶

To adjust the left and/or right indent, use the Left and Right boxes of the Paragraph dialog box (refer to Figure 15.10). To change the left indent only, in half-inch increments, you can also use the Increase Indent and Decrease Indent buttons on the Formatting Toolbar.

The type of indenting you're probably accustomed to, where the first line of a paragraph gets indented, is called a *first-line indent*. To create a first-line indent, select the paragraphs you want to indent, choose Format, Paragraph, and select First Line in the Special box.

Tip from

EQ & Woody

Don't indent paragraphs by typing tabs at the beginning of each paragraph. Instead, let Word do the work. If you want to indent the first line of all paragraphs in all new documents, you must change the Normal style. To do so, choose Format, Styles and Formatting. In the Styles and Formatting task pane, hover your mouse over the Normal style, and in the drop-down list, click Modify. Choose Format, Paragraph, and select First Line in the Special box. Click OK. Check the Add to Template box. Click OK, and then Apply. You might think Microsoft would make this easier, but...

The other type of indenting you'll see—where the first line juts out to the left—is called a *hanging indent*. Used sparingly, it's a good way to emphasize the first few words of a paragraph. (It's also common for bulleted and numbered paragraphs, which are discussed later in this chapter.) To create a hanging indent, select the paragraphs you want to indent, choose Format, Paragraph, and in the Special box select Hanging.

ADJUSTING LINE AND PARAGRAPH SPACING

Word has controls for three kinds of spacing:

- The amount of blank space before the first line of a paragraph
- The amount of blank space after the last line of a paragraph
- The amount of space internally, between the lines of a paragraph

The spacing between paragraphs adds up just as you would think: The "after" from the first paragraph is combined with the "before" of the second paragraph. Word ignores the "after" space if a paragraph will fit at the end of a page; but it includes the "before" space when a paragraph starts on a new page.

Internal line spacing isn't so simple:

- If you set Line Spacing to Exactly (say, Exactly 12 points), Word makes the distance between all the lines in the paragraph equal to whatever measurement you choose. If you put a large character on a line—say, an 18-point character—the top of the character might be cut off.
- If you set Line Spacing to Single, 1.5 lines, Double, or some other Multiple, Word calculates the distance between each line of the paragraph separately. It takes the tallest character (or graphic) on each line and adjusts to single, 1.5, or double spacing, as appropriate. If you have one 18-point character in the middle of a paragraph consisting

of 12-point characters, the distance to the line containing the 18-point character will be 50% greater than the distance between the other lines.

> **Note**
>
> With one exception, the height of "invisible" characters—spaces, paragraph marks, tabs, and the like—is not taken into account when calculating Single, 1.5, Double, or Multiple spacing. The exception: If the paragraph is empty or contains only invisible characters, the height of those characters counts.

- If you set Line Spacing to At Least (say, At Least 12 points), Word treats it the same as single spacing, but pretends at least one character of the given height is in each line.

Generally, you'll want to use Exactly spacing if you use two or more fonts in a paragraph: By setting the internal spacing to Exactly a given figure, all the lines will be equally spaced, even if the different font normally calls for more whitespace.

CONTROLLING PAGE BREAKS

Each paragraph can also be formatted to control the way Word breaks pages. The Line and Page Breaks tab in the Paragraph dialog box (see Figure 15.12) holds these settings:

- Widow/Orphan Control, when checked, keeps Word from printing *widows* (the last line of a paragraph all by itself at the top of a new page) and *orphans* (the first line of a paragraph all by itself at the bottom of a page). It's on by default.

Figure 15.12
You can control each paragraph, individually, to determine whether it flops onto a new page.

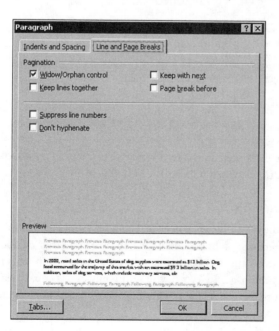

- Keep Lines Together ensures that all the lines of the paragraph appear on a single page.
- Keep with Next forces Word to put this paragraph and the next paragraph on the same page.
- Page Break Before makes Word start the paragraph on a new page.

Note

Word can't always follow your instructions, of course: If you format all the paragraphs in a long document to Keep with Next, the pages have to break somewhere. Word makes a valiant effort to follow your instructions but, if they're impossible, lays out the pages as best it can.

In almost all cases, you'll want to enforce widow and orphan control. If you have a paragraph in a report whose visual impact depends on the whole paragraph appearing on one page (say, a mission statement, or a quotation), you will probably want to keep the lines together. And headings should almost always be formatted Keep with Next so they don't get separated from the text they head.

USING DROP CAPS FOR EMPHASIS

Drop caps add emphasis and distinction to a paragraph. Used sparingly, they make a good visual break at the beginning of major sections in a report. Word makes drop caps easy: Click once inside the paragraph that's to have its initial letter turned into a drop cap, and then choose Format, Drop Cap (see Figure 15.13).

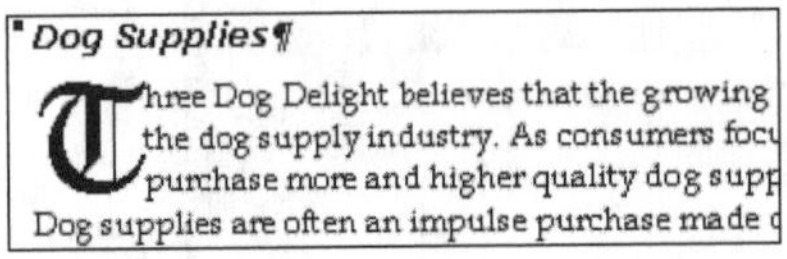

Figure 15.13
Drop caps work best in decorative fonts. Fonts that you wouldn't normally use in a business report make eye-catching drops.

Some fonts are particularly well-suited to drop-cap treatment. Take a look at the Algerian font, which ships with Office, or Old English MT.

POSITIONING TEXT WITH TABS

To fully understand the way tabs work in Word, you first must realize that a "tab" consists of two parts. First, there's the tab character—which, like any other character, is placed in a document when you press the Tab key. Second, there's the tab stop, which is a location, or series of locations, on the page. In Word, you set up tab stops for each paragraph, not for each line; in other words, every line in a paragraph must have identical tab stops.

Tip from

It's nearly impossible to work with tabs unless you make them visible on the screen. To do so, choose Tools, Options to open the Options dialog box. Then check the Tab Characters box on the View tab.

When Word encounters a tab character in a document, it advances to the next defined *tab stop*. Tab stops come in four different varieties: left-aligned, right-aligned, centered, and decimal-aligned (which aligns numbers so the decimal point appears at the tab location). In addition, you can specify a *leader* character (pronounced "leeder")—a character that will appear, repeated, in the blank area leading up to the tab stop. You've no doubt seen them in tables of contents.

```
This is a leader of periods........<Tab stop>
```

When working with tabs, it's always much easier to plan on having just one line per paragraph, and one paragraph per line. You'll see how that makes a big difference in the example in the next section.

To set a tab stop, do the following:

1. Select the paragraph(s) you want to have the new tab stops.

2. Choose Format, Tabs, and you'll see the Tabs dialog box as shown in Figure 15.14.

Figure 15.14

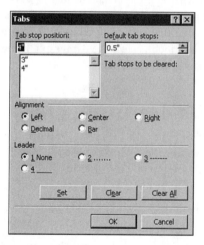

3. Type the location of the first tab stop in the Tab Stop Position box. (The "location" is the distance from the left margin of the document to the position of the tab stop, regardless of where the left edge of the paragraph might fall.)

Note

Paragraphs start out with left-aligned tab stops every half inch. If you specify your own tab stops, Word deletes the built-in tab stops preceding the ones you create. So, if you create a tab stop at 3 inches, and another at 4 inches, Word eliminates all the default tab stops up to 4 inches, but has left-aligned tab stops at 4.5 inches, 5.0, 5.5, 6.0, and so on, to the right edge of the page.

4. Choose the alignment and leader you want for the tab stop. Click the Set button and Word establishes a tab stop at the location you specify.

Caution

The Bar tab type in the Tabs dialog box creates a vertical rule—an up-and-down line—in the paragraph at the indicated tab location. This setting is a throwback to an early version of Word that didn't have borders. If you need a vertical line, use tables or borders, but avoid this setting.

The next section contains a detailed example, showing how leaders can be used to create a fill-in-the-blanks form.

The tab stops you create are stored in the paragraph mark; copy or move a paragraph mark, and the tab stops go with it. If the insertion point is in a normal paragraph with custom tab stops and you press Enter, the new paragraph inherits the same tab stops. Many Word users—even advanced Word users—find that confusing. To restore a paragraph to the default (left-aligned tab stops every half inch), select the paragraph, bring up the Styles and Formatting task pane, and click the original style's name.

USING THE RULER TO SET TAB STOPS AND INDENTS

Although the Tabs dialog box (refer to Figure 15.14) gives you much greater control over the location and characteristics of tab stops, many people use the Word ruler to set and move tab stops. To set a left-aligned tab stop at 2 inches using the ruler, you might try this approach:

1. Select the paragraphs that need tab stops. (You'll be able to see the results of setting tab stops immediately if you've already put the tab characters in the paragraphs.)

2. Bring up the ruler at the top of the screen by choosing View, Ruler or, if you want the ruler invisible most of the time, just "hover" your mouse directly below the Formatting toolbar.

3. The icon on the far left of the ruler tells you what kind of tab is available: left-, center-, right-, or decimal-aligned. Click the icon until you get the type of tab you need.

4. Click the ruler where you want the new tab to appear. All default tabs to the left of the new tab are destroyed in the process. Click and drag the tab icon to position it precisely where you want it. To get rid of a tab, click it and drag it off the ruler.

You can also use the ruler to adjust paragraph margins. Unfortunately, all these little icons can get confusing quickly—and it's impossible to set the leader character from the ruler—so use the Paragraph and Tabs dialog boxes for accurate settings. The ruler, however, can be handy for fine-tuning tab stops after they're established.

USING TABS TO CREATE A USER-INPUT FORM

Suppose you want to create a fill-in-the-blanks form, with room for a respondent to write (or type) her name and address.

If you've used Word for any time at all, you have probably tried to create just such a form, most likely by typing underscore (_) characters and trying to line up columns that never look right. By far the easiest way to create such a form is by using tabs, with the underscore leader:

1. Type the text, including tab characters, which will comprise the final form. In this case:

   ```
   Last Name <tab> First Name <tab>

   Address <tab>

   City <tab> State <tab> Zip <tab>
   ```

2. Position the insertion point inside the first paragraph, and choose Format, Tabs. Set two tab stops—a left-aligned tab at 3 inches, with underscore leader (Type 4); and a right-aligned tab at 6 inches with underscore leader.

Tip from

EQ & Woody

The default Word page layout—8.5-inch paper width, with 1.25-inch margins left and right—places the right margin at 6 inches, using the tab-measurement method.

3. Position the insertion point inside the second paragraph, and set a right-aligned tab at 6 inches, with underscore leader.

4. Position the insertion point in the third paragraph and set three tabs: left-aligned at 3 inches, left-aligned at 4.5 inches, and right-aligned at 6 inches, all with underscore leader.

5. Your form should look like Figure 15.15. If you want to fine-tune individual lines, click inside the line and bring up the ruler. Click and drag the tab stop icon to whatever position you like.

Word also enables you to double-click a "hot" spot on a line and insert a tab stop at the double-click location. This variant of click and type is notoriously inaccurate and much harder to use than either the Tabs dialog box or the ruler.

→ To learn more about Click and Type, **see** "Adjusting Paragraph Alignment and Outline Level," **p. 384**.

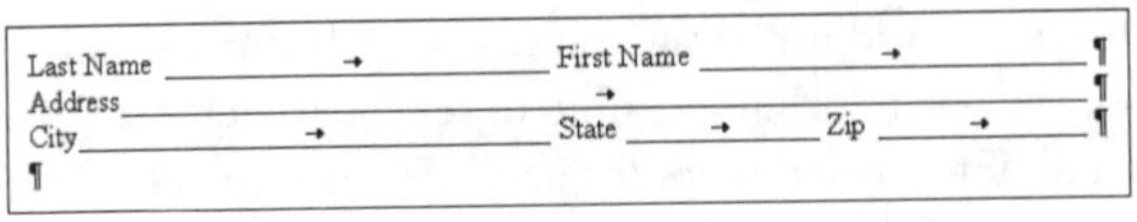

Figure 15.15
Word makes it surprisingly difficult to create a simple fill-in-the blanks form.

Last Name _____ → _____ First Name _____ → ____ ¶
Address _____ → _____ ¶
City _____ → _____ State _____ → ____ Zip _____ → ____ ¶
¶

FORMATTING SIMPLE LISTS WITH BULLETS AND NUMBERS

By far, the simplest way to create a bulleted or numbered list is to use one of the many shortcuts for starting and continuing such lists. For example, if you type a number or letter, followed by a period, a space, and then text, Word begins a numbered list, provided that you haven't disabled the options on the AutoFormat As You Type tab in the AutoCorrect dialog box. Dozens of combinations are available.

→ To have Word handle some of the formatting chores for you, **see** "Automatic Formatting," **p. 343**.

Numbering and bulleting are paragraph properties. As such, they're stored in the paragraph mark and travel if the paragraph mark is copied, cut, or pasted. Position the insertion point inside a numbered or bulleted paragraph and press Enter, and the bulleting or numbering is "inherited" by the new paragraph.

Note

AutoNumbered and AutoBulleted lists are slightly different because Word lets you bail out of bulleting or numbering by pressing Enter twice in succession. In other words, if the insertion point is inside a bulleted or numbered paragraph, and the paragraph is empty, when you press Enter, Word removes the bulleting and formatting from both the old and new paragraphs.

Bullets and numbers maintained by Word aren't "real" characters. You can't select them, much less delete or change them. Instead, they are generated automatically by Word, as a consequence of their paragraph formatting.

Many advanced Word users disable Word's AutoBulleting and AutoNumbering feature and apply bullets or numbers to lists by using simple toolbar buttons or—in more complex situations—using the dialog box.

→ AutoFormat driving you crazy? The good news is that you can disable it. **See** "Disabling AutoFormat Settings," **p. 358**.

You can always create a simple bulleted or numbered list by selecting the paragraphs you want to bullet or number, and clicking the Bullets icon or Numbering icon on the Formatting toolbar.

To take advantage of Word's extensive bulleting and numbering options, select the paragraphs you want to bullet or number, and choose Format, Bullets and Numbering (or right-click and choose Bullets and Numbering). You'll get the Bullets and Numbering dialog box shown in Figure 15.16.

Figure 15.16
From simple bullets to complex outline-style numbering schemes, Word has a solid (but far from complete) array of options.

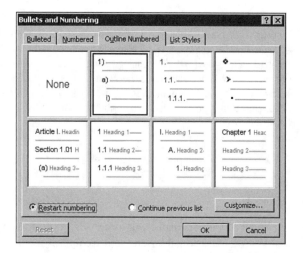

Select from the prebuilt bullet or numbering schemes, or click the Customize button to establish your own.

Tip from

EQ & Woody

You can manually construct intricate numbering schemes—often required by law offices—by using the {ListNum} field. For example, you can put together numbering sequences such as IV (31) A, and have the paragraphs renumber themselves when moved. Moreover, if you have a reference to a {ListNum}-generated number ("see paragraph IV (31) A"), and the paragraph is moved and renumbered, the reference changes as well.

→ To learn more about constructing complicated numbering schemes, **see** "Managing Custom Numeric Sequences," **p. 504**.

Consecutive paragraphs need not be numbered consecutively. For example, you could have paragraphs numbered 1, 2, 3, then two paragraphs with no numbering, and pick back up at 4, 5 and so on. To stop the numbering sequence, select the paragraph(s) you don't want to have numbered, choose Format, Bullets and Numbering and, on the Numbered or Outline Numbered tab, click the None box in the upper-left corner. To continue numbering where you last left off, select the first paragraph after the break, and on the Numbered or Outline Numbered tab, click the Continue Previous List button. You can get the same effect by right-clicking on a paragraph and choosing Restart numbering or Continue numbering.

Because bulleting and numbering is a paragraph property, if you place the insertion point inside a bulleted or numbered paragraph and press Enter, the newly created paragraph "inherits" the bulleting or numbering.

It also means that you can move, drag, or rearrange numbered paragraphs at will, and Word renumbers them, on-the-fly, as appropriate.

Tip from

EQ & Woody

You can associate numbering with a specific paragraph style, making Word put a sequential number in front of each paragraph formatted with that style. If your chapter headings are formatted with the Heading 1 style, for example, associating numbering with the Heading 1 style automatically generates chapter numbers. To make the association, choose Format, Bullets and Numbering, bring up the Outline Numbered tab, click a numbering style, and then click Customize, More. In the Link Level to Style box, choose the style.

FORMATTING ALL OR PART OF A DOCUMENT AUTOMATICALLY

If you feel intimidated by all of Word's formatting options, you can leave your document's destiny in the hands of Word's (occasionally useful, but frequently awful) batch AutoFormat capability.

When you run it, AutoFormat scans your document, identifies the "AutoFormat As You Type" kinds of changes—curling quotes, creating headings, AutoNumbering and AutoBulleting lists, and the like—adds some general formatting changes (one that is particularly despicable: changing Normal paragraphs to Body Text), and then allows you to review those changes, one by one.

→ To learn more about the evils of AutoFormatting, **see** "Automatic Formatting," **p. 343**.

Because you do have the ability to review the changes onscreen and vote yea or nay on each, you really have nothing to lose by running AutoFormat. An AutoFormat run can be useful if you've just opened a plain text document and need to format it quickly, or if you're having trouble getting the hang of Word's formatting capabilities. AutoFormatting email messages can remove extra carriage returns and emphasize marked reply text. To run AutoFormat

1. Save a copy of the file you are going to AutoFormat.

2. Choose Format, AutoFormat. Word gives you the option of running AutoFormat, or running it and reviewing each change. You should always opt to review changes.

3. Tell Word whether you're AutoFormatting a plain document, a letter, or an email message. Slightly different rules are applied in each case. Click OK to run.

4. When AutoFormat is complete, it gives you the option of reviewing the changes (always a good idea), accepting, or rejecting all of them (see Figure 15.17). It also lets you get to the Style Gallery, which permits wholesale (and frequently disastrous) substitution of styles.

Figure 15.17

Avoid the Style Gallery. Microsoft has made it difficult to find the Style Gallery in Word 2002, and for good reason. Although it was once touted as a godsend for people wanting to incorporate professional design into their documents, it in fact tramples over every bit of formatting you might have applied and, in all but the simplest situations, renders your documents virtually illegible.

CHECKING SPELLING AND GRAMMAR

Word contains one of the most sophisticated spell checkers you can find. The spell-checking module, which Word shares with the rest of Office, contains rich tools for custom dictionaries and "exclude" dictionaries, and easy right-click access to suggested spellings for words highlighted with the infamous red squiggly line.

→ To find out how to supercharge Word's spell checker, **see** "Setting Up Spell-Checking Options," **p. 46**.

Some people find the red squiggly lines distracting—as if they're being forced to correct spelling mistakes as they type. Word includes a batch spell checker, so you can turn off the squiggly lines and run a spell check after you're done typing. To turn off the squiggly lines, choose Tools, Options, bring up the Spelling & Grammar tab, and then uncheck the Check Spelling As You Type box. To run a batch spell check, choose Tools, Spelling and Grammar—or press F7.

Tip from	If you don't want Word to spell check a specific word or paragraph, select the text or paragraph, choose Tools, Language, Set Language, and check the Do Not Check Spelling or Grammar box.

The Grammar Checker's advice, on the other hand, can be overly simplistic. Why? Because it's rule-based, and English grammar is far too complex to fit neatly into a small set of rules. If you know you need help with basic grammar issues, you can get a great deal of benefit from the grammar checker. Most advanced users, however, find the squiggly green lines distracting and turn them off (choose Tools, Options, and on the Spelling & Grammar tab, uncheck the Check Grammar As You Type box).

If you want the grammar checker to help improve specific aspects of your writing (such as flagging sentences that are too long, or those in passive voice, or their/there mistakes), you can customize Grammar Checker to respond only to violations of those rules. To do so, choose Tools, Options and click the Settings button on the Spelling & Grammar tab. There you'll find dozens of different grammatical problem areas, and you can instruct Word to watch for the ones most important to you.

To use Word's built-in Thesaurus, position the insertion point inside the word you want to look up, and choose Tools, Language, Thesaurus. Alternatively you can bring up the spell checker by hitting F7, and the Thesaurus with Shift+F7.

SHARING DOCUMENTS

Word is often used in a business environment with groups of users who need to work together. To accommodate the need for users to create documents as a team, Word has workgroup features that make it easier to track and protect changes in documents.

TRACKING REVISIONS

When more than one person can make changes to a document, pandemonium can ensue. The surest way to maintain the integrity of a document is to ensure that changes—if they're allowed at all—are clearly identified so that anyone reviewing the edited document can trace specific changes back to their originator. That's at the heart of Word's Track Changes (frequently called "Revision tracking") capability.

When Word tracks changes made to a document, text that is added, deleted, or modified is marked to emphasize the changes made. You can subsequently go through those changes, one at a time, and accept or reject them.

To have Word track changes made to a document, choose Tools, Track Changes, or double-click the grayed-out TRK button on the Status bar. That brings up the Reviewing Toolbar, and changes made from that point on are explicitly shown by Word.

The Reviewing Toolbar (which can be moved anywhere on the screen, see Figure 15.18) gives you one convenient location for working with all document changes. In particular, the toolbar lets you look at any of the following:

- **Original**—What the document looked like before Change Tracking was turned on.
- **Original Showing Markup**—Shows the original document, with insertions noted in a manner similar to comments, out in the right margin, and deletions marked with an overstrike.
- **Final Showing Markup**—The final state of the document, inserted text appearing as underlined and deleted text noted in the margin.
- **Final**—The end result.

Shifting back and forth among the different views gives you a quick idea of the effect of changes.

On the Reviewing Toolbar, you'll find icons for jumping from revision to revision, accepting or rejecting individual changes as you go. There's also an icon for making your own comments, in case you need to follow up on a change, and for bringing up a pane that lists changes in order. Overall, it's a powerful and useful feature.

Figure 15.18
If Word has been told to track changes, you can review the changes easily, one at a time, with this dialog box.

Tip from

The trick, of course, is to ensure that all the people working on a document have Word track changes. Otherwise, their changes won't be explicitly shown, and you'll have to go through the additional step of comparing your original document with their modified versions to figure out what has changed. To force everyone making changes to a document to have Word track their changes, choose Tools, Protect Document, check the Tracked Changes button, enter an optional password, and click OK. From that point on, anyone who opens the document (except you) has to allow Word to track changes.

If you didn't set Word to track revisions, and somebody has made changes to a document, you still have one last resort, a feature called Compare Documents. To invoke it, open the original document, choose Tools, Compare and Merge Documents. Follow along as Word has you open the modified document. The feature automatically generates revision marks, noting the pieces that have been added or deleted from the original document, along with formatting changes. You can then use the normal accept or reject changes routines on the Reviewing Toolbar described earlier to decide which changes you want to accept into your original document.

ADDING COMMENTS TO DOCUMENTS

When making changes to a document, it's helpful to leave comments along the way, explaining the reasons behind the changes or suggesting additional changes to the author. Comments should be considered an adjunct to making revisions, as a means to help explain what has been done, or could be done, to a document. If your editors or reviewers make revisions to a document (with revision tracking turned on; see the preceding section), it's relatively easy to accept or reject their revisions. But if the reviewers add comments, rolling the comments into the document is a multistep task that takes a fair amount of time.

To enter a comment, highlight the text that pertains to the comment and choose Insert, Comment. Type your comment in the comment box.

Or you can cycle through all the comments in a document by using the Next button on the Reviewing Toolbar.

You can print all the comments attached to a document by choosing File, Print, and selecting Document showing markup in the Print What drop-down box.

SAVING DOCUMENT VERSIONS

Keeping backup copies and early versions of important documents should be a regular part of your daily Office routine. In addition to the normal backup cycle, Word 2002 enables you to keep multiple versions of a document in a single file.

If you're sharing documents and need to keep track of who made changes to what, you should consider saving versions of the document from time to time. Word makes version saving automatic, if you choose File, Save As, and then choose Tools, Save Version. The Save Version dialog box (which is also accessible by choosing File, Versions) lets you make comments about each specific version. Three caveats with Save versions:

- All the versions are stored in a single file. Although only the "deltas"—changes— between versions are saved (it's all invisible to you, of course), file size can become a significant problem, quickly.

- The Save Version dialog box lets you delete versions as they become obsolete. Use it.

- Never, ever send a versioned file to a customer, or someone else who might take offense at (or advantage of!) full knowledge of intermediate drafts. It happens more often than you might think.

TROUBLESHOOTING

WHICH BOOKMARK IS WHICH?

I have a couple of bookmarks that are right next to each other. When I show bookmarks by choosing Tools, Options and checking Bookmarks on the View tab, I get a jumbled mess that looks like this:

...and now [for [something] completely] different...

In fact, Word doesn't give you enough information to tell where one bookmark ends and another begins. In this example, you could have a bookmark that covers "for something completely" and another one that covers "something," or a bookmark that covers "for something" and another bookmark that covers "something completely." There's no way to tell which of these two interpretations is correct by viewing bookmarks.

The only way to be sure which bookmark covers what text is to navigate to the bookmark and see which text is selected. Choose Edit, Go To, and then choose Bookmark in the Go To What box, and select a bookmark. Click Go To, and Word highlights the contents of the bookmark you have chosen.

REMOVING MENU SHORTCUTS

When I press Ctrl+Alt+- (the hyphen/minus sign to the right of the zero on the keyboard, not the Number pad), the pointer changes to a thick, dark horizontal line.

If you intended to insert an em-dash, you used the wrong hyphen—press the minus key on the numeric keypad instead. Pressing the key combination Ctrl+Alt+- on the keyboard enables one of Word's most obscure and dangerous features, which goes by the awkward name ToolsCustomizeRemoveMenuShortcut. When you enable this feature and click a menu item, Word deletes the selected item immediately.

To restore the pointer to its normal function, press Esc. The next time you want to add an em-dash, remember to hold down Ctrl+Alt, and then use the minus key on the Number pad instead.

SECRETS OF THE OFFICE MASTERS: COMBINING REVISION MARKS AND COMMENTS

Few editors take advantage of both of the two major reviewing tools at their disposal: revision marking and comments. As you can see in Figure 15.19, the combination of the two is far more effective than using either individually.

The general rule of thumb for editing a Word document is straightforward:

- Make sure revision marking is turned on (choose Tools, Track Changes, or double-click the grayed-out TRK button in the Status Bar). Then go ahead and make the changes you want directly in the text. You can toggle the changes on and off by clicking the Highlight Changes on Screen box.
- If you want to explain why you want the indicated change, use a comment (Insert, Comment).

If you conscientiously stick to this approach—make the changes directly and explain why in comments—it's easy to review the comments at the same time you accept or reject the changes.

The alternatives aren't nearly as efficient. If editors type comments in the document, the comments have to be deleted manually. Conversely, if editors put changes in the comments but not in the document itself, the changes have to be copied out of the comment and applied to the document.

Remember: Changes are changes, and comments are comments. Keep the two separate and you'll make everyone's work easier.

Figure 15.19

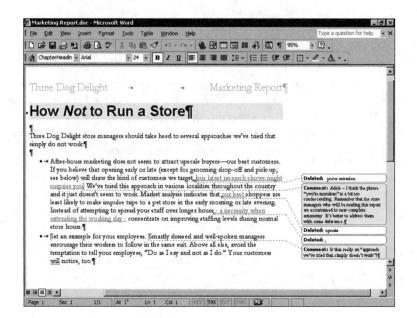

CHAPTER 16

ADVANCED DOCUMENT FORMATTING

In this chapter

ADJUSTING MARGINS

Word's margins look straightforward, but some of the settings work in strange ways. To view and change the margin settings for a document with a single section, choose File, Page Setup, and click the Margins tab. Word responds with the Page Setup dialog box shown in Figure 16.1.

Figure 16.1
Margins appear to be simple, but they're not.

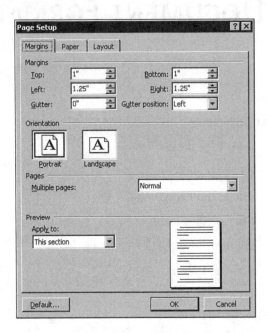

Note

This is the first time Word's margins have been correctly documented—the interaction between paper size, margin, and header and footer areas gets quite complex. If you've been having trouble with margins, follow along closely.

The Left margin setting works as you would expect: It specifies the distance from the left edge of the paper to the left margin of text. So, if you set a left margin of 1 inch, any left-aligned paragraph with an indent of 0 inches will start precisely 1 inch from the left edge of the paper. Similarly, the Right margin setting gives the distance from the right edge of the paper to the rightmost character in right-aligned or fully justified paragraphs, with 0 right indent.

→ For an explanation of how indents work, **see** "Indenting Paragraphs for Emphasis," **p. 385**.

If you're going to print on both sides of each sheet of paper (called *duplex printing*), and bind the sheets in a book or some kind of binder, you might want to allow extra room along the bound side—the left side on odd-numbered pages, and the right side on even-numbered pages. If you look at this book, you'll see how the additional whitespace, alternating left and right, improves the balance of the pages. To allow extra room, alternating left and right, choose Mirror Margins from the Multiple Pages drop-down list. Word adjusts the Page Setup dialog box to reflect Inside and Outside margins—the inside margin being closer to the binding (see Figure 16.2).

Figure 16.2
Use mirror margins when you create a bound document with printing on both sides of each sheet of paper.

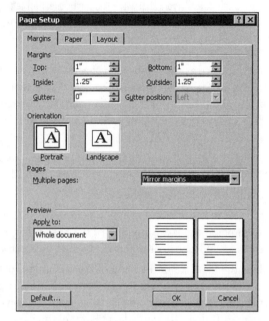

Similarly, you can choose the 2 Pages per Sheet option from the Multiple Pages drop-down list to print two half-size pages on a sheet (turned vertically, if you like, with Landscape orientation) or to "Book fold" print in booklet sequence so the pages can be stapled down the middle.

Note

If you choose "Book fold" for a document, the pages print in landscape orientation, two to a page. If you change your mind and choose Normal in the Multiple pages drop-down box, Word leaves your document in landscape orientation. You'll have to change it back to portrait manually.

A *gutter* is the additional amount of space left on each sheet for binding pages. If you're going to print on only one side of each sheet of paper, the Gutter distance is added to the left edge of each sheet. If you're going to print on both sides of each sheet of paper, and have chosen Mirror Margins in the Multiple Pages drop-down list, Word adjusts the gutter accordingly—adding it to the left margin on odd-numbered sheets and the right margin on even-numbered sheets.

Note

Word also has a provision for gutters at the top of each sheet; just choose Top in the Gutter Position drop-down list. This is a rather odd setting, because it won't be "mirrored" if you plan to print on the front and back of each sheet. (You might expect the gutter to appear at the top of odd-numbered pages and at the bottom of even-numbered pages, but it doesn't work that way.) You might use it for legal briefs that are bound at the top, or for single-sided pages that are destined for flip-top binders.

To control the amount of whitespace at the top of each sheet, you have to juggle three different settings: the Top setting on the Margins tab in the Page Setup dialog box, the Header setting on the Layout tab, and the contents of the header itself. After exhaustive testing, it has been determined that Word lays out the top of each document by using the following rules:

- Word takes the Header measurement in the Layout tab of the Page Setup dialog box and goes down that far on the page, placing the top of the first line of the header (if a header exists) that distance from the top of the paper.

- Word then lays out the rest of the header, including pictures, before and after spacing, and the like. So, for example, if the last paragraph of the header has an After spacing of 24 points, Word reserves an additional 24 points of space at the bottom of the header.

- Finally, Word assembles the first line in the body of the document, placing it below the header in the location it would normally occupy if there were no distinction between header and body text. Word then measures the distance from the top of this first body line to the top of the paper. If that distance is less than the Top value on the Margins tab of the Page Setup dialog box, Word moves the line down so at least the Top amount of space is between the top of the first line and the top of the sheet.

Using the terminology commonly associated with paragraph distances, the Header distance is an "exactly" measurement; and the Top distance is an "at least" measurement.

Bottom margins work precisely the same way, with the bottom of the last line of the footer "exactly" the Footer distance from the bottom of the sheet, and the bottom of the last line of body text "at least" the Bottom distance.

Click the Default button at the bottom of the Page Setup dialog box, and Word offers to alter the template attached to the current document, giving it all the page-formatting options specified on this three tabs in the dialog box.

You can also change margins for individual sections within a document.

→ For more information about your options when setting up a document, **see** "Page/Section Setup Options," **p. 340**.

CHANGING PAPER SIZE AND ORIENTATION

The Paper tab on the Page Setup dialog box (see Figure 16.3) allows you to choose from several common paper sizes (Letter, Legal, or A4, for example). The Margins tab lets you pick whether you want the printing to run along the short edge of the paper (Portrait orientation) or the long edge (Landscape orientation).

Figure 16.3
Word gives you complete control over paper size and the printer bin.

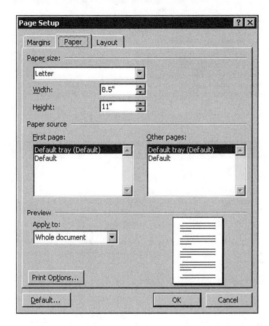

As with margins, the settings for paper size and orientation apply to sections. If your document has only one section, the size and orientation you choose applies to the entire document.

By judiciously choosing the page size, you can use a few tricks for special effects.

Tip from

EQ & Woody

Word can print to within 1/8 inch of the bottom of the sheet on a LaserJet printer—an important discovery if you're trying to print labels that extend to the bottom of the sheet. On the Paper tab, select a Paper Size of Legal 8 1/2×14 in. Then in the Paper Source box, pick Manual Feed. If you manually feed a regular letter-sized sheet, the print nearly touches the bottom of the sheet.

Other effects are possible as well. For example, when printing envelopes, adjust the page size to extend beyond the borders of the envelope, and you can frequently print all the way up to the edge, or even "bleed" over the edge. Experiment a bit. Remember that envelopes can often be fed either short-end first or long-end first.

INSERTING AND DELETING MANUAL PAGE BREAKS

If you want to force Word to start a new page, click once where you want the new page to begin; then choose Insert, Break, Page Break, and click OK (see Figure 16.4). (Alternatively, you can press Ctrl+Enter.)

Figure 16.4
Manually inserted page breaks are visible as dotted lines, like this, in all views.

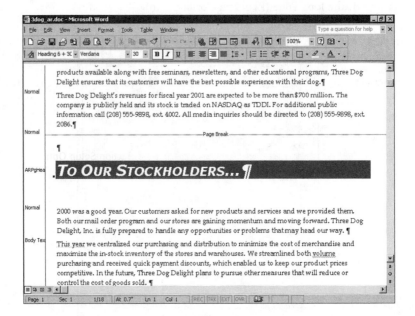

In general, it's easiest and cleanest to control page breaks with paragraph styles—set a page break before each paragraph with the Chapter Heading style, for example, or force all the text in a Quote style paragraph to appear on one page. That kind of page break setting belongs in the paragraph style—choose Format, Style, and select the style you want to adjust; then click the Modify button, choose Format, Paragraph, and click Line and Page Breaks tab. Even with well-designed paragraph styles, however, sometimes you'll want to force Word to start a new page at a location of your choosing.

The problem with manually inserted page breaks, of course, is that they don't change when the text changes: If you add or delete a few lines in several places in a document, you might need to adjust every manual page break—a dreary prospect indeed.

To delete all manual page breaks, follow these steps:

1. Choose Edit, Replace (or press Ctrl+H).

2. Clear the Find What and Replace With boxes, if necessary, and then click the More button. Clear all check boxes and all formatting.

3. Click the Special button and choose Manual Page Break. Word adds the ^m character to the Find What box.

4. Choose Replace All to remove every manual page break in the document.

FORMATTING DOCUMENTS BY SECTION

Although most Word documents contain only one section, if you want to change headers or footers, page size or orientation, margins, line numbers (used in some legal documents), page borders, or the number of newspaper-like columns in different parts of a document, you have to use sections.

Perhaps the most common situation arises when you want to change headers or footers in the middle of a document. In that case, you have to add a new section; there's no other alternative. Likewise, you might need to add a section if you have a wide table in the middle of a long report. Most of your pages will be printed in portrait orientation, but you'll need to add a section break before and after the table so that you can print it in landscape orientation. You could print the table separately and collate it by hand, but using section breaks removes your layout hassles with just a few clicks.

→ For a description of other page setup settings, **see** "Page/Section Setup Options," **p. 340**.

TYPES OF SECTIONS

Word recognizes four different types of section breaks:

- **Continuous**—Defines a new section, but does not force a page break. Continuous section breaks are used almost exclusively for changing the number of newspaper-like columns in a document, or resetting line numbering (typically in legal documents).

- **Next Page**—The most common type of section break, a Next Page section break not only defines a new section, it forces Word to start the section on a new page.

- **Odd Page**—Like the Next Page break, except Word can add one additional blank page to force the new section to begin on an odd-numbered page.

- **Even Page**—Like the Odd Page break, but Word starts on an even-numbered page.

Section breaks are visible in all views.

Just as paragraph formatting is stored in the paragraph mark at the end of a paragraph, Word stores section formatting in the section break mark at the end of the section. Formatting for the final section in a document is stored in the last paragraph mark in the document. If a document has only one section, the document's final paragraph mark holds the section formatting for the entire document.

INSERTING AND DELETING SECTION BREAKS

To insert a new section break into a document:

1. If the document does not yet include one, it's strongly recommended that you put a dummy manual section break at the end of the document. To do so, click once in front of the final paragraph mark in the document. Press Enter a few times. Then choose Insert, Break. In the Break dialog box (see Figure 16.5), choose Continuous, and click OK.

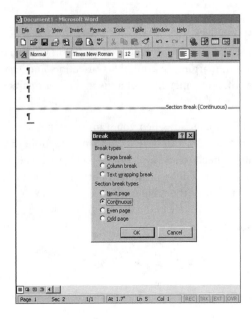

Figure 16.5
Before you insert that first section break, you can save yourself hours—days!—of trouble by placing a dummy section break at the end of the document.

2. If all the headers and footers in the document will be the same, you'll find it much easier to establish them now. Follow the instructions in the "Creating and Editing Headers and Footers" section later in this chapter for creating and editing headers and footers.

3. Carefully determine what section breaks you'll need in your document, what type they should be, and where they will occur. In particular, if you plan to change the number of newspaper-like columns for a short run in the middle of the document, you'll want Continuous section breaks both before and after the change.

4. Starting at the beginning of the document, create the section breaks, one at a time, by using the Break dialog box (choose Insert, Break).

The dummy section break at the end of the document can help you salvage important formatting information, because you can copy or move the section break, although copying or moving the final paragraph mark won't have any effect on section formatting. See the next section for details.

After establishing all sections, carefully go back into each section and apply the section formatting you require.

Tip from

EQ & Woody

> You'll find it much easier to work with sections if you've planned ahead, and can go through each section in order, from beginning to end, applying the section formatting. By working from beginning to end, you simplify problems—massive problems—associated with changing headers and footers, and whether a section is linked to the previous one or not. If you start at the beginning, you can see the effect each change has on subsequent sections. If you start in the middle, it can be infuriatingly difficult to see why or how a header or footer has changed.

PART

III

CH

16

If you must delete a section break, select the break and press Delete. The newly merged section takes on the settings of the section break at the end. Immediately examine the document for odd formatting changes. If you find any unwelcome formatting, press Ctrl+Z or click the Undo button to restore the section break.

COPYING FORMATTING BETWEEN SECTIONS

Section breaks store the settings for the section. You can select, delete, copy, or move these settings at will.

By far, the simplest way to copy section formatting from one section to another is by copying the section break. If you want to copy the section formatting from, say, section number 6 to section number 3, follow these steps:

1. Select the section break at the end of section 6 and press Ctrl+C to copy it to the Clipboard.
2. Click just in front of the section break at the end of section 3.
3. Press Ctrl+V to paste the section break you copied previously.
4. Press Delete to delete the old section break at the end of section 3.

Tip from

EQ & Woody

> If you created an extra dummy section break at the end of the document, all the document's original section formatting is stored in that section break. To restore a specific section to the document's original formatting, copy that dummy section break to the end of that specific section.

ADDING LINES, BORDERS, SHADING, AND BACKGROUNDS

Word lets you draw border lines and apply colors and other forms of shading to specific pieces of text, cells in tables, paragraphs, entire tables, or entire pages. When you draw a line around a page, it's called a *page border*. When you apply colors or shading to an entire page, it's called a *background*. And when you place a picture or text "behind" the text on a page—say, to print DRAFT diagonally across the page, or CONFIDENTIAL—that picture or text is called a *watermark*.

Tip from

To add a watermark to a document, choose Format, Background, Printed Watermark. The watermark is inserted as part of the document's (actually, the section's) header. By working directly with the header (View, Header and Footer), you can manually change the watermark—move it, resize it, or even delete it.

QUICK WAYS TO CREATE LINES

The easiest way to draw a horizontal line across a page is to type any of the horizontal line AutoFormat characters (see Table 16.1) three times and press Enter. The line will appear above the characters you typed.

TABLE 16.1   AUTOFORMAT CHARACTERS FOR HORIZONTAL LINES

Character	Type of Line
- (hyphen)	Light single line
_ (underscore)	Heavy single line
= (equal)	Heavy double line
# (number sign)	Thick line with thin lines above and below
~ (tilde)	Wavy line
* (asterisk)	Horizontal line of small squares

The horizontal line (also called a *rule*) is actually a lower border for the paragraph above the one where you typed. If you click once on that paragraph, and then choose Format, Borders and Shading, you'll see what formatting has taken effect. If you find this behavior annoying, you can turn it off in the AutoFormat dialog box.

→ To eliminate unwanted AutoFormat behaviors, **see** "Automatic Formatting," **p. 343**.

You can also use the tools on the Drawing toolbar to draw lines, or choose Table, Draw Table, and use Word's table drawing tool; however, neither of these approaches quickly creates lines that extend all the way across a page and move with their associated text.

BORDERS AND BOXES

You can draw borders—essentially rectangles—around characters, paragraphs, table cells, or pages. To create a border for characters, paragraphs, or cells:

1. Select the character(s), paragraph(s), table cell(s), or table(s) you want to format.

2. Choose Format, Borders and Shading. On the Borders tab (see Figure 16.6), make sure the Apply To box shows the correct setting: Paragraph, Text, Cell, or Table.

Figure 16.6
The Borders and Shading dialog box lets you draw lines around characters, paragraphs, or cells.

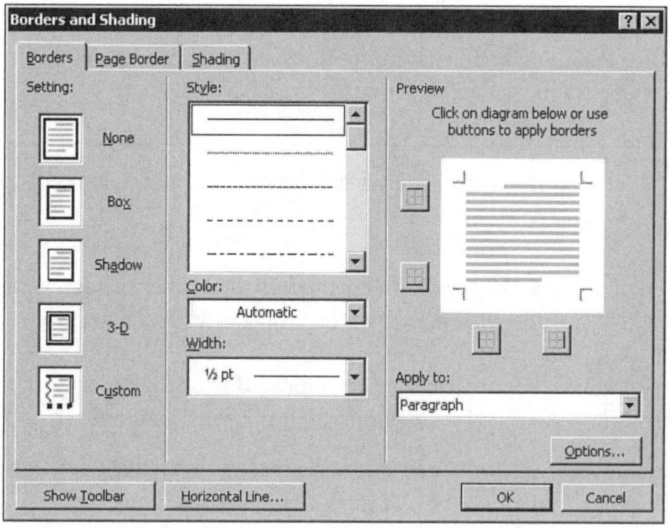

3. Choose from the common settings along the left, or draw your own border in the Preview pane on the right. You might want to use the Preview pane if, say, you want to have lines appear to the left and above a paragraph, but not to the right or below. Choose the line style, color, and width in the center pane.

Tip from

If you want borders of different types (to add double lines on the top and bottom, but single lines at the left and right, for example), start by clicking the Custom box. Then build the first border type by selecting from the Style, Color, and Width boxes. Finally, tell Word where you want this particular border type to appear by selecting the location(s) in the Preview pane. Go back and build your second border type, apply it in the Preview pane, and repeat as needed.

4. To set the distance between the text and the border, click Options and fill in the amounts. Click OK and the border appears.

Note

If the Tables and Borders toolbar is hidden, click the Show Toolbar button in the Borders and Shading dialog box to quickly display it.

The procedure for applying page borders is similar:

1. If you want only a specific page (or pages) in your document to have a border, set up section breaks at the beginning and end of the page (or pages). Then click once inside the section you want to have page borders.

2. Choose Format, Borders and Shading, and click the Page Border tab.

3. To choose from a fairly large selection of border options, click the down arrow in the Art box. Page Border formatting options are similar to general Border formatting, except pages can also use artwork for their borders.

Note
Unfortunately, you can't add your own page borders to Word's collection.

4. If you don't want the border to encompass the header or footer, click the Options button. Click OK and the border will be visible in Print Layout view.

To understand how borders can move around a document and appear suddenly as if out of nowhere, it's important to know where the formatting is stored:

- Character borders are stored in the characters themselves. If you move or copy a character with a border, the border goes along with it.
- Paragraph borders are stored in the paragraph mark. If you copy, move, or delete a paragraph mark, the border goes with it. If you press Enter while inside a paragraph with a border, the new paragraph mark—and thus the new paragraph—"inherits" the border settings from the previous paragraph.
- Table cell borders are stored in the individual cell's end-of-cell marker. Borders that apply to the entire table are in the final end-of-row marker.
- Page borders are stored in the section break mark. If your document has only one section, page borders are stored in the final paragraph mark in the document.

→ For an explanation of how to format cells, rows, and tables, **see** "Working with Tables," **p. 449**.

SHADING CHARACTERS, PARAGRAPHS, AND PAGES

A little shading goes a long way. Black text on a light shade of gray (or pale color) can be quite legible, and actually enhance the appearance of forms, in particular. White text on a very dark background can be striking, too. But avoid the middle ground: Dark shading with dark characters can be virtually illegible, even if you never print the document—colors vary widely from monitor to monitor, as well.

Character, paragraph, table cell, and entire table shading works much like borders. Select the item(s) you want to shade, choose Format, Borders and Shading, and then click the Shading tab. You see the Shading options shown in Figure 16.7.

The interaction of the various parts of the Shading dialog box can be confusing. Think of it this way: If you want to apply a solid color, use the Fill box at the top of the dialog box. If you want to apply a shade—say, a 5% gray background—use the Pattern box at the bottom.

"No Fill" in the Fill box on the top means there's no solid background color. "Clear" in the Style box near the bottom means there's no shading.

Figure 16.7
Color and shading are both applied from the Shading tab.

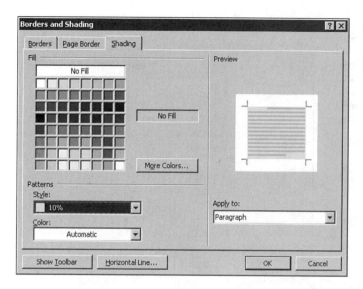

If you absolutely must have a background color, with a shade of gray on top of the color, pick the color in the Fill box and the shade in the Pattern box. Finally, just to guarantee that you stay thoroughly confused, shades aren't confined to shades of gray. In fact, you can "shade" with any color; choose it in the Color box at the bottom.

If you want to apply a shade or a fill color to the entire page, you're in the wrong place. You'll have to go back to your document, and then choose Format, Background. At that point, you can choose a solid color background, or you can choose Fill Effects to bring up the Fill Effects dialog box shown in Figure 16.8.

Fill effects include the capability to perform one- or two-color gradient fills; use a repeating picture called a "texture"; create cross-hatched patterns in a wide variety of styles and any color; or bring in your own picture, which will be repeated like a tiled Windows wallpaper.

Note

Page backgrounds show up onscreen only in Web Layout view and do not appear if you print the document. If you choose a page background, Word automatically shifts to Web Layout view.

Page backgrounds apply to the entire document; they cannot be changed from section to section, like page borders. In addition, the fill effects available on pages are not available to characters, table cells, or paragraphs. Page fill effects have few uses for anything but Web pages.

Figure 16.8
Word has an extensive collection of fill effects, but they can be applied only to pages, and all the pages in a document must have the same effects.

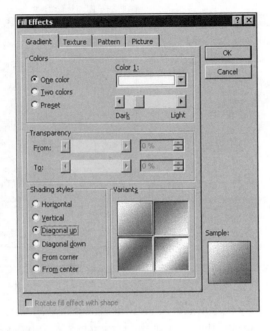

FORMATTING A DOCUMENT WITH COLUMNS

Another section-formatting option controls the number of newspaper-like snaking columns within the section. You might be tempted to use multiple columns for laying out newsletters and brochures, or (not surprisingly) newspapers. But before you try, take a closer look at the nuances.

Snaking newspaper-like columns might not work the way you're expecting: They run from top to bottom, and there's no rebalancing for a page break. If you have, say, 12 items in a section that's set up with three columns, they'll appear arranged as in Table 16.2.

TABLE 16.2 SEQUENCE OF SNAKING COLUMNS

Item 1	Item 5	Item 9
Item 2	Item 6	Item 10
Item 3	Item 7	Item 11
Item 4	Item 8	Item 12

However, if you add a page break between, say, the second and third lines in Table 16.2, items 2, 6, and 10 will appear on the first page, and items 3, 7, and 11 will end up on the second page.

If you need greater control over the appearance and layout of snaking columns, use tables instead of column formatting. Place each item in its own table cell and hide the table's gridlines. With Word's capability to draw custom tables with any number of cells, including nested cells, it makes little sense to work with columns if the layout is complicated.

Tip from

El & Woody

If tables won't do, you can also give yourself much greater control over your pages by using linked text boxes (see the next section).

PART

III

CH

16

To set up snaking columns in the middle of a document, follow these steps:

1. Switch to Normal view, and then choose Insert, Break. Add a Continuous section break immediately before the first item in the list and another Continuous section break immediately after the last item in the list.

2. Click once between the two section break marks.

3. Choose Format, Columns, and choose the column layout you like (see Figure 16.9). Note that you can set column widths and inter-column whitespace manually.

Figure 16.9
To avoid confusion, set up the "before" and "after" section breaks manually: click inside the area you want to format in snaking columns, and choose This Section from the Apply To box.

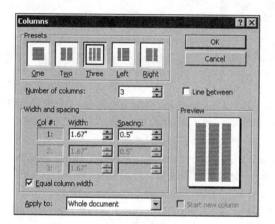

FAKING COLUMNS WITH LINKED TEXT BOXES

You can simulate column formatting in your document by constructing text boxes and filling the text boxes with text. In fact, if you want to create true newspaper-like columns in a document—where the last entry in a column says "See rest of story on page xxx"—your only choice is to create a series of linked text boxes. Word refers to the contents of a single set of linked text boxes as a *story*; the text in a story flows from one text box into the next, as needed.

The following is a common way to set up linked text boxes:

1. Click the Text Box button on the Drawing toolbar to draw the text boxes you want to contain the story. The text boxes appear in the drawing layer, and you can add them anywhere in the document.

→ For more details on how the drawing layer works, **see** "Adding Text to a Drawing," **p. 116**.

2. As soon as you draw the first text box, Word's Text Box toolbar appears (see Figure 16.10). Click once inside the first text box in the chain.

Figure 16.10
The key to linking text boxes is the link icon at the beginning of the Text Box toolbar.

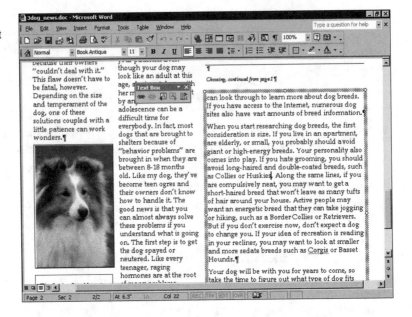

3. Click the Create Text Box Link button at the beginning of the Text Box toolbar. The pointer changes to the shape of a pitcher, with characters pouring out of the spout. Click inside the second text box in the chain.

4. After creating the link, either copy and paste ("pour") the story into the first box, or begin typing the story in the first box. In either case, Word uses all the room in the first text box, and then automatically flows the story into the second box.

5. If you need a third linked text box to hold the story, click inside the second text box in the chain. Click the Create Text Box Link icon on the Text Box toolbar, and then click inside the third linked text box. If you need more than three boxes, continue in this manner, linking all the boxes in the chain.

To add a jump line ("See rest of story on page xxx") at the end of a linked text box, first create a bookmark on the linked-to text box. Then choose Insert, Cross-Reference to construct a reference to the page number of the bookmark.

→ For step-by-step instructions on how to create bookmarks, **see** "Using Bookmarks," **p. 432**.

Linked text boxes might appear to be simple, but in most real-world situations they aren't:

■ Getting the boxes set up for precisely the correct width, and aligning them on column boundaries, requires some juggling with the Size and Layout (Advanced) tabs of the Format Text Box dialog box (choose Format, Text Box).

- The margins inside text boxes might conflict with the margins established in the column. To adjust the internal margins of the text box, choose Format, Text Box and click the Text Box tab.

- Text boxes float in the drawing layer. That can cause problems with constructing indexes, tables of contents, fields, and much more.

→ For an explanation of the limitations of the drawing layer, **see** "Working with the Drawing Layer," **p. 108**.

PART

III

CH

16

Tip from

EQ & Woody

You can also link any kind of AutoShape that can hold text. Although the AutoShapes aren't literally "text boxes," they behave much like text boxes.

CREATING AND EDITING HEADERS AND FOOTERS

Headers appear at the top of each page; footers at the bottom. Word lets you specify "first page only" headers and footers, so the first page of a report or letter can have headers and footers that are different from those in the body of the report. In addition, Word enables you to set up different headers and footers for odd-numbered and even-numbered pages. That comes in handy if you're going to be printing on the front and back of each sheet of paper. (Look at the headers in this book for an example.)

CREATING HEADERS AND FOOTERS

Headers and footers exist on every page in a Word document. Until you put something in them, however, they're invisible. Word reserves room for them, but doesn't print anything (or show anything on the screen) in the reserved area.

To create a header, follow these steps:

1. Choose View, Header and Footer. Word switches to Print Layout view (if you aren't there already), displays the Header and Footer toolbar, turns the body text of the document gray, and highlights the header area of the page (see Figure 16.11).

Figure 16.11
You "view" a header, in Word parlance, because the header already exists—even if you haven't put anything into it.

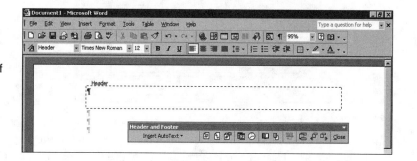

2. Enter anything you want in the header. Note that the paragraph is formatted with the Header style, which includes two tab stops: a centered stop at the middle of the page and a right-aligned stop on the right margin. (If you've changed margins, you also need to change the locations of these tab stops.)

3. When you're finished with the header, click the Switch Between Header and Footer button on the Header and Footer toolbar. Word moves the insertion point to the footer for the current page.

4. Enter text, graphics, or whatever else you want in the footer.

5. Click the Close button on the Header and Footer toolbar to return to your document.

If you have created a header or footer for a page, you can see it when you're in Print Layout view, as a grayed-out shadow of how the header or footer will appear on the final printed page. To edit a header or footer that you can see on the screen, double-click it.

To force Word to use a different header and footer on the first page than the one in the rest of the document, or to alternate headers and footers for odd- and even-numbered pages, click the Page Setup icon on the Header and Footer toolbar. That displays the Layout tab in the Page Setup dialog box (see Figure 16.12), where you can check the Different Odd and Even, and the Different First Page boxes.

Figure 16.12
Specify whether you want different headers for the first page and odd/even pages in this dialog box.

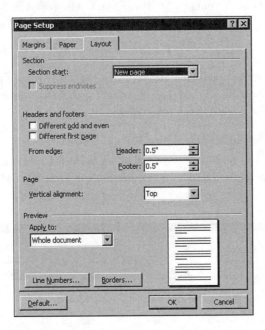

After checking the Different First Page box, you can navigate to the first page in your document, choose View, Header and Footer, and customize the first page header and footer as you like.

After checking the Different Odd and Even box, any changes you make in the header or footer of an even-numbered page will appear on all even-numbered pages; thus, if you change the header on page 6, your changes appear on all even-numbered pages. Similarly, changing the header or footer on an odd-numbered page changes all the odd-numbered pages, with the possible exception of page 1, which remains unaltered if you've checked the Different First Page box.

The actual locations of a header or footer on the page are determined by the margins.

→ For an explanation of how headers and margins work together, **see** "Adjusting Margins," **p. 402**.

NUMBERING PAGES

By far the most common use for a header or footer is to show the page number. Word gives you several options:

- To place a plain page number in the header or footer, with no additional text (a simple 14 instead of Page 14), choose Insert, Page Numbers. You'll see the Page Numbers dialog box (see Figure 16.13) which allows you to position the number at the top or bottom of the page—left, middle, or right.

Figure 16.13

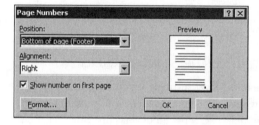

- While editing the header or footer, use the Header and Footer toolbar buttons to insert the current page number, or the total number of pages. To use the format Page x of xx, for example, follow these steps: Type Page, followed by a space; click the Insert Page Number icon; type a space, the word of, and another space; and click the Insert Number of Pages icon.

- The Insert Page Number icon actually places a {Page} field in the header or footer; the Insert Number of Pages icon adds a {NumPages} field. By inserting your own fields, you can create and edit custom page number formats.

→ For more details on how to number pages in long documents, **see** "Page Numbering," **p. 498**.

Tip from

EQ & Woody

If you choose Insert, Page Number, Word actually puts a {Page} field *inside a frame*, and tucks that frame into the header or footer. Frames can cause all sorts of problems, especially when you're formatting other header or footer entries. For example, if you select the entire footer and apply some sort of font formatting, the formatting will not "take" inside the frame. Unless you're in a big hurry, it's smarter and cleaner to use the icons on the Header and Footer toolbar.

ADDING DATES AND DOCUMENT DETAILS

The Header and Footer toolbar also includes icons that let you insert the current date or time. You can accomplish the same result manually by choosing Insert, Date and Time, or by creating your own fields to show, say, the document's filename, or the date and time it was last printed.

One of the most important fields—called {StyleRef}—allows you to put text from the document into a header or footer. You can use {StyleRef} to add the title or number of the current chapter to a header, for example, or to produce "Able–Autry" page indexes in the header, as in a telephone book.

→ For step-by-step instructions on how to create custom headers and footers for catalogs and other long documents, **see** "Referring to Document Contents," **p. 498**.

HOW SECTION BREAKS AFFECT HEADERS AND FOOTERS

Headers and footers are section-level settings; if you have more than one section in a document, each section can have its own set of headers and footers. Headers and footers are stored in the section break marks. If a document has just one section, the headers and footers are stored in the final paragraph mark in the document; that is an important detail if you find yourself trying to unravel inscrutable headers and footers in a multisection document.

→ To decipher the mysteries of sections, **see** "Formatting Documents by Section," **p. 407**.

To format a section so that it uses the same headers and footers as the preceding section, you don't need to do anything more than insert a section break. Word automatically formats the headers and footers in the new section by using the Same As Previous option.

If you want to break the Same As Previous link between the current section and the preceding section, click the Same As Previous button on the Header and Footer toolbar.

When you break the Same As Previous link, you effectively break the document into two separate pieces. With this setting in effect, any changes to a header or footer in the first section affect pages only in that section. Likewise, changes to a header or footer in the second section affect only that section.

> **Caution**
>
> When you break and restore the Same As Previous link, or add, delete, move, or copy section breaks on-the-fly, the effects on existing headers and footers can be extremely unpredictable. It's always best to lay out your document and establish section breaks first, before you begin modifying text, headers, or footers.

Sometimes you need to restart the page numbers in a section. Perhaps you want to start the numbering at 1 once again. Maybe you need to advance a handful of numbers to accommodate sheets you plan to print and interleave manually.

To restart page numbers, follow these steps:

1. Switch to Normal view and choose Insert, Break, Next Page to create a section break where you want the new page-numbering sequence to begin.

→ For an explanation of how each type of section works, **see** "Types of Sections," **p. 407**.

2. Click once immediately after the Next Page section break.

3. Choose Insert, Page Numbers. In the Page Numbers dialog box, click the Format box.

> **Note**
>
> The Format Page Number icon also appears on the Header and Footer toolbar.

4. In the Page Numbering Start At box, specify the section's starting page number.

CREATING AND EDITING LETTERS

It sounds so easy: In theory, the Letter Wizard walks you step-by-step through the process of addressing, writing, and formatting a personal or business letter, with perfect results. In practice, the Letter Wizard and its connection to the Outlook Contacts list suffer from dozens of frustrating flaws—unless you know the secrets.

> **Tip from**
>
> *EQ & Woody*
>
> Although you might think the Letter Wizard is about as straightforward as they come, you'll be surprised at what you don't know about this seemingly innocuous wizard. In this book, you'll find some of its quirks documented for the first time—anywhere.

USING THE LETTER WIZARD

The key to making the Word Letter Wizard generate decent-looking letters lies in understanding what it can and cannot do, and how it interacts with the letter itself.

The least effective way to use the Letter Wizard is to start with a blank document and choose Tools, Letters and Mailings, Letter Wizard. The results, as shown in Figure 16.14, will surely be unsatisfactory—even if you choose a superb custom template in the Choose a Page Design box.

Figure 16.14
When you run the Letter Wizard on a blank document, the wizard throws away almost all the contents of the template you choose, generating an amateurish-looking letter.

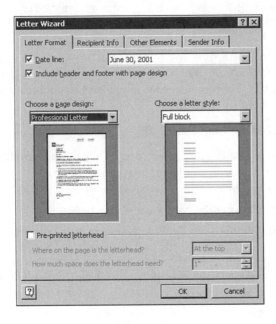

Be vigilant: Word can trick you into running the Letter Wizard on a blank (or nearly blank) document in any number of ways. If you type Dear John, for example, the Office Assistant might pop up and ask whether it can help you type a letter. Say yes, and you'll be running the Letter Wizard on a nearly blank document. If you select an item in Outlook's Contacts folder and choose Actions, New Letter to Contact, you'll end up running the Letter Wizard on a blank document. If you choose File, New, choose General Templates, and pick the Letter Wizard from the Letters & Faxes tab, once again you'll end up running the Letter Wizard on a blank document. All these approaches doom you to a poorly constructed, amateurish letter.

Tip from

EQ & Woody

The only way to get a professional-looking letter out of Word's Letter Wizard is to start with a document that's been specifically designed to work with the Letter Wizard. The three templates on the Letter Format tab include all the right elements, but you need to replace generic text and graphics with your own content for best results.

The fundamental trick to using the Letter Wizard is this: Create a new document first—one that is specifically designed to work with the Letter Wizard. *Then* run the Letter Wizard.

Word ships with three templates that produce documents for use with the Letter Wizard. To see what they'll do, choose File, New, General Templates; click the Letters Format tab; and pick Contemporary Letter, Elegant Letter, or Professional Letter. Click OK to create the new document, and then click anywhere within the document itself and choose Tools, Letters and Mailings, Letter Wizard.

As you can see from the Letter Wizard's Recipient Info tab shown in Figure 16.15, the Letter Wizard actually picks up information from the letter itself—in this case the Dear Sir or Madam: salutation generated by the Elegant Letter template—and presents that information in the Letter Wizard dialog box.

Figure 16.15
The Letter Wizard picks up text from the letter template, such as the salutation shown here.

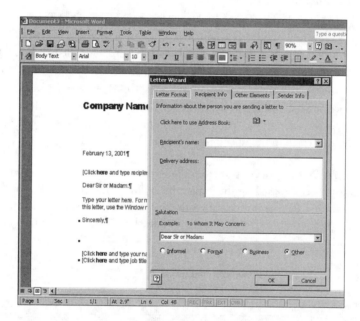

Tip from

EQ & Woody

If you create a template that's designed to be used with the Letter Wizard, you can have Word run the Letter Wizard immediately after creating a new document based on the template. Create a Document_New() macro with this line:

```
ActiveDocument.RunLetterWizard
```

For detailed instructions on how to create a macro that runs each time you create a new document, turn to Chapter 40, "Building Custom Applications with VBA."

CUSTOMIZING LETTER TEMPLATES

The easiest way to make a template that will generate documents designed to work with the Letter Wizard is to start with one of Word's three built-in letter templates—Contemporary

Letter, Elegant Letter, or Professional Letter—and save the modified template under a new name.

→ For details on how to work with Word templates, **see** "Customizing Word Templates," **p. 482**.

If you prefer to create a new template from scratch or modify one of your company's existing letter templates, follow these guidelines to ensure that the documents it creates are compatible with the Letter Wizard:

- Use a {CreateDate} field for the date. The Date line box shown previously in Figure 16.14 automatically finds the field and changes its formatting, based on the sample you choose from the drop-down box.

→ For a detailed explanation of how date and time fields work, **see** "Showing Dates and Times," **p. 496**.

- If you're printing on letterhead paper, draw an empty text box around the area where a logo or other graphic appears. The Letter Wizard adds the text box and flows the letter text around it. This technique is much simpler than trying to jury-rig a setting in the Pre-printed Letterhead section on the Letter Format tab.

- In spite of what you see in the three prebuilt letter templates, don't use any "click here and type your letter" or "click here and type your name" placeholders. Instead, use the Styles described in the upcoming Table 16.3.

The Letter Wizard retrieves text from the letter and displays it on the wizard tabs. It identifies the text it needs based on the paragraph styles in the letter itself. For example, if you enter the text Ed Bott and format it with the Signature style, and then run the Letter Wizard, it places that text in the Sender's Name box on the Sender Info tab, as shown in Figure 16.16.

Figure 16.16
The Letter Wizard picks up the Sender's Name for the Sender Info tab by looking in the letter for a paragraph formatted with the Signature style.

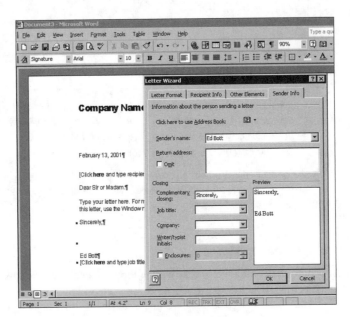

Conversely, if you type the name Woody Leonhard in the Sender's Name box on the Letter Wizard's Sender Info tab, and then click OK, the Letter Wizard removes any lines in the letter that happen to be formatted in the Signature style, and replaces them with one containing the text Woody Leonhard.

In short, the Letter Wizard picks up data from the letter based on certain predefined styles, and it puts data back into the letter using those styles. The styles are listed in Table 16.3.

TABLE 16.3   STYLES RECOGNIZED BY THE LETTER WIZARD

Style in Letter	Tab in Wizard	Box in Wizard
Inside Address Name	Recipient Info	Recipient's Name
Inside Address	Recipient Info	Delivery Address
Salutation	Recipient Info	Salutation
Reference Line	Other Elements	Reference Line
Mailing Instructions	Other Elements	Mailing Instructions
Attention Line	Other Elements	Attention
Subject Line	Other Elements	Subject
Cc List	Other Elements	Cc:
Signature	Sender Info	Sender's Name
Return Address	Sender Info	Return Address
Closing	Sender Info	Complimentary Closing
Signature Job Title	Sender Info	Job Title
Signature Company	Sender Info	Company
Reference Initials	Sender Info	Writer/Typist Initials
Enclosure	Sender Info	Enclosures

In addition, the main part of the letter should appear in a style called Body Text. The Letter Wizard modifies the Body Text, Closing, Signature, Signature Job Title, and Signature Company styles on-the-fly, depending on the option you select in the Choose a Letter Style box (Full block, Modified block, Semi-block) on the Letter Format tab.

If you construct your own templates using these styles, you should be able to use the Letter Wizard with excellent results.

ADDRESSING LETTERS WITH THE OUTLOOK CONTACTS LIST

If you try to use the Outlook Address Book from inside the Letter Wizard, you'll quickly discover that Outlook insists on inserting a country line into every address that doesn't explicitly include a country. Thus, if you live in the United States, every address you insert follows this format:

> Bill Gates
>
> One Microsoft Way
>
> Redmond, WA 98052
>
> United States of America

When you use the Letter Wizard with Outlook's Address Book, no easy way exists to get around this problem. If you don't want the country line in the address, you have to delete it manually.

You can customize Word so that it imports names and addresses directly from your Outlook Address Book into any document, without requiring the Letter Wizard. Unfortunately, this feature, too, brings along the unnecessary country line. To add an Insert Address button to a toolbar, choose Tools, Customize, and click the Commands tab. From the Categories list on the left, choose Insert. Scroll through the list on the right until you find the Address Book command, and then click and drag it onto a convenient toolbar.

When you click the Insert Address button, Word opens your Address Book and waits for you to select a name. After you click OK, it inserts the contact's name and address into your document.

There's a trick you can use to get rid of the stray "United States of America" line that appears at the end of addresses you import by using the Insert Address button. If you use this trick, however, country names won't appear even when you want them to: If you select the name of a contact who lives in Thailand, for example, Word inserts their address properly, but the country won't appear at the end of the address.

To customize the format of names and addresses imported with the Insert Address icon:

1. Start with a new blank document. Carefully type these three lines in the document:
   ```
   <PR_DISPLAY_NAME>
   <PR_STREET_ADDRESS>
   <PR_LOCALITY>, <PR_STATE_OR_PROVINCE> <PR_POSTAL_CODE>
   ```

2. Select all three lines. Choose Insert, AutoText, New, and create a new AutoText entry with the name AddressLayout (all one word).

3. The next time Word inserts an address using the Insert Address icon, it will look for an AutoText entry called AddressLayout. If it finds such an entry, it uses the codes in the entry as a template for the imported name and address.

If you use the three-line AutoText entry codes in step 1 in the previous list, you'll start getting names and addresses that look like this:

> Bill Gates
>
> One Microsoft Ave
>
> Redmond, WA 98052

Word and Outlook recognize all the formatting codes defined in Table 16.4.

TABLE 16.4 VALID FORMATTING CODES FOR THE AddressLayout AutoText Entry

Code	Corresponding Field from Contact Form
PR_DISPLAY_NAME	Full Name
PR_GIVEN_NAME	First name
PR_SURNAME	Last name
PR_STREET_ADDRESS	Street address (one or more lines, from the designated mailing address)
PR_LOCALITY	City
PR_STATE_OR_PROVINCE	State or province
PR_POSTAL_CODE	ZIP or postal code
PR_COUNTRY	Country
PR_TITLE	Job title
PR_COMPANY_NAME	Company name
PR_DEPARTMENT_NAME	Department name (Details tab)
PR_OFFICE_TELEPHONE_NUMBER	Business number
PR_BUSINESS_FAX_NUMBER	Business fax number
PR_OFFICE2_TELEPHONE_NUMBER	Business 2 number
PR_HOME_TELEPHONE_NUMBER	Home number
PR_CELLULAR_TELEPHONE_NUMBER	Mobile number
PR_BEEPER_TELEPHONE_NUMBER	Pager number
PR_EMAIL_ADDRESS	First listed e-mail address
PR_COMMENT	Text in the Notes box

PART III
CH 16

You can write a macro to insert an address from Outlook into a Word document. The macro uses the formatting codes listed in Table 16.4 to determine how it should format the name and address it retrieves from Outlook.

For example, the macro in Listing 16.1 tells Word that you want to retrieve the name, company name, address, city/state/postal code, and country. It then lets you pick the name and address you want from the Outlook Address Book. Finally, the macro removes "United States of America," if it exists, and closes up any blank lines (if, for example, no company name is used), before depositing the name and address in your document.

LISTING 16.1 InsertAddressFromOutlook()

```
Public Sub InsertAddressFromOutlook()
Dim strCode, strAddress As String
Dim iDoubleCR As Integer
`Set up the formatting codes in strCode
```

LISTING 16.1   CONTINUED

```
strCode = "<PR_DISPLAY_NAME>" & vbCr
strCode = strCode & "<PR_COMPANY_NAME>" & vbCr
strCode = strCode & "<PR_STREET_ADDRESS>" & vbCr
strCode = strCode & "<PR_LOCALITY>, <PR_STATE_OR_PROVINCE> <PR_POSTAL_CODE>" &
ÂvbCr
strCode = strCode & "<PR_COUNTRY>" & vbCr
`Let the user choose the name in Outlook
strAddress = Application.GetAddress("", strCode, False, 1, , , True, True)
`Strip away the final "United States of America", if any
If Right(strAddress, 25) = "United States of America" & vbCr Then
strAddress = Left(strAddress, Len(strAddress) - 25)
End If
`Eliminate blank lines by looking for two carriage returns in a row
iDoubleCR = InStr(strAddress, vbCr & vbCr)
While iDoubleCR <> 0
strAddress = Left(strAddress, iDoubleCR - 1) & Mid(strAddress, iDoubleCR + 1)
iDoubleCR = InStr(strAddress, vbCr & vbCr)
Wend
`Insert the modified address at the current insertion point
Selection.TypeText strAddress
End Sub
```

Note

> WOPR 2002 includes a utility called the Popup Contacts List that lets you right-click in a document and insert any name and address from your Outlook Contacts. See Appendix B, "What's on Que's WOPR XP/2002 Pack," for details.

CREATING ENVELOPES AND LABELS

Word includes an extensive set of features that allow you to address and print a single envelope, use mail merge to generate a large number of properly addressed envelopes, or format single and multiple labels using addresses from a variety of sources.

Tip from

EQ & Woody

> WOPR, the Office add-in distributed exclusively on this book's companion CD, has a much more versatile envelope printer called Enveloper. Although it takes a few minutes to set up Enveloper, you'll find it useful if you want to print your company's logo or other design, or messages on the envelope; if you want to place the POSTNET bar code in a location of your choosing; or if you commonly print more than one kind of envelope.

PRINTING ENVELOPES

To print an envelope, choose Tools, Letters and Mailings, Envelopes and Labels. Fill in the Envelopes and Labels dialog box shown in Figure 16.17, and then click the Print button.

Insert a blank envelope in your printer's manual feed, and you should get the results you expect.

Figure 16.17
To pull a delivery or return address for an envelope from the Outlook Address Book, click the Insert Address icon.

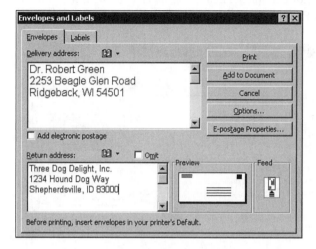

The first time you print an envelope, make sure you click the Options button to set up the proper envelope size, fonts, paper source, and other printing options.

Tip from

EQ & Woody

Although Word usually does a good job of figuring out what kind of printer you're using—and thus how to orient an envelope so it prints properly—it rarely (if ever) correctly identifies an envelope paper tray. If you have an envelope tray for your printer, you'll need to click the Options button and specify that your printer includes this tray.

If you select an address before choosing Tools, Letters and Mailings, Envelopes and Labels, that address appears in the Delivery Address box. In addition, Word is frequently smart enough to identify an address, if it appears near the beginning of the document.

When you click the Add to Document button in the Envelopes and Labels dialog box, Word attaches a special section to the beginning of the document that includes the envelope. When you subsequently print the letter, both the letter itself and the envelope will print. That can be helpful if you aren't ready to print the letter, but want to set the envelope up ahead of time. It can also be helpful in creating a template with an envelope attached to the document. Finally, you can use this technique to place a logo, text box, or other graphic element on the envelope prior to printing.

→ For more details on how to merge addresses with envelopes, **see** "Merge Envelopes," **p. 523**.

PRINTING LABELS

When you choose Tools, Letters and Mailings, Envelopes and Labels, and then click the Labels tab, Word displays the dialog box shown in Figure 16.18, which allows you to create single labels or an entire sheet of labels. Click the Options button to tell Word what kind of label position (row and column) you're using. (The dialog box includes settings for virtually all Avery labels, for example.) Then fill in the label number if you want to print only one label, and click Print.

Figure 16.18
Word's label format includes grids for all the major label (and business card) sizes.

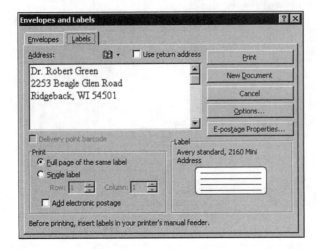

You can also generate mailing labels for an entire list of recipients, via a mail merge.

→ For details on how to merge data and labels, **see** "Merge Labels," **p. 525**.

CUSTOMIZING LABELS

The major shortcoming in Word's bag of labeling tricks is its inability to let you customize what gets printed on labels. If you're running standard Avery 5260 labels, with 3 labels per row and 10 rows per sheet, there's no room on the label to print anything interesting. But if you have larger labels (or business cards), you don't have to limit yourself to plain-vanilla name and address.

Tip from
EQ & Woody

If you have an odd-sized label, Word makes it easy to add it to the list of available labels, with extensive tools to help you get the layout just right. On the Labels tab of the Envelopes and Labels dialog box, choose Options. Then on the Label Options dialog box, choose New Label. A plethora of options await you.

For example, the Avery 8154 (and related) labels run six to the page. More than enough room is available on a label that big to include your return address, your company's logo, and just about anything you can imagine.

If you want to print larger, fancier labels, your best choice is to create a template that includes all the design elements—logo, return address, and so on—except the addressee's name and address. If you have such a template handy, you can create a new document based on the template, then copy the addressee's name and address into it, and print. If you want to get even fancier, and let yourself print just one label at a time, you can create a collection of templates, each with the design elements for just one label. Give the template a descriptive name ("AV5164 lower-right label") and you can generate precisely the right document for the right location.

The easiest way to make a template for a specific type of label is to use the Envelopes and Labels dialog box. In Figure 16.18 shown previously, leave the Address box blank, choose the Full Page of the Same Label option, pick the label type you want from the Options button, and then click New Document. Word creates a grid of labels for you, completely blank and ready for your customizing. Add your return address, logo, and other custom details, then choose File, Save As, and save it as a Document Template.

PART

III

CH

16

Tip from

EQ & Woody

Because the Labels are just a table, you can use all the table formatting tricks, including dividing the label into "sub cells" to better place graphics and text.

→ To read more about how to create and modify templates, **see** "Customizing Word Templates," **p. 482**.

KEEPING LONG DOCUMENTS UNDER CONTROL

Effectively using Word to handle long documents—100 pages or more—requires a great deal of forethought and planning. After document file sizes exceed a megabyte or two, they become unwieldy, slow to load, and susceptible to corruption.

ONE FILE OR MANY?

There's no easy cure for long documents. Adding more RAM usually helps improve Word's response time on large and small documents, and Windows NT, 2000, or XP definitely provides a more stable environment than Windows 95, 98 or Me. But at some point, generally in the vicinity of 1MB–5MB file sizes, any PC will have trouble handling a big Word document.

As your documents get larger, you have three choices:

- **Continue to work with a single large file**—If you should opt to do so, take extra precautions to back up the file regularly, and work as frequently as you can in Normal view, to minimize system overhead.

Caution

Make absolutely sure you disable Word's Fast Save option, to decrease the chances of scrambling the file's contents.

→ To turn off Fast Saves, **see** "Options Settings," **p. 355**.

■ **Remove some of the contents of the large file**—There are two easy strategies for doing this: Cut and remove portions of text, storing them in a separate file and replacing them only as needed (for example, to run a Table of Contents); or save pictures in separate files and create links to those graphics instead of *embedding* them.

→ To learn more about when embedding is better than linking, **see** "Embedding Versus Linking," **p. 143**.

Tip from

EQ & Woody

You can use a macro to replace figures with text placeholders (such as [Insert file Corprep.pcx here]) and use a second macro to replace the text with the correct figure. Run the first macro to temporarily remove the figures so you can work with a compact file; run the second macro to restore the figures for printing and page layout tasks. That's the premise behind *Go Figger!*, a free utility from Woody and friends. For details, see Appendix B.

■ **Break them down into smaller files**—You can do that manually, employing techniques described in this chapter to keep them working together, or you can use Word's *Master Documents* feature, also described later in this chapter.

Unfortunately, none of these three approaches is clearly superior to the others.

Caution

All the approaches that involve linking pictures, moving them out of a document, or using multiple documents (including Master Documents) depend on hard-coded filenames. That can pose problems when moving a large document from one machine to another. For example, if all the linked pictures files on the first machine reside in a folder called c:\My Documents\Annual Report\Pictures, they must be placed in an *identically* named folder on the second PC. Replicating folder structures is almost a prerequisite for moving large documents from one machine to another.

USING BOOKMARKS

One of the largest problems facing those who maintain large documents is maintaining the integrity of references. For example, the title of Chapter 3 in an annual report might be "Evaluating Business Practices." When you refer to Chapter 3 in other parts of the document, you might be tempted to type that text. But if you later change the title of Chapter 3, you'll have to search through your document and change every reference. For a long, complex document that undergoes many changes, keeping cross-references synchronized manually is a nightmare.

The simplest way to keep text in sync is to use bookmarks.

→ To create and work with bookmarks, **see** "Bookmarks," **p. 367**.

In this example, you could select the text "Evaluating Business Practices" and give the bookmark the name Chapter3Title. Then, anyplace you wanted to refer to the title of

Chapter 3, you could choose Insert, Field, click the REF field, and add Chapter3Title to tell Word you want to insert the field {Ref Chapter3Title}.

→ For details on the {Ref} field, **see** "Referring to Document Contents," **p. 498**.

That way, anytime the title changes—that is, anytime the contents of the Chapter3Title bookmark changes—all the {REF} field references to the title will change, too, automatically.

You can maintain page number references in the same way, using the {PAGEREF} field. For example, the field {PAGEREF Chapter3Title} gives the page number of the bookmark Chapter3Title. So a line such as "See {Ref Chapter3Title} on page {PageRef Chapter3Title}" will yield a valid reference, no matter what the bookmark Chapter3Title might contain, or where it might be located, as long as the bookmark, {Ref} field, and {PageRef} field are all in the same document, or are both parts of the same Master Document.

PART

III

CH

16

If you break a long document into multiple files, the bookmark options aren't quite as good: You can reference bookmarks in other documents, by using the {IncludeText} field, but the references will retrieve only the contents of the bookmarks; you can't get at the page number.

For example, this field

```
{INCLUDETEXT "C:\\My Documents\\Annual Report.doc" Chapter3Title}
```

will retrieve the contents of the Chapter3Title bookmark in the indicated file, and place it in the current document.

INSERTING CROSS-REFERENCES

Word includes extensive support for *cross-referencing*—everything from "See Figure x-y above" kinds of references to "as defined in paragraph IV.B.7.a." Each type of cross-reference has its own requirements and quirks, so a little bit of planning will go a long way.

These references persist even if the document changes. That's what makes them so powerful and useful. Say you have a reference in a contract that says "as defined in paragraph IV.B.7.a." Then one of the attorneys working on the contract realizes it needs an additional numbered paragraph, and that new paragraph has to go ahead of the current paragraph IV.A. All you need to do is insert the paragraph, select the document, and press F9 to update fields. Automatically, the old paragraph IV.B.7.a becomes paragraph IV.C.7.a, and the old reference to it turns into "as defined in paragraph IV.C.7.a."

Many kinds of cross-references interact with captions (see the next section for details on how to set up the captions correctly). Say you have a picture in a document with a caption that says "Figure 17," and a reference to it such as "See Figure 17." Your editor decides to add a figure immediately before figure number 17. If you used cross-references and captions correctly, the next time you update fields, the old figure number 17 will get the caption "Figure 18," and the old reference will be updated so it says "See Figure 18." The connections persist even in the face of complex restructuring in the document. So, if you moved this new Figure 18 to the beginning of the document, for example, it would get the caption

"Figure 1" and the reference would change to "See Figure 1." Captions and references throughout the document would change to match the new numbering scheme—and all you have to do is update fields.

To see Word's Cross-reference dialog box (see Figure 16.19), click Insert, Reference, Cross-reference.

Figure 16.19
Word's cross-reference capabilities key off of precisely defined styles, bookmarks, and sequences located inside the document.

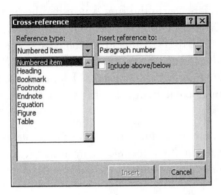

Choices in the Reference Type drop-down list are linked to specific elements in the document.

Reference Type: Numbered item refers exclusively to paragraphs formatted with Word-applied numbering. (If you number your paragraphs manually, they won't appear here.) There's a fair amount of native intelligence in the cross-reference: For example, if you refer to paragraph IV.B.7.a from inside paragraph IV.B.6.c, you can tell Word to use the reference "7.a."

> **Note**
>
> For a detailed discussion of these "full context" and "no context" numbering references, see the online Help topic "In the Cross-reference dialog box, what do "no context" and "full context" mean?"

Reference Type: Heading choices include only those paragraphs marked with the built-in Word heading styles: Heading 1, Heading 2, Heading 3, and so on.

Say you have a product catalog where each product's name appears in a paragraph formatted as Heading 2. To insert a reference such as, "See Retractable Dog Chains on page 77." in your document, you would follow these steps:

1. Click once where you want the reference to appear. Type "See " (don't forget the trailing space), and then choose Insert, Cross-reference. Choose Heading in the Reference Type drop-down list (see Figure 16.20).

Figure 16.20
It's easy to insert a reference to a heading, if you use the built-in tools.

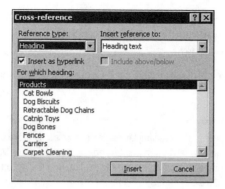

2. In the For Which Heading box, choose Retractable Dog Chains. Click Insert, and then Close.

3. Type " on page " (with a leading and a trailing space) and then choose Insert, Cross-reference again.

4. In the Reference Type drop-down list, choose Heading; in the Insert Reference To drop-down list, choose Page Number. In the For Which Heading list box, choose Retractable Dog Chains. Click Insert, and then Close.

Your document would read, "See Retractable Dog Chains on page 77."

> **Note**
>
> Again, the reference persists, even if the name of the product changes, or its page number changes. If you update the product catalog next year, change the name of the product to "Retractable Safety Dog Chains," and rearrange products so that it now falls on page 396, the reference automatically changes to "See Retractable Safety Dog Chains on page 396."

Reference Type: Bookmark includes any bookmarks you've defined in the document. By using the Insert, Cross-reference feature, you can put the bookmarked text or the bookmark's page number in the document, and it will be updated should the contents of the bookmark—or its location—change.

Reference Type: Footnote, Endnote are tied to footnotes and endnotes in the document. If you want to create two references in a document to the same footnote, choose Insert, Cross-reference, and in the Reference Type drop-down list, choose Footnote.

→ To work with footnotes in general, **see** "Inserting Footnotes," **p. 376**.

Reference Type: Figure refers exclusively to paragraphs in the document that contain the {SEQ Figure} field. When you choose Insert, Cross-reference, and select Figure from the Reference Type drop-down list, Word scans the document for {SEQ Figure} fields, and puts the paragraphs containing those fields in the For Which Heading list. See the next section for several examples of how to use figure cross-references. In particular, when you use Word's built-in Insert, Caption feature, it can generate an {SEQ Figure} field that's picked up by the Insert Cross-reference feature.

Reference Type: Equation, Table similarly refers exclusively to {SEQ Equation} and {SEQ Table} fields.

Caution

Captions that appear in the drawing layer aren't detected by Word's Insert Cross-reference feature. If you have a caption in a text box, or if your figures "float over text" with an attached caption, you must first move the caption into the document itself before Insert Cross-reference can find it.

The Insert Cross-reference feature works only on references inside the current document, or inside one Master Document.

CREATING INDEXES

Creating an index for your document is a straightforward two-step process:

1. Mark index entries in the document by using Insert, Reference, Index and Tables (see Figure 16.21), and then click Mark Entry. Proceed through the entire document, marking index entries where they occur.

Figure 16.21
The Index tab allows you to both mark index entries and generate the index itself.

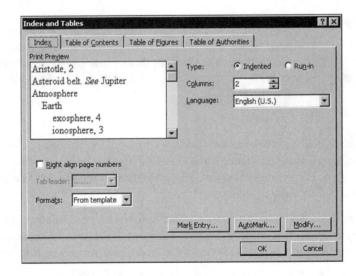

2. When you're done marking the entries, generate the index by placing the insertion point where you want the index to appear, bring up the Index and Tables dialog box (refer to Figure 16.21), and click OK.

Like so many other advanced Word features, indexing is driven by field codes. In this case, the {XE} field code, generated previously in step 1, marks the location of index entries. The index itself, generated in step 2, is really just an {Index} field. To understand how indexes are built, you first must understand Word fields.

→ To learn more about fields, **see** "Using Fields Intelligently," **p. 488**.

Unfortunately, Word's indexing feature is not as intuitive as one might hope. Although it appears that indexes built with the Standard Mark Index Entry dialog box can run only two entries deep, there is a workaround. Although the Mark Entry dialog box has only two boxes for entry levels (Main Entry and Sub Entry), you can enter up to seven levels in either of these boxes by separating your entries with colons—for example, you could enter Flowers:Roses:Red.

With that caution in mind, there are a few tricks you can use to make indexing faster and easier.

To create an index entry for a particular word in a document, double-click the word to select it, and then press Alt+Shift+X. If you want to use the word as the main (highest level) entry, press Enter. If you want to use something different for the main entry, press Ctrl+X to cut the selected word, type in your main entry, press Tab, and then press Ctrl+V to make the selected word a subentry.

For example, if you see the word Rose in a document and want to create an entry for Flowers:Rose, here's a quick way to do it:

1. Double-click Rose to select it.
2. Press Alt+Shift+X to bring up the Mark Index Entry dialog box.
3. Press Home to move the cursor to the beginning of the Main Entry box.
4. Type the word Flowers: (note the colon).
5. Press Enter twice and an {XE "Flowers:Rose"} field will be inserted into your document.

Although the key sequence is a bit convoluted, with practice it can be mastered.

{XE} fields are hidden. If you insert them via the Mark Index Entry dialog box, Word turns on the Show All feature so you not only can see the fields, but you also get dots for spaces. To turn off Show All, choose Tools, Options, click the View tab, and clear the All box.

If you want to see your {XE} fields, choose Tools, Options, and on the View tab check the Hidden Text box.

If you're willing to trust the computer to construct your index, consider using a concordance file. You set up the concordance file as a two-column table, with entries you want to index in the first column (say, Roses), and the index you want to use in the second column (say, Flowers:Rose). You apply an index concordance file to a document via the AutoMark button in the Index and Tables dialog box, as shown in Figure 16.21. For more information, see the Word help file entry "Create a concordance file."

When Word updates the {Index} field, you're given two options: Update the page numbers only (in which case new index entries are ignored); or update the entire index (in which case any entries or formatting you've entered manually into the index get wiped out). Talk about being caught between Scylla and Charybdis.

Fortunately, you can pour Word documents into high-end desktop-publishing programs, which include all the tools necessary to generate decent indexes. Quark XPress, PageMaker, and Ventura Publisher all do much better jobs than Word.

 If you're frustrated because your edits to the compiled index are lost whenever you update the index, see "Updating Index Entries" in the "Troubleshooting" section at the end of this chapter.

If you've spell-checked your index but still find spelling errors, see "Spell Checking an Index" in the "Troubleshooting" section at the end of this chapter.

CREATING A TABLE OF CONTENTS

By comparison, the Table of Contents (TOC) generator in Word works quite well:

1. Make sure you've applied styles to all the heading paragraphs you want to appear in the TOC. You can use Word's default "Heading n" styles, or you can create your own.

2. If you want to add more entries—say, freeform text entries that will appear in the TOC even if they aren't in paragraphs with appropriate styles—use Insert, Field to put {TC} fields in your document.

   {TC} fields can include much more than plain text. For detailed reference information on how to use this type of field, see "Field codes: TC (Table of Contents Entry) field" in online help.

3. Put the insertion point where you want the TOC to appear, and choose Insert, Reference, Index and Tables, Table of Contents. The Index and Tables dialog box appears with the Table of Contents tab in front (see Figure 16.22).

Figure 16.22
You can build a Table of Contents based on any set of styles.

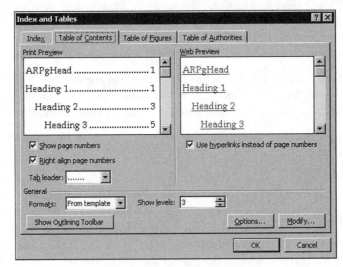

4. If you're using styles other than the standard "Heading n" set, click Options and map each style to a TOC heading level. When you're done, click OK and Word builds the TOC.

A Table of Contents (even a large one) is just a Word field—a {TOC} field, to be precise. To see the field, choose Tools, Options, click the View tab, and check Field Codes.

Tip from

If you regularly work with field codes, memorize the ViewFieldCodes keyboard short-cut, Alt+F9. Or assign the command to a toolbar button, so you can toggle it on and off.

{TOC} behaves just like any other field, with one exception. When you update it, Word might ask you whether you want to Update Page Numbers Only, or Update the Entire Table. Although the default response is Update Page Numbers Only, you should accept this choice only if you are absolutely certain that none of the TOC entries has been deleted, and no new entries have been added.

Word generally keeps good track of your headings, and if it detects that a heading has been added or deleted it won't even ask whether you want to Update Page Numbers Only.

Word can also produce TOC-like tables for figures, or any of the special {SEQ} fields discussed under the preceding section, "Making Captions Work." Choose Insert, Reference, Index and Tables, and click the Table of Figures tab.

The entire Table of Figures engine is based on the labels in {SEQ} fields, in a manner similar to the Insert, Cross-reference hooks described earlier in this chapter. In fact, a Table of Figures is nothing more than a {TOC} field, with switches added to indicate which {SEQ} field should be indexed.

A Table of Contents, Index, or other kind of table, can be generated only for entries inside the current document, or inside one Master Document.

WRAPPING TEXT AROUND GRAPHICS

Word makes it easy to wrap text around a graphic. Insert the graphic into your document (for example, by choosing Insert, Picture), right-click the graphic, and choose Format Picture (or Format AutoShape). Click the Layout tab (see Figure 16.23) and choose how you want the text to wrap.

If you want to wrap text tightly around an odd-shaped graphic, start with the Tight option in the Format Picture (or Format AutoShape) dialog box shown in Figure 16.23.

But if you need to wrap text even tighter, you have to turn to a totally different part of Word—the Drawing toolbar.

Figure 16.23
Word does a decent job of wrapping text tightly around a picture, but you can do better.

Tip from

EQ & Woody

To adjust the wrapping points—the points Word uses to judge how closely it should move text to the graphic—select the graphic, and then bring up the Drawing toolbar. Click Draw, Text Wrapping, Edit Wrap Points. (Edit Wrap Points also appears as an icon on the Picture toolbar.) Click and drag any of the text-wrapping points—you can even have text wrap onto the graphic itself. When you're finished, click outside the graphic, and Word rearranges the text.

SUMMARIZING A DOCUMENT AUTOMATICALLY

Word includes a feature called AutoSummarize that can, under just the right circumstances, help you create a summary of a document. Word does that by coming up with a word frequency list, and then rating each sentence in the document according to how many frequently used words appear in the sentence. You then assign a cutoff point, and any sentence that exceeds the cutoff point is included in the summary.

You might want to try AutoSummarize on highly structured, repetitive documents, just to see whether it generates anything other than gibberish. To use it, choose Tools, AutoSummarize. Specify whether you want to highlight the high-scoring sentences or extract those sentences and use them to create a free-standing summary.

Assign the cutoff point by choosing a percentage size for the summary (say, you want the summary to be 10% as long as the document itself). Optionally, you can have Word automatically update the file properties, placing the most frequently encountered words in the Keywords and Comments boxes.

→   For a description of how to use Office file properties, **see** "Storing Document Details," **p. 67**.

If the summary proves less than enlightening, you can always delete it—providing you told Word to extract the sentences.

TROUBLESHOOTING

UPDATING INDEX ENTRIES

After inserting the index, I edited the entries by directly typing over them within the index itself. But when I updated the index, all those edits were lost.

Always make changes to the index entries in the body of the document—that is, change the contents of the {xe} fields themselves. That way, when you update the index (or table of contents), your changes will be reflected in the new index.

SPELL-CHECKING AN INDEX

Even though I spell-checked my index, there are still spelling errors in the index.

Index entries—that is, {xe} fields—normally are hidden. Word doesn't check hidden text when you run a spell-check. To spell-check your index entries, first display hidden characters (choose Tools, Options, click the View Tab, and check the Hidden Text box). Next, run the spell-check. Misspelled words in {xe} fields will appear with a red squiggly underline.

SECRETS OF THE OFFICE MASTERS: CREATIVE NEWSLETTER LAYOUTS

Creating a visually attractive newsletter involves many technical tricks. In Figure 16.24, a main page with four columns has been assembled using standard section formatting. But a linked text box has been added in the lower-right corner and adjusted to match the width of two columns. Breaking up the page "teases" the reader to look more closely.

Figure 16.24

CHAPTER 17

USING TABLES

In this chapter

USING TABLES TO ORGANIZE INFORMATION

Most people think of Word tables as repositories for rows and columns of numbers. In fact, Word has few tools for working with numbers—and the tools that exist are error-prone and sometimes buggy. If you want to do any sort of arithmetic on rows or columns of numbers—anything more complex than an occasional sum or product on a small handful of data—you're far better off working in Excel, even if you have to learn Excel to do it. An embedded or linked Excel table inside a Word document will give you a lot more peace of mind, if your primary concern is performing calculations.

In addition to the obvious uses for tables to organize and present tabular data, Word tables are perfect for placing and organizing items (words, numbers, pictures) on a page. In Figure 17.1, it might be obvious to you that the list of paid holidays should fall in a table—after all, each cell has a line around it and the data is classically tabular. But it might not be so obvious that a table provides a simple way to organize the top lines of the memo, as well.

Figure 17.1
A table, without the gridlines, makes it easy to create and maintain the "To/From/Re/Date" part of this memo. Dotted lines appear onscreen, but no lines print.

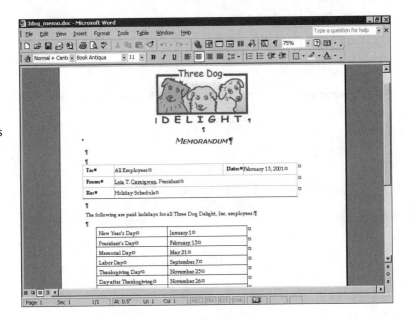

You should also consider using tables when you need to

- Line up paragraph headings on the left with text on the right. Many résumés use this format.
- Draw intersecting horizontal and vertical lines. Using tables is generally much simpler than trying to establish borders on words or paragraphs.
- Create forms that will be filled out by hand, or on a typewriter. In addition, tables are the most common way to arrange fields on a Word data-entry form.

→ To learn more about entering data in Word forms, **see** "Creating a Data-Entry Form," **p. 509**.

- Place text in a fixed location on a page. Anytime you're thinking about using tab stops to arrange text or graphics on a page, also consider using tables, and printing them without the gridlines. In general, tables are faster and easier to set up, and much simpler to maintain.

→ For a full description of how to use the drawing layer, **see** "Working with the Drawing Layer," **p. 108**.

Tables can be drawn inside tables—a very handy trick if you use tables for page layouts. Each "nested table" appears, in its entirety, within a single cell in the larger outer table.

ADDING A TABLE TO A DOCUMENT

When creating a new table, you have two basic choices: Either Word can draw the table for you, or you can draw it yourself. When Word draws the table for you:

- Either the table stretches from the left to the right margin, each column has the same width, or each column adjusts to fit the widest cell.

- Rows start out one line tall, but automatically get taller, if necessary, to hold text or graphics.

PART

III

CH

17

If you can live with those two restrictions, Word will make your table quickly. In any other situation—if the table can only take up part of a page, or if you have complex cell patterns— you can draw your table freehand.

CREATING QUICK TABLES

To have Word draw a table for you, follow these steps:

1. Click in an empty paragraph where you want the upper-left cell of the new table to be located.

2. Choose Dra<u>w</u> Table, Insert, Table. You see the Insert Table dialog box (see Figure 17.2). Click the AutoFormat button to choose from dozens of prefab formats for your new table.

3. Choose the number of columns and rows, and tell Word how to determine the width of the table and its columns. Click OK and Word creates the table you specify (see Figure 17.3).

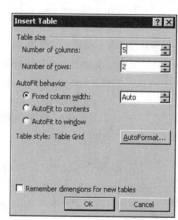

Figure 17.2

Tip from

EQ & Woody

You can choose default table settings in the Insert Table dialog box—even an AutoFormat—and click Remember Dimensions for new tables. From that point on, the Insert Table button on the Standard toolbar inserts precisely that type of table into your document.

Figure 17.3
Quick, cookie-cutter tables are easy with the Insert Table dialog box.

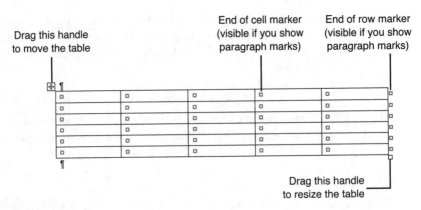

Drag this handle to move the table

End of cell marker (visible if you show paragraph marks)

End of row marker (visible if you show paragraph marks)

Drag this handle to resize the table

Although you can use Word's Table menu and the right-click context-sensitive menu for manipulations on tables and inside table cells, you'll find it much easier to work with tables if you bring up the Tables and Borders toolbar. To do so, click the Tables and Borders button on the Standard toolbar.

DRAWING A COMPLEX TABLE

Unless you specifically want a table that conforms to Word's Insert Table restrictions, drawing one by hand is the best option. To do so:

1. Choose Table, Draw Table, or click the Draw Table icon on the Tables and Borders toolbar. The mouse pointer turns into a pencil.

2. Click where you want the upper-left corner of the table to appear. (You can even click inside a table cell, to create a table within a table—what Word calls a *nested table*. See the section later in this chapter on "Nesting Tables Within Tables.")

3. Drag the pencil down and to the right, to the lower-right corner of the new table. Word creates a table with a single, large cell.

4. Using the pencil, click an existing table line and drag to the opposite edge to form a row, column, or individual cell. You can even click a cell corner and drag to the opposite corner to create a diagonal line.

If you don't like the position or size of your cells, you can always use the Erase button on the Tools and Borders toolbar. Position the "eraser" mouse pointer on the line you want to erase and click. To restore your usual mouse pointer, press Esc or click the Erase button again.

CONVERTING TEXT TO A TABLE

Frequently, as you're typing text, you'll decide that what you've been typing would work better as a table. You might be tempted to create the table, and then cut and paste the text into the table—but before you do, consider using Word's built-in text to table converter:

1. Select the text you want to convert. Your text has to use a *delimiter* (paragraph mark, tab, comma, or some other character) consistently for Word to figure out what data goes in which cell. For example, the lines shown in Figure 17.4, which have tab characters delimiting cells, will work fine.

Figure 17.4
If you're careful about using delimiting characters (such as the tab here), Word will readily convert text to a table.

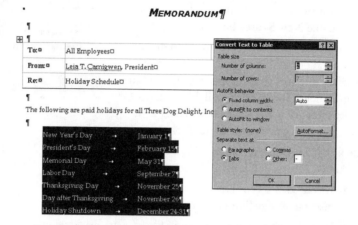

PART
III

CH
17

Tip from

EQ & Woody

By far the simplest and most reliable way to delimit text for easy conversion to a table is with tabs separating the cells, and paragraph marks at the end of each row. You can use commas (or any other character, for that matter), but be cautious of stray commas in the data that can throw off the conversion.

2. Choose Table, Convert, Text to Table. Word presents the Convert Text to Table dialog box shown previously in Figure 17.4.

3. Choose the delimiter in the Separate Text At box at the bottom of the dialog box. If the figure in the Number of Columns box doesn't match your expectations, look carefully at the first selected line. Chances are good something went wrong.

4. Format the table as you like, and then click OK.

If you can't make the last row of your table match the last row of your data, see "Check for Stray Delimiters" in the "Troubleshooting" section at the end of this chapter.

CONVERTING DATA TO A TABLE

Word also lets you fill a table with data from a simple text file, Word document, Excel worksheet range, Access table, dBASE, FoxPro, ODBC or SQL Server database, or just about any database—local or remote—you can imagine.

To add data from another application to your Word table, follow these steps:

1. Click in the document where you want the table to appear. You can click inside a table cell and create a nested table within a table, if you want.

2. Bring up the Database toolbar (right-click any toolbar or the main menu bar and check the Database box). Click the Insert Database icon. You get the Database dialog box (see Figure 17.5), which lets you select data from a document, spreadsheet, or almost any kind of database via the New Source button.

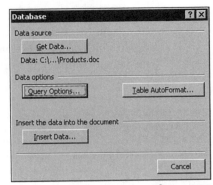

If you frequently insert databases into documents and don't have any other use for the Database toolbar, consider putting this icon on your Standard toolbar. It's available under the Insert category in the Customize dialog box, which appears when you choose Tools, Customize, Commands.

Figure 17.5

3. Click the Get Data button, find the file you want to use (text, Word document, Excel workbook, Access database) and click Open.

   - If you open a Word document, you are asked to specify the delimiters (see the discussion of delimiters in the preceding section).

   - If you select an Excel workbook file, you are asked whether you want entire specific sheets or just one of the named ranges.

   - If you open an Access database, you get to choose from among the defined tables or queries. After the file is opened, click Query Options, and specify filters, sort fields (up to three), and the fields you want to include in the table.

4. Click Insert Data, select the records you want (by record number), optionally tell Word whether you want to Insert the Data as a Field (thus automatically updating it each time fields are updated), and the data appears in a table in your document.

NESTING TABLES WITHIN TABLES

Word lets you create tables within tables. These *nested tables* can be handy if you're using tables for some other formatting trick (for example, creating side-by-side headings, as you might for a résumé) in which you need to put a table inside one of the cells.

> **Note**
>
> Keep in mind that you can always move a table on a page by clicking and dragging the handle in the upper-left corner of the table. So you don't need to create a table inside a table, for example, to put two tables side-by-side. Just drag them.

To create a table within a table, click in the desired cell and use the menu or freehand drawing tool as explained earlier in this section.

For an example of nested tables and their application in a common business document, see "Secrets of the Office Masters" at the end of this chapter.

WORKING WITH TABLES

Table cells behave much like Word paragraphs: They can be formatted, centered, indented and spaced, bulleted and numbered, with borders and shading, and can have tab stops. The formatting is stored in the end-of-cell marker, which you can see only when paragraph marks are showing (choose Tools, Options, View tab, check the Paragraph Marks box).

SELECTING CELLS, ROWS, AND COLUMNS

Select data within a cell just as you select data in a paragraph; make sure you pick up the end-of-cell marker, just as you pick up the paragraph mark, if you want to transfer paragraph formatting. Alternatively, you can select everything in a cell (including the end of cell marker) by letting the mouse pointer hover over the left side of the cell. When it turns into a thick arrow pointing to the right, click to select the whole cell. Or you can click inside the cell and choose Table, Select, Cell.

Other selection techniques include the following:

PART
III
CH
17

- To select an entire row, including the end-of-row marker, move the mouse pointer to the left of the row. When it turns into the shape of a hollow arrow pointing to the upper right, click. Equivalently, click once inside the row and choose Table, Select, Row.

- To select an entire column, let the mouse pointer hover near the top of the column. When it turns into a black solid arrow pointing down, click. Or you can choose Table, Select, Column.

- To select the whole table, let the mouse pointer hover in the upper-left edge of the table until it turns into a four-headed arrow, and then click to select the table. Alternatively, choose Table, Select, Table.

ENTERING AND EDITING DATA

You can type in a table cell precisely the same way you would type in a paragraph. If you press Enter, Word creates a new paragraph for you—in the same cell. Single cells can contain text, graphics, linked and embedded items—basically anything you can put in a document.

To move from one cell to the next, press Tab. To move back one cell, press Shift+Tab. To move backward or forward one character at a time, jumping from cell to cell at the end, use the left- and right-arrow keys. To move up or down one cell, press the up- or down-arrow keys.

Tip from

EQ & Woody

To enter the Tab character in a table cell, press Ctrl+Tab.

If the insertion point is in the last cell in a table, pressing Tab creates a new row, formatted the same as the current row, and moves the insertion point to the first cell in that row.

Many of the special navigation key combinations described in Chapter 4, "Editing and Formatting Text," work inside tables. For example, Ctrl+Right Arrow selects text one character at a time, Ctrl+Shift+Right Arrow picks up a word at a time, and so on.

→   To learn about Word's extensive text-selection techniques, **see** "Selecting Text," **p. xx**.

Tip from	You can add text above a table at the top of a document. With the insertion point in the first row of the table, press Ctrl+Shift+Enter to insert a paragraph above the table, and then move the insertion point into that new paragraph. Use this same shortcut to split a table if the insertion point is in any row other than the first.

MOVING AND COPYING PARTS OF A TABLE

All the usual copy, cut, and paste routines you're accustomed to in Word work within tables and cells. If you've placed cells on the Clipboard, Word responds by adding new entries in the Edit menu: Paste Cells, Paste Columns, Paste Rows, and Paste as Nested Table.

Paste Cells replaces the existing cells with the contents of the copied cells; the table itself is only expanded if the there are too many copied rows or columns to fit in the existing table. If you choose Paste Columns, Rows, or Paste as Nested Table, Word creates a new column, row, or table as needed and fills it with the contents of the Clipboard. If you click inside a cell, and then insert directly from the Clipboard task pane, Word assumes you want to insert the columns, rows, or table on the Clipboard as a nested table, within the current cell.

Tip from	However, if you paste cells, Word overwrites the contents of the current cells--without warning, and without giving you an opportunity to change your mind. If that happens, click the Undo button (or press Ctrl+Z or choose Edit, Undo), and try again.

You can click and drag cells, columns, and rows, just as you do elsewhere in Word—with one exception. If you're going to move an entire row, you must select the end-of-row marker.

If you copy or move a cell, including the end-of-cell marker, to an area outside a table, Word creates a new table on the spot, with one cell, which matches the cell being copied or moved.

⚠ *If you are frustrated with cell contents or the row markers disappearing, see "Disappearing Cell Contents and Row Markers" in the "Troubleshooting" section at the end of this chapter.*

CHANGING COLUMN WIDTHS AND ROW HEIGHTS

To adjust a column's width, you have four choices:

- **Eyeball it**—Move your mouse pointer so it's near a vertical line in the table. When the pointer changes into a double-headed arrow, click and drag the line. If you move left, the column to the left gets narrower and the column to the right gets wider. If you move right, the column to the right gets narrower and the column to the left gets wider.

Tip from

EQ & Woody

If you want to change the width of the column only on the left (shrinking or expanding the size of the entire table as you go), hold down the Shift key as you drag.

- **Measure it**—Click inside the column you want to change, and then choose Table, Table Properties. In the Table Properties dialog box, click the Column tab (see Figure 17.6). From that point, you can precisely specify the width of each column.

Figure 17.6
To get precise column measurements, nothing beats the Table Properties dialog box.

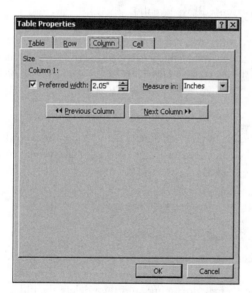

- **Fit the contents**—If you want the column width to grow or shrink, depending on the width of the contents, click once inside the row, and then choose Table, AutoFit, AutoFit to Contents.

Tip from

EQ & Woody

To AutoFit only selected columns you can double click on the border of the selection.

- **Fit the margins**—You can also have Word automatically calculate how wide a specific column must be to have the table extend all the way from the left to the right margin. To do so, click inside the column, and then choose Table, AutoFit, AutoFit to Window.

If you need to restore some uniformity to the table, you can always make all the columns the same width by choosing Table, AutoFit, Distribute Columns Evenly.

Tip from

Yes, you can use the ruler to adjust column widths. But trying to figure out the exact function of each little slider and triangle is more trouble than it's worth. It's much easier to manipulate a table directly.

By default, rows expand and contract to hold the tallest item in the row. Row heights can be adjusted in much the same way as column widths: eyeballing it with a click and drag; measuring it in the Table Properties dialog box's Row tab (where heights are either "At least" or "Exactly"); or making each row height the same to fill up the space occupied by the table (choose Table, AutoFit, Distribute Rows Evenly).

Tip from

If you're creating a Word form for data entry, using "Exactly" for the row height prevents the cell from expanding if the user types in too much text. That prevents entries from pushing information from one page onto the next.

To change the height and width of individual cells, select the entire cell (including the end-of-cell marker), and then click and drag. As long as you've selected an entire cell (or group of cells), only those cells are resized.

 If you can't see all the contents of a table cell, see "Properly Setting the Row Height for Your Word Tables" in the "Troubleshooting" section section at the end of this chapter.

ADDING AND DELETING ROWS AND COLUMNS

Sometimes, you want to keep your table formatting intact, but replace existing data in the table. For example, if you create the same sales report every month, you can copy the table from last month's report into a new document, and then delete the old data and replace it with this month's numbers. Here are a few tricks you need to know:

- If you select a cell and press Delete, the cell contents are deleted. If you include the end-of-cell marker and press Delete, the end-of-cell marker *with its formatting* stays intact.
- If you select a column or row and press Delete, the contents of all the cells in the column or row are deleted—but the column or row itself stays and, again, the end-of-cell markers and their formatting remain. It doesn't matter whether you select the end-of-row marker or not.

- If you select an entire table and press Delete, the contents of all the cells in the table are deleted, but the table skeleton remains, formatting intact.

- If you select an entire table plus one or more characters after the table (including, for example, a paragraph mark), and press Delete, the entire table and selected character(s) are deleted completely. No skeleton remains.

To truly delete a cell, row, column, or table, click in the cell, row, column, or table that you want to delete, and choose Table, Delete, and then select either Cells, Rows, Columns, or Table.

> **Note**
>
> Icons for performing all these actions are on the Tables and Borders toolbar. Or, you can get at them by using the right-click context menu from inside a table.

To insert a cell, row, or column (or table, for that matter), click in the cell, or in a row to the left or right of the place you want to put the new row or column, and then choose Table, Insert, and the appropriate entry.

ROTATING TEXT

It's easy to rotate text in a table by 90 degrees, clockwise or counterclockwise. To do so, select the cell(s) you want to rotate, and then choose Format, Text Direction. The Text Direction–Table Cell dialog box enables you to choose orientation (see Figure 17.7).

Figure 17.7
As long as you want your text aimed straight up or straight down, Word can accommodate.

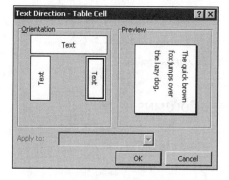

If you want table headings angled at something other than the nosebleed nineties, consider embedding or linking an Excel range. It's much easier to rotate text to any desired angle in an Excel worksheet.

MERGING AND SPLITTING CELLS AND TABLES

If you insert a table into a cell, you have two tables, one inside the other, which are nested tables. Most of the time you don't need—or want—two separate tables; usually, when you run out of room in a table, what you really need is the capability to split an existing cell into two, four, or six cells.

There are only a few subtle differences between, say, nesting a four-column one-row table inside a cell, and manually splitting the cell into four smaller cells. The main difference is in spacing—unless you change the spacing settings, nested tables take up an additional amount of space inside the cell to accommodate the outside of the table itself, whereas split cells require no additional spacing. Use a nested table when you want to manipulate the contents of a portion of the table as a unit: You can click and drag a nested table outside of its confining cell, for example, but moving four subcells is considerably more complex.

→ To learn more about using nested tables, **see** "Nesting Tables Within Tables," **p. 448**.

The easy way to split a cell into multiple cells is to use Word's table-drawing tools. Click the Draw Table button on the Tables and Borders toolbar (to display this toolbar, right-click any visible toolbar or the main menu bar and check the Tables and Borders box). Use the pencil-shaped pointer to draw horizontal or vertical lines inside the cell(s) you want to split.

You can use the Table, Split Cells menu command, but why bother?

To merge two cells together, use the Eraser icon on the Tables and Borders toolbar (see Figure 17.8).

Figure 17.8
You might want to merge all the cells in the top row of a table to accommodate a heading, as shown here.

BALANCE SHEET¤			
¤	Jan-2000¤	Jan-1999¤	Jan-1998¤
Cash¤	3.4¤	42.9¤	9.5¤
Net Receivables¤	10.9¤	7.2¤	4.3¤
Inventories¤	96.9¤	68.5¤	42.8¤
Total Current Assets¤	124.4¤	120.6¤	57.2¤
Total Assets¤	335.2¤	280.3¤	157.2¤
Short-Term Debt¤	8.4¤	4.6¤	2.3¤
Total Current Liabilities¤	91¤	66.8¤	42.7¤
Long-Term Debt¤	38¤	14.1¤	10.3¤
Total Liabilities¤	149.1¤	95.8¤	60.7¤
Common Stock Equity¤	186.1¤	184.6¤	96.4¤
Shares Outstanding (mil.)¤	21.1¤	18.6¤	12.7¤

To split a table horizontally—between two rows—click once in the row that will become the top row in the new table. Choose Table, Split Table. A paragraph mark appears between the two tables.

Tip from

EQ & Woody

You can easily split a table vertically as well. Select the columns you want to split away from the original table. Cut them (choose Edit, Cut or press Ctrl+X). Move the insertion point to wherever you want the new table to appear, and paste. You can then place the two tables side-by-side, if you want, by using their drag handles.

SORTING DATA WITHIN TABLES

Although it doesn't hold a candle to Excel's sorting capabilities, Word can sort up to three keys, including dates, and can handle case-sensitive sorts as well as nonstandard sorting sequences (for languages other than English).

Sorting in Word can come in handy in all sorts of situations. You might want to sort a table of names, to put it in alphabetical order, and then copy the table and sort it again by employee ID number. Or perhaps you created a table with the data sorted by region, but you later decide the data is more meaningful if sorted by product. That kind of sorting is easy in Word.

PART
III
CH
17

Note

In fact, you needn't put data in a table to sort it. Word does just fine if you have clean data with delimiters—precisely in the same way that's required for converting text to a table. You can also sort simple lists (say, a list of state names, each in a single paragraph), because the paragraph mark is a delimiter.

Tip from

EQ & Woody

Entire chapters and sections can be sorted (using their headings) in Outline view.

→ To learn more about automatically converting your text into a Word table, **see** "Converting Text to a Table," **p. 446**.

You can also sort by individual words within cells—for example, if you have a row with names in FirstName LastName order, you can tell Word to sort by LastName, the second word in the column, followed by FirstName, the first word in the column (see Figure 17.9).

To sort data, do the following:

1. Click once inside the table (or data).

2. Choose Table, Sort. You see the Sort dialog box shown in Figure 17.9.

3. If your table (or data) has a header row—that is, if the first row describes the data below it—start by clicking the My List Has Header Row option. That way, Word uses the header row's names instead of the generic "Column 1," "Column 2," and so on.

Figure 17.9
Although not as comprehensive as Excel's sorting capabilities, Word does rather well—it even has a LastName FirstName sorting capability—and you needn't convert your data to a table to sort it.

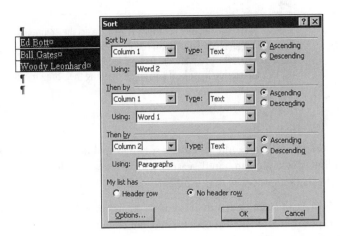

4. Choose your sort conditions. If you need to select field delimiters (for nontable data only), specify a case-sensitive sort, or choose a sorting sequence other than standard English, and click Options. When you're ready to perform the sort, click OK, and the table is sorted.

> **Tip**
>
> In unusual circumstances, you might want to sort just one column of a table, while leaving the other columns untouched. A teacher might construct a table with two columns, one containing scientific terms, the other containing definitions. By sorting just one column, the teacher could create a "connect the definitions" test, in which the students have to associate terms with definitions. To sort just one column of a table, select the column prior to choosing Table, Sort. Click Options, and check the Sort Column Only box. Click OK, and the single column is sorted independently.

PERFORMING CALCULATIONS IN A TABLE

Word contains rudimentary (and historically buggy) features for performing standard math calculations in tables—Sum, Average, Min, Max, Product, and the like.

To put a formula in a cell, select the cell and choose Table, Formula. Then enter the formula, and click OK.

When you use a Word table as a worksheet in this fashion, cells are numbered using Excel's standard A1 format, with a colon separating addresses that identify a range. For example:

- =A1+A2 calculates the sum of the first and second cells in the first column.
- =AVERAGE(B1:C4) calculates the average of eight contiguous cells.
- Special ranges called ABOVE, BELOW, LEFT, and RIGHT represent precisely what you would expect. =SUM(RIGHT) calculates the sum of all the cells to the right of the current cell.

Tip from

EQ & Woody

All these calculations use the {=} field. The results of those fields can be formatted by using the \# picture switch.

→ To learn more about using Word to perform mathematical operations, **see** "Performing Mathematical Calculations," **p. 502**.

→ For a list of all the ways you can format the results of a mathematical operation, **see** "Numeric \# Picture Switches," **p. 492**.

POSITIONING TABLES ON THE PAGE

Although you might think that tables exist in the drawing layer—click the dragging handle to move them around—in fact, they are in the main part of the document. Thus, you can put captions inside tables and reference them via the Cross-reference dialog box, which appears when you choose Insert, Cross-reference; paragraphs can be numbered and the numbering continues from the main part of the document, through the table, and into the rest of the document; and entries in tables are picked up for indexes and tables of contents.

PART

III

CH

17

Although you'll most often want a table to appear flush left with text above and below it (not wrapping around), from time to time, you'll want the table to appear flush right or centered. You also might want main body text in the document to wrap around the table, especially with smaller tables. Follow these steps to make it happen:

1. Create the table by using any of the methods explained in this chapter.

2. Click once inside the table, and then choose Table, Table Properties. You see the Table Properties dialog box (see Figure 17.10).

Figure 17.10
The Table Properties dialog box lets you align tables on a page, and specify whether you want text to wrap around.

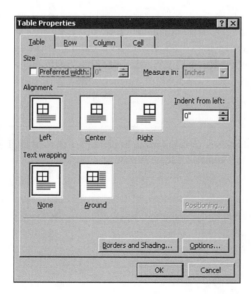

3. Set Left, Center, or Right alignment in the Alignment section. If you want to control the distance from the left edge of the box to the left margin of the page, use the Indent from Left spinner.

4. Allow document body text to flow around the table by clicking the Around box. If you want finer control over, for example, the distance from text to the table edges, click the Positioning button.

ADVANCED TABLE FORMATTING OPTIONS

A properly formatted table helps the reader (or surfer) absorb and understand the contents. You know your table hasn't been formatted well when a reader has to pull out a ruler to tell which numbers belong on what rows.

LETTING WORD DO THE WORK WITH AUTOFORMAT

Word provides more than three dozen AutoFormat options that give you a good start on your way to table perfection. To use AutoFormatting, click once inside the table, and then choose Table, Table AutoFormat. (You can also bring up the AutoFormat dialog box when you create a table by choosing Table, Insert, Table.)

Table AutoFormatting comes in handy when you want to make your tables stand out—give them a personality, beyond the standard font—but you don't want to go to a lot of trouble creating and applying your own custom formatting. AutoFormatting is a good first choice when creating any type of table that includes rows or columns of numbers, such as a price list or an income statement.

The Table AutoFormat dialog box (see Figure 17.11) contains dozens of predefined formats, with a preview of each.

If your data doesn't match the preview's format, don't worry; AutoFormat gives you a lot of options. For example, all the previews assume you have column headings in the first row. If you don't, uncheck the Heading Rows box. Several of the formats include color, but if you're going to be printing in black-and-white, uncheck the Color box to see what you'll get on the printer.

Tip from

EQ & Woody

Tables of numbers on Web pages can be particularly challenging. Take a look at the three Web AutoFormats for some interesting ideas.

You can create your own Table AutoFormat Style by clicking the New button and assembling the formatting you want.

Figure 17.11
Although Table AutoFormat might not have the design you want, it does provide a good starting place for creatively formatting your own tables.

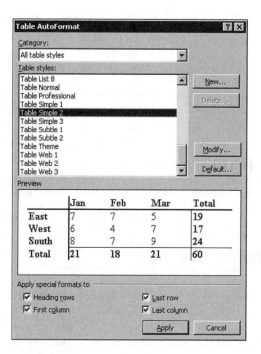

Tip from

The Styles that Word uses to create its built-in AutoFormat tables are available for your use, too. Bring up the Styles and Formatting task pane, in the Show box choose All styles, and then scroll down to the lengthy list that begins with the word "Table." When you pick a "Table" style, it's applied to the entire current table—all the rows and all the columns—even if you haven't selected the table.

USING BORDERS AND SHADING

Borders, shading, and background colors in table cells are identical to their counterparts in paragraphs. Click once inside a cell to change the border, shading, or background for that cell; select cells, rows, columns, or the entire table to change them.

→ To learn more about the common drawing tools used throughout Office, **see** "Adding Lines, Borders, Shading, and Backgrounds," **p. 409**.

Word normally displays a faint gray gridline on the screen, corresponding to cell borders, even if you format the cells so their borders are invisible.

Tip from

If you're creating a table that will be viewed on the screen in Word, you can hide the table gridlines by choosing Table, Hide Gridlines.

Tables viewed by a Web browser never show gridlines, regardless of the Show/Hide Gridlines setting.

ALIGNING TEXT IN CELLS

Left-aligned text in cells might work for certain types of text tables, or tables where the columns are narrow. Frequently, however, you'll want to right-align numbers, or center text. Right-aligned numbers are much easier to read and compare. If you're using a two-column table to simulate columns (in a résumé, for example), right-align the text in the left column to help show the connection with the matching blocks of text in the right column. For small amounts of text, centered text—even if it's just centered headings over a column—looks better than left-aligned almost anywhere in a table, except the first column.

You can click once in a cell, or select a series of cells, and change the alignment from left-justified to centered to right-justified by clicking the Align Left, Center, and Align Right buttons on the Formatting toolbar. Because end-of-cell markers behave much like paragraph marks, that formatting travels with the end of cell marker when it's copied or moved.

Word also allows you to center text vertically inside the cell. To do so, select the cells you want to format, and choose Table, Table Properties, and then click the Cell tab. There you can choose from Top, Center, or Bottom positioning. Click the Options button and you can even tell Word how much whitespace you want between the cell edge and the text inside the cell.

You can combine the actions of horizontal and vertical alignment in one easy step: Select the cells you want to align, right-click, and choose Cell Alignment from the context menu. All nine combinations appear (see Figure 17.12), ready for you to apply.

Figure 17.12
All nine combinations of left, right, center, and top, middle, bottom appear on the cell's context menu.

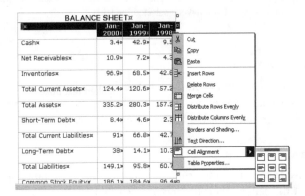

Tip from

EQ & Woody

If you click and drag on the horizontal bar above the nine alignment pictures shown in Figure 17.12, it turns into a tear-off menu (which is basically a floating toolbar, which appears in the right-click Tools shortcut menu until closed). There doesn't appear to be any other way to activate the Cell Alignment toolbar.

WORKING WITH BIG TABLES

When you work with large tables, you'll commonly encounter three distinct problems. Fortunately, each has a simple solution:

- **Too wide**—When adjusting column widths or adding columns, sometimes the table extends beyond the page margins. If you're working in Print Layout view, you won't be able to see (or work with) the rightmost columns.

 If you lose the final column, refer to "Can't See Final Column(s) in a Table" in the "Troubleshooting" section at the end of the chapter.

- **Repeating titles**—If your table will print on more than one page, frequently you'll want the title row(s) to appear at the top of each page. To do so, select the row(s) you want to repeat, and choose Table, Heading Rows Repeat.

- **Page breaks in cells**—By default, Word keeps all of a cell's contents on one page, allowing a page to break only when a new cell starts. If you're writing a résumé using a table, for example, you might want to relax that restriction, so page breaks can fall more naturally.

 If you want to relax the way Word breaks cells in a table, see "Allow Page Breaks in a Table Cell" in the "Troubleshooting" section at the end of the chapter.

Word has two significant alternatives to tables, which can be handy if you need to list a large amount of information in a small place (say, a list of vendors in an appendix, or a list of participating pharmacies in the back of a health plan brochure).

First, you can tell Word to create a page with more than one column; the text in each column "snakes," as in a newspaper, extending to the bottom of the first column, then continuing at the beginning of the second column, then the third, and so on. To create snaking newspaper-like columns, you'll have to work with section formatting—and be prepared for some surprises.

Second, you can create and position text boxes in the drawing layer, linking them so text poured into the linked boxes fills the first box, then the second, then the third, and so on.

→ To learn more about using snaking newspaper columns, or linked text boxes, **see** "Formatting a Document with Columns," **p. 414**.

TROUBLESHOOTING

DISAPPEARING CELL CONTENTS AND ROW MARKERS

I selected a row and dragged it to a new location, but instead of moving the whole row, as expected, Word replaced the contents of existing cells in the destination row.

Although you thought you selected the entire row, you actually selected all the cells in the rows. To make sure you select the entire row, you need to have Word show you the end-of-row markers—which are visible only if you show paragraph marks (choose Tools, Options, click the View tab, and check the Paragraph Marks box). If you want to click and drag a table row to a new location, select the entire row—including the end-of-row marker—and then click and drag, as you would with any other Word component.

PROPERLY SETTING THE ROW HEIGHT FOR WORD TABLES

When I insert a lot of text (or graphics) in a table cell, I can't see all of it. The bottom is chopped off.

Chances are good you did something to make Word set the row height using the "Exactly" option. To restore the default setting—in which rows grow and shrink to fit the contents—open the Table Properties dialog box (choose Table, Table Properties), click the Row tab, and uncheck the Specify Height box.

CHECK FOR STRAY DELIMITERS

When I use Word's Convert Text to Table feature, occasionally it does the conversion incorrectly, and the table is off by a cell or two.

Immediately after converting text to a table, look at the last row of the table and verify that it matches the last row of the selected data. If you're off by one or two cells (typically, one or two cells will be dangling at the bottom of the table), you probably have a stray delimiter character somewhere in the selected text. Scan the table to see whether you can locate it. Click the Undo button or press Ctrl+Z, fix the data, and try the conversion again.

Tip from

Ed & Woody

One of the hardest characters to find is a Tab character that's "squished" between two pieces of text—or, worse, two or more tab characters in succession that aren't entirely visible because text surrounds them. You can select the text and use Find to search for single or double tabs—look for ^t or ^t^t.

CAN'T SEE FINAL COLUMN(S) IN A TABLE

When I add a column to a table (or adjust the width of a column), I no longer can see the last column.

The table is too wide to fit in the defined margins, and if you try to view the document in Print Layout view, you won't see the portion that falls off the page. Switch into Normal view (choose View, Normal), and use the horizontal scrollbar to move to the right.

ALLOW PAGE BREAKS IN A TABLE CELL

Word insists on waiting until the end of a cell before it triggers a page break. As a result, my tables flip-flop all over the page: Some pages have only one row showing, and it looks horrible.

By default, Word generates a page break only at the bottom of a cell. If your cells are large, you might end up with an unsightly mess. To get Word to relax a bit, click once inside the table, and choose Table, Table Properties. In the Table Properties dialog box, click the Table tab, click the Options button, and clear the Allow Table to Break Across Pages box.

SECRETS OF THE OFFICE MASTERS: NESTED TABLES FOR SUPERIOR LAYOUT

Nested tables provide great flexibility in setting page layout. In Figure 17.13, the standard Word Professional Résumé has been modified with a table across from the Education entry, making it easy to enter multiple degrees.

The nested table's
drag handle

Figure 17.13

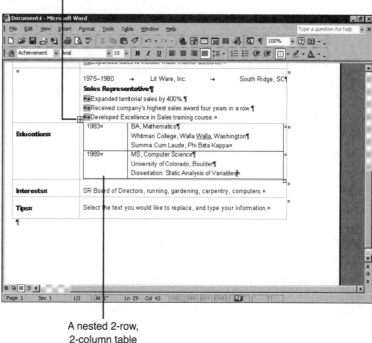

A nested 2-row,
2-column table

CHAPTER 18

USING STYLES, TEMPLATES, AND THEMES

In this chapter

USING STYLES AND TEMPLATES TO MANAGE FORMATS

Word's formatting behavior can be confusing, even to expert users. To understand formatting, it's important that you grasp several key concepts.

Word allows you to apply multiple formatting settings at one time by using *styles*. You gather the settings together and give them a name. Then when you want to use all the formatting at once, you apply the style. For example, you could tell Word that you want the ProductName style to consist of centered paragraphs, with Arial 18-point, italic blue characters. Then, every time you apply the style ProductName to a paragraph, Word formats it as centered, Arial 18 point, italic blue.

Think of styles as an easy and fast way to organize the format settings you see on the Styles and Formatting task pane. Although you can scroll through the task pane's Pick Formatting to Apply list, and ultimately find the Arial 18-point, italic blue entry, it's generally simpler to find a style called ProductName. Styles also tie parts of your document together, to ensure the formatting is consistent: If you decide to change formatting for all your ProductNames to Arial 18 point, bold blue, it's easy to change the style and have the change ripple through your document. Looking for the old formatting and replacing it by hand is a tedious, cumbersome, error-prone task.

The behavior of styles is tied closely to *templates*, the cookie-cutter prototypes for documents found in the New dialog box (choose File, New to get there). When you create a new document, you must base it on a template. Word dutifully copies all the text that resides in the template into the new document—even if the template contains only a single paragraph mark—before it presents the document to you for editing.

Behind every document sits an associated template. Unless you've taken steps to change it, a document's template is the same one you used to create the document in the first place. Choose Tools, Templates and Add-Ins, and you see the name of the associated template in the Document Template box (see Figure 18.1).

> **Note**
>
> A *global template* is a template that's available to all open documents. Specifying a global template gives you access to special-purpose macros and AutoText entries throughout Word, without having to change the template for a given document. Because the Normal document template (Normal.dot) is always loaded and made global each time Word starts, it's always available to every open document. You'll hear Normal.dot called "the" global template, but it isn't really: There can be many global templates available at any given moment.

Now say that you apply the style ProductName to a paragraph. Word first checks the document to see whether it includes a style by that name. If the style isn't there, Word looks in the document's template. If the style isn't in the template, Word looks in a special template, called Normal, which is always available.

Figure 18.1
Word tells you the name of the template attached to the current document, as well as the names of any "global" templates that were loaded when Word started. Normal.dot is always loaded, and thus doesn't appear here.

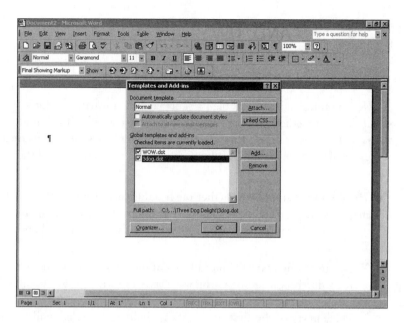

The Normal document template includes dozens of predefined styles, including the ubiquitous "Heading 1," "Heading 2," "Heading 3" styles, the "Normal" paragraph style, and a plethora of styles used for formatting table of contents entries, footnotes, bulleted and numbered lists, index entries, tables, and more.

To make matters even more confusing, sometimes Word takes it upon itself to automatically apply a style to text you've typed. These automated escapades are discussed at various points throughout this chapter, but here are the major culprits:

- If you find Word is applying a Heading style to your short sentences or sentence fragments, choose Tools, AutoCorrect Options, and on the AutoFormat As You Type tab, clear the Built-in Heading Styles box.

- If you find Word is changing the properties of styles when you use the Style drop-down box, choose Tools, AutoCorrect Options, and on the AutoFormat As You Type tab, clear the Define Styles Based on Your Formatting box.

- If Word insists on changing text you've typed into hyperlinks—say, www.mcp.com turns blue and underlined—choose Tools, AutoCorrect, and on the AutoFormat As You Type tab, clear the Internet and Network Paths with Hyperlinks box.

Word, like PowerPoint and FrontPage, supports *themes*, which are prepackaged sets of background colors, graphical bullets, and other design elements, suitable only for Web pages. Themes originated with FrontPage, and aren't so much integrated with Word as they are tacked on—you can't create or change a theme using Word. If you want to create or modify a theme, you must use FrontPage. In general, themes can cause behavior that many experienced Word users will find perplexing. (Themes aren't stored in templates—they're in *.inf and *.elm files; they don't print.)

PART

III

CH

18

→ To learn how to modify your FrontPage themes, **see** "Applying Styles, Colors, and Images with a Theme,"
p. 953.

FORMATTING DOCUMENTS WITH STYLES

A style is nothing more or less than a shorthand for formatting: Put a bunch of formatting
specifications together, give it a name, and you have a style. If you find yourself applying
the same formatting to text throughout a document, use styles to ensure a consistent and
professional appearance that's easily modified. Use styles to control the formatting of the
following:

- **Heading paragraphs**—Whether the headings are chapter titles, section names, product
  numbers, department names, contract division subtitles—doesn't matter. If your document has a repeating kind of paragraph that's always formatted the same way, create a
  style for it.

- **Repeating body text**—If your document includes repeating body text that requires formatting different from the norm, use a style to format it. For example, if your company
  name always appears in Arial 12 point, bold, create a style for it. If you have a contract
  in which **party of the first part** is always bold, use a style. Similarly, use a style to format italicized telephone numbers in a company phone directory, to highlight company
  names in a marketing report, or to call attention to negative numbers in a corporate
  balance sheet.

Defining and using styles consistently provides two great benefits. First, it ensures that all
similar items in a document are formatted similarly—say, all the department names will
appear in Garamond 12 point, bold. Second, if you need to make a change to the appearance of a style—say, you decide that all the department names should appear in 14 point,
instead of 12 point—changing the style (which requires just a few clicks) changes the
appearance of everything formatted with that style, all the way through the document.

→ To learn when you should use direct formatting from the Styles and Formatting task pane's list and
when you should choose styles, **see** "Direct Formatting Versus Styles," **p. 338**.

PARAGRAPH VERSUS CHARACTER STYLES

Paragraph styles control all the characteristics of a paragraph. That includes centering, spacing, widows (i.e., whether a single line that begins a paragraph should be allowed to appear
at the bottom of a page), orphans (whether a single line that ends a paragraph should be
allowed to appear alone at the top of a page), and other settings in the Paragraph dialog box
that appears when you choose Format, Paragraph, as well as bullets and numbering, borders
and shading, tab stops, and the language Word uses for proofing tasks such as checking
spelling and grammar (choose Tools, Language).

In addition, paragraph styles define *character formatting* for all characters within the paragraph. When you establish a paragraph style, you must also specify the default character
format for the paragraph. Unless you specifically override the default character format
with direct formatting or a character style, all text within a paragraph will appear in the
paragraph's default character format.

Say you have a paragraph style called ProductName that specifies centered paragraphs, with Arial 18-point, italic blue characters. If you apply the ProductName style to a paragraph, all the characters turn Arial 18-point, italic blue. But if you then select the last word in the paragraph and make it red, the formatting you applied manually—the red—takes precedence over the default character formatting specified in the ProductName style.

Character styles behave similarly, except they carry only character formatting. That includes the font, font size and style, color, super/subscript, underscore, and other attributes available in the Font dialog box that appears when you choose Format, Font. It also includes borders and shading, and proofing language.

Say you have a character style called PhoneNumber that specifies the Courier New font in 10 point. If you apply the PhoneNumber style to some text, it loses its old formatting (which probably originated as the paragraph style's default character formatting), and picks up the formatting defined by the character style—Courier New 10 point.

When it comes to character formatting, Word's hierarchy is strict. First comes the paragraph style, which you can modify by applying formatting directly (for example, you can format a Normal paragraph to be right-aligned, without changing its style). Then comes the character style, which takes precedence over the paragraph style settings. Finally, you can apply formatting directly to a character. That formatting takes precedence over both the character and the paragraph styles.

You can see the hierarchy at work by bringing up the Reveal Formatting task pane as shown in Figure 18.2, and then clicking the Distinguish Style Source option at the bottom of the pane. The full hierarchy of formatting applied by both the paragraph and character styles, and by directly applied formatting is shown.

PART

III

CH

18

Figure 18.2
Using the Distinguish Style Source option on the Reveal Formatting task pane gives you all the formatting details about the selected text, along with an explanation of where the formatting originated.

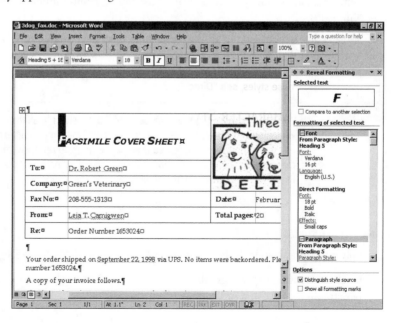

Tip from

EQ & Woody

Note to former WordPerfect users: In spite of what you might have read or expected, Word's "Reveal Formatting" isn't the least bit like WP's "Reveal Codes."

Every paragraph has exactly one paragraph style. Every character has exactly one character style. In many cases the character style will be "Default Paragraph Font" or "Clear Formatting," in which case Word applies the character formatting defined in the paragraph style.

LIST AND TABLE STYLES

Word has two built-in sets of styles that you might find useful when applying complex formatting:

Tip from

EQ & Woody

To see all the built-in styles available to you, bring up the Styles and Formatting task pane, and in the Show box, select All styles.

- List styles let you directly specify the level of a list item by choosing the style and applying it to your selected paragraph. For example, if you want a bulleted list item that appears at the third indent level, you can apply the List Bullet 3 style, and Word takes care of the details. List styles are available for standard indented lists with no bullets or numbering (called, simply, "List"), standard lists with extra space inserted below the list item ("List Continue"), bulleted lists ("List Bullet"), and numbered lists ("List Number").

- Table styles, which include all the formatting options available in Word's Table AutoFormat dialog. There are dozens of styles, all with names beginning with the word "Table."

Caution

Word makes some effort to apply selected "Table" styles to all the rows in a table, whether they've been selected or not. That's not what you would expect from Word, and it trips up many experienced users. Make sure you review formatting changes made by the "Table" styles before moving on to other parts of a document, making liberal use of the Undo button, if necessary.

APPLYING STYLES MANUALLY

To apply a paragraph style, follow these steps:

1. Click once inside the paragraph whose style you want to change, or select one or more paragraphs.

2. Choose the paragraph style from the Styles and Formatting task pane.

To apply a character style, follow these steps:

1. Select the characters whose style you want to change.
2. Choose the character style from the Styles and Formatting task pane.

If you select text and apply a paragraph style, Word looks at what you've selected before applying the style. If you have chosen all the text in a paragraph (with or without the paragraph mark), Word applies the paragraph style, just as you would expect. If one or more paragraph marks are in the selection, all the selected paragraphs have the chosen paragraph style applied.

It's easy to assign styles to toolbar buttons, the right-click context menu, or keyboard shortcut keys. Fresh out of the box, Word comes with the keyboard shortcuts shown in Table 18.1.

→ You can create customized buttons for frequently used styles and place them on toolbars; **see** "Customizing Toolbars," **p. 30**.

→ Word gives you the ability to assign keyboard shortcuts to frequently used styles; **see** "Bypassing Menus with Keyboard Shortcuts," **p. 42**.

PART

III

CH

18

TABLE 18.1   DEFAULT KEYBOARD COMBINATIONS FOR STYLES

Style	Shortcut Key
Normal	Ctrl+Shift+N
List Bullet	Ctrl+Shift+L
Heading 1	Ctrl+Alt+1
Heading 2	Ctrl+Alt+2
Heading 3	Ctrl+Alt+3

Tip from

EQ & Woody

If you use a lot of styles, consider assigning keyboard shortcuts to the styles, to make applying the style faster. To do so, choose Tools, Customize, and click the Keyboard button. In the Categories box pick Styles. Then in the Styles box, pick the style you want to assign a shortcut key to. Click once in the Press New Shortcut Key box, and hold down the key combination you want to assign to the style.

SAVING FORMATS AS NAMED STYLES

Although Word ships with more than 100 defined styles—they're built in to the Normal template—you'll quickly find that they don't always apply to your documents and your specific needs.

If your needs are simple, you can set up a paragraph style by formatting a paragraph the way you want, and telling Word the name of the style to be based on that formatting. To do so:

1. Format an entire paragraph to have all the attributes you want—both character and paragraph formatting apply.

2. Click once inside the paragraph.

3. Click New Style in the Style and Formatting task pane, and type in a name for the new paragraph style in the Name box (see Figure 18.3).

Figure 18.3
Creating a new style can be tricky. Make sure you understand what all the options mean before using them.

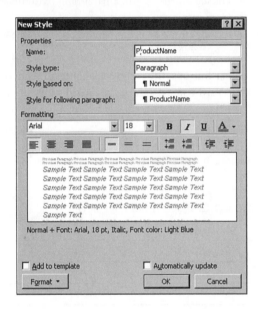

4. In the Style Type box, choose Paragraph to create a paragraph style, or Character for a character style.

5. In the Style Based On box, you can set up an inheritance scheme that can help you propagate changes quickly—or mess up a document mightily. Say your new style, ProductName, is "based on" the Normal style. If you change the Normal style to be right-justified with bold characters, the ProductName style takes on the formatting—that is, right-justified with bold characters. You can create complex hierarchies of styles this way. You can also create a mountain of spaghetti that takes hours to fix. If it all gets too messed up, your only recourse is to delete the file with the fancy styles, and start all over again with a new template.

6. The Style for Following Paragraph box lets you tell Word which style it should use for the next paragraph when you press Enter. For example, most heading styles have Normal as the style for the following paragraph—when you type a heading and press Enter, you usually want the next paragraph to be Normal. If you set up a style called Illustration, for example, you might want its Style for Following Paragraph setting to be Caption. And you might want the Style for Following Paragraph setting on Caption to

run back to Normal. That way, you can format a paragraph as Illustration, insert the illustration, press Enter, type the caption, and then press Enter again to return to Normal.

Caution

The style for Following Paragraph setting kicks in only if the insertion point is immediately in front of a paragraph mark when you press Enter. If you leave even a single space between the insertion point and the paragraph mark when you press Enter, Word gives you a new paragraph with the same formatting and style as the current paragraph.

7. If you leave the Add to Template box unchecked, the new style appears only in this particular document. If the Add to Template box is checked, however, the style is added to the document's template. That way, it's available to the current document and to any other document based on the template.

8. If you check the Automatically Update box, every change you make to a paragraph formatted with that particular style is automatically applied to every paragraph in the document with that style.

Caution

In almost all circumstances, Automatically Update is a disaster waiting to happen. Say you have a document and it includes dozens of paragraphs formatted with the ProductName style. If you accidentally select the paragraph mark at the end of any ProductName paragraph, and format the paragraph mark as bold, all the text in all the ProductName paragraphs immediately turns bold...*even if you can't see the paragraph mark!*

9. After you've waded through all the options in the New Style dialog box, choose the formatting you want to associate with the style. More complex formatting requires you to burrow through the Format button. For character styles, you can select Font (which brings up a dialog box identical to the one that appears when you choose Format, Font), Border (same as choosing Format, Borders and Shading), and Language (same as choosing Tools, Language, Set Language). For paragraph styles, you can also choose Paragraph (same as choosing Format, Paragraph), Tabs (same as choosing Format, Tabs), Frame (for old-fashioned frames that earlier versions of Word used to wrap text around pictures), and Numbering (same as Format, Bullets and Numbering). You can also pick a shortcut key from this direction, just as you would in the Customize Keyboard dialog box (choose Tools, Customize, Keyboard to get there) mentioned earlier in this chapter.

10. Click OK. If no style with that name exists, a new one is created for you and placed in the document.

Tip from

You can just type a new name into the Name box on the formatting toolbar and press Enter, to create a new paragraph style based on a selected paragraph's attributes.

If you want to modify a Style's definition, click the drop-down button next to the style's name in the Styles and Formatting task pane, and then choose Modify. You'll have all the foregoing formatting options at your disposal.

Tip from

WOPR, the Office add-in package that comes on this book's companion CD, includes a routine that allows you to duplicate styles—a feat that's time-consuming if attempted manually.

→Que's Special Edition WOPR XP/2002 Pack is packed with tools to help maximize your productivity and enjoyment with Office; **see** "WOPR XP/2002—Woody's Office POWER Pack," **p. 1007**.

 If your custom styles disappear when you open a document, see "Automatically Updating Styles" in the "Troubleshooting" section at the end of this chapter.

CUSTOMIZING THE NORMAL DOCUMENT TEMPLATE

When you create a new, blank document—either by clicking the New Blank Document icon on the Standard toolbar, or by choosing Blank Document in the New Document task pane—Word creates a new document based on the Normal document template, Normal.dot. The Normal template is always available when Word is running.

At the beginning of this chapter, you learned how Word finds styles, starting with the document, moving up to the document's template and, if the style name can't be found there, looking inside the Normal template.

Note

If the document is based on the Normal template, there's no intermediate step—the search progresses directly from the document to Normal.

Actually, the Normal document template is something of a misnomer. Normal.dot is no more "normal" than any other template. A more accurate name would be the default document template, the one Word uses when you create a new blank document without specifying a template. Normal.dot is frequently called the global template, because it's always available. Although other templates can be global in the sense that they're loaded when Word starts (refer to the Templates and Add-Ins dialog box, Figure 18.1, at the beginning of this chapter), no other template is tied directly to the New Blank Document icon on the Standard toolbar or the Blank Document choice in the New Document task pane.

Note

Although they share the same name, the Normal document template and the Normal style are quite different. The Normal document template—Normal.dot—is a file. Like any other template, it can be used to create new documents. The Normal style, on the other hand, is a paragraph style—a collection of paragraph and character formatting, which can be applied to a paragraph.

By default, Word 2002 starts new blank documents with the Times New Roman 12-point font, and no paragraph indenting or spacing. If you open Normal.dot, you'll see why: It contains a single paragraph mark formatted in the Normal style, and the Normal style is defined as Times New Roman 12 point, with no paragraph indenting or spacing. When Word creates a new document based on Normal.dot, it copies everything in the template into the new document—same as it does when creating a document from any template—and you end up with a new document with a single paragraph mark, with Normal style formatting.

Tip from

EQ & Woody

If you want to change the default font for new blank documents, you don't need to mess with Normal.dot. Instead, use this hidden shortcut: Create a new blank document, and then choose Format, Font. Choose the font you want (say, Garamond 11 point), and click the Default button. From that point on, any new blank document you create will use the Garamond 11-point font for its Normal style.

If you want to change more than the default font on new blank documents, the simplest way is this:

1. Create a new blank document by clicking the New Blank Document icon on the Standard toolbar.

2. Choose Format, Styles and Formatting. In the Styles and Formatting task pane, you should see Normal highlighted. Click the down-arrow next to Normal, and then click Modify to change the Normal style.

3. Make whatever changes you want to make to Word's defaults for new blank documents. More-complex formatting options sit underneath the Format button: You can change the font, paragraph formatting, tabs, borders and shading, proofing language, bullets, and numbering.

4. When you've made all the changes you want to make, check the Add to Template box, and click OK. Because you checked Add to Template, all the modifications you made to the Normal style are reflected in this document's template—which just happens to be the Normal document template, Normal.dot.

If you've made a colossal mess of your Normal document template and want to start over, see "Restoring the Default Normal Template" in the "Troubleshooting" section at the end of this chapter.

USING WORD'S BUILT-IN TEMPLATES

Word ships with scores of templates, and hundreds more are available for download from the Microsoft Web site. Choose Help, Office on the Web to search Microsoft's Web site for additional templates not included on the Office CD-ROM.

Although the generic "click here and type" templates can come in handy in a pinch, you'll want to customize any generic template that you expect to use more than a few times. It's well worth your while to replace the "click here" instructions with text appropriate to your particular situation—your company's name, your phone number, and so on. Here's how to customize Word's Professional fax template, and make it your own:

1. Choose File, New, click General Templates and on the Letters & Faxes tab, double-click Professional Fax.

2. Fill out the appropriate portions of the fax template—the information that won't change from fax to fax—such as the company name, address and phone number, and possibly the From: entry.

3. Choose File, Save, and in the Save as Type box, choose Document Template (see Figure 18.4). Give the template a descriptive name and click the Save button.

Figure 18.4
Customize the built-in templates that ship with Word. It's easy and fast to make them your own.

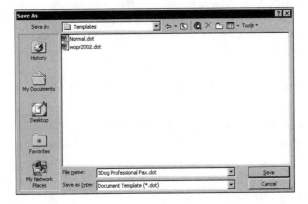

4. The next time you want to use the template, choose File, New, click General Templates on the New Document task pane, and select the template name you assigned from the offerings on the General tab.

Many of the built-in Word templates contain interesting examples of techniques discussed elsewhere in this book. The following are the ones you're likely to learn from, starting with the most instructive:

■ The Manual template (Publications tab) contains dozens of excellent hands-on examples that apply to any document more than a few pages long.

- The Résumé templatesMa and wizard (Other Documents tab) use tables, as you might expect. They show you how to set up text on a line so some is left-aligned, some centered, and some is right-aligned. (Hint: Use two tab stops, the one in the middle centered, the one on the right margin right-aligned.)

- The Pleading Wizard (Legal Pleadings tab) shows you how to use tables to construct and control horizontal and vertical lines.

- The various Report templates (Reports tab) contain several unusual examples of graphic elements in longer documents. These templates are also well worth studying.

- The various Fax templates (Letters & Faxes tab) all use tables to good advantage, with different kinds of borders. They also have macros you can use called CheckIt and UncheckIt that allow you to check and uncheck boxes in a document.

- The Brochure template (on the Publications tab) contains an interesting example of three-column section formatting, used to create a tri-fold brochure. Work with it long enough and you'll become convinced that Publisher handles simple tri-fold brochures much more easily.

- The Directory template (Publications tab) gets you started with a membership roster, or directory of organizations. This template is well worth examining closely for its deft use of styles. Unfortunately, it doesn't include a demonstration of the {styleref} field, which is an indispensable part of most rosters.

- If you have to prepare a thesis to complete your MBA, the Thesis template (Publications tab) comes in handy, providing your university conforms to the styles used in the template.

PART

III

CH

18

In addition, the Web Page tab includes almost a dozen examples of Web-related formatting that can be helpful if you're constructing Web pages with Word.

If you intend to use any of the built-in Letter templates, be sure to read the indispensable discussion of the Letter Wizard before you go any further. You'll find it in Chapter 16, "Advanced Document Formatting."

CHANGING DOCUMENT FORMATS GLOBALLY

When Word creates a new document, it copies the entire contents of the template to the new document—text, pictures, headers and footers, and so on—and then establishes a link between the document and template (so, for example, styles in the template become available in the document). With one possible exception, after a document is created, nothing from the template gets copied into the document. So, for example, if you change the Normal template so its default font is Garamond 11 point, all new blank documents will have Garamond 11 point—but all old documents based on the Normal template will stay just as they are.

Tip from

EQ & Woody

There's one huge exception to this rule: If you choose Tools, Templates and Add-Ins, and then check the Automatically Update Document Styles box in the Templates and Add-Ins dialog box, Word "updates" (that is, wipes out) a document style if one exists in the template with the same name. This option is good news if you always, without exception, want template styles to control the look of a document. But if you sometimes create styles within a document, avoid this option.

So unless the Automatically Update Document Styles box is checked, you can make all the changes you want to a template, and the documents associated with that template won't change a bit. Changes to the template affect only new documents based on the template.

How do you make global paragraph and character formatting changes to a document—that is, make global changes to the appearance of a document—without going into each style, each paragraph, and making the changes manually? Word gives you three options:

- Allow Word to make changes for you, either piece-by-piece (in the AutoFormat feature) or wholesale (by using the Style Gallery). Neither of these options is likely to improve the appearance of the document.

→ To learn how you can put Word's AutoFormatting features to work for you, **see** "Automatic Formatting," **p. 343**.

- Change the template applied to the document, and then force Word to update all the styles in the document so they conform to the styles in the new template. You might want to do this if, for example, a coworker comes up with a spectacular new template that handles all the styles you commonly use.

- Apply a theme. Because themes include background colors, and background colors rarely appear in professional documents, this approach is virtually unusable unless you're working with a Web page.

To attach a new template to a document and update the document's styles, follow these steps:

1. If the document has any styles defined inside it (that is, at the document level), save a copy of the document. This process can completely overwrite styles in the document, and you can't bring them back.

2. Choose Tools, Templates and Add-Ins. Click the Attach button, navigate to the template you want to attach to the document, and click Open.

3. Check the Automatically Update Document Styles box. Click OK.

4. Close and reopen the document. With the Automatically Update Document Styles box checked, this flushes out any styles with identical names in the document—overwriting the document's formatting with the new template's formatting.

5. If you don't want to update the document with future style changes in the attached template, immediately go back into the Templates and Add-Ins dialog box (choose Tools,

Templates and Add-Ins) and clear the Automatically Update Document Styles check box.

The Word documentation says you can leave that box checked "to ensure that your document contains up-to-date style formatting." That's true for documents based on standard corporate templates, where you absolutely, positively want the template to dictate every style choice. It's also the right choice if you fully understand the relationship between the document you're working with and the template to which it's attached, and you want to use only the styles in the template. If you're experimenting with styles in a document, however, leave this box unchecked. You'll avoid headaches caused by disappearing document styles.

Before you consider applying a theme to change the appearance of a document, make sure you understand what a theme entails. A theme contains

- A background pattern (few of the themes that come with Word have solid-color backgrounds)
- Style definitions for Heading 1, 2, 3, 4, 5, and 6, as well as the Normal style
- A graphic for bullets
- A graphic for horizontal lines
- AutoText entries specifically designed for Web pages—the "created by" entry puts the originator's name on the page; "created on" inserts the date

Themes can be handy if you're trying to create a Web page that matches the formatting generated in a different program—FrontPage or PowerPoint, for example. They're also reasonably useful if you're developing a Web page from scratch. But they're effectively unusable for any other kind of document.

When you apply a theme to a document (choose Format, Theme, per Figure 18.5), Word does the following:

- Changes the background of the document (choose Format, Background) to match the pattern in the theme.
- Replaces the document's (not the template's) style definitions for Normal and Heading 1, 2, 3, 4, 5, and 6.
- Sets up default bullets and horizontal lines to match the graphic in the theme.
- Puts the AutoText entries in the template (not the document).

Be careful when applying themes to existing documents. If you apply a theme to a document and then decide to remove it by setting the theme in the Themes dialog box to (No Theme), you'll find that the styles you defined in the document for Normal, Heading 1, and so on, don't work. Sadly, those styles you created are gone. There's nothing you can do.

Figure 18.5
Apply a theme to a
Word document by
choosing Format,
Theme, and choosing
from the list.

You should expect a lot of additional anomalies if you decide to work with themes. Animated graphics appear in themes, but they won't be animated in Word—you have to use your Web browser to see them move. You can't create or modify a theme in Word. You have to use FrontPage. They don't print.

Themes are clearly a "version 1.1" addition to Word. Use them with care.

MANAGING STYLES AND TEMPLATES

As you can see from the discussion in this chapter, styles and templates are inextricably related. Because many of the styles you use are stored in templates, managing styles boils down to managing the templates that contain them.

CREATING A NEW TEMPLATE FROM SCRATCH

To create a new template choose File, New, click the Template button, and then click OK.

A Word template is nearly identical to a Word document, except it also contains AutoText entries. (The Normal template also contains formatted AutoCorrect entries.) That's the only difference. Usually Word templates are identified with the filename extension *.dot, but that isn't a requirement.

WHERE DOES WORD STORE TEMPLATES?

When you save a new template, Word attempts to save it in your User templates folder— that's the location marked User Templates in the File Locations tab of the Options dialog box (choose Tools, Options), as shown in Figure 18.6.

Figure 18.6
The User Templates and Workgroup Templates folders should hold all the templates you intend to use.

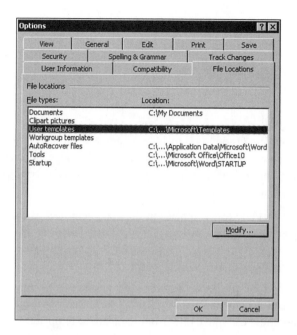

Unless you specifically change the location on the File Locations tab, user templates are stored in your Windows \Profiles folder. If you're working on a Windows NT, 95, 98, or ME machine with user profiles enabled, that's typically C:*<Windows folder>*\Profiles\ *<username>*\Application Data\Microsoft\Templates (where *<Windows folder>* is the name of the folder that contains the Windows program files and *<username>* is your logon ID); in Windows 2000, it's C:\Documents and Settings*<username>*\Application Data\Microsoft\ Templates. If you're working on a Windows 95, 98, or ME machine that doesn't distinguish among different users, you'll usually find user templates in C:*<Windows folder>*\Application Data\Microsoft\Templates. If you want to create a new tab for the New dialog box and place your template on that tab, choose File, Save, click the Create New Folder icon, give the new folder the same name you want to appear on the tab, and then choose Save.

When you bring up the New dialog box, Word combines the templates in the User Templates folder, the Workgroup Templates folder, and any predefined (possibly uninstalled) templates that ship with Office (in the U.S. English version of Word, those are stored in C:\Program Files\Microsoft Office\Templates\1033).

→ To learn the tricks of the trade when it comes to creating new files, **see** "Creating New Files," **p. 61**.

Templates stored in the \Startup folder (shown at the bottom of Figure 18.6) are automatically loaded by Word when it starts. If you have any VBA macros that you want to be available every time you run Word, they should be placed in templates located in the \Startup folder.

→ To learn about VBA's rather stringent requirements for the files that hold projects, **see** "Storing Projects," **p. 1034**.

> **Note**
>
> The Word documentation would have you believe that styles defined in templates in the \Startup folder are available in every open document. That isn't true. *Macros* in the \Startup templates are available in all the documents. Styles are not.

CUSTOMIZING WORD TEMPLATES

When you open a template (as opposed to creating a new document based on a template), you can modify it in precisely the same ways as you would change a document: You can add text, pictures, headers and footers, hyperlinks, macros—in short, everything that goes in a document (plus AutoText entries).

Remember, however, that any text you place in the document itself is considered to be "boilerplate," and is copied into any new documents you create based on that template.

COPYING STYLES AND SETTINGS BETWEEN TEMPLATES

Word includes a handy tool called the *Organizer* that allows you to copy styles, toolbars, and macro projects between documents and templates. The Organizer also lets you copy AutoText entries, but these can move only from template to template.

To make use of the Organizer, follow these steps:

1. Choose Tools, Templates and Add-Ins. Click the Organizer button. You see the Organizer dialog box (see Figure 18.7).

Figure 18.7
The Organizer copies, deletes, or renames styles, AutoText entries, custom toolbars, and macro projects.

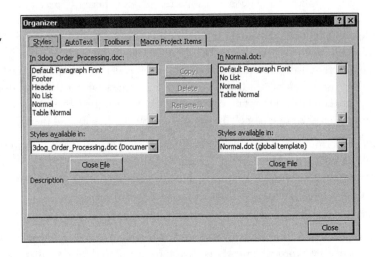

2. Make sure the "from" and "to" files—documents or templates—are referenced in the Styles Available In boxes. If you have the wrong files, click Close File, then Open File, and select the correct ones.

3. Select Styles, AutoText, Toolbars, or Macro Project Items, depending on which settings you want to manipulate. Note that AutoText items can reside only in templates.

4. Select the individual items and click Copy, Delete, or Rename, as appropriate.

TROUBLESHOOTING

REVEALING CHARACTER FORMATTING

As a former WordPerfect user, I'm accustomed to WordPerfect's "reveal codes" command, which displays formatting directives hidden in a document, much like HTML tags. When I search through online help, however, there's no mention of Word's reveal codes command.

Word doesn't use WordPerfect-style codes to apply formatting. Instead, it stores formatting for each character with the character itself, and it stores paragraph formatting in the paragraph mark. However, the Reveal Formatting task pane displays the names of styles and direct formatting applied to any character.

AUTOMATICALLY UPDATING STYLES

When I opened a document that contained a number of custom styles, the formatting changed unexpectedly, and clicking the Undo button didn't bring them back.

Styles in the document template are overwriting styles in the document itself. If you create a set of formats in named styles and save them in a document, you might find that your styles get wiped out by styles of the same name stored in the document template every time you open the document. To make sure you don't have the problem, choose Tools, Templates and Add-Ins, and clear the Automatically Update Document Styles box.

RESTORING THE DEFAULT NORMAL TEMPLATE

I've made a mess of the Normal template, and every new document I create inherits formatting I don't want.

You have two choices. The easy (but drastic) option is to exit Word, rename Normal.dot to something else (for example, Old-normal.dot), and start Word again. When Word can't find Normal.dot, it creates a new Normal document template; in the process, however, you'll lose all your toolbar customizations, keyboard shortcuts, formatted AutoCorrect entries, and much more.

The more tedious option is to choose Format, Style and use Format button options to work through every style in the template until you have the Normal style back to where it started. For U.S. installations, that includes the following defaults: Times New Roman, 12 point, English (U.S.), Flush left, Line spacing single, Widow/orphan control. Make sure you click Add to Template when you're done. It's more work, but you won't lose any of your customizing.

SECRETS OF THE OFFICE MASTERS: USING A MACRO TO REPLACE STRAIGHT QUOTES WITH CURLY QUOTES

Large writing projects demand special attention. The first order of business in undertaking a major project is to settle on a template. A template, as you've seen in this chapter, contains styles that define how the document will appear. Add to that AutoText entries, toolbars crafted for the work at hand, and custom macros to take over the most onerous, repetitive (or, if you're lucky, difficult) work, and you'll have a template that's an effective tool for everyone involved in the project.

Macros in big-project templates run the entire gamut of VBA/Word capabilities, but one of the most common requirements you'll see over and over again is the need to scan a document and convert "curly" quotes (Microsoft calls them "smart" quotes) to "straight" quotes. Somehow, page layout software still gets confused by simple curly quotes, and putting a curly quote in the body of an e-mail message is just an invitation to disaster.

This program saves the current document, changes all curly quotes to straight quotes, and then saves the revised document with an XXX Straight Quotes.doc filename (see the following code).

```
Public Sub Cleanup()
Dim bReplaceQuotes As Boolean
ActiveDocument.Save
bReplaceQuotes = Options.AutoFormatAsYouTypeReplaceQuotes
Options.AutoFormatAsYouTypeReplaceQuotes = False
With ActiveDocument.Range.Find
    .ClearFormatting
    .Text = Chr(145)
    With .Replacement
        .ClearFormatting
        .Text = Chr(39)
    End With
    .Execute Replace:=wdReplaceAll, Format:=False
    .Text = Chr(146)
    With .Replacement
        .ClearFormatting
        .Text = Chr(39)
    End With
    .Execute Replace:=wdReplaceAll, Format:=False
    .Text = Chr(147)
    With .Replacement
        .ClearFormatting
        .Text = Chr(34)
    End With
    .Execute Replace:=wdReplaceAll, Format:=False
    .Text = Chr(148)
    With .Replacement
        .ClearFormatting
        .Text = Chr(34)
    End With
    .Execute Replace:=wdReplaceAll, Format:=False
End With
Options.AutoFormatAsYouTypeReplaceQuotes = bReplaceQuotes
```

```
sFileName = ActiveDocument.Name
sFileName = WordBasic.[filenameinfo$](sFileName, 4)
ActiveDocument.SaveAs sFileName & " Straight Quotes.doc"
End Sub
```

To enter the macro, follow the instructions in Chapter 38, "Using Macros to Automate Office Tasks."

PART

III

CH

18

CHAPTER **19**

CREATING DYNAMIC DOCUMENTS WITH FIELDS AND FORMS

In this chapter

USING FIELDS INTELLIGENTLY

Behind many of Word's most powerful features sits a peculiar document element called a *field*. Word fields are placeholders whose contents change dynamically; they typically work in the background, invisibly, displaying the correct data onscreen and in print, based on information within the current document, in other documents, or from external sources. For example, if you put a {Date} field in your document, it displays the current date each time you open the document.

Word supports more than 70 different fields. Use them when you want to accomplish tasks such as these:

- Show the current day in a document ({date}, {time}), or the time the document was last printed ({printdate}).
- Construct a paragraph numbering scheme ({seq}, {AutoNum}, {AutoNumLgl}) more complex than those available in the dialog box that appears when you choose Format, Bullets and Numbering. A similar technique ({ref}, {styleref}) allows you to set up "Figure x-y" figure numbering captions that incorporate the chapter number.
- Set up a "hot" button ({macrobutton}) or picture that runs a macro when clicked.

→ To run a macro based on a click inside a document, **see** "'Hot' Linking to Macros," **p. 1006**.

- Refer to the contents of bookmarked text. For example, you can place a bookmark on a chapter title and refer to that title throughout your document by using the {Ref} field. If the title changes, all the references change, too.

→ For details on all the nuances of using bookmarks, **see** "Using Bookmarks," **p. 432**.

- Refer to the first or last occurrence of a particular style on a page. Use this type of field ({stylref}) in the header for a phone book, for example, listing the first and last entries ("Able, George to Alphonso, Chris") on each page.
- Insert information about a document into the document itself ({info})—total number of pages, filename, author, file size, number of words, date when the document was last saved, and so on.
- Perform calculations, comparisons, and even elementary arithmetic. For example, the {Page} field produces the number of the current page, whereas a {{Page}+1} field results in the number of the next page.

There's even a field that converts a postal ZIP Code to a USPS bar code!

Fields also drive such key built-in Word capabilities as tables of contents, figures, tables, equations, indexes, and mail merges. Although Word uses layers of wizards and dialog boxes to shield you from the field codes used to implement those features, sometimes the only way to tweak the feature—to limit a table of contents to a part of the document covered by a specific bookmark, for example—is by working with the field code itself.

Note

Fields are an enormous topic. In this book, you'll learn some of the more useful fields—ones that will increase your productivity—today. If you need a detailed fields reference, see *Special Edition Using Microsoft Word* 2002 (published by Que).

Caution

Many fields do not translate well into HTML-formatted files. If you need to use a field on a Web page, make sure you test it with all the commonly used browsers to ensure that it works properly.

SHOWING AND HIDING FIELD CODES

Word allows you to flip-flop between seeing the field codes themselves and field code results—for example, between seeing

```
{Date \@ "d-MMM-yyyy"}
```

and

```
1-JAN-2003
```

To show field codes, choose Tools, Options; choose the View tab; and then check the Field Codes box. To return to showing field code results, clear that same Field Codes box.

Tip from

Ed & Woody

If you're going to do much serious work with field codes, you might want to add the Field Codes button to the Standard or Formatting toolbar or memorize the View Field Codes keyboard shortcut, Alt+F9. Either one toggles between showing field codes and showing their results.

→ For detailed instructions, **see** "Customizing Toolbars," **p. 30**.

FIELD CODE SYNTAX

Field codes can take on many different forms, but generally they look like this, with the field name and required or optional parameters enclosed in curly braces:

```
{Author \* mergeformat}
```

In this case, the field {Author} has one parameter, called a *formatting switch*. The formatting switch, if present, controls the way the field result is formatted inside the document. Switches are discussed extensively in the "Formatting Field Results," section later in this chapter.

> **Note**
>
> In this book, you'll always see field codes as they appear onscreen, surrounded by curly braces—something like this:
>
>   {Seq Figures * mergeformat}
>
> Of course, you can't type curly braces into a document and get a field code. There are only three ways to insert field marks (braces): Choose Insert, Field; use one of the built-in Word functions that produces a field code; or press Ctrl+F9.

INSERTING A FIELD INTO A DOCUMENT

By far, the easiest way to put a field into a document is to use one of the built-in Word features to do the dirty work for you. For example, if you choose Insert, Date and Time, and then check the Update Automatically box, Word inserts a {Date} field into your document, adding a formatting switch for the date format you choose (see Figure 19.1).

Figure 19.1
Checking Update Automatically in this dialog box causes Word to insert a {Date} field, instead of the date itself.

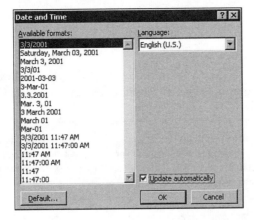

Similarly, putting a page number in a header or footer using the Insert Page Number button on the Header and Footer toolbar will insert a {Page} field, as will inserting a table of contents or index, creating a caption or cross-reference, or running a document merge.

If you want to build a field from scratch, you can do it the hard way, by pressing Ctrl+F9 to create the field marks, and then manually inserting the field name and parameters. If you make a mistake, of course, the field won't work as you expect. To be absolutely certain you get the syntax right, choose Insert, Field instead. This Field dialog box (see Figure 19.2) offers context-sensitive help and immediate access to the most common field switches (the terms "properties" and "options" are somewhat arbitrary; don't get hung up on the terminology). If you want to work with the raw field code, click the Field Codes button in the lower-left corner.

Figure 19.2
Word provides good support for fields via the Field dialog box.

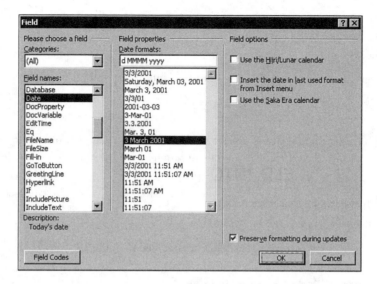

FORMATTING FIELD RESULTS

Unless you add a switch inside the field to change formatting, the field result takes on the formatting of the first nonblank character of the field.

For example, if you have a field that says {*A*uthor}, with the "A" in Times New Roman, 10-point italic, the result of the field takes on that formatting: *Douglas Adams*.

Word has three different field switches that control the appearance and formatting of field code results.

GENERAL * FORMAT SWITCHES

The most common field switch is the general formatting switch:

```
\* mergeformat
```

This switch tells Word to ignore the formatting of the first character of the field, and instead to use whatever formatting you apply to the field itself.

For example, say you're typing along in 12-point Garamond, and you insert a {NumWords} field (which shows the number of words in the document), using the Field dialog box. If you check the Preserve Formatting During Updates box, Word inserts a * mergeformat switch:

```
{NUMWORDS   \* MERGEFORMAT}
```

With that switch in place, every time you update the field, it takes on the original formatting—Garamond 12 point—unless you apply some different formatting directly on the field result.

PART

III

CH

19

Formatting switches gives you an enormous amount of flexibility in how a field appears in your document—for example

```
\* dollartext
```

converts a number—say, 123.45—into the kind of text you put on a check—one hundred twenty-three and 45/100.

```
\* caps
```

capitalizes the initial letters of each word in the field result. Combine the two formatting switches with the = field, which evaluates numeric expressions, to get the field:

```
{ = 123.45 \* dollartext \* caps }
```

which appears in your document as

```
One Hundred Twenty-Three And 45/100
```

The most useful formatting switches are detailed in Table 19.1.

TABLE 19.1   * FORMATTING SWITCHES

Switch	Action
* mergeformat	Retains the current formatting of the field result whenever it's updated.
* charformat	Uses the formatting applied to the first nonblank character of the field code.
* caps	Capitalizes the first letter of each word.
* firstcap	Capitalizes the first letter of the first word only.
* lower	Makes all letters lowercase.
* upper	Makes all letters uppercase.
* cardtext	Converts a number to text: 12 becomes twelve.
* ordtext	Converts a number to the ordinal text: 12 becomes twelfth.
* Roman	Displays a number in capitalized Roman numerals: 12 becomes XII.
* dollartext	Spells out the whole part of the number, then rounds the fraction and appends "and xx/100": 123.456 becomes one hundred twenty-three and 46/100.

NUMERIC \# PICTURE SWITCHES

Word also allows you to specify a numeric "picture" switch to be applied to numbers. This could come in handy if, for example, you calculate numbers in a table or bring them in for a merge, and you want to show negative numbers in parentheses.

The basic building blocks of field numeric pictures are as follows:

- Decimal point
- Thousands separator (typically a comma)

- Zero (digits that always appear)
- # sign (digits that are used only if necessary)
- Various combinations to format negative numbers; and literal text, which appears in the field result.

You could practically write an entire book on the nuances of numeric picture formatting. Rather than dwell on the details, examine the common numeric picture elements shown in Table 19.2.

TABLE 19.2 COMMON \# NUMERIC PICTURE ELEMENTS

Switch	Result
`\* 00.00`	Forces Word to display two digits to the left and two to the right of the decimal point, adding leading and trailing zeros as needed: 1.2 displays as 01.20 and –1.2 shows up as –01.20. Use this format when you want numbers in a column to line up perfectly.
`\* #0.000`	One or more digits might appear to the left of the decimal point, but three must appear after: 1.23 displays as 1.230, –12.3456 becomes –12.346, and 1234.5 shows 1234.500.
`\* $,#.00`	Shows a dollar sign, followed by the number with commas grouping each set of three digits, and two decimal places: .12 appears as $.12, 12345.678 shows $12,345.68.
`\* $,0.00`	Same as the preceding, but always shows at least one digit for dollars: .12 displays as $0.12.

Unless you specify a different format, Word always displays negative numbers with a leading minus sign. To force Word to show negative numbers in parentheses, you have to provide two formatting pictures, the first for positive numbers and the second for negatives, enclosed in quotes, separated by a semicolon. For example, this format

`\# "$,#.00;($,#.00)"`

will show 0.123 as $.12 and –1234.56 as ($1,234.56).

DATE-TIME \@ FORMAT SWITCHES

The date-time picture switch almost always appears in a {Date}, {Time}, {Createdate}, {Printdate}, or {Savedate} field. (The last three fields show when the document was created, last printed, or last saved.) The switch tells Word how to format the date or time. For example, add this field to a document:

`{Date \@ "MMMM d, yyyy - h:mm:ss AM/PM"}`

When you open the document on the morning of Bill Gates' fiftieth birthday, Word updates the field and displays text that looks like this:

`October 28, 2005 - 8:33:05 AM`

The most common date-time picture elements are shown in Table 19.3.

TABLE 19.3 \@ DATE-TIME PICTURE ELEMENTS

Element	Meaning
M	Month number without leading 0: August is 8
MM	Month number with leading 0: August is 08
MMM	Month as three-letter abbreviation: Aug
MMMM	Month spelled out: August
d	Day of the month without leading zero
dd	Day of the month with leading zero
ddd	Day of the week as three-letter abbreviation: Mon
dddd	Day of the week spelled out: Monday
yy	Last two digits of the year: 01
yyyy	Four-digit year: 2001
h	Hour on a 12-hour clock without leading zero
hh	Hour on a 12-hour clock with leading zero
H	Hour on a 24-hour clock without leading zero
HH	Hour on a 24-hour clock with leading zero
m	Minutes without leading zero
mm	Minutes with leading zero
s	Seconds without leading zero
ss	Seconds with leading zero
AM/PM	AM or PM (used with h and hh for 12-hour clock)
Text	Appears as text in the field result

DISPLAYING FIELD RESULTS CORRECTLY

When you first insert a field code into a document, or when you create a new document with a field code in it, Word calculates the value of the field code and displays its results.

After the first time, however, field codes are never updated automatically, except when a file is opened. So, for example, if you create a new letter based on a template that has a {Date} field code, Word puts the current date in the new document. When you close and reopen the document, Word updates the field if necessary, but if you leave the document open overnight, the date won't change.

When you open a document containing a field, the field is updated automatically. There are two common ways to update a field manually—that is, to have Word recalculate the field's value and display the new value in your document:

- Select the field, and then press F9.
- Select one or more fields, right-click, and choose Update Field.

You can also specify that Word should automatically update all fields in a document immediately before printing the document. To set this option, choose Tools, Options; click the Print tab; and check the Update Fields box. The setting is global, so it stays in effect for all documents until you change it.

You can permanently eliminate a field, and have it replaced with the text that's currently showing in the document. For example, if you've written a letter by using a {Date} field, you might want to replace the field with its results, so when you open the letter later, you'll see the date you sent the letter rather than the current date. This process is called "unlinking" a field, although it actually removes the field entirely, replacing it with the current value of the field.

For example, a purchase order might include a bookmark called DollarAmount, where the user enters the price of an item. Later in the document, you might refer to that number in check format, using a field like this:

```
{ = {REF DollarAmount} \* dollartext \* upper }
```

If the amount the user enters is 79.82, the field code result appears in the document as

```
SEVENTY-NINE AND 82/100
```

When you unlink the field, Word eliminates the field code entirely, replacing it with text that you can edit directly. Later, if you change the amount in the DollarAmount bookmark, the text won't change.

To unlink a field, do the following:

1. If you want to be certain the field result is current, update the field. (In some circumstances, you might choose not to update the field; for example, if it shows an old date and time that you want to preserve.)
2. Click to position the insertion point in the field. It doesn't matter whether field codes or field code results are showing.
3. Press Ctrl+6 (that's the 6 on the keyboard, not on the number pad) or Shift+Ctrl+F9.

Tip from

Ed & Woody

If you regularly work with fields, add an Unlink Fields button to a convenient toolbar, using the procedures described in Chapter 2, "Customizing the Office Interface."

To lock a field—that is, to prevent a field from being updated—select the field or place the insertion point in it and press Ctrl+F11. To allow the field to be updated again, select the field and press Shift+Ctrl+F11.

SOME USEFUL CUSTOM FIELDS

Word includes a wasp's nest of fields, many of which have become outdated over the years and remain available only so documents created in older versions of Word will still work in Word 2002. These fields and their switches and settings comprise an entire programming language unto itself, buried inside Word, and completely separate from the language used in macros: Visual Basic for Applications.

Tip from

Ed & Woody

Don't let the profusion of fields sway you. In general, if there's a way to accomplish your goal without using fields, that alternative is preferable. Many Word field codes are poorly documented, and you can expect to lose precious time trying to make them work properly.

Although you can use the Field properties and Field options lists in the Field dialog box to assemble a field, some options aren't listed at all, and interactions among options are complex and confusing. And because error messages are few and far between, debugging field codes is usually a tedious, repeated trial-and-error process.

SHOWING DATES AND TIMES

If you want to insert the current date and/or time in a document, choose Insert, Date and Time; if the choices in the Date and Time dialog box include the formatting you need, use the menu. Forget the field.

Tip from

Ed & Woody

The date and time formats that appear when you choose Insert, Date and Time are identical to the formats offered when you choose Insert, Field, and choose the Date field. If one of the formats listed in the Date and Time menu dialog box is close to the one you want, use the Date and Time entry, and check the Update Automatically box to insert the field code in your document. Then press Alt+F9 to show field codes and edit the field manually. It's much easier than constructing a field from scratch.

Word's date and time fields are listed in Table 19.4. They're all formatted by using the \@ date-time format switches, discussed earlier in this chapter.

TABLE 19.4   DATE AND TIME FIELDS

Field	Meaning
{Date}	The current date and time
{Time}	The current date and time
{CreateDate}	The date and time the file was created

TABLE 19.4   CONTINUED

Field	Meaning
{PrintDate}	The date and time the file was last printed
{SaveDate}	The date and time the file was last saved

So, for example, the field

```
{PrintDate \@ "d-MMM-yy h:mm A/P"}
```

in a document last printed on October 20, 2001 might have a field result that looks like this:

```
20-Oct-01 10:45 AM
```

The only significant difference between {Date} and {Time} is in the default formatting—that is, the format of the field result if no \@ date-time format switch is used:

- For the {Date} field, if you've set a default date format using the Default button on the Date and Time dialog box, Word uses that format. Otherwise, Word looks to the Windows Short Date style; to adjust this format, open the Windows Control Panel's Regional Settings option and click the Date tab.

- For the {Time} field, if you've set a default time format in the Date and Time dialog box, Word uses that format. Otherwise, Word uses the Windows Time style setting; open Control Panel's Regional Settings option and click the Time tab to adjust this format.

The {Date} field also takes an \l switch that isn't used in the {Time} field. When Word updates a {Date \l} field, it checks to see which date or time format you last used in the Date and Time dialog box and then applies that format to the field.

 If you enter a time field in your document, but when you update the field it displays a date, see "Time and Date Discrepancies" in the "Troubleshooting" section at the end of this chapter.

If there is no \@ date-time switch in the {CreateDate}, {PrintDate}, or {SaveDate} fields, they will show the date and time, formatted according to Date and Time defaults, as described previously, or the Control Panel's Regional Settings option.

PART

III

CH

19

Caution

> Be careful using {Date} fields in templates. When you create a new letter based on the template, Word puts the {Date} field in the document, and then updates the field so it shows the current day. A week later, when you discover that you need an extra copy of the letter, you open the saved file and Word dutifully updates the {Date} field—leaving you no idea when you actually created the letter.

To avoid allowing Word to insert the current date in a document each time you open it, you should use the {CreateDate} field in templates, and explicitly supply the \@ date-time format switch for it. That way, the date won't change if you open or print a letter sometime after it was originally created.

For example, this field

`{CreateDate \@ "MMMM d,yyyy"}`

produces a result reflecting the day the document was created, with formatting like this:

`July 17, 2002`

Caution Don't use the {PrintDate} field in a template. Word always updates this field immediately prior to printing, regardless of the setting you specify on the Print tab of the Options dialog box.

PAGE NUMBERING

To show the current page number or the total number of pages in a document's header or footer, don't bother entering the {Page} and {NumPages} fields manually. The Header and Footer toolbar has buttons for each.

If you aren't in a header or footer, however—or you need to use the {SectionPages} field, which displays the total number of pages in the current section—you should start by choosing Insert, Field. You'll find {Page}, {SectionPages}, and {NumPages} in the Field Names box.

REFERRING TO DOCUMENT CONTENTS

Certain fields allow you to pluck text out of a document and use it someplace else, or refer to its location—for example

- You can create cross-references to bookmarked pieces of text. In a catalog of pet products, for example, using {Ref} and {PageRef} fields lets you automatically insert this text: "See Retractable Dog Chains on page 77." The simplest and most reliable way to create these fields is to choose Insert, Cross-reference and use that dialog box.

→ To use Word's built-in cross-reference support, **see** "Inserting Cross-References," **p. 433**.

  - Similarly, you can refer to paragraph numbers—for example, "as defined in paragraph IV.B.7.a"—by using the {Ref} field, preferably by using the Cross-reference dialog box.
  - Use the {StyleRef} field to put the first and last entries on a page in the header or footer, just as you would in a dictionary or telephone book. The {StyleRef} field also allows you to put the name of a chapter (or section, or anything else that's formatted with a style) in a header or footer.

The {Ref Bookmark} field retrieves bookmarked text from elsewhere inside the document. For example, if you have a bookmark called TotalSales and it currently covers the text 123.45, a {Ref TotalSales} field in the document displays the field result 123.45.

{Ref} has a half-dozen switches, but for most situations, the switches are obsolete: You can control every nuance of every switch more easily by using the Cross-reference dialog box or the Insert Hyperlink dialog box. There's one obscure exception: If you need to remove the alphabetic text from a paragraph number, consult online Help about the \t switch.

The {StyleRef} field, on the other hand, has many applications in Word. In the simplest situation, a field code such as:

```
{StyleRef "Heading 1"}
```

causes Word to look backward in the document, to find the most recent use of the style Heading 1. If, for example, the nearest paragraph formatted with the Heading 1 style contains the text "Executive Summary," the field code result shows that text.

Note

The {StyleRef} field works with both character and paragraph styles.

Although you can use {StyleRef} in the body of a document to repeat the last text formatted with a particular style, it's most useful in headers and footers, where these rules apply:

- When Word encounters a {StyleRef} field in a header or footer, it finds the first occurrence of that particular style on the page, and the field result is the text in that paragraph.
- When Word encounters a {StyleRef \l} field in a header or footer (which you can create by checking the Search from Bottom of Page to Top box in the Field dialog box), it uses the last paragraph formatted with the particular style.

Say you have a corporate telephone book with phone extensions that looks something like this:

Aaron, Ron	3319		Ambray, Jill	9937		Astron, Deb	3826
Able, Janey	1766		Antone, Phil	7635		Autry, Gene	5311
Actor, John	4113		Appley, Anne	5539		Azure, Irene	7631

To construct a header that uses the format "Aaron, Ron to Azure, Irene," you need to set up the telephone book carefully, because each employee's name must be formatted with its own style. In this case, if you create and apply a character style called EmpName to all the employee names, you could use fields in the header like this:

```
{StyleRef "EmpName"} to {StyleRef "EmpName" \l}
```

to produce the correct header format.

On each subsequent page, Word will update the header to include the first and last occurrence of the EmpName style on that particular page.

PART

III

CH

19

Likewise, to place chapter (or section) names in headers and footers, use the {StyleRef} field:

1. Ensure that the text you want to go in the headers (or footers) is all formatted with the same style. For example, if all the chapter names in your document are formatted with the "Heading 1" style, you're set.

2. Choose View, Header and Footer to display the header or footer. Place the insertion point where you want the chapter name to appear.

3. Choose Insert, Field. In the Field Names box, select StyleRef.

4. In the Style Name box, choose the name of the style that you want to link into the header. In this case, that's Heading 1 (see Figure 19.3). Click OK.

Figure 19.3
The StyleRef field can refer to any of the styles in the document.

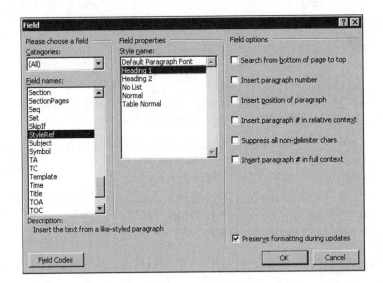

Word inserts a {STYLEREF "Heading 1"} field in the header (or footer). Every time Word encounters the field, it finds the first "Heading 1" paragraph on the page, and turns the text from the paragraph into the field result. If there is no "Heading 1" paragraph on the current page, Word scans backward through the document toward the beginning until it encounters that style, and uses that text as the field result.

DISPLAYING DOCUMENT PROPERTIES

Word provides dozens of additional fields that retrieve data associated with a document. You've already seen these fields:

■ {CreateDate}, {SaveDate}, and {PrintDate}, all discussed in the "Showing Dates and Times" section earlier in this chapter.

■ {Page}, {NumPages}, and {SectionPages}, all discussed in "Page Numbering" earlier in this chapter.

- The {Ref} and {StyleRef} fields, which retrieve bookmarked text and words or paragraphs formatted with specific styles, as described in the preceding section.

In addition, Word lets you retrieve all the information from the Properties dialog box that appears when you choose File, Properties (see Table 19.5).

TABLE 19.5   FILE PROPERTIES AVAILABLE VIA FIELDS

Field	Meaning
Author*	From the Summary tab.
Comments*	From the Summary tab.
EditTime	Total editing time from the Statistics tab.
FileName	Filename from the General tab. Check the Add Path to Filename box in the Field dialog box to show the filename with full path.
FileSize	Size of the file from the General tab. Check one of the boxes in the Field Options section to show the size in KB or MB.
Keywords*	From the Summary tab.
LastSavedBy	From the Statistics tab. Word keeps track of the last person to save the file by using the name in the User Information tab on the Options dialog box (choose Tools, Options to get there).
NumChars	Number of characters (excluding spaces) from the Statistics tab. Use DocProperty (described later in this section) to retrieve the number of characters with spaces.
NumWords	Number of words from the Statistics tab. Might or might not match your word count, because of the way Word defines a "word."
RevNum	"Revision" number from the Statistics tab. Actually has nothing to do with revisions and instead counts the number of times the document has been saved.
Subject*	From the Summary tab.
Template	Name of the file's template, from the Summary tab. Check the Add Path to Filename box to return full path as well. If the file is a template, returns the name of the file.
Title*	From the Summary tab.

Caution

The first time Word updates the NumChars field, it will be low by the number of characters in the NumChars field's result! To see a number identical to the one on the Statistics tab, you must update the field twice.

Fields that appear in Table 19.6 with an asterisk can be set, as well as referenced. For example, the field

```
{Author}
```

yields a field result that's identical to the contents of the Author box on the Summary tab of the File Properties dialog box. However, the field

```
{Author "Mark Twain"}
```

sets the Author value on the Summary tab to Mark Twain, *and* displays that result in the document.

Tip from

EQ & Woody

There's a tricky, effective, and thoroughly undocumented (until now anyway) method for prompting the user to fill in any of these modifiable file properties. For details, skip ahead to "Prompting for Input" later in this chapter.

Several of the values that appear in the File Properties dialog box don't have fields associated with them directly. Most of them can be accessed through the DocProperty field. For example, this field

```
{DocProperty "Paragraphs"}
```

shows the number of paragraphs in the current document, as it appears on the Statistics tab. (Like the NumChars field, this field must also be updated twice to get an accurate value.) To get to all the DocProperty settings, choose Insert, Field, and choose DocProperty in the Field Names box.

PERFORMING MATHEMATICAL CALCULATIONS

Word has dozens of operators and functions that let you perform (almost) any kind of mathematical calculation. But just because the capability exists, doesn't mean you should use it. In all but the most elementary cases, you're much better off working with a tool more suited to calculations, such as Excel 2002 or your trusty calculator. There are three general areas in which using fields to perform calculations makes sense:

- When you have a Word table that requires extremely simple mathematics, such as adding up a row or column of numbers. If you need anything more complex, use Excel.

- Inside simple data-entry forms, as discussed in "Creating a Data-Entry Form" later in this chapter. Note, however, that VBA/Word provides much more powerful and reliable calculation capabilities with its custom dialog boxes (UserForms).

→ For more information about creating custom dialog boxes with VBA and Word, **see** "Creating Custom Dialog Boxes," **p. 1026**.

- When you need to retrieve data that has been bookmarked in Word, to perform straightforward calculations.

The Word "Formula" field is indicated by an equal sign. When Word sees a field like this

```
{ = ....}
```

it knows to calculate the value inside the field.

Say you have a Word document that lists medical insurance reimbursements. The document prints on a preprinted form with a perforated check at the bottom. You want Word to generate the check amounts automatically, reflecting the total amount due, minus a $50 deductible. If the total amount due is covered by a bookmark called TotDue, this field could appear on the check, to print the amount due with a leading dollar sign

```
{ = TotDue - 50 \# $,0.00 }
```

and then this field could go on the next line, to print the amount due in words:

```
{ = TotDue - 50 \* dollartext \*caps }
```

To perform calculations, you can mix bookmark names with all the common mathematical symbols. All these are valid calculation fields, providing the referenced bookmarks exist, and will produce the results you expect:

```
{ = (3*Book1) + Book2 } { = Book79 ^ 2 } { = - Book15 + Book27 }
```

Tip from

EQ & Woody

If the bookmark covers a series of numbers, Word adds them together before applying the calculations in the field. If the bookmark covers characters, it's assigned a value of zero.

The most useful Word field operators are listed in Table 19.6.

TABLE 19.6   WORD FIELD OPERATORS

Operator	Meaning
Abs(x)	Absolute value of x
Int(x)	The integer part of x, discards the fractional part
Mod(x,y)	x modulo y, which is the remainder when x is divided by y
Round(x,y)	Round off x to y decimal places
Sign(x)	1 if x is > 0, –1 if x < 0, and 0 if x = 0
Average(x,y,…)	Average of items in the list
Count(x,y,…)	The number of items in the list
Max(x,y,…)	The largest value in the list
Min(x,y,…)	The smallest value in the list
Product(x,y,…)	Multiplies all the values in the list
Sum(x,y,…)	Adds all the values in the list

When you're working inside a table, you can use the special "bookmarks" listed in Table 19.7.

TABLE 19.7 BOOKMARKS AVAILABLE INSIDE A TABLE

Bookmark Name	Meaning
A1	Upper-left cell; cells are numbered as in Excel so you can refer to, for example, B4 and get the fourth row, second column.
B:B	The entire B column.
3:3	The entire 3rd row.
A2:C5	A 12-cell range, as in Excel.
Above	All cells above the current cell.
Below	All cells below the current cell.
Left	All cells to the left of the current cell.
Right	All cells to the right of the current cell.

So, for example, if this field appears in a table:

`{ = Sum(Left) }`

the field result is the sum of all the cells immediately to its left.

By far the easiest way to put formulas into tables is to choose Table, Formula and use the Formula dialog box (see Figure 19.4). This is the same box you'll see if you choose Insert, Field; bring up "= (Formula)" in the Field Names box; and then click Formula.

Figure 19.4
The Formula dialog box handles simple { = } Formula fields.

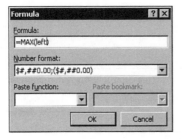

Although the dialog box helps keep you from misspelling the built-in functions and offers a little support for number formatting, it doesn't hold a candle to Excel's capabilities. You should rely on Excel for anything but the simplest calculations.

→ For detailed instructions on inserting an Excel worksheet range into a Word document, **see** "Combining Two or More Data Types in One Document," **p. 142**.

MANAGING CUSTOM NUMERIC SEQUENCES

Word supports a variety of built-in paragraph numbering schemes via the Bullets and Numbering dialog box. For custom numbering tasks, there are two fields you can use to create your own numbering schemes and maintain them throughout a document. If you work in a legal office, these capabilities might be the single most important feature in Word:

- The {ListNum} field works wonders in custom-generated paragraph numbering schemes, particularly the type of numbering schemes you'll find in legal documents.

- The {Seq} field, on the other hand, helps you maintain sequences of numbers that are (typically) independent of paragraph numbering.

USING {LISTNUM} TO CREATE SOPHISTICATED NUMBERING SCHEMES

{ListNum} fields can adhere to one of three numbering schemes, per Table 19.8.

TABLE 19.8   {LISTNUM} NUMBERING SCHEMES

Level	Number	Outline	Legal
1	1)	I.	1.
2	a)	A.	1.1.
3	i)	1.	1.1.1.
4	(1)	a)	1.1.1.1.
5	(a)	(1)	1.1.1.1.1.
6	(i)	(a)	1.1.1.1.1.1.
7	1.	(i)	1.1.1.1.1.1.1.
8	a.	(a)	1.1.1.1.1.1.1.1.
9	i.	(i)	1.1.1.1.1.1.1.1.1.

The {ListNum} field allows you to build complex and sophisticated numbering sequences, which are sensitive to both other {ListNum} fields and to the position of the {ListNum} field in a sentence. Detailing {ListNum}'s capabilities could take a chapter by itself, but to get a glimpse of its power, try these experiments:

- Put a {ListNum} field at the beginning of a blank paragraph. Select the field, and use the Increase Indent or Decrease Indent buttons to change the level of the field—and thus the format of the number.

- Insert several {ListNum} fields in a paragraph, interspersed with text. Click and drag the text with its associated {ListNum} field. All the fields will be renumbered automatically.

- Put a bookmark on a {ListNum} field, and use a {Ref} field (or Insert, Cross-Reference) to refer to the field. Then move the {ListNum} field and update the document. The reference will be updated as well. This is the kind of approach you can use to keep references such as "see paragraph III (173) A (3) iii" in sync. If you set up the reference to use a {Ref} field, and the {Ref} field points to a bookmark over a (potentially quite complex) {ListNum} or series of {ListNum} fields, if you move the fields, the reference changes automatically. So if the previously mentioned paragraph is moved and suddenly becomes paragraph III (172) A (3) iii, the reference will be automatically updated to say "see paragraph III (172) A (3) iii."

- The {ListNum} field has two switches. The \s switch tells Word what number to start at (so you can being numbering at any point). Usually, {ListNum} senses its level in the list by its position within a paragraph, and the presence of {ListNum} fields before it. The \l switch allows you to manually override {ListNum}'s level auto-sensing capabilities.

Note

To see more information about {ListNum} (but, tragically, only a small glimpse of its power), refer to Microsoft Knowledge Base article Q162895.

USING {SEQ} TO COUNT AUTOMATICALLY

By contrast, {Seq} fields are straightforward. You have to make up an "identifier" (or use one of the built-in identifiers provided by Word) to keep the various sequences in a document straight. For example, you might add this text with field codes at the start of a document:

```
Refer to folders {Seq FolderNumber} and {Seq FolderNumber}
```

The field results will look like this:

```
Refer to folders 1 and 2
```

Note

You cannot use {Seq} fields in headers or footers.

The next time Word encounters a {Seq FolderNumber} field, it will produce the value 3, then 4, and so on. This technique can be extremely useful if, for example, you want to number illustrations in a manuscript sequentially. If you use a field such as

```
Illustration Number {Seq IllustrationNo} - Monet
```

in the caption above or below each illustration, Word numbers the illustrations sequentially:

```
Illustration Number 77 - Monet
```

Then if you reorder the illustrations—move a few around, delete some, and add some others throughout the document—all you have to do is press Ctrl+A to select the entire document, and then press F9 to update the fields. Word renumbers the illustrations, starting at 1 and continuing sequentially throughout the document.

Moreover, if you use one of the three identifiers that Word recognizes—Figure, Table, or Equation—your {Seq Figure}, {Seq Table}, and {Seq Equation} fields can dovetail into Word's built-in features for generating cross-references, such as (See Figure 17 on page 22), and tables of figures.

Tip from

E & Woody

If you choose Insert, Field, and pick Seq from the list of Field names, you'll have to click the Field Codes button in the lower-left corner of the Field dialog box to get at the extensive {Seq} Options. Clicking the Caption button merely moves you to the Caption dialog box, which you would normally see if you chose Insert, Reference, Caption.

{Seq} fields recognize five switches; the three you'll commonly use are shown in Table 19.9.

TABLE 19.9   COMMON {SEQ} FIELD SWITCHES

Switch	Meaning
\c	Repeat the previous sequence number; don't increment the counter
\h	Hide the field and its results
\r val	Reset the sequence number to val

So, for example, this series of {Seq} fields starting at the beginning of a document:

{Seq MyId} {Seq MyId \c} {Seq MyId} {Seq MyId \r 8} {Seq MyId}

produces this as the field result:

1 1 2 8 9

Tip from

E & Woody

If you have a long document, with more than one chapter, and you want to reset the Figure sequence so it starts at Figure 1 at the beginning of each chapter, put a field that looks like this at the beginning of each chapter:

{Seq Figure \h \r 0 }

To see an innovative use for the \h switch, see the next section.

Note

There's extensive discussion of a Bookmark parameter for the {Seq} field in older versions of the online Help (and in most Office books, for that matter). The old online help is totally wrong, and any lazy author who parrots those help files deserves to be horsewhipped. If you want to refer to bookmarked information, use the {Ref} field, as described earlier in this chapter.

PROMPTING FOR INPUT

Word supports two fields that prompt for user input. Typically, you would use the {Ask} and {Fillin} fields in a template or a mail-merge master document to ask the person creating a new document or performing the merge for additional information:

PART
III

CH
19

- A {Fillin} field in a template, for example, can prompt the user to type in keywords or other data that can be placed in the File Properties dialog box. Each time a new document is created based on the template, the {Fillin} field is updated, and the user sees the prompt.

- An {Ask} field in a mail merge can pause the merge on every record, prompting the user to type in information specific to the record—say, a past-due amount, or a personalized message in a greeting card—and have that information repeated several places in the merged document.

→ To put {Fillin} and {Ask} fields to work, **see** "Customizing Form Letters with Fields," **p. 527**.

When you update an {Ask} field, it stores the results in a bookmark in the document. When you update a {Fillin} field, Word uses the typed text as the field result. So the field

```
{ Ask DueDate "Enter the due date:" }
```

replaces whatever was in the DueDate bookmark with what the user typed. And the field

```
{ Fillin "Enter account number" }
```

displays whatever the user types as the field code's result.

The {Fillin} field, in particular, can be manipulated in many useful ways. For example, the

```
{ KeyWords "new key words" }
```

field can set the value of the Keywords box in the Properties dialog box. Say you have a template that your company uses all the time, but people forget to fill out the Keywords box most of the time—making it difficult to search for documents. Put this field at the beginning of the template:

```
{Keywords {Fillin "Please provide document keywords:"}}
```

Every time a new document is created based on the template, Word first updates the {Fillin} field by prompting the user (see Figure 19.5).

Figure 19.5
When Word updates a {Fillin} field, it prompts the user for input.

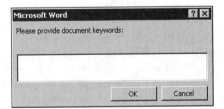

Then Word updates the {Keywords} field, inserting the keywords typed by the user into the Keywords box in File Properties. Unfortunately, the result of the {Fillin} field will show in the new document. Fortunately, you can use the {Seq} field to hide it. To prompt the user for keywords in a new document, all you need is this nested field in the template:

```
{Seq \h {Keywords {Fillin "Please provide document keywords:"}}}
```

You can do the same for any of the file properties listed with an asterisk in Table 19.5 earlier in this chapter.

TABLE OF CONTENTS AND INDEX FIELDS

Word creates Tables of Contents and Indexes using fields, as well. There's a wealth of information about those fields—{tc}, {toc}, {ie}, {xe}, and the like—in the online help.

In general, the Table of Contents options are handled so well with the built-in TOC tools (choose Insert, Reference, Index and Tables, and click the Table of Contents tab) that dealing with individual fields is time-consuming and won't buy you much.

By contrast, Word's indexing tools (Insert, Reference, Index and Tables, and click the Index tab) are so woefully inadequate that all the field codes in the world won't accomplish much. Avoid them if you possibly can. If you're serious about indexing, buy an add-on package that can read Word files.

CREATING A DATA-ENTRY FORM

Word contains extensive tools for building forms that you can use in a number of ways:

- You can create a form that's designed to be printed and subsequently filled out with a pen or a typewriter. Typically, you'll create and maintain such a form as a standard Word document.

- You can make a form that's designed to be filled out online (by using either Word or a Web browser). The user fills in the missing information—say, customer name and line items for an invoice, or payment instructions for a statement—and then prints the form. These kinds of forms are almost invariably set up as templates, with portions of the form (say, the return address) "locked" so the user can't alter them. When the form is filled out (as in Figure 19.6), it can be printed, saved, or handled like any other document.

Figure 19.6
A custom invoice form created and saved as a template can be filled out and mailed to a customer.

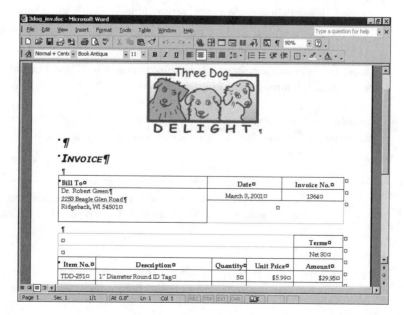

PART
III

CH
19

Tip from
EQ & Woody

> Although Word can certainly perform most of the functions required of these online forms, if the people filling out the forms will be using Word, you should consider using custom dialog boxes in VBA/Word for this type of work. VBA/Word has a great deal of power not available directly in Word forms, and has the added benefit of a full development and testing environment, which Word forms can't begin to match.

- You might post a more sophisticated online form on your company's Web site, so a potential customer could fill in her name and address, and request a catalog. The information would be sent by e-mail to someone inside your company. These forms exist as Word HTML documents, and must include a Submit or Image Submit button, so the form results can be transmitted by e-mail.

- At the highest end of the chain, you can create Word forms that interact directly with a database so, for example, a customer participating in your company's extranet can enter orders directly, and have your internal order database updated without any further human intervention.

The tools you use to create all four types of forms reside on the Forms toolbar and, perhaps, the Control Toolbox toolbar.

To create one of the more complex data-entry forms, which is designed to be filled out online by Word users, follow these steps:

1. To create a new template, choose File, New; click the General Templates item in the New from Template list in the New Document task pane; choose Template in the Create New box at the lower right of the Templates dialog box; and click OK.

2. Put together the form's static elements—the parts that won't change each time the form is used. This might include a logo, return address, tables, questions, and descriptions.

3. Use the Forms toolbar or the Control Toolbox toolbar to place form fields on the form.

4. When you're done, click the Protect Form button on the Forms toolbar. That will keep users from altering any static information in the form: They'll be limited to making changes in the form fields you have specified.

If you then save the template in some readily accessible location, users can create a new document based on the template, fill out the template, print it, and save it, much as they would any other document.

Tip from
EQ & Woody

> If you need to make changes to the template, you'll have to click the Protect Form button again before Word will allow you to change any static portions.

Data-entry form design techniques, and the characteristics of many individual controls on the Forms toolbar, are covered in detail in this book's discussion of Excel data-entry forms.

→ For details from an Excel point of view, **see** "Using Forms to Add and Edit List Data," **p. 691**.

Form controls available on the Control Toolbox toolbar—check boxes and option buttons, drop-down lists, list boxes, text boxes, and the like—are standard HTML form controls. As such, they have properties and generate events that can be controlled in VBScript and JScript applications. These properties and events are detailed in the online Help under the topic "Form controls you can use on a Web page."

TROUBLESHOOTING

TIME AND DATE DISCREPANCIES

I entered a {Time} field in my document, but when I update it, the field displays a date.

To solve the problem, remove the \l switches in your {date} and {time} fields. If you don't understand how the \l switch works, bizarre consequences like this are nearly inevitable. If you use the Date and Time dialog box to insert a time in a document, all the {Time \l} fields will, when updated, show a time. If you then use the same dialog box to insert a date in your document, all the {Date \l} fields, when updated, will show a date.

SECRETS OF THE OFFICE MASTERS: PUTTING THE {LISTNUM} FIELD TO WORK

The {ListNum} field offers a nearly infinite variety of formatting options. To see its most basic capability—that of consecutively numbered items inside paragraphs—consider the following figure.

The first time a {ListNum} field appears in a paragraph, it's at the highest numbering level—that's what creates a 1) in the first paragraph and a 2) in the second. The second (and subsequent) times a {ListNum} field appears, it's assumed to be at the second level—thus the a), b), c), and so on.

If you move any second-level phrases around in the paragraph, Word automatically renumbers the phrases to reflect their new location.

To create a third-level {ListNum} field, insert it into a paragraph, and then click the Increase Indent toolbar button. (You can use the \l switch in the field to increase the level, but clicking the Increase Indent button is much simpler.) Third-level {ListNum} fields increment until a second-level field is encountered.

Note

This figure also shows how turning off the Show Windows in Taskbar option will help in displaying more than one document onscreen at a time. To make room for more document and less overhead, choose Tools, Options; and on the View tab, clear the box marked Windows in Taskbar.

Figure 19.7

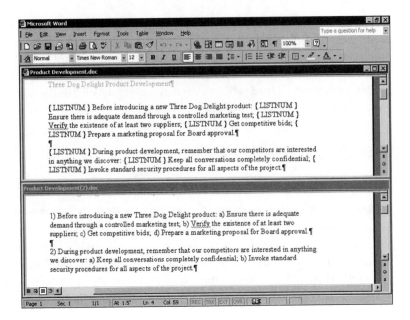

CHAPTER 20

MERGING DATA AND DOCUMENTS

In this chapter

MERGING DATA TO CREATE CUSTOM REPORTS AND LETTERS

Most Word users think of *mail merge* as a synonym for "form letters" or "junk mail." Although it's true that Word can churn out form letters and bulk mailings until the cows come home, the term *mail merge* only hints at what you can do with this capability.

At its most basic, a mail-merge operation consists of two parts—a database and a document—and the "merge" just brings the two together. The database can contain just about anything—names and addresses are the most common contents, of course, but you can also stuff the database with product names, court case citations, serial numbers, invoices, test scores, or anything else you can fit into a database record.

The document, too, can take just about any imaginable form—yes, the first thing you think of is likely to be a form letter, but you can also add fields from your database to an envelope, catalog, e-mail or fax message, telephone book, Web page, financial report, stock inventory, or time log. For that matter, the "document" could simply be a text file, enabling you to use a mail merge to create a new database from an old one.

Although Word doesn't have the extensive merging capabilities of a full-strength database manager such as Access, it's the best tool to choose when you need to produce a document or series of documents based on data in a reasonably clean list. On the other hand, if you need to manipulate data extensively, or your primary goal is to produce bare-bones printed reports, the tools in Access or Excel are more appropriate.

Word's mail-merge features come in handy in a variety of circumstances. When you're working with form letters going out to a mailing list, Word lets you

- Sort and/or filter the incoming data, removing records according to field-level criteria you establish (for example, you could specify "Only include people in New York or New Jersey").
- Print envelopes or mailing labels, with USPS Postnet postal bar codes. You can even interleave the form letters with envelopes—print an envelope, then its letter, then the next envelope and its letter, and so on—using an undocumented technique discussed under "Merge Envelopes" later in this chapter.
- Force the merge process to pause at each record, to enable you to type in custom information. Use this technique if you're producing a holiday newsletter, for example, and you want to add some unique content for each recipient.

When you move beyond basic form letters, Word's mail-merge capabilities let you

- Send similar, but customized, e-mail messages or faxes to a large number of people.
- Create a product catalog, parts list, or price sheet from a list (or database) of individual products.
- Create an organization membership roster or telephone book from a list (or database) of members.

Word contains extensive support for running mail merges, embodied in the Mail Merge Wizard (which looks just like a task pane). To get to it, click Tools, Letters and Mailings, Mail Merge Wizard. The wizard handles almost every merge problem you're likely to encounter (see Figure 20.1).

Figure 20.1
The Mail Merge Wizard—the first wizard Microsoft ever created—appears as a task pane.

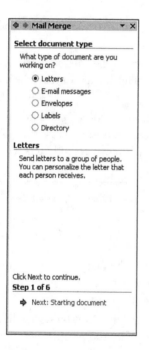

Although the wizard has its share of idiosyncrasies, it makes perfect sense after you've learned how to use it.

Each of the major types of mail merge is a bit different—Letters, E-mail messages, Envelopes, Labels, and Directories—so we're going to deal with each one separately.

USING MAIL MERGE TO PERSONALIZE FORM LETTERS

By far the most common mail merge scenario involves a form letter, a database, and a printer. You have a database of names and addresses, most likely in an Outlook Contacts list, but possibly in the form of an Access database, Excel list, or simple tab-delimited format. And you have a form letter (or at least an idea of what you want to write). That's all you need: In Word-speak, you have a data source and a main merge document. The rest is just juggling.

The general procedure goes like this (you'll get additional details and important suggestions for each of these steps in the rest of this chapter):

1. Bring up the Mail Merge Wizard by choosing Tools, Letters and Mailings, Mail Merge Wizard. In the wizard's first step, choose Letters.

2. Pick a document, or create a new one, to use as the "merge document"—the boilerplate skeleton that will drive the merge. Then attach a data source—the list or database to be merged—to the form letter.

3. Use the Mail Merge task pane, er, wizard, to put merge fields in the form letter. They'll appear something like this: <<Address Block>>, or <<First Name>> <<Last Name>>. Then use the wizard to preview how the first few merged letters will appear.

Note
You can't just type the << and >> marks: Word has to insert them for you, via buttons in the Mail Merge Wizard.

4. If you want to exclude certain records from the merge, or sort them so that the letters print in a particular sequence (ZIP Code order, for example), use the Mail Merge Wizard's Edit Recipient List option to set them up.

5. On the Mail Merge Wizard's final pane, click the Edit individual letters option so Word will merge the form letters to a new file, and save the new merged file. Before you print the file, go through it and make sure it doesn't contain any surprises. When you're satisfied that everything is correct, start printing.

Tip from
EQ & Woody

Long merge print jobs can pose all sorts of mechanical challenges, from toner cartridges running down to buffer overflows to massive paper jams. If the merged file contains more than a few hundred pages, consider printing a hundred or two at a time (choose File, Print, and enter a range in the Pages box).

For important mailings, keep the merged file handy until the mailing has been delivered to the post office—or better yet, until you're certain that most addressees have received their copies.

The merged document consists of multiple sections—one section per input record. That can cause unexpected problems if you try to use an advanced technique to get particular pages to print.

→ If you get stuck working on multiple sections, **see** "Formatting Documents by Section," **p. 407**.

CREATING THE FORM LETTER

When creating a main merge document, all Word's tools are at your disposal. You can adjust formatting, insert pictures, create headers and footers, add tables and fields, and work with objects in the drawing layer. For example, you might choose to insert your company's logo in the letter (see Figure 20.2), or use a callout AutoShape to draw attention to a specific selling point.

Figure 20.2
The second step of the Mail Merge Wizard, for form letters, has you put together a main merge document.

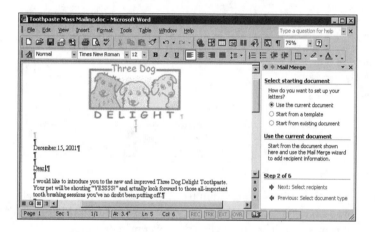

→ To work with AutoShapes, **see** "Working with AutoShapes," **p. 111**.

When you're satisfied with the content of your form letter, choose Next: Select Recipients at the bottom of the task pane, and start adding merge data.

SPECIFYING A SOURCE FOR NAMES AND ADDRESSES

After you have the static part of the form letter complete, you have to tell Word where to pick up the data that will be merged. In fact, at this point, Word just needs the data field names—last name, first name, address, and so on—but the Mail Merge Wizard takes advantage of the moment to have you select the data source.

Tip from

EQ & Woody

It's an often-overlooked point, but the biggest problem you're likely to encounter at this juncture is the lack of a specific data field, or a poorly defined field. For example, if your form letter demands an "Amount Due" in each letter, you better have a data file handy that includes an "Amount Due" for each customer.

The Mail Merge Wizard gives you three choices:

- **Use an Existing List**—If you have an existing data source, whether it's a table in a Word document, a list in an Excel workbook, or an Access database, use this option. If the first row of the Word table or Excel list includes field names (Last Name, First Name, and so on), you'll be able to merge immediately. Click Browse and retrieve the list.

- **Select from Outlook Contacts**—Make this choice and Word imports the data directly from Outlook. Click Choose Contacts Folder and pick the Contacts list that you want to use (see Figure 20.3).

Figure 20.3
The Mail Merge List of Recipients is generated from your Outlook Contacts list. Click the appropriate column heading to sort the list.

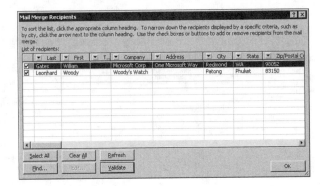

- **Type a New List**—This option (see Figure 20.4) brings up a useful Data Form that allows you to create your own merge database on-the-fly. If you want to modify the field names and their order, click the Customize button.

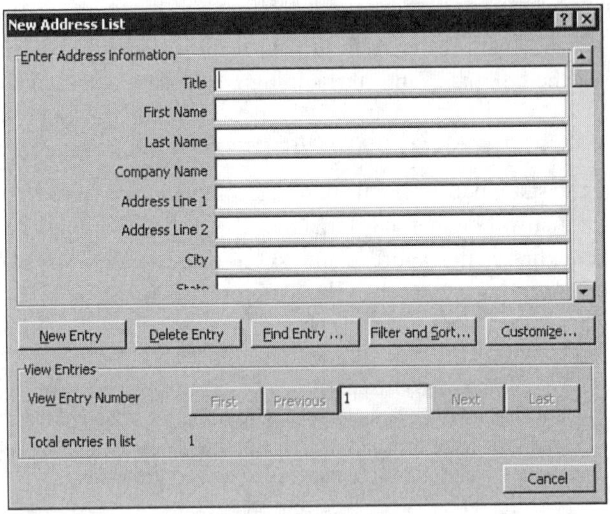

Figure 20.4
The New Address List allows you to build a merge data document on-the-fly. The address list is an .mdb file that you can edit with Access.

PLACING DATA FIELDS WITHIN YOUR DOCUMENT

Now that Word knows what data you're going to use, it can help you put merge data into your document. Data fields represent the link between your form letter and the data source. For example, if you have a data source field called Last Name, Word replaces every occurrence of the field <<Last Name>> in the form letter with the Last Name data in the current record of the data source.

The easiest way to insert data fields into your form letter is via Step 4 of the Mail Merge Wizard. Place the insertion point wherever you want a data field to appear, click Insert Merge Field, and choose the field you need. Word has a particularly helpful merge field called Address block, which you can use to overcome several problems that are commonly encountered when importing Outlook Contacts data into Word (see Figure 20.5).

Figure 20.5
Word now has the capability to suppress the country name for specific countries during a mail merge.

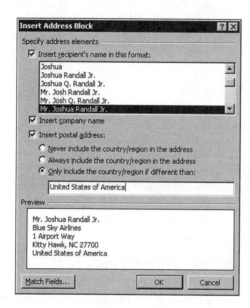

Remember that you have to provide the punctuation if it isn't included in the data source. A typical letter opening might look like this:

<<AddressBlock>>

Dear <<Title>> <<Last>>:

Tip from

EQ & Woody

You can put the same data field in the form letter as often as you like. If you're preparing a promotional letter to customers in a specific region, for example, you might include the <<City>> field in the address block and in the text of the letter itself: "All our customers who live in <<City>> are entitled to an extra discount this month only."

PREVIEWING MAIL MERGE RESULTS

To see how the merge will progress, start by having Word show you what the result will be when you merge live data with your form letter. To do so, go on to Step 5 of the Mail Merge Wizard, and click the Next Record button repeatedly to see how the records appear (see Figure 20.6).

Figure 20.6
Word lets you preview your form letter with live data, stepping through each data source record.

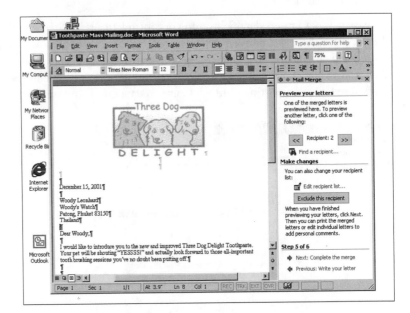

Use this preview to check for gross errors:

- Look for incorrect fields—for example, those using <<First>> where you really wanted <<Last>>.

- Identify unreliable data source information; if half of your data source records don't have an entry in the <<Title>> field, for example, you need to find a way to work around the problem.

- If you see any parts of the merge that just don't look right—if some of the merged letters flop over to two pages, for example—click Edit Recipient List and try to jury-rig the data so it fits.

When all looks well, go on to Step 6 in the wizard, and click Edit Individual Letters. Before you print the resulting document, which has all the merged letters head-to-toe, examine it closely for any unexpected and unwelcome merge results.

Tip from

EQ & Woody

In general, you should avoid merging directly to the printer. Creating a merge file first lets you easily recover from mechanical disasters—you can reprint letters 1378 to 1392, for example, if the printer runs out of toner or the person carrying the envelopes to the post office drops them in the mud.

MASS E-MAILING AND FAXING WITH OUTLOOK AND MAIL MERGE

If you use Outlook 2002, creating personalized mass e-mailings and faxes is almost as simple as creating and merging a form letter. Here's how:

1. For either mass e-mail or faxes, choose E-mail messages in the first step of the Mail Merge Wizard. Complete the e-mail message or fax as if it were a form letter, using the instructions in the preceding section.

2. Attach a recipient list and preview the messages or faxes with live data in Step 5 of the wizard.

3. In the final step of the Mail Merge Wizard, choose to merge to Electronic Mail. In the Merge to E-mail dialog box (see Figure 20.7), choose which Outlook Contact field you want to merge to. Most often, you'll either choose E-mail_Address or Business_Fax. Type a subject, if you like, and click OK.

Figure 20.7
If you want to send the same fax to many people, tell the Mail Merge Wizard that you want to create e-mail messages, and then choose Business_Fax in this very last step.

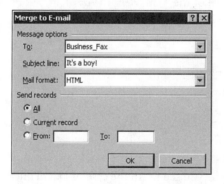

4. Word performs the merge, and transfers the merged e-mail messages or faxes to your Outlook outbox.

The next time you use Outlook to send mail, the e-mail messages or faxes will be sent in the usual way.

Tip from EQ & Woody

High-volume unsolicited e-mail—better known as spam—is almost universally detested, even when it's personalized. Sending unsolicited e-mail might violate local and federal laws.

CREATING DIRECTORIES

The only real difference between the way Word handles form letters and the way it handles merged "directories" (in previous versions of Word, they were called "catalogs") lies in the way Word uses page breaks. In a form letter, Word inserts a page break (actually, a "next page" section break) after it finishes processing a record from the data source. In a directory, Word doesn't add page breaks; as a result, one record follows another in the finished document.

→ You can also use Outlook's built-in printing capabilities to produce phone lists, even on Day-Timer sheets; for details, **see** "Printing Phone Lists from Your Contacts List," **p. 307.**

Say you want to print a custom report of all the people in your Outlook Contacts list, in which several records appear on a page—perhaps in your own version of a Day-Timer-like format. Here's how you do it:

1. Start a new document as described in the preceding sections, but in the first step of the Mail Merge Wizard, choose Directory. That tells Word you want to put more than one record on a page.
2. Add the fields by using Step 4 of the Mail Merge Wizard, as before. A typical MyTimer page might look like Figure 20.8.

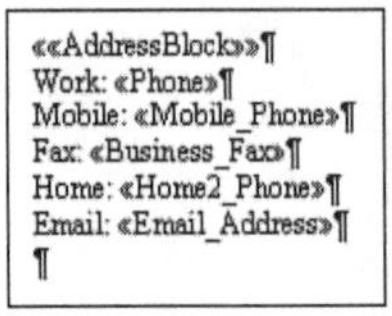
«AddressBlock»¶
Work: «Phone»¶
Mobile: «Mobile_Phone»¶
Fax: «Business_Fax»¶
Home: «Home2_Phone»¶
Email: «Email_Address»¶
¶

Figure 20.8
Custom Outlook Contacts reports are much easier to configure in Word than in Outlook itself—if you know how to merge.

3. Adjust the document any way you see fit. In the case of Day-Timer-like reports, you might want to create multiple columns, change the page size, and/or set the paper source to print on special drilled sheets.

Tip from EQ & Woody

To control page breaks in directory-style merges such as this one, use the paragraph formatting property Keep with Next. In this case, you might put an empty paragraph mark at the end of all the data lines. Then select the data lines (*not* the final paragraph mark); choose Format, Paragraph; click the Line and Page Breaks tab; and check the Keep with Next box to ensure records don't break across pages.

4. Have Word merge to a new document. You'll probably want to print in duplex style—that is, using both sides of each sheet of paper. To do so, choose File, Print, and check the Manual Duplex box in the Print dialog box.

ADVANCED MAIL MERGE TECHNIQUES

Mail merge works by using Word fields specially designed for implementing a merge. To see those fields, open a main merge document and press Alt+F9, or choose Tools, Options; click the View tab; and check the Field Codes box (see Figure 20.9).

Figure 20.9
Main merge docu-
ments contain fields
that dictate how the
merge should hap-
pen.

{ ADDRESSBLOCK \f "<< _TITLE0_ >><< _FIRST0_ >><< _LAST0_ >><< _SUFFIX0 >>¶
<< _COMPANY_ ¶
>><< _STREET1_ ¶
>><< _STREET2_ ¶
>><< _CITY_ >><<, _STATE_ >><< _POSTAL_ >><<¶
COUNTRY >>" \l 1033 \c 2 \e "United States of America" }¶
Work: { MERGEFIELD "Phone" }¶
Mobile: { MERGEFIELD "Mobile_Phone" }¶
Fax: { MERGEFIELD "Business_Fax" }¶
Home: { MERGEFIELD "Home2_Phone" }¶
Email: { MERGEFIELD "Email_Address" }¶
¶

In many cases, you'll be able to get satisfactory results with a merge by using the Mail Merge toolbar to manipulate these fields. In some more advanced cases, however, you might find yourself operating on the fields directly.

→ To learn how to manually manipulate fields, **see** "Some Useful Custom Fields," **p. 496**.

MERGE ENVELOPES

Running a merge to generate envelopes that match one-for-one with a form letter run isn't difficult, as long as you go to great pains to ensure that the data source doesn't change between the time you run the form letters and the time you print the envelopes, and that the filters you specify are identical.

Tip from
EQ & Woody

Beware of paper jams, because one missing or one extra letter or envelope can throw off the entire sequence. If a jam should occur, mark that point in the run—with a paper clip, for example. After you've finished running both letters and envelopes, go back to the marked points and ensure you have one—and only one—letter for each envelope.

To start an envelope run, use the Mail Merge Wizard and select Envelopes as the document type in the first step. If you use the Envelope Wizard and tell it you want to create envelopes for a mailing list, it launches the Mail Merge Wizard automatically. To start this wizard, choose File, New. On the New Document task pane, choose General Templates, and then on the Letters & Faxes tab, double-click Envelope Wizard.

Note

There's a much more powerful and flexible envelope mail merge routine built into Enveloper, one of the WOPR (see Appendix B, "What's on Que's WOPR XP/2002 Pack."

There's an alternative (and undocumented) method for generating envelopes at the same time you do the main form letter run. This method creates envelopes interleaved with the form letters—you get an envelope and its letter, the next record's envelope and its letter, and so on. As long as you have a printer with separate feeders for the form letter paper and the envelopes—most laser printers pull envelopes from a different location than the standard paper trays anyway—the technique works, and it could save you a great deal of frustration with mismatched envelopes and form letters. Here's how to do it:

1. Create your form letter, following the instructions in the preceding sections.

2. At the end of the Wizard's Step 2, before you select recipients, choose Tools, Letters and Mailings, Envelopes and Labels. On the Envelopes tab (see Figure 20.10), set up the return address the way you want it. Then click Options and make sure the correct paper tray has been set up for your envelopes. *Do not click Print.* Instead, click Add to Document. The envelope appears above your form letter on the Word screen.

Figure 20.10
If you "add" an enve-lope to your form let-ter, merged envelopes and letters will print interleaved.

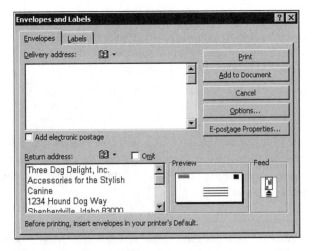

3. Attach the data source and place fields in your form letter as usual. When you're fin-ished with the letter, move up to the envelope and insert merge fields in the envelope, wherever you want them to appear (see Figure 20.11).

4. Merge to a file, as usual. When you print the file, envelopes appear before form letters, interspersed throughout the merge run.

Figure 20.11
Merge data fields go
into the envelope, just
as they would in the
form letter itself.

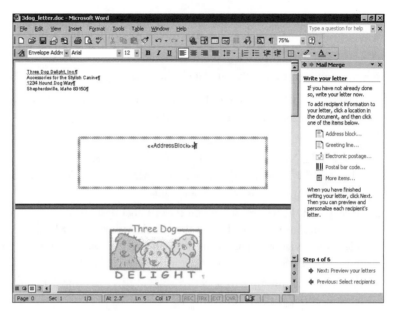

ADDING E-STAMPS TO ENVELOPES

Word has automatic hooks to several major vendors of electronic postage. If you sign up with one of these vendors, you can automatically generate electronic "stamps" for mail in general, and merged envelopes in particular. The electronic postage business is changing quickly, with companies altering their fees and payment structures almost as quickly as they can change their Web sites.

The simplest way to get the latest information about electronic postage firms that work with Word is to click the Electronic Postage option in Step 4 of the Mail Merge Wizard. You will be transported to the Microsoft Office Update page, which includes full details. Look for a heading that says "Print postage online" or some such; Microsoft places the topic in a general area called "eServices."

Tip from	Electronic postage is still in its infancy, and companies come and go. Make sure you don't pay for more postage than you can use in a reasonably short amount of time. And keep your ear to the ground to make sure the company you choose doesn't unexpectedly fold up shop.
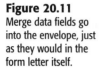	

MERGE LABELS

Word's features for creating mailing labels work well enough for small labels—that is, labels that are big enough to hold only the name and address. But if you're using preprinted labels, or if you have larger labels and want to print your return address or logo on them, or if you want to change the default font, you'll have nothing but problems (unless you know these tricks, of course).

To run a mail merge and generate labels the usual way:

1. Start the Mail Merge Wizard by choosing Tools, Letters and Mailings, Mail Merge Wizard, and then selecting Labels as the document type

   or

   choose File, New, on the New Document task pane, and click General Templates. Then, on the Letters & Faxes tab, select Mailing Label Wizard, and tell the Paper Clip that you want to create labels for a mailing list.

2. In Step 2 of the wizard, when you select Label options, you are prompted to supply the details for your mailing labels in the Label Options dialog box. In most cases, you can select a manufacturer and product number; most common preprinted labels, including those from Avery, the 800-pound gorilla of the industry, include built-in formats here.

3. Follow Word's prompts to select a recipient list. Place the data merge fields in the first label position, as shown in Figure 20.12.

Figure 20.12
Set up the first label with recipient information from the merge file.

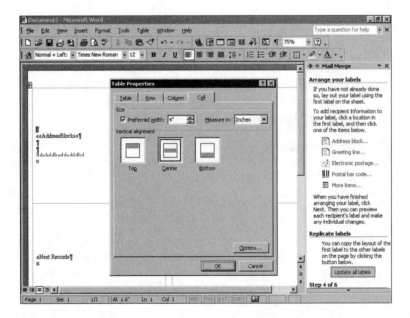

Note	Word automatically causes text in the label to "float up and down"—to be centered vertically. If you want the printing on your labels to always appear at the same location, choose Table, Properties, click the Cell tab, and choose Top or Bottom.

4. When you're happy with the first label, click the Update All Labels button at the bottom of the Mail Merge task pane. Finish the merge by using the techniques described earlier in this chapter. Preview the merge, merge to file, and print.

Tip from

EQ & Woody

Because the label form is just a table, you can divide the existing cells to better position text, graphics, or anything else on the label.

See "Secrets of the Office Masters: Professional Labels, Big Time" at the end of this chapter for an example of how Word's mail merge features can be used to create professional mailing labels.

CUSTOMIZING FORM LETTERS WITH FIELDS

Like so many other features in Word, merging occurs compliments of Word fields. All the various merge fields discussed in this chapter are just special types of Word fields—a small subset of all the fields available in Word. The Mail Merge Wizard simply puts a pretty face on the underlying fields: You get to use the merge fields without getting your hands dirty working with field codes, formatting switches, and the like. The fields themselves control all the nuances of merging. You can use any of Word's extensive collection of fields in mail merge documents.

Two fields come in handy if you want Word to pause the merge at each record, and let you type in custom data. Both {Ask} and {Fillin} request data for each merged record. The former places whatever you typed in a bookmarked location on the form letter; the latter replaces the field with what was typed.

To use the {Fillin} field:

1. Place the insertion point wherever you want the custom text to appear in the form letter.

2. Click Insert, Field, and then select Fill-in from the Field Name box (see Figure 20.13). Type in a suitable prompt and default text. (You can also use the Insert Word Field button on the Merge toolbar.)

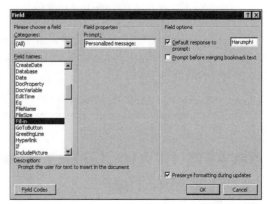

Figure 20.13

> **Note**
>
> Although the input box in the Field dialog box is small, you can type in lengthy default responses, providing they don't include carriage returns. There's a longer input box available if you use the Insert Word Field button on the Merge toolbar.

3. Perform the merge as usual. Each time Word encounters a {Fillin} field, once for each data source record, it prompts you for whatever custom text you want to provide.

For additional information on fields that apply specifically to mail merge, see the Help topic "Word fields for use in mail merge."

TROUBLESHOOTING

KEEPING TRACK OF LONG MERGES

When running a long mail merge, I need to make sure that letters were printed for everyone on my Contacts list.

As you'll soon discover, long merges are a horse of a different color. You'll find it very useful to put a record number on each merged item so, for example, you can look and see if the printer swallowed form letter number 2,481. To place a merge record number on a document, bring up the Mail Merge toolbar (right-click an empty area on any handy toolbar and choose Mail Merge). Click wherever you want the record number to appear in the document, choose Insert Word Field on the Mail Merge toolbar, and select Merge Record # from the list. See the following section for a suggestion on how to format merge record numbers.

My merged documents don't look right—the fields don't line up properly, or suddenly a line that should hold a person's name is showing a ZIP Code.

If your merge data file gets out of whack by one single entry, it can throw off an entire merge. The easiest way to do a quick check for data integrity is to run the Mail Merge Wizard through step 4 (so your merge document is set up), bring up the Mail Merge toolbar (right-click an empty area in a toolbar and pick Mail Merge), and click the Check for Errors button. Generally, if you ask Word to pause to report each error as it occurs, you'll find the problem in no time.

Check for Errors won't find fields that are improperly aligned. That still needs to be done by meticulously looking at every merged document.

SECRETS OF THE OFFICE MASTERS: PROFESSIONAL LABELS, BIG TIME

Use all the tricks in this chapter to create professional-looking mailing labels, and then add a few embellishments to create the ultimate label.

Use pictures, logos, or other catchy
material in the upper part of the label

Figure 20.14

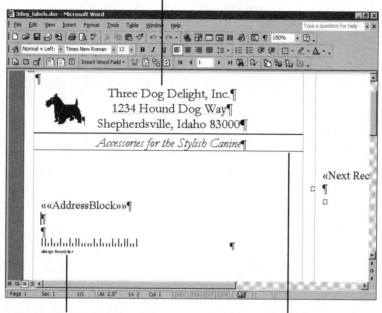

yourself some headaches on big
runs by placing the record number
e inconspicuous spot. In this case,
aced it at the bottom of the label
d formatted it as 4-point Arial

Word creates a table for labels,
and you can use any of the table
tools – drawing lines is a snap

USING EXCEL

CHAPTER 21

EXCEL ESSENTIALS

In this chapter

WORKING WITH WORKSHEETS AND WORKBOOKS

The basic building blocks of Excel haven't changed much in the past few versions of Office. Excel's default file format is still the *workbook* (file extension .xls), which can hold multiple *worksheets*. By default, each new Excel workbook starts out with three blank worksheets; an index tab at the bottom of each worksheet identifies the sheet by name. You can add a new worksheet, delete an existing worksheet, and rename or rearrange worksheets to suit your needs.

Multiple worksheets help keep complex projects organized within a single workbook. In a consolidated budget, for example, you might create a separate worksheet for each department's numbers, using identical templates to make sure each budget category appears in the same row and each month is in the same column; then use an identical template to create a summary worksheet that rolls up totals for the entire company. Placing related data tables on different sheets makes it easier to view, format, and print each type of data separately—for example, you might create a loan analysis form on one worksheet, and then generate an amortization table on a separate sheet. When you create new charts or *PivotTable* reports from a list, it's often convenient to give each of these elements its own sheet. That way, you can rearrange the data in the underlying list without having to worry about whether deleting a row or column will mess up the design of a PivotTable report.

WORKING WITH MULTIPLE WORKSHEETS

Working with multiple sheets simultaneously is how power users quickly create and format a complex workbook with a minimum of wasted effort. Use the following techniques to make working with multiple sheets easy:

- To select multiple worksheets, hold down the Ctrl key as you click each tab.

- To select a contiguous group of worksheets, click the first one in the group, and then hold down the Shift key and click the last one in the group.

- To select all the worksheets in the current workbook, right-click any worksheet tab and choose Select All Sheets from the shortcut menu.

- To quickly make any sheet active, click its index tab; to remove a sheet from a group, hold down Ctrl and click its tab.

- To remove the multiple selection and resume working with a single sheet, click any unselected sheet; if you've selected every sheet in the workbook, right-click any worksheet tab and choose Ungroup Sheets.

- If you've selected more than one sheet, you see the word Group in brackets in the title bar, and any data you enter appears in the corresponding cells on each worksheet in the group. So, if you have grouped Sheet1, Sheet2, and Sheet3, entering text in cell A1 on Sheet1 also enters the same text in the corresponding cells on Sheet2 and Sheet3.

- Likewise, any formatting choices you make—resizing columns, for example, or applying a numeric format—affect all the grouped worksheets identically. If you're building a budget workbook with identically formatted sheets for each department, you can use these techniques to quickly enter the budget categories in the first column and months along the top of each sheet.

- You can't use the Clipboard to enter data into multiple sheets simultaneously. When you paste data, it appears only in the active sheet, not in any other sheets you've selected. To quickly copy formulas, labels, or formats from a single worksheet to a group of sheets within a workbook, follow these steps:

  1. Select the sheet that contains the data you want to appear in each sheet.

  2. Use Ctrl+click or Shift+click to select the group of sheets to which you want to add the data.

  3. Select the data itself and choose Edit, Fill, Across Worksheets. An additional dialog box lets you choose whether to copy the formatted cell contents, just the data, or just the formats.

MOVING, COPYING, INSERTING, AND DELETING WORKSHEETS

In many cases, the easiest way to construct a workbook containing multiple sheets is to create the first sheet and then copy it. Although each new workbook starts with a set number of blank worksheets, you can add, copy, delete, and rearrange worksheets at will.

To add a new worksheet to an existing workbook, right-click any sheet tab and choose Insert, click the Worksheet icon in the Insert dialog box, and click OK. The new worksheet appears to the left of the sheet tab you clicked, with a generic name and a number one higher than the highest numbered sheet in the current workbook—Sheet4, Sheet5, and so on.

If that process feels too cumbersome, point to the sheet tab you want to copy, hold down the Ctrl key, and drag it left or right. As you drag, the mouse pointer changes shape and a small triangular marker with a plus sign appears above the sheet tab. When you release the mouse button, Excel creates a copy of the sheet you dragged, using its name followed by a copy number in parentheses: Sheet3 (2), for example.

Caution

When you copy a sheet that contains data, either within a workbook or to another workbook, Excel truncates the contents of any cell that contains more than 255 characters. If Excel detects that any cell in the sheet you're about to copy contains more than 255 characters, it displays a warning message; when you click OK, it copies the sheet anyway. To fix the copy, select all cells in the original worksheet and copy them to the Clipboard. Then, click cell A1 in the copy and paste the Clipboard contents.

PART

IV

CH

21

To delete a worksheet from a workbook, right-click the sheet tab of the worksheet you want to delete, and then choose Delete from the shortcut menu.

Tip from

EQ & Woody

In some workbooks, you might want to hide a worksheet rather than remove it. This technique is especially useful when a worksheet contains static data you use in formulas on other worksheets but rarely need to edit. Hiding a sheet also removes the temptation for other users to examine (and possibly change) the data on one of these sheets. To hide a sheet, choose Format, Sheet, Hide. To display a list of hidden sheets in the current workbook so you can make them visible again, choose Format, Sheet, Unhide.

To move a worksheet within a workbook, point to its sheet tab, click, and drag the triangular pointer along the sheet tabs until the black marker is over the location where you want to move the worksheet. Release the mouse button to drop the worksheet in its new location. Although it's possible to drag and drop worksheets between workbooks, it's much quicker and more accurate to use shortcut menus for this task. Follow these steps to move or copy a worksheet from one workbook to another:

1. Open the target workbook into which you plan to move or copy the worksheet. (Skip this step if you plan to move or copy the worksheet to a brand-new workbook.)

2. Switch to the workbook that contains the worksheet you want to move or copy. Point to the worksheet tab and right-click.

3. Choose Move or Copy from the shortcut menu.

4. In the Move or Copy dialog box (see Figure 21.1), select the name of the target workbook from the To Book drop-down list. To move or copy the sheet to a new, empty workbook, choose (new book) from the top of the list.

5. By default, Excel moves or copies sheets to the beginning of the target workbook. To select a different location, choose a sheet name from the Before Sheet list.

6. By default, using this dialog box moves the selected worksheet to the target workbook. To leave the original worksheet in place, select the Create a Copy check box.

7. Click OK.

Figure 21.1

RENAMING A WORKSHEET

To navigate more easily through workbooks with multiple worksheets, replace the generic default worksheet labels (Sheet1, Chart2, and so on) with descriptive names such as "Q3 Sales Forecasts," "Marketing Expenses," or "PivotTable." To rename a worksheet, double-click the worksheet tab (or right-click the tab and select Rename). Type a new name and press Enter.

Names you enter on worksheet tabs must conform to the following rules:

- Maximum length is 31 characters.
- Spaces are allowed.
- You can use parentheses anywhere in a worksheet's name; brackets ([ ]) are also allowed, except as the first character in the name.
- You cannot use any of the following characters as part of a sheet name: / \ ? * : (slash, backslash, question mark, asterisk, or colon). Other punctuation marks, including commas and exclamation points, are allowed.

If you plan to use references from one worksheet in formulas on another sheet, choose worksheet names carefully. Create names that are as short as possible without being needlessly cryptic; long names can make formulas particularly difficult to troubleshoot and edit.

Note

Worksheet tabs automatically resize to accommodate the name you enter.

Tip from

EQ & Woody

Excel 2002 allows you to color code worksheet tabs (right-click the worksheet tab and choose the Tab Color option). This option is best used sparingly. Colorizing each worksheet tab doesn't help organize data. Instead, try using colors to identify sheets that are part of the same group (yellow for East, green for West), or use colors to highlight summary sheets while leaving data input sheets with the default gray background.

NAVIGATING IN A WORKBOOK WITH KEYBOARD SHORTCUTS

For touch typists, Excel includes a wealth of keyboard shortcuts, as well as a couple of unusual ways to move through a worksheet and select cells:

- The Home key moves to the beginning of the current row.
- The Page Up/Page Down keys take you one window in their respective directions.
- Ctrl+Home returns to the top-left corner (cell A1) of the current sheet.
- Ctrl+End jumps to the bottom-right corner of the data-containing part of the worksheet—a useful technique when navigating through a lengthy list.
- If you've made a selection, you can move clockwise through all four corners of the selection by repeatedly pressing Ctrl+period.
- To move one worksheet at a time through the current workbook, press Ctrl+Page Up or Ctrl+Page Down.
- To select the current worksheet and the next or previous sheet, so you can work with them as a group, hold down the Shift key as you select them.

■ Pressing the End key turns on *End mode*, an unusual (and somewhat confusing) way to move through the current worksheet. Most of the End mode shortcuts are alternatives to Ctrl+*key* shortcuts that are appropriate for people who are unable to press two keys simultaneously (or just don't want to). Press End followed by an arrow key to jump along the current row or column in the direction of the arrow, to the next cell that contains data, skipping over any intervening empty cells. Press End and then Home to go to the last data-containing cell in the current worksheet. Press End and then Enter to move to the last cell in the current row, even if there are blank cells within the row—this is the most useful of the End mode shortcuts, because it has no matching Ctrl+*key* alternative. Press End again to turn off End mode.

USING CELL REFERENCES AND RANGE NAMES TO NAVIGATE IN A WORKBOOK

Excel's Name box (the combo box to the left of the Formula bar) lets you jump straight to a specific cell or named range. Click in this box, enter a cell reference (H4, for example), and press Enter to jump straight to that cell. To pick from a list of all named ranges in the current workbook, even on different worksheets, click the drop-down arrow to the right of the Name box.

Excel's Go To dialog box offers the same capabilities, with a few extra twists, including the capability to return to a cell you previously selected, or to select all cells on a worksheet that match criteria you specify.

To open the Go To dialog box shown in Figure 21.2, choose Edit, Go To, or use the keyboard shortcuts F5 or Ctrl+G. To jump to a specific cell or range, type its address or name in the Reference box. In general, it's easier to use the Name box to jump around a worksheet in this fashion. The advantage of the Go To dialog box is that Excel keeps track of the four most recent cell addresses you enter here, including the cell you started from. To return to any of these addresses, open the Go To dialog box and double-click the entry in the Go To list.

Figure 21.2
The Go To dialog box lets you jump to cells or named ranges you've visited recently, but its most useful feature is the Special button.

The list of references in the Go To dialog box also includes any named ranges in the current workbook. To jump to one of these ranges, select its name from the list and click OK. Because Excel saves range names with the workbook, that list is always available when you open the Go To dialog box. On the other hand, Excel discards the list of recent addresses each time you close the workbook.

Tip from

EQ & Woody

Using the Go To dialog box to jump to a specific cell or a named range is needlessly complex. Whenever possible, use the Name box instead. It's also easy to create a macro that jumps to a specific named range or cell address. Use the following code, for example, to jump to a range with the name ZipCodes (the Scroll parameter positions the window so that the top-left cell in the range is at the top-left corner of the window):

```
Sub GoToZipCodes()
Application.Goto
Reference:=Worksheets("Sheet1").Range("ZipCodes"),scroll:=Tr
ue
End Sub
```

→ For an explanation of how range names work in formulas, **see** "Using Range Names and Labels in Formulas," **p. 615.**

FILE COMPATIBILITY ISSUES

The standard binary format for an Excel 2002 workbook is the same as the format used for Excel 97 and Excel 2000. In an office where all users have access to either of those Excel versions, you should save and exchange files by using the Microsoft Excel Workbook format.

Excel 2002 is capable of opening and saving worksheets and workbooks using the file formats of all older Excel versions, including 2.x, 3.0, 4.0, and 5.0/95. You can also open and save files in the formats used by Lotus 1-2-3 (Release 1.x, 2.x, 3, 4), Quattro Pro for MS-DOS, and all versions of dBASE. Using Excel, you can open worksheets created by Microsoft Works 2.0, but you cannot save a worksheet in that format.

Excel 2002 also includes a hybrid format that allows users of Excel 5.0/95 to open files created in Excel 2002. If you regularly exchange files with users of this Excel version, save your files using the Microsoft Excel 97-2002 & 5.0/95 Workbook format. Although users of the older version will not be able to access all features of the workbook, they will be able to open and view it. Because this file format includes the equivalent of two full-sized files, it occupies roughly twice as much space as an ordinary Excel workbook file. This format is not appropriate if you want users of the older version to edit workbook files—the Excel 97-2002 version of the file disappears as soon as they save the edited workbook.

Saving files in an older data format invariably means giving up some features. In general, the older the format you choose, the more formatting and features you'll have to surrender. For example, saving in Excel 5.0/95 format will cause you to lose the following data and/or formatting:

- Any rows past 16,384 are deleted. Excel 97 and later can have as many as 65,536 rows per sheet.

- The contents of any cell after the first 255 characters will vanish. In Excel 97 and later, each cell can contain up to 32,767 characters.

- Rotated text changes to horizontal orientation, indented text becomes left aligned, and conditional formatting changes to Normal style.

- Merged cells are restored to their original size and shape, and the text that was in the merged cell appears in the top-left cell of the formerly merged range.

- In charts, gradient fills are converted to solid colors, rotated text is saved in horizontal orientation, and time-scale axes change to category axes.

- *PivotCharts*, which were introduced in Excel 2000, are displayed as regular charts.

Tip from	When you attempt to save a workbook in an alternate format, Excel doesn't identify the specific data and formatting you will lose. Instead, it displays a warning dialog box and offers to open the Help topic, "Formatting and features not transferred in file conversions." If you're uncertain of the limitations of the format you've chosen, save a backup copy in the default Microsoft Excel Workbook format first; then click the Help button and read the excellent description of the differences between file formats.

For exchanging information (especially lists) with databases and older spreadsheet programs (or even with Outlook 2000), use any of the universal conversion formats: CSV (Comma Separated Values), Text (Tab delimited), and Formatted Text (Space delimited). Each is appropriate for transferring lists minus any formatting or formulas. Each format uses a different delimiting character to separate rows and columns, but the transfer of data should be identical with all three choices.

USING RANGES TO WORK WITH MULTIPLE CELLS

Any selection of two or more cells is called a *range*. You can dramatically increase your productivity by using ranges to enter, edit, and format data. For example, if you highlight a range and click the Currency Style button, all the numeric entries in that range appear with dollar signs and two decimal places. Assigning a name to a range makes it easier to construct (and troubleshoot) formulas, and ranges make up the heart and soul of charts by defining *data series* and labels for values and categories.

Tip from	A rapid-fire data-entry technique lets you stuff the same data into multiple cells in one smooth operation. This trick comes in especially handy when you're entering a formula or a default value, such as zero, into a noncontiguous range. First, select the range into which you want to enter the identical data. Next, type the formula or data into the active cell, but hold down Ctrl when you press Enter.

The most common way to select multiple cells is to highlight a *contiguous range*—a rectangular region in which all cells are next to one another. But cells in a range don't have to be contiguous. You can also define a perfectly legal range by selecting individual cells or groups of cells scattered around a single worksheet.

Excel uses two addresses to identify a contiguous range, beginning with the cell in the upper-left corner and ending with the cell in the lower-right corner of the selection. A colon (:) separates the two addresses that identify the range—such as A1:G3. Commas separate the parts of a noncontiguous range, and you can mix individual cells and contiguous ranges to form a new range, as in the example A3,B4,C5:D8.

SELECTING RANGES

To select a contiguous range, click the cell at any corner of the range and drag the mouse pointer to the opposite corner. To select a noncontiguous range, select the first cell or group of cells, hold down the Ctrl key, and select the next cell or group of cells. Continue holding the Ctrl key until you've selected all the cells in the range. To select an entire row or column, click the row or column heading. To select multiple rows or columns, drag the selection or hold down the Ctrl key while clicking.

To select all cells in the current worksheet, click the unlabeled Select All button in the upper-left corner of the worksheet, above the row labels and to the left of the column labels.

Tip from

EQ & Woody

Use this shortcut to select a contiguous range that occupies more than one screen: Click the top-left cell in the range, and then use the scrollbars to move through the worksheet until you can see the lower-right corner of the range. Hold down the Shift key and click to select the entire range.

MOVING FROM CELL TO CELL WITHIN A RANGE

To enter data into a list in heads-down mode, select the range first. As you enter data, press the Enter key to move the active cell down to the next cell within the range, or press Tab to move to the right. (Press Shift+Enter or Shift+Tab to move in the opposite direction.)

When you reach the end of a row or column, pressing Enter or Tab moves the active cell to the next column or row in the selection. When you reach the lower-right corner of the range, pressing Enter or Tab moves you back to the upper-left corner.

ENTERING THE SAME DATA IN MULTIPLE CELLS

Occasionally, you'll want to fill a range of cells with exactly the same data in one operation, without using the Clipboard. For example, you might want to enter zero values in cells in which you intend to enter values later; you can also use this technique to enter a formula in several cells at once. To enter a formula in several cells at once, follow these steps:

1. Select the range of cells into which you want to enter data. The range need not be contiguous.

2. Type the text, number, or formula you want to use, and then press Ctrl+Enter. The data appears in all cells you selected.

Tip from

When you enter a formula using this technique, Excel inserts *relative cell references* by default. If you want the formula to refer to a constant value, select the cell reference and press F4 to convert it to an absolute reference before pressing Ctrl+Enter.

→ For a discussion of the differences between absolute and relative cell references, **see** "Using Cell References in Formulas," **p. 608**.

→ For instructions on how to automatically fill in data using Excel's AutoFill feature, **see** "Automatically Filling In a Series of Data," **p. 676**.

SELECTING RANGES OF DATA WITH THE GO TO DIALOG BOX

The Go To dialog box is especially useful when you're designing or troubleshooting a large worksheet and you want to quickly view, edit, format, copy, or move a group of cells with common characteristics. In fact, mastering this dialog box can make it possible to do things even most Excel experts swear can't be done, such as copying a range of data while ignoring hidden rows and columns. Open the Go To dialog box as usual, and then click the Special button to display the Go To Special dialog box shown in Figure 21.3. When you select one of these options and click OK, Excel selects all the cells that match that characteristic.

When you select cells using the Go To Special dialog box, the effect is the same as if you had selected a range by pointing and clicking. If you select all constants, for example, you can use the Tab and Enter keys to move through all the cells in your worksheet that contain data, skipping over any cell that contains a formula.

The following list describes the options available in the Go To Special dialog box:

Figure 21.3

- **Comments**—Selects all cells that contain *comments*. Use this option, and then press the Tab key to move from comment to comment instead of using the Previous Comment and Next Comment buttons on the Reviewing toolbar. This option is also useful if you want to remove all comments from a worksheet. Select all comments, and then right-click any of the selected cells and choose Delete Comment from the shortcut menu.

- **Constants**—Selects all cells that contain text, dates, or numbers, but not formulas. The Numbers and Text check boxes let you restrict the selection by data type (although the Logicals and Errors boxes are available, using these settings when searching for *constants* will always return an empty set). Select just text, for example, if you want to change the formatting of row and column labels while leaving the data area alone. Select all numbers and clear their contents to turn a worksheet into a template that contains only text labels and formulas.

- **Formulas**—The opposite of the Constants choice, this option selects only cells that begin with an equal sign. The Numbers and Text check boxes let you restrict the selection by data type. Use the Logicals check box to find cells that contain a TRUE or FALSE value. Check the Errors box to quickly select all cells that currently display an error value, and then use the Tab key to move from cell to cell and fix the misbehaving formulas.

- **Blanks**—A straightforward option that searches all cells between the top of the worksheet and the last cell that contains data, selecting those that do not contain data or formatting. This option is useful when you want to enter a default value or assign a default format to these cells.

- **Current Region**—Selects all cells around the active cell, up to the nearest blank row and column in any direction.

- **Current Array**—If the active cell is within an *array*, this option selects the entire array.

- **Objects**—Choose this option to select all charts, text boxes, AutoShapes, and other graphic objects on the current worksheet. This option is particularly useful when you want to change formatting for borders and shading, or when you want to group objects.

- **Row Differences**—Selects cells whose contents are different from those in a comparison cell. This is a challenging option to master: You must make a selection first, and then position the active cell in the column you want to use for comparison. If you select multiple rows, Excel compares each row independently to the value in the column that contains the active cell. The example in Figure 21.4 shows what happens when you select D11:I16 and then position the active cell in column D and use the Go To Special dialog box with the Row Differences option. The highlights readily identify two rows where expenses are different each month, but it also finds one out-of-the-ordinary value in cell F14.

- **Column Differences**—Like the previous option, except it works on a column-by-column basis. This option is extremely useful for finding unexpected differences in a list. Use a calculated column that determines whether a particular set of columns is within a normal range and returns a TRUE or FALSE result, and then use this option to find all cells that are FALSE.

- **Precedents**—Selects all cells to which the current selection refers. Use the Direct Only and All Levels options to find only direct references or all references. This option is useful when you're trying to trace the logic of a complex worksheet by working through a series of formulas.

- **Dependents**—Similar to the previous option, except it selects all cells that directly or indirectly refer to the active cell or range.

- **Last Cell**—Jumps to the last cell on the worksheet that contains data or formatting.

Select this range first...

Figure 21.4
Using the Row Differences command identifies values that are out of the ordinary; a cost-conscious business manager might ask why March cleaning bills are 25% higher than usual.

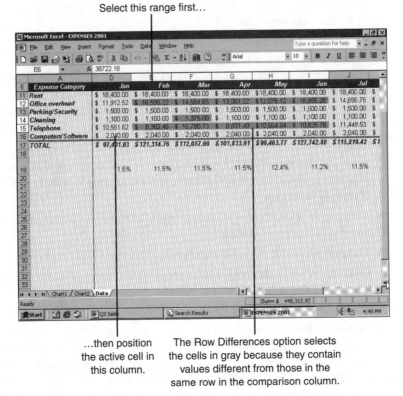

...then position the active cell in this column.

The Row Differences option selects the cells in gray because they contain values different from those in the same row in the comparison column.

- **Visible Cells Only**—Easily the most useful of all the options in the Go To Special dialog box. Use this type of selection to avoid the common problem of pasting more data than you expect. For example, if you copy a range of data that includes a hidden column, and then paste it into a new sheet, Excel pastes the hidden column as well. To avoid this problem, select the range you want to copy, and then use the Go To Special dialog box to select only visible cells. Copying and pasting that selection will have exactly the result you intend.

- **Conditional Formats**—Selects all cells that use any form of *conditional formatting*. Use the A11 option when you want to quickly find all cells that contain conditional formatting. Use the Same option if you just want to edit these options for cells that match the current cell.

- **Data validation**—Similar to the previous option, except it selects cells with *data validation* rules.

 If choosing the Last Cell option in the Go To Special dialog box causes you to jump to a blank cell far below your actual worksheet range, see "Resetting the Last Cell" in the "Troubleshooting" section at the end of this chapter.

HIDING ROWS AND COLUMNS

On some worksheets, you need to use rows or columns to hold data used in calculations, but you don't need to clutter up the rest of the worksheet by showing it. Click any cell within the row or column you want to hide (you don't need to select the entire row or column) and choose Format, Row, Hide or Format, Column, Hide.

To make a hidden row visible again, select cells in the row above and below the hidden row, and then choose Format, Row, Unhide. To display a hidden column, select cells in the columns to the left and right and choose Format, Column, Unhide.

If the first row or column of a worksheet is hidden, press F5 to open the Go To dialog box. Type A1 in the Reference box and click OK; then choose Format, Row (or Column), Unhide.

FINDING, REPLACING, AND TRANSFORMING DATA

Just as in other Office applications, you can use simple drag-and-drop techniques to move or copy the contents of a cell or range. Using the Windows Clipboard and the Paste Special menu, you can also change the format of information or perform mathematical transformations as you move or copy it. Most of the options are self-explanatory, but a handful are unique to Excel and truly useful.

→ For an overview of standard Clipboard techniques you can use within and between Office programs, **see** "How Office Extends the Windows Clipboard," **p. 132**.

FINDING AND REPLACING THE CONTENTS OF A CELL OR RANGE

In previous Excel versions, the Find and Replace dialog box offered no bells and whistles, just the capability to search for and replace strings of text. In Excel 2002, the Find and Replace dialog box add the capability to find and change formatting, as well as options to search across all sheets in a workbook or to restrict the search and subsequent changes to the current worksheet.

As in other Office programs, you use the Edit, Find and Edit, Replace menus (or the corresponding Ctrl+F and Ctrl+H shortcuts) to open the respective dialog boxes. Figure 21.5 shows the Replace dialog box with formatting options selected. (If the additional settings aren't visible, click the Options button.)

If you leave the Find What or Replace With boxes blank, Excel finds or replaces formatting in all cells where it finds a match. To enter formatting criteria using dialog boxes, click the Format button to the right of the Find What or Replace With text boxes. To find cells where formatting matches the settings of an existing cell, click the drop-down arrow to the right of the Format button and select the Choose Format from Cell option. After you select this option, the Find and Replace dialog box disappears and the mouse pointer changes to an eyedropper shape. Click the cell that contains the formatting you want to match.

Figure 21.5
The improved Find and Replace dialog boxes in Excel 2002 let you change formatting globally across an entire workbook.

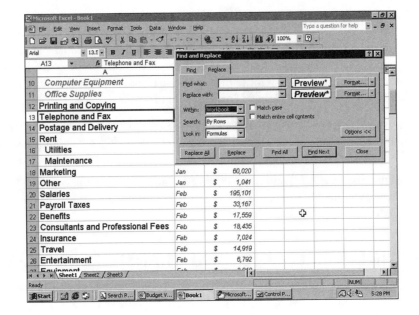

DRAGGING AND DROPPING TO CONVERT DATA

As is true elsewhere in Office, you can take control of the options available when dragging cells from one place to another. For instance, if you hold down the right mouse button and drag a cell or range of cells, a shortcut menu with paste options appears when you release the button. Two of these options are worth special note:

- Use the Copy Here as Formats Only option to quickly transfer cell formatting (fonts, shading, borders, and so on) without copying the contents of the cells.

- Choose Copy Here as Values Only to convert formulas to their results and paste the Clipboard contents as constants—numbers or text—rather than as formulas.

This technique is especially useful when you want to quickly convert a cell or range from a formula to a value. Say column A contains a list of product details, imported from an external database. All you really need from each is the six-digit part number it starts with, so you've filled column B with a range of formulas, each of which uses the LEFT() function to extract the first six characters from the original cell—for example, =LEFT(A2,6).

So far, so good. But if you now delete column A, your list of part numbers will shift to the left and turn into a column full of error messages. Before you can safely delete column A, you must convert column B to its results. To do so, select the entire range that contains the formula, right-click and drag it a short distance in any direction (without releasing the mouse button), and then drag it back and release it over the original cells. Choose Copy Here as Values Only from the shortcut menu. The column now contains just the part numbers, and you can safely delete column A.

You cannot use the Clipboard or drag-and-drop techniques to copy or move a noncontiguous range that consists of multiple selections.

TRANSFORMING DATA WITH PASTE OPTIONS

One of the most powerful ways to manipulate data on a worksheet is to copy it to the Clipboard first. Using the Clipboard, you can strip some or all formatting or manipulate values in the copied cells or range; you can then paste the data into the new location so it appears exactly as you want it.

Smart Tags (new in Excel 2002) let you quickly apply some common transformations. When you cut or copy data to the Clipboard and then use Edit, Paste or the Ctrl+V keyboard shortcut to paste the data, you see a Smart Tag in the lower-right corner of the pasted area. Click the Smart Tag to choose from the menu shown in Figure 21.6.

Figure 21.6
Smart Tag options let you tweak the appearance of data after pasting it; the Keep Source Widths option, for instance, fixes this common problem when pasting into a new worksheet.

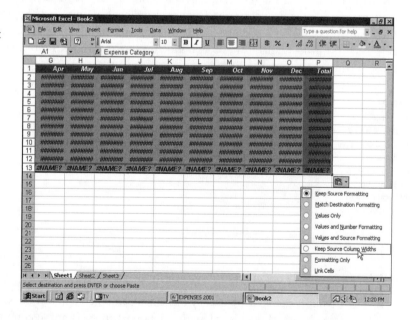

By default, data pasted from another Excel worksheet brings along its own formatting. If the data appears incorrectly when you paste it, click the Smart Tag and change the display of the pasted data in any of these ways:

- Choose Match Destination Formatting to strip all formatting but preserve formulas.
- Use one of the three Values options to convert formulas to their resulting values and paste them into the new location, with or without formatting.

PART
IV

CH
21

- Click Keep Source Column Widths to copy all formulas, number formatting, and cell formatting along with column widths. This option is most useful when pasting a highly formatted table into a new worksheet, where all columns are the standard width.

- Choose Formatting Only when you want to copy the format of a table to a new worksheet and then enter data manually in the new location.

- Click the Link Cells option to convert the pasted data into a link to the other worksheet.

→ For more details on how to use links between worksheets and workbooks, **see** "Using Links to Automatically Update or Consolidate Worksheet Data," **p. 552**.

Smart Tags are convenient for quick, uncomplicated transformations. But they have several limitations, most notably that each change undoes the changes from other Smart Tags. So if you paste in a range of formulas, you can use Smart Tags to convert formulas to values *or* to adjust column widths, but not both.

For more control over the results of a paste operation, use the Paste Special menu. Copy the contents of one or more cells to the Clipboard and choose Edit, Paste Special—you'll see the Paste Special dialog box shown in Figure 21.7. A handful of these options are also available using the plain-vanilla Edit, Paste option or Smart Tags, but Paste Special offers a much broader range of capabilities.

Figure 21.7
Use the Paste Special dialog box to add or subtract two columns of numbers, or to multiply or divide a range of numbers by a value you copy to the Clipboard.

Within or between workbooks, you can selectively paste in the following ways:

- The Formulas option is hopelessly misnamed, and the Help text does a terrible job of describing its actual function. Use this option when you want to copy all the data from one range to another, including formulas, without copying any formatting. This option is most useful when you're trying to copy data from another worksheet without destroying the formatting of your existing worksheet. Use the Formulas and Number Formats option (new in Excel 2000) to copy number formatting without carrying over other cell formatting, such as borders and colors.

- Select Values to convert formulas to their results and paste them as constant numbers or text. This has the same effect as the drag-and-drop technique described in the previous section. Use this option when you need to convert a noncontiguous range of formulas to its results. This option does not copy any formatting. Use the Values and Number Formats option (new in Excel 2002) to preserve number formatting without affecting other cell formatting.

■ Click Formats to copy all formatting from one cell or range to another. Use the All Except Borders option to skip cell borders, and the Column Widths option to duplicate column widths, especially from one worksheet to another.

Tip from

EQ & Woody

> Using Excel's Paste Special options can test your creativity. It's often possible to save a ton of work by combining several operations in consecutive Paste Special actions. For instance, choose All Except Borders to copy formulas and cell formatting without adding underlines and table borders from the original data; then repeat the Paste Special option and choose the Column Widths option. This duplicates an entire table on a new worksheet, leaving out only borders and underlines.

■ Choose the Comments option to transfer comments from one location to another.

■ Use the Validation option to duplicate data-entry rules, especially between different worksheets or workbooks.

The options in the Operation area are some of the most interesting of all, because they let you perform mathematical transformations on a group of numbers without having to tamper with your existing worksheet structure. To use this technique, enter a number in one cell and copy it to the Clipboard, select the range you want to transform, and use the Paste Special dialog box to add or subtract the value on the Clipboard from each entry in the selection; you can also multiply or divide the selection by that number. This technique might come in handy if you're beginning to plan next year's budget and you want to start by increasing this year's numbers by 6%. Follow these steps:

1. Click in any blank cell (even on another worksheet) and enter the value you want to use when transforming the existing data. In this case, enter 1.06 because you want to increase the values by 6%.

Tip from

EQ & Woody

> You can also use this technique to add or subtract two ranges of numbers, or to multiply one range of numbers by another. If you have two departmental worksheets formatted in exactly the same way, you can copy all the numbers from one worksheet and use this option to add them to the data in the other sheet, for example. Just make sure that the range you copy is the same size as the range you paste to.

2. Press Ctrl+C to copy the value to the Windows Clipboard.

3. Select the range of data you want to increase.

4. Click Edit, Paste Special. In the Paste Special dialog box, choose the Multiply option.

5. Click OK. Excel multiplies the selected range by the constant on the Clipboard, increasing each number by exactly 6%.

The final two check boxes in the Paste Special dialog box work with other options:

- Click the Skip Blanks option if you're performing a mathematical operation using two ranges of data. This setting skips pasting data for any cells that are blank in the original copy area.

- Check Transpose to flip a row of labels into a column, or vice versa. You can use this option to change the orientation of an entire region as well.

Tip from

EQ & Woody

Changing the orientation of an entire region is a trick that is especially useful when working with imported data. If your list has months along the side and categories along the top, for example, choose the Transpose option to rearrange the list so that each month's data appears in its own column and each category gets its own row.

CUSTOMIZING THE WORKSHEET WINDOW

Changing the size and configuration of a worksheet window can make it easier to work with data, especially in large worksheets. Zoom out or in to show more or less data, lock a row or column in place to maintain titles and headings, work in multiple panes, or open a new window on the same workbook.

USING THE ZOOM CONTROLS

Use the Zoom button on the Standard toolbar to change the view of your worksheet. Most of the options are self-explanatory: You can shrink the worksheet to as small as 10% of normal size for an overview of the sheet's design, or enlarge it to as much as 400% of normal. (This option is especially useful for close editing of complex grouped objects on a sheet.) If you choose a Zoom level of 39% or lower, your gridlines disappear. That's not a bug—at the lower magnification, the lines get in the way of your ability to edit, so Excel hides them on the screen.

The most useful option on the Zoom control is one that even some expert users don't know about. You can resize and reposition the editing window so that it includes the current selection; Excel chooses the proper Zoom percentage automatically. After you make a selection, choose Selection from the bottom of the Zoom drop-down list. Excel resizes the selection automatically. To return to normal view, click the Zoom button again and choose 100% from the drop-down list.

Tip from

EQ & Woody

If you have a Microsoft IntelliMouse, you can use the wheel to zoom in and out of your worksheet. Hold down the Ctrl key and spin the wheel down to zoom out; spin the wheel up to zoom back in. You might need to enable this feature before it works properly; choose Tools, Options, click the General tab, and check the Zoom on Roll with IntelliMouse box.

LOCKING ROW AND COLUMN LABELS FOR ONSCREEN VIEWING

In a typical worksheet, labels identify the type of data in each column or row. For example, a common design for budget worksheets arranges data into one row for each budget category, with values for each month appearing in columns from left to right. In this model, a label at the left edge of each row identifies the category, and a label at the top of each column identifies the month. If the data in your worksheet occupies more than a single screen, row and column labels can scroll out of view, making it difficult to identify which data goes in each row and column. The lack of labels also makes it difficult to enter data in the correct rows and columns, unless you want to continually scroll to see the heading labels.

To keep the row and column labels visible at all times, *freeze* them into position. In Figure 21.8, for example, notice that you can see the row titles in column A at the left, as well as the columns for July, August, and beyond at the right (starting at column H). As you click the horizontal scrollbar, columns on the left of the data area scroll out of view, but the labels in the first column remain visible.

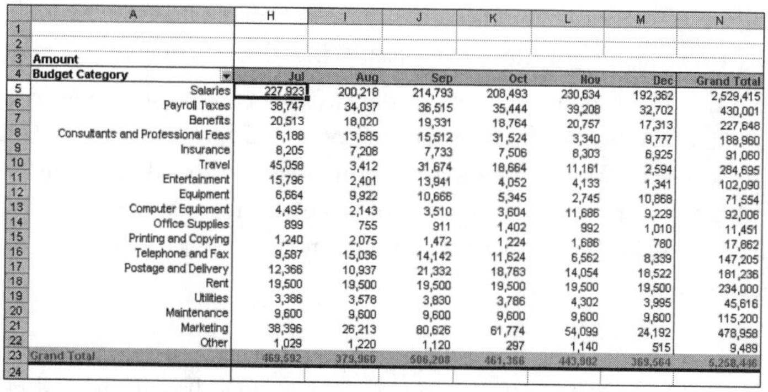

Figure 21.8
When you freeze rows or columns in place, you can scroll through the worksheet without losing identifying labels.

Budget Category	Jul	Aug	Sep	Oct	Nov	Dec	Grand Total
Salaries	227,923	200,218	214,793	208,493	230,834	192,362	2,529,415
Payroll Taxes	38,747	34,037	36,515	35,444	39,208	32,702	430,001
Benefits	20,513	18,020	19,331	18,764	20,757	17,313	227,648
Consultants and Professional Fees	6,188	13,685	15,512	31,524	3,340	9,777	188,960
Insurance	8,205	7,208	7,733	7,506	8,303	6,925	91,060
Travel	45,058	3,412	31,674	18,664	11,161	2,594	284,695
Entertainment	15,796	2,401	13,941	4,052	4,133	1,341	102,090
Equipment	6,664	9,922	10,666	5,345	2,745	10,868	71,554
Computer Equipment	4,495	2,143	3,510	3,604	11,686	9,229	92,006
Office Supplies	899	755	911	1,402	992	1,010	11,451
Printing and Copying	1,240	2,075	1,472	1,224	1,686	780	17,862
Telephone and Fax	9,587	15,036	14,142	11,824	6,562	8,339	147,205
Postage and Delivery	12,366	10,937	21,332	18,763	14,054	18,522	181,236
Rent	19,500	19,500	19,500	19,500	19,500	19,500	234,000
Utilities	3,386	3,578	3,830	3,786	4,302	3,995	45,616
Maintenance	9,600	9,600	9,600	9,600	9,600	9,600	115,200
Marketing	38,396	26,213	80,626	61,774	54,099	24,192	478,958
Other	1,029	1,220	1,120	297	1,140	515	9,489
Grand Total	469,592	379,960	506,208	461,366	443,982	369,564	5,258,446

To freeze rows, columns, or both, click in the cell below the row and to the right of the column that you want to lock into position. To freeze the first two columns and the first row, for example, click in cell C2. Choose Window, Freeze Panes. A solid line sets off the locked rows and columns from the rest of the worksheet.

Tip from

EQ & Woody

If your worksheet consists of a long list, lock in the labels for columns only. Click in column A, one row beneath the row that contains your column labels, and then choose Window, Freeze Panes.

To navigate in a worksheet whose panes are frozen, use the scrollbars to move through the data in your worksheet. The panes are locked only on the screen; if you print the worksheet, rows and columns appear in their normal positions. To unlock the row and column labels, choose Window, Unfreeze Panes.

→ To learn how to add row or column labels on each page of a printed worksheet, **see** "Using Repeating Titles for Multiple Page Printouts," **p. 563**.

SPLITTING THE WORKSHEET WINDOW

Split a worksheet into separate panes when you want to compare data in different regions of a worksheet side-by-side. A *split bar* divides the window into two panes, horizontally or vertically. You can drag both split bars onto the worksheet to create four panes. All changes you make in one pane are reflected in the other. You can drag cells and ranges between panes, and you can scroll and enter data in each pane independently.

To split a worksheet, use either of the following techniques:

- Click to select the cell below and/or to the right of where you want the split to appear, and then choose Window, Split. Select any cell in the column at the left of the current window to create side-by-side panes (also known as a vertical split). Select any cell in the top row to create a horizontal split, with one pane over another. If you choose the cell at the top left of the screen, Excel divides the window into four equal panes.

- Aim the mouse pointer at one of the two *split boxes*, which appear just above the vertical scrollbar and just to the right of the horizontal scrollbar, to create side-by-side panes (vertical split). When the mouse pointer changes to a double line with two arrows, click and drag in the direction of the worksheet to create a new pane. As you drag, the bar snaps into place at a row or column boundary. Release when you reach the right position.

To remove multiple panes and return to a single editing window, you can do any of the following: Choose Window, Remove Split; double-click the split bar; or click the bar and drag it off the worksheet window.

USING LINKS TO AUTOMATICALLY UPDATE OR CONSOLIDATE WORKSHEET DATA

Use *links* to share data between cells or ranges in one worksheet and another location in the same workbook or a different workbook. Just as a formula displays the results of a calculation, a link looks up data from another location and displays it in the active cell.

Links offer a powerful technique for consolidating data from different sources into one worksheet without requiring that you reenter or copy data. For example, you might use separate sales-tracking worksheets for each month of the year, with a single year-to-date worksheet that consolidates the monthly results. A business manager can use separate worksheets to analyze budget information for each division within a company, creating links to a master worksheet that ties all the numbers together.

Note

You can use *links* (also known as external references) within formulas as well.

After you establish a link, data you enter in one location automatically appears in all linked locations. To create a link, follow these steps:

1. Open all the workbooks you plan to link.

2. In the source workbook (the one that contains the data you want to reuse), select the cell or range to be linked, and press Ctrl+C to copy it to the Clipboard.

3. Switch to the dependent workbook (the one in which you want to insert the link), and select the cell where you want to create the link.

4. Choose Edit, Paste Special. In the Paste Special dialog box, click Paste Link.

→ Using hyperlinks provides yet another powerful option for linking your Excel worksheets; **see** "Working with Hyperlinks," **p. 167**.

Excel updates linked cells automatically if the worksheet that contains the link is open. If you change the data in the source workbook when the workbook that contains the link is closed, the links do not update automatically. When you reopen the workbook that contains the links, Excel will ask whether you want to update the links. To update or change the source of links manually, choose Edit, Links.

RESTRICTING AND VALIDATING DATA ENTRY FOR A CELL OR RANGE

When designing a worksheet, you'll occasionally want to restrict the type of data users can enter in a specific cell or range. Excel lets you define data-validation rules for cells and ranges to do exactly that. Examples of useful applications include the following:

- In a list of recent sales results formatted to show only month and date, restrict entry in a specific column to only dates within the last month. This technique prevents users from inadvertently entering a date in the wrong month or year, or in the future.

- On a budget worksheet, require that the user enter a department name and restrict allowed entries to a specific list. You can add a drop-down arrow to a cell with this type of restriction so users can pick from a list.

- For purchase orders, check the amount a user enters against his or her authorized spending limit—say, $500. If the amount is over the limit, display a message that directs them to talk to a supervisor or re-enter the amount.

- Ask a user to enter a description in a form; to keep data to a manageable length, restrict the total number of characters the user can enter and display a warning message if the description exceeds that length.

- On an invoice form, allow a salesperson to enter an optional discount for good customers, but only if the amount before sales tax is over $100. Compare the entry in the Discount field with a formula that calculates the total purchases to validate the entry.

DEFINING DATA-VALIDATION RULES

Each *data-validation* rule has three components: the criteria that define a valid entry; an optional message you can display to users when they select the cell that contains the rule; and an error message that appears when users enter invalid data. To begin creating a data-validation rule, first select the cell or range for which you want to restrict data entry, and then choose Data, Validation. You'll see a Data Validation dialog box similar to the one in Figure 21.9.

Figure 21.9
When defining data-validation rules, you can enter values or formulas that evaluate to the correct data type. This example restricts valid entries to dates within the last 30 days.

On the Settings tab, enter the criteria that define a valid entry. First, choose the required data type in the Allow drop-down list; then define specific criteria. The available options in the Allow drop-down list (described in Table 21.1) vary depending on the type of data you select. Keep in mind that the options shown in the Data Validation dialog box change depending on the criteria you've selected in the Allow drop-down list. The dialog box shown in Figure 21.9 represents just one example.

TABLE 21.1   DATA-VALIDATION SETTINGS

Data Type	Allowed Restrictions
Any Value	Default setting; no restrictions allowed. Select this option if you want to display a helpful input message only, without restricting data entry.
Whole Number, Decimal	Choose an *operator* (between, for example, or greater than) and values or formulas. The Whole Number data type produces an error if the user enters a decimal point, even if it's followed by zero. The Decimal choice allows any number after the decimal point.
List	In the Source box, enter the address or name of the range that contains the list of values you want to allow. The range can be on another worksheet (a hidden worksheet in the current workbook is your best choice) or in another workbook. For a short list, enter the valid items directly in this box, separated by commas (Acctg, Sales, Mktg). If you want users to be able to pick from a list, check the In-cell box.
Date or Time	Choose an operator and appropriate values. You can enter formulas here as well; for example, to allow only dates that have already occurred, choose Less Than from the Data box and enter =TODAY() in the End Date box.
Text Length	Choose an operator and then specify numbers that define the allowed length; you can also enter formulas or cell references that produce numbers as values for use with the selected operator.
Custom	Enter a formula that returns a *logical value* (TRUE or FALSE). Use this option when the cell that contains the rule is part of a calculation, and you want to test the results of that calculation rather than the cell value itself. On a purchase order with multiple items that you total in a cell named Total_PO, for example, enter =Total PO < 500 as the rule for each cell used in the SUM formula; that prevents the user from exceeding a $500 total limit even though each individual item is under the allowance.

DISPLAYING HELPFUL INPUT MESSAGES

Rules that stop users from entering invalid data are good, but helpful error messages are even better. As part of a data-validation rule, you can display messages that appear every time the user enters the cell that contains that rule. These messages appear in small pop-up windows alongside the cell. Use *input messages* to help users understand exactly what type of data they should enter in the cell, especially if you are designing a data-entry sheet for less-experienced Excel users.

Note

If the Office Assistant is visible, the user will see the message in a cartoon bubble next to the Assistant character.

To create an input message, choose Data, Validation. Click the Input Message tab (see Figure 21.10) and enter the title text and message you want to appear. Your message should be as helpful and brief as possible; if you've restricted the user to a particular type of data, make sure they know exactly what they're allowed to enter.

Figure 21.10
The message you enter here can explain the purpose of the cell and warn the user of data restrictions.

ALERTING THE USER TO ERRORS

How do you want Excel to respond when users enter invalid data? In all cases, you can display an error alert. If the data type is wrong, or if the date or value is not appropriate, you can refuse to accept the input and force users to enter an acceptable value. You can also choose to accept the value; this can be an effective way to force users to double-check values that might be valid but are outside of a normal range. On an expense report, for example, you might define valid entries as being below $2,000. If the amount users enter is over that amount, you could display a message that asks them whether they're sure the amount is correct. If they accidentally added an extra zero, the message will give them a chance to correct their mistake, or Excel can accept the input if they click OK.

To define an error message and set options for handling data that is outside the defined range, choose Data, Validation and click the Error Alert tab (see Figure 21.11).

Figure 21.11
You define the error message users see when they enter invalid data; you can reject the data or allow them to enter it with a warning.

Check the Show Error Alert After Invalid Data Is Entered box. Enter a title and text for the message you want users to see when they enter an invalid value. As with the Input Message, try to be as informative as possible so that the user knows exactly what he must do to correct the error. Then select one of the following choices from the Style box to define how Excel should handle the input:

- **Stop**—Displays a Stop dialog box and lets the user choose Retry or Cancel.

- **Warning**—Displays the error message and adds Continue? The user can choose Yes to enter the invalid data, No to try again, or Cancel.

- **Information**—Displays the error message. The user can click OK to enter invalid data or Cancel to back out.

DELETING, MOVING, OR COPYING DATA-VALIDATION RULES

To remove all validation rules from a cell or range, first select the cell(s) containing the validation rule; then choose Data, Validation, and click the Settings tab. Click the Clear All button and click OK. This option erases the input message, error alert, and validation settings.

When should you select the Apply These Changes to All Other Cells with the Same Settings check box? If you originally create a set of validation rules for a range of cells, Excel stores those settings with the range. If you later adjust the settings for an individual cell in that range, you break the link to the range. Check this box while editing data-validation settings for a single cell, and Excel extends the selection and applies your changes to the entire range you originally selected. The check box has no effect on other cells for which you defined rules individually, even if the rules are absolutely identical.

Tip from

When you copy or move a cell or range, data-validation rules travel with the cell's contents. To copy only data-validation rules from one cell to another, without affecting the contents or formatting of the target cell, use Paste Special. Select the cell whose rule you want to copy, and then choose Edit, Copy. Select the cells where you want to copy the rule, and choose Edit, Paste Special. Check the Validation option and click OK.

Are you still finding invalid data in a user form in which you've created validation rules to protect data? See "Data Validation Limitations" in the "Troubleshooting" section at the end of this chapter.

TROUBLESHOOTING DATA ERRORS

Data-validation rules are not perfect. Users can bypass the rules and enter invalid data by pasting from the Clipboard, or by entering a formula that results in an invalid value. Also, Excel does not check the existing contents of a cell or range when you create or copy a validation rule. When you *audit* a worksheet, Excel finds cells that contain values that are outside the limits you defined with data-validation rules. This technique is the only way to find incorrect values on a worksheet.

These auditing tools are not available from any menu. The only way to identify invalid data is to click a button on the Formula Auditing toolbar; curiously, this option never appears on the list of toolbars that Excel displays when you right-click an existing toolbar. To display the Auditing toolbar, choose Tools, Formula Auditing, Show Formula Auditing Toolbar. Click the Circle Invalid Data button to show any cells that are outside the rules, as shown in Figure 21.12; click the Clear Validation Circles button to clear the highlights.

Note

The Circle Invalid Data button will find a maximum of 255 cells. If you have more invalid entries, you'll need to correct the data in some of the invalid cells, and then click the Circle Invalid Data button again.

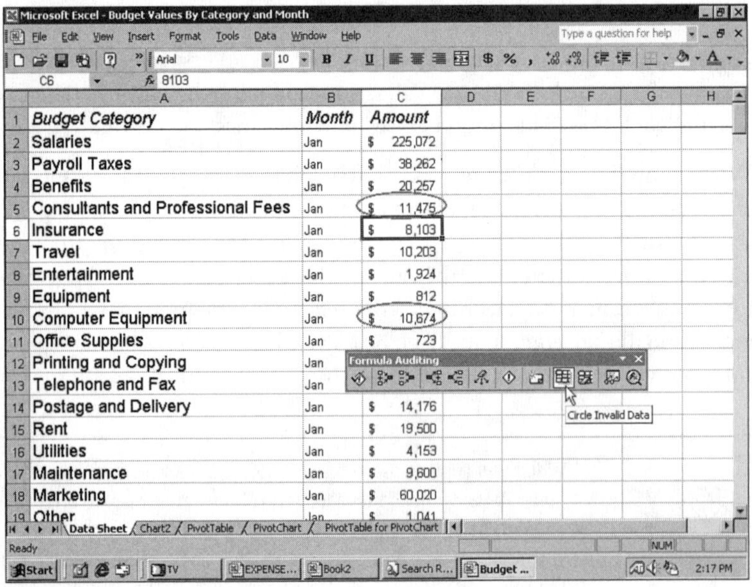

Figure 21.12
Click the Circle Invalid Data button to add these bold highlights around any cell whose contents violate a validation rule.

→ For an overview of other tools you can use to track down problems in formulas, **see** "Troubleshooting Formulas," **p. 634**.

PRINTING WORKSHEETS

Unlike Word documents, which typically are designed to fit on specific paper sizes, Excel worksheets are free-flowing environments that sprawl in every direction. If you click the Print button and leave the formatting to Excel, you'll end up with page breaks that appear at arbitrary locations in your worksheet, with no regard to content. To properly translate a large worksheet into printed output takes planning and a fair amount of creative formatting.

If you don't specifically define a print area, Excel assumes that you want to print all the data in the currently selected worksheet or worksheets, beginning with cell A1 and extending to the edge of the area that contains data or formatting. If necessary, you can divide a worksheet into smaller sections and print each region on its own page. As explained in this section, you can also shrink the print area to fit in a precise number of pages, and you can repeat row and column headings to make the display of data easier to follow.

Tip from	Don't overlook other techniques for rearranging data on a worksheet for the purpose of producing great printouts. On lists, AutoFilters can help you select and print only data that matches criteria you specify (see Chapter 25, "Working with Lists and Databases," for more details). Hiding rows and columns temporarily can help cut a large worksheet down to size. To print the quarterly sales totals for each sales rep without printing the monthly details, for example, hide the details before printing the selection. In some cases, the best way to print a complex selection from a worksheet is to translate it into another worksheet, using linked ranges or PivotTable reports (covered in Chapter 27, "Using PivotTables and PivotCharts").

USING RANGES TO DEFINE THE DEFAULT PRINT AREA

You can force Excel to use a defined print area as the default for a worksheet. (Excel bypasses all dialog boxes and uses this region when you click the Print button.) This technique is especially useful if you regularly print a complex worksheet that contains a number of nonprinting regions. On a worksheet that contains a list and a criteria range, for example, you'll typically want to print only the list. On a budget worksheet that includes monthly data by category and an executive summary region, you might want to define the summary as the default when you click the Print button.

Tip from	The Print button bypasses all dialog boxes and prints the default print area without allowing you to review any options. The results can be tremendously frustrating (and waste reams of paper, if you can't stop the print job fast enough). For that reason, we strongly recommend replacing the Print button with the Print… button (note the three dots to the right of the Print command). The Print… command uses an identical icon, but displays the Print dialog box when clicked instead of sending your job to the printer with current settings. Use the techniques described in Chapter 2, "Customizing the Office Interface," to make this switch. You'll use one extra click every time you print, but you'll significantly reduce the number of times you accidentally print the wrong selection.

Start by selecting the range you want to print. The range need not be contiguous, but if you select a noncontiguous range, keep in mind that each selection will print on its own page, and the results might not be what you intended. All parts of the range to be printed must be on the same worksheet; each worksheet in a workbook gets a separate print area.

To define the selection as the default print area, choose File, Print Area, Set Print Area. Excel creates a named range called Print_Area in the current worksheet.

To delete the current print area selection and start over, choose File, Print Area, Clear Print Area.

When you define a specific print area, Excel prints only that area when you click the Print button. If you define a print area and then add rows at the bottom or columns to the right of the data, the new data won't appear on the printed pages. Whenever you redesign a worksheet, make a special point to recheck the print area.

INSERTING YOUR OWN PAGE BREAKS

When you attempt to print a worksheet, Excel automatically inserts page breaks to divide it into sections that will fit on the selected paper size. (To see a dashed line that represents each break as you edit a workbook, choose Tools, Options, click the View tab, and check the Page Breaks box.) Excel doesn't analyze the structure of your worksheet before inserting page breaks; it simply adds a page break at the point where each page runs out of printable area. To make multipage worksheets more readable, you can and should position page breaks by hand.

To insert a manual page break, select the cell below and to the right of the last cell you want on the page; then choose Insert, Page Break. To remove the page break, select the same cell and choose Insert, Remove Page Break. To remove all manual page breaks from the current worksheet, select the entire sheet, and then choose Insert, Reset All Page Breaks.

Excel includes an unusual view option called Page Break Preview that lets you see all page breaks and adjust them by clicking and dragging. To switch to this view from a worksheet-editing window, choose View, Page Break Preview; from the Print Preview window, click the Page Break Preview button on the toolbar. As Figure 21.13 shows, this view lets you see your entire worksheet, broken into pages exactly as Excel intends to print it, with oversize page numbers laid over each block. (The numbers and lines don't appear on printed pages, of course.)

Dashed lines represent automatic page breaks inserted by Excel; solid lines represent manual page breaks. To adjust page breaks in this view, point to the thick line between two pages and drag it in any direction. To adjust the print area, drag the solid lines on any edge of the print area; cells that are not in the print area appear gray in Page Break Preview.

Figure 21.13
The page numbers show the order in which pages will print; drag the thick lines to adjust the print area and page breaks.

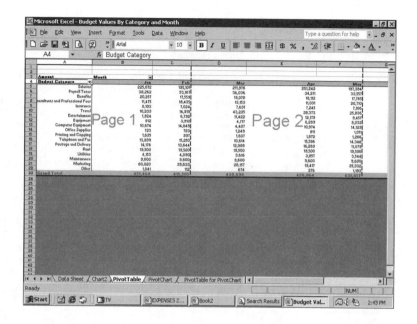

When using Page Break Preview, you'll have best results if you start at the top of the worksheet and work in the order it will print—normally from top to bottom and left to right, unless you've used the Page Setup dialog box to specify that you want to go across the worksheet before you work your way down. Move page breaks up or to the left only; moving them down or to the right can cause unpredictable results if you drag past the size of the page. In that case, Excel adds its own page breaks, undoing the effects of your painstaking page-breaking efforts.

EXTRA ITEMS YOU CAN PRINT

Use Excel's Print dialog box to specify that you want to print additional parts of a worksheet, such as comments, gridlines, and row or column headings. You can also control the way Excel translates colors into shades of gray. To see these additional printing options, choose File, Page Setup, and click the Sheet tab.

Table 21.2 lists the options available for each worksheet.

TABLE 21.2   WORKSHEET PRINT OPTIONS

Print Option	What It Does
Gridlines	It's okay to show gridlines on draft worksheets; for final output, however, turn off gridlines and use borders to set off data areas.
Comments	By default, comments are not printed; check this box to print them on a separate sheet or as they appear onscreen.
Draft Quality	Prints cell contents but skips gridlines and graphics. This option is unnecessary when using a laser printer but might be useful for speeding up printing on color output devices or slow inkjet printers.

PART
IV

CH
21

TABLE 21.2   CONTINUED

Print Option	What It Does
Black and White	Excel translates color backgrounds to shades of gray on the printed page. This option removes most gray shades; it can also speed up print jobs on color printers. Use Print Preview to print a small test page to check results before printing a large sheet with this option.
Row and Column Headings	Prints letters and numbers to help identify cell addresses. Use in combination with the option to view formulas (choose Tools, Options, click the View tab, and check the Formulas bar) when you want to print out the structure of a worksheet so you can study it.
Print Titles	If the data in your worksheet spans several pages, you might lose your points of reference, such as the headings above columns of data or to the left of each row. Identify the Rows to Repeat at Top of each page or the Columns to Repeat at Left of each page. (See the following section for more details.)
Page Order	The graphic to the right of this option shows whether your sheet will print sideways first, then down, or the other way around. Adjust this order if necessary to make page numbering work properly.

LABELING PRINTED PAGES WITH HEADERS AND FOOTERS

Any worksheet that spans more than one page should include a header or footer (or both). An assortment of preconfigured headers and footers lets you number pages, identify the worksheet, specify the date it was created, list the author, and so on. Choose File, Page Setup, and then click the Header/Footer tab to add or edit a header and footer. Click the Custom Header or Custom Footer button to build either of these elements with text of your choosing. Buttons on both dialog boxes let you add fields, such as the name of the current workbook or sheet or the current date and time.

Unlike every previous version, Excel 2002 allows you to include graphics in a header or footer. This is a feature that Excel users have been clamoring about for years, and it's a welcome addition. The most common application is to add a company logo to the top or bottom of each printed page. Click the Insert Picture button and browse to any graphic file supported by Office. You can insert one and only one graphic in each section—left, center, and right. Click the Format Picture button to crop, compress, resize, or scale a picture file in a header or footer.

→ For general-purpose advice on how to work with graphics in Office, **see** "Importing, Exporting, and Compressing Graphics," **p. 123**.

By default, Excel allows a half-inch for a worksheet's header or footer. If you want to maximize the amount of data on each page and you're not using a header or footer, open the Page Setup dialog box, click the Margins tab, and set the Header, Footer, Top, and Bottom boxes to 0. (On some printers, you might need to adjust the top and bottom margins to match the unprintable area on the page.)

 If your custom header or footer doesn't look right on the page, see "Adjusting Header and Footer Margins" in the "Troubleshooting" section at the end of this chapter.

Tip from

EQ & Woody

If you want a custom header or footer to appear on every worksheet you create, add headers and footers to each sheet in the template Excel uses when you create a new workbook. (The specific instructions for creating and saving this template appear later in this chapter.) Remember that each sheet has its own header and footer; if you want the same header to appear on each sheet in the template, you must create each one individually.

USING REPEATING TITLES FOR MULTIPLE PAGE PRINTOUTS

For worksheets that span multiple pages, you can repeat one or more rows or columns (or both) as titles for the data on each new page. On a typical budget worksheet, for example, the first column might contain income and expense categories, with columns for each month's data extending to the right across several pages. In this case, follow these steps to repeat the entries in the first column as titles at the left of each page:

1. Choose File, Page Setup, and click the Sheet tab.

2. To specify a column for titles, click in the Columns to Repeat at Left box. To use a row as titles on each new page, click in the Rows to Repeat at Top check box.

3. Click in any cell in the column or row you want to specify as the title. You need not select the entire row or column. If you select multiple cells, Excel uses all selected rows or columns as titles. If necessary, use the Collapse Dialog button to move the dialog box out of the way as you select.

4. Click the Print Preview button to ensure that you've configured the titles correctly. Click Print to send the worksheet to the printer immediately.

FORCING A WORKSHEET TO FIT ON A SPECIFIED NUMBER OF PAGES

Just as you can use the Zoom control to change the size of cells in a worksheet window, you can also reduce the size of data on a printout. Making the scale smaller lets you squeeze more rows and columns onto each page. If you want your printed worksheet to fit in a specific number of pages, Excel can calculate the *scaling percentage* for you:

1. Click File, Page Setup, and click the Page tab.

2. To scale the page to a fixed percentage, enter a value between 10 and 400 in the Adjust to % Normal Size box.

Caution

Choosing a number that's too low can result in a completely unreadable printout. In general, you should choose a scaling percentage lower than 40 only when you want to see the overall structure of your worksheet, not when you want to actually read and analyze data.

3. To adjust the printout to a fixed height or width, select the Fit To option. Use the spinner controls to adjust the number of pages you want the printout to occupy; leave one number blank if you want Excel to adjust only the width or height of the printout. The settings in Figure 21.14, for example, will scale the worksheet to no more than one page in width but allow the sheet to print additional rows on multiple pages.

Figure 21.14
These settings force Excel to scale the current worksheet to one page wide for printing.

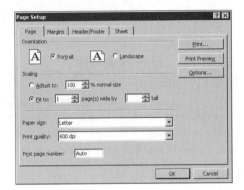

4. Click Print Preview to verify that your worksheet's print settings are correct.

5. Click Print to send the worksheet to the printer.

PUBLISHING EXCEL DATA IN WEB PAGES

Like Word and PowerPoint, Excel allows you to save files in HTML format so that you or anyone else can view them in a Web browser. You can save a simple range of data, a chart, a worksheet, or an entire workbook in HTML format; when opened in a Web browser, the resulting file will closely resemble the worksheet as seen in an Excel window. Some differences in formatting and appearance are inevitable because of the way that browsers display HTML code.

→ For an overview of some of the compatibility issues you'll face with different browsers, **see** "Browser-Compatibility Issues," **p. 163**.

When saving a workbook as a Web page, you must deal with the following noteworthy restrictions:

- HTML pages represent a static snapshot of the worksheet data; if you view worksheet data in a browser, you can't edit or rearrange cells or their contents unless you use *interactive Web components*.

- Gridlines and row or column headings do not appear in the browser window.

Tip from

To set off rows and columns in an Excel-generated Web page, don't rely on gridlines; instead, use borders to separate cells within the data area. Use shading and font formatting to set off headings, totals, and other distinctive elements.

- Some advanced features don't translate properly to HTML pages; for example, if you've saved multiple scenarios in a workbook, they'll be lost in translation, as will rotated text and some other forms of custom formatting.

 You'll see an error message if you try to publish a password-protected workbook as a Web page; see "Passwords Don't Work on Web Workbooks" in the "Troubleshooting" section at the end of this chapter.

- The first cell that contains data in your workbook always moves to the top-left corner of the HTML page, even if you've left blank rows or columns as part of the design.

- All sheets in your workbook appear on the resulting Web page, even those containing no data; the sheet tabs are visible in browsers that support *dynamic HTML*.

To save an entire workbook as an HTML page, choose File, Save As Web Page. Give the page a name, choose a destination folder (on a local hard drive, a network server, or a Web server), and click Save. If you want the Web page to be updated automatically whenever you update the underlying worksheet, choose File, Save As Web Page, and then click the Publish button. Check the AutoRepublish Every Time This Workbook Is Saved box and click Publish to save the Web page. (This option is new in Excel 2002.)

Tip from

Don't forget the title. In the Save As Web Page dialog box, just above the File Name box, you'll see a space for the page title, which appears in the browser title bar and on the page itself. Excel doesn't add a title by default; click the Change button to add or edit the title.

To save a chart or a range from a worksheet, make a selection first, and then click the Selection option in the Save As Web Page dialog box. To save a single sheet instead of an entire workbook, make sure only a single cell is active before you choose Save As Web Page, and then choose Selection: Sheet from the resulting dialog box.

To select multiple named items from a workbook, such as two sheets, a sheet and a chart, or multiple named ranges, click the Publish button in the Save As Web Page dialog box. That in turn displays the Publish As Web Page dialog box shown in Figure 21.15.

Choose a sheet name or another category, such as Range of Cells or Previously Published Items, from the Choose drop-down list. Then click an item from the list below your selection.

PART

IV

CH

21

Figure 21.15
To save individual items from a workbook to a Web page, select them by using this dialog box.

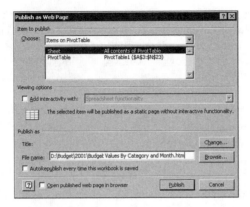

To give viewers of HTML pages the ability to manipulate data, including PivotTables and *AutoFilter lists*, select the Add Interactivity With check box; then choose any of the available options. Note that only viewers using Internet Explorer 4.01 or later are able to manipulate data in pages you create this way.

Customizing Excel

You can choose from dozens of options for adjusting the way Excel looks, acts, and works. Most are accessible in the Options dialog box that appears when you click Tools, Options. The settings on the 13 tabs here are generally self-explanatory, and many of them are variations on common features found in other Office applications. In this section, we highlight only the most useful:

→ For details of Office-wide configuration options, **see** "Configuring Common Office Features," **p. 44.**

- Options on the View tab enable you to hide or show interface elements, such as the Formula bar, status bar, gridlines, scrollbars, and the startup task pane. Unlike Word, which allows you to set many such options on a document-by-document basis, the settings you check here apply to every workbook you open.

- The Calculation tab enables you to change the default settings Excel uses for calculating formulas. In the days when 286 and 386 computers ruled the Earth, setting *manual calculation* was a survival tactic, because calculating a large worksheet could literally take hours. In an era when processor speed is measured in gigahertz, this option is necessary only for scientific applications when you need to control the precise order of calculations. In general, the overwhelming majority of users should accept the default options on this tab.

- Most of the options on the Edit tab are the same as those found in other Office programs. If you routinely select a range and fill in list values, consider changing the Move Selection After Enter box from its default selection of Down to Right. If you find Smart Tags annoying, clear the Show Paste Options and Show Insert Options boxes.

Tip from

Ed & Woody

When entering currency values, such as entries in a check register, people with an accounting background often prefer to let Excel fill in the decimal point. If you choose the Fixed Decimal option on this tab and leave it at the default setting of 2, entering 14398 will result in a value of 143.98. It's extremely unlikely you'll want to set this option permanently. If you use it frequently, however, create this simple toggle macro and assign it to a toolbar button so that you can switch into and out of fixed decimal mode on demand:

```
Sub ToggleFixedDecimal()
        Application.FixedDecimal = Not Application.FixedDecimal
End Sub
```

- The Transition tab is most useful for those who are comfortable with 1-2-3 menus and keystrokes. If your organization prefers that you save files in an alternative format, you can choose that format as your default here as well.

→ For a discussion of the Chart and Color tabs, **see** "Editing and Formatting Chart Elements," **p. 662**.

→ To learn when file compatibility issues might dictate choosing an alternate file format, **see** "File Compatibility Issues," **p. 539**.

- Click the General tab to display the options shown in Figure 21.16. The Sheets in New Workbook setting enables you to change the number of blank sheets in each new workbook to any number between 1 and 255. Choose a smaller setting if you rarely use multiple sheets in a workbook or a larger one if you regularly create complex workbooks, such as consolidated budgets. You can also adjust the font that Excel uses for text and numbers in new worksheets from the default of 10-point Arial. Choose a new font from the Standard Font list; specify a new size by using the drop-down list to its right.

Figure 21.16
Use these options to adjust the default font size, number of worksheets per workbook, and other key Excel options.

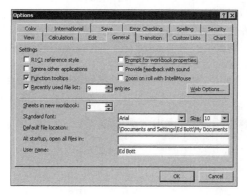

Tip from

With Excel 2002, Microsoft made it a bit less likely that you'll fall into a common trap. A box on the General tab used to allow you to specify an Alternate Startup File Location. In this version, the wording is clearer: At Startup, Open All Files In the specified directory. Most users should leave this box blank. Templates and workbooks you want to load automatically should go in the Xlstart folder in your personal profile instead. If you specify an alternative location, Excel loads any workbooks stored in that folder as well as those from Xlstart. This feature is typically used in corporate settings to run macros and install Excel add-ins automatically.

- Options on the International tab let you override system settings for date and currency formats, default paper size, and right-to-left orientation.

- Set AutoRecover options on the Save tab. Note that this feature, borrowed from Word, is new in this version of Excel.

→ For a discussion of Office AutoRecover features, **see** "Setting Up Automatic Backup and Recovery Options," **p. 76**.

- Use the Spelling tab to set spell-checking settings. These options were available on a separate dialog box in earlier versions.

- The Error Checking tab includes settings that let you control background checking for common worksheet errors, including those in formulas. These options, new in Excel 2002, include check boxes that let you locate numbers stored as text (which can cause problems with formulas) and text dates containing two-digit years (which can result in Y2K-style date arithmetic errors).

→ For more details on how to check for errors in formulas, **see** "Troubleshooting Formulas," **p. 634**.

- Look on the Security tab (see Figure 21.17) for file encryption and file sharing boxes, where you can specify a password that locks a file for modifications or encrypts it so the data can only be seen by authorized users. Click the Macro Security button to access options that affect how Visual Basic macros and scripts work with all workbooks.

→ Office XP includes a broad array of new security settings; for a complete overview and important details, turn to "Setting Security Options," **p. 49**.

Figure 21.17
If you enter a password here, the security option applies only to the current workbook. Click the Macro Security button to set options that apply to all workbooks.

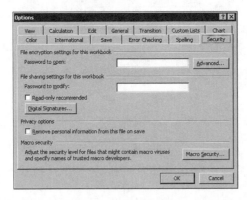

CHANGING DEFAULT FORMATTING FOR NEW WORKBOOKS AND WORKSHEETS

Every time you start Excel or create a new workbook without using a custom template, Excel uses its default settings. To change settings for the default workbook, create a new template called Book.xlt and save it in the XLStart folder. Follow these steps:

1. Create or open the workbook whose settings you want to use as Excel's defaults.

2. To change the style of all cells in the workbook, modify the Normal style. Add other named styles, macros, text, and other content or formatting. If you want to change the number of sheets or add headers and footers, go right ahead.

3. Choose File, Save As. In the Save As Type box, choose Template.

4. In the File Name box, enter Book. (Excel adds the .xlt extension automatically.) Do not save the file in the Templates folder; instead, save it in the XLStart folder. The exact location of this folder varies depending on your version of Windows. On a Windows 98 system, with user profiles enabled, navigate to C:\Windows\Profiles*Username*\Application Data\Microsoft\Excel\XLStart, substituting your Windows or network logon name for *Username*. (Windows NT or Windows 2000 users might need to substitute \Winnt for \Windows in this location.)

5. Click OK to save the template. Any future workbooks you create will include the formats and content in this template.

> **Note**
>
> What's the difference between an Excel template and a worksheet? Structurally, the two file types are identical. Like a workbook, a template can include as many sheets as you want, with or without text, charts, and formatting. The key difference is this: When you open a workbook template, from within Excel or from an Explorer window, Excel leaves the original template file undisturbed and creates a new, unnamed document that is an identical copy of the template.

INSTALLING EXCEL ADD-INS

Excel includes a variety of special-purpose *add-ins*—compiled macros that add new functions beyond those already available. The Analysis ToolPak adds a broad range of worksheet functions to Excel's list of built-in functions, and the Solver add-in offers a wizard-based alternative to trial-and-error formula solving. Both add-ins are described in more detail in Chapter 23, "Using Formulas and Functions." You need to supply the main Office CD (or point to a network install point) to add any of these add-ins.

By default, most of Excel's default add-ins are configured to be installed on first use. That means you'll have to hunt down the main Office CD each time you use an add-in for the first time—an annoying distraction, especially if you're in the middle of a deadline and the CD isn't close at hand.

If you think you might use any of Excel's add-ins in the future, open Control Panel's Add/Remove Programs option, double-click the Microsoft Office XP entry, and launch the

Windows Installer in maintenance mode. Go through the list of add-ins under the Excel group and change their status from Installed on First Use to Run from My Computer.

EXCEL STARTUP SWITCHES

When you start Excel, it normally opens a new workbook using the default settings, runs any AutoStart macros in the Personal Macro workbook, and switches to the default location for data files. To change any of these settings, use one of the following startup switches with the Excel.exe command line. You can use any of these switches as part of a shortcut or type them directly at the command line.

Switch	Function
/e	Forces Excel to start in embedded mode, without creating a new workbook (Book1).
/I	Forces Excel to start with a maximized window, ignoring previous window size settings.
/p <folder>	Sets the active path to a folder other than the default file location; enter the folder name (with its complete path) in quotes.
/r <filename>	Forces Excel to open the specified file in read-only mode.
/s	Forces Excel to start in safe mode, bypassing all files in the Xlstart and Alternate Startup Files folders. Use this switch when debugging startup problems.

Note

To learn more about using command line switches with Excel, see *Special Edition Using Microsoft Excel 2002* by Patrick Blattner (published by Que).

TROUBLESHOOTING

RESETTING THE LAST CELL

I pressed Ctrl+End to go to the last cell in my worksheet, but I ended up with the insertion point in a blank cell below and to the right of the actual end of the sheet. How do I convince Excel to jump to the actual end of the sheet?

When you select the last cell in a worksheet, either by using the Go To Special dialog box or by pressing Ctrl+End, Excel actually jumps to the last cell that has ever contained data or formatting. As you've seen, that can produce unexpected results, especially if you've deleted a large number of rows or columns (or both) from a list or worksheet model, or if you once placed a range of data in an out-of-the-way location and then moved or deleted it. In that case, selecting the Last Cell option might position the insertion point in a cell that's far beyond the actual end of the sheet. To reset the sheet so that you can truly jump to the last cell, delete all rows that are between the actual end of the sheet and the location that Excel insists on identifying as the last cell, and then repeat the process for all columns that match that definition.

If this is a common occurrence, you can create a one-line macro that will reset the last-cell location in the current sheet. Press Alt+F11 to open the Visual Basic Editor and enter the following code:

```
Sub ResetRange()
    ActiveSheet.UsedRange
End Sub
```

Be sure to save the ResetRange macro in an easily accessible location, such as your Personal macro workbook; then run it whenever you encounter a worksheet that needs this type of cleanup.

ADJUSTING HEADER AND FOOTER MARGINS

I created a complex custom footer for a worksheet, but when I try to print, the footer runs into data at the bottom of the sheet.

By default, Excel positions headers and footers a half-inch from the edge of the page and another half-inch from the worksheet's data. That's ideal for a one-liner, but if you try to add too much information in either place—for example, if you insert a long boilerplate paragraph required by a government agency at the bottom of each sheet—you'll quickly overrun that margin. If you decrease the Top or Bottom margins without also adjusting the Header or Footer margins, your data might also collide. You can enter an exact measurement for any of these margins by using the Margins tab on the Page Setup dialog box. If you've already created the header and footer, however, it's much easier to set the margins visually. Choose File, Print Preview; click the Margins button, if necessary, to display the margin markers along each edge of the preview window, and drag the indicators up or down until the preview looks right.

PASSWORDS DON'T WORK ON WEB WORKBOOKS

When I try to save a workbook as a Web page, I get an error message warning that the workbook or sheet is password-protected.

For security reasons, Excel won't let you save a password-protected workbook or worksheet in HTML format. If the entire workbook is protected, you can still save an individual sheet. If any sheet is protected, however, you cannot publish that sheet or even a selection from it in HTML format. Temporarily remove the password protection by choosing Tools, Protection, Unprotect Sheet. After entering the correct password, you can publish the Web page and then restore the protection.

DATA VALIDATION LIMITATIONS

I created a set of validation rules to protect data entry, but when users returned the filled-in worksheet, I found invalid data in those cells. I've triple-checked the data-validation rules, and I'm certain they're working properly. What's the problem?

Validation settings apply only when the user types data into a cell. If the user copies or cuts data from another source and pastes it into the cell via the Clipboard, Excel ignores the rule. There is no workaround for this problem, so you'll have to train your users not to use the Clipboard when filling in forms. Also, if any cell contains a formula as well as a data-validation rule, Excel ignores the rule.

If you want to triple-check the values in cells protected by data-validation rules to make sure they're correct, use the Go To dialog box. Press F5 and click the Special button, and then check the Data Validation option. Click All to see all cells with data-validation rules, or Same to see only cells whose rules match the currently selected cell.

SECRETS OF THE OFFICE MASTERS: BEWARE OF UNDO

Like all Office applications, Excel includes an Undo button and a corresponding keyboard shortcut—Ctrl+Z. Unlike Word, however, which stores an unlimited number of changes, Excel can undo only the 16 most recent actions. When the Undo buffer is full, the oldest entry in the list vanishes to make room for your most recent formatting change, move, copy, data entry, or other action. In previous Excel versions, a simple change in the Registry could expand the Undo buffer significantly; however, that Registry hack no longer works in Excel 2001.

Excel's Undo feature has other significant limitations. For example, if you delete rows from a list and then remove outlining, you cannot undo any changes. Likewise, adding a chart or other object to a sheet clears the Undo history completely. You have absolutely no warning before Excel clears the Undo buffer, and you cannot recover its contents afterwards.

If you're used to working with Word, where the Undo capability gives you a nearly limitless ability to "roll back" a document to a previous version, Excel's considerably less powerful Undo feature might result in a rude surprise. When making extensive changes to the structure or design of an important worksheet, we recommend saving interim versions of the worksheet as you work. This file-saving routine doesn't have to be complex; for instance, you might tack on a version extension—v1, v2, v3, and so on—at the end of the filename each time you save. This simple precaution can make it possible for you to experiment with a worksheet while still preserving the ability to retreat to an earlier version if necessary.

CHAPTER 22

ADVANCED WORKSHEET FORMATTING

In this chapter

HOW CELL FORMATTING WORKS

In an Excel worksheet, what you see in a cell is not necessarily what's stored in that cell. If you enter a formula, for example, Excel stores the formula but displays its result. When entering numbers, dates, and text, you can go as quickly as you want, without too much regard for how they'll look in your worksheet; afterwards, use cell formatting instructions to specify how you want the cells' contents to display, including such details as decimal places, currency symbols, and how many digits to use for the year. Other cell formatting options let you adjust fonts, colors, borders, and other attributes of a cell or range.

A handful of buttons on the Formatting toolbar let you bypass dialog boxes for some common tasks, such as choosing a font or changing a range of cells to bold. If you're building a financial worksheet, click the Currency button to ensure that every number in a given range lines up properly and includes the correct currency symbol. To see the full assortment of Excel formatting options, select a range and choose Format, Cells, or right-click a cell or selection and choose Format Cells from the shortcut menu. All available cell formatting options are arranged on six tabs in the Format Cells dialog box.

USING THE GENERAL NUMBER FORMAT

On a new worksheet, every cell starts out using the General format. When the cell contains a constant value, Excel usually displays the exact text or numbers you entered; in cells that contain a formula, the General format displays the results of the formula using up to 11 digits—the decimal point counts as a digit. (Date and time values follow a special set of rules, as you'll see shortly.) If the cell is not wide enough to show the entire number, Excel rounds the portion of the number to the right of the decimal point, for display purposes only; if the portion of the number to the left of the decimal point won't fit in the cell or contains more than 11 digits, the General format displays the number in scientific notation.

To remove all number formats you've applied manually and restore a cell to its default General format, right-click and choose Format Cells, and then click the Number tab and choose General from the Category list. Although it's not particularly intuitive, there's also a keyboard shortcut that applies the General format instantly to the active cell or current selection: Press Ctrl+Shift+~ (tilde) to reset cells to General format.

CONTROLLING AUTOMATIC NUMBER FORMATS

When you enter data in a format that resembles one of Excel's built-in formats, Excel automatically applies formatting to the cell. In some cases, the results might be unexpected or unwelcome:

■ If you enter a number that contains a slash (/) or hyphen (-) and matches any of Windows' date and time formats, Excel converts the entry to a date serial value and formats the cell using the closest matching Date format. If the date you enter includes only the month and date, Excel adds the current year.

→ In some cases, Excel 2002 picks up formatting from your Windows version; for details of how this interaction works, **see** "Setting Date and Time Formats," **p. 582**.

⚠️ *If you import data into a worksheet, Excel might convert values that look like dates or times. For suggestions on how to prevent this from occurring, see "Stopping Automatic Conversions" in the "Troubleshooting" section at the end of this chapter.*

- If you enter a number preceded by a dollar sign, Excel applies the Currency style, with two decimal places, regardless of how many decimal places you entered. (If you've used the Regional Settings option in Control Panel to specify a different currency symbol, Excel applies the Currency style when you enter data using that symbol.)

Note

As explained later in this chapter, the Currency style is actually a variation of the Accounting format.

- If you enter a number that begins or ends with a percent sign, Excel applies the Percent style with up to two decimal places.

Tip from

EQ & Woody

Excel supports fraction formats as well, but entering data in this format is tricky. If you enter 3/8, for example, Excel interprets your entry as a date—March 8—and formats it accordingly. To enter a fraction that Excel can recognize automatically, start with 0 and a space: 0 3/8. Excel correctly enters that number as 0.375 and changes the cell format to Fraction. Although Excel stores the number as 0.375, it is displayed as 3/8.

Tip from

EQ & Woody

Excel also supports *compound fractions*—fractions that include a whole number and a fractional number, such as 12 1/8. Enter the whole number part (in this case, 12) followed by a space and then the fraction part. Excel displays the entry as 12 1/8 but stores it as 12.125. You'll find this technique invaluable if you ever have to perform calculations involving stock market prices; although more and more markets are moving to decimal pricing, some exchanges still use archaic fractional pricing—16ths, 32nds, even 64ths of a dollar!

- When you enter a number that contains a colon (:), or if the number is followed by a space and the letter A or P, Excel converts it to a time format.
- If the number you enter contains leading zeros (as in part numbers, for example, which might need to fill a precise number of characters), Excel drops the leading zero.
- When you enter a number that contains the letter E anywhere in the middle (3.14159E19, for example), Excel formats the cell using the Scientific option, using no more than two decimal places. In this case, Excel would display 3.14E+19.
- If you enter a number that includes a comma to set off thousands or millions, Excel applies the Number format using the default thousands separator as defined in Windows' Regional Settings. If the number you entered contains more than two decimal places, Excel stores the number you entered but rounds it for display purposes to no more than two decimal places.

To override any of these automatic number formats, you have four choices:

- After entering the data, choose Format, Cells and select a new format. (Press Ctrl+1 to quickly open this dialog box.) This is your best choice if the underlying data stored in the cell is correct and you just want to use a different display format.

- Enter an apostrophe before entering the number. When you do this, Excel formats the number as text and displays it exactly as entered. Note that this solution might have unintended consequences in formulas that use the value shown in that cell!

- Enter a space character before entering the number. This prefix also tells Excel to format the number as text and display it exactly as entered. Note that this technique will not prevent Excel from converting a number to scientific notation nor will it preserve leading zeros. It will, however, work with all other automatic formatting described in the previous list.

- Format the cell as text (choose Format, Cells, click the Number tab, and select Text) before entering the data. This option might also have unintended side effects, as explained a bit later in this chapter.

AVOIDING ROUNDING ERRORS

It's tempting to assume that because numbers look so orderly in Excel's row-and-column grids, they're also unfailingly accurate. That's not exactly so. To squeeze data so that it fits in a cell, Excel *rounds* numbers and *truncates* cell contents, usually without telling you. And there's an absolute limit on the precision of Excel calculations that affects every calculation you make.

Note

What's the difference between rounding and truncating? When Excel rounds a number, it changes the value displayed in the cell without affecting the underlying number stored in the cell. If you enter 3.1415926 in a cell and format it to display two decimal points, Excel displays 3.14. If you later change the display format to show all seven decimal points, your number will appear exactly as you entered it. When Excel truncates data, on the other hand, it chops off digits permanently. If you enter a number with more than 15 decimal places, for example, Excel lops off the 16th and any subsequent numbers to the right of the decimal point. Likewise, if you copy a worksheet that contains cells with more than 255 characters, Excel discards all characters after the first 255.

When Excel alters the display of a number, the most common cause is that the number is too long to fit in the active cell. Excel deals with this sort of data in one of the following three ways:

- When you enter data that is wider than the current cell, Excel automatically resizes the column. It does not resize a column if you have already set the column width manually. If the cell is formatted using General format, this automatic resizing stops when the number reaches 11 digits, at which point Excel converts it to scientific notation. If the cell is formatted using Number format, automatic resizing continues until the number reaches 30 digits.

- In cells using the default General format, Excel uses scientific notation to display large numbers if possible. The General format rounds numbers expressed this way to no more than six *digits of precision* (8.39615E+13, for example).

Note

It's no accident that the total number of characters in the preceding example—including the decimal point, plus sign, and E—is 11. Regardless of column width, cells using the General format are always limited to 11 digits.

- In cells using any number format other than General, Excel displays a string of number signs (####) if the column is too narrow to display the number in scientific notation. You must change the cell's number format or make the column wider before Excel can display the number correctly.

The second most common cause of apparent errors in a worksheet occurs when the number of decimal cells you specify in a number format doesn't match the number of decimal places stored in that cell or range. Figure 22.1, for example, shows two identical columns of numbers. Because column A uses the General format, each number appears exactly as entered. Column B, on the other hand, is formatted with the Number format to show zero decimal places. When Excel performs the calculation on the numbers in column B, it uses the actual amount stored in the cell, not the rounded version you see here. It then displays the result without any decimal places, exactly as specified in the cell format. Although the sum of the rounded numbers in column B appears to be 16, Excel rounds the actual result to 15 for display purposes. Because of the mismatch between the numbers and their formatting, Excel (and, by extension, the author of this worksheet) appears incapable of basic arithmetic.

Figure 22.1
The values in these two columns are identical, with different formatting. Because of cumulative rounding errors, the numbers in column B appear to add up to 16, despite what the SUM formula suggests.

	A	B
1	2.3	2
2	2.5	3
3	2.5	3
4	3.1	3
5	2.75	3
6	2.2	2
7	15.35	15

That's a simple and obvious example, but subtle rounding errors can wreak havoc in an environment where you require precise results. To prevent rounding from making it look like your worksheet contains errors, always match the number of decimal places displayed with the number of decimal places you've entered in the row or column in question.

Tip from

EQ & Woody

If you must use rounded numbers in a worksheet, indicate that fact in a footnote on charts and reports you plan to present to others. Rounding can cause apparent mistakes, and anyone who sees your worksheet—or a chart or presentation slide based on those numbers—might make unflattering judgments about your accuracy if totals in a pie chart, for example, don't add up to 100%.

THE LIMITS OF PRECISION

There's an overriding limit to the degree of precision you can achieve with Excel. If you enter a number that contains more than 15 significant digits, Excel permanently and irrevocably converts the 16th and subsequent digits to 0. (It doesn't matter which side of the decimal point the digits appear on—the total number of digits allowed includes those on both sides of the decimal point.) Although you can display numbers with up to 30 decimal places, your calculations will not be accurate if Excel has to store more than 15 digits.

Excel includes a useful, but extremely dangerous, option to permanently store numbers using the displayed precision. If you've increased the numbers in a budget worksheet by 8.25%, for example, you might end up with three decimal places for some entries, even though only two are displayed using the Currency format. If you choose Tools, Options, and click the Calculation tab, you can check the Precision As Displayed box to convert all stored numbers in the current workbook to the values actually displayed.

Caution

When you use the Precision As Displayed option, Excel displays a terse dialog box warning you that your data will permanently lose accuracy. Believe it. This option affects every cell on every sheet in the current workbook, and it remains in force until you explicitly remove the check mark from this box. If you forget you turned on this option, even simple formatting choices like changing the display of decimal places will permanently change stored data. Unless you're absolutely certain that using this option will have no unintended consequences, you should treat it like dynamite.

Tip from

EQ & Woody

The Precision As Displayed option affects all cells in the current workbook, and there's no way to apply it just to a selected range. If you want to change the precision of a selection, use the Windows Clipboard to control this option precisely—in the process, you can also avoid any unintended ill effects. Open a new, blank workbook, copy the range you want to change from the original workbook, and paste it into the blank workbook. In the blank workbook, choose Tools, Options, click the Calculation tab, and check the Precision As Displayed box. Click OK when you see the warning dialog box. Now copy the changed data to the Clipboard and paste it over the original data. Close the blank workbook without saving it, and you're finished.

WORKING WITH NUMBERS IN SCIENTIFIC NOTATION

Scientific (or exponential) *notation* displays large numbers in a shorthand form that shows the first few digits along with instructions on where to place the decimal point. To convert a number written in scientific notation to its decimal equivalent, move the decimal to the right by the number that appears after "E+"; if there's a minus sign after the *E*, move the decimal to the left. In either case, add extra zeros as needed. Thus, 8.23E+06 is actually 8,230,000, and 3.82E-07 is .000000382.

Numbers expressed in scientific notation are often rounded. When you see numbers in General format expressed in scientific notation, you'll see a maximum of six significant digits, even if the cell is wide enough to hold more. To display a number in scientific notation using more digits of precision, choose Format, Cells, and choose the Scientific option from the Category list. Use the spinner control to set a fixed number of decimal places, between 0 and 30.

ENTERING NUMBERS AS TEXT

Hands down, the most confusing option on the Number tab of the Format Cells dialog box is Text. Use this format when you want to enter numbers in a cell, but you want Excel to treat them as though they were text. You might use this format, for example, when entering a list of part numbers that you will never use in calculations.

If you apply the Text format to a cell and then enter or paste a numeric value into that cell, Excel adds a small green triangle in the top-left corner of the cell, indicating a possible error. Selecting that cell reveals a Smart Tag that gives you the option to convert the cell to number format.

→ For more information about Smart Tags, **see** "Common Formatting Options," **p. 100**.

→ To learn how to check an Excel workbook for errors, **see** "Checking for Errors in a Worksheet," **p. 636**.

When you format numbers as Text, Excel ignores them in formulas such as SUM() and AVERAGE(). It also aligns the cell's contents to the left rather than the right. Unfortunately, applying the Text format requires that you work around an admitted bug that still exists in Excel 2002. If you format the cells first, then apply the Text format, and finally enter the numbers, Excel treats the data as text, just as you intended. However, if you try to apply the Text format to numbers that are already in your worksheet, Excel changes the alignment of the cell, but not the data stored there. After applying the Text format, you must click in each reformatted cell, press F2, and then press Enter to store the number as text. The new error-checking tools in Excel 2002 do not identify cells formatted this way, either.

CHANGING FORMATTING FOR A CELL OR RANGE

In general, as noted previously, Excel stores exactly what you type in a cell. You have tremendous control over how that data appears, however. Number and date formats, for example, give you precise control over commas, decimal points, and whether months and days are spelled out or abbreviated. And if you can't find the precise format you're looking for, Excel lets you create your own custom format.

SETTING NUMBER FORMATS

How should Excel display the contents of a cell? You have dozens of choices, all neatly organized by category on the Number tab of the Format Cells dialog box. To specify exactly how you want the contents of a cell or range to appear, follow these steps:

1. Click the cell you want to format, or select a range, and then choose Format, Cells. Use the keyboard shortcut Ctrl+1 to open this dialog box instantly.

Tip from

EQ & Woody

Few keyboard shortcuts in all of Office are as useful as Ctrl+1, which opens Excel's Format Cells dialog box. When you're formatting a large or complex worksheet, this key combination can save a startling number of mouse clicks. Even if you generally don't use keyboard shortcuts, this one is worth memorizing. Note that you must use the number 1 on the top row of the keyboard; the 1 on the numeric keypad won't work.

---

2. In the Format Cells dialog box, choose an entry from the Category list on the left.

3. If the category you selected includes predefined display options, select one from the Type list. Adjust other format options (currency symbol, decimal point, and so on), if necessary.

Tip

To quickly adjust the number of decimal points in a cell or range, make a selection and click the Increase Decimal or Decrease Decimal buttons on the Formatting toolbar. Each click adds or subtracts one decimal point from the selection.

---

4. Inspect the Sample box in the upper-right corner of the dialog box to see how the active cell will appear with the format settings you've selected. Click OK to accept the settings and return to the editing window.

The following number format categories are available:

- General, the default format, displays numbers as entered, using as many decimal places as necessary, up to a maximum of 11 digits. It does not include separators between thousands. No additional options are available.

- Number formats let you specify the number of decimal places, from 0 to 30 (the default is 2), as well as an optional separator for thousands, based on the Windows Regional Settings. You can also choose one of four formats for negative numbers (**see** Figure 22.2).

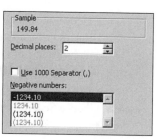

Figure 22.2

- Choices in the Currency category display values using the default currency symbol, as specified in the Regional Settings options of Control Panel. You can adjust the number of decimal places from its default of 2 to any number between 0 and 30 and select a format for negative values (see Figure 22.3).

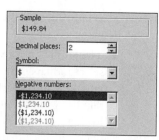

Figure 22.3

- Accounting formats are similar to those in the Currency category, except that currency symbols and decimal points align properly in columns and you can't choose a format for negative values. With Accounting formats, the currency symbol ($ in U.S. English installations) sits at the left edge of the cell. This effect can be odd in wide columns that contain small numbers; in that case, choose a Currency format instead, if possible (see Figure 22.4).

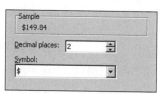

Figure 22.4

- The Date category includes 15 formats that determine whether and how to display day, date, month, and year. Excel 2000 and 2002 include two Year-2000–compatible date formats that use four digits for the year (see Figure 22.5).

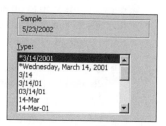

Figure 22.5

- The Time category includes eight formats that determine whether and how to display hours, minutes, seconds, and AM/PM designators (see Figure 22.6).

- Applying the Percentage format multiplies the cell value by 100 for display purposes and adds a percent symbol; the only option here lets you specify the number of decimal places, from 0 to 30 (the default is 2).

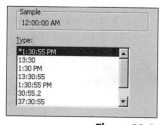

Figure 22.6

PART

IV

CH

22

■ Fraction formats store numbers in decimal format but displays cell contents as fractions using any of 9 predefined settings; to display stock prices using 8ths, 16ths, and 32nds, click Up to Two Digits in the Type list (see Figure 22.7).

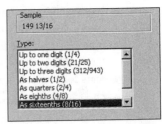

Figure 22.7

■ Choose Scientific to display numbers in scientific notation; you select the number of decimal places, from 0 to 30.

■ Applying the Text format displays cell contents exactly as entered, even if the cell contains numbers or a formula.

■ The four choices in the Special category allow you to select formats for long and short U.S. ZIP codes, phone numbers, and Social Security numbers. You enter the number without any punctuation, and Excel adds hyphens and parentheses as necessary for display purposes only (see Figure 22.8).

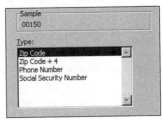

Figure 22.8

■ Choose the Custom option to define your own display rules. Start with a built-in format and use symbols in the formatting instructions; see "Custom Number Formats" later in this chapter for more details on custom number formats.

SETTING DATE AND TIME FORMATS

Normally, Excel stores exactly what you type into a cell. That's not the case when you type a recognizable date or time, however; when storing date and time information, Excel first converts the value you enter into *serial date format*. This numeric transformation explains how Excel can perform calculations using date and time information. Understanding the following facts is crucial to working effectively with serial date formats:

■ Excel converts the date to a whole number that counts the number of days that have elapsed since January 1, 1900. Thus, the serial date value of December 31, 2001 is 37256.

■ When you enter a time (hours, minutes, and seconds), Excel converts it to a fractional decimal value between 0 (midnight) and 0.999988 (11:59:59 PM). If you enter a time of 10:00 AM, for example, Excel stores it as 0.416667.

■ If you combine a date and time, Excel combines the serial date and time values. Thus, Excel saves December 31, 2001 10:00 AM as 37256.416667.

Note

When you enter only a date, Excel converts it to a serial value and uses 0 (or 12:00 AM) as the time value. If you enter only a time, Excel tacks on a date value of 1; if you later format this cell to show the date and time, Excel displays the nonsense date 1/0/1900.

The transformation to a serial value happens as soon as you enter a date or time value in a cell; at the same time, Excel automatically applies the default Date or Time format to your cell so that the data you enter displays correctly. You can choose a different Date or Time format to change the display format of date or time values. If you change the format of the cell to General or Number, however, you will see the serial values instead of the dates you expect.

Conversely, if you accidentally apply the Date format to a cell that contains a number, the result is likely to be nonsense, especially if the number is relatively low. Choose the General or Number format to display the cell's contents correctly.

Tip from

EQ & Woody

If the display of dates is important to you, be aware of the unusual interaction between Excel's date and time formats and those you define in Windows' Regional Options Control Panel (in some Windows versions, this appears as Regional Settings). These linked formats appear at the top of the Date and Time lists in the Format Cells dialog box, with an asterisk in front of the format. When you change the date format in Windows, the format in your worksheet changes too—if you've used one of these formats.

Excel transforms dates and times to serial values so that you can use them in calculations. Because date and time values are stored as numbers, you can easily enter formulas that calculate elapsed time. If you include an employee's hire date as part of a list, for instance, you can use a simple formula to compare that value to today's date and determine whether the employee has qualified for participation in a profit-sharing or stock-option program. If you enter start and end times for each participant in a road race, you can easily calculate the total elapsed time and determine the top finishers.

After you enter the employee's start date in C1 and your report date in C2, for example, you can quickly calculate the difference between the two dates by using the formula =C1-C2.

Tip from

EQ & Woody

Unfortunately, Excel outsmarts itself when you use this type of formula. Because it sees dates in both cells used in the formula, it automatically applies a date format to the cell containing the formula. As a result, the cell contents display as a nonsense date. Reset the cell's format to General or Number to correctly display the difference between the dates.

To use a date directly in a formula, enclose it in quotation marks first: =Today()-"1/1/2001" counts the number of days that have elapsed since January 1, 2001, for instance.s

Note

Excel's Options dialog box includes a setting for the 1904 date system. This obscure option is necessary only when exchanging files with users of old versions of Excel for the Macintosh, which started the calendar at the beginning of 1904 rather than 1900. Recent Mac Excel versions, including Excel 98, handle this conversion seamlessly. Under normal circumstances, this option should not be necessary.

EXCEL AND YEAR 2000 ISSUES

The much-feared global Y2K crisis never happened. Planes continued to fly, power stations hummed along, and banks didn't run out of money. Yes, the world successfully entered the new Millennium, but that doesn't let you off the hook when it comes to Year 2000 (Y2K) issues. Excel's default settings correctly handle most formulas that include dates from different centuries. But a few "gotchas" linger for the unwary:

■ When you enter a date before January 1, 1900 in an Excel worksheet, the date appears as text. As far as Excel is concerned, dates before the 20th Century simply don't exist—that's bad news for historians hoping to use Excel to plot dates that go back more than a century.

■ On the other hand, dates after December 31, 1999 don't represent a problem. In fact, Excel worksheets will accept any date through December 31, 9999 (that's a serial date value of 2958465, if you want to try it for yourself).

Tip from

EQ & Woody

If you need to track timelines and perform calculations for dates before the beginning of 1900 (to chart long-term records of earthquake activities, for example), don't use Excel. Instead, fire up Access, which can correctly handle dates as early as January 1, 100 (Common Era). If you're a student of ancient history, you'll need to use another program—or perhaps you can make do with clay tablets.

Because Excel stores dates as serial values, it is unaffected by most garden-variety Y2K problems. In practice, however, you might encounter Y2K problems if you enter or import data that includes only two digits for the year. When Excel encounters dates in this format, it has to convert the year to four digits; in the process, it's possible to select the wrong century. When translating two-digit years, Excel uses the following rules:

■ Excel automatically converts dates entered using the two-digit years 00 through 29 to the years 2000 through 2029. Thus, if you enter or import the value 5/23/02, Excel stores it as serial value 37399, or May 23, 2002.

■ When you enter the two-digit years 30 through 99 as part of a date, Excel converts the dates using the years 1930 through 1999. Thus, when you enter or import the value 9/29/55, Excel stores it as serial value 20361, or September 29, 1955.

If you're using a display format that shows only two years, you might not realize that Excel has stored the wrong data, but any calculations you make might be off by a full century. To avoid inadvertently entering or importing incorrect data, get in the habit of entering all dates using four-digit formats for the year: 5/23/2002. Excel stores this date correctly regardless of the Date format you've chosen for display purposes.

When importing data that includes dates with two-digit years, check the format of the original data carefully. You might need to manually edit some dates after importing. Pay special attention to worksheets that were originally created using older versions of Excel for Windows or the Macintosh, because the algorithms those programs use to convert two-digit years are different from those in Excel 2000 and 2002.

The automatic date conversion routine is a clever workaround, but don't rely on it. Entering or importing two-digit years is guaranteed to cause problems in the following circumstances:

- In the banking industry, in which dates beyond 2029 are common in 30-year mortgages that begin in the year 2000 or later. If you enter the start date as 2/1/00 and the end date as 2/1/30, your loan will start out 70 years overdue.

- In any group that includes milestone dates—birthdays, graduation dates, and so on—for an older population. If you enter a birthdate of 6/19/27, your worksheet might assume that the person in question isn't born yet.

Tip from

E Q & Woody

This can't be said strongly enough or repeated too often: Get in the habit of using four-digit years whenever you enter or display a date in a worksheet.

CREATING CUSTOM CELL FORMATS

If the exact number format you need isn't in Excel's collection of built-in formats, create a custom format. Custom formats let you specify the display of positive and negative numbers as well as zero values; you can also add text to the contents of any cell.

Tip from

E Q & Woody

Excel saves custom number formats in the workbook in which you create them. To reuse formats, add them to the template on which you base new workbooks. To copy cell formats from one workbook to another, copy the cell that contains the custom format, click in the workbook where you want to add the format, and choose Edit, Paste Special, Formats.

The list of 35 custom formats in the Type box includes some that are already available within other categories, as well as a few you won't find elsewhere. It's almost always easier to design a custom format if you start with one that already exists. To create a custom number format, open the Format Cells dialog box and choose the format you want to start with.

Then click Custom at the bottom of the Category list. Excel displays the codes for the format you just selected in the Type box, ready for you to modify. The example shown in Figure 22.9, for example, shows the results when we chose a Currency format and changed the symbol from the U.S. dollar sign to the Euro. Although the switches for these codes are undocumented, this technique adds them to the Type box, making it easy to define a new format that uses this symbol correctly.

Figure 22.9
Enter custom format codes here. Note the Sample area, which shows how the contents of the active cell will appear.

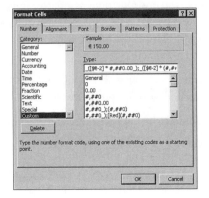

Custom formats use format codes to tell Excel how to display digits, decimal places, dates and times, and other details. Each custom format can include up to four sections, separated by semicolons, as shown in the example in Figure 22.10. Using all four sections defines display formats for positive numbers, negative numbers, zero values, and text, respectively. If you enter only two sections, Excel uses the first set of instructions for positive numbers and zero values and the second for negative numbers. If you enter only one section, that format will apply to all numbers you enter. You don't need to enter a format for each section, but if you plan to skip a format option (specifying formats only for positive numbers and zero values, for example), insert a semicolon for each section you skip.

Figure 22.10
Custom number formats can contain up to four sections.

`_($* #,##0_);_($* (#,##0);_($* "-"_);_(@_)`

Tip from
EQ & Woody

When creating an extremely complex custom format, working with the narrow text box in the Format Cells dialog box can be difficult. To make life easier, select the contents of this box, and then copy them to a friendlier editor, such as Notepad or Word. Edit the format codes, and then use the Clipboard to paste the results back into the dialog box.

Creative use of custom number formats can help you deal with tricky data-entry challenges. For example, how do you make it easy to enter a serial number with leading zeros? Say your company uses invoice or part numbers that must be exactly seven digits, with no exceptions. If the number you enter includes fewer than seven digits, you want Excel to pad the beginning of the entry with as many zeros as it takes to reach that magic number. Entering a number like 0001234 won't work, because Excel considers the leading zeros insignificant digits and strips them before storing the value in the cell.

The solution is to create a custom format that includes a zero for each digit you want to include in the displayed result—in this case, 0000000.

Tip from

EQ & Woody

To guarantee that only correct data appears in the cell, combine this custom format with a data-validation rule, as described in Chapter 21, "Restricting and Validating Data Entry for a Cell or Range." If your company policy says the number must be larger than 1000, create a validation rule that restricts data entry to whole numbers (to prevent stray decimal points or text from messing up the list) between 1001 and 9999999. The all-zeros display format guarantees that any data within this range will display as exactly seven digits, with leading zeros if necessary.

CUSTOM NUMBER FORMATS

Custom number formats let you round or truncate numbers, control the number of decimal places or significant digits, and make sure amounts line up properly in columns. Use the codes shown in Table 22.1 to define the display format.

TABLE 22.1 CUSTOM NUMBER FORMAT CODES

Code	What It Does	How You Use It
#	Display significant digit	Using the format #.# displays all significant (nonzero) digits to the left of the decimal point and rounds to one digit on the right of the decimal point; if you enter 0.567, this format displays .6.
0	Display zero if the number has fewer digits than the number to format	The format 0.000 always displays exactly three decimal points; for numbers below 1, it includes a 0 to the left of the decimal point.
?	Align decimal points or fractions	Click any of Excel's built-in Fraction formats, and then choose Custom to see an example of how to use this placeholder.
.	Decimal point	To round the cell's contents to a whole number, leave off the decimal point.
,	Display thousands separator or scale number by multiple of 1,000	Inserting two commas after a number scales it by a million; to display a large number (163,200,000) in an easier-to-read style (163.2 MM), enter this format: #0.0,," MM".
%	Display the number as a percentage of 100	If you enter 8, Excel displays it as 800%. To enter 8%, start with a decimal point and a zero: .08.

TABLE 22.1   CONTINUED

Code	What It Does	How You Use It
[*color*]	Show the cell contents in specified color	Choose one of eight colors—Black, Blue, Cyan, Green, Magenta, Red, White, Yellow—for any section; you must use brackets and enter the color as the first item in each section, like this: `[Blue]#,##0;[Red]#,##0;[Black]0`.

CUSTOM DATE AND TIME FORMATS

Excel's selection of ready-made date and time formats is extensive, but there are several situations in which you might want to create your own. For example, if your company uses a special date format to identify dates on an invoice, you can enter a format such as yyyymmdd to display a date as 19990321.

Custom date and time formats are also useful on billing worksheets for professionals who charge by the minute or hour, or if you've captured data from time sheets filled out by hourly workers. Table 22.2 includes examples of date and time codes you can add to custom formats.

TABLE 22.2   CUSTOM DATE/TIME FORMAT CODES

Code	What It Does	How You Use It
d, dd m, mm	Day or month in numeric format, with or without leading zero	Use the leading zero when you want columns of dates to line up properly; to add a zero to the date only, use this format: m/dd/yyyy.
ddd, mmm dddd, mmmm	Day or month in text format, abbreviated or full	Use ddd or mmm to show abbreviations such as Wed or Jan; use dddd and mmmm for the fully spelled out month or day: January and Wednesday.
mmmmm	Month as first letter only	Potentially confusing, because it's impossible to distinguish between January, June, and July, or between March and May.
yy, yyyy	Year, in two- or four-digit format	If you're concerned about possible confusion caused by the Year 2000, specify four-digit years.
h, hh m, mm s, ss	Hours, minutes, or seconds, with or without leading zero	Use a leading zero with minutes and seconds; to store precise times, add a decimal point and extra digits after the format: `h:mm:ss.00`.
A/P, AM/PM	Show AM/PM indicator	Insert after time code to use 12-hour clock and display AM or PM (6:12 PM); otherwise, Excel displays the time in 24-hour format (18:12).

Table 22.2 Continued

Code	What It Does	How You Use It
[h], [m], [s]	Show elapsed time in hours, minutes, or seconds	Add brackets to display elapsed time rather than a time of day. Add decimals for seconds; for instance, for a worksheet containing race times, use this format: [m]:ss.00.

Adding Text to a Cell

To display text in a cell that contains numbers, Excel includes a selection of special format codes. Use this type of format to add a word like "shortage" or "deficit" after a negative number, for example. Because the format doesn't change the contents of the cell, the number you entered will still work in formulas that reference that cell.

You can add the space character, left and right single quotation mark, and any of the following special characters without enclosing them in double quotation marks:

$ - + / ( ) : ! [ct] & ~ { } = < >

To add other text to a cell, use the codes in Table 22.3.

Table 22.3 Custom Text Format Codes

Code	What It Does	How You Use It
*	Repeat characters to fill cell to column width	Enter an asterisk followed by the character you want to repeat. Use *- in the third position of a custom format to replace zero values with a line of hyphens, for example.
_ (underscore character)	Add a space the width of a specified character	Enter an underscore followed by the character whose width you want to use. Several built-in formats use _)) with positive number formats, for example, to make sure they line up properly with negative numbers that use parentheses.
\	Display the character that follows the backslash	To add a space and the letter P or L after a positive or negative value, use this format: `#,##0_)\P;[Red](#,##0) \L.`
"text"	Display the text you enter inside the double quotation marks	Remember to add a space inside the quotes when necessary. For example, to display a negative amount as $514.32 Loss in red, enter this format: `$0.00"Profit";[Red] $0.00"Loss".`
@	Display the text entered in the cell	Use this code only in the fourth (text) section in a custom format to combine the entered text with other text. If you include a text section without the @ character, Excel hides any text in the cell.

Tip from

Ed & Woody

When creating a custom number format, first click in a cell that contains data you want to see in the new format. As you edit the custom format, the Preview region of the Custom Format dialog box shows you how the active cell's contents will appear in the new format.

ADDING CONDITIONS TO A DISPLAY FORMAT

You can also use *conditions* as part of custom number formats. Conditions use comparison operators and are contained in brackets as part of a format definition. Look at the built-in Phone Number format (in the Special category) to see how this option works:

`[<=9999999]###-####;(###) ###-####`

If you enter a number of seven or fewer digits in a cell that uses this format, Excel treats it as a local phone number and adds a hyphen where the prefix appears. If you enter a number greater than seven digits, Excel uses the second part of the format, displaying the last seven digits as a phone number and any number of digits prior to that number as an area code in parentheses.

The results of this format can be absurd if you enter a number that's smaller than 7 digits or larger than 10 digits. Here's how to use conditions to customize this format. The example shown here assumes you work in the 212 area code and want to add that code to the beginning of any 7-digit (local) number; if the number uses more than 10 digits, the default condition at the end kicks in, adding the international dialing prefix (+011) and splitting the digits before the number into country and city codes.

`[<=9999999](212) ###-####;[<=9999999999](###) ###-####;"+011 "(#-##) ###-####`

Tip from

Ed & Woody

Don't confuse these custom formats with conditional formatting, which is described later in this chapter. If you want to change the font or color of text based on values displayed in the cell, use the Conditional Formatting option on the Format menu (described later in this chapter). The conditional display formats shown here are most useful when you want to subdivide a number with punctuation marks or change the number of digits displayed. You can effectively combine this type of format with conditional formatting—for example, if the user enters a phone number with six or fewer digits, you might display it in red to help it stand out as a possibly invalid number.

DESIGNING AND FORMATTING A WORKSHEET FOR MAXIMUM READABILITY

If you simply enter data into a new worksheet without adjusting any formatting first, every cell will look exactly the same, and anyone reading the worksheet will be forced to work to pick out the important details. Want to make it easier on your audience? Set off different regions of a worksheet by using custom cell formatting—larger, bolder fonts for headings, for example, plus borders around the data area with a double line to mark where the data range ends and the totals begin. Carefully resetting row heights and column widths, wrapping and slanting text, and adding background shading can make the entire sheet easier to follow.

CHANGING FONTS AND CHARACTER ATTRIBUTES

The default worksheet font (10-point Arial) is fine for basic data entry, but for any worksheet more complex than a simple list you'll probably want to adjust fonts to squeeze more data onto printed pages while beefing up titles, totals, and category headings with larger, bolder fonts.

→ If you're entering data in a list, some cells format themselves automatically; for details, **see** "Speeding Up Repetitive Data Entry with AutoComplete," **p. 675**.

If you select a cell or range, you can apply font formatting to the entire contents of the selection. You can also apply different fonts, font sizes, colors, and font attributes to different words or characters in the same cell. In either case, you can use the Font and font size lists on the Formatting toolbar. Open the Format Cells dialog box and click the Font tab (see Figure 22.11) for access to all font formats, including some options you won't find on the toolbar, such as strikethrough and double underline attributes.

Figure 22.11
Options on the Font tab let you format an entire cell or selected words or characters within a cell.

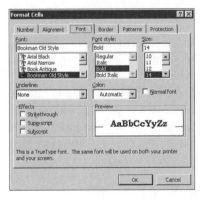

Most of the options on the Font tab of this dialog box are fairly straightforward. One check box deserves some explanation, however. When you add custom font formatting, you automatically clear the Normal Font check box. Check this box again to remove all font formatting from the current cell or selection and restore Excel's default style.

 If you're having trouble restoring default font formatting to a cell, see "Click Twice for Normal" in the "Troubleshooting" section at the end of this chapter.

You'll find countless uses for rich formatting within cells. The range shown in Figure 22.12, for example, uses different font formatting for the product number and name in a list of products. This feature is also a useful way to insert trademark and copyright symbols and other special characters within a cell.

Figure 22.12
Mix and match font formatting within a cell to emphasize one type of data over another.

Note

To enter a manual line break within a cell, position the insertion point at the spot where you want the break to appear and press Alt+Enter. Unfortunately, there's no easy way to copy rich formatting from one cell to another. If you use the Format Painter or the Clipboard to copy formats, only the first font is copied.

An obscure check box on the Alignment tab of the Format Cells dialog box actually has a major effect on formatting. Check the Shrink to Fit box when you want Excel to automatically adjust the font size when the contents of a cell are too wide to fit. This option doesn't change the formatting applied to the cell; it changes the scaling instead, going up or down in 1-point increments. If you enter more text or adjust the width of the column, Excel changes the size of the font automatically so that you can continue to see its contents. Use this option with care—if you format an entire column as Shrink to Fit and then fill it with data that varies in length, the results can look like a ransom note.

ALIGNING, WRAPPING, AND ROTATING TEXT AND NUMBERS

When you use the default General format, cells containing text align to the left, and those with numbers align to the right. You can change the alignment of any cell or range by using the Align Left, Center, and Align Right buttons on the Formatting toolbar.

Use the Wrap Text option on the Alignment tab to handle long strings of text that don't fit in a cell. Wrapped text is useful for column headings that are much longer than the data in the column. You can also use wrapped text to create tables, where each cell in a row holds an entire paragraph. Excel wraps text to additional lines automatically, maintaining the column width you specified. To control the location of each break, press Alt+Enter. To use text wrapping, follow these steps:

1. Select the cell or range that contains the text you want to wrap. Right-click and choose Format Cells.

2. Click the Alignment tab on the Format Cells dialog box and check the Wrap Text box.

3. Adjust the vertical alignment if needed. For column headings with long and short entries, for example, choose Center from the Vertical drop-down list. Headings formatted this way seem to "float" instead of sitting on the bottom of the cell. For text in a table, choose the Top format so that each paragraph begins at the same point.

4. Click OK to apply the new format. Now, instead of disappearing from view when they reach the right edge of the cell, the text you enter begins filling additional lines in the same cell.

Two other alignment options can help make worksheets easier to read. You can change the orientation of a column heading to any angle, including straight up or down. Slanting column headings can save space and give tables a professional look when you have narrow columns with lengthy titles. To help set off groups of items in a column, indent the cells in second and subsequent levels. (See the before and after worksheets at the end of this chapter for examples of all these alignment options.) This option is especially useful when you want to distinguish subheadings from headings at the beginning of a row.

To indent a cell or range of cells, follow these steps:

1. Select the cell or range you want to format, right-click, and choose Format Cells.

2. Click the Alignment tab. In the Text Alignment section, click the Horizontal drop-down list and choose Indent (Left).

3. Use the Indent spinner to select the indent level for the selection. For each number, Excel adds approximately as much space as a capital M. For the outline levels in column A of Figure 22.13, we used settings of 1 and 2, respectively.

4. Click OK to accept the changes and return to the worksheet.

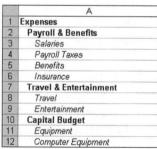

Figure 22.13

Use the Format Cells dialog box to change the orientation of column headings so that they slant up or down:

1. After entering the text for the headings, select one or more cells, right-click, and choose Format Cells.

2. Click the Alignment tab, and then point to the control in the Orientation section of the dialog box and drag it up or down to the desired angle, as shown in Figure 22.14, or use the spinner to specify a precise angle by degrees.

3. Click OK to accept the changes and return to the worksheet.

Figure 22.14
Click the line between the word Text and the red square; then drag it up or down to arrange text at a space-saving angle.

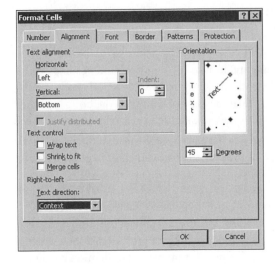

Word and PowerPoint don't allow you to position headings using any orientation except horizontal or vertical. If you want to add a table with slanted headings to a Word document or PowerPoint presentation, create the table in Excel, and then use Paste Special and choose "Microsoft Excel Worksheet object" to embed the worksheet range, complete with slanted headings.

Vertical headings use little column width, but they can be difficult to read. You have two choices when changing a heading to vertical orientation. Click the skinny box just under the word Orientation to stack letters one over another. This option is most effective with short words in all capitals. You can also change the orientation to 90[dg] to turn the cell on its side, so the contents read from bottom to top.

USING BORDERS, BOXES, AND COLORS

You can create a distinctive identity for sections of a worksheet by using borders, boxes, and background colors. Dark backgrounds and white type help worksheet titles stand out. Soft, light background colors make columns of numbers easier to read. Use alternating colors or shading to make it easy for the eye to tell which entries belong in each row, even on a wide worksheet that contains many columns of data.

When preparing a worksheet that you intend to print on a black-and-white printer, test different color combinations. Use the printout to decide which colors are best for you. Sometimes, for example, it's easier to read black type on a light yellow background (which appears gray) than on a background on which you specify a shade of gray.

The Borders, Fill Color, and Font Color buttons on the Formatting toolbar work much as you would expect. After selecting a cell or range, click the arrow to the right of each button to choose a specific option from the drop-down list.

These toolbars don't give you access to every formatting option, however. For maximum control over borders and colors, first select the cells or range you want to format; then right-click and choose Format Cells. Click the Border tab (see Figure 22.15) to add and remove lines around the selection.

Figure 22.15
Use borders to distinguish sections of your worksheet. Note that this range includes three different line styles.

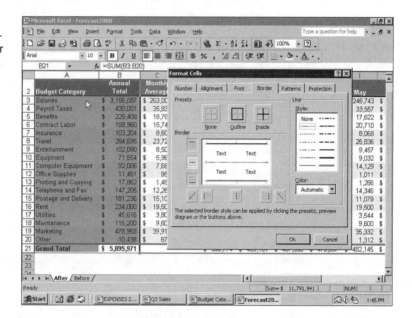

To create custom borders, follow these steps:

1. Before you add any lines, choose a line style—thick, thin, doubled, dotted, or dashed—from the Style box at the right.

2. Choose a different border color, if you like, from the Color drop-down list. Colors are most effective with thick lines.

3. Click the Outline button to add lines in the thickness and color you specified on all four sides of the active cell. If you selected a range, click Outline to draw a box around the range, and click Inside to draw borders around every cell in the selection.

4. Click any of the buttons in the Border section to add one line at a time, on the left, right, top, or bottom of the cell, or diagonally. Click again to remove the line. The preview area shows which edges currently have borders.

Note

You can also click directly on lines in the preview area to add or remove borders.

5. You can mix and match line styles and colors, even on different borders of the same cell. Click the line style or change the color, and then click the button in the Border area to change the style.

6. Click OK to close the Format Cells dialog box and return to the worksheet.

Getting borders just right on a complex worksheet often takes multiple iterations. The trick is figuring out which regions need separate formatting and which have common borders. For example, you might need to select the entire data area first to add a thick border around the outside. Then select the heading rows to adjust their borders, which might be thinner and lighter. Select the data area next, to add, remove, and format interior rules between rows and columns that contain data. Finally, if your data area contains a totals row at the bottom, select that row (or the last row of data) to add a double line between the end of the data range and the totals.

MERGING CELLS

On a highly structured worksheet, merging cells can help you show the relationship between headings and subheadings. In a list where two or three rows have the same value in the first column, for example, you could merge those cells to make the common nature of those rows truly stand out. You can combine adjacent cells in a row, a column, or any contiguous range.

To quickly merge two or more cells, select the cells and click the Merge and Center button on the Formatting toolbar. Excel displays a dialog box warning you that when you merge cells, you will lose all data except the contents of the top-left cell in the selection. Click OK to continue or Cancel if you want to back out and move the data before you lose it.

→ Merged cells can cause problems when you create scenarios on a worksheet; for details, **see** "Storing Multiple Scenarios in a Single Workbooks," **p. 715.**

To edit text in a merged cell, click in the cell and begin typing. You can also change the alignment of the merged cells to left or right, without changing the merge.

You might encounter problems when you try to cut and paste merged cells, or when you attempt to sort a list that contains a merged cell. To restore the merged cells to their normal position on the grid, click to make the merged cell active, and then click the Merge and Center icon on the Formatting toolbar. You can also use Excel's menus: Right-click and choose Format Cells. Click the Alignment tab and clear the check mark from the Merge Cells box.

CHANGING ROW HEIGHT AND COLUMN WIDTH

On a new worksheet, every row is exactly 12.75 points high, and every column is 8.43 characters wide. (If the default font for Normal style is a proportional one such as Arial, Excel uses a lowercase x as the character to measure.) As you design a worksheet and fill it with data, however, you'll need to change the size of rows and columns. A column that contains only two-digit numbers doesn't need to be as wide as one that's filled with category headings, for example.

Some of these adjustments happen automatically. If you change the font size of text in a cell, the row automatically changes height to accommodate it. Likewise, when you enter data that's too wide to fit in the default column width, Excel expands the column.

→ For an explanation of how columns expand to accommodate data you enter, **see** "Avoiding Rounding Errors," **p. 576**.

You can also adjust row heights and column widths manually in any of three ways:

- Use Excel's AutoFit feature to set column widths and row heights automatically. Double-click the right border of a column heading to adjust column width to fit the widest entry in the column. Double-click the bottom border of a row heading to resize a row to accommodate the tallest character in that row. If you select multiple rows or columns, you can adjust them all at once.

- Click and drag any column or row to a new size. Point to the thin line at the right of the column heading or the bottom of a row heading until the pointer changes to a two-headed arrow. Click and drag the column or row to the desired width or height, and release the mouse button.

Tip from

EQ & Woody

When you use the mouse to adjust column widths and row heights, ScreenTips show the exact height and width, in characters (for columns) or points (for rows). Curiously, both ScreenTips also show the measurements in *pixels*—use this scale if you're optimizing a worksheet for viewing in a browser at a specific resolution, say, 800×600 pixels.

- To set a precise height or width, use a dialog box. Choose Format, Row, Height and enter any number between 0 and 409 (points). Or choose Format, Column, Width and enter any number between 0 and 255 (characters).

To adjust more than one row or column, select the group of rows or columns first. Then point to the border of any row or column heading in the selection and drag to the desired size. When you release the mouse button, Excel adjusts all selected rows or columns to the height or width of the column you selected. This technique is especially useful when you're putting together a budget worksheet with 12 columns, one for each month. After entering data, select all 12 columns and drag them to the correct width.

Here are some expert tips to help you when working with row heights and column widths:

- To hide any row or column, set its height or width to 0 (drag a column heading to the left or a row heading to the bottom, for example). To make a hidden column or row visible, select the columns or rows on either side of the hidden one; then choose Format, Row or Column, and click Unhide.

- To resize a column according to the contents of one or more specific cells in that column, make a selection and then choose Format, Column, AutoFit Selection.

- To automatically change the size of a group of columns or rows without the mouse, use AutoFit from the menus. Select the rows or columns, and then click Format, Row or Column, and choose AutoFit Selection.

- If you've customized column widths and/or row heights and you want to copy this information along with data, copy and paste the entire row or column, not just the individual cells. Use the Column Widths option on the Paste Special dialog box to duplicate the arrangement of columns from one worksheet to another.

- To change the standard width for all columns in the current worksheet, choose Format, Column, and then enter the new column width (in characters) in the dialog box. The new width will not apply to columns whose width you have already reset.

USING CONDITIONAL FORMATTING TO IDENTIFY KEY VALUES

Conditional formatting lets you set font attributes, colors, and other formatting options that cause data to appear differently based on the value displayed in a cell. Most often, you'll use this feature to set an alarm that highlights data that is outside of an expected range. For example, you might attach conditional formatting to a row of totals on a daily sales report, displaying each cell's contents in bold red letters if it falls below a target level and in bright green if the number is significantly above average. In an employee roster, you might use bold formatting to identify the names of employees who are overdue for a formal evaluation.

Tip from

EQ & Woody

Conditional formats are most effective when used sparingly. If every cell in a worksheet has "special" formatting, nothing stands out. The best use of this option is to highlight truly unusual conditions that require action—when you open a worksheet and see one or two items in bright red, they get your full attention.

Some predefined number formats automatically display negative numbers in red, but conditional formatting gives you somewhat greater control. For cells whose contents match one or more conditions you define, you can specify a new font style (bold italic, for example), use the underline or strikethrough attributes, or change the borders and color of the selection. You cannot use conditional formatting to change fonts or font sizes.

To use conditional formatting, select a cell or range, and then choose Format, Conditional Formatting; fill in the dialog box shown in Figure 22.16.

Use drop-down lists in the Condition section to compare the cell values with the contents of another cell, a value, or a formula. For example, you could define a condition "Cell value is greater than or equal to 20000," and Excel would apply the special formatting if the value is 30,000 but leave the standard format in place if the value is only 15,000. If you enter a formula in this box, it must use a logical function that evaluates to True or False. For most garden-variety conditions, you should choose Cell Value Is.

Figure 22.16
Use conditional formatting to change the appearance of certain cells based on comparisons you define.

Formulas in conditional formats can apply to any data on the worksheet, not just the data in the current cell, or even to external data. For example, in a list where Column A contains dates and Columns B, C, and D contain sales figures, you might want to automatically apply shading to each row that contains data for a Monday; this trick helps you pick out each new week at a glance. If the data begins in row 2, create a conditional format using theformula =WEEKDAY($A2)=2, using the shading you want to see. Copy that format to all cells in the data range, using the Paste Special dialog box or the Format Painter (described in the following section), to automatically shade every Monday row in the entire list.

To create a conditional format, follow these steps:

1. In the box labeled Condition 1, use the drop-down lists to define the comparison you want to make.

2. Click the Format button to open a stripped-down version of the Format Cells dialog box, and then define the special format you want to use when the cell's contents match that condition. If you want the highlighted cells to be noticeable on a printed page, use bold italic, underline, or other text formatting rather than color.

3. To create a second or third conditional format, click the Add button and repeat the previous steps for Condition 2 and Condition 3.

 Is conditional formatting producing unexpected results? For possible solutions, see "Working with Multiple Conditions" in the "Troubleshooting" section at the end of this chapter.

4. Click OK to apply the new formatting options to the selected cell or range.

→ To prevent out-of-the-ordinary data from appearing in a worksheet in the first place, use data-validation rules; **see** "Restricting and Validating Data Entry for a Cell or Range," **p. 553**.

COPYING FORMATS WITH THE FORMAT PAINTER

Use the Format Painter button to quickly copy all formats—fonts, colors, borders, alignment...the works—from one cell to another. Select a cell that has the formatting you want to copy, and then click the Format Painter button and click the cell to which you want to copy the formatting. (If you select a range of cells to copy from, Excel repeats the formatting in your selection.)

If you want to copy formatting to multiple cells, select the cell whose formats you want to copy, and then double-click the Format Painter button to lock it in position. Click each destination cell to copy formatting. When you're finished, click the button again or press Esc to turn off the Format Painter.

Tip from

EQ & Woody

If you select an entire column or row, you can use the Format Painter to copy column widths and row heights. After the pointer turns to the paintbrush shape, click the heading of the row or column you want to change. Note that this technique will also copy other formats (fonts, colors, and so on) from the selected row or column.

SAVING FORMATS AS NAMED STYLES

Although Excel's *named styles* are considerably less versatile than their equivalents in Word, you can still use this feature to reuse favorite formats. By default, every new workbook includes a set of predefined formats in the following named styles: Normal, Percent, Currency, Comma, Currency [0], and Comma [0]. (The two styles followed by [0] show whole numbers only rather than two decimal places.)

Tip from

EQ & Woody

The Currency, Percent, and Comma buttons on Excel's Formatting toolbar actually apply the corresponding named styles. If you want to redefine any of these buttons, just redefine that style. The Currency button, for example, applies the Accounting format with two decimal places to the selected cell or range. To change the way the Currency button works, redefine the Accounting named style so that it uses a Currency format, if you want. Likewise, you can change the named Percent style to include one or two decimal places, if you prefer. See Chapter 21, "Excel Essentials," for instructions on how to save these changes as part of the default workbook format so that they are available for every new workbook you create.

You can create named styles using any format you want. This technique is a great time-saver if you continually find yourself applying the same formatting options to new worksheets:

1. Format a cell using the number, font, and other formatting options you want to save. Click to make this the active cell.

2. Choose Format, Style to display the Style dialog box shown in Figure 22.17.

Figure 22.17
To reuse a complicated cell format, save it as a named style and then apply it when you need it.

3. Type a descriptive name in the Style Name box. Use any combination of letters, numbers, and spaces; to make sure you can read the full name, keep its total length to 30 characters or fewer.

4. By default, all cell formatting options are included with the style. Clear the check mark from any of the boxes below the style name to remove that option from the style.

5. Click the Modify button to open the Format Cells dialog box and adjust any formatting options, if necessary.

6. Click the Add button to save the style in the current workbook.

To use a named style instead of direct formatting options, choose Format, Style. Choose a style name from the drop-down list and click OK.

Styles are available only to worksheets in the workbook in which you save them. To save named styles so that they're available for all new worksheets, save them in a template. To copy styles between two open workbooks, switch to the workbook you want to copy the styles to, and choose Format, Style. In the Style dialog box, click the Merge button. In the Merge Styles dialog box, pick the name of the workbook that contains the styles you want to reuse, and then click OK.

Tip from

EQ & Woody

If you regularly use named styles in worksheets, you can dramatically increase your productivity by adding the Style list to the Formatting toolbar. You'll find step-by-step instructions for this task in Chapter 2, "Customizing the Office Interface." Make sure you do this with the default workbook template, as defined in Chapter 21, so the new toolbar is available to all workbooks you create.

→ For more details on how to create and customize toolbars, **see** "Customizing Toolbars," **p. 30**.

→ For step-by-step instructions on how to customize the default Excel workbook template, **see** "Changing Default Formatting for New Workbooks and Worksheets," **p. 569**.

USING AUTOFORMAT

Like the Word feature of the same name, Excel's AutoFormat promises to turn your worksheet into a work of art, instantly and effortlessly. When you apply AutoFormatting to simple worksheet ranges with easily identifiable headings, totals, and other elements, the feature works pretty much as advertised. In fact, the AutoFormat options available with PivotTables are exceptionally useful because the format of a PivotTable is always the same. For more complex worksheets, however, it's likely that you'll need to clean up after AutoFormat. In general, we recommend trying the AutoFormat options; you can always undo the results if you don't like them, and in many cases the formatting gives you a good start.

When you use AutoFormat and other table-based options (such as sorting a list), Excel tries to apply your instructions to the current selection. If you don't make a selection, Excel uses the current region, which is the block of filled-in cells that extends in all directions from the insertion point to the next empty row or column or the edge of the worksheet. For that reason, when you design a worksheet, you should always include at least one blank row and column to mark the border of every separate data entry block.

To use AutoFormat, follow these steps:

1. Select a range. If you skip this step, Excel selects the current region.

2. Choose Format, AutoFormat. The dialog box shown in Figure 22.18 appears.

Figure 22.18
AutoFormat is most effective when you use it on small, well-defined ranges. Choose the options at the bottom of the dialog box to determine what types of changes to apply automatically.

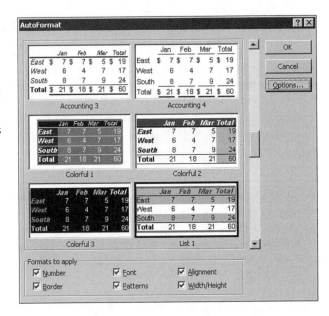

3. Pick one of the built-in formats. Each entry in the list includes a sample that gives you a general idea of the formats you can expect. The Simple and Accounting formats are the most conservative and are best for lists that you plan to include as tables in financial reports. The 3D choices at the end of the list are good for Web pages.

4. To enable or disable specific types of automatic formatting, such as borders or fonts, click the Options button and add or remove check marks.

5. Click OK to apply the formats.

→ For an overview of other Office-wide formatting options, **see** "Common Formatting Options," **p. 100**.

TROUBLESHOOTING

STOPPING AUTOMATIC CONVERSIONS

After importing data into a worksheet from text files and databases, I noticed that Excel converts some data to date serial values and other data to scientific notation. I want the information to appear in my worksheet exactly as it did in the database. Is there any way to change it back?

No, unfortunately. When Excel sees a value that looks like a date or time or scientific notation, either when you type a value into a cell or when you import a database, it converts the value automatically as you type or import. There is no way to reverse this conversion. If you have serial numbers that use the format ##X####, where each # is a number and the X is a letter, Excel converts any serial number that contains the letter E in that position to scientific notation. Your best option is to edit the text or database file, adding an apostrophe to the beginning of each field that contains values Excel will try to convert. In that case, Excel imports the data in text format exactly as it appears.

CLICK TWICE FOR NORMAL

I formatted text in a cell using more than one font, and I want to restore Excel's default font format. I opened the Format Cells dialog box, clicked the Font tab, and checked the Normal Font box once, but my formatting stays exactly as it was. What's the secret?

When you have multiple font formats applied to different words or characters in a cell, the Normal Font check box is checked, but it's grayed out. To restore the default formatting, click once to clear the box (exactly the opposite of what you normally do), and then click OK to close the dialog box. Now reopen the dialog box and check the Normal Font box again. This time your change will stick.

WORKING WITH MULTIPLE CONDITIONS

I applied conditional formatting to a cell, but the formatting doesn't appear on some cells, even though the data in those cells meets the conditions I specified.

If you specify multiple conditions and more than one is true for a given cell, Excel applies the formats of the first true condition it encounters and ignores the second and third conditions. If you've defined conditions that have the potential to overlap, arrange them in order so that the most important one (or the one least likely to be true) is first in the list.

SECRETS OF THE OFFICE MASTERS: REDESIGNING A WORKSHEET CLARIFIES THE INFORMATION

When you first create a worksheet, every cell uses the same fonts, every row is the same height, and there's no distinction between headings and the data they describe. With Excel's extensive selection of formatting tools, you can redesign a worksheet to make its organization crystal clear.

When we imported data from a database into a worksheet, the results looked like a data disaster, as the "Before" example in Figure 22.19 illustrates.

Figure 22.19

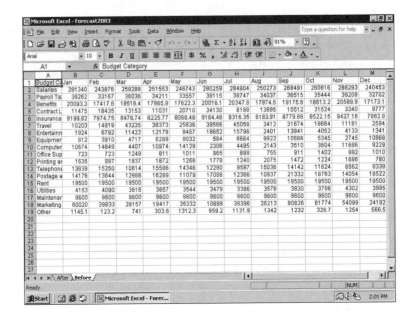

After some careful formatting, however, the results are much easier to read and follow. Here are the basic principles we followed when formatting the "After" worksheet shown in Figure 22.20:

- Adjust the formatting for every cell, especially those that contain numbers, dates, and dollar amounts. Pay particular attention to fonts, font size, and the number of decimal places displayed.

- Enter totals, averages, and other formulas as needed for analytical purposes.

- Make sure that all columns align properly and that rows and columns are the proper width.

- Make headings and titles bigger and bolder so that they clearly define what type of data is in each row and column. Bold white type on a dark background is especially effective in column headings. Excel also uses this formatting to identify headings for sorting purposes.

- Turn on text wrapping and merge cells as needed, especially in headings.

- To unclutter the worksheet, choose File, Page Setup, click the Sheet tab, and clear the check mark from the Gridlines box.

- Use the Borders button to add grid elements as necessary. Notice the double underline above a row of totals and the thin single borders along the bottom of each row of data that help the reader follow along from left to right in each row.

- Use the Fill Color drop-down menu to add light shading throughout the data section. In this worksheet, a soft green shading was added to alternate rows to make long rows easier to follow.

- Freeze worksheet panes to make it easier to scroll through columns and rows without losing track of data.

- Add graphics as needed to give the worksheet the proper corporate identity.

Figure 22.20

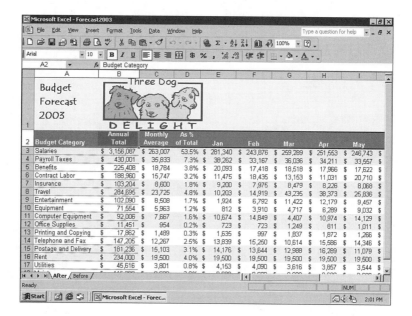

CHAPTER 23

USING FORMULAS AND FUNCTIONS

In this chapter

ENTERING AND EDITING FORMULAS

Formulas add intelligence to a workbook. Use formulas to manipulate values (text, numbers, or dates), perform simple or complex calculations, and display alternative results based on logical tests. A formula can be as simple as a reference to another cell, or it can go on for hundreds of characters, with as many as seven functions nested within other functions; regardless of its complexity, however, a formula must begin with an equal sign (=). If you start a formula with a plus sign (+) or minus sign (–), Excel adds an equal sign to the beginning of the formula.

Formulas consist of three basic building blocks: *operands* (the elements to be calculated), *operators*, and worksheet functions:

- **Operands**—The data to be calculated in a formula can include any combination of the following: *constant values* (numbers, text, or dates you enter directly in a cell or formula, for example); cell or range references; names that refer to cells or ranges; labels that define the intersection of a specific row and column, used in *natural language formulas*; or worksheet functions. When you use a cell or range reference in a formula, Excel substitutes the contents of that address just as if you had typed it in directly.

- **Operators**—Formulas can use any of six basic arithmetic operators: addition (+), subtraction (–), multiplication (*), division (/), percent (%), or exponentiation (^). You can also use comparison operators to compare two values and produce the logical result TRUE or FALSE. The list of comparison operators consists of equal to (=), greater than (>), less than (<), greater than or equal to (>=), less than or equal to (<=), and not equal to (<>). Use an ampersand (&) to combine, or concatenate, two pieces of text into a single value.

- **Worksheet functions**—Predefined formulas that allow you to perform calculations on worksheet data by entering a constant value or a cell or range reference as the *argument* that a named function transforms. You can use a worksheet function as the complete contents of a cell, or you can use a function as an operand in another formula.

→ For a detailed discussion of how to use natural language formulas, **see** "Using Natural Language Formulas," **p. 616**.

→ For a full discussion of worksheet functions and arguments, **see** "Manipulating Data with Worksheet Functions," **p. 620**.

USING CELL REFERENCES IN FORMULAS

You can enter any cell or range address directly in a formula. These addresses are not case-sensitive; if you enter a2:b8 in a formula, Excel converts the entry to A2:B8 when you press Enter. You can also point and click to enter any cell or range reference.

One of the simplest Excel formulas is a direct reference to another cell. If you click in cell I24, for example, and enter the formula =A5, Excel displays the current value of cell A5 in cell I24. This technique is most commonly used with worksheets that contain input cells in which you type data that you'll use throughout the worksheet. For example, cell A5 might contain the current interest rate you plan to use as part of a series of loan and payment calculations. If you use custom views to display different portions of your worksheet, this technique lets you see the underlying assumptions at a glance.

To enter a reference to an entire row or column, use the row number or column letter as both halves of the range reference: B:B for column B, 2:2 for row 2. You can also use this syntax for multiple rows or columns—B:K includes every cell in columns B through K, just as 10:13 includes every cell in rows 10 through 13.

USING 3D REFERENCES TO CELLS ON OTHER WORKSHEETS

Sometimes it's helpful to use references to cells and ranges on other worksheets within the same workbook—known as *3D references*. For example, you might include a lookup table that lists sales tax rates for different counties or states on a separate sheet. Using this table to determine the correct tax rate for an invoice makes your data accurate, yet keeps the invoice sheet uncluttered. Likewise, in a loan worksheet you might want to perform all the data-entry and payment calculations on one sheet, but place the amortization table on its own sheet for display and printing.

To enter a 3D address, preface the cell address with the name of the sheet followed by an exclamation point. (If the sheet name contains a space, enclose it within single quote marks.) If you have a sheet named Amortization Table, for example, you can refer to the top-left cell of that sheet by entering ='Amortization Table'!A1 on any other sheet in the same book. You can also click the appropriate sheet tab and then select the desired cell or range of cells to add references to cells or ranges on other sheets. When you use this technique, Excel automatically enters the sheet name, exclamation point, and cell references.

CONTROLLING THE ORDER AND TIMING OF CALCULATIONS IN FORMULAS

If a formula contains more than one operator, Excel performs calculations in the following order (if you remember high school algebra, this list will be familiar):

- Percent (%)
- Exponentiation (^)
- Multiplication (*) and division (/)
- Addition (+) and subtraction (–)
- Concatenation (&)
- Comparison (=, <, >, <=, >=, <>)

To control the order of calculation, use parentheses; Excel evaluates all items within parentheses first, from the inside out, using the same order as listed previously. If a formula contains operators with the same precedence, such as addition and subtraction or any two comparison operators, Excel evaluates the operators from left to right. The number of levels of nested parentheses you can use within a single formula is not limited, although you are limited to seven levels of nesting for a function.

Tip from

EQ & Woody

> When you're trying to figure out the structure of a complex formula with many sets of nested parentheses, let Excel help. Click to make the cell that contains the formula active, and then use the arrow keys to move back and forth through the formula. As you move the insertion point to the right of a left parenthesis or to the left of a right parenthesis, Excel highlights its mate in bold. When you make any change to the formula, Excel displays each matched set of parentheses in a different color, making it easier for you to see which is which.

Normally, Excel recalculates all formulas every time you open or save a workbook. When you change a value in a cell, Excel recalculates all formulas that refer to that cell on any worksheet in the current workbook. Calculation takes place in the background, and on a typical uncomplicated worksheet, the process is essentially instantaneous.

You might want to control when Excel recalculates formulas in at least two circumstances:

- If your worksheet contains a large number of complex formulas, recalculation can cause annoying pauses when you try to enter data. This is especially noticeable on systems with slow CPUs and low-memory configurations.

- When your formula contains cells that refer to themselves, as in some scientific and engineering formulas, Excel must repeat (iterate) the calculation—by default, each time you recalculate this type of formula, Excel goes through 100 iterations.

Under normal circumstances, most users should leave recalculation settings alone. If you must turn off automatic recalculation, follow these steps:

1. Choose Tools, Options, and click the Calculation tab. You see the dialog box shown in Figure 23.1.

Figure 23.1
Adjust recalculation options with care. For most situations, the default automatic options are appropriate.

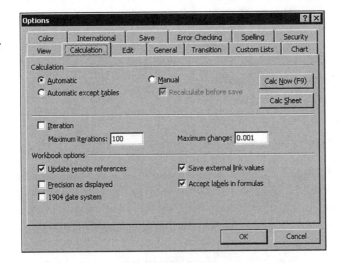

2. Choose the Manual option in the Calculation section. (The Automatic Except Tables option is for use with worksheets that include a relatively obscure Excel feature called data tables. If your worksheet includes a one- or two-variable data table, Excel recalculates the entire table every time you edit any cell in the worksheet; checking this option lets you recalculate the table manually.)

3. If you want Excel to recalculate the workbook only when you explicitly choose to do so, remove the check mark from the Recalculate Before Save check box.

4. Click OK to save the setting and return to your worksheet.

When you turn off automatic recalculation, you need to specify when Excel should recalculate formulas. To calculate all formulas in the current workbook, press F9. To recalculate only formulas in the current worksheet, press Shift+F9.

PART

IV

CH

23

Tip from

Excel 97 includes several well-documented calculation bugs that can cause incorrect results under some circumstances. Beginning with Excel 2000, Microsoft made major changes to Excel's recalculation engine intended to fix these bugs. The first time you use Excel 2000 or Excel 2002 to open a worksheet created in Excel 97, the program completely recalculates the worksheet. When you close the worksheet, you'll be asked whether you want to save your changes, even if you've done nothing more than look at the worksheet. We strongly recommend that you click Yes when you see this dialog box, to avoid the possibility of being bitten by those old recalculation bugs.

ABSOLUTE VERSUS RELATIVE CELL REFERENCES

Normally, Excel interprets cell and range references within a formula as *relative references*. When you copy or move the formula, Excel automatically adjusts cell references to reflect their position relative to the new location. This capability is useful when you need to quickly copy a formula across several rows or columns. In the worksheet shown in Figure 23.2, for example, the formula in cell B7 totals the contents of column B. When you copy that formula across to the right, Excel assumes you want to total the numbers in the same relative position in each column, so it adjusts the formula accordingly, from =SUM(B2:B6) to =SUM(C2:C6), =SUM(D2:D6), and so on.

Figure 23.2
Relative cell addresses are automatically updated as they are copied from cell to cell.

	A	B	C	D	E	F
1	Year	North	South	East	West	Grand Total
2	2002	5,630	5,880	6,600	4,760	22,870
3	2001	6,120	4,810	6,610	5,790	23,330
4	2000	3,650	5,520	5,870	3,360	18,400
5	1999	6,590	6,470	5,120	4,660	22,840
6	1998	5,600	6,530	4,830	4,180	21,140
7	Total	27,590	29,210	29,030	22,750	108,580

→ The easiest way to copy a row or column of formulas is with the help of Excel's AutoFill feature; **see** "Automatically Filling In a Series of Data," **p. 676**.

In some cases, however, you want to copy a formula so that a cell or range reference in the copied formula points to the same cell or range as in the original. For example, if you enter the current interest rate in a cell near the top of a loan worksheet, you can refer to that cell in any formula that makes an interest-related calculation. To convert a relative reference to an *absolute reference*, which does not adjust when copied or moved, use dollar signs within the cell address. For example, when you copy the formula =B4*$A$5 to the right, Excel adjusts the first cell reference relative to its new location, but leaves the second reference unchanged: =B5*$A$5, =B6*$A$5, and so on.

Tip from

EQ & Woody

When you want to include a reference to an input cell in several formulas, you're generally better off using a named range, which is always an absolute reference. If cell A5 contains an interest rate, name the cell Interest_Rate and use that name in formulas—=B6*Interest_Rate, for example. If you move or copy the formula, the reference to the named range will not change.

You can mix and match relative and absolute addresses in a formula, or even in the same address. Using a dollar sign in front of the column portion of the address ($A5) tells Excel to change only the row reference when the formula is moved or copied; likewise, a dollar sign in front of the row (A$5) changes only the column portion of the cell reference. In Figure 23.3, for example, you could enter the formula =B2/$F2 in cell B10 and then copy the formula down and to the right. The *mixed reference* to $F2 adjusts the references so that they always point to the Grand Total formula in Column F for the correct row.

Figure 23.3

Formulas in the bottom table use mixed references; that allows each percentage to be divided by the result in the Grand Total column as you copy the formula down and across.

	A	B	C	D	E	F
1	Year	North	South	East	West	Grand Total
2	2002	5,630	5,880	6,600	4,760	22,870
3	2001	6,120	4,810	6,610	5,790	23,330
4	2000	3,650	5,520	5,870	3,360	18,400
5	1999	6,590	6,470	5,120	4,660	22,840
6	1998	5,600	6,530	4,830	4,180	21,140
7	Total	27,590	29,210	29,030	22,750	108,580
8						
9	Year	North	South	East	West	
10	2002	24.6%	25.7%	28.9%	20.8%	
11	2001	26.2%	20.6%	28.3%	24.8%	
12	2000	19.8%	30.0%	31.9%	18.3%	
13	1999	28.9%	28.3%	22.4%	20.4%	
14	1998	26.5%	30.9%	22.8%	19.8%	

Use the F4 keyboard shortcut to switch quickly between relative, mixed, and absolute references in a formula. Click in the active cell to enable editing; then place the insertion point in a cell or range reference (either in the Formula bar or in the cell itself) and press F4 to convert a relative reference to absolute. Press F4 again to enter a mixed reference. Keep pressing F4 to cycle through all four variations for the selection.

PREVENTING FORMULAS FROM DISPLAYING IN THE FORMULA BAR

When you design a worksheet that you intend other people to use for data entry, you might want to hide the formulas themselves and show their results. This technique can be useful if your formula contains confidential or proprietary information that you don't want to share with others. It's also a useful way to prevent other users from attempting to edit a formula.

To prevent a formula from appearing in the Formula bar, you must first set a specific formatting option for that cell, and then turn on *protection* for the entire worksheet:

1. Right-click the cell that contains the formula you want to hide (to hide multiple formulas, select a range) and choose Format Cells from the shortcut menu.

2. Click the Protection tab and check the Hidden box.

> **Caution**
>
> Make sure you leave the check mark next to the Locked box as well. If you clear this box and check Hidden, anyone who can open the worksheet can replace the hidden formula with another formula or a constant value, undoing your attempt at protection.

3. Select other cells on the worksheet, if necessary, and adjust whether their contents are hidden or locked.

4. Choose Tools, Protection, Protect Sheet. Make sure there's a check next to the Contents box.

5. Click OK to close the Protect Sheet dialog box. Users will no longer be able to see hidden formulas in the Formula bar or in the cell itself, nor will they be able to edit formulas. The results of a hidden formula will display in the cell and on printouts.

→ For more details on how to prevent unauthorized changes to a workbook or worksheet, **see** "Protecting a Worksheet," **p. 704**.

USING ARRAY FORMULAS

Array formulas let you perform multiple calculations across a range of cells (an array) by using a function that normally works only on a single cell. To enter an array formula, construct the formula just as you normally would, and then press Ctrl+Shift+Enter. Excel enters the formula in curly braces to indicate that it is an array formula.

An array formula can return either a single result or multiple results. Array formulas are a common way to combine the SUM and IF functions, for example. Under normal circumstances, an IF function compares one cell with another cell or a constant value. An array formula, on the other hand, lets you compare a single value to every cell in an array and return a result you can work with, so you can compare a condition in an IF function and use all matching results in a SUM function, all in one formula.

⚠ *If you're having trouble editing an array formula, see "Editing an Array Formula" in the "Troubleshooting" section at the end of this chapter.*

For example, say you keep a list of invoice information in an Excel worksheet with header information in row 1 and the first record in row 2, as in the example in Figure 23.4. If column B contains the amount of each invoice and column C contains the name of the salesperson who prepared that invoice, you can use an array formula to keep a running total of all invoice amounts by salesperson. Assuming column D is blank, click in cell D2 and type this formula: =SUM(IF($C$2:C2=C2,$B$2:B2)). Press Ctrl+Shift+Enter to enter it as an array formula, and then use AutoFill to copy the formula to the remainder of the cells in column D. (Excel automatically adds curly braces at the beginning and end to indicate that this is an array formula. Do not enter the curly braces yourself, or the array formula will fail.)

Figure 23.4
In this example, the array formula allows you to keep a running total of all invoice amounts by salesperson.

	A	B	C	D
				Running Total
1	Inv_Num	Amount	Salesperson	per Salesperson
2	1001	$ 85.60	Bianca Merrill	$ 85.60
3	1002	$ 70.50	Dolores Calderon	$ 70.50
4	1003	$ 80.00	Ed Bott	$ 80.00
5	1004	$ 68.10	Ed Bott	$ 148.10
6	1005	$ 178.50	Woody Leonhard	$ 178.50
7	1006	$ 166.30	Ed Bott	$ 314.40
8	1007	$ 65.60	Woody Leonhard	$ 244.10
9	1008	$ 204.50	Bianca Merrill	$ 290.10
10	1009	$ 121.30	Ed Bott	$ 435.70
11	1010	$ 61.60	Ed Bott	$ 497.30
12	1011	$ 183.00	Woody Leonhard	$ 427.10
13	1012	$ 80.50	Woody Leonhard	$ 507.60
14	1013	$ 115.80	Dolores Calderon	$ 186.30
15	1014	$ 103.80	Bianca Merrill	$ 393.90
16	1015	$ 107.80	Ed Bott	$ 605.10
17	1016	$ 92.30	Woody Leonhard	$ 599.90
18	1017	$ 84.10	Bianca Merrill	$ 478.00
19	1018	$ 99.70	Ed Bott	$ 704.80
20	1019	$ 201.70	Dolores Calderon	$ 388.00
21	1020	$ 195.90	Bianca Merrill	$ 673.90

D2 fx {=SUM(IF($C$2:C2=C2,$B$2:B2))}

The first argument in this array formula compares each previous cell in column C to the contents of column C in the current row. The second argument returns an invoice amount to the SUM function for each cell in column C if the condition in the IF function is true. The copy of this formula in cell D11, for example, looks like this:
{=SUM(IF($C$2:C11=C11,$B$2:B11))}. This formula looks in the range from C2 to C11 for cells that match the contents of C11—the name "Ed Bott." It finds matching contents in C4, C5, C7, C10, and C11, so it adds the invoice amounts in B4, B11, and B12 to produce its result, a running total of all amounts up to and including row 11 for Ed.

USING THE WATCH WINDOW TO MONITOR CALCULATIONS

Normally, as you enter and edit values in a worksheet, formulas that reference those values change as well. If the formula is close to the cells you're editing, you can see the results immediately. But it's more difficult to track formula results when the formulas are widely separated—on the same worksheet or even on linked sheets in a different workbook.

Thanks to a new feature in Excel 2002, you can keep an eye on the results of specific cells, even when those cells are on different sheets. Use the *Watch Window* to track a list of cells; this window floats above the current worksheet, as shown in Figure 23.5. With this window open, you don't have to continually switch between worksheets to monitor your work.

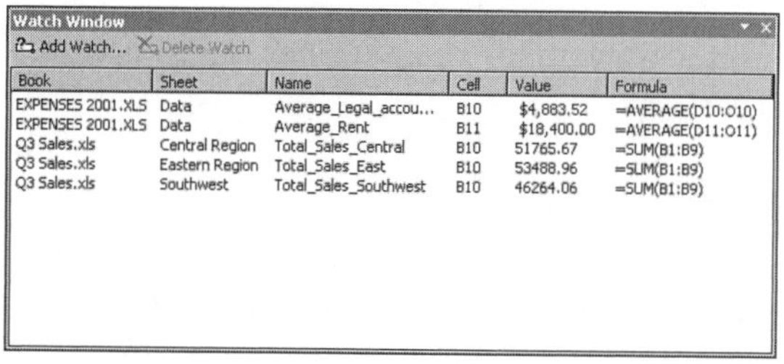

Figure 23.5
The Watch Window lets you track formula results across multiple workbooks. Range names make it easier to identify why you added a cell to the list.

To add a single cell to the Watch Window, select the cell, right-click, and choose Add Watch. (If the selected cell is already on the Watch list, the menu changes to Delete Watch.) As soon as you add a cell address, the Watch Window appears. The Watch Window is resizable. And just as with any list-based control, you can click a column heading to sort by that column, or resize columns by dragging the line between column headings.

In a strange programming decision, Microsoft chose to implement the Watch Window as a toolbar. If the Watch Window is currently hidden, you can make it visible by choosing View, Toolbars, Watch Window. Because it's a toolbar, you can also drag the window to any edge of the screen, where it will dock. (If you want to dock the Watch Window, try the bottom of the screen; that gives you the ability to view information in all columns and doesn't interfere with task panes.) You can't minimize the Watch Window; the down arrow to the left of the Close box in the upper-right corner leads to a basically useless Customize menu.

→ For more details about using and customizing Office toolbars, see "Customizing Toolbars," **p. 30**.

After the Watch Window is open, use the Add Watch button to select a group of cells and quickly add them to the list.

Tip from

If you use the Watch Window a lot, we recommend that you define names for the cells you include on the Watch list. The Name column appears in the list, and a meaningful name like Jan_Sales_Total makes it much easier to identify the value you're tracking than a cell address like B10.

USING RANGE NAMES AND LABELS IN FORMULAS

Understanding the logic of a complex formula can be a challenge, even when you entered the formula yourself. This form of amnesia is especially common when you haven't opened a particular workbook in months or years.

To make it easier for you to understand a formula's purpose just by looking at it, you can enter cell references by using *named ranges*. This technique is especially useful with cells that contain constant values such as interest rates, loan amounts, sales tax rates, and discount formulas, because you can define a handful of input cells and then plug the contents of those cells into formulas on any worksheet within the workbook.

You can define range names explicitly, or you can enter cell references that are defined by the labels on rows and columns.

USING NATURAL-LANGUAGE FORMULAS

If your worksheet includes headings above columns and to the left of rows, Excel lets you include cell references within formulas by referring to the intersections of rows and columns rather than entering addresses. Microsoft calls this feature a *natural-language formula*, because you describe data by using descriptive labels.

Caution

In this section, we explain exactly how to use natural-language formulas; before you use them in an important worksheet, however, we recommend reading the next section, which reveals the hidden traps that can cause natural-language formulas to display the wrong result without any warning to you.

The worksheet in Figure 23.6, for example, uses months of the year as column labels and expense categories as row labels. To refer to the value at the intersection of a row and column, enter the two labels (the order doesn't matter), separated by the *intersection operator*, a space. Thus, =Jan Insurance refers to cell D9, which is at the intersection of the column labeled Jan and the row labeled Insurance.

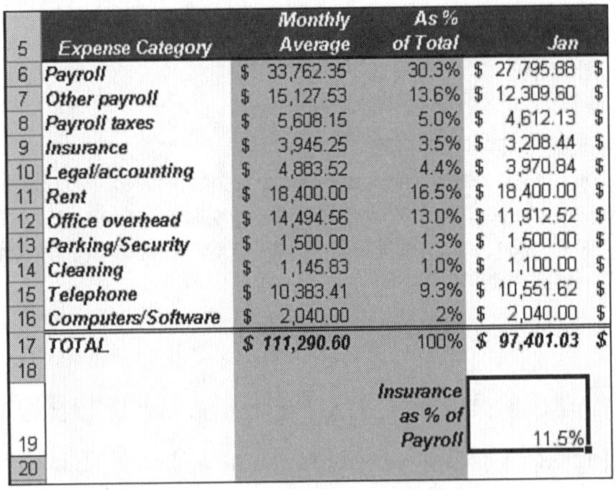

Figure 23.6
The natural-language formula shown here divides the contents of D6 by D9; using row and column labels makes understanding its purpose much easier.

5	Expense Category	Monthly Average	As % of Total	Jan	
6	Payroll	$ 33,762.35	30.3%	$ 27,795.88	$
7	Other payroll	$ 15,127.53	13.6%	$ 12,309.60	$
8	Payroll taxes	$ 5,608.15	5.0%	$ 4,612.13	$
9	Insurance	$ 3,945.25	3.5%	$ 3,208.44	$
10	Legal/accounting	$ 4,883.52	4.4%	$ 3,970.84	$
11	Rent	$ 18,400.00	16.5%	$ 18,400.00	$
12	Office overhead	$ 14,494.56	13.0%	$ 11,912.52	$
13	Parking/Security	$ 1,500.00	1.3%	$ 1,500.00	$
14	Cleaning	$ 1,145.83	1.0%	$ 1,100.00	$
15	Telephone	$ 10,383.41	9.3%	$ 10,551.62	$
16	Computers/Software	$ 2,040.00	2%	$ 2,040.00	$
17	TOTAL	$ 111,290.60	100%	$ 97,401.03	$
18					
19			Insurance as % of Payroll	11.5%	
20					

As Figure 23.6 illustrates, row and column labels can contain spaces. To use these labels in formulas, be sure to enclose them in single quotation marks ('). If you use double quotation marks, Excel's Formula AutoCorrect feature offers to correct the entry for you.

→ For a full description of how Formula AutoCorrect works, **see** "How Formula AutoCorrect Works," **p. 634**.

Although it's easy to use a natural-language formula, you should be aware of some quirks in this feature that can affect the results of formulas you enter:

- If your worksheet includes a label that appears to be a cell address (Q4 or FY99, for example), you must enclose the label in single quotation marks in your formula.

- Likewise, you must enclose a label in single quotation marks if it contains a space: ='Marketing Department' Aug, for example, identifies the cell at the intersection of the row labeled Marketing Department and the column labeled Aug.

- If you move or copy a natural-language formula from one cell to another, the labels change to reflect the relative locations. In the previously shown Figure 23.6, for example, 'Jan Insurance' changes to 'Feb Insurance' if you copy the formula to the right. If you change a row or column label, any formulas that include that label change automatically.

- Numbers used as row or column labels must be between 1900 and 9999.

- If your row or column headings contain duplicate labels and you enter a natural-language formula that could refer to two or more cells, Excel generally uses the one above and to the left of the formula. If your worksheet includes two or more tables that contain the same headings, Excel displays the Identify Label dialog box and prompts you to pick the correct label.

- If you use only one heading for a label, Excel assumes you mean all cells in that row or column. In Figure 23.6, for example, the natural-language formula =Sum(Jan) would total all the entries in the column under the heading Jan.

LIMITATIONS OF NATURAL-LANGUAGE FORMULAS

Natural-language formulas have several serious limitations, some of them obscure, others quite common:

- Be extremely careful if you modify a worksheet that contains natural-language formulas, especially by adding or deleting rows or columns at the edge of a range. Excel does not redefine existing natural-language formulas when you revise your worksheet, nor does it give you a clue your formulas could be wrong. In the previous Figure 23.6, for example, if you enter =SUM(Jan) at the bottom of the first column and then add a new row just above the formula, Excel doesn't include the new row in your total. Even carefully examining every formula won't reveal this problem, because the natural-language formula appears to reference every cell under the heading Jan. After adding rows or columns or otherwise modifying a sheet, you must delete and reenter the formula for it to work properly.

- If you use more than 32,764 natural-language formulas, Excel displays an out-of-memory message and might stop responding altogether. Although that sounds like an absurd number, it's not difficult to reach if you define a single natural-language formula and use AutoFill to extend it across several columns and down a lengthy list.

- Natural-language formulas produce unexpected results if you merge cells in the headings above a column. In that case, the heading refers only to the column at the left of the selected range, because the contents of merged cells are actually stored in the top-left cell of the merged range.

- Finally, natural-language formulas choke when you use any of the following reserved terms as a row or column label: Complex, Imaginary, Workday, Convert, LCM, Yield, Delta, Multinomial, Disc, Networkdays, Duration, Quotient, Effect, or Received.

If you're sufficiently frightened by the potential for data loss or miscalculation caused by natural-language formulas, you should disable this feature. Choose Tools, Options, click the Calculation tab, and clear the check mark from the Accept Labels in Formulas box. If you turn off labels in formulas, Excel substitutes absolute cell or range references for any existing natural-language formulas; as a result, your formulas continue to work.

USING NAMED RANGES IN FORMULAS

For absolute control over cell and range references in formulas, use a range name instead of its row-and-column address. Unlike natural-language formulas, which rely on row and column headings, you explicitly define range names. When you refer to a named range in a formula, the effect is the same as if you had entered the absolute address of the named cell or range.

Using named ranges makes it easier for anyone looking at a worksheet to understand exactly how a formula works. That comes in handy when you share a workbook with a coworker, or when you look at a worksheet you designed long ago. On an invoice worksheet, for example, the following formula is instantly understandable:

```
=Quantity_Ordered*Unit_Price*(1+Sales_Tax_Rate)
```

The easiest way to name a cell or a range is to use the Name box, located just to the left of the Formula bar (see Figure 23.7). Select the cell or range you want to name, and then click in the Name box to highlight the entire cell address. Type a legal name for the cell or range, and press Enter to store the range name in the workbook.

The rules for assigning a *legal name* to a cell or a range are completely different from (and much more restrictive than) those that apply to the names of files and worksheet tabs:

- You can use a total of up to 255 characters in a range name.

Tip from

EQ & Woody

The point of range names is to make worksheets and formulas easier to understand. For clarity's sake, try to keep range names under 15 characters—the width of the Name drop-down list.

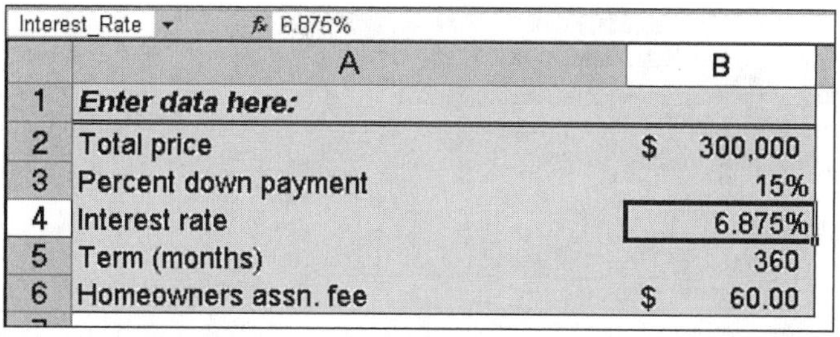

Figure 23.7
Select a range, and then click in the Name box and type the name you want to use for that range.

Interest_Rate ▾	*fx* 6.875%	
	A	B
1	**Enter data here:**	
2	Total price	$ 300,000
3	Percent down payment	15%
4	Interest rate	6.875%
5	Term (months)	360
6	Homeowners assn. fee	$ 60.00

- The first character must be a letter or the underline character. You can't legally name a cell or range 4thQuarterBudget, but Q4Budget is acceptable.

- The remaining characters can be letters, numbers, periods, or the underline character. No other punctuation marks are allowed in range names. Spaces are forbidden; use the underscore character instead to form a legal name that's also easy to read.

- A cell or range name cannot be the same as a cell reference or a value, so you can't name a cell Q4, FY2001, or W2, nor can you use a single letter or enter a number without any punctuation or letters.

Note

When you name a cell or range, that name attaches itself to the absolute address you specify. If you move or copy a formula containing a reference to the named range, the reference continues to point to the original address rather than adjust to a new relative address. For this reason, you should use named ranges in formulas only when you want the formula to refer to an absolute address.

When constructing a formula, you can choose from a list of all defined names in the current workbook. After typing an equal sign or clicking in an existing formula, choose Insert, Name, Paste to display a dialog box that lists all defined names on all sheets in the current workbook. If the name you select is on a different worksheet, Excel automatically enters it by using the correct syntax, including the sheet name.

If you insert a cell or range reference in a formula by clicking a cell or range, Excel enters the defined name of the cell or range, if one exists. If you don't want this automatic substitution to take place, type the cell address directly, rather than clicking to enter it.

MANAGING RANGE NAMES

To manage names of cells or ranges stored in a workbook, choose Insert, Name. The Define Name dialog box (see Figure 23.8) lets you add a new name to an existing range, delete one or more range names, or change the reference for an existing name.

Figure 23.8
Use this list to manage named ranges in a workbook; to redefine an existing name, select a new cell or range in the Refers To box.

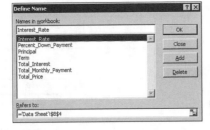

You can assign more than one name to the same cell or range. Use different names if you intend to refer to the contents of a cell in several different formulas, and you want the names to match the purpose of each formula. For example, on a loan worksheet, you might refer to the same cell as AmountFinanced and AmountBorrowed, and then use either name in formulas on that worksheet.

It's relatively easy to change the location that a cell or range name refers to: Choose Insert, Name, Define to open the Define Name dialog box, and then select the cell or range name from the Names in Workbook list. Select the contents of the Refers To box and click in the worksheet to select the new cell or range. When you use this technique, any worksheet formulas that refer to the range name automatically use the new location you defined.

Surprisingly, however, it's impossible to change a defined name in one step. Instead, you have to create a new name for an existing range, and then delete the old name. Open the Define Names dialog box, select the existing name, enter a new name in the Names in Workbook box, and click the Add button. Then select the old name and click the Delete button.

 If some of the formulas in your workbook display error messages after you change or delete a range name, see "Check Formulas Before Deleting Range Names" in the "Troubleshooting" section at the end of this chapter.

MANIPULATING DATA WITH WORKSHEET FUNCTIONS

Worksheet functions handle a broad array of tasks, from simple arithmetic to complex financial calculations and intricate statistical tests. Regardless of its complexity, every function consists of two parts: the function name and its *arguments*—the specific values the function uses to calculate a result. The *syntax* of a function defines what type of arguments it uses: text, numbers, dates, and logical values, for example. In most cases, you can substitute a cell or range address or another formula or function as an argument, as long as the data evaluates to the required data type. Some arguments are required, and others are optional. Arguments always appear to the right of the function name, inside parentheses; Excel uses commas to separate multiple arguments.

The following examples illustrate the syntax of some commonly used functions. Bold type means the argument is required. An ellipsis (...) means that the function accepts an unlimited number of arguments.

```
=TODAY()
=AVERAGE(number1,number2,...)
=IPMT(rate,per,nper,pv,fv,type)
```

TODAY() is one of the simplest of all worksheet functions. Whenever you open, save, or otherwise recalculate a worksheet that contains this function, Excel updates the value of the cell that contains this formula to display the current date, as stored in your computer's clock chip. This function is extremely common in formulas that calculate elapsed time, such as the number of days that have passed since you mailed an invoice or received a payment.

AVERAGE accepts up to 30 arguments (but requires only 1) and calculates the arithmetic mean of all values in the list, ignoring text and logical values. Although you can enter constant values in this formula, it's most commonly used to calculate the average of a range of numbers, such as monthly sales or budget results. If you calculate a year's worth of monthly sales totals in cells B20 through M20, for example, =AVERAGE(B20:M20) displays the average of the 12 monthly totals.

To calculate the amount of interest you pay each month on a mortgage, use the IPMT function. As the syntax description shows, you must supply a minimum of four values as arguments. This function requires (in order) the interest rate per period (rate), the specific payment period for which you want to calculate interest (per, a number between 1 and nper), the number of payment periods (nper), and the present value (pv, the amount of the loan). The final two arguments—future value (fv) and the type of loan (type)—are optional. Here, too, you're more likely to include a reference to a cell than the actual number in a formula that uses this function.

Note

Although the Formula bar and Excel's help screens always display function names in capital letters, the names are not case sensitive. Use any combination of capital and lowercase characters; when you enter the formula, Excel converts the function's name to capitals.

ENTERING ERROR-FREE FORMULAS

For some functions, especially those with only a single argument, the easiest course of action is often to type them into a cell directly, using the mouse to select the cell or range address of any arguments.

When you begin to enter a new function or edit an existing one, Excel 2002 displays a ScreenTip just below the Formula bar. This yellow box displays all required arguments in bold type, with optional arguments in lighter type. After you enter an argument, the argument name serves as a link—click it to select the entire argument.

For functions with multiple arguments, however, especially those where you're not certain of the exact syntax, a fill-in-the-blanks form often ensures the proper results. The Insert Function dialog box in Excel 2002 allows you to enter any function and all its arguments quickly and accurately, by using a series of dialog boxes. The Insert Function dialog box is an expert Excel user's best friend: It makes errors nearly impossible, it provides constant feedback as you build a formula, and it includes hooks to surprisingly advanced help, including useful examples of some complex formulas.

Note

Excel 2000 included two tools for automatically inserting functions—the Formula Palette and the Paste Function dialog box. Although their workings are generally similar, these two functions have been combined and extensively redesigned to create the Insert Function dialog box in Excel 2002.

You can use the Insert Function dialog box to build a function from scratch: You choose a function from a categorized list and then fill in the arguments using input boxes. Or you can enter part or all of the function and its arguments and use the Insert Function dialog box to edit specific arguments or debug a formula that isn't working as you expect.

To build a function from scratch, follow these steps:

1. Click to select the cell in which you want to add a formula, and then click the Insert Function button (the fx just to the left of the Formula bar). Excel inserts an equal sign in the Formula bar, positions the insertion point to its right, and opens the Insert Function dialog box.

Note

Opening the Insert Function dialog box replaces the Name box (just to the left of the Formula Bar) with the Function box. When you first use Excel, this list includes the 10 most popular functions; as you use the Insert Function dialog box, Excel replaces the entries on this list with the 10 functions you've used most recently. The last function you used is always the top selection in the Function box.

2. If the name of the function you want to use appears in the Select a Function box, click to select it. If the function you want to use is not on the Most Recently Used list, choose a category. If you're not certain of the exact name of the function, enter a brief description or keyword in the Search box and click the Go button (see Figure 23.9).

Figure 23.9

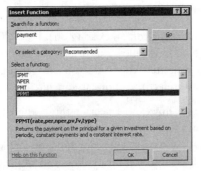

3. The text at the bottom of the Insert Function dialog box offers a brief explanation of the selected function and its syntax (click the Help on This Function link for a more detailed explanation). When you've selected the correct function, click OK. Excel adds the function to the Formula bar and opens a new dialog box with separate input boxes for each argument, as shown in Figure 23.10.

Figure 23.10

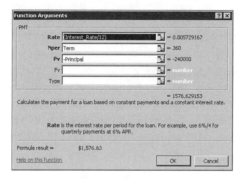

4. Click within the first argument box and fill in the required data. Note that the help text at the bottom of the dialog box is specific to the argument you're currently working with, and the data type required for each argument appears to the right of the input box.

- Type text, numbers, and other constants directly in the input box.

- To add cell references by pointing and clicking, first click the Collapse Dialog button (at the right side of each argument input box) to roll most of the Insert Function dialog box up and out of the way. Next, select the cell or range to use for the selected argument, and then click the Collapse Dialog button again to continue.

- To use a function as an argument within another function, click to position the insertion point within the box for that argument and then select the function from the Function box to the left of the Formula bar. (See "Secrets of the Office Masters: Nesting Functions Within Functions" at the end of this chapter for more details.)

- When entering constant values, you can include the percent operator (%) and minus signs (–) with numeric data. Look to the right of the input box to see the current value of each argument you enter. If the data is not of the type required by the argument, Excel displays the word Invalid to the right of the input box.

5. Repeat step 4 for other required and optional arguments. Look to the right of the equal sign for each argument to see its current value, using the data you've entered so far. To see the result of the formula itself, look at the text along the bottom of the dialog box.

6. After entering all required arguments, click OK to paste the complete function into the current cell, or click Cancel to start over.

Tip from

Ed & Woody

Debugging a formula can be frustrating, especially when working with complex formulas containing several nested functions. Here's a backup strategy that allows you to freely experiment with formulas and functions without fear of losing your work or damaging a worksheet. Before editing a formula, remove the equal sign from the beginning of the formula and press Enter; then copy the formula to another cell. Without the equal sign, Excel treats the cell's contents as plain text and copies the formula exactly as it appears, with no adjustments. If your experiments are unsuccessful, copy the backed-up formula to the original cell and then restore the equal sign.

To use the Insert Function dialog box as a proofreading and reference tool, begin constructing your formula as usual, starting with an equal sign and the function name. After entering the first parenthesis, click the Insert Function button to open the Insert Function dialog box with the current function selected. Any arguments you've already entered will be in the dialog box as soon as it opens.

TOTALING ROWS AND COLUMNS AUTOMATICALLY

The most commonly used functions are also the easiest to enter. To insert a formula that adds a column or row of numbers automatically, click in a blank cell beneath any column of numbers (or at the end of a row of numbers), and then click the AutoSum button. Excel inserts the SUM function with the argument already filled in and selected. Adjust the selected range, if necessary, and then click the Enter box in the Formula bar or press Enter to store the formula in the active cell.

Use the drop-down arrow to the right of the AutoSum button to select the AVERAGE, COUNT, MAX, or MIN functions for the adjacent row or column. Select the More Functions option from the bottom of the list to open the Insert Function dialog box with the adjacent row or column selected as the default argument.

Two quirks in AutoSum are worth noting:

- First, if the range above or to the left of the cell containing the SUM formulas contains any blank cells, the range to be totaled stops there.
- Second, when the cell that holds the SUM function is at the end of a row and a column, AutoSum always selects the column. In either case, the moral is the same: When using AutoSum, always check to be certain that the correct range is selected.

To automatically add totals for several adjacent rows or columns, select the cells directly beneath the columns or to the right of the rows and then choose an AutoSum function. Excel plugs in the selected formula for each row or column, just as if you had added each one individually. When you use the AutoSum button this way, you do not see a confirmation dialog box.

If you use AutoSum below an AutoFiltered list, the resulting formula uses the SUBTOTAL function instead. This syntax allows you to see a correct sum using only the filtered data; if you used the SUM function, the result would show all cells, including those hidden by the filter.

Tip from

EQ & Woody

> You don't need to enter a formula to make quick calculations. When you select two or more numbers in a worksheet, Excel displays a summary of the selected cells in the status bar along the bottom of the worksheet window. The default calculation is a simple total; look at the right side of the status bar and you'll see SUM=, followed by the total of the selected cells. Right-click anywhere on the status bar to display a shortcut menu that lets you choose a different calculation, including Average, Max, Min, Count (which counts the number of selected cells), and Count Nums (which counts only the number of selected cells that contain numbers). Use this feature in conjunction with selecting a column in a list, for example, to quickly spot the largest and smallest values in that field.

PUTTING WORKSHEET FUNCTIONS TO USE

Excel has over 300 functions, including those available in various add-ins. The following sections list some of the tasks you can accomplish by using functions in each category.

CALCULATING FINANCIAL FORMULAS

Excel includes a large number of financial functions—52 in all—covering everything from simple household budget problems, such as calculating a house payment, to complex tasks such as figuring the bond-equivalent yield for a U.S. Treasury bill (TBILLEQ) or the accrued interest for a security that pays interest at maturity (ACCRINTM).

Most of the more advanced financial functions, including those that calculate depreciation schedules (DB, DDB, SLN, SYD, and VDB) and internal rates of return (IRR, MIRR) are useful only if you have enough of an accounting or finance background to understand the underlying principles. However, a number of general-purpose functions are useful for a wide variety of calculations involving loans and investments. You can calculate the periodic payment for a loan or annuity using PMT, figure the net present value of an investment or loan with NPV, determine the interest and principal portion of a periodic payment with IPMT and PPMT, and calculate the future value of an investment (FV). These functions, and several more that cover the same ground, use some or all of the following common arguments:

- Future value (fv) is the amount that an investment or loan will be worth after all payments have been made. When dealing with investments, fv is usually positive; in the case of loans, fv is typically 0.

- Number of periods (nper) is the total number of payments or periods of an investment. Make sure the unit of measurement is consistent with the payment period; if you pay a 30-year mortgage monthly, nper is equal to 360 (30*12).

- Payment (pmt) is the amount paid periodically to an investment or loan. It cannot change over the life of the annuity. Typically, pmt includes principal and interest but no other fees or taxes. For a loan or investment, in which you are the one making payments, you typically enter pmt as a negative number; if you receive dividends or other payments (in other words, if you're the bank), pmt is generally a positive number.

- Present value (pv) is the value of an investment or loan at the beginning of the investment period. When you are the borrower, the present value of a loan is the principal amount that is borrowed, expressed as a negative number.

- Rate (rate) is the interest rate or discount rate for a loan or investment. Pay particular attention that nper and rate use the same scale as pmt. If you make monthly payments on a 30-year loan at 7.5% annual interest, use 7.5%/12 for rate (to convert the annual rate to a monthly rate, such as the payments) and 30*12 for nper (360, the number of monthly payments in a 30-year loan).

- Type (type) is the interval at which payments are made during the payment period, such as at the beginning of a month or the end of the month. In interest rate calculations over a long period of time, the difference can be substantial.

WORKING WITH DATE AND TIME FUNCTIONS

Use date and time functions for simple tasks, such as displaying today's date or the day of the week for a given date. If you run an organization whose members pay dues annually on their birthday, how do you create a list of birthdays sorted by month? If you sort by birthday, you'll end up with a list that's sorted by the members' ages. To create a column that you can sort by, you'll have to add a formula that uses the MONTH function to convert a date to a month.

> **Note**
> There is a profound difference between using a function to convert a value and using cell formats to change the display of a value. Functions return a different value from the value you use as an argument; when you change formats, on the other hand, the underlying value stored in the cell remains exactly the same.

→ For an overview of how Excel enters and manipulates dates as serial values, **see** "Setting Date and Time Formats" **p. 582**.

Date functions can help you perform even the most sophisticated calculations. For example, U.S. tax laws require that participants in some types of retirement accounts begin withdrawing funds and paying taxes as soon as they turn 70 1/2 years old. To calculate the first day of the month after a person reaches that age, enter the account holder's birthday in a cell named Birth_date, and then use the following formula to calculate the retirement date:

```
=DATE(YEAR(Birth_date)+70,MONTH(Birth_date)+7,1)
```

Table 23.1 lists the most useful date and time functions, along with examples of how to use each one.

TABLE 23.1   DATE AND TIME FUNCTIONS

Function Name	Description	How to Use It
TODAY(), NOW()	Return the current date or time as a serial value	No argument required; enter =NOW() to plug the current date and time into a cell; use TODAY() to enter only the current date.
YEAR(serial_number) MONTH(serial_number) DAY(serial_number)	Convert a serial date value to its year, month, or date	Useful when you need to separate the components of a date entered in a cell to create a list of all birthdays for all employees and sort it by month, for example.
WEEKDAY(serial_number)	Convert a serial date value to a weekday	Useful in formulas in which you want to calculate paydays or due dates. The result is a number from 1 (Sunday) to 7 (Saturday). Format the result using the "ddd" or "dddd" format to see the results as a day of the week.
HOUR(serial_number) MINUTE(serial_number) SECOND(serial_number)	Convert a serial date value to its hour, minute, or second	Useful when you need to separate the components of a time entered in a cell—to create a list of all starting times for a golf tournament, for example, grouped by hour.

You'll find an interesting collection of special-purpose date and time formats in the Analysis ToolPak, an Excel add-in. EOMONTH(TODAY(),0), for example, returns the last day of the current month—a useful calculation when working with payments that are due on the last day of the month. (Change the second argument to 1 to return the last day of next month, or -1 for the previous month.) Other date/time functions in the Analysis ToolPak include WORK-DAYS and NETWORKDAYS, which are useful when you're calculating project timelines. To install the Analysis ToolPak, choose Tools, Add-Ins, and check the Analysis ToolPak box.

PERFORMING STATISTICAL ANALYSES

Excel includes 78 statistical functions, including such widely used measures as standard deviation (STDEV), normal distribution (NORMDIST), Chi test (CHITEST), and Student's t-test (TTEST). As with the financial functions, these are most useful to people who have a firm grounding in the principles of statistical analysis, but a handful are applicable to users with a general business background.

Excel includes not one but three functions for working with a set of values. AVERAGE returns the arithmetic mean (the total of all values, divided by the number of entries in the list); MEDIAN returns the value in the middle of the list; and MODE returns the value that occurs most frequently. Depending on the distribution of data in a sample, any one of these three functions might be more or less appropriate.

MIN, MAX, and COUNT are straightforward functions that calculate the minimum, maximum, and number of entries in a list. These functions (and several others) have variations that end in the letter A—MINA, MAXA, and COUNTA. Use COUNTA, for example, when you want to work with not just numeric values in a list, but all arguments, including text and those that evaluate to a logical result such as TRUE or FALSE.

USING THE LOOKUP WIZARD TO FIND INFORMATION IN LISTS

The 16 functions in the Lookup and Reference category are intended for use with lists and tables. HLOOKUP and VLOOKUP, for example, are designed to help you track down specific information in a table—by row or column—based on the contents of a cell that contains another value to use for comparison. (LOOKUP, which sounds like a simpler version of both functions, is actually included only for compatibility with other spreadsheet programs and is not recommended for use with Excel.) MATCH, INDEX, and OFFSET are other functions in this category that are useful for reference tasks, such as locating information in tax tables.

The syntax of all these functions is hideously complicated and rarely worth the effort. If you must add this type of function to a worksheet, do yourself a favor and use the Lookup Wizard, an Excel add-in specifically designed to generate these formulas with minimal effort on your part. For example, if you store a list of part numbers, product names, and prices in an Excel table, you might want to create a data-entry area at the top of the table that lets you enter a specific part number and quickly look up the corresponding product name and price.

Before you can use the Lookup Wizard, you have to install it. Choose Tools, Add-Ins, click the Lookup Wizard option, and supply the Office XP CD or point the Installer to a network installation point. After installing the wizard, you can use it to create lookup formulas that work properly without any debugging.

The worksheet in Figure 23.11 contains one such lookup formula. You enter a part number in cell A2, and Excel finds that value in the corresponding column in the list below, reads across to the value in the Price and Product Name columns in that row, and displays the results in cells C2 and D2. The formulas in cells C2 and D2 that actually perform the lookup are fairly complex, including nested MATCH and INDEX functions.

Figure 23.11
Use the Lookup Wizard to add the data-entry cell (A2) and lookup formulas (C2 and D2) to a worksheet.

	D2			f_x	=INDEX($A$4:$E$1039, MATCH(A2,$A$4:$A$1039,), MATCH(D1,$A$4:$E$4,))	
	A	B	C	D		E
1	Part #	Category	Price	Product Name		In Stock
2	RE900101		$ 8.45	Zoo Med Repti Cave with Cactus		
3						
4	Part #	Category	Price	Product Name		In Stock
5	BI816908	Bird	$1.68	3 Toy Value Pack		8
6	MI048685	Misc.	$1.73	3M Vetrap Bandaging Tape		0
7	DO060957	Dog	$2.56	5" Paw Print Stoneware		3
8	DO060933	Dog	$1.79	5" Short Bowl Paw Print Stoneware		5
9	DO014608	Dog	$7.25	7 in 1 Nylon Leash (1 inch)		2
10	DO014592	Dog	$6.97	7 in 1 Nylon Leash (3/4 inch)		3
11	DO060971	Dog	$4.35	7" Paw Print Stoneware		9
12	DO060995	Dog	$6.29	9" Paw Print Stoneware		6
13	RE296980	Reptiles	$3.09	A Step by Step Book About Lizards		1
14	RE245995	Reptiles	$3.09	A Step-By-Step Book About Iguanas		1

To add a lookup formula to a worksheet that contains a list, start by creating the list itself. You must include a header row that contains column labels for each field in the list, and the first column must consist of unique values that serve as row labels. The data does not need to be sorted in any order. Leave several blank rows at the top of the list to allow room for placing the lookup cells. After verifying that the list is arranged properly, follow these steps:

Tip from
EQ & Woody

If you plan to create a lookup form on a worksheet, position it above the list or on a separate sheet. If you position cells that contain the formula and parameters alongside or below a list, you could accidentally hide or erase them when you filter or delete records.

1. Select the entire range that contains the list, including the header row. (Although this step is not required, it's easier to select this range before running the wizard.)

2. Choose Tools, Lookup. (If this command is not available, you need to load the Lookup Wizard first, by choosing Tools, Add-Ins.) In the first step of the wizard, verify that the entire list is selected; if necessary, adjust the selection. Click Next to continue.

3. In the next step (see Figure 23.12), choose the name of the column that contains the value you want to look up—in this case, Product Name. At the bottom of the dialog box, select any row from the drop-down list. Because this value will appear in an input cell, the exact value doesn't matter. Click Next to continue.

Figure 23.12

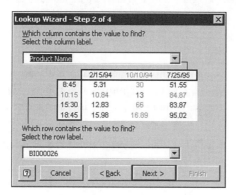

4. Specify that you want to copy the formula and lookup parameters to your worksheet, as shown in Figure 23.13.

Figure 23.13

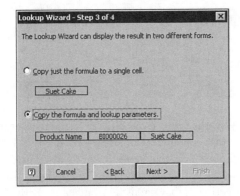

5. Follow the wizard's prompts to position lookup formulas and related cells on the worksheet. The first value the Lookup Wizard produces is the label over the lookup column; it goes in D1. The second value is the one you'll change later to lookup values; in this case, it goes in cell A2. The third value contains the lookup formula and goes in D2.

6. Repeat steps 2–5 to add the formula that looks up information for other columns. For example, to look up information in the Price column, create a lookup formula and add it to cell C2.

Tip from

EQ & Woody

Add just the lookup formula to your worksheet when you want to perform a different lookup in every row of your table. For example, a golf tournament coordinator might keep a list of each player's current handicap on one worksheet. Using a list on a separate worksheet for each tournament, the coordinator could enter the date, the player's name, and the raw score in the first three columns. A lookup formula in the fourth column of every row would find the current handicap on the other worksheet, based on the member's name in the first column. Use an additional calculated field to figure the net score by subtracting the looked-up handicap from today's score.

USING DATABASE FUNCTIONS

Excel includes a dozen functions you can incorporate into formulas to analyze information in a list. These functions work with the same techniques as advanced *filters*—for each function, you define a criteria range, specify the location of a list, and select a column on which to perform calculations.

→ For details on how to use advanced filters in Excel lists, **see** "Finding and Filtering Data in a List," **p. 683**.

To work with any of these functions, choose Insert, Function, or click the Insert Function button on the Standard toolbar. In the Insert Function dialog box, select Database from the Function Category list. Choose any entry from the list on the right to see a brief description in the same dialog box, or click the Help button for step-by-step instructions on how to use the function and enter parameters.

Note that all 12 of these functions begin with the letter D (for *database*). All the D-functions take three arguments:

- `database`—The first argument is the range that contains your list; it must include the header row that contains column labels.
- `field`—The second argument is the label over the column you want to summarize.
- `criteria`—The final argument is the range that contains a condition you specify.

Use these functions to analyze whether values in a list meet specific criteria. For example, in a list that contains product information organized by category, you can count all the rows in which the category is "Cat" and the price is greater than $20.

PERFORMING MATHEMATICAL OPERATIONS

Given Excel's extensive mathematical capabilities, it's only natural that the list of worksheet functions includes 60 mathematical functions. Several handle advanced trigonometry calculations (`COS`, `TAN`, `SIN`, `ACOS`, `ATAN`, and `ASIN`, for example), and the `PI` function displays the value of Pi to 15 decimal places.

Use the `ROUND` and `TRUNC` functions to transform values for use in calculations. For example, if cell C16 contains the value 23.5674, use `=ROUND(C16,2)` to convert that value to 23.57; the second argument defines the number of decimal places. Use `=TRUNC(C16,2)` to lop off all digits beyond the number of decimal places you specify in the second argument. Because this function truncates the value rather than rounding it, the result is 23.56 rather than 23.57.

Note

> Although you can use cell formats to change the way information is displayed in a cell, these formats don't change the underlying information stored in the cell. Use the `ROUND` and `TRUNC` functions when you want to perform calculations based on a specific level of precision.

The MOD function divides one value by another and returns a remainder. One interesting use of this formula is to determine whether a given year is a leap year. If cell A1 contains the year to be tested, enter this formula:

```
=IF(OR(MOD(A1,400)=0,AND(MOD(A1,4)=0,MOD(A1,100)<>0)),"Leap Year", "Not a Leap
Year")
```

This tricky formula uses the logical operators IF, OR, and AND to test whether cell A1 is divisible by 400 or is both divisible by 4 and not divisible by 100. If either condition is true, it returns the text "Leap Year"; otherwise, it returns the text "Not a Leap Year."

To display the *absolute value* of a formula, so the result is always a positive number, use the ABS function. =ABS(A14-A16), for example, always returns the difference between the values in these two cells as a positive number, even if A16 is larger than A14.

One of the most interesting functions in this group is SUMIF(range,criteria,sum_range); use it to total a range of numbers based on whether they meet criteria you define. For example, if the range B2:B20 contains the names of salespeople and the range C2:C20 contains invoice amounts, use the following formula to calculate the total for all invoices from Debbie McKenna:

```
=SUMIF(B2:B20,"Debbie McKenna",C2:C20)
```

COMBINING AND SEPARATING TEXT VALUES

It's easy to think of functions in mathematical terms, but some of the most useful functions work strictly with text. You can use text functions to pull specific information from a single *text value*, split a text value into multiple cells, combine text values into a single string, or convert one type of data (such as a number or date) into text, using a specific format.

When you want to combine (or *concatenate*) the text from two cells, use an ampersand. The following formula adds a space between the values in two adjacent cells:

```
=A1&" "&A2
```

For more sophisticated manipulation of strings of text, use any of Excel's 23 text functions. These functions are especially useful when you've imported text from another program or file. Simple text functions let you convert text from all capitals to lowercase letters (and vice versa) or convert a date value to text in a specific format. The following formula, for example, combines three functions to pull out just the last name from a complete name in cell A17:

```
=RIGHT(A17,LEN(A17)-FIND(" ",A17))
```

The task isn't as easy as it might first appear. Because the last name can be any length (Bott or Leonhard, for example), you first need to calculate the correct number of characters. For starters, use the FIND function to locate the space separating the first and last names. If the first name contains five letters, the formula FIND(" ",A17) returns the value 6. Next, use the LEN function to determine the total length of the name; by subtracting the value determined in the first step from this value, you can determine the exact length of the last name. Finally, use the RIGHT function to extract that number of characters from the input cell (A17), starting at the right side.

Table 23.2 lists the most useful text functions.

TABLE 23.2   COMMON TEXT FUNCTIONS

Function Name	Description	How to Use It
CONCATENATE(text1, text2,...)	Combine two or more text items	Generally, an ampersand (&) is easier.
UPPER(text), LOWER(text), PROPER (text)	Convert case of text, to all capitals, all lowercase letters, or initial capitals	`=PROPER('macmillan computer publishing')` changes the first letter of each word to a capital letter—in this case, `Macmillan Computer Publishing`.
FIND(find_text, within_text,start_num) SEARCH(find_text, within_text,start_num)	Find text in a cell	`FIND` is case-sensitive; `SEARCH` allows wildcard characters.
LEFT(text, num_chars) RIGHT(text, num_chars) MID(text,start_num, num_chars)	Extract text from a cell	Use with `FIND` and `SEARCH` to extract part of a text string for example, a part number from a lengthy product code.
TEXT(value,format _text) FIXED(number, decimals, no_commas) DOLLAR(number, decimals)	Convert number to text	For the `TEXT` function, specify any number format (except General) from the Category box on the Number tab in the Format Cells dialog box. Be sure to enclose the format in quotation marks: `=TEXT(TODAY(), "mmmm d,yyyy")`.
CLEAN() TRIM()	Remove unwanted characters from text	`TRIM` removes extra spaces from imported text, and `CLEAN` removes unprintable characters, such as might be found at the top or bottom of a file that contains formatting informa tion that Excel can't interpret.

If you have trouble concatenating two values, see "Convert Values to Text Before Concatenating" in the "Troubleshooting" section at the end of this chapter.

G LOGICAL AND INFORMATION FUNCTIONS

Excel includes six *comparison functions*, which you can use to compare two values and define actions based on the comparison. Far and away the most popular and useful logical function is *IF*. The following is the syntax of the *IF* function:

`=IF(`**logical_test**`,value_if_true,value_if_false)`

Excel also includes 18 *information functions*, which give you information about cells, worksheets, and your system itself. For the most part, you'll use these functions to build error-handling and data-validation routines into a worksheet. Nine of these functions belong in a subgroup called the IS functions: ISTEXT, ISERROR, ISNUMBER, and so on.

By combining the IF function and the ISERROR function, you can avoid seeing error codes in a worksheet. The formula =IF(ISERROR(A5/A8),"",A5/A8), for example, tests the value of the formula A5/A8 before displaying a result. If A8 is equal to 0, Excel displays nothing in the cell rather than the annoying #DIV/0! error message; if the value of A8 is other than 0 and the formula returns a valid result rather than an error message, Excel displays that result.s

Tip from

Ed & Woody

In many cases, *conditional formatting* is a better way to suppress error messages than using formulas. Select the cell in which you want to suppress error messages—A9, for instance—then choose Format, Conditional Formatting. In the Conditional Formatting dialog box, click the Condition 1 drop-down list and choose Formula Is. In the edit box to the right, enter the formula =ISERROR(A9). Next, click the Format button, and in the Format Cells dialog box, click the Color drop-down list and choose the white square. Click OK to close the Format Cells dialog box and click OK to close the Condition Formatting dialog box. Now, any error messages in that cell will appear as white text on a white background and will be invisible.

→ For a detailed discussion of conditional formatting, **see** "Using Conditional Formatting to Identify Key Values," **p. 598**.

TROUBLESHOOTING FORMULAS

The more complex the formula, the more likely you are to need time to get it working properly. Excel 2002 includes a variety of tools you can use to troubleshoot errors in formulas and in worksheets. Excel 2002 adds several new error-checking tools that can make your worksheets more accurate. This section discusses the most useful options.

HOW FORMULA AUTOCORRECT WORKS

Under most circumstances, Excel won't let you enter a formula using incorrect syntax. If you make one of many common mistakes in formula syntax or punctuation, Excel offers to correct the mistake for you, and generally the correction is appropriate. This feature, called Formula AutoCorrect, can detect and repair any of the following errors:

■ Unmatched parentheses, curly braces, or single or double quotation marks.

■ Reversed cell references (14C instead of C14, for example) or comparison operators (=< instead of <=).

■ Extra operators, such as an equal sign or plus sign, at the beginning or end of a formula.

■ Extra spaces in cell addresses (A 14 instead of A14), between operands, or between a function name and its arguments.

- Extra decimal points or operators—in general, Excel uses the decimal point or operator farthest to the left and removes all others, so 234.56.78 becomes 234.5678, and =23*/34 becomes =23*34.

- Incorrect range identifiers, such as a semicolon or an extra colon between the column and row identifiers.

- Implied multiplication—if you omit the multiplication sign and enter 2(A14+B14), for example, or use an x instead, Excel adds the correct sign.

RESOLVING COMMON ERROR MESSAGES

All Excel error messages begin with a number sign (#); in all, you might see any of seven possible error codes. To remove the error message and display the results you expect, you have to fix the problem either by editing the formula or changing the contents of a cell to which the formula refers.

Excel 2002 offers greatly improved tools for resolving error messages. If the cell in question contains an error message, you see a small green triangle in the upper-left corner of the cell. Click to select that cell and a Smart Tag with a yellow exclamation point appears. Click that Smart Tag to display a menu like the one shown in Figure 23.14.

Figure 23.14
Click the Smart Tag to find clues to the cause of an error message and possible solutions.

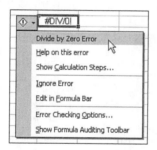

The top line in the Smart Tag menu displays the name of the error and is not clickable. Use additional menu choices to find possible causes and solutions for the error.

Table 23.3 lists the seven error codes you're likely to see when an Excel formula isn't working properly, along with suggested troubleshooting steps.

TABLE 23.3   COMMON FORMULA ERROR CODES

Error Code Displayed	What It Means	Suggested Troubleshooting Steps
#DIV/0!	Formula is trying to divide by a zero value or a blank cell.	Check the divisor in your formula and make sure it does not refer to a blank cell. You might want to add an error-handling =IF() routine or conditional format to the cell, as described earlier in this chapter.

TABLE 23.3 CONTINUED

Error Code Displayed	What It Means	Suggested Troubleshooting Steps
#N/A	Formula does not have a valid value for argument passed.	#N/A means "No value is available." Check to see whether you have problems with LOOKUP functions. You can also manually enter the #N/A value in cells in which a value is temporarily unavailable, to prevent #DIV/0! Errors.
#NAME?	Formula contains text that is neither a valid function nor a defined name on the active worksheet.	You've probably misspelled a function name or a range name. Check the formula carefully. In a natural-language formula, this error means Excel cannot identify one or both labels.
#NULL!	Refers to intersection of two areas that don't intersect.	You're trying to calculate a formula by using labels for a column and row that have no common cells. Choose new labels for the row or column or both.
#NUM!	Value is too large, too small, imaginary, or not found.	Excel can handle numbers as large as 10^308 or as small as 10^-308. This error usually means you've used a function incorrectly—for example, calculating the square root of a negative number.
#REF!	Formula contains a reference that is not valid.	Did you delete a cell or range originally referred to in the formula? If so, you see this error code in the formula as well.
#VALUE!	Formula contains an argument of the wrong type.	You've probably mixed two incompatible data types in one formula—trying to add text with a number, for example. Check the formula again.

CHECKING FOR ERRORS IN A WORKSHEET

As noted in the previous section, Excel tracks formula errors automatically as you work, displaying a green triangle in the upper-left corner of any cell that contains an error. You can also check for errors on a sheet manually, by choosing Tools, Error Checking. When you choose this option, Excel finds the first error (on the current sheet only) and displays a dialog box like the one shown in Figure 23.15. Use the Previous and Next buttons to highlight additional errors on the sheet.

Figure 23.15
Click the Evaluate button to step through each operation and debug a complex formula.

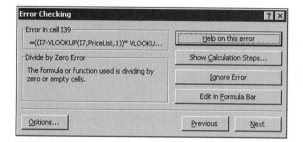

If the error is harmless and you don't want Excel to nag you about it any further, click the Ignore Error button. For simple errors where the fix is immediately obvious (a typographical error or a misplaced divisor, for instance), click the Edit in Formula Bar button to make the change directly, without closing the Error Checking dialog box.

For complex formulas, in which an error can be difficult to track down, click the Show Calculation Steps button. This button opens the Evaluate Formula dialog box (Figure 23.16), which lets you drill down into a formula to find and fix the problem.

Figure 23.16
Use the Step In button to drill down into a formula in search of errors from another cell.

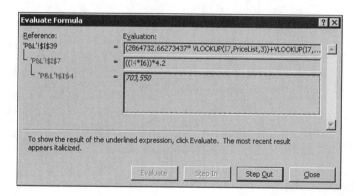

The initial view shows each element in the formula, evaluated to the result just before the error. Click the Evaluate button to step through the error. Keep clicking and you'll eventually return to the formula as entered, where you can walk through each element of the formula, moving from left to right. With each click, Excel evaluates another part of the formula.

For formulas that refer to other formulas in other cells, click the Step In button to follow the chain of references through as many steps as it takes to find the error.

Tip from 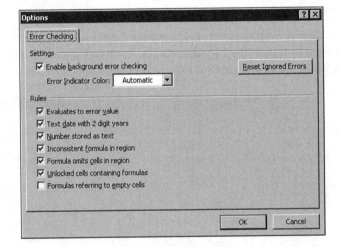 *Ed & Woody*	If you inherit a worksheet that someone else has developed and you want to quickly check it for errors, take this precautionary step: Open the Error Checking dialog box, click the Options button, and click the Reset Ignored Errors button. This option ensures that you'll see all possible errors that Excel can detect, even if a previous user hid the error indicators.

Click the Options button on the Error Checking dialog box to specify which errors Excel should look for. For instance, Excel normally flags dates with two-digit years as errors (because of possible date arithmetic problems) and also calls out any formula that is inconsistent with other formulas in the same row or column. If you get tired of false alarms, uncheck any of the boxes shown in Figure 23.17.

Figure 23.17
Use these options to prevent Excel from checking for certain types of errors.

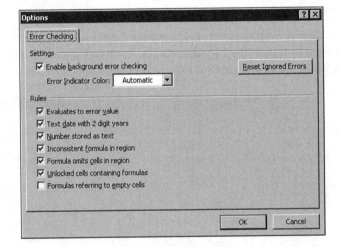

USING THE RANGE FINDER TO LOCATE PARTS OF A FORMULA

When a cell that contains a summary formula doesn't display the correct result, the first place to look is at the cell and range references in that formula. If you've added new rows or columns, it's possible that the formula references the old range and doesn't include the new cells.

To match cell references in any formula with the actual worksheet cells, use Excel's Range Finder. When you select any cell that contains a formula and make it available for editing, Excel highlights each cell or range reference in that formula with a different color, and then adds an identically color-coded outline around the cells to which the range refers.

If you discover that a formula includes an incorrect cell or range reference, use the Range Finder to add or remove cells from the reference, or to select a completely different group of cells. Click the color-coded border on any cell edge to move the reference to a different cell; click and drag the square handle in any corner of the colored border to extend the selection. To record your changes, press Enter or click the green Enter Formula button next to the formula bar.

USING GOAL SEEK TO FIND VALUES

After you've constructed a worksheet and built several intricate formulas, you might discover that you can't easily get the answer you're looking for. A formula that uses the PMT function, for example, is designed to produce the total monthly payment when you enter the price and loan details. But what if you want to start with a specific monthly payment and interest rate, and then calculate the maximum loan amount you can afford based on those values? Rather than construct a new formula or use trial-and-error methods to find the right result, use Excel's Goal Seek tool to perform the calculations in one operation:

1. Start by opening the worksheet that contains the formula you want to work with, and then choose Tools, Goal Seek. Excel displays the Goal Seek dialog box shown in Figure 23.18.

Figure 23.18

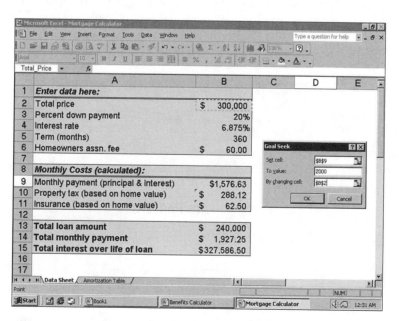

2. Fill in the three boxes to match the results you're trying to achieve. In the Set Cell box, enter the address of the formula whose results you want to control. In the To Value box, enter the amount the formula specified in the previous cell should equal. Finally, in the By Changing Cell box, enter the cell that contains the single value you want to change.

3. When you click OK, Excel runs through all possibilities and displays the Goal Seek Status dialog box, as shown in Figure 23.19. If you look at the worksheet itself, you'll see the values have changed to reflect the result shown here.

Figure 23.19

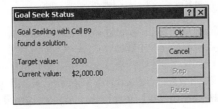

4. Click OK to incorporate the changed data into your worksheet; click Cancel to close the dialog box and restore the original data.

If your problem is more complex and can't be solved by changing a single cell, use the Solver add-in. Like other Excel add-ins, you must install this option before it's available on the Tools menu; choose Tools, Add-Ins, and click the Solver option to install it for the first time. Then choose Tools, Solver to display the Solver Parameters dialog box, as shown in Figure 23.20.

Figure 23.20
Use the Solver Parameters dialog box to specify more complex conditions for working backward to a formula's solution.

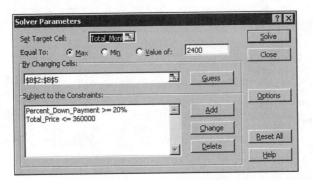

Select the cell that you want to adjust in the Set Target Cell box, click the Max, Min, or Value Of box, and enter a comparison amount. In the By Changing Cells box, select the cells you want to adjust. Note that unlike the Goal Seek feature, you can specify multiple cells here. Finally, enter any constraints you want to impose on the solution; for example, you can specify a maximum or minimum value for one or more of the changing cells. Click the Solve button to begin calculating.

When the Solver utility completes its calculation, it displays the Solver Results dialog box, shown in Figure 23.21. If Solver reports an error message, adjust the constraints and try again. If Solver successfully found a solution, you have three choices: Select the Keep Solver Solution option and click OK to change the values in your worksheet; choose the Restore Original Values option and click OK to cancel all changes; or click the Save Scenario button to create a worksheet scenario using the Solver results.

Figure 23.21
The Solver Results dialog box shows the results of a formula's calculations.

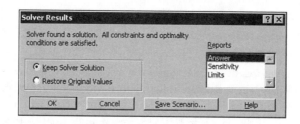

→ For a detailed discussion of workbook scenarios, **see** "Storing Multiple Scenarios in a Single Workbook," **p. 715**.

TROUBLESHOOTING

EDITING AN ARRAY FORMULA

I entered an array formula, but when I try to edit or copy it, the results change or I get an error message.

Editing an array formula is tricky. If the array formula was entered across multiple cells, you must select every cell that contains the array before you can edit it. If the array formula is contained in a single cell, you can edit it just as you would a conventional formula, but you must remember to press Ctrl+Shift+Enter to store your changes as an array formula. If you forget and press Enter, Excel stores it as a standard formula, with the wrong results. Finally, you'll notice some restrictions when you try to copy an array formula. If the destination range you select also contains the array formula, you'll get an error message; select a new destination range, or use AutoFill to copy the formula. Oh, and don't try to cheat by adding your own curly braces to create an array formula—the only way to enter an array formula is to press Ctrl+Shift+Enter and let Excel add the curly braces.

CHECK FORMULAS BEFORE DELETING RANGE NAMES

After I deleted a range name in my worksheet, some of my formulas displayed error messages.

It's a frustrating fact of life: When you delete a range name from a worksheet, Excel does not automatically adjust any formulas that contain that range name. Even though it should, logically, be able to substitute the old cell address for the range name, it leaves the name there to torture you. After deleting a range name, you will see a #NAME? error in any cell that contains a formula with a reference to the deleted range name. Unfortunately, there's no easy way to determine which cell goes with the defunct name. If you spot these errors immediately after deleting the range name, press Ctrl+Z to undo your change. If you remember this possibility before deleting a range name, you can easily change any cells before deleting or changing the defined name. Press Ctrl+F to open the Find dialog box, enter the name of the cell or range, choose Formulas from the Look In box, and click Find Next to jump to and edit each cell that contains that name.

CONVERT VALUES TO TEXT BEFORE CONCATENATING

When I try to combine a cell that contains text with one that contains a date, the result is nonsense. The cell that holds the date is correctly formatted, but the resulting text says something like "Today is 36232" instead of displaying a date.

As you've seen, Excel ignores the formatting of the original cell when concatenating the two values and instead displays the serial date value. Before concatenating a date with text, you must convert the date to text and choose a format. Use the TEXT function followed by a format in quotation marks. If the date is in cell A15, for example, use this formula to get the result you're looking for: `="Today is "&TEXT(A15,"mmmm d, yyyy")`.

SECRETS OF THE OFFICE MASTERS: NESTING FUNCTIONS WITHIN FUNCTIONS

In some cases, it's necessary to use one function as the argument for another. *Nesting* functions within functions this way is common with logical functions such as IF, for example. In a sales worksheet that you use to calculate commissions at a regular rate of 5%, you might want to pass along an extra 2% bonus to salespersons who beat their quota in every quarter and pay no commission to those who averaged 10% or less than their target number for the year. If the quarterly quota for the first salesperson is in cell B3 and the actual sales for each quarter are in B4:B7, enter the following formula to perform the full calculation in a single step:

```
=IF(MIN(B4:B7)>B3,SUM(B4:B7)*7%,IF(AVERAGE(B4:B7)<B3,0,SUM(B4:B7)*5%))
```

Note that this example includes three levels of nesting, with the final SUM and AVERAGE functions nested within an IF function, which in turn is the final argument of the first IF function. The MIN and SUM functions comprise the first two arguments within the first IF function. You can nest functions within functions within functions to create some clever effects. Say you want to add a date stamp to a worksheet, so whenever you print the worksheet, you'll see a large text label that includes your name and the current date. Enter this formula in a cell that is within the print range, substituting your name in the text string that begins the formula:

```
="Prepared by John Q. Smith, "&TEXT(TODAY(),"mmmm d, yyyy")
```

When nesting functions, note that the nested function must return the same value type (text, number, date, true/false) as the argument it's replacing. Unlike formulas containing constants or cell references, which can contain an unlimited number of nesting levels, Excel enables you to nest a maximum of seven levels of functions. If you need to perform more calculations than this, you'll have to break the formula into multiple steps and place each step in its own cell.

You can use the Insert Function dialog box to enter a nested function within another function. Begin entering the first function by using the Insert Function dialog box, as described earlier in this chapter. Click in the input box for any argument, and then choose another function from the Function box (this box is located to the left of the Formula Bar, where the Name box normally appears; it is visible only when the Function Arguments dialog box is open). As you enter the formula, you can switch between functions at any time by clicking the function's name in the Formula bar. If you choose a function that contains a nested function as an argument (as in the example shown here), the entire function appears in the input box, and the result of the function using current values appears to its right.

Figure 23.22

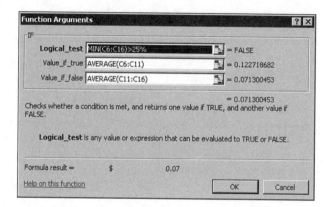

CHAPTER 24

CREATING AND EDITING CHARTS

In this chapter

ANATOMY OF AN EXCEL CHART

The basic row-and-column worksheet grid is essential in helping you organize data and perform calculations, but it's difficult—and sometimes impossible—to analyze information and see patterns by staring at a sea of numbers.

Charts help you turn numeric data into visual displays in which you can identify trends and pick out patterns at a glance. By using lines, columns, bars, and pie slices to compare series of data over time and across categories, charts often provide clear answers to tough questions, such as these:

- **Which Sales Region and Which Product Lines Have Been Most Successful in the Past 12 Months?**—A stacked column chart lets you see both sets of data in a single display.

- **Does Your Small Business Have Seasonal Variations in Cash Flow or Inventory?**—You might not be able to tell from an accounting statement packed with hundreds of individual data points, but a line chart can help you clearly see the highs and lows.

- **Just Where Does the Money Go?**—If you've broken out a year's worth of expenditures by category, a pie chart helps you see which categories are taking more than their fair share—and devise strategies for reining in those expenses.

When you create a new chart, Excel allows you to place it on its own chart sheet or embed a chart object within the worksheet that contains the data you want to chart. Working with a chart on its own sheet gives you the maximum working room for editing and formatting; embedding a chart within a worksheet lets you easily see the data and chart side by side.

Excel automatically maintains links between worksheet data and its graphic representation on the chart; if you change the numbers or text in the data range, the columns, pie slices, and other graphic elements on the chart change, too.

To create a chart, use either of these two basic techniques:

- To create a chart and adjust all its options in four easy steps, click the Chart Wizard button on the Standard toolbar.

- To instantly create a chart on its own chart sheet using the default chart type, chart options, and formatting, open the worksheet that contains the data you want to chart. Select the range that contains the data you want to chart, and then press F11.

If the data you select is in a PivotTable, pressing F11 creates a new PivotChart on its own sheet using default formats.

You can choose from dozens of Excel chart types, ranging from basic bar charts appropriate in almost any business situation to exotic data displays suited only for specialized scientific or engineering applications. Regardless of chart type, however, most charts include a set of standard elements and a palette of common options. Each row or column that contains numbers to be plotted, for example, makes up a data series. Each value within the series is called a *data point*. If the range you select for your chart includes worksheet headings, Excel uses them as labels along the category axis or value axis. The stacked-column chart in Figure 24.1 shows most of the common elements you'll encounter as you work with charts.

Figure 24.1
Most Excel charts include some or all of these standard elements.

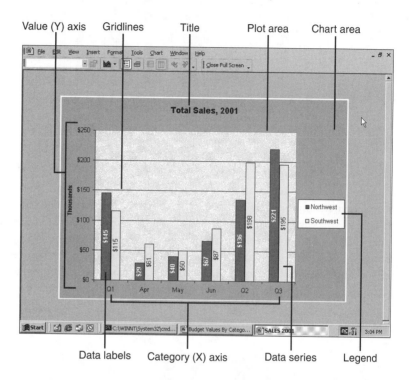

Tip from

EQ & Woody

To identify elements on an Excel chart, use the ScreenTips that pop up when the mouse pointer passes over objects. Even if you never use ScreenTips elsewhere, pay attention here because they are invaluable aids in identifying even the most obscure chart elements. Within the plot area, they identify the name of the data series and data points, as well as the precise value of each data point. If you don't see these ScreenTips, this feature might have been disabled; to turn them back on, select Tools, Options, click the Chart tab, and check both boxes in the Chart Tips area.

DATA SERIES

Each group of related data points in a chart is called a *data series*. In almost all cases, a series consists of a row or column on a worksheet, and when plotted in the chart each data series has a unique color or pattern. You can plot one or more data series in a chart. Bar charts, area charts, and column charts, like the one shown in Figure 24.2, typically contain multiple series. Pie charts consist of only one data series, in which the total always adds up to 100%. A line chart might contain one or multiple series.

Figure 24.2
This ScreenTip identifies the name of the data series and the name and value of the data point under the mouse pointer.

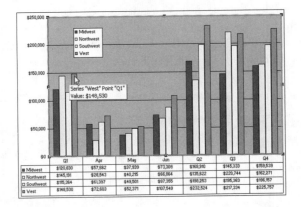

DATA MARKERS

Each point in a data series becomes a single *data marker* on a chart. In column, bar, and pie charts, each column, bar, or pie slice is a marker that represents one data point. In stacked column charts, each segment within each column or bar is a marker. In line, xy (scatter), and radar charts, you can use dots or symbols to identify all the data points on a series. For example, a line chart that compares the trends of two or more stock prices over time might use a triangle, a diamond, and a square to mark data points on different series. Marker characters appear in the legend, as shown in Figure 24.3.

Figure 24.3
When you're printing in black and white, you can't tell that each line is a different color. Instead, use data markers to differentiate series; the marker characters appear in the legend.

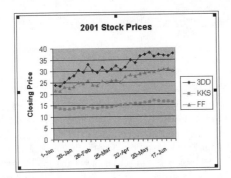

Tip from

EQ & Woody

Data markers are usually unnecessary when you're creating a chart that will be viewed online—instead of marker characters, use colors to differentiate between series. Markers are most useful when you intend to print a line chart in black and white and you want each line to be easily identifiable.

AXES AND GRIDLINES

Axes are the lines along each side of the plot area, which provide the scale for measurement or comparison of plotted data. The *category (X) axis* (usually horizontal) arranges your data by category—by time, for example, or by division or employee. The *value (Y) axis* (usually vertical) defines how you want to plot the worksheet data. In the default column chart, for example, taller columns represent bigger numbers. In combination charts (discussed later in this chapter), it's not unusual to see two value axes, both vertical. When you create a secondary value axis, the labels appear on the right of a column chart.

> **Note**
>
> In the default column chart type, the Y-axis is vertical and the X-axis is horizontal. Direction isn't important, however; what matters most is the type of data you plot along each axis. In any chart, the X-axis contains categories. On a 2D chart, the Y-axis is for values; in a 3D chart the values go on the Z-axis, with the Y-axis reserved for different series of data.

PART

IV

CH

24

Gridlines are horizontal or vertical lines that extend through the plot area to help you visualize the connections between data points and values or categories. Gridlines start with the tick marks on an axis and extend through the plot area.

DATA LABELS, LEGENDS, AND TITLES

Data labels identify items on the category axis and define the scale of the value axis; you can also add labels to a single data marker, an entire data series, or all data markers in a chart. Depending on the chart type, data labels can show values, names of data series or categories, percentages, or a combination of these elements. Because of their tendency to clutter a chart, you should use data labels sparingly.

A *legend* is a color-coded key that identifies the colors or patterns that correspond to data series or categories. If you've defined data marker characters (as on a line chart), the legend includes the marker character as well.

Titles consist of descriptive text that identifies the chart or an axis. By default, titles are aligned to an axis or centered at the top of the chart.

Tip from

EQ & Woody

> Add a chart title when you want to provide a descriptive label for the entire graphic. If you plan to paste the chart in a highly formatted Word document or PowerPoint presentation, however, you might want to leave the title off the chart while working in Excel and add the text in Word or PowerPoint instead. That way, when you change your document or presentation design, the title will change as well.

PLOT AREA

In a 2D chart, the *plot area* is the region enclosed by the axes; it includes all data series. In a 3D chart, the plot area also includes category names, tick-mark labels, and axis titles. Right-click and select Format Plot Area to add borders or background colors, textures, and fill effects behind the plotted data.

CHART AREA

The *chart area* includes all chart elements. When you select the chart area, you'll see eight small black squares—one in each corner and one in the middle of each side. Right-click and select Format Chart Area to change all text elements to a specific font or to add a background color or texture behind the entire chart.

Tip from

EQ & Woody

Many Excel experts don't even know this secret: After selecting any part of a chart, you can move in rapid succession to other parts of the same chart by pressing the arrow keys. Use the up- and down-arrow keys to select major chart elements. Use the left- and right-arrow keys to select every available chart element in succession, including individual points within each data series, as well as every color key and text entry in the legend. The Name box (just to the left of the Formula bar) identifies which element is selected.

WORKING WITH EMBEDDED CHARTS

If you chose to insert the chart as an object in an existing worksheet, it sits in its own layer on top of your data. Select the chart by clicking anywhere on it, and then point to one of its edges until the pointer turns into a four-headed arrow. Click and drag to slide the chart object into a new position. As you slide to any edge of the window, the worksheet scrolls in that direction.

When you move or resize cells underneath a chart object on a worksheet, Excel moves or resizes the chart as well. To change this link between chart and cells, right-click the chart area and select Format Chart Area from the shortcut menu. Click the Properties tab and select one of the three options in the Object Positioning section. Select Move but Don't Size with Cells, for example, if you want the proportions of a chart and all objects on it to remain exactly the same even if you move it.

To change an *embedded chart* to a *chart sheet*, and vice versa, right-click the plot area or chart area and select Location from the shortcut menu. The two choices on this dialog box let you enter a name for a new chart sheet or select the name of an existing sheet on which to place an embedded chart.

You can view an embedded chart in a window without moving it to its own chart sheet—a handy option when you want to edit or format an embedded chart without accidentally moving it or changing the zoom level of the worksheet. Right-click anywhere on the plot area or chart area of the embedded chart, and then select Chart Window from the shortcut menu. You can resize the window without affecting the position of the original embedded sheet. Right-click the title bar to print the chart, set page options, or run a spelling check. Click the Close (X) button to return to the worksheet window.

To resize an embedded chart, click once on the chart border to select the chart area. You'll see eight small sizing handles along the border—one on each side and one in each corner. Point to any of these black squares and drag the pointer—a two-headed arrow—in any direction to adjust the size and shape of the chart. As you drag, Excel adjusts the scale of all elements on your chart to match the new size and shape.

Excel doesn't add sizing handles to a chart on a chart sheet; instead, the default settings for the chart sheet use your default paper size and expand the chart area to fit the entire page. So, if you select a zoom level of 100%, you see the entire chart. To resize the chart area of a chart sheet for printing, select File, Page Setup, and then click the Chart tab. Select the Custom option to display sizing handles so you can change the dimensions of the chart, and then click OK to return to the chart sheet. You can now move or resize the chart.s

USING THE CHART WIZARD FOR QUICK RESULTS

Expert users might be tempted to dismiss Excel's Chart Wizard as just another tool for beginners, to be avoided at all costs. Big mistake. Don't think of the Chart Wizard as a set of training wheels—instead, think of it as a highly structured, superbly organized interface that lets you efficiently deal with every chart option in four steps.

PART
IV
CH
24

Tip from

EQ & Woody

Each of the four steps in the Chart Wizard corresponds to one of four choices on the shortcut menu that appears when you right-click the plot area or chart area of any chart. If you want to change only the data source of a chart, it takes fewer clicks to use the shortcut menus than to restart the Chart Wizard.

- In Step 1, use the Chart Type dialog box (see Figure 24.4) to select any of Excel's built-in chart types or select a custom chart type you've defined previously. Select a category from the Chart Type list, and then click the icon for the corresponding chart subtype that best represents the type of chart you want to create. If you selected a range of data before starting the Chart Wizard, click and hold the button below the chart types to see a preview of your data. Click Next.

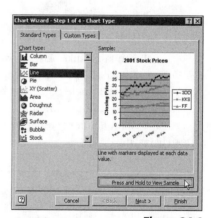

Figure 24.4

- In Step 2, fill in or edit the Source Data dialog box to define the location of data series and values for use with labels and axes. If you selected data before starting the Chart Wizard, most of these decisions are already made for you.

→ Choosing the best chart design for your data is a crucial step many Excel users overlook; **see** "Choosing a Standard Chart Type," **p. 654**.

- In Step 3, enter title text and configure the appearance of legends, gridlines, and other chart elements. Use any of the categories in the multitabbed Chart Options dialog box shown in Figure 24.5. (The exact options available depend on the chart type you

selected in Step 1.) As you
add title text and adjust
other chart options, the
preview window changes to
show how your chart will
look.

■ In Step 4, use the Location
dialog box to specify
whether you want to create
a new chart sheet or embed
a chart object in an existing
worksheet. If you want to
review your choices or
make any changes, click the
Back button. Click Finish to close the wizard and add the chart to your worksheet.

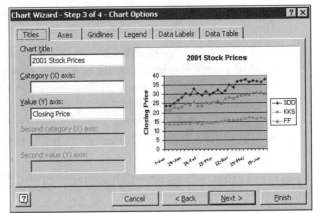

Figure 24.5

You can agonize over every detail of a chart, but sometimes it's more effective to breeze
through the Chart Wizard first, using its default settings and ignoring most of the fine
details. After you've created a solid foundation for your chart, you can tweak individual elements. You can also click the Chart Wizard button to restart the wizard any time after
you've created your chart. Many of the choices will be much clearer when you see what the
first draft of the chart looks like.

SELECTING DATA TO PLOT

Excel maintains links between worksheet data and the data series on a chart. When you create a chart, Excel automatically detects the data to be charted based on the current selection.
If you select a single cell, Excel bases the chart data on the current region—an area that
extends in each direction until you encounter the edge of the worksheet or a blank row or
blank column. On the other hand, if you select a range of cells, Excel uses that range for the
chart data.

Note

The number of points per series is limited to 32,000, and the total number of points
per chart is limited to 256,000. The maximum number of series you can use in a chart
is 255. If you have more series than this, you must filter your list before creating your
chart. You should also seriously reconsider the point you're trying to make because
even Stephen Hawking would have trouble absorbing that much information at once.

Be sure the range you select includes all the data to be charted, as well as the labels you'll
use for the categories. The range does not have to be contiguous. For example, to create a
pie chart, you might want to select a row of column labels and a row of totals, ignoring the
detail rows in between. Nor do you need to select all the data in a table, if all you want to

chart is a subset of the data—for example, on a 12-month budget worksheet, you might want to show sales totals only for the months of October through December.

If the range you plan to chart ends with a row or column of totals, don't include those totals in your selection; otherwise, the totals will create one column or pie slice that overwhelms all the others in the chart.

When you select the data source, Excel attempts to identify category headings, value axis labels, and data series; it also chooses whether to plot data by rows or by columns. This choice is based on the number of items—if there are more columns than rows, Excel plots the data by column, placing the column headings along the category axis; if there are more rows than columns, or an equal number of rows and columns, Excel plots by row.

Changing the way data is plotted can help emphasize different trends and patterns. For example, Figure 24.6 shows a worksheet that contains a small range of data. When plotted by row, the data emphasizes the full year's results for each region, and you can see at a glance that the Northwest had a great Q3. When plotted by column, however, the chart encourages comparing how each region did on a quarter-by-quarter basis, and it's easy to see that the West was dominant throughout the year.

Figure 24.6
Changing the way data is plotted—by rows or columns—can change the story a chart tells.

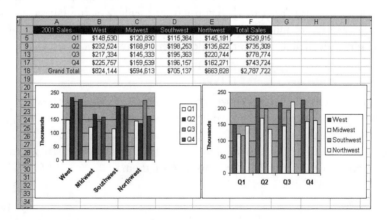

To reverse the order in which Excel plots the selected data, use one of two buttons on the Chart toolbar (if this toolbar is not visible, right-click the menu bar or any visible toolbar and choose its entry from the list). Click the Series in Rows or Series in Columns button to shift orientation. (This option is also available when you right-click the plot area and select Data Series, or in Step 2 of the Chart Wizard).) With some chart types and data, making this switch could render the chart incomprehensible; click the Undo button if that happens.

Normally, Excel plots data series from left to right and top to bottom. What do you do if your data source is arranged in alphabetical order, but you want to display the series in a different order—say, with the two most productive regions listed first, or with dates in reverse order? If you don't want to change the arrangement of data on the worksheet, you can change the plotting order of the data series:

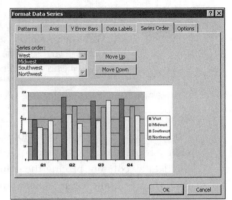

1. Click any data series in the chart you want to change.

2. Select Format, Selected Data Series (or press Ctrl+1), and click the Series Order tab.

3. In the Series Order box (see Figure 24.7), select the series you want to move, and then click Move Up or Move Down. Repeat this step for each additional series you want to move. Watch the display in the Preview window to see the effect of your changes.

4. Click OK to apply your changes to the chart.

Figure 24.7

SELECTING AND CUSTOMIZING A CHART TYPE

When you create a new chart, Excel lets you select from 73 chart types in 14 categories (although a significant number of these choices are actually just minor variations of others in the same category). You can also choose from a gallery of 20 built-in custom chart types, and you can create and save your own chart types as well. The type of data you're planning to plot usually dictates which type of chart you should choose.

CHOOSING A STANDARD CHART TYPE

When you start the Chart Wizard, the first step is to specify what type of chart you want to create. After you create a chart, you can easily change it to a new type; right-click the chart area or plot area and select Chart Type, or click the Chart Type button on the Chart toolbar to display the Chart Type dialog box. The following sections discuss all the standard Excel chart types and describe how you can best use them.

COLUMN

This type of chart shows a comparison between values in one or more series, often over time. For example, you can show how your company's sales compare with its competitors over the past five years. Stacked column charts further divide the total for each column, so you can also measure how each geographic region performed for each company. Select a column chart when you want to show comparisons between different data points, especially those that change over time. Avoid this chart type if each series includes so many data points that you'll be unable to distinguish individual columns.

BAR

Think of a bar chart as a column chart turned on its side, with values along the horizontal axis and categories on the vertical axis. It de-emphasizes time comparisons and highlights winners and losers. Figure 24.8, for example, graphically illustrates how well each region has performed in a competition where the goal is to hit $150,000 in sales.

Figure 24.8
Bar charts highlight winners and losers. In this example, it's easy to see which region is in the lead.

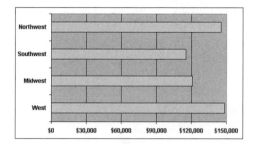

LINE

This chart type displays a trend, or the relationship between values over a time period. For example, Figure 24.9 plots a year's worth of monthly high temperatures for four U.S. cities. By placing temperatures on the value axis and using the category axis as the time scale, the dips and rises in the line show when the weather is getting cooler or warmer. Select a line chart when you have many data points to plot and want to show a trend over a period of time. Avoid this chart type when you're trying to show the relationship between numbers without respect to time, and when you have only a few data points to chart.

Figure 24.9
Line chars are most useful for showing trends over a period of time.

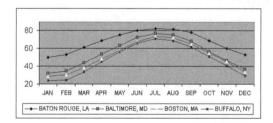

PIE

Pie charts show the relative size of all the parts in a whole—for example, the ethnic composition of a city. Pie charts have no x- or y-axis, and only one data series can be plotted. Use pie charts when you have only a few numbers to chart and want to show how each number contributes to the whole. Avoid this chart type when your data series includes many low numbers that contribute a very small percentage to the total. In this case, individual pie slices will be too small to compare.

XY (SCATTER)

use a scatter chart to show correlations between different series of values when the element of time is unimportant—usually used for scientific analyses. For example, plotting daily high temperatures and ice cream sales over the course of a year will no doubt show clusters of high sales on hot days. Figure 24.10 shows a scatter chart that measures the correlation between risk and reward in stock investments (note the use of trendlines in both series). You can also create charts that plot two groups of numbers as one series of XY coordinates; this is the principle behind the price-performance charts you sometimes see in computer magazines. The correct arrangement of data on the worksheet, especially sorting, is crucial when creating this chart type.

Figure 24.10
Scatter charts help to illustrate correlations between two sets of data. We've used trendlines in this example to make the relationship even clearer.

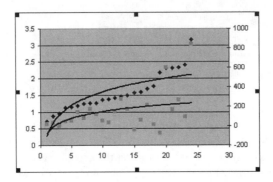

AREA

This chart type shows lines for parts of a series, adding all the values together to illustrate cumulative change. Unlike line charts, which emphasize the rate of change, area charts show the amount and magnitude of change. The area chart in Figure 24.11, for example, shows how much each division of a company contributes to total profits over the course of a year.

Figure 24.11
Area charts graphically illustrate cumulative changes–this example shows the year-long contribution of four company divisions.

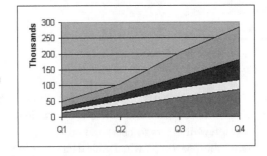

DOUGHNUT

The doughnut chart is similar to a pie chart, except that it can contain more than one data series. Each ring of the doughnut chart represents a data series.

RADAR

Each category in a radar chart has its own value axis that extends from the center of the chart. Lines connect all the values in the same series.

Tip from
EQ & Woody

Are you baffled by some of these chart types? You're not alone. According to Microsoft, both doughnut and radar chart types are popular among Excel users in the Far East but are rarely used in the United States and Europe.

SURFACE

Select this chart type to add a topographic layer over a column or area chart. Instead of assigning a color to each series, this chart type assigns different colors to similar values. The result resembles a topographic map, which can be used to show relationships among large amounts of data that might otherwise be hard to see.

PART
IV
CH
24

BUBBLE

Bubble charts are similar to scatter charts, except they contain three series of data rather than two. Instead of placing a uniform-sized dot at the point where each pair of x- and y-values intersect, the data markers are bubbles whose size is determined by the values in a third series. Bubble charts often are used to present financial or market research information.

STOCK

Four built-in chart types make tracking open/high/low/close prices over time possible, as in the example in Figure 24.12. Combination chart types in this category enable you to plot volume traded as well. You also can adapt these chart types for scientific use, to show high-low values in experimental data. When choosing one of these chart types, read the text under the Sample window carefully to ensure you've arranged your data correctly. The Office Assistant displays an error message if you have too many or too few columns, or if they are in the wrong order.

Figure 24.12
Each line in this stock chart shows the high, low, and closing prices for a selected ticker symbol on a specific day.

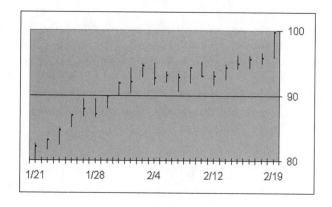

CONE/CYLINDER/PYRAMID

For the most part, these are simply glitzy versions of standard 3D column and bar charts. Options enable you to control whether each data marker tapers to a point or is tapered to the highest value in the series.

USING COMBINATION CHARTS

The list of standard Excel chart types includes several *combination charts*, which mix two chart types in a single graphic. The Line-Column chart type, for example, lets you format one series of data along a line and another in columns; you'll find this versatile chart type on the Custom Types tab of the Chart Types dialog box, along with other built-in custom designs.

In the Stock category on the Standard Types tab of the same dialog box, you'll find combination charts that let you plot high, low, and closing stock prices on a line, with trading volume in columns. In this case, you use two value axes, one to the left of the chart area and the other on the right.

The Pie-of-Pie and Pie-of-Bar combination charts, both available as subtypes in the Pie category, offer a clever solution when you have so many data points that your chart is difficult to read. As the example in Figure 24.13 shows, you can use a Pie-of-Bar chart to combine several smaller slices into a single large slice, and then show the detail in a separate chart connected to the original.

Figure 24.13
Use a Pie-of-Bar chart to keep small slices of the pie from getting lost.

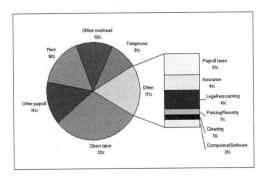

If you're having trouble formatting your combination chart, see "Formatting Combination Charts" in the "Troubleshooting" section at the end of this chapter.

To create either of these combination chart types, open the Chart Type dialog box and select the Pie type; then select the appropriate chart subtype from the list on the right and click OK. To adjust which slices of the pie will go in the secondary (pie or bar) chart, right-click either pie and select Format Data Series. Then click the Options tab and adjust the settings as shown in Figure 24.14.

Figure 24.14
Use this dialog box to shift slices of a pie from the primary chart to the secondary chart.

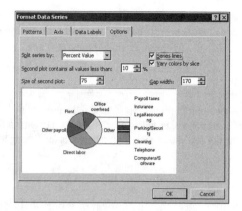

Using the Split Series By list, you can tell Excel to use a specific number of slices, or all slices below a certain value or percent. To move slices from the primary to the secondary chart, select the Custom option in this list; then close the Options dialog box and drag slices directly on the chart.

CREATING AND SAVING CUSTOM CHART TYPES

If you've extensively customized a chart, you can save its formatting settings and chart options in a named format. All the custom chart types you save appear on the Custom Types tab of the Chart Type dialog box. When you choose a custom chart from this list, Excel applies all the saved options and format settings from the selected chart type to the current chart. This is an especially effective technique for managing a collection of format charts you use regularly. It's also an effective way to maintain a consistent style across charts within a company.

The Custom Types tab actually shows two groups of custom charts, drawn from a built-in gallery and a user-defined gallery:

■ Click the Built-in option to see all the chart types in the Excel gallery, a collection of mostly combination charts. This file, Xl8galry.xls, is added to your system as part of the default Excel installation. On a typical installation for a U.S. English system, you'll find the built-in gallery in C:\Program Files\Microsoft Office\Office10\1033.

Note

The filename in the previous paragraph is not a typo. Even though Excel 2000 was version 9.0 and Excel 2002 is version 10, the collection of built-in chart types uses the same format as those found in Excel 97 (version 8.0); to maintain compatibility, the file uses the Xl8 prefix.

→ For an explanation of the default storage location of this and other Office files, **see** "Choosing a Default Local Storage Location," **p. 56**.

- Click the User-defined option to see a list of all user-defined charts. These details are stored in a file called Xlusrgal.xls, which Excel creates the first time you define a custom chart type. You'll find this file in the Application Data\Excel folder in your personal profile.

Tip from

EQ & Woody

When you save a custom chart type, your entry in the user-defined gallery stores all formatting and chart options, including titles. If you want to enter a new title each time, replace the title text with a generic placeholder before saving the custom chart type.

To create a custom chart type, first select the chart sheet or embedded chart object whose format settings and options you want to save, and then follow these steps:

1. Click the Chart Type button on the Chart toolbar, or right-click the chart area or plot area and select Chart Type from the shortcut menu.

2. In the Chart Type dialog box, click the Custom Types tab; in the area labeled Select From, select User-defined. Excel filters the list to display only the Default chart type and other custom chart types you've previously created, as shown in Figure 24.15.

Figure 24.15
Click the User-defined option to see a list of all custom chart types you've previously created.

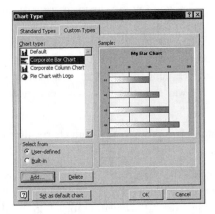

3. Click the Add button to display the Add Custom Chart Type dialog box shown in Figure 24.16.

4. Enter a name and description for your chart type. Then click OK to save your changes in the User-defined gallery.

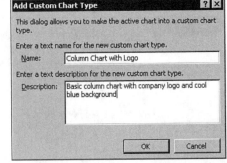

Figure 24.16

Excel's built-in gallery of chart types is a wildly inconsistent collection of several good-looking examples mixed with others that are staggeringly ugly. Although most users don't know it, you can edit this collection, and you also can add your own custom charts to the built-in gallery. Customizing the built-in gallery is a particularly good way to distribute standard chart types throughout a department or an entire corporation, while preventing users from modifying or deleting the chart types.

Tip from
Ed & Woody

> To delete a custom chart type you've created, select its entry in the Custom Types tab, and then click the Delete button. You can't directly rename or modify a saved custom chart type; instead, apply the chart type to a new chart, modify it as necessary, save the resulting chart type under a new name, and then delete the existing chart type.

PART

IV

CH

24

Custom chart types are stored as individual chart sheets in Xl8galry.xls (for built-in custom chart types) and Xlusrgal.xls (for user-defined chart types). Use the following techniques to manage the contents of the chart gallery:

- To rename or delete one or more chart types from the built-in gallery, open Xl8galry.xls, right-click the sheet you want to delete, and then click Rename or Delete.

- To add a new chart type to the built-in gallery, first save the new chart type in the user-defined gallery, being sure to give it a name and description. Then open Xl8galry.xls and Xlusrgal.xls and copy the chart tab from Xlusrgal.xls to Xl8galry.xls. Save both files.

If you cannot open the chart gallery, see "Opening the Chart Gallery" in the "Troubleshooting" section at the end of this chapter.

CREATING A DEFAULT CHART

The absolute quickest way to create an Excel chart is to select a data range and press F11. This creates a chart using all Excel's default chart options—on a clean installation of Office 2002, this is the Column chart type. If you prefer to use a different chart type as your default, open the Chart Type dialog box, select the chart type you want to use from either the Standard or Custom tab, and click the Set As Default Chart button. The next time you press F11, Excel will create a chart sheet using the current region or selected data with the chart options in your default chart type.

To reset the default chart type, open the Chart Types dialog box and click the Custom Type tab. Select the User-defined option in the Select From box; then click Default in the Chart Type list, and click the Delete button.

EDITING AND FORMATTING CHART ELEMENTS

Although the default chart settings are often good enough to get you started, Excel offers a broad range of chart options that give you complete control over the look of the chart and plot area. The easiest way to change many chart options is to rerun the Chart Wizard. The wizard's dialog boxes pick up your current chart settings and let you change chart types, edit the source data, apply new formatting, or change the location of your chart.

Note

All the techniques described in this section work equally well with embedded chart objects, chart sheets, and PivotCharts.

To adjust individual chart objects, first select the object (the chart title or the category axis, for example), and then change its properties.

Tip from

EQ & Woody

Selecting a specific chart object by pointing to it can be difficult, especially on a small chart with many elements crowding one another for space. Try this simple shortcut: Use the Chart Objects drop-down list at the left of the Chart toolbar. Selecting any item from this list selects that item in the current chart. Then click the Format button just to its right to display the Format dialog box for the selected object.

Excel also lets you add an enormous number of attention-getting elements in the drawing layer on top of a chart. For example, you can add text boxes to data markers to explain anomalies in your data or call attention to key numbers. If you select the chart or plot area and start typing, Excel begins creating a text box immediately. After you've added the desired text, you can then move it anywhere on the chart and reformat it to your liking.

→ To add, edit, and format text boxes, AutoShapes, callouts, and other drawn elements in charts, use the Office drawing tools; **see** "Using Office Drawing Tools," **p. 108**.

ADJUSTING CHART OPTIONS

Step 3 of the Chart Wizard displays a tabbed dialog box that lets you adjust various chart options. After you create a chart, you can display the same dialog box by right-clicking the chart area or plot area and selecting Chart Options from the shortcut menu. The following six categories of options might be available, depending on the chart type.

TITLES

Create titles that appear on the top of the chart or next to any axis. If the nature of data along each axis isn't immediately apparent, you can add explanatory text here, too. Click this tab and enter the text for the chart title and any available axes. In both locations, titles are nothing more than text boxes. The default font size for titles and other text objects on a chart is 10 point. Typically, that results in chart titles that are too small and legends that are too large. Use the Font tab on the Format dialog box to adjust the size of each object.

AXES

Check Automatic to allow Excel to format and display the axes that are appropriate for the chart type you've chosen. Normally, Excel is capable of analyzing the data type and using the correct settings. If your category axis includes dates, the Format Axis dialog box allows you to set the options shown in Figure 24.17. Adjust the Minimum and Maximum settings if you want to restrict the charted portion of your data; for example, in a list of daily sales results that encompasses several years, you might want to see just a few months' results. Change the Base Unit option to chart time data using a different scale. For example, in a list that includes data for many days, select Month(s) or Year(s) to let Excel group the data before plotting.

Figure 24.17
Time-scale axes let you control the start and stop dates as well as the interval for the plotted data.

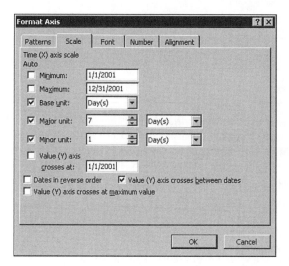

Use the Category and Time-scale options to solve a particularly annoying charting problem: If you select a time series that skips some dates, Excel might leave gaps in the category axis. If you construct a stock chart using daily high, low, and closing prices, for instance, your time series will be missing values for Saturdays, Sundays, and holidays, when the market is closed. Unfortunately, Excel insists on adding phantom markers for those days, messing up the smooth line you expect to see.

The solution is to convert the Time-scale axis to a Category axis. Right-click the chart axis and select Chart Options. Click the Axes tab and select the Category option under the primary Category (X) Axis. When you close the dialog box, Excel changes the display of data to a simple series, with no gaps. If you open the Format Axis dialog box, you'll see a different set of options, as shown in Figure 24.18.

This dialog box also lets you control the placement of tick marks, which are the small lines that indicate where each item on the category axis is plotted.

Figure 24.18

If your time-scale axis includes some gaps in dates, convert it to a category axis. You might need to check the Categories in Reverse Order box to display the dates correctly.

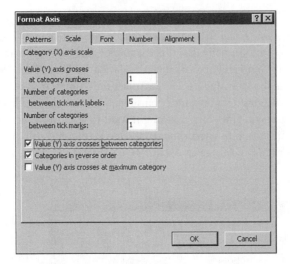

If you have more items on your category axis than will fit, use the Number of Categories Between Tick-mark Labels option to suppress some of them. Enter a value of 2 here to see every other label on this axis; enter 3 to see every third label. You can also use the settings on the Alignment tab to rotate the text on the category axis labels and make extra room.

GRIDLINES

Gridlines help readers see where data points cross category or value axes. You can set major and minor gridlines for each axis. Normally, Excel does a decent job of setting intelligent defaults, but you often can clean up a chart and make it easier to read by adjusting these settings. In general, you should try to use as few gridlines as you can get away with. Watch the Preview window to see the effect as you add or remove gridlines.

LEGEND

A chart legend identifies each data marker according to its color or pattern on a chart. Options on this tab let you move or reformat the legend. If you don't need to show a legend (perhaps because you want to label each column or pie slice individually), uncheck the Show Legend box. The Placement options control where the legend first appears within the chart: Bottom, Corner, Top, Right, or Left. You can drag to position it more precisely later.

DATA LABELS

Use data labels when you want to display charted worksheet values, category labels, or percentages next to each point in a data series. Check the Legend Key Next to Label box to add a color-coded key at the beginning of each label. The options in this dialog box control the placement and appearance of data labels for every data series. However, if you want to add labels for just one series, or even a single point, you can do so. Skip the Chart Options dialog box and instead open the Format dialog box for the series or point you want to label. Check the appropriate option on the Data Labels dialog box for that item.

DATA TABLE

Display a worksheet-style table directly in your chart to show the plotted worksheet data alongside the chart itself. Each row in the data table represents a data series. If your chart includes a relatively small amount of data, a data table can make an effective addition, as the example in Figure 24.19 shows.

Figure 24.19
Data tables give your audience both views of the data–the visual display as well as the underlying numbers.

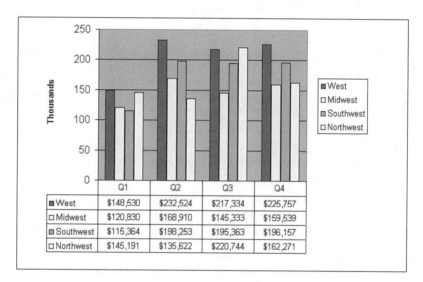

	Q1	Q2	Q3	Q4
■ West	$148,530	$232,524	$217,334	$225,757
□ Midwest	$120,830	$168,910	$145,333	$159,539
■ Southwest	$115,364	$198,253	$195,363	$196,157
□ Northwest	$145,191	$135,622	$220,744	$162,271

> **Note**
>
> Data tables are available only in column, bar, line, area, and stock charts. You cannot add a data table to a pie, XY (scatter), doughnut, radar, surface, or bubble chart.

CHANGING NUMBER FORMATS

Use the right-click shortcut menus to change the number format of any item on a chart; to adjust the value axis, for example, right-click and select Format Axis. Click the Number tab in the Format Axis dialog box, and then select a format from the Category list. You can select a built-in number format or create a custom format, just as you can when formatting worksheet data. Click OK to apply the new format to your chart data.

→ To learn more about altering Excel's number formatting, **see** "Setting Number Formats," **p. 580**.

Normally, numbers that appear in Excel charts use the same format as the source data in the worksheet to which they're linked. If you change the format of the numbers in the chart, you break the link to the format in the worksheet. Under many circumstances you'll want to do exactly that—for example, if numbers in your worksheet use the Currency format with two decimal places, but you don't want to see a dollar sign or decimals in your chart. To reestablish the link so the data on the chart uses the same number format as the data on the worksheet, select the chart object (for instance, the Value axis), select its Format option, click the Number tab, and check the Linked to Source box.

CHANGING TEXT FORMATS

You can change the appearance of any text item on a chart. As with worksheet cells, Excel lets you change fonts as well as font sizes and character attributes. You can choose different colors for the text and its background. To keep labels from running into one another on any axis, rotate text to an angle.

Tip from
EQ & Woody

When you use the Chart Options dialog box to enter text for titles, Excel doesn't let you enter line breaks or change formatting within the title. After you place the title on the chart, however, you can select and format individual words or characters as well as the entire title. To add a line break to a title, click to position the insertion point within the title on the chart, and then press Enter.

To adjust font options for all text in your chart, right-click the chart area and select Format Chart Area. Click the Font tab of the resulting dialog box and adjust formatting as necessary. This dialog box is a great way to apply the same font to all text in your chart, but avoid the temptation to choose a standard size as well. In most cases, you'll want to specify different font sizes for different items, such as the chart title, axes, and legend.

To change text formatting for any text object on the chart, right-click the object and select its Format option. Click the Font tab and adjust options as desired.

Tip from
EQ & Woody

By default, text in an Excel chart is *scalable*—that is, as you resize the entire chart, the text gets larger or smaller so it remains in proportion with the rest of the chart elements. If you have carefully designed a text element and don't want its font size to change, turn off automatic scaling. Right-click the object and click the Format menu. On the Font tab, clear the check mark from the Auto Scale box.

Are the category axis labels crowding the axis itself? Use the Offset box to specify the distance between the axis labels and the axis itself; the higher the number, the more distance between the two points.

ADDING BACKGROUND COLORS, TEXTURES, AND PICTURES

The default background for charts is plain white, but you can add background colors, textures, pictures, and gradient fills to an entire chart, to just the plot area, or to individual items such as data markers. In 3D charts, you also can add images to the walls and the floor.

These features use the Drawing tools shared by all Office programs. If you've used Word to design a Web page or created a presentation with PowerPoint, you can use the same backgrounds in Excel charts as in those files and then paste the charts into your Web page or presentation with confidence that they'll match the existing design.

→ To learn how to change background colors in any Office document, **see** "Changing Background Colors and Line Formats," **p. 114**.

→ The Office Drawing tools enable you to easily add interesting visual effects; **see** "Adding Shadows and 3D Effects," **p. 115**.

CHANGING THE SCALE AND SPACING OF AXES

To make a chart easier to read, you might also want to adjust the scale on the value axis. Normally, the values on this axis start with 0 and extend to a number past the highest number in your data series. You might want to change the scale to start at a higher number, so you can more easily see the difference between data points. You can also adjust the display of large numbers:

1. Right-click the value axis and select Format Axis.

2. Click the Scale tab to display the dialog box shown in Figure 24.20.

3. Enter the high and low values for the axis in the Minimum and Maximum boxes. Note that changing the default numbers automatically clears the check marks in the Auto column.

4. If you want to make large numbers—thousands or millions, for example—easier to read, select an option from the Display Units drop-down list. If you select Millions, for example, Excel will display $85,000,000 as $85.

5. Click OK to apply the changes to your chart.

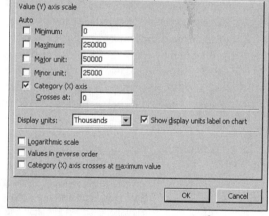

Figure 24.20

PART
IV

CH
24

CHANGING THE DATA SOURCE FOR AN EXISTING CHART

How do you add, edit, or remove data series, category names, and axis labels when you've already created the chart? Use one of the following three techniques:

■ If the *data source* is simple and straightforward, with easy-to-identify headings for categories and values, right-click the chart area or plot area and select Source Data. Click the Data Range tab of the Source Data dialog box and select the new data range. If necessary, specify whether the series is in rows or columns. Click OK to apply the changes to the current chart.

- To add, remove, or change an individual data series or the range that defines labels or names, click the Series tab on the Data Source dialog box and adjust the options there. For example, if your current chart includes five data series, one for each year from 1997 through 2001, you might want to remove the first two years and add the years 2002 and 2003 to bring the chart up to date. Select the 1997 entry from the Series list and click Remove, and then do the same for the 1998 series. Note that the category name and value labels adjust automatically when you use this option.

- To add or remove a single series from a chart embedded on a worksheet, select the data range that contains the headings and values you want to plot and drop it directly on the chart. Excel adds the data to the plot area, complete with new category labels and legend items, if necessary.

Tip from

EQ & Woody

If you copy a worksheet range to the Clipboard, you can right-click the plot area or chart area and select Edit, Paste to add the series to an existing chart.

When you select a data series on an embedded chart, the Range Finder displays a colored line around the corresponding range within the data source; the Range Finder also adds a border around the value axis labels and category labels, using different colors for each. Drag the selection by using the rectangular handle in the lower-right corner of each selection to extend or move the data range for each series. On a chart where the data source consists of a single contiguous range, selecting the chart area causes the Range Finder to highlight all the data series in one color, the value axis labels in another color, and category names in still another color.

Tip from

EQ & Woody

Excel uses the Range Finder only when the chart and its corresponding data range are on the same worksheet. Take advantage of this feature to debug problems in charts. If your chart is on a separate sheet, right-click the chart area and select Location; then click the As Object In option and select the worksheet that contains the charted data. Resize and reposition the chart object so it's near the corresponding range within the data source and use the color-coding to identify which data series is causing the problem. After you've fixed the chart, use the Location shortcut menu to move it back to its own chart sheet.

When using the Range Finder with charts, you should be aware of the following limitations:

- The Range Finder works only with a chart object that is embedded on the same worksheet as the data. It does not work with charts on chart sheets.

- You can drag to expand the data range or a given series to include new data in either direction; however, this technique works only for contiguous series. If any series consists of a noncontiguous range, you must use the wizard or the Data Source dialog box to select the data.

- When you click an individual data point, the Range Finder highlights the series that contains that point.

ADVANCED CHART OPTIONS

Excel's advanced chart options let you add details that help you spot trends more easily. For example, in a line chart that plots daily closing stock prices over time, you can add a trendline and a moving average that smooth out some of the peaks and valleys in the data. You can do the same with a column chart to show a smooth trend over time. Select the series, right-click, and select Add Trendline. For charts that project data, you can also add error bars that define the upper- and lower-error limits of your projections by using standard statistical measures. You'll find these options on the Error Bars tab of the Format Data Series dialog box.

Note

For more information on how you can display detailed analyses in Excel charts, see *Special Edition Using Microsoft Excel 2002*, by Patrick Blattner and Laurie Ulrich (published by Que, ISBN 0-7897-2511-8).

TROUBLESHOOTING

FORMATTING COMBINATION CHARTS

I created a Pie-of-Pie or Pie-of-Bar chart, but I'm having trouble formatting it.

These combination chart types follow some fairly rigid rules. You cannot select either pie individually. They are always side by side, and you cannot move them, although you can change their relative size. To show the link between the two charts, you can add or remove Series lines; however, you cannot reformat these connecting lines.

OPENING THE CHART GALLERY

I tried to open one of the chart type galleries, but the file wouldn't open or I received an error message.

If you've already worked with a custom chart, Excel might have opened and hidden one or both workbooks. To make sure you can open and view both files, close all open workbooks and exit Excel; then restart the program and immediately open these two workbooks.

SECRETS OF THE OFFICE MASTERS: CREATING A CUSTOM CHART LIBRARY

Why reinvent the wheel every time you create and format a chart? Build a library of good-looking custom charts, save them in your User-defined chart gallery, and call on them whenever you need them. The process is simple and straightforward:

1. Start with a blank worksheet. Enter a basic table of dummy data, like the range shown here. (Note we've hidden gridlines and added formatting to the range, just to make the sheet look good.)

Figure 24.21

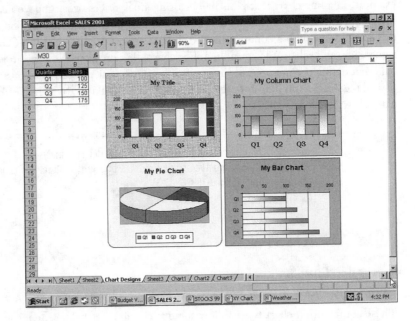

2. Click anywhere in the worksheet outside the range you just created and click the Chart Wizard button. Breeze through the process of creating a basic column chart without any titles or additional formatting. Place this generic chart on the same sheet with your dummy data.

3. Use the Clipboard to make three, four, or more copies of this chart, and arrange them on the sheet. Now you're ready to begin customizing.

4. Right-click each chart in turn and set any or all of the following options:
   - Adjust the chart type if necessary.
   - Change the background colors for the chart area, plot area, fill area, gridlines, and data series. Choose a variety of complementary colors, including gradient fills and textures available when you click the Fill Effects button on the Patterns tab of the Format dialog box for each item.

- Right-click the chart area, select Format Chart Area, and adjust the fonts for the entire chart. Then adjust the sizes of individual chart elements, such as axis labels and legends.

- Add chart titles and adjust the size and position of each. Because the title is just a text box, you can move it anywhere, including inside the plot area. Don't be afraid to make extra copies of the basic chart and experiment with them.

- If corporate policy dictates certain elements, such as logos or disclaimer text, add them to each basic chart design now.

5. Save the workbook that contains the charts so you can reuse them any time. If you're certain you'll want to use one or more chart designs, add them to the User-defined chart gallery.

PART

IV

CH

24

CHAPTER **25**

WORKING WITH LISTS AND DATABASES

In this chapter

CREATING A LIST ON A WORKSHEET

Excel's row-and-column structure makes it an ideal tool for organizing related information into a *list*. On an Excel worksheet, a list is a group of consecutive rows of related data. Conceptually, an Excel list is identical to a table in Access (or any other database management program). Each *column* within a list is a *field*, and each *row* is a *record* of data; headings in the top row represent the names of the fields. Within each field, you can enter text, numbers, dates, formulas, or hyperlinks. Excel does not impose any additional restrictions on the type of data that you can enter in a list.

You can sort list data in nearly any order, search for a specific bit of information, or use filters to find groups of data that match criteria that you specify. For complex lists, Excel can automatically create *outlines* that let you summarize and subtotal groups of records. Large, complex lists are a perfect starting point for PivotTable and PivotChart reports, which let you drag fields on a layout page to perform complex data-analysis tasks without having to construct a single formula.

→ For more details on how to use external data in an Excel list, **see** "Creating Links to External Databases," **p. 695.**

→ For a full discussion of the wonders of PivotTables, **see** "How PivotTable and PivotChart Reports Work," **p. 724**.

Excel uses column labels in the first row of a list (also called the *header row*) to identify the names of fields. Although you can create a list without a header row, we highly recommend that you include column labels for every list that you create or import. You must have a header row if you want to enter data using forms or use the AutoFilter feature to find groups of records.

Tip from

EQ & Woody

You don't need a header row to sort a range of data; to sort a selection that doesn't include column labels, be sure to check the No Header Row option when you sort.

When creating a list, follow these basic guidelines:

- Create only one list per worksheet. Many of Excel's list features (including its Auto-Filter capability) depend on being able to identify one list per sheet. If you need to create multiple lists in a workbook, put them on different sheets.

→ For more details on how to manage multiple worksheets in a single workbook, **see** "Working with Multiple Worksheets," **p. 534.**

- Create a single header row with a unique label for each column. Apply distinctive formatting to make the column labels stand out from the data area. Use a larger font size with bold attributes, for example, and add a border beneath the header row. Excel uses this formatting to identify the header information in lists when sorting and creating reports.

- Don't leave any blank rows or columns in your list. When you sort or search, Excel ignores data that appears below a blank row or to the right of a blank column. You can safely leave individual cells in a row or column blank, however.

→ To prevent yourself or other users of a worksheet from entering invalid data, including blank cells, create data validation rules; **see** "Restricting and Validating Data Entry for a Cell or Range," **p. 553**.

- Although you can start a list at any cell, you should avoid leaving any blank columns to the left of the list. You might want to leave five or six blank rows above the header row of the list, to create a criteria range or add a title. Remember to leave at least one blank row between any such data and the start of the list.

- To make it easier to enter data, freeze the worksheet panes just below the header row.

→ For instructions on how to freeze worksheet panes, **see** "Locking Row and Column Labels for Onscreen Viewing," **p. 551**.

When you enter new data in an existing list, Excel automatically picks up formatting and formulas from the previous rows, without requiring you to explicitly format cells in the new row. For example, if the first cell in the previous row is formatted in bold italic, Excel automatically applies that formatting as soon as you enter the data into the first cell in the new row. If the last cell in the previous row contains a formula that multiplies the values in the two previous cells, Excel adds that formula as soon as you enter data in the second of the two cells that make up that formula.

This feature isn't foolproof. For some inexplicable reason, Excel won't automatically pick up date formatting from the previous row, although it will consistently copy font formatting and attributes. Likewise, new rows pick up colors and shading consistently, but borders don't always extend as you expect. Although the documentation claims that Excel will pick up formatting and formulas that match three of the previous five rows, we found that this automatic feature works consistently only if the formatting appears in four of the previous five rows.

Part
IV
Ch
25

Tip from

EQ & Woody

If you don't want Excel to automatically pick up formatting and formulas from previous rows, turn off this capability. Choose Tools, Options, and click the Edit tab. To automatically format new items that you add to the end of a list to match the format of the rest of the list, check the Extend List Formats and Formulas box.

Speeding Up Repetitive Data Entry with AutoComplete

Excel's default setup enables an option called *AutoComplete*, which is designed to speed up entering data in lists. As you type, Excel compares each character that you enter with other entries in cells directly above the active cell. If the opening characters match those of any other entry, Excel assumes that you want to repeat that entry and fills in the rest of the label. (This comparison applies only to cells that contain text; AutoComplete ignores numbers, dates, and times.)

If you want to repeat the previous entry, press Enter (or Tab or any arrow key) to insert the AutoComplete entry in the cell. Keep typing to enter a new value in the cell. Excel will not suggest an AutoComplete entry unless the string that you have entered identifies a unique entry in the list above the active cell.

Tip from

Ed & Woody

Instead of waiting for Excel's suggestion, you can select from a list of entries already in the column. To display the list, press Alt+down arrow, or right-click the cell and then choose Pick from List from the shortcut menu.

Some users find AutoComplete disconcerting, dangerous, or merely annoying because if you don't pay close attention, you risk accidentally entering the wrong data. You can easily disable AutoComplete: Choose Tools, Options, and click the Edit tab. Clear the check mark from the Enable AutoComplete for Cell Values box. Click OK to save the new setting and continue editing.

If you have a love-hate relationship with AutoComplete, create a macro that toggles this feature on and off. Assigning the macro to a toolbar button lets you turn on AutoComplete when you're entering data in a list where its capabilities are useful, and turn it off at all other times. Here's all the code you need:

```
Sub ToggleAutoComplete()
    Application.EnableAutoComplete = Not Application.EnableAutoComplete
End Sub
```

→ For instructions on how to assign the macro to a toolbar button, **see** "Adding Macros to a Toolbar," **p. 36**.

→ Don't confuse AutoComplete with AutoCorrect; for more details about this and other Office-wide Auto-features, **see** "Using AutoCorrect to Automate Documents," **p. 91**.

AUTOMATICALLY FILLING IN A SERIES OF DATA

One common and tedious data-entry task is entering a sequence of numbers or dates in a column or row. Excel's *AutoFill* feature can handle this chore automatically by filling in information as you drag the mouse along a column or row. Use AutoFill to copy formulas or values; enter the days of the week, months of the year, or any series of numbers or dates; and even fill in custom lists of departments, category names, part numbers, and other information that you define.

Because of its tremendous number of options, even Excel experts sometimes have trouble coaxing the correct results out of AutoFill. The addition of Smart Tags in Excel 2002 makes this task somewhat easier. If using AutoFill has the wrong result, click the AutoFill Smart Tag to see a list of other options that enable you to select a different result, such as changing a simple copy to a series.

→ For more details about Smart Tags, see "Changes in the Office Interface," **p. 12**.

In general, using AutoFill will have one of the following results:

- **Copy Data from One or More Cells**—If the selection is not a sequence that Excel recognizes—for example, if you select a cell that contains text—AutoFill copies the selection in the direction that you drag.

Tip from

EQ & Woody

> Using AutoFill is an excellent way to copy a formula from one cell across a row or down a column. This technique is especially useful for copying formulas that total columns or rows. As you drag, AutoFill copies the formula, adjusting relative references as needed.

- **Copy Formatting or Values Across a Row or Down a Column**—Normally, AutoFill copies both formats and values from the cells that you start with. To choose one, make a selection and then hold down the right mouse button while dragging. When you release the mouse button, choose Fill Formats or Fill Values. Don't be confused by the latter option; if you select a formula in the starting cell, this option copies the formula without formatting.

- **Fill in a Series of Dates**—If you enter a date in any recognizable format, such as 4/10 or 5-23-02, AutoFill will extend the series in one-day increments. AutoFill also recognizes long and short versions of days of the week and months. If you enter Jan in the first cell, for example, AutoFill will continue the list with Feb, Mar, Apr, and so on; start with Wednesday, and AutoFill will extend the list with Thursday, Friday, Saturday, and so on. Excel also recognizes calendar quarters. If you enter Q1 in a cell and use AutoFill, you get Q2, Q3, and Q4, at which point the series starts over with Q1.

Tip from

EQ & Woody

> When you reach the end of a finite AutoFill sequence, such as days of the week or months of the year, the sequence repeats. If you start with Monday, for example, the sequence starts over again after the seventh cell.

- **Fill in a Series of Numbers**—This is probably the trickiest AutoFill option. If you start with a single cell that contains the number 1 and use AutoFill to extend it, Excel will copy the number 1 to the rest of the cells that you select. To instruct Excel to AutoFill a series instead of copying the number, hold down the Ctrl key as you drag.

Tip from

EQ & Woody

> When you insert a sequence of numbers, Excel assumes that you want to increment them by 1. Thus, if you start with 100, the sequence continues with 101, 102, and so on. To use a different sequence, enter values in at least two cells so that the sequence is apparent, and then select those cells and use AutoFill. For example, if you enter 100 and 200 in the first two cells and then select those cells and use AutoFill, Excel continues the series with 300, 400, and so on. You can also use this technique to enter a date

series, such as every other day (Monday, Wednesday, Friday), every third month (Feb, May, Aug), or the 10th of each month (1/10, 2/10, 3/10). Enter the first two or three cells in the sequence, select the cells that you entered, and then extend the selection using AutoFill.

- **Fill in a Series of Numbered Items**—If you enter any text plus a number (Chapter 1, Item 1, or Area 51, for example), AutoFill extends the selection by 1 (Chapter 2, Chapter 3, and so on). Confusingly, this option works exactly the opposite on a series of numbers without text: Hold down Ctrl to prevent Excel from extending the selection and copy the values instead.

- **Fill in a Custom List**—If you've created a custom list (see the following section for step-by-step instructions), enter the first item from that list in any cell, and then use AutoFill to add the remaining items in the list.

- **Fill in a Trend Series**—For this option, you must select a number of cells first and then drag with the right mouse button for more options. You can choose a *linear* series, in which Excel calculates the average difference between each value in the series that you selected and then adds it to (or subtracts it from) each succeeding value in the AutoFill range. Choose a *geometric* series to have Excel calculate the percentage of difference between items in the series and apply that amount to each new value. These options are useful when you're trying to project future patterns, such as sales or revenue growth, based on existing data.

To use AutoFill, follow these steps:

1. First, enter the initial value or values for the range. If the list begins a unique sequence—months of the year, for example, starting with Jan or January—you need to enter a value in only one cell. To AutoFill a sequence of numbers or dates with an increment value other than 1, enter the first two or three values in the series.

2. Point to Excel's *fill handle*—the small black square in the lower-right corner of the currently selected cell or range. When you point at the fill handle, the mouse pointer turns into a thin black cross.

3. Drag in any direction (up or down in a column, left or right in a row) to begin filling in values (see Figure 25.1). Hold down the Ctrl key as you extend the selection to switch the AutoFill action from copy to fill series, or vice versa.

Note

AutoFill works only in one row or column at a time. To extend a selection down and to the right, you must perform the AutoFill action in two steps.

Figure 25.1
As you drag, Excel automatically fills in values in your series— dates, in this example.

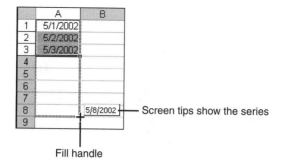

Screen tips show the series

Fill handle

4. ScreenTips display the value that will appear in each new cell as you extend the series. When you reach the final cell, release the mouse button to fill in the data.

5. If the AutoFill results are not what you expected, click the AutoFill Smart Tag to display a menu with additional options (see Figure 25.2).

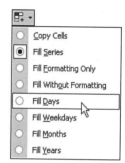

Figure 25.2

Tip from

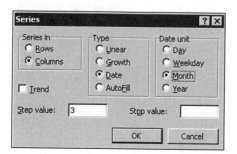

You can also use AutoFill to remove items from a range without removing formatting. Select the range that contains the series, and then grab the fill handle and drag into the range.

For maximum control over AutoFill options, hold down the right mouse button while dragging. Choose the Series option at the bottom of the shortcut menu to display a dialog box that lets you choose any option, including starting points and step values for a series, as in Figure 25.3.

Figure 25.3
If Excel can't recognize the progression in an AutoFill series, use this dialog box to specify series settings manually.

CREATING CUSTOM AUTOFILL LISTS TO FIT YOUR PROJECTS

You can also create a custom list, such as company divisions, budget categories, or product codes, and add the list to Excel. Excel adds custom lists to the Windows Registry, with each list appearing in the precise order in which you enter individual items. The result can be tremendous time savings for you if you regularly insert the same list into worksheets, such as names of regional offices or budget categories. AutoFill can insert any custom list in any row or column, anytime (and, as we'll demonstrate in the next section, you can also use a custom list as a sort key for the rest of your list).

Tip from

EQ & Woody

How do you copy a custom list from one machine to another? Because this information is stored in a Windows Registry key, it's not easy. You can use a hideously complicated 18-step process to export the information from the Registry of one machine and import it to another. Believe it or not, Microsoft expects you to wipe out all your Excel preferences except the one that contains the custom lists, export the Registry file, restore the deleted keys to your machine, and then finally merge the exported file into the Registry on the other machine. Are they serious? The entire process is needlessly complex and dangerous. (The gory details are in Microsoft Knowledge Base article Q212245, if you insist on reading them.) But why go through all that pain? To share one or two lists with another Excel user, add them to a worksheet and let the other user import the lists by using the simple two-step process described next. It takes a few minutes at most, and it's foolproof.

To add a custom list to Excel, use either of the following procedures:

- If the list is short, you can type it directly into a dialog box. Choose Tools, Options, click the Custom Lists tab, select New List, and start entering items in the List Entries box, as shown in Figure 25.4. Be sure to enter each item in the correct order, and press Enter at the end of each line. When the list is complete, click the Add button.

- If the list is already available in a worksheet, the process is even easier. Say that you've created a worksheet that contains all budget categories in the exact order that you want to enter them every time. Open that sheet and select the worksheet range (column or row) that contains the list. Choose Tools, Options, click the Custom Lists tab, and click Import.

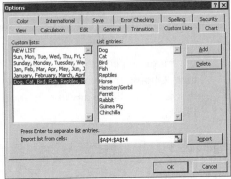

Figure 25.4

Your list is now available in any Excel worksheet that you open on this machine. To automatically add the custom list to a worksheet range, enter the first list item, use the fill handle to complete the list, and click OK.

SORTING LISTS

Excel's sorting capabilities let you view data in almost any order, regardless of the order in which you entered it. To quickly sort a list, first click a single cell in the column by which you want to sort, and then click the Sort Ascending button. Excel selects all the data in your list and sorts it alphabetically, using the column that contains the active cell. Click the Sort Descending button to sort in reverse order, using the same column. If you want to sort only a portion of the list, make a selection first, and then use the Tab key to move the active cell to the correct column. This option, used incorrectly, can make a mess of your database, so use it with caution.

Tip from

ED & Woody

If the order in which you enter data is important, create a numeric field that you can use to identify each row, and then increment it by 1 for each new record. Re-sort using the values in this field to return the list to its original order. Don't use a formula for this field, however—when you sort the list, the values will change and you won't be able to return to the original sort order.

When you choose ascending order, Excel always sorts numbers first, then most punctuation characters, and then letters, in ascending (A–Z) order, without regard to whether the letters are uppercase or lowercase. Excel generally ignores apostrophes and hyphens when sorting; if two entries are otherwise identical but one contains a hyphen, it will appear after the one that does not contain a hyphen. The precise order for punctuation is as follows:

(space) ! " # $ % & (°) * , . / : ; ? @ [\ ] [ct] _ [ag] { | } [td] + < = >

SORTING BY MULTIPLE FIELDS

By using the two sort buttons on the Standard toolbar, you can perform a multicolumn sort without ever using a dialog box. Perform each column sort in sequence, using the reverse of the final order that you want to see; Excel preserves the order of other columns in the list when you sort each succeeding column. In a sales results worksheet, for example, you might click in the Salesperson column and click a sort button, and then do the same with the Month column and finally with the Region column. The result is to sort your list by region, then by month, and then by salesperson.

If sorting your list has unexpected results, see "Sorting Out Sorting Problems" in the "Troubleshooting" section at the end of this chapter.

The Sort dialog box lets you sort by up to three fields at one time; choose Data, Sort to open the Sort dialog box, as shown in Figure 25.5. Excel lets you specify up to three fields for your sort order, using ascending or descending order for each one.

Figure 25.5
This Sort dialog box shows three sort fields, each corresponding to a column label in the list.

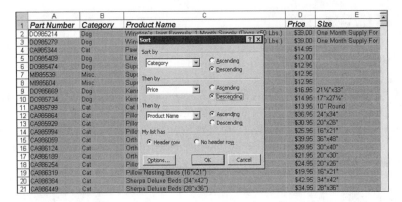

SORTING BY DATES OR CUSTOM SERIES

By default, Excel's sort options reorder data alphabetically or numerically. However, a basic A–Z or 1–10 sort isn't always appropriate. Dates and weekdays in text format represent a particular problem. For example, a list of bonds or mortgage loans might include a text field that identifies the month in which an investment matures. Or, a list of shift assignments for employees might include a column of weekdays. Using the default sort order would put the month names and weekdays in alphabetical order—April, August, December, February, or Mon, Sat, Sun, Thu—when you actually want to sort the list in calendar order. You might also want to sort your list using a custom AutoFill list—by region, for example, or by budget category (see the previous section for details about how to create one of these lists).

Sorting by date or a custom series is available only when you use the Sort dialog box. To sort by text dates or using a custom series, follow these steps:

1. Click in the list that you want to sort, or select the region to be sorted.

2. Choose Data, Sort, and identify up to three field names for sorting. The field that contains the dates or custom list must be the first field in the list.

3. Click the Options button in the lower-left corner of the Sort dialog box to open the Sort Options dialog box (see Figure 25.6).

4. Click the down arrow in the First Key Sort Order list box and select the appropriate series. The default selection includes four built-in lists—days of the week and months, in long and short versions. In addition, any custom

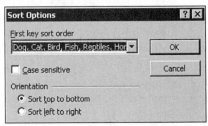

Figure 25.6

lists that you've created will appear here. You can also choose a different orientation here—for most lists, the default column sort is the correct choice.

5. Click OK to confirm the sort order that you selected; then click OK again to perform the sort.

Note

> By default, Excel does not distinguish between lowercase and capital letters when sorting. To change this setting, click the Options button in the Sort dialog box and check Case Sensitive. With this option enabled, Excel sorts lowercase letters ahead of capital letters.

As you can see, this option has one significant limitation—it is available only for the first sort key that you specify. If you're willing to sort in several steps, however, you can sort with a custom list or dates series in the second or third key. Perform each sort one column at a time. Remember to sort using the reverse of the order in which you want the final list to appear. To sort by year and then by product category, for example, first use the Sort dialog box to sort by a single column, using the custom series that you've defined for product categories. Then perform a sort using only the year column. The results will be in perfect order.

FINDING AND FILTERING DATA IN A LIST

When working with lists, you can use the Find shortcut (Ctrl+F) to search for any value in the list. That technique is useful if you want to jump quickly to a specific unique value in the list. More often, however, you'll want to extract details from a list instead of simply jumping to a single record. In that case, use *filters* to hide all records except those that match criteria that you specify. In a list that contains hundreds or thousands of rows, defining a filter helps you see a small number of related records together, making it easier to compare data and identify trends.

For example, in a list of daily high, low, and closing stock prices that includes data for many companies, you might want to see only those records in which the entry in the Symbol field is equal to KO (that's the Coca-Cola Company, for those who don't know ticker symbols by heart). Or, if you import product inventory information from a database into an Excel list, you can use filters to show only items that are currently out of stock, making it easy to build a reorder list.

AutoFilter options let you select information by choosing from drop-down lists of unique items in each column. You can also create custom filters using multiple criteria and combining criteria from multiple columns, or you can display only the top 10 (or bottom 10) entries in a list, by number or percentage, based on the contents of a single field.

Note

> Unlike sorts, which rearrange data in a list, filters do not change the underlying data. When you define a filter, you hide records that don't match the criteria that you define.

→ For an overview of Office-standard Find and Replace tools, **see** "Finding and Replacing Text," **p. 87**.

→ For details on database functions that let you analyze with data in lists, **see** "Using Database Functions," **p. 630**.

USING AUTOFILTER TO FIND SETS OF DATA

The easiest way to build a filter is with the help of Excel's AutoFilter capability. When you enable this option for a list, you can define criteria by choosing values from drop-down lists; as the name implies, an AutoFilter applies the filter to your list automatically, as soon as you select the criteria. When you understand how AutoFilters work, you can use them to narrow even massive lists. To create an AutoFilter, follow these steps:

1. Click anywhere in your list. (This step isn't necessary if Excel recognizes that your worksheet contains a single list with headings.)

2. Choose Data, Filter, AutoFilter. A drop-down arrow appears to the right of each column heading in your list, as shown in Figure 25.7.

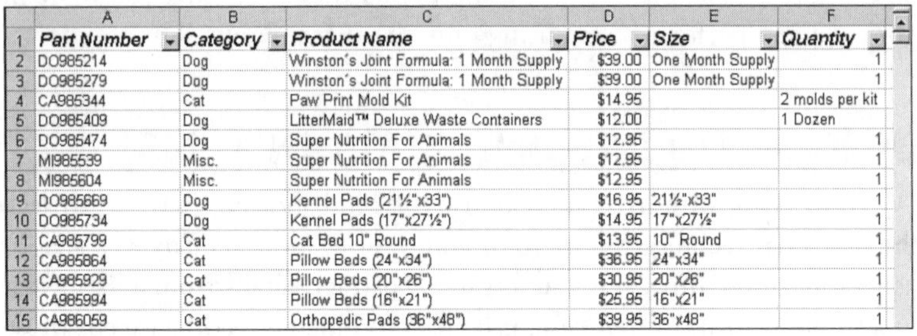

Figure 25.7

Drop-down AutoFilter lists let you narrow your selection by choosing from all unique values in that column.

	A	B	C	D	E	F
1	Part Number	Category	Product Name	Price	Size	Quantity
2	DO985214	Dog	Winston's Joint Formula: 1 Month Supply	$39.00	One Month Supply	1
3	DO985279	Dog	Winston's Joint Formula: 1 Month Supply	$39.00	One Month Supply	1
4	CA985344	Cat	Paw Print Mold Kit	$14.95		2 molds per kit
5	DO985409	Dog	LitterMaid™ Deluxe Waste Containers	$12.00		1 Dozen
6	DO985474	Dog	Super Nutrition For Animals	$12.95		1
7	MI985539	Misc.	Super Nutrition For Animals	$12.95		1
8	MI985604	Misc.	Super Nutrition For Animals	$12.95		1
9	DO985669	Dog	Kennel Pads (21½"x33")	$16.95	21½"x33"	1
10	DO985734	Dog	Kennel Pads (17"x27½")	$14.95	17"x27½"	1
11	CA985799	Cat	Cat Bed 10" Round	$13.95	10" Round	1
12	CA985864	Cat	Pillow Beds (24"x34")	$36.95	24"x34"	1
13	CA985929	Cat	Pillow Beds (20"x26")	$30.95	20"x26"	1
14	CA985994	Cat	Pillow Beds (16"x21")	$25.95	16"x21"	1
15	CA986059	Cat	Orthopedic Pads (36"x48")	$39.95	36"x48"	1

3. Click the arrow to the right of the column label that you want to use as the first condition in the filter. Choose an item from the drop-down list to restrict the display to only rows that contain that item, or choose any of the options shown in the following bulleted list. Excel applies your criteria immediately, filtering out all rows except those that contain the value that you selected.

Note

Excel generates the drop-down list of AutoFilter values for each field automatically, by pulling out all unique values from that column. As a result, every item on the drop-down list is guaranteed to be in that column, making it impossible to select an incorrect value. AutoFilter lists always display in ascending order.

Excel offers several AutoFilter choices:

- **Top 10**—Show the highest or lowest numeric values in a list, by number or by percentage. Don't be misled by the name—when you choose this option, you see a dialog box that lets you select any number between 1 and 500; you can choose Bottom or Top, and you can specify percent as well. Use the settings in Figure 25.8, for example, to display the top 5% of all products in a list, based on the amount in the selected column. If the list contains 2,000 items, this setting will show only the top 100.

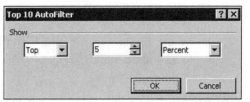

Figure 25.8

 If Excel beeps or displays unexpected results when you try to use the Top 10 option, see "Top 10 Is for Numbers Only" in the "Troubleshooting" section at the end of this chapter.

- **Custom**—Use comparison operators (covered in the next section) to define criteria. You can combine up to two criteria using this option.

- **Blanks**—Display only records that contain no data in the selected column. This option is available only if the selected column contains one or more blank cells.

- **NonBlanks**—Display all records that contain data in the selected column, hiding blank records. This option is available only if the selected column contains one or more blank cells.

- **All**—Show all records in the list. Use this option to remove AutoFilter criteria from a column.

AutoFilter criteria are cumulative; by combining criteria in different columns, you can successively filter a list to display an increasingly selective group of records. Although you can choose filter criteria in any order, it's best to start with columns that include the fewest options because the list of choices for succeeding columns will be narrower and easier to scroll through.

When you apply a filter to a list, Excel changes the color of the drop-down arrow for the field that you selected to blue. That is your only indication that a particular column is filtered. As the list in Figure 25.9 shows, Excel maintains the row numbers of the underlying list when you use an AutoFilter, hiding all rows that don't match the criteria that you specified.

PART
IV
CH
25

Figure 25.9
Because an AutoFilter does not change the data in the underlying list, you'll see gaps in row numbering when you filter a list.

	A Part Number	B Category	C Product Name	D Price	E Size	F Quantity
1	Part Number	Category	Product Name	Price	Size	Quantity
150	FE806308	Ferret	Oasis Heavy Duty Water Bottles 16oz. Fe	$3.09	16 Ounces	1
233	FE621358	Ferret	Super Pet Ferret Couch Pouch	$9.14		1
466	FE262220	Ferret	Ferrets As A New Pet	$3.64		1
525	FE211587	Ferret	Your First Ferret	$1.19		1
936	FE006147	Ferret	Ferret Tent	$14.97		1
941	FE006031	Ferret	Ferret Hide-N-Sleep Sack	$8.50		1
979	FE004103	Ferret	FerretVite High Calorie Vitamin Concentrat	$3.21	4.25 Ounces	1
980	FE004080	Ferret	Vita-Sol: Ferret	$2.21	4 Ounces	1
981	FE004073	Ferret	Ferretone Food Supplement	$3.99	8 Ounces	1
982	FE004042	Ferret	Ultra Blend Select Advanced Nutrition Diet	$3.07		1
1027	FE001098	Ferret	Ferret Combo Hammock	$6.65		1
1047						

To change AutoFilter criteria, click the blue arrow and select another value. To remove AutoFilter criteria for a single column, choose All from the AutoFilter list for that column. To remove all AutoFilter criteria from the list, choose Data, Filter, Show All. To restore a list to its original, unfiltered Display All view, choose Data, Filter, AutoFilter. The drop-down arrows disappear.

Excel stores AutoFilter criteria only in memory. When you turn off the AutoFilter option, Excel discards any custom criteria that you've created. To reapply those same AutoFilter criteria, you have to reenter them.

USING COMPARISON CRITERIA TO CREATE CUSTOM FILTERS

The drop-down AutoFilter list for each column allows you to select one and only one specific value. In some cases, that limitation gets in the way of finding the information that you need. For example, what if you want to search through your product list and find all items whose price is less than $10? Or, what if you want to find items whose name includes the text "puppy"? To create complex criteria in an AutoFiltered list, click the AutoFilter arrow for the field that you want to use, and then select the Custom option.

The Custom AutoFilter dialog box (see Figure 25.10) enables you to use any of the following *comparison operators*:

Figure 25.10
Use the Custom AutoFilter dialog box to combine criteria; if you need more than two criteria, use an Advanced Filter instead.

- Equals/does not equal
- Is greater than/is less than
- Is greater than or equal to/is less than or equal to
- Begins with/does not begin with
- Ends with/does not end with
- Contains/does not contain

You can also combine two criteria for a single field using the logical operator AND, or use the OR operator to tell Excel that you want to see records that match either of the criteria that you specify for that field.

Select a comparison operator for the first set of criteria, and then click in the box to the right of the comparison operator and enter the value that you want to use in your criteria. Or, use the drop-down list to select from all unique values in the field. If you add a second set of criteria for the same field, click And to select only records in which both criteria are true; click Or to create a filter that shows records in which either set of criteria is true.

Tip from	Although you're limited to only two criteria when you use AutoFilter's Custom option, you can easily work around this limitation by using Excel's capability to filter on criteria for two or more columns at once. Make a copy of the column that you want to use in your filter, and specify a separate set of criteria in the AutoFilter box for that column.
EQ & Woody	

FILTERING WITH ADVANCED CRITERIA

Compared with the one-click ease of AutoFilters, Excel's advanced filters are downright cumbersome. Still, they're the only way to accomplish some tasks, such as defining more than three criteria for a single column or finding only unique values within a list that contains duplicate entries. Advanced filters also let you specify more complex criteria than you can use with AutoFilters, including criteria based on formulas.

To use advanced filters, start by creating a *criteria range* on the same worksheet that contains the list. Although you can add this range anywhere on the list, we strongly recommend that you place it directly above the list, where it's unlikely to be affected by any changes that you make to the sheet's design. Allow a minimum of three rows in the criteria range—one for the column labels, one for the criteria, and one to serve as a separator between the list and the criteria range.

PART

IV

CH

25

Tip from	Add one extra row for each set of criteria that you expect to use when filtering the list. In almost all circumstances, you can get by with a criteria range of five rows, which allows you to add up to three sets of criteria for each column while still maintaining a one-row separation between the criteria range and the list.
EQ & Woody	

Copy the column labels from the list to the first row of the criteria range. The resulting range should look something like the example shown in Figure 25.11, which also includes several criteria.

→ For more details on working with named ranges, **see** "Using Named Ranges in Formulas," **p. 618**.

Begin entering criteria in the row just below the column labels. You can enter text, numbers, dates, or logical values using comparison operators such as > and <. To find values that are greater than or equal to a specific value, use the >= operator. For example, >=1000 finds all values greater than or equal to 1000 in the specified column; in a text column, <C finds all entries that begin with A or B.

Figure 25.11
Always create the criteria range above the list, not below or alongside it; that placement keeps it from being scrambled when you extend or sort the list.

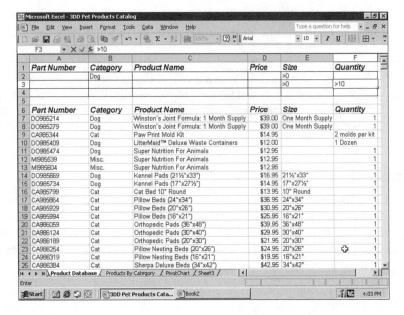

You can enter values in more than one field and in more than one row. When you do, Excel interprets your input as follows:

- For values in more than one field within a single row, Excel looks for records that match all values that you specify in the row, the equivalent of a logical AND.

- For values in the same field in separate rows, Excel displays records that match any of the values, the equivalent of a logical OR.

In essence, each row in the criteria range equals a single *condition*. By mixing and matching conditions, you can filter a list in many different ways, including the following:

- **Multiple Conditions for One Column**—Enter each condition in a separate cell under the column label in the criteria range. In the example shown in Figure 25.12, any row containing the value Dog, Cat, or Fish in the Category column will match.

	A	B
1	*Part Number*	*Category*
2		Dog
3		Cat
4		Fish

Figure 25.12

- **One Condition in Each of Several Columns**—Enter each condition under its respective column label in the same row. The example in Figure 25.13 will match rows in which the value in the Category column is Dog and the price is less than $10. Generally, this type of filter is much easier to apply using an AutoFilter.

	A	B	C
1	*Part Number*	*Category*	*Price*
2		Dog	<10

Figure 25.13

- **Multiple Conditions in Multiple Columns**—Enter each set of conditions in its own row of the criteria range, and Excel will find rows in the list that match either set. Figure 25.14 finds any item in the Dog category whose price is less than $10, or any item in the Fish category whose price is greater than $20. This type of condition is nearly impossible to match with an AutoFilter.

	A	B	C
1	*Part Number*	*Category*	*Price*
2		Dog	<10
3		Fish	>20

Figure 25.14

Tip from

EL & Woody

To specify multiple criteria for the same field in the same row, add another column heading in the criteria range, using the same column label (extend the criteria range, if necessary, or replace the label for an existing column for which you're not defining conditions). For example, if you have a field called Amount, add a second column label, also called Amount, to your criteria range. Then, when you enter >3000 in one cell and <6000 in the other, both in the same row, Excel finds only records in which the Amount is between 3000 and 6000.

Caution

If you enter text in a criteria range, Excel finds all matching records that begin with that text. Thus, if you enter the letter F under the Category label, Excel finds all records whose category begins with F. To find only records that match the exact text that you specify, you must enter the value using the following format: `="=texti`. Make sure to include both equals signs.

Finally, you can create conditions based on formulas. Although formulas can be a powerful way to filter a list, they are extremely challenging to enter, and the syntax is confusing. Unlike other conditions, which must appear under a column label that matches the corresponding label in the list, you must not use a column label with a formula; enter the formulas in a cell beneath a blank label, or change the label above it so that it does not match a label in the list. Individual references in the formula should come from the column label or the first record of the list, and the formulas must evaluate to TRUE or FALSE.

In the example in Figure 25.15, note that we've changed the label in cell E1 to read Inventory. As you can see from the formula bar, the formula in cell E2 multiplies the quantity in the In Stock field by the value in the Price field for the first row of the list (E7*C7) to see whether it's greater than 300. The result of this filter finds 14 matching rows.

Figure 25.15
The formula in cell E2 contains relative references to values in the first row of the database (row 7); note that the label above it does not match a label in the list itself.

	A	B	C	D	E	F
	Part Number	Category	Product Name	Price	Size	Inventory
2						FALSE
3						
4						
5						
6	Part Number	Category	Product Name	Price	Size	In Stock
8	DO985279	Dog	Winston's Joint Formula: 1 Month Su	$39.00	One Month Supply	96
25	CA986384	Cat	Sherpa Deluxe Beds (34"x42")	$42.95	34"x42"	76
33	DO986904	Dog	Deluxe Rectangular Beds (36"x48")	$37.95	36"x48"	91
41	DO987424	Dog	Zodiac® 6-Pak Protection Kit for Dog	$39.95		76
46	CA987749	Cat	Zodiac® 6-Pak Protection Kit for Cat	$39.95		89
59	DO988594	Dog	Bowser Bag Original	$41.99	18" x 24" x 4"	94
123	BI829588	Bird	Cockatiel Starter Kit	$48.05	approx. 23.50"H x !	93
271	GU604000	Guinea Pig	Hagen Guinea Pig Starter Kit	$45.60		67
316	DO537876	Dog	Comfort Ride Pet Seat	$49.99	20"L x 14"W x 6"H	77
791	CA030169	Cat	Professional Clipper Kit with Video	$39.75		92
880	DO010002	Dog	American Tourister Pet Traveler	$43.80	19"Lx10.75"Hx10"W	88
1008	CA002932	Cat	Midwest Econo Cage-Small	$41.62	24" x 20" x 21"	96
1022	DO002043	Dog	Radio Fence Wire & Flag Kit	$34.84		98
1043	DO000027	Dog	Scat Mat (30"x16")	$49.95	30"x16"	92
1052						

After you've created the criteria range and entered criteria, apply the filter to your list by following these steps:

1. Choose Data, Filter, Advanced Filter. The Advanced Filter dialog box appears (see Figure 25.16). Note that the values shown here correspond to values in Figure 25.15.

2. Click in the List Range box and then select the entire list, including the header row.

3. Click in the Criteria Range box and select the portion of the criteria range that contains data. At a minimum, this must include one column label and one cell beneath that label. If your criteria include multiple rows, make sure that you select each row. The portion of the criteria range that you select must be a contiguous range.

Figure 25.16

If your advanced filter doesn't work as you expect, see "Debugging Advanced Filters" in the "Troubleshooting" section at the end of this chapter.

4. To filter the list in place, as an AutoFilter does, accept the default option under Action. To extract records to another location, click the Copy to Another Location option; then click in the Copy To box and select the cell at the top-left corner of the range where you want the extracted records to appear (logically, this location is called the *extract range*). This location must be on the same worksheet as the list itself; if you want to extract specific fields, you must include column labels that correspond to the fields you want to extract. You do not need to extract every column from the list.

5. To filter out duplicate records, select the Unique Records Only check box. If you filter the list in place, this option excludes in which where every field is identical. If you extract the results to a new location and specify a subset of fields, Excel defines duplicates based only on the fields in the extract range.

Tip from

EQ & Woody

By extracting unique records, you can quickly build a list of categories from a much larger list like the one in the examples shown here. Use no conditions in the criteria range. For the extract range, pick a cell below the list and enter the label of the column that you want to extract (Category, in this case). When you run the Advanced Filter, Excel displays a list of all the unique values in your Category column, with no duplicates.

6. Click OK to apply the filter.

Tip from

EQ & Woody

Use range names to skip some steps in this process. If you create named ranges called Database and Extract, Excel automatically selects them in the Advanced Filter dialog box each time you use it. Excel automatically creates a named criteria range each time you use the Advanced Filter dialog box.

Advanced filters don't update automatically when you enter new values in the criteria range. To apply the new criteria, you need to reopen the Advanced Criteria dialog box and click OK. To remove an in-place filter from a list, choose Data, Filter, Show All.

USING FORMS TO ADD AND EDIT LIST DATA

Data forms provide a simple method for entering data into an Excel list. When you open a data form, Excel creates a dialog box on the fly, based on your list's column headings. When you enter data in the form, Excel fills in the correct columns, adding rows to the end of the list, if necessary.

Tip from

EQ & Woody

Although you can also use data forms to view and search for information in lists, this technique is rarely worth it. Sorts, filters, and PivotTables are much easier ways to browse a list. The advantage of using a data form for data entry is that Excel automatically adds each row that you enter to the end of the list without requiring you to reposition the active cell.

To add records to an existing list with a data form, choose Data, Form to display a dialog box like the one in Figure 25.17. (The exact arrangement of fields, of course, depends on the header row in your list.) Click the New button to add a record to the list. When you press Enter, Excel stores the new row at the end of the list and displays a blank form for the next new record. Click Close or press Esc to return to the worksheet.

Figure 25.17
When you add a new record using a data form like this one, Excel automatically adds a new row at the end of the list.

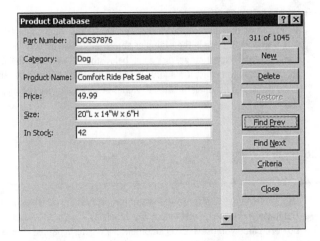

In general, using data forms to search for information is inefficient. In one specific circumstance, however, this technique is useful. Say that you have a list that contains a large number of fields, some of which are extremely wide. Editing information in this type of list is a hassle because you have to continually scroll to the right to see all the fields in your list and then scroll back to see the beginning of the next row. If you need to edit a group of related records in a list like this, use the data form to locate specific records by entering criteria that identify data in your list:

1. Choose Data, Form to open a new data form. Click the Criteria button. Excel clears the data from the form and displays a blank box for each field in the list.

2. Enter your criteria for each field that you want to search. You can enter text or numbers. You can also use comparison operators, such as less than (<) and greater than (>) in the criteria that you enter in a form. To find records in which a particular field is blank, enter an equals sign (=) with no other text in that field. To narrow your search, enter criteria in multiple fields.

> **Note**
>
> If you search for a text string using a data form, Excel searches for fields that contain the entire string you entered. Use wildcards such as * and ? to search for fields that include a particular string. For example, type *puppy* in the Product Name field, and Excel will find any record that contains that word anywhere within its name.

3. Click Find Next to move through the list looking for records that match the criteria you entered. If Excel can't find a matching record, you'll hear a beep. Click Find Prev to search in reverse order through the list.

 If you've used a data form to add several new records to a list, but now that list doesn't work, see "No Room at the End" in the "Troubleshooting" section at the end of this chapter.

After locating records with a form, you can change any data except calculated fields. Excel inserts your changes into the list as soon as you move to another row. When you use a data form to change a value that is used in a calculated field, you won't see the change in the calculated result immediately because Excel waits to recalculate fields until you move to another record. To update the calculation, press Enter to store your changes and then (if necessary) click Find Prev to return.

To delete the record currently visible in the form, click the Delete button. The effect is the same as if you had deleted all cells from that record in the list and then shifted the remainder of the list up.

Note

Using a data form, you can delete only one record at a time. Return to the list and select multiple rows to delete more than one record at once.

Caution

If you delete a row by mistake in Data Form view, you'll see a confirmation message warning you that you're about to delete the record permanently. Take this message seriously! When you delete a record using a data form, the Undo command is not available to restore the original data. The Restore button lets you discard changes that you've made to the current row, but only if you haven't moved to the next record and entered the changes on the worksheet.

PART
IV
CH
25

IMPORTING AND EXPORTING DATA

Excel enables you to create a list using data from a *text file*; you can also save a list to a text file. You import and export text files when you want to share lists between programs, such as mailing-list management software and database programs that cannot read Excel 2000/2002 worksheet files.

Note

In some cases, you can extract data directly from a database without having to convert it to a file. See the following section for details on how to connect to an external database.

To import a text file as a list, first position the insertion point in the cell where you want the data to appear. Make sure that no data appears below or to the right of the location that you select, or it could be overwritten. Then follow these steps:

1. Choose Data, Import External Data, Import Data.

2. In the Open dialog box, choose Text Files from the Files of Type list, and select the file that you want to import. The Text Import Wizard appears.

3. Specify how Excel should separate fields in your import file. Pick Delimited if the list uses characters such as commas or tabs to identify each field; choose Fixed Width if each field starts at the same position in each row.

Note

> If the settings look correct here and you're confident that you don't need to adjust any other import options, click Finish to skip the remainder of the Import Text Wizard.

4. Click Next to display Step 2 of the wizard. If you're importing a *delimited* file, check that Excel has selected the correct options for your file. (In the example shown in Figure 25.18, we had to check the Comma box before the wizard would correctly identify each field.) With a fixed-width file, click in the ruler to identify the beginning of each new column. Click Next again.

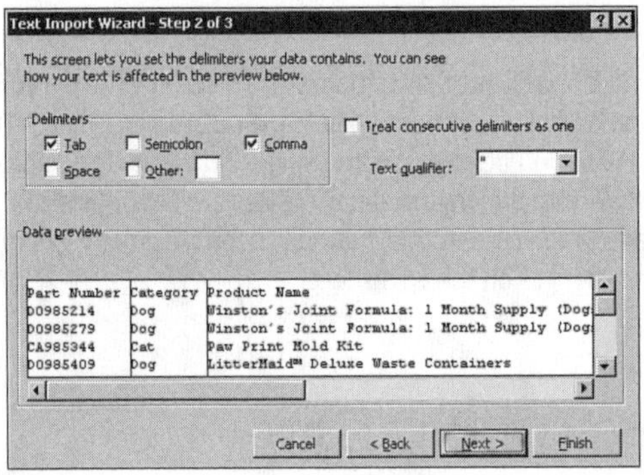

Figure 25.18

Be sure to specify the correct delimiters when importing a text file. Scroll through the Data Preview window, if necessary, to check a sufficient sample of records.

5. In the next step of the wizard, which is optional, choose formatting options for date and time fields, or specify any fields that you don't want to import. Click Finish to move to the last step of the process. Excel displays the Import Data dialog box.

6. Select the cell that you want to use as the top-left corner of the list on the current worksheet, or click New Worksheet to create the list without disturbing existing sheets.

7. Click OK to add the new list to your worksheet.

To save an existing list in a text file that you can import into a database program, select the list, choose File, Save As, and choose one of Excel's compatible delimited formats: CSV (comma-delimited) or Text (tab-delimited).

After importing data into a worksheet, you might end up with some blank cells. In some situations, you might want to replace those blanks with a value, such as "NA" or zero. To do so, follow these steps:

1. Select the range that contains the blank cells that you want to change. Don't select any other cells.

2. Press F5 to display the Go To dialog box.

3. Click the Special button and choose Blanks from the list of options in the Go To Special dialog box. Click OK to select all blank cells in the range.

4. Type the number or text that you want to enter in the blank cells, and then hold down the Ctrl key and press Enter. Excel enters that value in every formerly blank cell.

CREATING LINKS TO EXTERNAL DATABASES

For basic list-management tasks, such as sorting, searching, grouping, and summarizing, Excel is an appropriate, easy-to-use tool. For large and complex databases, however, you have better choices, including Microsoft Access. Choose Access over Excel if any of the following statements is true:

- You need to combine data from multiple tables.

- You want to create custom data-entry forms and highly formatted reports.

- You want to create a secure application that multiple users can work with simultaneously.

- Your list contains more than 65,536 records.

- You want to store sounds, pictures, or other data besides text and numbers.

If your database needs have outgrown Excel's list-management capabilities, let a more powerful program (such as Access) manage the data; then use Excel to chart and analyze the subset of data that you selected.

PART

IV

CH

25

> **Note**
>
> Live queries to external databases are especially useful with PivotTable reports and PivotCharts. For a full discussion of how to combine queries with these powerful analytical tools, see Chapter 27, "Using PivotTables and PivotCharts."

Use Microsoft Query to pull information from an external database—a group of tables in Access, for example, or a companywide database such as Oracle or SQL Server. Use the Query Wizard to create simple *queries* and place a reference to an external data range on your worksheet. Use MS Query directly to create more complex queries.

> **Note**
>
> The most attractive part of Microsoft Query is that it uses *Open Database Connectivity (ODBC) drivers* to directly access data files in other formats. You do not need to have a particular database program installed; all you need is a copy of the data file or access to the server that contains the data you want to use.

USING THE QUERY WIZARD

To launch the Query Wizard and create a new query, follow these steps:

1. Choose Data, Import External Data, New Database Query. If this is the first time you've used the Query Wizard, the Windows Installer will prompt you to complete the installation. The Choose Data Source dialog box appears, as shown in Figure 25.19.

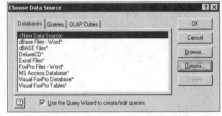

Figure 25.19

2. If the data that you want to connect with is in a relational database, such as dBASE, FoxPro, or Access, click the Databases tab and choose the correct entry from the list. If the data is in another data source, such as Paradox, SQL Server, or Oracle, choose <New data source>. Make sure Use the Query Wizard to Create/Edit Queries is selected, and click OK.

3. If you chose the <New data source> option, Excel displays the dialog box shown in Figure 25.20. Give the data source a descriptive name, choose the correct ODBC driver, and click the Connect button to enter server names and other login information. If you chose one of the database formats in Step 2, you'll bypass this step.

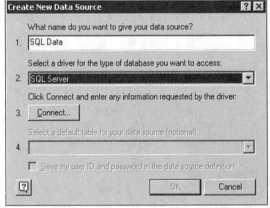

Figure 25.20

4. When the Select Database dialog box appears, choose the database file that contains the table or tables that you want to use. Click OK.

5. After you've finished these preliminaries, you'll see the Query Wizard. Work through each step, choosing options appropriate to the database format that you selected. If you chose Microsoft Access format, for example, you'll see the Choose Columns dialog box shown in Figure 25.21. Pick the fields that you want to add to the query, and click Next. Succeeding steps enable you to filter your query and set sorting options.

Figure 25.21
Select the fields that you want to add to your query.

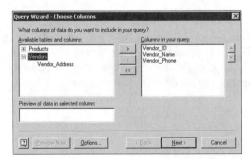

6. In the wizard's final step, click the Save Query button to save your query settings under a descriptive name. This entry appears on the Queries tab of the Choose Data Source dialog box. The next time you need to access this data, you can rerun this query directly rather than going through the Query Wizard again.

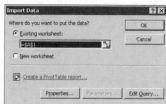

7. Select the Return Data to Microsoft Excel check box, and click OK. A dialog box (see Figure 25.22) lets you choose whether to add the data to a location on the existing worksheet, to a new worksheet, or to a PivotTable. Make your choice and click OK.

Figure 25.22

For maximum flexibility, choose a PivotTable as the location for the data your query returns, and then manipulate it using the techniques described in Chapter 27.

INTEGRATING EXTERNAL DATA INTO A WORKSHEET

When you use the Query Wizard to add data from an external source to a worksheet, you can edit it just as though you had typed it in yourself. But the data that you see is not a simple static display; instead, Excel maintains a live connection between the source database and the worksheet data. Use the buttons on the External Data toolbar to update the data and edit the query, if necessary. The advantage of this connection is that you can refresh your data at any time. For example, if your company keeps its current product inventory and sales records on a SQL Server database, you can create a query that downloads sales results for the past six months and identifies products that are low on inventory. By using charts and PivotTables to analyze the sales for each product, you can decide whether, when, and how much of each product to reorder.

■ If you saved your query, you can reuse it in a new worksheet at any time. Choose File, Open, and select Queries from the Files of Type list (each saved query has the extension .dqy).

■ When you reopen a worksheet that contains a query, use the Refresh button on the External Data toolbar to make sure that your worksheet contains the most up-to-date data.

■ For maximum control over query options, click the Data Range Properties button. In the External Data Range Properties dialog box (see Figure 25.23), you can choose a variety of useful options. For example, if the data is constantly updated, check the Refresh Control options to tell Excel that you want to update it regularly and automatically. If the quantity of data is unpredictable and you've added your own formulas at the end of each row, adjust the Data Formatting and Layout options. To completely replace the existing contents of the sheet and add your custom formulas to each new row, choose the Overwrite Existing Cells and Fill Down Formulas options.

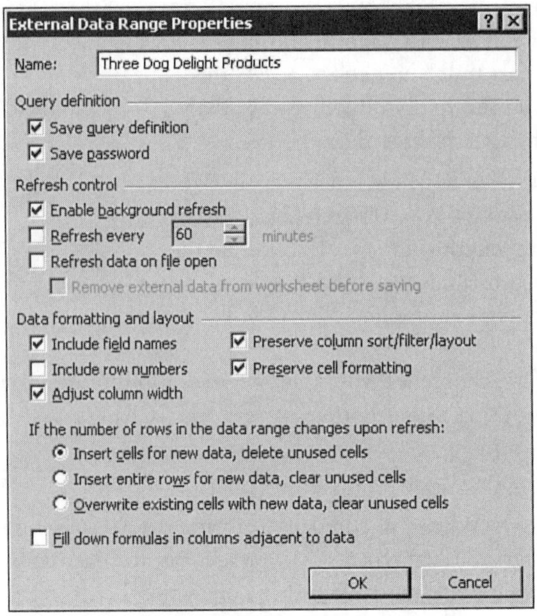

Figure 25.23
Use this dialog box to
set data refresh
options.

USING MICROSOFT QUERY TO CREATE CUSTOM QUERIES

For some situations, a fixed query is perfectly acceptable. But in other instances, you want the query to be flexible. For example, you might want to be able to enter the name of a particular customer when you open the query so that you can see all the data associated with that customer. Or, maybe you want to view information about a salesperson or product category. One of the most powerful ways to customize a query is to add parameters—when you run or refresh the query, you see a prompt asking you to fill in the specific information that you want to look for. To create a *parameter query*, follow these steps:

1. Use the Query Wizard to define the database, tables, and fields for your query. Skip the step that enables you to define a filter for your query.

2. In the final step of the Query Wizard, choose the View Data or Edit Query in Microsoft Query option. Microsoft Query opens.

3. If necessary, choose View, Criteria to display a list of Criteria fields below the table or tables.

4. Drag the name of the field that you want to use for the parameter from the Table box above to the criteria list below. Click in the Value box just below the field name, and enter the prompt that you want to appear each time you run the query, enclosing the prompt text in brackets.

5. Choose File, Save, and give the query a descriptive name. Then choose File, Return Data to Microsoft Excel.

The next time you click the Refresh button, you'll see a dialog box in which you can enter the data that you want to use as the query parameter (for instance, the name of a company or product). Click OK to kick off the search.

When you click the Edit Query button, Microsoft Query opens. If you've used Microsoft Access, this application will look extremely familiar. The basic controls are the same as those in the Query By Example builder in Access. Use the same basic techniques to add and remove tables, edit query parameters, and adjust the layout of data returned to the worksheet.

→ For a detailed discussion of Access queries, **see** "Using Queries for Extract Data from a Database," **p. 899**.

Note

> Microsoft Query is a surprisingly complex application that includes dozens of sophisticated options, and there isn't room to cover all of them here. For much more detail about connecting an Excel workbook to external databases, see *Special Edition Using Microsoft Excel 2002 ISBN: 0-7897-2511-8*, also from Que.

CREATING AND USING WEB QUERIES

PART
IV
CH
25

Excel and your Web browser can work together to gather information from a source on the Web. Microsoft Excel Web Query files are simple text documents that include a pointer to a Web page, plus a few lines that define parameters for the query. When you run a Web Query, Excel opens a connection to the Internet, connects with the specified Web page, executes the query, and returns the data to Excel.

Writing a Web Query from scratch takes specialized development skills, but you can pull in a surprising amount of useful data using sample Web Query files that come with Excel. For example, you can connect with Microsoft Investor to download current prices for stocks and mutual funds. To open any of the three sample Web queries, choose Data, Import External Data, Import Data.

You don't have to write a single line of code to bring data from the Web into an Excel worksheet, however. If the original data is contained in a table on any Web page, you can copy the table's data to the worksheet and specify that you want to transform it into a refreshable Web query. Follow these steps:

1. Click to select the cell where you want the table data to appear.

2. Choose Data, Import External Data, New Web Query.

3. In the New Web Query dialog box (see Figure 25.24), enter or paste the URL of the page that contains the data that you want to add to the worksheet. Click the Go button to load that page.

4. The New Web Query dialog box identifies each table in the page with a small arrow. Click the arrow next to the table (or tables) that you want to add. The box turns to a green check mark after you've selected it.

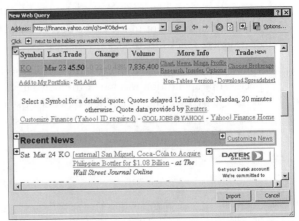

Figure 25.24

5. By default, Excel pulls your data in with no formatting. If you want to pick up text formatting from the Web page, click the Options button. In the Web Query Options dialog box (see Figure 25.25), check the Rich Text Formatting Only option. Use the Full HTML Formatting option if you want all table properties to be preserved.

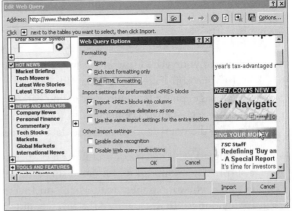

Figure 25.25

6. Click the Import button to open the Import Data dialog box. The cell that you selected in Step 1 is highlighted. Change this location, if necessary, and click the Properties button if you want to adjust the refresh times for the live data.

7. Click OK to add the Web data to your worksheet. (Click the Save Query button first if you want to save the query settings as a separate file that you can open in another worksheet.)

8. Repeat Steps 1–7 to add data from another Web page to your worksheet.

Tip from

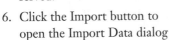

If this process seems too cumbersome, you can speed things up by using the Clipboard. From an Internet Explorer window, select the data that you want to add to your worksheet, right-click, and choose Copy. Paste the data into your worksheet, and click the Paste Options Smart Tag. Click the Create Refreshable Web Query menu option to convert the pasted data to a live link. This option is available only if you have selected a full table.

TROUBLESHOOTING

SORTING OUT SORTING PROBLEMS

I tried to run a multicolumn sort on my list, but the result came out scrambled and my column labels disappeared.

The most likely cause of this problem is that Excel couldn't identify the header row in your list. If you use the Sort dialog box, you can check a box that tells Excel that your list has a header row. Other common sorting problems are caused by blank rows or columns in the list, in which case Excel doesn't sort the records below the blank row or to the right of the blank column.

TOP 10 IS FOR NUMBERS ONLY

After turning on AutoFilter, I chose the Top 10 option for one field in my list. Instead of displaying the dialog box that lets me select further options, however, Excel simply beeped or displayed a list that didn't contain nearly as many items as I specified.

The Top 10 option works only with numeric values. If you've selected a field that contains text, Excel balks and refuses to even display an error message. If the column includes a mix of text and numbers, Excel ignores the text values and bases the Top 10 selection only on numbers in that column.

DEBUGGING ADVANCED FILTERS

I've set up an Advanced Filter, but Excel keeps returning the entire set of records from my list, and I know that the filter should return only a small number of records.

Check the reference for the criteria range in the Advanced Filter dialog box. The most likely explanation is that you've entered criteria in one row but selected two or more rows. If your criteria are only in a single column, select just that label and its criteria. If you've used a formula, make sure that the references in the formula refer to the first row in the list or to the labels above the list. For formulas only, make sure that the label above the formula does not match the label of a column in your list.

NO ROOM AT THE END

I used a data form to successfully add several new records to a list, but it no longer works. When I try to add a new row, I get an error message instead.

If your list has 65,536 rows, you've run out of room completely. If not and you see the error message `Cannot Extend List or Database`, Excel can't add a new record because you've run out of blank rows below your list. Select one or more rows beneath the list, right-click the selection, and choose Insert from the shortcut menu. Better yet, move the data from beneath the list to a separate worksheet so that you don't encounter this problem again.

SECRETS OF THE OFFICE MASTERS: COMBINE DATA FROM SEVERAL WEB SOURCES IN A CUSTOM PAGE

Do you regularly check several Web pages during the day to gather information? Excel's capability to create live links to Web data might let you combine parts of each Web page into a single worksheet. You can then save the resulting worksheet as a Web page and put all those bits and pieces of data into a single easy-to-update location.

The page shown in Figure 26.26, for example, consists of tables drawn from Yahoo!'s Finance page and the home pages of MSN Investor and Thestreet.com. We added headings to identify each block, hid several columns that contained nonessential information, and formatted the top two blocks as Full HTML.

By saving the resulting worksheet in HTML format, we now have a clean Web page that combines all three data sources in a single location.

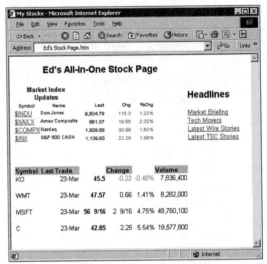

Figure 25.26

CHAPTER 26

USING EXCEL IN A WORKGROUP

In this chapter

PROTECTING A WORKSHEET

If you store Excel workbooks only on your own PC, you can control exactly how and when you change the data and structure of each worksheet. In a typical workgroup environment, however, you'll often save a workbook to a shared folder on your company's network. How do you maintain the confidentiality of sensitive data? And how do you allow co-workers to view the contents of a workbook without changing crucial data or formulas, either deliberately or by accident?

If you must store sensitive workbook files in shared network folders that are accessible to everyone, lock them up with passwords. Excel lets you create two levels of access to limit an unauthorized user's ability to opening or modifying a workbook. For finer control over the contents of a workbook, you can lock down individual cells, password-protect ranges, hide formulas, and prevent changes to the formatting or structure of your workbook.

USING PASSWORDS TO RESTRICT ACCESS TO A WORKBOOK

The simplest form of protection uses passwords to prevent unauthorized users from opening or modifying a workbook. You can specify this option at any time.

By setting up two passwords and carefully restricting access to them, you can allow access to information while maintaining the integrity of data in a workbook. For example, you might assign different Open and Modify passwords to a budget workbook, and then give each department manager the Open password while allowing only your trusted assistant to have the Modify password. Department managers can view the budget data, but they'll have to forward requests for changes to you or your assistant.

→ For instructions on how to assign and modify passwords, **see** "Keeping Shared Documents Secure," **p. 172**.

Tip from

If you leave the Open password blank but assign a Modify password, anyone with access to the folder in which the workbook file is stored can view, but not change, its contents.

Anyone who attempts to open a password-protected workbook will first have to enter the correct password. If the workbook is protected by a Modify password, you'll see the dialog box shown in Figure 26.1.

Figure 26.1
If you don't know the password, click the Read Only button to view the workbook's contents. Without the password, you cannot save changes to the workbook unless you give it a new name.

> **Password**
> 'Sales Results Q3.xls' is reserved by Ed Bott
> Enter password for write access, or open read only.
> Password: [   ]
> OK   Cancel   Read Only

Workbook passwords are an all-or-nothing proposition. After entering the correct Modify password, a user can make any changes. That unrestricted freedom can be disastrous in the hands of a sloppy or untrained user if you've carefully designed a worksheet and entered complex formulas. You can even do irreparable damage to your own workbooks or worksheets if you're distracted or you simply don't notice that you're working with an original when you meant to create a copy. The following two sections describe how to protect yourself.

PROTECTING THE STRUCTURE OF A WORKBOOK

After you've assigned a password to a workbook, locked important cells, and turned on worksheet protection, your worksheet is perfectly safe, right? Wrong. A malicious or clumsy user can destroy all your careful work by deleting a worksheet from a workbook, even when it's otherwise fully protected. To keep your data out of harm's way, you need to add one more level of protection.

To prevent users from changing the design of your workbook, select Tools, Protection, Protect Workbook (see Figure 26.2), and then check one or both of these options:

Figure 26.2
Use workbook protection options to prevent users (including yourself) from deleting a worksheet or closing a window.

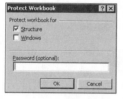

- By default, the Structure option is checked. This setting prevents users from adding or deleting worksheets, renaming sheets, or displaying sheets you've hidden.

- Check the Windows box if your worksheet contains more than one sheet and you've arranged them in a particular order. When you select this setting, users can select Arrange from the Window menu, but these options no longer work.

- Add a password to prevent users from removing protection.

To restore the capability to make changes to a workbook, select Tools, Protection, Unprotect Workbook.

PREVENTING CHANGES TO A WORKSHEET

Excel 2002 gives you many more workbook and worksheet protection options than earlier Excel versions. You can prevent cell formatting and stop users from inserting or deleting rows and columns, for example (but only if the user opens the file in Excel 2002).

To apply protection options to the current worksheet, select Tools, Protection, Protect Sheet. In the Protect Sheet dialog box (see Figure 26.3), select options you want to apply to all users (including yourself). The Protect Worksheet and Contents of Locked Cells box turns protection on or off for the current sheet.

Figure 26.3
You can require users to enter a password before entering data in specified ranges. To impose this level of control on a worksheet, select Tools, Protection, Allow Users to Edit Ranges. The resulting dialog box (see Figure 26.4) lists currently protected ranges and allows you to specify which users can edit those ranges.

Figure 26.4
After you assign a password, click the Permissions button to specify which users (including yourself) can edit data without a password.

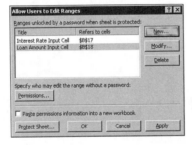

To add a new range to this list, first unprotect the worksheet, if necessary, and then follow these steps:

1. From the Allow Users to Edit Ranges dialog box and click the New button.

2. In the New Range dialog box (see Figure 26.5), replace the generic description (Range1) in the Title box with a descriptive name.

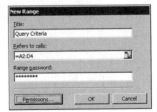

3. Adjust the range shown in the Refers to Cells box, if necessary. By default, this box shows the address of the current selection.

4. Enter a password if you want only specific users to be able to enter data in the locked cells.

Figure 26.5

5. Click the Permissions button to choose the names of users who can enter data without supplying a password. For files stored on an NTFS drive in a Windows NT/2000/XP network, this option hooks directly into file system permissions.

The biggest advantage of setting data-entry protection by range is that you can assign varying levels of protection to a worksheet. Lock especially important data with a supervisors-only password, while opening the data-entry ranges with a password that's more widely distributed. After defining ranges that are locked for editing, you must protect the worksheet (Tools, Protection, Protect Sheet).

You can also use cell formatting to protect cells; this attribute prevents changes to data and formulas in individual cells. This option allows you to lock a cell, which prevents all users from deleting or changing the contents of that cell.

You can also hide formulas within a cell; *hidden cells* allow any user to see the results of the formula without being able to see the formula that produced that result. This option lets you protect proprietary calculations and prevent users from being confused by particularly long and complex formulas.

→ To learn more about formatting numbers and text in your worksheets, **see** "How Cell Formatting Works," **p. 574**.

By default, all cells in a worksheet are locked but not hidden; however, these formats take effect only when you specifically enable protection for a worksheet. To unlock a cell or range and allow editing, or to hide formulas within a cell or range, you first must make a selection and adjust its cell formatting. Because the Locked and Hidden formats are independent, you can lock a cell that contains a formula while still allowing the user to see that formula.

Caution

Although you can hide a formula without locking the cell in which it's stored, it's hard to imagine a scenario in which this option makes sense; with this formatting, the user could inadvertently wipe out the formula by typing in another value.

To protect the contents of the current worksheet, follow these steps:

1. Select the cells you want to unlock for editing, typically those used for data entry or notes. (Remember that all cells are locked by default on a worksheet.)

2. Select Format, Cells, click the Protection tab, and clear the check mark from the Locked box.

3. Select all cells that contain formulas you want to hide.

4. Select Format, Cells, click the Protection tab, and check the Hidden box.

5. Repeat steps 1–4 for other worksheets you want to protect. Click OK to close the dialog box, and then save the workbook.

To enable protection for the selected worksheet, select Tools, Protection, Protect Sheet.

→ For an explanation of how to protect scenarios on a worksheet, **see** "Storing Multiple Scenarios in a Single Workbook," **p. 715**.

SHARING A WORKBOOK

When you try to open a workbook another user is currently viewing or editing, Excel displays the polite File in Use dialog box shown in Figure 26.6. Just as with a Word document or PowerPoint presentation, you can choose to open a read-only copy; and just as you can with Word (but not PowerPoint), you can ask Excel to notify you when the other user has finished working with the file.

Figure 26.6
Normally, you'll see this dialog box if you try to open a workbook another user is currently viewing or editing.

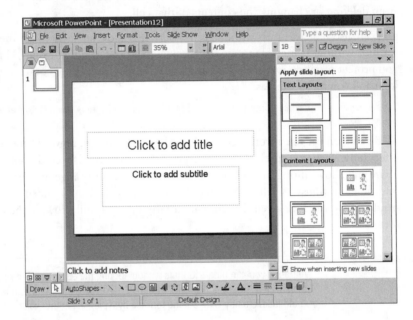

But unlike Word and PowerPoint, Excel allows you to flag a workbook as *shared*, so multiple users can open it simultaneously and store their changes in the same file. If you work in an office where you regularly collaborate with other Excel users, this capability can be extremely handy. For example

- When you're under a deadline to produce a companywide budget, create a shared workbook with multiple worksheets, one for each department. Then allow each department head to work on his or her numbers without waiting for others to finish.

- Keep a shared list of contacts, products, or parts in a network folder so any user can open, view, and update information anytime.

When you set up a shared workbook, you define how often Excel checks for changes, and you also determine whether Excel should maintain a history of changes to the current workbook—a useful option if you must maintain an audit trail showing the who, what, and when of all revisions. If you change the contents of a cell after another user has changed the same cell, Excel warns you and then lets you decide how to resolve the conflict.

SETTING UP A WORKSHEET FOR SHARED USE

There's no way to accidentally share a workbook with another user. You must explicitly enable this capability. Excel prompts you to turn on workbook sharing if you choose File, Send To, Mail Recipient (for Review). To enable sharing manually, select Tools, Share Workbook, click the Editing tab, and check the Allow Changes by More Than One User at the Same Time box. You see the dialog box displayed in Figure 26.7. (The parenthetical reference to "exclusive" in the Who Has This Workbook Open Now section of this dialog box will disappear after you turn on sharing.)

Figure 26.7
Check this box to allow multiple users to open and edit a workbook simultaneously.

Note

You cannot share a workbook if another user already has it open. Ask the other user to save changes and close the file so you can enable sharing.

When you enable sharing, Excel saves the workbook (including all recent changes) under the current name. If you have not previously saved the file, Excel prompts you to give it a name and location. If you want the file to be accessible to other users, be sure to specify a shared network location.

Note

To enable workbook sharing, you must save your file in Excel 97 format or later. Excel 95/5.0 users can't work with a shared workbook.

How do you know when a workbook is shared? Look at the title bar, where you'll see the word "Shared" in brackets after the workbook's name. You can continue to edit the workbook as before; however, you will not be able to complete some worksheet actions. Here's a partial list of actions that are impossible in a shared workbook (for a complete list of actions that are not permitted in shared workbooks, search for the Help topic "Limitations of Shared Workbooks"):

PART
IV

CH
26

- You cannot move, copy, delete, or rename worksheets.

- Most options on the Properties dialog box are grayed out.

- You can't insert a chart, picture, AutoShape, object, or hyperlink.

- Although you can add or delete rows and columns, you can't insert or delete cells and ranges.

- You can't merge cells in a shared workbook, although cells you merge before sharing the workbook will display correctly.

- Many options on the Data menu are grayed out. Specifically, you can't group, outline, add subtotals, or create validation rules.

- You cannot apply conditional formats or work with scenarios on a shared workbook.

- When you create a PivotTable and then share the workbook that contains it, the PivotTable will work correctly; however, you can't create a new PivotTable or change the design of an existing one.

- You can't write, edit, or record macros in a shared workbook. You can run existing macros, although they might fail if a command is not available.

Tip from

Ed & Woody

Excel lets you save personal printing and filter settings for a shared workbook. That option is especially useful when multiple users are working with different regions on a single worksheet. If you prefer to have all users share the same settings, select Tools, Share Workbook, click the Advanced tab, and uncheck either or both boxes (Print Settings and Filter Settings) at the bottom of the dialog box.

DISABLING WORKBOOK SHARING

To remove the shared status from a workbook and restore it to exclusive use, follow these steps:

1. Select Tools, Share Workbook, click the Editing tab, and check the list of users in the Who Has This Workbook Open Now box.

2. If other users have the workbook open, ask them to close the workbook and save their changes. To disconnect another user immediately, select the name from the list and click the Remove User button.

Has Excel told you (incorrectly) that another user already has a workbook open? See the "Troubleshooting" note, "The Case of the Nonexistent User," at the end of this chapter.

3. When the only name left in the list of users is yours, clear the check mark from the Allow Changes by More Than One User at a Time box. Click OK.

4. Excel displays a dialog box warning you that you're about to disconnect other users and clear the change history (see the following section for more information about tracking the change history). If you're certain you want to proceed, click Yes.

TRACKING WORKBOOK REVISIONS IN A WORKGROUP

When you enable revision tracking, Excel keeps track of most changes you and other users make to the current workbook. This change history becomes a part of the workbook file. You can view all changes, on the worksheet itself or in a separate list. You can filter the list of changes to see only those made at a certain time or by a specific person. And like the equivalent feature in Word, you can review changes and accept or reject them.

If you manage a workgroup, revision tracking can be a powerful way to distribute work without losing the ability to see who did what to a workbook. Unfortunately, the procedures for tracking and reviewing changes are not as straightforward as they should be, and there are several significant (and potentially confusing) quirks in the way this feature works.

To turn on revision tracking, follow these steps:

1. Open or switch to the workbook in which you want to track changes.

2. Select Tools, Track Changes, Highlight Changes. You'll see the dialog box shown in Figure 26.8.

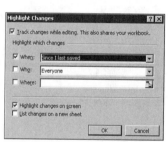

3. Check the Track Changes While Editing box. If necessary, this option also enables sharing for the workbook.

   By design, you can track changes only in a shared workbook, and sharing a workbook also turns on revision tracking. Although you can share a workbook without tracking changes, there's no way to track changes in a workbook that's reserved for exclusive use. By default, Excel tracks changes for 30 days.

Figure 26.8

4. Use the When, Who, and Where drop-down lists to restrict which changes you'll see in the current workbook. These options do not affect the change history; they simply define which changes are visible.

5. Click OK to close the dialog box and return to the workbook.

Excel tracks a wide variety of actions in the change history: If you change the contents of a cell, insert a new sheet, or add or delete columns or rows, Excel makes a note in the change history. Some actions are not tracked, however—most notably formatting. No record exists in the change history if you change fonts or attributes for a cell or range, for example, or if you rearrange the size and position of individual worksheet windows.

Removing the shared status of a workbook permanently deletes the change history. If you return a workbook to exclusive use and save the file, there is no way to recover the change history.

Keeping a change history can dramatically increase the size of a file, especially in workbooks that you use over a period of months or years. To reduce the size of the workbook file, consider reducing the number of days for which you track changes (select Tools, Sharing, Advanced tab). To eliminate the entire change history, remove sharing from the workbook, and then reenable it.

VIEWING CHANGES TO A SHARED WORKBOOK

Every time you save a shared workbook, Excel compares the contents of the file currently stored on the disk with the contents of the workbook you're about to save. If the only changes are yours, Excel simply saves the file. However, if another user has saved changes to the workbook since the last time you saved the file, Excel adds those changes to the change history, updates the workbook you see onscreen, and displays a dialog box warning you that the workbook now contains changes saved by other users.

The previous section explained how to set the options that determine which changes you see in the open workbook. By default, changes are visible on the worksheet itself. Look in the upper-left corner of any changed cell or range and you'll see a small, triangular marker. If you let the mouse pointer hover over that cell, a pop-up note similar to the one in Figure 26.9 describes the change.

Flowers Total
$20,898.03
Gardening Equipmen Q1
$677.44
Gardening Equipmen Q2
$2,012.66
Gardening Equipmen Q3
$5,284.33
Gardening Equipmen Q4
$4,696.87
Gardening Equipment Total
$12,671.30
Landscape Services Q1
$3,000.15
Landscape Services Q2
$2,080.03
Ed Bott, 4/1/2001 11:55 AM:
Changed cell D17 from '$1,677.44 ' to '$677.44 '.

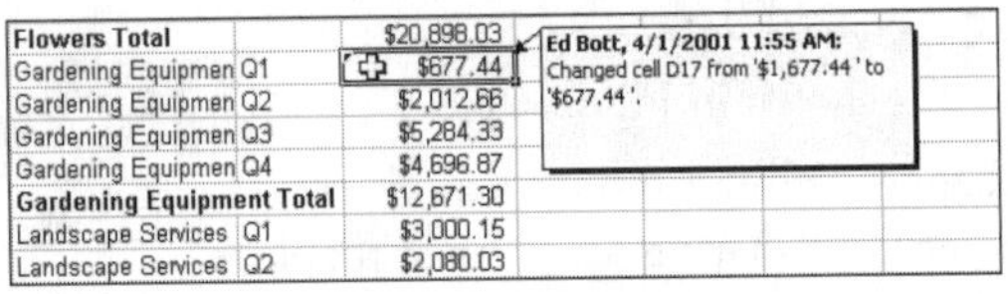

Figure 26.9
Look for the small marker in the upper-left corner of a changed cell. Let the mouse pointer hover over the cell to see this pop-up note.

Normally, Excel updates an open, shared workbook with other users' changes only when you save the workbook. Likewise, other users see your changes only when they save the file after you save your work. In a fast-paced environment in which several users are editing a workbook simultaneously, you might want to see and save changes more often. Follow these steps to adjust automatic update options:

1. Open or switch to the shared workbook and select Tools, Share Workbook.
2. Click the Advanced tab to display the dialog box shown in Figure 26.10.

Share Workbook
Editing
Advanced
Track changes
Keep change history for: 30 days
Don't keep change history
Update changes
When file is saved
Automatically every: 1440 minutes
Save my changes and see others' changes
Just see other users' changes
Conflicting changes between users
Ask me which changes win
The changes being saved win
Include in personal view
Print settings
Filter settings
OK
Cancel

Figure 26.10
Use this dialog box to update changes to a shared workbook automatically.

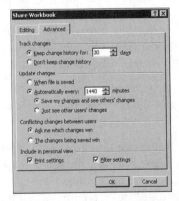

3. In the Update Changes section, check the Automatically Every option, and select an interval between 5 and 1,440 minutes. (We cover resolving change conflicts in the next section.)

Note

Why 1,440? That's the number of minutes in one day. Enter this value to automatically update your shared workbook exactly once a day.

4. To save your copy of the workbook automatically at the specified interval, select the Save My Changes and See Others' Changes option. To pull in other users' changes without also saving your changes, select Just See Other Users' Changes.

5. Click OK to close the dialog box and return to your worksheet.

If you don't see all the changes you expect, check the revision-tracking settings to see whether you're inadvertently hiding recent changes. Select Tools, Track Changes, Highlight Changes, and select from the following options:

- **When**—Click to filter changes by time. Select all changes, restrict by date, hide changes you've already reviewed, or show only changes since the last time you saved.

- **Who**—Click to filter by username. Select Everyone, or select from a list of users who have made changes to the workbook. To see only changes from others, select Everyone but Me.

- **Where**—Click and specify a cell or range to show only changes in a specific part of the workbook.

The easiest way to see all changes by all users is to clear all three of the previous check boxes:

- To hide changes in the current workbook, clear the check next to the Highlight Changes on Screen option. Excel continues to track changes without displaying them.

- To see all changes to the current workbook in a list, check the List Changes on a New Sheet option. When you select this option, Excel creates a History worksheet and adds it to the current workbook. You can see and AutoFilter all changes from all users of a shared workbook on the History sheet.

Although the History worksheet looks like an ordinary worksheet, it's definitely not. You can't edit, move, copy, or rename this sheet, although you can select data on the sheet and copy it to the Clipboard. The History sheet shows only changes you've saved, and it uses the When, Who, and Where filters you define. Use the drop-down arrows to the right of each column heading to filter the display of changes.

Each time you save or close the workbook, Excel wipes out the History sheet. To re-create it, select Tools, Track Changes, Highlight Changes.

RESOLVING CONFLICTS IN SHARED WORKBOOKS

Let's say another user changes the value in cell A15 and saves the workbook. You then change the same cell to a different value. When you save your changes, Excel detects the conflict. So what happens when changes collide?

By default, Excel displays the dialog box shown in Figure 26.11, which lets you review each conflicting change and decide which one to keep.

Figure 26.11
When two users try to save changes to the same cell, Excel asks you to resolve the conflict.

To automatically save your own changes in the event of a conflict without having to slog through dialog boxes, select Tools, Share Workbook, click the Advanced tab, and check the option labeled The Changes Being Saved Win.

Cooperation is the key to successfully collaborating on a workbook. If you and a co-worker both insist on automatically saving changes, neither of you will ever know that the other person has made conflicting changes to the worksheet. Both changes will be saved in the change history, however, making this option appropriate if you plan to review all changes later.

INCORPORATING CHANGES INTO A WORKBOOK

When two or more users make changes to a workbook, Excel displays only the changes most recently saved. But the change history keeps a record of all changes, going back 30 days by default (although you can roll this number up or down). At any time, you can step through each of the changes in a workbook and accept or reject them.

To review changes, follow these steps:

1. Select Tools, Track Changes, Accept or Reject Changes. You'll see the dialog box shown in Figure 26.12.

2. Select options from the When, Who, and Where boxes. You can see all changes, just changes from a specific user, those made since a specific date, or those made within a specific workbook region.

Figure 26.12

3. Click OK to begin reviewing changes. Excel displays each change in the Accept or Reject Changes dialog box. If a particular cell has been changed more than once, a dialog box will show all such changes (see Figure 26.13).

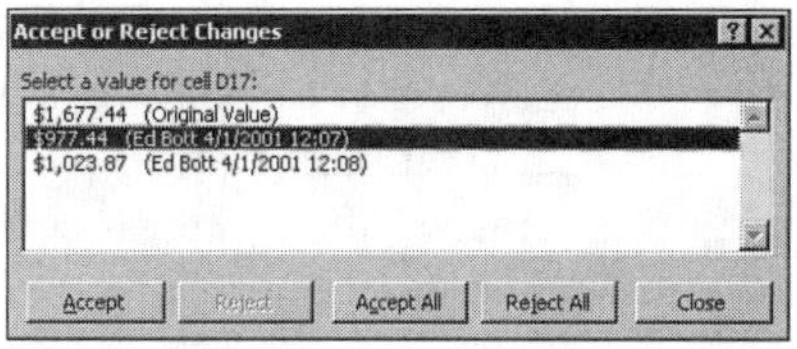

Figure 26.13

4. Click Accept or Reject to move to the next change in the list. Click Accept All to deal with all changes at once; click Reject All to roll back the workbook so it looks like it did when you first began tracking changes.

PROTECTING A SHARED WORKBOOK

When you enable sharing for a workbook, Excel lets you prevent other users from removing the shared status of the workbook and wiping out the change history. This step is particularly important when you're dealing with inexperienced or unsophisticated users. Turn on protection using either of these techniques:

Note

Don't confuse this protection option with your choices for protecting worksheets and workbooks. If you want to lock the contents of cells, hide formulas, or protect the structure of a workbook, you must do so before you share the workbook.

■ To share a worksheet and protect it in one operation, select Tools, Protection, Protect and Share Workbook, and check the Sharing with Track Changes box. If you also specify a password in this dialog box, no one will be able to remove sharing unless they supply the correct password.

■ To protect a worksheet that is already shared, select Tools, Protection, Protect Shared Workbook, and check the Sharing with Track Changes box. This option does not allow you to specify a password.

PART
IV

CH
26

STORING MULTIPLE SCENARIOS IN A SINGLE WORKBOOK

One of Excel's most valuable hidden features is its capability to store multiple scenarios within a single workbook. Creating scenarios helps you plan for a future in which you can't be certain that your worksheet model is accurate, especially when a change in one assumption will have a ripple effect on other values that affect the bottom line. Scenarios are useful in these two circumstances:

■ When the underlying assumptions depend on external factors out of your control, such as the weather or the economy. For example, if you sell heating oil or umbrellas, you might create a P&L forecast using multiple scenarios to compare the results of strong sales in cold, wet weather and weak sales if the winter is mild.

- When you want to perform what-if analyses that test the bottom-line effect of price increases or capital expenditures. For instance, the classic demand curve from Econ 101 says that raising prices past a certain point might reduce demand so much that profits actually suffer, whereas cutting prices might cause sales to grow tremendously and swell the bottom line. Use scenarios in combination with market research to test the bottom-line impact of a 10% price cut, a 5% price hike, and a 10% increase.

Tip from
EQ & Woody

> You often can accomplish the same goal by creating multiple workbooks within a single worksheet, starting with a basic model and creating a copy for each scenario—best case, worst case, and so on. For simple analyses, where the underlying assumptions remain the same and you simply need to show revised totals, you also can add an extra row or column using slightly different formulas. Reserve scenarios for complex analyses where the changing assumptions include many related factors.

Adding scenarios to a worksheet is a three-step process. First, create a worksheet that includes all the data and formulas you want to use in your comparison. Next, select specific cells you want to change as part of each scenario. (The changing cells typically contain values used in one or more formulas in the sheet.) Finally, create named scenarios and enter the data in the changing cells for each one. By switching between scenarios, you can watch the bottom line change—and even change the bars and columns in charts based on data in the worksheet.

When putting together a fiscal forecast, for example, you might want to test the impact of various growth scenarios on your expenses. In the first scenario, you increase the number of employees (and thus salaries, payroll taxes, benefits, and other expenses tied to head count) to handle anticipated new business. In the second scenario, you freeze hiring and outsource the increased workload instead (keeping salaries at their current level but increasing expenses for contract labor). In the third scenario, you analyze what happens if you kick off a major hiring program and rent new office space (besides the increases in labor costs, you'll have to adjust for higher rent, utilities, and maintenance).

To create a worksheet that includes multiple scenarios, follow these steps:

1. Create the basic worksheet containing all the data and formulas you want to use in your first scenario.

2. Select up to 32 cells that will change in each scenario. Although you can select the changing cells and enter data at the same time you create a scenario, it is much, much easier to build scenarios in this order.

3. Select Tools, Scenarios. In the Scenario Manager dialog box, click the Add button to display the Add Scenario dialog box shown in Figure 26.14.

Figure 26.14
Give each scenario a name and add a descriptive comment; if you selected the changing cells before displaying this dialog box, your selection appears here.

Caution

There's no requirement that you select the same set of changing cells in each scenario; however, we strongly recommend that you do so. The purpose of creating scenarios is to show you various outcomes when you control specific input assumptions. If you use different changing cells in each scenario, your workbook essentially becomes an uncontrolled experiment, and the same data could result in different results for a given scenario depending on which scenarios you view first.

---

4. In the Scenario Name box, enter a name that describes the scenario you're creating. You'll use this name to view and edit scenarios later, so keep the name short and meaningful: Best case and Worst case, for example. By default, the Comment box at the bottom of this dialog box contains your name and the date you created the scenario. If your scenario includes assumptions that aren't readily apparent, add a detailed description here.

5. Select protection options for the scenarios on the current worksheet. (By default, the Prevent Changes option is checked and the Hide option is unchecked.) Click OK. The Scenario Values box appears, as shown in Figure 26.15.

PART
IV
Cʜ
26

Figure 26.15
Use this dialog box to enter values for the changing cells in each scenario.

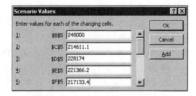

 If you've enabled protection for scenarios but other users are able to change your data, see the "Troubleshooting" note, "Protection Is a Two-Step Process," at the end of this chapter.

6. Check the values you want to use for each of the changing cells in this scenario, and change any of them, as necessary.

Tip from

EQ & Woody

Normally, the Scenario Values dialog box displays cell references. However, if you use range names for the changing cells, those names will appear in this dialog box, making entering data and verifying that the values in each changing cell make sense much easier.

7. If your other scenarios are relatively uncomplicated, with only a handful of changing cells, click the Add button and enter the numbers for each scenario directly in this dialog box. If the underlying worksheet is complex, however, you'll probably find it easier to close the Scenario Manager dialog box, enter your data, and repeat steps 2–6 to create additional scenarios. When you finish, the dialog box should look something like the one in Figure 26.16.

Figure 26.16
Select a scenario and click the Show button to display the worksheet with that scenario's values.

To view different scenarios, open the Scenario Manager dialog box, select a scenario name, and click the Show button (or double-click the scenario name). You can drag the Scenario Manager dialog box out of the way to see the changed values in your worksheet. If you want to scroll or edit the worksheet, however, you must close this dialog box.

Tip from

EQ & Woody

Viewing a worksheet that contains scenarios can be confusing. Unless the Scenario Manager dialog box is open, how do you know which scenario you're looking at? Use text labels to solve this problem elegantly. Although it's most common to select cells with numeric values as the changing cells in a worksheet with scenarios, you can also enter text in a changing cell. Set aside one cell on your worksheet to contain a description of the current scenario and make it a changing cell as well. When you create each scenario, be sure the contents of this cell are accurate. Using this technique, you'll always be able to see which scenario is on display, just by looking at this cell.

⚠ *If you get a cryptic error when you try to view a scenario, there's probably a simple explanation. See "Merged Cells and Scenarios Don't Mix" in the "Troubleshooting" section at the end of this chapter.*

After creating scenarios, you can add, remove, or change scenarios by using the same basic procedures. Two options in the Scenario Manager dialog box are particularly interesting for advanced users:

- **Merge Button**—Click this to consolidate the data from changing cells into a new worksheet. Start in a new worksheet and open the workbooks that contain the scenarios you want to merge. The Merge Scenarios dialog box lists all open workbooks, and when you select one, you can pick from a list of worksheets within that workbook (the status bar tells you whether any scenarios exist in the sheet you've selected). Click OK to open the Scenario Manager dialog box, and then click Show to add the data from the changing cells to the current sheet. This technique is especially useful when you've passed out several copies of a worksheet template and you want to copy some but not all of the scenarios to the new sheet.

- **Summary Button**—Click this to produce a report that arranges the values from the changing cells in all scenarios into a new sheet in the current workbook. Select the Scenario Summary option to display the data in a neatly formatted table; use the Scenario PivotTable option to display data in a format in which you can manipulate it further.

CONSOLIDATING DATA FROM MULTIPLE USERS INTO A SINGLE WORKBOOK

So far, we've discussed sharing workbooks and tracking revisions on a shared workbook file users open from a central location on a company network. But revision tracking can be useful in another set of circumstances as well. You can create a workbook, turn on revision tracking, and then make copies and distribute them to a group of people. If you want a group of department heads to work on draft budgets, for example, give each one an identical workbook with revision tracking turned on. When they return the copies with their changes, you can merge the copies into a single workbook, and then review and accept or reject individual changes.

PART

IV

CH

26

Tip from

EQ & Woody

If there is any chance that the process of distributing, collecting, and merging workbooks will take longer than 30 days, be sure to change the time period you specify to maintain the merge history. Select Tools, Share Workbook, click the Advanced tab, and enter a number of days in the Keep Change History For box. To be extra safe, set this value to its maximum of 32767.

When creating the worksheet for distribution, follow these steps to be certain the merge process will work properly:

1. Create the workbook model you want users to fill in, complete with formulas and headings. If you want to lock cells or hide formulas, do so now.

2. Select Tools, Protection, Protect and Share Workbook, and check the Sharing with Track Changes box. To force all users to track changes and prevent them from disabling revision tracking, enter a password in this dialog box and click OK.

3. Confirm the password you just entered and click OK. Excel displays the Save As dialog box.

4. Give the file a name and click Save. This is your master workbook.

5. Without making any changes to the workbook, click File, Save As, and make a new copy for each person to whom you plan to distribute the workbook. Make sure each copy is identical, and save each one under a different name.

After you receive the filled-in copies from each co-worker, follow this procedure to merge the workbooks:

1. Open the master workbook you created before distributing the copies.

2. Select Tools, Merge Workbooks. If you've made any changes to the workbook since opening it, Excel prompts you to save the file now.

3. In the Select Files to Merge into Current Workbook dialog box, click the name of the first workbook whose changes you want to merge. Hold down the Ctrl key and click to select multiple files.

4. Click OK to merge the workbooks.

5. Repeat steps 2–4 for other workbooks you want to merge.

Tip from

EQ & Woody

There are many ways that merging workbooks can go wrong. If you get an error message when attempting to merge one or more workbooks, try copying the information from one workbook and pasting it into the master copy. Be certain you're not overwriting important data when you use this technique.

TROUBLESHOOTING

THE CASE OF THE NONEXISTENT USER

When I try to open a shared workbook, Excel tells me it's already in use, but I'm certain it's not true.

Excel might report that another user has a workbook open even though this is no longer true; in fact, you might see your own name more than once in the list of users. This situation occurs most often after a system crashes while the workbook is open. In this circumstance, select the user's name and click the Remove User button. If you see your own name listed twice, one of the listings is correct. If Excel won't let you remove one of these entries, try the other one.

PROTECTION IS A TWO-STEP PROCESS

I've created a shared workbook that contains multiple scenarios, but even after checking the Prevent Changes box, I find that other users are able to change my data.

Protecting scenarios from inadvertent changes is a crucial step when you plan to share workbooks with other people, but these options are confusing if you don't understand how Excel protects workbooks. Checking the Prevent Changes box tells Excel you don't want anyone to be able to change or delete a given scenario. Checking the Hide box removes a scenario from the Scenario Manager, without removing the scenario itself. After enabling these options, however, you must turn on protection for your entire worksheet. Select Tools, Protection, Protect Sheet, and make sure the Scenarios box is checked in the Protect Sheet dialog box. Add a password if you want to prevent experienced but unauthorized users from overriding this option and making changes anyway.

MERGED CELLS AND SCENARIOS DON'T MIX

When I try to view a scenario on a particular worksheet, Excel displays the cryptic error message Some changing cells are part of an array or table and cannot be changed. *What's that all about?*

One or more of your changing cells includes a merged cell. Excel enables you to create a scenario that includes a merged cell and even enter data into it, without warning you that you won't be able to view the scenario you just created. The only solution is to unmerge the changing cell.

SECRETS OF THE OFFICE MASTERS: CREATING CUSTOM VIEWS OF WORKSHEET DATA

When you share workbooks within an organization, it's always a challenge to help other users see the data in its best light. A complex workbook can contain several worksheets, charts, and various regions containing data. By selecting the correct worksheet, hiding rows and columns, freezing panes, setting zoom levels, and defining print areas, you can focus on exactly the data you want to. But it's a huge waste of time to repeat all those actions every time you open the worksheet.

Although you can create both custom views and scenarios for use with your own workbooks, these tools are most useful when you want other members of your workgroup to see a workbook exactly as you do.

Instead, after you set up the workbook exactly the way you want to view or print it, save the current arrangement as a custom view so you can quickly return to it. After arranging the workbook, select View, Custom Views. In the Custom Views dialog box shown here, click the Add button and enter a descriptive name for the view.

When you create a custom view, you can include any of the following options:

- Which sheet is active and which cells are selected.
- Column widths, row heights, and hidden rows or columns.
- Zoom settings. Note that different Zoom settings have different effects, depending on the display resolution the user has selected; at 800×600, for example, a chart at 68% Zoom might fill the entire window, although at 1024×768 resolution a significant empty space appears around the same chart.
- Display options, including those that appear when you select Tools, Options, and select the View tab.

Tip from

Ed & Woody

For a particularly striking "clean" custom view, hide all distracting interface elements: scrollbars, row and column headings, gridlines, the formula bar, and the status bar. Save the resulting custom view to let anyone else who opens the workbook see this uncluttered view.

- Window details, including size, position, splits, and frozen panes.
- Outline and grouping settings.
- Filter settings, including AutoFilter and Advanced Filter options.
- Print settings, including defined print areas.

To display a custom view, select View, Custom Views. Select a view from the list and click Show.

To make it extremely easy for anyone to navigate around a workbook using custom views, create a simple macro using this snippet of code:

```
ActiveWorkbook.CustomViews("Viewname").Show
```

Replace *Viewname* with the exact name of the view you want to use. Assign the macro to a toolbar button, drawing object, or keyboard shortcut to make switching to a custom view truly a one-click process.

CHAPTER 27

USING PIVOTTABLES AND PIVOTCHARTS

In this chapter

HOW PIVOTTABLE AND PIVOTCHART REPORTS WORK

PivotTables and PivotCharts are powerful tools for automatically summarizing and analyzing data without ever having to add a formula or function. As the name implies, you start with a list in table format, snap the rows and columns into position on a grid, and end up with a sorted, grouped, summarized, totaled, and subtotaled report. PivotTable reports are best for cross-tabulating lists—the more categories, the better. You can reduce a list of thousands of items to a single line, showing totals by category or quarter. Or you can create complex, multilevel groupings that show total sales by employee, grouped by product category and by quarter. You can hide or show detail for each group with a quick double-click. You can change the view or grouping in literally seconds, just by dragging items on or off the sheet and moving them between row, column, and page fields.

Start with a list that contains multiple fields, and then use Excel's PivotTable Wizard to set up a blank PivotTable page with just a few clicks. Instead of sorting your list and entering formulas and functions, you drag fields around on the PivotTable page to create a new view of your list—Excel groups the data and adds summary formulas automatically. PivotCharts are the visual equivalent of PivotTables, letting you create killer charts just as quickly, by dragging fields on a chart layout page.

→ For more details on how to create and work with lists, **see** Chapter 25, "Working with Lists and Databases," **p. 673**.

→ PivotCharts add a new dimension to PivotTable reports, **see** "Creating and Editing PivotCharts," **p. 737**.

If you used PivotTables in Excel 2000, you'll barely notice the difference in Excel 2002 (although you'll probably like the usability tweaks). If you tried to create or edit a PivotTable in Excel 97 and gave up in frustration, try again. The process of creating and editing PivotTables is dramatically easier in Excel 2000/2002 than in Excel 97, especially when it comes to changing a PivotTable on-the-fly. PivotCharts were introduced in Excel 2000.

Unlike subtotals and outlines, which modify the structure of your list to display summaries, PivotTables and PivotCharts create new, independent elements in your workbook. When you add or edit data in a list, the changes show up in your PivotTables and PivotCharts as well; because they're separate elements, you can easily change the structure of a PivotTable or PivotChart, too, and your changes won't mess up the data in the underlying list. Using *interactive Web components*, you can also make PivotTables available to other people via a Web browser.

Figure 27.1 shows the four main *drop zones* on a blank PivotTable page. The PivotTable toolbar includes buttons for every field in your list. Use row fields and column fields to define how you want Excel to group your list. Data items define which fields contain the information you want to summarize. Page fields let you further refine your view by displaying a separate PivotTable for each item in a group, as though the table were on its own virtual page. You can use multiple row fields, column fields, or both, and you can specify which summary action you want Excel to perform on data items—the sum, average, or count of all related values, for instance.

Figure 27.1
Drag field buttons from the toolbar and drop them on the layout to build a PivotTable on-the-fly.

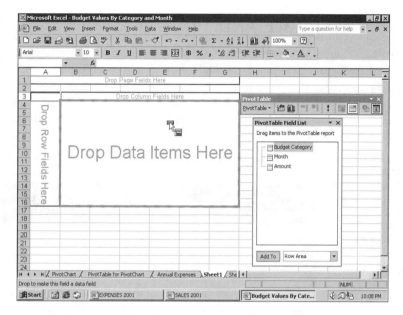

What can you do with a PivotTable? The number of uses is limited only by your imagination. Despite their dramatically different structures, for example, each of the following four PivotTables started with the same list of information about publicly traded stocks. In its raw form, with its grand total of 37,400 separate data points, the list is a prescription for information overload. Each of the 2,200 rows contains 17 data fields for an individual publicly traded company, including its name, ticker symbol, and industry category, the exchange on which it trades, its high and low stock price for the past year, and financial measurements such as net profit margin and return on equity.

Figure 27.2 shows a simple PivotTable that lets you see at a glance how many companies are in each industry category, along with the average increase in stock price from companies in that category over the past year. This PivotTable consists of a single row field and two data items.

Figure 27.2
With no column fields and only one row field, this PivotTable quickly counts the number of companies in each category and calculates the average price change for the year.

	A	B	C
		Number of	% Price Chg Last Yr
3	Industry Name	Companies	(Avg)
28	Gas Utilities	19	17.47
29	Regional - Southeast Banks	18	27.12
30	Aerospace/Defense Products & Services	18	25.84
31	Regional - Southwest Banks	17	18.89
32	Drug Manufacturers - Other	16	44.73
33	Drug Manufacturers - Major	16	32.84
34	Waste Management	15	44.19
35	Investment Brokerage - Regional	15	43.35
36	REIT - Diversified	14	23.97
37	Processing Systems & Products	14	30.82
38	Information Technology Services	14	29.42
39	Biotechnology	14	30.62
40	Wireless Communications	13	77.88
41	Textile Manufacturing	13	35.55

In Figure 27.3, more detail is added, displaying individual statistics for each company, and grouping the detail rows in alphabetical order by industry name. For this PivotTable, the data is arranged in report format, similar to the banded database reports Access and other database management programs produce. Note that this PivotTable includes four data items instead of two, and a slew of Excel formatting options are used to make the report more readable—changing fonts and font sizes, aligning type and adding background shading, and standardizing the number of decimal points in each column.

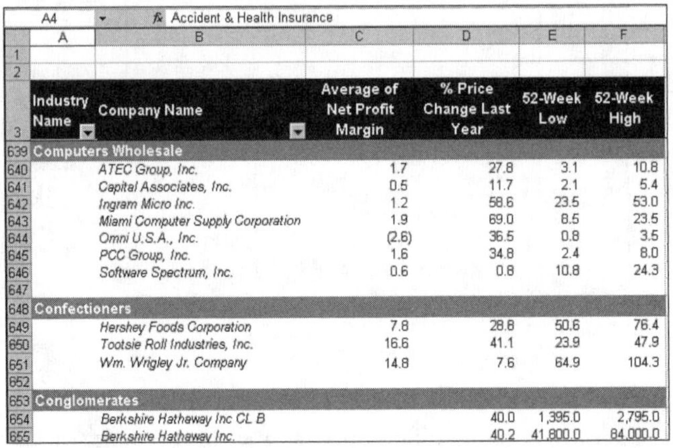

Figure 27.3
To hide gridlines and group-related items in bands such as these, choose a report format instead of the default table layout.

A4	▼	*fx* Accident & Health Insurance				
	A	B	C	D	E	F
1						
2						
3	Industry Name ▼	Company Name ▼	Average of Net Profit Margin	% Price Change Last Year	52-Week Low	52-Week High
639	Computers Wholesale					
640		ATEC Group, Inc.	1.7	27.8	3.1	10.8
641		Capital Associates, Inc.	0.5	11.7	2.1	5.4
642		Ingram Micro Inc.	1.2	58.6	23.5	53.0
643		Miami Computer Supply Corporation	1.9	69.0	8.5	23.5
644		Omni U.S.A., Inc.	(2.6)	36.5	0.8	3.5
645		PCC Group, Inc.	1.6	34.8	2.4	8.0
646		Software Spectrum, Inc.	0.6	0.8	10.8	24.3
647						
648	Confectioners					
649		Hershey Foods Corporation	7.8	28.8	50.6	76.4
650		Tootsie Roll Industries, Inc.	16.6	41.1	23.9	47.9
651		Wm. Wrigley Jr. Company	14.8	7.6	64.9	104.3
652						
653	Conglomerates					
654		Berkshire Hathaway Inc CL B		40.0	1,395.0	2,795.0
655		Berkshire Hathaway Inc.		40.2	41,800.0	64,000.0

→ For details on how to create similar reports from an Access database, **see** "Building Great Forms and Reports," **p. 883**.

To slice the data even more finely and add an extra analytical dimension, you can drag more buttons from the PivotTable toolbar to the row and column fields. Each row in the PivotTable is grouped using unique values in two categories, and there are two column headings as well, one for each unique value in the "Split in Last Year" column field. (To make the PivotTable easier to read, the column headings were renamed from Yes and No to Split and No Split.) At the intersection of each row and column in the PivotTable, Excel counts the number of companies and calculates the average income per employee for all rows that match the row and column fields.

The resulting PivotTable, shown in Figure 27.4, is a concise and crystal-clear cross-tabulation, giving you a side-by-side analysis of the number of stocks that split in the past year versus those that didn't, broken down by industry category and exchange.

There are literally hundreds of options in even a modestly complex PivotTable, but a PivotTable doesn't have to be large or complex to be effective. The PivotTable in Figure 27.5, for example, neatly summarizes all 37,400 data points in just a few rows and columns.

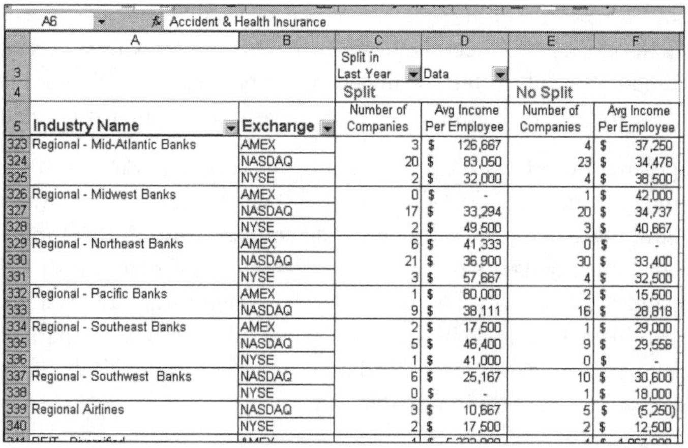

A6 | Accident & Health Insurance

	Industry Name	Exchange	Split: Number of Companies	Split: Avg Income Per Employee	No Split: Number of Companies	No Split: Avg Income Per Employee
323	Regional - Mid-Atlantic Banks	AMEX	3	$ 126,667	4	$ 37,250
324		NASDAQ	20	$ 83,050	23	$ 34,478
325		NYSE	2	$ 32,000	4	$ 38,500
326	Regional - Midwest Banks	AMEX	0	$ -	1	$ 42,000
327		NASDAQ	17	$ 33,294	20	$ 34,737
328		NYSE	2	$ 49,500	3	$ 40,667
329	Regional - Northeast Banks	AMEX	6	$ 41,333	0	$ -
330		NASDAQ	21	$ 36,900	30	$ 33,400
331		NYSE	3	$ 57,667	4	$ 32,500
332	Regional - Pacific Banks	AMEX	1	$ 80,000	2	$ 15,500
333		NASDAQ	9	$ 38,111	16	$ 28,818
334	Regional - Southeast Banks	AMEX	2	$ 17,500	1	$ 29,000
335		NASDAQ	5	$ 46,400	9	$ 29,556
336		NYSE	1	$ 41,000	0	$ -
337	Regional - Southwest Banks	NASDAQ	6	$ 25,167	10	$ 30,600
338		NYSE	0	$ -	1	$ 18,000
339	Regional Airlines	NASDAQ	3	$ 10,667	5	$ (5,250)
340		NYSE	2	$ 17,500	2	$ 12,500

Figure 27.4
Add a column field to quickly compare related data points. Notice that the worksheet pane is frozen to keep headings visible when scrolling, just as with an ordinary worksheet.

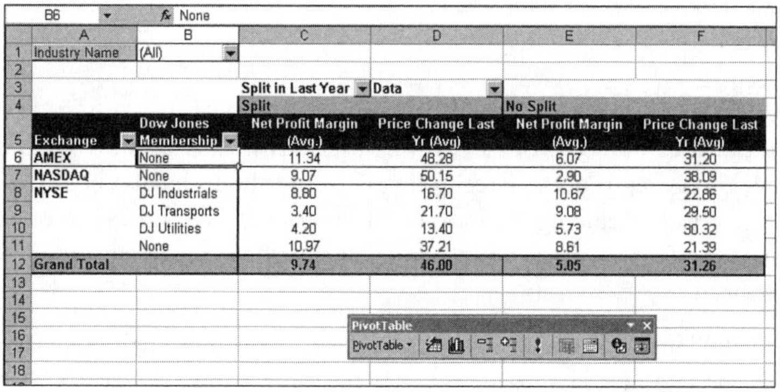

B6 | None

Industry Name: (All)

Exchange	Dow Jones Membership	Split: Net Profit Margin (Avg.)	Split: Price Change Last Yr (Avg)	No Split: Net Profit Margin (Avg.)	No Split: Price Change Last Yr (Avg)
AMEX	None	11.34	48.28	6.07	31.20
NASDAQ	None	9.07	50.15	2.90	38.09
NYSE	DJ Industrials	8.80	16.70	10.67	22.86
	DJ Transports	3.40	21.70	9.08	29.50
	DJ Utilities	4.20	13.40	5.73	30.32
	None	10.97	37.21	8.61	21.39
Grand Total		9.74	46.00	5.05	31.26

Figure 27.5
Notice the grand totals under the rows in this PivotTable. Use the page field in the top-left corner to filter the entire list.

To produce this example, we used two column fields, two row fields, and one page field—a drop-down list that lets us filter the records in the entire table. Choosing (All) from the page field shows a summary of all data in the list; by selecting a different entry from the drop-down list, you can show the same breakdown for each industry name. Select one category at a time to flip through a series of otherwise identical PivotTables that focus on each category.

The layout Excel produced automatically included totals for each row and column; we kept only the grand total at the bottom of the PivotTable. We had to modify other default settings as well, including changing the default formula to calculate the average of our data items. To make the headings and totals easier to read, we did some rewording, and then changed fonts and alignment, added shading, and wrapped text.

WHEN SHOULD YOU USE A PIVOTTABLE?

PivotTables have several advantages over other worksheet models. Using the PivotTable Wizard, it's easy to create a PivotTable that summarizes all or part of a list in dozens of different ways. Trying to accomplish the same task by entering formulas manually would take days. Also, because PivotTables and PivotCharts do not change your existing data or its arrangement on the worksheet, you can freely experiment with different PivotTable layouts. Use the Undo button to roll back any changes you make in a PivotTable layout. If you want to start over, you can delete the PivotTable page and run the wizard again.

PivotTables are the correct choice when all your data is in a list or in an external database you can query from Excel. PivotTables are not appropriate for structured worksheet models that include data-entry cells, subtotals, and summary rows. A PivotTable won't do much good on an annual budget worksheet, for example, because it already includes rows, columns, and subtotals. On the other hand, if you enter the raw data in a list (or import it from an external database), with each row containing a month, department, budget category, and amount, you can easily re-create that same layout in PivotTable form—and you'll have many more analytical options available to you later.

→ For more details on how to use Microsoft Query to pull data from an external database, **see** "Creating Links to External Databases," **p. 695**.

CREATING A PIVOTTABLE

To create a PivotTable from an existing list, start with Excel's PivotTable Wizard. In this simple three-step process, Excel prompts you for basic details about the PivotTable you want to create, including the location of the data source and where you want the PivotTable to appear. After you finish with the wizard, you'll be able to lay out your data directly on the worksheet.

Excel 2000 introduced the capability to create and edit a PivotTable layout directly on the sheet—an enormous improvement over the same feature in Excel 97, which required that you edit PivotTable layouts in a dialog box. The Layout dialog box is still available, however, and on slow machines or with extremely large lists, you might prefer to use this technique, because it doesn't actually begin rearranging data until you click OK. To open the Layout dialog box, click the Layout button in Step 3 of the PivotTable and PivotChart Wizard.

To build a new PivotTable, open the workbook that contains the list on which you plan to base the PivotTable. Then follow these steps:

1. Click anywhere in your list. To build a PivotTable from a subset of the data in your list, select the range that contains the data.

2. Choose Data, PivotTable and PivotChart Report. The PivotTable Wizard appears, as shown in Figure 27.6.

3. Specify the location of your data—typically an Excel list. If you choose the Multiple Consolidation Ranges option, Excel lets you select a group of data ranges from one or more worksheets. Click Next to move on.

Figure 27.6
If you don't select a range first, the PivotTable Wizard assumes you want to base the new PivotTable on the entire list. Change the selection, if necessary, in the next step.

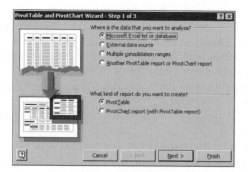

Using External Databases with PivotTables

In a corporate setting, it's often useful to base a PivotTable on the result of a query to an external database. If you choose the External Data Source option, Excel starts the Query Wizard and prompts you for details about the format and location of the database. Excel then uses this query as the source for the PivotTable or PivotChart. Each time you refresh the data in the PivotTable, Excel runs the saved query and updates the PivotTable with the most recent information.

Excel 2000 and 2002 also offer the option to build PivotTables from special data structures called On-Line Analytical Processing (OLAP) databases. Instead of rows and columns, these files organize data into dimensions and levels. Instead of forcing Excel to chug through massive amounts of data, the server does the summarizing first and sends the summary values directly to your report.

When you connect to an OLAP database, Excel lets you save your data in local files called *OLAP cubes* and use them as the source for a PivotTable. There are some substantial differences in the way PivotTables based on OLAP data work compared with those based on Excel lists or non-OLAP databases.

4. The wizard asks you to specify the range in which your data is located. The default selection is your current list, or any range you selected before starting the wizard. Adjust the selection, if necessary, and click Next.

 If the wizard starts in Step 3 instead of Step 1, see "Adding Extra PivotTables" in the "Troubleshooting" section at the end of this chapter.

5. In its final step, the wizard asks you where you want to place the PivotTable. Choose the default option, New Worksheet.

Caution

The PivotTable Wizard offers the option to place a PivotTable or PivotChart on an existing worksheet. In general, you should always choose to place a PivotTable on its own sheet. Adding a PivotTable to a sheet that contains data exposes you to the risk that changes you make to the list design will affect your PivotTable, or vice versa.

6. Click Finish to close the wizard and create a blank PivotTable page. Excel jumps to the new worksheet you just created and displays the PivotTable toolbar.

7. Drag field buttons from the PivotTable Field List and drop them into the appropriate regions in the layout. You must have at least one row or column field, and you must specify a data item.

PART

IV

CH

27

Tip from	If you're uncertain about exactly where to drop field buttons, watch the screen for two important clues. As the mouse pointer passes over each region of the PivotTable, Excel displays informative ScreenTips. When dragging fields around, watch the mouse pointer—it changes shape to match the PivotTable layout, and a blue highlight in the pointer shows which of the four regions (row, column, data, or page) is under the pointer at any given moment.

Don't be surprised if the PivotTable doesn't display properly at first. In particular, summary fields in the data area default to the SUM function. If you want to use COUNT, AVERAGE, or another summary function instead, see the next section.

EDITING AND UPDATING A PIVOTTABLE

After you create a PivotTable, it's easy to rearrange fields and data items. Drag fields from one place to another to change the display of data—from a row field to a column field, for example, if you want to see values side by side rather than one above the other. Right-click to display shortcut menus that let you adjust formatting and other options for each field. This section describes common procedures for editing PivotTables.

If you've upgraded from Excel 2000, you should notice a significant change in the arrangement of PivotTable editing tools. The assortment of menu options on the PivotTable toolbar is expanded, and the PivotTable Field List is now a separate control, as shown in Figure 27.7.

Figure 27.7
Bold type in the Field List indicates fields you've already placed on the PivotTable layout.

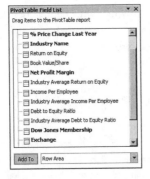

If you're uncomfortable with drag-and-drop operations, use the Add To drop-down list to choose where you want the field to appear. If the Field List isn't visible, right-click the PivotTable layout area and choose View Field List from the bottom of the shortcut menu. To make changes to the PivotTable report, use any or all of these techniques:

- To change the list or data source on which the PivotTable is based, click the PivotTable Wizard button on the PivotTable toolbar. Click Back twice to return to the beginning of the wizard and make the required changes, and then click Finish. If you add new rows or columns to a list, you might need to perform this step before the data or fields will be available.

⚠ *If you've added new fields or data to a list, but your PivotTable doesn't reflect the changes, see "Refresh to Update a PivotTable" in the "Troubleshooting" section at the end of this chapter.*

- To add a new field to the layout, drag a field button from the PivotTable toolbar and drop it on the layout. If you're replacing an existing field, remove the old field first to reduce unnecessary calculations. When you drop a new field in the row or column area, Excel adds it as part of the hierarchy of fields that are already there and automatically groups items in the order in which they appear. Be careful to arrange these fields in the proper order. For example, if you have a list of product categories, each of which contains multiple products, place the category field to the left of the product name field, or the results will be nonsense.

Tip from

EQ & Woody

If your list includes two fields that have an absolute one-to-one correspondence, such as part numbers and part names, you can add them to the row area in either order and your list will appear correctly.

- To remove a field from any part of the PivotTable layout, drag the field button off the layout; when the pointer icon changes to include a red X, release the mouse button.
- To change the order of fields in rows, columns, or the data area, drag the field button and drop it in the correct location on the layout. Make sure you're pointing to the field button and not its label; you'll know you've aimed correctly when the mouse button turns to a four-headed pointer. Drag to another location and watch the mouse pointer and thick black lines for feedback on the correct "drop" location.

Tip from

EQ & Woody

Using the mouse to rearrange the order of data items on a PivotTable can be frustrating. It's usually easier to right-click the field button you want to move, and then choose any of the options on the Order menu. Typically, you can move the item left or right one position, or move it to the beginning or end of the list.

- To change the summary function used in the data area (from SUM to COUNT or AVERAGE, for example), right-click the field button in the PivotTable and choose Field Settings from the shortcut menu. That action opens the PivotTable Field dialog box, shown in Figure 27.8. Select a function from the Summarize By list; if you want to change the name from its default, do so in the Name box, and then click OK to save the change.

Figure 27.8

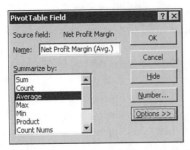

When you drag and drop buttons to arrange fields on a PivotTable page, Excel makes all sorts of decisions on your behalf. If these defaults aren't correct, the following sections will help you change them.

CHANGING SORT ORDER AND OTHER DISPLAY OPTIONS

The *default sort order* for rows and columns is usually alphanumeric. You can change the order of individual items by dragging them up or down (in the case of rows) or left or right (for columns). In other cases, you might want to adjust the default sort order. For example, if your PivotTable counts the number of items in each category, you might want to see categories with the highest number of items at the top of the list. To change the sort order, follow these steps:

1. Right-click the PivotTable button for the row or column field and choose Field Settings.

2. Click the Advanced button to display the dialog box shown in Figure 27.9.

Figure 27.9

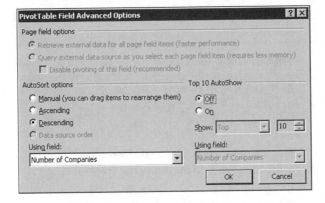

3. Choose a sort order and the column by which to sort. The settings in Figure 27.9, for example, produce the list shown earlier in Figure 27.2, moving categories that contain the largest number of companies to the top of the list.

4. To show a specific number of records, choose Automatic from the AutoShow options section. This is a good way to create a "top 10" list, for example, showing only the

categories that have the most items. Choose Top or Bottom from the Show drop-down list, and select a number between 1 and 255. Excel chooses records based on the sort order you defined in step 3.

→ AutoFilter can save a tremendous amount of time, if you know how to use it properly; **see** "Using AutoFilter to Find Sets of Data," **p. 684**.

5. Click OK to close the Advanced Options dialog box, and click OK again to close the PivotTable Field dialog box and return to the worksheet.

Adding and Removing Column and Row Subtotals

You can add subtotals to rows, columns, or both in a list. In some cases, Excel adds them automatically, even if they're not appropriate. Subtotals can add a useful way to see the impact of groupings in your PivotTable, or they can add clutter between rows and columns. Depending on the design of your PivotTable and what Excel did automatically, you might need to add or remove these subtotals. In some cases, you can remove subtotals with the right-click shortcut menu. Right-click any of the subtotals and choose Hide. To add subtotals, you need to use the dialog boxes. To work with subtotals, follow these steps

1. Right-click the PivotTable button for the row or column heading that contains the subtotal, and choose Field Settings from the shortcut menu. Excel displays the PivotTable Field dialog box, as shown in Figure 27.10.

Figure 27.10
Use the Subtotals options to add, edit, or hide subtotals for a row or column.

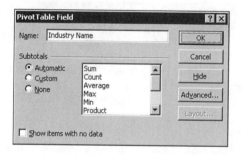

2. In the Subtotals section, choose Automatic to let Excel create subtotals for all items. Choose Custom and click a summary function to add one or more specific type of subtotals, such as Count and Average. Click None to remove all subtotals.

3. Click OK to exit the dialog box and make the changes you specified.

Switching Between Table and Outline Layouts

The default layout for a PivotTable, as the name implies, is a tabular format. But that grid-style arrangement is not always the most effective way to present data. When you're grouping a PivotTable by one row field and displaying data for a second row field, you probably want to use outline format instead; in that layout, the top-level row field appears in its own row, followed by each group of items. Which one should you choose? The question is partly dictated by the data in your table and partly by aesthetics; there is no right answer. Figure 27.11, for example, shows a table format. Figure 27.12 shows the same data arranged in outline format. In this case, the outline format is probably more appropriate, because each break in the grouping functions as a header for the list of details beneath it.

Industry Name	Company Name	Average of Net Profit Margin	% Price Change Last Year	52-Week Low	52-Week High
Accident & Health	Citizens Financial Corporation	12.5	86.5	5.6	30.3
	UNUM Corporation	8.3	4.8	40.9	59.6
Advertising Agencies	Cordiant Communications Group plc	0.6	70.1	5.4	24.5
	Lamar Advertising Company	(2.4)	71.1	17.7	41.5
	Leap Group, Inc.	(12.3)	1.2	0.9	7.9
	Obie Media Corporation	8.0	82.1	5.9	35.0
	Omnicom Group Inc.	7.1	47.8	32.8	58.4
	TMP Worldwide Inc.	4.1	32.0	15.0	39.2
	WPP Group plc	7.0	27.0	40.3	77.3
Aerospace/Defense - Major Diversified	General Dynamics Corporation	7.7	11.9	38.0	98.9
	Gulfstream Aerospace Corporation	12.6	19.6	26.5	51.5
	Sequa Corp CL A	1.7	21.3	52.9	75.9
	Sequa Corp CL B		33.8	59.0	85.8
	AAR CORP.	4.6	0.5	21.8	64.9
	Aerosonic Corporation	6.3	51.8	8.5	20.1

Figure 27.11
In tabular format view, the categories are arranged in a column to the left of the items to which they belong.

Industry Name	Company Name	Average of Net Profit Margin	% Price Change Last Year	52-Week Low	52-Week High
Accident & Health Insurance					
	Citizens Financial Corporation	12.5	86.5	5.6	30.3
	UNUM Corporation	8.3	4.8	40.9	59.6
Advertising Agencies					
	Cordiant Communications Group plc	0.6	70.1	5.4	24.5
	Lamar Advertising Company	(2.4)	71.1	17.7	41.5
	Leap Group, Inc.	(12.3)	1.2	0.9	7.9
	Obie Media Corporation	8.0	82.1	5.9	35.0
	Omnicom Group Inc.	7.1	47.8	32.8	58.4
	TMP Worldwide Inc.	4.1	32.0	15.0	39.2
	WPP Group plc	7.0	27.0	40.3	77.3
Aerospace/Defense - Major Diversified					
	General Dynamics Corporation	7.7	11.9	38.0	98.9
	Gulfstream Aerospace Corporation	12.6	19.6	26.5	51.5
	Sequa Corp CL A	1.7	21.3	52.9	75.9

Figure 27.12
In Outline view, the categories appear more like headers, and you can use space on the page or screen more efficiently.

To switch between tabular and outline formats, follow these steps:

1. Right-click the PivotTable button for the row field that's farthest to the left, and choose Field Settings from the shortcut menu.
2. In the PivotTable Field dialog box, click the Layout button to display the dialog box shown in Figure 27.13.

Figure 27.13

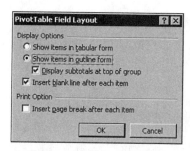

3. To use a tabular layout, select the Show Items in Tabular Form option. To use an outline-style layout, select the Show Items in Outline Form option.

4. Adjust any other options—to add a blank line or a page break after each group, for example—and click OK.

To make the tabular view in Figure 27.11 easier to read, a hidden option was used. Right-click anywhere on the table, choose Table Options, and then check the Merge Layout option. The effect is to merge all cells for the outside row and column labels.

Tip from

EQ & Woody

Excel includes a broad selection of PivotTable AutoFormats, divided more or less equally between table and outline (report) layouts. Use AutoFormats to quickly switch between table and outline layouts while also adjusting formatting options.

REMOVING BLANK CELLS AND ERROR MESSAGES

Because PivotTables automatically summarize all data, it's common to see blank cells and error messages in the data area. #DIV/0 errors, for example, are especially common when calculating averages because in a long list, it's almost certain that some items will have no matches in a particular row-and-column intersection. For example, if you're calculating average sales with regions in the column area and product categories in the row area, some regions will have no sales for a particular category. These aren't really errors; instead, you want the table to display a label such as NA, for "Not Applicable."

Careful attention to blanks and error messages can make your PivotTable easier to read and make it look more professional. Here's how to adjust the appearance of blank cells and errors:

1. Right-click any part of the PivotTable and choose Table Options from the shortcut menu. Excel displays the PivotTable Options dialog box, as shown in Figure 27.14.

PART
IV

CH
27

Figure 27.14
Use the options at the right of this dialog box to change the way a PivotTable displays blank cells and error messages.

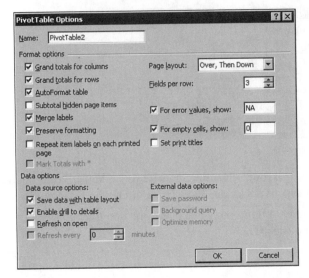

2. Select the For Error Values, Show check box. Click in the box to the right and fill in the information you want to display instead of the error message, such as NA.

3. Select the For Empty Cells, Show check box. If the field contains numeric data, enter 0 here; for a text field, enter the value you want Excel to display (NA, for instance) instead of leaving the cell blank.

4. Click OK to save your changes.

REFRESHING DATA IN A PIVOTTABLE

When you change the layout of a PivotTable, Excel automatically recalculates the resulting display of data. If you add or edit data in the underlying list, however, your changes do not appear immediately in the associated PivotTable. For PivotTable reports based on Excel lists, you must manually refresh the data in the PivotTable whenever you add, remove, or edit data. To be certain that the PivotTable reflects all recent changes, click the Refresh Data button on the PivotTable toolbar. If this toolbar isn't visible, choose Data, Refresh Data.

Tip from

EQ & Woody

For PivotTable reports based on external data queries, you should refresh the query every time you open the workbook to make sure the report is using the most current data. To automate the process of refreshing external queries, right-click anywhere on the PivotTable and choose Table Options from the shortcut menu. Select the Refresh on Open option to update the query every time you open the workbook that contains the PivotTable. Use the Refresh Every *n* Minutes option to automatically update the query at regular intervals.

CREATING AND EDITING PIVOTCHARTS

A PivotChart is a chart based on data in a PivotTable. Like its row-and-column-based counterpart, you can rearrange a PivotChart by dragging field labels on a chart sheet. When you change the layout of a PivotChart, Excel automatically rearranges the corresponding data in your PivotTable, and vice versa.

PivotCharts were introduced in Excel 2000, and they're a welcome addition. In general, anytime you can use a PivotChart instead of a conventional chart, you should jump at the opportunity, because they're so much easier to create and edit.

PivotCharts follow almost exactly the same rules as charts you create from a conventional worksheet. The default chart type for a PivotChart is a stacked column chart, but you can change this to any chart type except X-Y (scatter) charts, bubble charts, and stock chart types. Chart options are identical to those found in regular charts, although you'll discover that it's impossible to move certain items, including the plot area, chart title, and axis titles.

Note

> Every PivotChart requires a PivotTable, which it uses as its data source. You cannot create a PivotChart without adding a PivotTable to your worksheet as well.

To instantly create a PivotChart from an existing PivotTable, first click in the PivotTable, and then click the Chart Wizard button. (You'll find this button on Excel's Standard toolbar and on the PivotTable toolbar.) The PivotChart appears on a new chart sheet, as shown in Figure 27.15.

Figure 27.15
To change the layout of a PivotChart, drag field buttons from the toolbar and drop them on the appropriate area.

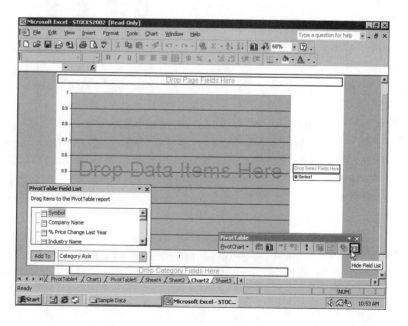

PART

IV

CH

27

Of course, a chart doesn't include rows or columns, so the available drop zones on a blank PivotChart page are slightly different from their counterparts on a PivotTable. When you create a PivotChart from a PivotTable, row fields become category fields, and column fields become series fields. To change the arrangement of data in the PivotChart, drag field buttons from the PivotTable toolbar and drop them in one of four areas on the PivotChart. Category fields go below the chart, and series fields appear at the right of the chart. Drop data items directly into the body of the chart. If you want to add a page field, drag it to the region above the chart. Page fields are especially effective on a PivotChart, because they allow you to chart a subset of your data without having to remove or change data series. Click the drop-down arrow to the right of the page field to choose which item you want to display in the chart. The chart shown in Figure 27.16, for example, allows you to quickly compare data for each company within an industry category. If you used the All option for this chart, the display of more than 2,200 companies would be gibberish.

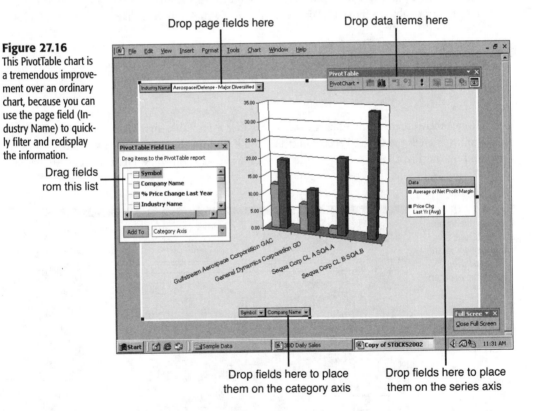

Figure 27.16
This PivotTable chart is a tremendous improvement over an ordinary chart, because you can use the page field (Industry Name) to quickly filter and redisplay the information.

Drop page fields here

Drop data items here

Drag fields from this list

Drop fields here to place them on the category axis

Drop fields here to place them on the series axis

With PivotCharts, you can use the same formatting and editing options as with conventional charts. In particular, use right-click shortcut menus to choose a different chart type; format data series, axes, and the plot area; and add or edit colors and backgrounds to your chart.

→ For instructions on how to edit charts, **see** "Editing and Formatting Chart Elements," **p. 662**.

FORMATTING AND PRINTING PIVOTTABLES

When you first create a PivotTable, it picks up the generic look of a default worksheet, with plain 10-point Arial formatting for details and headings alike. To make your PivotTable more compelling, use Excel's formatting features to add emphasis to text and backgrounds or shading to cells, rows, and columns. You can also adjust the number format of data items.

→ For an overview of Excel's many formatting options, **see** Chapter 22, "Advanced Worksheet Formatting," **p. 573**.

You can format numbers and text in the data area of a PivotTable by selecting cells individually and choosing formatting options as you would in a normal worksheet. However, if you redefine your PivotTable later, you will lose this formatting. That can be exasperating if you're constantly losing, say, the number of decimal points you want to see in each data item. To apply number formatting that lasts, right-click any cell in the data items area and choose Field Settings from the shortcut menu. Click the Number button and choose a format from the dialog box.

Tip from

EQ & Woody

When you create a PivotTable or PivotChart on a new worksheet, Excel assigns a generic name to the new sheet. To make your worksheets easier to understand, right-click the tab, choose Rename, and give the sheet a new name that helps identify it. (You can also double-click the existing tab name to make it available for editing.) Right-click the PivotTable itself and choose Table Options to give the PivotTable itself a name, which you can use in dialog boxes and in the PivotTable Wizard.

Sometimes you need to adjust other formatting options as well. For example, you might want to change the alignment of a column of numbers, change to a new font, or add a background shade behind the column. Here, too, you have two options: If you right-click the cells in question and choose Format Cells, you'll have access to all common cell formatting options—Number, Alignment, Font, and so on. But as soon as you rearrange your PivotTable, those custom formats vanish.

To lock cell formatting in place regardless of what you do with your PivotTable, right-click the PivotTable button for the field you want to format and choose Format Cells from the shortcut menu. Adjust desired formatting options and click OK.

To make PivotTables look their best, take advantage of Excel's AutoFormat capability. After you've created a PivotTable, click the Format Report button on the PivotTable toolbar. You see a dialog box containing more than 20 ready-made formats. Select any format and click OK to apply the changes to your PivotTable.

If you don't like the AutoFormat you've applied to a PivotTable, it's easy to undo the changes. First, right-click any cell in the PivotTable, choose Table Options from the shortcut menu, and clear the check mark from the AutoFormat Table check box. Next, click the Format Report button to open the AutoFormat dialog box again. Scroll to the bottom of the list. Select the None option and click OK.

TROUBLESHOOTING

ADDING EXTRA PIVOTTABLES

I wanted to create a new PivotTable, so I chose Data, PivotTable and PivotChart Report. Instead of starting at the beginning of the wizard, however, Excel started at the third step. Why is this happening?

You've already created a PivotTable in your worksheet. Because the active cell is within that PivotTable, Excel assumes you want to use the wizard to modify the existing table. To create a new PivotTable, switch to the sheet that contains the list of data you want to use. If you want to create a second or third PivotTable based on the same data as another PivotTable, choose the Another PivotTable or PivotChart option in Step 1; doing so conserves memory and improves performance.

REFRESH TO UPDATE A PIVOTTABLE

I've updated data in the list on which my PivotTable is based, but when I view the PivotTable, I don't see the changes. What's wrong?

Click in the PivotTable, rerun the PivotTable Wizard, and check the data source shown in Step 1 to make sure the data source is specified correctly. If you've changed data in the table, you might need to refresh the PivotTable manually—PivotTables don't automatically update with those changes. Position the insertion point anywhere in the PivotTable, right-click, and choose Refresh Data from the shortcut menu. When the data updates, Excel displays a dialog box warning you that the data has changed.

If you've added new fields to the list, those fields might not show up on the PivotTable toolbar until you refresh.

SECRETS OF THE OFFICE MASTERS: GROUPING ITEMS IN A PIVOTTABLE

Excel PivotTables are capable of splitting data into groups, even when you haven't organized your data in advance. This is a powerful feature that's useful in a variety of circumstances. When you choose to group data in a PivotTable, Excel analyzes the field you've chosen and displays a dialog box with choices that are appropriate for that type of data. For example, if you have a year's worth of daily sales figures, you might want to group them by week, by month, or by quarter. If you have a product catalog in which each row contains a product name, its category, and a price, you might want to group the list of products by category, and then by price within groups: $1.00–$10.00, $10.01–$20.00, and so on.

In the example shown here, a simple worksheet has just two columns: Date and Sales Volume. Each row contains a date and the total sales for that date, in dollars. In total, the sheet contains three years' worth of data. Here's how to create a report that shows monthly trends for all three years:

1. Create a PivotTable using the Date field in the Row area and the Sales Volume field in the Data area.

2. Right-click any entry in the Date column and choose Group and Outline, Group from the shortcut menu. Note that Excel correctly determines these are dates and offers to group by month. Because the sample extends over several years, choose Months and Years, and then click OK.

3. Drag two more copies of the Sales Volume button into the Data area and format each one to show a different summary: Sum, Average, and Min. Adjust the names of each summary as well. This step allows you to see the total sales, average sales, and minimum daily sales for each month during the three-year period.

4. Use the AutoFormat option to choose one of the Report formats. Adjust column formatting and number formats for each summary cell.

The results, shown in the following Figure, give a month-by-month snapshot of total sales, even though we started with nothing more than a daily list.

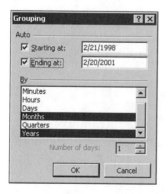

Notice the final frill in this useful table: We hid the taskbar and chose View, Full Screen to make as much information as possible visible on the screen, hiding distracting toolbars and title bars.

File   Edit   View   Insert   Format   Tools   Data   Window   Help   _ ☐ ×

	A	B	C	D	E	F	G
3	Years ▾	Date ▾	Total Monthly Sales	Average Sales Volume	Lowest Sales Volume		
28		Nov	$394,895.51	$19,744.78	$12,960.00		
29		Dec	$456,434.69	$21,734.99	$10,853.24		
31	**2000**						
32		Jan	$317,149.96	$13,789.13	$9,768.17		
33		Feb	$202,268.42	$10,645.71	$6,525.70		
34		Mar	$241,356.95	$10,970.77	$6,532.98		
35		Apr	$228,593.20	$10,885.39	$5,759.57		
36		May	$235,633.96	$11,220.66	$4,896.18		
37		Jun	$314,546.45	$14,297.57	$7,367.43		
38		Jul	$335,077.44	$15,956.07	$3,055.83		
39		Aug	$180,027.59	$9,475.14	$6,659.13		
40		Sep	$220,204.22	$10,485.92	$5,037.27		
41		Oct	$212,045.15	$9,638.42	$5,587.43		
42		Nov	$149,435.46	$7,471.77	$4,579.93		
43		Dec	$168,433.97	$7,656.09	$4,801.81		
45	**2001**						
46		Jan	$189,877.97	$9,041.81	$5,994.03		
47		Feb	$114,255.88	$8,161.13	$5,964.33		
48							
49	**Grand Total**		**$9,922,762.40**	**$13,090.72**	**$1,754.56**		
50							

Data / Chart2 \ **Daily CrossTab Report** / Sheet2 / Chart1 / Sheet3 /

Using PowerPoint

CHAPTER **28**

PowerPoint Essentials

In this chapter

ANATOMY OF A POWERPOINT PRESENTATION

Putting together a basic PowerPoint presentation takes little more than the spark of an idea and a few minutes with the AutoContent Wizard. Assembling an effective, persuasive presentation, on the other hand, demands much more.

Although the next few chapters deal with the mechanics of creating a dynamite presentation, one thought should remain uppermost in your mind: Content rules. A poorly conceived and executed PowerPoint presentation will leave your audience cold, no matter how many fancy transitions, animations, or Web links you employ. Conversely, a compelling story, well told, will stick with your audience even if it's presented exclusively in 14-point Times New Roman.

Note

> Although PowerPoint can help you create effective presentations, becoming a better public speaker is largely up to you. If you want to hone your presentation skills, we recommend picking up a copy of *Special Edition Using Microsoft PowerPoint 2002* by Patrice Rutledge (also by Que, ISBN: 0-7897-2519-3).

Figure 28.1 illustrates the basic components of a PowerPoint presentation—slides, notes, and a panel on the left side that can be switched between a text outline and slide thumbnails.

Figure 28.1
PowerPoint's Normal view includes most of the information you need to assemble a presentation.

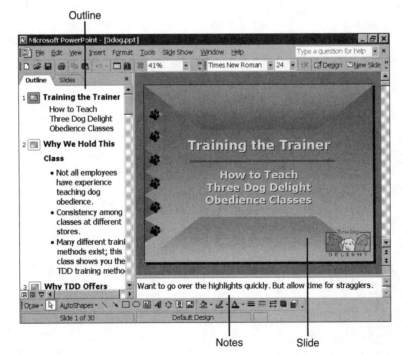

A fully loaded slide (see Figure 28.2) has at most six parts:

Figure 28.2
All the components of a PowerPoint slide are shown here, with slide thumbnails in place of a text outline.

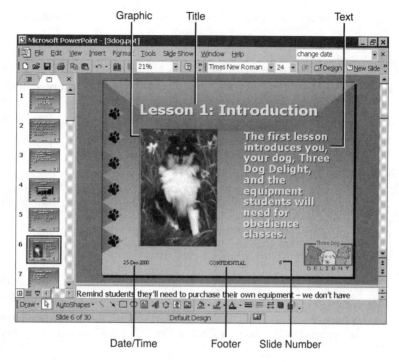

- The *title*, which usually sits at the top of the slide.
- *Body text*, the main part of the slide. The text on a slide frequently appears as a series of bulleted or numbered phrases. In fact, any kind of text can appear in this part of a slide—bullets and numbers are not required. The text sits inside a resizable and movable container, called a *placeholder*, which you can see if you click any of the bulleted text in the slide pane.

Note

PowerPoint help screens sometimes refer to the text and its surrounding placeholder as a "text object."

- Some slides contain one or more *graphics*—pictures or video clips that, in the best circumstances, serve to illuminate your presentation. Each graphic resides in its own resizable placeholder, too.

Note

You will also see references to "graphic objects" in the online help. The term is meant to include a graphic and its surrounding placeholder.

PART

V

CH

28

- The *date and time* which, if they show up on the slide at all, generally appear at the lower-left corner.
- The *footer* usually appears at the bottom of the slide, in the middle.
- And finally, a *slide number* might sit in the lower-right corner.

Most presentations begin with a *title slide*, which includes the title of the presentation, the speaker's name, and other introductory details. Other slides in a presentation can also be title slides—you might use a title slide to introduce different portions of a long presentation, for example—but in most cases, you'll have just one title slide in a presentation, and it will serve as the first slide.

> **Note**
>
> Don't be confused by the terminology. A *title slide* is, in most cases, a slide that introduces a presentation. A *slide title*, on the other hand, is usually the first line on a slide.

FILE COMPATIBILITY ISSUES

Microsoft changed the format of PowerPoint presentation files between PowerPoint 95 and PowerPoint 97. PowerPoint 2000 and PowerPoint 97 use the same file format. Using PowerPoint 2002, you can open and edit files created in any version of PowerPoint; however, files created in PowerPoint 2000 or PowerPoint 97 cannot be opened in PowerPoint 95.

If you need to share files with users of PowerPoint 95, you must save them in an alternate format. To do so, choose File, Save As and select PowerPoint 97-2002 & 95 Presentation (*.ppt) in the Save as Type box. When you choose this option, PowerPoint saves two copies of your presentation in the same file—one in PowerPoint 95 format, the other in PowerPoint 2000 format—and anyone can open, view, and edit the presentation by using PowerPoint 95, 97, 2000, or 2002.

 When you save a PowerPoint 2002 presentation in PowerPoint 95 format, you lose many components of your presentation. Animated chart elements, hyperlinks, and macros, among other elements, all disappear. In addition, file size usually swells: PowerPoint 95 has comparatively crude picture-compression capabilities. See "PowerPoint 2000-97 & 95 Format Changes" in the "Troubleshooting" section at the end of this chapter.

CREATING A PRESENTATION

When PowerPoint starts, it presents you with a variety of options for creating or opening presentations (see Figure 28.3).

Figure 28.3
PowerPoint lets you choose whether you want to open an existing presentation, create a new presentation with or without content, or pull in a template.

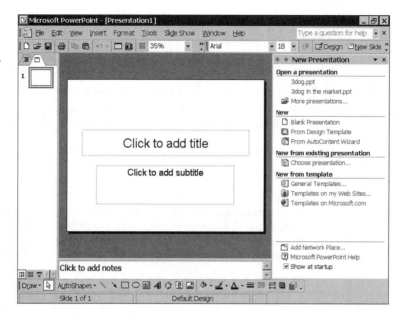

CREATING A BLANK PRESENTATION

When you create a new, blank presentation—by choosing Blank Presentation in the New Presentation pane (refer to Figure 28.3); by choosing File, New; or by clicking the New icon on the Standard toolbar—PowerPoint generates a new presentation and places you in the Slide Layout pane (see Figure 28.4).

Figure 28.4
Whenever you have a new, blank slide, PowerPoint prompts you to pick a slide layout and to determine which placeholders will go on a slide and where they will sit.

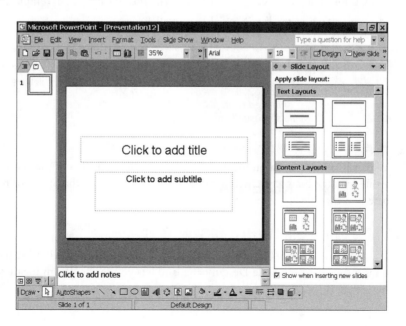

PART
V

CH
28

Like the Design Template approach mentioned in the preceding section, PowerPoint starts with a single slide. You have to choose what kind of slide you want by using the choices in the Slide Layout pane.

→ For tips on negotiating the layout maze, **see** "Picking the Best Slide Layout," **p. 769**.

Unlike the Design Template approach—which leaves you with something resembling a respectable slide—this blank PowerPoint presentation starts with a white background, Arial 44- and 32-point (for titles and body text, respectively), and standard, dull, round bullets.

To apply a new design to any presentation, click the Design icon on the Formatting toolbar, and the Slide Design pane (see Figure 28.5) appears.

Tip from
EQ & Woody

PowerPoint doesn't install all of its Design Templates unless you specifically ask for them. To pull all the templates off the Office installation CD, go into the Slide Design pane, scroll all the way to the bottom of the Apply a Design Template box, and click Install More Templates. Have your Office CD handy.

If your company has certain standards for all presentations—logo in a specific location, identification of title slides, and so on—you might want to change PowerPoint's "blank" presentation so it reflects your standards.

To replace the PowerPoint default blank presentation with one of your own design, follow these steps:

1. Create the presentation you want to use as the "blank" presentation.
2. Choose File, Save As. In the Save as Type box, click Design Template.
3. Type Blank in the File Name box and click Save.

Tip from
EQ & Woody

To make this change for all the users in your organization, you must create a Blank Presentation design template file for each user and place it in the correct custom template folder.

→ For details on organizing files, **see** "Creating New Files," **p. 61**.

With a Blank Presentation file in the correct location, all "blank" presentations—whether created via the New Presentation pane or the New icon on the Standard toolbar—will be based on that file.

STARTING POWERPOINT WITH A DESIGN TEMPLATE

If you choose Design Template from the PowerPoint New Presentation pane, PowerPoint transports you to the Slide Design pane, and lets you pick a design for the presentation (see Figure 28.5).

A *design*, in this case, includes a background, font specifications for the title slide and other slides in the presentation, default bullets, and a handful of lesser settings—title locations, footers, slide numbering, and the like.

If you choose Apply to All Slides, PowerPoint sets things up so the single slide in your new presentation, which you can see in the large window, has the desired design, as well as any new slides you might add.

Figure 28.5
Creating a new presentation from a Design Template leaves you with a single slide, but all new slides will take on the same design.

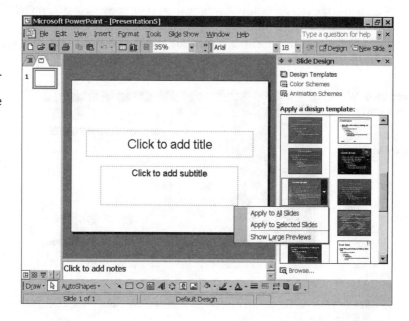

Tip from

Several design templates were lost in the transition from PowerPoint 97 to PowerPoint 2002. If you can't find your favorite "classic" template in PowerPoint 2002's current lineup, check the Office update Web site, officeupdate.microsoft.com, for links to all the old designs.

ADDING YOUR OWN PRESENTATIONS TO THE AUTOCONTENT WIZARD

PowerPoint ships with dozens of prefabricated presentations, many of which combine decent visual effects with reasonable suggestions for presenting your own content. The AutoContent Wizard guides you through creating presentations conforming to the built-in templates.

Although PowerPoint ships with great templates (providing they cover the topic you want), most advanced PowerPoint users will find that their own custom presentations provide a better starting point.

PART
V

CH
28

You can add your own presentations to the AutoContent Wizard by following these steps:

1. Create and save a presentation that you want to put in the AutoContent Wizard. (In particular, you can start with one of PowerPoint's built-in presentations, available by choosing File, New, and selecting from the files listed on the Presentations tab.) You can save it in either Presentation format (*.ppt) or Design Template format (*.pot).

2. Start the AutoContent Wizard by clicking From AutoContent Wizard on the New Presentation pane (refer to Figure 28.3).

3. Click Next to jump to the second step, Presentation type.

4. Choose the category most appropriate to your presentation. General, Corporate, Projects, and Sales/Marketing work; All and Carnegie Coach do not—no doubt because "All" includes all presentations present, and the Carnegie presentations are under license. Click Add (see Figure 28.6).

Figure 28.6
Add your own presentations to the AutoContent Wizard using the Add button here.

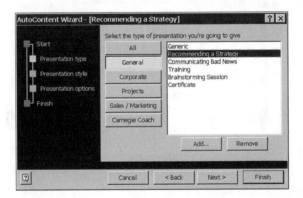

5. Select your presentation or design template file, and click OK. When you return to the wizard, click Cancel.

Presentations added in this manner work just like the built-in templates, except the full filename, including the .ppt or .pot filename extension, appears in the wizard's second pane.

RETRIEVING CLASSIC MICROSOFT TEMPLATES

Experienced PowerPoint 2000 users might discover that not all the templates they've seen in previous versions ship with 2002. That's by design—Microsoft is constantly picking and pruning the template collection, shipping only the ones felt to be most popular.

Additional templates, including many of the "classic" templates you might remember from earlier versions of PowerPoint, are on the Microsoft Web site. To get there, choose Help, Office on the Web, and follow the links to the PowerPoint templates.

COPYING THE DESIGN OF AN EXISTING PRESENTATION

Frequently, you'll find an existing presentation with just the right design elements, even if the content is completely different from what you need.

PowerPoint makes it easy to recycle the design of an existing presentation, providing you have the original presentation file, and you can "borrow" the design without changing the content of your presentation in any way.

Just choose Format, Apply Design Template. In the Files of Type box, scroll down to Presentations and Shows. Choose the presentation you like, and click Apply.

The design of the chosen presentation is applied automatically to your current presentation.

IMPORTING FROM A WORD OUTLINE

How many times have you been asked to give a presentation based on an existing report or other document? If you can import the document into Word and convert its headings to Word's default "Heading 1" style, the rest is a snap.

Outlines in Word can be imported directly into PowerPoint in either of two ways. From inside Word, choose File, Send To, Microsoft PowerPoint. From inside PowerPoint, choose File, Open, and in the Files of Type box choose All Outlines, as shown in Figure 28.7.

Figure 28.7
Import outlines from other documents in the Open dialog box.

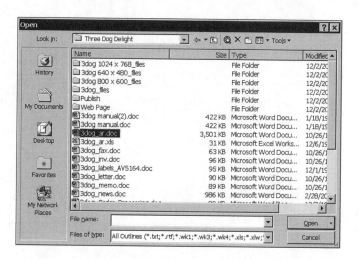

When you import a Word document, Level 1 headings (formatted "Heading 1" in Word) turn into the titles of new slides. Level 2 headings turn into top-level bullet points. Level 3 headings become second-level bullet points, and so on. In essence, the outline that you see in Word's Outline view is translated into a PowerPoint outline.

Each time PowerPoint encounters a level 1 heading in Word, it starts a new slide and uses the level 1 heading text for the slide's title.

PART
V

CH
28

> **Note**
>
> In other words, your presentation will include exactly one slide for each level 1 heading in the Word document.

You can insert an outline into the middle of an existing presentation. Select the slide you want the outline to follow, and then choose Insert, Slides from Outline. PowerPoint offers to insert an outline (refer to Figure 28.7), and the inserted outline appears as slides after the selected slide.

VIEWING A PRESENTATION

It's never been easier to stay on top of your PowerPoint presentation. PowerPoint 2002 allows you to see either a text outline of your presentation or thumbnails of all the slides in the left-most pane. The current slide appears in the main pane, and the slide's notes sit below (see Figure 28.8).

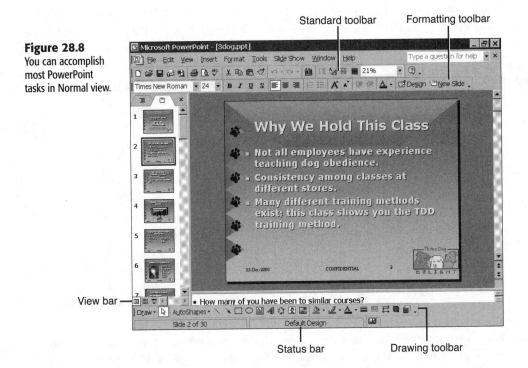

Figure 28.8
You can accomplish most PowerPoint tasks in Normal view.

PowerPoint starts in Normal view. You can return to this view at any time by choosing View, Normal, or by selecting the Normal View icon on the View Bar.

Normal view includes the presentation's outline in the left pane, a preview of the current slide in the upper-right pane, and speaker notes at the bottom right. Click and drag on the edge of any pane to resize that portion of the view.

Tip from

EQ & Woody

> The outline and notes that appear in Normal view's two respective panes aren't formatted correctly. For example, if you have a bold word in a particular slide's title, that formatting does not appear in Normal view's outline pane.
>
> To force the outline and notes panes to display formatting correctly, click the Show Formatting icon on the Standard toolbar.

Although Normal view gives quick and easy access to most of the options you'll typically want to use, each of the individual views available via the View Bar comes in handy for specific tasks.

ORGANIZING IDEAS IN THE OUTLINE PANE

You can do most of the important work on a presentation—that is, content, content, content—without ever leaving the outline pane.

Tip from

EQ & Woody

> The Outline pane becomes much more useful when it's accompanied by the Outlining toolbar: Choose Tools, Customize, Toolbars, select the Outlining check box, and click OK.

Any text you type in the outline pane immediately to the right of a slide number becomes the title of the slide; subsequent outline points turn into bulleted items in the slide's text placeholder. Highlight, click, and drag to move outline text or entire slides. To select an entire slide, move the mouse pointer under the slide number until it turns into a "northwest arrow"—meaning that the arrow points upward and to the left. Click and the slide is selected.

→ Details on setting outline levels are given in the next chapter; **see** "Editing Slides," **p. 772**.

USING SLIDE SORTER VIEW TO REARRANGE A PRESENTATION

Slide Sorter view (see Figure 28.9) gives you an opportunity to see the entire presentation all at once, move slides around, control the transition effects that bind the slides and animation together on an individual slide, and perform easy, one-click previews of animations and transitions.

Move to Slide Sorter view by selecting the Slide Sorter view icon in the View Bar, or by choosing View, Slide Sorter.

PowerPoint transitions control how a slide makes its appearance onscreen. Animations, on the other hand, control how components of the slide appear, after the slide is onscreen.

Bring up the Slide Transition pane by choosing the Transition icon on the Slide Sorter toolbar. Or, you can bring up the Animation schemes on the Slide Design pane by clicking the Design icon on the Slide Sorter toolbar and then choosing Animation schemes.

PART
V

CH
28

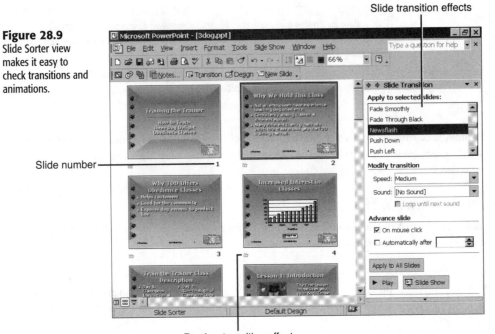

Slide transition effects

Figure 28.9
Slide Sorter view makes it easy to check transitions and animations.

Slide number —

Preview transition effect

Slide Sorter view is the easiest place to

- **Rearrange slides**—Just click and drag.
- **Add slides**—Click in the space between two slides and select Insert, New Slide.
- **Delete slides**—Click a single slide or hold down the Ctrl key and click several slides, and then press the Delete key.
- **Set transition effects**—Click a slide or hold down the Ctrl key and click several slides, and then use the Slide Transition pane to pick and fine-tune the transition you like.
- **Preview transition effects**—Click the Preview button to the left of the slide number, or click Play at the bottom of the Slide Transition pane.
- **Apply a built-in PowerPoint animation to the contents of the slide**—Click a slide or Ctrl+click several slides, and then use the Slide Design pane's Animation Schemes list to pick the animation you like, or the Custom Animation pane to build an animation from the ground up.

Previewing Your Slides in Slide Show View

At any point in the process of developing a presentation, you can preview the show itself.

To see the presentation starting with the currently selected slide, just pick a slide (in any view) and click the Slide Show View icon on the View Bar. This starts the show and all the usual show navigation techniques apply (for example, click to advance the slide, press Esc to exit). When the show is over, you return to the view you were using before starting the slide show.

Tip from

EQ & Woody

> If you want to see the entire presentation, starting with the first slide, click Slide Show, View Show. Alternatively, press F5. Again, you return to the original view after the show is done.

ADDING NOTES

The simplest way to add or modify notes is via the Normal or Outline views, where the notes pane can be expanded if necessary to accommodate lengthy notes.

PowerPoint has a Notes view (also called Notes Page view) although, oddly, you can't get to it via a button on the View Bar. Instead, you have to choose View, Notes Page (see Figure 28.10.)

Figure 28.10
Notes view shows one slide at a time, and the notes attached to that single slide.

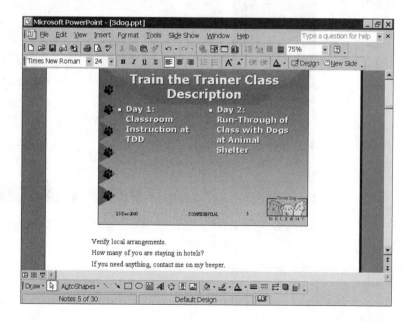

If the notes for any particular slide extend beyond one page, Notes view expands the text area downward to accept what you type. If you print the notes for that particular slide, however, they'll be truncated at one page. Multipage notes appear in Normal view.

Although the text formatting in Normal views' notes pane might not be correct, it should appear correctly in Notes view.

Caution

Trying to export multipage notes to Word (choose File, Send To, Microsoft Word) might trigger a *general protection fault* (GPF) error, meaning that PowerPoint could crash and cause you to lose your presentation. Always save your presentation before attempting this operation.

VIEWING PRESENTATIONS IN A WEB BROWSER

If you save your presentation as a Web page, either on the World Wide Web, or on your company's intranet, the entire presentation can be viewed with a Web browser (see Figure 28.11). The person looking at your presentation need not have PowerPoint installed to see all the details and navigate the presentation fully.

Figure 28.11
This PowerPoint presentation is being viewed through Internet Explorer 5.5.

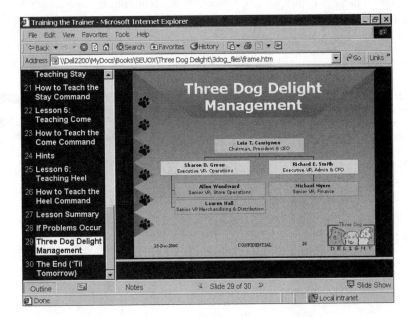

→ For details on viewing your HTML-based presentation, **see** "Using a Browser for Your Presentation," **p. 845**.

To get full effect of the browser-viewing option, the person viewing the presentation should be running Internet Explorer version 4 or later, or Netscape Navigator version 4 or later. Although you can create presentations that show up on earlier versions of both browsers, there are extensive limitations on what they can do.

This browser-viewing capability might not perform precisely the way you expect. In particular, you might be disappointed with the way diagonal lines (for example, in AutoShape callouts), WordArt, and Organization Charts appear when viewed from a browser (refer to Figure 28.11 for an example).

Before you expend a lot of effort developing a presentation for the Web, flesh out a few of the most complex graphics, stick them in a slide, and choose File, Web Page Preview. That will give you a good indication of how the final presentation will appear, at least when using the browser installed on your PC.

MANAGING SLIDE SHOWS

PowerPoint has several useful tools and techniques you can use to manage presentations. If you work in Slide Sorter view, it's easy to copy, move, insert, or delete slides. But there are some tricks. To paste a slide at the beginning of a presentation, go into Slide Sorter view and click to the left of the first slide, and then paste.

If you want to copy slides from one presentation and put them in another, select the slide you want the imported slides to appear after (in Slide Sorter view, click between the slides), and then choose Insert, Slides from Files. The Slide Finder dialog box appears, as shown in Figure 28.12.

Figure 28.12
Slide Finder lets you pick and choose which slides to copy into the current presentation.

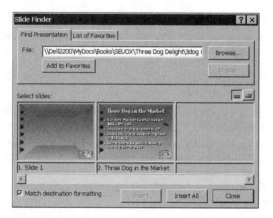

Find the file containing the slides you want to copy, and then click the Display button. Click each slide in turn and click Insert.

The Slide Finder's List of Favorites tab is maintained independently of Windows' (and Office's) Favorites folder.

Caution

When you bring a slide into a presentation via the Slide Finder, and you have the Match Destination Formatting box checked, PowerPoint modifies each slide to take on the design of the current presentation. That certainly changes the background of the imported slides; it might also change fonts, bullets, and much more, and imported hyperlinks might not behave as expected.

Check immediately after importing slides in this manner to make sure that the imported slides hold no surprises.

PowerPoint lets you mark specific slides as *hidden*. Hidden slides appear in all views except Slide Show view and they don't show up when the presentation is run.

To hide a slide, go into Slide Sorter view, select the slide to be hidden, and click the Hide Slide icon. You'll know that the slide won't be shown in the presentation because a "not" sign appears over the slide number.

Caution

You can hide slides while working in other views—select the slide, and then choose Slide Show, Hide Slide. When you use this technique, Normal View will show the slide number with a slash through it. That tells you the slide is hidden.

When you add a new slide to a presentation, you must specify what kind of slide you want (unless you paste one in). To specify the type of new slide, choose a *thumbnail* sketch from the Slide Layout pane (refer to Figure 28.6).

→ For tips on getting the slide layout right, **see** "Picking the Best Slide Layout," **p. 769**.

If you deliver PowerPoint presentations regularly, you might have a main presentation that needs only a bit of tweaking for use with a variety of audiences. For example, you might have one version for executives and a slightly different version for technical professionals. PowerPoint makes it easy to keep all your slides together in one file, but build separate, custom slide shows for specific audiences.

To create a custom show, choose Slide Show, Custom Shows, New. The Define Custom Show dialog box appears, as shown in Figure 28.13.

Select the slides you want to appear in the custom show and click Add. Note that you can move a slide—so it appears in a different sequence in the custom show—by clicking the up arrow or down arrow. Type in a name for the custom show, and click OK.

To preview a custom show, click the name of the show and click Show.

Move to the slide in your presentation where you want to branch out to one of these custom shows. Select a location for the link (perhaps in the body text, or in a drawing), and click the Hyperlink icon. In Link To, pick Existing File or Web Page. Type the text you want to have displayed on the slide, and click Bookmark, as shown in Figure 28.14. The Select Place in Document dialog box appears.

Figure 28.13
Pick and arrange existing slides to be incorporated in a custom show.

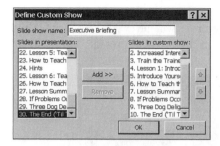

Figure 28.14
Hyperlink to one of the custom shows—for example, Executive Briefing.

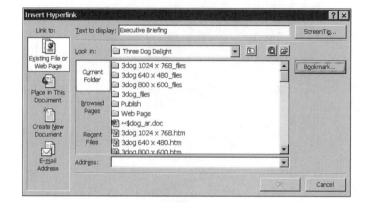

Choose the custom show you want to link to, and click OK. From that point on, whenever you encounter the slide with the hyperlink, click it to display the custom show.

Note that there is no automatic facility to "return to the main presentation" after a custom show is over. For that reason, you might find it easiest to put all the remaining slides in a presentation in your custom show.

Tip from

Alternatively, you can create a hyperlink on the last slide in the custom show to take you back to whatever point in the main presentation you like.

→ For details about hyperlinking inside your presentation, **see** "Using Hyperlinks," **p. 763**.

You can tell PowerPoint that you want it to run a custom show, instead of the "normal" show, whenever you start a slide show. To do so, choose Slide Show, Set Up Show and the Set Up Show dialog box appears (see Figure 28.15). Select the custom show you like in the Custom Show box in the Show Slides area.

Custom shows can be a powerful feature. For example, you can put all your slides relating to a given topic inside one PowerPoint file, and then pick and choose the slides you want to give for your main presentation. Set up a custom show called Main, and then choose Main as the default show in the dialog box shown in Figure 28.15. That way, all your slides stay in one .ppt file, the Main presentation runs whenever you start a slide show, and you can easily and quickly add and remove slides from the Main presentation.

Figure 28.15
Have PowerPoint run a custom show automatically by using the Custom Show setting.

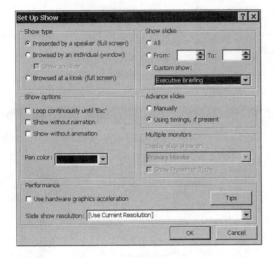

NAVIGATING THROUGH A PRESENTATION

PowerPoint presents myriad ways to navigate in a presentation.

MOUSE AND KEYBOARD SHORTCUTS

In addition to the navigation methods you've probably used (left mouse button to advance, Backspace key to back up, Esc to end), PowerPoint also supports a wide variety of mouse and keyboard shortcuts:

- To advance from one slide to another, or perform the next animation on the current slide, you can click the left mouse button—but you can also press Enter, N (for Next), page down, right arrow, down arrow, or the spacebar. You can also right-click the screen during a presentation and choose Next.

- To move to the previous slide, or activate the preceding animation on the current slide, you can press Backspace—but you can also try P (for Previous), page up, left arrow, or the up arrow. Or you can right-click the screen and choose Previous.

- To end a presentation, in addition to the Esc key, you can right-click and choose End Show.

An almost-complete list of navigation controls is available by right-clicking the screen during a presentation and choosing Help, by pressing F1, or by referring to the Help topic "Slide Show Controls." Most of the controls are obscure, but a few might be worth memorizing:

- B (for Black) or pressing the period key toggles between displaying a black screen and showing the current slide
- Similarly, W (for white) or pressing the comma key toggles a white screen
- Tab cycles among all the hyperlinks on a slide

This doesn't appear to be documented anywhere, but pressing the Home key during a presentation returns you to the first slide.

Tip from

E Q & Woody

Similarly (and this one doesn't appear to be documented anywhere, either), pressing the End key sends you to the final slide.

USING HYPERLINKS

Hyperlinks allow you to turn text, graphics, pictures, or almost anything else on a slide, into a "hot" link. Those hot links can point just about anywhere—a specific slide, the first or last slide in a presentation, the next or previous slides, files (whether on the local hard drive, or accessible through the network), specific locations inside Word documents or Excel workbooks, and much more. As shown previously in Figure 28.14, you can even link to a custom show within the current presentation, by using the Bookmark button in the Insert Hyperlink dialog box.

If the PC you're using for the presentation is connected to the Web (or if the presentation itself is on the Web), hyperlinks can also connect to Web pages.

The easiest way to establish a hyperlink is to start by selecting whatever you want to hyperlink from (that is, the text, drawing, picture, and so on, that will be "hot" during the presentation), and then click the Hyperlink icon on the Standard toolbar. That brings up the Insert Hyperlink dialog box shown in Figure 28.16.

Figure 28.16
Specify the location you want to hyperlink to.

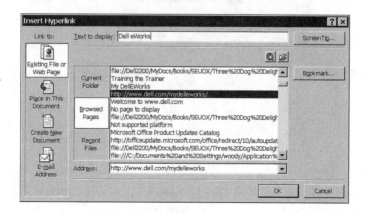

The problem with hyperlinking to an object that requires another application, of course, is how to hyperlink back to the point in your presentation where you left. If you hyperlink out to an object that requires a program other than PowerPoint—to a Web page, say, or a Word document—when you close that program, PowerPoint is still there, with the "linked from" slide still visible.

Tip from

If you hyperlink to an entire PowerPoint presentation, you can run through that presentation and, when it's done, you are back where you started, at the "link from" slide.

ADVANCED NAVIGATION WITH ACTION SETTINGS

Action Settings are an older variation on Hyperlinks that let you link to a few unusual locations in a presentation—in particular, the "previously viewed" (or "linked from") slide. Action Settings also let you start a program, run a macro, and/or combine sounds with all the preceding.

If you want to be able to "jump back" to the previously viewed slide, your best bet is to set up an Action Button (see next section) with an Action Setting that moves to the previously viewed slide. Action Settings allow you to navigate in powerful ways that aren't possible with hyperlinks.

To open the Action Settings dialog box (see Figure 28.17), select the text or graphic you want to make "hot," and then click Slide Show, Action Settings.

Figure 28.17
Action Settings provide the only (easy) way to return to the previously viewed slide.

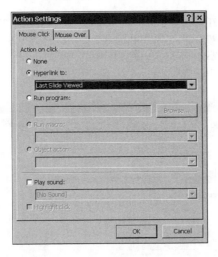

Note that you can specify separate actions for a mouse over—where you move the mouse pointer over the "hot" area—and for a mouse click.

NAVIGATION SHORTHAND WITH ACTION BUTTONS

PowerPoint makes some kinds of hyperlinking easy by attaching predefined hyperlinking information to a group of AutoShapes called Action Buttons.

If you want to add a button that allows you to immediately move to the end of the presentation, use an Action Button. If you're creating a presentation for the Web and want to create your own Next Slide and Previous Slide buttons, instead of relying on PowerPoint's built-in navigation bar, Action Buttons make it easy.

To place an Action Button on a slide, select the slide and, on the Drawing toolbar, choose AutoShapes, Action Buttons. (Equivalently, you can choose Slide Show, Action Buttons.) The buttons look just like AutoShapes (see Figure 28.18).

Figure 28.18
Predefined Action Buttons cover many of the common hyperlinking bases.

Several of the Action Buttons (for example, the question mark, information sign, video camera) don't hyperlink to anything in particular; they just put the picture on the slide and bring up the Action Settings dialog box.

Most of the Action Buttons, however, have predefined actions associated with them. You can insert buttons on your slides to move to the first or last slide in the presentation, to go to the next or previous slide, or to return to the last viewed slide.

TROUBLESHOOTING

POWERPOINT 2002-97 & 95 FORMAT CHANGES

A coworker used PowerPoint 95 to open and edit a presentation that had been saved in "PowerPoint 2002-97 & 95" format. The next time I opened the presentation in PowerPoint 2000, the animated charts wouldn't work.

PowerPoint 95 doesn't support animated charts, so when you saved the file in PowerPoint 95, you lost that feature. There's no way to retrieve it, so you'll have to rebuild the animation from scratch.

CHAPTER 29

EXPERT PRESENTATION-BUILDING TECHNIQUES

In this chapter

EDITING THE PRESENTATION OUTLINE

The fastest, easiest, and safest way to edit the text of your presentation is by working with the outline. Flip into Normal view, and concentrate on the outline pane down the left side of the screen for building content.

EDITING SLIDES IN OUTLINE VIEW

If you have a good idea of what you want to say—or if you're willing to use one of Microsoft's default presentations to suggest content—the simplest way to get a presentation on its feet in no time is to work directly on the outline. Enter text for the slide's title and body, and then you can select, click and drag, copy, move, and delete, just as you would in any other Office application.

Tip from

EQ & Woody

Before you start working with an outline, bring up the Outlining toolbar and click the Show Formatting icon (at the bottom of the Outlining toolbar; see Figure 29.2) so you can see formatted text in your outline.

You can use the Tab key while in Outline view to demote one outline level. When you press the Tab key, PowerPoint demotes the current line of text—moves it down one level lower in the hierarchy. (You can accomplish the same result by clicking the Demote icon on the Outlining toolbar.)

Similarly, you can promote a line by one level by pressing Shift+Tab (essentially the "back tab" key). Clicking the Promote icon on the Outlining toolbar does the same thing.

When you promote a line in the outline to the highest level, it becomes the title of a new slide. Thus, a quick and easy way to insert a new slide in a presentation is to repeatedly press the Shift+Tab key, or click the Promote icon.

You can type your entire presentation this way, promoting and demoting as you go: When you type a line at the highest level of the hierarchy, it automatically becomes the title of a new slide; any line below the top level turns into a bullet point (nested however deep you might want) in the slide's text placeholder.

Tip from

EQ & Woody

If your slides start getting too wordy and you want to turn high-level bullet points into slides of their own, select the points and promote them to the highest level. PowerPoint automatically turns all of them into slides, with the old high-level bullet points now serving as titles.

REORDERING SLIDES

Use the Move Up and Move Down arrows to rearrange text in the outline, and thus in the slides. To do so, click inside the line you want to move, or select a group of lines. Then click the Move Up or Move Down arrows until the lines are positioned correctly.

Note

> You can select any group of lines, even if they appear in different slides, as long as they are contiguous.

Tip from

EQ & Woody

> You might find it easier to use Slide Sorter view to perform extensive reordering, or to reorder a large presentation. Slide Sorter view gives you a lot more flexibility for drag and drop; it also shows you more of the presentation at one time.

→ For a detailed discussion of Slide Sorter view, **see** "Using Slide Sorter View to Arrange a Presentation," p. 755.

EXPANDING AND COLLAPSING

PowerPoint also makes it easy to hide all the bullets under a slide's title—commonly called *collapsing*—or display every line (*expanding*). Collapsing an outline to just the titles lets you see the overall organization and flow of your presentation, without being distracted by details. Expanding allows you to work on all the bullet points, and compare them across slides. Click inside the slide you want to change (or select a number of contiguous slides) and click the Collapse button to hide all the detail, or Expand to show all the detail.

Note

> PowerPoint does not have the capability to expand or collapse to a particular level in the hierarchy: It's an all-or-nothing setting. Either you see all the lines in a slide, or you see just the title.

If you want to collapse or expand all the slides in the presentation in one fell swoop, click the Collapse All or Expand All icons on the Outlining toolbar.

PICKING THE BEST SLIDE LAYOUT

Although it's easy to add a new slide to a presentation, choosing the right slide layout isn't always so simple.

PowerPoint supports two broad categories of slides: *title slides* (typically the first slide in a presentation), and "regular" slides (which, confusingly, are usually just called "slides"). PowerPoint has one predefined layout for title slides, and almost two dozen predefined layouts for regular slides.

Slide layouts aren't static: You can change a slide's layout by selecting the slide, choosing Format, Slide Layout, and applying a layout (by clicking it) from the Slide Layout pane

CHOOSING A SLIDE LAYOUT

Whether you're applying a layout to a brand-new slide, or changing the layout of an existing slide, PowerPoint presents you with the Slide Layout choices shown in Figure 29.1.

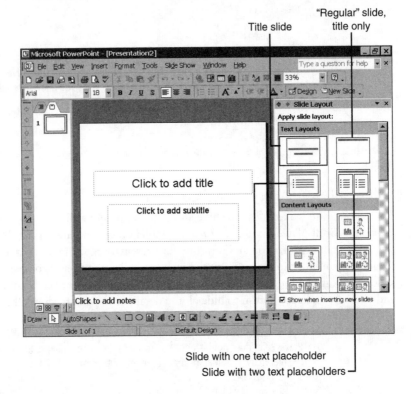

Figure 29.1
The Slide Layout pane gives you more than two dozen different ways to organize a slide.

If you choose the first thumbnail in the Slide Layout pane, PowerPoint turns the new slide (or selected slide) into a title slide. Title slides are treated differently from other slides in a presentation—they're formatted independently of the rest of the slides, using the *Title Master*. They generally don't have bullet points and they generally do have a subtitle, so make sure you really want a title slide before making this choice.

→ For more information on editing title slides, **see** "Using the Title Master," **p. 793**.

Note

The distinction between a title slide and a "regular" slide comes into play because of the way master formatting changes ripple through a presentation. The only way you can manually turn a "regular" slide into a title slide is by applying this first layout, the one called "Title Slide" in the Slide Layout pane.

Other slide thumbnails in the Slide Layout dialog box (refer to Figure 29.1) contain one or more of the following:

- **Text placeholders**—Typically for bulleted and numbered lists.

- **A general "content" placeholder**—Ties into PowerPoint's Insert Object function. The standard content on offer here includes a simple grid (that is, a table), a Microsoft Chart chart, clip art from the gallery, a picture (from a file), a diagram/org chart, or a media clip.

→ For instructions on using the chart drawing tool, **see** "Creating and Editing Charts and Diagrams," **p. 128**.

→ To use Office's Org Chart drawing system, **see** "Organization Charts," **p. 128**.

- **Combinations of "content" and text**—The placeholders are arranged in various configurations.

Tip from

EQ & Woody

Placeholders can be resized or dragged to fit your requirements. You need not settle for the size or placement established in the Slide Layout dialog pane.

The general "content" placeholder is a superset of the individual clip art, chart, media clip, and org chart placeholders. In general, you do not limit your choices by using the Slide Layout pane's Content Layouts, as opposed to the Other Layouts.

USING PLACEHOLDERS

With few exceptions, every slide layout has a title placeholder, which reserves space for the title of the slide; this text also appears at the highest hierarchical level in the presentation's outline.

Most slides also have at least one text placeholder. The contents of the text placeholder appear in the outline as points underneath the highest hierarchical level.

Slides that have two text placeholders generate separate outline sections for each placeholder. As you can see in Figure 29.2, PowerPoint gives each placeholder a number, which is used in the outline to keep track of what text belongs in which placeholder.

All the other kinds of slide layout placeholders are special kinds of graphic placeholders: table, chart, org (organizational) chart, clip art, media clip, and general "content" placeholders all contain graphics that don't appear in the outline. The only real difference among all these graphic placeholders, in fact, is the kind of link they provide to retrieve the graphic.

Note

You cannot manually insert a placeholder on a slide. Instead, you have to use the Slide Layout pane shown previously in Figure 29.1. In particular, you cannot add a third text placeholder to a slide.

Figure 29.2
Multiple text place-holders receive separate numbers, as indicated in the outline pane.

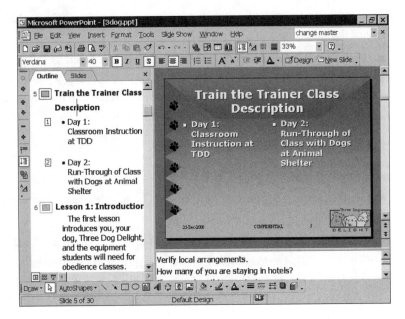

GOING OUTSIDE THE PLACEHOLDERS

Not all slide activity takes place within placeholders. In fact, any of the items that can go in one of the many graphic placeholders can also be placed directly on the slide—no placeholder required.

There are two benefits to using the graphic placeholders: First, as the name implies, they hold a place open on the slide so PowerPoint can scale the inserted graphic properly and move other placeholders out of the way as needed. Second, they provide easy links to specific kinds of graphics. If neither of these characteristics matters on a given slide, consider bypassing graphic placeholders entirely.

Graphics and drawings (for example, items generated by the Drawing toolbar, or any graphic from the Insert menu) that are placed directly on a slide go in the drawing layer.

→ To learn more about how the drawing layer stores graphics and drawings for your presentation, **see** "Working with the Drawing Layer," **p. 108**.

Note, in particular, that text entered in the drawing layer (say, inside a callout or a text box generated by the Drawing toolbar or by choosing Insert, Text Box) does not appear in the outline.

EDITING SLIDES

Slides can contain text, bulleted and numbered lists, tables, and other content such as clip art and charts. In most cases, you can make changes to each of these elements directly on the slide itself, in Normal view.

ADDING AND EDITING TEXT

The highest-level points in a presentation's outline appear as slide titles. Everything else in the outline appears in the slides' text placeholders. The outline links to the slide strictly and exclusively via the title placeholder and the text placeholder.

If you try to enter more text than a placeholder can accommodate, PowerPoint automatically tries to shrink the text to fit within the confines of the placeholder. First, it tries to reduce the spacing between lines. If that doesn't work, it shrinks the size of the font.

→ To work from the outline, **see** "Editing the Presentation Outline," **p. 768**.

Whenever PowerPoint shrinks text to fit in a placeholder, a "shrink" icon appears (it's a variant of an AutoCorrect icon). If you don't want PowerPoint to squeeze the text into the placeholder, click the button marked Stop Fitting Text to This Placeholder, and it will spill over onto the face of the slide. This same button also gives you an alternative to split the current slide into two slides, to continue on a new slide, or to change to two columns (which rarely helps matters).

Tip from

EQ & Woody

On presentations that adhere to strict design guidelines, auto-fitting text damages the integrity of the design; it might also make the slide too hard to read.

Also, if you have strict design guidelines, consider establishing a single companywide policy for style-checking rules.

→ For more on the style-checking feature, **see** "Checking for Inconsistencies and Style Errors," **p. 786**.

If you choose to continue on a second slide, the final bullet point on the overextended slide becomes the first bullet point on the new slide. If you opt to split the text between two slides, PowerPoint tries to balance the quantity of text on each slide. In both cases, titles and any other modifications you might have made to the original slide carry forward onto the new slides.

PowerPoint includes a rudimentary indenting and tabbing capability, but this feature is available only when the ruler is visible. (By contrast, Word and Outlook allow you to finely adjust tabs, specify leaders, and much more.) To adjust tabs and indents, follow these steps:

1. Choose View, Ruler to display the ruler.

2. Using the ruler, slide the triangle at the top left edge of the ruler to set the left margin for each line in a text placeholder.

3. You can also set left-aligned, centered, decimal-aligned, and right-aligned tab stops. The method for doing so parallels the method in Word: Click the tab button at the far left edge of the ruler to select a tab type, and then click inside the ruler to set the tab.

Tip from

In a bulleted list, the top triangle controls the bullet, the bottom triangle moves the text, and the lower square moves both top and bottom concurrently.

→ For more on Word's paragraph-formatting features, **see** "Changing Paragraph Formatting," **p. 383**.

Default tab stops appear every inch inside the title and text placeholders. They can be adjusted; consult the Help topic "Tab stops" for details.

Note

The Tab key behaves differently in the outline pane, where it promotes and demotes lines in the presentation's hierarchy. When you're working in the slide pane, a tab is just a tab.

Tip from

In a bulleted list, you should use Ctrl+Tab. A regular tab changes the bullet level.

You might also place text anywhere in the drawing layer—which is to say, on "top" of the slide—by using the Drawing toolbar's text box, and many different kinds of AutoShapes.

→ To get text into the drawing layer, **see** "Adding Text to a Drawing," **p. 116**.

In the case of AutoShapes, PowerPoint lets you type in text that extends beyond the ends of the shape. In text boxes, PowerPoint expands the text box downward to accommodate all the text you care to add. In both cases, any text that extends beyond the edge of a slide does not show up on the slide—even if it shows in the slide pane.

You can apply formatting to any text on a slide by selecting the text and then choosing the formatting. If you want to change the formatting on all slides, however—say, change all the titles on all the slides to a new font, or make all the first-level bullet points on all the slides green—you should use the Slide Master.

Tip from

You can change all instances of a font (typeface) with another font by choosing Format, Replace Fonts.

→ To edit all the slides at once, **see** "Using the Slide Master," **p. 795**.

Tip from

In general, if you want to make a change to all the slides in a presentation—move the titles, or put a graphic on all the slides—you should use the Slide Master.

PowerPoint applies AutoFormatting while you type, changing fractions (1/4 to ¼), ordinals (1st to 1ˢᵗ), "smart" curly quotes, dashes, and the like. It will also change a single quote in front of a number into a curly quote ('99 to '99), with the curl pointing in the correct direction, change (c) into a copyright symbol, and change several different combinations of : and) into a smiley face (☺).

 If you're frustrated because some of your Word AutoCorrect entries don't work in PowerPoint, see "Not All AutoCorrect Entries Work in PowerPoint" in the "Troubleshooting" section at the end of this chapter.

→ For advice on making AutoCorrect work the way you want—and to turn the vexing changes off—**see** "Using AutoCorrect to Automate Documents," **p. 91.**

WORKING WITH BULLETED AND NUMBERED LISTS

Most of the text you enter on slides appears as bulleted—or possibly numbered—items.

You can pick bullets or a numbering scheme when the insertion point is in any text, whether in the title placeholder, text placeholder, or even on the drawing layer.

To change a bullet—say, to use a picture as a bullet—go through the Bullets and Numbering dialog box:

1. Click within the line you want to change, or select all the lines to change.

2. Choose Format, Bullets and Numbering. (Equivalently, right-click and select Bullets and Numbering.) The Bullets and Numbering dialog box appears (see Figure 29.3).

Figure 29.3
PowerPoint lets you choose any character or picture as a bullet.

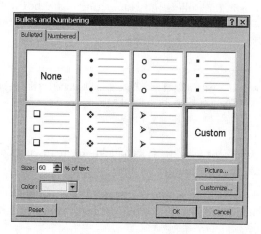

3. You can use a picture in any Office-compatible graphics format—PCX, GIF, and JPEG, for example—as a bullet. To do so, click Picture (see Figure 29.4), and use one of the built-in bullets, or click Import Clips to bring in a picture of your own.

Figure 29.4
Choose a picture from among the ones offered, or import your own.

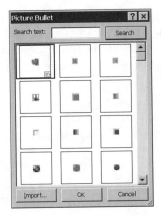

The Size % of Text spin box in the Bullets and Numbering dialog box (refer to Figure 29.3) adjusts the size of the bullet (whether picture or character), scaling it to the point size of the text. Settings between 25% and 400% are permitted.

Note

The Color drop-down list box in the Bullets and Numbering dialog box applies only to characters; it does not affect the color of a picture used as a bullet.

Numbered paragraphs renumber themselves as you add new items and delete or move existing ones. Follow these steps to number the lines in a slide:

1. Click within the line you want to number, or select a range of lines to be numbered. Auto numbering is supported only for the highest-level paragraphs; if you select lower-level paragraphs, they are ignored.

2. Choose Format, Bullets and Numbering. (Equivalently, right-click and select Bullets and Numbering from the shortcut menu.)

3. In the Bullets and Numbering dialog box (refer to Figure 29.3), click the Numbered tab.

4. Pick the type of numbering you want—fairly simple Roman, Arabic, and lettered "numbers" are supported on the Numbered tab.

5. If you have a long numbered list that extends over multiple slides, you can specify a starting value other than 1.

The size and color formatting options mentioned for bullets earlier in this section apply to numbers, too.

If you want to construct multiple-level numbering schemes (for example, 1.1, 1.2, 1.3, 2.1, 2.2), you have to type and maintain the numbers manually.

WORKING WITH TABLES

PowerPoint supports two different methods for constructing tables. Using the older Insert Table approach, you specify the number of rows and columns, and then place the table in the slide. The freeform Draw Table feature lets you draw custom tables by using the mouse.

> **Note**
>
> Although tables created in PowerPoint look a lot like Word tables, there are fundamental differences, both in options and in implementation–the version in PowerPoint isn't nearly as powerful. If you need advanced cell formatting (for example, rotating text within cells), consider using the Draw Table feature in Word, and then pasting the resulting table into your presentation.

> **Tip from**
>
>
>
> Don't forget to use the Clipboard! Pasting a Word table into a slide brings the table in as a graphic. That gives you the opportunity to scale the table by simply clicking and dragging the sizing handles.

To place a simple table on your slide, choose Insert, Table, or click the Insert Table icon on the Standard toolbar. Specify how many rows and columns you want in the table and click OK; the table appears at the insertion point. You can click and drag the resizing handles on the outer edge of the table to resize it. You can also adjust each line in the table by letting the mouse pointer hover until it turns into a parallel line pointer, and then click and drag.

> **Tip from**
>
> If you specified a slide layout that includes a table, or you chose "content" in the layout and clicked to bring in a table, PowerPoint inserts this more rigidly formatted kind of table.

To draw your own table freehand, do the following:

1. Start by clicking the Tables and Borders icon on the Standard toolbar. The Tables and Borders toolbar appears.

2. On the Tables and Borders toolbar, click the Draw Table icon. Your mouse pointer turns into a pencil.

3. Immediately draw a rectangle that defines the outer boundaries of your new table. From that point, you can

- Use the pencil to draw horizontal or vertical lines within the table wherever you want.
- Enter text in a table cell by clicking inside the cell and typing.
- Erase a line by clicking the Eraser icon and moving it over the unwanted line.
- Align text, split and merge cells, set border and fill colors, insert cells, and more by using the other options on the Tables and Borders toolbar.

4. When you're done drawing, press the Esc key to turn the pencil back into a normal mouse pointer.

Tip from

EQ & Woody

The simpler Insert Table approach changes the mouse pointer into the Draw Table tool. Press Esc to restore the normal mouse pointer.

Caution

If you create a freehand table in PowerPoint 2002, you can view it in PowerPoint 97. However, if you change a freehand table in PowerPoint 97 (by ungrouping and then editing) and save the presentation, PowerPoint 2002 no longer recognizes the results as a table. Instead, you'll see each table element as a separate shape in the drawing layer.

Of course, you can import tables from Word, Excel, or other sources by using simple copy and paste, or PowerPoint's Insert, Object, or Edit, Paste Special options. Word's table functions are somewhat more powerful than those in PowerPoint: They include the capability to rotate text, sort, and sum, for example.

To maintain control over the look of the pasted results, always use Paste Special when inserting tables. As explained later, Office uses HTML as its default format when you choose a simple Paste, and the results will generally be unsatisfactory.

→ For details, **see** "Inserting an Excel Chart or Range," **p. 780**.

⚠ *If you can't see all the cells in your Excel table after pasting it into a PowerPoint slide, see "Excel Tables Don't Display Properly" in the "Troubleshooting" section at the end of this chapter.*

ADDING PICTURES, DIAGRAMS, AND CLIP ART

Use the full array of Office drawing tools (available on the Drawing toolbar) to insert pictures and text boxes, add WordArt and AutoShapes, set colors, connect AutoShapes with lines, draw shadows, and so on.

→ To work in the drawing layer, **see** "Using Office Drawing Tools," **p. 108**.

Grids and guidelines help you line up drawing items; you can be a little imprecise and, if you choose, the computer will do the hard work of lining things up precisely. When working with pictures and other drawing tools, it's helpful to show gridlines on the screen. To do so, choose View, Grid and Guides (see Figure 29.5).

Figure 29.5
PowerPoint lets you control the granularity of its grid, and whether drawings should be snapped to the grid.

Sometimes you want to know how far a picture lies from dead center. That's where drawing guides come in handy. If you choose to Display drawing guides onscreen, you'll get horizontal and vertical lines that you can use to gauge how far any particular item on the slide sits, compared to dead center (see Figure 29.6). Click the guide, and its distance from center appears as a Tooltip.

Figure 29.6
PowerPoint's gridlines—one horizontal, one vertical—are shown here. Note how pictures can be parked in the unoccupied area around the slide.

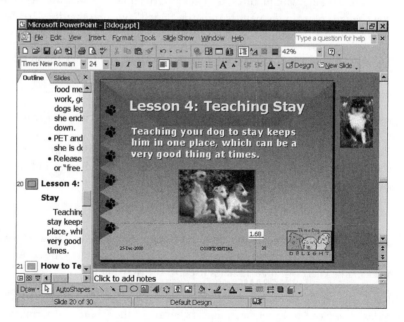

PowerPoint offers one more "snap" option: snap to shape. This feature allows you to line up shapes so they abut each other, or so they share a common axis.

PowerPoint also allows you to park pictures in the gray area outside of a slide, but still in the slide pane. This option can come in handy if you have a few different pictures you're considering for the slide, but can't make up your mind which one would be best: Parking them in the margin lets you swap them in and out quickly. To get a picture into the margin, click and drag on the picture, moving it to the edge of the pane. It takes a little practice to get a picture positioned this way, but the picture remains handy without appearing on the slide itself.

Many presentations can benefit from the addition of a few simple diagrams. When you go fishing for clip art, don't forget that PowerPoint—like all the Office applications—has a small, powerful diagram builder that lets you construct Organization Charts, Cycle diagrams, Radial diagrams (with arms emanating from a core), Pyramids, Venn diagrams, and Bullet/Target charts. There are extensive facilities for adding text to the charts and for applying different colors and designs. To get at the diagramming tools, click the Insert Diagram or Organization Chart button on the Drawing toolbar.

CHANGING COLORS IN WMF PICTURES

If you're working with pictures in Windows Metafile format(.wmf files), PowerPoint lets you change colors in the picture to better match your presentation. To change a picture's colors, follow these steps:

1. After the picture has been inserted on the slide, right-click it and select Show Picture Toolbar.

2. On the Picture toolbar, click the Recolor Picture icon.

3. From that point, you can change any color in the picture, or the background fill.

PowerPoint 2002 properly displays animated GIFs in a normal presentation. They also show up correctly when you save the presentation as a Web page and view it in a browser that supports animated GIFs.

INSERTING AN EXCEL CHART OR RANGE

You can place an Excel chart or a range of worksheet data on a PowerPoint slide through the usual methods—primarily Paste, Paste Special, and Insert Object. Any slide layout works: The chart or range attaches itself to the drawing layer.

→ If you want to learn more about the Office Clipboard, **see** "Using the Office Clipboard," **p. 132**.

When you paste an Excel data range, be aware of these potential formatting issues:

■ **ColumnWidths Can Be Problematic**—For columns that consist primarily of numbers, PowerPoint decides what column width to use. Adjusting the width after the table has been imported, although possible (by choosing View, Ruler), can be frustrating and time consuming.

- **Fonts and Font Sizes Might Not Translate to PowerPoint Properly**—For cells that use the default formats, PowerPoint converts the imported data to a new font and point size, based on the Slide Master. If you formatted the worksheet cells manually, that formatting might or may not carry across.

After you paste an Excel data range into a PowerPoint slide, the data is converted to items on the drawing layer. The pasted range or chart is treated as an embedded object. You can click it and use all of Excel's tools. However, there's no remaining link to the original spreadsheet: If you change values or formatting in the spreadsheet, those changes are not reflected in the presentation.

Tip from

In many cases, you might want to use Edit, Paste Special (or Insert, Object) to link an Excel data range or chart to a slide. This has the advantage of keeping the underlying data synchronized: Change the data in the spreadsheet, and the slide changes. On the other hand, it also carries across formatting changes: If you adjust the width of the columns in Excel, for example, the column widths in PowerPoint change as well. That can have unexpected consequences, especially in a carefully constructed slide.

To use Paste Special, follow these steps:

1. Start Excel and open the workbook that contains the range (or chart) you want to paste onto your slide.
2. Select the range and choose Edit, Copy.
3. Move to PowerPoint and select the slide you want to receive the range (or chart). Make sure you click once on the slide itself (inside the slide pane); otherwise, the range might be interpreted as text for the outline pane, and each cell's worth of data will turn into a bullet point on the slide.
4. In PowerPoint, click Edit, Paste Special. The Paste Special dialog box appears, as shown in Figure 29.7.

Figure 29.7
When you use Paste Special, you have to tell PowerPoint how to interpret the data on the Clipboard.

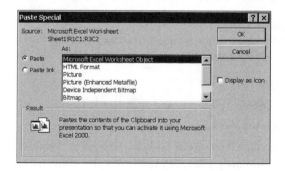

5. If you want PowerPoint to automatically update the data from Excel every time you open your presentation, click the Paste Link button. Otherwise, click Paste.

6. Select Microsoft Excel Worksheet Object and click OK.

7. The pasted range (or chart) appears on the slide. From that point, you can resize and move the range as you like. Double-click the range to activate Excel and make changes to the range, with the full power of Excel available to you.

Using this technique gives you the ability to format the range easily, using Excel's considerably more powerful formatting capabilities. PowerPoint maintains the fidelity of inserted objects: An Arial 20-point cell in Excel looks like an Arial 20-point entry on the slide.

Excel charts, PivotTables, and PivotCharts behave much the same way. Avoid pasting this type of object unless it's your only choice for reasons of performance or availability.

Tip from

EQ & Woody

If you use Insert, Object to place an Excel range on a slide, the Excel cell gridlines show on the slide. To get rid of them, double-click the embedded object, choose Tools, Options, click the View tab, and clear the Gridlines check box.

Finally, you can import an entire worksheet into PowerPoint and place it on a slide; however, the method for resizing the image is a bit odd. Choose Insert, Object, Create from File. If you can't see all the information you wanted from the spreadsheet, double-click it to start Excel, and then resize the spreadsheet "window" by using the resizing handles. Excel will show more of the spreadsheet. (Oddly, this doesn't happen when you try to resize the object from PowerPoint itself.) Click outside the spreadsheet to return to PowerPoint.

CREATING A SUMMARY SLIDE

PowerPoint offers a quick way to create a summary slide (also known as an *agenda slide*). You can use this slide at the beginning of a presentation, as its name implies, but it's also effective at the end of a presentation, to quickly recap your main points. You can also print out the summary slide and use it as a leave-behind.

In essence, you select the slides you want to summarize, and then PowerPoint gathers the titles from all those slides and turns them into bullet points on a new slide.

Follow these steps for the easiest way to set up a summary slide:

1. Go into Slide Sorter view by clicking the Slide Sorter icon on the View Bar.

2. Select the slides you want to summarize by Ctrl+clicking each in turn.

3. Click the Summary Slide icon on the Slide Sorter toolbar. PowerPoint creates a new slide, with the title Summary Slide, listing all the titles of the selected slides as bullet points (see Figure 29.8).

Figure 29.8
An automatically generated summary slide lists all the main points of the presentation.

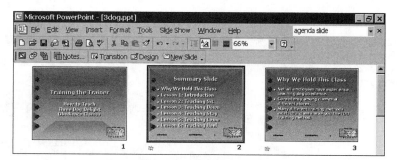

If there are too many bullet points to fit on one slide, PowerPoint automatically creates two (or more) slides, with the title "Summary Slide (cont.)."

The new summary slide appears immediately in front of the first slide you selected. From that point, you can easily click and drag the summary slide or slides wherever you want in your presentation. Because the summary slide is text, without links to existing slide titles, it won't automatically update when you change your presentation.

> **Note**
> You can also create a summary slide from Normal view's outline pane—there's even an icon on the Outlining toolbar to do so.

COLLABORATING ON A PRESENTATION

PowerPoint offers several powerful tools to help you build a presentation as a collaborative effort.

ADDING AND EDITING COMMENTS

You can attach yellow sticky-note *comments* to slides in your presentation. These notes can be helpful when you're passing around a presentation file for comments. They don't appear during the presentation, and you can use View, Comments and Changes to either show them or hide them when you're working on the slide.

To create a comment, do the following:

1. Pick the slide you want to contain your comment.

2. Choose Insert, Comment. PowerPoint creates a sticky note, places your name on it (taken from the Tools, Options, General, User Information box), and the date, and displays the Reviewing toolbar.

3. Type whatever information you like inside the sticky note (see Figure 29.9).

Reviewing toolbar

Figure 29.9
PowerPoint lets you
put yellow sticky-note
comments on slides.

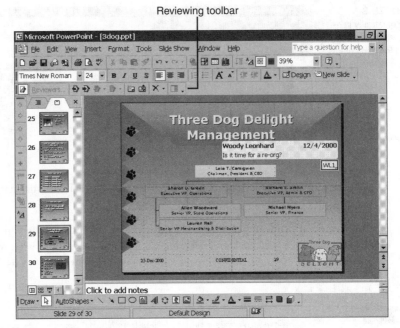

4. You can move the comment by dragging the small box with your initials. Hover your mouse over the small box to see the entire comment. You can also delete it or copy the comment text by right-clicking the small box.

If you pass the file around, other users can add their own comments; each author's name appears at the top of his or her comment. If someone changes a comment, his initials appear in the small box. That prevents one reviewer from making untracked changes to another's comments.

Use the Reviewing toolbar to jump from one comment to the next, or to make edits.

To show all comments in the current presentation, choose View, Comments; the comments only appear in Normal view: you can't see them in Slide Sorter view.

PowerPoint comments are different from the comments you can insert during Web Discussions. For example, PowerPoint comments can be positioned anywhere on the slide, although Web Discussion comments appear only at the end of a specific slide. In most situations, PowerPoint comments are easier to use; but if you have access to a Web Discussion server (see the next section), you can post the presentation there, as opposed to sending out copies to individuals, and if you need comments from many people in a short period of time, Web Discussions work better.

PowerPoint supports almost all the features of Office Web Discussions, including threaded conversations, e-mail notification of changes, filtering by the author of the comments or date, show/hide individual comments or discussions, and the rest. Inline comments—where threaded conversations can be attached to specific points within a file—aren't available: In PowerPoint Web Discussions, comments apply to an entire slide.

TRACKING CHANGES

PowerPoint also has powerful tools for comparing versions of a presentation. You can send a presentation via e-mail to one or many reviewers by choosing File, Send To Mail Recipient (for Review), or (As Attachment), or maintain a list of reviewers via the Routing Recipient option. PowerPoint automatically generates a message and attaches a copy of the presentation, if you request one (see Figure 29.10).

Figure 29.10
When you send a presentation out for comments using PowerPoint's File/Send To Mail Recipient, the program does all the heavy lifting.

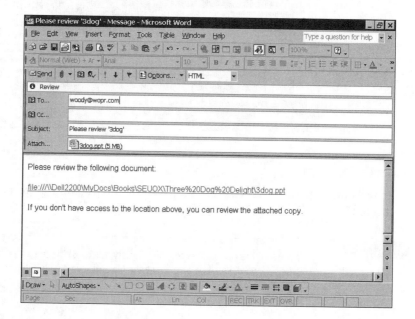

When the file comes back, you can compare the revised presentation with your original by choosing Tools, Compare and Merge Presentations. PowerPoint will ask you to locate the original presentation, then present you with an overview of the changes, complete with a Revisions pane that helps you go over all the changes that have been made, filtering out individual reviewers, if you so desire (see Figure 29.11).

After you're done going over the revisions, click the End Review button on the Reviewing toolbar. If you want to mail a copy of the new presentation back to the person who made the comments, use File, Send To, Original Sender.

Figure 29.11
PowerPoint's file comparison feature includes a powerful Revisions Pane.

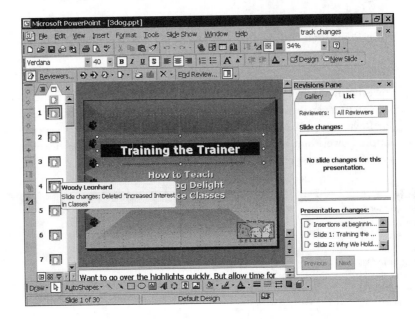

PASSWORD PROTECTION

PowerPoint supports both read and write passwords. To password-protect a presentation, choose File, Save As, Tools, Security Options, and type in the password(s).

Caution

If you lose the read password, you've pretty much lost the presentation. If you lose the write password, you'll be able to see the file and save it with a different name, but you won't be able to edit or save changes directly to the file.

CHECKING FOR INCONSISTENCIES AND STYLE ERRORS

Just as Word checks constantly for spelling and grammar mistakes, so, too, does PowerPoint. If you see a squiggly red line underneath a word, that means the word doesn't appear in the Office common dictionaries. Right-click the word and either correct the spelling or add it to a dictionary.

→ To work with the Office spell checker, **see** "Setting Up Spell-Checking Options," **p. 46**.

PowerPoint can also be set up to look for common presentation transgressions, rather than grammar errors—and PowerPoint can be downright pushy when it comes to recommending corrections.

PowerPoint can flag the following common problems:

- Fonts that are too small.
- "Ransom note" combinations of too many different fonts on a single slide.
- Too many bullets, or too many lines, on a slide.
- Bullets that don't start with capital letters.
- Violations of punctuation rules that you specify.

To enable style checking, choose Tools, Options, and check the box marked Check style. PowerPoint will warn you that it uses the old Office Assistant for style checking. (And you thought the old Clippit was dead!)

With style checking turned on, PowerPoint displays a light bulb next to parts of a presentation that clash with one of its style rules. To see more details, click the light bulb. The Office Assistant character appears, and offers to correct the mistake, ignore it, or let you take a look at the style option that triggered the light bulb. If you choose the latter (see Figure 29.12), you can change the rule if you like.

Figure 29.12
The Style Options dialog box lets you set the options for PowerPoint's style checker.

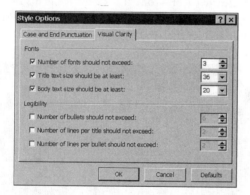

The default values on both the Case and End Punctuation and Visual Clarity tabs ensure that your presentation is both legible and consistent. You should consider enabling any of the Legibility settings that might have been turned off.

You can also look at the style options anytime; choose Tools, Options, click the Spelling & Style tab, and then click the Style Options button.

TROUBLESHOOTING

NOT ALL AUTOCORRECT ENTRIES WORK IN POWERPOINT

An AutoCorrect entry works fine in Word, but the exact same entry doesn't work in PowerPoint.

Any AutoCorrect entry in Word that produces a formatted result will not be available in PowerPoint. If you need the AutoCorrect entry, open Word, delete the entry, and replace it with one that doesn't produce a formatted result.

EXCEL TABLES DON'T DISPLAY PROPERLY

After using Paste Special to put an Excel table in a slide, the placeholder is big enough, but the table doesn't line up correctly. As a result, I can't see all the cells on the slide.

Double-click the table to open it in Excel 2000. Use the arrow keys to make the top-left cell in the range active. Click anywhere outside the table to return to the PowerPoint editing window. In most cases, this technique will line up your table properly.

SECRETS OF THE OFFICE MASTERS: ADVANCED TRICKS FOR SHOWING GRAPHS

Many presentations include graphs, but most of them try to show too much in too little space. The most important trick for getting your graphs to tell their story is to allow them enough room so that they're clearly visible—or cut back the elements in the graph to let the message through. Also important is using colors that stand out from the slide's background and choosing a font that's clear and easy to read.

Figure 29.13

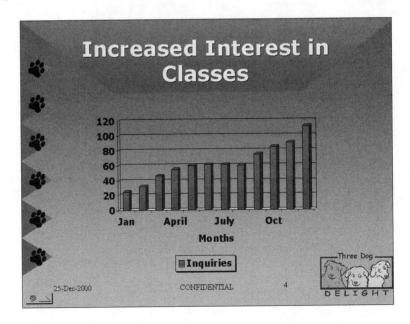

CHAPTER 30

ADVANCED FORMATTING OPTIONS

In this chapter

POWERPOINT FILE TYPES

PowerPoint uses three main file types: Presentation, Template, and Slide Show. For the most part, you can construct and deliver simple presentations without ever having to deal with the differences among these types of files. But before you can effectively use PowerPoint's advanced formatting options, you have to understand its file formats.

The Office XP Setup program registers a collection of PowerPoint file types. When you view the list of registered file types in Windows Explorer, you'll see the three major types listed in Table 30.1 (there are also some variant HTML file types which work much the same as these).

TABLE 30.1   POWERPOINT FILE TYPES

File Type	File Extension	Default Action
PowerPoint Presentation	*.ppt	Open
PowerPoint Template	*.pot	New
PowerPoint Slide Show	*.pps	Show

Thus, from an Explorer window, if you double-click an icon whose file type is Presentation (.ppt), PowerPoint opens the file for editing. When you double-click an icon whose file type is Template (.pot), however, PowerPoint creates a new presentation, based on the template, and takes you to the first slide so you can begin editing. Finally, if you launch an icon whose type is Slide Show (.pps), PowerPoint runs the show without ever showing you any of its slide-editing tools.

Surprisingly, the internal structure of all three file formats is exactly the same: You can save any presentation as a Template or Slide Show file, and the contents of the file remain the same.

> **Note**
>
> You will find many inconsistent references to these three file types scattered throughout PowerPoint's Help files and dialog boxes. In this book, the three terms defined in this section are used—Presentation, Template, and Slide Show—to differentiate among the three file types.

When should you use each file type? Follow these general guidelines:

- Use the Presentation file type (.ppt) when you plan to edit the presentation and/or work with its design. To save a file as file type Presentation, choose Presentation in the Files of Type box in the Save As dialog box.
- Use the Template file type (.pot) when you create a presentation that you want to use as the basis for creating new presentations, or if you will "borrow" the presentation's design for use in other presentations. To save a file as a Template, choose Design Template in the Save As dialog box.

■ Use the Slide Show file type (.pps) for presentations that you no longer need to edit or design. (Although it's possible to open this type of file from within PowerPoint, this is not the default action when you double-click its icon on the desktop or in an Explorer window.) Choose this file type if you want to be able to start a slide show directly from the desktop, or if you want a coworker to be able to double-click a file icon and see the show. To save a file as a Slide Show, choose PowerPoint Show in the Save As dialog box.

Tip from	Because all three file types are internally identical, it's easy to change file types. Just choose a different format from the Save As dialog box. If you're comfortable working with file extensions in an Explorer window or at a command prompt, you can change a file type by changing the file's extension; for example, changing the file extension from .ppt to .pps converts a Presentation into a Slide Show.

ORGANIZING FORMATS WITH MASTER SLIDES

Behind every great PowerPoint presentation lurk masters that control the presentation's appearance: the Title Master, Slide Master, Notes Master, and Handouts Master. Each provides detailed formatting information for title slides, "regular" slides, speaker's notes, and hardcopy handouts, respectively.

These masters control many facets of the slides themselves—backgrounds, fonts (typeface, point sizes, colors, and the like), bullets, locations for all the main components, tabs, and indents. You can also use masters to specify pictures—a logo, for example—and "boiler-plate" text that appears on all slides.

Tip from 	If you want to put a graphic, a piece of text, or any other type of object on a bunch of slides, add it to the Slide Master. Repeat the process with the Title Master, too, if you want the same object to appear on title slide(s).

Masters ensure a uniform appearance for your entire presentation. Your company might have a standard slide show template. If so, use it. If not, ask your boss if you can borrow her latest.

CREATING MULTIPLE MASTER SLIDES

Every slide in a presentation has an associated set of four masters. In most cases, one set of masters—that is, one Title Master, one Slide Master, one Notes Master, and one Handouts Master—suffices for the entire presentation.

In some cases, however, you might want to associate certain slides in your presentation with a different set of masters. For example, you might want to set up a "point/counterpoint" presentation, where the "point" slides all look the same, but they're different from the "counterpoint" slides. The main part of the presentation would flip-flop between point and counterpoint slides, with the point slides showing, say, a woman facing to the right, and the counterpoint slides showing a man facing to the left. In a situation like that, you would establish one set of masters for the point slides, and another set of masters for the counterpoint slides.

When you create a new presentation from scratch, all the slides are associated with one set of masters. If you want to use a second set of masters, you have to manually choose the slides that will be associated with the second set, and apply the new set of masters to those slides. Here's how:

1. Make sure you have the second set of masters ready. If you don't have a presentation at hand that includes the second set of masters, you can create new masters inside the current presentation. Choose View, Master, Slide Master. PowerPoint goes into Master View (see Figure 30.1).

2. Choose Insert, New Slide Master or New Title Master and format the masters as desired. Click the Close Master View button when you're done.

Figure 30.1
Use Master View to create your own set of four masters. The gray bar between slides 1 and 2 in the left pane connect a Slide Master and Title Master that are related.

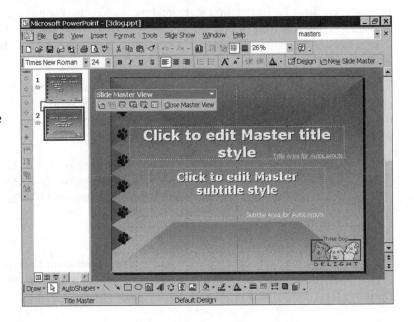

3. In Normal view, click the Design button on the Formatting toolbar. This brings up the Slide Design pane.

4. Select the slides that you want to associate with the second set of masters. In the Apply a Design Template box, click the down-arrow next to the design that includes the second set of masters, and choose Apply to Selected Slides (see Figure 30.2). If you created

a second set of masters in the current presentation using the method in step 1, the design belonging to the second set of masters appears immediately to the right of the current design.

Figure 30.2
Apply a second set of masters to selected slides by using the Slide Design pane.

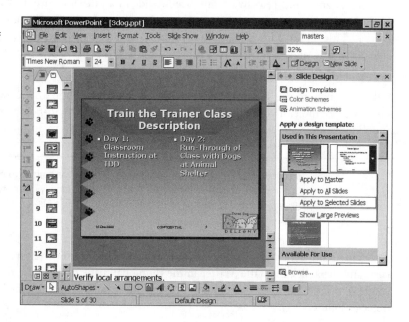

5. Verify that there are two sets of masters in the current presentation by going back into Slide Master View (View, Master, Slide Master).

This is the only way you can apply more than one set of masters to a presentation: You must choose individual slides to be associated with the new set of masters, use the Slide Design pane, and choose Apply to Selected Slides from the drop-down box next to the design associated with the second set of masters. Any other combination results in the old set of four masters being completely replaced by a new set of four masters.

Using a similar technique, you can apply any number of sets of masters to a particular presentation—PowerPoint does not limit you to two sets of masters. Caution is advised, however: the logistics of serving many masters can be daunting.

For the remainder of this chapter, assume that the presentation has only one set of masters. To work with multiple sets of masters, go into Slide Master View (View, Master, Slide Master), and choose the specific master you want to manipulate.

USING THE TITLE MASTER

The *Title Master* controls "title" slides—typically just the first slide of your presentation. If you create a presentation using the AutoContent Wizard or any of the presentation templates that ship with PowerPoint, your presentation includes one title slide, at the beginning.

Many presentations can benefit from multiple title slides: They can help you organize long presentations, emphasize when you're making a transition from one topic to another, or provide cues to you for custom presentations. You can insert a title slide anywhere in a presentation at any time. To convert any specific slide to a title slide, use the Slide Layout pane, select the slide you want to anoint as a title slide, and apply the first layout on the pane (marked Title Slide). This is the only method PowerPoint supports to convert a "regular" slide into a title slide.

→ For help on setting slide layouts, **see** "Choosing a Slide Layout," **p. 770**.

Making changes to the Title Master automatically changes all the title slides in your presentation. For example, if you change the Title Master's subtitle to 36-point Arial bold, all the title slides in your presentation will have their subtitles changed to 36-point Arial bold.

Tip from

EQ & Woody

If your presentation has only one title slide, and you don't intend to use the presentation to create new presentations—or use its design to modify other presentations' designs—there is absolutely no reason to change the Title Master.

To bring up the Title Master, choose View, Master, Slide Master to move into Slide Master view, and then click the Title Master in the thumbnail pane on the left. You can tell when you have a Title Master because the top placeholder reads, "Click to edit Master title style" (refer to Figure 30.1).

A typical Title Master includes placeholders for the title and subtitle, and a background design that consists of some sort of color treatment, possibly with a picture. Some Title Masters also have placeholders for a date, footer, and/or slide number.

To change the formatting of the title or subtitle, click inside the placeholder and apply font or paragraph formatting. Similarly, you can click inside the date, footer or slide number placeholders—if they exist—and adjust their formatting.

For example, if you want the title on all title slides to be left-aligned (instead of centered), click once inside the title placeholder and click the Align Left icon on the Formatting toolbar.

Similarly, you can resize or move any of the placeholders on the Title Master. If you move the subtitle placeholder down a half inch on the Title Master, the subtitles on all title slides will move down half an inch.

PowerPoint ignores any text you type into the title or subtitle placeholders. But if you type text into the date, footer, or slide number placeholders, PowerPoint repeats the text on all title slides. So if you want the slide number on each title slide to say "Slide *n*", click the slide number placeholder and type the text "Slide" in front of the <#>.

Tip from

EQ & Woody

If you accidentally delete one of the five placeholders, you can restore it. Choose Format, Master Layout, pick the desired placeholder, and click OK. You might have to click and drag on the new placeholder to return it to its original location.

Note

It's important to realize that you can override Title Master settings on each individual title slide. For example, to move the subtitle on a slide or to add a picture to just one title slide, jump to the slide and make the change.

When you override a Title Master setting on an individual slide, you break the link between that setting and the master; subsequent changes won't affect that setting. For example, if you change formatting for the subtitle on the first slide in your presentation, and later change formatting for the subtitle on the Title Master, the subtitle on the first slide won't change. Even changing the Title Master entirely using Apply Design Template won't restore the link.

To bring the link back, you have to reapply the layout by using the Slide Layout pane, re-applying the Title Slide layout.

USING THE SLIDE MASTER

Whenever you want to change all the slides in your presentation (except the title slides) in exactly the same way, you should change the *Slide Master*. If you want to put a logo on all your slides, for example, work with the Slide Master, not the individual slides. The same is true if you want to put identical text on all the slides—or change a color, modify a font, or use a different kind of bullet.

→ Using the Slide Master is much like using the Title Master; for help, **see** "Using the Title Master," **p. 793**.

With the following two exceptions, the Slide Master behaves in precisely the same fashion as the Title Master:

- Exception #1: The Slide Master applies to all "regular" slides in a presentation—that is, all slides other than title slides. The Title Master applies only to title slides, and in most presentations, that's just the first slide.

→ If you have multiple masters in a presentation with each Slide Master controlling its set of slides, **see** "Creating Multiple Master Slides," **p. 791**.

- Exception #2: The Slide Master includes a text placeholder designed primarily to hold bulleted lists, and thus the core of most presentations. By contrast, the Title Master includes the relatively mundane subtitle placeholder.

There's little consistency in PowerPoint terminology. In Figure 30.3, the phrase "Title Area for AutoLayouts" means "Title Placeholder." The phrase "Object Area for AutoLayouts" means "Text Placeholder." The phrase "Click to edit Master text styles" means "change appearance of highest-level items."

Figure 30.3
The Text Placeholder (confusingly called "Object Area for AutoLayouts" on the Slide Master) holds the textual part of each slide.

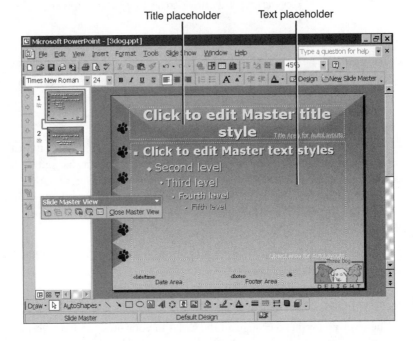

General instructions for the Slide Master mirror those for the Title Master, described in the previous section:

- Click inside a placeholder to change formatting.
- Resize or move placeholders at will.
- Type text into the date, footer, or slide number placeholders to have it appear on all slides.
- When you work on an individual slide and override settings on the Master—creating different settings for that slide—you break the link to the Master.

 Are you confused by PowerPoint's seeming reluctance to update some of the slides in your presentation when you update the slide master? See "Slide Master Link Damage" in the "Troubleshooting" section at the end of this chapter.

The primary formatting difference between the Title Master and Slide Master is that when working with a Slide Master, you must set formatting and bullets for each level of text in the body of your presentation.

To change the formatting of the bullet points in your presentation, do the following:

1. Choose View, Master, Slide Master to go into Slide Master view. Then click the Slide Master thumbnail for editing.

2. To change the formatting of text in the highest-level bullet points, click the line that says "Click to enter Master text styles" and apply the formatting. For example, if you want all highest-level bullet points in your presentation to appear in 24-point Arial, click "Click to enter Master text styles" and set the font to 24-point Arial, using Format, Font.

3. Similarly, to change the bullet used at the highest level, click "Click to edit Master text styles," then choose Format, Bullet, and choose the bullet you like.

4. To change the font or bullet for the second-highest-level items in your presentation, click "Second level," and apply whatever formatting you like, or change the bullet.

5. Similarly, change formatting or bullets for third-, fourth-, and fifth-level bullet items by clicking the appropriate line and applying the formatting.

PART

V

CH

30

Tip from

EQ & Woody

To "tighten up" the distance between the bullet and text, choose View, Ruler, and adjust the tab stops (see Figure 30.4). PowerPoint aligns each level's bullet and text with the stops shown on the ruler.

Figure 30.4
To change the location of bullets and text in the body of a presentation, adjust tab stops in the Slide Master.

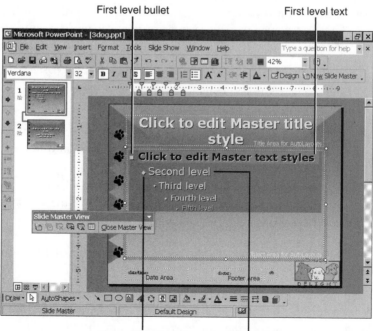

First level bullet   First level text

Second level bullet   Second level text

Caution

Changing font formatting of the title placeholder on the Slide Master also changes the title placeholder on the Title Master. So, for example, if you change the Slide Master to make the title on all "regular" slides 36-point Arial, PowerPoint changes your Title Master, too, so *its* title is 36-point Arial.

The Slide and Title masters do not share paragraph formatting, however; if you right-align the Slide Master's title, for example, the Title Master's title remains unchanged.

Tip from

EQ & Woody

The PowerPoint Help file admonishes you to "Finish working on the Slide Master before changing the Title Master, because any text formatting that's changed on the Slide Master also changes on the Title Master." That simply isn't true. The only shared formatting on the Slide Master and the Title Master is font and paragraph formatting for the title placeholder.

CHANGING THE BACKGROUND OF EVERY SLIDE

If you want a logo, a graphic, or a drawing item to appear on all "regular" slides, place it on the Slide Master. Items in the Slide Master's drawing layer appear in the drawing layer of all nontitle slides in the same location it occupies on the Slide Master.

Text you place on the Slide Master behaves the same way. For example, in a presentation that contains sensitive data, you might want to add the word CONFIDENTIAL to every slide; for a presentation that's under construction, you might want to stamp DRAFT on every slide. To put identical pieces of text on every "regular" slide, follow these steps:

1. Go into Slide Master view (choose View, Master, Slide Master).

2. Click the Text Box icon in the Drawing toolbar. Draw a text box on the Slide Master.

3. Resize and move the box, as necessary.

4. Click in the text box and enter the text you want to repeat on all slides. This text will appear in the drawing layer on all the "regular" slides in your presentation, and thus will not show up in the outline.

5. To apply formatting to the box itself, right-click the edge of the box and choose Format Text Box. You might want to draw a thick line around the box, for example, or change its background color.

Similarly, if you want a logo, fixed text, or other drawing item to appear on all title slides, put it on the Title Master.

You'll find by far the richest vein of background customizing options when you learn how to develop, modify, and apply designs. Use these techniques to modify Microsoft's prebuilt Master Slides, or devise your own masters and store them for future use.

→ To work with designs, **see** "Applying and Modifying Designs," **p. 802.**

WORKING WITH HEADERS AND FOOTERS

In PowerPoint's often confusing terminology, the phrase "Headers and Footers" refers exclusively to the three placeholders designed to hold the date, the footer, and the slide number. Don't be confused by this label: You can move any of these three placeholders to any location on a slide—you don't have to confine them to the top or bottom of a slide.

The date placeholder can show the current date—the date the slide show is being presented— or any fixed date you choose. Many advanced PowerPoint users take advantage of the field as a versioning tool, assigning different dates to different versions of the presentation.

The footer placeholder can carry any text you want. Because it need not stay at the bottom of the slide, some advanced PowerPoint users move it to, say, the upper-left corner, and use it to "brand" each slide with the name of the presentation, or perhaps the name of a company or client.

The slide number placeholder can be confusing if it appears near other numbers on a slide. Slide numbers are rarely useful (you might rely on them as a visual reminder of how many slides are left), and they're frequently distracting. If you decide to use slide numbers, keep them subtle, and remember that you can always make the font smaller than the default provided by PowerPoint.

If you look closely at a Slide Master, you'll see that these three placeholders all have dummy values enclosed in angle brackets (< >):

- The date placeholder includes a dummy value called `<date/time>`.
- The footer placeholder includes a dummy value called `<footer>`.
- The slide number placeholder includes a dummy value called `<#>`.

To show (or hide) the date/time, footer, or slide number placeholders and their contents, do the following:

1. Choose View, Header and Footer to open the PowerPoint Header and Footer dialog box, shown in Figure 30.5.

Figure 30.5
Use this dialog box to specify which placeholders appear, and replacements for the three Slide Master dummy values.

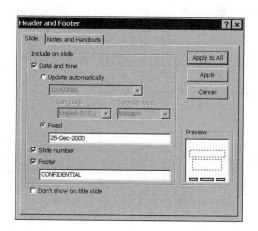

2. Check the appropriate box to display each of the three placeholders on all slides; clear the check mark to hide the selected placeholder.

3. Use the entries under the check boxes to define what, if anything, replaces the dummy entries—the current date or a footnote, for example.

4. Click Apply to change the setting for the currently selected slide only. Click Apply to All to make the change to all "regular" slides in your presentation. To apply the same change to title slides, too, clear the check mark from the Don't Show on Title Slide box.

Note

If you don't plan to use one (or more) of these placeholders, you can safely delete it.

Tip from

EQ & Woody

If you are likely to use the same headers or footers or other master elements in additional presentations, save a copy of the presentation as a template.

REMOVING SLIDE MASTER ELEMENTS FROM A SINGLE SLIDE

You can have the slide number appear on every slide except one. You might need to do this if one slide includes a big chart, and you need every square inch of slide space to hold it, for example. You might think that you could select the slide number placeholder on a single slide and press the Delete key to remove it. If you try it, however, you'll see that this approach doesn't work.

In fact, removing elements of the Slide Master from an individual slide is an all-or-nothing proposition: You get all of them, or you get none of them. This can be particularly vexing when the design you've chosen includes graphics—and most of the designs provided by Microsoft include graphics—or when you have a graphic element, such as a logo, that's supposed to appear on all slides.

To remove *all* the Slide Master elements (except the title placeholder and text placeholder) from a single slide:

1. Select the slide.

2. Choose Format, Background.

3. Check the Omit Background Graphics from Master box.

4. Click Apply.

Caution

Do *not* click Apply to All. Doing so will remove all the elements from all the regular slides in your presentation.

If this method is too drastic—you want to remove only one element, for example, on just one slide—you can cover the element up, instead of removing it:

1. Create a small rectangle by clicking the Rectangle icon on the Drawing toolbar.

2. Make the rectangle just slightly larger than the Master Slide element you want to eliminate. If you need to adjust the size in finer increments than the tool normally allows, press the Alt key while making the adjustments.

3. Drag the rectangle over the Master Slide element.

4. Click the down arrow next to the Fill Color icon. There should be a color very close to the background color available at the beginning of the first or second line of color swatches. Choose the color closest to the background color.

5. Click the down arrow next to the Line Color icon. Choose the same color you just chose for the fill color.

PART
V

CH
30

If you match the colors carefully, your audience will never know.

CREATING SPEAKER NOTES AND AUDIENCE HANDOUTS

The *Notes Master* and *Handout Master* behave differently from the Title and Slide Masters; their only function is to provide extremely rudimentary instructions for printing speaker notes and audience handouts.

Speaker notes, in PowerPoint, typically hold one slide per page: The slide appears at the top of the page, and the notes are at the bottom. Audience handouts, again, from PowerPoint's point of view, consist solely of printed copies of the slides. They might have two, three, four, six, or nine slides per page. There are no options in PowerPoint to print blank lines next to the slides, so the audience can take notes.

In fact, experienced presenters frequently use printed PowerPoint speaker notes as handouts: If you want your audience to walk away with printed notes about each slide, there's no better way to construct them. PowerPoint "handouts" rarely suffice for anything other than a hardcopy backup record of a presentation.

Tip from

Ed & Woody

Compared with PowerPoint, Word offers much better formatting and printing options for notes and handouts. To send a PowerPoint presentation to Word, choose File, Send To, Microsoft Word. Word creates a document with blank lines next to the thumbnails, in a format suitable for handouts.

To set PowerPoint printing options for speaker notes:

1. Go into Notes Master view by choosing View, Master, Notes Master. You will almost always want to adjust the Zoom factor, using the Zoom icon on the Standard toolbar.

2. Apply formatting to the Notes Body Area just as you would to the Slide Master's text placeholder: Click the desired bullet level, and apply text formatting.

3. Resize and/or move the slide placeholder and the Notes Body Area.

4. Move the header placeholder, footer placeholder, date/time placeholder, and page number placeholder (marked "Number Area"). Note that you can type text into any of these placeholders and the text will appear on the notes.

5. Control the appearance and contents of those four placeholders by choosing View, Header and Footer, Notes and Handouts, and setting the check boxes accordingly.

When you're satisfied with the formatting, print the speaker notes—choose File, Print, choose Notes Pages in the Print What box, and click OK.

Tip from

EQ & Woody

Color slides–particularly those with dark backgrounds–invariably print better on a black-and-white printer if you check the Grayscale box in the Print dialog box. Choose the View Color/Grayscale icon on the standard toolbar to preview the presentation in Black and White.

There are considerably fewer options for handouts:

1. Choose View, Master, Handout Master to go into Handout Master view.

2. Move the header placeholder, footer placeholder, date/time placeholder, and page number placeholder ("Number Area"). Here, too, you can type text into any of these placeholders and the text will appear on the handouts.

3. To control the appearance and contents of these four placeholders, choose View, Header and Footer, Notes and Handouts, and set the check boxes accordingly.

The Handout Master view toolbar lets you choose between one, two, four, six, or nine slides on a page. It also lets you control how the outline is printed, using a makeshift grid instead of tabs.

Tip from

EQ & Woody

Seriously consider how your audience will use your handout before you hand them out! Audience members will find it difficult to stay focused on what you're saying, if they can look at your handout and jump ahead to a topic that specifically concerns them. Presenters all too frequently steal their own thunder by letting the audience see the entire presentation before it's presented.

APPLYING AND MODIFYING DESIGNS

PowerPoint designs control the appearance of a presentation. By letting you save, modify, and reuse designs—including dozens of Microsoft-supplied samples—PowerPoint makes it easy to create presentations that are visually appealing and consistent. Consistency is especially important when you want a group of presenters from the same organization to share a common look.

You might think of a presentation design as something Microsoft hired professional designers to create—a set of perfectly tuned and balanced elements that shouldn't be altered by those of us with less-than-perfect artistic skills. Nothing could be further from the truth. In fact, if your audience includes anyone who has ever used PowerPoint, they'll be able to spot one of the ready-made designs from the back row of the auditorium.

The designs that Microsoft provides are only a starting point. If you find pieces of a design you like, swipe them and put them in your presentations. If you come up with a presentation that really gets your point across, save the presentation as a template and use it to design new presentations.

Tip from

EQ & Woody

If you're developing a presentation for a PowerPoint-savvy audience–that includes anybody who views more than a couple of presentations a week–be careful: You'll distract your audience if you use a standard design. ("Man, that's the fourth Dad's Tie presentation this month!") Besides, some of the designs by Microsoft are just plain bad: They make text hard to read, printouts dark and murky, and, in general, can get in the way of you making a great presentation. You will get your point across better if you use a simple, plain design that isn't part of the Microsoft prefab kit.

A design is a set of four masters—a Title Master, Slide Master, Notes Master, and Handout Master—along with a group of color settings called Standard color schemes. Between them, the four masters completely control the look and feel of a presentation: background design, color, and pictures; fonts, sizes, and attributes; bullet points; and location and contents of placeholders. In other words, it includes practically everything except the content itself. The color schemes make it easy to change groups of color settings.

→ To change every slide in a presentation, **see** "Organizing Formats with Master Slides," **p. 791**.

→ To modify the colors of all the slides, **see** "Using Color Schemes," **p. 809**.

PowerPoint's dialog boxes and Help files use a variety of design-related terms to describe variations on templates. As you work with advanced formatting options, you might encounter any of the four terms defined in Table 30.2. In every case, these refer to files whose type is PowerPoint Template and whose extension is *.pot.

TABLE 30.2   TEMPLATE TERMINOLOGY

PowerPoint Term	Definition
Design template	Typically, "design" templates include only design elements (that is, four masters and the color scheme), with no other slides.
Presentation design	Same as a design template.
Content template	Typically, "content" templates contain a group of slides with title text and bullets.
Presentation template	Same as a content template.

You'll find PowerPoint's collection of content templates in the AutoContent Wizard; typi-cally, the text on these slides includes content-related tips that you replace with your own text. You can create your own templates, using your own original content, and place them in the AutoContent Wizard (just click the Add button on the second dialog in the wizard). That content becomes the starting point for each new presentation based on that template. For instance, if every presentation you create includes three boilerplate slides that describe your company and its mission, consider adding those slides to the templates you use regu-larly.

→   To make templates work for you, **see** "PowerPoint File Types," **p. 790**.

CHOOSING THE BEST DESIGN FOR YOUR PRESENTATION

Nothing detracts more from a good presentation than a poor design. To choose the best possible design for a presentation, weigh the following, conflicting factors:

- **Your audience**—The single most crucial factor, a design that's great for one audience (vibrant colors and animated bullets for a bunch of programmers and computer book authors, perhaps) might fall on its face for another (subtle gradient fills or textures and richer colors for the Board, say). Remember that PowerPoint-savvy audiences will respond better to seeing something that isn't straight out of the box.

- **Your image**—Although a presentation isn't quite "Dress for Success," the image you project onscreen shouldn't conflict with the image you project in person. If you're wear-ing a pinstripe Armani suit, you don't want a LaVerne presentation; if you're in jeans and a T-shirt, Romanesque will leave your audience bewildered.

- **Your point**—If you're trying to get information across, stick to the no-nonsense designs (for example, Pulse, Fireball, or High Voltage). If you're trying to sway group opinion, add a bit of panache (maybe Mountain, or Soaring, or even Whirlpool). And if you're trying to sell something, well, the sky's the limit.

After you have a clear vision of the image you want to project, you're ready to choose a design. To pick a design for your presentation, follow these steps:

1. Start with a new blank presentation, or click the File New button, and choose Insert, New Slide a few times. Bring up the Slide Design pane by clicking Design on the Formatting toolbar.

2. In the Apply a Design Template list, choose a design you like (see Figure 30.6).

Tip from

Ed & Woody

If you can't quite make out the designs, click the down-arrow to the right of one of the offered designs, and choose Show Large Preview. PowerPoint enlarges the thumbnails so they take up the entire width of the pane.

Figure 30.6
Some designs—but by no means all—are available through the Apply Design pane. Applying a design to an entire presentation is as easy as double-clicking the design.

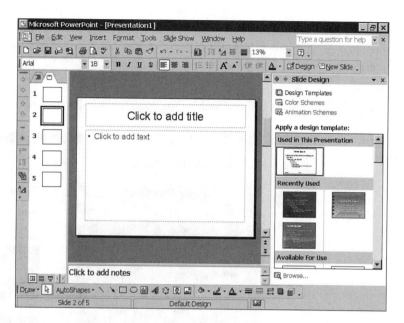

3. If you haven't installed all the designs that came with Office (which is the case if you performed a standard install), the last design template will read Additional Design Templates. Click that box, insert your Office XP CD, and PowerPoint will bring in the rest of the templates that ship with Office.

Tip from

EQ & Woody

Serious PowerPoint users should install all the templates. Few designs are over 50KB in size, and most presentations are under 150KB. Adding all the available templates only takes up a few megabytes of disk space.

→ Why quibble? To add it all, **see** "Adding and Removing Office Features," **p. 1069**.

4. If you still haven't found a design you like, click the Browse button at the bottom of the Slide Design pane. From that point you can look for designs on your hard drive, your network, or even the Web.

Tip from

EQ & Woody

There are thousands of sites on the Web that have PowerPoint designs, many for a small fee. Use the Browse button at the bottom of the Slide Design pane, click the Web icon, and search for the phrase "PowerPoint design."

---

5. When you've found a design that you like, double-click it. PowerPoint throws away the masters it's currently using, replacing them with those in the design or presentation that you've chosen, rippling those changes through your presentation.

MODIFYING AN EXISTING DESIGN FOR YOUR PRESENTATION

Many PowerPoint designs include groups of drawing objects that you can move, resize, and otherwise modify to suit the needs of a particular presentation.

For example, the Fireworks design (see Figure 30.7) consists of a picture of a firework burst on a black background. The rectangle in the upper right holds the fireworks.

Figure 30.7
You can move or delete components of a design.

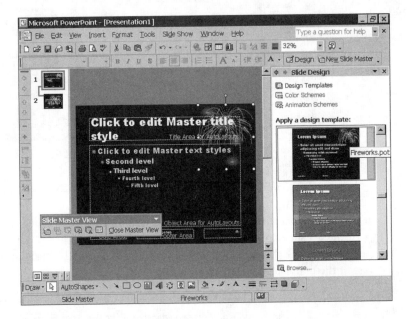

At first glance, this might not appear to have much bearing on the quality of your presentations. Think of it this way: Every single graphic element in every single PowerPoint presentation—whether it's from Microsoft or any other source—can be lifted and moved to your presentations. So, for example, if you see a color-layering technique in a presentation, but you don't like the colors, you can lift the design (see the preceding section), and then work element-by-element on the Slide Master to retouch each piece. Or you can selectively add, remove, copy, or move any element to any location you like. That comes in handy if you need more room on an existing design.

For example, if you wanted to emphasize the fireworks in Figure 30.7, and trim back a bit on the title placeholder, this is how you would do it:

1. To apply the Fireworks design, bring up the Slide Design pane by clicking Design in the Formatting toolbar. Select Fireworks from the list, and double-click it.

2. Choose View, Master, Slide Master to go into Slide Master view.

3. To select the rectangle with the picture of the fireworks on it, click the fireworks. You might have to jockey around a bit to get outside of the title placeholder.

Tip from

Some of the more complex designs have many different elements. If you think that might be the case with the design you're using, click the design, click Draw on the Drawing toolbar, and choose Ungroup. If you do that with the fireworks you just selected, you'll find that there are many components to the fireworks—it isn't a simple, single drawing.

4. Drag the sizing handle on the lower left to expand the fireworks. Then click and drag to move the title placeholder to the right a bit. Then resize the text placeholder so it matches up with the title placeholder. When you're done, click Close Master View on the Slide Master view toolbar, and the changes will take effect.

Use this same technique to resize, move, or delete any of the drawings that appear on the background in this (or any other) design.

Tip from

To maintain design uniformity in the presentation, you might want to make the same changes to the Title Master. Unfortunately, PowerPoint has no automated tools to help; you must make the changes manually.

CHOOSING THE BEST BACKGROUND COLOR

The background color itself—the "canvas" that sits beneath the design's background pictures—offers an entirely different set of possibilities. The background might include gradient-filled colors, textures, or patterns, or you can import a graphic file (in GIF, JPEG, Windows Metafile, or any compatible graphics format) to use as the background.

All the considerations you give to choosing a good design also apply to the background color (see the preceding two sections). There's one more influence, however, that should guide your color selection: the medium you'll use for the presentation.

If you're going to make the presentation in a darkened room on a large, high-contrast screen, you can get away with just about any combination of colors. But if you're making your presentation in a low-contrast situation (in a room where ambient light will fall on the screen, for example, or on a portable in which some members of your audience might not be able to view the screen directly), make sure you use light letters on a dark background, or vice versa. Those who have trouble discerning colors in low-contrast situations (not to mention the colorblind, who most frequently have trouble distinguishing green and red) will thank you.

Finally, if you intend to print the presentation—or show it on an overhead projector—stick to very light backgrounds. Although there are tricks for improving the printed appearance of almost any presentation, if your most important destination is hardcopy, you should design the presentation from the ground up to comply.

→ For tips on getting the most out of hardcopy, **see** "Printing Your Presentation," **p. 851**.

To change the background, do the following:

1. Apply the design you want and go into Slide Master view (View, Master, Slide Master).
2. Choose Format, Background. You see the Background dialog box (see Figure 30.8).

Figure 30.8
Apply quick background changes, or select Fill Effects in the drop-down list to use PowerPoint's extensive set of tools for changing backgrounds.

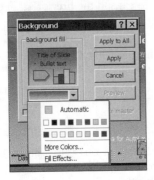

3. To make simple changes to the background color, select the new color from the drop-down list. There's a more extensive selection if you choose More Colors from the drop-down list.
4. Choose Fill Effects in the drop-down list to take advantage of the Fill Effects dialog box (see Figure 30.9), which has extensive tools for controlling color gradients, textures (you can import your own textures), or patterns. You can also import a picture to use as the background; the picture will be stretched to fit the slide.

Figure 30.9
The Fill Effects dialog box offers comprehensive tools for creating the "canvas" behind your slides.

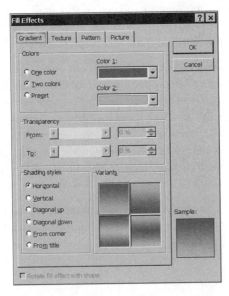

→ For tips on graphics, **see** Chapter 5, "Creating and Editing Professional-Quality Graphics," **p. 107**.

5. When you've constructed the background you want, click Apply to update the Slide Master, and have the changes take effect throughout your presentation.

For consistency's sake, you might want to make the same changes to the Title Master.

CHANGING THE BACKGROUND ON SELECTED SLIDES

Sometimes your presentation will include one or two slides that absolutely demand a different background. Maybe the colors in a photo clash with the background color. Perhaps the bars of a chart don't stand out well enough against a color that's otherwise perfect for the rest of the presentations.

If you don't want to change the background for every slide in your presentation, use the same techniques described in the preceding section on individual slides. Select the slide you want to change, and follow the instructions. In the last step, make sure you click Apply. (If you click Apply to All, you'll change the Slide Master, and every slide in the presentation will take on the new background.)

USING COLOR SCHEMES

A *color scheme* (see Figure 30.10) consists of eight colors, one for each major type of element in a presentation. Each of PowerPoint's ready-made color schemes consists of foreground and background colors that work well together.

Figure 30.10
A color scheme has
eight defining colors.

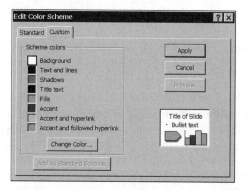

The problem is that sometimes you don't want the colors to work together all that well. From time to time, a little bit of clash can be a good thing. For example, the color schemes that ship with PowerPoint can be very soothing when applied to text and backgrounds. But when you have a chart on the screen, you want the bars to stand apart from each other: The viewer should be able to tell at a glance where one data bar ends and another begins.

Further, you can use color schemes to subtle advantage. You don't have to be as obvious as, say, setting off your competitor's product specs in red, while showing your product's specs in green. But choosing a high-contrast color for your product and a washed-out, low-contrast color for your competitor can have an impact.

You can create your own color schemes by using any colors that your video settings will support (refer to Figure 30.10 and see Table 30.3).

TABLE 30.3   COLOR SCHEME COMPONENTS

Component	Description
Background	The color behind all text and objects on the slide; on slides with gradient-filled backgrounds, it's the primary color.
Text and Lines	The color of the font in the text placeholder, and the outline color for items in the drawing layer.
Shadows	The second color in a gradient-filled background; it doesn't appear to have anything to do with the "shadow" color of shadowed text.
Title Text	The color of the font of text in the title placeholder. It's also the color of the highest-level bullet in the text placeholder. This setting doesn't affect the color of any text on a title slide.
Fills	The background color of items in the drawing layer, and the color of the bars for the first set of data in a chart. It has nothing to do with gradient fills.
Accent	The only use found for the *Accent* color is for the bars representing the second set of data in a chart.
Accent and Hyperlink	The color of the text of hyperlinks that haven't been "followed" (that is, clicked and activated). It's also the color of the third bars in charts.
Accent and Followed Hyperlink	The color of hyperlinked text that has been "followed," and it's the color of the fourth bars in charts.

Just as you can change any detail on a master slide, you can change the colors in the current presentation by changing the color scheme of any master. PowerPoint saves color schemes along with the design; if you apply a new design, PowerPoint discards any previous color changes and applies the color scheme from the new design to your presentation.

PowerPoint uses colors from the color scheme in many different places. For example, the Background dialog box (refer to Figure 30.8) offers colors from the current color scheme as its first choice.

CHOOSING A NEW COLOR SCHEME

To apply a color scheme to your presentation:

1. Apply the design you want. Then choose View, Master, Slide Master to go into Slide Master view.

2. Click the Design button on the Formatting toolbar, and choose Color Schemes. You'll see the Edit Color Scheme dialog box shown in Figure 30.11.

Figure 30.11
Standard color schemes vary depending on the design.

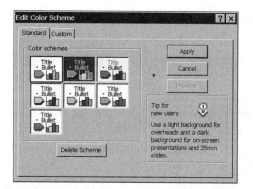

3. Choose from among the color schemes offered on the Standard tab, or click the Custom tab (shown earlier in Figure 30.10) to create your own scheme. Select the scheme you want, and then click Apply.

Note

To save a color scheme, click the Add As Standard Scheme button on the Custom tab. From that point on, the new scheme shows up on the Standard tab.

The Standard color schemes for a presentation are saved with the masters. Thus, if you create a new Standard color scheme, and save it as a Design Template or Presentation, that Standard color scheme will be available whenever you apply the design to a different presentation.

CHANGING COLORS ON SELECTED SLIDES

If you decide you need to change one color on a slide—perhaps it clashes with a picture or doesn't contrast enough with a chart—you might want to consider changing the entire color scheme for that slide.

The procedure for changing the color scheme for a single slide is nearly identical to the procedure outlined in the preceding section. Just select the slide you want to change before starting with step 1. In step 3, be careful to click Apply, and not Apply to All.

COPYING A COLOR SCHEME

It's easy to create, store, and modify color schemes; use the Standard color scheme technique described in the preceding two sections. Unfortunately, it's difficult to copy a color scheme from one presentation to another, or from one design to another. That can pose a problem if you want to use the same color scheme (or a group of color schemes) across many different designs—for example, if your company (or your boss) prefers a specific set of colors. You can re-create the color schemes manually in each design or presentation, but the process is time-consuming and error-prone.

Fortunately, there is an undocumented method for transferring a color scheme from one presentation (or design) to another:

1. Open or create a presentation with at least one slide that contains the color scheme you want to copy. Call this slide the "from slide." Click the Slider Sorter icon to switch to Slide Sorter view.

2. Open the presentation to which you want to transfer the color scheme. Call this the "to presentation." Switch to Slide Sorter view in this presentation, too.

3. Click the "from slide," and then click the Format Painter icon on the Standard toolbar.

4. Switch to the "to presentation" by clicking its icon in the Windows taskbar. Then click once on any slide in the "to presentation." The colors of the "from slide" are transferred to this slide in the "to presentation."

5. Bring up the Edit Color Scheme dialog (refer to Figure 30.10) by choosing Design on the Formatting toolbar, clicking Color Scheme on the Slide Design pane, and then clicking Edit Color Scheme. The custom settings you will see match the color scheme on the "from slide."

6. Click the Add As Standard Scheme button on the Custom tab. Flip over to the Standard tab and verify that the "from slide" color scheme is now a Standard color scheme for this slide.

7. Click the Apply to All button so that this new Standard color scheme will be applied to the Slide Master. The "to presentation" now has a copy of the "from slide" color scheme.

You can then save the presentation (or its design) by choosing File, Save, or File, Save As.

If you want to restore the original formatting to the "to presentation," open the Slide Master, bring up the Edit Color Scheme dialog box, and click the first Standard color scheme.

CHANGING PARAGRAPH AND TEXT FORMATTING

Not all presentation text is created equal, and not all text falls into PowerPoint's relentless and presumed point-by-point-by-point format. Sometimes you might want to center a line of text, to make it stand out. In other presentations, you might want to ensure each top-level bullet point has an extra bit of space after it, to make the presentation more readable from the back of the room. Then there's the inevitable bold text, and italic, and even the fontographer's nightmare, bold italic. All these treatments have a place in your repertoire of presentation tricks.

In general, PowerPoint paragraph and text formatting options mirror those available in Word. This section covers the few notable exceptions:

■ To change paragraph or text formatting for all the "regular" slides in your presentation (that is, all slides except title slides), change the Slide Master.

- To change paragraph or text formatting for a title slide, it's generally easier to change the slide directly—providing your presentation has just one title slide.

- The normal rules of Windows apply: Select whatever you want to change—paragraphs, words, characters—and then apply the change.

→ To change all the slides, **see** "Using the Slide Master," **p. 795**.

→ To change the title slide(s), **see** "Using the Title Master," **p. 793**.

USING PARAGRAPH FORMATTING

All the standard paragraph formatting settings found in Word are at your disposal, including alignment (right, center, and left), spacing (double and triple), and so on. These options are accessible directly from the Format menu.

Note

To remove bullets from a paragraph, click inside the paragraph, choose Format, Bullets and Numbering, and click None.

To change tab stops and adjust the behavior of tab characters, you must use the ruler.

→ To tackle the ruler, **see** "Adding and Editing Text," **p. 773**.

Some tab formatting options you might use in other Office applications do not exist in PowerPoint. For example, there is no easy way to put a tab stop in every cell of a table; you have to enter them all manually.

USING FONTS

Professional designers recommend you stick with one font for titles and another for text—better yet, use the same font for both. Using too many fonts detracts from a presentation.

To adjust any font effects, select some text, right-click, and choose Font from the shortcut menu. All standard effects are available in the Font dialog box: color, bold, italic, bold italic, underline, shadow, emboss, and superscript/subscript. You can also adjust the elevation of superscripts and subscripts in the Offset box.

If you're planning to deliver your presentation on a large screen, avoid italicized fonts, which often end up looking like wavy blobs. You can use underline instead, to emphasize a word or phrase, but underlining is traditionally reserved as a substitute for italic. If you absolutely must emphasize a word, bold is probably your best choice.

REPLACING FONTS THROUGHOUT A PRESENTATION

If you're trying to change all the Times New Roman in a presentation to Garamond, you might be tempted to change the Title Master and Slide Master, and call it a day.

Unfortunately, if you've applied any manual formatting to individual slides, the "link" between the slide and its master might be broken. In that case, even if the master is updated, the slide might not make the switch.

→ To change every slide in your presentation, **see** "Using the Title Master," **p. 793**.

To truly change all occurrences of Times New Roman to Garamond, choose Format, Replace Fonts. Choose Times New Roman from the Replace drop-down list; choose Garamond from the With list. Click OK to apply the change throughout the presentation— even in the masters.

> **Note**
>
> Unfortunately, this technique changes only the font; you can't use the dialog box to change point size.

TROUBLESHOOTING

SLIDE MASTER LINK DAMAGE

I changed the Slide Master, but some of the slides in my presentation haven't been updated with the changes.

If you do something odd (for example, delete one of the placeholders in a slide), it's possible to break the link between a slide and the Slide Master. After the link has been broken, changes to the Slide Master are no longer propagated to the slide. To reset the link, select the slide, bring up the Slide Layout pane by choosing Format, Slide Layout, and apply the layout that's most appropriate for the slide.

SECRETS OF THE OFFICE MASTERS: TWEAKING THE SLIDE MASTER

If you need extra space for the text placeholder in your presentation, consider modifying the Slide Master by using the method described in this chapter's section, "Modifying an Existing Design for Your Presentation." If you move the graphic elements around just a bit, and expand the main text area on three or four sides, you can squeeze a substantial amount of additional room for text into each slide.

Contrast the Slide Master shown in Figure 30.12 with the one shown earlier in Figure 30.7 (this one has had a couple of elements moved just a bit, with the graphic on the upper right squished slightly, using the techniques described earlier in this chapter). Although this slide isn't as aesthetically pleasing as the earlier slide, there's considerably more room for slide text—and chances are good your audience will never notice the difference between the two.

Figure 30.12

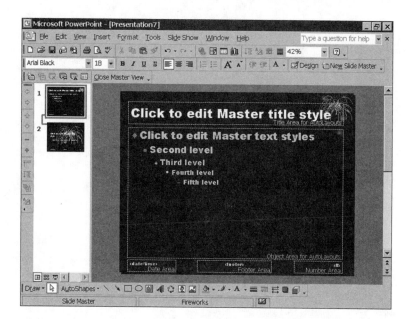

CHAPTER 31

ADDING GRAPHICS, MULTIMEDIA, AND SPECIAL EFFECTS

In this chapter

USING TRANSITIONS TO CONTROL PACING

PowerPoint makes it easy to control what your audience sees on the screen when you move from one slide to another. You can arrange things so that one slide replaces another onscreen, just as it would if you clicked through a carousel of 35mm slides. Or you can add wipes, dissolves, and other varieties of eye-catching (and frequently distracting) transitions. Properly done, transitions (sometimes also called *transition effects* or *slide transitions*) provide a breathing space between slides. Improperly done, your presentation will look amateurish and detract from making your point—which, after all, is the purpose of PowerPoint.

The nature of that breathing space lies totally at your control—a subtle, quick fade to black; a pixelated dissolve that leaves the old slide in view for quite some time; shutters and checkerboards; and dozens more. Transitions can help add an ambience to your presentation. You might want a more abrupt transition if you're trying to project a snappy, rapid-fire image, and a more relaxed transition when the situation calls for a less formal approach.

Most experts agree that you should select one transition, and use it exclusively throughout your presentation, with perhaps a few slides here and there getting "special treatment"—just to keep the audience awake. Mixing and matching transitions, however, jars the audience every bit as badly as ransom-note mixed fonts.

When dealing with transitions, it's always easiest to work in Slide Sorter view.

→ For tips on using Slide Sorter view, **see** "Using Slide Sorter View to Rearrange a Presentation," **p. 755**.

Note

Although you might think that a transition is defined between slides—showing how to *fade out* on the first slide and *fade in* on the next—PowerPoint doesn't work that way. Instead, you assign a transition to a slide, and that particular transition takes place when the slide is shown—it's a fade-in effect.

Tip from

EQ & Woody

Although PowerPoint has most of the animation bases covered, in a few instances, animation can't be applied. For example, you might have a picture of a product that you're building in your presentation, but you want some elements to disappear after two or more mouse clicks, perhaps to de-emphasize the old pieces as you add new ones. PowerPoint doesn't offer a "hide after *N* mouse clicks" animation option, so you can't animate it directly. In these cases, use a transition to fake animation: Build two slides—one to show the "before" image and the other for the "after" image—and then run a quick transition between the two. Your audience will be impressed.

APPLYING A TRANSITION TO ONE SLIDE

To set a transition for a slide, first switch to Slide Sorter view, and then follow these steps:

1. Click the Transition button on the Formatting toolbar. This brings up the Slide Transition pane (see Figure 31.1).

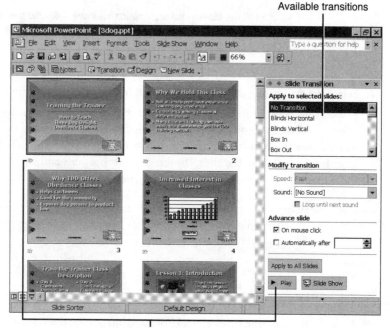

Figure 31.1
The Slide Transition pane makes it easy to apply and modify transitions.

PART

V

CH

31

2. Select the slide you want to have a particular transition, and then select the transition effect you want from the Apply to Selected Slides list.

3. PowerPoint shows you a preview of the transition you selected and adds a small icon just below the bottom-left corner of the slide, as shown in Figure 31.1. To see the transition again, click this icon, or click Play at the bottom of the Slide Transition pane.

Tip from

EQ & Woody

If you want your transitions and animations to appear when your presentation is viewed from a Web browser, you must choose Tools, Options, General, Web Options, and check the Show Slide Animation While Browsing box.

APPLYING A TRANSITION TO A GROUP OF SLIDES

To assign the same transition to a group of slides

1. In Slide Sorter view, select the slides you want to have the same transition. Ctrl+click to select single slides, or Shift+click to select a contiguously numbered group.

Tip from

EQ & Woody

To select all the slides in the presentation, click one slide, and then press Ctrl+A.

2. Select the transition you want from the list on the Slide Transition pane.

3. PowerPoint goes through a preview of the transitions and animations on all the selected slides. To stop it, press the Stop button at the bottom of the Slide Transition pane. To see the transition and animation on an individual slide, click the Preview Transition icon below the slide. To repeat the transitions and animations for all the slides, press Play on the Slide Transition pane.

Caution

When you apply a transition to a slide, PowerPoint replaces any transitions you previously applied to that slide.

CONTROLLING SLIDE TRANSITION SPEED

The Slide Transition pane gives you additional control over the transition between slides. You can

- Set the speed of most transitions to slow, medium, or fast.
- Tell PowerPoint whether you want to be able to advance to the next slide during a presentation by clicking the mouse. Note that this is a "fade out" setting—one that controls how the slide exits—and is thus different from most other transition settings.
- Specify that you want to advance to the next slide automatically after a preset interval. Again, this is a "fade out" setting.
- Make PowerPoint play a sound during the transition.

Tip from

EQ & Woody

In general, resist the temptation to check the Loop Until Next Sound box, which is certain to distract almost any audience, unless you have a specific impression in mind: a suspenseful tick-tick-tick leading up to the next slide, for example, might be appropriate. But consider the reaction if a question from the audience takes you 10 minutes to answer—with the tick-tick-tick going all the time.

The two Advance settings—On Mouse Click and Automatically After—operate independently. If you activate both options, PowerPoint shows the next slide when the timer expires, or when you click the slide, whichever comes first. If you leave both boxes unchecked, the slide advances only when you press the spacebar, the Enter key, or one of PowerPoint's other keyboard presentation *control keys*.

→ For a definitive list of presentation control keys, **see** "Mouse and Keyboard Shortcuts," **p. 762**.

ANIMATING TEXT AND OBJECTS ON A SLIDE

Just as you use transition effects to control how a slide fades in, you use *animations* to control how the individual elements of a slide make their appearance. By showing one bullet point at a time, for example, you can make sure your audience concentrates on what you're saying now rather than reading the rest of the bullets on your slide and mentally calculating how much longer you're going to speak.

The most rudimentary form of slide animation displays each bullet point on a slide one at a time: You click the mouse and the slide's title appears. Click again, and the first bullet point appears onscreen. Keep clicking to display each bullet point on the list. Other animations let you specify that bullet points fly in or zoom from any direction. You can also choose fades, dissolves, wipes, and other visual effects.

You can apply animations to almost any part of a slide, and then activate the animations by clicking the mouse or using PowerPoint's built-in timers. Used sparingly, these animations can add punch to your presentation, augmenting your spoken words with powerful visuals. Say you have a graph that illustrates how sales have taken off in the past year. You could show the whole graph, all at one time, and emphasize the spike in the final number verbally. Much more effectively, however, you could have the bars fly onto the graph one at a time—building up, in your narration, to the spike in the final quarter.

You can use animations to coordinate sounds, so they play as predetermined parts of the slide appear. You can also place text on a slide, one character, word, or paragraph at a time. For example, use animations to start movies and other types of video clips at predetermined intervals after the slide first appears. Or use them to dim or change the color of items on the slide, in conjunction with the appearance of a new item.

Tip from

EQ & Woody

For sophisticated animation effects, break the clip-art objects apart, and then animate each element separately. Duplicating elements and using flying effects can also create the illusion of motion.

ANIMATING BULLET POINTS

Animating the arrival of bullet points on a slide gives you control over how much information your audience sees, and when. Moving one bullet point at a time onto the slide lets you keep your audience running at your pace, particularly if you know that people in the audience have a tendency to read ahead. Also consider using bullet animation if you want to save some surprising or emphatic points for the end of the slide.

Caution

If you remove the capability to advance a slide based on mouse clicks (by unchecking the On Mouse Click box shown earlier in Figure 31.1), you also remove the capability to animate bullet points with a mouse click. Instead, if you've provided an automatic advance time (in the Automatically After box), PowerPoint divides that time equally among the bullet points, and presents each in turn, automatically.

If you check the Automatically After box in Figure 31.1, PowerPoint will show each of the bullet points automatically if you don't click soon enough. Here, too, each bullet point is given an equal amount of time.

Tip from

EQ & Woody

If you have animated bullet points, don't forget to show them as you're making the presentation! You would be amazed how many presenters talk "to" multiple animated bullet points on a slide, show the first point, and then forget to click to put the other bullet points on the screen so their audience can follow along.

To animate "flying" bullet points the easiest way, choose from the Animation Schemes on the Slide Design pane:

1. Bring up the Slide Design panel's Animation Schemes by choosing Slide Show, Animation Schemes (see Figure 31.2).

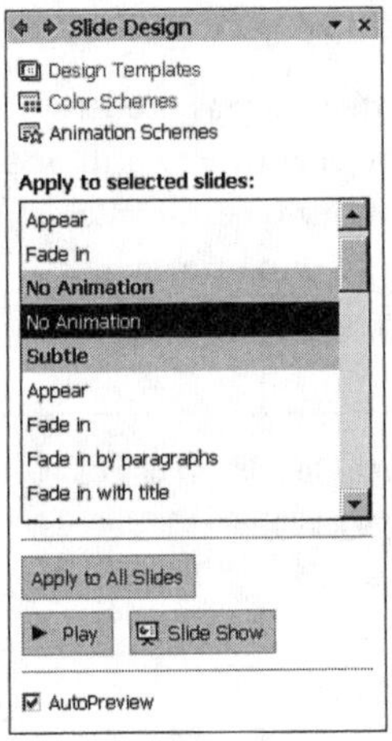

Figure 31.2
Animation schemes are on the Slide Design pane.

2. Select the slide or slides you want to take on the specified animation. Ctrl+click to select single slides, Shift+click to select a contiguous group, or press Ctrl+A to select all the slides. Select the animation you prefer from the Apply to Selected Slides list.

3. Look at the first slide you selected to see a preview of the slide's transition, followed by the animation. If you want to see the transition and animation again, click the slide's Preview transition and animation button, which is just below the slide on the left.

PowerPoint's collection of built-in animation effects is impressive, but if you don't see the animation effect you want, you can create your own. For example, you can bring in second- and lower-level bullet points one at a time, or specify that bullet-point text should appear onscreen one word or character at a time. To build your animation from scratch, use the Custom Animation pane.

→ To go it on your own, **see** "Advanced Animation," **p. 824**.

Tip from	If you want your transitions and animations to appear when your presentation is viewed from a Web browser, you must choose Tools, Options, General, Web Options, and check the Show Slide Animation While Browsing box.
Ed & Woody	

ANIMATING TITLES

The trickiest part of animating a title lies in understanding precisely when the animation will take place. When you click to advance to a slide with an animated title using preset animations, your presentation proceeds in one of two ways (assuming the Slide Master itself isn't animated):

- **If the Bullet Points Are Not Animated**—The background appears, along with all the slide's bullet points. Shortly thereafter, the title appears, using the chosen animation. You don't have to click.

- **If the Bullet Points Are Animated**—The slide background appears. Shortly thereafter, the title appears, using the animation you specified. Click to display the first bullet on the slide. Click again to show each succeeding bullet.

It's easy to animate titles by using most of the preset animations available on the Slide Design pane's Animation Schemes list.

The easiest way to apply one of these preset animations to a slide's title is via Animation Schemes:

1. In Normal or Slide view, select the slide whose title you want to animate.

2. If the Slide Design pane is not visible, click the Design button on the Formatting toolbar. Click Animation Schemes.

3. Choose one of the dozens of effects in the Apply to Selected Slides list. As soon as you choose the animation, watch the selected slide to see what the animation entails.

By creating a custom title animation, you can go far beyond the preset choices here: Arrange for the title to appear after the bullet points, for example, or have the characters or words in the title appear, one after the other. To create your own, use the Custom Animation pane.

→ For details on animations, **see** "Advanced Animation," **p. 824**.

ADVANCED ANIMATION

In the preceding two sections, you saw how to apply PowerPoint's prebuilt animations with titles and bullet points. This section shows you how to build custom animations, again concentrating on bullets and titles.

PowerPoint offers an enormous variety of ways to animate items on a slide. For example, what if you want top-level bullet points to appear onscreen first, followed one at a time by second-level bullets? Every one of PowerPoint's preset animations displays an entire high-level bullet point and all the lower-level points below it at the same time. Follow these steps to create a custom effect:

1. In Normal view, bring up the slide that contains the bullet points you want to animate. This exercise is more effective if you have bullet points at both the first and second levels.

2. Choose Slide Show, Custom Animation. The Custom Animation pane appears (see Figure 31.3).

Figure 31.3
To build a custom animation from the ground up, start with the Custom Animation pane.

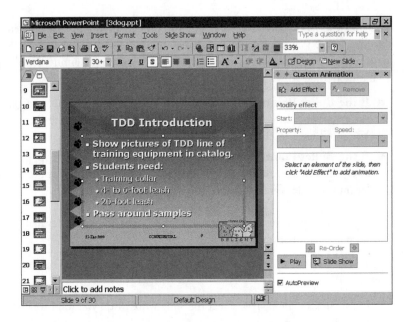

3. Select the items on the slide you want to animate. In Figure 31.3, the slide's body text is animated, but the slide's title is not, so the text placeholder (which contains all the bullet points) is selected.

4. Click the Add Effect button and choose the effect you want. An Entrance effect called Fly In is used in Figure 31.4.

Figure 31.4
PowerPoint has hundreds of animation effects. For each element of a slide, you can pick the entrance motion, font effects (marked Emphasis), exit motion, or you can apply any motion that you can draw.

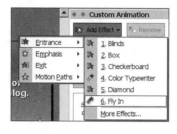

5. PowerPoint shows the first animation—in this case, the bullet point that starts with "Show pictures of TDD..."—in the timing review list. Click the downward-pointing chevron below the first animation, and PowerPoint shows you all the bullet points and their sequence (see Figure 31.5). The timing review list indicates that on the first mouse click, the first bullet ("Show pictures of TDD...") appears. On the second mouse click, four more bullet points appear. And on the third click, the last bullet point appears.

Figure 31.5
The timing review list shows what each mouse click will do. Sequence numbers to the left of the bullet points repeat that information.

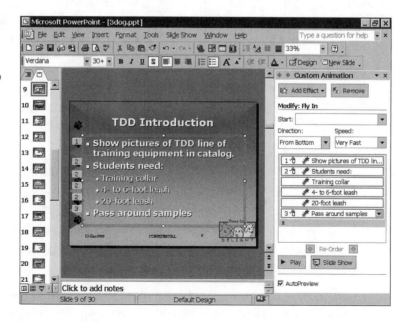

6. Each bullet point should appear in turn—six mouse clicks, each of which is to bring up one bullet point. Click the first unnumbered bullet point ("Training collar"), select the down-arrow to the right, and choose Start On Click (see Figure 31.6).

Figure 31.6
You can adjust the appearance of each bullet item individually.

7. Continue in this manner until all the bullet points have their own sequence numbers, 1 through 6 (see Figure 31.7).

Figure 31.7
Each bullet point appears in turn, as indicated by the numbers 1 through 6.

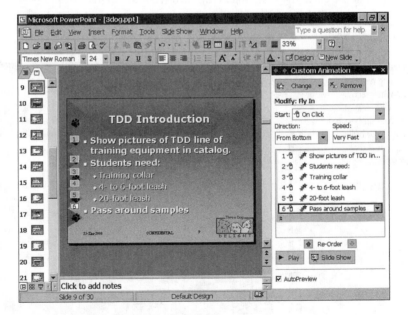

8. Finally, to verify your choices, click the Slide Show button at the bottom of the Custom Animation pane. The heading should come up as soon as the slide appears. Click once, and the first bullet point comes up. Click again and you get the second bullet point, and so on. This level of control is not available in any of the standard Animation Schemes.

Note

There is no way to apply separate animations to individual bullet points on a slide. For example, you can't have the first bullet point wipe from the left, and have the second spiral from the top.

Tip from

EQ & Woody

Of course, if you absolutely must make bulleted list items fly from all directions, you can create pictures that look just like bulleted items. Then you can animate each, any way you like. That increases the size of the presentation, which can be a problem if your presentation has to be sent via e-mail, or shown over the Web.

When you make a presentation, any item on the slide that isn't animated shows up as soon as the slide hits the screen. Animated items appear next, normally in top-to-bottom order. Sometimes you don't want the slide's elements to appear from top to bottom, however; you might have a picture that you want to appear before the bullets, or a video clip that should show before the title comes up. Using the Custom Animation pane, you can control the order in which animated items appear.

PART

V

CH

31

To arrange the order in which animations appear

1. In Normal view, select the slide with the animations that need to be ordered.

2. Choose Slide Show, Custom Animation. You'll see the Custom Animation pane.

3. Choose the items on the slide you want to animate, as in Figure 31.3.

4. To change the order of any animated item in the list, click to select the item and then use the Re-Order arrows at the bottom of the timing review list.

On slides with two text placeholders, you must animate each placeholder separately. That poses a slight restriction on your ability to design a presentation, because it means all the bullets in one placeholder must go up on the screen before you can start showing bullets from the other placeholder. But this feature also offers a clever way to use different animation effects for each set of bullets on a slide: Just use a different animation for each placeholder.

→ To alter slide layouts, **see** "Choosing a Slide Layout," **p. 770**.

If one of PowerPoint's preset Animation Schemes is close to the effect you want, use it as a starting point for customization. Apply the Animation Scheme, and then open the Customize Animation pane to modify it slightly.

For example, if you like the Boomerang and exit Animation Scheme, but want it to apply to both first- and second-level bullets, try this:

1. In Normal view, select the slide you want to animate.

2. Choose Slide Show, Animation Schemes. On the Animation Schemes pane, choose the Boomerang and exit scheme.

3. Change to the Custom Animation pane (by, say, clicking the down arrow to the right of Animation Scheme and choosing Custom Animation). You'll see all the components of the Fly in and fade in scheme, detailed in the timing review list.

4. Click to the right of the first bullet point you want to Fly in, and choose Start On Click.

5. Adjust the remaining bullet points. When you're ready, click Slide Show and make sure the animation does what you want.

 If you're frustrated because you can't copy custom animation effects from slide to slide, see "Custom Animation Tricks" in the "Troubleshooting" section at the end of this book.

Tip from

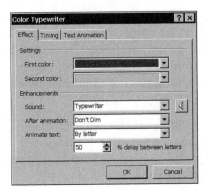

To add a custom animation to every slide, animate the Slide Master. You can apply any animation effect to any item on the Slide Master—title, text, background pictures, date/time, footer, and slide number. You can also animate the Title Master.

To coordinate the arrival of each character in a title with a sound (say, a typewriter clacking), here's how you coordinate sounds with characters:

1. In Normal view, select the slide whose bullet points you want to animate. Bring up the Custom Animation pane (choose Slide Show, Custom Animation).

2. Choose the item you want to animate—for example, the title. Click Effects, and choose Entrance, Color Typewriter.

3. In the timing review list, click the down arrow to the right of the title, choose Effect Options, and choose Typewriter in the Sound box (see Figure 31.8).

Figure 31.8
The Color Typewriter Animation Scheme allows you to play a sound announcing the arrival of each character.

When the title appears on the slide, each character flies in, accompanied by the sound of a typewriter.

ANIMATING THE DRAWING LAYER

PowerPoint lets you animate any items in the drawing layer—text boxes, drawings, AutoShapes, clip art, charts, embedded Excel or Word objects, org charts, and more. Before you try, however, it's important that you understand how the drawing layer works, and how to use it in conjunction with the Custom Animation dialog box.

→ To add pictures to the drawing layer, **see** "Working with the Drawing Layer," **p. 108**.

→ For an overview of animation, **see** "Advanced Animation," **p. 824**.

Say you've created a dramatic slide that features the company's mascot, a collie. You've scanned a photo of the mascot, and you want the photo to "dissolve" onto the screen with applause—and you hope the audience will join in. Here's how:

1. Select the slide and add the new picture.

2. Select the picture and choose Slide Show, Custom Animation. The Custom Animation pane appears.

3. Click Add Effect, Entrance, More Effects, and then choose Fade (see Figure 31.9).

Figure 31.9
If you select an item on a slide and then choose an animation, PowerPoint applies only the animation to the selected item.

4. Click the down arrow in the timing review list next to the picture. Choose Effect Options. In the Sound box, pick Applause. Now when the slide appears on the screen, the picture of the dog will "fade in," accompanied by the sounds of four paws clapping.

Use similar techniques to animate any object on the drawing layer. For example, you might want to have a text box that says "Met Year 2002 Goals!" on top of a slide showing financial information, animated to appear after you've had a chance to talk about the numbers.

Custom animations also let you introduce text in AutoShape callouts or text boxes one word or letter at a time.

HIDING AND UNCOVERING SLIDE CONTENTS

There's a trick to using items in the drawing layer that all too frequently escapes PowerPoint users. If you carefully match the color of a shape in the drawing layer to the color of the background, you can use animation on these shapes to *hide* parts of your presentation.

Say you have a slide that includes an organizational chart, and you want to unveil each member of the organization, one at a time. PowerPoint offers only basic options when it comes to organizational charts, in noteworthy comparison to the long list of fancy effects you can accomplish with charts you create with Excel or Microsoft Graph. Here's how to use animations to show one piece of the org chart at a time:

1. Create the slide and organizational chart. For best results, make sure the slide's background is a solid color.

2. Click the Rectangle tool on the Drawing toolbar. Draw a rectangle around the top box in the org chart, extending down so that it covers the vertical line at the bottom of the box. If you have trouble covering the rectangle precisely and need more control, hold down the Alt key as you drag.

3. Click the Fill Color icon. Select the color that most nearly matches the background color.

4. Click the Line Color icon. Select the same color you selected in the preceding step.

5. Repeat steps 2, 3, and 4 to draw rectangles around each box, including appropriate sections of the connecting lines.

6. Choose Slide Show, Custom Animation, and bring up the Custom Animation pane. Click all the Rectangles and choose whatever Animation Effect suits your fancy. In the timing review sequence list, arrange the order so the first Rectangle is the last in order. Use the Effect Options choices to add any additional effects (applause, for example).

The presentation will now reveal each piece of the org chart when you click the mouse.

ANIMATING CHART COMPONENTS

You can animate every piece of a chart separately. For example, to dramatically demonstrate five years of steady growth, try sliding each bar in the chart up from the bottom of the slide, one after the other. To focus on your progress versus a competitor, show the bars for the competitor first, and then reveal the corresponding bars for your company.

Before you undertake this advanced animation, make sure you understand how to create a chart in Excel or Microsoft Graph, how to insert a chart into a slide, and how to use the Custom Animation dialog box.

→ To create a chart in Excel, **see** Chapter 24, "Creating and Editing Charts," **p. 645**.

→ To put a chart in a slide, **see** "Inserting an Excel Chart or Range," **p. 780**.

→ For tips on Custom Animation, **see** "Animating Text and Objects on a Slide," **p. 821**.

To animate an Excel chart, you must put the chart in a slide's chart placeholder—charts inserted in an object placeholder, or put on the drawing layer, can't have their components animated. To put an Excel chart in a chart placeholder

1. Create the chart in Excel. It's easiest if you put it on its own Chart Sheet.

2. Bring up the slide in PowerPoint, and use the Slide Layout pane to apply a Content or Content & Text layout.

3. Click the chart placeholder in the middle of the upper row. PowerPoint responds by creating a dummy chart and spreadsheet using Microsoft Chart.

4. Choose Edit, Import File, and navigate to the workbook that includes the chart. Click Open.

5. In the Select Sheet from Workbook box, choose the sheet that includes the chart. Click OK.

6. PowerPoint places your chart in the chart placeholder, and imports the associated data into its Datasheet. At this point, you can animate the chart.

Note

Bringing an Excel chart into PowerPoint in this way severs all ties with Excel. You cannot double-click the chart and edit it in Excel.

→ For the most elementary type of charts, **see** "Creating and Editing Charts and Diagrams," **p. 128**.

→ To take full advantage of your animation options, **see** "Advanced Animation," **p. 824**.

To make each bar of a bar chart appear independently on the screen

1. Open the slide that contains the chart. Select the chart and choose Slide Show, Custom Animation. You'll get the Custom Animation pane.

2. Choose Add Effect and pick an Entrance effect such as Diamond.

3. Click the down arrow next to the Chart in the timing review list and choose Effect Options. On the Chart Animation tab, choose the method you want to use to Introduce Chart Elements: The chart can come in all at once; by Series (that is, all similarly colored bars appear, followed by all bars with the next color, and so on); by

PART

V

CH

31

Category (each group of bars that falls into one group on the y-axis appears, and then the next group); or by individual bars within each Series or Category (see Figure 31.10).

Figure 31.10
Individual bars in a chart appear in the sequence defined on the Chart Animation tab.

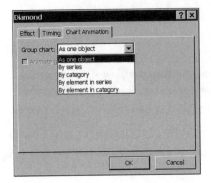

4. Test your animation by clicking the Play button.

Because PowerPoint gives you the capability to present data by Series or Category, the animation sequence for chart effects can be complex. Use the Play button as you work to make sure the order is correct.

ADDING MULTIMEDIA TO YOUR PRESENTATION

PowerPoint puts you in the director's chair when it comes to adding sounds, clip art (including pictures with movement such as animated GIFs), extended musical accompaniment, and even movie clips. But just because it *can* be done doesn't necessarily mean it *should* be done. Multimedia components in a presentation tend to overwhelm the audience. Be sure you really want to draw your audience's attention away from what you're saying before you insert a multimedia clip.

ADDING MUSIC, SOUNDS, AND VIDEO CLIPS

The easiest way to add multimedia to a presentation combines the Slide Layout pane's content placeholder and Office's Clip Gallery:

1. In Normal view, select the slide on which you want to include a media clip (sound or movie).
2. Bring up the Slide Layout pane by choosing Format, Slide Layout.
3. In the Slide Layout pane, select one of the Content Layouts, Text and Content Layouts, or one of the Other Layouts that includes the "321" clapboard.

→ To change the layout of the slide, **see** "Choosing a Slide Layout," **p. 770**.

4. Back in the slide, rearrange the placeholders as necessary to fit both the clip and text (if any) on the slide. (If you don't want text on the slide, make the text placeholder as small as possible and move it to the side.)

5. If you used a content layout, click the video camera in the lower-right corner. If you used a clapboard layout, double-click the clapboard icon. The Media Gallery appears, with the Sound and Motion Clips tabs visible.

6. Choose the sound or motion clip you want, and then click OK. The Media Gallery inserts the clip you selected into the media clip placeholder on your slide, and then asks: "Do you want your movie (or sound) to play automatically in the slide show? If not, it will play when you click it." Choose Yes if you want the movie/sound to begin as soon as the slide appears. If you choose No, you'll have to click the picture (or the speaker that symbolizes a sound) to play the sound or show the video during the presentation.

> **Note**
>
> You'll find animated GIFs in the Media Gallery. Office XP does not include any tools that allow you to edit an animated GIF; to change one of these images, you must use a program specifically designed to handle this graphic format, such as Magic Viewer from Crayonsoft (www.crayonsoft.com/).

Other methods for adding multimedia to a slide include the following:

- To place a clip in the drawing layer, choose Insert, Picture, Clip Art (or equivalently, click the Clip Art icon on the Drawing toolbar). This brings up the Insert Clip Art pane—thus giving you the widest latitude in choosing what kind of clip you want to use.

- To bypass the Media Gallery and choose a picture from files stored on your computer or network, choose Insert, Picture, From File.

- Use Insert, Movies and Sounds if you know what kind of multimedia clip you want to insert: Movie from Media Gallery brings up the Media Gallery with Motion Clips alone available; Sound from Media Gallery does the same, with Sounds.

- Also use Insert, Movies and Sounds if you want to play a CD track, or if you want to record a custom sound to go with the slide.

→ For more information on sounds, **see** "Using CD Audio and Recorded Audio," **p. 836**.

All the preceding methods insert a multimedia clip into your presentation for playback by PowerPoint itself. For maximum control over media objects, embed a Windows Media Player object on a slide. The following guidelines can help you decide when you should use this option:

- Do you want anyone viewing the presentation to be able to start, stop, and jump through the media clip? PowerPoint includes only basic controls for starting, ending, and looping. Media Player includes extensive capabilities for fast forward, marking and jumping to segments, editing, and the like. A Media Player Object can even display a working "Play/Stop" slider on the slide.

- Some versions of Media Player on machines running Windows 95 were unstable and rendered clips with poor fidelity. On such a system, clips that perform well with PowerPoint alone might appear grainy or streaked with Media Player.

- You cannot adjust the PowerPoint animation multimedia effects of a Media Player object (see next section).

- If you test a presentation with one version of Media Player and then run it on a machine that uses a different version of Media Player, you might notice significant differences.

To embed a Windows Media Player object in a slide, choose Insert, Object, and then choose Media Clip, MIDI Sequence, Video Clip, or Wave Sound. Any of those choices will embed an object that plays back with the Windows Media Player.

CONTROLLING A VIDEO OR SOUND CLIP

To change the behavior of a video or sound clip after you place it on a slide—whether it's in a placeholder, or in the drawing layer—right-click the clip (or the bullhorn icon representing a sound) and choose Custom Animation. Click the Multimedia Settings tab to see options that apply only to sounds and media clips.

Use these options to create a video introduction to a slide with bullet points. The slide should appear first, with the title and background. Then, as quickly as PowerPoint can manage, the video clip should play. Finally, after the clip is over, the video should disappear and your bullet points should slide onto the screen.

Here's how to do it:

1. Select the slide you plan to use, and enter its title and bullet points.

2. To place the video clip in the drawing layer, click the Clip Art icon on the Drawing toolbar; you can also choose Picture or Movies and Sounds from the Insert menu.

3. When PowerPoint asks, "Do you want your movie to play automatically in the slide show? If not, it will play when you click it," click Yes.

4. Resize the movie clip window and position it where you want the movie to appear. Ignore the bullet points for the time being—they won't be there when the video runs—and concentrate on getting the movie clip right.

5. Right-click the movie clip window and select Custom Animation. You'll see the movie file appear at the top of the timing review list, with a 0 next to it (indicating that the movie will run as soon as the slide appears).

6. Click the Text placeholder, and then click the Add Effect box on the Custom Animation pane to assign an effect for the slide's bullet points. In Figure 31.11, the Fly in effect is used. The bullet points appear in the timing review list directly below the animation.

Figure 31.11
The timing review list indicates that the Firework.avi animation will run before the bullet points appear.

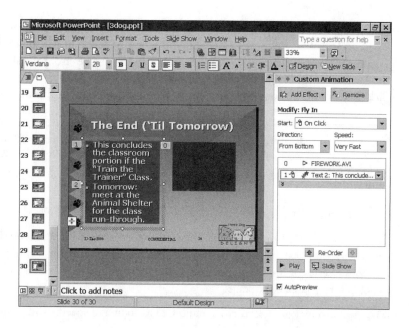

PART

V

CH

31

7. Click the down arrow next to the media clip at the top of the timing review list. Choose Effect Options. In the Play Movie dialog box (see Figure 31.12), check the box to Hide While Not Playing, and choose Hide After Animation from the After Animation drop-down list. That ensures that the movie clip will play and then disappear, before the bullet points arrive.

Figure 31.12
Tell the movie clip to disappear when it's done playing.

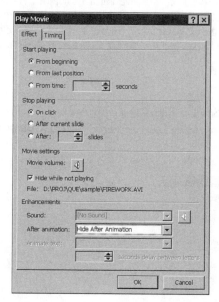

8. Click the down arrow next to the Text 2 bullet point in the timing review list, and select Start After Previous. This ensures that the first bullet point will appear immediately after the movie clip finishes, and the movie itself vanishes from the slide.

Click Play on the Custom Animation pane and you'll see how all this ties together.

Tip from	Loop and rewind options vary depending on the type of multimedia clip you select. To work with these settings, click the Effect and Timing tabs in the Play Movie dialog box.

USING CD AUDIO AND RECORDED AUDIO

You can use recorded audio (such as a narration) or a track from a music CD as a dramatic way to introduce a slide or a presentation. You could even use this technique in combination with a series of timed animations to run a dramatic series of slides, complete with audio, before you take the stage.

If you want to play a track from an audio CD as soon as a specific slide appears during a presentation, try this:

1. In Normal view, select the slide. Insert the CD you want to use in the PC's CD-ROM drive.

Tip from	If you have enabled CD AutoPlay on your system, Windows will begin playing an audio CD as soon as you insert it into the drive. When this happens, PowerPoint won't be able to take control of the CD to let you select a track. To give control back to PowerPoint, open the CD Player applet (choose Start, Programs, Accessories, Entertainment, CD Player), and stop the CD. Close the CD Player to let PowerPoint use the CD.

2. Choose Insert, Movies and Sounds, Play CD Audio Track. PowerPoint responds with the Movie and Sound Options dialog box (see Figure 31.13). Choose the track(s) you want to play and click OK.

Figure 31.13
As long as you have the CD in your PC's drive, PowerPoint automatically calculates how much time it will take to play the tracks you select.

3. PowerPoint asks whether you want your movie to play automatically in the slide show. If you want the CD track to start the moment this slide hits the screen, select Yes. If you select No, you'll have to click the slide's CD icon (which looks just like a CD) before the track(s) will play.

4. If you want to make any more changes to the animation, right-click the CD icon and select Custom Animation. Use any of the options described earlier in this chapter.

CD tracks have all the flexibility of any other kind of animation. PowerPoint can launch a CD audio track automatically, and individual tracks can appear in any order, before or after other animated elements on a slide.

Note

> PowerPoint doesn't identify the actual CD in the CD-ROM drive; it knows only to play the tracks you've specified, no matter which CD might be in there. If you forget to put a CD in the drive when running a presentation, PowerPoint continues as if there were no track(s) to be played.

Similarly, if your PC has a functioning microphone, you can record a sound to be played with slides—you can even prerecord narration for every slide and, using timed advancing on the slides, deliver an entire presentation without being physically present. Choose Insert, Movies and Sounds, Record Sound, and follow the instructions.

Caution

> Audio clips in presentations viewed over the Web can slow down the process horribly, unless the viewer has a very high speed connection.

USING ACTION LINKS TO COMBINE EFFECTS

You can tie each animated element on a slide to a hyperlink or action setting. When you click a hyperlinked element or an item that includes an action setting, the animation takes place before the hyperlink or action setting kicks in.

→ For hyperlink information specific to PowerPoint, **see** "Using Hyperlinks," **page 763**.

Combining custom animation and action settings needn't be overly confusing because they typically operate on different slide components. For example, you can apply a sound "animation" to the appearance of bullet points on a slide, but you can apply the sound "action setting" only to the words (and characters) in the bullet point.

Surprisingly, however, there's one action that you can implement only through hyperlinks and action settings: the mouse over. All the fancy animation techniques discussed in this chapter are tied to mouse clicks, or internal timers.

For example, if you want to make a video clip start by passing the mouse over the clip, you *must* use action settings. Select the clip, and then choose Slide Show, Action Settings, Mouse Over.

TROUBLESHOOTING

CUSTOM ANIMATION TRICKS

I created a slick custom animation for one slide, but I can't figure out how to copy the animation effects to other slides in my presentation.

Although PowerPoint has no built-in way to copy a custom animation from one slide to another, here's an undocumented trick that lets you reuse custom animations: Make a copy of a slide, and then change the title and bullets on the copy. The copy includes all the custom animation settings of the original.

For example, if you've created a nifty custom animation on slide 20, how do you move it to slides 17, 18, and 19? You could edit the animation settings for each of the other three slides, but that's a cumbersome process. Instead, make three copies of slide 20, and then move the existing text from the old slides to the copies. Delete the old slides when you've finished.

SECRETS OF THE OFFICE MASTERS: ANIMATE CHARTS TO EMPHASIZE DATA

Almost every chart can benefit from some animation. In the simplest case, shown in the following figure, you can set up the bars to appear one at a time, cumulatively from left to right, by using the Flash Once/Fast entry animation. After you get the hang of clicking to advance the animation while you speak, your point will be all the more forceful.

Figure 31.14

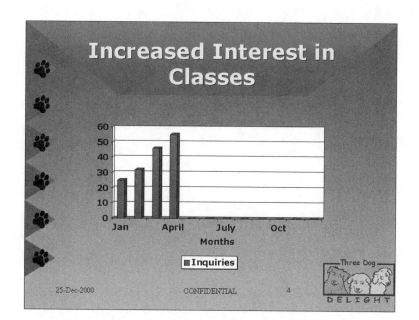

CHAPTER 32

PLANNING AND DELIVERING A PRESENTATION

In this chapter

PLANNING YOUR PRESENTATION

Far too many presentations crash in flames because the presenter fails to anticipate what could reasonably go wrong, or doesn't prepare for questions that can be answered with a few facts, figures, or slides.

On the other hand, some less-than-flashy presenters with solid but uninspired slides regularly draw raves from appreciative audiences. Why? Because they step through points logically and in sequence, and when questions arise, they have solid answers, ready and waiting—and right at hand in their speaker notes.

THE IMPORTANCE OF PREPARATION

It's no secret, and no coincidence, that the best presenters rehearse their presentations over and over, in front of different groups that closely parallel the target audience. Before they stand up on stage, they take apart their presentation, slide by slide, and then edit, reorganize, put it back together, and test it again.

You might be tempted to practice in front of a mirror, and if your primary concern is the mechanics of the presentation, that's a reasonable approach. But if you want to get a point across, nothing beats jumping into the lion's den. Practice delivering the presentation to people who are willing to stop you when they don't understand, and make suggestions when your points miss their mark.

PowerPoint includes a number of tools that will help you prepare, refine, and ultimately deliver the presentation. But in the final analysis, they won't help a bit unless you have the content down pat. The best presentations practically deliver themselves.

ORGANIZING YOUR REMARKS WITH SPEAKER NOTES

Some people are capable of delivering a perfect presentation without notes. But what if you don't have a photographic memory or weeks to rehearse? For those of us who are chronically short on spare time and brain cells, there's no substitute for PowerPoint's *speaker notes*.

→ For an overview of notes, **see** "Adding Notes," **p. 757**.

The easiest way to construct and maintain notes is in PowerPoint's Normal view, where the Notes pane appears below the slide. Normally, this window displays only a few lines; to look at all the notes for a given slide, go to Notes view by choosing View, Notes Page.

You can do little to change the appearance of the Notes page, except for adjusting tab stops. Because default tab stops start at one inch, you might find yourself running out of room if you indent text on a note page that contains lots of text; follow these steps to adjust the tabs and give the indented text a little extra room:

1. In Normal or Slide Sorter view, select the slide with the notes that you want to change.

2. Choose View, Notes Page. Then bring up the ruler by choosing View, Ruler.

3. Click once to position the insertion point in the notes placeholder below the slide. Then click and drag on the bottom of the ruler to adjust the tab stops.

To change the tab spacing on all your Notes pages, bring up the Notes Master (choose View, Master, Notes Master), adjust the tab stops on the ruler, and save your changes to the master.

Tip from

* EQ & Woody*

If you can anticipate any questions your audience might ask when a particular slide is on the screen, consider typing the question (and a possible answer, of course) at the bottom of the Notes page for that slide. To make it easier to identify the questions while you're flipping through your notes, set them off in bold or italic.

USING POWERPOINT'S TIMER TO REHEARSE A PRESENTATION

When you practice a presentation, PowerPoint can start a timer to keep track of the amount of time you spend on each slide and on the presentation as a whole. These timings can be useful in several situations:

- Timing your presentation helps you identify slides that are too complex or contain too much detail. If you find yourself spending five minutes explaining a single slide, consider simplifying the slide or splitting it into two or more. Likewise, if you discover you're racing through one part of your presentation, taking only a few seconds on each slide, that might be a clue that those slides are too elementary.

- PowerPoint timers help you set up the presentation so that slides advance automatically. This capability might be useful if, for example, you need to have both hands free to demonstrate a product. In this case, you can use the timings from your rehearsals to specify how long PowerPoint should display each slide before advancing.

- With the help of a special timer on the Rehearsal dialog box, you can plan your presentation so you don't overrun a tight time slot. The Rehearsal's timer appears onscreen to tell you how long you've spent on each slide. Although few people use the Rehearsal timer during a final presentation, it can help you keep on top of timing during rehearsals.

To rehearse a presentation using the timer, follow these steps:

1. Gather all the notes you'll need to step through the slides, and open the presentation in PowerPoint, preferably using the same PC you'll use when you actually deliver the presentation.

2. Choose Slide Show, Rehearse Timings. As your presentation begins, the Rehearsal dialog box appears onscreen (see Figure 32.1).

3. Run through your presentation normally. Try to speak at a natural pace, using your notes if necessary, and click your way through slides and animations.

4. Watch the Slide Time box to see how much time you've spent on the current slide. If you bump into an unexpected snag—you lose your place in your notes, for example— click the Pause button to stop the clock. Click Next to proceed.

PART

V

CH

32

Figure 32.1
Keep track of the time spent on each slide by using the Slide Meter.

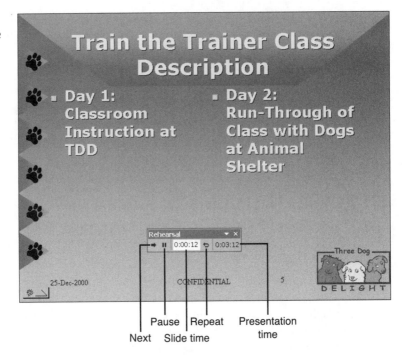

5. If you get flustered, click Repeat to "turn back the clock"—that is, reset the time on the current slide to zero, and subtract the appropriate amount of time from the Presentation Time counter. Resume your presentation at that slide.

Note

Clicking the Repeat button causes animations to repeat, starting with the first animation on the slide, but you must click once on the screen before the first repeat animation appears.

6. When you finish the presentation, PowerPoint tells you how long the entire presentation took, and asks whether you want to update the times associated with each slide to reflect the latest numbers. If you click Yes, the timing numbers appear in Slide Sorter view, to the lower left of each slide (see Figure 32.2).

Figure 32.2
The results of the last (accepted) timing run appear to the lower left of each slide.

Timing number

Unfortunately, there is no way to keep a history of timing runs, or to selectively adjust timings on a slide-by-slide basis. You must either accept all the new times, or reject them all.

> **Note**
>
> If you show the same slide more than once (such as if you back up or use it in a custom show), the timer keeps statistics only for the final time it appears.

To set an individual slide so that it advances automatically after a specific amount of time, you must use the Slide Transition dialog box.

→ For details on timing, **see** "Using Transitions to Control Pacing," **p. 818**.

DELIVERING A PERFECT PRESENTATION

The perfect presentation makes your point. It's that simple. Ultimately, of course, you control the quality of your presentation, but a few tricks can help you master the mechanics of presenting.

RUNNING A SLIDE SHOW

PowerPoint contains an enormous—even overwhelming—variety of options to help you run a slide show. One piece of advice rises above all others: If you're not sure what to do next during a presentation, right-click the screen. Don't press Escape. Right-click.

The right-click context menu available from the presentation screen gives you instant access to nearly every option you'll ever need to run a slide show. For example, you can jump to any slide if you know the title; you can move backward, or blank the screen, or perform a dozen other important gyrations—even if you don't remember the shortcut key for a particular obscure option. Unless you need to create a new slide in the middle of your presentation (it happens), right-click to steer your way out of trouble.

USING A BROWSER FOR YOUR PRESENTATION

The fact that Web browsers are practically ubiquitous might tempt you to save your PowerPoint presentation as a Web page and hit the road with only a browser to make the presentation (see Figure 32.3).

In many situations, saving your presentation as a Web page is a good idea:

- Internet Explorer 4 and 5 and/or Netscape 4 are widely available, so you needn't worry whether PowerPoint is installed on the PC you'll use for your presentation.

→ Some presentation details might not make the transition to a browser, however; **see** "Browser Compatibility Issues," **p. 163**.

Figure 32.3
A PowerPoint presentation, saved as a Web page at 800×600 resolution, looks like this from within Internet Explorer 5.0.

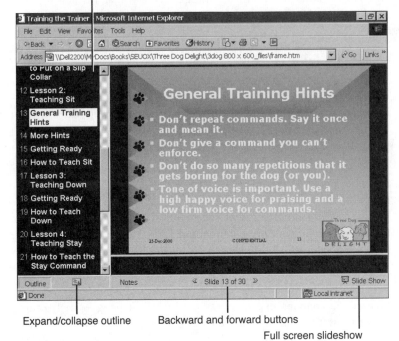

Outline (that is, titles of all the slides)

Expand/collapse outline

Backward and forward buttons

Full screen slideshow

- Running in a browser in full screen mode—with toolbars and menus hidden—your presentation will look almost exactly the same as if you were using PowerPoint for the show.

- It's a great "Road Warrior" fallback. If your notebook dies suddenly in Denver and you have to give the presentation a few hours later in Orlando, you can easily connect to the Net from another PC and be right back in business.

- The outline shown in the browser (on the left side of Figure 32.3) can actually make presenting easier—although viewers might find it distracting. For example, if you forget which slide contains a specific bullet point, you can expand and collapse the outline dynamically to find the point, and then jump to the slide in question with one click.

But there are also potential problems when you rely on a Web server and a browser for your presentation:

- Unless there's a wide communications pipeline straight from your presentation PC to the Web server, a browser-based presentation always runs slower than a PowerPoint presentation—in many cases, much, much slower. You can reduce this performance penalty by saving the Web page to disk and running it from a local drive.

- When you're running in a browser, some of the PowerPoint presentation navigation techniques don't work. Pressing the Enter key and the spacebar doesn't advance slides. Pressing B doesn't blank the screen. And, if you right-click a slide, you get the browser's context menu, not PowerPoint's.

If you decide to use a browser to make your presentation, always practice with the browser you're going to use.

 If you're having problems getting your transition and/or animation effects to display in a Web browser, see "Viewing Transition and Animation Effects in a Browser" in the "Troubleshooting" section at the end of this chapter.

USING TWO MONITORS

If you will be running your presentation on Windows 98, ME, or 2000 (or later), and you have dual monitors set up and recognized by the operating system, you can tell PowerPoint to show the presentation on one monitor, while you control the presentation in a normal-like view on the other monitor.

Note

> Hardware requirements for Multiple Monitor Support in Windows 2000 are extensive: See support.microsoft.com/support/kb/articles/Q238/8/86.ASP for details.

PART
V

CH
32

The primary monitor, which you use to control the presentation, displays the presentation in Normal view. Alternatively, you can have PowerPoint display "presenter tools," which give you slide thumbnails, buttons for showing the next and previous slide, a timer, speaker notes, and a black screen button. The secondary monitor shows the usual presentation full-screen.

To set up a presentation for dual monitors, choose Slide Show, Set Up Show, and in the Multiple monitors box point PowerPoint to the secondary monitor. If you want "presenter tools" to appear on the primary screen, check the Show Presenter Tools box.

USING HIDDEN SLIDES TO ANTICIPATE QUESTIONS

If you anticipate a question and have the answers handy in your presentation notes, your audience will be impressed. If you can cut immediately to a new slide that answers that question, your audience will sit up and take notice.

Hidden slides offer a marvelous, tricky (and undocumented) way to prepare for topics that you want to bring up only if someone asks. If you anticipate that someone in your audience might ask a question about slide 4, for example, here's how to be ready with a slide that answers the question:

1. Switch to Slide Sorter view and click after the final slide in the presentation. Click New Slide on the Slide Sorter toolbar, and create the slide that answers the question.

2. At the bottom of the slide, add a text box (saying, perhaps, "Back to presentation") or a picture to use as a button to return to the originating slide.

Tip from

EQ & Woody

On the Drawing toolbar, if you choose AutoShapes, Action Buttons, and select the "return" action button in the lower-left corner, it will do exactly what you want.

3. Right-click the picture or text box and select Action Settings. In the Action Settings dialog box, click Hyperlink To, and choose Last Slide Viewed from the offered drop-down list. During the presentation, you'll be able to click this hyperlink, and return to the originating slide.

→ For details on action settings, **see** "Advanced Navigation with Action Settings," **p. 764**.

4. Back in Slide Sorter view, make sure you select the slide you just added, and then click the Hide Slide button. Because the slide is hidden, it never appears in the normal course of a presentation.

5. Return to slide 4 and create a hyperlink to this new, hidden slide. Attach the hyperlink to a small picture or piece of text—anything that will jog your memory without alerting your audience that you've prepared a "hidden" answer to a specific question.

→ For more about hyperlinks inside PowerPoint, **see** "Using Hyperlinks," **p. 763**.

When you deliver the presentation, if a member of the audience asks the question, click the hyperlink, discuss the issues on the hidden slide, and then click the "Back to presentation" button at the bottom of the hidden slide to return to the main presentation. To see this hidden slide technique in action, see "Secrets of the Office Masters: Anticipating Questions with Hidden Slides" at the end of this chapter.

Tip from

EQ & Woody

You can use the same technique if the answer to a question requires more than one slide. Instead of creating a hyperlink that jumps to a specific slide, however, create one that jumps to a custom presentation. You can branch back from the end of the custom presentation with yet another hyperlink that's specifically tied to the originating slide—just remember to use it during the presentation!

→ For more on custom shows, **see** "Creating a Presentation," **p. 748**.

WRITING OR DRAWING ON SLIDES

Sometimes in the course of delivering a presentation, you might want to "draw" on a slide: Like a commentator on a TV football broadcast, you can use circles and arrows to drive home a point. Here's how:

1. Right-click the screen and choose Pointer Options, Pen. Click the pen-shaped pointer to draw on the slide.

2. To change pen colors, right-click the screen, choose Pointer Options, Pen Color, and choose among the colors offered.

3. Because you're now using the mouse pointer to draw, press Enter or the spacebar to advance to the next animation or slide.

Note

As soon as you move on to the next (or previous) screen, the drawings disappear, and cannot be retrieved.

To erase all that you have drawn on a slide, press E on the keyboard.

USING POWERPOINT WITH A PROJECTOR

Experienced presenters know this scenario too well: You try to connect a portable computer to a projector, an external monitor, or the A/V system in a large conference room, but things don't go the way you expect. The video port doesn't work, the slides appear too narrow, the colors you see don't match the design you created, or the volume is barely audible.

PowerPoint includes detailed step-by-step instructions for troubleshooting projector problems. Type `troubleshoot projector` in the Standard toolbar's Ask a Question box, and look at the Help item called Troubleshoot running a slide show on a laptop and a projector.

PART

V

CH

32

TAKING NOTES DURING A SLIDE SHOW

PowerPoint offers two different ways to take notes during a presentation. The first, and much simpler, way is by modifying the speaker notes for an individual slide. To do so, right-click the slide in question during a presentation and select Speaker Notes.

The second option, although more complex, lets you take full minutes as you make the presentation, assign follow-up tasks—and even link them all to your Outlook calendar should you so desire. It's an entire subsystem in PowerPoint called *Meeting Minder*. To take notes with Meeting Minder, follow these steps:

1. Right-click the slide as you're making the presentation and select Meeting Minder.

2. Jot down a record of points raised during the presentation on the freeform Meeting Minutes tab (see Figure 32.4).

3. To assign specific follow-up items to a responsible individual and add a due date, click the Action Items tab (see Figure 32.5).

Figure 32.4
Take minutes during a meeting, and then export the notes to Word for formatting and printing.

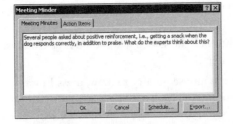

Figure 32.5
To record action items, type in a description, the person responsible for follow-up, and the due date, and then click Add.

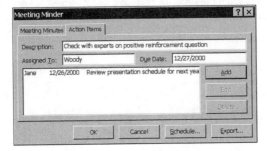

4. To link an action item to your Outlook calendar, click the Schedule button on the Action Items tab. If Outlook is running on that machine, you can set up an appointment on the spot.

PowerPoint gathers all Action Items as you type and automatically generates a slide that appears at the end of your presentation (see Figure 32.6).

Figure 32.6
As you enter Action Items, PowerPoint gathers them on this slide at the end of the presentation.

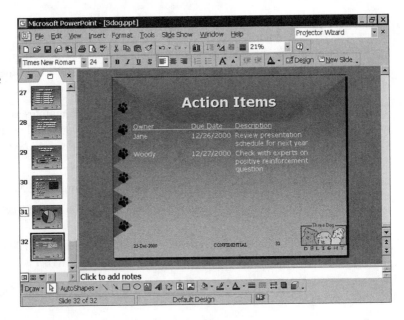

PowerPoint saves your Meeting Minder data with the presentation itself. To view Meeting Minder entries in your presentation, open the presentation and choose Tools, Meeting Minder.

Tip from

To convert Meeting Minder items into a formal document, click the Export button. This action sends the minutes and action items to Word, where you can use that program's complete set of formatting and editing tools.

PRINTING YOUR PRESENTATION

Eventually, you'll want to print out a presentation. Print options let you generate speaker notes for you, handouts for your audience, and copies of the slides for you to study and revise while you're sitting on a plane or stuck in traffic.

CHOOSING WHICH ELEMENTS TO PRINT

When you choose File, Print, PowerPoint offers four different choices in the Print What box as shown in Table 32.1.

TABLE 32.1   PRINTING OPTIONS

Print What	Means
Slides	One slide per page, portrait, the slide fills up the whole page
Handouts	Multiple slides per page, based on the number in the Slides Per Page box, formatted according to the Handout Master that has the same number of slides per page
Notes Pages	One slide per page, formatted according to the Notes Master
Outline View	No slides, only outline text, formatted according to the Outline setting on the Handout Master

→ For details on notes and handouts formatting, **see** "Creating Speaker Notes and Audience Handouts," **p. 801**.

Tip from

To print one or two slides per page with either speaker's notes or blank lines next to the slides, choose File, Send To, Microsoft Word, and print from Word.

PREPARING A COLOR PRESENTATION FOR A BLACK-AND-WHITE PRINTER

When you print PowerPoint slides on a black-and-white printer, you might be disappointed at the way Windows translates color to black-and-white pages. Shadowing in graphs loses much of its definition. All but the lightest backgrounds completely obliterate any nuances in the foreground—to the point of obscuring text, in many cases.

For the best-quality printed output, use PowerPoint's built-in grayscale converter, which is optimized for the colors in presentation designs. By taking liberties with your slides—converting dark backgrounds to light when needed, for example—it produces extremely readable black-and-white output.

To preview what your slides look like when viewed through this special grayscale converter, click the Grayscale Preview button on the Standard toolbar. You'll be sent into Color/Grayscale View, with a toolbar that lets you tweak the grayscale settings.

You can also see how your slides will look by using PowerPoint's Print Preview: Just choose File, Print Preview.

To print using the Grayscale converter, click the Print button while in Print Preview, or choose File, Print, and print with the Grayscale box checked at the bottom of the Print dialog box.

TURNING A PRESENTATION INTO 35MM SLIDES

Given a choice, few people want to deliver a presentation with 35mm slides—they're expensive, bulky, get smudged and rearranged too easily, and Heaven help you if you dump the carousel on your way to the big show. Sometimes, however, you have no choice. That's when PowerPoint's fast and easy online connections can make a huge difference.

Many service bureaus around the world now accept PowerPoint files, and turn them into 35mm slides. If the service bureau accepts files via e-mail, the process is as easy as choosing File, Send To, Mail Recipient (As Attachment).

The original PowerPoint service bureau, Genigraphics, is still going strong. They can have your slides back to you first thing in the morning—and arrange to have an InFocus projector sent to just about any site in North America, in around the same amount of time. See www.genigraphics.com for details, or check with your favorite Web search engine for the words "PowerPoint slides overnight."

TROUBLESHOOTING

VIEWING TRANSITION AND ANIMATION EFFECTS IN A BROWSER

I've added transitions and animation effects to my slides, but they don't appear when I view my presentation in a Web browser.

If none of your transition or animation effects appear in the browser, open the presentation and choose Tools, Options. On the General tab of the Options dialog box, click the Web Options button. On the General tab of the Web Options dialog box, select the Show Slide Animation While Browsing check box. Click OK to close each dialog box, and save your presentation.

SECRETS OF THE OFFICE MASTERS: ANTICIPATING QUESTIONS WITH HIDDEN SLIDES

If you can anticipate a question from your audience, you'll be miles ahead if you have a slide ready to answer it. For example, this first slide might elicit the question, "What percentage of the people attending are employees?"

Figure 32.7

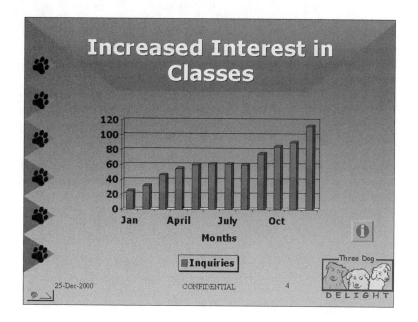

In anticipation of the question, you could construct a slide like the one shown next, and place it in the presentation immediately after the first slide. Then make the second slide hidden (Slide Show, Hide Slide), add an action button to the first slide that shows the hidden slide, and add an action button to the hidden slide that returns to the presentation.

→ For details on linking to a hidden slide and returning to the main presentation, **see** "Using Hidden Slides to Anticipate Questions," **p. 847**.

By constructing the presentation in this way, if someone asks the question, "What percentage of the people attending are employees?" you can click the (i) information icon, give the answer, and continue with your presentation. If nobody asks the question, you don't click the (i) icon, and the presentation proceeds normally—the second slide will never appear.

Figure 32.8

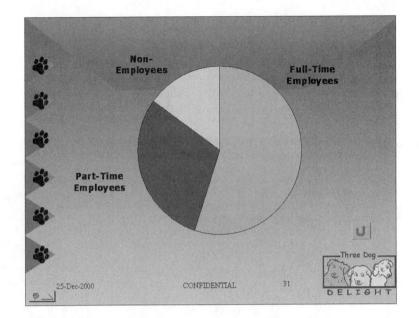

Other Office Applications

CHAPTER 33

ACCESS ESSENTIALS

In this chapter

PLANNING AN ACCESS DATABASE

Of all the Office applications, Microsoft Access is by far the most demanding and conceptually challenging. Anyone who's ever composed an interoffice memo or put together a budget can relate to Word and Excel instantly; an Access database, on the other hand, is made up of many individual objects, each of which must be built individually. With a wizard's help, it's possible to put together a simple database application in a relatively short time—to handle everything from tracking the contents of a wine cellar to managing inventory. Access applications can also scale up to enormous sizes, serving the information needs of large organizations and acting as a front end to data stored on mainframes and other network databases.

> **Note**
>
> Access is truly an enormous application, and it's impossible to do more than introduce the essentials in this book. For the most part, we've focused on the tasks that ordinary business users face when building simple interactive databases. If you want to learn more about using Access with larger databases, or you want detailed information about building Access applications with VBA, we suggest you pick up a copy of *Special Edition Using Microsoft Access 2002*, by Roger Jennings, also published by Que (ISBN: 0-7897-2510-X).

Using an Access database, you can store and manage large quantities of data for a wide variety of business and personal activities. Before you begin laying out the structure of a database, however, it helps to understand the components that make up Access:

- The *database engine* is the (generally invisible) software that actually stores, indexes, and retrieves data. When you create a standalone database, Access uses its own engine (called Jet...get it?) to manage data. If you choose File, New and select one of the Project options, you can use the Microsoft Data Engine (MSDE) instead. MSDE is compatible with Microsoft's enterprise-wide database program, SQL Server.

 If you cannot connect to your SQL Server, see "How to Install MSDE" in the "Troubleshooting" section at the end of this chapter.

- *Database objects* provide the interface you use to view, enter, and extract information from a database. The most common database objects are tables, forms, queries, and reports.

- Access includes a full set of *design tools* that you use to create objects. The reports designer, for example, enables you to sort data, group by fields, and add headers and footers to each page as well as the entire report.

- Finally, Access includes a rich set of *programming tools* you can use to automate routine tasks. Confusingly, the Access database window includes an object type called *macros*; these automation tools are completely different from the Visual Basic for Applications code you can add to most database objects.

The basic file type in Access is a *database*, which uses the extension *.mdb. Curiously, an Access database file doesn't have to contain any data at all; if you use Access strictly as a front end to retrieve information from a SQL Server database, the *.mdb file need contain only form, report, and query objects. If you design your database to hold data, you must create one or more table objects to hold the data, and those objects as well as the data itself are stored in the database file.

Tip from

EQ & Woody

Access wizards make it relatively easy to create and work with database objects, but don't underestimate the challenges of building a robust, easy-to-use database application. Access applications have a way of creeping up in complexity, and it's all too easy to get in over your head. Adding error-handling routines and setting up security for multiple users are just two of the significant challenges you'll face as you build an application. Don't even consider using Access to handle mission-critical data, such as the accounting system for your business, unless you're a skilled programmer. And even then, chances are good that a commercial program will handle the job more smoothly and safely than anything you can build on your own.

The basic building blocks of an Access database are objects. Although Access supports many types of objects, the most common by far are tables, queries, forms, and reports. A database can contain any number of objects. The database window, which is visible by default when you open a new database, lets you create and edit objects contained in the current database. As you can see in Figure 33.1, the Access database window closely resembles the Outlook interface, with a column of buttons on the left side of the database window representing each type of database object. Click a button to see a list of the existing objects in the current database.

Figure 33.1
Use the database window to see a list of all database objects, arranged by type.

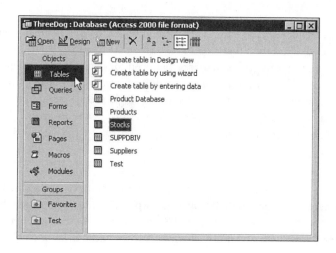

TABLES

A *table* is the basic unit for storing a collection of data in an Access database. A table's definition consists of a list of *fields*, each of which stores a discrete piece of information for a single *record*. For example, an Employees table might contain the fields LastName, FirstName, Position, DateHired, and HourlyRate. Because each record consists of one complete set of fields, a single record in the Employees table contains all available fields for a single employee.

The arrangement of fields and records is most obvious in *Datasheet* view, which displays data in rows and columns. When you open a table in Datasheet view, each record consists of a single row, and each column represents a single field.

→ For simple database applications, Excel lists are often easier to work with than Access tables; for an introduction to Excel lists, **see** "Creating a List on a Worksheet," **p. 674**.

QUERIES

Queries enable you to extract a subset of data from a single table, from a group of related tables, or from other queries, using criteria you define. By saving a query as a database object, you can run the query at any time, using the current contents of the database. When you display a query in Datasheet view, it looks exactly like a table; the crucial difference is that each row of the query's results can consist of fields drawn from several tables. A query can also contain *calculated fields*, which display results based on the contents of other fields.

> **Caution**
>
> Be careful when working with queries. Queries typically contain "live" data. If you change data in a query datasheet or form, it changes in the underlying table as well, without any warning.

FORMS

Access *forms* enable users to enter, view, and edit information, generally one record at a time. You can design forms that closely resemble paper forms such as invoices and time sheets, or you can create forms that are organized for data entry, complete with *data-validation* rules. A form window can also include a *subform* that displays information from a related table. For example, a form that shows a single record from the Departments table might include a subform that displays all the employees who work in a given department, allowing you to edit information about those employees.

REPORTS

Reports enable you to present data from one or more tables or queries in a readable style and a professional format, generally for printed output. A report might include detailed lists of specific data, with each row consisting of a single record, or it might provide a statistical summary of a large quantity of information. A report design can include grouping and sorting options; for example, you might create a weekly sales summary that runs a query, groups the query results by salesperson, and displays details of each sale in a list beneath each name.

Tip from

EQ & Woody

Access reports transfer well to other Office applications, where you can use more powerful editing and analysis tools to create good-looking documents and charts. For example, buttons on the Access toolbar enable you to export a report to Microsoft Word, edit the page, and then print it or save it on a Web server. You can also send a report to Excel, perhaps to create a chart or PivotTable report for use in another document.

DATA ACCESS PAGES

Pages—also known as *data access pages*—enable you to publish database information on a corporate intranet or (with some difficulty) on the Web. You can design pages that present data, enable users to edit the contents of a database—including changing data and appending new data to a table—or provide tools for data analysis. It's relatively easy to create a data access page, thanks to the Page Wizard; however, editing a data access page and managing its security settings require advanced skills. Unlike all other database objects, a data access page is stored on disk as a separate HTML file; icons in the database window are shortcuts to the actual file.

Note

For a detailed discussion of how to create and manage data access pages, see Chapter 38, "Data Access Pages," in *Platinum Edition Using Microsoft Office 2000*, by Laura Stewart (published by Que, ISBN: 0-7897-1841-3).

MACROS AND MODULES

The final two selections in the database window allow you to automate actions in an Access database:

- *Macros* enable you to define a sequence of actions in an Access database. Macros are generally easy to create, even for users who have no programming background. You select each action by name, fill in the appropriate *action arguments*, and optionally supply a condition under which the action will be performed. For example, you can specify that a particular macro is to run every time you open a specific form, or you can attach the macro to a command button in a form. To run a macro, select the object in the Macros list and click the Run button on the Access toolbar.

- *Modules* are collections of Visual Basic procedures and declarations, designed to perform specific tasks in the context of your database. Unlike Word, Excel, and PowerPoint, Access does not have a macro recorder that can generate VBA code automatically.

PART

VI

CH

33

Tip from

EQ & Woody

> If you're determined to write Visual Basic code in Access, you can use one less-than-ideal shortcut. Create a macro object by opening the Macros pane of the database window and clicking the New button. Define the conditions and actions for the macro, and then choose Tools, Macros, Convert Macros to Visual Basic. The resulting code is unlikely to be perfect, but you might be able to edit it and learn something about the Access object model in the process.

→ For more details on Access\VBA and its object model, **see** "How Office Applications Store Macros," **p. 966**.

CHOOSING THE RIGHT FILE FORMAT

With each new release of Access, Microsoft has changed the underlying file format. Access 2002 is no exception. If you create a new database using Access 2002, you might be confused by your file format options.

Access 2000 format is the default for all new databases. This option assumes that you will be using the database in a large organization where some users are still running Access 2000. This option allows all Access 2000/2002 users (with the correct permissions, of course) to modify the design and content of the database.

Access 2002 format includes a handful of new functions, methods, and properties, and its method for storing objects within the database file is more efficient. If you're certain you will use a database only on systems running Access 2002, you can convert it to the new format by choosing Tools, Database Utilities, Convert Database, To Access 2002 Format. (If you choose this menu option with no database open, you'll be prompted to supply the name of the database to convert.)

Tip from

EQ & Woody

> Access 2000 refuses to open a database saved in Access 2002 format. To make sure you don't inadvertently create an incompatibility headache in your organization, always check the Access title bar when working with a database. Access 2002 displays the current file format here, after the name of the database file.

If you use Access strictly for personal use, or in a small workgroup where you're absolutely certain that all other users will be running Access 2002, you can configure Access to create all new databases using Access 2002 format. Choose Tools, Options, click the Advanced tab, and select either Access 2000 or Access 2002 from the Default File Format list.

WORKING WITH DATABASE OBJECTS

As noted earlier, all the objects in a given database are available for browsing in the database window. In addition, you can visit this location and create a new object with a single click.

The default action for database objects is Open—if you double-click a query icon, for example, Access executes that query and returns its result in Datasheet view. Likewise, double-clicking a form or report icon opens the selected object using the current contents of the database. The effect is the same if you select an object and click the Open button at the top of the database window. (If you select a Report object, the Open button is replaced by the Preview button.)

To view and edit the definition and structure of an object, select any object and click the Design button. In Design view, you can modify the appearance of an object (the fonts and colors on a form, for example), change the table or query from which it derives data, or adjust any of hundreds of other properties for the selected object.

CREATING NEW OBJECTS

To create a new table, query, form, or report, use either of the following techniques:

■ Click the New button on the toolbar at the top of the database window, and select one of the options listed in the resulting dialog box. For example, Figure 33.2 shows the New Form window, listing a variety of wizard and AutoForm tools for creating new forms. In addition, the first entry in the list enables you to go directly to the Design view for a form, and begin your work on a new form object from scratch.

Figure 33.2

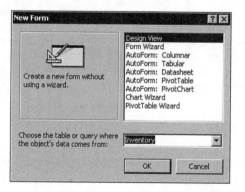

PART

VI

CH

33

■ Double-click any of the template icons shown at the beginning of any object list. These icons (which resemble a scratchpad with a key icon on it) offer multiple ways to create a new object, including various wizards and the option to create an object from scratch in Design view. As Figure 33.3 demonstrates, the "canned" choices available from the New Table Wizard can be a useful starting point for business and personal databases.

When used judiciously, wizards can be enormously helpful in the initial design of any database object. Some wizards are valuable mainly as introductory tools for newcomers to Access, whereas others are consistently useful even for experienced database developers. The Table and Query Wizards, for example, are acceptable for generic databases, but in both cases, Design view represents a far more efficient way to develop individual objects that precisely match specific requirements. On the other hand, the Form and Report Wizards almost always provide an excellent starting point for creating new forms and reports. When working with forms and reports in Design view, it's usually easier to move or modify existing objects than it is to add and edit new controls.

Figure 33.3

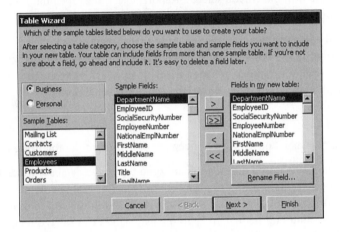

Tip from

When you use a wizard to create the initial version of an Access object, always expect to switch over to Design view to fine-tune the result. A wizard seldom produces the exact object that you need; in particular, the Design views for forms and reports offer direct access to important design elements such as controls, properties, fields, sections, and groups—and enable you to make detailed changes in the appearance and behavior of database objects.

MANAGING DATABASE OBJECTS

To see a concise list of available options for existing objects, select any object in the database window and use the right-click shortcut menus. Many of these options are also available from buttons on the Access toolbar, or from Access menus. You can open any object to view its content or its design; you can also rename or delete an object, cut or copy it to the Windows Clipboard, or add it to a group of favorite shortcuts for quick access.

Tip from

Unlike Access 97, Access 2000/2002 is "smart" about handling changes to the names of objects. When you rename a field in a table, Access automatically changes any references to that field in queries, forms, reports, and other objects. If you change the name of a field, you shouldn't need to edit any other objects. However, any captions that reference those fields on an existing form or report are unchanged.

MODIFYING OBJECT PROPERTIES

Confusingly, every database object has two sets of *properties*. If you right-click the object's icon in the database window and choose Properties, you see a bare-bones dialog box that lists the object's General properties. These include the object's name, a text description, the date the object was created, and the date it was last modified. Ho-hum.

By contrast, if you open an object in Design view and click the Properties button, you see a complete list of properties that enable you to control the appearance and behavior of that object. Figure 33.4, for example, shows the Properties dialog box for a form, with all available settings organized by category on five tabs.

Figure 33.4
The Design view properties of a database object include a much more important list of settings that can dramatically change the way you see and use an object.

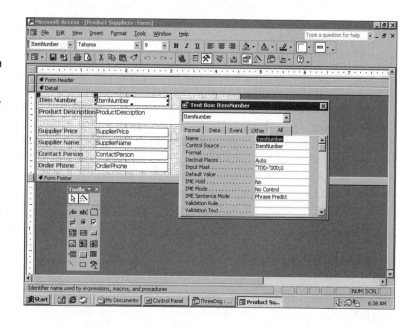

PART

VI

CH

33

Tip from

EQ & Woody

Because the Properties dialog box is modeless, you can leave it open as you work with different objects. The contents of the dialog box always match the currently selected object. Rather than closing and reopening the dialog box as you edit a form, for example, move it off to the side, where you can see its contents without hiding fields or controls on the form. This technique is the most efficient way to adjust the properties of text boxes, subforms, labels, and other parts of a form or report.

USING EXPRESSIONS IN DATABASE OBJECTS

When designing database objects, you don't have to limit yourself to data stored in a table. Extend the power of a database by writing expressions to transform that data on-the-fly. An *expression* is a combination of symbols, values, and identifiers (the name of a field, control, or property) that calculates a numeric result, combines text, or produces a logical value. Some of the *operators* you'll use in expressions include everyday arithmetic operators: + (plus), – (minus), * (multiplication), and / (division). Other operators used in expressions might be less familiar.

Expressions are useful throughout Access in many types of objects. The following are a few examples:

- In a query, you might include calculated fields, in which each entry is the result of an expression. The operands in the expression might include other fields in the same table or in a related table. You can use an expression to calculate a due date for an invoice ([SaleDate]+30) or to produce a total, such as [Qty]*[UnitPrice]. You supply the expression for the column and Access performs the operation for each record in the resulting datasheet.

→ Access performs operations for each record; **see** "Creating and Applying Filters," **p. 910**.

- The design of an individual field in a table might include a *validation rule*, which specifies a range of acceptable entries in the field itself. You might create a rule that prohibits users from entering a value in the SaleDate field that is in the future or more than 30 days in the past, for example. If a given data entry does not meet the condition expressed in the rule, Access rejects the entry. To create a validation rule, write an expression that will evaluate to True or False for each new entry. If the result is True, the entry is accepted; if False, it is not.

→ To learn more about creating validation rules, **see** "Defining Validation Rules," **p. 896**.

- A *criterion* is an expression that you can use to select a target group of records for a particular operation. Any record that meets the criterion becomes part of the group; a record that does not meet the criterion is excluded from the group. Again, a criterion expression results in a value of True or False for each record examined.

In these and other examples, you use specific types of operators in expressions to produce the appropriate types of values. The following categories of operators are commonly used:

- **The Arithmetic Operators**—In addition to the familiar four (+, -, *, and /), these include ^ (exponentiation), \ (integer division), and MOD (the remainder from the division of two integers). These operators require numeric operands and produce numeric results.
- **The Comparison Operators**—< (less than), <= (less than or equal), <> (not equal), > (greater than), >= (greater than or equal), and Between (expressing a numeric range). These operators produce *logical* values, indicating whether a comparison is True or False.

- **The Logical Operators**—These take logical operands and produce logical results. For example, a logical operator might combine the values of two comparison expressions. Among these operators, the most commonly used are And (true if both operands are true), Or (true if one or both operands are true), and Not (produces the opposite value of an operand). Other logical operators include Eqv (true if both operands have the same value), Imp (true if the first operand is true and the second is false), and Xor (true if the operands have different values).

- **A String Operator**—The & symbol represents *concatenation*, the process of combining two text values.

Because expressions are so central to the design of database objects, Access provides a special tool called the Expression Builder to help you write expressions quickly and accurately. As you can see in Figure 33.5, the Expression Builder contains buttons representing operands, along with other categories of identifiers that might become part of an expression.

Figure 33.5
Use the Expression Builder to build an expression one element at a time by clicking the operand buttons and selecting from categories of identifiers.

PART

VI

CH

33

You can generally open the Expression Builder by clicking the Build button (labeled ...) next to the box where the expression is entered. Or, right-click inside the box and choose Build from the shortcut menu.

Tip from

When working with forms and reports, use the Expression Builder to quickly add page numbers and date/time information. Scroll to the bottom of the left column and select Common Expressions to see these useful shortcuts.

USING WIZARDS TO CREATE DATABASES AND OBJECTS

As noted earlier, Access offers a collection of wizards to help you create individual objects in a database that you're developing. In addition, Access includes another set of wizards that create complete, special-purpose databases, devoted to specific business procedures. These wizards create fully developed database applications designed to handle common business tasks, such as expense accounting, time- and billing management, and order entry.

The wizard-generated databases create a full set of tables, queries, forms, and reports, as well as a sophisticated database application. The centerpiece of each of these canned databases is a form called a *switchboard*, which offers one-click options for viewing tables, opening data-entry forms, running queries, and producing reports. The menus and forms are tied together with VBA code, which you can easily inspect and borrow for other applications.

Tip from

Ed & Woody

If you're planning to develop a database that covers any of these application areas, it is strongly recommended that you experiment with the corresponding wizard. Even if you find that you can't use the resulting database application exactly as it is created, you'll undoubtedly discover some productive ideas about how to structure your own database.

To build a new database by using any of the database wizards, follow these steps:

1. Click the New button on the Access toolbar, or choose File, New. In the New File task pane, click the General Templates option.

2. Click the Databases tab and select any of the database wizard icons. Don't expect any help from the preview window on the right—all it shows is an abstract illustration intended to represent the functions of the corresponding database application.

3. Click OK to start the wizard. In the File New Database window, enter a name for the database file the wizard will generate, choose a new location if necessary, and click the Create button.

4. Follow each step of the wizard to read a brief description of the database application, select fields for specific tables, and choose formatting options, such as background images and presentation styles.

5. After you've completed all the steps, click Finish. The wizard generates the database and all its objects and opens the main switchboard, such as the one shown in Figure 33.6.

To begin entering or editing data, click any of the buttons on the switchboard form. Some buttons open submenus of additional options. To edit the Switchboard itself, choose Tools, Database Utilities, Switchboard Manager.

Figure 33.6
The wizard-generated databases are actually menu-driven applications. This Switchboard form shows your options when you first open one of these databases.

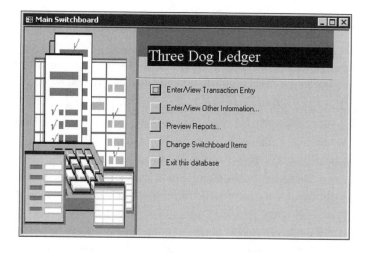

EXPORTING AND IMPORTING DATA

Sooner or later—probably sooner—you'll want to transfer information stored in an Access database to some other software environment, or move data originally created in another program into Access. In some cases, you'll want to move entire tables between database programs for use in different applications. For example, you might want to copy a table of supplier names and addresses from Access so that another database developer can incorporate that data into an application created with SQL Server or Oracle. Or, if you're building an Access database to replace an application created in an older program, such as dBASE, FoxPro, or Paradox, you might need to import data twice—once when you begin designing the database, so you can test forms, reports, and queries using real data, and a second time when you're ready to switch from the old system to the new one.

Even when you're extremely careful, exporting and importing information between database formats runs a serious risk of creating duplicate data sets. If you keep information about customers and products in Access and in an SQL Server database, for example, whoever is responsible for data entry has to enter changes in two places, and it's almost certain that some records will be out of sync or contain errors and inconsistencies. When you must use the same data in two different database programs, you should choose one program to store the data, and then create a link to that data from the other database program so that you can add or edit records or run queries. Because Access can link to data stored in a variety of formats—including dBASE, SQL Server, and Paradox—you will most often want to store shared data in another program and create links to it from Access.

In other cases, your need for Access data is strictly temporary. For instance, if you've created a report or query in Access, you can transfer the data to Word to incorporate it into a larger report, or send it to Excel, where you can easily analyze it with the help of PivotTables and charts.

PART

VI

CH

33

The simplest and most efficient tools in this category are known as *OfficeLinks*; these short-cuts are designed to send Access data directly to another Office application. To use one of the three OfficeLink options, first select a target object in the current database window, or open a form, report, or query; then choose Tools, Office Links, or click the OfficeLinks drop-down list on the Access toolbar. The list includes the following three items:

- **Merge It with MS Word**—This option sends a table of data to a new or existing mail-merge document in Word. When the transfer is complete, you can insert fields from the Access table as merge fields in the Word document itself.

- **Publish It with MS Word**—This option creates a text file on disk—in RTF format—from a selected Access object, and immediately opens the file in Microsoft Word. This file might become the starting point for a longer business document or report.

- **Analyze It with MS Excel**—This option creates a worksheet file on disk (in XLS format) from a selected Access object, and immediately opens the file in Excel. In the worksheet environment, you can perform mathematical, statistical, and other analytical operations that might not be possible in Access. You can also make use of Excel's versatile charting capabilities. If the report you start with includes grouping, the resulting Excel worksheet will include subtotals as well.

You can also create a Word or Excel file by selecting an object in the database window and then choosing File, Export. In the resulting Export dialog box, you can choose a specific format (including formats for previous versions of Office), and you can supply a nondefault name for the file that will be created. You might prefer this approach to the OfficeLink options if you need more control over the format or the name of the resulting file.

Tip from

EQ & Woody

If you're tempted to try the Publish It with MS Word button from an Access report, keep your expectations low. In general, the formatting in the exported file will only approximate the report formatting, and you'll have to do significant editing to get satisfactory results. It's often easier and more productive to use the Clipboard.

Another important use for Export and Import options is to exchange data between Access and other database-management programs. Access can produce files that can be read by a number of popular database applications, including most versions of dBASE, Paradox, and Lotus 1-2-3. To create a file in one of these formats, first open or select a database object, and then choose File, Export. To read files produced by these and other applications, choose File, Get External Data, Import.

CREATING ACCESS APPLICATIONS

An Access database can also include code modules, written in the programming language known as Visual Basic for Applications. Although you won't learn how to write code in the chapters ahead, you might be interested in exploring some of the locations where code can be of use in a database application.

→ For a thorough introduction to VBA as used throughout Office, **see** "VBA Basics," **p. 986**.

Note

For a more comprehensive look at creating your own code modules, see Chapter 40, "Building Basic Applications," in *Platinum Edition Using Microsoft Office 2000*. If your needs are more advanced, we suggest picking up a copy of *Special Edition Using Microsoft Access 2002*.

In general, a programmer writes code modules to simplify the use of a database—to automate procedures, to provide intuitive database objects and tools, to create and implement menus, to perform complex background operations, and to expand the functional options of a database.

A central characteristic of the Visual Basic language is its *event-driven programming model*. This means that certain procedures in code are designed to be performed when triggered by specific events. Events are often associated with user-initiated actions such as a click of the mouse or an entry from the keyboard. For example, a procedure you write for a command button might define the action that will take place when the user clicks the button with the mouse.

The windows in Figure 33.7 illustrate one combination of elements involved in an event-driven procedure. At the left side of the figure, you can see the Design view of the Main Switchboard form from the Northwind database, one of the sample applications included with Access. The form includes a button that closes the switchboard and displays the database window; this button appears as a command button control in Design view. In the Properties box for this control, you can see the list of event properties, including a property named On Click. The setting for this property is, in turn, a call to a function named CloseForm. In the code window at the lower-right corner of the figure, you can see the actual code for CloseForm. When the user clicks the OK button, the On Click event is triggered, resulting in a call to CloseForm.

⚠ *The Northwind sample database included with Access is filled with ideas and code that you can borrow for your own applications. Can't find it? See "Installing the Sample Databases" in the "Troubleshooting" section at the end of this chapter.*

Note

If you want to learn the basics of VBA, turn to Chapters 38–41 in Part VII, "Automating Office with Macros and VBA." If you want to learn how to use VBA with Access, pick up a copy of *Special Edition Using Microsoft Access 2002*.

PART

VI

CH

33

Figure 33.7
In this example, clicking the OK button is the triggering action. The On Click property specifies the VBA procedure that will be called when the click occurs.

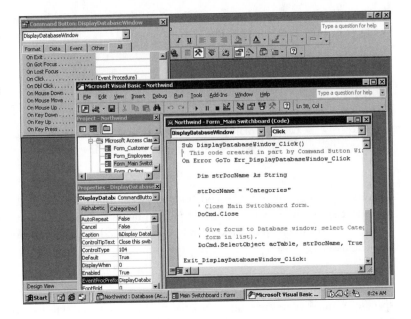

TROUBLESHOOTING

HOW TO INSTALL MSDE

When I choose File, New and click the Project (New Database) icon, Access asks me to fill in details about my SQL Server connection, but I can't connect successfully.

You need to install the Microsoft SQL Server Desktop Engine. Find the Office XP CD1 and run the Setup program in the MSDE2000 folder. This option is not installed by default, and it will not install automatically like other Office features. If you're creating a new project from scratch, choose File, Connection; in the Data Link Properties dialog box, enter your computer name as the name of the SQL server, but don't include any backslashes in front of it. You must have administrative rights, or be an authorized user as defined by the SQL Server manager. After completing these steps, you should be able to connect your Access project to the Microsoft Data Engine.

INSTALLING THE SAMPLE DATABASES

I want to look through the Access sample databases to see whether I can glean any ideas or borrow any objects or code, but the Open dialog box doesn't include shortcuts for the samples, and I can't find them anywhere on my hard disk.

Before you can open the sample files, you have to install them. If you click a shortcut, the Windows Installer handles this chore automatically, but as you've discovered, the shortcuts to the sample files are available only when you first begin using Access. After you've worked with a few files, those shortcuts drop off the bottom of the list. To make the files available, run the Office Setup program (from Control Panel, choose Add/Remove Programs, choose your Office version, click Change, and choose the Add or Remove Features option). Drill down through the Microsoft Access options until you find the Sample Databases group, and configure the sample applications by using the Run from My Computer option. By default, the Northwind files are installed in the Program Files\Microsoft Office\Office 10\Samples folder.

SECRETS OF THE OFFICE MASTERS: A DATABASE DESIGN CHECKLIST

Before you begin creating database objects, think carefully about who will use the database and what kind of reports you'll need to produce from the data stored within it. Use the following checklist to define your design:

- **Storing data**—How much data do you plan to enter? How much training and expertise will be required of those who are responsible for that data entry? Will you need to create systems to ensure accurate and reliable data entry?

- **Retrieving data**—What relationships do you need to establish among the different sets of data that you produce? How can you exploit these relationships to create new combinations of data from different sources? Do you need to subtotal or summarize the data in any way?

- **Modifying data**—Who will be responsible for editing data, and what level of understanding will be required of them? What safeguards will you need to create to ensure that changes in your database do not result in duplicate records or inconsistent data? If several people are using the database, how do you prevent unauthorized changes to data, while still allowing users to retrieve the information they need?

CHAPTER 34

CUSTOMIZING TABLES, FORMS, AND REPORTS

In this chapter

CREATING AND CUSTOMIZING TABLES

A *table* is the basic unit for storing and organizing information in an Access database. One database can contain any number of tables, as well as links to tables stored in other locations and other formats. Data within a table is arranged in a basic grid: Each row contains all the data *fields* in a single *record*, and each column represents a *field*, where similar information (first name and last name, for instance) is stored in all the records. In turn, tables directly or indirectly form the basis for all other objects within an Access database, including queries, forms, and reports.

As a general rule, however, each field definition has four elements, all of them visible when you open a table in Design view and select a field, as in Figure 34.1.

Figure 34.1
By selecting a field, you can edit its properties (see the following list). The descriptions for each field help document the structure of the table.

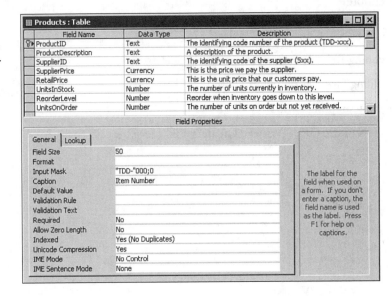

- The *field name* must follow the same rules as those for other database objects: It can consist of up to 64 characters, including letters, numbers, spaces, and any special characters except a period, exclamation point, accent grave (`` ` ``), or brackets. Spaces are allowed within object names, but not as the first character.

Tip from

EQ & Woody

Although Access allows you to use spaces in the names of Access objects, we strongly recommend that you avoid doing so—especially if you plan to use the field names with VBA code. Instead of naming a field Postal Code, for example, try PostalCode or Postal_Code. Get into this habit and you'll have a much smoother time with Access.

- Each field definition also includes a *data type*; this setting controls formats for display and input and also serves as a way of validating data entry. (See the following section for a detailed list of available data types.)

- The field *description* is optional; if you choose to enter text here, it helps to document the database. It also helps when viewing a table's contents in Datasheet view; the Description text for the current column appears in the lower-left side of the status bar. Maximum length is 255 characters.

- Finally, the *field properties* for the selected field appear at the bottom of the table window. The exact properties for each field vary, depending on the data type you've selected. Use these properties to define more details about the type of data permitted in each field, as well as its display format and the default caption that appears when you place the field on a form or report.

CHOOSING A FIELD'S DATA TYPE

By default, every new field you create uses the Text data type, with a maximum length of 50 characters. More often than not, that setting will be inappropriate for the type of data you plan to store in a field. The Text field enables you to enter nearly any type of data, including numbers, currency, dates, and times. In many cases, however, another data type is a better choice. For example, if you intend to enter invoice dates in a field, specify Date/Time as the field type; this option prevents you from inadvertently entering a value that isn't a legal date, such as 2/30/2001. You can choose from the following data types for any field:

- **Text**—Enables you to enter a maximum of 255 characters, including letters, numbers, and punctuation. This data type is also appropriate for entering numeric data that you don't want to use for calculations or sorting, such as Social Security numbers and phone numbers.

Tip from

EQ & Woody

To set the maximum length of a Text field, adjust the Field Size property. You can also reset the default field size from 50 to a more reasonable number—say, 10 or 12. Choose Tools, Options, click the Tables/Queries tab, and enter the desired number in the Text box under Default Field Sizes.

PART

VI

CH

34

- **Memo**—This data type allows for long blocks of text, up to 64,000 characters. Memo fields do not allow formatting; they're most useful for notes and descriptions that exceed 255 characters.

- **Number**—Allows entry of numeric characters only. Choose an entry from the Field Size property box to further define the format. Byte is the most efficient and most limited choice, permitting you to enter whole numbers from 0 to 255. To store whole numbers, positive or negative, without fractions, choose Integer (–32,768 to 32,767) or Long Integer (–2,147,483,648 to 2,147,483,647). Single, Double, and Decimal formats allow increasingly more precise numbers with fractions.

- **Date/Time**—This data type enables you to enter dates and times by using a variety of formats and date separator characters. Use the Format property to control the display of data in Datasheet view.

- **Currency**—Like Number formats, except these values always display using the default Currency symbol, as defined in Control Panel's Regional Settings option. A Currency field is accurate to 15 digits to the left of the decimal point and 4 digits to the right; this option cannot be adjusted.

- **AutoNumber**—This data type results in a field of consecutive integers, supplied by Access as you add new records to your database. AutoNumber fields are commonly used for invoice numbers and for primary keys.

Tip from

EQ & Woody

Although the default AutoNumber field properties generate sequential values, you can also specify that you want an AutoNumber field to randomly generate numbers that are unique within the current table. Choose Random from the New Values property for that field. This option might be useful if you want to avoid creating the impression that the data-entry order in a given table is significant.

- **Yes/No**—Use this data type for fields that have only one of two values. Use a Yes/No field to identify customers who are exempt from sales tax, for example. Use the Format property to change the value displayed from Yes/No to True/False or On/Off.

- **OLE Object**—Enables you to create a field for storing pictures, documents, or OLE objects developed in other programs. Note that you can't sort, index, or group by any field that uses this data type.

- **Hyperlink**—Enables you to enter clickable links to Web addresses, folders, files, and other objects.

→ For a detailed description of how Office hyperlinks work and how to create and manage them, **see** "Working with Hyperlinks," **p. 167.**

 If you imported a list that included a column of hyperlinks, Access should automatically create a Hyperlink field; if you encounter problems, see "Importing Hyperlinks into Access" in the "Troubleshooting" section at the end of this chapter.

SETTING A PRIMARY KEY

Every time you create a new table, Access prompts you to create a *primary key*. This step isn't mandatory, but it's highly recommended. For starters, a primary key is required if you ever want to create a relationship for the table. By definition, the primary key contains nonduplicate entries for each record; as a result, Access can use this unique identifier to positively identify each record, making searches easier and faster.

Access gives you three options for the primary key:

- *AutoNumber primary keys* are your safest choice. Under some circumstances, Access creates this type of primary key automatically. Using the AutoNumber data type guarantees that values are unique.

- A *single-field primary key* is a good choice when you're certain that the contents of the selected field will always be unique. Examples of useful single-field keys include unequivocal identification codes such as an employee badge number, Social Security number, part ID, or license plate number.

- *Multiple-field primary keys* are most common in junction tables used to link two tables in a many-to-many relationship. In an Invoices table, for example, each unique InvoiceID value might contain several ProductID values; likewise, each unique ProductID value in the Products table might be part of several invoices, each with its own InvoiceID number. By creating a third table (Order_Details) that combines these two values to create a primary key, you can be certain that the table will not contain any duplicate records and that you'll always find the record you need.

To define a single field as the primary key, click the Primary Key button on the toolbar. The primary key field is identified in Design view by a small key icon, displayed just to the left of the field name.

SPEEDING UP SORTS AND QUERIES WITH INDEXES

Indexes help make short work of searching and sorting. When you build an index for a field or combination of fields, Access creates a sorted data structure that it can search through to find unique values. Without an index, Access has to step through every record to complete a query or sort; with an index, Access can find a unique value and jump directly to the rows that contain that value. The performance difference can be astounding.

By default, the primary key in every table is indexed. As part of the process of defining field settings, you can also create an index for a specific field. In Design view, select the field and change the Indexed property to Yes from its default setting of No. In addition, you can choose the Yes (No Duplicates) setting to ensure that each new entry in the field is unique. By definition, this is the Indexed setting for a table's primary key.

You can also create an index that covers multiple fields. This technique is useful when you have a query that sorts and searches on a group of fields. Click the Indexes button and fill in the name of the index, the fields it should include (up to 10), and the sort order for each one. This same dialog box lets you view and edit or delete existing indexes.

Tip from

EQ & Woody

Access creates some indexes automatically, and if you follow some common-sense naming conventions, you can guarantee that the right fields are indexed. By default, any field name that begins or ends with ID, num, code, or key will be indexed. Use field names such as ProductID and EmployeeNum as the primary key when possible. When you use the same field names in related tables where another field is the primary key, Access automatically indexes these fields, making queries that use these fields as fast as possible.

DEFINING RELATIONSHIPS BETWEEN TABLES

A well-designed Access database typically contains many interrelated tables, with each table containing a specific, narrowly defined set of data, without any duplicate information. This type of design is crucial to maintaining *referential integrity*—when you change a name, address, or other piece of data in one record, your change automatically appears in all related tables.

Imagine a database application that tracks customer purchases based on invoices. A proper design stores this information in four separate tables, as shown in Figure 34.2:

Figure 34.2
Note that each of the relationships between these four tables is tied to the primary key in one of the tables, shown in bold in the field list.

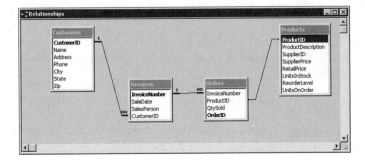

- The Customers table contains one record for each of your customers, with their name, address, and phone number, plus a CustomerID field that uniquely identifies that customer.

- The Products table contains one record for each unique product you sell, containing the name and description of the product, its wholesale and retail prices, and a unique ProductID field that identifies that product.

- The Invoices table contains one record for each invoice you create, with an InvoiceNumber field that automatically creates a new, unique number when you start a new invoice, plus fields for the date and the name of the salesperson who filled in the invoice; each record also contains a CustomerID field that enables you to look up information from the matching record in the Customers table.

- The Orders table contains one record for each item on each invoice; fields include InvoiceNumber, ProductID, and QuantitySold.

By storing information in multiple related tables, each of which has a specific purpose, you can extract results and produce reports that combine data in a wide variety of ways. For instance, by starting with the Invoices table, you can print out an invoice that includes the customer's name and address (drawn from the Customers table) and all the details for each product in that sale (drawn from the Products and Orders tables). If you start with the Customers table, you can prepare a monthly report that shows details and a grand total for each customer's orders that month. Or, by starting with the Products table, you can generate reports for each product showing sales by month and by customer, which might help you target advertising and promotions more effectively.

Before you can work with multiple tables in a database, you have to define a *relationship* between the tables. A relationship defines the fields that two tables have in common, so Access can combine information from the two tables into a logical result. In general, establishing a relationship between two tables requires that each table have a field in common with the other. Usually, the two common fields include the *primary key* for one table; the corresponding field in the second table is called the *foreign key*.

Tip from

Ed & Woody

Although it's common for the fields that define a relationship to have the same name, it certainly isn't required. All that's necessary is that the two fields contain the same type of data. Thus, you could define a relationship between two tables by using the PostalCode field from one table and the ZipCode field from another table. Wherever the values match, Access combines the values in a query.

The most common type of relationship between tables is a *one-to-many* relationship, in which each record in a primary table can correspond to many records in a related table. Each record in the Suppliers table (the primary table) corresponds to one or more records in the Products table. Conversely, each product record must correspond to exactly one supplier record. No product can be recorded without a supplier. One-to-many relationships are common in everyday life: In a classroom, one teacher has many students; in a business, one customer has many orders and each invoice has many items.

Two other types of relationships are less common, but still occasionally useful:

- As the name implies, *one-to-one* relationships store information in which a single record in one table corresponds to one and only one record in the second table.

- *Many-to-many* relationships actually consist of multiple one-to-many relationships, with an intermediate table (sometimes called a *junction table*) pulling the results together. At a university, for example, each class consists of one teacher and many students, and each student's schedule includes multiple classes. By using a third table, you can produce a query or report showing the many-to-many relationship between a group of students and a group of teachers.

Tip from

Ed & Woody

One-to-one relationships are useful when data security is an issue. In a business, for example, you might have an employee table that contains contact information such as e-mail addresses, phone numbers, department names, and locations. Another table contains information about salaries, performance reviews, and other sensitive information. Although only one record exists for each employee in each table, it would be foolish to combine the two tables and make the sensitive information visible to everyone. In this case, you set restrictions on user access to the second table, and then use a one-to-one relationship between the tables to create salary and benefits reports for authorized users.

PART

VI

CH

34

Carefully defined *table relationships* are among the most important structural elements of a database. The Relationships window provides a clear graphic representation of all existing tables and queries for a database and enables you to define and edit the relationships between them. In the Relationships window, you can establish logical links between any combination of these objects.

 If some of the relationships you define here don't appear in query windows, see "Juggling Multiple Relationships" in the "Troubleshooting" section at the end of this chapter.

Before attempting to edit or create relationships, first close any open tables. To open the Relationships window, choose Tools, Relationships. If you have not yet defined any relationships between tables in the current database, the Show Table dialog box appears automatically over the top of the Relationships window. If it doesn't appear, choose Relationships, Show Table. The Show Table dialog box displays a list of existing table objects in your database.

DEFINING A ONE-TO-MANY RELATIONSHIP

To define a one-to-many relationship, you must first make sure the two tables are visible in the Relationships window. Next, drag the related field from one table and drop it onto the other. Finally, use the Edit Relationships dialog box to define the properties of the relationship itself. Follow these steps:

1. If the two tables are not visible, use the Show Table dialog box to select the first table— Suppliers, for instance—and click Add. A field list for the Suppliers table appears inside the Relationships window. Repeat this step until all tables are visible in the Relationships window. Then click the Close button.

2. Make sure the fields that define the relationship are visible in both field lists. Click the field in the first table and drag it on top of the matching field in the second table. When you release the mouse button, the Edit Relationships dialog box appears on the desktop, as shown in Figure 34.3. The Edit Relationships dialog box identifies the matching fields that link two tables. It also tells you the type of relationship that is being created.

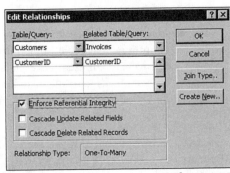

Figure 34.3

3. Examine the information displayed in the Edit Relationships dialog box to confirm that the definition is correct: In this example, Access is about to create a relationship between the Suppliers and Products tables, based on the SupplierID field in each table. Access has determined that this is a one-to-many relationship, as you can see in the Relationship Type box.

 If the Relationship Type box identifies the relationship as Indeterminate, you'll need to make a few small repairs; see "Firming Up a Relationship" in the "Troubleshooting" section for some suggestions.

4. If you want to ensure consistency in your data, check the Enforce Referential Integrity box.

5. Click Create to define the relationship. Access adds a bold line connecting the fields in each table. The symbols displayed above the line indicate the direction of the one-to-many definition.

6. Click the Close button to close the Relationships window and save the layout you've created.

WORKING WITH ONE-TO-MANY RELATIONSHIPS

After creating a one-to-many relationship, you can see one important effect of the new relationship when you open the primary table (the table on the "one" side of the relationship) in Datasheet view. Access automatically creates a *subdatasheet* in this table, enabling you to view corresponding records from the Products table. The only visible sign of the subdatasheet, at least initially, is a column of plus signs (known as *expand indicator icons*) at the left side of the Suppliers table. Click any one of these icons to see details from the related table (the "many" side of the relationship) for the selected record. As you can see in the example in Figure 34.4, Access displays all the Products records for the selected record in the Suppliers table.

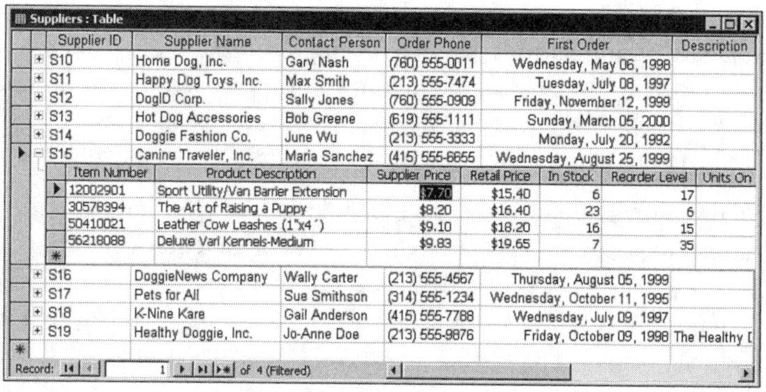

Figure 34.4
When you open a primary table that is part of a one-to-many relationship, you can expand or collapse the subdatasheet to control the display of data from the related table.

BUILDING GREAT FORMS AND REPORTS

Access provides a design and development environment that gives you extensive control over the appearance and functionality of forms and reports. The tools you use for either task are remarkably similar. The differences typically reflect the different design goals of forms and reports, as explained here:

■ A *form* is a formatted database object, generally used to display one record at a time in an onscreen window. Forms are most commonly used to create convenient fill-in-the-blanks windows for entering or editing data; in this case, you use a table or query as the data source for the form.

- Access *reports* typically organize data in a format suited for printing or publishing. Although you can also use a form to view data onscreen, reports are better suited for this task and often represent the most important end product of a database.

When designing a form or report, you start by specifying a *data source*—one or more tables or queries, or a statement written in SQL—and position controls on a design grid. Although you can create a report or form from scratch in Design view, using a wizard is often a better starting point. The wizard produces the basic structure, and you then open the form or report in Design view to make detailed changes to its content and appearance.

As with other database objects, Access provides several ways to create a form or report. After selecting Forms or Reports from the database window, click New to open the New Form or New Report dialog box. The options shown here let you create a new form or report by opening a blank form in Design view, or by choosing wizards and AutoForm/AutoReport options that enable you to create a default form with a single click.

To open an existing form or report in Design view, select it from the database window and click the Design button. If the form or report is already open, click the Design button to switch into Design view.

DESIGN 101: WORKING WITH CONTROLS

The building blocks of any form or report are objects called *controls*, which include text boxes, labels, option buttons, lists, command buttons, toggles, and other familiar Windows interface elements. Controls have their own property settings, as do individual sections of the form or report; by changing the settings of these properties, you can modify the appearance and content of the form or report. Controls can take any of three forms:

- Some controls are directly tied to a field in a table or query. In the peculiar jargon of Access, these are called *bound controls*. When you enter data in a control that is bound to a particular field, Access adds the data to that field; when you view data by using a form or report, Access checks the Control Source property for each control to see which data it should display. Figure 34.5 shows the Properties dialog box for a text box bound to the ItemNumber field in the underlying table.

- Some controls are *unbound*—that is, not tied to any data source. For example, a line, box, or freestanding text label is an unbound control.

- When you enter an expression in the Control Source property box, Access creates a *calculated control*. The expression `=[SupplierPrice]*2`, for example, multiplies the contents of the SupplierPrice field by 2 and displays the result.

→ For an overview of Access expressions, **see** "Using Expressions in Database Objects," **p. 865.**

When you open a form or report in Design view, you can change the font, font size, color, borders, and other formatting properties of any control. In Design view, Access lets you position controls on a grid for precise alignment. You can also group and align controls.

Figure 34.5

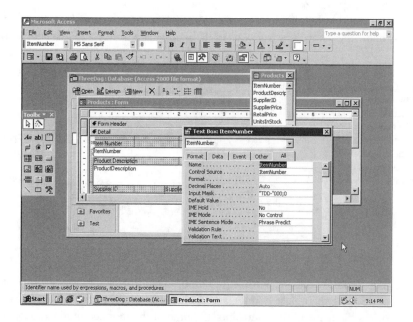

When you work with a form or report in Design view, three interface elements are essential:

- Use the Toolbox to add new controls or change existing controls. You can customize the Toolbox buttons just as you can any other Office toolbars; to toggle it on or off while you work, click the Toolbox button or choose View, Toolbox.

- The Field List displays a list of all the fields in the source query or table, which you can use to add new controls. To show or hide this list in Design view, click the Field List button or choose View, Field List.

- To adjust the appearance or behavior of a control, section, or the form itself, open the Properties dialog box. You can keep the Properties dialog box open while you work; as you select different objects, the properties displayed in this dialog box change to reflect the available choices.

PART

VI

CH

34

Tip from

Ed & Woody

Tabs in the Properties dialog box make it easier to find the exact function you're looking for. All the tabs that affect the appearance of a control, for example, are on the Format tab. Click the All tab to scroll through a list of all the properties that apply to the selected object.

ADDING A NEW CONTROL TO A FORM OR REPORT

If you drag a field name from the Field list onto a form or report, Access automatically creates a text box control bound to that field. If you click another Toolbox button first, and then drag a field onto the form, Access launches a wizard that creates the control type you selected. Figure 34.6, for example, shows one step of the Option Group Wizard. Follow the wizard's instructions to define the data source and behavior of the control.

Figure 34.6
If the Control Wizards button on the Toolbox is selected when you add a new control to the form, Access lets you fill in the control's properties with a wizard.

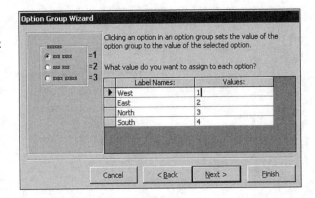

The Toolbox contains buttons for common controls you might want to add to a form. By positioning the mouse pointer over a button in the Toolbox, you can view a ScreenTip that shows the name of the control itself. Some of the more common and useful controls include the following: check boxes, which let users enter data in a Yes/No field or an option group; combo boxes and list boxes, which let users select from lists of data items; and labels, which add descriptive text to a control or a form or report.

Note •

Labels are always unbound, and they don't change as you move from one record to another. Access automatically adds labels to new fields you place on a form or report; you might also use labels for titles and instructions.

POSITIONING CONTROLS AND LABELS

When you use the Form Wizard to build a form, the default type for all controls is a text box with a label attached to its left. In some cases, however, you'll want the labels to appear above the text box, and you might want to change the position, alignment, size, or grouping of controls on the form. After you learn the secrets of working with Access controls, you'll find it easy to position controls precisely where you want them. It does take some practice, however.

Access displays *handles*—small black rectangles—around the outside of a selected control, as shown in Figure 34.7; these handles are a visual indication that you've selected the control. The eight small black squares are *size handles*—you'll find one on each corner and one in the middle of each side of the selected control. When you position the mouse pointer over a size handle, it takes the shape of a double-headed arrow, at which point you can drag the handle in any direction to change the size and shape of the control itself.

Figure 34.7
Note that both the control and its label are selected here. The "open hand" pointer means that you can move both the control and the label at once.

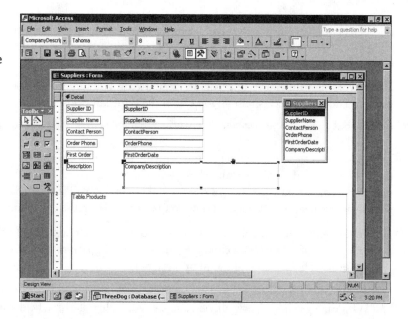

The large black square at the upper-left corner of a selected control lets you move the object to a new position within the form. When you drag this handle, the mouse pointer takes the shape of a hand with one finger pointing up; as you move the selected control, you see only its outline, making it easier to position on the form grid. When you release the mouse button, the control itself moves to the location you've selected.

For the most part, every control you add to a form actually consists of two controls: the bound or unbound control (text box or combo box, for example), and a matching label. If you know the techniques, it's easy to position these controls correctly:

- Use the large square in the upper-left corner of either the control or the label to move either one independently. This technique is effective if you want to move a label from the left of a text box so that it sits above the control.

- To move both the control and its label at once, point to any border of the control or the label, until the mouse pointer takes the shape of an open hand. Drag to position the control-label combination in its new location.

Tip from

EQ & Woody

Do you want to position an object precisely on a form? If you plan to print out an Access form and use it as an invoice, you might want a graphic to appear in a fixed location at the top of the form. To add the graphic, choose the Image button from the Toolbox. Then click and drag to define a region on the form, in the general location where you want it to appear. Select the image file from the Open dialog box. Finally, click the Format tab on the Properties dialog box for the image you embedded, and set the Left, Top, Width, and Height properties to define the exact size and location on the page.

To delete any control, select it and press the Delete key. If you select a control, Access also selects its label; if you click the label itself, Access does not select the matching control.

GROUPING AND ALIGNING CONTROLS

When working with a form or report in Design view, you can group, distribute, and align controls and other objects, just as you can in the Office drawing layer.

→ For a full discussion of basic techniques for working with the drawing layer in Office programs, **see** "Using Office Drawing Tools," **p. 108.**

In all cases, you start by selecting all the controls you want to work with simultaneously. To do so, hold down the Shift key and click each selection in succession. Or use the mouse to draw a rectangle around a group of objects and select them all at once. Say you've quickly added six new fields to a form, and now you want to tidy up the collection:

1. To distribute the controls into two groups of three, each distributed equally, select the first group of controls and choose Format, Vertical Spacing, Make Equal. Then repeat the process for the second group of three fields.

2. To align each group of fields, select the controls and choose Format, Align, Left.

3. With each group properly aligned and spaced, gather all three fields and choose Format, Group. This option locks the current position of all the elements so that you can move them as one unit. Repeat for the second group of three fields.

MAKING FORMS EASIER TO USE

A well-designed form makes data entry easier and more accurate, especially when you want other people to enter data into a database. By limiting the data the user sees, carefully arranging input boxes, and providing explanatory text, you can guide the user through the data-entry process.

A form can include as many as five sections. The data itself typically appears in the Details section; in addition, each form can have up to two headers and two footers, with one header/footer combination for the form itself and another for individual pages. Use the View menu to hide or show headers and footers.

Simple forms generally show the contents of one record at a time, but you can also design a form that includes a *subform*, which displays information from a related table or query. If you choose a table that includes a subdatasheet and then create an AutoForm, Access adds a subform automatically. Using this type of form, you can scroll through groups of records, or search for information by using filters and other search tools. Figure 34.8, for example, shows a form and subform combination in which the main form is bound to the Suppliers table, with a subform bound to the related Products table. Note the two sets of navigation buttons at the bottom of the form. Use the Next and Previous record buttons for the main form to jump through the Suppliers table; use the navigation buttons within the subform to move through the list of products for each supplier.

Figure 34.8
This form, based on the Suppliers table, contains a subform that displays data from the related Products table. The one-to-many relationship determines which data appears in the subform.

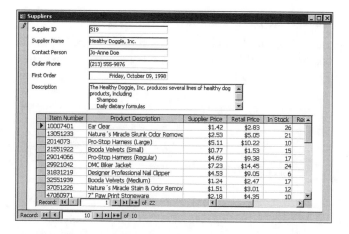

For special-purpose forms, one powerful area to explore is the Properties dialog box for the form itself. This list contains settings that affect important characteristics of a form's appearance and behavior. For example, in the Data tab (see Figure 34.9), you can set three properties that determine whether the form is available for reading alone or can be used for editing, deleting, and appending records.

Figure 34.9
Set the Allow Edits, Allow Deletions, and Allow Additions form properties to No if you want your form to be used only for viewing data.

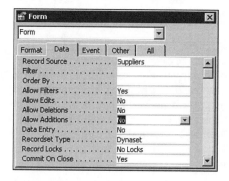

PART
VI

CH
34

Tip from
EQ & Woody

If the Properties dialog box is open, but it currently displays the properties of a control or section, you can easily switch to a view of the form properties: Use the drop-down list at the top of the Properties dialog box; this list is a usability improvement that's new in Access 2002.

When you create a form from a single table, the Allow Edits, Allow Deletions, and Allow Additions properties are set to Yes. As a result, the user can add, edit, and delete records using nothing but this form. Depending on who will be using the form, you might want to restrict this capability. Change the property setting to No on one or more of these important properties if you want to restrict the user's ability to revise the data.

MAKING REPORTS EASIER TO UNDERSTAND

Access reports are organized into horizontal sections that are laid out in a specific order. Understanding how to work with each section is a crucial step in designing an effective report. Figure 34.10 shows a basic report that illustrates some commonly used sections.

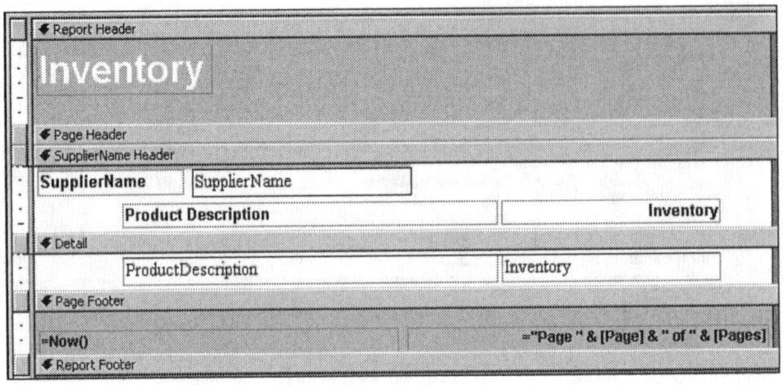

Figure 34.10
Each section in an Access report contains a different type of data. Headers and footers set off groups of data and pages; items you place in the Details section repeat as needed.

- The Report Header and Footer appear at the beginning and end of the report. A report header often includes the title of the report and a calculated control that contains the expression =Date() to display the date the report was printed. Report footers often contain grand totals or averages for the data within a report. To hide either section, change its Visible property to No.

Tip from

With a modest amount of creativity, you can turn a report header into a dramatic title page for a report. If the report header isn't visible in Design view, choose View, Report Header/Footer to make it appear. Next, drag the bottom border of the Report Header section to make it occupy as much of the page as you need. In the Properties dialog box for the section, set the Force New Page property to After Section. Finally, add any text labels and graphics you want, and set the background color if necessary.

- The Page Header and Footer appear at the top and bottom of each page, even if the Detail section is a continuation of data from the previous page. Page headers are commonly used for column headings, so readers can follow a lengthy list, and page footers are useful for dates and page numbers.

Tip from

If you've grouped data using a field that contains date information, use the Group On option to arrange it by interval—month, quarter, or year, for example. By combining this header with other groupings, you can see a list of all sales by customer by month, even if the data appears only by day.

- Group Header and Group Footer sections appear automatically when you define grouping and sorting options for a report. By placing calculated fields in either of these sections, you can display summaries of the data within each group.

Tip from

ED & Woody

If you want to start a new page for each grouping, open the Properties dialog box for the Group Footer section and set the Force New Page property to After Section. If this section is not visible, set this property for the Detail section instead.

- The Detail section includes fields from each record in your data source. Each field in the Detail section appears once for each record in your data source, making this the right place to specify how you want a list to appear.

GROUPING AND SORTING RECORDS IN A REPORT

In complex presentations of Access data, *groups* are the essence of report design. A group defines how records are organized in the output of a report, and how information can be summarized in statistical calculations, such as totals and averages. In the Design view of a report, groups are represented by a hierarchy of Header, Detail, and Footer sections.

Using the Report Wizard, you can choose the fields you want to use for grouping in a report, and you can specify how you want groups to be summarized by specific calculations. To adjust grouping and sorting options, however, you need to flip into Design view and click the Sorting and Grouping button. This option displays a dialog box such as the one shown in Figure 34.11, which gives you control over virtually all grouping options.

Figure 34.11
Use this dialog box to specify which fields should be used for grouping and whether you want to show or hide headers and footers for each section.

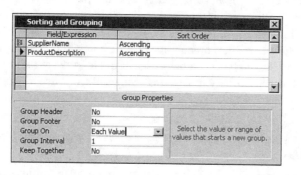

For example, in a report that you plan to use as a product catalog, you might want to group records by Supplier, in alphabetical order, with the product names listed under each supplier's name, also in alphabetical order. In this example, you would include the Supplier's name in a Group Header, with the ProductDescription, SupplierPrice, and UnitsInStock fields in the Detail section; optionally, for an inventory report, you might add a calculated field in the Group Footer section, using the expression =SUM([SupplierPrice]* [UnitsInStock]).

To tell Access you want to sort by Supplier, and then by ProductDescription, open the Sorting and Grouping dialog box and use the drop-down arrows to select those two columns in order. By default, Access offers to sort in Ascending order; if you want to use Descending order, adjust the setting here.

By choosing these two fields, you tell Access that you want to sort records in this order, but you need to go one extra step to group records: In the Sorting and Grouping dialog box, select the row that contains the Supplier field and change the Group Header property to Yes. If you want to add a footer for this section, change the Group Footer property to Yes as well.

Tip from

E.Q. & Woody

When you've added two or more levels of grouping, you can change the order of the group headings. Click the left edge of the row to select the entire row, and then drag it up or down in the Sorting and Grouping dialog box. The group priority determines the ultimate heading locations and the nature of summary calculations: Groups at the top of the list can be used for grand totals, whereas those at the bottom of the list display subtotals for smaller groups.

TROUBLESHOOTING

IMPORTING HYPERLINKS INTO ACCESS

I imported a list filled with hyperlinks into an Access table, but none of my hyperlinks work properly. What happened?

When you create a table by importing data, Access automatically recognizes a column that contains URLs or UNC-style file addresses and uses the Hyperlink data type for that column. However, this conversion takes place only if all the values start with a recognized prefix, such as http: or \\. If even one value doesn't follow this format, Access refuses to convert the column into a Hyperlink field. Switch to Design view and change the data type for the field to Hyperlink; after you save this change, all your hyperlinks will work properly.

JUGGLING MULTIPLE RELATIONSHIPS

I defined relationships between two or more tables, but when I open the Query window to edit an existing query, Access doesn't connect the tables with lines. What's wrong?

The Relationships window enables you to define default relationships between tables. When you create a new query, Access picks up those settings and uses them. Changing the default relationship in the Relationships window has no effect on existing objects, such as queries; likewise, you can change the relationship between two tables in a query without affecting the default relationship. Re-create the relationship in the Query window so that it matches the default relationship for the two tables.

FIRMING UP A RELATIONSHIP

According to the Edit Relationships dialog box, a relationship I established between two tables is of "Indeterminate" type. Is this a problem?

Check the design of your database. You're probably trying to create a many-to-many relationship without using a junction table. If neither field is a primary key or has a unique index, Access knows that you can enter duplicate values on both sides of the relationship; as a result, it's impossible to define the relationship properly. If necessary, define a unique index for one of the fields.

SECRETS OF THE OFFICE MASTERS: CREATING LINKS TO EXTERNAL DATABASES

In some cases, you might want to incorporate the contents of an external database file (or a collection of related files) into an Access database. If the external file is available on your system or network, and if the data is stored in a format that Access can use, you can incorporate the data into your Access application in either of two ways: You can *import* a copy of the data, creating a new table in your Access database. You can also create a *link* to the external table, without actually importing it into your current database. When you create a link, Access allows you to work with the data just as if it were stored within the Access file—you can establish relationships between the external data and existing table objects in your database, and you can create new queries to extract combinations of data from related tables.

Links are always the preferred option when you have multiple database programs maintaining identical data stores. For example, suppose that your office uses an accounting program that stores data about customers and suppliers in dBASE IV file format. Your accounting manager doesn't plan to switch from the dBASE application, because it suits the department's needs. You want to build a contact-tracking database in Access, and the information about suppliers and customers is a key part of it. If you import the information into Access, you will have no way of knowing when a record has been updated in the accounting program, and as time goes on, the two sets of records will develop more and more inconsistencies.

Instead, create a link to the Suppliers table; you can use the data the table contains in queries involving other tables stored directly in your Access database. To create the link, choose File, Get External Data, Link Tables. In the Files of Type list at the bottom of the Link dialog box, choose dBASE IV. Browse to the location where the external database file is stored, select its name, and click Link. If the dBASE file includes an index file, choose its name when prompted; if no index file exists, click Cancel to continue. Click OK when Access notifies you that the import was successful, and then close the Import dialog box.

The linked file appears in the database window, alongside other table objects, with an arrow to the left that lets you know it's a linked file and is not stored in the database itself. The icon is also different, depending on the original format of the data file. In general, you can view, edit, add, and delete data in a linked file, just as if it were stored locally.

CHAPTER **35**

ENTERING, FINDING, AND FILTERING DATA

In this chapter

RESTRICTING DATA ENTRY

Even the most carefully designed database is worthless if it contains inaccurate or inconsistent data. Unfortunately, the data-entry process is typically tedious, and even a highly motivated, well-trained worker can become tired or distracted. When fingers slip or the mind wanders, errors are inevitable. You can't prevent users from accidentally typing incorrect data, but you can define rules that prevent Access from storing errors.

Tip from

EQ & Woody

Some of the most effective data restrictions are side effects of the data type you specify for a field. Trying to enter text in a Numeric field or numbers in a Date/Time field, for example, results in an error message. Likewise, you can restrict the length of a Text string or control the number of decimal places allowed in a Number field by adjusting the Field Size property.

DEFINING VALIDATION RULES

Like Excel, Access enables you to write *validation rules*; you can attach a validation rule to a field or to an entire table. When a user attempts to save a new or changed record, Access checks the contents of each field in that record against any existing validation rules. If the record violates a rule, Access displays an error message, which you can customize. By creating validation rules, you can avoid entering data that is outside a reasonable range, inappropriate, or just plain wrong.

To attach a validation rule to a field, open the table in Design view, select the field, and edit the Validation Rule and Validation Text properties. In the input box for the Validation Rule property, enter a logical expression that must be evaluated as *true* for Access to accept an entry in the target field. In the Validation Text property, enter the error message that Access will display for any entry that does not pass the rule. (If you leave this property empty, Access will display a default error message.)

To build complex validation rules, including those that incorporate Access functions, use the Expression Builder. To open the Expression Builder, open a table in Design view, select the Validation Rule property for a target field, and click the Build button (...) to the right of the setting box. For simple validation rules, however, you can enter an expression directly in the Validation Rule property box.

For example, in a Products table that consists exclusively of low-cost items, you might anticipate one common data-entry error—if the user inadvertently drops the decimal point in a unit price, they might try to enter $399 instead of the correct value, $3.99. By comparing the value in the RetailPrice field to the expression >0 And <100, you can ensure that only positive values under 100 make it into the database. As part of this rule, create a helpful error message for users: In the Validation Text box, enter Unit Price must be less than $100. Figure 35.1 shows the validation rule and accompanying error message as they appear in Design view.

Figure 35.1
To prevent users from accidentally entering invalid or inappropriate data, set the Validation Rule property. Use the Validation Text property to display a friendly error message.

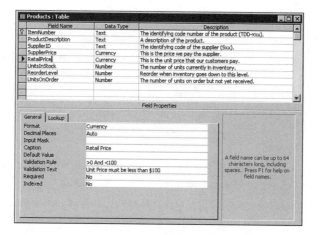

Click the Save button to save the rule as part of the table. When you add a validation rule to a table that already contains data, Access walks you through a two-step process: First, the program asks whether you want to test the existing data in your table against the new rule; if you want the rule to apply to newly entered data only, click No. You might choose this option in an invoice database, for example, where you want to restrict numbers and dates for new invoices only.

If you specify that you want the rule to be applied to existing data, Access applies the rule to the existing table and warns you if it finds any data that violates the rule. This option is especially useful after you've imported a table from another source. If errors exist, you can then choose to keep the validation rule and allow the incorrect data to remain in the database; if the error-checking turns up a problem in your rule, you can reset the contents of the Validation Rule property to its previous setting and start over.

Tip from

ED & Woody

In some cases, you might want to allow existing data to remain in the database, even if it violates a validation rule you've defined. This strategy is proper if you want the rule to control data entry only in new records. For example, if you want to preserve historical data about customer accounts but you don't want to enter any new records with a date earlier than January 1, 2002, define a validation rule, but don't apply it to existing data.

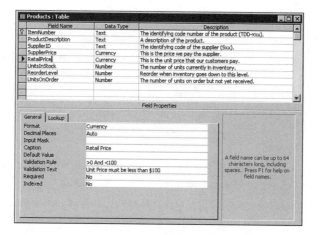 *If Access tells you that some data in a table violates a validation rule but you can't find the offending records, see "Tracking Down Data Integrity Problems" in the "Troubleshooting" section at the end of this chapter.*

PART

VI

CH

35

The following examples illustrate some useful validation rules:

- `>0` in a numeric field specifies that the value must be positive and not zero.

- `<= Date()` compares the value in a date field to today's date to make sure the date is not in the future; you might use this rule when you want to ensure that employees don't accidentally enter an invoice date that is in the future.

- `[ShipDate]<=[OrderDate]+30` displays an error message if you enter a ship date that is more than 30 days past the order date. (As this example illustrates, field names are enclosed in brackets.)

- `Like "S???"`, when used in a Text field, requires the user to enter a value that is exactly four characters long and begins with S.

- `StrComp(UCase([TickerSymbol]),[TickerSymbol],0) = 0` uses several Access functions to ensure that the value (in this case, a stock ticker symbol) is entered in all caps.

- `>=#1/1/1999# And <Date()` allows the user to enter a date that is greater than January 1, 1999, but before today's date; note that date values must be enclosed between number signs (#).

- `>=1001 And <=9999`, when used in a field that is set to an Integer data type, guarantees that the value you enter is exactly four digits.

→ For more details on how to use the Expression Builder, **see** "Using Expressions in Database Objects," **p. 865**.

You can also define validation rules for an entire table, rather than for an individual field. This technique is useful when you want to establish rules that involve more than one field. For instance, you might want to define an input rule that specifies that the RetailPrice field can never be greater than twice the value of the SupplierPrice field in the same record. Defining this rule for the table allows Access to check the contents of both fields at once.

To enter a validation rule for a table, open the table in Design view and choose View, Properties. In the Table Properties dialog box, enter the expression `[RetailPrice]<=2*[SupplierPrice]` in the Validation Rule box. (Note that you must enclose the field names in square brackets in this expression.) If the user enters a SupplierPrice of $1.95 and a RetailPrice of $3.99, Access displays an error message; the user must change one or both values before saving the record.

USING AN INPUT MASK TO DEFINE DATA FORMATS

When you're concerned with the appearance of data rather than its value, use an *input mask*. This field property supplies an input template consisting of blank spaces and literal characters (parentheses or hyphens, for example) that force a field's contents into the correct format. You can use this property to simplify standard-format entries such as phone numbers, vehicle identification codes, and Social Security numbers. The mask can include special characters such as parentheses and dashes, providing visual clues for the data entry itself.

Tip from

EQ & Woody

For an exhaustive list of the special characters used in input masks, along with a selection of useful examples, search for the Help topic "Examples of Input Masks."

Caution

Although it's possible to define an input mask for a date value, think twice before choosing this option. By default, Access enables users to enter data in a Date\Time field by using any recognizable format; by defining an input mask, you eliminate the option to use formats with which a user might be comfortable.

Setting a Default Value

The Default Value property supplies the starting value for any field. Whenever a field has a typical or common value, you can use this property to supply that value; the user can override it with a different entry, if necessary. The default value can be a *constant*, such as 0 or California or #12/31/2001#, or an expression from the Expression Builder. If you want a field to default to a value of today's date, for example, use Date() as the Default Value property. In an invoice table, you might set the PaymentDue field to a default value of [InvoiceDate]+30; to specify a different date, click in the field and replace the default value.

Note

When you create a new field by using the Number or Currency data types, Access automatically uses a default value of 0.

Requiring a Value

The Required property determines whether the user must enter a value for a particular field to complete a record entry. The setting for this property is either Yes or No. If the property is No, the field can be left blank in a new record entry. Set this property to Yes if you do not want to allow the user to skip an important field.

Using Queries to Extract Data from a Database

Queries are database objects that enable you to extract data from a database to use in another way—as the source of data used in a printed report, for example, or to produce a list of items for use in a lookup control on a data-entry form. A query can be based on a single table or on multiple related tables. In addition to fields drawn directly from tables, a query can also contain *calculated fields* that transform data—adding sales tax to an invoice amount, for example, or performing statistical analysis (totals, averages, and the like) on groups of records drawn from multiple tables.

Like other Office wizards, the Access query wizards are efficient at guiding you smoothly through the steps of a complex process, providing detailed explanations of the choices you need to make, and enabling you to view graphic representations of the results.

Although Design view is a more versatile environment in which to create queries, it's often easier to begin by using a wizard to create a basic query. After you finish with the wizard, you can then open the query in Design view to modify the result.

To view a list of available query wizards, press F11 to open the database window, and then choose Insert, Query. The New Query dialog box lists four query wizards. Double-click any of these options to launch a wizard.

Tip from

EQ & Woody

In their efforts to simplify tasks, query wizards sometimes unnecessarily restrict your choices. In the Crosstab Query Wizard, for example, you must base your new query on a single existing table or query. If you want to use fields from more than one table, you must first create a query that contains all the target fields. By contrast, if you create a crosstab query in Design view, you can add fields from two or more related tables.

The first step in designing a query from scratch in Design view is to select the tables or queries on which the new query will be based. You can add any combination of existing tables and queries to the upper pane of the query design window. Choose View, Show Table, or click the Show Table button on the Access toolbar to open this box. The Show Table dialog box provides lists of all objects available for building a new query.

CHOOSING THE RIGHT QUERY TYPE

Access enables you to create several types of queries. The most common is a *select* query, which extracts information from one or more tables. You can also create *crosstab* queries, which group and summarize information in row-and-column formats such as an Excel PivotTable. Some of the most powerful (and potentially dangerous) things you can do with Access involve *action queries*, which actually change the data in an underlying table based on the criteria you define in the query.

Like queries, *filters* enable you to work with a subset of records in a database. Filters offer a quick way to temporarily limit the display of records in Datasheet or Form views. You can create a filter by entering data in a form or by making a selection in Datasheet view. Even though the display of data is filtered, it still represents "live" data, not a separate copy as in a report. If you enter changes in a Datasheet view based on a query, Access changes the data in the underlying table.

Tip from

EQ & Woody

Filters represent an excellent way to create a query without diving into the sometimes-confusing Query Design view. For instance, you can open a table in Datasheet view and select a fragment of data in a single field (the word Nylon, for instance). Create a filter based on the selection, and then switch to Advanced Filter/Sort view to save the filter as a query (Products That Contain the Word Nylon) that you can reuse anytime. Detailed instructions appear later in this chapter.

To create a new query, choose Insert, Query. The New Query dialog box (see Figure 35.2) lets you start from scratch in Design view or use a wizard to build one of several specific types of queries.

Figure 35.2
Use this dialog box to create queries based on a wizard or from scratch, in Design view.

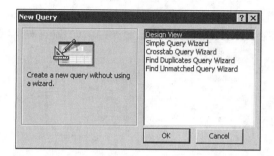

SELECT QUERIES

When you use Design view to create a new query from scratch, Access creates a select query by default. As the name implies, the purpose of a select query is to gather data from one or more tables, and to present it in a format that you save as part of the query itself. Select queries can include any of the following elements:

- Fields drawn from one or more tables or queries. You can base a query on another query, a common technique when you want to create a summary view of data gathered from multiple tables. Access uses defined relationships to match records from different sources and to find relevant connections between the data. You can also define new relationships between tables and/or queries and define them as part of the query.

→ For an explanation of how to define and save relationships, **see** "Defining Relationships Between Tables," **p. 880**.

- Calculated fields, which display the results of expressions using fields from one or more source tables.
- Totals, which perform statistical operations, such as sum and average, on fields from a source table.
- Selection criteria, which define the specific set of records the query will return. For example, in an Invoices table you might define criteria for the InvoiceDate field to return only invoices prepared in the past 30 days.
- Sorting instructions, which arrange the query results in numerical, alphabetical, or chronological order by one or more columns.
- Hidden fields, which are included for the purpose of defining criteria or sorting instructions, but are not actually shown in the query's results.

PART
VI

CH
35

When you save a query, you save the instructions for retrieving and displaying records from a database, not the records themselves. As a result, running a saved query always displays the current data set.

Figure 35.3 shows a select query that combines data from two tables and is designed to produce a summary of the value of products on hand. Note the first column, which contains a calculated field that multiplies the wholesale price (the value in the SupplierPrice field) by the current inventory for each product (as stored in the UnitsInStock field). The label in front of the formula in the third column defines the name of the calculated field. Use a colon to separate the label from the formula used to calculate the field results.

Figure 35.3
This select query combines data from two tables, along with totals; the third column is a calculated column.

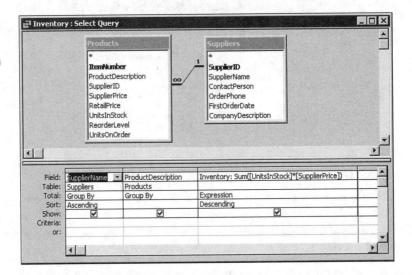

In Design view, a query includes two panes: The top pane contains field lists for each table and query used as a data source; this pane also shows relationships between the data sources. The lower pane contains a grid with one column for each field that makes up the query. When you design a query, you can drag any field reference directly from the lists in the upper pane, or you can choose from drop-down lists that appear when you activate a given column in the grid. (Double-click a field name to quickly add it to the grid.) You can enter calculated columns manually or with the help of the Expression Builder.

→ For details about how to use the Expression Builder, **see** "Using Expressions in Database Objects," **p. 865**.

In the rows below each field name, you can see specifications that explicitly determine the content of the query:

- The Table row shows the source of each field. This row is visible by default.

- The Total row lets you specify operations to be performed on that field—Sum, Average, and so on. This row is normally hidden. The default selection is Group By, which displays all values in the selected field without performing a calculation.

- The Sort row specifies whether a particular column will be used for sorting, and if so, whether the sort is in ascending or descending order. If you specify a sort order in multiple columns, Access sorts by each column, going in order from left to right.

- The Show row contains a check for each field that will be displayed as part of the query's results. Clear this check box when you want to use a field for sorting or filtering but you don't want it to appear in Datasheet view.

- The Criteria rows contain one or more criterion expressions for determining which records will be included in the query.

→ For an explanation of how to use criteria in queries, **see** "Defining Criteria," **p. 909**.

CROSSTAB QUERIES

Another kind of query, known as a *crosstab*, transforms record-oriented data into a summary view that resembles an Excel PivotTable.

The Design window for a simple crosstab query appears in Figure 35.4. The grid in the lower pane of the window includes a Crosstab row not found in select queries, where the contents of the selected fields are identified as the Row Heading, Column Heading, and Value of the crosstab query. To add the Crosstab row to the design grid of a select query, choose Query, Crosstab Query.

Figure 35.4
In the Design window of a crosstab query, select fields for row headings, column headings, and values. The Crosstab Query Wizard fills in these values automatically.

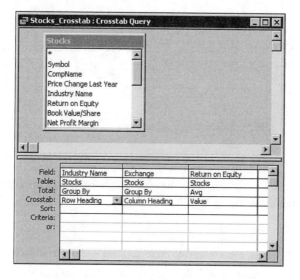

Creating a crosstab query from scratch in the Design window is a fairly straightforward process, but it's much easier when you use the Crosstab Query Wizard.

PARAMETER QUERIES

Normally, saving a query includes all the criteria you've defined for that query. If you want to see all sales results by product for all vendors, it's easy to save a query that extracts those results from the current contents of the database each time you run it. But what do you do when you want to specify slightly different criteria every time you run the query? For instance, what if you want to enter a specific vendor number or a maximum price when you run a query? For that task, you need a *parameter* query.

Each time you open a parameter query, Access displays a dialog box asking you to enter a piece of data to be used in the selection criteria for the query. You define the input prompt as part of the query's definition.

To create a parameter query, open the query in Design view and click in the Criteria box for the field in which you want to add selection criteria. The expression should include the text you want to display as the input prompt, enclosed in square brackets where you would normally enter a constant value. For example, Figure 35.5 shows a parameter query that prompts you to enter the minimum retail price you want to use as the selection criterion in a select query.

Figure 35.5
To create a parameter query, you write an expression that replaces part of the selection criterion with an input prompt; the result is an interactive query.

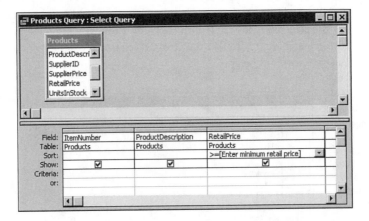

The value the user enters into the prompt becomes the parameter in the expression, which in this example specifies a selection criterion for the query. For example, if you enter 10 in the Enter Parameter Value dialog box, Access displays a list of products whose retail price is at least $10.00.

 If Access prompts you for a parameter when you try to run an ordinary select query, see "Is It a Parameter or a Typo?" in the "Troubleshooting" section at the end of this chapter.

The simplest parameter queries include a single value, but you can also use wildcards or multiple parameters as part of a query. The following examples should give you some ideas:

- To create an input dialog box that prompts the user to enter the beginning of a search string, use an asterisk with the parameter. For instance, entering Like [Enter beginning of product name] & "*" will search for all records in which the specified field begins with the value the user inputs.

- To search for a string anywhere in a given field, use two asterisks: `Like "*"&[Enter any text that appears in the product name]&"*"` will do the trick.
- To define a beginning and ending range of numbers or dates, use two parameters in a single expression, such as: `Between [Enter beginning date] And [Enter ending date]`. When you run a query with multiple parameters, Access displays an input dialog box for each one.

Tip from

EQ & Woody

> The expression you enter in the Criteria row of a parameter query can include a large amount of text, especially if you include more than one input prompt. That can make it difficult to enter and edit criteria in the query grid. If the expression is just a few characters wider than the current column width, expand the column that contains the expression by dragging the right border of its column heading. For extremely long and complicated expressions, press Shift+F2 to open a Zoom window for entering or editing the expression.

ACTION QUERIES

An *action query* potentially changes the data in an existing table, or creates a new table. Access enables you to create four kinds of action queries:

- An *update* query replaces data in existing records. In the design of an update query, you write selection criteria to identify the target records, and you provide an expression that generates the replacement data. Use an update query to change a group of records at once—when an area code changes, for example, or to make an across-the-board price increase. The example in Figure 35.6 shows the properties of an update query that include a parameter: It adds 5% to the amount in the RetailPrice field for all records that match the supplier code you enter.

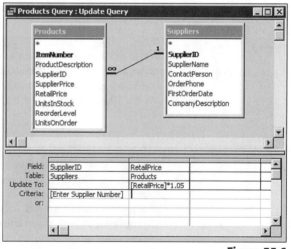

Figure 35.6

- A *make-table* query creates a new table object from the result of the query itself. For instance, you might build a query that produces a list of all customers who have not ordered products from you in the past year and copy those

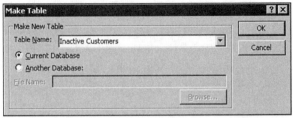

Figure 35.7

records into an Inactive Customers table. This type of query does not affect the underlying source data. As Figure 35.7 shows, you can choose a table from the current database or from another database file. If you enter the name of a table that does not currently exist, Access creates it for you.

- An *append* query adds new records to an existing table from a source query. This type of query is most commonly used when importing data from an external source. Append queries enable you to take some or all of the imported information and move it into an existing set of tables in the correct format. When you choose Query, Append Query, Access prompts you to enter a table name by using a dialog box that is identical to the one for a make-table query.

- A *delete* query removes records that match specified selection criteria for an existing table. You might use a delete query to prune outdated records from a database. When you create a delete query, Access adds a Delete row to the query's design grid.

Tip from

EQ & Woody

Want to archive information from a database table? Run a make-table query to copy records that meet specific criteria, such as customers who haven't placed an order in more than a year. Then, after running that query, use the same selection criteria as part of a delete query to remove the same records from the original table.

Caution

Running an action query can absolutely and irrevocably scramble your data, and in most cases the effect of an action query cannot be undone. If you inadvertently run an action query that doesn't behave as you expected, you might find it difficult or impossible to restore your original data. For this reason, you should proceed with great care when designing and running an action query. At a minimum, make a copy of the original table under another name, so that you can restore the data if your action query has unintended consequences.

Following are two fail-safe mechanisms that can prevent a data disaster:

- Before you begin designing an action query, create a copy of the table you intend to modify. In the database window, select the table icon, press Ctrl+C to copy it to the Clipboard, and then immediately press Ctrl+V. In the Paste Table As dialog box, enter a name such as Copy of Tablename, choose the Structure and Data option, and click

OK to create the copy. If the action query doesn't work properly, you can return to the original state by deleting the modified table and renaming the backup copy the same name as the original.

- Before running an action query, test its effects by designing a select query that uses the same selection criteria. When you open this query in Datasheet view, inspect the results carefully, because these records will ultimately be the same ones that change as a result of the action query. After inspecting the results, return to Design view and choose Query, followed by the menu choice for the type of query you want to create.

Tip from

EQ & Woody

You can save an action query for future use, or you can abandon it after a single use. If the purpose of the query is to perform a one-time maintenance chore, get rid of the query when you no longer need it. That way you don't risk accidentally corrupting your database. The only reason to save a query is if you expect to reuse it as part of ongoing database management—for example, in a monthly database cleanup routine.

SQL QUERIES

Structured Query Language (SQL) is a powerful, industry-standard database language that is available for use in a variety of software environments. In general, you can build Access queries interactively by checking dialog box options, and never have to deal with SQL. However, every Access query exists behind the scenes as an SQL statement, and in some cases you might find it useful to work directly with the SQL code.

Note

Microsoft's most powerful database product, designed to run on networks, is called SQL Server. Database experts typically pronounce each of the letters in this acronym: *S-Q-L* Server. Some old-timers prefer the more casual pronunciation, *Sequel Server*.

To view the SQL statement behind a query you've created in Access, open the query in Datasheet or Design view, and then choose View, SQL View. Access opens an SQL view window, showing the statement that matches the query you created in Design view. For example, the SQL equivalent of the make-table query shown previously in Figure 35.6 is

```
UPDATE Suppliers INNER JOIN Products ON (Suppliers.SupplierID =
Products.SupplierID) AND (Suppliers.SupplierID = Products.SupplierID) AND
(Suppliers.SupplierID = Products.SupplierID) AND (Suppliers.SupplierID =
Products.SupplierID) AND (Suppliers.SupplierID = Products.SupplierID)
SET Products.RetailPrice = [RetailPrice]*1.05
WHERE (((Suppliers.SupplierID)=[Enter Supplier Number]));
```

Why should you care about SQL code? Under normal circumstances, you don't need to. However, SQL code can be exceptionally useful in one specific circumstance: when you want to use a complex query as the data source for another object, such as a form or report. Open the underlying query in SQL view, copy its entire contents to the Clipboard, and then paste it into the Record Source property box for the form or report.

PART
VI

CH
35

> **Note**
>
> For a thorough discussion of how to use SQL statements with Access databases, see
> *Special Edition Using Microsoft Access 2002*, published by Que.

INSERTING, DELETING, AND REARRANGING FIELDS

To add a new field to a query, use any of the following techniques:

- Drag the field name directly from a list in the upper pane and drop it on the grid. When you release the mouse button, the new field appears in the grid to the left of the field on which you dropped it.

> **Tip from**
> *EQ & Woody*
>
> To select multiple fields in a field list, hold down Ctrl and click, and then drag the fields
> into the query design grid. Hold down Shift and drag to select contiguous fields.

- Double-click any field name in a list to add that field name in the next available column.
- Click the down-arrow button in the top cell of any empty column to choose from a drop-down list of all available fields. Note that fields and tables are identified by using the notation *TableName.FieldName*.

In some cases, you might want to add all the fields from a selected table to the query grid. If you don't need to work with the properties of individual fields in the grid, you can drag the asterisk from the top of a field list to a cell in the grid. When you do, Access represents the table in the notation *TableName.**. This notation means that all the table's fields will be shown in the output of the query. If you need to work with individual field settings in the design grid, double-click the title bar of the target table list to select all fields, and then drag the selection to the design grid.

To delete or move a field in the design grid, begin by selecting the field's column. Place the mouse pointer over the gray bar just above the column; the mouse pointer changes to a small black down arrow. Click to select the current column, and then drag the column to a new position or press the Delete key to remove the field from the query's design.

DEFINING A CALCULATED COLUMN

To define a calculated column, enter an expression in the Field row. You can enter an expression directly, such as [RetailPrice]*[UnitSales]; note that you must use brackets around field names. Or you can click the Build button to use the Expression Builder to create a calculated field.

If you enter an expression alone, Access adds a default name for the calculated field, using the generic *Expr1*, *Expr2*, and so on. To specify a more descriptive name, double-click this generic label and type a replacement name.

Did Access change the expression you entered as a calculated field in Design view? See "Cleaning Up After Expressions" in the "Troubleshooting" section at the end of this chapter.

DEFINING CRITERIA

Any expressions you enter in the Criteria row instruct Access to show only those records that satisfy the criteria. These expressions can be extremely simple: >10, for example, tells Access to display all records in which the value of the selected field is greater than 10. You can combine multiple criteria in a single column or across multiple columns, using the following logical rules:

- Expressions in multiple columns in a single row are treated as And criteria. To be selected as part of the query's results, a record must meet all the criteria in a given row.

- Expressions in different rows are treated as Or criteria. To be selected, a record needs to meet the criteria only in any one row.

When building an entry in the Criteria row, you can use any expression that evaluates to True or False. The most common building blocks for numeric and date fields are the comparison operators: < (less than), > (greater than), <= (less than or equal to), >= (greater than or equal to), <> (not equal), and = (equal). With Access, you can make an additional comparison by using the keyword Between, which expresses an inclusive range to compare with the value of a field.

You can also use the logical operators And, Or, and Not. If two expressions are connected by And, the operation is true only if both expressions are true. By contrast, the Or operation is true if either one or both of the expressions are true. The Not operation yields the opposite of the expression it modifies—true if the expression is false, or false if the expression is true.

Finally, for text fields, use the Like operator, with or without wildcards. If you enter a string of text in the Criteria box for a given field, Access automatically adds the Like operator and encloses the string in quotes.

Tip from

EQ & Woody

In Access criteria, spelling counts, but capitalization doesn't. If you enter an operator such as Between or And, Access automatically adjusts its spacing and capitalizes the keyword when you move out of the input box.

DEFINING QUERY PROPERTIES

In gs that are available in the design grid for a query, you can also adjust a host of settings that apply to the entire query. Open a query and switch to Design view. If necessary, click the Properties button to display the Properties dialog box, and then click anywhere in the background area of the query design window.

The Query Properties window contains a list of settings that apply to the specific type of query that you're creating. Although some of these settings are for specialized uses, the following are valuable in common situations in which you might use a query:

■ **Top Values**—Returns a specified number or percentage of records. This setting is most often used in conjunction with a sort setting; to see the 10 most expensive products, for example, click the RetailPrice column, and set Top Values to 10 and the Sort property to Descending.

■ **Unique Values**—Returns a query result in which no duplicate records exist. Choose Yes if you want to extract a unique set of values from a database, such as supplier names from a table filled with product names. Access eliminates duplicates from the result set based on records visible in the query's result, not on the contents of the underlying table or tables.

■ **Unique Records**—Returns a query result after eliminating duplicate records in the data source. Depending on the fields you choose to display, you might see duplicate values in the query results.

Tip from
EQ & Woody

You cannot set both the Unique Values and Unique Records properties to Yes—you must choose one or the other. If you set both properties to No, the query will return all records based on the criteria you specify.

■ **Column Headings**—This property, used only in crosstab queries, lets you limit the columns to be displayed. Separate entries with semicolons. In a data source that contains a RegionalOffice field, for example, you might specify East;West;Midwest in this property. Access ignores all other values when performing the crosstab query and displays these three columns in the specified order.

■ **Output All Fields**—Specifies that you want the query to return all fields from all tables included in the query, regardless of whether the field name is on the design grid or the Show box is checked. When you set this property, you need to add fields to the grid only to set Criteria and Sort properties.

■ **Link Child Fields, Link Master Fields**—Used to set the relationship between a main form and a subform or other embedded object. Normally, Access sets this property automatically based on relationships you define between the tables.

CREATING AND APPLYING FILTERS

When you use criteria in a query, Access displays a subset of records in the underlying data source. To revise the selection criteria, you have to open the query in Design view and enter one or more new expressions in the Criteria row of the design grid. You then have the option of saving these new criteria as part of the permanent design of your query.

A *filter* is a faster, more convenient way to temporarily focus on specific records in a query, table, or form. You can develop and apply filters quickly, without switching to Design view, and return to the unfiltered display whenever you want to see the entire set of records again.

The easiest way to create a filter is to base it on the contents of an existing record. When a query or table is open in Datasheet view or in a form, right-click and use the Filter by Selection or Filter Excluding Selection options (these options are also available via toolbar buttons or from the Records, Filter menu). When you choose one of these options, Access shows or hides records based on your selection. The exact filter action depends on which of the following three selections you make:

- If you select the entire contents of a field, or position the insertion point in a field without making any selection, the filter finds (or excludes) all records in which the contents of that field match the exact contents of the selected cell. This technique is especially effective when a field contains a category description or a name that is repeated in records throughout the data source.

- If you select a portion of the cell that includes the first character in the cell, the filter finds (or excludes) all records in which the field begins with the selection. If you want to see only those products that begin with the letter A, for example, find any product that begins with that letter, select the first character in its name, and click the Filter by Selection button.

- Finally, if you select a portion of a cell's contents that does not include the first character, the filter shows (or hides) all the records in the query that contain the selected string of characters or numbers anywhere in the target field. This technique is useful for finding records based on the contents of a field that contains variable text rather than consistent entries.

If no record that matches the filter is visible, click the Filter by Form button (or choose Records, Filter, Filter By Form). This option clears away the current contents of the query or table and displays a simple grid containing each of the columns in the query or table with a blank cell under each one. When you click in any of these blank cells, you can enter an expression or select from a drop-down list of unique items contained in each field of the query.

As you might guess, the Filter by Form option is an especially powerful way to search using a form you've created. Figure 35.8 shows the result when you open a form and click the Filter by Form button. If you start your query from a form, you can quickly switch between Form and Datasheet views to refine the display of data.

After entering criteria in the Filter by Form window, click the Toggle Filter button to apply the filter and see its results. If you need to refine the filter, click the Filter by Form button again, and add or remove criteria.

Figure 35.8
The Filter by Form option lets you enter expressions or choose from a drop-down list to refine the display of data from a query or table.

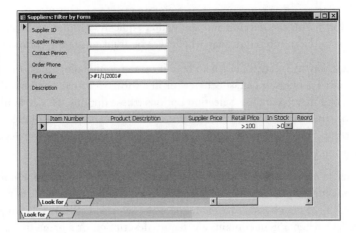

Tip from

EQ & Woody

The Filter by Form interface looks simple, but it can be surprisingly powerful. If you enter criteria in multiple fields, Access combines them by using the logical operator And—all the conditions must be true to display a result. Click the Or tab at the bottom of the window to create an additional set of conditions using the Or operator—Access will return records that match any of the sets of conditions you enter.

Regardless of how you create a filter, you can always restore the display of all records by clicking the Toggle Filter button again. Note that the ScreenTip for this button reads Apply Filter or Remove Filter, depending on its current state.

To create complex filters, or to edit an existing filter, choose Records, Filter, Advanced Filter/Sort. The resulting filter window contains a field list and a design grid, identical to the Design view for a query. To refine a filter, add one or more fields to the grid and write criteria expressions to select a subset of records; then click the Apply Filter button to see the result of your filter.

VIEWING OUTLOOK DATA IN PIVOTTABLES AND PIVOTCHARTS

In previous Access versions, you could view the contents of an Access database as a PivotTable by exporting it to Excel. Access 2002 builds PivotTable and PivotChart capabilities directly into Access. You can view any table, query, or form in either PivotTable or PivotChart view to analyze the data. You can also save PivotTable and PivotChart views as Data Access Pages viewable in a browser.

To create a PivotTable view of a table, open the table in Datasheet view and then choose View, PivotTable View. As shown in Figure 35.9, you can drag columns from the Field List to the "drop zones" on the PivotTable canvas to build the PivotTable.

Figure 35.9
Access PivotTables work much like their Excel counterparts. The Totals entry appears because the Inventory column heading was clicked to set up a summary value.

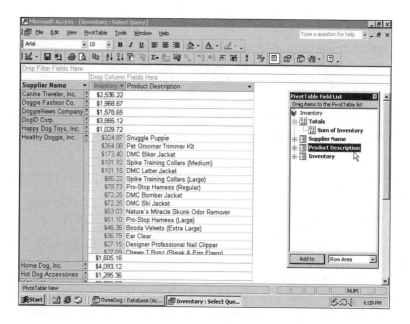

Access PivotTables are a powerful way to analyze data interactively, just as they are in Excel. Excel PivotTables are easier to use for simple lists; use Access PivotTables when you need to combine data from multiple sources for analysis.

TROUBLESHOOTING

TRACKING DOWN DATA INTEGRITY PROBLEMS

I applied a validation rule to a database that already contained data. When Access tested the contents of the database against the rule I created, it found that some data violated the rule, but I don't know which records need to be edited.

Frustrating, isn't it? Testing your validation rule tells you only that a problem exists; it doesn't tell you which records are incorrect. To find and fix the invalid data, copy the contents of the rule and create a query that uses the same criteria. If necessary, edit the values in the query result datasheet, and then re-create the rule.

IS IT A PARAMETER OR A TYPO?

I created a simple select query without parameters, but when I run it, Access displays an Enter Parameter Value dialog box. Regardless of what I enter, the query doesn't work properly.

This problem is almost always caused by a typo in a field name. Field names and parameters both appear inside brackets. If you misspell a field name, especially in an expression used with a calculated field, Access can't find the field and therefore assumes you want to display a parameter dialog box. Go through every expression in the query and see whether you can find (and fix!) the typo.

CLEANING UP AFTER EXPRESSIONS

I entered an expression to define a calculated field, and then chose Sum from the Total row. The query displays the results correctly, but when I look back at the query's design, I see that Access changed the Total row to Expression and also changed the syntax of my expression. Is this correct?

Yes, this is perfectly normal. It's more efficient to perform multiple calculations in one operation, so when you save a query, Access edits it. If you select Sum in the Total row, for instance, Access adds a SUM( ) function to the formula that defines your calculated field.

SECRETS OF THE OFFICE MASTERS: INPUT MASKS MADE EASY

Struggling with the Byzantine codes to define an input mask manually is a sucker's game. To create an input mask for common data types, such as phone numbers, ZIP codes, passwords, and popular date and time formats, it's much, much easier to use the well-hidden Input Mask Wizard. Click to position the insertion point in the Input Mask property box for a field, and then right-click and choose Build from the shortcut menu. The three-step wizard (the first step of which is shown here) lets you choose a built-in format from a list, specify the character to be used in blanks, and specify how you want the data stored.

You can also use this wizard to save and reuse your favorite input-mask formats. On the first screen of the Input Mask Wizard, click the Edit List button; then follow the wizard's prompts to add a custom input mask, give it a name, and save it for use in other tables— even if those tables are in other databases.

CHAPTER 36

FrontPage Essentials

In this chapter

HOW FRONTPAGE FITS INTO OFFICE

If you're new to FrontPage, or Web page design and management in general, you'll be able to leverage much of what you know about the traditional Office applications into FrontPage. Granted, you'll miss a few Office-wide features (such as AutoShapes connectors and the capability to tile all open windows), but experienced Office users generally will find the learning curve for FrontPage much lower than that for competing products.

Although the other Office applications can lay some claim to the "Web-enabled" marketing cheer, FrontPage is the real thing. If you're serious about designing and maintaining more than a few pages—a task easily handled by Word, Excel, PowerPoint, or Access, each in its own way—you need FrontPage.

USING THE INTEGRATED ENVIRONMENT

Before jumping headfirst into FrontPage, you should become familiar with its different views. Microsoft FrontPage is composed of multiple functions all integrated into a single *workspace*. You work in the workspace to manage your entire Web site, including the files and folders, user permissions, and tasks.

Tip from

Ed & Woody

> If you want to maximize the amount of room available to edit a page's HTML directly, choose Window, New Window to open a new window to the same Web site. Then hide the Views Bar and Folder List so that you'll have a full window for editing your pages.

The FrontPage workspace is divided into several screen areas. The Views Bar appears at the extreme left (see Figure 36.1). Use the Views Bar to quickly change between the major functions of FrontPage. You activate each view by clicking the appropriate icon in the Views Bar.

Tip from

Ed & Woody

> If you have a small monitor and want to optimize the layout of your workspace, you can right-click over the Views Bar and choose Small Icons. If you prefer not to display the Views Bar, right-click and choose Hide Views Bar: You can then switch among the different FrontPage views by using the View menu.

To the right of the Views Bar is the Folder List. It appears as soon as you open a Web site. Use the Folder List to navigate your Web site's files and folders. The Folder List is not used for the Reports view or the Tasks view, so it disappears when using those views.

When FrontPage communicates with the Web server, you'll see the arrow icon spin in the status bar. In Page view, the status bar indicates the expected download time of the page.

Figure 36.1
Select your function by using the view icons.

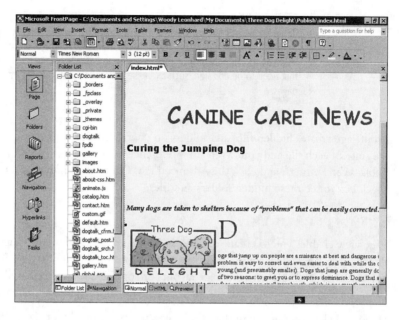

MANAGING FILES IN THE FOLDERS VIEW

Use the Folders view to manage the individual files and folders of your Web site (see Figure 36.2). In the Folders view, you perform Web site file operations, such as deleting files, moving files, and renaming files. You can also use the Folders view to visualize the overall file structure of your Web site.

Figure 36.2
Use the Folders view to manage the file structure of your Web site.

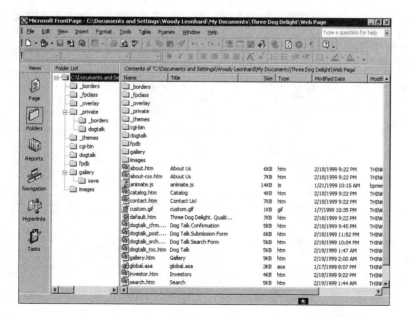

Note

Resist the urge to perform file operations on your Web site outside the FrontPage environment. When you perform the operations within FrontPage, FrontPage can actively help you manage the links between pages and can watch for dynamic components that need to be updated, such as the search engine index or the table of contents pages.

FrontPage creates hidden files and folders on your Web site to maintain information such as the state of each file and your Web site preferences. To see these files in Folder view, choose Tools, Web Settings, and click the Advanced tab. Check the Show Hidden Documents check box to see these hidden folders and files.

EDITING PAGES IN PAGE VIEW

Page view enables you to create and edit individual pages, and modify page formats and themes. You use Page view to design the page, choosing different styles and page layouts. You can choose simple page-by-page layouts or sophisticated frame-based layouts. In Page view, you also insert images, tables, hyperlinks, and automated components.

Double-click a page in any of the other views to open and edit a page in Page view. While editing in Page view, you can use three alternate views: Normal, HTML, and Preview. The Normal view enables you to edit pages directly, without digging into the HTML.

In Normal Page view, you can choose View, Reveal Tags (or press Ctrl+/) to illustrate the effect that each HTML tag has on the page content (see Figure 36.3). Reveal Tags mode is especially useful if you are new to HTML and want to see how each HTML tag affects the page.

Figure 36.3
Reveal Tags mode displays the effect that each HTML tag has on the formatted page.

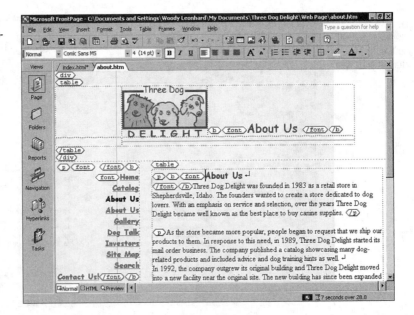

In HTML Page view, you can edit the HTML directly. HTML Page view also supports Dynamic HTML, JavaScript, VBScript, Active Server Pages scripts, and XML (see Figure 36.4).

Figure 36.4
Use the HTML Page view to edit the HTML directly.

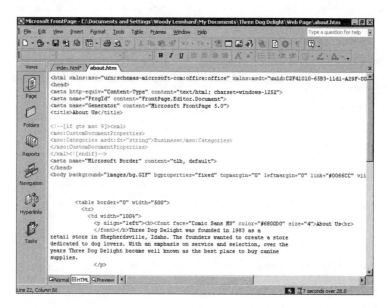

In the Preview Page view, you see how your page will actually look in the Internet Explorer Web browser. Although Normal view provides a what-you-see-is-what-you-get (WYSI-WYG) editing environment, the Preview Page view (see Figure 36.5) helps you visualize how some special effects and styles cooperate to format your page. In Preview Page view, you can actually interact with your page and browse to other linked documents.

Figure 36.5
Preview Page view shows you precisely how the page will look and act while inside Internet Explorer.

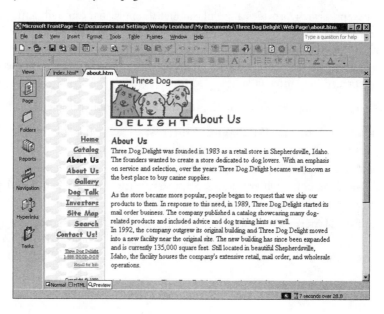

USING REPORTS VIEW

Reports view, shown in Figure 36.6, provides a comprehensive set of tabular reports about the status of your Web site. With Reports view, you can monitor important site information, such as the following:

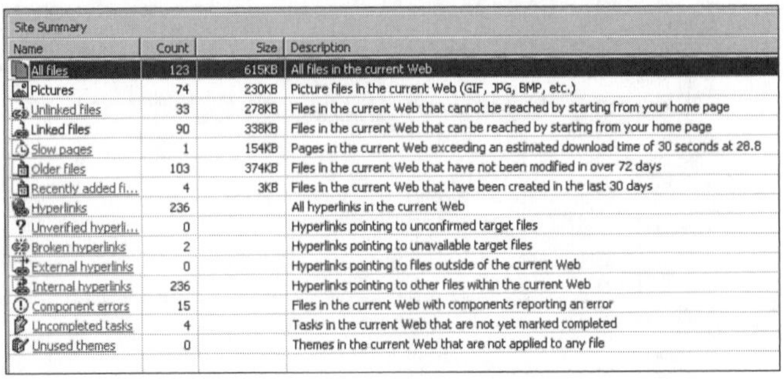

Site Summary

Name	Count	Size	Description
All files	123	615KB	All files in the current Web
Pictures	74	230KB	Picture files in the current Web (GIF, JPG, BMP, etc.)
Unlinked files	33	278KB	Files in the current Web that cannot be reached by starting from your home page
Linked files	90	338KB	Files in the current Web that can be reached by starting from your home page
Slow pages	1	154KB	Pages in the current Web exceeding an estimated download time of 30 seconds at 28.8
Older files	103	374KB	Files in the current Web that have not been modified in over 72 days
Recently added fi...	4	3KB	Files in the current Web that have been created in the last 30 days
Hyperlinks	236		All hyperlinks in the current Web
Unverified hyperli...	0		Hyperlinks pointing to unconfirmed target files
Broken hyperlinks	2		Hyperlinks pointing to unavailable target files
External hyperlinks	0		Hyperlinks pointing to files outside of the current Web
Internal hyperlinks	236		Hyperlinks pointing to other files within the current Web
Component errors	15		Files in the current Web with components reporting an error
Uncompleted tasks	4		Tasks in the current Web that are not yet marked completed
Unused themes	0		Themes in the current Web that are not applied to any file

Figure 36.6
Use the Reports view to find any hidden problems with your Web site.

- The total number of pages in your Web site
- The total size of your Web site
- Pages that are considered too slow for 28.8Kbps modem users
- Recently added or changed pages
- Old pages that might need updating
- Files that are not linked within your site
- Broken links to other pages within your Web site and locations to other sites
- Unfinished pages with assigned authors and each page's review status

The Reports view provides a useful Summary report that can highlight specific problem areas of your Web site, such as broken links or pages that might take too long to download. When you find a problem area or a specific report item that needs closer inspection, click the item to see further details. The Reports view can help you isolate specific problem pages and correct them interactively.

While in the Reports view, you can use the Reports toolbar to perform several actions:

- **Choose the Specific Report of Interest**—Each report offers multiple levels of information. The Summary report is a good place to start.
- **Choose a Report Setting**—Some reports enable you to refine the report criteria. For instance, in the Older Files report, you can select the age cutoff in days that divides older files from newer ones.
- **Edit Hyperlinks**—Some reports indicate broken links. In those reports, you can select a line of the report and choose the Edit Hyperlinks button. Doing so invokes a dialog box that enables you to perform sitewide corrections of the broken link.

- **Verify Hyperlinks**—To track the status of links to external locations, click the Verify Hyperlinks button. FrontPage tries to connect to each externally referenced page and test the success status. If the external page has been moved or deleted, the link is flagged as broken, and you can fix it in a sitewide fashion.

> **Note**
>
> In general, you should not rely solely on Preview mode. Instead, you should preview your Web pages in as many browsers as you can get your hands on, by choosing File, Preview in Browser. Each browser renders HTML differently. For example, Netscape Navigator and Internet Explorer do not display paragraphs with a background color the same: IE shows the color the full width of the window, whereas Netscape shows it only the width of the text.

COMMANDING YOUR SITE LAYOUT IN NAVIGATION VIEW

Use Navigation view to define how users will navigate through your Web site (see Figure 36.7). Navigation view does not actually rename your files or move them from folder to folder; it defines the hierarchical relationship of your pages.

Figure 36.7
Use Navigation view to define your Web site structure.

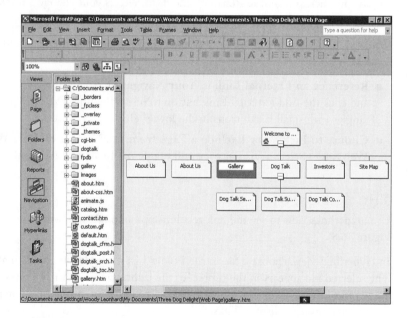

In Navigation view, the home page of your Web site appears as a rectangle at top center. To add other pages, drag them from the Folder List to the Navigation view. As you drag a new page to the view, a connecting line appears, illustrating the relationship to the other pages. Drag the page rectangle to the desired location, such as a sibling or child of the home page. You can reposition any page in a similar manner, drag it to the preferred location, and confirm the connecting-line relationship.

Navigation view works hand in hand with FrontPage link bars, the navigational aids that FrontPage supports to give a user access to the sites she needs most. A typical link bar might have links called Home, Search, Products, and Contact Us—clicking each of the links in the link bar would propel the viewer to the appropriate page in your Web.

You can build a custom link bar manually or have FrontPage create one for you, based on the structure shown in Navigation View.

Caution

If you want to create a link bar with Back and Next links, or if you want to create a custom link bar and have it maintained by FrontPage, your Web server must be running Microsoft FrontPage Server Extensions 2002.

→ For more information about link bars, **see** "Using Link Bars to Make Navigation Easier," **p. 936**.

If you maintain page titles in Navigation view religiously, you can use FrontPage's page banner feature to automatically generate titles for each page. To put a banner on a Web page, choose Insert, Page Banner. Then, when you change the page title within Navigation view (right-click and choose Rename), the page reflects your change automatically without you having to edit the page directly.

While in Navigation view, you can use the Navigation toolbar to perform two important actions:

- **Reference an External Link in Your Navigation Structure**—Select a current page and click the Add External Link button to insert the link. External links appear as rectangles with small Earth icons in the lower left.

- **Choose to Include or Exclude a Page from the Navigation Bars Within Your Web Site**—Select a current page and toggle the Include in Navigation Bars button.

USING HYPERLINKS VIEW

Use Hyperlinks view to see the link relationships among pages within your Web site (see Figure 36.8).

In Hyperlinks view, choose a file in the Folder List to display the links to and from the file. The selected file appears in the center To the right, you'll see arrows representing links going out of the page. To the left, you'll see arrows representing links going into the page. Dashed lines indicate broken links.

Tip from
EQ & Woody

Right-click a page icon and choose Move to Center to see all the hyperlinks going into and out of the chosen page. Click the + (plus) icon in the top left of a page icon to show the links to which that page links, and click the – (minus) icon to collapse those links. Using these selections, you can quickly navigate through your entire Web site.

Figure 36.8
Use Hyperlinks view to visualize how pages are linked together.

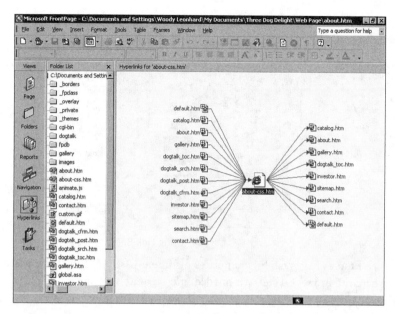

By default, Hyperlinks view displays the filenames of your pages. To change the information that is displayed, right-click and choose one of the following options:

- **Show Page Titles**—To display the page titles instead
- **Hyperlinks to Pictures**—To display links to image files
- **Repeated Hyperlinks**—To see whether a page has multiple links to the same file
- **Hyperlinks Inside Page**—To see links to bookmarks on the same page

→ For more about chasing down broken links, **see** "Maintaining Accurate Hyperlinks," **p. 945**.

CREATING AND EDITING WEB PAGES

In Page view, FrontPage provides an extensive set of HTML formatting and image-manipulation tools. When you first open a Web site and go to Page view, FrontPage displays a new blank page.

CREATING PAGES WITH TEMPLATES

Although you can certainly start with a blank page and build whatever suits your fancy, you will probably find it easier—at least, at first—to start with one of FrontPage's built-in templates. Choose File, New, and, on the New Page or Web task pane, select from the long list of prefabricated page or Web templates (see Figure 36.9).

Figure 36.9
Choose the template or wizard that best fits your new page's purpose.

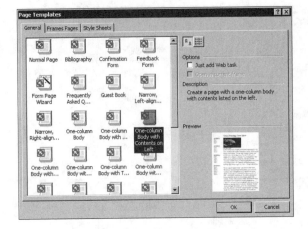

The Frames Pages tab lists templates for frame-based layouts. Frames are multipage layouts, where the browser window is divided into separate subpages.

→ For more about frames, **see** "Using Frames," **p. 932**.

The Page Templates dialog box also provides cascading style sheet templates in the Style Sheets tab.

→ To learn more about style sheets, **see** "Using Cascading Style Sheets," **p. 947**.

IMPORTING WEB PAGES

If you already have a Web site handy, or if you want to borrow one as the basis for forming your own Web, you can import it into FrontPage and take it from there (within the bounds of copyright protection, of course). Choose File, Import to display the Import dialog box. You can import individual files, such as documents, images, or style sheets, or you can import entire folders or other Web sites. When you import folders and other Web sites, the Import Wizard keeps the folder structure intact, as you might expect. After you select the files or folders, you can click Modify to change the destination location to where the content will be imported.s

MANAGING HYPERLINKS

Hyperlinks provide the interactive power for your Web documents. You can link to other documents or resources, to other Web sites, to resources within your own Web site, and even to locations *within* documents (known as bookmarks). Links do not always have to connect to other documents—you can link to interactive database queries, zip files, images, videos, sound files, or even executable programs on a server that returns HTML responses.

→ For general information about hyperlinks in Office, **see** "Working with Hyperlinks," **p. 167**.

CREATING LINKS TO OTHER PAGES WITHIN YOUR WEB

To create a link within your Web document to another page within your Web, select the text that will form your link and click the Hyperlink toolbar button. The Create Hyperlink dialog box appears, as shown in Figure 36.10.

Figure 36.10
Link to files within
your Web, on other
Webs, and to book-
marks within pages.

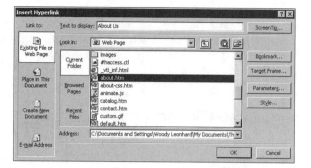

Tip from

It's easy to create a dynamic "rollover effect"–that is, to make the hyperlink text change its appearance whenever the mouse pointer goes over it. Right-click your page and choose Page Properties. On the Background tab, check Enable Hyperlink Rollover Effects and click Rollover Style. Then use the Font dialog box to define an alternative text style. When the user moves the mouse pointer over a hyperlink, the hyperlink text will change momentarily to your rollover style.

The Create Hyperlink dialog box displays the files and folders within your Web site. To link to another page in your Web, select it and click OK. If the destination page does not exist yet, you can create a new page and link to it in one operation. Click the Create a Page and Link to the New Page button. Using this technique, you can build a Web site page by page as your content grows.

Tip from

You can quickly create a hyperlink to another page within your Web site by dragging the target page from the Folder List and dropping it onto your page. FrontPage inserts the link, using the page's title.

USING BOOKMARKS TO LINK WITHIN A DOCUMENT

To have a hyperlink that jumps to a location within a page, the destination must be *book-marked*. When the user clicks a link to a bookmark, the bookmark's text scrolls to the top of the browser window.

To create a bookmark, select the text to which you want to link. Choose Insert, Bookmark; in the Bookmark dialog box, enter a unique name. In Page Normal view, FrontPage displays the bookmark text with a dashed underline.

To create a link to your new bookmark,, select the text that will form the link. Click the Hyperlink toolbar button to display the Edit Hyperlink dialog box, and choose the Bookmark to which the browser should jump.

To clear a bookmark, right-click the bookmark and choose Bookmark Properties. Click Clear in the Bookmark dialog box.

Tip from

To create a bookmark and hyperlink in one step, right-click and drag the target bookmark text, and drop it where you want the hyperlink. When you release the right mouse button, choose Link Here. FrontPage creates the bookmark and inserts the hyperlink using the bookmark text.

CREATING LINKS TO RESOURCES ON THE INTERNET

You can link to other files on other Web sites. All you need to know is the address (URL) of the destination.

To create a link within your Web document to another location on the Internet, select the text that will form your link, and click the Hyperlink toolbar button to display the Create Hyperlink dialog box. Next, type the full URL of the Internet resource if you know it, or click the Use Your Web Browser to Select a Page or File button. FrontPage launches your Web browser, and you can navigate to the intended location. When you close the browser, FrontPage enters the URL for you.

Tip from

To quickly create a hyperlink to an external page, browse to the location in Internet Explorer and drag the icon from the Address Bar, dropping it onto your page. FrontPage inserts the link by using the page's title.

FIXING BROKEN LINKS

To fix *broken links* (links that point to locations that no longer exist) throughout your entire Web site, use the Broken Hyperlinks report in Reports view. Right-click the hyperlink that is broken, and choose Edit Hyperlink. Use the Edit Hyperlink dialog box to fix the link in all the pages that reference it.

CREATING AND EDITING TABLES

Tables provide a useful way to organize information into rectangular columns and rows. In fact, you can use tables to organize the layout of your entire page. Most successful Web sites use tables to present a clean, professional, and organized look to their customers. You will find that FrontPage makes it easy to work with tables—and the techniques are nearly identical to those in Word.

→ Word's table capabilities are described in Chapter 17, "Using Tables," **p. 443**.

A few settings in FrontPage are different from those in Word. For example, if you want your table to have a border, choose Table, Table Properties, Table; in the Table Properties dialog box (see Figure 36.11), increase the Border Size to a value greater than 0. Values are listed in pixels. When using a nonzero border size, you also get borders around each cell.

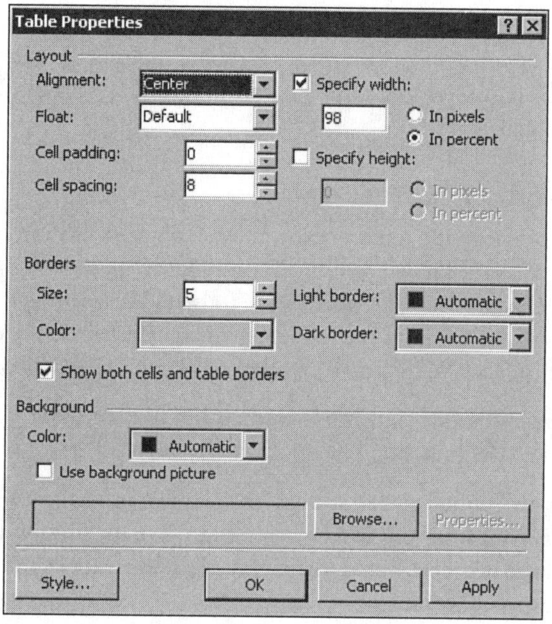

Figure 36.11
The Table Properties dialog box enables you to make some adjustments that you won't find in Word.

The Table Properties dialog box also enables you to modify the number of pixels that pad the contents of each cell by using the Cell Padding value. The Cell Spacing value determines the distance in pixels between adjacent cells.

Tip from

EQ & Woody

In Page Normal view, you can select complete blocks of HTML content by holding down the Alt key as you click. This is especially useful when selecting individual cells of a table.

In the Table Properties dialog box you can choose to have your entire table aligned to the left margin, centered, or aligned to the right margin. If you want text to flow around the table, you must *float* the table to the right or left. Right-click the table and choose Table Properties to make your adjustments.

If you want to apply a background image or texture for an interesting effect to your table or individual cells, right-click and choose Table Properties or Cell Properties. Check the Use Background Picture check box, and click Browse to locate the image to use.

For individual cells, you can adjust how the content is aligned within the cell. Select the cell that you want to adjust, right-click, and choose Cell Properties. For instance, if you want everything in the cell to be centered, choose Centered in the Horizontal Alignment option list.

If you want to prevent the contents of the cell from wrapping automatically, check the No Wrap check box. Additionally, if you want to declare specific cells as Header Cells, check the Header Cell check box. Browsers display Header Cells centered within the cell and in bold text automatically.

INSERTING IMAGES, CLIP ART, AND VIDEOS

You can improve the appearance of your pages by using multimedia components such as images and videos. Doing so creates a more compelling and captivating Web site, inviting users to return again and again.

CHOOSING THE RIGHT IMAGE FILE FORMAT

Although hundreds of image file formats exist, most Web browsers can natively display only two main image file formats, known as *GIF (Graphics Interchange Format)* and *JPEG (Joint Photographic Experts Group)* files. These are *native* formats because they can be displayed within the browser window without the assistance of an external viewer or plug-in. A new native image format called *PNG (Portable Network Graphic)* is slowly becoming popular.

The difference between the GIF and JPEG formats lies in their inherent compression and image quality:

- GIF image files are limited to 256 maximum colors in an image. Other colors must be simulated, or *dithered*, from the 256 lucky ones, to give the illusion that more colors are available. GIF format is best suited for images with few colors and for images that have large areas of the same color.

- JPEG image files can support up to 16.7 million colors per image. The JPEG compression algorithm can be adjusted to reduce image quality, producing much smaller files. JPEG format is best suited for natural scenes or scenes with many colors.

That said, the GIF format offers some worthwhile features that aren't available in JPEG:

- **Transparency**—You can identify one of the colors within the image that, upon display, maps to the color of the background of the window, thus rendering the chosen color "transparent."

- **Interlacing**—Every eighth row of the image appears first, then the next set of eight rows, and so on, so that the image appears onscreen with a Venetian blind effect.

- **Animation**—Multiple GIF files can be assembled together into one file as frames of the animation, and you control the delay between images and looping.

Also, if you have text superimposed on an image, GIF can be superior to JPEG because JPEG has a tendency to make the edges of the text fuzzy.

JPEG offers a *progressive* format, similar to GIF's interlacing, that creates the image fade-in over several passes, with each pass adding more detail than those before it.

A new image file format supported by some browsers is the PNG (Portable Network Graphic) format. PNG is an improvement over GIF in that it offers 16.7 million colors (24 bits) and transparency as well. Both FrontPage and Internet Explorer support PNG, but it will likely take some time before you see PNG used regularly on the Web.

On the video side, most formats are not supported natively by Web browsers—an external application (such as ActiveMovie on Windows platforms) is needed to view them. The three most popular video formats are *AVI (Audio Video Interleaved)*, *MPEG (Motion Picture Experts Group)*, and *QuickTime* files (an Apple Computer technology). Each format provides a trade-off in video quality, audio quality, and compression.

Compressing and viewing video requires the use of a *codec*, short for COmpressor-DECompressor. Codecs invariably result in some sound and image degradation or the introduction of *artifacts*—unwanted information inserted into the data by compression.

Because video files are large and time-consuming to download, the industry has developed video *streaming* technologies, in which the video application displays the video as it downloads over the network. Users run a decoder, or player, to decompress and play streaming video.

CONVERTING IMAGES

After you have placed an image on your Web page, you can convert it to the Web image format that you prefer.

FrontPage prompts you for details about graphic formats when you save a page. So if you want to change, say, the compression level of a JPEG, you must first change one of the images on the page (perhaps by cropping it a few pixels) and then save the page. During the course of the save, FrontPage prompts you with the Save Embedded Files dialog box, from which you can click the Picture Options button to modify picture layouts (see Figure 36.12).

Figure 36.12
Convert your image by using the Picture Options dialog box.

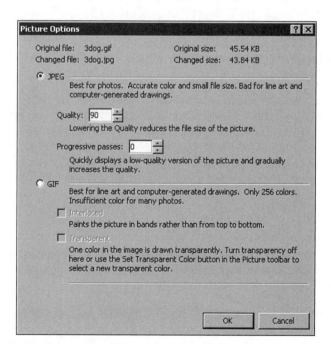

When converting to JPEG, choose the quality level in the Picture Options dialog box that gives the results that you want and still produces a compressed file for short download durations. Usually, a 75% quality setting is sufficient, but you might want to adjust it further—lower values yield smaller files at the expense of image clarity.

ADJUSTING IMAGES

FrontPage includes a number of useful image-manipulation tools that handle many of the simple image adjustments that you'll need to make. Open the Pictures toolbar to get access to these tools.

FrontPage provides the capability to overlay text onto GIF images.

To overlay text, select the image in Page Normal view and click the Text button on the Picture toolbar. A box appears in the middle of the image—type your text into the box and use text formatting to change the font, size, and color of the text. You can also align the text within the box, and you can change the box size by dragging the resize handles.

When you place an image on a page, you can adjust the alignment of the image relative to adjacent text, the spacing around the image, and the color and width of the border.

To set the alignment of an image, right-click the image, choose Picture Properties, and click the Appearance tab. Choose the alignment from the Alignment options list. Most of the choices determine how the image will align to adjacent text—that is, whether the top of the image follows the top of the text, or the bottom of the image along the text baseline, and so on.

If you want to fine-tune the spacing of the image with respect to adjacent text or other images, change the Horizontal Spacing and Vertical Spacing values. The spacing values are set in pixels.

Tip from

EQ & Woody

If you want to create an interesting layout that uses odd spacing of text and images, use the following image trick: Create a transparent single-pixel image (1×1) as a GIF file with one pixel's color set as the transparent color. Save the file to your Web site, and wherever you need to define odd spacing, insert the image into your page and use the Horizontal Spacing and Vertical Spacing values to create the spacing that you want. Because the image file is small and transparent, you can use it in every page with little degradation of performance.

When you resize an image, you actually define the preferred width and height values in HTML so that the browser scales the image upon display. In other words, if you have a 640×480-pixel image and you set the width and height values to 64 and 48, the browser actually downloads the large image and dynamically scales it to 64×48 when the image is displayed.

FrontPage provides two simple effects for Web images: You can convert an image to black and white (actually grayscale), which eliminates all the color information, and you can wash out the image, which combines brightness and contrast changes to create a subtle image suitable for page, table, or cell backgrounds. The washed-out appearance does not interfere with text on the page and can help to avoid a busy-looking page.

In Page Normal view, select the image, or, if you want to modify the background image, do not make any selection. Click the Black and White button on the Picture toolbar to convert the image to grayscale. To wash out the colors, click the Wash Out button. If you want to restore the image to its original state, click the Restore button.

Note

When you wash out a GIF image, any transparency information is lost. Reset the transparent color by using the Set Transparent Color toolbar button.

CREATING IMAGE THUMBNAILS

FrontPage provides a useful feature that enables you to make quick thumbnails of images. A thumbnail is a smaller version of an image. Users appreciate thumbnails; users are not burdened by extensive download times and can browse the thumbnails before clicking to load the image that they want to see in full size.

In Page Normal view, select the image and click the Auto Thumbnail button on the Picture toolbar. FrontPage creates a small version of the image and automatically hyperlinks it to the full-size version.

 If the Auto Thumbnail button is not available, see "Auto Thumbnail Feature Is Not Available" in the "Troubleshooting" section at the end of this chapter.

If you want to change how FrontPage creates the thumbnail, choose Tools, Page Options, and then click the AutoThumbnail tab (see Figure 36.13). Here, you can set the preferred height or width of new thumbnails, set the border size, and specify whether to bevel the thumbnail, too.

Figure 36.13
Specify the size and border of your thumbnail images in the Page Options AutoThumbnail tab.

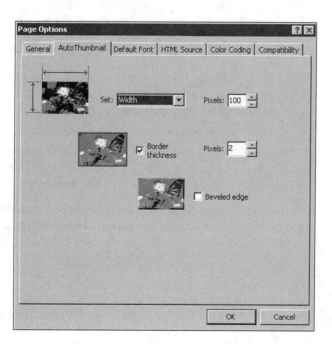

If you want to create thumbnails for many pictures, use the FrontPage Photo Gallery. Click wherever you want the Gallery to appear, and then choose Insert, Web Component, PhotoGallery. You have four different formats to choose from: horizontal, vertical, montage, and slideshow. Captions appear in all but the montage version. After you've chosen the format, click Add to gather all the pictures that you want to add to the Gallery. When you're done, click OK; FrontPage automatically generates the Gallery page for you.

LAYING OUT PAGES

You should consider several factors when designing the layout of your Web site so that the information is consistent, usable, and navigable. In addition to the layout of the actual content of your information, you need to decide where to display the page title, navigation buttons, copyright information, document author, last modified date of the document, and so on. Consistency counts.

FrontPage offers several tools to help you maintain a consistent page layout. Most important among these is the use of FrontPage templates to choose the best layout for your information. To maintain a consistent layout across your Web site, you must use the same template for each page.

USING FRAMES

Frames enable you to define separate regions of the Web browser window, such as a banner at the top, a navigation page at the side, and a footer section at the bottom, using the middle region for the content of your information. Each frame has its own underlying Web page, which, when displayed by the browser, shows as multiple independent pages that all fit within the browser window. Each frame can also appear with its own set of scrollbars, borders, and margins. Frames can save on page download time for your users, too, because only the body content needs to be loaded as users navigate your site; the other frames remain static.

Unfortunately, with frames, all the good comes with some bad. Frames are more difficult to manage and maintain. In addition, you'll find that many of the important Internet search engines do not index frame content—thus, Internet users may not be able to find your site easily.

Before you create a frame layout, you should first understand how frames work. Every frame document begins with a specially formatted HTML page that defines the divided regions of the browser window and the separate subpages to load into each region.

Each region of a frame layout is called a frame. Each frame has its own name, and you can define hyperlinks in one frame to load pages in another. Finally, each frame specifies the first page to load when the frame displays.

CREATING FRAMES

FrontPage provides powerful frame-editing tools. To create a frame, choose File, New, Page or Web; in the New Page or Web task pane, choose Page Templates and then click the

Frames Pages tab. Browse the available templates, and use the preview to visualize the layout of the frames. Find a layout that best fits your needs. If one doesn't match exactly, choose one that you can modify—you can later use tools to reshape your frames.

When the frames page is created from the template, FrontPage displays helper buttons to remind you what to do next. For each frame, use the helper buttons to define the underlying page. Click the New Page button to create a new blank page to fill that specific frame. Click Set Initial Page to browse for a current page within your Web site to use as the frame's page. Additionally, you can click Set Initial Page to create a new page by using one of the new page templates, such as the Table of Contents template.

EDITING FRAMES

If you want to improve the layout of your frames, you can adjust the size of each frame by dragging the frame border to your preferred location. If you want to remove a specific frame, click the mouse inside the frame and choose Frames, Delete Frame.

To split a current frame into two new frames, select the frame to split and choose Frames, Split Frame. Use the Split Frame dialog box to specify whether you want to split the frame into new columns or rows.

To further tune the layout of a frame, right-click the frame and choose Frame Properties. In the Frame Properties dialog box (see Figure 36.14), you can control the frame's attributes quite precisely.

Figure 36.14
Use Frame Properties to fine-tune your frame's settings.

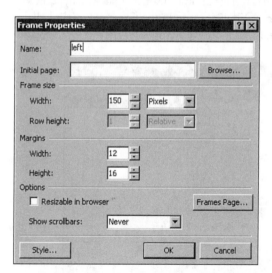

Note

If other frames share the same column or row of the edited frame, adjusting the width or height affects the other frames in the column or row.

If you want the user to be able to resize your frame, check the Resizable in Browser check box. Additionally, you can choose whether the frame displays scrollbars only if needed, always, or never.

To edit the settings of the page that defines the set of frames, click the Frames Page button. In the Page Properties dialog box, adjust the pixel spacing between all your frames, and choose whether to display frame borders.

Tip from

E.Q. & Woody

Use a common background color on your pages, and disable the frame borders to make your frames all appear as one document. Use this tactic if you want to cordon off part of your site as a navigational area, but you don't want the scrollbar to appear.

TARGETING HYPERLINKS TO FRAMES

You can *target* hyperlinks to display their destination page in different frames. Targeting hyperlinks enables you to load pages into other frames without affecting the frame in which the hyperlink resides. You've no doubt used this feature many times with navigational frames, typically on the left side of the page: When you click a hyperlink in the navigation frame, the destination page is loaded in a body frame, and the navigational frame remains. If you didn't have frame targets for your hyperlinks, the destination page would load inside the frame that originated the link.

To create a hyperlink that targets another frame, create the hyperlink as you would normally, but click the Target Frame button in the Create Hyperlink dialog box. The Target Frame dialog box appears, as shown in Figure 36.15.

Figure 36.15
Target your links to your frames, the entire current window, or a new browser window.

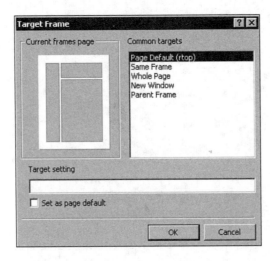

To target your link to a specific frame, click the frame in the Current Frames Page panel.

USING SHARED BORDERS

Frames can be a challenge to manage—and, if you are not careful, frames can impede your Web site's placement in search engines. If you want to provide a consistent layout to your pages without using frames and without many of the problems that frames impose, use *Shared Borders*. Shared Borders provide an easy way to add and maintain the same content at the top, left, right, or bottom of your Web pages. Use Shared Borders to provide a consistent layout for your Web pages and make it a snap to maintain when you have a change to the shared content.

> **Caution**
>
> To use Shared Borders, your server must be running Microsoft FrontPage 2002 Server Extensions.

When you edit a page using Shared Borders, FrontPage displays the shared regions with dashed lines in Page view. You can edit the Shared Border contents as you do any other page. When you save the page, the Shared Border is saved as well, and all other pages that reference that border are updated.

Shared Borders can be applied to individual pages or to your Web site as a whole. If you enable Shared Borders for your entire Web site, you can turn them off on a page-by-page basis. You can even create a background along the shared border that's different from the page background.

To use Shared Borders, choose Format, Shared Borders to display the Shared Borders dialog box, as shown in Figure 36.16. Click the All Pages option button to apply the Shared Borders to your entire Web site.

Figure 36.16
Choose from top, left, right, or bottom Shared Borders.

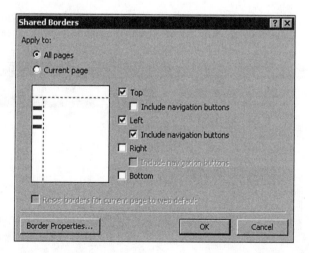

If you're frustrated because you cannot get the top and bottom shared borders to align with each other, see "Aligning Shared Borders" in the "Troubleshooting" section at the end of this chapter.

While editing a page, you can turn individual Shared Borders on or off in a similar fashion. Click the Current Page option button, and check or uncheck the borders that you want to affect. If you want to restore a page to use the Shared Borders used for your entire Web site, check the Reset Borders for Current Page to Web Default check box.

USING LINK BARS TO MAKE NAVIGATION EASIER

A link bar is a navigational aid that provides shortcuts to the important places in your Web. The hyperlinks that you place on your link bars generally reflect where you think the user is most likely to want to go next: Home, Search, Contact Us, Next Page, Previous Page, and the like.

FrontPage automatically maintains three different types of link bars:

- **Custom Link Bar**—Contains links to pages that you define, such as Home, Search, and Contact Us.

- **Custom with Next and Back Links**—Works just like a custom link bar, except that FrontPage also maintains Next and Back links on all "sibling" pages.

- **Full Navigation View-Based Link Bars**—Offers the full monty—these are link bars that can include automatically maintained links to the home page, other high-level pages, the parent of the current page, the children of the current page, the siblings of the current page, plus Next and Back buttons for the nearest siblings.

> **Caution**
>
> To use custom or custom with Next and Back link bars, your server must be running Microsoft FrontPage Server Extensions 2002.

To put a link bar in one of your pages, click where you want the bar to go, choose Insert, Web Components, and pick Link Bars from the Component Type list (see Figure 36.17).

Figure 36.17
FrontPage automatically generates three different kinds of link bars (although you'll need FrontPage Server Extensions 2002 to take advantage of the first two).

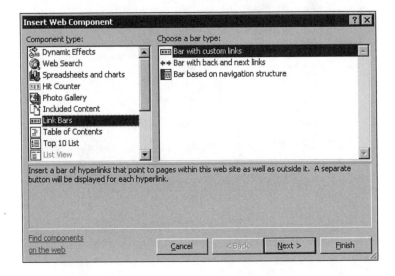

TROUBLESHOOTING

ALIGNING SHARED BORDERS

I'm using Shared Borders, and I can't get the top and bottom Shared Borders to line up with each other.

It is possible that you have different spacing defined for the content of your Shared Borders, such as table cell spacing or the spacing around images. The easiest way to fix the borders is to edit the borders individually. FrontPage maintains the Shared Border contents in separate files in the _borders folder. To edit the HTML of the Shared Borders independently, open the files in the _borders folder. If you cannot see the _borders folder, choose Tools, Web Settings, and click the Advanced tab. Check the Show Documents in Hidden Directories check box and click OK.

SENDING E-MAIL

I configured a form to send an e-mail message of the form input, but it won't work.

To use the Send to E-Mail Address feature, the FrontPage Server Extensions must be installed and configured properly for sending e-mail on the Web server. Contact the administrator of your Web server to install or update the Server Extensions Resource Kit to fix the problem.

CGI PROGRAMS

I imported a custom CGI program, but it won't execute when referenced by a form.

For security reasons, most Web servers restrict CGI programs from executing within the content area of a Web site. You might have to move the custom CGI program to another area of your Web server that will enable programs to run, such as /cgi-bin or /scripts. Contact your Web site administrator for help.

TABLE OF CONTENTS

I added a Table of Contents component to a page, but my pages aren't listed correctly.

The Table of Contents component uses the HTML title of each page rather than the name given in Navigation view. For the pages whose names do not display correctly, right-click and choose Page Properties. On the General tab, type the correct title of the page in the Title box.

UPDATING THE SEARCH INDEX

I'm using the FrontPage Search Form component, but it finds pages that no longer exist in my Web site.

For fast response to users' searches, the FrontPage Server Extensions maintain an index of all the Web site contents in a hidden database on the Web server. Normally, the FrontPage Server Extensions keep the index up-to-date whenever pages change within the Web site. Sometimes, however, the index can get out-of-date, especially if you remove or rename pages outside FrontPage. To manually regenerate the index, enter FrontPage and choose Tools, Recalculate Hyperlinks.

NAMING PARAMETERS

I'm using the Substitution component to display a parameter, but it does not work.

Make sure that you do not have a colon in the name of your parameter—that can confuse the FrontPage Server Extensions and prevent the substitution from working correctly. Choose Tools, Web Settings, and click the Parameters tab to modify the parameter. Then open each page that included the parameter and correct the reference in the Substitution components.

AUTO THUMBNAIL FEATURE IS NOT AVAILABLE

I want to create a thumbnail of my image map, but FrontPage does not allow me to use the Auto Thumbnail feature.

FrontPage prevents you from using Auto Thumbnail with images that are hyperlinked already or that have hotspots identified. Remove the links and hotspots, and try again.

You also cannot use Auto Thumbnail with images that are smaller than the thumbnail setting or that are animated GIF images.

SCHEDULED ELEMENTS

I'm using the Scheduled Include Page or Scheduled Picture component, and it does not change when the scheduled time expires.

These components check their start and end times only when a user modifies the current Web site in some way by using the FrontPage Server Extensions.

IIS MAXIMUM USERS ENCOUNTERED

I installed the IIS Web server onto my Windows NT Workstation system by using the default Web page, but when others browse to my Web site, some get an error page asserting that the maximum number of users has been exceeded.

The Windows NT Workstation version of IIS is restricted to 10 simultaneous connections. One solution is to install IIS and your Web pages onto Windows NT Server or onto Windows 2000, which has no user limitations.

SECRETS OF THE OFFICE MASTERS: USING FRONTPAGE COMPONENTS

Your first and most important task for creating excellent Web pages is to draw viewers in and give them what they want (or need, which might not be the same thing!). Do that by starting with an overall organization that's clean and consistent, with your primary message and important page elements at the top, where users will see them. For the Three Dog Delight main page, we used several FrontPage tools to get the user oriented quickly and to make the site as friendly as a lapdog.

Navigational links are clear, concise, and very accessible

Shared Borders keep the design uniform on all pages

Page banner lets the user know what site he's in and where he is on the site

Figure 36.18

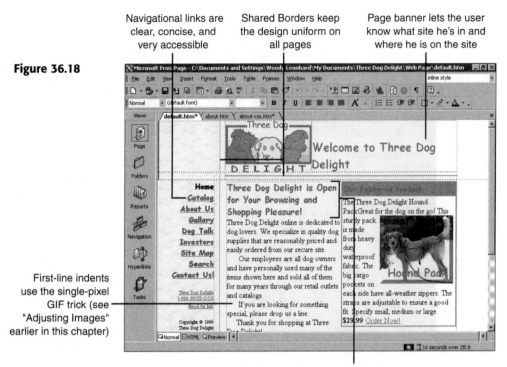

First-line indents use the single-pixel GIF trick (see "Adjusting Images" earlier in this chapter)

Headings are juxtaposed with their following paragraphs, with no vertical white space

CHAPTER 37

DEVELOPING AND MANAGING A WEB SITE

In this chapter

CREATING AND MANAGING WEB SITES

FrontPage contains all the tools you need to create, develop, publish, and maintain a Web site. You can create Web sites online connected to a Web server, offline on your local hard disk, or offline on a network drive. If you create your Web site offline, you must publish it to a Web server to make it available to users. Publishing your Web site entails copying the Web files to the Web server. After your Web site is online, you face the day-to-day challenges of managing it, and FrontPage can help you there, too.

Many of FrontPage's built-in features—searching features, hit counters, discussion groups, dynamic page components, live connections to databases, some kinds of link bars, and much more—require that your server be running FrontPage Server Extensions 2002. FrontPage Server Extensions 2002 is a subset of Office XP Server Extensions. If you don't have a server set up with FPSE or OSE, Microsoft will help you find one: Click File, Publish Web, and then click the indicated hyperlink.

If you have many people working on developing and maintaining a single site, you should consider installing SharePoint Team Services on your server. SharePoint is also a superset of FPSE.

→ For more information about SharePoint Team Services, see *Special Edition Using FrontPage 2002*, ISBN 0-7897-2512-6.

CREATING A WEB SITE ONLINE WITH A WEB SERVER

When you create a Web site, FrontPage can help you with a selection of templates and wizards that automate key tasks. The templates and wizards can create the entire file structure, navigation scheme, and consistent design for your new Web site. To create a new Web site, choose File, New, Page Web. The New Page or Web task pane appears; if you choose Web Site Templates, you'll be well on your way.

Tip from

EQ & Woody

After you've created your new Web site, but before developing the content, you should configure the Web compatibility settings to prevent you from using features that will not work on your target Web server or browsers. To do so, choose Tools, Page Options, and make your choices on the Compatibility tab.

→ For details on restricting features, **see** "Choosing Compatibility for Your Web," **p. 944**.

Several of the templates and wizards are quite sophisticated:

- **Corporate Presence**—Includes a home page, a table of contents, a "What's New" section, a press release, information on products and services, feedback, and a search feature.

- **Customer Support**—Includes a FAQ page, a suggestion box, downloads, a discussion area, a page for technical notes, and interactive forms for filing and responding to customer service questions.

- **Discussion**—Supports full threaded discussions, with a search feature and a table of contents.

Unlike other Office applications, you must specify a location for your new Web site before you create it (see Figure 37.1). In practice, any location—even a local hard drive—where you have write permission will suffice.s

Figure 37.1
Choose the template or wizard that best fits your new Web site's purpose.

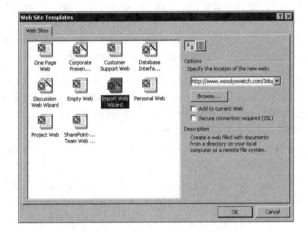

If you want to encrypt all information to and from FrontPage during your editing session, check the Secure Connection Required (SSL) check box. Your Web server must support SSL connections to use this feature, and the URL may start with `https://`. Using a secure connection can mitigate the chances of a hacker intercepting the dialogue between Front-Page and the Web server. If you have sensitive data on your Web site, such as credit card numbers or customer lists, use a secure connection if your Web server supports it.

Tip from

Many companies use a *proxy server*, which filters requests to the Web server. Proxy servers can be used to both improve performance and increase security. If you must connect through a proxy server to get to your Web server, chances are good that Internet Explorer is already set up to handle it (see the Internet applet in the Control Panel). If you have problems, though, choose Tools, Options; on the General tab, click Proxy Settings. You'll be working with the Control Panel's Internet applet.

Click OK, and FrontPage connects to the Web server to create the files. If the connection requires a username and password, FrontPage first prompts you for the necessary credentials.

CREATING AN OFFLINE WEB SITE

To create an *offline Web site* in a local folder or a folder on a network drive, enter the path to the folder in the Specify the Location of the New Web option list (refer to Figure 37.1).

For example, enter c:\Web\sales to create a Web site on your local c: hard drive. For network drives, you can enter the *Universal Naming Convention (UNC)* of the shared drive (for example, \\DELL2200\intranet).

CREATING SUBWEBS

Subwebs are subdirectories of the main Web site. Subwebs can be managed independently; each subweb can have its own access permissions, so you can effectively block authors from working on subwebs other than their own. You might find it useful, for example, to maintain an independent sales subweb that's restricted to sales support staff, who can then implement their own review and approval policies. Subwebs can have their own subwebs.

To create a subweb, you must be connected to a server running FrontPage Server Extensions 2002 (or Office XP Server Extensions, or SharePoint Team Services). Choose Tools, Server, Administration Home. In the Site Administration dialog box, click Create a Subweb. At that point, you can assign access permission.

 If you need help creating subwebs while offline, see "Creating Subwebs" in the "Troubleshooting" section at the end of this chapter.

FrontPage takes a few minutes to create the new subweb. When finished, the subweb appears as a folder with an Earth icon. To open a connection to the subweb, double-click the subweb's icon; FrontPage opens a separate window to the subweb. You now can create new Web pages as usual.

CONNECTING TO EXISTING FRONTPAGE WEB SITES

To connect to an existing FrontPage Web site, choose File, Open. The Open File dialog box appears.

Use the folder navigational tools to locate your folder, or type it in the Folder Name text box. For an online connection to a Web server, type the URL in the Folder Name text box. If required, FrontPage prompts you for the username and password before connecting to the Web server.

If you have used FrontPage with a Web site already, you can use File, Recent Webs to open the Web site again.

CHOOSING COMPATIBILITY FOR YOUR WEB

FrontPage enables you to design your Web sites for a specific browser, browser version, or server. For example, if you are creating an intranet for your sales force and your salespeople use Internet Explorer 5, you'll want to be sure that your Web site does not contain elements viewable only by Navigator.

Web server features can add even more constraints. For example, only Internet Information Server (IIS) supports *Active Server Pages*, and, if you plan to move your Web site to another host in the future, you must make sure that it supports your Web site. If you move an IIS-based Web site to a UNIX-based server, such as Linux running the Apache Web server, you might find that many features that you used under IIS need to be reworked for Apache—and conversely.

Choose Tools, Page Options, and click the Compatibility tab (see Figure 37.2) to define the browser and server capabilities that you want to include in your Web site. You can also customize the individual technologies that your targeted environments can support on an item-by-item basis.

Figure 37.2
Target the browser and server environments for your Web site.

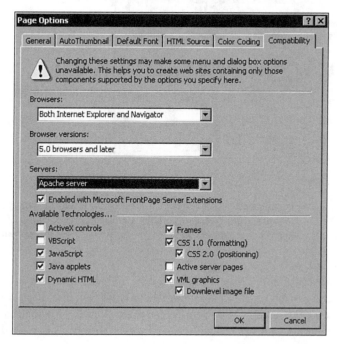

MAINTAINING ACCURATE HYPERLINKS

As your Web site grows and you begin to add more content, you must keep a close watch over the links within your Web site and to other sites. Often, Web pages on other sites move or are removed, and your links no longer work.

Use the FrontPage Broken Hyperlinks report in Reports view for verifying the links within your Web site, as well as the links to other sites. When the report displays, as shown in Figure 37.3, you see a listing of the pages on which FrontPage finds broken or unverified links.

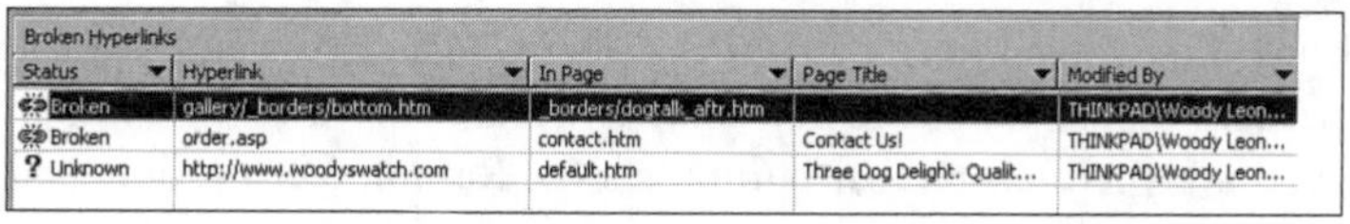

Figure 37.3
Use the Broken Hyperlinks report to identify pages with broken or unverified links.

Status	Hyperlink	In Page	Page Title	Modified By
Broken	gallery/_borders/bottom.htm	_borders/dogtalk_aftr.htm		THINKPAD\Woody Leon...
Broken	order.asp	contact.htm	Contact Us!	THINKPAD\Woody Leon...
Unknown	http://www.woodyswatch.com	default.htm	Three Dog Delight. Qualit...	THINKPAD\Woody Leon...

The *unverified links* are to those pages outside your Web site. You must ask FrontPage to check for them manually. This process can take a bit of time, depending on the number of unverified links and the speed of your network connection. To check the links, click the Verify Hyperlinks in the Current Web button on the Reports toolbar. The Verify Hyperlinks dialog box appears, as shown in Figure 37.4.

Figure 37.4
Choose Verify All Hyperlinks to perform an online test of the links.

Tip from

FrontPage can take a long time to complete the verification process, especially for links to slow servers. Whenever possible, schedule link verification during hours when the Internet is most responsive, usually in the wee hours of the morning.

Choose the Verify All Hyperlinks option button, and click Start. FrontPage connects to each of the pages and verifies the remote Web server's response. If you're unlucky enough to be watching the screen while FrontPage verifies, you can monitor FrontPage's progress as it does the work in the status bar. If the remote Web server indicates that the page has moved, FrontPage marks the page as broken.

You can stop verification at any point by clicking the Stop toolbar button. To pick up where you left off, click the Verify Hyperlinks toolbar button again and choose Resume Verification.

After FrontPage completes the link verification, double-click the broken links to repair the pages that contain them. If you have the same broken link on several pages, FrontPage can edit all the pages at once with the corrected link. When you double-click a broken link page, the Edit Hyperlink dialog box appears, as shown in Figure 37.5.

In the Edit Hyperlink dialog box, you can jump directly to Page view of the page with the broken link by clicking the Edit Page button.

For links that you edit manually or that FrontPage repairs automatically, the Broken Hyperlinks report marks the new links as Unknown. To verify your corrections, click the Verify Hyperlinks toolbar button, choose Resume Verification, and click Start.

Figure 37.5
Repair all pages that reference the same broken hyperlink at once.

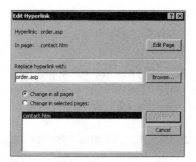

Tip from

Ed & Woody

Some pages in your Web site might have become stranded—that is, no pages link to them any longer. You can view a listing of the orphaned files in the Unlinked Files report. To reduce the overall space requirement of your Web site, remove these files. Select the files that you want to remove, right-click, and choose Delete.

Ensuring a Consistent Visual Style

After you have an understanding of HTML formatting and how to create and edit Web pages, you can apply more advanced capabilities to create pages that are easier to view, use, and maintain. You can also create pages that perform advanced functions, such as search the content of your site, automate your navigational buttons, process interactive forms, or perform database queries.

To make it easy for you to create advanced pages, FrontPage integrates several capabilities, such as cascading style sheets (CSS), themes, Shared Borders, frames, forms, and FrontPage components. Without this integrated approach, you would have to add these capabilities by hand, including the complex programming for the Web server.

Using Cascading Style Sheets

HTML uses a specification called *cascading style sheets* (CSS) to enable you to create and assign your own styles to paragraphs or characters, in much the same way that Word supports paragraph and character styles. The first version of the CSS specification, CSS 1, controls formatting. The second version, CSS 2, primarily relates to positioning.

Caution

Before you use style sheets, consider your Web site's audience. CSS 1 requires version 4 browsers (IE or Navigator) or later. CSS 2 requires version 5 or later. If you are sure that your users will be able to use style sheets, choose Tools, Page Options and click the Compatibility tab to enable style sheet support within FrontPage.

FrontPage enables you to assign CSS styles to any page element. The Style buttons found on nearly every property dialog box enable you to define and assign CSS styles. You can create new styles of your own, or change the default style of standard HTML tags. For example, if you want all Heading Level 1 paragraphs to use bold, sans serif text, in a light color, you can create a CSS style that overrides the default formatting of all H1 tags.

For an example of some of the CSS formatting that you can apply, consider the before and after snapshots of the Three Dog Delight About Us Web page, as shown in Figures 37.6 and 37.7. In the after view, notice the following CSS improvements:

Figure 37.6
Before: a simple page using standard HTML formatting.

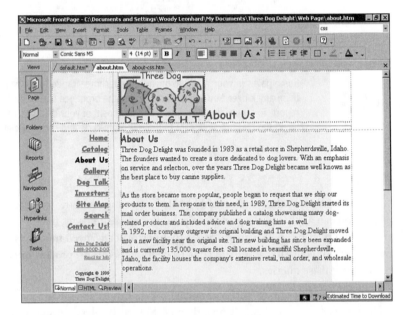

Figure 37.7
After: the same simple page as Figure 37.6, with additional *cascading style sheets* formatting applied.

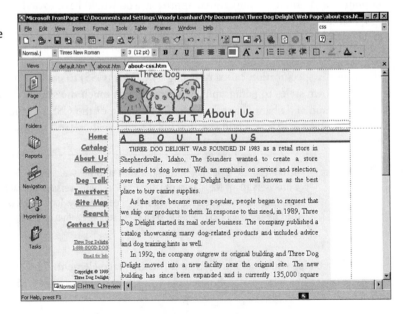

- **Letter Spacing**—The heading at the top of the text uses CSS expanded letter spacing for a more distinct look.

- **All Caps**—The heading style uses CSS to display in all capital letters.

- **Typeface and Size**—CSS defines the font typeface and size for the heading; in this case, we use Comic Sans in 12 point.

- **Top and Bottom Rules**—The heading uses CSS borders to produce horizontal rules that extend across the page.

- **Foreground and Background Colors**—The heading uses CSS to define foreground and background (or shading) colors.

- **Text Spacing**—The heading style sets the top and bottom spacing of 0, keeping the heading properly adjoined to its related text.

- **Line Spacing**—The body text uses CSS to open the line spacing a bit. In this example, the spacing is set to 140%.

- **Text Justification**—Using CSS, you can justify text to both the right and left margins.

- **First-Line Indentation**—Indent the first line of paragraphs using CSS indention setting.

- **Right-Margin**—The body text is padded to the right using the CSS right-indent capability.

- **Top and Bottom Spacing**—As with the heading, use CSS to define the spacing that you want before and after paragraphs. In this example, the spacing was set to 0.

- **Small Caps**—As in *The Wall Street Journal* newspaper, use CSS to format the first few words of a paragraph in small capital letters.

Tip from

EQ & Woody

If you are a novice text formatter, here are two tips that will put you above your coworkers. First, whenever possible, always keep headings juxtaposed (with no vertical space) with the following paragraph; the proximity improves the reader's association of the heading to the text. Second, when indenting the first line of paragraphs, do not use extra vertical whitespace above the paragraph. Indenting is a tried-and-true method to make your information more readable, and additional vertical spacing can interrupt the reader's flow while scanning the page.

PART

VI

CH

37

Cascading style sheets come in three flavors:

- At the lowest level, an *inline* CSS is applied directly to the characters or paragraphs in question. Formatting specified by the inline CSS takes precedence over formatting from the other two types of CSS. If you select text or paragraphs and apply a style from the drop-down Style list on the Formatting Toolbar, the result is an inline CSS.

- At the intermediate level, an *embedded* CSS is attached to one Web page and is accessible only from that Web page.

- At the highest level, a page can be linked to an *external* CSS. An external CSS is a page in and of itself.

When a browser attempts to resolve complex formatting on a page, it follows a simple hierarchy. Manually applied formatting overrides everything else. If there's no manually applied formatting on a particular chunk of text, the inline CSS takes over. If there's no inline CSS, the browser looks for a matching style definition inside the page—the so-called embedded CSS. If there's no definition embedded in the page, the browser looks to an external CSS, if there is one. Finally, if there is no style definition in the external CSS, the browser falls back on its own style definitions.

Actually, that's a bit of an oversimplification. In fact, any given Web page can have multiple external CSSs. When the browser attempts to resolve a style reference, it looks at all the external CSSs, in reverse order.

→ For more details about the search sequence, **see** "Using Cascading Style Sheets," **p. 947**.

Caution

FrontPage enables you to use spaces within your style names, but if you do, the style won't appear correctly in the Style drop-down list.

EMBEDDING A STYLE SHEET IN A WEB PAGE

Once in a blue moon, you'll want to create a style sheet that affects only one Web page. For example, you might want to create a style sheet that stores styles unique to the résumé page in your personal Web Site. In that case, you'll want to embed that style sheet in the résumé page so that the styles you create don't clutter the Style drop-down list on other pages. The styles that you define on an embedded style sheet aren't accessible to any other pages in your Web—or anywhere else, for that matter.

To create an embedded style sheet, open the page in Page Normal view and choose Format, Style. The Style dialog box appears, as shown in Figure 37.8. In this dialog box, you can modify the standard HTML styles or create your own new styles.

If you no longer need an embedded style, you can delete it from the embedded style sheet by choosing Format, Style; selecting the style from the list of styles; and clicking Delete.

Caution

When you remove an embedded style, FrontPage does not remove references to the style from your page. If you later add a style with the same name, those text elements inherit the new style's formatting. To avoid this behavior when you remove a style, use FrontPage's Find feature to search the HTML for the style reference and then remove the references manually in HTML view.

Figure 37.8
Using the Style dialog
box changes the style
definitions stored in an
embedded style sheet.

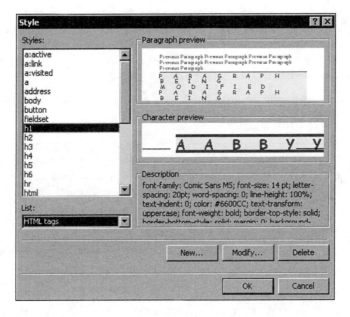

USING EXTERNAL STYLE SHEETS FOR MULTIPLE PAGES

To share styles with several Web pages within your Web site, create an *external style sheet* and link the pages to the external style sheet. As with embedded style sheets, styles that you create in an external style sheet become available in the Style toolbar option list so that you can apply the same style to multiple elements on the same page. You can also apply your styles together with standard HTML styles to produce a combined effect. When you change a style in the external CSS, all your pages inherit the new settings.

Note

You can use multiple external style sheets—when linked to the same page, the styles cascade and produce a combined effect. If you have conflicting formatting associated with the same style, the formatting of the last (not the first) style sheet linked to the page takes precedence.

When the browser downloads a page that references a style sheet, the browser downloads the style sheet, too. If the browser downloads a subsequent page referencing the same style sheet, it's smart enough to know that the style sheet has already been loaded and is available in cache. By using the same external style sheet, you accomplish two important goals: a consistent look among pages, and minimal download time.

To create an external style sheet, choose File, New, Page or Web. In the New Page or Web task pane, under New from Templates, pick Page Templates

Note

You must explicitly save the style sheet before it will be available for linking.

External style sheets are saved in files with the .css extension.

With your external style sheet open in Page view, choose Format, Style to modify the standard HTML styles or to create your own.

Tip from

Use a name that describes the style's purpose rather than its appearance. For example, type DogGalleryEntry rather than BoldDoubleBorder. This way, if you change the style's appearance later, your style name still makes sense.

Note

FrontPage does not have anything analogous to the Word Formatting and Styles task pane.

After you have saved your external style sheet, you need to link it to the pages within your Web site. In Folder view, select the Web pages to which you want to link the style sheet, and choose Format, Style Sheet Links. In the Link Style Sheet dialog box (see Figure 37.9), choose whether you want to link the style sheet to all pages within your Web site or only to the selected pages.

You must save the external style sheet before it's even available in the

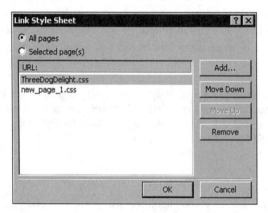

Tip from

Link Style Sheet dialog box. And you must explicitly, manually link pages to the external style sheet before styles defined in the sheet become available to your Web pages.

When you link multiple style sheets to a page, the order affects how browsers resolve conflicting style references. Use the Move Up and Move Down buttons to change the order. Contrary to what you might expect, the style sheet listed at the bottom of the list has higher precedence than those above it.

APPLYING STYLES, COLORS, AND IMAGES WITH A THEME

As with all Office applications, you can leverage *themes* to provide consistency to all the Web pages in your Web site. Office includes several themes to choose from—each theme has its own personality, assembling styles, images, colors, and fonts to provide a one-stop shop for a coordinated design for your Web pages.

To see the themes available for your Web site, choose Format, Theme. Browse the list of themes and view the samples to find one for your site. To change a theme before applying it to your presentation, click the Modify button and then change the basic colors, embedded graphics, or fonts (under the Text button—see Figure 37.10).

Figure 37.10
Make your own themes by using the Themes dialog box.

FrontPage does not enable some advanced capabilities unless you apply a theme to your Web site. For instance, without a theme applied, you cannot create graphical Page Banners or graphical buttons in Navigation Bars. Instead, you must settle for the text-only version or create these elements manually for each page.

If you prefer not to use cascading style sheets with your Web site, FrontPage can apply the theme formatting directly within the HTML. Uncheck the Apply Using CSS check box, in this case. If the check box is not available, you need to select the compatibility options for your Web site.

Each FrontPage theme includes 11 graphical elements to use for the bullets, buttons, banners, background, and horizontal rules. Also, each theme uses two sets of these graphical elements: one set for normal graphics, and the other to apply when using active graphics. You can change graphics by clicking the Graphics button, choosing the element that you want to work on in the Item list, and, for each picture listed in the Picture tab, clicking Browse to locate the image that you want to use for that purpose.

Tip from	In Active graphics mode, you'll need three images for your navigational buttons—one when not selected, another when the user hovers the mouse pointer over the button, and yet a third when the user clicks the button.

Most of the graphical elements can have their own text style. For instance, when you use the Banner Component in graphics mode, FrontPage overlays the title of the page on the banner image using your text style. This way, you can be assured that the banner text is consistent with the other text formatting of your Web site. Change fonts by clicking the Text button.

Tip from	You can type more than one font name, delimited by commas, for each text item. When a browser cannot find the first font listed, it looks for the second, and so on. If none is found, it displays the default font, which is usually Times New Roman.

PUBLISHING A WEB SITE

If you worked with FrontPage offline to develop your Web site, you must publish the Web files to a Web server to make them available to your users. FrontPage provides a set of complete tools for publishing your Web site, including support for Web servers that do not have FrontPage Server Extensions installed.

When FrontPage publishes your Web site, it copies your Web files to the Web server and corrects hyperlinks and document references for the new location.

Tip from	If you are publishing a personal Web site and need an inexpensive Web-hosting service, these two services will host your Web site free: see Yahoo! GeoCities at http://www.geocities.com and Lycos Tripod at http://www.tripod.com.

Note	If you set up an intranet Web server to be used for authoring your Web site and intend to publish that site to an Internet Web server at a later time, be sure to configure FrontPage to match the capabilities of the Internet server. For example, if your intranet server uses Windows NT and IIS, and the Internet server uses Linux and Apache, disable the features that cannot be used with Apache. To do so, choose Tools, Page Options, and make your choices on the Compatibility tab.

Before you publish your Web site, you should test it thoroughly. Make a complete pass through your Web site content before you publish it to a Web server. Typically, this entails navigating through your pages, confirming each link, and verifying the look and feel of your pages. If you find any discrepancies, it's better to fix them now than to publish the Web and have your users find the errors online.

CHOOSING WHICH FILES TO PUBLISH

Normally, you can let FrontPage decide which files need to be published. FrontPage compares the file dates with those on your Web server and sends only the files that have changed. By default, FrontPage attempts to publish all new or modified files in your Web site. If you do not want certain files or folders to be published, you can choose which files to exclude from publishing. For example, you might have unfinished content in some pages, but you want to publish the others anyway; or, you might want to publish a recently completed portion of the Web site.

PART

VI

CH

37

To choose the files to exclude from publishing, enter Reports view and bring up the Reporting toolbar. Choose Reports, Workflow, Publish Status. For each file that you want to exclude from publishing, right-click in the Publish column and select Don't Publish.

PUBLISHING TO A SERVER WITH FRONTPAGE SERVER EXTENSIONS

If your Web server supports FrontPage Server Extensions (or Office Server Extensions, or SharePoint Server Extensions), you should encounter little difficulty when publishing your Web site. FPSE assists FrontPage with file and link management, and can duplicate many of the actions that you took while offline, such as deleting, renaming, or moving files. For example, if you delete a page in your Web site while authoring offline and then you publish the Web site, FPSE will delete the page on the Web server, too.

To start the process of publishing your Web site, choose File, Publish Web.

> **Note**
>
> When using FrontPage Server Extensions, resist the urge to update files outside FrontPage, such as through an FTP program. Doing so can confuse FrontPage and limit its capability to track your links, update your table of contents, and maintain your search engine index. If you must do so—perhaps in an urgent situation in which you command your Web-hosting service to update a critical page—be sure to resynchronize the Web site when you return to FrontPage by choosing Tools, Recalculate Hyperlinks.

 If you find that some links become broken after you've published your Web, see "Broken Links After Publishing" in the "Troubleshooting" section at the end of this chapter.

PUBLISHING TO A SERVER WITH FTP

If your Web server does not use FPSE, you can publish your Web site using the *File Transfer Protocol (FTP)*. FTP provides a simple way for you to transfer the updated files from your local machine to the Web server.

To publish via FTP, you must first create an FTP Location shortcut. The FTP Location shortcut can remember your username and password for you. When you publish your Web site again in the future, FrontPage can supply your login information automatically. To create the FTP Location shortcut, choose File, Publish Web. and click Browse. In the Look In options list at the top of the Open Web dialog box, choose the FTP Locations folder. Double-click the Add/Modify FTP Locations icon. The Add/Modify FTP Locations dialog box appears, as shown in Figure 37.11.

Figure 37.11
Enter the location and login credentials for your FTP site.

In the Name of FTP Site text box, enter the server name , such as `ftp.threedogdelight.com`. If the server requires a specific username and password, choose the User option button and enter the username in the associated text box. Type the password into the Password text box, and click Add. You should see your new location in the FTP Sites list box. Click OK.

PUBLISHING TO A LOCAL DRIVE OR NETWORK SHARE

FrontPage enables you to publish your Web content to a local drive or a network drive (sometimes called a *network share*). This is a useful way to create a backup of your Web content. Instead of copying the files manually, publish the files to the backup location so that you also copy any of the important supporting files that FrontPage uses to maintain your Web site, including Shared Borders, Java applets, themes, and security information.

To enter the destination location of your Web site, choose File, Publish Web. The New Publish Location dialog box appears, and you can navigate to the appropriate location.

ADJUSTING PUBLISHING OPTIONS

In the Publish Web dialog box, click Options to display a set of publishing options (see Figure 37.12).

Figure 37.12
Control how your
Web site is published.

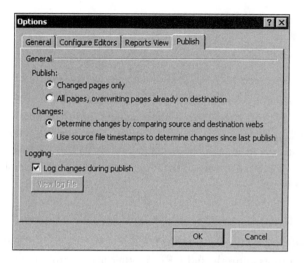

If you want all your Web files to be published, click the Publish All Pages, overwriting pages already on destination option button. Doing so overwrites any files currently hosted at your Web site. Never fear—any files that you might have identified to exclude from publishing will not be published.

To save time when you publish your Web site, choose the Publish Changed Pages Only option button. FrontPage compares the dates and times of the source and destination files, and updates only the changed files.

Tip from

If you work with a group of authors on a fairly busy site, you should consider setting up a *staging server*, where you can stage new content or updates to existing content before publishing it to the live Web server. Using a staging server also enables the new content to be tested thoroughly and reviewed by upper management before publishing it to the world at large.

TRANSFERRING WEB FILES

After you have selected your publishing options, click Publish to start the process of copying your content to the Web server. FrontPage connects to the server and updates your files. If the server requires a username and password to connect, you might see a Name and Password Required dialog box. Enter the proper credentials and click OK.

After FrontPage connects, a dialog box appears to display the progress of the publishing process. Watch, and you can see how FrontPage updates your Web server. In this dialog box, click the blue underlined text link to open a browser to your Web site. You can immediately test your Web site and verify that the changes that you made have been properly published.

If you publish your Web site and find that some files did not update, see "Some Files Not Updated" in the "Troubleshooting" section next.

TROUBLESHOOTING

SOME FILES NOT UPDATED

I published my Web site to another host, but some files were not updated.

It's possible that some files were updated on the destination Web server, and when you published your Web site, FrontPage decided not to update those files because they had more recent timestamps. In Reports view, use the Publish Status report to identify the pages that should not be published again, and choose File, Publish Web. This time, choose the Publish All Pages option to force the update of the files even though they have older timestamps than those on the server.

BROKEN LINKS AFTER PUBLISHING

I moved my Web site from one Web host to another, and now some links are broken.

Sometimes page authors enter the full URL to other pages within the same Web site. When you move the Web site to another host, these links can still point to the original location. Use the Broken Hyperlinks report to identify the links and make repairs.

CREATING SUBWEBS

I cannot create a subweb in my offline Web site.

FrontPage enables you to create subwebs only when online with the Office Server Extensions. As a workaround, create a separate folder on your local disk or network share, and create your new Web site there.

SECRETS OF THE OFFICE MASTERS: UNDERSTANDING FRONTPAGE'S STATISTICS

As long as you're using FrontPage Server Extensions, you'll automatically get a long list of useful statistics, covering almost every trackable nuance of your Web site. It helps to understand the terminology:

- A *hit* is a single access. If you have a page with nine graphics on it, every time a user waits around for the entire page to load, you'll log 10 hits.

- A *page view* or *impression* is the number of times a user initiates viewing of a page— whether or not that user waits around to download all of the graphics. Identifying your most-used pages can help focus your sales pitches; many sites put particularly enticing offers in their high-volume locations.

- *Referring URLs* are the URLs of the pages that your users were looking at immediately before viewing your page, and *referring domains* are the associated domains. Those can be handy if you're wondering how your viewers got to you, what search engines they're using, and how effective your advertising might be. They can also help you trace how your users are navigating your site internally. If the referrer field is empty, the user either typed your URL directly into the browser or used the Favorites list.

- You can also get reports on what browser your users were using, and what operating system was employed. That could help you feel more confident about using, for example, Internet Explorer-only features.

- One of the most useful reports (and one of the most frequently overlooked) tells you what search strings your users typed into the built-in FrontPage search engine. This report not only gives you insight into what your users think is important, but it also tells you how you need to improve your navigation capabilities.

To view your site's statistics, go into Reports view and choose Usage.

AUTOMATING OFFICE WITH MACROS AND VBA

CHAPTER 38

USING MACROS TO AUTOMATE OFFICE TASKS

In this chapter

HOW MACROS WORK

When you get right down to it, a *macro* is nothing more than a computer program. Macros can be surprisingly short—even a one-line macro can perform helpful tasks—or they can run for hundreds of lines, with loops and variables and input boxes, and other elements you normally associate with a full-fledged programming language. You don't need to be a programmer to automate much of your work with macros. All you need is a basic understanding of the underlying application and a willingness to step through a few lines of code.

With rare exceptions, you can create a macro to automate any task you can do manually in Word, Excel, PowerPoint, Outlook, FrontPage, or Access. Macros are ideal for automating routine drudge work—those everyday tasks that normally require multiple menu selections and mouse clicks.

For example, you can use macros to

- Print company letters and companion envelopes—routing the printout to the correct network printer, and selecting the correct paper trays for letterhead, additional pages, and envelopes—and then printing file copies on yet another printer, or with a different tray.

- Apply complex formatting rules—everything from scanning corporate reports to ensuring that all "Level 1" headings start with a number, to validating the searchable keywords in a memo, to correcting common typographical mistakes such as two spaces following a period.

- Collate and aggregate budgets, at any organizational level, complete with charts and custom pivot tables, based on Excel spreadsheets submitted by each work unit. When changes come, roll the new numbers into the divisional or corporate report in minutes.

- Retrieve data from an Access customer database and generate collection letters in Word for all customers whose accounts are 90 days or more past due.

All the major Office applications share a common programming language, *Visual Basic for Applications 6.0 (VBA)*. VBA is discussed in more detail in Chapter 39, "Working with Visual Basic for Applications"; in this chapter, the focus is on how you can record and edit macros to automate simple tasks. And if you don't think of yourself as a programmer, think again: When you record a macro, you are creating a full-fledged VBA program.

WHAT CAN YOU DO WITH MACROS?

Say your branch offices post their sales reports over the weekend on your company's intranet. Your boss expects you to download each report, format it according to company style, add your analysis, and then turn it into a memo that can go out under the boss's name to everyone else in the department. You can write a macro to automate much of the task. The sequence might go something like this:

- On Monday morning, you start Word; choose File, New; select the Memo based on sales statistics; and click OK. Then you go get a latte.

- Word creates the new memo, complete with distribution list and a Word table at the top of the memo. Then the macro kicks in and opens the intranet Web page with the sales information, viewing it as a Word document. The macro steps through the document, pulling data from predefined locations on the page.

- The macro takes the data from the Web page, performs whatever mathematical gymnastics might be required, and puts the resulting numbers in predefined locations in the table. It leaves the Web page open, so you can see that the correct data has been posted over the weekend.

- The macro then hops down to the bottom of the memo, attaches your boss's signature block, and then backs up a few lines—leaving room for your analysis—and exits. You return with your latte; verify the data is correct; type your analysis; choose File, Send To; and send it to your boss for approval.

If others in your company perform similar duties, you can easily distribute the memo template and the macro. Those using the macro only need to know that clicking the button, or choosing the menu item, creates the report. As long as the format of the Web page doesn't change, they needn't know a thing about macros or VBA, or even how to modify their toolbars or menus. You can do it all for them, easily, with a macro.

→ For more information about templates, **see** "Managing Styles and Templates," **p. 480**.

Macros aren't confined to a single Office application. A good programmer with a solid knowledge of Word, Excel, and Access could write a sophisticated program for generating reminder letters based on values in an Access database. Then the programmer could update the database, print the envelopes, send e-mail reports to the sales force with summaries of the actions taken, and crank up Excel to have it generate aged balances and a Web-based PivotChart based on the same data.

WHAT SHOULDN'T YOU DO WITH MACROS?

Each individual Office application includes features that help you automate tasks without having to use macros. When there's a good alternative to writing a custom macro, the alternative is almost always preferable:

- For inserting boilerplate text into documents, workbooks, or slides, it's usually more efficient to use AutoCorrect or AutoText entries.

- Before you write a custom macro to find and replace characters, try Word's extremely capable Find feature.

- If you want to add complex paragraph numbering to a Word document, try custom fields first.

- Excel's automatic data-entry and list-management features can help you accomplish many complex tasks without having to work with VBA code.

→ For hints on how to bring in boilerplate text, **see** "Using AutoCorrect to Automate Documents," **p. 91**.

→ To tailor a Find in Word, **see** "Finding and Replacing Text and Other Parts of a Document," **p. 370**.

→ For details on Word's overpowered and underappreciated {ListNum} field, **see** "Managing Custom Numeric Sequences," **p. 504**.

ELIMINATING MACROS ENTIRELY

Office XP allows system administrators to install Office so it can't run any macros, ever, under any circumstances. If the Visual Basic for Applications check box in Custom Setup is unchecked when Office gets installed, none of the VBA files—which are necessary for running macros—will be available on the machine.

This "scorched earth" approach might be appropriate for installations in which the threat of macro viruses outweighs the needs of users. In most cases, it severely limits Office's capabilities. In any case, neutralizing Visual Basic for Applications will not prohibit other (non-macro) types of viruses from spreading.

If you can't get macros to work under any circumstances, check with your system administrator to ensure that VBA is operating properly on your machine. You might have to re-run setup and ensure that the Visual Basic for Applications box is checked in Custom Setup.

HOW OFFICE APPLICATIONS STORE MACROS

No two Office applications handle macros the same way. Although the precise details are complex, here's a quick summary of how each Office application stores macros:

- **Word**—Word can store macros in documents, templates, or the global template known as Normal.dot. When you open a document, macros in its associated template become available. If you store templates in the \Startup folder, Word gives you access to macros stored in those templates whenever you start Word.

→ For details on template locations, **see** "Where Does Word Store Templates?," **p. 480**.

> **Note**
>
> Previously, Word used a macro language called *WordBasic*. You can no longer create WordBasic macros. You can, however, open old Word templates that contain WordBasic macros, and Word 2002 automatically converts them to VBA/Word.

- **Excel**—Excel stores macros in workbooks or templates. Unlike Word, Excel does *not* maintain a link between a workbook and the template you use to create it; if you add or edit a macro in a template, that macro is available only in new workbooks you create with that template. Excel automatically opens all workbooks in the \Xlstart folder when it starts, including the hidden workbook Personal.xls. Thus, all macros in Personal.xls are available all the time.

→ For details on templates, **see** "Customizing Excel," **p. 566**.

Excel also has an old macro language, sometimes referred to as *XLMacro*, or *XLM macros*, which executes commands in a special kind of spreadsheet cell. It, too, has been supplanted entirely by VBA/Excel.

■ **PowerPoint**—PowerPoint stores macros in presentations and templates. Like Excel, PowerPoint uses templates only to create new files, so adding or editing macros in a template will not affect existing presentations based on that template. PowerPoint does *not* have a Startup folder or anything resembling a global template.

→ To understand the role of templates in PowerPoint, **see** "PowerPoint File Types," **p. 790**.

Caution

Unless you're a skilled programmer, avoid trying to automate anything but the most routine PowerPoint tasks with VBA. Compared with Word and Excel, its object model is incomplete. There's no easy way to copy macros from one presentation to another. The lack of a global template makes it difficult to manage macros, and the documentation is apparently classified Top Secret, because you'll search in vain for explanations of even simple tasks.

PART
VII

CH
38

■ **Outlook**—Outlook stores all of its macros in one place, and all macros are available all the time. VBA/Outlook is a "version 2.0" product, and although there have been significant improvements made to its object model since Outlook 2000, you should anticipate significant problems working with it in this state.

■ **FrontPage**—Similarly, FrontPage stores all of its macros globally, and they're all available, all the time. VBA/FrontPage is also a "version 2.0" product, and suitable precautions are in order.

■ **Publisher**—New with Office XP, Publisher can store macros in each document. Oddly, the Visual Basic Editor only allows you to work with one document's macros at a time. This is definitely a "version 1.0" product—not for the faint of heart.

■ **Access**—Access stores VBA programs in modules for the database itself (visible in the Modules pane of Database view) and in forms or reports. You can also collect VBA routines in a library database (*.mda file).

Note

Access also has an old-fashioned macro language, one that's markedly different from VBA/Access. You can design and edit old-style macros, based on conditions and actions, using a database's Macros pane. You'll find VBA programs in the Modules pane. (The terminology is confusing. When Access macros are discussed in these chapters, they are referring exclusively to VBA programs. The old-fashioned "macros" aren't even discussed outside of this section.)

VBA/Access programs work with the Access interface: forms, reports, tables, and the like. You can also run old-fashioned "macros" by using the DoCmd command. Oddly, if you want to get at data stored by Access, you need to work directly with an Access database; for example, to bring live data from an Access database into an Excel worksheet or a Web page, use *Data Access Objects (DAO)*.

Note

For more information on Access databases, see *Special Edition Using Microsoft Access XP*, by Roger Jennings, published by Que.

USING OBJECT MODELS

The fundamental building blocks of VBA remain the same, no matter which application you're using. An IF statement in VBA/Word, for example, works like an IF statement in VBA/Excel. That's one of VBA's great strengths, for as soon as you learn VBA with one Office application, you can apply much of what you know to the other applications—or even to non-Microsoft applications, such as Visio and AutoCAD, which use VBA as their macro language.

Still, VBA has to accommodate the differences in each application. You work with words, sentences, and bookmarks in Word, you use formulas, cells, and ranges in Excel, and you work with tables and reports in Access. Those parts of VBA that differ between applications are embodied in the *object model* for that application. The object model provides the means for working with an application.

Word's object model, for example, includes objects that let you create and change documents, paragraphs, and footnotes. Excel's object model works with workbooks, charts, and pivot fields. PowerPoint's object model has presentations, slides, and sound effects. Outlook's object model includes contacts and e-mail messages. FrontPage actually has two object models, one for Web pages themselves (with tags, themes, Webs, and the like) and the other for the FrontPage editor (with styles, text, and tables). The Access object model has reports, forms, and images.

The object model is important because it defines precisely how VBA can interact with an application. That, in turn, imposes limitations on how the macro recorder can work, because the recorder must generate a valid VBA program.

RECORDING SIMPLE MACROS

Word, Excel, and PowerPoint all let you record macros. Access, and FrontPage do not have macro recording capabilities—a significant restriction, because you won't be able to use the recorder to capture VBA commands that correspond to typical user interactions. Although Outlook lacks a macro recorder, you can record macros while creating a message.

In theory, when you turn on the macro recorder, VBA "watches" as you perform some action or series of actions. When you turn off the recorder, you can replay the resulting recorded macro to replicate that series of actions.

In practice, you'll more often use the macro recorder to eliminate the tedious steps of creating a macro. Unfortunately, a recorded macro rarely solves a real-world problem by itself. After recording a macro, you'll typically need to make some modifications.

You can also use the recorder to capture the steps of a particular task, and then copy all or part of the recorded macro into a larger macro.

HOW THE MACRO RECORDER CAPTURES ACTIONS

As anyone who's used Office's *macro recorder* for more than a few minutes can tell you, the macro recorder can't record every single action you take. There are two fundamental reasons why the recorder can fail:

- The action you take might not have an exact translation in the application's object model. For example, if you record a macro in PowerPoint to change first-level bullet points in a presentation to 18-point bold, the macro won't work because PowerPoint's object model doesn't include commands for working with first-level bullet points.

> **Caution**
>
> This type of failure, generally completely undocumented, happens without any warning to you. The recorder doesn't stop; there's no other feedback. You know the failure occurred only because the macro fails to work when you play it back.

- The action you take might be ambiguous; in other words, the recorder might not be able to tell exactly what you want to do. For example, if you type this paragraph into a Word document and use the mouse to select it, the VBA/Word macro recorder has no way of knowing what you're trying to do. Are you selecting the current paragraph? Or are you selecting the first paragraph that starts with the word "The"? Maybe you really want to select the 10th paragraph in the document. Or the first one with more than a hundred words. That's why the recorder usually won't record mouse actions—there's just too much ambiguity, most of the time, when you use the mouse.

After you turn on the macro recorder, it records the effect of your actions, not the actions themselves. The full effect of your actions goes into the recorded macro, not the means you used to apply them. For example

- If you choose File, Open, type mydoc, and click OK, the recorder notes that you opened Mydoc.doc—not that you went through all the clicking.
- If you choose Format, Font, and change the font to Wingdings, the recorder records the fact that you changed the font to Wingdings—but it also picks up all the other formatting settings, including font size, bold, italic, underline, and so on.

- If your insertion point is inside a paragraph in a Word document, and you want to tell the recorder to select the first word in that paragraph, double-clicking the first word in the paragraph will not work. If you try to double-click the first word in the paragraph, the recorder won't let you do it. The recorder can't record your double-click action because it's ambiguous: You know that you want to select the first word in the current paragraph, but there's no way to specify that precisely by clicking with the mouse. For all the recorder knows, you might want to select the 50th word on the page, or the first word on the 10th line, or the last capitalized word in the paragraph.

When recording, instead of using the mouse, you'll frequently have to resort to obscure keyboard navigation keys. To move to the beginning of the current paragraph in Word, press Ctrl+↑. To select the first word in the paragraph, press Ctrl+Shift+→. To italicize the word, click Ctrl+I.

Tip from

EQ & Woody

Nobody, but nobody, memorizes all of Word's obscure key combinations. To create a 10-page document listing them all, click Tools, Macro, Macros, type `listcommands`, and press Enter. Click Current Menu and Keyboard Settings, and then OK. Unfortunately, there's no easy equivalent for PowerPoint or Excel.

RECORDING A MACRO

Word, Excel, and PowerPoint include simple macro recorders that work in essentially the same way. To record a macro in Word, for example, follow these steps:

1. Create a new document or open an existing document.
2. Choose Tools, Macro, Record New Macro. In the Record Macro dialog box (see Figure 38.1), click in the Macro Name box, and type a name (ItalicizeFirstWord, in this example).

Figure 38.1
Replace the generic Macro1 name with a descriptive macro name, but don't use spaces or punctuation marks.

Note

Macro names can contain up to 255 letters and numbers, but no spaces or other punctuation marks. Names must start with a letter, and cannot duplicate certain reserved names (for example, cell addresses in Excel).

3. Choose a location for the macro (the current document or a template, for example) and add a description (optional).

4. You'll see the Recording pointer, which has a picture of a cassette tape attached to the bottom. In addition, the Stop Recording toolbar appears on the screen (the Excel and PowerPoint versions of this toolbar are slightly different, but both include a Stop Recording button). Perform any actions you want to record in your macro.

5. Click the Stop Recording button on the Stop Recording toolbar.

To record macros in Excel and PowerPoint, follow the same steps.

TESTING THE MACRO

After recording a macro, it's essential that you test it to see whether it works the way you expect. To quickly run a Word macro, follow these steps:

1. Open a document or create a new document. If necessary, click to position the insertion point at an appropriate location in the document.

Caution

Don't use a "live" document when testing. Always work with a backup copy or a dummy document you create just for testing.

2. To run the macro, choose Tools, Macro, Macros. You'll see the Macros dialog box shown in Figure 38.2.

Figure 38.2
All available macros appear in the Macros dialog box.

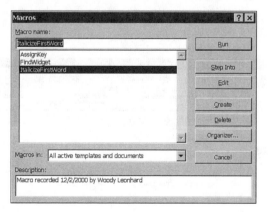

3. Click the name of the macro you want to run and press Enter or click Run. If all goes well, the macro performs the task you intended.

4. For more complete troubleshooting, click in another location within the document, and repeat steps 1–3.

Using the Macro dialog box lets you run all currently available macros, whether you're working in Word, Excel, PowerPoint, Outlook, Publisher, or FrontPage. If you're going to use the macro regularly, however, this procedure is cumbersome and slow; you'll learn faster methods for running macros later in this chapter.

TROUBLESHOOTING RECORDED MACROS

Macros rarely work right the first time. Recorded macros, in particular, frequently require some tweaking before they work as intended. If the macro you recorded doesn't work, re-record it and see whether you can use a different method for accomplishing the same result. Edit a recorded macro only when it works most of the time, but occasionally fails to work the way you expect, or triggers an error message.

STEPPING THROUGH AND EDITING RECORDED MACROS

Fortunately, Office makes it relatively easy to edit a recorded macro. It even supports you in your bug-extermination efforts by allowing you to run the macro program one line at a time, and see what the effect of each command might be. Here's how to use the VBA Editor to step through a macro recorded in Word (the steps in Excel, PowerPoint, Outlook, Publisher, and FrontPage are virtually identical):

1. Create a new document or open an existing document and position the insertion point as necessary. For example, to test a macro that italicizes the first word in a paragraph, be sure to click inside a paragraph in the current document.

2. Choose Tools, Macro, Macros. Select the name of the macro you want to troubleshoot, and click Step Into. The VBA Editor opens, with your macro visible in the right pane (see Figure 38.3). You'll see a large yellow arrow appear to the left of the Sub line, and the Sub line will be highlighted.

Figure 38.3
When you step into a macro for trouble-shooting, the line that's about to be run appears highlighted.

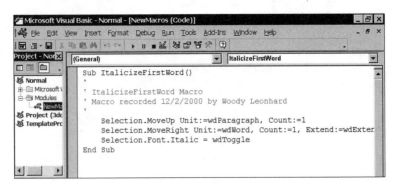

→ For details on the programming environment, **see** "Using the VBA Editor," **p. 992**.

3. Arrange the windows on your desktop so you can see both the application (in this case, Word) and the VBA Editor at the same time (see Figure 38.4). Click the window holding the VBA Editor.

Figure 38.4
By default, recorded VBA/Word macros show up as subroutines (beginning with the word Sub) in the Normal project's NewMacros module.

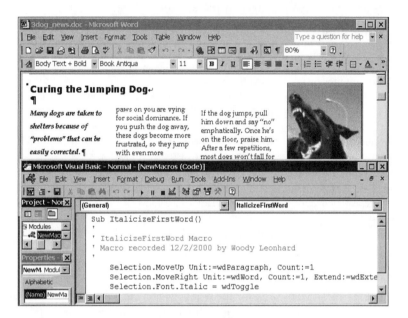

4. To begin executing the VBA code one step at a time, press F8, or choose Debug, Step Into. The first line of the macro—the Sub line—executes.

5. Press F8 again, and watch carefully as the macro performs the next actions; repeat this process, one command at a time.

6. When you run the End Sub line, the VBA Editor stops. You can start all over again, if you like, beginning with step 4.

Frequently, you'll be able to identify the location of the problem (or problems) in a macro by stepping through it in this way. Although the solution might not be at all clear—there are lots of VBA commands, and each one behaves in a different way—being able to narrow the problem down to a line or two can make a huge difference.

After you isolate the line that you suspect is causing the problem, position the insertion point within that line and press F1. That action brings up context-sensitive VBA Help, which might present a possible solution.

Follow the same procedures to step through VBA/Excel and VBA/PowerPoint macros; you'll find recorded macros in the current workbook or presentation, in a module called Module1. In Access, open the database that contains the VBA program, select the Modules pane, and double-click the name of the VBA program. Press F8 to step through the macro.

COMMON RECORDED MACRO MISTAKES

When a recorded macro doesn't work as you expect, chances are the problem is one of several common errors. Table 38.1 lists common mistakes and suggested troubleshooting steps.

TABLE 38.1   COMMON MACRO PROBLEMS

Macro Error	Troubleshooting Suggestion
A key combination doesn't work the way you thought it would.	Many navigation keys have easy-to-understand descriptions (select next word, or move down one paragraph), but they behave oddly in unusual circumstances—inside a Word table, cell, or at the end of a document, for example. Find a different key combination that accomplishes the same task in a slightly different way.
Formatting commands overwrite existing formatting.	When you apply formatting using the Format menu, the application might replace all formatting with the new format. If you want to add the new formatting—for example, boldfacing a word while leaving intact other attributes, such as italic—use shortcut keys to apply formatting (Ctrl+B to apply bold).
A repeating macro doesn't do the entire job.	Recorded macros rarely incorporate the kind of repetition you anticipate. To create a macro that loops properly, you almost always have to edit it manually. (One exception—Replace All will loop through an entire document, worksheet, or presentation.)

In addition, any number of unusual circumstances can trigger errors in recorded macros. For example, if you search for the word "widget" in a document where that word is in a footer and not in the body of the document, the search will succeed. When you record that action in a VBA/Word macro, everything appears to work just fine. But when you play back the recorded macro in the same document, Word won't find the word you're looking for no matter how many times you run it—in fact, it will trigger a Run Time Error. The recorded version of the Find operation works differently from the interactive version when it comes to footers.

TESTING AND BULLET-PROOFING MACROS

Will your recorded macro work properly every time you run it? Frankly, there's no way to know for sure—VBA macros hardly fall into the category of "provably correct" computer programs—but you can improve the odds of a macro working correctly by employing two time-honored testing techniques:

- Trace through the logic. In most cases, that means stepping through the macro, as explained earlier in this section. Watch for behavior or settings that you don't understand.

- Test it in a wide variety of circumstances. Try to think of odd situations that might make the macro fail, and then see whether it does. Enlist the aid of fellow workers to test a macro, if possible, because testers will think of situations that just don't occur to you.

For example, the ItalicizeFirstWord macro example (in the "Recording a Macro" section earlier in this chapter) should italicize the first word in the current paragraph, but it doesn't. Instead, when the insertion point is at the beginning of a paragraph, this macro italicizes the first word of the *preceding* paragraph. Running through the macro a step at a time reveals that the culprit is the MoveUp command; when you point to that command and press F1, the context-sensitive help suggests several examples. The first example contains the solution to the problem: It shows how you have to MoveRight once before performing a MoveUp, to stay in the original paragraph.

The recorded ItalicizeFirstWord macro contains a second problem as well. When you run the macro, and then leave the insertion point in the same paragraph and run the macro again, it *removes* the italic formatting from the first word. Stepping through the macro again lets us see the problem: The Selection.Font.Italic line toggles the italic attribute on and off. According to the Help file, the Italic property "can be set to True, False, or wdToggle." Changing the value from wdToggle to True causes it to work properly.

When you modify the ItalicizeFirstWord macro so that it looks like the one in Figure 38.5, you'll find that both problems have disappeared.

PART
VII
CH
38

Figure 38.5
Compare this code to the contents of Figure 38.4; two small changes had to be made before the recorded macro would work properly.

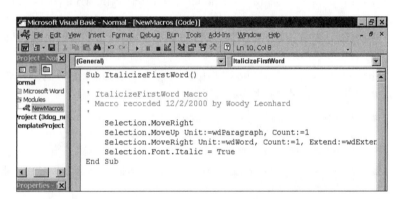

RUNNING MACROS

Although each of the Office applications offers myriad ways to run macros, three simple methods in Word, Excel, PowerPoint, Outlook, Publisher, and FrontPage will get you going:

- Choose Tools, Macro, Macros to open the Macros dialog box, which contains a list of all currently available macros. Use this technique for macros you run only infrequently.
- Before you start recording a macro, you can choose to assign the macro to a menu (Word only) or a specific key combination (Word or Excel).
- After recording a macro, you can assign it to a menu, a toolbar button, or a key combination.

→ For details on setting up macros as menu items, **see** "Customizing Built-In Menus," **p. 40**.

In addition, you can set macros to run each time you start an application. For example, you can record a macro that maximizes the Excel window whenever you start Excel. Or you can set up a macro to run every time you open or close a specific document. You might use this technique to run a macro that queries a database and updates a letter with current customer information. You can assign a macro to a picture or a piece of text, or to run at a specific time. Your macros can even take over built-in Office functions such as printing. For example, if you want to track printer usage in your office, create a macro that counts the number of pages in a document or worksheet, adds a new row to an Excel list with the user's name, the date and time, and the number of pages, and then sends the job to the printer.

MACRO SECURITY

Macros can save time and energy, but an ill-conceived macro can (intentionally or unintentionally) destroy data and otherwise wreak havoc on your system or network. For example, a macro that automates file management tasks by deleting old files could inadvertently wipe out a whole folder full of files if you don't define its parameters carefully.

You can have a high degree of confidence in macros you write yourself, but you should never trust a macro you receive from someone you've never met. Thousands of macro viruses exist, and you run the risk of encountering one of them every time you open a document, workbook, presentation, or Access database.

What is a *macro virus*, and how likely are you to encounter one? Here are some simple facts every Office user should know:

- A computer "virus" is just a program that propagates. A macro virus uses a macro language (such as VBA or VBScript) as the means of propagating. A large percentage of macro viruses aren't harmful in any way.

- Some viruses corrupt data in subtle ways by rearranging words and phrases in documents, or adding the word "not" in random locations. These are the most insidious viruses because, without full and detailed backups, it's nearly impossible to restore documents to their original state.

- Other serious macro viruses erase selected files or groups of files from your hard drive. You can often recover from these destructive viruses by using the Windows Recycle bin, well-maintained backups, or third-party software such as Norton's Unerase.

- Some nasty macro viruses prevent you from using Office, or Windows itself, by deleting key files or rearranging the Windows Registry. Sometimes the cure is as simple as reinstalling the software, but a well-written virus can make even this cure impossible.

- The most sophisticated virus-writing techniques often appear in Office macro viruses before they show up anywhere else. Some use "stealth" technology (for example, the virus might take over the Office components that let you see macros, thereby hiding themselves), or "polymorphism" (where the virus mutates each time it replicates, making it much harder to identify and catch).

■ Viruses can propagate from application to application. For example, you might introduce a virus to your system by opening an infected Word document, and then the infection can spread to Excel workbooks. Because Outlook and other clients support scripting languages, it is theoretically possible to spread viruses through e-mail messages, even without file attachments.

■ You're far more likely to receive an infected file from a coworker, a friend, or a network server than by downloading documents from the Internet. Similarly, you are far more likely to lose data due to a dumb mistake or a hardware problem than to a macro virus.

■ Almost all virus scares are precisely that—scares—with little or no foundation in reality.

The vast majority of macro viruses rank as amateurish and poorly written, and can hardly survive in the wild. Some, however, have proven themselves robust—and destructive.

Tip from

EQ & Woody

For the latest unbiased information on macro viruses, threats, and solutions, subscribe to the free weekly e-mail newsletter called Woody's Office Watch by sending a message to wow@wopr.com.

USING DIGITAL SIGNATURES TO VERIFY A MACRO'S SOURCE

Office XP includes a number of innovative methods to help protect you from macro viruses. *Digital signatures* lie at the heart of the approach most frequently encountered by Office users.

A digital signature identifies the source of a macro. Developers must apply for digital signatures from *certifying authorities*, which verify the identity of developers before issuing them a signature. Certifying authorities can revoke a certificate after issuing it, if they discover evidence that a developer is distributing viruses or unsafe software.

A digital signature identifies the company (or person) that claims to have written a macro. It does *not* tell you anything about the author. A macro signed "A-Z Developers Inc." could have originated with a terrorist in Timbuktu. Similarly, certificates can be generated with any name, so if you find a macro signed "Bill Gates" on the Web site www.virusheaven.com, you should doubt its veracity. It's up to you to decide whether you trust the company (or person) that signed the macro.

When you open a digitally signed macro in Word, Excel, PowerPoint, Outlook, or FrontPage, you'll see a dialog box that contains information about the signature and asks whether you want to run the program (see Figure 38.6).

If you click the box marked Always Trust Content from *Source*, Office will add that digital signature to its "trusted sites" list. From that point on, you will be able to open signed macros from that source without having to click through a dialog box.

Figure 38.6
A digital signature verifies only the source of the macro—not its safety.

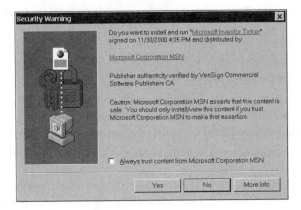

CONFIGURING OFFICE SECURITY LEVELS

Digital signatures work in conjunction with each application's *security level* to determine which macros will or will not run. Word, Excel, PowerPoint, Outlook, and Publisher (but, surprisingly, not FrontPage) enable you to set three different security levels (see Table 38.2). For example, you might want to run any macro on your company's intranet, because you know your company's information technology specialists have tested it carefully before putting it there. On the other hand, you probably never want to run a macro you receive from a completely unknown source on the Internet. To open the Security dialog box (see Figure 38.7), choose Tools, Macro, Security.

Figure 38.7
If you understand the implications of digital code signing and the possible threat from macro viruses, the Medium setting will generally suffice.

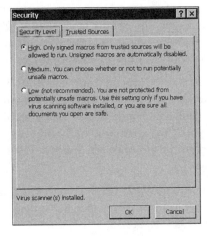

TABLE 38.2 OFFICE XP SECURITY LEVELS

Security Level	Macro Restrictions
High	Only valid digitally signed macros from a previously identified "trusted source" will run automatically. If the macro is signed, but the source isn't listed as a "trusted source," you will be given the opportunity to accept or reject the certificate (refer to Figure 38.7) and add the source to the trusted list. In all other cases, macros are disabled.
Medium	Much like the High setting, except that users have the option to enable or disable macros if there's a problem with the signature (for example, it was incorrectly applied), or if there's no signature at all.
Low	All macros are enabled, without regard to the presence of a digital signature.

The default security setting in Word, Excel, PowerPoint, Outlook, and Publisher is High.

Tip from

EQ & Woody

Consider setting Word and Excel security to Medium. If you leave it on High, Word and Excel discards unsigned macros, and you'll never know they existed.

When you receive HTML messages, Outlook 2002 uses the same zone-based security model as Internet Explorer. In fact, the security options you specify in Outlook apply to Internet Explorer and Outlook Express, and vice versa. From Outlook, choose Tools, Options, click the Security tab, and click the Zone Settings button; you'll see the dialog box shown in Figure 38.8.

Figure 38.8
Outlook 2002 uses the same security settings as those you'll find in Internet Explorer.

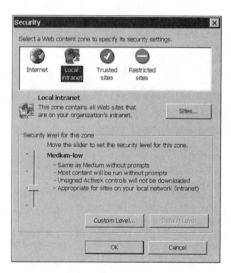

Internet Explorer and Outlook define four zones:

- The Local Intranet zone, which covers Web sites maintained on your company's internal intranet. Default security setting is Medium-Low.

- The Trusted Sites zone, which includes only those URLs you have specifically designated as "trusted." Use this setting if you're certain that a site's security substantially exceeds Web norms; by default, Internet Explorer allows you to add only sites that require server verification (https) to this zone. To add a URL to this list, click Add Sites. Default security setting is Low.

- The Internet zone, an "all other" category that includes any site not designated Local, Trusted, or Restricted. Default security setting is Medium.

- The Restricted Sites zone, where you should definitely place any "hacker" or "cracker" sites you visit. To add a URL to this list, select Restricted Sites zone from the list, and then click Add/Remove Sites. Default security setting is High.

You can customize individual security settings—dozens of them—by choosing the zone you want to restrict, and then clicking Custom Level (see Figure 38.9).

Figure 38.9
Internet Explorer offers dozens of custom security choices.

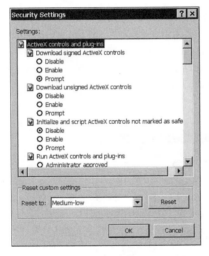

Many of these custom settings are complex, with consequences not at all apparent based strictly on the descriptions in the dialog box.

Note

To learn more about customizing the Windows security settings, see *Special Edition Using Microsoft Windows XP, Home Edition,* or *Special Edition Using Windows 98.*

BLOCKING ACCESS TO THE VISUAL BASIC PROJECT

Most macro viruses propagate by creating copies of themselves: They build macros attached to documents, which, in turn, infect other Office users. To create a copy, the virus has to be able to get at the part of VBA that's used to write new programs. The virus then proceeds in a manner that's similar to what you would use to write or record a macro, except the virus does it all by using programs.

The part of VBA that's used to build new macros (and modify old ones) is called the Visual Basic Project.

Office automatically prevents programs from getting into the Visual Basic Project unless you specifically, deliberately allow macros to get in. You can only allow macros access to the Visual Basic Project if you choose Tools, Macro, Security, click the Trusted Sources tab, and check the box marked Trust Access to Visual Basic Project (see Figure 38.10).

PART

VII

CH

38

Figure 38.10
Unless you have a specific reason to allow macros to create and modify other macros, leave the box marked Trust Access to Visual Basic Project unchecked.

It's rare that anyone—even professional macro programmers—will grant programmatic access to the Visual Basic Project. Although leaving this box unchecked won't protect you from all macro viruses, it effectively neutralizes a large percentage of all the viruses created before December, 2000.

PROTECTING YOUR PC AND NETWORK FROM VIRUSES

Office 2002 incorporates virus-detection technology that allows antivirus programs to "hook into" Office; an up-to-date antivirus program that includes this hook can examine a file for viruses before allowing an Office program to open the file. (That's why you'll frequently see the message "Requesting a virus scan" at the bottom of an application's window whenever you open a file.) This antivirus scan operates independently of digital signatures, and it has been proven effective in reducing the impact of Office macro viruses.

It's impossible to stop every macro virus, but you can dramatically reduce the risks to your system and network by following these procedures:

■ For Word, Excel, PowerPoint, Outlook, and Publisher, keep the digital security setting on Medium for users who understand the implications of macro viruses, and High for all others.

■ Purchase, install, and regularly update one of the major antivirus software packages. Make sure the program you select is compatible with Office 2002.

■ Stay informed of the latest virus (and antivirus) developments. All the major antivirus software vendors maintain Web sites with up-to-the-minute news: The Symantec Anti-Virus Research Center (Norton AntiVirus) is at www.symantec.com/avcenter; Network Associates' (McAfee VirusScan) site is at www.nai.com/vinfo.

Tip from

EQ & Woody

How many times this week have you received a breathless e-mail warning you about a deadly new virus? Is the latest warning real, or the figment of someone's grossly over-active imagination? For the definitive answer, head directly to Rob Rosenberger's Virus Myths Home Page at http://www.vmyths.com. Rob's voice of reason stands in stark contrast to much of the mindless virus-clamoring you'll hear on the Net. And, he knows his stuff.

SECRETS OF THE OFFICE MASTERS: GETTING READY TO TACKLE VBA

Ready to start working with VBA? Good. Take a few moments to organize your screen and customize the VBA Editor. That way, you won't have to hunt and click so much to get going. (To start the VBA Editor, just start your favorite Office application and press Alt+F11.)

Most VBA aces believe that the best way to arrange VBA and any Office application is by putting the application in the top half of the screen and the VBA Editor in the bottom half, as you can see in this figure. That way, you can step through your program, keeping track of the active command in the bottom window, while watching the effects of your program in the top window.

As you become more proficient, you might want to add VBA's Immediate Window (choose View, Immediate Window) so that you can change variable values as the program runs and test unfamiliar VBA commands. You might also want to get rid of the Properties window (in the lower-left corner; View, Properties Window) if you won't be working with custom-built dialog boxes.

Remember, the behavior of the VBA Editor is controlled by choosing Tools, Options and clicking the Editor tab. In particular, consider checking the Require Variable Declaration box. That will protect you from the single most common source of programming errors—misspellings.

Figure 38.11

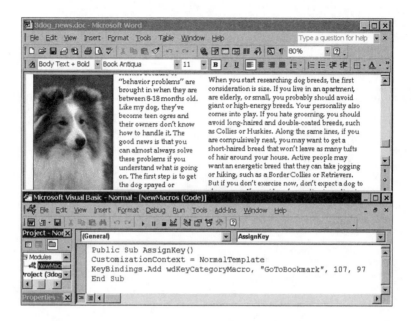

CHAPTER **39**

WORKING WITH VISUAL BASIC FOR APPLICATIONS

In this chapter

VBA BASICS

Microsoft estimates that more than three million people use Visual Basic for Applications (VBA). Although the precise figure certainly remains open to debate, it's fair to say that Visual Basic and VBA, taken together, constitute the most popular programming language in the history of computing.

Visual Basic for Applications version 6.0 is a key component of Office XP. It bears a striking resemblance to Visual Basic 6.0 (VB), Microsoft's mainstream full-strength programming language, which creates executable programs (although it isn't yet up to the standards of Visual Basic 7). Most notably, the *development environment*—the place where you write and test program—is almost indistinguishable in VB 6 and VBA. The same tools are available in both products, the same commands work in both, and many of the language constructs are identical.

Some noteworthy differences exist, however, between VB and VBA:

- VB has much more extensive tools for binding data to dialog boxes, designing databases, and interacting with a server in client/server or Web-based applications.

- VBA, on the other hand, lets you use direct links to the object models of the underlying Office applications. Although VB can interact with objects in Office applications, it's a little more difficult to get at the objects (see the following example). In VBA, all the capabilities of the associated Office applications are immediately at hand.

→ For a description of the various Office object models, **see** "Using Object Models," **p. 968**.

A simple example helps illustrate the difference between the two programming models. In VBA/Word, you can work directly with the Word *object model* to create a new Word document with a simple command:

```
Documents.Add
```

If you try to create a new Word document from Visual Basic, however, it's a little more difficult:

```
Dim objWord as Object
Set objWord = CreateObject("Word.Application")
objWord.Documents.Add
```

The object model in VBA/Word makes it easier to get at Word's underlying capabilities, just as the object models in VBA/Excel, VBA/PowerPoint, VBA/Outlook, VBA/Publisher, VBA/FrontPage, and VBA/Access make it easier to control the capabilities of those applications. In all other respects, the six variants of VBA are virtually identical.

And then there's VBScript—the "scripting" language used to write programs for Web pages. Although VB and VBA are so close that learning to use one gives you an enormous advantage in learning the other, VBScript hardly resembles VB at all. Some of the commands look the same, but VBScript doesn't work like VBA, doesn't respond like VBA, and the development environment (Microsoft Script Editor) bears only a vague semblance to VB's editor.

PART

VII

CH

39

Note

> You use VBA (or VB) to write macros (or programs) that will run with the Office applications. You use VBScript to write programs that run from Web pages (and, in unusual circumstances, HTML e-mail messages). VBScript is a language and environment unto itself; it's not covered in this book.

In general, you'll find it easier to work with Windows itself using VB, but it's much easier to automate individual Office applications through VBA. Unlike VB, which costs hundreds of dollars, VBA is included with Office, at no additional cost. Even if you have no programming experience, you can leverage your knowledge of Office applications to learn VBA (and VB) programming techniques on the side.

VBA contains an internal hierarchy that enables you to organize and manage your programs. At the lowest level, the individual *macros* (more accurately, *procedures*: snippets of programming code in subroutines and functions) do the work. Groups of procedures get organized into modules. Modules can then combine with custom dialog boxes that you create (VBA calls them *UserForms*) to make up a *project*. When things happen to a dialog box (say, the user types something, or clicks a button), procedures respond to the actions. In addition, procedures can change the contents of the dialog boxes, and make them appear and disappear (see Figure 39.1).

Figure 39.1
VBA's basic internal hierarchy enables you to organize and manage your programs.

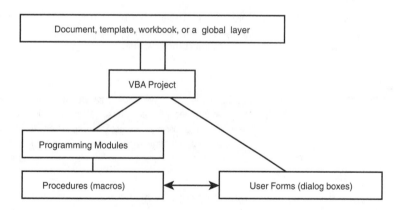

The project is then attached to a document, template, workbook, Publisher publication, or presentation—depending on which Office application you're using. In Word, Excel, Publisher, and PowerPoint, VBA projects don't have an independent existence; they're always attached to a document, template, workbook, or presentation. In Outlook and FrontPage, they all float around in a universal global layer.

With that bottom-up preview, let's take a much closer look at the components, starting at the top and working down.

PROJECTS

To understand some VBA terminology, it's important to keep in mind that VBA evolved as an offshoot of Visual Basic (VB). In VB, a *project* amounts to what many people would call a system or an application—a collection of programs, dialog boxes, program libraries, system declarations, and so on that, taken together, perform some sort of task. In VB, you try to store all the pieces of a project together so they're easy to find and use.

In VBA, all the pieces have to be stored together, of course, but Office users customarily attach macros to documents, templates, worksheets, and other data files. Storing VBA code independently, in VB-style projects, isn't a natural fit, so Office applications use this simple compromise: In Office, a project is the VBA part of a document, template, workbook, or presentation. The following shows what this means in each application of Office:

- In Word, there is one (and only one) VBA project in each document or template.
- In Excel, there is one (and only one) VBA project in each workbook.
- In PowerPoint, there is one (and only one) VBA project in each presentation.
- In Publisher, there is one (and only one) VBA project in each Publisher publication.
- In Outlook, there can be many projects, and they are always open.
- In FrontPage, there is only one project, called Microsoft_FrontPage, and it is always open.
- In Access, the terminology gets confusing because project has an altogether different meaning. Suffice it to say that an Access project contains one and only one VBA project.

Note

Unfortunately, the archaic "project" terminology can be confusing when you work with Office and VBA, and it appears in dialog boxes, Help files, and even inside the VBA Editor itself, notably in the so-called Project Explorer. When you see the term *project*, think of it as a document, template, worksheet, or presentation that contains VBA code.

For example, if you want to move or copy a few macros to a new VBA project—say, to split a large project into two smaller pieces—you first need to create a new document, template, worksheet, publication, or presentation.

The author of a VBA project can choose a "locked for viewing" option—that is, define a password to protect other users from viewing or modifying the VBA code. But this option is an all-or-nothing decision: Either you password-protect the entire project, or you allow other people to look at everything in the project.

MODULES

Modules, on the other hand, are just collections of macros (or, more accurately, collections of procedures; see the next section for a definition). A project can have any number of modules, and a module can contain any number of procedures.

Typical uses for modules include the following:

- **To Distinguish Among Groups of Programs**—For example, you might want to set up one module for VBA macros that you're testing, while maintaining "production" macros in a second module.

- **To Group Subroutines and Functions That Call Each Other**—As long as you stay within one module, the methods for calling other procedures are simpler.

You cannot password-protect individual modules.

Note
When you open the VBA Editor or use the Help files, you'll see occasional references to *class modules*. Think of class modules as super modules that hold self-contained pieces of code, which can be reused throughout a project. Class modules are not covered in this book. To learn more about class modules, see *Special Edition Using Visual Basic 6*, published by Que (ISBN: 0-7897-1542-2).

PROCEDURES: SUBROUTINES AND FUNCTIONS

The actual work of a VBA program takes place in the collection of procedures, or chunks of code, that make up the program. Procedures live in modules, and come in two different varieties:

- **Subroutines**—Generally constructed to perform a specific task. For example, a subroutine might loop through a PowerPoint presentation and replace the word "cheap" with "inexpensive."

- **Functions**—Work just like subroutines, except they return a value. A function might loop through a PowerPoint presentation, replacing "cheap" with "inexpensive," and then return the number of times it made a replacement.

Subroutines start with the keyword Sub and a name, and end with End Sub. Functions start with the keyword Function and a name, and end with End Function.

Note
If you've used Excel functions, you already know how VBA functions operate: They take arguments, and produce a value. VBA subroutines can also take arguments, but they don't turn out values.

MACROS

In Word, Excel, PowerPoint, Outlook, Publisher, and FrontPage, a macro is just a subroutine. When you open an Office application and run a macro with a given name, it runs the subroutine that goes by that same name.

→ For details on locating the macros, **see** "How Office Applications Store Macros," **p. 966**.

In Access, the term *macro* has a completely different meaning. Access's old-fashioned "macros" are rigidly defined commands stuck in a matrix; they don't have anything in common with macros in the other Office applications.

USERFORMS

Don't let the similar terminology throw you—VBA UserForms have nothing in common with Word forms or Access forms. In VBA, UserForms are custom dialog boxes. You build UserForms when you write a VBA program. They let the user enter information that the routine can use, or click buttons that activate specific subroutines.

MANAGING MACROS

Word, Excel, PowerPoint, Outlook, Publisher, and FrontPage include built-in tools for creating and deleting macros. In all six applications:

1. Choose Tools, Macro, Macros, and you'll see the Macros dialog box (see Figure 39.2).

Figure 39.2
If more than one document, template, workbook, or presentation is open, you can narrow down the list of macros by making a choice in the Macros In box.

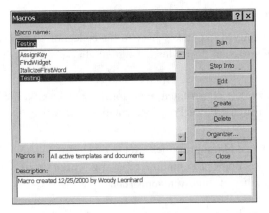

2. To create a new, empty macro, type a name for the new macro, choose a location for it in the Macros In box, and click Create. VBA creates a new subroutine with the given name, and puts you in the VBA Editor (discussed in the next section), ready to start typing your macro.

   Word places newly created macros in a module called NewMacros. Excel and PowerPoint put them in modules called Module1, Module2, and so on. If you want to place your new macro in a specific module, use the VBA Editor.

Tip from

EQ & Woody

If you want to easily copy and move individual macros in Word, you'll want to move them out of the NewMacros module and give them their own module.

3. To delete a macro, click the macro's name and click Delete.

Of all the Office applications, only Word provides any tools for copying and moving macros—and even then, you have to move or copy an entire module full of macros at a time. To copy a VBA/Word module or UserForm (custom dialog box) from one document or *template* to another, or to delete or rename a module or UserForm:

1. Choose Tools, Macro, Macros, and click the Organizer button. The Word Organizer opens (see Figure 39.3).

Figure 39.3
The Word Organizer can copy or move modules or UserForms—so-called "macro project items"—but not individual macros.

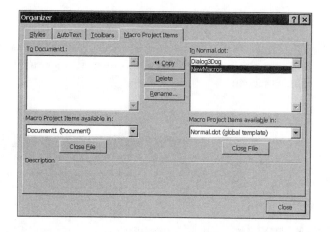

2. Click the Macro Project Items tab. You'll see a list of all modules and UserForms in the current document (on the left side of the dialog box) and in the Normal "global" template (on the right side of the dialog box).

→ For detailed information on how to work with Normal.dot, **see** "Customizing the Normal Document Template," **p. 474**.

3. If necessary, select different "from" and "to" documents or templates from the Macro Project Items Available In boxes. (Note that you can copy in either direction, left-to-right, or right-to-left.) If the document or template isn't available in these lists, click Close File, and then click Open File and select the correct document or template.

4. Click once to select the module or UserForm you want to copy, delete, or rename, and then click the appropriate button to copy, delete, or rename it (the arrows on the Copy button show you which file you'll copy from and to). Note that you cannot move a module in a single action: You must copy it, and then delete it.

Modules often contain more than one macro, and the Word Organizer won't tell you the names of the macros in a module. Be careful that you don't copy or delete the wrong macros, or rename the wrong module.

Caution

If you use macros that are confidential or proprietary, be sure you know what macros are in a module before you copy and distribute it. Because the individual macro names never appear in the Organizer, it's easier to make a mistake than you might think.

To copy, move, delete, or rename an individual macro in Word, Excel, PowerPoint, Outlook, Publisher, or FrontPage, you have to use the Visual Basic Editor, as described in the next section.

USING THE VBA EDITOR

The *VBA Editor* (see Figure 39.4) is a true work of art. It's easily the equal of any programming editor ever devised, although it also has some noteworthy shortcomings, which you'll learn about later in this section.

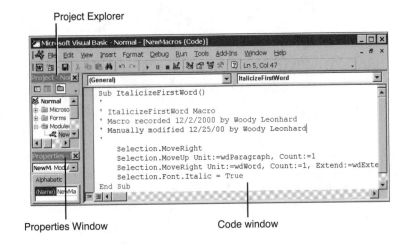

Project Explorer

Figure 39.4
The VBA Editor usually contains two "dockable," resizable panes, plus a large open area for writing programs and creating custom dialog boxes.

Properties Window

Code window

To open the VBA Editor in Word, Excel, PowerPoint, Outlook, FrontPage, or Access, choose Tools, Macro, Visual Basic Editor. The VBA Editor sits in its own window, separate from the Office application that opened it.

MANAGING VBA COMPONENTS WITH PROJECT EXPLORER

Although you can drag and dock the Project Explorer window anywhere—even, surprisingly, outside the VBA Editor window—it usually sits in the upper-left corner of the VBA Editor.

At the highest level, the *Project Explorer* provides a list of projects. In VBA/Word, for example, that's a list of all open documents and templates. Because Normal.dot is always open when Word runs, it always appears in the VBA/Word Project Explorer as the *Normal project*.

Tip from

EQ & Woody

> If you want to open a new project, you must switch back to the original application—in the case of Figure 39.4, Word—and open the project's document or template. After you open the file using the correct application, the associated project appears in Project Explorer.

Renaming a macro in the VBA Editor is a snap:

1. In the application (Word, Excel, PowerPoint, Outlook, or FrontPage), choose Tools, Macro, Macros to open the Macro dialog box.

2. Click to select the macro whose name you want to change, and click Edit.

3. The VBA Editor appears, with the insertion point at the beginning of the Sub line that corresponds to the macro you've chosen. For example, if you picked Macro3, the insertion point should be on the line that says Sub Macro3(), as in Figure 39.5.

Figure 39.5

If you ask to edit the macro called Macro3, you'll end up in the subroutine called Macro3().

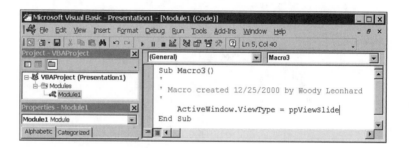

4. To change the name of the macro, delete the old macro name and type in a new one. In the case of Figure 39.5, you could delete the name Macro3 and type the name `ChangeToSlideView`.

Tip from

EQ & Woody

> Don't worry about the parentheses after the macro name. If you forget to type them, VBA puts them in for you.

5. To verify that the macro name has changed—and it will change, even if you don't save the template—switch back to the application, choose Tools, Macro, Macros, and look for the new name in the list of macro names.

Although changing a macro name is easy—if you don't mind working directly with the subroutine program code—copying, moving, and deleting individual macros with the VBA Editor can be a frustrating and error-prone process.

Say you have a macro called ItalicizeFirstWord in Normal.dot's (er, "the Normal Project's") NewMacros module, and you want to move it into a new Normal.dot module called Production:

1. Start the VBA Editor (choose Tools, Macro, Visual Basic Editor). In the Project Explorer, navigate to the Normal project's Modules folder and click it.

2. Add the new module by choosing Insert, Module. A new module called Module1 appears (see Figure 39.6). (If you already have a module called Module1, each new module is called Module2, Module 3, and so on.)

Figure 39.6
When you create a new VBA module, Office gives it the generic name Module1. It's a good idea to change this name to something more descriptive.

3. Click Module1. In the Properties window, find the entry marked (Name), double-click to select Module1, and type `Production` (see Figure 39.7). Press Enter to change the name in the Project Explorer.

4. To retrieve the ItalicizeFirstWord macro, double-click the NewMacros module, and then scroll or use the Procedure drop-down list (see Figure 39.8) to find ItalicizeFirstWord.

Tip from

It's always a good idea to rename a module as soon as you create it. Renaming modules after you've started to build a program can be difficult, because many hidden references to the module names are scattered throughout VBA programs.

Tip from

You can switch between seeing a single procedure (Procedure view) at a time and all procedures, one after the other (Full Module view) by clicking the appropriate buttons as shown previously in Figure 39.8.

Figure 39.7
Use the Properties window to change the name of a module.

Procedure drop-down list

Figure 39.8
To see a list of all macros in the current module, use the Procedure drop-down list.

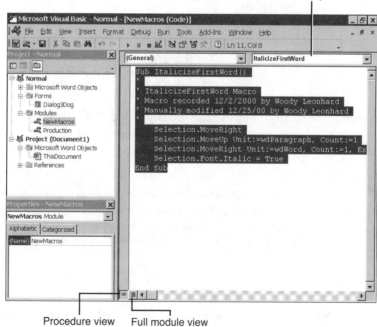

Procedure view   Full module view

5. At this point, you might think there would be a way to drag and drop ItalicizeFirstWord into the Production module, but the VBA Editor isn't that smart. Instead, you have to select the entire subroutine, from the Sub ItalicizeFirstWord() line all the way through End Sub, and then choose Edit, Cut.

6. Double-click the Production module in the Project Explorer, and then choose Edit, Paste (see Figure 39.9).

Figure 39.9
There is no way to drag and drop macros from one module to another. Instead, use the Clipboard to cut the macro out of the NewMacros module, and then paste it into the Production module.

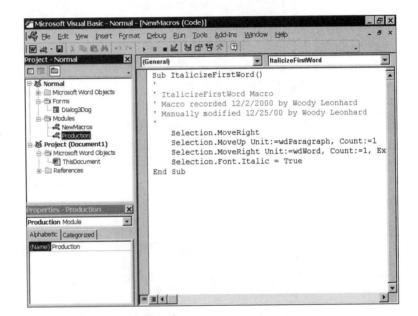

Other familiar Explorer-like actions aren't possible in Project Explorer, either. For example, you can't click a module and press the Delete key to delete it. Instead, you must right-click the module name and choose Remove.

Tip from

EQ & Woody

> You can click and drag within Project Explorer to copy a module from one project to another. Unfortunately, the right mouse button doesn't work the way it does in Office applications, so you can't right-click and drag to move a module, for example. (However, you can always click and drag to copy, and then delete the original.)

PROGRAMMING IN THE CODE WINDOW

The VBA Editor's *Code window* houses a sophisticated development and debugging system. Among its many features:

- **Auto Quick Info**—When typing a command in the Code window, you'll find that the VBA Editor offers *ScreenTips* and *parameter lists* (which arguments have to be provided to subroutines and functions, and in what order). They help you type faster and remember the (often lengthy) details of how each command is fashioned. Press the Tab key to accept the offered auto entry.

- **Stepped Execution**—The VBA Editor lets you step through programs, one line at a time, and watch the results of each command. You can even "hover" the mouse pointer over a variable and the VBA Editor displays a ScreenTip that shows the current value of the variable.

→ For more details on stepped execution, **see** "Stepping Through and Editing Recorded Macros," **p. 972**.

- **Context-Sensitive F1 Help**—If you're ever stuck on a command and can't figure out what it should do, press F1 and VBA's extensive (but far from exhaustive) Help system appears.

- **Quick Access to Subroutines**—Click the down arrow next to the Procedure drop-down list (see Figure 39.10), select a subroutine, and the VBA Editor takes you right to it.

Figure 39.10
All the procedures (subroutines and functions) in a module appear in the Procedure drop-down list.

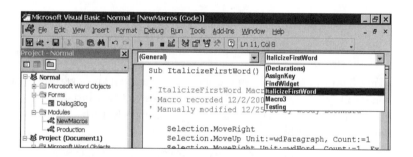

PART

VII

CH

39

- **Object Browser**—Although it will take a while for you to get accustomed to it, the VBA *Object Browser* lets you look at all the commands available in the object models, not only for the version of VBA that you're using (for example, all the VBA/Word commands), but for other applications that you can control via VBA (such as Excel). To see the Object Browser, press F2 (see Figure 39.11).

Tip from

EQ & Woody

To make commands for other applications visible in the Object Browser, choose Tools, References and check any applications that interest you. At a minimum, consider checking the boxes for: Office, Word, Excel, PowerPoint, Outlook, the FrontPage Editor and Microsoft FrontPage Web Objects Reference, the Microsoft Windows Scripting Host, and (if you'll be working with databases) Access and DAO.

Adding applications to the References list won't seriously affect performance, although it can make lookups more difficult. If you look for the Find command, for example, and you have References for both Word and Excel, you'll have to tell the Object Browser whether you want to look up Word's Find or Excel's Find. In practice, this rarely causes a problem.

Figure 39.11
The Object Browser lists every command available, and includes hot links at the bottom of Help file entries.

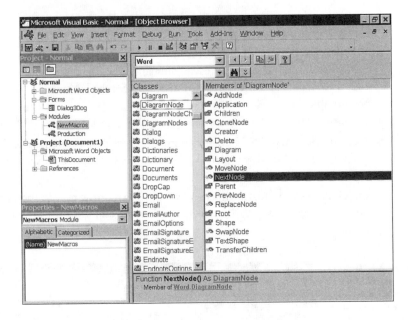

Many, but by no means all, of the applications listed include version numbers. In general, you should pick the versions of the applications you have installed on your machine (which usually means the latest versions). When you upgrade, go back into the References list, uncheck the old version, and check the new one.

If you write a program with one flavor of VBA—for example, VBA/Word—and it calls Excel, that program will run only on machines with both Word and Excel installed. Depending on the details of the program, you might actually need to run the same versions of Word and Excel that were used to develop the program. But the person running the program need not go into VBA and change the References list to add Excel. (One subtle exception to that final point: If the program contains named variables that are unique to the application—for instance, wdAlignParagraphCentered in Word, or xlToLeft in Excel—the Reference list for the affected application must be active.)

A host of programming settings appear if you choose Tools, Options. Among the most important is syntax checking (the Auto Syntax Check box), which controls whether VBA will check the syntax of every line as it is typed; and strict variable checking (the Require Variable Declaration box), which forces you to declare all your variables in Dim statements. Most experienced programmers turn the former off and the latter on—precisely the opposite of the default values.

BUILDING INTERACTIVE VBA PROGRAMS

Some macros work by themselves, with no user intervention required. The ItalicizeFirstWord macro, which you recorded in the previous chapter, falls into the "no hands required" category. It runs from start to finish and, except for starting it, the user doesn't have to do a thing. In fact, all recorded macros run without any user intervention, because the recorder doesn't have the intelligence necessary to know when to pause for user input when it's required.

More powerful macros interact with the outside world—for example, a macro might stop and let you select a file from a browse box, or display a message and wait for you to click OK. You can also set up timers to let a macro pause for a predetermined amount of time—to display a message without requiring the user to click OK, for example.

Here's how to create a simple macro that requires user intervention. It just counts to five:

1. In Word, Excel, PowerPoint, Outlook, Publisher, or FrontPage, choose Tools, Macro, Macros. In the Macro Name box type Counter and click Create. VBA creates a subroutine called Counter, as shown in Figure 39.12.

Figure 39.12
VBA (in this case, VBA/Publisher) puts together all the details you need to get started with the macro called Counter.

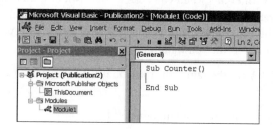

PART

VII

CH

39

2. Type the code you see in Figure 39.13. Take advantage of the Auto features of the VBA Editor, when you have a chance.

Figure 39.13
The program loops five times, each time showing the current value of i in a message box.

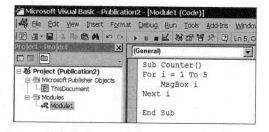

3. Now run the program by clicking the Run Sub/User Form button.

The Office application should respond by displaying a series of five message boxes, with the numbers between 1 and 5, as in Figure 39.14.

Figure 39.14
When run in Publisher, Counter's message boxes all display the title "Microsoft Publisher."

Each time the box appears, the macro stops and waits for the user to click OK. After the message box has been cleared, the macro picks back up where it left off.

In VBA parlance, clicking OK is an *event*—something that happens outside the macro program itself. In this case, the Counter macro responds to the event of an OK click by continuing in its loop.

Windows lives and dies by events. In fact, events lie at the heart of interactive Windows programs in general, and VBA programs in particular: If the user clicks *this* (say, a Cancel button), the program should do *that* (perhaps clear out the dialog box); if the user types something over here (such as a filename), the program should do something over there (maybe open the file). Events, and responses to events, are of paramount importance when designing and programming VBA systems that interact with a user.

You'll most often work with events when you design your own custom dialog boxes to enable the user to interact with a macro. VBA contains an extensive toolkit for constructing custom dialog boxes. You can choose from a wide variety of items—VBA calls them *controls*—and place them wherever you want on a custom dialog box.

The controls used by VBA are the same controls you use when working with Windows dialog boxes.

The more useful VBA controls are listed in Table 39.1.

TABLE 39.1   CUSTOM DIALOG BOX CONTROLS

Name	Description
Label	Static piece of text on a custom dialog box that the user can't change.
Text Box	Location set aside on a custom dialog box where the user is permitted to type in text.
Command Button	A button the user can click. OK and Cancel are the two most common kinds of command buttons, but you can create command buttons of any size, containing any descriptive text.
Check Box	A box the user can check or clear to make a yes-or-no choice.
Option Button	Also known as a radio button, designed to enable the user to pick one and only one option from several alternatives. You set up option buttons in a group on your custom dialog box: As soon as the user clicks one of the option buttons in the group, all the others get cleared out automatically by VBA.
List Box	Drop-down list of several options. The user clicks the down arrow to the right of the list, and can pick, at the most, one.
Image	A picture. VBA lets you put pictures anywhere on a custom dialog box.

In short, any control you've ever seen in a Windows dialog box (including scrollbars, spin buttons, drop-down combo boxes, and more) are available for your use in building custom dialog boxes.

Table 39.2 lists some of the more common events that VBA tracks inside custom dialog boxes, and makes available to your programs. You can write pieces of VBA code to respond to the events as they occur.

TABLE 39.2   VBA EVENTS

Name of Event	What It Means
Click	If you ask it to, VBA notifies your program when the user clicks a command button, picture, or some other part of the custom dialog box.
Double-click	VBA determines when a double-click (as opposed to two single clicks) has occurred, and notifies your program accordingly.
Mouse Move	You can set up the dialog box so that VBA tells your program when the mouse has moved over a command button, picture, or anywhere else on a custom dialog box.
Key Press	When the user presses a key—generally while the insertion point sits in a text box—you can have VBA notify your program of the fact, and tell the program which key has been pressed.

That's just the tip of the event iceberg. VBA can track and log almost any event you can conceive—anything the user might do on or to a custom dialog box that you've constructed—and send a notification to your program. In the next chapter, you'll see how to write programs that work with controls and events to interact effectively with a user.

PART

VII

CH

39

CONTROLLING AN OFFICE APPLICATION FROM VBA

So far in this chapter, we've focused on the components inside VBA—projects, modules, custom dialog boxes, controls, events, and the like. Ultimately, however, almost every VBA program interacts with the underlying application: For example, you usually write a VBA/Word macro to perform some sort of action on a Word document. That isn't an absolute requirement—you can write a VBA/Excel macro that doesn't interact with any workbooks—but in most cases you will want your program to control the underlying application.

That's where the object model comes in. When a VBA/Word macro controls Word, it does so by using the Word object model. When a VBA/PowerPoint macro changes a slide, it uses the PowerPoint object model.

→ For an overview of the object models, **see** "Using Object Models," **p. 968**.

Application object models can be enormously complex: It would take at least 100 pages to describe just the highlights of the Word object model, for example—and you could devote an encyclopedia to its many nuances. But if you understand the application itself, you've won half the battle. In fact, it's far, far easier for a Word, Excel, PowerPoint, Outlook, Publisher, or FrontPage expert to learn VBA than for a VB (or VBA) expert to learn Word, Excel, PowerPoint, Outlook, Publisher, or FrontPage.

To get started with the object model in a particular application, look through the Object Browser, and try typing a few commands. If you get stuck, press F1 and VBA's context-sensitive help will appear, with extensive details and a few working samples.

That said, here's a thumbnail introduction to the object models in each of the Office applications. We'll go over the fundamental ways of using these object models in the next chapter. Note that initial capitals are used to identify the names of objects and methods.

→ For a quick comparison of object models, **see** "Opening, Closing, and Creating New Documents," **p. 1016**.

- The foundation of all Word objects is the document: You can add them (that is, create a new document), save them, and open, close, and print them. The current active document is known as the ActiveDocument. When you get inside a document, you're most likely to use the Selection object (in other words, whatever text, pictures, tables, and so on, are currently selected).

- Excel, on the other hand, starts with a workbook. Inside an individual workbook, you'll most likely run with the Sheets object (or Worksheets if you want to limit yourself to just worksheets). Within Sheets, Ranges do most of the work.

- Presentations rule in PowerPoint. Inside a presentation, there are Slide objects, and the TextFrame and TextRange objects on the slides hold the text. Master objects control the Slide, Title, Handout, and Notes masters.

- Publisher bears many similarities to Word, except there's more emphasis on the predefined objects available in Publisher—for example, Layout guides and Connector formats.

- Outlook objects run the gamut of Outlook applications, from contacts to e-mail to Calendar items to to-do lists.

- FrontPage has two independent object models, one for the editor itself, and the other for HTML constructs (tags and the like).

- Access, always the oddball, doesn't have a Project object (although there is an OpenAccessProject command). Instead, it deals with Forms, Reports, Modules, and Screens—where the Screen object is just the currently active form, report, or control.

There are also object models for Data Access Objects (DAO), and even the VBA Editor itself. The DAO and VBA Editor object models are robust, and a skilled VBA programmer can practically work miracles with them.

SECRETS OF THE OFFICE MASTERS: ELEMENTS OF PROGRAMMING STYLE FOR THE NONPROGRAMMER

Even if you're new to programming and have only just begun writing your first VBA programs, you should always keep several tips in mind:

- Use lots of comments. Yes, you can remember precisely what each line of code in your program does, and what each variable's duty in life might be. But when you look at your program a year from now, it will all be gibberish unless you add a lot of comments now, while it's still fresh in your mind.

- Don't be afraid to experiment. You aren't going to break anything. The real beauty of VBA is that you can try something, see how (or whether) it works, and then try something else. Amazing things have been discovered by trial and error.

- Remember that nothing is perfect, and VBA certainly follows that rule. Although VBA itself is reasonably stable and predictable, the underlying object models in all the Office applications have lots and lots (and lots and lots) of rough edges. Go slowly, step through all your programs, and be observant.

- Test. Then test some more. Then give your program to 10 friends, and have them all test it even more. Everyone has a slightly different configuration, and odd settings can throw off even the most well-conceived program.

- Keep your sense of humor. Programming is fun. But it's also hard work. The machine isn't out to get you—even though there will certainly be days when you think it is.

- Ask questions. Nobody knows it all. And even if they did, by the time they figured out the last nuance of the last feature, they would've forgotten what they knew in the first place.

- No matter what happens, there's always another revision. VBA is a dynamic language and every new version brings some exciting new capabilities. Stay on top of the wave, and you'll be able to solve problems that would curl the hair of mere mortals.

PART

VII

CH

39

CHAPTER 40

BUILDING CUSTOM APPLICATIONS WITH VBA

In this chapter

CONTROLLING HOW VBA APPLICATIONS START

There are countless ways to run a macro. The most direct way, of course, is to choose from the pull-down menus. But there are far more productive ways to automate work processes, especially when you're creating a document, workbook, or presentation that you want to pass along to other users.

You can create a macro that runs automatically every time a user opens a specific Word document or Excel workbook, for example. Excel keeps track of 20 workbook-related events (Before Print, Before Save, when a Sheet is Activated), and you can write macros that run when any of those events "fire." Use these Auto macros to ask the user for initial information for a report, or to update a worksheet with up-to-the-minute data off the Web every time a user opens a workbook.

You can also set up "hot" areas within a document, worksheet, or PowerPoint slide, so clicking a bit of text or graphics will run a macro. PowerPoint lets you run a macro by passing the mouse pointer over a "hot" spot on a slide.

In Outlook, you can specify that a macro be run when the application starts or quits, new mail arrives, a message gets sent, or a Reminder shows up onscreen.

FrontPage and Publisher have the least developed macro-triggering capabilities of all the Office applications. Without a lot of work, the most you can do is put a macro on the menu or a toolbar.

At the high end, you can even replace Word's built-in functions with macros of your own devising. For example, you can create your own File Open routine to run in place of Word's File Open. That solution might come in handy if your company uses nonstandard file extensions and you want to see a list of those files every time you choose File, Open.

"HOT" LINKING TO MACROS

Word, Excel, and PowerPoint include their own variations on a *macro hot link*—a picture or piece of text that runs a macro when clicked. Surprisingly, however, the technique you use to implement these hot links varies widely from application to application.

HOT LINKING IN WORD

In Word, you can implement hot links with MacroButton fields.

→ For details on Word fields in general, **see** "Using Fields Intelligently," **p. 488**.

→ To learn more about building your own interactive VBA programs, **see** "Building Interactive VBA Programs," **p. 998**.

Say you want to add the sentence "Double-click HERE to run Counter," so that double-clicking the word HERE will run the macro called Counter, which was created in the preceding chapter:

1. In a Word document, type the sentence "`Double-click to run Counter`" (without quotes). Don't include the word HERE yet.

2. Position the insertion point where you want to add the hot word HERE.

3. Choose Insert, Field. You'll see the Field dialog box shown in Figure 40.1. In the Categories box, select Document Automation; and then select MacroButton from the Field Names box.

Figure 40.1
When the user double-clicks a MacroButton field, the indicated macro runs.

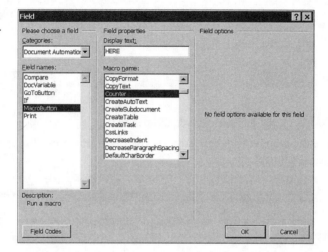

4. In the Display Text field type the word HERE. Then in the Macro Name field select Counter and click OK.

5. After returning to the document, verify that the macro runs every time you double-click the hot text.

Word doesn't limit you to text in a MacroButton field; you can use pictures as well. After you have the field set up with text using the preceding steps, it's easy to convert to a picture. Use this two-step method to make a picture in Word "hot" (first, create a MacroButton field with text, and then replace the text with a picture). It's much less error-prone than trying to type in the field from scratch.

1. With the sentence `Double-click HERE to run Counter` showing, choose Tools, Options. Click the View tab, select the Field Codes check box, and click OK. You should be able to see the MacroButton field (see Figure 40.2).

PART

VII

CH

40

Figure 40.2
The MacroButton field
enables the "hot
spot" in this Word
document.

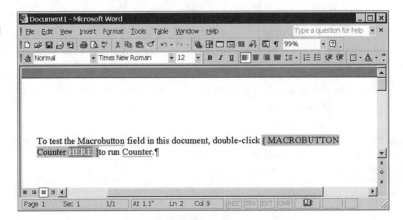

2. Select the word HERE inside the field, and delete it.

3. To replace the hot text with a picture, choose Insert, Picture, Clip Art, and choose a picture (see Figure 40.3).

Figure 40.3
You can use a picture
for the "hot spot"–in
this case, a photo-
graph–by replacing
the text in the
MacroButton field
with a picture.

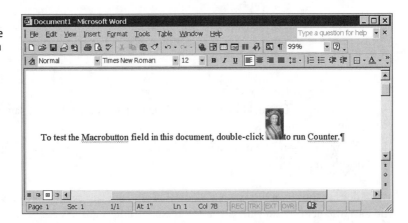

Tip from

Any of the Insert Picture options will work—From File, From Scanner, and so on.

4. Choose Tools, Options; on the View tab, clear the Field Codes check box. Click OK, and your document returns to showing the results of field codes, instead of the codes themselves.

In Word, you can also run macros on entry or exit to a data-entry form field. When the user fills out a data-entry form and uses the Tab key to move into or out of a field defined on the form, you can have a specific macro run.

→ For details on Word data-entry forms, **see** "Creating a Data Entry Form," **p. 509**.

In summary, in all situations except data-entry forms, Word documents can have hot text or pictures. It always takes a double-click to activate the hot link.

HOT LINKING IN EXCEL

Excel, surprisingly, has two entirely different ways to make text and pictures "hot":

■ You can assign a macro to a control on a data-entry form. The controls come from the Form toolbar. When you place a command button on an Excel data-entry form, Excel immediately prompts you to assign a macro to it. To make other controls "hot," right-click and select Assign Macro.

■ You can also assign a macro to a picture in the drawing layer.

→ For the definitive guide to drawing in Office documents, **see** "Working with the Drawing Layer," **p. 108**.

Working with the Excel drawing layer gives you an enormous amount of flexibility in designating hot areas, because you can place drawings directly on top of cells, charts, or even other drawings. For example, let's assume you have a VBA/Excel macro called DistributeSheets that works with Outlook and creates email messages for everyone in your department, attaches the current worksheet to the messages, and mails all the messages. Use this technique to assign the macro DistributeSheets to the word Distribute in the Excel sentence, **Distribute** to department:

1. If the Drawing toolbar isn't visible, right-click any toolbar and choose Drawing from the list of available toolbars.

2. Click the Text Box icon, and then click and drag on the worksheet to add the text box. Type the text Distribute to department in the text box, as shown in Figure 40.4.

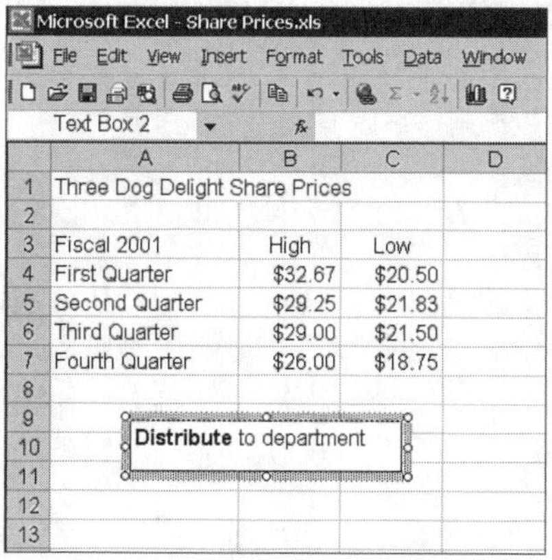

PART

VII

CH

40

Figure 40.4
Use layered drawings to make Excel text hot. Start with a text box that includes the hot text.

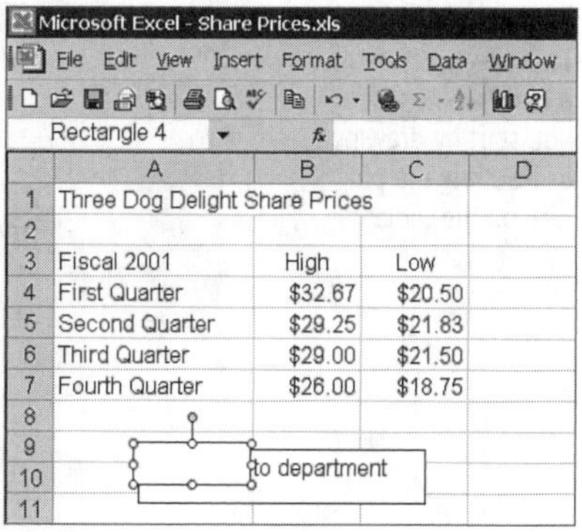

Figure 40.5
Then draw a rectangle that completely covers the hot text.

3. Now draw a rectangle *on top of* the word Distribute—click the Rectangle icon, and draw the rectangle so that it completely covers the word Distribute (see Figure 40.5).

4. Right-click the rectangle and select Format AutoShape. In the Format AutoShape dialog box, choose No Fill in the Fill Color box, and No Line in the Line Color box. Click OK, and you'll be able to see the text `Distribute` through the now-transparent rectangle.

5. Right-click the rectangle once more and select Assign Macro. In the Assign Macro dialog box, select DistributeSheets (assuming you have a macro with that name) and click OK.

6. The text `Distribute` should now be hot.

HOT LINKING IN POWERPOINT

PowerPoint can also use the drawing layer to make text or drawings hot. Unlike Excel, however, you can make a PowerPoint macro run by merely passing your mouse over it.

Say you have a presentation with a slide that includes your company's current market capitalization (market capitalization = current stock price × number of shares outstanding). The PC you're using to make the presentation is connected to the Web, so you write a VBA/PowerPoint macro called GetMarketCap that retrieves your company's current stock price from the Web, calculates market capitalization, and puts that number in the slide.

Now you want to set up a hot drawing on the slide so that every time you pass your mouse pointer over the drawing, the market capitalization figure gets updated with up-to-the-second information from the Web. Here's how:

1. In PowerPoint, bring up the slide where you want to have a hot link.

2. Use the Drawing toolbar to create the picture you want to be hot. In Figure 40.6, an AutoShape has been drawn that looks like a lightning bolt.

Figure 40.6
To make a picture on a PowerPoint slide hot, start by drawing or inserting the picture on the slide.

3. Right-click the drawing and select Action Settings. In the Action Settings dialog box, you can choose from hyperlinks, programs, sounds, and other options.

4. Click the Mouse Over tab, and then click the Run Macro button. Choose GetMarketCap from the offered list, and click OK.

→ For details about all these options, **see** "Advanced Navigation with Action Settings," **p. 764**.

In summary, PowerPoint, too, can have hot pictures, but only in the drawing layer. The hot text trick works in PowerPoint, same as it does in Excel. But in PowerPoint, the hot link can work with either a single click, or by moving your mouse over the link.

USING AUTO MACROS

Word, Excel, PowerPoint, and Outlook all enable you to create macros that will run when the applications start or quit, or when you open or close a specific document, workbook, or presentation. In all cases, the trick lies in putting the macro in the right place, and giving the macro the correct name. (In PowerPoint, you must clear a couple of additional hurdles.)

These so-called *Auto macros* can come in handy when you want to modify the application itself when it starts—to load the most recently used document, for example. This technique is also effective when you need to modify a document before the user starts working on it— to automatically calculate an invoice number, for example.

USING AUTO MACROS IN WORD

Word responds to a number of different Auto events, but we generally recommend you stick to one of these five events:

- AutoExec() and AutoExit(), which run when Word starts and quits, respectively. These macros have to be placed in a module in Normal.dot.

- Document_Open() and Document_Close(), which fire when the document containing the macros is opened or closed. If you store macros with either of these names in a Word template, they'll also run when you open or close documents based on the template.

  The Document_Close() macro runs before Word asks whether you want to save changes.

- Document_New(), which fires when you create a new document based on the template (or document) containing the name.

Although you might place AutoExec and AutoExit macros in any module in Normal.dot, Document_Open(), Document_Close(), and Document_New() must all be created in a special area called Microsoft Word Objects.

Say your boss has taken a stance against the paperless office and decreed that you need to print an additional hard copy of every memo and deliver it to the filing clerk. You can easily create a macro that reminds people of the new requirement, and attach it to your company's memo template. Here's how:

PART

VII

CH

40

1. In Word, open your company's memo template. In this example, Memo.dot was chosen.

2. Start VBA/Word by choosing Tools, Macro, Visual Basic Editor (or by pressing Alt+F11).

→ For details on the VBE, **see** "Using the VBA Editor," **p. 992**.

3. In the Project Explorer, navigate to the Memo project, called TemplateProject (Memo). Then double-click Microsoft Word Objects, and double-click ThisDocument.

   In Word, projects attached to templates are called TemplateProject(*Template name*). So, for example, the project attached to Letterhead.dot is called TemplateProject(Letterhead).

4. To have the warning message appear whenever a user creates a new memo based on this template, click the Object drop-down list and choose Document. Then, in the Procedure drop-down list, choose New. VBA/Word provides the Sub Document_New()/End Sub pair (see Figure 40.7).

Figure 40.7
The Document_Open(), Document_Close(), and Document_New() Auto macros go in the project's Microsoft Word Objects folder.

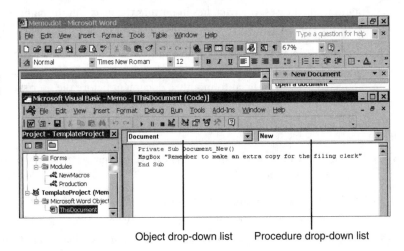

Object drop-down list   Procedure drop-down list

5. Type this one line between Sub and End Sub:

```
MsgBox "Remember to make an extra copy for the filing clerk."
```

That's all there is to it. (Surprisingly, you don't even need to save your changes.) To see the macro in action, create a new document based on Memo.dot. The reminder appears before the user can even start typing.

USING AUTO MACROS IN EXCEL

Although Word handles just three document-oriented Auto events, Excel keeps track of 20 events—Before Close, Before Save, New Sheet, Sheet Activate, and many more—and you can write pieces of code to be invoked whenever one of these 20 events occurs. To see a complete list of these events and a discussion of how to write code for them, consult the online Help topic "Workbook Object Events."

It's relatively easy to follow the instructions in online Help to create Auto macros that corre-spond to most workbook events, but it's not at all obvious how to create Auto macros that run when Excel starts or exits. For example, let's assume that you want to maximize the Excel window every time Excel starts. Follow these steps:

1. Start Excel and press Alt+F11 to open the VBA Editor. Look in the Project Explorer for a VBAProject(Personal.xls) entry.

 If you can't locate your Personal.xls file, see "Missing Personal.xls" in the "Troubleshooting" section at the end of this chapter.

2. Double-click Personal.xls and choose Modules, Module1. That puts you in Module1 of your Personal Macro Workbook.

3. Choose Insert, Procedure to bring up Excel's Add Procedure dialog box (see Figure 40.8). Type Auto_Open (note the required underscore character), and click OK.

Figure 40.8
An Auto_Open() subroutine in Excel's Personal Macro Work-book (Personal.xls) will run every time Excel starts.

4. In the newly created Auto_Open() subroutine, type the one-line program you see in Figure 40.9.

Figure 40.9
This one-line program maximizes the Excel application window.

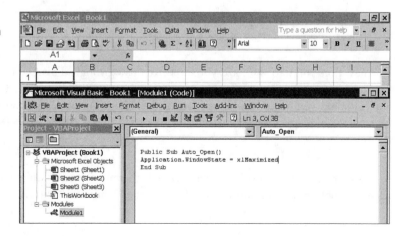

PART

VII

CH

40

5. Close Excel. When asked whether you want to save changes to your personal workbook, click Yes.

Every time you start Excel, the Auto_Open() macro in Personal.xls kicks in and maximizes Excel.

USING AUTO MACROS IN POWERPOINT

PowerPoint, by contrast, requires that you use class modules to house macros that react to the application's Auto events. Then you have to run a separate program that activates those events before the events will "fire." The procedure is complicated. For details, look in the PowerPoint Help topic "Application Events."

USING AUTO MACROS IN OUTLOOK

Outlook makes it easy to run macros automatically when the application starts and ends, as long as you have your macro security setting at Medium or Low (Tools, Macro, Security). Say you want to have Outlook put a message on the screen every time you start it that says, "Remember to back up!" Here's how:

1. Start Outlook. Choose Tools, Macro, and then pick Visual Basic Editor (or press Alt+F11) to bring up the VBA/Outlook editor.

2. In the Project Explorer window, navigate to Project1 Microsoft Outlook Objects/ThisOutlookSession. Double-click ThisOutlookSession.

3. In the Object drop-down list, choose Application. In the Procedure drop-down list, choose Startup. VBA/Outlook responds by creating the procedure pair:
   ```
   Private Sub Application_Startup()
   End Sub
   ```

4. Complete the following VBA/Outlook program. Exit Outlook and tell it to save changes to ThisOutlookSession.

   ```
   Private Sub Application_Startup()
   MsgBox "Remember to back up!"
   End Sub
   ```

The next time you start Outlook, you'll receive this warning: "This OutlookSession contains macros. Macros might contain viruses. It is always safe to disable macros, but if the macros are legitimate, you might lose some functionality." If you respond by choosing Enable Macros, the backup message appears.

USING AUTO MACROS IN ACCESS

Access sports a similar AutoExec capability, but it's limited to old-fashioned macros—VBA need not apply. For more information, look for the Help topic "AutoExec."

CREATING TOOLBAR BUTTONS, MENUS, AND KEY COMBINATIONS

To make your macros more accessible, consider placing those you use most often on tool-bars or menus. Office lets you place toolbar or menu entries on existing toolbars or menus. For example, you could put a toolbar button for a custom macro print routine right next to the Print button on the Standard toolbar, or you could stick it between Print Preview and Print on the File menu.

You can also create your own toolbars or top-level menus, and arrange buttons and menu items where you like. This approach is particularly useful if you have a substantial number of macros associated with a particular template: By keeping them off the built-in toolbars and menus, you lessen the potential for confusion.

Tip from

EQ & Woody

Give related custom menu items a uniform "look" by placing the same icon on the menu. Say you have a memo template with a dozen different macros, assigned to sev-eral different menus. If all of the menu items have the same "M" icon, users will be able to easily tell, visually, which menu items go with the memo template.

→ For details on making customized toolbars, menus, and keyboard shortcuts appear, **see** "Customizing Toolbars," "Customizing Built-In Menus," and "Bypassing Menus with Keyboard Shortcuts," **pp. 30, 40, and 42**.

Surprisingly, the mechanics for assigning a macro to a menu item or toolbar button differs slightly among the Office applications. In Word, PowerPoint, and Outlook, for example, you can drag a macro straight from the macro list (choose Tools, Customize, Commands) directly onto a menu or toolbar. In Excel and FrontPage, however, you have to drag a placeholder onto the menu or toolbar, and then right-click to select the macro. The net result is the same.

SUBSTITUTING FOR BUILT-IN COMMANDS

Word—and Word alone—allows you to take over the built-in commands used by the appli-cation itself. You can preempt every single one of more than 1,000 commands, from AcceptAllChangesInDoc to WordUnderline. The macro you write will run instead of the built-in Word command, and it doesn't matter how you invoke the built-in command: by clicking a menu choice or toolbar button, pressing a key combination, or even using exter-nal means (for example, via Object Linking and Embedding from Visual Basic). Your macro takes precedence.

Where you place the macro controls the extent of its influence. For example

- If you place a macro called FilePrint in a document, it will run whenever you (or an-other user) print that document. You might use such a macro on a corporate network to keep a running list of who has printed the document, and when.

- If you place a macro called ToolsWordCount in a template, your ToolsWordCount macro will run whenever someone runs a word count in a document based on that tem-plate. You might want to attach such a macro to a catalog product description template and have it plug the numbers into a table at the top.

PART

VII

CH

40

■ If you place a ViewZoom macro in the Normal.dot project—the global template—your macro will run in place of the standard View Zoom (for example, by choosing View, Zoom) all the time. Such a macro might prompt you and ask whether you want to use your favorite zoom factor.

The hardest part of writing macros to supplant built-in Word commands lies in figuring out the name of the macro: FilePrint and ViewZoom are pretty obvious, but ToolsWordCount isn't. There are two undocumented tricks that can help:

■ To see which built-in command sits behind a Word menu item or toolbar button, press and hold the Ctrl and Alt keys simultaneously and press the "plus" sign on the numeric keypad. The mouse pointer turns into a shape that resembles a cloverleaf. Click the menu item or toolbar button in question to display the Customize Keyboard dialog box, with the correct command name highlighted. In Figure 40.10, for example, Ctrl+Alt+NumPad Plus (+) was pressed, and Tools, Word Count was clicked.

Figure 40.10
To find the built-in command behind a menu item or toolbar button, press Ctrl+Alt+NumPad Plus and click the item.

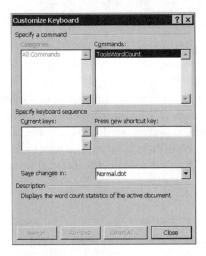

■ To display a complete list of built-in Word commands, choose Tools, Macro, Macros; then choose Word Commands from the Macros In drop-down list.

OPENING, CLOSING, AND CREATING NEW DOCUMENTS

The most fundamental VBA commands look similar in Word, Excel, PowerPoint, and FrontPage—and very different in Outlook and Access.

USING VBA TO OPEN, CLOSE, AND CREATE WORD DOCUMENTS

In Word, the command to create a new document based on the normal document template (Normal.dot) looks like this:

```
Documents.Add
```

If you want to base the new document on a different template, add the full path to the template:

```
Documents.Add "c:\Program Files\Microsoft Office\Templates\Company\Invoice.dot"
```

To open an existing file—C:\My Documents\Invoice1049.doc, for example—use the Open method:

```
Documents.Open "C:\My Documents\Invoice1049.doc"
```

The Open method not only opens the document, it makes the newly opened document the active document—just as Word would, if you opened it by choosing File, Open.

There are three common ways to save a document. If you just want to save the currently active document, use

```
ActiveDocument.Save
```

On the other hand, if you know you want to save the document called "Memo to Justin.doc"—but you don't know whether it's the currently active document, you can activate it, and then close it, like this:

```
Documents("Memo to Justin.doc").Activate
ActiveDocument.Save
```

In fact, VBA/Word doesn't require you to activate the document before you save it. This will save "Memo to Justin.doc," too:

```
Documents("Memo to Justin.doc").Save
```

The Close method works just like the Save method. All three of these are valid:

```
ActiveDocument.Close
```

```
Documents("Memo to Justin.doc").Activate
ActiveDocument.Close
```

```
Documents("Memo to Justin.doc").Close
```

That looks pretty simple, but there's a lot behind the different commands. In VBA parlance, a Document is an *object*. In this case, the Document object is exactly what you would expect: a Word document. The Documents object is a *collection* of Document objects; more precisely, it's the collection of open Word documents. Documents("Invoice.doc") is the Document object called Invoice.doc.

Add is a *method*, an action that can be applied to the Documents collection. It adds a new Document object to the Documents collection (a nonprogrammer would say that Add creates a new document). Similarly, Open is a method that applies to the Documents collection.

Save and Close are methods, but they can be applied to either a single Document object or to the entire Documents collection. For example,

```
Documents.Save
```

saves all open documents.

USING VBA TO OPEN, CLOSE, AND CREATE EXCEL WORKBOOKS

Excel works similarly to Word. The following VBA/Excel statements are all analogous to their VBA/Word counterparts:

```
Workbooks.Add

Workbooks.Add "C:\Program Files\Microsoft Office\Templates\Company\Scores.xlt"

Workbooks.Open "C:\My Documents\Scores20001217.xls"

Workbooks("Scores20001217.xls").Activate
ActiveWorkbook.Save

Workbooks("Scores20001217.doc").Save
```

USING VBA TO CREATE A NEW OUTLOOK E-MAIL MESSAGE OR CONTACT

Outlook's approach to creating new e-mail messages and Contacts doesn't involve the Add method. Instead, Outlook uses something called CreateItem. There's almost no similarity at all between Outlook and Word or Excel.

The following creates a new message and displays it, so the user can fill it out:

```
Set message = CreateItem(olMessageItem)
message.Display
```

And this creates a new Contact, again displaying the Contact so the user can complete it:

```
Set message = CreateItem(olContactItem)
message.Display
```

The documentation claims you have to mess around with MAPI calls, create all sorts of odd objects, and the like, but that's not true. The preceding examples work perfectly well.

USING VBA TO CREATE A NEW FRONTPAGE WEB FILE

FrontPage resembles Word and Excel in using the Add method to create new Web files. The command looks something like this:

```
WebFiles.Add "http://mysite.com/somepage"
```

Note that the URL must be included with an Add.

USING VBA TO OPEN, CLOSE, AND CREATE POWERPOINT PRESENTATIONS

PowerPoint lives in a world of its own away from Word and Excel. All these commands work:

```
Presentations.Add
Presentations.Add "C:\Program Files\Microsoft Office\Templates\Company\Sales.pot"
Presentations.Open "C:\My Documents\Sales Presentation.ppt"
ActivePresentation.Save
Presentations("Sales Presentation.ppt").Save
```

However, there's no reasonable way to activate any particular open presentation. (Yes, it's theoretically possible, but the method is too convoluted to be practical.)

Using VBA to Open, Close, and Create Access Files

In Access, there's no `Projects` collection, and no `Add` method to go with it. Instead, you must deal with methods with names such as NewAccessProject, CreateAccessProject, and OpenAccessProject, which work only with the `Application` object. Look in the Access help files for the topic "Application Object."

Using VBA to Add Text

You would think that something as simple as adding text to a document, spreadsheet cell, slide body, or an e-mail message should be fairly uniform, and that all the Office applications would behave in more or less the same way.

Not a chance.

Adding Text to a Word Document with VBA

In VBA/Word, the simplest way to add text to a document is with the `TypeText` method. For example, the small program in Listing 40.1 creates a new document, adds a return address and date, and then exits, allowing the typist to continue where the macro left off.

LISTING 40.1   TypeReturnAddress

```
Public Sub TypeReturnAddress()
Documents.Add
Selection.TypeText "Ed & Woody's Widgets"
Selection.TypeParagraph
Selection.TypeText "123 Anyplace"
Selection.TypeParagraph
Selection.TypeText "Hometown, CO 12345"
Selection.TypeParagraph
Selection.TypeParagraph
Selection.TypeText Format(Now, "mmmm d, yyyy")
Selection.TypeParagraph
Selection.TypeParagraph
Selection.TypeText "PAST DUE NOTICE"
Selection.TypeParagraph
Selection.TypeParagraph
End Sub
```

Note that paragraph marks must be explicitly "typed" for them to appear in the document.

The `Format()` function takes a value (in the case of Listing 40.1, `Now` is the current date and time), and a formatting pattern ("`mmmm d, yyyy`" specifies the name of the month, date, and then a comma followed by the four-digit year). It produces a string formatted according to the pattern—for example, January 23, 2001. For more details, open the VBA Editor, click to position the insertion point inside the `Format()` command, and press F1.

ADDING TEXT TO AN EXCEL WORKBOOK WITH VBA

Adding text to Excel cells similarly requires little effort as shown in Listing 40.2.

LISTING 40.2   TYPECOLUMNHEADINGS

```
Public Sub TypeColumnHeadings()
Cells(1, 1) = "A Column Head"
Range("B1") = "B Column Head"
Cells(1, 3) = "C Column Head"
Range("D1") = "D Column Head"
End Sub
```

Both the `Cells()` property and the `Range()` property work equally well: With the former, you must specify the numeric location of the cell (with the column first, then the row, so B3, for example, becomes Cells(2,3)); with the latter, you have to refer to the range with a standard address, such as A1:C3.

A Range designation might include $ (dollar signs)—you can use the dollar signs as you would to indicate an absolute cell or range reference—but VBA/Excel ignores them.

ADDING TEXT TO AN OUTLOOK E-MAIL MESSAGE WITH VBA

Outlook works entirely differently from the rest of the Office suite. In an Outlook e-mail message, the contents of the Subject and Body are properties of the message itself.

This program creates a new e-mail message, inserts the "To:" and "Subject:" fields, types text into the body of the message, and then sends it:

```
Set Message = CreateItem(olMailItem)
Message.Recipients.Add ("billg@microsoft.com")
Message.Subject = "Meeting tonight at 8:00"
Message.Body = "Is that OK with you?"
Message.Send
```

Any attempt to access the Contacts list—in this case, running the Message.Recipients.Add command—triggers the macro virus warning shown in Figure 40.11. The user must click OK to proceed. This protection was built into Outlook as a response to the infamous ILOVEYOU virus, which uses this approach to send e-mail messages to everyone on an infected computer's Contacts list. The virus caused untold embarrassment when it swept like wildfire through Microsoft's Redmond campus—among people who should, supposedly, know better.

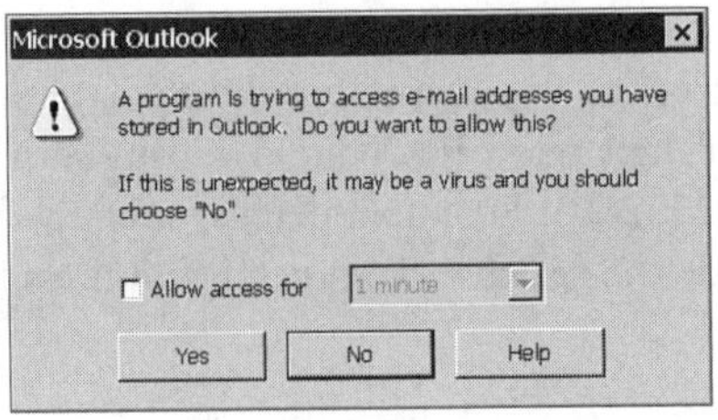

Figure 40.11
Outlook warns you when a macro attempts to get at entries in the Contacts list.

Unfortunately, there's no way to disable this particular warning message: If you run a macro that hits the Contacts list repeatedly, the most any user can do is disable the message for a specified number of minutes. The protection is particularly vexing for people who synchronize handheld computers with their Outlook Contacts list—you can't turn the message off. Outlook's security lockdown has been roundly criticized as a draconian, simplistic solution to a complex problem.

Outlook also warns the user each time a program attempts to add a message to the Outbox— another legacy of the ILOVEYOU debacle. The statement Message.Send in the previous macro triggers this warning: "A program is trying to automatically send e-mail on your behalf. Do you want to allow this? If this is unexpected, it might be a virus and you should choose 'No'." The user has to click Yes before the message will be deposited in the Outbox.

Tip from

EQ & Woody

It's important that you be aware of these severe limitations before you attempt to write an Outlook macro. Any time your program tries to access Contacts data, the user will have to manually grant permission. Any time your program tries to put a message in the Outbox, permission must be given as well. Until some enterprising virus writer figures out a way to bypass these severe security restrictions, people using your macros will have no choice but to click away.

→ Outlook has no analog to the Trusted Sources list, nor does it recognize digital signatures, **see** "Macro Security," **p. 976**.

Adding Text to a PowerPoint Presentation with VBA

PowerPoint uses the InsertBefore and InsertAfter methods to place text on a slide. Unfortunately, PowerPoint's objects work completely differently from Word's or Excel's, so you'll have an interesting time trying to get off the ground.

For example, to insert text before the currently selected text on a slide, you have to use this monstrosity:

```
ActiveWindow.Selection.TextRange.InsertBefore "Some text"
```

Word has a Selection object—but it doesn't require the ActiveWindow. or .TextRange you see here. Unfortunately, VBA/PowerPoint won't work without all the extra baggage.

Strike another blow for consistency across the Office applications.

Displaying Messages

All the versions of VBA in the Office suite include three quick and easy ways to present messages to the user:

- A simple message box, which displays a message and an OK button. Typically, you would use a simple message box to notify the user of an action.
- A more complex message box, which has a message and includes two or three buttons (for example, Yes, No, Cancel), requiring the user to make a choice. These message

boxes can come in handy if you can pose a simple question that can be answered in a Yes/No or Yes/No/Oops fashion.

■ An input box, which also displays a message, and allows the user to type an answer. Use this type of box when you want the user to provide specific information rather than a Yes/No/Oops style answer. Input boxes always have two buttons: OK and Cancel.

The simplest message box just contains the text of the message. Follow these steps to display a short message:

1. From any Office application, press Alt+F11 to bring up the VBA Editor.

2. If there are no modules, create a new one (choose Insert, Module). Then start a new procedure (choose Insert, Procedure) and give it a name—WarningMessage, for example.

3. VBA provides the first and last lines of the new subroutine. You add the middle one:

```
Public Sub WarningMessage()
MsgBox "Your Message Here"
End Sub
```

4. To run the WarningMessage macro, click the Run Sub/User Form button (or press F5). The message box appears. Click OK in the message box and the macro finishes.

DISPLAYING MESSAGES IN WORD WITH VBA

A more complex message box includes the message text, a title, and a description of the buttons that should appear. For example, let's assume you want to create a message that asks, "Do you want to print the current document?" with buttons for Yes and No. Follow this procedure to add that message box to a Word document:

1. Start Word and press Alt+F11 to bring up the VBA Editor. In the Project Explorer, navigate to a module in the Normal project, Normal.dot.

2. Choose Insert, Procedure, type OKToPrint, and press Enter. You'll have a new subroutine called OKToPrint(), with the Sub/End Sub pair provided by VBA.

3. Start typing the following program. Note how the ScreenTip appears (see Figure 40.12) to show you the components available in MsgBox().

Figure 40.12
VBA's ScreenTip follows along as you type, giving you hints for the parameters valid in a MsgBox().

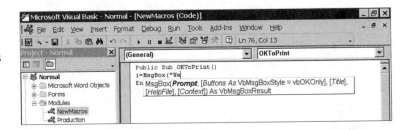

```
Public Sub OKToPrint()
i = MsgBox("Want to print the current document?", vbYesNo)
If i = 6 Then ActiveDocument.PrintOut
End Sub
```

4. To run OKToPrint, click the Run Sub/User Form button (or press F5). Test it several times by clicking Yes and No, pressing Enter, tabbing between the Yes and No buttons, and even pressing the Esc key to abort the message box (see Figure 40.13).

Figure 40.13

MsgBox() returns a value of 6 if the user clicks Yes. To see a complete list of all valid MsgBox() return values, position the insertion point within MsgBox() and press F1.

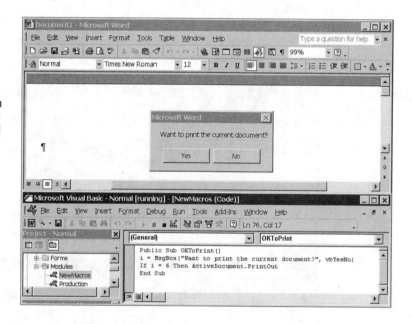

InputBox() has all sorts of applications. For example, do you forget to type the File Properties information in your new documents and workbooks?

→ To see what this refers to, **see** "Storing Document Details," **p. 67**.

There's an easy way to remind yourself—and others in your office—to fill in the Properties information: Use an InputBox(). Here's how to remind users to enter the Subject information, every time they create a new blank document in Word:

1. Start Word and press Alt+F11 to bring up the VBA Editor.

2. Navigate to the Normal project, Microsoft Word Objects, This Document. Click the Object drop-down list and select Document; then click to display the Procedure drop-down list and select New. That creates a subroutine called Document_New() that will run whenever the user creates a new blank document based on the Normal document template (Normal.dot).

3. Type this program:

```
Private Sub Document_New()
strSubject = InputBox("Document Subject", "File Properties")
```

```
If strSubject <> "" Then
    BuiltInDocumentProperties(wdPropertySubject) = strSubject
End If
End Sub
```

Note

In VBA/Word, `BuiltInDocumentProperties` refers to the contents of the File Properties box.

4. Create a new blank document by clicking the New button on the Standard Toolbar. The `InputBox()` should appear (see Figure 40.14). Fill in a new subject and click OK.

Figure 40.14
If the user cancels an InputBox, the returned value is blank.

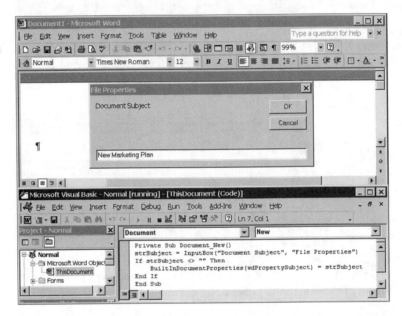

5. Choose File, Properties, and look at the Summary tab. Was the Subject updated properly?

DISPLAYING MESSAGES IN EXCEL WITH VBA

You can create a similar macro for Excel, but there's no corresponding `Document_New()` event to hook into. In Excel, you access the Subject text through this snippet of code:

```
ActiveWorkbook.BuiltinDocumentProperties("Subject")
```

`MsgBox()` and `InputBox()` comprise the two major ways of displaying messages for users. There's a third, often overlooked, way: You can also display a message in the status bar, at the bottom of the Word or Excel window. In Word, use the following code:

```
Statusbar = "Text to appear in the status bar"
```

For no apparent reason, Excel uses a slightly different syntax:

```
Application.Statusbar = "Text to appear in status bar"
```

PowerPoint does not have a status bar.

DISPLAYING OFFICE-STANDARD DIALOG BOXES

Word and Excel let you display, alter, and retrieve data from any of their built-in dialog boxes. (There is no comparable capability in Outlook, PowerPoint, FrontPage, or Access.) These techniques can come in handy if you just want to tweak a built-in dialog box and you don't want to go through the considerable hassle of trying to completely re-create the dialog box.

USING BUILT-IN EXCEL DIALOG BOXES WITH VBA

Say you want to write a VBA/Excel macro that displays the Open dialog box, but instead of the default list of various Excel file types, you only want to look for Web pages (those with an .htm extension). Here's how:

1. Start Excel and press Alt+F11 to bring up the VBA Editor.

2. Navigate to a convenient module (possibly in the Personal Macro Workbook, Personal.xls) and double-click its entry.

3. To create a new macro, choose Insert, Procedure, type OpenHTM, and press Enter. VBA provides the Sub/End Sub pair.

4. Type this one-line program:
   ```
   Application.Dialogs(xlDialogOpen).Show "*.htm"
   ```

5. To run the macro, click the Run Sub/User Form button (or press F5). Excel's Open dialog box shows only *.htm files (see Figure 40.15).

Figure 40.15
By putting a wildcard pattern in the File Name box, Excel looks only for files with the indicated name.

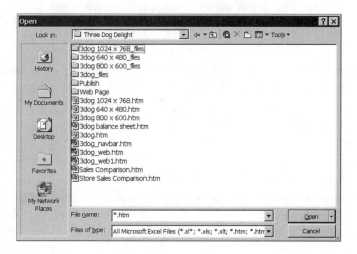

Excel enables you to replace parameters in built-in dialog boxes, but only by using positional arguments: The first argument after the .Show method must be the filename, the second argument concerns updating links, and so on. To see a full list of all the positional parameters available in all Excel dialog boxes (200+ of them), search for the Help topic "Built-In Dialog Box Argument Lists."

USING BUILT-IN WORD DIALOG BOXES WITH VBA

Word, on the other hand, doesn't suffer from Excel's archaic positional fixations. The equivalent program in Word looks like this:

```
Dialogs(wdDialogFileOpen).Name = "*.htm"
Dialogs(wdDialogFileOpen).Show
```

The .Show method in both Word and Excel displays the dialog box and interacts with the user in precisely the same way as if the user had brought up the dialog box.

Word uses a second method, .Display, that enables the user to make a selection from a dialog box but doesn't actually complete the normal operation of the dialog box. For example, you can use the .Display method with the Open dialog box to retrieve a filename; when the user selects a file and clicks Open, your program can use the specified filename without opening the file itself.

```
With Dialogs(wdDialogFileOpen)
     .Name = "*.htm"
     .Display
     MsgBox "You chose File " & .Name
End With
```

> **Note**
> The With/End With command pair saves you a lot of typing. When you add a parameter after the With command, VBA tacks that parameter onto the beginning of every statement inside the With/End With block, if it begins with a dot. Thus, in the example here, VBA interprets .Name just as if you had entered
> Dialogs(wd.DialogFileOpen).Name.

These tricks all apply to standard, built-in Office dialog boxes—the dialog boxes you use every day, from Open to Save As to Find.

You need to open an entirely different bag of tricks to build and manipulate your own dialog boxes, working from scratch. That's the subject of the next section.

CREATING CUSTOM DIALOG BOXES

All the Office VBAs contain extensive tools for creating and controlling custom dialog boxes. VBA calls them *UserForms* but they have absolutely nothing to do with Word or Excel data-entry forms.

VBA custom dialog boxes can do anything any Windows dialog boxes or Office dialog boxes can do, without exception. You can create custom dialog boxes to ask for user input, have the user make choices, let them navigate to a file or folder, or warn them of questionable actions, for example.

All the items you're accustomed to seeing on Windows dialog boxes (they're called "controls") are available in VBA: pushbuttons, check boxes, radio buttons (option buttons), pictures, text boxes, tabs, and so on.

In general, when you want to build a custom dialog box, the general process looks like this:

1. Start with a blank dialog box.
2. Add controls to the box.
3. Write programs to handle various events associated with the controls: what should happen when the user clicks a button, types text, or checks a box, for example.
4. Test the custom dialog box to make sure it contains the controls you specified and that the programs attached to the controls work properly.
5. Repeat and refine.

Say you want to build a custom Word dialog box to handle printing letters. It contains two check boxes: One tells Word to print the current document; the other tells Word to print an envelope. Here's how:

1. Start Word and press Alt+F11 to bring up the VBA Editor. In Project Explorer, navigate to the Normal project.
2. Choose Insert, UserForm. A custom dialog box called UserForm1 appears in the code window, along with a toolbox containing controls you can place on the custom dialog box (see Figure 40.16).

PART
VII

CH
40

Figure 40.16
VBA calls its custom dialog boxes UserForms. This new one gets the name UserForm1.

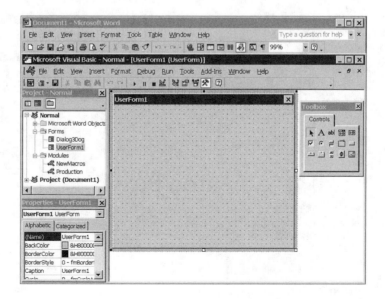

3. To change the name "UserForm1," move down to the Properties window, select the text to the right of the entry (Name), and type a new name—say, PrintLetterEnvelope.

4. To change the title of the UserForm1 window, select the text next to Caption in the Properties window, and replace it with Print Letter and/or Envelope (see Figure 40.17).

Figure 40.17
In the Properties window, the name of the custom dialog box is stored in (Name), and the window title is in Caption.

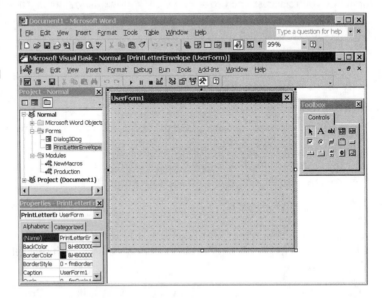

5. Click once on the check box icon in the toolbox. Then click and draw on the blank custom dialog box, as shown in Figure 40.18. Click CheckBox1 and type the text you want to appear in the custom dialog box—for example, Print letter.

Figure 40.18
Draw controls on the custom dialog box by clicking once in the toolbox, and then clicking and dragging on the dialog box.

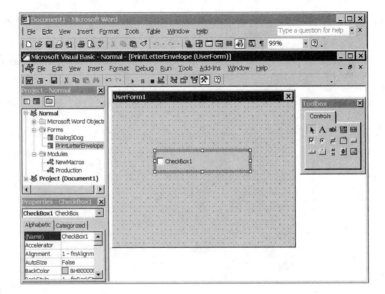

6. Click once more on the check box icon in the toolbox, draw another check box on the custom dialog box, and add the following text: Print envelope.

7. Click once on the Command Button icon in the toolbox. Click and draw a button at the top of the custom dialog box; then click the face of the button and type the text OK.

8. Repeat the procedure and draw a Cancel button, typing the text Cancel on the face of the button. Then, in the Properties window, change the Cancel property to True (see Figure 40.19).

Figure 40.19
Setting the Cancel property for a button to True makes the button work like a Windows-standard Cancel button—click once to dismiss the dialog box, or press Escape to achieve the same result.

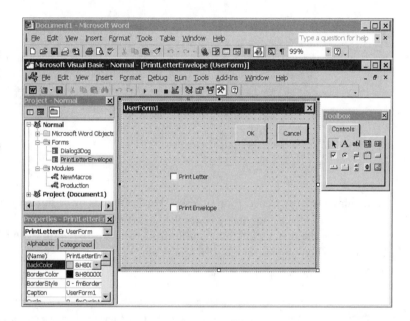

Although the custom dialog box doesn't do anything yet, now's a good time to test it, just to make sure the controls look right. To get the custom dialog box started, you have to create a macro that runs the dialog box. Here's how:

1. Find a convenient module in the Normal project.

2. Choose Insert, Procedure to insert a new macro. Name it PrintLetterOrEnvelope and press Enter. As usual, VBA provides the Sub/End Sub pair.

3. Type this one-line program: PrintLetterEnvelope.Show.

4. To run the macro, press F5. VBA finds the PrintLetterEnvelope custom dialog box, and shows it on the screen (see Figure 40.20). To end the test, click the Close (X) button in the upper-right corner of the custom dialog box.

When you finish running the test, VBA/Word should look like Figure 40.19, shown previously, with the PrintLetterEnvelope custom dialog box showing. To add some intelligence to the custom dialog box:

Figure 40.20
Custom dialog boxes have to be launched—in this case, by a macro. When launched, the dialog box's internal programs take over.

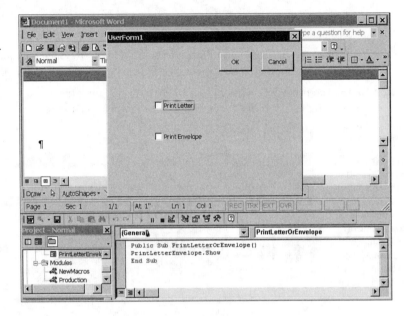

1. Double-click the Cancel button. VBA/Word responds by creating a new subroutine, attached to the custom dialog box, called CommandButton2_Click(). This subroutine will run when the user clicks CommandButton2, which is the button you labeled Cancel. As always, VBA supplies the Sub/End Sub pair.

2. Type this one-line program: End.

> **Note**
>
> The End command removes the custom dialog box from the screen, closes all open files, releases any memory being held for variables, and stops the macro.

3. Bring back the custom dialog box by choosing View, Object. Again, the screen should look like Figure 40.19.

4. Double-click the OK button. VBA/Word creates the subroutine called CommandButton1_Click(). It runs when the user clicks CommandButton1—the one you marked OK. You'll see the Sub/End Sub pair.

5. Type this three-line program:

```
If CheckBox1 Then ActiveDocument.PrintOut
If CheckBox2 Then ActiveDocument.Envelope.PrintOut
End
```

That's it. The custom dialog box is complete. Anytime you want to use this custom dialog box, just run the PrintLetterOrEnvelope macro, using any of the techniques discussed in the first section of this chapter.

TROUBLESHOOTING

MISSING PERSONAL.XLS

I've looked in the Project Explorer, but I can't find my Personal Macro Workbook.

If you don't have a Personal Macro Workbook (stored as Personal.xls), the simplest way to create one is to flip back to Excel and record a do-nothing macro: click Tools, Macro, Record New Macro, and make sure you choose Personal Macro Workbook in the Store Macro In box. Click OK, and then click the Stop button. Excel automatically creates Personal.xls to store the recorded macro.

SECRETS OF THE OFFICE MASTERS: CUSTOM DIALOG BOXES IN VBA

Custom dialog boxes in VBA can successfully mimic any dialog boxes you've ever seen in Windows.

In the Three Dog Orders dialog box in Figure 40.21, you see the familiar file tabs that let you flip back and forth between multiple dialog box divisions. There's nothing particularly magical about them—you can draw them yourself, or steal them from, for example, the Support.dot file that's supplied with Office. (Although you wouldn't want to steal a copyrighted picture or duplicate a copyrighted program, dialog box layouts are fair game.) To get all the Word template goodies Microsoft ships with Office, put the installation CD in your drive, choose Add/Remove Programs, expand the Microsoft Word list, and choose More Templates and Macros.

Figure 40.21

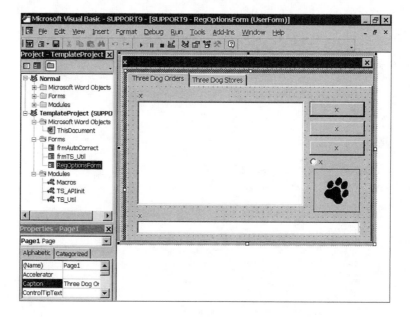

CHAPTER 41

ADVANCED VBA TOOLS AND TECHNIQUES

In this chapter

MANAGING VBA PROJECTS

The preceding three VBA chapters gave you an eagle's-eye view of how to put macros to work in your office. After you move beyond the fundamentals of VBA, becoming truly productive is mostly a question of mastering the vocabulary. In the case of Office XP, that means learning the underlying object models of each of the Office applications. Like any language, VBA gets easier with practice. As you work with VBA and build up a library of macros and code that you want to reuse, managing the collection becomes a challenge.

STORING PROJECTS

When you begin writing macros in Word and Excel, it's easiest to store them in the projects provided by the macro recorder. In Word, that's the Normal project (by default), stored in Normal.dot, or in the current document. Excel reverses the defaults: A recorded macro goes into either the currently open workbook (by default), or the Personal Workbook known as Personal.xls.

Although those locations might be convenient for novices, they're far from optimal. If you want to move your macros from one machine to another, for example, copying Normal.dot or Personal.xls to the new machine will change settings, wipe out existing recorded macros, and generally cause all sorts of headaches.

> **Caution**
>
> Here's another good reason not to use the default macro storage locations. Some viruses actually lock Normal.dot and Personal.xls with a password. (In fact, an old Microsoft *antivirus* product, called Scanprot, password protects Normal.dot.) If you have important macros stored in either of these files and you can't open the file because a virus encrypted them with a password, your macros are lost—and there's nothing you can do to retrieve them.

It's strongly recommended that you store your VBA projects outside of Normal.dot and Personal.xls.

To create a new Word template for macros and make it available for all documents, follow these steps:

1. Choose File, New. Click the Blank Document icon, and choose the Template option under Create New. Click OK. Word creates a new template.

2. Choose File, Save. Navigate to Word's Startup folder (look in Tools, Options, File Locations for the folder's location), give the template a name, and save the file (see Figure 41.1).

3. Exit and restart Word. Choose File, Open, and open the new macros template. Press Alt+F11 to start the VBA Editor and verify that you can place macros in the new template.

Figure 41.1
Create a new template in the Startup directory to hold all your macros. Give it a descriptive name such as Macros.dot.

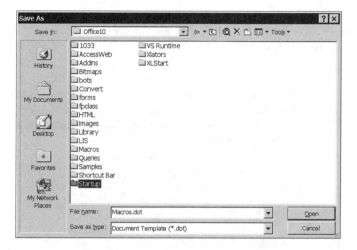

Remember that you must open this new template in Word before the VBA Editor will enable you to make changes to it.

Follow these steps to create a default workbook for storing Excel macros:

1. Start with a clean, empty workbook.

2. Choose File, Save. Navigate to the XlStart folder (typically C:\Program Files\Microsoft Office\Office10\Xlstart), give the workbook a name such as Macros.xls, and save the file (see Figure 41.2).

Figure 41.2
After creating a workbook to store Excel macros, file it in the XlStart folder and mark it as hidden.

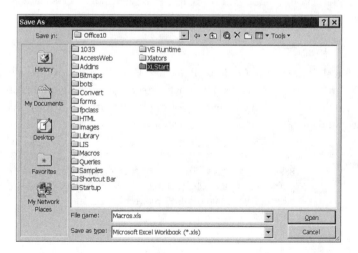

3. Excel automatically opens any workbook in XlStart. To make sure the new workbook doesn't get in the way when you're working with Excel, choose Window, Hide.

4. Exit and restart Excel (you'll be prompted to save Macros.xls again). Press Alt+F11 to start the VBA Editor and verify that you can create macros in this new hidden, autoloading workbook.

Tip from

EQ & Woody

Before you can record or edit macros in this new location, you have to explicitly unhide and select Macros.xls. After you've finished working with your macros, you have to hide the sheet again. Add the following macro code to Macros.xls to make it easier to manage this sheet:

```
Sub SaveAndHideMacrosWorkbook()
' Hides the workbook.
ThisWorkbook.Windows(1).Visible = False
' Saves the workbook after it is hidden.
ThisWorkbook.Save
End Sub
```

Next, choose Tools, Customize. Click the Commands tab, scroll through the Categories list, and choose Macros. Under Commands, click Custom Menu Item. Drag this item onto the Window menu and place it just below the Unhide choice. Right-click the new menu item and change its Name to Save/Hide Macros Workbook. Right-click again and choose Assign Macro from the bottom of the shortcut menu. Assign the macro you just created to the new menu item and click OK. Now, to make macros available for editing, choose Window, Unhide; after you've finished working with the code in this worksheet, choose Window, Save/Hide Macros Worksheet to save your changes and hide the sheet again.

Neither PowerPoint, Outlook, FrontPage, Publisher, nor Access has analogous startup capabilities.

LOCKING VBA PROJECTS

Word, Excel, PowerPoint, Outlook, Publisher, FrontPage and Access all have provisions for password-protecting VBA code. The Lock Project for Viewing option prevents users from seeing, modifying, or even copying any of the VBA source code for procedures, modules, and custom dialog boxes in a given project.

Caution

Before locking VBA source code, it's always a good idea to save a copy of the original project without password protection, in a safe location. That way, if you forget the password, you can reconstruct your work.

To lock a project in Word, Excel, PowerPoint, Outlook, FrontPage, or Access, follow these steps:

1. In Word, Excel, Publisher, or PowerPoint, open the project (template, document, workbook, or presentation). In Access, open the database. In Outlook and FrontPage, you need only start the application.

2. Press Alt+F11 to start the VBA Editor.

3. In Project Explorer, right-click the project and select Project Properties. Click the Protection tab.

4. Check the Lock Project for Viewing box (see Figure 41.3), and provide a password. Click OK, and close the project in the application.

Figure 41.3

Tip from

Ed & Woody

When you lock a project for viewing, the macros still run, but you'll need to supply the password to view, edit, or copy the macros or custom dialog boxes.

Caution

The Lock Project for Viewing password protection scheme is relatively easy to crack. If you really need to keep your source code out of competitors' hands, consider writing your sensitive programs (or parts of programs) in Visual Basic. A compiled VB program has no remnants of source code, and only the most determined and technically proficient hacker can reverse-engineer it.

Access includes the capability to save a database as an MDE file that doesn't include VBA source code. This type of file (which uses the *.mde extension) runs like the original database, but users can't change the VBA modules (or forms or reports, for that matter).

Caution

After converting a database to an MDE file, you can't change it back to a regular database.

To convert a database to an MDE file, first make a copy of the original database, and then choose Tools, Database Utilities, Make MDE File.

CODE SIGNING

Digital signatures form the backbone of Office XP's macro security—in Word, Excel, and PowerPoint, anyway. Digital signatures are also available in Outlook and FrontPage, although they're of limited benefit in those applications because Outlook and FrontPage VBA projects are rarely moved from machine to machine.

A digital signature verifies the identity of the person or organization that created a macro; Office includes features that enable you to preapprove signatures from a particular source.

→ For more information about using digital signatures, **see** "Using Digital Signatures to Verify a Macro's Source," **p. 977**.

If you are writing VBA programs to distribute within your organization, or for general distribution, you must

- Acquire a digital certificate
- "Sign" your VBA project
- Tell the people who will be using your macros what your signature looks like, and what they need to do to get your macros working

> **Note**
>
> If your users have their security setting on High—the default for all Office applications—they won't be able to use your macros, and they won't be told why unless you sign your macros.

→ For more details on setting up security levels to manage macros, **see** "Configuring Office Security Levels," **p. 978**.

You have three options for obtaining a digital certificate:

- You can create an *unauthenticated certificate* by running Selfcert.exe (see Figure 41.4). If you can't find SelfCert.exe on your hard drive, rerun Office XP Setup from the Office CD and click Add or Remove Features. Click the plus sign (+) next to Office Shared Features; click Digital Signature for VBA Projects and then click Run from My Computer. Click Update. This certificate is Stored in the Registry and is required to get past Office Applications' Medium Security Setting. An unauthenticated certificate represents

Figure 41.4

no security at all: Anybody can create an unauthenticated certificate claiming to be Bill Gates, for example. When a user opens a VBA project that's signed with an unauthenticated certificate, he will always be asked to verify that he trusts the source of the project.

- If you work for a large organization, you might be able to get a certificate from your group's certification authority (your network administrator will use Microsoft Certificate Server to generate the file for you).

- You can buy an authenticated certificate from VeriSign (`http://www.verisign.com`) or Thawte (`http://www.thawte.com`)—look for "developer certs" or "software signing Ids." Avoid Class 2 IDs, which certify the existence of a particular e-mail address—Selfcert.exe works just as well. Class 3 IDs, for organizations, costs $200–$400 per year for the first year (subsequent years are half that price). Microsoft maintains links to other certification authorities at `http://officeupdate.microsoft.com/office/redirect/fromOffice9/cert.htm`.

To sign a VBA project, follow these steps:

1. Open the project (template, document, workbook, publication, or presentation) using the associated application.

2. Press Alt+F11 to start the VBA Editor.

3. In Project Explorer, highlight the project you want to sign.

4. Choose Tools, Digital Signatures, Choose (see Figure 41.5). Select either a new signature or change an existing one; click OK.

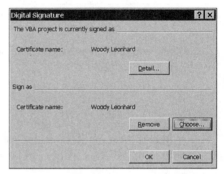

Figure 41.5

> **Note**
>
> You can't sign Excel workbooks (that is, projects) that contain old-fashioned Excel "macro" (XLM) code. Digital signatures are valid only with VBA projects. Because the old XLM macros exist only in spreadsheets (and not in VBA), they can't be signed.

Access does not support the use of digital signatures.

VARIABLE NAMING CONVENTIONS

If you're recording a macro, or making adjustments to a short macro, you probably won't have much trouble following the logic of the code. As macros grow longer, they become increasingly inscrutable, even with extensive inline comments.

Years ago, Microsoft adopted a *variable naming convention* which, if applied religiously, can help you keep track of a program's logic. Often called *Hungarian notation* (in a bit of homage to its inventor, Charles Simonyi), it simplifies the process of scanning through programs by applying consistency to the assignment of variable names.

The part of Hungarian notation that's most useful—and the style you'll see in this book—assigns prefixes to variable names that describe the data type. For example, a variable called `intNumberOfPlaces` is an integer, `strResponse` is a string, and `objExcelWorksheet` is an object. Some of the more common Hungarian notation prefixes are listed in Table 41.1.

TABLE 41.1   COMMON PREFIXES FOR VARIABLE NAMES

Prefix	Meaning	Value
i or int	Integer	–32,768 to 32,767
str	String	A string of almost any length
var	Variant	Number or string; VBA figures out which (notoriously slow and error prone, variants are usually best avoided)
f	Boolean	False (zero) or True (any other value)
cur	Currency	–922,337,203,685,477.5808 to 922,337,203,685,477.5807
byt	Byte	0–255
obj	Object	An object—for example, a reference to an application

Thus, you're likely to see variable declarations at the beginning of well-written programs that look like this:

```
Dim intPointSize as Integer
Dim objExcelWorkbook as Object
Dim strLastName as String
```

Where the `Dim` (or "Dimension") statement tells VBA to set aside storage locations for variables with the given names and attributes.

Arrays of variables follow similar naming conventions. For example, you could set up an array of three different store names like this:

```
Dim strStoreName(3)
strStoreName(1) = "Downtown"
strStoreName(2) = "Woodland Park"
strStoreName(3) = "Westminster"
```

CALLING PROCEDURES IN OTHER PROJECTS

Many developers create libraries of little programs that they like to use over and over again. You can set up program libraries with reusable routines, but there are two tricks:

- The *routines* in the libraries have to be declared *Public*—that is, accessible to programs outside the immediate module—so they have Public Sub or Public Function as their first lines.

- You must explicitly link the calling project to the library project.

Say you've created a Word template called Library.dot, and you've stored it in the \Startup folder so it loads automatically every time Word starts. Library.dot contains a few programs that are declared Public—perhaps a

```
Public Sub Register(strCourseName, strStudent)
```

or a

```
Public Function Calculate(intCourseHours)
```

Further, let's say you have a Word template called Signup.dot, and you want it to be able to use commands from the library, such as

```
Register("ECON 101", "John Adams")
curFee = Calculate(4)
```

Here's how you link the Signup project (that is, template) to the Library project, so those commands will work:

1. In Word, open Signup.dot. Press Alt+F11 to bring up the VBA Editor.

2. In the Project Explorer, double-click the project in which you want to use the external commands—in this example, double-click Signup.

3. Choose Tools, References. Check the box next to the name of the project that contains the code you want to use—in this example, that's Library. (If you can't find the file, click Browse to search through other folders.)

With this link manually established between Signup and Library, the commands that refer to the Library will work.

REJUVENATING VBA

In previous Office versions, VBA would occasionally go out to lunch for no apparent reason—mysterious General Protection Faults occurred, projects wouldn't save correctly, and sometimes entire modules became irretrievably scrambled. Although VBA 6 is not so badly afflicted, three precautions are in order:

- If you're using Windows 95, 98, or Me, restart Windows frequently. With hard VBA work, two or three restarts a day is not out of the question. Constant use of VBA seems to make Windows 95 and 98 unstable, and more prone to General Protection Faults. (If you do a lot of program development, consider switching to Windows 2000, which is far more stable.)

- If VBA starts producing random, inexplicable errors, uninstall and then reinstall the entire Office suite from the original CDs.

- From time to time, create text backups of all your modules and UserForms and save them in a safe place. To do so, select the module or UserForm and choose File, Export File. Choose *Basic Files* (*.bas) format for modules or *Form Files* (*.frm) format for UserForms. Both of these formats produce standard text files that you can import into VBA 6 by choosing Files, Import.

CODE SNIPPETS YOU CAN USE

Although it would take a book this size to explore the VBA object model for just one of the Office applications, most of the programming chores you'll encounter boil down to a handful of common techniques. This section gives you working code you can plug into your macros to overcome the most common problems.

Tip from

ED & Woody

If you want to see more examples of VBA code in action, we recommend that you purchase *Platinum Edition Using Microsoft Office XP*, also published by Que. You'll find real-world, premade code snippets, which you can drop in and use today. Used in tandem with this book, you truly can take control of Office and make it work your way.

USING VBA TO NAVIGATE OFFICE DOCUMENTS

One of the first tasks most beginning VBA programmers undertake is to figure out how to move around a document using VBA commands. Navigation is a fundamental capability of all the versions of VBA in Office XP.

NAVIGATING WORD DOCUMENTS WITH VBA

In Word, you will frequently want to move the insertion point (VBA calls it the "Selection") within a document. It's easiest to understand how VBA/Word accomplishes this navigation by trying a few different VBA/Word commands, and watching what happens on the screen:

1. Open (or create) a Word document that has several paragraphs of text as a test document, so you can see what is going on with each of the different commands.

2. Bring up the VBA Editor by pressing Alt+F11. Arrange the screen so that you can see both the VBA Editor and the Word document at the same time.

3. Find a convenient project in the Project Explorer (say, MyMacros.dot or Normal) and double-click it. Navigate down to a Module. Use Insert, Procedure and create a new subroutine called Navigate.

4. In between the Sub/End Sub pair, type each of these commands, one at a time. Press F8 to step through the subroutine. Watch where your cursor ends up in the Word document:

```
Selection.HomeKey unit:=wdStory, Extend:=wdMove    'Moves to the beginning
➥of the doc
Selection.EndKey unit:=wdStory, Extend:=wdMove     'Moves to the end of the
➥doc
Selection.MoveLeft unit:=wdCharacter, Count:=1, Extend:=wdMove 'Move left
➥one char
Selection.MoveRight unit:=wdWord, Count:=1, Extend:=wdMove 'Move right one
➥word
Selection.MoveUp unit:=wdParagraph, Count:=1, Extend:=wdMove ' Move up one
➥para
ActiveDocument.Bookmarks("test").Select  'Selects the bookmark "test"
```

NAVIGATING EXCEL WORKBOOKS WITH VBA

In Excel, you're less likely to use the insertion point, and will most frequently refer to cells by name or location. Use the method in the preceding section (working with a project such as Personal.xls or Macros.xls) to write and test each of these commands:

```
Range("A1") = "First Cell" 'Put the text "First Cell" in cell A1
Cells.SpecialCells(xlLastCell) = "Last Cell" 'Put the text "Last cell" in the last
➥used cell
```

```
Range("test").Rows(1) = "First Row" 'Put "First Row" in top cells of the range
➥"test"
Range("test").Rows(1).Columns(1) = "First Cell in test"
➥Upper left cell of "test"
```

NAVIGATING POWERPOINT PRESENTATIONS WITH VBA

With the possible exception of Publisher, PowerPoint presents the greatest challenge in navigating the object model. For example, to change the title of the third slide to "Hello," you have to resort to this kludgy technique:

```
ActivePresentation.Slides(3).Shapes.Title.TextFrame.TextRange = "Hello"
```

NAVIGATING PUBLISHER PUBLICATIONS WITH VBA

Publisher's nascent object model makes it difficult to navigate through a publication, unless you know in advance what the publication looks like, which text boxes appear in what sequence, what the text boxes contain, and so on. This command, for example, replaces the text in the currently selected text box with "Hello Publisher!":

```
Selection.TextRange.Text = "Hello Publisher!"
```

USE VBA TO AUGMENT FIND AND REPLACE

Another common activity, Finding and Replacing text from a VBA program, can be challenging. The primary difficulty lies in figuring out precisely when VBA performs the Find (or Replace). Much of the work in implementing a Find is in setting up all the parameters properly.

USING FIND AND REPLACE VBA CODE IN WORD

In Word, if you want to find and replace all occurrences of one string with another, you needn't resort to looping through the document. Instead, the simple VBA snippet in Listing 41.1 will suffice.

LISTING 41.1   REPLACEOLDWITHNEWSTRING

```
With ActiveDocument.Content.Find
    .ClearFormatting
    .Replacement.ClearFormatting
    .Text = "old string"
    .Replacement.Text = "new string"
    .Execute Replace:=wdReplaceAll
End With
```

PART

VII

CH

41

Note

Be sure to use the `.ClearFormatting` property to modify both the `Find` and `Replacement` objects. Otherwise, you might inadvertently search for formatted text using leftover settings from a previous search.

Because this succinct piece of code doesn't refer to the Selection, the user won't see the document scroll and the mouse pointer move while the macro runs. That has its advantages and disadvantages. On the plus side, the macro will run faster because the screen isn't updated each time you find the string. On the minus side, the user might think the macro has frozen her PC because there's no visible sign of life until the macro finishes (unless the macro writes updates to, for example, the status bar).

If you want to loop through a document and count the number of occurrences of, say, "string," moving the selection as you go, use a program like that in Listing 41.2.

LISTING 41.2 COUNTOCCURRENCESOFSTRING

```
intCount = 0
'Move to the beginning of the document
Selection.HomeKey unit:=wdStory
With Selection.Find
    .ClearFormatting
    .Text = "string"
'    Find the first occurrence of "string"
    .Execute
'    Loop while "string" is found
    While .Found
'        Increment the counter
        intCount = intCount + 1
'        And look for another occurrence
        .Execute
    Wend
End With
MsgBox "Found " & Str$(intCount) & " occurrences"
```

USING FIND AND REPLACE VBA CODE IN EXCEL

In Excel, the general approach is similar. For example, to replace "old string" with "new string" in all the cells of the active worksheet, use this:

```
Cells.Replace What:="old string", Replacement:="new string", LookAt:= xlPart,
SearchOrder:=xlByRows, MatchCase:=False
```

Always explicitly include values for LookAt (whether Excel must match the contents of the entire cell, or if only a partial match suffices), SearchOrder, and MatchCase, to avoid picking up leftover settings from a previous Find/Replace operation.

If you want to restrict the replacing to a specific named range (such as Database), try this technique:

```
Range("Database").Replace What:="old string", Replacement:="new string",
➥LookAt:=xlPart, SearchOrder:=xlByRows, MatchCase:=False
```

USING VBA TO APPLY FORMATTING

VBA gives you full control over formatting, although the mechanics of applying formatting can be obscure. For example, if you want to change a selection of text to italic in Word or Excel, this command does the trick:

```
Selection.Font.Italic = True
```

But to turn selected text italic in PowerPoint, you have to jump through this hoop:

```
ActiveWindow.Selection.TextRange.Font.Italic = True
```

Similarly in Publisher:

```
Selection.TextRange.Font.Italic = True
```

Formatting text as you place in it a document, spreadsheet, or presentation is a more complex process. Say you want to insert this sentence into a Word document:

> Please join us at the *Three Dog Delight* gala.

It's easiest to "type" text into the document, interrupting the macro's typing to switch to italic and back. Listing 41.3 has the code that will do it.

LISTING 41.3   TYPEWORDFORMATTEDSTRING

```
With Selection
    .TypeText "Please join us at the "
    .Font.Italic = True
    .TypeText "Three Dog Delight"
    .Font.Italic = False
    .TypeText " gala."
End With
```

Excel's in-cell formatting works in a completely different way. Instead of interrupting the typing to switch to italic and back, Excel requires you to dump all the text into the cell, and then go back and make selected characters italic. To put that same sentence in the selected Excel cell, use the code in Listing 41.4.

LISTING 41.4   INSERTEXCELFORMATTEDSTRING

```
With Selection
    .Value = "Please join us at the Three Dog Delight gala."
    .Characters(23, 17).Font.Italic = True
End With
```

The same concepts apply in PowerPoint as in Excel, although the actual commands vary a bit, as in Listing 41.5.

LISTING 41.5   INSERTPOWERPOINTFORMATTEDSTRING

```
With ActiveWindow.Selection.TextRange
    .Text = "Please join us at the Three Dog Delight gala."
    .TextRange.Characters(23, 17).Font.Italic = True
End With
```

Publisher works similarly:

```
.TextRange.Characters(23, 17).Font.Italic = True
```

Sometimes you want to use formatting as a *selection criterion*. Say you want to loop through a Word document and make sure that all the `"Heading 4"`-style paragraphs start with the text `"(d)"`. The program in Listing 41.6 will do it.

LISTING 41.6   ADDDTOHEADING4

```
'Move to the beginning of the document
Selection.HomeKey unit:=wdStory
With Selection.Find
    .ClearFormatting
    .Style = "Heading 4"
    .Format = True
    .Text = ""
'   Find the first occurrence of "Heading 4"
    .Execute
'   Loop while "Heading 4" is found
    While .Found
'       Move to the beginning of the paragraph
        Selection.Collapse
'       Select the first three characters
        Selection.MoveRight unit:=wdCharacter, Count:=3, Extend:=wdExtend
        If Selection.Text <> "(d)" Then
            Selection.Collapse
            Selection.TypeText "(d)"
        End If
'       Move on to the next paragraph
        Selection.MoveDown unit:=wdParagraph, Count:=1
'       And look for another occurrence
        .Execute
    Wend
End With
```

The `.Format = True` setting in the `Find` loop in Listing 41.6 ensures that Word looks for paragraphs with the specified formatting.

USING VBA TO LOOP THROUGH COLLECTIONS

VBA abounds with *collections*. All the files currently open in an application, for example, define one common collection. Other collections include all the bookmarks in a document, or all the named ranges in a workbook.

Sometimes you know exactly which member of a collection you're trying to find. For example, the VBA/Excel command

```
Workbooks("Book1.xls").Activate
```

scans the `Workbooks` collection, and brings up the workbook called Book1.xls.

At other times, however, you want your program to look at all the members of a collection, one at a time, to see which one meets certain criteria. For example, you might want to loop through all the slides in a presentation to select the one with the most verbiage in a text placeholder.

The VBA command For Each enables you to step through all the members of a collection. In Word, the FontNames collection contains a list of all the fonts available in Word. Listing 41.7 shows you how to loop through the collection, displaying the name of each font in its own message box (see Figure 41.6).

Figure 41.6
Use the VBA/Word FontNames collection to display the names of all available fonts.

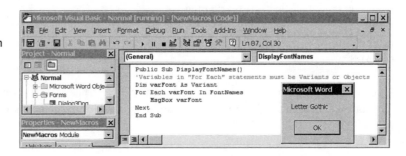

LISTING 41.7   DISPLAYFONTNAMES

```
'Variables in "For Each" statements must be Variants or Objects
Dim varFont As Variant
For Each varFont In FontNames
    MsgBox varFont
Next
```

After you see how For Each works, it's only a small step to write a VBA/Word program that prints a list of all the fonts available on your machine. Taking input from the user for point size and a test sentence, Listing 41.8 shows you how that might be done.

→ To add VBA code that asks the user to enter information, **see** "Displaying Messages," **p. 1021**.

LISTING 41.8   PRINTFONTNAMES

```
Dim varFont As Variant
Dim intPoints As Integer
Dim strTestString As String
intPoints = 11
intPoints = InputBox("Print list at what point size?", "PrintFontNames",
➥intPoints)
If intPoints <= 0 Then GoTo Cancel
strTestString = "The quick brown fox jumped over to greet the lazy
➥poodle."
strTestString = InputBox("Test print text:", "PrintFontNames",
➥strTestString)
Documents.Add
Selection.TypeText "Samples at " & Str$(intPoints) & " points."
Selection.TypeParagraph
Selection.TypeParagraph
For Each varFont In FontNames
    Selection.Font.Size = 11
    Selection.Font.Name = "Arial"
```

PART

VII

CH

41

LISTING 41.8   CONTINUED

```
    Selection.TypeText varFont & ": "
    Selection.TypeParagraph
    Selection.Font.Name = varFont
    Selection.Font.Size = intPoints
    Selection.TypeText strTestString
    Selection.TypeParagraph
    Selection.TypeParagraph
Next
Cancel:
```

If you run the program shown in Listing 41.8, you'll be struck by one severe shortcoming: The font names aren't alphabetized. That problem is solved in the next section.

USING VBA TO SORT AN ARRAY

Unfortunately, collections aren't sorted. When you retrieve items from a collection, as in the preceding section, they can appear randomly. In many cases, that won't do. If you print a list of fonts, especially on a machine with hundreds of installed fonts, you expect to see a neat, alphabetized list. If you present a list of open workbooks and invite the user to choose one, it makes the user's job much easier if you alphabetize the list.

Adding insult to injury, only Word has a built-in Sort function, and it's so well hidden that you're unlikely to find it on your own. The command to sort an array called strFonts() looks like this:

```
WordBasic.sortarray strFonts()
```

VBA/Word's Sort works only on arrays, so if you want to sort a collection (such as the FontNames collection), you first must transfer all the members of the collection into an array. It isn't as complicated as it sounds, as Listing 41.9 demonstrates.

LISTING 41.9   TRANSFERCOLLECTIONTOARRAY

```
Dim i As Integer
Dim varFont As Variant
Dim strFonts() As String
'Adjust the size of the array so it will hold all the font names
ReDim strFonts(FontNames.Count)
i = 1
For Each varFont In FontNames
'    Add each font, in turn, to the array
    strFonts(i) = varFont
'    Then boost the array index by one
    i = i + 1
Next
```

If you combine this technique for transferring a collection to an array with the sort method and the PrintFontNames routine shown earlier in Listing 41.8, and put the "With Selection" command into service, you'll come up with the macro called PrintSortedFontNames, shown in Listing 41.10.

LISTING 41.10   PRINTSORTEDFONTNAMES

```
Dim i As Integer
Dim varFont As Variant
Dim strFonts() As String
Dim intPoints As Integer
Dim strTestString As String
ReDim strFonts(FontNames.Count)
intPoints = 11
intPoints = InputBox("Print list at what point size?", "PrintFontNames",
➥intPoints)
If intPoints <= 0 Then GoTo Cancel
strTestString = "The quick brown fox jumped over to greet the lazy poodle."
strTestString = InputBox("Test print text:", "PrintFontNames", strTestString)
Documents.Add
i = 1
For Each varFont In FontNames
    strFonts(i) = varFont
    i = i + 1
Next
WordBasic.sortarray strFonts()
With Selection
    .TypeText "Samples at " & Str$(intPoints) & " points."
    .TypeParagraph
    .TypeParagraph
    For i = 1 To FontNames.Count
        .Font.Size = 11
        .Font.Name = "Arial"
        .TypeText strFonts(i) & ": "
        .TypeParagraph
        .Font.Name = strFonts(i)
        .Font.Size = intPoints
        .TypeText strTestString
        .TypeParagraph
        .TypeParagraph
    Next
End With
Cancel:
```

CONTROLLING OTHER APPLICATIONS

VBA enables you to control other Office applications—in fact, any application that uses VBA as a macro language, or any application that has been designed to make its internal functions available to other programs (or "exposed"), can be controlled directly via VBA. For example, it's possible (but difficult) to control Outlook 2002 from Word, because Outlook has "exposed" parts of its interface.

What should you call applications that can be controlled by other programs? Microsoft has a long history of terminology changes in this arena. You might hear the terms *OLE Automation Server*, *ActiveX Object*, *ActiveX Container*, or *COM Server* and they all more or less refer to this type of application. If you hear that an application is "exposed," that means you can manipulate it by using the techniques discussed here.

PART

VII

CH

41

STARTING EXCEL WITH A VBA/WORD MACRO

Say you want to create a VBA/Word macro that starts Excel and places some information in a worksheet. For your entrance into Excel, use the `CreateObject()` function, as in Listing 41.11.

LISTING 41.11   RUNEXCELFROMWORD

```
Dim ExcelSheet As Object
Set ExcelSheet = CreateObject("Excel.Sheet")
With ExcelSheet.Application
'    Show Excel with the open sheet
     .Visible = True
     .Cells(1, 1) = "Hello, Excel!"
     .ActiveWorkbook.SaveAs "Excel Test.xls"
     .Quit
End With
Set ExcelSheet = Nothing
```

STARTING WORD WITH A VBA/EXCEL MACRO

Similarly, if you want to create a VBA/Excel macro that starts Word and places information in a document, try the `CreateObject()` function shown in Listing 41.12.

LISTING 41.12   RUNWORDFROMEXCEL

```
Dim objWord As Object
Set objWord = CreateObject("Word.Document")
With objWord.Application
     .Selection.TypeText "Hello, Word!"
     .ActiveDocument.SaveAs "Word Test.doc"
End With
Set objWord = Nothing
```

STARTING POWERPOINT WITH A VBA/WORD MACRO

In the same vein, the VBA/Word program in Listing 41.13 creates and saves a new PowerPoint presentation.

LISTING 41.13   RUNPOWERPOINTFROMWORD

```
Dim objPPT As Object
Set objPPT = CreateObject("PowerPoint.Application")
With objPPT
     .Visible = True
     .Presentations.Add
     .Presentations(1).SaveAs "PowerPoint Test.ppt"
     .Quit
End With
Set objPPT = Nothing
```

COMMONALITIES IN CONTROLLING ONE APPLICATION WITH ANOTHER

All the methods for controlling one application with another have several details in common:

- You have to set up a variable of type "Object" and then Set that variable to the application generated by the CreateObject() function.

- The parameter used in CreateObject() follows a precise format. Word.Document creates a new Word document; Excel.Sheet creates a new Excel workbook; PowerPoint.Application merely invokes PowerPoint, without creating a new presentation.

Caution
> Each Office application includes its own collection of valid CreateObject() strings. No uniformity and precious little documentation exists. Sometimes the application's Help file will tell you; many times, you just have to guess.

- When you're finished working with an object, you should set it to Nothing, to free up any lingering allocations, and dislodge any hidden copies of the program that might be running.

Tip from
EQ & Woody
> It's crucial that you set the object to Nothing because that's the only way Windows knows it should clean up after your application. Windows allocates memory space and other system resources to your program so that it can run. By setting to Nothing, you give Windows a chance to reclaim all the resources it has allocated.

In almost all other respects, Word, Excel, and PowerPoint behave entirely differently when controlled via CreateObject():

- Word, for example, becomes visible as soon as you run a CreateObject("Word.Document"). Excel and PowerPoint, on the other hand, run hidden—you can't see them at all—unless you set the .Visible value to True.

- When you leave a procedure that's been manipulating Word via CreateObject(), Word stays visible on the screen, and any documents you have opened remain open. Excel, on the other hand, disappears.

- Most frustrating of all, Word documents that have been created or opened via CreateObject() remain open after the program finishes. In Excel, if the program stops, all the open workbooks disappear. You must save Excel workbooks before exiting or all the changes will be lost.

Office isn't the only "exposed" application. Windows 98 and Windows 2000 include the Windows Scripting Host, which offers a huge library of file-related routines that you can call from any VBA program.

USING THE OBJECT BROWSER

Learning the nuances of VBA can be as difficult as learning the details of any human language. Fortunately, VBA includes an extremely thorough dictionary that lists all valid commands. Granted, the dictionary doesn't have descriptions of what all those commands mean, but you can often deduce those meanings by seeing the commands themselves.

Microsoft calls the giant dictionary an *object browser*, and it opens up the entire world of object models—not just the ones for Office and your favored variety of VBA, but for any program that can be called from VBA, using the CreateObject() function.

To use the VBA Object Browser

1. Select the programs you want to browse by choosing Tools, References (see Figure 41.7).

Figure 41.7
Check the box for any application you might want to manipulate from VBA, either with programs inside the Office application itself, or via the CreateObject() function.

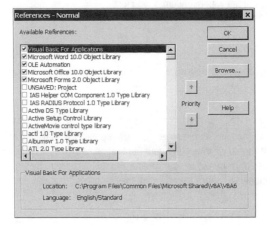

2. Press F2 to display the Object Browser (see Figure 41.8).

3. Select the application that interests you in the Library box, and all the valid commands for that application appear. You can even look for a specific word or string of characters, by typing them in the Search box and clicking the Search button.

If you double-click an object, all the valid properties, methods, and events associated with the object appear on the right. In Figure 41.8, Document.Close shows up as a valid Object.Method pair, and its parameters appear at the bottom of the screen. Choose an object, property, method, or event and press F1 to see context-sensitive help.

To dismiss the Object Browser, press F7 or choose View, Code.

Search for a particular
word or phrase.

Library—select
your application here.

Objects appear
with this icon.

Figure 41.8
The Object Browser
brings up an exhaus-
tive list of all the valid
components of the
underlying object
model.

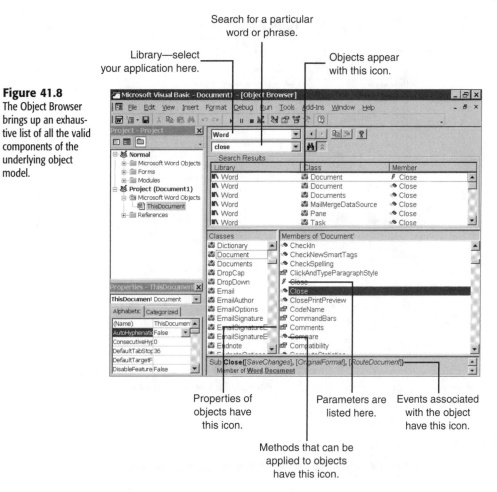

Properties of
objects have
this icon.

Parameters are
listed here.

Events associated
with the object
have this icon.

Methods that can be
applied to objects
have this icon.

SECRETS OF THE OFFICE MASTERS: STUCK ON A LINE OF VBA CODE?

If you get stuck while writing a line of VBA code and don't quite know where to turn, consider right-clicking the command or parameter that's giving you problems, as shown in the
following figure.

PART

VII

CH

41

Figure 41.9

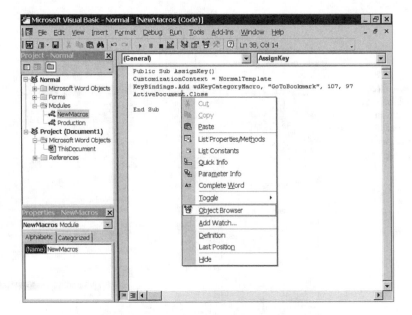

You have these options:

- **List Properties/Methods** gives you a list of all the properties and methods that can replace the property or method you clicked. Pick this option only if you think you've chosen the wrong command.

Figure 41.10

- **List Constants** tells you which other predefined constants can be used to replace the current constant. This can come in handy if you discover you've chosen the wrong constant, and you don't want to use F1 to review all the details about a command.

Figure 41.11

- **Quick Info** summarizes all parameters for a particular command. Use this option if you've somehow switched parameters around on the command line.

Figure 41.12

```
KeyBindings.Add wdKeyCategoryMacro, "GoToBookmark", 107, 97
                  Add(KeyCategory As WdKeyCategory, Command As String,
                  KeyCode As Long, [KeyCode2], [CommandParameter]) As
End Sub            KeyBinding
```

- Parameter Info duplicates the information from Quick Info, except it highlights the parameter where you right-clicked. That can come in handy if you're working with a command (such as MsgBox or InputBox, for example) where it's easy to lose track of which parameter you're working on.

Figure 41.13

```
KeyBindings.Add wdKeyCategoryMacro, "GoToBookmark", 107, 97
                  Add(KeyCategory As WdKeyCategory, Command As String,
                  KeyCode As Long, [KeyCode2], [CommandParameter]) As
End Sub            KeyBinding
```

- Complete Word brings up the auto-completion box you're accustomed to using. It can help if you're backspacing or retyping a command, and the VBA Editor isn't popping up the choices automatically.

Figure 41.14

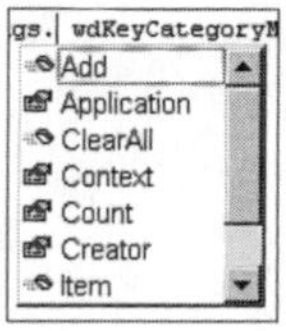

```
gs. | wdKeyCategoryN
     Add
     Application
     ClearAll
     Context
     Count
     Creator
     Item
```

Don't forget to use the Object Browser if you're completely stuck on what objects, properties, and methods might be available. And don't hesitate to hit F1 to bring up the full-blown Help system. Examples in the Help system, in particular, can give you hints that the text never approaches.

PART VIII

APPENDIXES

ADVANCED SETUP OPTIONS

In this appendix

USING THE WINDOWS INSTALLER

If you're installing Office XP on an individual computer at home or in a small office, you don't need any documentation, because the Setup process is almost fully automated. However, if you want to control what actually happens during Setup, or if you're responsible for installing Office on multiple computers, you'll need the information in this appendix. The Office Installer program was introduced with Office 2000, and even expert Office users can be baffled by its intricacies—at least until they have some experience with it.

The easiest way to install Office XP on an individual PC is to insert the first disc in the Office package into the system's CD-ROM drive. If AutoPlay is enabled on the PC in question, Office launches its Setup program automatically and displays the dialog box shown in Figure A.1. If you're upgrading over an existing version of Office, the top button will read Upgrade Now; if Setup does not find an existing version of Office, the button will read Install Now.

Figure A.1
Choose the Custom option to specify a different location for program files. Note that Setup requires space on your system drive even if you specify a different drive.

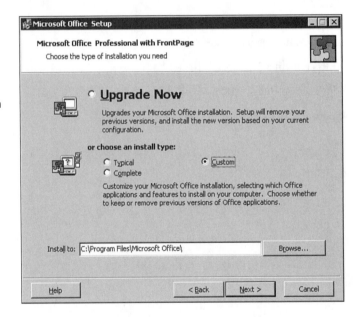

Note
If Setup doesn't run automatically, the most likely reason is that CD-ROM AutoPlay is disabled. In that case, display the contents of the CD and run Setup, or click the Start button, choose Run, and enter <d:>\Setup, substituting the letter of the drive that contains the CD-ROM for <d:>.

The Windows Installer used in Office 2000/XP uses a program called Setup.exe to run the actual installation routine. Besides the name, however, this version of Setup has nothing in common with the Acme Setup program used in Office 97 and other pre-2000 Microsoft programs. Instead, Setup.exe is a small *bootstrap program* whose only purpose is to perform some basic system checks and then pass *command-line parameters* based on its findings to the Windows Installer, which actually does the work of setting up Office.

> **Note**
>
> For an abbreviated list of command-line parameters for Setup.exe, open a Command Prompt window and type Setup /?. For a detailed explanation of how each switch works, search the Office section of Microsoft's Knowledge Base using the string "setup switches."

When you run Setup for the first time, it checks to see whether the Windows Installer, Msiexec.exe, is present; if this program is not available, Setup installs it in the System folder. The Windows Installer is a standard part of Windows 2000/Me/XP; if necessary, Setup will install or upgrade this program and some support files on a system running Windows 95/98/NT 4.0.

> **Caution**
>
> If you are running Setup on a Windows NT 4.0 system, you must log in with administrative privileges before Setup will add the installer components. If the Installer program is installed on the computer already, it isn't necessary to log in as administrator to run the Office XP Setup program.

After you run Setup, it hands off control to the Windows Installer, which uses a variety of files to control how Office XP is installed:

- *Installer package files* are the most important pieces. These files, which use the *.msi extension, contain all the information necessary to install Office XP. Information in this package includes a list of the component files and Registry settings in each feature, the proper installation sequence, destination folder paths, system dependencies, and installation options. The default installer package for Office XP Professional with FrontPage is called Proplus.msi. Depending on your version of Office, it's possible that some installer packages will be found on other CDs or will use a different name.

> **Note**
>
> It's important to note that the package file does not actually contain any Office program files. Instead, it points to the location where the Windows Installer can find those files—on a CD or a network share, for example. After installation, the Windows Installer uses the package file to add, remove, repair, or replace features and components.

- *Transform files*, which use the *.mst extension, contain custom settings that tell Setup to modify the default parameters defined in the package file. If you use the Custom Installation Wizard, for example, you create a transform file that contains all your custom settings. (The Custom Installation Wizard is covered in detail later in this appendix.)

APP

A

- *Configuration files*, which use the *.ini extension, contain instructions that Setup can use to define which package and transform files to use, and can also contain a long list of custom options. By default, Setup looks for a file called Setup.ini and uses its settings; if you want to use a custom configuration file, run Setup with the /Settings switch followed by the name and full path of the .ini file you want to use.

 If you encounter an error message when you first run Setup, see "Some Features Not Available" in the "Troubleshooting" section at the end of this appendix.

ACTIVATING YOUR COPY OF OFFICE

After you complete the Setup process from a retail or OEM version of Office XP, Office is available for immediate use. However, you may be required to complete one final step before you can continue using Office past an initial trial period. For these copies, you must *activate* the product by contacting Microsoft over the Internet or by phone. This measure is intended to stop piracy by refusing to activate a copy of Office XP that has already been installed on another computer already.

For most users with an Internet connection, product activation happens automatically and takes only a few seconds. The activation process generates a "fingerprint" based on the hardware in your system and then associates that ID code with your 25-character Product ID. If you reinstall the software on the same system (after reformatting the hard drive, for instance), reactivation should be automatic. If you try to install the software on another machine with substantially different hardware, however, you may have to call Microsoft to get a new activation code.

Adding a new hard drive or video card will not trigger a demand for reactivation, but substantially upgrading a PC (by swapping the motherboard and switching hard drives and replacing the network card) probably will. In any case, you can reinstall Office XP an unlimited number of times on the same hardware.

A product activation reminder pops up each time you start a new Office program. If you don't have ready access to the Internet, you can delay activation, but don't wait too long. Without activating the product, you can use individual Office programs a maximum of 50 times (each time you launch a different program counts as a single use, even if you are forced to restart after a crash); after you use your 50 free starts, a process that can take less than a week, Office switches into a limited mode that allows you to open files but not edit or save them.

PERFORMING A CUSTOM INSTALLATION

When you click Install Now or Upgrade Now to install Office XP, Setup uses the following default options:

- Program files go in a default location, and you do not have an opportunity to specify a different location.

- Setup removes your previous Office installation (if any) and replaces all installed programs, which migrates your personal settings and preferences to Office XP.

- On systems running Internet Explorer 4.0 or earlier, the current default browser is replaced with Internet Explorer 5.01 with Service Pack 1. This option affects only users of Windows 95, Windows 98 (original release), and Windows NT 4.0, and then only if they have not already upgraded to any version of IE5. This step eliminates previous versions of Internet Explorer; however, it does not remove Netscape Navigator or other non-Microsoft browsers.

- Setup installs a standard set of features. In the case of an upgrade, it automatically replaces all previously installed components with new versions, even if they're not part of the standard install.

Tip from

Ed & Woody

If you're not sure whether to use the Custom Installation option, choose it anyway. When you do, Setup lets you review all options, and if you accept the default settings at every opportunity, the effect is the same as if you had performed a standard installation.

⚠ *If you performed a default installation and some Office features are missing, see "No Packages for You" in the "Troubleshooting" section at the end of this appendix.*

SELECTING AN INSTALLATION LOCATION

We strongly recommend that you accept the default location for installing Office XP, if practical. Normally, this is the Program Files folder on the same drive as Windows—usually C:. If you installed Windows on a different drive, the Program Files folder will be on that drive instead.

Two good reasons to specify a different location from the default include the following:

- You do not have sufficient free space on the default drive. In this case, choose another drive that does have enough space for Office and its program files. Note, however, that Office still insists on putting some files on the same drive with Windows.

- You want to continue to use your previous version of Office. In that case, as explained in the following section, you must specify a different location or Setup overwrites all your existing Office files.

To choose an alternative location for Office XP, use the Customize option and select a new location in the dialog box shown previously in Figure A.1.

Caution

Be careful when installing Office on systems with limited free drive space. The Setup program requires a considerable amount of free space to extract and work with temporary files. Even if you have room for all the options you select, you might encounter a disk-space error if there isn't extra working space for Setup.

CONFIGURING INDIVIDUAL OFFICE PROGRAMS

To perform a custom setup, you'll use two dialog boxes that allow you to change which pieces of Office are installed. The Windows Installer distinguishes between *applications*, which are major pieces of the package, and *installation options*, which comprise the files, programs, *dynamic link libraries* (DLLs), and Registry entries that make up each feature.

The wizard screen shown in Figure A.2 lets you choose not to install specific programs. By default, all boxes are checked; clear the check mark to the left of a program to specify that you want to skip that application.

Figure A.2
For maximum control over how Office programs are installed, choose the option at the bottom of this dialog box.

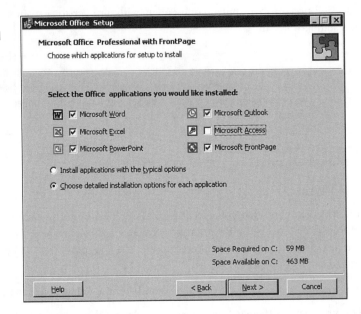

If you select Choose Detailed Installation Options for Each Application, clicking Next displays the dialog box shown in Figure A.3. The icon to the left of each feature shows how it will be installed. A white box with a drive icon means all options will be installed using the method you've specified; a gray box with a drive icon means that some of the options available in that feature will not be installed. Click the plus sign to the left of each feature to see a list of options and adjust each one as needed.

In Office XP, as in Office 2000, you can configure each Office feature separately, saving considerable disk space. For example, if you use Word and Excel regularly but you rarely use PowerPoint or Access, you can set up Word and Excel to run from your local computer but run PowerPoint and Access from the network server.

Figure A.3
By using a custom installation, you can select installation options for each Office application.

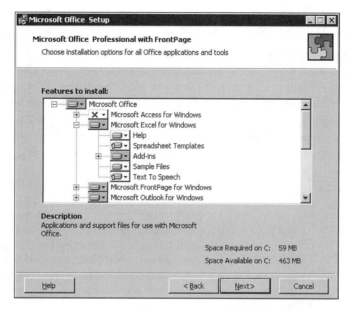

Four settings are available for most features and options. Click the drop-down arrow to the left of any feature to see a full list of options, as shown in Figure A.4.

Figure A.4
When setting up Office, you can choose whether and how to run each feature.

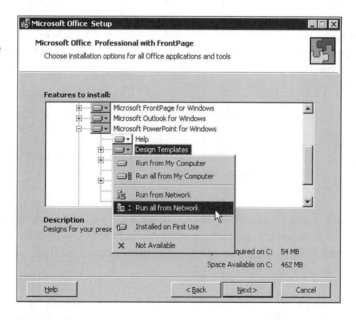

- When you choose Run from My Computer, Setup copies all associated program files to the specified location on the user's hard disk, and the application runs the feature locally. This option results in the best performance. Choose Run All from My Computer to apply this setting to all options under the selected feature.

- Depending on how you install, you can choose either Run from CD or Run from Network for some features. In this configuration, Setup leaves all associated program files on the source CD or on the network installation point. When you run a feature installed by using this option, Office uses the CD or network connection to load program files. This option minimizes the amount of disk space used on the local PC, but it also decreases performance. Use this installation option only for features that are rarely used, and only when the user has a persistent and reliable network connection or easy access to the Office CD-ROM. Choose Run All from Network or Run All from CD to apply this setting to all options under the selected feature.

Tip from	Run from CD or Run from Network are excellent choices for Help files and other options you don't use often. For example, the VBA Help files take up well over a megabyte of disk space and are configured by default to install on first use. If you rarely need access to these Help files and have ready access to a network installation point, reset this option to Run from Network to prevent Setup from adding the files to your local hard disk.

- When you specify Installed on First Use for a feature, Setup creates a menu item or shortcut for the specified feature, but does not install the files associated with the feature. When you first use that menu choice or shortcut, the Windows Installer copies the necessary files to the local hard disk just as if you had chosen the Run from My Computer option. You might be prompted to insert the Office CD to complete the installation.

Tip from	Be extremely careful when using this option on portable computers. If you configure a system option to Installed on First Use, the Windows Installer must be able to access the CD-ROM or network installation point to complete the installation. If you're on an airplane and the CD is on your desk back at the office, you will be unable to use this feature until you return home.

- Choose Not Available when you do not want to install a feature or create shortcuts that refer to it. In some cases, built-in menus include options that refer to features you've chosen not to install; if you select one of these menus, you'll see an error message that instructs you to rerun Setup.

Note that you can set an entire application to be installed on first use. This option might be useful in a setup in which disk space is at a premium and some users are unlikely to need specific applications. If you're installing Office XP on a PC whose primary user is unlikely to need to create PowerPoint presentations, for example, you can save disk space by setting that application up as Installed on First Use. The first time the user clicks the PowerPoint icon on the Start menu, PowerPoint installs itself automatically if the shared network distribution point is available; otherwise, the Windows Installer prompts the user to supply the Office XP CD-ROM.

SAVING YOUR PREVIOUS OFFICE VERSION

If you have sufficient free disk space and you want to preserve the capability to run previous versions of Office programs, choose Customize at the initial Setup screen. When you see the dialog box that asks whether you want to remove previously installed applications (Figure A.5), inspect the list of available programs and clear the check mark next to the box for any program you want to keep. Note that you cannot run two versions of Outlook on the same computer. If you install Outlook 2002, you must uninstall any previous version of Outlook.

Figure A.5
If you want to continue to use previous versions of any Office programs, clear the check marks in this dialog box. This example keeps the previous versions of Word and Excel.

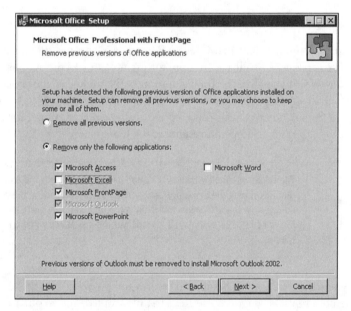

Tip from
EQ & Woody

In Office 2000, keeping separate versions of Office applications required that you specify a different location for program files. Office XP does not require any such rigmarole. Leave the default directory in the initial dialog box; the Windows Installer will sort out files appropriately.

In general, Office XP does a good job of respecting earlier versions of Office. All your preferences, for example, are stored in separate branches of the Registry based on the version number, so customizations you make in one program will not affect the other. However, some unavoidable side effects are caused by using multiple Office versions:

APP

A

- Launching document icons (by double-clicking icons in an Explorer window, for example) launches the Office XP version of the program. If you want to open a document in Word 2000, for instance, you must open the program first and then open the file.

- Some incompatibilities exist between file formats, and using an Office 97 program to edit a file created in Office XP might expose these differences.

- Because of changes in VBA object models or capabilities, macros you create in Office XP might not work properly when opened in earlier Office versions. This is especially true of Outlook macros, because Outlook 97 and Outlook 98 do not support VBA. Although Outlook 2000 and Outlook 2002 use VBA, previous versions of Outlook used VBScript.

→ For a discussion of file-format options, **see** "Using Alternative File Formats," **p. 66**.

FIXING SETUP PROBLEMS

Thanks to the Windows Installer, Office XP Setup is a far more robust process than in previous Office versions. A "rollback" option, for example, tracks the actions of the Setup program as it works. If you click the Cancel button in the middle of the process, Setup uses this feature to undo any Registry changes or delete any files you've copied so far. If Setup is interrupted for any other reason—by a system crash or power failure, for example—you should be able to restart Setup and resume at the place where it stopped previously.

Tip from	The Windows Installer creates a hidden folder called Config.msi to store files it removes during the Setup process so that you can roll back to the previous installation if necessary. If you find this folder on your computer after successfully installing Office XP, you can safely eliminate it and recover the disk space without any dire consequences.

Unless you specify otherwise, Setup also creates and saves log files that contain information on all Setup actions—changes to the Registry, files copied, and so on. You can locate these files in your system's Temp directory; each one begins with the name of the Office version, followed by the word Setup and a number. You can open each file by using WordPad or any text editor.

USING SETUP IN MAINTENANCE MODE

When you run Setup on a system that has Office installed already, you'll see the Maintenance Mode Options dialog box shown in Figure A.6. Use this dialog box when you want to add or remove features, when you need to repair an Office installation that is not functioning properly, or when you want to completely uninstall Office XP.

Figure A.6
After you install Office XP, running Setup displays the Maintenance Mode Options dialog box.

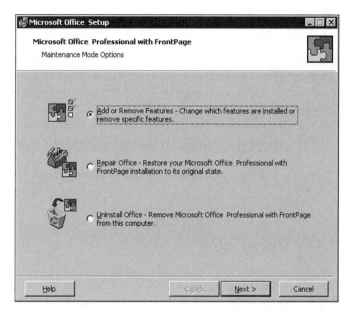

You can start Setup in Maintenance Mode by running Setup from the CD or network installation point, or by using the Add/Remove Programs option in Control Panel.

ADDING AND REMOVING OFFICE FEATURES

To change the list of installed Office features after running Setup for the first time, run Setup in Maintenance Mode and click the Add or Remove Features button. The resulting dialog box is nearly identical to the list of features available when you perform a custom installation, as described previously. You can also use this dialog box to change the configuration of a feature—for example, to change a feature that is installed to run from the local computer so that it runs from a CD or the network instead, using one of these techniques:

- To add a feature so that it is available at all times, check the Run from My Computer, Run from CD, or Run from Network check boxes.

- To configure a feature so that it is available for installation when needed, select the Installed on First Use option.

- To remove a feature, select Not Available.

REPAIRING AN OFFICE INSTALLATION

The Windows Installer maintains a complete record of all Office components you've installed. If you accidentally delete a file or a Registry entry becomes corrupted after installation, the Windows Installer can automatically reinstall the component the next time you try to use it. In most cases, these repairs are automatic: If a key DLL for Publisher is missing when you attempt to launch the program, for example, the Installer starts automatically

APP

A

and reinstalls the missing file from the original installation source. You might need to supply the Office CD to continue.

If you suspect that some features of an application might be damaged, you can force Setup to inspect all essential files for that application and reinstall any files that are missing or corrupted. To use this option, choose Help, Detect and Repair. You'll see the dialog box shown in Figure A.7; click Start to continue.

Figure A.7
If you've inadvertently deleted one or more shortcuts for an application, use the Detect and Repair option to restore the shortcuts and any missing program files.

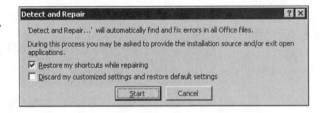

The Detect and Repair option works only on the application from which you run it. If you're unable to start that application, or if you suspect that several programs are damaged, rerun Setup in Maintenance Mode and choose Repair Office. This option lets you choose whether to completely reinstall Office using all the settings you originally specified, or whether the Windows Installer should look for missing or corrupted files and Registry settings and repair them as needed.

UNINSTALLING OFFICE XP

The final option in the Maintenance Mode dialog box, Uninstall Office, lets you completely uninstall Office XP and all associated features and components. When you choose this option, you see one and only one dialog box asking you to confirm that you want to remove Office completely. If you click OK, the Windows Installer begins the uninstall process immediately.

Tip from
EQ & Woody

Thanks to the Windows Installer's rollback capability, you can abort the uninstall process at any time before completion, and Setup restores your system to its previous state. A progress bar moves from left to right as the Windows Installer removes components; if you click the Cancel button, watch the progress bar move from right to left as the Windows Installer undoes its actions and restores the original configuration.

You should be aware of three caveats when uninstalling Office:

- Uninstalling Office XP does not remove Internet Explorer 5. Depending on your system configuration, you might not be able to uninstall IE5 by using the Add/Remove Programs option in the Windows Control Panel, although you will still be able to remove Office. If IE5 was included with your operating system rather than installed as an upgrade to IE4, for example, it cannot be removed.

- Using the Uninstall Office option effectively deletes virtually all program files and associated Registry entries. However, it leaves behind a considerable number of Registry entries associated with user settings and preferences, as well as some files that contain user settings. If you attempt to reinstall Office later, the new installation will use these settings. For instance, if you've defined alternate locations for documents, these will appear in your new installation, as will Excel macros in a leftover Personal Macro Workbook.

- If you upgraded over an earlier version of Office, removing Office XP will not bring back the previous version. The only way to preserve older Office versions is to specifically choose that option by performing a custom install of Office XP in the first place.

INSTALLING OFFICE FROM A NETWORK

If you have access to a network and you have purchased a Select or Enterprise version of Office XP, you can set up Office so that users install from a shared folder on a network server. This approach has significant advantages over the tedious alternative of performing a CD-based install for each user:

Note

This option was previously available with the retail and OEM versions of Office 2000. With Office XP, attempting to use the administrative setup option with a retail or OEM CD will produce an error message.

- Users can install Office on their schedule. Administrators can make it even easier by providing a custom shortcut that runs the Setup program when double-clicked.

- When you access a feature that is set to be installed on first use, you'll reconnect with the administrative installation point automatically instead of having to find and insert the CD-ROM.

- Experienced administrators can create custom installations with different sets of features and options for different groups of users.

CREATING A NETWORK INSTALLATION POINT

Before you can install Office XP over a network, you must create an *administrative installation point*—a server share that contains all the Office files. After completing this step, you can customize installation options if necessary, and then run Setup directly from each user's computer.

To create an administrative installation point for Office, follow these steps:

1. Create a share on a network server to use as the administrative installation point. For Office XP Professional with FrontPage, this share must have at least 650MB of free disk space. Adjust permissions so you have write access to this folder and other users have read access to it.

APP

A

Tip from

EQ & Woody

When creating a shared folder, give it a name that makes its purpose obvious. For example, you might create a folder called D:\MSO-XP and share it using the same name. Users can connect to the share by using UNC (Universal Naming Convention) syntax (*server**share*). If the shared folder is on a server called Marketing, for example, users will be able to open a window showing the shared files by clicking the Start button, choosing Run, and entering the command \\Marketing\MSO-XP.

2. On a computer running Windows 95/98/Me, Windows NT/2000, or Windows XP, connect to the share you just created and verify that you can write files to this location.

3. Insert the Office XP CD into the CD-ROM drive on your computer, click the Start button, and choose Run. In the Run box, enter the command `<d:>\setup.exe` `/a packagename`, substituting the drive letter of your CD-ROM for `<d:>` and the name of the installed package you're trying to install for `packagename`. (Proplus.msi, for example, is the package file for Office XP Professional with FrontPage; the /a switch runs Setup in Administrative Mode.) Click OK.

4. In the Administrative Mode Setup dialog box, follow the wizard's prompts and enter all required information, including the CD key and the organization name you want to define for all users who install Office from this location.

5. When you reach the Microsoft Office XP Location box, enter the name of the server and share you created in step 1.

6. Click Install Now to begin copying files to the share. Setup creates a hierarchy of folders in the share you created, and then copies all files from the Office CD to their respective locations. Setup also creates the package file (Proplus.msi) that tells the Windows Installer that this is an administrative installation point.

Tip from

EQ & Woody

If you have a large network and you want users to be able to choose from several administrative installation points, you can run Setup again for each administrative installation point. However, it's easier to copy the complete folder hierarchy and files to multiple servers, and then create a network share for the copy.

RUNNING SETUP FROM THE NETWORK

To customize the installation process and adjust default settings, you can use either of two options:

- Run Setup with a custom command line. There are dozens of switches and parameters you can tack onto the end of the command line. If the parameter requires that you enter information (such as a username or company name), add an equal sign after the parameter and enclose the custom information in quotes. For example, use this command to run Setup in "quiet" mode, without displaying any dialog boxes, rebooting automatically, and not upgrading Internet Explorer:

```
Setup /qn REBOOT="Force" NOIE
```

- Edit the Settings.ini file in the root of the shared folder so that anyone who runs Setup from this location uses the settings you specify here. Available options here are the same as those you can use at the command line. You can also create a custom settings file and specify it on a command line using the /settings switch after the Setup command; this technique is useful if you want to create multiple custom configurations for different types of users.

Table A.1 lists some useful *parameters* you can add as part of the Setup command line. For parameters that require an additional value, follow the parameter with an equal sign and then the value. You can also enter these parameters in Settings.ini, under the [Options] heading.

TABLE A.1 COMMON CUSTOM SETUP PARAMETERS

Parameter	Values
COMPANYNAME	Enter the organization name in quotes.
USERNAME	Enter the username in quotes.
NOCOMPANYNAME,NOUSERNAME	Use either or both of these parameters when setting up Office on a multiuser system; each user will be prompted to enter his username and company name at the beginning of Setup.
INSTALLLOCATION	Enter the full path of the folder where you want to install Office program files.
REBOOT	Use any of the following settings after this parameter:
	OnlyIfNeeded Setup reboots if required.
	Force Setup always reboots after completing.
	Suppress Setup does not reboot to update system files but can reboot for other startup functions.
	ReallySuppress Setup does not reboot under any circumstances.
SOURCELIST	Specify a list of network shares to search for install packages; separate individual share names with semicolons.
TRANSFORMS	Enter the name and path of the transform file to use during Setup.
NOIE	TRUE (the default) means do not upgrade to IE5; enter FALSE to force upgrade.

APP

A

Note

> For a complete list of setup switches and the syntax for editing settings files, look in the Office XP Resource Kit. Full documentation should be available for download from Microsoft's Office Web site, http://www.microsoft.com/office.

USING THE CUSTOM INSTALLATION WIZARD

For the absolute maximum in control over all details of Office XP Setup, use the Office Custom Installation Wizard. This utility, available free as part of the Office Resource Kit on Microsoft's Web site, is a 17-step wizard that lets you specify the exact mix of features you want to install and options you want to use in an Office installation. Although it takes some time to run through each step, the results are well worth it. You can choose exactly which features to install, define the names and locations of shortcuts, configure IE5 options, install other programs or add data files and templates to a user's machine, and even configure Outlook accounts and profiles (see Figure A.8).

Figure A.8
The Custom Installation Wizard lets you define literally every aspect of an Office XP installation, including Outlook setup options.

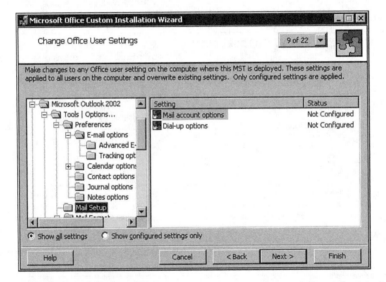

Tip from
EQ & Woody

> Although most people think of the Custom Installation Wizard as a tool for use in organizations, you can benefit from it even if the only machine you administer is your own. Before you set up Office XP for the first time, run through the Custom Installation Wizard and select each option carefully; when you're finished, you'll be able to install the entire program in full confidence that your configuration will appear exactly the way you want it. Run the Setup program from the CD, but specify the full path for the transform file in a command-line switch. Save the transform file in a safe place so you can reuse it if you ever need to reinstall Office.

After running through the wizard, save the results as a Windows Installer transform file with the *.mst extension. When you run Setup, add the TRANSFORMS option on the command line or in a settings file; for example, if you create a transform file called Custom.mst, use the following command line to install Office exactly as you defined it in the Custom Installation Wizard:

```
Setup.exe TRANSFORMS="Custom.mst"
```

Using a transform file does not affect the original package file. As a result, you can create as many different transforms as you want, one for each type of custom configuration you want to install.

BACKING UP USER SETTINGS

One of the most frustrating aspects of configuring Office is the lengthy set of customization options you have to go through when you first install the software. If you're particular about user preferences, such as those found in the Options dialog box for virtually all Office programs, installing Office on a new computer is particularly vexing. It can take days or weeks to reset all preferences so the programs work the way you want them to work. And some settings—such as custom dictionaries, AutoCorrect and AutoText entries, and macros—require painstaking backup and restore routines to transfer from one computer to another.

If you want to back up your preferences and settings once and for all so you can restore them on demand, use an Office tool called the Save My Settings Wizard. This wizard backs up your settings and saves them to a file or to secure, protected storage on Microsoft's Web site. As Figure A.9 shows, the wizard lets you save a file and restore it to a new or existing Office installation, enabling you to quickly transfer preferences on demand, without having to wade through dialog boxes.

Figure A.9
Use the Save My Settings Wizard to back up and restore your Office settings and preferences.

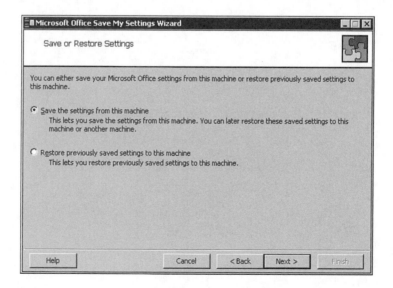

APP

A

TROUBLESHOOTING

No Packages for You

When I run Setup, I see an error message that says the program couldn't find a package to install.

It's unlikely you'll see this message when running Setup from the CD. If you're running Setup from a shortcut on a local hard disk, check the parameters on the command line; there's a good chance they refer to a settings file that is unavailable. If you're running Setup from a network share, open the Setup.ini file and make sure the line that begins MSI= points to the correct package file. You will also see this error message if two or more package files are in the same folder and you have not specified which one to use, either in Setup.ini or in a custom settings file.

Some Features Not Available

After upgrading a previous version of Office, some programs or features are not available.

If you click the Upgrade Now option, Setup installs Office XP components only when the corresponding earlier program or feature is already on the computer. If you performed a custom install of Office 97 and opted not to install a particular feature, the Office XP Setup program uses those options rather than the defaults for a new installation. To install the missing pieces, rerun Office XP Setup.

WHAT'S ON QUE'S WOPR XP/2002 PACK

In this appendix

WOPR XP/2002

Because of the security model in Microsoft Office XP, it is possible that the security settings in Office might prevent some of the applications on the web site from running. Many of these applications are based on macros in templates. Although all the macros and templates on this site are virus-free, Office security settings might prevent them from running anyway. If your Office security settings are set to High, unsigned macros will not run and you will not be given a prompt to change them. You can change this option by following the directions discussed in this book. If your company has "locked" your copy of Office to prevent you from changing this setting, you will need to contact your Office XP administrator where you work to change this setting to allow these to run.

> **Caution**
>
> Some of the macros have been signed with a digital certificate to authenticate who the creator was. With these, you might be prompted whether or not to run them and asked whether you "trust" the signer. You should accept the prompt to allow the template or macro to work correctly.

Of course, the centerpiece of *WOPR XP/2002 software* is WOPR (pronounced "whopper") XP/2002 itself. WOPR XP/2002 is available exclusively through Que books and Pearson Technology Group. If you've never used WOPR before, you'll be impressed with the wide array of new features it brings to Office XP. If you have used WOPR before, you'll love the speed and flexibility of this improved version. WOPR XP/2002 takes full advantage of all the Office XP improvements, including task panes and Smart Tags. It now loads and runs faster than ever before. And, many of the features of WOPR are now available not only in Word but also Excel and the other Office applications.

The copy of WOPR XP/2002 on *Que's Office XP Web Site* is *fully licensed* at no additional cost to you. This isn't shareware, freeware, trialware, demoware, or limited in any other way. Previous versions of WOPR cost more than the price of this book, and now you are getting WOPR and *Special Edition Using Microsoft Office* XP for less than the cost of the software. No other Office book gives you a value like this at no extra charge.

As with any other software, however, WOPR XP/2002 does have a license agreement. Be sure to read that and agree to it before using the software.

What Does WOPR XP/2002 Do?

Many individual modules make up WOPR XP/2002. These are the key modules:

- **WOPR Commander**—This feature is new for Office XP. This system tray component runs down in the Windows taskbar—right next to the clock—and allows you to control and configure all aspects of WOPR from one convenient location.

- **Enveloper**—With Enveloper, you create envelope templates that define exactly how your envelopes will look. You can have as many envelope templates as you want, formatted any way you like with graphics and fonts and notes—and, yes, you can put the bar code down at the bottom (or anywhere else for that matter).

- **City2Airport Smart Tags**—Get the airport name or code for any city typed into your documents (using Microsoft Word's all new Smart Tags interface), view online maps of the city or its airport region, and get driving directions to or from the city's airport.

- **Task Pane Controller**—Quickly and easily control all the Word task pane's advanced features.

- **Lookup ZIP+4**—Look up ZIP+4 Codes from the United States Postal Service (USPS) Web site.

- **Pop-up Contacts List**—Insert a contact from Outlook's contacts list, quickly and easily.

- **Insert Picture**—Get quick access to your graphics images, with more options and flexibility than Word's Insert Picture tool.

- **Lil' WOPRs**—These are small, fast tools that you'll use every day for managing files, adding digital signatures to your documents, printing, viewing special characters, fixing ASCII line breaks, removing potentially embarrassing personal information from your documents, and much more.

These are just a few of the fabulous WOPR XPtools.

DOWNLOADING AND INSTALLING WOPR XP/2002

To download WOPR XP/2002, do the following:

1. Download the WOPR-XP/2002 software directly from the Que's online Office XP resource. Just follow the prompts you see onscreen.

2. You are asked to select which WOPR components you want to install. By default, all options are selected. (You might want to go ahead and install all WOPR tools because you can easily remove any unneeded components later.)

3. Click Next to finish the first stage of the installation.

   The Install Wizard starts Word to finish the installation. After it has completed the installation, Word will close.

Most of the WOPR components install with no further prompts, but some, such as Enveloper, have their own additional installers, which run when you first attempt to use them.

ADDING COMPONENTS

If you performed a partial installation, and you want to install any component that you missed, 'select Add/Remove WOPR Components from the WOPR Commander system tray menu. Select any component that wasn't installed, and follow the prompts.

UNINSTALLING

WOPR XP/2002 has two uninstall options. You can do a complete uninstall or a partial uninstall.

UNINSTALLING WOPR XP/2002 COMPLETELY

To uninstall WOPR XP/2002 completely, follow these steps:

1. Close all Office XP applications.
2. Click Start, Settings, Control Panel. Double-click Add/Remove programs.
3. Scroll down to WOPR XP/2002 and click the Add/Remove button. Follow the prompts.

UNINSTALLING SOME WOPR XP/2002 COMPONENTS

To perform a partial uninstall, follow these steps:

1. Run the WOPR-XP.EXE program. Click Next until you get to the Select Components dialog box.
2. Uncheck any component you want to uninstall, and click the Next button.
3. Follow the prompts.

UPDATING WOPR XP/2002 TO THE LATEST VERSION

WOPR XP/2002 includes a sophisticated update program, which ensures that you always have the latest version. If you want to use the automated WOPR XP/2002 software updating system, do the following:

1. Connect to the Internet with your dial-up connection.
2. From the WOPR Commander system tray, choose Help, WOPR on the Web, and then select Check for Updated Software.
3. Your version of WOPR is updated automatically.

To perform a manual update, do the following:

1. From the WOPR Commander system tray menu, choose About WOPR. Note your version number.

2. Find the latest version of WOPR XP/2002 on our Web site at
   `http://www.wopr.com/wopr-xp`.

3. If the version displayed is a later version than what you have installed, download it into a temporary directory; then run the WOPR-XP.EXE file and follow the prompts. You do not have to uninstall WOPR before installing the new version.

TECH SUPPORT

> **Note**
>
> The technical support options listed here are for WOPR XP/2002 only!

For technical support:

- Visit the FAQ (Frequently Asked Questions) page on our Web site at `http://www.wopr.com/wopr-xp/support/woprsupportfaq.htm`, and you'll likely find your answer.

- Follow the instructions on the FAQ site to submit a support question, using our tech support system.

WOW, Woody's Office Watch, is Woody's free, weekly e-mail bulletin on all things related to Microsoft Office. We run the very latest information on WOPR in this free bulletin, so be sure you send e-mail to `wow@wopr.com` to get your copy each week.

INDEX